Merriam-Webster's
Pocket
Dictionary

D0029551

Merriam-Webster's
Pocket
Dictionary

Merriam-Webster, Incorporated
Springfield, Massachusetts

A GENUINE MERRIAM-WEBSTER

The name *Webster* alone is no guarantee of excellence.
It is used by a number of publishers and may serve
mainly to mislead an unwary buyer.

Merriam-Webster™ is the registered trademark you
should look for when you consider the purchase of
dictionaries or other fine reference books. It carries the
reputation of a company that has been publishing since
1831 and is your assurance of quality and authority.

Copyright © 2006 by Merriam-Webster, Incorporated

Library of Congress Cataloging-in-Publication Data

Merriam-Webster's pocket dictionary.
    p.   cm.
  ISBN-13   978-0-87779-530-8
  ISBN-10   0-87779-530-4
1. English language—Dictionaries.   I. Merriam-Webster, Inc.
PE1628.M38   2006
423—dc22

                                        2005026276

Printed in Canada
26th Printing   Marquis   Toronto, ON   11/2021

Preface

This new edition of *Merriam-Webster's Pocket Dictionary* contains new words and senses that have become established in the language in the decade since publication of the previous edition. Yet, while the vocabulary has been updated, users will find that the book has a familiar feel since the easy-to-use format has not changed significantly.

This book remains an extremely concise reference to those words that form the very core of the English vocabulary. It is intended to serve as a quick reference, especially for questions of spelling, pronunciation, and hyphenation of the most common words in everyday use. While this is the smallest of the family of dictionaries published by Merriam-Webster, it shares many details of presentation with the more comprehensive dictionaries on which it draws, such as *Merriam-Webster's Collegiate Dictionary, Eleventh Edition.* However, conciseness of presentation necessarily requires special treatment of entries, and this book has a number of special features uniquely its own. Users need to be familiar with the following major features of this dictionary.

Main entries follow one another in alphabetical order. Centered periods within the entries show points at which a hyphen may be put when the word is broken at the end of a line.

Homographs (words spelled the same but having different meanings) are run in to a single main entry when they are closely related. Second and succeeding homographs are represented by a swung dash: ~ Homographs of distinctly different origin (as **¹perch** and **²perch**) are given separate entries with preceding raised numerals.

Variant spellings that are quite common appear at the main entry following a comma (as **the•ater, the•atre**) and following other boldface entry words, such as inflected forms and run-on entries.

Inflected forms of nouns, verbs, adjectives, and adverbs are shown when they are irregular—as when requiring the dropping of a final *e* or changing a final *y* to *i* before the suffix: (as **prat•ed; prat•ing** at **prate**) or when the form of the base word itself changes: (as **swam...; swum** at **swim**)—or when there might be doubt about their spelling: (as *pl* **twos** at **two**). They are given either in full (as **worse...; worst** at **bad**) or cut back to a convenient point of division (as **-mat•ed; -mat•ing** at **es•ti•mate**). Common variants of inflected forms are shown even if they are regular (as **bused** *or* **bussed** at **bus**). When the inflected forms of a verb involve no irregularity except the doubling of a final consonant, the double consonant is shown instead of full or cutback inflected forms (as **vb** **-gg-** at **hug**). A variant or inflected form whose alphabetical place is distant from the main entry is entered at its own place with a cross-reference in small capital letters to the main entry (as **laid** *past of* **LAY**).

Several other kinds of entries are also found in this dictionary. A **run-in entry** is a term related to a main entry that appears within a definition (as **cacao beans** at **ca•cao**). It is set off by parentheses. Derivative words, made up usually of the main entry and a common word element, such as a suffix, are shown as **undefined run-on entries** following all definitions of a main entry. These are set off by a dash (as — **man•u•al•ly** at **man•u•al** or — **hill•top** at **hill**). The meaning of an undefined run-on entry can be inferred from the meaning of the main entry where it appears and that of the added word element, shown elsewhere in the book. A **run-on phrase** is a group of two or more words having the main entry as a major element and having a special meaning of its own (as **knock out** at **knock** or **set forth** at **set**). Run-on phrases are always defined.

Lists of undefined words formed by the addition of a common English prefix to a word entered in the dictionary and having meanings that can be inferred from the meaning of the root word and that of the prefix will be found in a separate section at the bottom of the page at entries for the following prefixes: *anti-, bi-, co-, counter-, extra-, hyper-, in-, inter-, mini-, multi-, non-, over-, post-, pre-, re-, self-, sub-, super-, un-,* and *vice-.*

Pronunciation information is either given explicitly or implied for every entry in the dictionary. Pronunciation respellings are placed within reversed slanted lines (as \ˌjenəˈralətē\ at **ge•ner•al•i•ty**). Where the pronunciation is not indicated at a particular entry, or is indicated in a cutback form, the full pronunciation is to be inferred from an earlier indicated pronunciation. A full list of the pronunciation symbols used is shown on the page following this Preface.

The grammatical function of entry words is indicated by an italic **functional label** (as *vb, n,* or *prefix*).

A **hyphen** that is a fixed part of a hyphenated expression (such as *water-soluble* at the entry **acid**) is converted to a special "double hyphen" (⹀) when the compound expression appears in lightface type and when the fixed hyphen comes at the end of a line in this dictionary. This indicates to you that the hyphen is to be retained when the word is not at the end of a line. Fixed hyphens in boldface entry words are shown as short boldface dashes, which are a bit larger than ordinary hyphens. These short dashes or long hyphens in boldface words are retained at the end of a line in this dictionary.

Guide words are used at the top of pages to indicate the range of entries on those pages. In choosing guide words for a page, we select the alphabetically first and last spelled-out boldface words or phrases on that page. This means that any boldface entry—main entry, variant spelling, inflected form, run-in or run-on entry—can be used as a guide word. Please keep this in mind if the word used as a guide word does not happen to be the first or last main entry on the page. The guide words themselves are in alphabetical order throughout the book, so occasionally it has been necessary to modify this rule. When the alphabetically last entry on one page would come later than the alphabetically first entry on the following page, a different word is chosen as guide word. On pages that contain a substantial number of undefined words derived from a prefix entry, the undefined words are not considered when choosing guide words.

All **abbreviations** used in this book are listed, along with a number of other common abbreviations, in a special section immediately following the dictionary proper.

Pronunciation Symbols

ə banana, collide, abut; raised \\ᵊ\\ in \\ᵊl, ᵊn\\ as in battle, cotton; in \\lᵊ, mᵊ, rᵊ\\ as in French table, prisme, titre

ˈə, ˌə humbug, abut

ər operation, further

a map, patch

ā day, fate

ä bother, cot, father

à father as pronounced by those who do not rhyme it with *bother*

aủ now, out

b baby, rib

ch chin, catch

d did, adder

e set, red

ē beat, nosebleed, easy

f fifty, cuff

g go, big

h hat, ahead

hw whale

i tip, banish

ī site, buy

j job, edge

k kin, cook

k̲ German ich, Buch

l lily, cool

m murmur, dim

n nine, own; raised \\ⁿ\\ indicates that a preceding vowel or diphthong is pronounced through both nose and mouth, as in French bon \\bōⁿ\\

ŋ sing, singer, finger, ink

ō bone, hollow

ò saw, cork

œ French bœuf, German Hölle

œ̄ French feu, German Höhle

òi toy, sawing

p pepper, lip

r rarity

s source, less

sh shy, mission

t tie, attack

th thin, ether

t̲h̲ then, either

ü boot, few \\ˈfyü\\

ủ put, pure \\ˈpyủr\\

ue German füllen

ūē French rue, German fühlen

v vivid, give

w we, away

y yard, cue \\ˈkyü\\; raised \\ʸ\\ indicates that a preceding \\l\\, \\n\\, or \\w\\ is modified by the placing of the tongue tip against the lower front teeth, as in French digne \\dēnʸ\\

z zone, raise

zh vision, pleasure

\\ slant line used in pairs to mark the beginning and end of a transcription

ˈ mark at the beginning of a syllable that has primary (strongest) stress: \\ˈpenmən͵ship\\

ˌ mark at the beginning of a syllable that has secondary (next-strongest) stress: \\ˈpenmən͵ship\\

A

¹**a** \'ā\ *n, pl* **a's** *or* **as** \'āz\ : 1st letter of the alphabet

²**a** \ə, 'ā\ *indefinite article* : one or some — used to indicate an unspecified or unidentified individual

aard·vark \'ärd‚värk\ *n* : ant-eating African mammal

aback \ə'bak\ *adv* : by surprise

aba·cus \'abəkəs\ *n, pl* **aba·ci** \'abə‚sī, -‚kē\ *or* **aba·cus·es** : calculating instrument using rows of beads

abaft \ə'baft\ *adv* : toward or at the stern

ab·a·lone \‚abə'lōnē\ *n* : large edible shellfish

¹**aban·don** \ə'bandən\ *vb* : give up without intent to reclaim — **aban·don·ment** *n*

²**abandon** *n* : thorough yielding to impulses

aban·doned \ə'bandənd\ *adj* : morally unrestrained

abase \ə'bās\ *vb* **abased; abas·ing** : lower in dignity — **abase·ment** *n*

abash \ə'bash\ *vb* : embarrass — **abashment** *n*

abate \ə'bāt\ *vb* **abat·ed; abat·ing** : decrease or lessen

abate·ment \ə'bātmənt\ *n* : tax reduction

ab·at·toir \'abə‚twär\ *n* : slaughterhouse

ab·bess \'abəs\ *n* : head of a convent

ab·bey \'abē\ *n, pl* **-beys** : monastery or convent

ab·bot \'abət\ *n* : head of a monastery

ab·bre·vi·ate \ə'brēvē‚āt\ *vb* **-at·ed; -at·ing** : shorten — **ab·bre·vi·a·tion** \ə‚brēvē'āshən\ *n*

ab·di·cate \'abdi‚kāt\ *vb* **-cat·ed; -cat·ing** : renounce — **ab·di·ca·tion** \‚abdi'kāshən\ *n*

ab·do·men \'abdəmən, ab'dōmən\ *n* **1** : body area between chest and pelvis **2** : hindmost part of an insect — **ab·dom·i·nal** \ab'dämən²l\ *adj* — **ab·dom·i·nal·ly** *adv*

ab·duct \ab'dəkt\ *vb* : kidnap — **ab·duc·tion** \-'dəkshən\ *n* — **ab·duc·tor** \-tər\ *n*

abed \ə'bed\ *adv or adj* : in bed

ab·er·ra·tion \‚abə'rāshən\ *n* : deviation or distortion — **ab·er·rant** \a'berrənt\ *adj*

abet \ə'bet\ *vb* **-tt-** : incite or encourage — **abet·tor, abet·ter** \-ər\ *n*

abey·ance \ə'bāəns\ *n* : state of inactivity

ab·hor \ab'hȯr, əb-\ *vb* **-rr-** : hate — **ab·hor·rence** \-əns\ *n* — **ab·hor·rent** \-ənt\ *adj*

abide \ə'bīd\ *vb* **abode** \-'bōd\ *or* **abid·ed; abid·ing 1** : endure **2** : remain, last, or reside

ab·ject \'ab‚jekt, ab'-\ *adj* : low in spirit or hope — **ab·jec·tion** \ab'jekshən\ *n* — **ab·ject·ly** *adv* — **ab·ject·ness** *n*

ab·jure \ab'jùr\ *vb* **1** : renounce **2** : abstain from — **ab·ju·ra·tion** \‚abjə'rāshən\ *n*

ablaze \ə'blāz\ *adj or adv* : on fire

able \'ābəl\ *adj* **abler** \-blər\; **ablest** \-bləst\ **1** : having sufficient power, skill, or resources **2** : skilled or efficient — **abil·i·ty** \ə'bilətē\ *n* — **ably** \'āblē\ *adv*

-able, -ible \əbəl\ *adj suffix* **1** : capable of, fit for, or worthy of **2** : tending, given, or liable to

ab·lu·tion \ə'blüshən, a'blü-\ *n* : washing of one's body

ab·ne·gate \'abni‚gāt\ *vb* **-gat·ed; -gat·ing 1** : relinquish **2** : renounce — **ab·ne·ga·tion** \‚abni'gāshən\ *n*

ab·nor·mal \ab'nȯrməl\ *adj* : deviating from the normal or average — **ab·nor·mal·i·ty** \‚abnər'malətē, -nȯr-\ *n* — **ab·nor·mal·ly** *adv*

aboard \ə'bōrd\ *adv* : on, onto, or within a car, ship, or aircraft ∼ *prep* : on or within

abode \ə'bōd\ *n* : residence

abol·ish \ə'bälish\ *vb* : do away with — **ab·o·li·tion** \‚abə'lishən\ *n*

abom·i·na·ble \ə'bämənəbəl\ *adj* : thoroughly unpleasant or revolting

abom·i·nate \ə'bämə,nāt\ *vb* **-nat·ed; -nat·ing** : hate — **abom·i·na·tion** \ə,bämə'nāshən\ *n*

ab·orig·i·nal \,abə'rijənəl\ *adj* **1** : original **2** : primitive

ab·orig·i·ne \-'rijənē\ *n* : original inhabitant

abort \ə'bȯrt\ *vb* : terminate prematurely — **abor·tive** \-'bȯrtiv\ *adj*

abor·tion \ə'bȯrshən\ *n* : spontaneous or induced termination of pregnancy

abound \ə'baund\ *vb* : be plentiful

about \ə'baut\ *adv* : around — *prep* **1** : on every side of **2** : on the verge of **3** : having as a subject

above \ə'bəv\ *adv* : in or to a higher place — *prep* **1** : in or to a higher place than **2** : more than

above·board *adv or adj* : without deception

abrade \ə'brād\ *vb* **abrad·ed; abrad·ing** : wear away by rubbing — **abra·sion** \-'brāzhən\ *n*

abra·sive \ə'brāsiv\ *n* : substance for grinding, smoothing, or polishing — *adj* **1** : tending to abrade **2** : causing irritation — **abra·sive·ly** *adv* — **abra·sive·ness** *n*

abreast \ə'brest\ *adv or adj* **1** : side by side **2** : up to a standard or level

abridge \ə'brij\ *vb* **abridged; abridg·ing** : shorten or condense — **abridg·ment, abridge·ment** *n*

abroad \ə'brȯd\ *adv or adj* **1** : over a wide area **2** : outside one's country

ab·ro·gate \'abrə,gāt\ *vb* **-gat·ed; -gat·ing** : annul or revoke — **ab·ro·ga·tion** \,abrə'gāshən\ *n*

abrupt \ə'brəpt\ *adj* **1** : sudden **2** : so quick as to seem rude — **abrupt·ly** *adv*

ab·scess \'ab,ses\ *n* : collection of pus surrounded by inflamed tissue — **ab·scessed** \-,sest\ *adj*

ab·scond \ab'skänd\ *vb* : run away and hide

ab·sent \'absənt\ *adj* : not present — **ab·sent** \ab'sent\ *vb* : keep oneself away — **ab·sence** \'absəns\ *n* — **absen·tee** \,absən'tē\ *n*

ab·sent-mind·ed \,absənt'mīndəd\ *adj* : unaware of one's surroundings or action — **ab·sent-mind·ed·ly** *adv* — **ab·sent-mind·ed·ness** *n*

ab·so·lute \'absə,lüt, ,absə'-\ *adj* **1** : pure **2** : free from restriction **3** : definite — **ab·so·lute·ly** *adv*

ab·so·lu·tion \,absə'lüshən\ *n* : remission of sins

ab·solve \əb'zälv, -'sälv\ *vb* **-solved; -solv·ing** : set free of the consequences of guilt

ab·sorb \əb'sȯrb, -'zȯrb\ *vb* **1** : suck up or take in as a sponge does **2** : engage (one's attention) — **ab·sor·ben·cy** \-'sȯrbənsē, -'zȯr-\ *n* — **ab·sorbent** \-bənt\ *adj or n* — **ab·sorb·ing** *adj*

ab·sorp·tion \əb'sȯrpshən, -'zȯrp-\ *n* : process of absorbing — **ab·sorp·tive** \-tiv\ *adj*

ab·stain \əb'stān\ *vb* : refrain from doing something — **ab·stain·er** *n* — **ab·sten·tion** \-'stenchən\ *n* — **ab·sti·nence** \'abstənəns\ *n*

ab·ste·mi·ous \ab'stēmēəs\ *adj* : sparing in use of food or drink — **ab·ste·mi·ous·ly** *adv* — **ab·ste·mi·ous·ness** *n*

ab·stract \ab'strakt, 'ab,-\ *adj* **1** : expressing a quality apart from an object **2** : not representing something specific — \'ab,-\ *n* : summary — \ab'-, 'ab,-\ *vb* **1** : remove or separate **2** : make an abstract of — **ab·stract·ly** *adv* — **ab·stract·ness** *n*

ab·strac·tion \ab'strakshən\ *n* **1** : act of abstracting **2** : abstract idea or work of art

ab·struse \əb'strüs, ab-\ *adj* : hard to understand — **ab·struse·ly** *adv* — **ab·struse·ness** *n*

ab·surd \əb'sərd, -'zərd\ *adj* : ridiculous or unreasonable — **ab·sur·di·ty** \-ətē\ *n* — **ab·surd·ly** *adv*

abun·dant \ə'bəndənt\ *adj* : more than enough — **abun·dance** \-dəns\ *n* — **abun·dant·ly** *adv*

abuse \ə'byüz\ *vb* **abused; abus·ing** **1** : misuse **2** : mistreat **3** : attack with words — \-'byüs\ *n* **1** : corrupt practice **2** : improper use **3** : mistreatment **4** : coarse and insulting speech — **abus·er** *n* — **abu·sive** \-'byüsiv\ *adj* — **abu·sive·ly** *adv* — **abu·sive·ness** *n*

abut \ə'bət\ *vb* **-tt-** : touch along a border — **abut·ter** *n*

abut·ment \ə'bətmənt\ *n* : part of a bridge that supports weight

abys·mal \ə'bizməl\ *adj* **1** : immeasurably deep **2** : wretched — **abys·mal·ly** *adv*

abyss \ə'bis\ *n* : immeasurably deep gulf

-ac \ak\ *n suffix* : one affected with

a·ca·cia \ə'kāshə\ *n* : leguminous tree or shrub

ac·a·dem·ic \ˌakə'demik\ *adj* **1** : relating to schools or colleges **2** : theoretical — **academic** *n* — **ac·a·dem·i·cal·ly** \-ik'lē\ *adv*

acad·e·my \ə'kadəmē\ *n, pl* **-mies** **1** : private high school **2** : society of scholars or artists

acan·thus \ə'kanthəs\ *n, pl* **acanthus** **1** : prickly Mediterranean herb **2** : ornament representing acanthus leaves

ac·cede \ak'sēd\ *vb* **-ced·ed; -ced·ing** **1** : become a party to an agreement **2** : express approval **3** : enter upon an office

ac·cel·er·ate \ik'selə,rāt, ak-\ *vb* **-at·ed; -at·ing** **1** : bring about earlier **2** : speed up — **ac·cel·er·a·tion** \-,selə'rāshən\ *n*

ac·cel·er·a·tor \ik'selə,rātər, ak-\ *n* : pedal for controlling the speed of a motor vehicle

ac·cent \'ak,sent\ *n* **1** : distinctive manner of pronunciation **2** : prominence given to one syllable of a word **3** : mark (as ´, `, ˆ) over a vowel in writing or printing to indicate pronunciation ∼ \'ak,-, ak'-\ *vb* : emphasize — **ac·cen·tu·al** \ak'senchəwəl\ *adj*

ac·cen·tu·ate \ak'senchə,wāt\ *vb* **-at·ed; -at·ing** : stress or show off by a contrast — **ac·cen·tu·a·tion** \-,senchə'wāshən\ *n*

ac·cept \ik'sept, ak-\ *vb* **1** : receive willingly **2** : agree to — **ac·cept·abil·i·ty** \ik,septə'bilətē, ak-\ *n* — **ac·cept·able** \-'septəbəl\ *adj* — **ac·cep·tance** \-'septəns\ *n*

ac·cess \'ak,ses\ *n* : capability or way of approaching — **ac·ces·si·bil·i·ty** \ik,sesə'bilətē, ak-\ *n* — **ac·ces·si·ble** \-'sesəbəl\ *adj*

ac·ces·sion \ik'seshən, ak-\ *n* **1** : something added **2** : act of taking office

ac·ces·so·ry \ik'sesərē, ak-\ *n, pl* **-ries** **1** : nonessential addition **2** : one guilty of aiding a criminal — **accessory** *adj*

ac·ci·dent \'aksədənt\ *n* **1** : event occurring by chance or unintentionally **2** : chance — **ac·ci·den·tal** \ˌaksə'dent³l\ *adj* — **ac·ci·den·tal·ly** *adv*

ac·claim \ə'klām\ *vb or n* : praise

ac·cla·ma·tion \ˌaklə'māshən\ *n* **1** : eager applause **2** : unanimous vote

ac·cli·mate \'aklə,māt, ə'klīmət\ *vb* **-mat·ed; -mat·ing** : acclimatize — **ac·cli·ma·tion** \ˌaklə'māshən, -,klī-\ *n*

ac·cli·ma·tize \ə'klīmə,tīz\ *vb* **-tized; -tiz·ing** : accustom to a new climate or situation — **ac·cli·ma·ti·za·tion** \-,klīmətə'zāshən\ *n*

ac·co·lade \'akə,lād\ *n* : expression of praise

ac·com·mo·date \ə'kämə,dāt\ *vb* **-dat·ed; -dat·ing** **1** : adapt **2** : provide with something needed **3** : hold without crowding

ac·com·mo·da·tion \ə,kämə'dāshən\ *n* **1** : quarters — usu. pl. **2** : act of accommodating

ac·com·pa·ny \ə'kəmpənē\ *vb* **-nied; -ny·ing** **1** : go or occur with **2** : play supporting music — **ac·com·pa·ni·ment** \-nəmənt\ *n* — **ac·com·pa·nist** \-nist\ *n*

ac·com·plice \ə'kämpləs, -'kəm-\ *n* : associate in crime

ac·com·plish \ə'kämplish, -'kəm-\ *vb* : do, fulfill, or bring about — **ac·com·plished** *adj* — **ac·com·plish·er** *n* — **ac·com·plish·ment** *n*

ac·cord \ə'kord\ *vb* **1** : grant **2** : agree ∼ *n* **1** : agreement **2** : willingness to act — **ac·cor·dance** \-'kord³ns\ *n* — **ac·cor·dant** \-³nt\ *adj*

ac·cord·ing·ly \ə'kordinlē\ *adv* : consequently

according to *prep* **1** : in conformity with **2** : as stated by

ac·cor·di·on \ə'kordēən\ *n* : keyboard instrument with a bellows and reeds ∼ *adj* : folding like an accordion bellows — **ac·cor·di·on·ist** \-nist\ *n*

ac·cost \ə'kost\ *vb* : approach and speak to esp. aggressively

ac·count \ə'kaunt\ *n* **1** : statement of business transactions **2** : credit arrangement with a vendor **3** : report **4** : worth **5** : sum deposited in a bank ∼ *vb* : give an explanation

ac·count·able \ə'kauntəbəl\ *adj* : responsible — **ac·count·abil·i·ty** \-,kauntə'bilətē\ *n*

ac·coun·tant \ə'kaunt³nt\ *n* : one skilled in accounting — **ac·coun·tan·cy** \-³nsē\ *n* ac·count·ing \ə'kaůntiŋ\ n : financial record keeping

ac·cou·tre, ac·cou·ter \ə'kütər\ vb -tred or -tered; -tring or -ter·ing \-'kütəriŋ, -'kütriŋ\ : equip

ac·cou·tre·ment, ac·cou·ter·ment \ə'kütrəmənt, -'kütər-\ n 1 : accessory item — usu. pl. 2 : identifying characteristic

ac·cred·it \ə'kredət\ vb 1 : approve officially 2 : attribute — ac·cred·i·ta·tion \-,kredə'tāshən\ n

ac·crue \ə'krü\ vb -crued; -cru·ing : be added by periodic growth — ac·cru·al \-əl\ n

ac·cu·mu·late \ə'kyümyə,lāt\ vb -lat·ed; -lat·ing : collect or pile up — ac·cu·mu·la·tion \-,kyümyə'lāshən\ n

ac·cu·rate \'akyərət\ adj : free from error — ac·cu·ra·cy \-rəsē\ n — ac·cu·rate·ly adv — ac·cu·rate·ness n

ac·cursed \ə'kərst, -'kərsəd\ ac·curst \ə'kərst\ adj 1 : being under a curse 2 : damnable

ac·cuse \ə'kyüz\ vb -cused; -cus·ing : charge with an offense — ac·cu·sa·tion \,akyə'zāshən\ n — ac·cus·er n

ac·cused \ə'kyüzd\ n, pl -cused : defendant in a criminal case

ac·cus·tom \ə'kəstəm\ vb : make familiar through use or experience

ace \'ās\ n : one that excels

acer·bic \ə'sərbik, a-\ adj : sour or biting in temper, mood, or tone

acet·amin·o·phen \ə,sētə'minəfən\ n : pain reliever

ace·tate \'asə,tāt\ n : fabric or plastic derived from acetic acid

ace·tic acid \ə'sētik-\ n : acid found in vinegar

acet·y·lene \ə'set³lən, -³l,ēn\ n : colorless gas used as a fuel in welding

ache \'āk\ vb ached; ach·ing 1 : suffer a dull persistent pain 2 : yearn — ache n

achieve \ə'chēv\ vb achieved; achiev·ing : gain by work or effort — achieve·ment n — achiev·er n

ac·id \'asəd\ adj 1 : sour or biting to the taste 2 : sharp in manner 3 : of or relating to an acid ~ n : sour water-soluble chemical compound that reacts with a base to form a salt — acid·ic \ə'sidik\ adj — acid·i·fy \ə'sidə,fī\ vb — acid·i·ty \-ətē\ n — acid·ly adv

ac·knowl·edge \ik'nälij, ak-\ vb -edged; -edg·ing 1 : admit as true 2 : admit the authority of 3 : express thanks for — ac·knowl·edg·ment n

ac·me \'akmē\ n : highest point

ac·ne \'aknē\ n : skin disorder marked esp. by pimples

ac·o·lyte \'akə,līt\ n : assistant to a member of clergy in a religious service

acorn \'ā,kórn, -kərn\ n : nut of the oak

acous·tic \ə'küstik\ adj : relating to hearing or sound — acous·ti·cal \-stikəl\ adj — acous·ti·cal·ly \-klē\ adv

acous·tics \ə'küstiks\ n sing or pl 1 : science of sound 2 : qualities in a room that affect how sound is heard

ac·quaint \ə'kwānt\ vb 1 : inform 2 : make familiar

ac·quain·tance \ə'kwānt³ns\ n 1 : personal knowledge 2 : person with whom one is acquainted — ac·quain·tance·ship n

ac·qui·esce \,akwē'es\ vb -esced; -esc·ing : consent or submit — ac·qui·es·cence \-'es³ns\ n — ac·qui·es·cent \-³nt\ adj — ac·qui·es·cent·ly adv

ac·quire \ə'kwīr\ vb -quired; -quir·ing : gain

ac·qui·si·tion \,akwə'zishən\ n : a gaining or something gained — ac·qui·si·tive \ə'kwizətiv\ adj

ac·quit \ə'kwit\ vb -tt- 1 : pronounce not guilty 2 : conduct (oneself) usu. well — ac·quit·tal \-³l\ n

acre \'ākər\ n 1 pl : lands 2 : 4840 square yards

acre·age \'ākərij\ n : area in acres

ac·rid \'akrəd\ adj : sharp and biting — acrid·i·ty \a'kridətē, ə-\ n — ac·rid·ly adv — ac·rid·ness n

ac·ri·mo·ny \'akrə,mōnē\ n, pl -nies : harshness of language or feeling — ac·ri·mo·ni·ous \,akrə'mōnēəs\ adj — ac·ri·mo·ni·ous·ly adv

ac·ro·bat \'akrə,bat\ n : performer of tumbling feats — ac·ro·bat·ic \,akrə'batik\ adj

across \ə'krós\ adv : to or on the opposite side ~ prep 1 : to or on the opposite side of 2 : on so as to cross

acryl·ic \ə'krilik\ n 1 : plastic used for molded parts or in paints 2 : synthetic textile fiber

act \'akt\ n 1 : thing done 2 : law 3 : main division of a play ~ vb 1

: perform in a play **2** : conduct oneself **3** : operate **4** : produce an effect

ac·tion \'akshən\ *n* **1** : legal proceeding **2** : manner or method of performing **3** : activity **4** : thing done over a period of time or in stages **5** : combat **6** : events of a literary plot **7** : operating mechanism

ac·ti·vate \'aktə,vāt\ *vb* **-vat·ed; -vat·ing** : make active or reactive — **ac·ti·va·tion** \,aktə'vāshən\ *n*

ac·tive \'aktiv\ *adj* **1** : causing action or change **2** : lively, vigorous, or energetic **3** : erupting or likely to erupt **4** : now in operation — **active** *n* — **ac·tive·ly** *adv*

ac·tiv·i·ty \ak'tivətē\ *n, pl* **-ties 1** : quality or state of being active **2** : what one is actively doing

ac·tor \'aktər\ *n* : one that acts

ac·tress \'aktrəs\ *n* : woman who acts in plays

ac·tu·al \'akchəwəl\ *adj* : really existing — **ac·tu·al·i·ty** \,akchə'walətē\ *n* — **ac·tu·al·iza·tion** \,akchəwələ-'zāshən\ *n* — **ac·tu·al·ize** \'akchəwə,līz\ *vb* — **ac·tu·al·ly** *adv*

ac·tu·ary \'akchə,werē\ *n, pl* **-ar·ies** : one who calculates insurance risks and premiums — **ac·tu·ar·i·al** \,akchə'werēəl\ *adj*

ac·tu·ate \'akchə,wāt\ *vb* **-at·ed; -at·ing** : put into action — **ac·tu·a·tor** \-,wātər\ *n*

acu·men \ə'kyümən\ *n* : mental keenness

acu·punc·ture \'akyù,pəŋkchər\ *n* : treatment by puncturing the body with needles — **acu·punc·tur·ist** \,akyù'pəŋkchərist\ *n*

acute \ə'kyüt\ *adj* **acut·er; acut·est 1** : sharp **2** : containing less than 90 degrees **3** : mentally alert **4** : severe — **acute·ly** *adv* — **acute·ness** *n*

ad \'ad\ *n* : advertisement

ad·age \'adij\ *n* : old familiar saying

ad·a·mant \'adəmant, -,mant\ *adj* : insistent — **ad·a·mant·ly** *adv*

adapt \ə'dapt\ *vb* : adjust to be suitable for a new use or condition — **adapt·abil·i·ty** \ə,daptə'bilətē\ *n* — **adapt·able** *adj* — **ad·ap·ta·tion** \,ad,ap-'tāshən, -əp-\ *n* — **adapt·er** *n* — **adap·tive** \ə'daptiv\ *adj*

add \'ad\ *vb* **1** : join to something else so as to increase in amount **2** : say further **3** : find a sum — **ad·di·tion** \ə'dishən\ *n*

ad·der \'adər\ *n* **1** : poisonous European snake **2** : No. American snake

ad·dict \'adikt\ *n* : one who is psychologically or physiologically dependent (as on a drug) ~ \ə'dikt\ *vb* : cause to become an addict — **ad·dic·tion** \ə'dikshən\ *n* — **ad·dic·tive** \-'diktiv\ *adj*

ad·di·tion·al \ə'dishənəl\ *adj* : existing as a result of adding — **ad·di·tion·al·ly** *adv*

ad·di·tive \'adətiv\ *n* : substance added to another

ad·dle \'ad³l\ *vb* **-dled; -dling** : confuse

ad·dress \ə'dres\ *vb* **1** : direct one's remarks to **2** : mark an address on ~ \ə'dres, 'ad,res\ *n* **1** : formal speech **2** : place where a person may be reached or mail may be delivered

ad·duce \ə'düs, -'dyüs\ *vb* **-duced; -duc·ing** : offer as proof

ad·e·noid \'ad,nöid, -²nöid\ *n* : enlarged tissue near the opening of the nose into the throat — usu. pl. — **ade·noid, ade·noi·dal** \-²l\ *adj*

adept \ə'dept\ *adj* : highly skilled — **adept·ly** *adv* — **adept·ness** *n*

ad·e·quate \'adikwət\ *adj* : good or plentiful enough — **ad·e·qua·cy** \-kwəsē\ *n* — **ad·e·quate·ly** *adv*

ad·here \ad'hir, əd-\ *vb* **-hered; -her·ing 1** : remain loyal **2** : stick fast — **ad·her·ence** \-'hirəns\ *n* — **ad·her·ent** \-ənt\ *adj or n*

ad·he·sion \ad'hēzhən, əd-\ *n* : act or state of adhering

ad·he·sive \-'hēsiv, -ziv\ *adj* : tending to adhere ~ *n* : adhesive substance

adieu \ə'dü, -'dyü\ *n, pl* **adieus** *or* **adieux** \-'düz, -'dyüz\ : farewell

ad·ja·cent \ə'jāsᵊnt\ *adj* : situated near or next

ad·jec·tive \'ajiktiv\ *n* : word that serves as a modifier of a noun — **ad·jec·ti·val** \,ajik'tīvəl\ *adj* — **ad·jec·ti·val·ly** *adv*

ad·join \ə'jöin\ *vb* : be next to

ad·journ \ə'jərn\ *vb* : end a meeting — **ad·journ·ment** *n*

ad·judge \ə'jəj\ *vb* **-judged; -judg·ing 1** : think or pronounce to be **2** : award by judicial decision

ad·ju·di·cate \ə'jüdi,kāt\ *vb* **-cat·ed; -cat·ing** : settle judicially — **ad·ju·di·ca·tion** \ə,jüdi'kāshən\ *n*

ad·junct \'aj,əŋkt\ *n* : something joined or added but not essential

ad·just \ə'jəst\ *vb* : fix, adapt, or set right — **ad·just·able** *adj* — **ad·just·er, ad·jus·tor** \ə'jəstər\ *n* — **ad·just·ment** \-mənt\ *n*

ad·ju·tant \'ajətənt\ *n* : aide esp. to a commanding officer

ad–lib \'ad'lib\ *vb* **-bb-** : speak without preparation — **ad–lib** *n or adj*

ad·min·is·ter \əd'minəstər\ *vb* 1 : manage 2 : give out esp. in doses — **ad·min·is·tra·ble** \-strəbəl\ *adj*

ad·min·is·tra·tion \əd,minə'strāshən, ad-\ *n* 1 : process of managing 2 : persons responsible for managing — **ad·min·is·tra·tive** \əd'minə,strātiv\ *adj* — **ad·min·is·tra·tive·ly** *adv*

ad·min·is·tra·tor \əd'minə,strātər\ *n* : one that manages

ad·mi·ra·ble \'admərəbəl\ *adj* : worthy of admiration — **ad·mi·ra·bly** \-blē\ *adv*

ad·mi·ral \'admərəl\ *n* : commissioned officer in the navy ranking next below a fleet admiral

ad·mire \əd'mīr\ *vb* **-mired; -mir·ing** : have high regard for — **ad·mi·ra·tion** \,admə'rāshən\ *n* — **ad·mir·er** *n* — **ad·mir·ing·ly** *adv*

ad·mis·si·ble \əd'misəbəl\ *adj* : that can be permitted — **ad·mis·si·bil·i·ty** \-,misə'bilətē\ *n*

ad·mis·sion \əd'mishən\ *n* 1 : act of admitting 2 : admittance or a fee paid for this 3 : acknowledgment of a fact

ad·mit \əd'mit\ *vb* **-tt-** 1 : allow to enter 2 : permit 3 : recognize as genuine — **ad·mit·ted·ly** *adv*

ad·mit·tance \əd'mit°ns\ *n* : permission to enter

ad·mix·ture \ad'mikschər\ *n* 1 : thing added in mixing 2 : mixture

ad·mon·ish \əd'mänish\ *vb* : rebuke — **ad·mon·ish·ment** \-mənt\ *n* — **ad·mo·ni·tion** \,admə'nishən\ *n* — **ad·mon·i·to·ry** \əd'mänə,tōrē\ *adj*

ado \ə'dü\ *n* 1 : fuss 2 : trouble

ado·be \ə'dōbē\ *n* 1 : sun-dried building brick

ad·o·les·cence \,ad°l'es°ns\ *n* : period of growth between childhood and maturity — **ad·o·les·cent** \-°nt\ *adj or n*

adopt \ə'däpt\ *vb* 1 : take (a child of other parents) as one's own child 2 : take up and practice as one's own — **adop·tion** \-'däpshən\ *n*

adore \ə'dōr\ *vb* **adored; ador·ing** 1 : worship 2 : be extremely fond of —

ador·able *adj* — **ador·ably** *adv* — **ado·ra·tion** \,adə'rāshən\ *n*

adorn \ə'dórn\ *vb* : decorate with ornaments — **adorn·ment** *n*

adrift \ə'drift\ *adv or adj* 1 : afloat without motive power or moorings 2 : without guidance or purpose

adroit \ə'dróit\ *adj* : dexterous or shrewd — **adroit·ly** *adv* — **adroit·ness** *n*

adult \ə'dəlt, 'ad,əlt\ *adj* : fully developed and mature ~ *n* : grown-up person — **adult·hood** *n*

adul·ter·ate \ə'dəltə,rāt\ *vb* **-at·ed; -at·ing** : make impure by mixture — **adul·ter·a·tion** \-,dəltə'rāshən\ *n*

adul·tery \ə'dəltərē\ *n, pl* **-ter·ies** : sexual unfaithfulness of a married person — **adul·ter·er** \-tərər\ *n* — **adul·ter·ess** \-tərəs\ *n* — **adul·ter·ous** \-tərəs\ *adj*

ad·vance \əd'vans\ *vb* **-vanced; -vanc·ing** 1 : bring or move forward 2 : promote 3 : lend ~ *n* 1 : forward movement 2 : improvement 3 : offer ~ *adj* : being ahead of time — **ad·vance·ment** *n*

ad·van·tage \əd'vantij\ *n* 1 : superiority of position 2 : benefit or gain — **ad·van·ta·geous** \,ad,van'tājəs, -vən-\ *adj* — **ad·van·ta·geous·ly** *adv*

ad·vent \'ad,vent\ *n* 1 *cap* : period before Christmas 2 : a coming into being or use

ad·ven·ti·tious \,advən'tishəs\ *adj* : accidental — **ad·ven·ti·tious·ly** *adv*

ad·ven·ture \əd'venchər\ *n* 1 : risky undertaking 2 : exciting experience — **ad·ven·tur·er** \-chərər\ *n* — **ad·ven·ture·some** \-chərsəm\ *adj* — **ad·ven·tur·ous** \-chərəs\ *adj*

ad·verb \'ad,vərb\ *n* : word that modifies a verb, an adjective, or another adverb — **ad·ver·bi·al** \ad'vərbeəl\ *adj* — **ad·ver·bi·al·ly** *adv*

ad·ver·sary \'advər,serē\ *n, pl* **-sar·ies** : enemy or rival — **adversary** *adj*

ad·verse \ad'vərs, 'ad-,\ *adj* : opposing or unfavorable — **ad·verse·ly** *adv*

ad·ver·si·ty \əd'vərsətē\ *n, pl* **-ties** : hard times

ad·vert \ad'vərt\ *vb* : refer

ad·ver·tise \'advər,tīz\ *vb* **-tised; -tis·ing** : call public attention to — **ad·ver·tise·ment** \,advər'tīzmənt, əd-'vərtəzmənt\ *n* — **ad·ver·tis·er** *n*

ad·ver·tis·ing \'advər,tīziŋ\ *n* : business of preparing advertisements

ad·vice \əd'vīs\ *n* : recommendation with regard to a course of action

ad·vis·able \əd'vīzəbəl\ *adj* : wise or prudent — **ad·vis·abil·i·ty** \-ˌvīzə'bilətē\ *n*

ad·vise \əd'vīz\ *vb* -**vised; -vis·ing** : give advice to — **ad·vis·er, ad·vis·or** \-'vīzər\ *n*

ad·vise·ment \əd'vīzmənt\ *n* : careful consideration

ad·vi·so·ry \əd'vīzərē\ *adj* : having power to advise

ad·vo·cate \'advəkət, -ˌkāt\ *n* : one who argues or pleads for a cause or proposal ~ \-ˌkāt\ *vb* -**cat·ed; -cat·ing** : recommend — **ad·vo·ca·cy** \-vəkəsē\ *n*

adze \'adz\ *n* : tool for shaping wood

ae·gis \'ējəs\ *n* : protection or sponsorship

ae·on \'ēən, 'ēˌän\ *var of* EON

aer·ate \'arˌāt\ *vb* -**at·ed; -at·ing** : supply or impregnate with air — **aer·a·tion** \ˌar'āshən\ *n* — **aer·a·tor** \'arˌātər\ *n*

ae·ri·al \'arēəl\ *adj* : inhabiting, occurring in, or done in the air ~ *n* : antenna

ae·rie \'arē, 'irē\ *n* : eagle's nest

aer·o·bic \ar'ōbik\ *adj* : using or needing oxygen

aer·o·bics \-biks\ *n sing or pl* : exercises that produce a marked increase in respiration and heart rate

aero·dy·nam·ics \ˌarōdī'namiks\ *n* : science of bodies in motion in a gas — **aero·dy·nam·ic** \-ik\ *adj* — **aero·dy·nam·i·cal·ly** \-iklē\ *adv*

aero·nau·tics \ˌarə'nòtiks\ *n* : science dealing with aircraft — **aero·nau·ti·cal** \-ikəl\ *adj*

aero·sol \'arəˌsäl, -ˌsòl\ *n* **1** : liquid or solid particles suspended in a gas **2** : substance sprayed as an aerosol

aero·space \'arōˌspās\ *n* : earth's atmosphere and the space beyond — **aerospace** *adj*

aes·thet·ic \es'thetik\ *adj* : relating to beauty — **aes·thet·i·cal·ly** \-iklē\ *adv*

aes·thet·ics \-'thetiks\ *n* : branch of philosophy dealing with beauty

afar \ə'fär\ *adv* : from, at, or to a great distance — **afar** *n*

af·fa·ble \'afəbəl\ *adj* : easy to talk to — **af·fa·bil·i·ty** \ˌafə'bilətē\ *n* — **af·fa·bly** \'afəblē\ *adv*

af·fair \ə'far\ *n* : something that relates to or involves one

¹af·fect \ə'fekt, a-\ *vb* : assume for effect — **af·fec·ta·tion** \ˌafˌek'tāshən\ *n*

²affect *vb* : produce an effect on

af·fect·ed \ə'fektəd, a-\ *adj* **1** : pretending to some trait **2** : artificially assumed to impress — **af·fect·ed·ly** *adv*

af·fect·ing \ə'fektiŋ, a-\ *adj* : arousing pity or sorrow — **af·fect·ing·ly** *adv*

af·fec·tion \ə'fekshən\ *n* : kind or loving feeling — **af·fec·tion·ate** \-shənət\ *adj* — **af·fec·tion·ate·ly** *adv*

af·fi·da·vit \ˌafə'dāvət\ *n* : sworn statement

af·fil·i·ate \ə'filēˌāt\ *vb* -**at·ed; -at·ing** : become a member or branch — **af·fil·i·ate** \-ēət\ *n* — **af·fil·i·a·tion** \-ˌfilē'āshən\ *n*

af·fin·i·ty \ə'finətē\ *n, pl* -**ties** : close attraction or relationship

af·firm \ə'fərm\ *vb* : assert positively — **af·fir·ma·tion** \ˌafər'māshən\ *n*

af·fir·ma·tive \ə'fərmətiv\ *adj* : asserting the truth or existence of something ~ *n* : statement of affirmation or agreement

af·fix \ə'fiks\ *vb* : attach

af·flict \ə'flikt\ *vb* : cause pain and distress to — **af·flic·tion** \-'flikshən\ *n*

af·flu·ence \'af,lüəns; a'flü-, ə-\ *n* : wealth — **af·flu·ent** \-ənt\ *adj*

af·ford \ə'ford\ *vb* **1** : manage to bear the cost of **2** : provide

af·fray \ə'frā\ *n* : fight

af·front \ə'frənt\ *vb or n* : insult

af·ghan \'afˌgan, -gən\ *n* : crocheted or knitted blanket

afire \ə'fīr\ *adj or adv* : being on fire

aflame \ə'flām\ *adj or adv* : flaming

afloat \ə'flōt\ *adj or adv* : floating

afoot \ə'fùt\ *adv or adj* **1** : on foot **2** : in progress

afore·said \ə'forˌsed\ *adj* : said or named before

afraid \ə'frād, *South also* ə'fred\ *adj* : filled with fear

afresh \ə'fresh\ *adv* : anew

aft \'aft\ *adv* : to or toward the stern or tail

af·ter \'aftər\ *adv* : at a later time ~ *prep* **1** : behind in place or time **2** : in pursuit of ~ *conj* : following the time when ~ *adj* **1** : later **2** : located toward the back

af·ter·life \'aftər‚līf\ *n* : existence after death

af·ter·math \-‚math\ *n* : results

af·ter·noon \‚aftər'nün\ *n* : time between noon and evening

af·ter·thought *n* : later thought

af·ter·ward \'aftərwərd\, **af·ter·wards** \-wərdz\ *adv* : at a later time

again \ə'gen, -'gin\ *adv* 1 : once more 2 : on the other hand 3 : in addition

against \ə'genst\ *prep* 1 : directly opposite to 2 : in opposition to 3 : so as to touch or strike

agape \ə'gäp, ə'gap\ *adj or adv* : having the mouth open in astonishment

ag·ate \'agət\ *n* : quartz with bands or masses of various colors

age \'āj\ *n* 1 : length of time of life or existence 2 : particular time in life (as majority or the latter part) 3 : quality of being old 4 : long time 5 : period in history ~ *vb* : become old or mature

-age \ij\ *n suffix* 1 : aggregate 2 : action or process 3 : result of 4 : rate of 5 : place of 6 : state or rank 7 : fee

aged *adj* 1 \'ājəd\ : old 2 \'ājd\ : allowed to mature

age·less \'ājləs\ *adj* : eternal

agen·cy \'ājənsē\ *n, pl* **-cies** 1 : one through which something is accomplished 2 : office or function of an agent 3 : government administrative division

agen·da \ə'jendə\ *n* : list of things to be done

agent \'ājənt\ *n* 1 : means 2 : person acting or doing business for another

ag·gran·dize \ə'gran‚dīz, 'agrən-\ *vb* **-dized; -diz·ing** : make great or greater — **ag·gran·dize·ment** \ə'grandəzmənt, -‚dīz-; ‚agrən'dīz-\ *n*

ag·gra·vate \'agrə‚vāt\ *vb* **-vat·ed; -vat·ing** 1 : make more severe 2 : irritate — **ag·gra·va·tion** \‚agrə'vāshən\ *n*

ag·gre·gate \'agrigət\ *adj* : formed into a mass ~ \-‚gāt\ *vb* **-gat·ed; -gat·ing** : collect into a mass ~ \-gət\ *n* 1 : mass 2 : whole amount

ag·gres·sion \ə'greshən\ *n* 1 : unprovoked attack 2 : hostile behavior — **ag·gres·sor** \-'gresər\ *n*

ag·gres·sive \ə'gresiv\ *adj* 1 : easily provoked to fight 2 : hard working and enterprising — **ag·gres·sive·ly** *adv* — **ag·gres·sive·ness** *n*

ag·grieve \ə'grēv\ *vb* **-grieved; -grieving** 1 : cause grief to 2 : inflict injury on

aghast \ə'gast\ *adj* : struck with amazement or horror

ag·ile \'ajəl\ *adj* : able to move quickly and easily — **agil·i·ty** \ə'jilətē\ *n*

ag·i·tate \'ajə‚tāt\ *vb* **-tat·ed; -tat·ing** 1 : shake or stir back and forth 2 : excite or trouble the mind of 3 : try to arouse public feeling — **ag·i·ta·tion** \‚ajə'tāshən\ *n* — **ag·i·ta·tor** \'ajə‚tātər\ *n*

ag·nos·tic \ag'nästik, əg-\ *n* : one who doubts the existence of God

ago \ə'gō\ *adj or adv* : earlier than the present

agog \ə'gäg\ *adj* : full of excitement

ag·o·nize \'agə‚nīz\ *vb* **-nized; -niz·ing** : suffer mental agony — **ag·o·niz·ing·ly** *adv*

ag·o·ny \'agənē\ *n, pl* **-nies** : extreme pain or mental distress

agrar·i·an \ə'grerēən\ *adj* : relating to land ownership or farming interests — **agrar·i·an·ism** *n*

agree \ə'grē\ *vb* **agreed; agree·ing** 1 : be of the same opinion 2 : express willingness 3 : get along together 4 : be similar 5 : be appropriate, suitable, or healthful

agree·able \-əbəl\ *adj* 1 : pleasing 2 : willing to give approval — **agree·able·ness** *n* — **agree·ably** *adv*

agree·ment \-mənt\ *n* 1 : harmony of opinion or purpose 2 : mutual understanding or arrangement

ag·ri·cul·ture \'agri‚kəlchər\ *n* : farming — **ag·ri·cul·tur·al** \‚agri'kəlchərəl\ *adj* — **ag·ri·cul·tur·ist** \-rist\, **ag·ri·cul·tur·al·ist** \-rəlist\ *n*

aground \ə'graünd\ *adv or adj* : on or onto the bottom or shore

ague \'āgyü\ *n* 1 : fever with recurrent chills and sweating 2 : malaria

ahead \ə'hed\ *adv or adj* 1 : in or toward the front 2 : into or for the future 3 : in a more advantageous position

ahead of *prep* 1 : in front or advance of 2 : in excess of

ahoy \ə'hói\ *interj* — used in hailing

aid \'ād\ *vb* : provide help or support ~ *n* : help

aide \'ād\ *n* : helper

AIDS \'ādz\ *n* : serious disease of the human immune system

ail \'āl\ *vb* 1 : trouble 2 : be ill

ai·le·ron \'ālə,rän\ n : movable part of an airplane wing

ail·ment \'ālmənt\ n : bodily disorder

aim \'ām\ vb 1 : point or direct (as a weapon) 2 : direct one's efforts ~ n 1 : an aiming or the direction of aiming 2 : object or purpose — **aim·less** adj — **aim·less·ly** adv — **aim·less·ness** n

air \'ar\ n 1 : mixture of gases surrounding the earth 2 : melody 3 : outward appearance 4 : artificial manner 5 : compressed air 6 : travel by or use of aircraft 7 : medium of transmission of radio waves ~ vb 1 : expose to the air 2 : broadcast — **air·borne** \-,bōrn\ adj

air–condition vb : equip with an apparatus (**air conditioner**) for filtering and cooling the air

air·craft n, pl aircraft : craft that flies

Aire·dale terrier \'ar,dāl-\ n : large terrier with a hard wiry coat

air·field n : airport or its landing field

air force n : military organization for conducting warfare by air

air·lift n : a transporting of esp. emergency supplies by aircraft — **airlift** vb

air·line n : air transportation system — **air·lin·er** n

air·mail n : system of transporting mail by airplane — **airmail** vb

air·man \-mən\ n 1 : aviator 2 : enlisted man in the air force in one of the 3 ranks below sergeant

airman basic n : enlisted man of the lowest rank in the air force

airman first class n : enlisted man in the air force ranking just below sergeant

air·plane n : fixed-wing aircraft heavier than air

air·port n : place for landing aircraft and usu. for receiving passengers

air·ship n : powered lighter-than-air aircraft

air·strip n : airfield runway

air·tight adj : tightly sealed to prevent flow of air

air·waves \'ar,wāvz\ n pl : medium of transmission of radio waves

airy \'arē\ adj **air·i·er, -est** 1 : delicate 2 : breezy

aisle \'īl\ n : passage between sections or rows

ajar \ə'jär\ adj or adv : partly open

akim·bo \ə'kimbō\ adj or adv : having the hand on the hip and the elbow turned outward

akin \ə'kin\ adj 1 : related by blood 2 : similar in kind

-al \əl\ adj suffix : of, relating to, or characterized by

al·a·bas·ter \'alə,bastər\ n : white or translucent mineral

alac·ri·ty \ə'lakrətē\ n : cheerful readiness

alarm \ə'lärm\ n 1 : warning signal or device 2 : fear at sudden danger ~ vb 1 : warn 2 : frighten

alas \ə'las\ interj — used to express unhappiness, pity, or concern

al·ba·tross \'albə,tròs, -,träs\ n, pl **-tross** or **-tross·es** : large seabird

al·be·it \ol'bēət, al-\ conj : even though

al·bi·no \al'bīnō\ n, pl **-nos** : person or animal with abnormally white skin — **al·bi·nism** \'albə,nizəm\ n

al·bum \'albəm\ n 1 : book for displaying a collection (as of photographs) 2 : collection of recordings

al·bu·men \al'byümən\ n 1 : white of an egg 2 : albumin

al·bu·min \-mən\ : protein found in blood, milk, egg white, and tissues

al·che·my \'alkəmē\ n : medieval chemistry — **al·che·mist** \'alkəmist\ n

al·co·hol \'alkə,hól\ n 1 : intoxicating agent in liquor 2 : liquor — **al·co·hol·ic** adj

al·co·hol·ic \,alkə'hólik, -'häl-\ : person affected with alcoholism

al·co·hol·ism \'alkə,hól,izəm\ n : addiction to alcoholic beverages

al·cove \'al,kōv\ n : recess in a room or wall

al·der·man \'óldərmən\ n : city official

ale \'āl\ n : beerlike beverage — **ale·house** n

alert \ə'lərt\ adj 1 : watchful 2 : quick to perceive and act ~ n : alarm ~ vb : warn — **alert·ly** adv — **alert·ness** n

ale·wife n : fish of the herring family

al·fal·fa \al'falfə\ n : cloverlike forage plant

al·ga \'algə\ n, pl **-gae** \'al,jē\ : any of a group of lower plants that includes seaweed — **al·gal** \-gəl\ adj

al·ge·bra \'aljəbrə\ n : branch of mathematics — **al·ge·bra·ic** \,aljə'brāik\ adj — **al·ge·bra·i·cal·ly** \-'brāəklē\ adv

alias \'ālēəs, 'ālyəs\ *adv* : otherwise called ∼ *n* : assumed name

al·i·bi \'alə,bī\ *n* 1 : defense of having been elsewhere when a crime was committed 2 : justification ∼ *vb* **-bied; -bi·ing** : offer an excuse

alien \'ālēən, 'ālyən\ *adj* : foreign ∼ *n* 1 : foreign-born resident 2 : extraterrestrial

alien·ate \'ālēə,nāt, 'ālyə-\ *vb* **-at·ed; -at·ing** : cause to be no longer friendly — **alien·ation** \,ālēə'nā-shən, ,ālyə-\ *n*

alight \ə'līt\ *vb* : dismount

align \ə'līn\ *vb* : bring into line — **align·er** *n* — **align·ment** *n*

alike \ə'līk\ *adj* : identical or very similar ∼ *adv* : equally

al·i·men·ta·ry \,alə'mentərē\ *adj* : relating to or functioning in nutrition

al·i·mo·ny \'alə,mōnē\ *n, pl* **-nies** : money paid to a separated or divorced spouse

alive \ə'līv\ *adj* 1 : having life 2 : lively or animated

al·ka·li \'alkə,lī\ *n, pl* **-lies** *or* **-lis** : strong chemical base — **al·ka·line** \-kələn, -,līn\ *adj* — **al·ka·lin·i·ty** \,alkə'linətē\ *n*

all \'ȯl\ *adj* 1 : the whole of 2 : greatest possible 3 : every one of ∼ *adv* 1 : wholly 2 : so much 3 : for each side ∼ *pron* 1 : whole number or amount 2 : everything or everyone

Al·lah \'älə, 'al-\ *n* : God of Islam

all-around *adj* : versatile

al·lay \ə'lā\ *vb* 1 : alleviate 2 : calm

al·lege \ə'lej\ *vb* **-leged; -leg·ing** : assert without proof — **al·le·ga·tion** \,ali'gāshən\ *n* — **al·leg·ed·ly** \ə'lej-ədlē\ *adv*

al·le·giance \ə'lējəns\ *n* : loyalty

al·le·go·ry \'alə,gōrē\ *n, pl* **-ries** : story in which figures and actions are symbols of general truths — **al·le·gor·i·cal** \,alə'gȯrikəl\ *adj*

al·le·lu·ia \,alə'lüyə\ *interj* : hallelujah

al·ler·gen \'alərjən\ *n* : something that causes allergy — **al·ler·gen·ic** \,alər-'jenik\ *adj*

al·ler·gy \'alərjē\ *n, pl* **-gies** : abnormal reaction to a substance — **al·ler·gic** \ə'lərjik\ *adj* — **al·ler·gist** \'alərjist\ *n*

al·le·vi·ate \ə'lēvē,āt\ *vb* **-at·ed; -at·ing** : relieve or lessen — **al·le·vi·a·tion** \ə,lēvē'āshən\ *n*

al·ley \'alē\ *n, pl* **-leys** 1 : place for bowling 2 : narrow passage between buildings

al·li·ance \ə'līəns\ *n* : association

al·li·ga·tor \'alə,gātər\ *n* : large aquatic reptile related to the crocodiles

al·lit·er·a·tion \ə,litə'rāshən\ *n* : repetition of initial sounds of words — **al·lit·er·a·tive** \-'litə,rātiv\ *adj*

al·lo·cate \'alə,kāt\ *vb* **-cat·ed; -cat·ing** : assign — **al·lo·ca·tion** \,alə'kā-shən\ *n*

al·lot \ə'lät\ *vb* **-tt-** : distribute as a share — **al·lot·ment** *n*

al·low \ə'laù\ *vb* 1 : admit or concede 2 : permit — **al·low·able** *adj*

al·low·ance \-əns\ *n* 1 : allotted share 2 : money given regularly for expenses

al·loy \'al,ȯi\ *n* : metals melted together — **al·loy** \ə'lȯi\ *vb*

all right *adv or adj* 1 : satisfactorily 2 : yes 3 : certainly

all·spice \'ȯlspīs\ *n* : berry of a West Indian tree made into a spice

al·lude \ə'lüd\ *vb* **-lud·ed; -lud·ing** : refer indirectly — **al·lu·sion** \-'lü-zhən\ *n* — **al·lu·sive** \-'lüsiv\ *adj*

al·lure \ə'lùr\ *vb* **-lured; -lur·ing** : entice ∼ *n* : attractive power

al·ly \ə'lī, 'al,ī\ *vb* **-lied; -ly·ing** : enter into an alliance — **al·ly** \'al,ī, ə'lī\ *n*

-al·ly \əlē\ *adv suffix* : -ly

al·ma·nac \'ȯlmə,nak, 'al-\ *n* : annual information book

al·mighty \ȯl'mītē\ *adj* : having absolute power

al·mond \'ämənd , 'am-, 'alm-, 'älm-\ *n* : tree with nutlike fruit kernels

al·most \'ȯl,mōst, ȯl'-\ *adv* : very nearly

alms \'ämz, 'älmz, 'almz\ *n, pl* **alms** : charitable gift

aloft \ə'lȯft\ *adv* : high in the air

alo·ha \ə'lōhä\ *interj* — used to greet or bid farewell

alone \ə'lōn\ *adj* 1 : separated from others 2 : not including anyone or anything else — **alone** *adv*

along \ə'lȯn\ *prep* 1 : in line with the direction of 2 : at a point on or during ∼ *adv* 1 : forward 2 : as a companion

along·side *adv or prep* : along or by the side

alongside of *prep* : alongside

aloof \ə'lüf\ *adj* : indifferent and reserved — **aloof·ness** *n*

aloud \ə'laùd\ *adv* : so as to be heard

al·paca \al'pakə\ n **1** : So. American mammal related to the llama **2** : alpaca wool or cloth made of this

al·pha·bet \'alfə,bet, -bət\ n : ordered set of letters of a language — **al·pha·bet·i·cal** \,alfə'betikəl\, **al·pha·bet·ic** \-'betik\ adj — **al·pha·bet·i·cal·ly** \-klē\ adv

al·pha·bet·ize \'alfəbə,tīz\ vb **-ized; -iz·ing** : arrange in alphabetical order — **al·pha·bet·iz·er** n

al·ready \ol'redē\ adv : by a given time

al·so \'olsō\ adv : in addition

al·tar \'oltər\ n : structure for rituals

al·ter \'oltər\ vb : make different — **al·ter·a·tion** \,oltə'rāshən\ n

al·ter·ca·tion \oltər'kāshən\ n : dispute

al·ter·nate \'oltərnət, 'al-\ adj **1** : arranged or succeeding by turns **2** : every other ∼ \-,nāt\ vb **-nat·ed; -nat·ing** : occur or cause to occur by turns ∼ \-nət\ n : substitute — **al·ter·nate·ly** adv — **al·ter·na·tion** \,oltər'nāshən, ,al-\ n

alternating current n : electric current that regularly reverses direction

al·ter·na·tive \ol'tərnətiv, al-\ adj : offering a choice — **alternative** n

al·ter·na·tor \'oltər,nātər, 'al-\ n : alternating-current generator

al·though \ol'thō\ conj : even though

al·tim·e·ter \al'timətər, 'altə,mētər\ n : instrument for measuring altitude

al·ti·tude \'altə,tüd, -,tyüd\ n **1** : distance up from the ground **2** : angular distance above the horizon

al·to \'altō\ n, pl **-tos** : lower female choral voice

al·to·geth·er \,oltə'gethər\ adv **1** : wholly **2** : on the whole

al·tru·ism \'altrü,izəm\ n : concern for others — **al·tru·ist** \-ist\ n — **al·tru·is·tic** \,altrü'istik\ adj — **al·tru·is·ti·cal·ly** \-tiklē\ adv

al·um \'aləm\ n : crystalline compound containing aluminum

alu·mi·num \ə'lümənəm\ n : silver-white malleable ductile light metallic element

alum·na \ə'ləmnə\ n, pl **-nae** \-,nē\ : woman graduate

alum·nus \ə'ləmnəs\ n, pl **-ni** \-,nī\ : graduate

al·ways \'olwēz, -wāz\ adv **1** : at all times **2** : forever

am pres 1st sing of BE

amal·gam \ə'malgəm\ n **1** : mercury alloy **2** : mixture

amal·gam·ate \ə'malgə,māt\ vb **-at·ed; -at·ing** : unite — **amal·ga·ma·tion** \-,malgə'māshən\ n

am·a·ryl·lis \,amə'riləs\ n : bulbous herb with clusters of large colored flowers like lilies

amass \ə'mas\ vb : gather

am·a·teur \'amə,tər, -,tür, -,tyür, -,chür, -chər\ n **1** : person who does something for pleasure rather than for pay **2** : person who is not expert — **am·a·teur·ish** \,amə'tərish, -'tür-, -'tyür-\ — **am·a·teur·ism** \'amə,tər,izəm, -,tür-, -,tyür-, -,chür-, -chər-\ n

am·a·to·ry \'amə,tōrē\ adj : of or expressing sexual love

amaze \ə'māz\ vb **amazed; amaz·ing** : fill with wonder — **amaze·ment** n — **amaz·ing·ly** adv

am·a·zon \'amə,zän, -zən\ n : tall strong woman — **am·a·zo·ni·an** \,amə'zōnēən\ adj

am·bas·sa·dor \am'basədər\ n : representative esp. of a government — **am·bas·sa·do·ri·al** \-,basə'dō-rēəl\ adj — **am·bas·sa·dor·ship** n

am·ber \'ambər\ n : yellowish fossil resin or its color

am·ber·gris \'ambər,grēs, -,grēs\ n : waxy substance from certain whales used in making perfumes

am·bi·dex·trous \,ambi'dekstrəs\ adj : equally skilled with both hands — **am·bi·dex·trous·ly** adv

am·bi·ence, am·bi·ance \'ambēəns, 'ämbē,äns\ n : pervading atmosphere

am·big·u·ous \am'bigyəwəs\ adj : having more than one interpretation — **am·bi·gu·i·ty** \,ambə'gyüətē\ n

am·bi·tion \am'bishən\ n : eager desire for success or power — **am·bi·tious** \-shəs\ adj — **am·bi·tious·ly** adv

am·biv·a·lence \am'bivələns\ n : simultaneous attraction and repulsion — **am·biv·a·lent** \-lənt\ adj

am·ble \'ambəl\ vb **-bled; -bling** : go at a leisurely gait — **amble** n

am·bu·lance \'ambyələns\ n : vehicle for carrying injured or sick persons

am·bu·la·to·ry \'ambyələ,tōrē\ adj **1** : relating to or adapted to walking **2** : able to walk about

am·bush \'am,bush\ n : trap by which

a surprise attack is made from a place of hiding — **ambush** *vb*

ame·lio·rate \ə'mēlyə,rāt\ *vb* **-rat·ed; -rat·ing** : make or grow better — **ame·lio·ra·tion** \-,mēlyə'rāshən\ *n*

amen \'ā'men, 'ä-\ *interj* — used for affirmation esp. at the end of prayers

ame·na·ble \ə'mēnəbəl, -'men-\ *adj* : ready to yield or be influenced

amend \ə'mend\ *vb* **1** : improve **2** : alter in writing

amend·ment \-mənt\ *n* : change made in a formal document (as a law)

amends \ə'mendz\ *n pl* : compensation for injury or loss

ame·ni·ty \ə'menətē, -'mē-\ *n, pl* **-ties** **1** : agreeableness **2** *pl* : social conventions **3** : something serving to comfort or accommodate

am·e·thyst \'aməthəst\ *n* : purple gemstone

ami·a·ble \'āmēəbəl\ *adj* : easy to get along with — **ami·a·bil·i·ty** \,āmēə'bilətē\ *n* — **ami·a·bly** \'āmēəblē\ *adv*

am·i·ca·ble \'amikəbəl\ *adj* : friendly — **am·i·ca·bly** \-blē\ *adv*

amid \ə'mid\, **amidst** \-'midst\ *prep* : in or into the middle of

amino acid \ə'mēnō-\ *n* : nitrogen-containing acid

amiss \ə'mis\ *adv* : in the wrong way ~ *adj* : wrong

am·me·ter \'am,ētər\ *n* : instrument for measuring electric current

am·mo·nia \ə'mōnyə\ *n* **1** : colorless gaseous compound of nitrogen and hydrogen **2** : solution of ammonia in water

am·mu·ni·tion \,amyə'nishən\ *n* **1** : projectiles fired from guns **2** : explosive items used in war

am·ne·sia \am'nēzhə\ *n* : sudden loss of memory — **am·ne·si·ac** \-zē,ak, -zhē-\, **am·ne·sic** \-sik, -sik\ *adj or n*

am·nes·ty \'amnəstē\ *n, pl* **-ties** : a pardon for a group — **amnesty** *vb*

amoe·ba \ə'mēbə\ *n, pl* **-bas** *or* **-bae** \-,bē\ : tiny one-celled animal that occurs esp. in water — **amoe·bic** \-bik\ *adj*

amok \ə'mək, -'mäk\ *adv* : in a violent or uncontrolled way

among \ə'məŋ\ *prep* **1** : in or through **2** : in the number or class of **3** : in shares to each of

am·o·rous \'amərəs\ *adj* **1** : inclined to love **2** : being in love **3** : indicative

of love — **am·o·rous·ly** *adv* — **am·o·rous·ness** *n*

amor·phous \ə'mórfəs\ *adj* : shapeless

amor·tize \'amər,tīz, ə'mór-\ *vb* **-tized; -tiz·ing** : get rid of (as a debt) gradually with periodic payments — **amor·ti·za·tion** \,amərtə'zāshən, ə,mórt-\ *n*

amount \ə'maúnt\ *vb* **1** : be equivalent **2** : reach a total ~ *n* : total number or quantity

amour \ə'múr, ä-, a-\ *n* **1** : love affair **2** : lover

am·pere \'am,pir\ *n* : unit of electric current

am·per·sand \'ampər,sand\ *n* : character & used for the word *and*

am·phib·i·ous \am'fibēəs\ *adj* **1** : able to live both on land and in water **2** : adapted for both land and water — **am·phib·i·an** \-ən\ *n*

am·phi·the·ater \'amfə,thēətər\ *n* : oval or circular structure with rising tiers of seats around an arena

am·ple \'ampəl\ *adj* **-pler** \-plər\; **-plest** \-pləst\ **1** : large **2** : sufficient — **am·ply** \-plē\ *adv*

am·pli·fy \'amplə,fī\ *vb* **-fied; -fy·ing** : make louder, stronger, or more thorough — **am·pli·fi·ca·tion** \,ampləfə'kāshən\ *n* — **am·pli·fi·er** \'amplə,fīər\ *n*

am·pli·tude \-,tüd, -,tyüd\ *n* **1** : fullness **2** : extent of a vibratory movement

am·pu·tate \'ampyə,tāt\ *vb* **-tat·ed; -tat·ing** : cut off (a body part) — **am·pu·ta·tion** \,ampyə'tāshən\ *n* — **am·pu·tee** \,ampyə'tē\ *n*

AMOK \ə'mək\ *var of* **AMOK**

am·u·let \'amyələt\ *n* : ornament worn as a charm against evil

amuse \ə'myüz\ *vb* **amused; amus·ing** **1** : engage the attention of in an interesting and pleasant way **2** : make laugh — **amuse·ment** *n*

an \ən, 'an\ *indefinite article* : a — used before words beginning with a vowel sound

-an \ən\, **-ian** \ēən\, **-ean** \ēən\ *n suffix* **1** : one that belongs to **2** : one skilled in ~ *adj suffix* **1** : of or belonging to **2** : characteristic of or resembling

anach·ro·nism \ə'nakrə,nizəm\ *n* : one that is chronologically out of place — **anach·ro·nis·tic** \ə,nakrə-'nistik\ adj

an·a·con·da \anə'kändə\ n : large So. American snake

ana·gram \'anə,gram\ n : word or phrase made by transposing the letters of another word or phrase

anal \'ān³l\ adj : relating to the anus

an·al·ge·sic \an³l'jēzik, -sik\ n : pain reliever

anal·o·gy \ə'naləjē\ n, pl **-gies** 1 : similarity between unlike things 2 : example of something similar — **an·a·log·i·cal** \an³l'äjikəl\ adj — **an·a·log·i·cal·ly** \-iklē\ adv — **anal·o·gous** \ə'naləgəs\ adj

anal·y·sis \ə'naləsəs\ n, pl **-y·ses** \-,sēz\ 1 : examination of a thing to determine its parts 2 : psychoanalysis — **an·a·lyst** \'an³l'ist\ n — **an·a·lyt·ic** \an³l'itik\, **an·a·lyt·i·cal** \-ikəl\ adj — **an·a·lyt·i·cal·ly** \-iklē\ adv

an·a·lyze \'an³l,īz\ vb **-lyzed; -lyz·ing** : make an analysis of

an·ar·chism \'anər,kizəm, -,när-\ n : theory that all government is undesirable — **an·ar·chist** \-kist\ n or adj — **an·ar·chis·tic** \,anər'kistik\ adj

an·ar·chy \'anərkē, -,när-\ n : lack of government or order — **an·ar·chic** \a'närkik\ adj — **an·ar·chi·cal·ly** \-iklē\ adv

anath·e·ma \ə'nathəmə\ n 1 : solemn curse 2 : person or thing accursed or intensely disliked

anat·o·my \ə'natəmē\ n, pl **-mies** : science dealing with the structure of organisms — **an·a·tom·ic** \,anə'tämik\, **an·a·tom·i·cal** \-ikəl\ adj — **an·a·tom·i·cal·ly** adv — **anat·o·mist** \ə'natəmist\ n

-ance \əns\ n suffix 1 : action or process 2 : quality or state 3 : amount or degree

an·ces·tor \'an,sestər\ n : one from whom an individual is descended

an·ces·tress \-trəs\ n : female ancestor

an·ces·try \-trē\ n 1 : line of descent 2 : ancestors — **an·ces·tral** \an-'sestrəl\ adj

an·chor \'aŋkər\ n 1 : heavy device that catches in the sea bottom to hold a ship in place 2 : anchorperson ∼ vb : hold or become held in place by or as if by an anchor — **an·chor·age** \-kərij\ n

an·chor·per·son \'aŋkər,pərsən\ n : news broadcast coordinator

an·cho·vy \'an,chōvē, an'chō-\ n, pl **-vies** or **-vy** : small herringlike fish

an·cient \'ānshənt\ adj 1 : having existed for many years 2 : belonging to times long past — **ancient** n

-ancy \ənsē\ n suffix : quality or state

and \ənd, 'and\ conj — used to indicate connection or addition

and·iron \'an,dīərn\ n : one of 2 metal supports for wood in a fireplace

an·drog·y·nous \an'dräjənəs\ adj 1 : having characteristics of both male and female 2 : suitable for either sex

an·ec·dote \'anik,dōt\ n : brief story — **an·ec·dot·al** \anik'dōt³l\ adj

ane·mia \ə'nēmēə\ n : blood deficiency — **ane·mic** \ə'nēmik\ adj

anem·o·ne \ə'nemənē\ n : small herb with showy usu. white flowers

an·es·the·sia \,anəs'thēzhə\ n : loss of bodily sensation

an·es·thet·ic \,anəs'thetik\ n : agent that produces anesthesia — **anesthetic** adj — **anes·the·tist** \ə'nesthətist\ n — **anes·the·tize** \-thə-,tīz\ vb

an·eu·rysm, an·eu·rism \'anyə-,rizəm\ n : blood-filled bulge of a blood vessel

anew \ə'nü, -'nyü\ adv : over again

an·gel \'ānjəl\ n : spiritual being superior to humans — **an·gel·ic** \an-'jelik\, **an·gel·i·cal** \-ikəl\ adj — **an·gel·i·cal·ly** adv

an·ger \'aŋgər\ n : strong feeling of displeasure ∼ vb : make angry

an·gi·na \an'jīnə\ n : painful disorder of heart muscles — **an·gi·nal** \an'jīn³l\ adj

¹**an·gle** \'aŋgəl\ n 1 : figure formed by the meeting of 2 lines in a point 2 : sharp corner 3 : point of view ∼ vb **-gled; -gling** : turn or direct at an angle

²**angle** vb **an·gled; an·gling** : fish with a hook and line — **an·gler** \-glər\ n — **an·gle·worm** n — **an·gling** n

an·go·ra \aŋ'gōrə, an-\ n : yarn or cloth made from the hair of an Angora goat or rabbit

an·gry \'aŋgrē\ adj **-gri·er; -est** : feeling or showing anger — **an·gri·ly** \-grəlē\ adv

an·guish \'aŋgwish\ n : extreme pain or distress of mind — **an·guished** \-gwisht\ adj

an·gu·lar \'aŋgyələr\ *adj* **1** : having many or sharp angles **2** : thin and bony — **an·gu·lar·i·ty** \ˌaŋgyə'larətē\ *n*

an·i·mal \'anəməl\ *n* **1** : living being capable of feeling and voluntary motion **2** : lower animal as distinguished from humans

an·i·mate \'anəmət\ *adj* : having life ~ \-ˌmāt\ *vb* **-mat·ed; -mat·ing** **1** : give life or vigor to **2** : make appear to move — **an·i·mat·ed** *adj*

an·i·ma·tion \ˌanə'māshən\ *n* **1** : liveliness **2** : animated cartoon

an·i·ma·tron·ic \ˌanəmə'tränik\ *adj* : relating to an electrically animated mechanical figure

an·i·mos·i·ty \ˌanə'mäsətē\ *n, pl* **-ties** : resentment

an·i·mus \'anəməs\ *n* : deep-seated hostility

an·ise \'anəs\ *n* : herb related to the carrot with aromatic seeds (**ani·seed** \-ˌsēd\) used in flavoring

an·kle \'aŋkəl\ *n* : joint or region between the foot and the leg — **an·kle·bone** *n*

an·nals \'anəlz\ *n pl* : chronological record of history — **an·nal·ist** \-°list\ *n*

an·neal \ə'nēl\ *vb* **1** : make less brittle by heating and then cooling **2** : strengthen or toughen

an·nex \ə'neks, 'anˌeks\ *vb* : assume political control over (a territory) ~ \'anˌeks, -iks\ *n* : added building — **an·nex·a·tion** \ˌanˌek'sāshən\ *n*

an·ni·hi·late \ə'nīəˌlāt\ *vb* **-lat·ed; -lat·ing** : destroy — **an·ni·hi·la·tion** \-ˌnīə'lāshən\ *n*

an·ni·ver·sa·ry \ˌanə'vərsərē\ *n, pl* **-ries** : annual return of the date of a notable event or its celebration

an·no·tate \'anəˌtāt\ *vb* **-tat·ed; -tat·ing** : furnish with notes — **an·no·ta·tion** \ˌanə'tāshən\ *n* — **an·no·ta·tor** \'anəˌtātər\ *n*

an·nounce \ə'nauns\ *vb* **-nounced; -nounc·ing** : make known publicly — **an·nounce·ment** *n* — **an·nounc·er** *n*

an·noy \ə'noi\ *vb* : disturb or irritate — **an·noy·ance** \-əns\ *n* — **an·noy·ing·ly** \-'noiiŋlē\ *adv*

an·nu·al \'anyəwəl\ *adj* **1** : occurring once a year **2** : living only one year — **annual** *n* — **an·nu·al·ly** *adv*

an·nu·i·ty \ə'nüətē, -'nyü-\ *n, pl* **-ties**

: amount payable annually or the right to such a payment

an·nul \ə'nəl\ *vb* **-ll-** : make legally void — **an·nul·ment** *n*

an·ode \'anˌōd\ *n* **1** : positive electrode **2** : negative battery terminal — **an·od·ic** \a'nädik\ *adj*

anoint \ə'nóint\ *vb* : apply oil to as a rite — **anoint·ment** *n*

anom·a·ly \ə'näməlē\ *n, pl* **-lies** : something abnormal or unusual — **anom·a·lous** \ə'nämələs\ *adj*

anon·y·mous \ə'nänəməs\ *adj* : of unknown origin — **ano·nym·i·ty** \ˌanə'nimətē\ *n* — **anon·y·mous·ly** *adv*

an·oth·er \ə'nəthər\ *adj* **1** : any or some other **2** : one more ~ *pron* **1** : one more **2** : one different

an·swer \'ansər\ *n* **1** : something spoken or written in reply to a question **2** : solution to a problem ~ *vb* **1** : reply to **2** : be responsible **3** : be adequate — **an·swer·er** *n*

an·swer·able \-rəbəl\ *adj* : responsible

ant \'ant\ *n* : small social insect — **ant·hill** *n*

-ant \ənt\ *n suffix* **1** : one that performs or causes an action **2** : thing that is acted upon ~ *adj suffix* **1** : performing an action or being in a condition **2** : causing an action or process

ant·ac·id \ant'asəd\ *n* : agent that counteracts acidity

an·tag·o·nism \an'tagəˌnizəm\ *n* : active opposition or hostility — **an·tag·o·nist** \-ənist\ *n* — **an·tag·o·nis·tic** \-ˌtagə'nistik\ *adj*

an·tag·o·nize \an'tagəˌnīz\ *vb* **-nized; -niz·ing** : cause to be hostile

ant·arc·tic \ant'ärktik, -'ärtik\ *adj* : relating to the region near the south pole

antarctic circle *n* : circle parallel to the equator approximately 23°27' from the south pole

an·te·bel·lum \ˌanti'beləm\ *adj* : existing before the U.S. Civil War

an·te·ced·ent \ˌantə'sēd°nt\ *n* : one that comes before — **antecedent** *adj*

an·te·lope \'ant°lˌōp\ *n, pl* **-lope** or **-lopes** : deerlike mammal related to the ox

an·ten·na \an'tenə\ *n, pl* **-nae** \-ˌnē\ or **-nas** **1** : one of the long slender paired sensory organs on the head of an arthropod **2** *pl* **-nas** : metallic device for sending or receiving radio waves

an·te·ri·or \an'tirēǝr\ *adj* : located before in place or time

an·them \'anthǝm\ *n* : song or hymn of praise or gladness

an·ther \'anthǝr\ *n* : part of a seed plant that contains pollen

an·thol·o·gy \an'thäləjē\ *n, pl* **-gies** : literary collection

an·thra·cite \'anthrǝ,sīt\ *n* : hard coal

an·thro·poid \'anthrǝ,pȯid\ *n* : large ape — **anthropoid** *adj*

an·thro·pol·o·gy \,anthrǝ'pälǝjē\ *n* : science dealing with humans — **an·thro·po·log·i·cal** \-pǝ'läjikǝl\ *adj* — **an·thro·pol·o·gist** \-'pälǝjist\ *n*

anti- \,antē, -,tī\ *or* **ant-**, *or* **anth-** *prefix* **1** : opposite in kind, position, or action **2** : opposing or hostile toward **3** : defending against **4** : curing or treating

an·ti·bi·ot·ic \,antēbī'ätik, -bē-\ *n* : substance that inhibits harmful microorganisms — **antibiotic** *adj*

an·ti·body \'anti,bädē\ *n* : bodily substance that counteracts the effects of a foreign substance or organism

an·tic \'antik\ *n* : playful act ~ *adj* : playful

an·tic·i·pate \an'tisǝ,pāt\ *vb* **-pat·ed; -pat·ing 1** : be prepared for **2** : look forward to — **an·tic·i·pa·tion** \-,tisǝ'pāshǝn\ *n* — **an·tic·i·pa·to·ry** \-'tisǝpǝ,tōrē\ *adj*

an·ti·cli·max \,antē'klī,maks\ *n* : something strikingly less important than what has preceded it — **an·ti·cli·mac·tic** \-klī'maktik\ *adj*

an·ti·dote \'anti,dōt\ *n* : remedy for poison

an·ti·freeze \'anti,frēz\ *n* : substance to prevent a liquid from freezing

an·ti·his·ta·mine \,anti'histǝ,mēn\ *n* : drug for treating allergies and colds

an·ti·mo·ny \'antǝ,mōnē\ *n* : brittle white metallic chemical element

an·tip·a·thy \an'tipǝthē\ *n, pl* **-thies** : strong dislike

---

List of self-explanatory words with the prefix anti-

antiabortion	anticigarette	antifatigue
antiacademic	anticlerical	antifemale
antiadministration	anticollision	antifeminine
antiaggression	anticolonial	antifeminism
antiaircraft	anticommunism	antifeminist
antialien	anticommunist	antifertility
antiapartheid	anticonservation	antiforeign
antiaristocratic	anticonservationist	antiforeigner
antiart	anticonsumer	antifraud
antiauthoritarian	anticonventional	antigambling
antiauthority	anticorrosion	antiglare
antibacterial	anticorrosive	antigovernment
antibias	anticorruption	antiguerrilla
antiblack	anticrime	antigun
antibourgeois	anticruelty	antihijack
antiboycott	anticult	antihomosexual
antibureaucratic	anticultural	antihuman
antiburglar	antidandruff	antihumanism
antiburglary	antidemocratic	antihumanistic
antibusiness	antidiscrimination	antihunting
anticancer	antidrug	anti–imperialism
anticapitalism	antidumping	anti–imperialist
anticapitalist	antiestablishment	anti–inflation
anti–Catholic	antievolution	anti–inflationary
anticensorship	antievolutionary	anti–institutional
anti–Christian	antifamily	anti–integration
anti–Christianity	antifascism	anti–intellectual
antichurch	antifascist	anti–intellectualism

an·ti·quar·i·an \\,antə'kwerēən\\ *adj*
: relating to antiquities or old books
— **antiquarian** *n*

an·ti·quary \\'antə,kwerē\\ *n, pl* **-quar·ies** : one who collects or studies
antiquities

an·ti·quat·ed \\'antə,kwātəd\\ *adj* : out-
of-date

an·tique \\an'tēk\\ *adj* : very old or out-
of-date — **antique** *n*

an·tiq·ui·ty \\an'tikwətē\\ *n, pl* **-ties 1**
: ancient times **2** *pl* : relics of ancient
times

an·ti·sep·tic \\,antə'septik\\ *adj* : killing
or checking the growth of germs —
antiseptic *n* — **an·ti·sep·ti·cal·ly**
\\-tiklē\\ *adv*

an·tith·e·sis \\an'tithəsəs\\ *n, pl* **-e·ses**
\\-,sēz\\ : direct opposite

ant·ler \\'antlər\\ *n* : solid branched
horn of a deer — **ant·lered** \\-lərd\\ *adj*

ant·onym \\'antə,nim\\ *n* : word of opposite meaning

anus \\'ānəs\\ *n* : the rear opening of the
alimentary canal

an·vil \\'anvəl\\ *n* : heavy iron block on
which metal is shaped

anx·i·ety \\aŋ'zīətē\\ *n, pl* **-eties** : uneasiness usu. over an expected misfortune

anx·ious \\'aŋkshəs\\ *adj* **1** : uneasy **2**
: earnestly wishing — **anx·ious·ly**
adv

any \\'enē\\ *adj* **1** : one chosen at random **2** : of whatever number or quantity ~ *pron* **1** : any one or ones **2**
: any amount ~ *adv* : to any extent or
degree

any·body \\-bədē, -,bäd-\\ *pron* : anyone

any·how \\-,haù\\ *adv* **1** : in any way **2**
: nevertheless

any·more \\,enē'mōr\\ *adv* : at the present time

any·one \\-'enē,wən\\ *pron* : any person

any·place *adv* : anywhere

any·thing *pron* : any thing whatever

any·time *adv* : at any time whatever

any·way *adv* : anyhow

---

antijamming	antiprofiteering	antisuicide
anti–Jewish	antiprogressive	antitank
antilabor	antiprostitution	antitax
antiliberal	antirabies	antitechnological
antiliberalism	antiracketeering	antitechnology
antilitter	antiradical	antiterrorism
antilittering	antirape	antiterrorist
antilynching	antirealism	antitheft
antimale	antirecession	antitobacco
antimanagement	antireform	antitotalitarian
antimaterialism	antireligious	antitoxin
antimaterialist	antirevolutionary	antitraditional
antimicrobial	antiriot	antitrust
antimilitarism	antiromantic	antituberculosis
antimilitarist	antirust	antitumor
antimilitary	antisegregation	antityphoid
antimiscegenation	antisex	antiulcer
antimonopolist	antisexist	antiunemployment
antimonopoly	antisexual	antiunion
antimosquito	antishoplifting	antiuniversity
antinoise	antislavery	antiurban
antiobesity	antismoking	antiviolence
antiobscenity	antismuggling	antiviral
antipapal	antismut	antivivisection
antipersonnel	antispending	antiwar
antipolice	antistrike	anti–West
antipollution	antistudent	anti–Western
antipornographic	antisubmarine	antiwhite
antipornography	antisubversion	antiwoman
antipoverty	antisubversive	

any·where adv : in or to any place

aor·ta \ā'ortə\ n, pl **-tas** or **-tae** \-ē\ : main artery from the heart — **aor·tic** \ā'ortik\ adj

apart \ə'pärt\ adv **1** : separately in place or time **2** : aside **3** : to pieces

apart·heid \ə'pär,tāt, -,tīt\ n : racial segregation

apart·ment \ə'pärtmənt\ n : set of usu. rented rooms

ap·a·thy \'apəthē\ n : lack of emotion or interest — **ap·a·thet·ic** \,apə-'thetik\ adj — **ap·a·thet·i·cal·ly** \-iklē\ adv

ape \'āp\ n : large tailless primate ∼ vb **aped**; **ap·ing** : imitate

ap·er·ture \'apər,chur, -chər\ n : opening

apex \'ā,peks\ n, pl **apex·es** or **api·ces** \'āpə,sēz, 'apə-\ : highest point

aphid \'āfid, 'a-\ n : small insect that sucks plant juices

aph·o·rism \'afə,rizəm\ n : short saying stating a general truth — **aph·o·ris·tic** \,afə'ristik\ adj

aph·ro·di·si·ac \,afrə'dēzē,ak, 'diz-\ n : substance that excites sexual desire

api·a·rist \'āpēərist\ n : beekeeper — **api·ary** \-pē,erē\ n

apiece \ə'pēs\ adv : for each one

aplen·ty \ə'plentē\ adj : plentiful or abundant

aplomb \ə'pläm, -'pləm\ n : complete calmness or self-assurance

apoc·a·lypse \ə'päkə,lips\ n : writing prophesying a cataclysm in which evil forces are destroyed — **apoc·a·lyp·tic** \-,päkə'liptik\ adj

apoc·ry·pha \ə'päkrəfə\ n : writings of dubious authenticity — **apoc·ry·phal** \-fəl\ adj

apol·o·get·ic \ə,pälə'jetik\ adj : expressing apology — **apol·o·get·i·cal·ly** \-iklē\ adv

apol·o·gize \ə'pälə,jīz\ vb **-gized**; **-giz·ing** : make an apology — **apol·o·gist** \-jist\ n

apol·o·gy \ə'päləjē\ n, pl **-gies 1** : formal justification **2** : expression of regret for a wrong

apo·plexy \'apə,pleksē\ n : sudden loss of consciousness caused by rupture or obstruction of an artery of the brain — **apo·plec·tic** \,apə'plek·tik\ adj

apos·ta·sy \ə'pästəsē\ n, pl **-sies** : abandonment of a former loyalty — **apos·tate** \ə'päs,tāt\ adj or n

apos·tle \ə'päsəl\ n : disciple or advocate — **apos·tle·ship** n — **ap·os·tol·ic** \,apə'stälik\ adj

apos·tro·phe \ə'pästrə,fē\ n : punctuation mark ' to indicate the possessive case or the omission of a letter or figure

apoth·e·cary \ə'päthə,kerē\ n, pl **-car·ies** : druggist

ap·pall \ə'pol\ vb : fill with horror or dismay

ap·pa·ra·tus \,apə'ratəs, -'rāt-\ n, pl **-tus·es** or **-tus 1** : equipment **2** : complex machine or device

ap·par·el \ə'parəl\ n : clothing

ap·par·ent \ə'parənt\ adj **1** : visible **2** : obvious **3** : seeming — **ap·par·ent·ly** adv

ap·pa·ri·tion \,apə'rishən\ n : ghost

ap·peal \ə'pēl\ vb **1** : try to have a court case reheard **2** : ask earnestly **3** : have an attraction — **appeal** n

ap·pear \ə'pir\ vb **1** : become visible or evident **2** : come into the presence of someone **3** : seem

ap·pear·ance \ə'pirəns\ n **1** : act of appearing **2** : outward aspect

ap·pease \ə'pēz\ vb **-peased**; **-peas·ing** : pacify with concessions — **ap·pease·ment** n

ap·pel·late \ə'pelət\ adj : having power to review decisions

ap·pend \ə'pend\ vb : attach

ap·pend·age \ə'pendij\ n : something attached

ap·pen·dec·to·my \,apən'dektəmē\ n, pl **-mies** : surgical removal of the appendix

ap·pen·di·ci·tis \ə,pendə'sītəs\ n : inflammation of the appendix

ap·pen·dix \ə'pendiks\ n, pl **-dix·es** or **-di·ces** \-də,sēz\ **1** : supplementary matter **2** : narrow closed tube extending from lower right intestine

ap·pe·tite \'apə,tīt\ n **1** : natural desire esp. for food **2** : preference

ap·pe·tiz·er \-,tīzər\ n : food or drink to stimulate the appetite

ap·pe·tiz·ing \-ziŋ\ adj : tempting to the appetite — **ap·pe·tiz·ing·ly** adv

ap·plaud \ə'plod\ vb : show approval esp. by clapping

ap·plause \ə'ploz\ n : a clapping in approval

ap·ple \'apəl\ *n* : rounded fruit with firm white flesh

ap·ple·jack \-,jak\ *n* : brandy made from cider

ap·pli·ance \ə'plīəns\ *n* : household machine or device

ap·pli·ca·ble \'aplikəbəl, ə'plikə-\ *adj* : capable of being applied — **ap·pli·ca·bil·i·ty** \,aplikə'bilətē, ə,plikə-\ *n*

ap·pli·cant \'aplikənt\ *n* : one who applies

ap·pli·ca·tion \,aplə'kāshən\ *n* 1 : act of applying or thing applied 2 : constant attention 3 : request 4 : computer program that performs a major task

ap·pli·ca·tor \'aplə,kātər\ *n* : device for applying a substance

ap·pli·qué \,aplə'kā\ *n* : cut-out fabric decoration — **appliqué** *vb*

ap·ply \ə'plī\ *vb* -plied; -ply·ing 1 : place in contact 2 : put to practical use 3 : devote (one's) attention or efforts to something 4 : submit a request 5 : have reference or a connection

ap·point \ə'pȯint\ *vb* 1 : set or assign officially 2 : equip or furnish — **ap·poin·tee** \ə,pȯin'tē, ,a-\ *n*

ap·point·ment \ə'pȯintmənt\ *n* 1 : act of appointing 2 : nonelective political job 3 : arrangement for a meeting

ap·por·tion \ə'pȯrshən\ *vb* : distribute proportionally — **ap·por·tion·ment** *n*

ap·po·site \'apəzət\ *adj* : suitable — **ap·po·site·ly** *adv* — **ap·po·site·ness** *n*

ap·praise \ə'prāz\ *vb* -praised; -prais·ing : set value on — **ap·prais·al** \-'prāzəl\ *n* — **ap·prais·er** *n*

ap·pre·cia·ble \ə'prēshəbəl\ *adj* : considerable — **ap·pre·cia·bly** \-blē\ *adv*

ap·pre·ci·ate \ə'prēshē,āt\ *vb* -ated; -at·ing 1 : value justly 2 : be grateful for 3 : increase in value — **ap·pre·cia·tion** \-,prēshē'āshən\ *n*

ap·pre·cia·tive \ə'prēshətiv, -shē,āt-\ *adj* : showing appreciation

ap·pre·hend \,apri'hend\ *vb* 1 : arrest 2 : look forward to in dread 3 : understand — **ap·pre·hen·sion** \-'henchən\ *n*

ap·pre·hen·sive \-'hensiv\ *adj* : fearful — **ap·pre·hen·sive·ly** *adv* — **ap·pre·hen·sive·ness** *n*

ap·pren·tice \ə'prentəs\ *n* : person learning a craft ~ *vb* -ticed; -tic·ing : employ or work as an apprentice — **ap·pren·tice·ship** *n*

ap·prise \ə'prīz\ *vb* -prised; -pris·ing : inform

ap·proach \ə'prōch\ *vb* 1 : move nearer or be close to 2 : make initial advances or efforts toward — **approach** *n* — **ap·proach·able** *adj*

ap·pro·ba·tion \,aprə'bāshən\ *n* : approval

ap·pro·pri·ate \ə'prōprē,āt\ *vb* -at·ed; -at·ing 1 : take possession of 2 : set apart for a particular use ~ \-prēət\ *adj* : suitable — **ap·pro·pri·ate·ly** *adv* — **ap·pro·pri·ate·ness** *n* — **ap·pro·pri·a·tion** \ə,prōprē'āshən\ *n*

ap·prov·al \ə'prüvəl\ *n* : act of approving

ap·prove \ə'prüv\ *vb* -proved; -prov·ing : accept as satisfactory

ap·prox·i·mate \ə'präksəmət\ *adj* : nearly correct or exact ~ \-,māt\ *vb* -mat·ed; -mat·ing : come near — **ap·prox·i·mate·ly** *adv* — **ap·prox·i·ma·tion** \-,präksə'māshən\ *n*

ap·pur·te·nance \ə'pərtnəns\ *n* : accessory — **ap·pur·te·nant** \-'pərtnənt\ *adj*

apri·cot \'aprə,kät, 'ā-\ *n* : peachlike fruit

April \'āprəl\ *n* : 4th month of the year having 30 days

apron \'āprən\ *n* : protective garment

ap·ro·pos \,aprə'pō, 'aprə,pō\ *adv* : suitably ~ *adj* : being to the point

apropos of *prep* : with regard to

apt \'apt\ *adj* 1 : suitable 2 : likely 3 : quick to learn — **apt·ly** *adv* — **apt·ness** *n*

ap·ti·tude \'aptə,tüd, -tyüd\ *n* 1 : capacity for learning 2 : natural ability

aqua \'akwə, 'äk-\ *n* : light greenish blue color

aquar·i·um \ə'kwarēəm\ *n*, *pl* -i·ums *or* -ia \-ēə\ : glass container for aquatic animals and plants

aquat·ic \ə'kwätik, -'kwat-\ *adj* : of or relating to water — **aquatic** *n*

aq·ue·duct \'akwə,dəkt\ *n* : conduit for carrying running water

aqui·line \'akwə,līn, -lən\ *adj* : curved like an eagle's beak

-ar \ər\ *adj suffix* **1** : of, relating to, or being **2** : resembling

ar·a·besque \ˌarə'besk\ *n* : intricate design

ar·a·ble \'arəbəl\ *adj* : fit for crops

ar·bi·ter \'ärbətər\ *n* : final authority

ar·bi·trary \'ärbəˌtrerē\ *adj* **1** : selected at random **2** : autocratic — **ar·bi·trari·ly** \ˌärbə'trerəlē\ *adv* — **ar·bi·trari·ness** \'ärbəˌtrerēnəs\ *n*

ar·bi·trate \'ärbəˌtrāt\ *vb* **-trat·ed; -trat·ing** : settle a dispute as arbitrator — **ar·bi·tra·tion** \ˌärbə'trāshən\ *n*

ar·bi·tra·tor \'ärbəˌtrātər\ *n* : one chosen to settle a dispute

ar·bor \'ärbər\ *n* : shelter under branches or vines

ar·bo·re·al \är'bōrēəl\ *adj* : living in trees

arc \'ärk\ *n* **1** : part of a circle **2** : bright sustained electrical discharge ∼ *vb* **arced** \'ärkt\; **arc·ing** \'ärkiŋ\ : form an arc

ar·cade \är'kād\ *n* : arched passageway between shops

ar·cane \är'kān\ *adj* : mysterious or secret

¹arch \'ärch\ *n* : curved structure spanning an opening ∼ *vb* : cover with or form into an arch

²arch *adj* **1** : chief — usu. in combination **2** : mischievous — **arch·ly** *adv* — **arch·ness** *n*

ar·chae·ol·o·gy, ar·che·ol·o·gy \ˌärkē'äləjē\ *n* : study of past human life — **ar·chae·o·log·i·cal** \-kēə'läjikəl\ *adj* — **ar·chae·ol·o·gist** \-kē-'äləjist\ *n*

ar·cha·ic \är'kāik\ *adj* : belonging to an earlier time — **ar·cha·i·cal·ly** \-iklē\ *adv*

arch·an·gel \'ärkˌānjəl\ *n* : angel of high rank

arch·bish·op \ärch'bishəp\ *n* : chief bishop — **arch·bish·op·ric** \-ə,prik\ *n*

arch·di·o·cese \-'dīəsəs, -ˌsēz, -ˌsēs\ *n* : diocese of an archbishop

ar·chery \'ärchərē\ *n* : shooting with bow and arrows — **ar·cher** \-chər\ *n*

ar·che·type \'ärkiˌtīp\ *n* : original pattern or model

ar·chi·pel·a·go \ˌärkə'peləˌgō, ˌärchə-\ *n, pl* **-goes** *or* **-gos** : group of islands

ar·chi·tect \'ärkəˌtekt\ *n* : building designer

ar·chi·tec·ture \'ärkəˌtekchər\ *n* **1**

: building design **2** : style of building **3** : manner of organizing elements — **ar·chi·tec·tur·al** \ˌärkə'tekchərəl, -'tekshrəl\ *adj* — **ar·chi·tec·tur·al·ly** *adv*

ar·chives \'ärˌkīvz\ *n pl* : public records or their storage place — **archi·vist** \'ärkəvist, -ˌkī-\ *n*

arch·way *n* : passageway under an arch

arc·tic \'ärktik, 'ärt-\ *adj* **1** : relating to the region near the north pole **2** : frigid

arctic circle *n* : circle parallel to the equator approximately 23°27' from the north pole

-ard \ərd\ *n suffix* : one that is

ar·dent \'ärd³nt\ *adj* : characterized by warmth of feeling — **ar·dent·ly** *adv*

ar·dor \'ärdər\ *n* : warmth of feeling

ar·du·ous \'ärjəwəs\ *adj* : difficult — **ar·du·ous·ly** *adv* — **ar·du·ous·ness** *n*

are *pres 2d sing or pres pl of* BE

ar·ea \'arēə\ *n* **1** : space for something **2** : amount of surface included **3** : region **4** : range covered by a thing or concept

area code *n* : 3-digit area-identifying telephone number

are·na \ə'rēnə\ *n* **1** : enclosed exhibition area **2** : sphere of activity

ar·gon \'ärˌgän\ *n* : colorless odorless gaseous chemical element

ar·got \'ärgət, -ˌgō\ *n* : special language (as of the underworld)

argu·able \'ärgyəwəbəl\ *adj* : open to dispute

ar·gue \'ärgyü\ *vb* **-gued; -gu·ing 1** : give reasons for or against something **2** : disagree in words

ar·gu·ment \'ärgyəmənt\ *n* **1** : reasons given to persuade **2** : dispute with words

ar·gu·men·ta·tive \ˌärgyə'mentətiv\ *adj* : inclined to argue

ar·gyle \'ärˌgīl\ *n* : colorful diamond pattern in knitting

aria \'ärēə\ *n* : opera solo

ar·id \'arəd\ *adj* : very dry — **arid·i·ty** \ə'ridətē\ *n*

arise \ə'rīz\ *vb* **arose** \-'rōz\; **aris·en** \-'riz³n\; **aris·ing** \-'rīziŋ\ **1** : get up **2** : originate

ar·is·toc·ra·cy \ˌarə'stäkrəsē\ *n, pl* **-cies** : upper class — **aris·to·crat** \ə'ristəˌkrat\ *n* — **aris·to·crat·ic** \ə,ristə'kratik\ *adj*

arith·me·tic \ə'rithməˌtik\ *n* : mathematics that deals with numbers — **ar·ith·met·ic** \ˌarith'metik\, **ar·ith·met·i·cal** \-ikəl\ *adj*

ark \ärk\ *n* : big boat

¹arm \ärm\ *n* **1** : upper limb **2** : branch — **armed** \ärmd\ *adj* — **arm·less** *adj*

²arm *vb* : furnish with weapons ∼ *n* **1** : weapon **2** : branch of the military forces **3** *pl* : family's heraldic designs

ar·ma·da \är'mädə, -'mäd-\ *n* : naval fleet

ar·ma·dil·lo \ˌärmə'dilō\ *n, pl* **-los** : burrowing mammal covered with bony plates

ar·ma·ment \'ärməmənt\ *n* : military arms and equipment

ar·ma·ture \'ärmə,chúr, -chər\ *n* : rotating part of an electric generator or motor

armed forces *n pl* : military

ar·mi·stice \'ärməstəs\ *n* : truce

ar·mor \'ärmər\ *n* : protective covering — **ar·mored** \-mərd\ *adj*

ar·mory \'ärmərē\ *n, pl* **-mor·ies** : factory or storehouse for arms

arm·pit *n* : hollow under the junction of the arm and shoulder

ar·my \'ärmē\ *n, pl* **-mies** **1** : body of men organized for war esp. on land **2** : great number

aro·ma \ə'rōmə\ *n* : usu. pleasing odor — **ar·o·mat·ic** \ˌarə'matik\ *adj*

around \ə'raúnd\ *adv* **1** : in or along a circuit **2** : on all sides **3** : near **4** : in an opposite direction ∼ *prep* **1** : surrounding **2** : along the circuit of **3** : to or on the other side of **4** : near

arouse \ə'raúz\ *vb* **aroused; arous·ing** **1** : awaken from sleep **2** : stir up — **arous·al** \-'raúzəl\ *n*

ar·raign \ə'rān\ *vb* **1** : call before a court to answer to an indictment **2** : accuse — **ar·raign·ment** *n*

ar·range \ə'rānj\ *vb* **-ranged; -rang·ing** **1** : put in order **2** : settle or agree on **3** : adapt (a musical composition) for voices or instruments — **ar·range·ment** *n* — **ar·rang·er** *n*

ar·ray \ə'rā\ *vb* **1** : arrange in order **2** : dress esp. splendidly ∼ *n* **1** : arrangement **2** : rich clothing **3** : imposing group

ar·rears \ə'rirz\ *n pl* : state of being behind in paying debts

ar·rest \ə'rest\ *vb* **1** : stop **2** : take into legal custody — **arrest** *n*

ar·rive \ə'rīv\ *vb* **-rived; -riv·ing** **1** :

reach a destination, point, or stage **2** : come near in time — **ar·riv·al** \-əl\ *n*

ar·ro·gant \'arəgənt\ *adj* : showing an offensive sense of superiority — **ar·ro·gance** \-gəns\ *n* — **ar·ro·gant·ly** *adv*

ar·ro·gate \-,gāt\ *vb* **-gat·ed; -gat·ing** : to claim without justification

ar·row \'arō\ *n* : slender missile shot from a bow — **ar·row·head** *n*

ar·royo \ə'róiō, -ə\ *n, pl* **-royos** **1** : watercourse **2** : gully

ar·se·nal \'ärsᵊnəl\ *n* **1** : place where arms are made or stored **2** : store

ar·se·nic \'ärsᵊnik\ *n* : solid grayish poisonous chemical element

ar·son \'ärsᵊn\ *n* : willful or malicious burning of property — **ar·son·ist** \-ist\ *n*

art \ärt\ *n* **1** : skill **2** : branch of learning **3** : creation of things of beauty or works so produced **4** : ingenuity

ar·te·rio·scle·ro·sis \ärˌtirēōsklə'rōsəs\ *n* : hardening of the arteries — **ar·te·rio·scle·rot·ic** \-'rätik\ *adj or n*

ar·tery \'ärtərē\ *n, pl* **-ter·ies** **1** : tubular vessel carrying blood from the heart **2** : thoroughfare — **ar·te·ri·al** \är'tirēəl\ *adj*

art·ful \-fəl\ *adj* **1** : ingenious **2** : crafty — **art·ful·ly** *adv* — **art·ful·ness** *n*

ar·thri·tis \är'thrītəs\ *n, pl* **-ti·des** \-'thritə,dēz\ : inflammation of the joints — **ar·thrit·ic** \-'thritik\ *adj or n*

ar·thro·pod \'ärthrə,päd\ *n* : invertebrate animal (as an insect or crab) with segmented body and jointed limbs — **arthropod** *adj*

ar·ti·choke \'ärtə,chōk\ *n* : tall thistlelike herb or its edible flower head

ar·ti·cle \'ärtikəl\ *n* **1** : distinct part of a written document **2** : nonfictional published piece of writing **3** : word (as *an, the*) used to limit a noun **4** : item or piece

ar·tic·u·late \är'tikyələt\ *adj* : able to speak effectively ∼ \-,lāt\ *vb* **-lated; -lat·ing** **1** : utter distinctly **2** : unite by joints — **ar·tic·u·late·ly** *adv* — **ar·tic·u·late·ness** *n* — **ar·tic·u·la·tion** \-,tikyə'lāshən\ *n*

ar·ti·fact \'ärtə,fakt\ *n* : object of esp. prehistoric human workmanship

ar·ti·fice \'ärtəfəs\ *n* **1** : trick or trickery **2** : ingenious device or ingenuity

ar·ti·fi·cial \,ärtə'fishəl\ *adj* **1** : manmade **2** : not genuine — **ar·ti·fi·ci·al·i·ty** \-,fishē'alətē\ *n* — **ar·ti·fi·cial·ly** *adv* — **ar·ti·fi·cial·ness** *n*

ar·til·lery \är'tilərē\ *n, pl* **-ler·ies** : large caliber firearms

ar·ti·san \'ärtəzən, -sən\ *n* : skilled craftsman

art·ist \'ärtist\ *n* : one who creates art — **ar·tis·tic** \är'tistik\ *adj* — **ar·tis·ti·cal·ly** \-iklē\ *adv* — **ar·tist·ry** \'ärtəstrē\ *n*

art·less \'ärtləs\ *adj* : sincere or natural — **art·less·ly** *adv* — **art·less·ness** *n*

arty \'ärtē\ *adj* **art·i·er; -est** : pretentiously artistic — **art·i·ly** \'ärt'lē\ *adv* — **art·i·ness** *n*

-ary \,erē\ *adj suffix* : of, relating to, or connected with

as \əz, ,az\ *adv* **1** : to the same degree **2** : for example ～ *conj* **1** : in the same way or degree as **2** : while **3** : because **4** : though ～ *pron* — used after *same* or *such* ～ *prep* : in the capacity of

as·bes·tos \as'bestəs, az-\ *n* : fibrous incombustible mineral

as·cend \ə'send\ *vb* : move upward — **as·cen·sion** \-'senchən\ *n*

as·cen·dan·cy \ə'sendənsē\ *n* : domination

as·cen·dant \ə'sendənt\ *n* : dominant position ～ *adj* **1** : moving upward **2** : dominant

as·cent \ə'sent\ *n* **1** : act of moving upward **2** : degree of upward slope

as·cer·tain \,asər'tān\ *vb* : determine — **as·cer·tain·able** *adj*

as·cet·ic \ə'setik\ *adj* : self-denying — **ascetic** *n* — **as·cet·i·cism** \-'setə,sizəm\ *n*

as·cribe \ə'skrīb\ *vb* **-cribed; -crib·ing** : attribute — **as·crib·able** *adj* — **as·crip·tion** \-'skripshən\ *n*

asep·tic \ā'septik\ *adj* : free of disease germs

¹ash \'ash\ *n* : tree related to the olives

²ash *n* : matter left when something is burned — **ash·tray** *n*

ashamed \ə'shāmd\ *adj* : feeling shame — **asham·ed·ly** \-'shāmədlē\ *adv*

ash·en \'ashən\ *adj* : deadly pale

ashore \ə'shōr\ *adv* : on or to the shore

aside \ə'sīd\ *adv* **1** : toward the side **2** : out of the way

aside from *prep* **1** : besides **2** : except for

as·i·nine \'as²n,īn\ *adj* : foolish — **as·i·nin·i·ty** \,as²n'inətē\ *n*

ask \'ask\ *vb* **1** : call on for an answer or help **2** : utter (a question or request) **3** : invite

askance \ə'skans\ *adv* **1** : with a side glance **2** : with mistrust

askew \ə'skyü\ *adv or adj* : out of line

asleep \ə'slēp\ *adv or adj* **1** : sleeping **2** : numbed **3** : inactive

as long as *conj* **1** : on condition that **2** : because

as of *prep* : from the time of

as·par·a·gus \ə'sparəgəs\ *n* : tall herb related to the lilies or its edible stalks

as·pect \'as,pekt\ *n* **1** : way something looks to the eye or mind **2** : phase

as·pen \'aspən\ *n* : poplar

as·per·i·ty \a'sperətē. ə-\ *n, pl* **-ties** **1** : roughness **2** : harshness

as·per·sion \ə'spərzhən\ *n* : remark that hurts someone's reputation

as·phalt \'as,folt\ *n* : dark tarlike substance used in paving

as·phyx·ia \as'fiksēə\ *n* : lack of oxygen causing unconsciousness

as·phyx·i·ate \-sē,āt\ *vb* **-at·ed; -at·ing** : suffocate — **as·phyx·i·a·tion** \-,fiksē'āshən\ *n*

as·pi·ra·tion \,aspə'rāshən\ *n* : strong desire to achieve a goal

as·pire \ə'spīr\ *vb* **-pired; -pir·ing** : have an ambition — **as·pir·ant** \'aspərənt, ə'spīrənt\ *n*

as·pi·rin \'asprən\ *n, pl* **aspirin** *or* **as·pirins** : pain reliever

ass \'as\ *n* **1** : long-eared animal related to the horse **2** : stupid person

as·sail \ə'sāl\ *vb* : attack violently — **as·sail·able** *adj* — **as·sail·ant** *n*

as·sas·si·nate \ə'sas²n,āt\ *vb* **-nat·ed; -nat·ing** : murder esp. for political reasons — **as·sas·sin** \-'sas²n\ *n* — **as·sas·si·na·tion** \-,sas²n'āshən\ *n*

as·sault \ə'solt\ *n or vb* : attack

as·say \'as,ā, a'sā\ *n* : analysis (as of an ore) to determine quality or properties — **as·say** \a'sā, 'as,ā\ *vb*

as·sem·ble \ə'sembəl\ *vb* **-bled; -bling** **1** : collect into one place **2** : fit together the parts of

as·sem·bly \-blē\ *n, pl* **-blies** **1** : meeting **2** *cap* : legislative body **3** : a fitting together of parts

as·sem·bly·man \-mən\ n : member of a legislative assembly

as·sem·bly·wom·an \-ˌwu̇-mən\ n : woman who is a member of a legislative assembly

as·sent \ə'sent\ vb or n : consent

as·sert \ə'sərt\ vb 1 : declare 2 : defend — **as·ser·tion** \-'sərshən\ n — **as·ser·tive** \-'sərtiv\ adj — **as·sert·ive·ness** n

as·sess \ə'ses\ vb 1 : impose (as a tax) 2 : evaluate for taxation — **as·sess·ment** n — **as·ses·sor** \-ər-\ n

as·set \'asˌet\ n 1 pl : individually owned property 2 : advantage or resource

as·sid·u·ous \ə'sijəwəs\ adj : diligent — **as·si·du·i·ty** \ˌasə'düətē, -'dyü-\ n — **as·sid·u·ous·ly** adv — **as·sid·u·ous·ness** n

as·sign \ə'sīn\ vb 1 : transfer to another 2 : appoint to a duty 3 : designate as a task 4 : attribute — **as·sign·able** adj — **as·sign·ment** n

as·sim·i·late \ə'simə,lāt\ vb -lat·ed; -lat·ing 1 : absorb as nourishment 2 : understand — **as·sim·i·la·tion** \-ˌsimə'lāshən\ n

as·sist \ə'sist\ vb : help — **assist** n — **as·sis·tance** \-'sistəns\ n — **as·sis·tant** \-tənt\ n

as·so·ci·ate \ə'sōshē,āt, -sē-\ vb -at·ed; -at·ing 1 : join in companionship or partnership 2 : connect in thought — **as·so·ci·ate** \-shēət, -sēət\ n — **as·so·ci·a·tion** \-ˌsōshē'āshən, -sē-\ n

as soon as conj : when

as·sort·ed \ə'sòrtəd\ adj : consisting of various kinds

as·sort·ment \-mənt\ n : assorted collection

as·suage \ə'swāj\ vb -suaged; -suag·ing : ease or satisfy

as·sume \ə'süm\ vb -sumed; -sum·ing 1 : take upon oneself 2 : pretend to have or be 3 : take as true

as·sump·tion \ə'səmpshən\ n : something assumed

as·sure \ə'shu̇r\ vb -sured; -sur·ing 1 : give confidence or conviction to 2 : guarantee — **as·sur·ance** \-əns\ n

as·ter \'astər\ n : herb with daisylike flowers

as·ter·isk \'astə,risk\ n : a character * used as a reference mark or as an indication of omission of words

astern \ə'stərn\ adv or adj 1 : behind 2 : at or toward the stern

as·ter·oid \'astə,ròid\ n : small planet between Mars and Jupiter

asth·ma \'azmə\ n : disorder marked by difficulty in breathing — **asth·mat·ic** \az'matik\ adj or n

astig·ma·tism \ə'stigmə,tizəm\ n : visual defect — **as·tig·mat·ic** \ˌastig-'matik\ adj

as to prep 1 : concerning 2 : according to

as·ton·ish \ə'stänish\ vb : amaze — **as·ton·ish·ing·ly** adv — **as·ton·ish·ment** n

as·tound \ə'staund\ vb : fill with confused wonder — **as·tound·ing·ly** adv

astrad·dle \ə'strad'l\ adv or prep : so as to straddle

as·tral \'astrəl\ adj : relating to or coming from the stars

astray \ə'strā\ adv or adj : off the right path

astride \ə'strīd\ adv : with legs apart or one on each side ∼ prep : with one leg on each side of

as·trin·gent \ə'strinjənt\ adj : causing shrinking or puckering of tissues — **as·trin·gen·cy** \-jənsē\ n — **as·trin·gent** n

as·trol·o·gy \ə'sträləjē\ n : prediction of events by the stars — **as·trol·o·ger** \-əjər\ n — **as·tro·log·i·cal** \ˌas-trə'läjikəl\ adj

as·tro·naut \'astrə,nòt\ n : space traveler

as·tro·nau·tics \ˌastrə'nòtiks\ n : construction and operation of spacecraft — **as·tro·nau·tic** \-ik\, **as·tro·nau·ti·cal** \-ikəl\ adj

as·tro·nom·i·cal \ˌastrə'nämikəl\ adj 1 : relating to astronomy 2 : extremely large

as·tron·o·my \ə'stränəmē\ n, pl -mies : study of the celestial bodies — **as·tron·o·mer** \-əmər\ n

as·tute \ə'stüt, -'styüt\ adj : shrewd — **as·tute·ly** adv — **as·tute·ness** n

asun·der \ə'səndər\ adv or adj 1 : into separate pieces 2 : separated

asy·lum \ə'sīləm\ n 1 : refuge 2 : institution for care esp. of the insane

asym·met·ri·cal \ˌāsə'metrikəl\, **asym·met·ric** \-trik\ adj : not symmetrical — **asym·me·try** \ˌā'simə-trē\ n

at \ət, 'at\ prep 1 — used to indicate a point in time or space 2 — used to indicate a goal **3** — used to indicate condition, means, cause, or manner

at all \ə'l\ *: without restriction or under any circumstances

ate *past of* EAT

-ate \ət, ˌāt\ *n suffix* **1** : office or rank **2** : group of persons holding an office or rank ~ *adj suffix* **1** : brought into or being in a state **2** : marked by having

athe·ist \'āthēist\ *n* : one who denies the existence of God — **athe·ism** \-ˌizəm\ *n* — **athe·is·tic** \ˌāthē-'istik\ *adj*

ath·ero·scle·ro·sis \ˌathərōsklə'rō-səs\ *n* : arteriosclerosis with deposition of fatty substances in the arteries — **ath·ero·scle·rot·ic** \-'rätik\ *adj*

ath·lete \'athˌlēt\ *n* : one trained to compete in athletics

ath·let·ics \ath'letiks\ *n sing or pl* : exercises and games requiring physical skill — **ath·let·ic** \-ik\ *adj*

-ation \'āshən\ *n suffix* : action or process

-ative \ˌātiv, ətiv\ *adj suffix* **1** : of, relating to, or connected with **2** : tending to

atlas \'atləs\ *n* : book of maps

ATM \ˌāˌtē'em\ *n* : computerized machine for performing basic bank functions

at·mo·sphere \'atməˌsfir\ *n* **1** : mass of air surrounding the earth **2** : surrounding influence — **at·mo·spher·ic** \ˌatmə'sfirik, -'sfer-\ *adj* — **at·mo·spher·i·cal·ly** \-iklē\ *adv*

atoll \'aˌtól, 'ā-, -ˌtäl\ *n* : ring-shaped coral island

at·om \'atəm\ *n* **1** : tiny bit **2** : smallest particle of a chemical element that can exist alone or in combination

atom·ic \ə'tämik\ *adj* **1** : relating to atoms **2** : nuclear

atomic bomb *n* : bomb utilizing the energy released by splitting the atom

at·om·iz·er \'atəˌmīzər\ *n* : device for dispersing a liquid as a very fine spray

atone \ə'tōn\ *vb* **atoned; aton·ing** : make amends — **atone·ment** *n*

atop \ə'täp\ *prep* : on top of ~ *adv or adj* : on, to, or at the top

atri·um \'ātrēəm\ *n, pl* **atria** \-trēə\ *or* **atriums** **1** : open central room or court **2** : heart chamber that receives blood from the veins

atro·cious \ə'trōshəs\ *adj* : appalling or abominable — **atro·cious·ly** *adv* — **atro·cious·ness** *n*

atroc·i·ty \ə'träsətē\ *n, pl* **-ties** : savage act

at·ro·phy \'atrəfē\ *n* : wasting away of a bodily part or tissue — **at·ro·phy** *vb*

at·ro·pine \'atrəˌpēn\ *n* : drug used esp. to relieve spasms

at·tach \ə'tach\ *vb* **1** : seize legally **2** : bind by personalities **3** : join — **at·tach·ment** *n*

at·ta·ché \ˌatə'shā, ˌaˌta-, əˌta-\ *n* : technical expert on a diplomatic staff

at·tack \ə'tak\ *vb* **1** : try to hurt or destroy with violence or words **2** : set to work on ~ *n* **1** : act of attacking **2** : fit of sickness

at·tain \ə'tān\ *vb* **1** : achieve or accomplish **2** : reach — **at·tain·abil·i·ty** \ə'tānə'bilətē\ *n* — **at·tain·able** *adj* — **at·tain·ment** *n*

at·tempt \ə'tempt\ *vb* : make an effort toward — **attempt** *n*

at·tend \ə'tend\ *vb* **1** : handle or provide for the care of something **2** : accompany **3** : be present at **4** : pay attention — **at·ten·dance** \-'ten-dəns\ *n* — **at·ten·dant** \-dənt\ *adj or n*

at·ten·tion \ə'tenchən\ *n* **1** : concentration of the mind on something **2** : notice or awareness — **at·ten·tive** \-'tentiv\ *adj* — **at·ten·tive·ly** *adv* — **at·ten·tive·ness** *n*

at·ten·u·ate \ə'tenyəˌwāt\ *vb* **-at·ed; -at·ing 1** : make or become thin **2** : weaken — **at·ten·u·a·tion** \-ˌtenyə'wāshən\ *n*

at·test \ə'test\ *vb* : certify or bear witness — **at·tes·ta·tion** \ˌaˌtes'tā-shən\ *n*

at·tic \'atik\ *n* : space just below the roof

at·tire \ə'tīr\ *vb* **-tired; -tir·ing** : dress — **attire** *n*

at·ti·tude \'atəˌtüd, -ˌtyüd\ *n* **1** : posture or relative position **2** : feeling, opinion, or mood

at·tor·ney \ə'tərnē\ *n, pl* **-neys** : legal agent

at·tract \ə'trakt\ *vb* **1** : draw to oneself **2** : have emotional or aesthetic appeal for — **at·trac·tion** \-'trakshən\ *n* — **at·trac·tive** \-'traktiv\ *adj* — **at·trac·tive·ly** *adv* — **at·trac·tive·ness** *n*

at·tri·bute \'atrə,byüt\ n : inherent characteristic ~ \ə'tribyət\ vb **-trib·ut·ed; -trib·ut·ing 1** : regard as having a specific cause or origin **2** : regard as a characteristic — **at·trib·ut·able** adj — **at·tri·bu·tion** \,atrə-'byüshən\ n

at·tune \ə'tün, -'tyün\ vb : bring into harmony

au·burn \'óbərn\ adj : reddish brown

auc·tion \'ókshən\ n : public sale of property to the highest bidder — **auc·tion** vb — **auc·tion·eer** \,ókshə'nir\ n

au·dac·i·ty \ó'dasətē\ n : boldness or insolence — **au·da·cious** \ó'dā-shəs\ adj

au·di·ble \'ódəbəl\ adj : capable of being heard — **au·di·bly** \-blē\ adv

au·di·ence \'ódēəns\ n **1** : formal interview **2** : group of listeners or spectators

au·dio \'ó'dē,ō\ adj : relating to sound or its reproduction ~ n : television sound

au·dio·vi·su·al \ódēō'vizhəwəl\ adj : relating to both hearing and sight

au·dit \'ódət\ vb : examine financial accounts — **audit** n — **au·di·tor** \'ódətər\ n

au·di·tion \ó'dishən\ n : tryout performance — **audition** vb

au·di·to·ri·um \,ódə'tōrēəm\ n, pl **-ri·ums** or **-ria** \-'rēə\ : room or building used for public performances

au·di·to·ry \'ódə,tōrē\ adj : relating to hearing

au·ger \'ógər\ n : tool for boring

aug·ment \og'ment\ vb : enlarge or increase — **aug·men·ta·tion** \,ógmən'tāshən\ n

au·gur \'ógər\ n : prophet ~ vb : predict — **au·gu·ry** \'ógyərē, -gər-\ n

au·gust \ó'gəst\ adj : majestic

Au·gust \'ógəst\ n : 8th month of the year having 31 days

auk \'ók\ n : stocky diving seabird

aunt \'ant, 'ánt\ n **1** : sister of one's father or mother **2** : wife of one's uncle

au·ra \'órə\ n **1** : distinctive atmosphere **2** : luminous radiation

au·ral \'órəl\ adj : relating to the ear or to hearing

au·ri·cle \'órikəl\ n : atrium or ear-shaped pouch in the atrium of the heart

au·ro·ra bo·re·al·is \ə'rōrə,bórē'aləs\

n : display of light in the night sky of northern latitudes

aus·pic·es \'óspəsəz, -,sēz\ n pl : patronage and protection

aus·pi·cious \ó'spishəs\ adj : favorable

aus·tere \ó'stir\ adj : severe — **aus·tere·ly** adv — **aus·ter·i·ty** \ó'ster-ətē\ n

au·then·tic \ə'thentik, ó-\ adj : genuine — **au·then·ti·cal·ly** \-iklē\ adv — **au·then·tic·i·ty** \,óthen'tisətē\ n

au·then·ti·cate \ə'thenti,kāt, ó-\ vb **-cat·ed; -cat·ing** : prove genuine — **au·then·ti·ca·tion** \-,thenti'kā-shən\ n

au·thor \'óthər\ n **1** : writer **2** : creator — **au·thor·ship** n

au·thor·i·tar·i·an \ò,thärə'terēən, ə-, -,thór-\ adj : marked by blind obedience to authority

au·thor·i·ta·tive \ə'thärə,tātiv, ó-, -'thór-\ adj : being an authority — **au·thor·i·ta·tive·ly** adv — **au·thor·i·ta·tive·ness** n

au·thor·i·ty \ə'thärətē, ó-, -'thór-\ n, pl **-ties 1** : expert **2** : right, responsibility, or power to influence **3** pl : persons in official positions

au·tho·rize \'óthə,rīz\ vb **-rized; -riz·ing** : permit or give official approval for — **au·tho·ri·za·tion** \,óthərə-'zāshən\ n

au·tism \'ó,tizəm\ n : mental disorder marked by impaired ability to communicate and form social relationships and by repetitive behavior patterns

au·to \'ótō\ n, pl **autos** : automobile

au·to·bi·og·ra·phy \,ótəbī'ägrəfē, -bē-\ n : writer's own life story — **au·to·bi·og·ra·pher** \-fər\ n — **au·to·bio·graph·i·cal** \-,bīə'grafikəl\ adj

au·toc·ra·cy \ó'täkrəsē\ n, pl **-cies** : government by one person having unlimited power — **au·to·crat** \'ótə,krat\ n — **au·to·crat·ic** \,ótə-'kratik\ adj — **au·to·crat·i·cal·ly** \-iklē\ adv

au·to·graph \'ótə,graf\ n : signature ~ vb : write one's name on

au·to·mate \'ótə,māt\ vb **-mat·ed; -mat·ing** : make automatic — **au·to·ma·tion** \,ótə'māshən\ n

au·to·mat·ic \,ótə'matik\ adj **1** : involuntary **2** : designed to function without human intervention ~ n

: automatic device (as a firearm) — **au·to·mat·i·cal·ly** \-iklē\ adv

au·tom·a·ton \ȯ'tämətən, -,tän\ n, pl -**atons** or -**a·ta** \-tə, -,tä\ : robot

au·to·mo·bile \,ȯtəmō'bēl, -'mō,bēl\ n : 4-wheeled passenger vehicle with its own power source

au·to·mo·tive \,ȯtə'mōtiv\ adj : relating to automobiles

au·ton·o·mous \ȯ'tänəməs\ adj : self-governing — **au·ton·o·mous·ly** adv — **au·ton·o·my** \-mē\ n

au·top·sy \'ȯ,täpsē, 'ȯtəp-\ n, pl -**sies** : medical examination of a corpse

au·tumn \'ȯtəm\ n : season between summer and winter — **au·tum·nal** \ȯ'təmnəl\ adj

aux·il·ia·ry \ȯg'zilyərē, -lərē\ adj 1 : being a supplement or reserve 2 : accompanying a main verb form to express person, number, mood, or tense — **auxiliary** n

avail \ə'vāl\ vb : be of use or make use ~ n : use

avail·able \ə'vāləbəl\ adj 1 : usable 2 : accessible — **avail·abil·i·ty** \-,vālə-'bilətē\ n

av·a·lanche \'avə,lanch\ n : mass of sliding or falling snow or rock

av·a·rice \'avərəs\ n : greed — **av·a·ri·cious** \,avə'rishəs\ adj

avenge \ə'venj\ vb **avenged; aveng·ing** : take vengeance for — **aveng·er** n

av·e·nue \'avə,nü, -,nyü\ n 1 : way of approach 2 : broad street

av·er·age \'avrij\ adj 1 : being about midway between extremes 2 : ordinary ~ vb 1 : be usually 2 : find the mean of ~ n : mean

averse \ə'vərs\ adj : feeling dislike or reluctance — **aver·sion** \-'vər-zhən\ n

avert \ə'vərt\ vb : turn away

avi·ary \'āvē,erē\ n, pl -**ar·ies** : place where birds are kept

avi·a·tion \,āvē'āshən, ,av-\ n : operation or manufacture of airplanes — **avi·a·tor** \'āvē,ātər, 'av-\ n

av·id \'avəd\ adj 1 : greedy 2 : enthusiastic — **avid·i·ty** \ə'vidətē, a-\ n — **av·id·ly** adv

av·o·ca·do \,avə'kädō, ,äv-\ n, pl -**dos** : tropical fruit with green pulp

av·o·ca·tion \,avə'kāshən\ n : hobby

avoid \ə'vȯid\ vb 1 : keep away from 2

: prevent the occurrence of 3 : refrain from — **avoid·able** adj — **avoid·ance** \-ⁿs\ n

av·oir·du·pois \,avərdə'pȯiz\ n : system of weight based on the pound of 16 ounces

avow \ə'vaů\ vb : declare openly — **avow·al** \-'vaůəl\ n

await \ə'wāt\ vb : wait for

awake \ə'wāk\ vb **awoke** \-'wōk\; **awok·en** \-'wōkən\ or **awaked; awak·ing** : wake up — **awake** adj

awak·en \ə'wākən\ vb -**ened; -en·ing** : wake up

award \ə'wȯrd\ vb : give (something won or deserved) ~ n 1 : judgment 2 : prize

aware \ə'war\ adj : having realization or consciousness — **aware·ness** n

awash \ə'wȯsh, -'wäsh\ adv or adj : flooded

away \ə'wā\ adv 1 : from this or that place or time 2 : out of the way 3 : in another direction 4 : from one's possession ~ adj 1 : absent 2 : distant

awe \'ȯ\ n : respectful fear or wonder ~ vb **awed; aw·ing** : fill with awe — **awe·some** \-səm\ adj — **awe·struck** adj

aw·ful \'ȯfəl\ adj 1 : inspiring awe 2 : extremely disagreeable 3 : very great — **aw·ful·ly** adv

awhile \ə'hwīl\ adv : for a while

awk·ward \'ȯkwərd\ adj 1 : clumsy 2 : embarrassing — **awk·ward·ly** adv — **awk·ward·ness** n

awl \'ȯl\ n : hole-making tool

aw·ning \'ȯniŋ\ n : window cover

awry \ə'rī\ adv or adj : wrong

ax, axe \'aks\ n : chopping tool

ax·i·om \'aksēəm\ n : generally accepted truth — **ax·i·om·at·ic** \,ak-sēə'matik\ adj

ax·is \'aksəs\ n, pl **ax·es** \-,sēz\ : center of rotation — **ax·i·al** \-sēəl\ adj — **ax·i·al·ly** adv

ax·le \'aksəl\ n : shaft on which a wheel revolves

aye \'ī\ adv : yes ~ n : a vote of yes

aza·lea \ə'zālyə\ n : rhododendron with funnel-shaped blossoms

az·i·muth \'azəməth\ n : horizontal direction expressed as an angle

azure \'azhər\ n : blue of the sky — **azure** adj

B

b \'bē\ *n, pl* **b's** *or* **bs** \'bēz\ : 2d letter of the alphabet

bab·ble \'babəl\ *vb* **-bled; -bling 1** : utter meaningless sounds **2** : talk foolishly or too much — **babble** *n* — **bab·bler** *n*

babe \'bāb\ *n* : baby

ba·bel \'bābəl, 'bab-\ *n* : noisy confusion

ba·boon \ba'bün\ *n* : large Asian or African ape with a doglike muzzle

ba·by \'bābē\ *n, pl* **-bies** : very young child ∼ *vb* **-bied; -by·ing** : pamper — **baby** *adj* — **ba·by·hood** *n* — **ba·by·ish** *adj*

ba·by·sit *vb* **-sat; -sit·ting** : care for children while parents are away — **baby-sit·ter** *n*

bac·ca·lau·re·ate \,bakə'lòrēət\ *n* : bachelor's degree

bac·cha·na·lia \,bakə'nālyə\ *n, pl* **-lia** : drunken orgy — **bac·cha·na·lian** \-yən\ *adj or n*

bach·e·lor \'bachələr\ *n* **1** : holder of lowest 4-year college degree **2** : unmarried man — **bach·e·lor·hood** *n*

ba·cil·lus \bə'siləs\ *n, pl* **-li** \-ˌī\ : rod-shaped bacterium — **bac·il·lary** \'basəˌlerē\ *adj*

back \'bak\ *n* **1** : part of a human or animal body nearest the spine **2** : part opposite the front **3** : player farthest from the opponent's goal — *adv* **1** : to or at the back **2** : ago **3** : to or in a former place or state **4** : in reply ∼ *adj* **1** : located at the back **2** : not paid on time **3** : moving or working backward **4** : not current ∼ *vb* **1** : support **2** : go or cause to go back **3** : form the back of — **back·ache** *n* — **back·er** *n* — **back·ing** *n* — **back·less** *adj* — **back·rest** *n*

back·bite *vb* **-bit; -bit·ten; -bit·ing** : say spiteful things about someone absent — **back·bit·er** *n*

back·bone *n* **1** : bony column in the back that encloses the spinal cord **2** : firm character

back·drop *n* : painted cloth hung across the rear of a stage

back·fire *n* : loud noise from the wrongly timed explosion of fuel in an engine ∼ *vb* **1** : make or undergo a backfire **2** : have a result opposite of that intended

back·gam·mon \'bak,gamən\ *n* : board game

back·ground *n* **1** : scenery behind something **2** : sum of a person's experience or training

back·hand *n* : stroke (as in tennis) made with the back of the hand turned forward — **backhand** *adj or vb* — **back·hand·ed** *adj*

back·lash *n* : adverse reaction

back·log *n* : accumulation of things to be done — **backlog** *vb*

back·pack *n* : camping pack carried on the back ∼ *vb* : hike with a backpack — **back·pack·er** *n*

back·slide *vb* **-slid; -slid** *or* **-slid·den** \-ˌslid'n\; **-slid·ing** : lapse in morals or religious practice — **back·slid·er** *n*

back·stage *adv or adj* : in or to an area behind a stage

back·up *n* : substitute

back·ward \'bakwərd\, **back·wards** *adv* **1** : toward the back **2** : with the back foremost **3** : in a reverse direction **4** : toward an earlier or worse state — *adj* **1** : directed, turned, or done backward **2** : retarded in development — **back·ward·ness** *n*

back·woods *n pl* : remote or isolated place

ba·con \'bākən\ *n* : salted and smoked meat from a pig

bac·te·ri·um \bak'tirēəm\ *n, pl* **-ria** \-ēə\ : microscopic plant — **bac·te·ri·al** \-ēəl\ *adj* — **bac·te·ri·o·log·ic** \-ˌtirēə'läjik\, **bac·te·ri·o·log·i·cal** \-əl\ *adj* — **bac·te·ri·ol·o·gist** \-ē'äləjist\ *n* — **bac·te·ri·ol·o·gy** \-jē\ *n*

bad \'bad\ *adj* **worse** \'wərs\; **worst** \'wərst\ **1** : not good **2** : naughty **3** : faulty **4** : spoiled — **bad** *n or adv* — **bad·ly** *adv* — **bad·ness** *n*

bade *past of* BID

badge \\'baj\\ n : symbol of status

bad·ger \\'bajər\\ n : burrowing mammal ∼ vb : harass

bad·min·ton \\'bad,mint³n\\ n : tennislike game played with a shuttlecock

bad–mouth \\'bad,mau̇th\\ vb : criticize severely

baf·fle \\'bafəl\\ vb -fled; -fling : perplex ∼ n : device to alter flow (as of liquid or sound) — **baf·fle·ment** n

bag \\'bag\\ n : flexible usu. closable container ∼ vb -gg- 1 : bulge out 2 : put in a bag 3 : catch in hunting

bag·a·telle \\,bagə'tel\\ n : trifle

ba·gel \\'bāgəl\\ n : hard doughnut-shaped roll

bag·gage \\'bagij\\ n : traveler's bags and belongings

bag·gy \\'bagē\\ adj -gi·er; -est : puffed out like a bag — **bag·gi·ness** n

bag·pipe n : musical instrument with a bag, a tube with valves, and sounding pipes — often pl.

¹bail \\'bāl\\ n : container for scooping water out of a boat — **bail** vb — **bail·er** n

²bail n 1 : security given to guarantee a prisoner's appearance in court 2 : release secured by bail ∼ vb : bring about the release of by giving bail

bai·liff \\'bāləf\\ n 1 : British sheriff's aide 2 : minor officer of a U.S. court

bai·li·wick \\'bāli,wik\\ n : one's special field or domain

bail·out \\'bā,lau̇t\\ n : rescue from financial distress

bait \\'bāt\\ vb 1 : harass with dogs usu. for sport 2 : furnish (a hook or trap) with bait ∼ n : lure esp. for catching animals

bake \\'bāk\\ vb baked; bak·ing : cook in dry heat esp. in an oven ∼ n : party featuring baked food — **bak·er** n — **bak·ery** \\'bākərē\\ n — **bake·shop** n

bal·ance \\'baləns\\ n 1 : weighing device 2 : counteracting weight, force, or influence 3 : equilibrium 4 : that which remains ∼ vb -anced; -anc·ing 1 : compute the balance 2 : equalize 3 : bring into harmony or proportion — **bal·anced** adj

bal·co·ny \\'balkənē\\ n, pl -nies : platform projecting from a wall

bald \\'bȯld\\ adj 1 : lacking a natural or usual covering (as of hair) 2 : plain — **bald·ing** adj — **bald·ly** adv — **bald·ness** n

bal·der·dash \\'bȯldər,dash\\ n : nonsense

bale \\'bāl\\ n : large bundle ∼ vb baled; bal·ing : pack in a bale — **bal·er** n

bale·ful \\'bālfəl\\ adj 1 : deadly 2 : ominous

balk \\'bȯk\\ n : hindrance ∼ vb 1 : thwart 2 : stop short and refuse to go on — **balky** adj

¹ball \\'bȯl\\ n 1 : rounded mass 2 : game played with a ball ∼ vb : form into a ball

²ball n : large formal dance — **ballroom** n

bal·lad \\'baləd\\ n 1 : narrative poem 2 : slow romantic song — **bal·lad·eer** \\,balə'diər\\ n

bal·last \\'baləst\\ n : heavy material to steady a ship or balloon ∼ vb : provide with ballast

bal·le·ri·na \\,balə'rēnə\\ n : female ballet dancer

bal·let \\'ba,lā, ba'lā\\ n : theatrical dancing

bal·lis·tics \\bə'listiks\\ n sing or pl : science of projectile motion — **ballistic** adj

bal·loon \\bə'lün\\ n : inflated bag ∼ vb 1 : travel in a balloon 2 : swell out — **bal·loon·ist** n

bal·lot \\'balət\\ n 1 : paper used to cast a vote 2 : system of voting ∼ vb : vote

bal·ly·hoo \\'balē,hü\\ n : publicity — **ballyhoo** vb

balm \\'bäm, 'bȧlm\\ n 1 : fragrant healing or soothing preparation 2 : spicy fragrant herb

balmy \\'bämē, 'bȧlmē\\ adj balm·i·er; -est : gently soothing — **balm·i·ness** n

ba·lo·ney \\bə'lōnē\\ n : nonsense

bal·sa \\'bȯlsə\\ n : very light wood of a tropical tree

bal·sam \\-səm\\ n 1 : aromatic resinous plant substance 2 : balsam-yielding plant — **bal·sam·ic** \\bȯl'samik\\ adj

bal·us·ter \\'baləstər\\ n : upright support for a rail

bal·us·trade \\-,strād\\ n : row of balusters topped by a rail

bam·boo \\bam'bü\\ n : tall tropical grass with strong hollow stems

bam·boo·zle \\bam'büzəl\\ vb -zled; -zling : deceive

ban \\'ban\\ vb -nn- : prohibit ∼ n : legal prohibition

ba·nal \bə'näl, -'nal; 'bān³l\ *adj* : ordinary and uninteresting — **ba·nal·ity** \bə'nalətē\ *n*

ba·nana \bə'nanə\ *n* : elongated fruit of a treelike tropical plant

¹**band** \'band\ *n* **1** : something that ties or binds **2** : strip or stripe different (as in color) from nearby matter **3** : range of radio wavelengths ~ *vb* **1** : enclose with a band **2** : unite for a common end — **band·ed** *adj* — **band·er** *n*

²**band** *n* **1** : group **2** : musicians playing together

ban·dage \'bandij\ *n* : material used esp. in dressing wounds ~ *vb* : dress or cover with a bandage

ban·dan·na, ban·dana \ban'danə\ *n* : large colored figured handkerchief

ban·dit \'bandət\ *n* : outlaw or robber — **ban·dit·ry** \-dətrē\ *n*

band·stand *n* : stage for band concerts

band·wag·on *n* : candidate, side, or movement gaining support

¹**ban·dy** \'bandē\ *vb* **-died; -dy·ing** : exchange in rapid succession

²**bandy** *adj* : curved outward

bane \'bān\ *n* **1** : poison **2** : cause of woe — **bane·ful** *adj*

¹**bang** \'baŋ\ *vb* : strike, thrust, or move usu. with a loud noise ~ *n* **1** : blow **2** : sudden loud noise ~ *adv* : directly

²**bang** *n* : fringe of short hair over the forehead — usu. pl. ~ *vb* : cut in bangs

ban·gle \'baŋgəl\ *n* : bracelet

ban·ish \'banish\ *vb* **1** : force by authority to leave a country **2** : expel — **ban·ish·ment** *n*

ban·is·ter \-əstər\ *n* **1** : baluster **2** : handrail

ban·jo \'ban,jō\ *n, pl* **-jos** : stringed instrument with a drumlike body — **banjo·ist** *n*

¹**bank** \'baŋk\ *n* **1** : piled-up mass **2** : rising ground along a body of water **3** : sideways slope along a curve ~ *vb* **1** : form a bank **2** : cover (as a fire) to keep inactive **3** : incline (an airplane) laterally

²**bank** *n* : tier of objects

³**bank** *n* **1** : money institution **2** : reserve supply ~ *vb* : conduct business in a bank — **bank·book** *n* — **bank·er** *n* — **bank·ing** *n*

bank·rupt \'baŋ,krəpt\ *n* : one required by law to forfeit assets to pay off debts ~ *adj* **1** : legally a bankrupt **2** : lacking something essential — **bankrupt** *vb* — **bank·rupt·cy** \-,krəpsē\ *n*

ban·ner \'banər\ *n* : flag ~ *adj* : excellent

banns \'banz\ *n pl* : announcement in church of a proposed marriage

ban·quet \'baŋkwət\ *n* : ceremonial dinner — **banquet** *vb*

ban·shee \'banshē\ *n* : wailing female spirit that foretells death

ban·tam \'bantəm\ *n* : miniature domestic fowl

ban·ter \'bantər\ *n* : good-natured joking — **banter** *vb*

ban·yan \'banyən\ *n* : large tree that grows new trunks from the limbs

bap·tism \'bap,tizəm\ *n* : Christian rite signifying spiritual cleansing — **bap·tis·mal** \bap'tizmal\ *adj*

bap·tize \bap'tīz, 'bap,tīz\ *vb* **-tized; -tiz·ing** : administer baptism to

bar \'bär\ *n* **1** : long narrow object used esp. as a lever, fastening, or support **2** : barrier **3** : body of practicing lawyers **4** : wide stripe **5** : food counter **6** : place where liquor is served **7** : vertical line across the musical staff ~ *vb* **-rr-** **1** : obstruct with a bar **2** : shut out **3** : prohibit ~ *prep* : excluding — **barred** *adj* — **bar·room** *n* — **bar·tend·er** *n*

barb \'bärb\ *n* : sharp projection pointing backward — **barbed** *adj*

bar·bar·ian \bär'bareən\ *adj* **1** : relating to people considered backward **2** : not refined — **barbarian** *n*

bar·bar·ic \-'barik\ *adj* : barbarian

bar·ba·rous \'bärbərəs\ *adj* **1** : lacking refinement **2** : mercilessly cruel — **bar·bar·ism** \-bə,rizəm\ *n* — **bar·bar·i·ty** \bär'baratē\ *n* — **bar·ba·rous·ly** *adv*

bar·be·cue \'bärbi,kyü\ *n* : gathering at which barbecued food is served ~ *vb* **-cued; -cu·ing** : cook over hot coals or on a spit often with a highly seasoned sauce

bar·ber \'bärbər\ *n* : one who cuts hair

bar·bi·tu·rate \bär'bichərət\ *n* : sedative or hypnotic drug

bard \'bärd\ *n* : poet

bare \'bar\ *adj* **bar·er; bar·est** **1** : naked **2** : not concealed **3** : empty **4** : leaving nothing to spare **5** : plain ~ *vb* **bared; bar·ing** : make or lay bare — **bare·foot, bare·foot·ed** *adv or adj* — **bare·hand·ed** *adv or adj*

— **bare·head·ed** adv or adj — **bare·ly** adv — **bare·ness** n

bare·back, bare·backed adv or adj : without a saddle

bare·faced adj : open and esp. brazen

bar·gain \'bärgən\ n 1 : agreement 2 : something bought for less than its value ~ vb 1 : negotiate 2 : barter

barge \'bärj\ n : broad flat-bottomed boat ~ vb **barged; barg·ing** : move rudely or clumsily — **barge·man** n

bari·tone \'barə,tōn\ n : male voice between bass and tenor

bar·i·um \'barēəm\ n : silver-white metallic chemical element

¹bark \'bärk\ vb 1 : make the sound of a dog 2 : speak in a loud curt tone ~ n : sound of a barking dog

²bark n : tough corky outer covering of a woody stem or root ~ vb : remove bark or skin from

³bark n : sailing ship with a fore-and-aft rear sail

bark·er \'bärkər\ n : one who calls out to attract people to a show

bar·ley \'bärlē\ n : cereal grass or its seeds

barn \'bärn\ n : building for keeping hay or livestock — **barn·yard** n

bar·na·cle \'bärnikəl\ n : marine crustacean

barn·storm vb : tour through rural districts giving performances

ba·rom·e·ter \bə'rämətər\ n : instrument for measuring atmospheric pressure — **baro·met·ric** \,barə-'metrik\ adj

bar·on \'barən\ n : British peer — **bar·on·age** \-ij\ n — **ba·ro·ni·al** \bə-'rōnēəl\ adj — **bar·ony** \'barənē\ n

bar·on·ess \-ənəs\ n 1 : baron's wife 2 : woman holding a baronial title

bar·on·et \-ənət\ n : man holding a rank between a baron and a knight — **bar·on·et·cy** \-sē\ n

ba·roque \bə'rōk, -'räk\ adj : elaborately ornamented

bar·racks \'barəks\ n sing or pl : soldiers' housing

bar·ra·cu·da \,barə'küdə\ n, pl **-da** or **-das** : large predatory sea fish

bar·rage \bə'räzh, -'räj\ n : heavy artillery fire

bar·rel \'barəl\ n 1 : closed cylindrical container 2 : amount held by a barrel 3 : cylindrical part ~ vb **-reled** or **-relled; -rel·ing** or **-rel·ling** 1 : pack in a barrel 2 : move at high speed

bar·ren \'barən\ adj 1 : unproductive of life 2 : uninteresting — **bar·ren·ness** n

bar·rette \bä'ret, bə-\ n : clasp for a woman's hair

bar·ri·cade \'barə,kād, ,barə'-\ n : barrier — **barricade** vb

bar·ri·er \'barēər\ n : something that separates or obstructs

bar·ring \'bäriŋ\ prep : omitting

bar·ris·ter \'barəstər\ n : British trial lawyer

bar·row \'barō\ n : wheelbarrow

bar·ter \'bärtər\ vb : trade by exchange of goods — **barter** n

ba·salt \bə'sȯlt, 'bā,-\ n : dark fine-grained igneous rock — **ba·sal·tic** \bə'sȯltik\ adj

¹base \'bās\ n, pl **bas·es** 1 : bottom 2 : fundamental part 3 : beginning point 4 : supply source of a force 5 : compound that reacts with an acid to form a salt ~ vb **based; bas·ing** : establish — **base·less** adj

²base adj **bas·er; bas·est** 1 : inferior 2 : contemptible — **base·ly** adv — **base·ness** n

base·ball n : game played with a bat and ball by 2 teams

base·ment \-mənt\ n : part of a building below ground level

bash \'bash\ vb : strike violently ~ n : heavy blow

bash·ful \-fəl\ adj : self-conscious — **bash·ful·ness** n

ba·sic \'bāsik\ adj 1 : relating to or forming the base or essence 2 : relating to a chemical base — **ba·si·cally** adv — **ba·sic·i·ty** \bā'sisətē\ n

ba·sil \'bazəl, 'bās-, 'bāz-\ n : aromatic mint

ba·sil·i·ca \bə'silikə\ n : important church or cathedral

ba·sin \'bās²n\ n 1 : large bowl or pan 2 : region drained by a river

ba·sis \'bāsəs\ n, pl **ba·ses** \-,sēz\ 1 : something that supports 2 : fundamental principle

bask \'bask\ vb : enjoy pleasant warmth

bas·ket \'baskət\ n : woven container — **bas·ket·ful** n

bas·ket·ball n : game played with a ball on a court by 2 teams

bas·re·lief \,bäri'lēf\ n : flat sculpture with slightly raised design

¹bass \'bas\ n, pl **bass** or **bass·es** : spiny-finned sport and food fish

²**bass** \'bās\ n 1 : deep tone 2 : lowest choral voice

bas·set hound \'basət-\ n : short-legged dog with long ears

bas·si·net \,basə'net\ n : baby's bed

bas·soon \bə'sün, ba-\ n : low-pitched wind instrument

bas·tard \'bastərd\ n 1 : illegitimate child 2 : offensive person ~ adj 1 : illegitimate 2 : inferior — **bas·tard·ize** vb — **bas·tardy** n

¹**baste** \'bāst\ vb **bast·ed; bast·ing** : sew temporarily with long stitches

²**baste** vb **bast·ed; bast·ing** : moisten at intervals while cooking

bas·tion \'baschən\ n : fortified position

¹**bat** \'bat\ n 1 : stick or club 2 : sharp blow ~ vb **-tt-** : hit with a bat

²**bat** n : small flying mammal

³**bat** vb **-tt-** : wink or blink

batch \'bach\ n : quantity used or produced at one time

bate \'bāt\ vb **bat·ed; bat·ing** : moderate or reduce

bath \'bath, 'báth\ n, pl **baths** \'bathz, 'baths, 'báthz, 'báths\ 1 : a washing of the body 2 : water for washing the body 3 : liquid in which something is immersed 4 : bathroom 5 : large financial loss — **bath·tub** n

bathe \'bāth\ vb **bathed; bath·ing** 1 : wash in liquid 2 : flow against so as to wet 3 : shine light over 4 : take a bath or a swim — **bath·er** n

bath·robe n : robe worn around the house

bath·room n : room with a bathtub or shower and usu. a sink and toilet

ba·tiste \bə'tēst\ n : fine sheer fabric

ba·ton \bə'tän\ n : musical conductor's stick

bat·tal·ion \bə'talyən\ n : military unit composed of a headquarters and two or more companies

bat·ten \'bat°n\ n : strip of wood used to seal or reinforce ~ vb : furnish or fasten with battens

¹**bat·ter** \'batər\ vb : beat or damage with repeated blows

²**batter** n : mixture of flour and liquid

³**batter** n : player who bats

bat·tery \'batərē\ n, pl **-ter·ies** 1 : illegal beating of a person 2 : group of artillery guns 3 : group of electric cells

bat·ting \'batiŋ\ n : layers of cotton or wool for stuffing

bat·tle \'bat°l\ n : military fighting ~ vb **-tled; -tling** : engage in battle — **battle·field** n

bat·tle–ax n : long-handled ax formerly used as a weapon

bat·tle·ment \-mənt\ n : parapet on top of a wall

bat·tle·ship n : heavily armed warship

bat·ty \'batē\ adj **-ti·er; -est** : crazy

bau·ble \'bóbəl\ n : trinket

bawdy \'bódē\ adj **bawd·i·er; -est** : obscene or lewd — **bawd·i·ly** adv — **bawd·i·ness** n

bawl \'ból\ vb : cry loudly ~ n : long loud cry

¹**bay** \'bā\ adj : reddish brown ~ n : bay-colored animal

²**bay** n : European laurel

³**bay** n 1 : compartment 2 : area projecting out from a building and containing a window (**bay window**)

⁴**bay** vb : bark with deep long tones ~ n 1 : position of one unable to escape danger 2 : baying of dogs

⁵**bay** n : body of water smaller than a gulf and nearly surrounded by land

bay·ber·ry \-,berē\ n : shrub bearing small waxy berries

bay·o·net \'bāənət, ,bāə'net\ n : dagger that fits on the end of a rifle ~ vb **-net·ed; -net·ing** : stab with a bayonet

bay·ou \'bīü, -ō\ n : creek flowing through marshy land

ba·zaar \bə'zär\ n 1 : market 2 : fair for charity

ba·zoo·ka \-'zükə\ n : weapon that shoots armor-piercing rockets

BB n : small shot pellet

be \'bē\ vb **was** \'wəz, 'wäz\, **were** \'wər\; **been** \'bin\; **be·ing** \'bēiŋ\; **am** \əm, 'am\, **is** \'iz, əz\, **are** \ər, 'är\ 1 : equal 2 : exist 3 : occupy a certain place 4 : occur — verbal auxiliary — used to show continuous action or to form the passive voice

beach \'bēch\ n : sandy shore of a sea, lake, or river ~ vb : drive ashore

beach·comb·er \-,kōmər\ n : one who searches the shore for useful objects

beach·head n : shore area held by an attacking force in an invasion

bea·con \'bēkən\ n : guiding or warning light or signal

bead \'bēd\ n : small round body esp. strung on a thread ~ vb : form into a bead — **bead·ing** n — **beady** adj

bea·gle \'bēgəl\ *n* : small short-legged hound

beak \'bēk\ *n* : bill of a bird — **beaked** *adj*

bea·ker \'bēkər\ *n* 1 : large drinking cup 2 : laboratory vessel

beam \'bēm\ *n* 1 : large long piece of timber or metal 2 : ray of light 3 : directed radio signals for the guidance of pilots ~ *vb* 1 : send out light 2 : smile 3 : aim a radio broadcast

bean \'bēn\ *n* : edible plant seed borne in pods

¹bear \'bar\ *n, pl* **bears** 1 *or pl* **bear** : large heavy mammal with shaggy hair 2 : gruff or sullen person — **bear·ish** *adj*

²bear *vb* **bore** \'bōr\; **borne** \'bōrn\; **bear·ing** 1 : carry 2 : give birth to or produce 3 : endure 4 : press 5 : go in an indicated direction — **bear·able** *adj* — **bear·er** *n*

beard \'bird\ *n* 1 : facial hair on a man 2 : tuft like a beard ~ *vb* : confront boldly — **beard·ed** *adj* — **beard·less** *adj*

bear·ing *n* 1 : way of carrying oneself 2 : supporting object or purpose 3 : significance 4 : machine part in which another part turns 5 : direction with respect esp. to compass points

beast \'bēst\ *n* 1 : animal 2 : brutal person — **beast·li·ness** *n* — **beast·ly** *adj*

beat \'bēt\ *vb* **beat**; **beat·en** \'bēt²n\ *or* **beat**; **beat·ing** 1 : strike repeatedly 2 : defeat 3 : act or arrive before 4 : throb ~ *n* 1 : single stroke or pulsation 2 : rhythmic stress in poetry or music ~ *adj* : exhausted — **beat·er** *n*

be·atif·ic \,bēə'tifik\ *adj* : blissful

be·at·i·fy \bē'atə,fī\ *vb* **-fied**; **-fy·ing** : make happy or blessed — **be·at·i·fi·ca·tion** \-,atəfə'kāshən\ *n*

be·at·i·tude \-'atə,tüd, -,tyüd\ *n* : saying in the Sermon on the Mount (Matthew 5:3-12) beginning "Blessed are"

beau \'bō\ *n, pl* **beaux** \'bōz\ *or* **beaus** : suitor

beau·ty \'byütē\ *n, pl* **-ties** : qualities that please the senses or mind — **beau·te·ous** \-ēəs\ *adj* — **beau·te·ous·ly** *adv* — **beau·ti·fi·ca·tion** \,byütəfə'kāshən\ *n* — **beau·ti·fi·er** \'byütə,fīər\ *n* — **beau·ti·ful** \-ifəl\

adj — **beau·ti·ful·ly** *adv* — **beau·ti·fy** \-ə,fī\ *vb*

bea·ver \'bēvər\ *n* : large fur-bearing rodent

be·cause \bi'kóz, -'kəz\ *conj* : for the reason that

because of *prep* : by reason of

beck \'bek\ *n* : summons

beck·on \'bekən\ *vb* : summon esp. by a nod or gesture

be·come \bi'kəm\ *vb* **-came** \-'kām\; **-come**; **-com·ing** 1 : come to be 2 : be suitable — **be·com·ing** *adj* — **be·com·ing·ly** *adv*

bed \'bed\ *n* 1 : piece of furniture to sleep on 2 : flat or level surface ~ *vb* **-dd-** : put or go to bed — **bed·spread** *n*

bed·bug *n* : wingless bloodsucking insect

bed·clothes *n pl* : bedding

bed·ding *n* 1 : sheets and blankets for a bed 2 : soft material (as hay) for an animal's bed

be·deck \bi'dek\ *vb* : adorn

be·dev·il \-'devəl\ *vb* : harass

bed·lam \'bedləm\ *n* : uproar and confusion

be·drag·gled \bi'dragəld\ *adj* : dirty and disordered

bed·rid·den \'bed,rid²n\ *adj* : kept in bed by illness

bed·rock *n* : solid subsurface rock — **bedrock** *adj*

¹bee \'bē\ *n* : 4-winged honey-producing insect — **bee·hive** *n* — **bee·keep·er** *n* — **bees·wax** *n*

²bee *n* : neighborly work session

beech \'bēch\ *n, pl* **beech·es** *or* **beech** : tree with smooth gray bark and edible nuts (**beech·nuts**) — **beech·en** \-ən\ *adj*

beef \'bēf\ *n, pl* **beefs** \'bēfs\ *or* **beeves** \'bēvz\ : flesh of a steer, cow, or bull ~ *vb* : strengthen — used with *up* — **beef·steak** *n*

bee·line *n* : straight course

been *past part of* BE

beep \'bēp\ *n* : short usu. high-pitched warning sound — **beep** *vb* — **beep·er** *n*

beer \'bir\ *n* : alcoholic drink brewed from malt and hops — **beery** *adj*

beet \'bēt\ *n* : garden root vegetable

bee·tle \'bētəl\ *n* : 4-winged insect

be·fall \bi'fól\ *vb* **-fell**; **-fall·en** : happen to

be·fit \bi'fit\ *vb* : be suitable to

be·fore \bi'fōr\ adv **1** : in front **2** : earlier ~ prep **1** : in front of **2** : earlier than ~ conj : earlier than
be·fore·hand adv or adj : in advance
be·friend \bi'frend\ vb : act as friend to
be·fud·dle \-'fəd°l\ vb : confuse
beg \'beg\ vb **-gg-** : ask earnestly
be·get \bi'get\ vb **-got; -got·ten** or **-got; -get·ting** : become the father of
beg·gar \'begər\ n : one that begs ~ vb : make poor — **beg·gar·ly** adj — **beg·gary** n
be·gin \bi'gin\ vb **-gan** \-'gan\; **-gun** \-'gən\; **-gin·ning 1** : start **2** : come into being — **be·gin·ner** n
be·gone \bi'gȯn\ vb : go away
be·go·nia \-'gōnyə\ n : tropical herb with waxy flowers
be·grudge \-'grəj\ vb **1** : concede reluctantly **2** : look upon disapprovingly
be·guile \-'gīl\ vb **-guiled; -guil·ing 1** : deceive **2** : amuse
be·half \-'haf, -'hȧf\ n : benefit
be·have \-'hāv\ vb **-haved; -hav·ing** : act in a certain way
be·hav·ior \-'hāvyər\ n : way of behaving — **be·hav·ior·al** \-əl\ adj
be·head \-'hed\ vb : cut off the head of
be·hest \-'hest\ n : command
be·hind \bi'hīnd\ adv : at the back ~ prep **1** : in back of **2** : less than **3** : supporting
be·hold \-'hōld\ vb **-held; -hold·ing** : see — **be·hold·er** n
be·hold·en \-'hōldən\ adj : indebted
be·hoove \-'hüv\ vb **-hooved; -hoov·ing** : be necessary for
beige \'bāzh\ n : yellowish brown — **beige** adj
be·ing \'bēiŋ\ n **1** : existence **2** : living thing
be·la·bor \bi'lābər\ vb : carry on to absurd lengths
be·lat·ed \-'lātəd\ adj : delayed
belch \'belch\ vb **1** : expel stomach gas orally **2** : emit forcefully — **belch** n
be·lea·guer \bi'lēgər\ vb **1** : besiege **2** : harass
bel·fry \'belfrē\ n, pl **-fries** : bell tower
be·lie \bi'lī\ vb **-lied; -ly·ing 1** : misrepresent **2** : prove false
be·lief \bə'lēf\ n **1** : trust **2** : something believed
be·lieve \-'lēv\ vb **-lieved; -liev·ing 1** : trust in **2** : accept as true **3** : hold as an opinion — **be·liev·able** adj — **be·liev·ably** adv — **be·liev·er** n

be·lit·tle \bi'lit°l\ vb **-lit·tled; -lit·tling 1** : disparage **2** : make seem less
bell \'bel\ n **1** : hollow metallic device that rings when struck ~ vb : provide with a bell
bel·la·don·na \,belə'dänə\ n : poisonous herb yielding a drug
belle \'bel\ n : beautiful woman
bel·li·cose \'beli,kōs\ adj : pugnacious — **bel·li·cos·i·ty** \,beli'käsətē\ n
bel·lig·er·ent \bə'lijərənt\ adj **1** : waging war **2** : truculent — **bel·lig·er·ence** \-rəns\ n — **bel·lig·er·en·cy** \-rənsē\ n — **belligerent** n
bel·low \'belō\ vb : make a loud deep roar or shout — **bellow** n
bel·lows \-ōz, -əz\ n sing or pl : device with sides that can be compressed to expel air
bell·weth·er \'bel'wethər, -,weth-\ n : leader
bel·ly \'belē\ n, pl **-lies** : abdomen ~ vb **-lied; -ly·ing** : bulge
be·long \bi'lȯŋ\ vb **1** : be suitable to **2** : be owned **3** : be a part of
be·long·ings \-iŋz\ n pl : possessions
be·loved \bi'ləvəd, -'ləvd\ adj : dearly loved — **beloved** n
be·low \-'lō\ adv : in or to a lower place ~ prep : lower than
belt \'belt\ n **1** : strip (as of leather) worn about the waist **2** : endless band to impart motion **3** : distinct region ~ vb **1** : put a belt around **2** : thrash
be·moan \bi'mōn\ vb : lament
be·muse \-'myüz\ vb : confuse
bench \'bench\ n **1** : long seat **2** : judge's seat **3** : court
bend \'bend\ vb **bent** \'bent\; **bend·ing 1** : curve or cause a change of shape in **2** : turn in a certain direction ~ n **1** : act of bending **2** : curve
be·neath \bi'nēth\ adv or prep : below
bene·dic·tion \,benə'dikshən\ n : closing blessing
bene·fac·tor \'benə,faktər\ n : one who gives esp. charitable aid
be·nef·i·cence \bə'nefəsəns\ n : quality of doing good — **be·nef·i·cent** \-sənt\ adj
ben·e·fi·cial \,benə'fishəl\ adj : being of benefit — **ben·e·fi·cial·ly** adv
ben·e·fi·cia·ry \,benə'fishē,erē, -'fishərē\ n, pl **-ries** : one who receives benefits
ben·e·fit \'benə,fit\ n **1** : something

that does good **2** : help **3** : fundraising event — **benefit** vb

be·nev·o·lence \bə'nevələns\ n **1** : charitable nature **2** : act of kindness — **be·nev·o·lent** \-lənt\ adj — **be·nev·o·lent·ly** adv

be·night·ed \bi'nītəd\ adj : ignorant

be·nign \bi'nīn\ adj **1** : gentle or kindly **2** : not malignant — **be·nig·ni·ty** \-'nignətē\ n

be·nig·nant \-'nignənt\ adj : benign

bent \'bent\ n : aptitude or interest

be·numb \bi'nəm\ vb : make numb esp. by cold

ben·zene \'ben,zēn\ n : colorless flammable liquid

be·queath \bi'kwēth, -'kwēth\ vb **1** : give by will **2** : hand down

be·quest \bi'kwest\ n : something bequeathed

be·rate \-'rāt\ vb : scold harshly

be·reaved \-'rēvd\ adj : suffering the death of a loved one — n, pl **be·reaved** : one who is bereaved — **be·reave·ment** n

be·reft \-'reft\ adj : deprived of or lacking something

be·ret \bə'rā\ n : round soft visorless cap

beri·beri \,berē'berē\ n : thiamine-deficiency disease

berm \'bərm\ n : bank of earth

ber·ry \'berē\ n, pl **-ries** : small pulpy fruit

ber·serk \bər'sərk, -'zərk\ adj : crazed — **berserk** adv

berth \'bərth\ n **1** : place where a ship is anchored **2** : place to sit or sleep esp. on a ship **3** : job ∼ vb : to bring or come into a berth

ber·yl \'berəl\ n : light-colored silicate mineral

be·seech \bi'sēch\ vb **-sought** \-'sòt\ or **-seeched**; **-seech·ing** : entreat

be·set \-'set\ vb **1** : harass **2** : hem in

be·side \-'sīd\ prep **1** : by the side of **2** : besides

be·sides \-'sīdz\ adv **1** : in addition **2** : moreover ∼ prep **1** : other than **2** : in addition to

be·siege \-'sēj\ vb : lay siege to — **be·sieg·er** n

be·smirch \-'smərch\ vb : soil

be·sot \-'sät\ vb **-tt-** : become drunk

be·speak \bi'spēk\ vb **-spoke**; **-spo·ken**; **-speak·ing 1** : address **2** : indicate

best \'best\ adj, superlative of GOOD

1 : excelling all others **2** : most productive **3** : largest ∼ adv superlative of WELL **1** : in the best way **2** : most ∼ n : one that is best ∼ vb : outdo

bes·tial \'beschəl, 'bēs-\ adj **1** : relating to beasts **2** : brutish — **bes·ti·al·i·ty** \,beschē'alətē, ,bēs-\ n

be·stir \bi'stər\ vb : rouse to action

best man n : chief male attendant at a wedding

be·stow \bi'stō\ vb : give — **be·stow·al** \-əl\ n

bet \'bet\ n **1** : something risked or pledged on the outcome of a contest **2** : the making of a bet ∼ vb **bet**; **bet·ting 1** : risk (as money) on an outcome **2** : make a bet with

be·tide \bi'tīd\ vb : happen to

be·to·ken \bi'tōkən\ vb : give an indication of

be·tray \bi'trā\ vb **1** : seduce **2** : report or reveal to an enemy by treachery **3** : abandon **4** : prove unfaithful to **5** : reveal unintentionally — **be·tray·al** n — **be·tray·er** n

be·troth \-'träth, -'tròth, -'tròth, or with th\ vb : promise to marry — **be·troth·al** n — **be·trothed** n

bet·ter \'betər\ adj, comparative of GOOD **1** : more than half **2** : improved in health **3** : of higher quality ∼ adv comparative of WELL **1** : in a superior manner **2** : more ∼ n **1** : one that is better **2** : advantage ∼ vb **1** : improve **2** : surpass — **bet·ter·ment** \-mənt\ n

bet·tor, bet·ter \'betər\ n : one who bets

be·tween \bi'twēn\ prep **1** — used to show two things considered together **2** : in the space separating **3** — used to indicate a comparison or choice ∼ adv : in an intervening space or interval

bev·el \'bevəl\ n : slant on an edge ∼ vb **-eled** or **-elled**; **-el·ing** or **-el·ling 1** : cut or shape to a bevel **2** : incline

bev·er·age \'bevrij\ n : drink

bevy \'bevē\ n, pl **bev·ies** : large group

be·wail \bi'wāl\ vb : lament

be·ware \-'war\ vb : be cautious

be·wil·der \-'wildər\ vb : confuse — **be·wil·der·ment** n

be·witch \-'wich\ vb **1** : affect by witchcraft **2** : charm — **be·witch·ment** n

be·yond \bē'yänd\ adv **1** : farther **2** : besides ∼ prep **1** : on or to the farther side of **2** : out of the reach of **3** : besides

bi- \\'bī, ,bī\ *prefix* **1** : two **2** : coming or occurring every two **3** : twice, doubly, or on both sides

bi·an·nu·al \,bī'anyəwəl\ *adj* : occurring twice a year — **bi·an·nu·al·ly** *adv*

bi·as \'bīəs\ *n* **1** : line diagonal to the grain of a fabric **2** : prejudice ∼ *vb* **-ased** *or* **-assed; -as·ing** *or* **-as·sing** : prejudice

bib \'bib\ *n* : shield tied under the chin to protect the clothes while eating

Bi·ble \'bībəl\ *n* **1** : sacred scriptures of Christians **2** : sacred scriptures of Judaism or of some other religion — **bib·li·cal** \'biblikəl\ *adj*

bib·li·og·ra·phy \,biblē'ägrəfē\ *n, pl* **-phies** : list of writings on a subject or of an author — **bib·li·og·ra·pher** \-fər\ *n* — **bib·li·o·graph·ic** \-lēə'grafik\ *adj*

bi·cam·er·al \'bī'kamərəl\ *adj* : having 2 legislative chambers

bi·car·bon·ate \-'kärbə,nāt, -nət\ *n* : acid carbonate

bi·cen·ten·ni·al \,bīsen'tenēəl\ *n* : 200th anniversary — **bicentennial** *adj*

bi·ceps \'bī,seps\ *n* : large muscle of the upper arm

bick·er \'bikər\ *vb or n* : squabble

bi·cus·pid \bī'kəspəd\ *n* : double-pointed tooth

bi·cy·cle \'bī,sikəl\ *n* : 2-wheeled vehicle moved by pedaling ∼ *vb* **-cled; -cling** : ride a bicycle — **bi·cy·cler** \-klər\ *n* — **bi·cy·clist** \-list\ *n*

bid \'bid\ *vb* **bade** \'bad, 'bād\ *or* **bid; bid·den** \'bid°n\ *or* **bid; bid·ding 1** : order **2** : invite **3** : express **4** : make a bid ∼ *n* **1** : act of bidding **2** : buyer's proposed price — **bid·da·ble** \-əbəl\ *adj* — **bid·der** *n*

bide \'bīd\ *vb* **bode** \'bōd\ *or* **bid·ed; bided; bid·ing 1** : wait **2** : dwell

bi·en·ni·al \bī'enēəl\ *adj* **1** : occurring

once in 2 years **2** : lasting 2 years — **biennial** *n* — **bi·en·ni·al·ly** *adv*

bier \'bir\ *n* : stand for a coffin

bi·fo·cals \'bī,fōkəlz\ *n pl* : eyeglasses that correct for near and distant vision

big \'big\ *adj* **-gg-** : large in size, amount, or scope — **big·ness** *n*

big·a·my \'bigəmē\ *n* : marrying one person while still married to another — **big·a·mist** \-mist\ *n* — **big·a·mous** \-məs\ *adj*

big·horn *n, pl* **-horn** *or* **-horns** : wild mountain sheep

bight \'bīt\ *n* **1** : loop of a rope **2** : bay

big·ot \'bigət\ *n* : one who is intolerant of others — **big·ot·ed** \-ətəd\ *adj* — **big·ot·ry** \-ətrē\ *n*

big shot *n* : important person

big·wig *n* : big shot

bike \'bīk\ *n* : bicycle or motorcycle

bi·ki·ni \bə'kēnē\ *n* : woman's brief 2-piece bathing suit

bi·lat·er·al \'bī'latərəl\ *adj* : involving 2 sides — **bi·lat·er·al·ly** *adv*

bile \'bīl\ *n* **1** : greenish liver secretion that aids digestion **2** : bad temper

bi·lin·gual \bī'lingwəl\ *adj* : using 2 languages

bil·ious \'bilyəs\ *adj* : irritable — **bil·ious·ness** *n*

bilk \'bilk\ *vb* : cheat

¹bill \'bil\ *n* : jaws of a bird together with their horny covering ∼ *vb* : caress fondly — **billed** *adj*

²bill *n* **1** : draft of a law **2** : list of things to be paid for **3** : printed advertisement **4** : piece of paper money ∼ *vb* : submit a bill or account to

bill·board *n* : surface for displaying advertising bills

bil·let \'bilət\ *n* : soldiers' quarters ∼ *vb* : lodge in a billet

bill·fold *n* : wallet

bil·liards \'bilyərdz\ *n* : game of driving balls into one another or into pockets on a table

bil·lion \'bilyən\ *n, pl* **billions** *or*

List of self-explanatory words with the prefix *bi-*

bicolored	bicultural	binational
biconcave	bidirectional	biparental
biconcavity	bifunctional	bipolar
biconvex	bimetal	biracial
biconvexity	bimetallic	

billion : 1000 millions — **billion** *adj* — **bil·lionth** \-yənth\ *adj or n*

bil·low \'bilō\ *n* **1** : great wave **2** : rolling mass ∼ *vb* : swell out — **bil·lowy** \'bilə̇wē\ *adj*

billy goat *n* : male goat

bin \'bin\ *n* : storage box

bi·na·ry \'bīnərē\ *adj* : consisting of 2 things — **binary** *n*

bind \'bīnd\ *vb* **bound** \'baund\; **bind·ing 1** : tie **2** : obligate **3** : unite into a mass **4** : bandage — **bind·er** *n* — **binding** *n*

binge \'binj\ *n* : spree

bin·go \'biŋgō\ *n, pl* **-gos** : game of covering numbers on a card

bin·oc·u·lar \bī'näkyələr, bə-\ *adj* : of or relating to both eyes ∼ *n* : binocular optical instrument —usu. pl.

bio·chem·is·try \,bīō'kemə̇strē\ *n* : chemistry dealing with organisms — **bio·chem·i·cal** *adj or n* — **bio·chem·ist** *n*

bio·de·grad·able \,bīōdi'grādəbəl\ *adj* : able to be reduced to harmless products by organisms — **bio·de·grad·abil·i·ty** *n* — **bio·deg·ra·da·tion** *n* — **bio·de·grade** *vb*

bi·og·ra·phy \bī'ägrəfē, bē-\ *n, pl* **-phies** : written history of a person's life — **bi·og·ra·pher** \-fər\ *n* — **bio·graph·i·cal** \,bīə'grafikəl\ *adj*

bi·ol·o·gy \bī'äləjē\ *n* : science of living beings and life processes — **bi·o·log·ic** \,bīə'läjik\, **bi·o·log·i·cal** \-əl\ *adj* — **bi·ol·o·gist** \bī'äləjist\ *n*

bi·on·ic \bī'änik\ *adj* : having normal biological capabilities enhanced by electronic or mechanical devices

bio·phys·ics \,bīō'fiziks\ *n* : application of physics to biological problems — **bio·phys·i·cal** *adj* — **bio·phys·i·cist** *n*

bi·op·sy \'bī,äpsē\ *n, pl* **-sies** : removal of live bodily tissue for examination

bio·tech·nol·o·gy \,bīōtek'näləjē\ *n* : manufacture of products using techniques involving the manipulation of DNA

bi·par·ti·san \bī'pärtəzən, -sən\ *adj* : involving members of 2 parties

bi·ped \'bī,ped\ *n* : 2-footed animal

birch \'bərch\ *n* : deciduous tree with close-grained wood — **birch, birch·en** \-ən\ *adj*

bird \'bərd\ *n* : warm-blooded egg-laying vertebrate with wings and feathers — **bird·bath** *n* — **bird·house** *n* — **bird·seed** *n*

bird's-eye \'bardz,ī\ *adj* **1** : seen from above **2** : cursory

birth \'bərth\ *n* **1** : act or fact of being born or of producing young **2** : origin — **birth·day** — **birth·place** *n* — **birth·rate** *n*

birth·mark *n* : unusual blemish on the skin at birth

birth·right *n* : something one is entitled to by birth

bis·cuit \'biskət\ *n* : small bread made with leavening other than yeast

bi·sect \'bī,sekt\ *vb* : divide into 2 parts — **bi·sec·tion** \'bī,sekshən\ *n* — **bi·sec·tor** \-tər\ *n*

bish·op \'bishəp\ *n* : clergy member higher than a priest

bish·op·ric \-shə,prik\ *n* **1** : diocese **2** : office of bishop

bis·muth \'bizməth\ *n* : heavy brittle metallic chemical element

bi·son \'bīsᵊn, 'bīz-\ *n, pl* **-son** : large shaggy wild ox of central U.S.

bis·tro \'bēstrō, 'bis-\ *n, pl* **-tros** : small restaurant or bar

¹**bit** \'bit\ *n* **1** : part of a bridle that goes in a horse's mouth **2** : drilling tool

²**bit** *n* **1** : small piece or quantity **2** : small degree

bitch \'bich\ *n* : female dog ∼ *vb* : complain

bite \'bīt\ *vb* **bit** \'bit\; **bit·ten** \'bitᵊn\; **bit·ing** \'bītiŋ\ **1** : to grip or cut with teeth or jaws **2** : dig in or grab and hold **3** : sting **4** : take bait ∼ *n* **1** : act of biting **2** : bit of food **3** : wound made by biting — **bit·ing** *adj*

bit·ter \'bitər\ *adj* **1** : having an acrid lingering taste **2** : intense or severe **3** : extremely harsh or resentful — **bit·ter·ly** *adv* — **bit·ter·ness** *n*

bit·tern \'bitərn\ *n* : small heron

bi·tu·mi·nous coal \bə'tümənəs-, -'tyü-\ *n* : coal that yields volatile waste matter when heated

bi·valve \'bī,valv\ *n* : animal (as a clam) with a shell of 2 parts — **bivalve** *adj*

biv·ouac \'bivə,wak\ *n* : temporary camp ∼ *vb* **-ouacked; -ouack·ing** : camp

bi·zarre \bə'zär\ *adj* : very strange — **bi·zarre·ly** *adv*

blab \'blab\ *vb* **-bb-** : talk too much

black \'blak\ *adj* **1** : of the color black

2 : dark-skinned **3** : soiled **4** : lacking light **5** : wicked or evil **6** : gloomy ∼ *n* **1** : black pigment or dye **2** : something black **3** : color of least lightness ∼ *n* : person of a dark-skinned race ∼ *vb* : blacken — **black·ing** *n* — **black·ish** *adj* — **black·ly** *adv* — **black·ness** *n*

black–and–blue *adj* : darkly discolored from bruising

black·ball \'blak‚ból\ *vb* **1** : ostracize **2** : boycott — **blackball** *n*

black·ber·ry \'blak‚berē\ *n* : black or purple fruit of a bramble

black·bird *n* : bird of which the male is largely or wholly black

black·board *n* : dark surface for writing on with chalk

black·en \'blakən\ *vb* **1** : make or become black **2** : defame

black·guard \'blagərd, -‚ärd\ *n* : scoundrel

black·head *n* : small dark oily mass plugging the outlet of a skin gland

black hole *n* : invisible extremely massive celestial object

black·jack *n* **1** : flexible leather=covered club **2** : card game ∼ *vb* : hit with a blackjack

black·list *n* : list of persons to be punished or boycotted — **blacklist** *vb*

black·mail *n* **1** : extortion by threat of exposure **2** : something extorted by blackmail — **blackmail** *vb* — **black·mail·er** *n*

black·out *n* **1** : darkness due to electrical failure **2** : brief fainting spell — **black out** *vb*

black·smith *n* : one who forges iron

black·top *n* : dark tarry material for surfacing roads — **blacktop** *vb*

blad·der \'bladər\ *n* : sac into which urine passes from the kidneys

blade \'blād\ *n* **1** : leaf esp. of grass **2** : something resembling the flat part of a leaf **3** : cutting part of an instrument or tool — **blad·ed** \'blādəd\ *adj*

blame \'blām\ *vb* **blamed; blam·ing 1** : find fault with **2** : hold responsible or responsible for — **blam·able** *adj* — **blame** *n* — **blame·less** *adj* — **blame·less·ly** *adv* — **blame·worthy** *adj*

blanch \'blanch\ *vb* : make or become white or pale

bland \'bland\ *adj* **1** : smooth in man-

ner **2** : soothing **3** : tasteless — **bland·ly** *adv* — **bland·ness** *n*

blan·dish·ment \'blandishmənt\ *n* : flattering or coaxing speech or act

blank \'blaŋk\ *adj* **1** : showing or causing a dazed look **2** : lacking expression **3** : empty **4** : free from writing **5** : downright ∼ *n* **1** : an empty space **2** : form with spaces to write in **3** : unfinished form (as of a key) **4** : cartridge with no bullet ∼ *vb* : cover or close up — **blank·ly** *adv* — **blank·ness** *n*

blan·ket \'blaŋkət\ *n* **1** : heavy covering for a bed **2** : covering layer ∼ *vb* : cover — *adj* : applying to a group

blare \'blar\ *vb* **blared; blar·ing** : make a loud harsh sound — **blare** *n*

blar·ney \'blärnē\ *n* : skillful flattery

bla·sé \blä'zā\ *adj* : indifferent to pleasure or excitement

blas·pheme \blas'fēm\ *vb* **-phemed; -phem·ing** : speak blasphemy — **blas·phem·er** *n*

blas·phe·my \'blasfəmē\ *n, pl* **-mies** : irreverence toward God or anything sacred — **blas·phe·mous** *adj*

blast \'blast\ *n* **1** : violent gust of wind **2** : explosion ∼ *vb* : shatter by or as if by explosive — **blast off** *vb* : take off esp. in a rocket

bla·tant \'blātᵊnt\ *adj* : offensively showy — **bla·tan·cy** \-ᵊnsē\ *n* — **bla·tant·ly** *adv*

¹**blaze** \'blāz\ *n* **1** : fire **2** : intense direct light **3** : strong display ∼ *vb* **blazed; blaz·ing** : burn or shine brightly

²**blaze** *n* **1** : white stripe on an animal's face **2** : trail marker esp. on a tree ∼ *vb* **blazed; blaz·ing** : mark with blazes

blaz·er \-ər\ *n* : sports jacket

bleach \'blēch\ *vb* : whiten — **bleach** *n*

bleach·ers \-ərz\ *n sing or pl* : uncovered stand for spectators

bleak \'blēk\ *adj* **1** : desolately barren **2** : lacking cheering qualities — **bleak·ish** *adj* — **bleak·ly** *adv* — **bleak·ness** *n*

bleary \'blirē\ *adj* : dull or dimmed esp. from fatigue

bleat \'blēt\ *n* : cry of a sheep or goat or a sound like it — **bleat** *vb*

bleed \'blēd\ *vb* **bled** \'bled\; **bleed·ing 1** : lose or shed blood **2** : feel distress **3** : flow from a wound **4**

: draw fluid from **5** : extort money from — **bleed•er** n

blem•ish \\'blemish\\ vb : spoil by a flaw ~ n : noticeable flaw

¹blench \\'blench\\ vb : flinch

²blench vb : grow or make pale

blend \\'blend\\ vb **1** : mix thoroughly **2** : combine into an integrated whole — **blend** n — **blend•er** n

bless \\'bles\\ vb **blessed** \\'blest\\; **bless•ing 1** : consecrate by religious rite **2** : invoke divine care for **3** : make happy — **bless•ed** \\'blesəd\\, **blest** \\'blest\\ adj — **bless•ed•ly** \\'blesədlē\\ adv — **bless•ed•ness** \\'blesədnəs\\ n — **bless•ing** n

blew past of BLOW

blight \\'blīt\\ n **1** : plant disorder marked by withering or an organism causing it **2** : harmful influence **3** : deteriorated condition ~ vb : affect with or suffer from blight

blimp \\'blimp\\ n : airship holding form by pressure of contained gas

blind \\'blīnd\\ adj **1** : lacking or quite deficient in ability to see **2** : not intelligently controlled **3** : having no way out ~ vb **1** : to make blind **2** : dazzle ~ n **1** : something to conceal or darken **2** : place of concealment — **blind•ly** adv — **blind•ness** n

blind•fold vb : cover the eyes of — **blindfold** n

blink \\'bliŋk\\ vb **1** : wink **2** : shine intermittently ~ n : wink

blink•er n : a blinking light

bliss \\'blis\\ n **1** : complete happiness **2** : heaven or paradise — **bliss•ful** adj — **bliss•ful•ly** adv

blis•ter \\'blistər\\ n **1** : raised area of skin containing watery fluid **2** : raised or swollen spot ~ vb : develop or cause blisters

blithe \\'blīth, 'blith\\ adj **blith•er; blith•est** : cheerful — **blithe•ly** adv — **blithe•some** \\-səm\\ adj

blitz \\'blits\\ n **1** : series of air raids **2** : fast intensive campaign — **blitz** vb

bliz•zard \\'blizərd\\ n : severe snowstorm

bloat \\'blōt\\ vb : swell

blob \\'bläb\\ n : small lump or drop

bloc \\'bläk\\ n : group working together

block \\'bläk\\ n **1** : solid piece **2** : frame enclosing a pulley **3** : quantity considered together **4** : large building divided into separate units **5** : a city square or the distance along

one of its sides **6** : obstruction **7** : interruption of a bodily or mental function ~ vb : obstruct or hinder

block•ade \\'blä'kād\\ n : isolation of a place usu. by troops or ships — **block•ade** n — **block•ad•er** n

block•head n : stupid person

blond, blonde \\'bländ\\ adj **1** : fair in complexion **2** : of a light color — **blond, blonde** n

blood \\'bləd\\ n **1** : red liquid that circulates in the heart, arteries, and veins of animals **2** : lifeblood **3** : lineage — **blood•ed** adj — **blood•less** adj — **blood•stain** n — **blood-stained** adj — **blood•suck•er** n — **blood•suck•ing** n — **bloody** adj

blood-cur•dling adj : terrifying

blood•hound n : large hound with a keen sense of smell

blood•mo•bile \\-mō,bēl\\ n : truck for collecting blood from donors

blood•shed n : slaughter

blood•shot adj : inflamed to redness

blood•stream n : blood in a circulatory system

blood•thirsty adj : eager to shed blood — **blood•thirst•i•ly** adv — **blood•thirst•i•ness** n

bloom \\'blüm\\ n **1** : flower **2** : period of flowering **3** : fresh or healthy look ~ vb **1** : yield flowers **2** : mature — **bloomy** adj

bloo•mers \\'blümərz\\ n pl : woman's underwear of short loose trousers

bloop•er \\'blüpər\\ n : public blunder

blos•som \\'bläsəm\\ n or vb : flower

blot \\'blät\\ n **1** : stain **2** : blemish ~ vb -**tt- 1** : spot **2** : dry with absorbent paper — **blot•ter** n

blotch \\'bläch\\ n : large spot — **blotch** vb — **blotchy** adj

blouse \\'blaus, 'blauz\\ n : loose garment reaching from the neck to the waist

¹blow \\'blō\\ vb **blew** \\'blü\\; **blown** \\'blōn\\; **blow•ing 1** : move forcibly **2** : send forth a current of air **3** : sound **4** : shape by blowing **5** : explode **6** : bungle ~ n **1** : gale **2** : act of blowing — **blow•er** n — **blowy** adj

²blow n **1** : forcible stroke **2** pl : fighting **3** : calamity

blow-out n : bursting of a tire

blow•torch n : small torch that uses a blast of air

¹blub•ber \\'bləbər\\ n : fat of whales

²**blubber** vb : cry noisily

blud·geon \'bləjən\ n : short club ~ vb : hit with a bludgeon

blue \'blü\ adj **blu·er; blu·est** **1** : of the color blue **2** : melancholy ~ n : color of the clear sky — **blu·ish** \-ish\ adj

blue·bell n : plant with blue bell-shaped flowers

blue·ber·ry \-,berē\ n : edible blue or blackish berry

blue·bird n : small bluish songbird

blue·fish n : bluish marine food fish

blue jay n : American crested jay

blue·print n **1** : photographic print in white on blue of a mechanical drawing **2** : plan of action — **blueprint** vb

blues \'blüz\ n pl **1** : depression **2** : music in a melancholy style

¹**bluff** \'bləf\ adj **1** : rising steeply with a broad flat front **2** : frank ~ n : cliff

²**bluff** vb : deceive by pretense ~ n : act of bluffing — **bluff·er** \-ər\ n

blu·ing, blue·ing \'blüiŋ\ n : laundry preparation to keep fabrics white

blun·der \'bləndər\ vb **1** : move clumsily **2** : make a stupid mistake ~ n : bad mistake

blun·der·buss \-,bəs\ n : obsolete short-barreled firearm

blunt \'blənt\ adj **1** : not sharp **2** : tactless ~ vb : make dull — **blunt·ly** adv — **blunt·ness** n

blur \'blər\ n **1** : smear **2** : something perceived indistinctly ~ vb **-rr-** : cloud or obscure — **blur·ry** \-ē\ adj

blurb \'blərb\ n : short publicity notice

blurt \'blərt\ vb : utter suddenly

blush \'bləsh\ n : reddening of the face — **blush** vb — **blush·ful** adj

blus·ter \'bləstər\ vb **1** : blow violently **2** : talk or act with boasts or threats — **bluster** n — **blus·tery** adj

boa \'bōə\ n **1** : a large snake (as the **boa con·stric·tor** \-kən'striktər\) that crushes its prey **2** : fluffy scarf

boar \'bōr\ n : male swine

board \'bōrd\ n **1** : long thin piece of sawed lumber **2** : flat thin sheet esp. for games **3** : daily meals furnished for pay **4** : official body ~ vb **1** : go aboard **2** : cover with boards **3** : supply meals to — **board·er** n

board·walk n : wooden walk along a beach

boast \'bōst\ vb : praise oneself or one's possessions — **boast** n —

boast·er n — **boast·ful** adj — **boast·ful·ly** adv

boat \'bōt\ n : small vessel for traveling on water — **boat** vb — **boat·man** \-mən\ n

boat·swain \'bōs²n\ n : ship's officer in charge of the hull

¹**bob** \'bäb\ vb **-bb-** **1** : move up and down **2** : appear suddenly

²**bob** n **1** : float **2** : woman's short haircut ~ vb : cut hair in a bob

bob·bin \'bäbən\ n : spindle for holding thread

bob·ble \'bäbəl\ vb **-bled; -bling** : fumble — **bobble** n

bob·cat n : small American lynx

bob·o·link \'bäbə,liŋk\ n : American songbird

bob·sled \'bäb,sled\ n : racing sled — **bobsled** vb

bob·white \'bäb'hwīt\ n : quail

bock \'bäk\ n : dark beer

¹**bode** \'bōd\ vb **bod·ed; bod·ing** : indicate by signs

²**bode** past of BIDE

bod·ice \'bädəs\ n : close-fitting top of dress

bod·i·ly \'bädⁿlē\ adj : relating to the body ~ adv **1** : in the flesh **2** : as a whole

body \'bädē\ n, pl **bod·ies** **1** : the physical whole of an organism **2** : human being **3** : main part **4** : mass of matter **5** : group — **bod·ied** adj — **bod·i·less** \-iləs, -ⁿ ləs\ adj — **body·guard** n

bog \'bäg, 'bog\ n : swamp ~ vb **-gg-** : sink in or as if in a bog — **bog·gy** adj

bo·gey \'bugē, 'bō-\ n, pl **-geys** : someone or something frightening

bog·gle \'bägəl\ vb **-gled; -gling** : overwhelm with amazement

bo·gus \'bōgəs\ adj : fake

bo·he·mi·an \bō'hēmēən\ n : one living unconventionally — **bohemian** adj

¹**boil** \'boil\ n : inflamed swelling

²**boil** vb **1** : heat to a temperature (**boiling point**) at which vapor forms **2** : cook in boiling liquid **3** : be agitated — **boil** n

boil·er \'boilər\ n : tank holding hot water or steam

bois·ter·ous \'boistərəs\ adj : noisily turbulent — **bois·ter·ous·ly** adv

bold \'bōld\ adj **1** : courageous **2** : insolent **3** : daring — **bold•ly** *adv* — **bold•ness** *n*

bo•le•ro \bə'lerō\ *n, pl* **-ros 1** : Spanish dance **2** : short open jacket

boll \'bōl\ *n* : seed pod

boll weevil *n* : small grayish weevil that infests the cotton plant

bo•lo•gna \bə'lōnē\ *n* : large smoked sausage

bol•ster \'bōlstər\ *n* : long pillow ~ *vb* **-stered; -ster•ing** : support

bolt \'bōlt\ *n* **1** : flash of lightning **2** : sliding bar used to fasten a door **3** : roll of cloth **4** : threaded pin used with a nut ~ *vb* **1** : move suddenly **2** : fasten with a bolt **3** : swallow hastily

bomb \'bäm\ *n* : explosive device ~ *vb* : attack with bombs — **bomb•proof** *adj*

bom•bard \bäm'bärd, bəm-\ *vb* : attack with or as if with artillery — **bom•bard•ment** *n*

bom•bar•dier \ˌbämbə'dir\ *n* : one who releases the bombs from a bomber

bom•bast \'bäm‚bast\ *n* : pretentious language — **bom•bas•tic** \bäm-'bastik\ *adj*

bomb•er \'bämər\ *n* **1** : one that bombs **2** : airplane for dropping bombs

bomb•shell *n* **1** : bomb **2** : great surprise

bona fide \'bōnə‚fīd, 'bän-; ˌbōnə-'fīdē\ *adj* **1** : made in good faith **2** : genuine

bo•nan•za \bə'nanzə\ *n* : something yielding a rich return

bon•bon \'bän‚bän\ *n* : piece of candy

bond \'bänd\ *n* **1** *pl* : fetters **2** : uniting force **3** : obligation made binding by money **4** : interest-bearing certificate ~ *vb* **1** : insure **2** : cause to adhere — **bond•hold•er** *n*

bond•age \'bändij\ *n* : slavery

¹**bonds•man** \'bändzmən\ *n* : slave

²**bondsman** *n* : surety

bone \'bōn\ *n* : skeletal material ~ *vb* **boned; bon•ing** : to free from bones — **bone•less** *adj* — **bony** \'bōnē\ *adj*

bon•er \'bōnər\ *n* : blunder

bon•fire \'bän‚fīr\ *n* : outdoor fire

bo•ni•to \bə'nētō\ *n, pl* **-tos** *or* **-to** : medium-sized tuna

bon•net \'bänət\ *n* : hat for a woman or infant

bo•nus \'bōnəs\ *n* : extra payment

boo \'bü\ *n, pl* **boos** : shout of disapproval — **boo** *vb*

boo•by \'bübē\ *n, pl* **-bies** : dunce

book \'bük\ *n* **1** : paper sheets bound into a volume **2** : long literary work or a subdivision of one ~ *vb* : reserve — **book•case** *n* — **book•let** \-lət\ *n* — **book•mark** *n* — **book•sell•er** *n* — **book•shelf** *n*

book•end *n* : support to hold up a row of books

book•ie \-ē\ *n* : bookmaker

book•ish \-ish\ *adj* : fond of books and reading

book•keep•er *n* : one who keeps business accounts — **book•keep•ing** *n*

book•mak•er *n* : one who takes bets — **book•mak•ing** *n*

book•worm *n* : one devoted to reading

¹**boom** \'büm\ *n* **1** : long spar to extend the bottom of a sail **2** : beam projecting from the pole of a derrick

²**boom** *vb* **1** : make a deep hollow sound **2** : grow rapidly esp. in value ~ *n* **1** : booming sound **2** : rapid growth

boo•mer•ang \'bümə‚raŋ\ *n* : angular club that returns to the thrower

¹**boon** \'bün\ *n* : benefit

²**boon** *adj* : congenial

boon•docks \'bün‚däks\ *n pl* : rural area

boor \'bur\ *n* : rude person — **boor•ish** *adj*

boost \'büst\ *vb* **1** : raise **2** : promote — **boost** *n* — **boost•er** *n*

boot \'büt\ *n* **1** : covering for the foot and leg **2** : kick ~ *vb* : kick

boo•tee, boo•tie \'bütē\ *n* : infant's knitted sock

booth \'büth\ *n, pl* **booths** \'büthz, 'büths\ : small enclosed stall or seating area

boot•leg \'büt‚leg\ *vb* : make or sell liquor illegally — **bootleg** *adj or n* — **boot•leg•ger** *n*

boo•ty \'bütē\ *n, pl* **-ties** : plunder

booze \'büz\ *vb* **boozed; booz•ing** : drink liquor to excess ~ *n* : liquor — **booz•er** *n* — **boozy** *adj*

bo•rax \'bōr‚aks\ *n* : crystalline compound of boron

bor•der \'bōrdər\ *n* **1** : edge **2** : boundary ~ *vb* **1** : put a border on **2** : be close

¹**bore** \'bōr\ *vb* **bored; bor•ing 1** : pierce **2** : make by piercing ~ *n* : cylindrical hole or its diameter — **bor•er** *n*

²**bore** *past of* BEAR

³**bore** \n : one that is dull ~ vb **bored; bor·ing** : tire with dullness — **bore·dom** \'bȯrdəm\ n

born \'bȯrn\ adj 1 : brought into life 2 : being suited by birth

borne past part of BEAR

bo·ron \'bȯr,än\ n : dark-colored chemical element

bor·ough \'bərō\ n : incorporated town or village

bor·row \'bärō\ vb 1 : take as a loan 2 : take into use

bo·som \'būzəm, 'büs-\ n : breast ~ adj : intimate — **bo·somed** adj

boss \'bȯs\ n : employer or supervisor ~ vb : supervise — **bossy** adj

bot·a·ny \'bät,nē\ n : plant biology — **bo·tan·i·cal** \bə'tanikəl\ adj — **bot·a·nist** \'bät,nist\ n — **bot·a·nize** \-ə²n,īz\ vb

botch \'bäch\ vb : do clumsily — **botch** n

both \'bōth\ adj or pron : the one and the other ~ conj — used to show each of two is included

both·er \'bäthər\ vb 1 : annoy or worry 2 : take the trouble — **bother** n — **both·er·some** \-səm\ adj

bot·tle \'bät²l\ n : container with a narrow neck and no handles ~ vb **bot·tled; bot·tling** : put into a bottle

bot·tle·neck n : place or cause of congestion

bot·tom \'bätəm\ n 1 : supporting surface 2 : lowest part or place — **bot·tom** adj — **bot·tom·less** adj

bot·u·lism \'bächə,lizəm\ n : acute food poisoning

bou·doir \'bü,dwär, 'bü-, ,bü²-, ,bü²-\ n : woman's private room

bough \'baù\ n : large tree branch

bought past of BUY

bouil·lon \'bü,yän; 'bùl,yän, -yən\ n : clear soup

boul·der \'bōldər\ n : large rounded rock — **boul·dered** adj

bou·le·vard \'bùlə,värd, 'bü-\ n : broad thoroughfare

¹**bounce** \'baùns\ vb **bounced; bounc·ing** 1 : spring back 2 : make bounce — **bounce** n — **bouncy** \'baùnsē\ adj

¹**bound** \'baùnd\ adj : intending to go

²**bound** n : limit or boundary ~ vb : be a boundary of — **bound·less** adj — **bound·less·ness** n

³**bound** adj 1 : obliged 2 : having a

binding 3 : determined 4 : incapable of failing

⁴**bound** n : leap ~ vb : move by springing

bound·ary \'baùndrē\ n, pl **-aries** : line marking extent or separation

boun·ty \'baùntē\ n, pl **-ties** 1 : generosity 2 : reward — **boun·te·ous** \-ēəs\ adj — **boun·te·ous·ly** adv — **boun·ti·ful** \-ifəl\ adj — **boun·ti·ful·ly** adv

bou·quet \bō'kā, bü-\ n 1 : bunch of flowers 2 : fragrance

bour·bon \'bərbən\ n : corn whiskey

bour·geoi·sie \,bùrzh,wä'zē\ n : middle class of society — **bour·geois** \'bùrzh,wä, bùrzh'wä\ n or adj

bout \'baùt\ n 1 : contest 2 : outbreak

bou·tique \bü'tēk\ n : specialty shop

bo·vine \'bō,vīn, -,vēn\ adj : relating to cattle — **bovine** n

¹**bow** \'baù\ vb 1 : submit 2 : bend the head or body ~ n : act of bowing

²**bow** \'bō\ n 1 : bend or arch 2 : weapon for shooting arrows 3 : knot with loops 4 : rod with stretched horsehairs for playing a stringed instrument ~ vb : curve or bend — **bow·man** \-mən\ n — **bow·string** n

³**bow** \'baù\ n : forward part of a ship — **bow** adj

bow·els \'baùəls\ n pl 1 : intestines 2 : inmost parts

bow·er \'baùər\ n : arbor

¹**bowl** \'bōl\ n : concave vessel or part — **bowl·ful** \-,fùl\ n

²**bowl** n : round ball for bowling ~ vb : roll a ball in bowling — **bowl·er** n

bowl·ing n : game in which balls are rolled to knock down pins

¹**box** \'bäks\ n, pl **box** or **box·es** : evergreen shrub — **box·wood** \-,wùd\ n

²**box** n 1 : container usu. with 4 sides and a cover 2 : small compartment ~ vb : put in a box

³**box** n : slap ~ vb 1 : slap 2 : fight with the fists — **box·er** n — **box·ing** n

box·car n : roofed freight car

box office n : theater ticket office

boy \'bȯi\ n : male child — **boy·hood** n — **boy·ish** adj — **boy·ish·ly** adv — **boy·ish·ness** n

boy·cott \-,kät\ vb : refrain from dealing with — **boycott** n

boy·friend \'bȯi,frend\ n 1 : male friend 2 : woman's regular male companion

brace \'brās\ n 1 : crank for turning a

bit **2** : something that resists weight or supports **3** : punctuation mark { or } — ~ vb **braced; brac·ing 1** : make taut or steady **2** : invigorate **3** : strengthen

brace·let \'brāslət\ n : ornamental band for the wrist or arm

brack·et \'brakət\ n **1** : projecting support **2** : punctuation mark [or] **3** : class — ~ vb **1** : furnish or fasten with brackets **2** : place within brackets **3** : group

brack·ish \-ish\ adj : salty

brad \'brad\ n : nail with a small head

brag \'brag\ vb **-gg-** : boast — **brag** n

brag·gart \'bragərt\ n : boaster

braid \'brād\ vb : interweave — ~ n : something braided

braille \'brāl\ n : system of writing for the blind using raised dots

brain \'brān\ n **1** : organ of thought and nervous coordination enclosed in the skull **2** : intelligence — ~ vb : smash the skull of — **brained** adj — **brain·less** adj — **brainy** adj

braise \'brāz\ vb **braised; brais·ing** : cook (meat) slowly in a covered dish

brake \'brāk\ n : device for slowing or stopping — ~ vb **braked; brak·ing** : slow or stop by a brake

bram·ble \'brambəl\ n : prickly shrub

bran \'bran\ n : edible cracked grain husks

branch \'branch\ n **1** : division of a plant stem **2** : part ~ vb **1** : develop branches **2** : diverge — **branched** adj

brand \'brand\ n **1** : identifying mark made by burning **2** : stigma **3** : distinctive kind (as of goods from one firm) ~ vb : mark with a brand

brand–new adj : unused

bran·dy \'brandē\ n, pl **-dies** : liquor distilled from wine

brash \'brash\ adj **1** : impulsive **2** : aggressively self-assertive

brass \'bras\ n **1** : alloy of copper and zinc **2** : brazen self-assurance **3** : high-ranking military officers — **brassy** adj

bras·siere \brə'zir\ n : woman's undergarment to support the breasts

brat \'brat\ n : ill-behaved child — **brat·ti·ness** n — **brat·ty** adj

bra·va·do \brə'vädō\ n, pl **-does** or **-dos** : false bravery

¹brave \'brāv\ adj **brav·er; brav·est**
: showing courage — ~ vb **braved; brav·ing** : face with courage — **brave·ly** adv — **brav·ery** \-ərē\ n

²brave n : American Indian warrior

bra·vo \'brävō\ n, pl **-vos** : shout of approval

brawl \'brȯl\ n : noisy quarrel or violent fight — **brawl** vb — **brawl·er** n

brawn \'brȯn\ n : muscular strength — **brawny** \-ē\ adj — **brawn·i·ness** n

bray \'brā\ n : harsh cry of a donkey — **bray** vb

bra·zen \'brāz²n\ adj **1** : made of brass **2** : bold — **bra·zen·ly** adv — **bra·zen·ness** n

bra·zier \'brāzhər\ n : charcoal grill

breach \'brēch\ n **1** : breaking of a law, obligation, or standard **2** : gap ~ vb : make a breach in

bread \'bred\ n : baked food made of flour — ~ vb : cover with bread crumbs

breadth \'bredth\ n : width

bread·win·ner n : wage earner

break \'brāk\ vb **broke** \'brōk\; **broken** \'brōkən\; **break·ing 1** : knock into pieces **2** : transgress **3** : force a way into or out of **4** : exceed **5** : interrupt **6** : fail — ~ n **1** : act or result of breaking **2** : stroke of good luck — **break·able** adj or n — **break·age** \'brākij\ n — **break·er** n — **break in** vb **1** : enter by force **2** : interrupt **3** : train — **break out** vb **1** : erupt with force **2** : develop a rash

break·down n : physical or mental failure — **break down** vb

break·fast \'brekfəst\ n : first meal of the day — **breakfast** vb

breast \'brest\ n **1** : milk-producing gland esp. of a woman **2** : front part of the chest

breast·bone n : sternum

breath \'breth\ n **1** : slight breeze **2** : air breathed in or out — **breath·less** adj — **breath·less·ly** adv — **breath·less·ness** n — **breathy** \'brethē\ adj

breathe \'brēth\ vb **breathed; breathing 1** : draw air into the lungs and expel it **2** : live **3** : utter

breath·tak·ing adj : exciting

breech·es \'brichəz\ n pl : trousers ending near the knee

breed \'brēd\ vb **bred** \'bred\; **breeding 1** : give birth to **2** : propagate **3** : raise — ~ n **1** : kind of plant or animal usu. developed by humans **2** : class — **breed·er** n

breeze \'brēz\ n : light wind ~ vb
  breezed; breez·ing : move fast —
  breezy adj

breth·ren \'brethrən, -ərn\ pl of
  BROTHER

bre·via·ry \'brēvərē, 'bre-, -vyərē,
  -vē̇erē\ n, pl **-ries** : prayer book used
  by Roman Catholic priests

brev·i·ty \'brevətē\ n, pl **-ties** : short-
  ness or conciseness

brew \'brü\ vb : make by fermenting or
  steeping — **brew** n — **brew·er** n —
  brew·ery \'brüərē, 'brürē\ n

bri·ar var of BRIER

bribe \'brīb\ vb **bribed; brib·ing** : corrupt or influence by gifts ~ n : something offered or given in bribing —
  brib·able adj — **brib·ery** \-ərē\ n

bric–a–brac \'brikə‚brak\ n pl : small
  ornamental articles

brick \'brik\ n : building block of
  baked clay — **brick** vb — **brick·lay·
  er** n — **brick·lay·ing** n

bride \'brīd\ n : woman just married or
  about to be married — **brid·al** \-ᵊl\
  adj

bride·groom n : man just married or
  about to be married

brides·maid n : woman who attends a
  bride at her wedding

¹**bridge** \'brij\ n 1 : structure built for
  passage over a depression or obstacle
  2 : upper part of the nose 3 : compartment from which a ship is navigated 4 : artificial replacement for
  missing teeth ~ vb : build a bridge
  over — **bridge·able** adj

²**bridge** n : card game for 4 players

bri·dle \'brīdᵊl\ n : headgear to control
  a horse ~ vb **-dled; -dling** 1 : put a
  bridle on 2 : restrain 3 : show hostility or scorn

brief \'brēf\ adj : short or concise ~ n
  : concise summary (as of a legal case)
  ~ vb : give final instructions or essential information to — **brief·ly** adv
  — **brief·ness** n

brief·case n : case for papers

¹**bri·er** \'brīər\ n : thorny plant

²**brier** n : heath of southern Europe

¹**brig** \'brig\ n : 2-masted ship

²**brig** n : jail on a naval ship

bri·gade \brig'ād\ n 1 : large military
  unit 2 : group organized for a special
  activity

brig·a·dier general \‚brigə'dir-\ n : officer ranking next below a major general

brig·and \'brigənd\ n : bandit — **brig-
  and·age** \-ij\ n

bright \'brīt\ adj 1 : radiating or reflecting light 2 : cheerful 3 : intelligent — **bright·en** \-ᵊn\ vb — **bright-
  en·er** \'brītᵊnər\ n — **bright·ly** adv
  — **bright·ness** n

bril·liant \'brilyənt\ adj 1 : very bright
  2 : splendid 3 : very intelligent —
  bril·liance \-yəns\ n — **bril·lian·cy**
  \-yənsē\ n — **bril·liant·ly** adv

brim \'brim\ n : edge or rim ~ vb : be
  or become full — **brim·less** adj —
  brimmed adj

brim·ful \-'fu̇l\ adj : full to the brim

brim·stone n : sulfur

brin·dled \'brindᵊld\ adj : gray or
  tawny with dark streaks or flecks

brine \'brīn\ n 1 : salt water 2 : ocean
  — **brin·i·ness** n — **briny** adj

bring \'briŋ\ vb **brought** \'brȯt\;
  bring·ing 1 : cause to come with one
  2 : persuade 3 : produce 4 : sell for
  — **bring·er** n — **bring about** vb
  : make happen — **bring up** vb 1
  : care for and educate 2 : cause to be
  noticed

brink \'briŋk\ n : edge

bri·quette, bri·quet \bri'ket\ n
  : pressed mass (as of charcoal)

brisk \'brisk\ adj 1 : lively 2 : invigorating — **brisk·ly** adv — **brisk·
  ness** n

bris·ket \'briskət\ n : breast or lower
  chest of a quadruped

bris·tle \'brisᵊl\ n : short stiff hair ~ vb
  -tled; -tling 1 : stand erect 2 : show
  angry defiance 3 : appear as if covered with bristles — **bris·tly** adj

brit·tle \'britᵊl\ adj **-tler; -tlest** : easily
  broken — **brit·tle·ness** n

broach \'brōch\ n : pointed tool (as for
  opening casks) ~ vb 1 : pierce (as a
  cask) to open 2 : introduce for discussion

broad \'brȯd\ adj 1 : wide 2 : spacious 3 : clear or open 4 : obvious 5
  : tolerant in outlook 6 : widely applicable 7 : dealing with essential points
  — **broad·en** \-ᵊn\ vb — **broad·ly**
  adv — **broad·ness** n

broad·cast n 1 : transmission by radio
  waves 2 : radio or television program
  ~ vb **-cast; -cast·ing** 1 : scatter or
  sow in all directions 2 : make widely
  known 3 : send out on a broadcast —
  broad·cast·er n

broad·cloth n : fine cloth

broad·loom *adj* : woven on a wide loom esp. in solid color

broad–mind·ed *adj* : tolerant of varied opinions — **broad–mind·ed·ly** *adv* — **broad–mind·ed·ness** *n*

broad·side *n* **1** : simultaneous firing of all guns on one side of a ship **2** : verbal attack

bro·cade \brō'kād\ *n* : usu. silk fabric with a raised design

broc·co·li \'bräkəlē\ *n* : green vegetable akin to cauliflower

bro·chure \brō'shur\ *n* : pamphlet

brogue \'brōg\ *n* : Irish accent

broil \'broil\ *vb* : cook by radiant heat — **broil** *n*

broil·er *n* **1** : utensil for broiling **2** : chicken fit for broiling

¹broke \'brōk\ *past of* BREAK

²broke *adj* : out of money

bro·ken \'brōkən\ *adj* : imperfectly spoken — **bro·ken·ly** *adv*

bro·ken·heart·ed \-'härtəd\ *adj* : overcome by grief or despair

bro·ker \'brōkər\ *n* : agent who buys and sells for a fee — **broker** *vb* — **bro·ker·age** \-kərij\ *n*

bro·mine \'brō,mēn\ *n* : deep red liquid corrosive chemical element

bron·chi·tis \brän'kītəs, bräŋ-\ *n* : inflammation of the bronchi

bron·chus \'bräŋkəs\ *n, pl* **-chi** \-,kī, -,kē\ : division of the windpipe leading to a lung — **bron·chi·al** \-kēəl\ *adj*

bronze \'bränz\ *vb* **bronzed; bronz·ing** : make bronze in color ~ *n* **1** : alloy of copper and tin **2** : yellowish brown — **bronzy** \-ē\ *adj*

brooch \'brōch, 'brüch\ *n* : ornamental clasp or pin

brood \'brüd\ *n* : family of young ~ *vb* **1** : sit on eggs to hatch them **2** : ponder ~ *adj* : kept for breeding — **brood·er** *n* — **brood·ing·ly** *adv*

¹brook \'bruk\ *vb* : tolerate

²brook *n* : small stream

broom \'brüm, 'brum\ *n* **1** : flowering shrub **2** : implement for sweeping — **broom·stick** *n*

broth \'brȯth\ *n, pl* **broths** \'brȯths, 'brȯthz\ : liquid in which meat has been cooked

broth·el \'bräthəl, 'brȯth-\ *n* : house of prostitutes

broth·er \'brəthər\ *n, pl* **brothers** *also* **breth·ren** \'brethrən, -ərn\ **1** : male sharing one or both parents

with another person **2** : kinsman — **broth·er·hood** *n* — **broth·er·li·ness** *n* — **broth·er·ly** *adj*

broth·er–in–law *n, pl* **brothers–in–law** : brother of one's spouse or husband of one's sister or of one's spouse's sister

brought *past of* BRING

brow \'braú\ *n* **1** : eyebrow **2** : forehead **3** : edge of a steep place

brow·beat *vb* **-beat; -beat·en** *or* **-beat; -beat·ing** : intimidate

brown \'braún\ *adj* **1** : of the color brown **2** : of dark or tanned complexion ~ *n* : a color like that of coffee ~ *vb* : make or become brown — **brown·ish** *adj*

browse \'braúz\ *vb* **browsed; brows·ing 1** : graze **2** : look over casually — **brows·er** *n*

brows·er \'braúzər\ *n* : computer program for accessing Web sites

bru·in \'brüən\ *n* : bear

bruise \'brüz\ *vb* **bruised; bruis·ing 1** : make a bruise on **2** : become bruised ~ *n* : surface injury to flesh

brunch \'brənch\ *n* : late breakfast, early lunch, or combination of both

bru·net, bru·nette \brü'net\ *adj* : having dark hair and usu. dark skin — **bru·net, brunette** *n*

brunt \'brənt\ *n* : main impact

¹brush \'brəsh\ *n* **1** : small cut branches **2** : coarse shrubby vegetation

²brush *n* **1** : bristles set in a handle used esp. for cleaning or painting **2** : light touch ~ *vb* **1** : apply a brush to **2** : remove with or as if with a brush **3** : dismiss in an offhand way **4** : touch lightly — **brush up** *vb* : renew one's skill

³brush *n* : skirmish

brush–off *n* : curt dismissal

brusque \'brəsk\ *adj* : curt or blunt in manner — **brusque·ly** *adv*

bru·tal \'brüt²l\ *adj* : like a brute and esp. cruel — **bru·tal·i·ty** \brü'talətē\ *n* — **bru·tal·ize** \'brüt²l,īz\ *vb* — **bru·tal·ly** \-²lē\ *adv*

brute \'brüt\ *adj* **1** : relating to beasts **2** : unreasoning **3** : purely physical ~ *n* **1** : beast **2** : brutal person — **brut·ish** \-ish\ *adj*

bub·ble \'bəbəl\ *vb* **-bled; -bling** : form, rise in, or give off bubbles ~ *n* : globule of gas in or covered with a liquid — **bub·bly** \-əlē\ *adj*

bu·bo \'bübō, 'byü-\ *n, pl* **buboes** : inflammatory swelling of a lymph gland — **bu·bon·ic** \bü'bänik, 'byü-\ *adj*

buc·ca·neer \ˌbəkə'nir\ *n* : pirate

buck \'bək\ *n, pl* **buck** *or* **bucks** 1 : male animal (as a deer) 2 : dollar ～ *vb* 1 : jerk forward 2 : oppose

buck·et \'bəkət\ *n* : pail — **buck·et·ful** *n*

buck·le \'bəkəl\ *n* 1 : clasp (as on a belt) for two loose ends 2 : bend or fold ～ *vb* -**led; -ling** 1 : fasten with a buckle 2 : apply oneself 3 : bend or crumple

buck·ler \'bəklər\ *n* : shield

buck·shot *n* : coarse lead shot

buck·skin *n* : soft leather (as from the skin of a buck) — **buckskin** *adj*

buck·tooth *n* : large projecting front tooth — **buck·toothed** *adj*

buck·wheat *n* : herb whose seeds are used as a cereal grain or the seeds themselves

bu·col·ic \byü'kälik\ *adj* : pastoral

bud \'bəd\ *n* 1 : undeveloped plant shoot 2 : partly opened flower ～ *vb* -**dd-** 1 : form or put forth buds or 2 : develop like a bud

Bud·dhism \'büˌdizəm, 'bù-\ *n* : religion of eastern and central Asia — **Bud·dhist** \'büdist, 'bùd-\ *n or adj*

bud·dy \'bədē\ *n, pl* -**dies** : friend

budge \'bəj\ *vb* **budged; budg·ing** : move from a place

bud·get \'bəjət\ *n* 1 : estimate of income and expenses 2 : plan for coordinating income and expenses 3 : money available for a particular use — **budget** *vb or adj* — **bud·get·ary** \-əˌterē\ *adj*

buff \'bəf\ *n* 1 : yellow to orange yellow color 2 : enthusiast ～ *adj* : of the color buff ～ *vb* : polish

buf·fa·lo \'bəfəˌlō\ *n, pl* -**lo** *or* -**loes** : wild ox (as a bison)

¹buff·er \'bəfər\ *n* : shield or protector

²buffer *n* : one that buffs

¹buf·fet \'bəfət\ *n* : blow or slap ～ *vb* : hit esp. repeatedly

²buf·fet \ˌbə'fā, bü-\ *n* 1 : sideboard 2 : meal at which people serve themselves

buf·foon \ˌbə'fün\ *n* : clown — **buf·foon·ery** \-ərē\ *n*

bug \'bəg\ *n* 1 : small usu. obnoxious crawling creature 2 : 4-winged sucking insect 3 : unexpected imperfec-

tion 4 : disease-producing germ 5 : hidden microphone ～ *vb* -**gg-** 1 : pester 2 : conceal a microphone in

bug·a·boo \'bəgəˌbü\ *n, pl* -**boos** : bogey

bug·bear *n* : source of dread

bug·gy \'bəgē\ *n, pl* -**gies** : light carriage

bu·gle \'byügəl\ *n* : trumpetlike brass instrument — **bu·gler** \-glər\ *n*

build \'bild\ *vb* **built** \'bilt\; **build·ing** 1 : put together 2 : establish 3 : increase ～ *n* : physique — **build·er** *n*

build·ing \'bildiŋ\ *n* 1 : roofed and walled structure 2 : art or business of constructing buildings

bulb \'bəlb\ *n* 1 : large underground plant bud 2 : rounded or pear-shaped object — **bul·bous** \-əs\ *adj*

bulge \'bəlj\ *n* : swelling projecting part ～ *vb* **bulged; bulg·ing** : swell out

bulk \'bəlk\ *n* 1 : magnitude 2 : indigestible food material 3 : large mass 4 : major portion ～ *vb* : cause to swell or bulge — **bulky** \-ē\ *adj*

bulk·head *n* : ship's partition

¹bull \'bùl\ *n* : large adult male animal (as of cattle) ～ *adj* : male

²bull *n* 1 : papal letter 2 : decree

bull·dog *n* : compact short-haired dog

bull·doze \-ˌdōz\ *vb* 1 : move or level with a tractor (**bull·doz·er**) having a broad blade 2 : force

bul·let \'bùlət\ *n* : missile to be shot from a gun — **bul·let·proof** *adj*

bul·le·tin \'bùlətən\ *n* 1 : brief public report 2 : periodical

bull·fight *n* : sport of taunting and killing bulls — **bull·fight·er** *n*

bull·frog *n* : large deep-voiced frog

bull·head·ed *adj* : stupidly stubborn

bul·lion \'bùlyən\ *n* : gold or silver esp. in bars

bul·lock \'bùlək\ *n* 1 : young bull 2 : steer

bull's-eye *n, pl* **bull's-eyes** : center of a target

bul·ly \'bùlē\ *n, pl* -**lies** : one who hurts or intimidates others ～ *vb* -**lied; -ly·ing** : act like a bully toward

bul·rush \'bùlˌrəsh\ *n* : tall coarse rush or sedge

bul·wark \'bùlˌwərk, -ˌwòrk; 'bəl-ˌwàrk\ *n* 1 : wall-like defense 2 : strong support or protection

bum \'bəm\ *vb* -**mm-** 1 : wander as a

tramp **2** : get by begging ~ *n* : idle worthless person ~ *adj* : bad

bum-ble-bee \'bəmbəl‚bē\ *n* : large hairy bee

bump \'bəmp\ *vb* : strike or knock forcibly ~ *n* **1** : sudden blow **2** : small bulge or swelling — **bumpy** *adj*

¹**bum-per** \'bəmpər\ *adj* : unusually large

²**bump-er** \'bəmpər\ *n* : shock-absorbing bar at either end of a car

bump-kin \'bəmpkən\ *n* : awkward country person

bun \'bən\ *n* : sweet biscuit or roll

bunch \'bənch\ *n* : group ~ *vb* : form into a group — **bunchy** *adj*

bun-dle \'bənd²l\ *n* **1** : several items bunched together **2** : something wrapped for carrying **3** : large amount ~ *vb* **-dled; -dling** : gather into a bundle

bun-ga-low \'bəŋgə‚lō\ *n* : one-story house

bun-gle \'bəŋgəl\ *vb* **-gled; -gling** : do badly — **bungle** *n* — **bun-gler** *n*

bun-ion \'bənyən\ *n* : inflamed swelling of the first joint of the big toe

¹**bunk** \'bəŋk\ *n* : built-in bed that is often one of a tier ~ *vb* : sleep

²**bunk** *n* : nonsense

bun-ker \-ər\ *n* **1** : storage compartment **2** : protective embankment

bun-kum, bun-combe \'bəŋkəm\ *n* : nonsense

bun-ny \'bənē\ *n, pl* **-nies** : rabbit

¹**bunt-ing** \'bəntiŋ\ *n* : small finch

²**bunting** *n* : flag material

buoy \'būē, 'bȯi\ *n* : floating marker anchored in water ~ *vb* **1** : keep afloat **2** : raise the spirits of — **buoy-an-cy** \'bȯiənsē, 'būyən-\ *n* — **buoy-ant** \-yənt\ *adj*

bur, burr \'bər\ *n* : rough or prickly covering of a fruit — **bur-ry** *adj*

bur-den \'bərd²n\ *n* **1** : something carried **2** : something oppressive **3** : cargo ~ *vb* : load or oppress — **bur-den-some** \-səm\ *adj*

bur-dock \'bər‚däk\ *n* : tall coarse herb with prickly flower heads

bu-reau \'byûrō\ *n* **1** : chest of drawers **2** : administrative unit **3** : business office

bu-reau-cra-cy \byù'räkrəsē\ *n, pl* **-cies** **1** : body of government officials **2** : unwieldy administrative system — **bu-reau-crat** \'byûrə‚krat\ *n*

— **bu-reau-crat-ic** \‚byûrə'kratik\ *adj*

bur-geon \'bərjən\ *vb* : grow

bur-glary \'bərglərē\ *n, pl* **-glar-ies** : forcible entry into a building to steal — **bur-glar** \-glər\ *n* — **bur-glar-ize** \'bərglə‚rīz\ *vb*

bur-gle \'bərgəl\ *vb* **-gled; -gling** : commit burglary on or in

Bur-gun-dy \'bərgəndē\ *n, pl* **-dies** : kind of table wine

buri-al \'berēəl\ *n* : act of burying

bur-lap \'bər‚lap\ *n* : coarse fabric usu. of jute or hemp

bur-lesque \bər'lesk\ *n* **1** : witty or derisive imitation **2** : broadly humorous variety show ~ *vb* **-lesqued; -lesqu-ing** : mock

bur-ly \'bərlē\ *adj* **-li-er; -est** : strongly and heavily built

burn \'bərn\ *vb* **burned** \'bərnd, 'bərnt\ *or* **burnt** \'bərnt\: **burn-ing 1** : be on fire **2** : feel or look as if on fire **3** : alter or become altered by or as if by fire or heat **4** : cause or make by fire ~ *n* : injury or effect produced by burning — **burn-er** *n*

bur-nish \'bərnish\ *vb* : polish

burp \'bərp\ *n or vb* : belch

bur-ro \'bərō, 'bûr-\ *n, pl* **-os** : small donkey

bur-row \'bərō\ *n* : hole in the ground made by an animal ~ *vb* : make a burrow — **bur-row-er** *n*

bur-sar \'bərsər\ *n* : treasurer esp. of a college

bur-si-tis \bər'sītəs\ *n* : inflammation of a sac (**bur-sa** \'bərsə\) in a joint

burst \'bərst\ *vb* **burst** *or* **burst-ed; burst-ing 1** : fly apart or into pieces **2** : enter or emerge suddenly ~ *n* : sudden outbreak or effort

bury \'berē\ *vb* **bur-ied; bury-ing 1** : deposit in the earth **2** : hide

bus \'bəs\ *n, pl* **bus-es** *or* **bus-ses** : large motor-driven passenger vehicle ~ *vb* **bused** *or* **bussed; bus-ing** *or* **bus-sing** : travel or transport by bus

bus-boy *n* : waiter's helper

bush \'bûsh\ *n* **1** : shrub **2** : rough uncleared country **3** : a thick tuft or mat — **bushy** *adj*

bush-el \'bûshəl\ *n* : 4 pecks

bush-ing \'bûshiŋ\ *n* : metal lining used as a guide or bearing

busi-ness \'biznəs, -nəz\ *n* **1** : vocation **2** : commercial or industrial

enterprise **3** : personal concerns —
busi·ness·man \-ˌman\ n — **busi·ness·wom·an** \-ˌwu̇mən\ n

¹**bust** \ˈbəst\ n **1** : sculpture of the head and upper torso **2** : breasts of a woman

²**bust** vb **1** : burst or break **2** : tame ~ n **1** : punch **2** : failure

¹**bus·tle** \ˈbəsəl\ vb **-tled; -tling** : move or work briskly ~ n : energetic activity

²**bustle** n : pad or frame formerly worn under a woman's skirt

busy \ˈbizē\ adj **busi·er; -est 1** : engaged in action **2** : being in use **3** : full of activity ~ vb **bus·ied; busy·ing** : make or keep busy — **busi·ly** adv

busy·body n : meddler

but \ˈbət\ conj **1** : if not for the fact **2** : that **3** : without the certainty that **4** : rather **5** : yet ~ prep : other than

butch·er \ˈbu̇chər\ n **1** : one who slaughters animals or dresses their flesh **2** : brutal killer **3** : bungler — **butcher** vb — **butch·ery** \-ərē\ n

but·ler \ˈbətlər\ n : chief male household servant

¹**butt** \ˈbət\ vb : strike with a butt ~ n : blow with the head or horns

²**butt** n **1** : target **2** : victim

³**butt** vb : join edge to edge

⁴**butt** n : large end or bottom

⁵**butt** n : large cask

butte \ˈbyüt\ n : isolated steep hill

but·ter \ˈbətər\ n : solid edible fat churned from cream ~ vb : spread with butter — **but·tery** adj

butter·cup n : yellow-flowered plant

but·ter·fat n : natural fat of milk and of butter

but·ter·fly n : insect with 4 broad wings

but·ter·milk n : liquid remaining after butter is churned

but·ter·nut n : edible nut of a tree related to the walnut or this tree

but·ter·scotch \-ˌskäch\ n : candy made from sugar, corn syrup, and water

but·tocks \ˈbətəks\ n pl : rear part of the hips

but·ton \ˈbətⁿn\ n **1** : small knob for fastening clothing **2** : buttonlike object ~ vb : fasten with buttons

but·ton·hole n : hole or slit for a button ~ vb : hold in talk

but·tress \ˈbətrəs\ n **1** : projecting structure to support a wall **2** : support — **buttress** vb

bux·om \ˈbəkəm\ adj : full-bosomed

buy \ˈbī\ vb **bought** \ˈbȯt\; **buy·ing** : purchase ~ n : bargain — **buy·er** n

buzz \ˈbəz\ vb : make a low humming sound ~ n : act or sound of buzzing

buz·zard \ˈbəzərd\ n : large bird of prey

buzz·er n : signaling device that buzzes

buzz·word \ˈbəzˌwərd\ n : word or phrase in vogue

by \ˈbī\ prep **1** : near **2** : through **3** : beyond **4** : throughout **5** : no later than ~ adv **1** : near **2** : farther

by·gone \ˈbīˌgȯn\ adj : past — **bygone** n

by·law, bye·law n : organization's rule

by·line n : writer's name on an article

by·pass n : alternate route ~ vb : go around

by·prod·uct n : product in addition to the main product

by·stand·er n : spectator

by·way \ˈbīˌwā\ n : side road

by·word n : proverb

C

c \ˈsē\ n, pl **c's** or **cs** \ˈsēz\ : 3d letter of the alphabet

cab \ˈkab\ n **1** : light closed horse-drawn carriage **2** : taxicab **3** : compartment for a driver — **cab·bie, cab·by** n — **cab·stand** n

ca·bal \kəˈbal\ n : group of conspirators

ca·bana \kəˈbanə, -nyə\ n : shelter at a beach or pool

cab·a·ret \ˌkabəˈrā\ n : nightclub

cab·bage \ˈkabij\ n : vegetable with a dense head of leaves

cab·in \-ən\ n **1** : private room on a ship **2** : small house **3** : airplane compartment

cab·i·net \ˈkabnət\ n **1** : display case or cupboard **2** : advisory council of a head of state — **cab·i·net·mak·er** n — **cab·i·net·mak·ing** n — **cab·i·net·work** n ca·ble \'kābəl\ n 1 : strong rope, wire, or chain 2 : cablegram 3 : bundle of electrical wires ～ vb -bled; -bling : send a cablegram to

ca·ble·gram \-,gram\ n : message sent by a submarine telegraph cable

ca·boose \kə'büs\ n : crew car on a train

ca·cao \kə'kaù, -'kāō\ n, pl cacaos : So. American tree whose seeds (ca·cao beans) yield cocoa and chocolate

cache \'kash\ n 1 : hiding place 2 : something hidden — cache vb

ca·chet \ka'shā\ n : prestige or a feature conferring this

cack·le \'kakəl\ vb -led; -ling : make a cry or laugh like the sound of a hen — cackle n — cack·ler n

ca·coph·o·ny \ka'käfənē\ n, pl -nies : harsh noise — ca·coph·o·nous \-nəs\ adj

cac·tus \'kaktəs\ n, pl cac·ti \-,tī\ or -tus·es : drought-resistant flowering plant with scales or prickles

cad \'kad\ n : ungentlemanly person — cad·dish \-ish\ adj — cad·dish·ly adv

ca·dav·er \kə'davər\ n : dead body — ca·dav·er·ous \-ərəs\ adj

cad·die, cad·dy \'kadē\ n, pl -dies : golfer's helper — caddie, caddy vb

cad·dy \'kadē\ n, pl -dies : small tea chest

ca·dence \'kād³ns\ n : measure of a rhythmical flow — ca·denced \-³nst\ adj

ca·det \kə'det\ n : student in a military academy

cadge \'kaj\ vb cadged; cadg·ing : beg — cadg·er n

cad·mi·um \'kadmēəm\ n : grayish metallic chemical element

cad·re \-rē\ n : nucleus of highly trained people

ca·fé \ka'fā, kə-\ n : restaurant

caf·e·te·ria \,kafə'tirēə\ n : self-service restaurant

caf·feine \ka'fēn, 'ka,fēn\ n : stimulating alkaloid in coffee and tea

cage \'kāj\ n : box of wire or bars for confining an animal ～ vb caged; cag·ing : put or keep in a cage

ca·gey \-ē\ adj -gi·er; -est : shrewd — ca·gi·ly adv — ca·gi·ness n

cais·son \'kā,sän, -sən\ n 1 : ammunition carriage 2 : watertight chamber for underwater construction

ca·jole \kə'jōl\ vb -joled; -jol·ing : persuade or coax — ca·jol·ery \-ərē\ n

cake \'kāk\ n 1 : food of baked or fried usu. sweet batter 2 : compacted mass ～ vb caked; cak·ing 1 : form into a cake 2 : encrust

cal·a·bash \'kalə,bash\ n : gourd

cal·a·mine \'kalə,mīn\ n : lotion of oxides of zinc and iron

ca·lam·i·ty \kə'lamətē\ n, pl -ties : disaster — ca·lam·i·tous \-ətəs\ adj — ca·lam·i·tous·ly adv

cal·ci·fy \'kalsə,fī\ vb -fied; -fy·ing : harden — cal·ci·fi·ca·tion \,kalsəfə'kāshən\ n

cal·ci·um \'kalsēəm\ n : silver-white soft metallic chemical element

cal·cu·late \'kalkyə,lāt\ vb -lat·ed; -lat·ing 1 : determine by mathematical processes 2 : judge — cal·cu·la·ble \-ləbəl\ adj — cal·cu·la·tion \,kalkyə'lāshən\ n — cal·cu·la·tor \'kalkyə,lātər\ n

cal·cu·lat·ing adj : shrewd

cal·cu·lus \'kalkyələs\ n, pl -li \-,lī\ : higher mathematics dealing with rates of change

cal·dron var of CAULDRON

cal·en·dar \'kaləndər\ n : list of days, weeks, and months

¹calf \'kaf, 'kàf\ n, pl calves \'kavz, 'kàvz\ : young cow or related mammal — calf·skin n

²calf n, pl calves : back part of the leg below the knee

cal·i·ber, cal·i·bre \'kaləbər\ n 1 : diameter of a bullet or shell or of a gun bore 2 : degree of mental or moral excellence

cal·i·brate \'kalə,brāt\ vb -brat·ed; -brat·ing : adjust precisely — cal·i·bra·tion \,kalə'brāshən\ n

cal·i·co \'kali,kō\ n, pl -coes or -cos 1 : printed cotton fabric 2 : animal with fur having patches of different colors

cal·i·pers \'kaləpərz\ n : measuring instrument with two adjustable legs

ca·liph \'kāləf, 'kal-\ n : title of head of Islam — ca·liph·ate \-,āt, -ət\ n

cal·is·then·ics \,kaləs'theniks\ n sing or pl : stretching and jumping exercises — cal·is·then·ic adj

calk \'kók\ var of CAULK

call \'kol\ vb 1 : shout 2 : summon 3 : demand 4 : telephone 5 : make a visit 6 : name — call n — call·er n

— **call down** vb : reprimand — **call off** vb : cancel

call·ing n : vocation

cal·li·ope \kə'līə,pē, 'kalē,ōp\ n : musical instrument of steam whistles

cal·lous \'kaləs\ adj **1** : thickened and hardened **2** : unfeeling — callous ~ vb : make callous — **cal·los·i·ty** \ka'läsətē\ n — **cal·lous·ly** adv — **cal·lous·ness** n

cal·low \'kalō\ adj : inexperienced or innocent — **cal·low·ness** n

cal·lus \'kaləs\ n : callous area on skin or bark ~ vb : form a callus

call-waiting n : telephone service by which during a call in progress an incoming call is signaled

calm \'käm, 'kälm\ n **1** : period or condition of peacefulness or stillness ~ adj : still or tranquil ~ vb : make calm — **calm·ly** adv — **calm·ness** n

ca·lor·ic \kə'lôrik\ adj : relating to heat or calories

cal·o·rie \'kalərē\ n : unit for measuring heat and energy value of food

ca·lum·ni·ate \kə'ləmnē,āt\ vb **-at·ed; -at·ing** : slander — **ca·lum·ni·a·tion** \-,ləmnē'āshən\ n

cal·um·ny \'kaləmnē\ n, pl **-nies** : false and malicious charge — **ca·lum·ni·ous** \kə'ləmnēəs\ adj

calve \'kav, 'käv\ vb **calved; calv·ing** : give birth to a calf

calves pl of CALF

ca·lyp·so \kə'lipsō\ n, pl **-sos** : West Indian style of music

ca·lyx \'kāliks, 'kal-\ n, pl **-lyx·es** or **-ly·ces** \-lə,sēz\ : sepals of a flower

cam \'kam\ n : machine part that slides or rotates irregularly to transmit linear motion

ca·ma·ra·de·rie \,käm'rädərē, ,kam-, -mə'-, -'rad-\ n : fellowship

cam·bric \'kāmbrik\ n : fine thin linen or cotton fabric

came past of COME

cam·el \'kaməl\ n : large hoofed mammal of desert areas

ca·mel·lia \kə'mēlyə\ n : shrub or tree grown for its showy roselike flowers or the flower itself

cam·eo \'kamē,ō\ n, pl **-eos** : gem carved in relief

cam·era \'kamrə\ n : box with a lens for taking pictures — **cam·era·man** \-,man, -mən\ n

cam·ou·flage \'kamə,fläzh, -,fläj\ vb : hide by disguising — **camouflage** n

camp \'kamp\ n **1** : place to stay temporarily esp. in a tent **2** : group living in a camp ~ vb : make or live in a camp — **camp·er** n — **camp·ground** n — **camp·site** n

cam·paign \kam'pān\ n : series of military operations or of activities meant to gain a result — **campaign** vb

cam·pa·ni·le \,kampə'nēlē, -'nēl\ n, pl **-ni·les** or **-ni·li** \-'nēlē\ : bell tower

cam·phor \'kamfər\ n : gummy volatile aromatic compound from an evergreen tree (**cam·phor tree**)

cam·pus \'kampəs\ n : grounds and buildings of a college or school

¹**can** \kən, 'kan\ vb, past **could** \kəd, 'kúd\; pres sing & pl **can 1** : be able to **2** : be permitted to by conscience or feeling **3** : have permission or liberty to

²**can** \'kan\ n : metal container ~ vb **-nn-** : preserve by sealing in airtight cans or jars — **can·ner** n — **can·nery** \-ərē\ n

ca·nal \kə'nal\ n **1** : tubular passage in the body **2** : channel filled with water

can·a·pé \'kanəpē, -,pā\ n : appetizer

ca·nard \kə'närd\ n : false report

ca·nary \-'nerē\ n, pl **-nar·ies** : yellow or greenish finch often kept as a pet

can·cel \'kansəl\ vb **-celed** or **-celled; -cel·ing** or **-cel·ling 1** : cross out **2** : destroy, neutralize, or match the force or effect of — **cancel** n — **can·cel·la·tion** \,kansə'lāshən\ n — **can·cel·er, can·cel·ler** n

can·cer \'kansər\ n **1** : malignant tumor that tends to spread **2** : slowly destructive evil — **can·cer·ous** \-sərəs\ adj — **can·cer·ous·ly** adv

can·de·la·bra \,kandə'läbrə, -'lab-\ n : candelabrum

can·de·la·brum \-rəm\ n, pl **-bra** \-rə\ : ornamental branched candlestick

can·did \'kandəd\ adj **1** : frank **2** : unposed — **can·did·ly** adv — **can·did·ness** n

can·di·date \'kandə,dāt, -dət\ n : one who seeks an office or membership — **can·di·da·cy** \-dəsē\ n

can·dle \'kand°l\ n : tallow or wax molded around a wick and burned to give light — **can·dle·light** n — **can·dle·stick** n

can·dor \'kandər\ n : frankness

can·dy \-dē\ n, pl **-dies** : food made

from sugar ∼ vb **-died; -dy·ing :** encrust in sugar

cane \'kān\ n **1 :** slender plant stem **2 :** a tall woody grass or reed **3 :** stick for walking or beating ∼ vb **caned; can·ing 1 :** beat with a cane **2 :** weave or make with cane — **can·er** n

ca·nine \'kā,nīn\ adj **:** relating to dogs ∼ n **1 :** pointed tooth next to the incisors **2 :** dog

can·is·ter \'kanəstər\ n **:** cylindrical container

can·ker \'kaŋkər\ n **:** mouth ulcer — **can·ker·ous** \-kərəs\ adj

can·na·bis \'kanəbəs\ n **:** preparation derived from hemp

can·ni·bal \'kanəbəl\ n **:** human or animal that eats its own kind — **can·ni·bal·ism** \-bə,lizəm\ n — **can·ni·bal·is·tic** \,kanəbə'listik\ adj

can·ni·bal·ize \'kanəbə,līz\ vb **-ized; -iz·ing 1 :** take usable parts from **2 :** practice cannibalism

can·non \'kanən\ n, pl **-nons** or **-non 1 :** large heavy gun — **can·non·ball** n — **can·non·eer** \,kanə'nir\ n

can·non·ade \,kanə'nād\ n **:** heavy artillery fire ∼ vb **-ad·ed; -ad·ing :** bombard

can·not \'kan,ät; kə'nät\ **:** can not — **cannot but :** be bound to

can·ny \'kanē\ adj **-ni·er; -est :** shrewd — **can·ni·ly** adv — **can·ni·ness** n

ca·noe \kə'nü\ n **:** narrow sharp-ended boat propelled by paddles — **canoe** vb — **ca·noe·ist** n

¹**can·on** \'kanən\ n **1 :** regulation governing a church **2 :** authoritative list **3 :** an accepted principle

²**canon :** clergy member in a cathedral

ca·non·i·cal \kə'nänikəl\ adj **1 :** relating to or conforming to a canon **2 :** orthodox — **ca·non·i·cal·ly** adv

can·on·ize \'kanə,nīz\ vb **-ized \-,nīzd\; -iz·ing :** recognize as a saint — **can·on·iza·tion** \,kanənə-'zāshən\ n

can·o·py \'kanəpē\ n, pl **-pies :** overhanging cover — **canopy** vb

¹**cant** \'kant\ n **1 :** slanting surface **2 :** slant ∼ vb **1 :** tip up **2 :** lean to one side

²**cant** vb **:** talk hypocritically ∼ n **:** jargon **:** insincere talk

can't \'kant, 'känt\ **:** can not

can·ta·loupe \'kant³l,ōp\ n **:** muskmelon with orange flesh

can·tan·ker·ous \kan'taŋkərəs\ adj **:** hard to deal with — **can·tan·ker·ous·ly** adv — **can·tan·ker·ous·ness** n

can·ta·ta \kən'tätə\ n **:** choral work

can·teen \kan'tēn\ n **1 :** place of recreation for service personnel **2 :** water container

can·ter \'kantər\ n **:** slow gallop — **can·ter** vb

can·ti·cle \'kantikəl\ n **:** liturgical song

can·ti·le·ver \'kant³l,ēvər, -,ev-\ n **:** beam or structure supported only at one end

can·to \'kan,tō\ n, pl **-tos :** major division of a long poem

can·tor \'kantər\ n **:** synagogue official who sings liturgical music

can·vas \'kanvəs\ n **1 :** strong cloth orig. used for making tents and sails **2 :** set of sails **3 :** oil painting

can·vass \-vəs\ vb **:** solicit votes, orders, or opinions from ∼ n **:** act of canvassing — **can·vass·er** n

can·yon \'kanyən\ n **:** deep valley with steep sides

cap \'kap\ n **1 :** covering for the head **2 :** top or cover like a cap **3 :** upper limit ∼ vb **-pp- 1 :** provide or protect with a cap **2 :** climax — **cap·ful** \-,fûl\ n

ca·pa·ble \'kāpəbəl\ adj **:** able to do something — **ca·pa·bil·i·ty** \,kāpə-'bilətē\ n — **ca·pa·bly** \'kāpəblē\ adv

ca·pa·cious \kə'pāshəs\ adj **:** able to contain much

ca·pac·i·tance \kə'pasətəns\ n **:** ability to store electrical energy

ca·pac·i·tor \-sətər\ n **:** device for storing electrical energy

ca·pac·i·ty \-sətē\ n, pl **-ties 1 :** ability to contain **2 :** volume **3 :** ability **4 :** role or job ∼ adj **:** equaling maximum capacity

¹**cape** \'kāp\ n **:** point of land jutting out into water

²**cape :** garment that drapes over the shoulders

¹**ca·per** \'kāpər\ n **:** flower bud of a shrub pickled for use as a relish

²**caper** vb **:** leap or prance about ∼ n **1 :** frolicsome leap **2 :** escapade

cap·il·lary \'kapə,lerē\ adj **1 :** resembling a hair **2 :** having a very small bore ∼ n, pl **-lar·ies :** tiny thin-walled blood vessel

¹**cap·i·tal** \'kapət³l\ *adj* **1** : punishable by death **2** : being in the series A, B, C rather than a, b, c **3** : relating to capital **4** : excellent ~ *n* **1** : capital letter **2** : seat of government **3** : wealth **4** : total face value of a company's stock **5** : investors as a group

²**capital** *n* : top part of a column

cap·i·tal·ism \-ˌizəm\ *n* : economic system of private ownership of capital

cap·i·tal·ist \-ist\ *n* **1** : person with capital invested in business **2** : believer in capitalism — *adj* **1** : owning capital **2** : practicing, advocating, or marked by capitalism — **cap·i·tal·is·tic** \ˌkapət³l'istik\ *adj*

cap·i·tal·ize \-ˌīz\ *vb* -ized; -iz·ing **1** : write or print with a capital letter **2** : use as capital **3** : supply capital for **4** : turn something to advantage — **cap·i·tal·iza·tion** \ˌkapət³lə'zāshən\ *n*

cap·i·tol \'kapət³l\ *n* : building in which a legislature sits

ca·pit·u·late \kə'pichəˌlāt\ *vb* -lat·ed; -lat·ing : surrender — **ca·pit·u·la·tion** \-ˌpichə'lāshən\ *n*

ca·pon \'kāˌpän, -pən\ *n* : castrated male chicken

ca·price \kə'prēs\ *n* : whim — **ca·pri·cious** \-'prishəs\ *adj* — **ca·pri·cious·ly** *adv* — **ca·pri·cious·ness** *n*

cap·size \'kapˌsīz, kap'sīz\ *vb* -sized; -siz·ing : overturn

cap·stan \'kapstən, -ˌstan\ *n* : upright winch

cap·sule \'kapsəl, -sül\ *n* **1** : enveloping cover (as for medicine) **2** : small pressurized compartment for astronauts ~ *adj* : very brief or compact — **cap·su·lar** \-sələr\ *adj* — **cap·su·lat·ed** \-səˌlātəd\ *adj*

cap·tain \'kaptən\ *n* **1** : commander of a body of troops **2** : officer in charge of a ship **3** : commissioned officer in the navy ranking next below a rear admiral or a commodore **4** : commissioned officer (as in the army) ranking next below a major **5** : leader ~ *vb* : be captain of — **cap·tain·cy** *n*

cap·tion \'kapshən\ *n* **1** : title **2** : explanation with an illustration — **caption** *vb*

cap·tious \'kapshəs\ *adj* : tending to find fault — **cap·tious·ly** *adv*

cap·ti·vate \'kaptəˌvāt\ *vb* -vat·ed; -vat·ing : attract and charm — **cap·ti·va·tion** \ˌkaptə'vāshən\ *n* — **cap·ti·va·tor** \'kaptəˌvātər\ *n*

cap·tive \-tiv\ *adj* **1** : made prisoner **2** : confined or under control — **captive** *n* — **cap·tiv·i·ty** \kap'tivətē\ *n*

cap·tor \'kaptər\ *n* : one that captures

cap·ture \-chər\ *n* : seizure by force or trickery ~ *vb* -tured; -tur·ing : take captive

car \'kär\ *n* **1** : vehicle moved on wheels **2** : cage of an elevator

ca·rafe \kə'raf, -'räf\ *n* : decanter

car·a·mel \'karəməl, 'kärməl\ *n* **1** : burnt sugar used for flavoring and coloring **2** : firm chewy candy

¹**carat** *var of* KARAT

²**car·at** \'karət\ *n* : unit of weight for precious stones

car·a·van \'karəˌvan\ *n* : travelers journeying together (as in a line)

car·a·way \'karəˌwā\ *n* : aromatic herb with seeds used in seasoning

car·bine \'kärˌbēn, -ˌbīn\ *n* : short-barreled rifle

car·bo·hy·drate \ˌkärbō'hīˌdrāt, -drət\ *n* : compound of carbon, hydrogen, and oxygen

car·bon \'kärbən\ *n* **1** : chemical element occurring in nature esp. as diamond and graphite **2** : piece of carbon paper or a copy made with it

¹**car·bon·ate** \'kärbəˌnāt, -nət\ *n* : salt or ester of a carbon-containing acid

²**car·bon·ate** \-ˌnāt\ *vb* -at·ed; -at·ing : impregnate with carbon dioxide — **car·bon·ation** \ˌkärbə'nāshən\ *n*

carbon paper *n* : thin paper coated with a pigment for making copies

car·bun·cle \'kärˌbəŋkəl\ *n* : painful inflammation of the skin and underlying tissue

car·bu·re·tor \'kärbəˌrātər, -byə-\ *n* : device for mixing fuel and air

car·cass \'kärkəs\ *n* : dead body

car·cin·o·gen \kär'sinəjən\ *n* : agent causing cancer — **car·ci·no·gen·ic** \ˌkärs³nō'jenik\ *adj*

car·ci·no·ma \ˌkärs³n'ōmə\ *n*, *pl* -mas *or* -ma·ta \-mətə\ : malignant tumor

¹**card** \'kärd\ *vb* : comb (fibers) before spinning ~ *n* : device for carding fibers — **card·er** *n*

²**card** *n* **1** : playing card **2** *pl* : game played with playing cards **3** : small flat piece of paper

card·board *n* : stiff material like paper

car·di·ac \'kärdē,ak\ *adj* : relating to the heart

car·di·gan \'kärdigən\ *n* : sweater with an opening in the front

¹car·di·nal \'kärd²nəl\ *n* 1 : official of the Roman Catholic Church 2 : bright red songbird

²cardinal *adj* : of basic importance

cardinal number *n* : number (as 1, 82, 357) used in counting

car·di·ol·o·gy \,kärdē'äləjē\ *n* : study of the heart — **car·di·ol·o·gist** \-jist\ *n*

car·dio·vas·cu·lar \-ō'vaskyələr\ *adj* : relating to the heart and blood vessels

care \'ker\ *n* 1 : anxiety 2 : watchful attention 3 : supervision ~ *vb* **cared; car·ing** 1 : feel anxiety or concern 2 : like 3 : provide care — **care-free** *adj* — **care·ful** \-fəl\ *adj* — **care·ful·ly** *adv* — **care·ful·ness** *n* — **care·giv·er** \-,givər\ *n* — **care·less** *adj* — **care·less·ly** *adv* — **care·less·ness** *n*

ca·reen \kə'rēn\ *vb* 1 : sway from side to side 2 : career

ca·reer \kə'rir\ *n* : vocation ~ *vb* : go at top speed

ca·ress \kə'res\ *n* : tender touch ~ *vb* : touch lovingly or tenderly

car·et \'karət\ *n* : mark ∧ showing where something is to be inserted

care·tak·er *n* : one in charge for another or temporarily

car·go \'kärgō\ *n, pl* **-goes** *or* **-gos** : transported goods

car·i·bou \'karə,bü\ *n, pl* **-bou** *or* **-bous** : large No. American deer

car·i·ca·ture \'karikə,chür\ *n* : distorted representation for humor or ridicule — **caricature** *vb* — **car·i·ca·tur·ist** \-ist\ *n*

car·ies \'karēz\ *n, pl* **caries** : tooth decay

car·il·lon \'karə,län\ *n* : set of tuned bells

car·jack·ing \'kär,jakiŋ\ *n* : theft of an automobile by force or intimidation — **car·jack·er** *n*

car·mine \'kärmən, -,mīn\ *n* : vivid red

car·nage \'kärnij\ *n* : slaughter

car·nal \'kärn²l\ *adj* : sensual — **car·nal·i·ty** \kär'nalətē\ *n* — **car·nal·ly** *adv*

car·na·tion \kär'nāshən\ *n* : showy flower

car·ni·val \'kärnəvəl\ *n* 1 : festival 2 : traveling enterprise offering amusements

car·ni·vore \-,vōr\ *n* : flesh-eating animal — **car·niv·o·rous** \kär'nivərəs\ *adj* — **car·niv·o·rous·ly** *adv* — **car·niv·o·rous·ness** *n*

car·ol \'karəl\ *n* : song of joy — **carol** *vb* — **car·ol·er, car·ol·ler** \-ələr\ *n*

car·om \'karəm\ *n or vb* : rebound

ca·rouse \kə'rauz\ *vb* **-roused; -rous·ing** : drink and be boisterous — **ca·rouse** *n* — **ca·rous·er** *n*

car·ou·sel, car·rou·sel \,karə'sel, 'karə,-\ *n* : merry-go-round

¹carp \'kärp\ *vb* : find fault

²carp *n, pl* **carp** *or* **carps** : freshwater fish

car·pel \'kärpəl\ *n* : modified leaf forming part of the ovary of a flower

car·pen·ter \'kärpəntər\ *n* : one who builds with wood — **carpenter** *vb* — **car·pen·try** \-trē\ *n*

car·pet \'kärpət\ *n* : fabric floor covering ~ *vb* : cover with a carpet — **car·pet·ing** \-iŋ\ *n*

car·port *n* : open-sided automobile shelter

car·riage \'karij\ *n* 1 : conveyance 2 : manner of holding oneself 3 : wheeled vehicle

car·ri·on \'karēən\ *n* : dead and decaying flesh

car·rot \'karət\ *n* : orange root vegetable

car·ry \'karē\ *vb* **-ried; -ry·ing** 1 : move while supporting 2 : hold (oneself) in a specified way 3 : support 4 : keep in stock 5 : reach to a distance 6 : win — **car·ri·er** \-ēər\ *n* — **carry on** *vb* 1 : conduct 2 : behave excitedly — **carry out** *vb* : put into effect

cart \'kärt\ *n* : wheeled vehicle ~ *vb* : carry in a cart — **cart·age** \-ij\ *n* — **cart·er** *n*

car·tel \kär'tel\ *n* : business combination designed to limit competition

car·ti·lage \'kärt²lij\ *n* : elastic skeletal tissue — **car·ti·lag·i·nous** \,kärt²l'ajənəs\ *adj*

car·tog·ra·phy \kär'tägrəfē\ *n* : making of maps — **car·tog·ra·pher** \-fər\ *n*

car·ton \'kärt²n\ *n* : cardboard box

car·toon \kär'tün\ *n* 1 : humorous drawing 2 : comic strip — **cartoon** *vb* — **car·toon·ist** *n*

car·tridge \'kärtrij\ *n* 1 : tube containing powder and a bullet or shot for a firearm 2 : container of material for insertion into an apparatus

carve \'kärv\ *vb* **carved; carv·ing** 1 : cut with care 2 : cut into pieces or slices — **carv·er** *n*

cas·cade \kas'kād\ *n* : small steep waterfall ∼ *vb* **-cad·ed; -cad·ing** : fall in a cascade

¹**case** \'kās\ *n* 1 : particular instance 2 : convincing argument 3 : inflectional form esp. of a noun or pronoun 4 : fact 5 : lawsuit 6 : instance of disease — **in case** : as a precaution — **in case of** : in the event of

²**case** *n* 1 : box 2 : outer covering ∼ *vb* **cased; cas·ing** 1 : enclose 2 : inspect

case·ment \-mənt\ *n* : window that opens like a door

cash \'kash\ *n* 1 : ready money 2 : money paid at the time of purchase ∼ *vb* : give or get cash for

ca·shew \'kashü, kə'shü\ *n* : tropical American tree or its nut

¹**ca·shier** \ka'shir\ *vb* : dismiss in disgrace

²**cash·ier** *n* : person who receives and records payments

cash·mere \'kazh,mir, 'kash-\ *n* : fine goat's wool or a fabric of this

ca·si·no \kə'sēnō\ *n, pl* **-nos** : place for gambling

cask \'kask\ *n* : barrel-shaped container for liquids

cas·ket \'kaskət\ *n* : coffin

cas·se·role \'kasə,rōl\ *n* : baking dish or the food cooked in this

cas·sette \kə'set, ka-\ *n* : case containing magnetic tape

cas·sock \'kasək\ *n* : long clerical garment

cast \'kast\ *vb* **cast; cast·ing** 1 : throw 2 : deposit (a ballot) 3 : assign parts in a play 4 : mold ∼ *n* 1 : throw 2 : appearance 3 : rigid surgical dressing 4 : actors in a play

cas·ta·nets \,kastə'nets\ *n pl* : shells clicked together in the hand

cast·away \'kastə,wā\ *n* : survivor of a shipwreck — **castaway** *adj*

caste \'kast\ *n* : social class or rank

cast·er \'kastər\ *n* : small wheel on a chair

cas·ti·gate \'kastə,gāt\ *vb* **-gat·ed; -gat·ing** : chastise severely — **cas·ti-**

ga·tion \,kastə'gāshən\ *n* — **cas·ti·ga·tor** \'kastə,gātər\ *n*

cast iron *n* : hard brittle alloy of iron

cas·tle \'kasəl\ *n* : fortified building

cast-off *adj* : thrown away — **cast-off** *n*

cas·trate \'kas,trāt\ *vb* **-trat·ed; -trat·ing** : remove the testes of — **cas·tra·tion** \ka'strāshən\ *n*

ca·su·al \'kazhəwəl\ *adj* 1 : happening by chance 2 : showing little concern 3 : informal — **ca·su·al·ly** \-ē\ *adv* — **ca·su·al·ness** *n*

ca·su·al·ty \-tē\ *n, pl* **-ties** 1 : serious or fatal accident 2 : one injured, lost, or destroyed

ca·su·ist·ry \'kazhəwəstrē\ *n, pl* **-ries** : rationalization — **ca·su·ist** \-wist\ *n*

cat \'kat\ *n* 1 : small domestic mammal 2 : related animal (as a lion) — **cat·like** *adj*

cat·a·clysm \'katə,klizəm\ *n* : violent change — **cat·a·clys·mal** \,katə-'klizməl\, **cat·a·clys·mic** \-'klizmik\ *adj*

cat·a·comb \'katə,kōm\ *n* : underground burial place

cat·a·log, cat·a·logue \'kat³l,óg\ *n* 1 : list 2 : book containing a description of items ∼ *vb* **-loged** *or* **-logued; -log·ing** *or* **-logu·ing** 1 : make a catalog of 2 : enter in a catalog — **cat·a·log·er, cat·a·logu·er** *n*

ca·tal·pa \kə'talpə\ *n* : tree with broad leaves and long pods

ca·tal·y·sis \kə'taləsəs\ *n, pl* **-y·ses** \-,sēz\ : increase in the rate of chemical reaction caused by a substance (**cat·a·lyst** \'kat³list\) that is itself unchanged — **cat·a·lyt·ic** \,kat³l-'itik\ *adj*

cat·a·ma·ran \,katəmə'ran\ *n* : boat with twin hulls

cat·a·mount \'katə,maúnt\ *n* : cougar

cat·a·pult \'katə,pəlt, -,púlt\ *n* : device for hurling or launching — **catapult** *vb*

cat·a·ract \'katə,rakt\ *n* 1 : large waterfall 2 : cloudiness of the lens of the eye

ca·tarrh \kə'tär\ *n* : inflammation of the nose and throat

ca·tas·tro·phe \kə'tastrə,fē\ *n* 1 : great disaster or misfortune 2 : utter failure — **cat·a·stroph·ic** \,katə-'sträfik\ *adj* — **cat·a·stroph·i·cal·ly** \-iklē\ *adv*

cat·bird *n* : American songbird

cat·call *n* : noise of disapproval

catch \'kach, 'kech\ *vb* **caught** \'kȯt\; **catch·ing** **1** : capture esp. after pursuit **2** : trap **3** : detect esp. by surprise **4** : grasp **5** : get entangled **6** : become affected with or by **7** : seize and hold firmly ~ *n* **1** : act of catching **2** : something caught **3** : something that fastens **4** : hidden difficulty — **catch·er** *n*

catch·ing \-iŋ\ *adj* : infectious

catch·up \'kechəp, 'kach-; 'katsəp\ *var of* KETCHUP

catch·word *n* : slogan

catchy \-ē\ *adj* **catch·i·er; -est** : likely to catch interest

cat·e·chism \'katə,kizəm\ *n* : set of questions and answers esp. to teach religious doctrine

cat·e·gor·i·cal \,katə'gȯrikəl\ *adj* : absolute — **cat·e·gor·i·cal·ly** \-klē\ *adv*

cat·e·go·ry \'katə,gȯrē\ *n, pl* **-ries** : group or class — **cat·e·go·ri·za·tion** \,katigərə'zāshən\ *n* — **cat·e·go·rize** \'katigə,rīz\ *vb*

ca·ter \'kātər\ *vb* **1** : provide food for **2** : supply what is wanted — **ca·ter·er** *n*

cat·er·cor·ner \,katē'kȯrnər, ,katə-, ,kītē-\, **cat·er·cor·nered** *adv or adj* : in a diagonal position

cat·er·pil·lar \'katər,pilər\ *n* : butterfly or moth larva

cat·er·waul \'katər,wȯl\ *vb* : make the harsh cry of a cat — **caterwaul** *n*

cat·fish *n* : big-headed fish with feelers about the mouth

cat·gut *n* : tough cord made usu. from sheep intestines

ca·thar·sis \kə'thärsəs\ *n, pl* **ca·thar·ses** \-,sēz\ : a purging — **ca·thar·tic** \kə'thärtik\ *adj or n*

ca·the·dral \-'thēdrəl\ *n* : principal church of a diocese

cath·e·ter \'kathətər\ *n* : tube for insertion into a body cavity

cath·ode \'kath,ōd\ *n* **1** : negative electrode **2** : positive battery terminal — **ca·thod·ic** \ka'thädik\ *adj*

cath·o·lic \'kathəlik\ *adj* **1** : universal **2** *cap* : relating to Roman Catholics

Cath·o·lic *n* : member of the Roman Catholic Church — **Ca·thol·i·cism** \kə'thälə,sizəm\ *n*

cat·kin \'katkən\ *n* : long dense flower cluster

cat·nap *n* : short light nap — **catnap** *vb*

cat·nip \-,nip\ *n* : aromatic mint relished by cats

cat's-paw *n, pl* **cat's-paws** : person used as if a tool

cat·sup \'kechəp, 'kach-; 'katsəp\ *var of* KETCHUP

cat·tail *n* : marsh herb with furry brown spikes

cat·tle \'kat³l\ *n pl* : domestic bovines — **cat·tle·man** \-mən, -,man\ *n*

cat·ty \'katē\ *adj* **-ti·er; -est** : mean or spiteful — **cat·ti·ly** *adv* — **cat·ti·ness** *n*

cat·walk *n* : high narrow walk

Cau·ca·sian \kȯ'kāzhən\ *adj* : relating to the white race — **Caucasian** *n*

cau·cus \'kȯkəs\ *n* : political meeting — **caucus** *vb*

caught *past of* CATCH

cauldron \'kȯldrən\ *n* : large kettle

cau·li·flow·er \'kȯli,flaůər, 'käl-\ *n* : vegetable having a compact head of usu. white undeveloped flowers

caulk \'kȯk\ *vb* : make seams watertight — **caulk** *n* — **caulk·er** *n*

caus·al \'kȯzəl\ *adj* : relating to or being a cause — **cau·sal·i·ty** \kȯ'zalətē\ *n* — **caus·al·ly** \'kȯzəlē\ *adv*

cause \'kȯz\ *n* **1** : something that brings about a result **2** : reason **3** : lawsuit **4** : principle or movement to support ~ *vb* **caused; caus·ing** : be the cause of — **cau·sa·tion** \kȯ-'zāshən\ *n* — **caus·ative** \'kȯzətiv\ *adj* — **cause·less** *adj* — **caus·er** *n*

cause·way *n* : raised road esp. over water

caus·tic \'kȯstik\ *adj* **1** : corrosive **2** : sharp or biting — **caustic** *n*

cau·ter·ize \'kȯtə,rīz\ *vb* **-ized; -iz·ing** : burn to prevent infection or bleeding — **cau·ter·i·za·tion** \,kȯtərə'zāshən\ *n*

cau·tion \'kȯshən\ *n* **1** : warning **2** : care or prudence ~ *vb* : warn — **cau·tion·ary** \-shə,nerē\ *adj*

cau·tious \'kȯshəs\ *adj* : taking caution — **cau·tious·ly** *adv* — **cau·tious·ness** *n*

cav·al·cade \,kavəl'kād, 'kavəl,-\ *n* **1** : procession on horseback **2** : series

cav·a·lier \,kavə'lir\ *n* : mounted soldier ~ *adj* : disdainful or arrogant — **cav·a·lier·ly** *adv*

cav·al·ry \'kavəlrē\ *n, pl* **-ries** : troops on horseback or in vehicles — **cav·al·ry·man** \-mən, -,man\ *n*

cave \'kāv\ *n* : natural underground chamber — **cave in** *vb* : collapse

cav•ern \'kavərn\ *n* : large cave — **cav•ern•ous** *adj* — **cav•ern•ous•ly** *adv*

cav•i•ar, cav•i•are \'kavē,är, 'käv-\ *n* : salted fish roe

cav•il \'kavəl\ *vb* **-iled** *or* **-illed; -il•ing** *or* **-il•ling** : raise trivial objections — **cavil** *n* — **cav•il•er, cav•il•ler** *n*

cav•i•ty \'kavətē\ *n, pl* **-ties** **1** : unfilled place within a mass **2** : decay in a tooth

ca•vort \kə'vört\ *vb* : prance or caper

caw \'kö\ *vb* : utter the harsh call of the crow — **caw** *n*

cay•enne pepper \,kī'en-, ,kā-\ *n* : ground dried fruits of a hot pepper

CD \,sē'dē\ *n* : compact disc

cease \'sēs\ *vb* **ceased; ceas•ing** : stop

cease•less \-ləs\ *adj* : continuous

ce•dar \'sēdər\ *n* : cone-bearing tree with fragrant durable wood

cede \'sēd\ *vb* **ced•ed; ced•ing** : surrender — **ced•er** *n*

ceil•ing \'sēliŋ\ *n* **1** : overhead surface of a room **2** : upper limit

cel•e•brate \'selə,brāt\ *vb* **-brat•ed; -brat•ing** **1** : perform with appropriate rites **2** : honor with ceremonies **3** : extol — **cel•e•brant** \-brənt\ *n* — **cel•e•bra•tion** \,selə'brāshən\ *n* — **cel•e•bra•tor** \'selə,brātər\ *n*

cel•e•brat•ed \-əd\ *adj* : renowned

ce•leb•ri•ty \sə'lebrətē\ *n, pl* **-ties** **1** : renown **2** : well-known person

ce•ler•i•ty \sə'lerətē\ *n* : speed

cel•ery \'selərē\ *n, pl* **-er•ies** : herb grown for crisp edible stalks

ce•les•ta \sə'lestə\ **ce•leste** \sə'lest\ *n* : keyboard musical instrument

ce•les•tial \sə'leschəl\ *adj* **1** : relating to the sky **2** : heavenly

cel•i•ba•cy \'seləbəsē\ *n* **1** : state of being unmarried **2** : abstention from sexual intercourse — **cel•i•bate** \'seləbət\ *n or adj*

cell \'sel\ *n* **1** : small room **2** : tiny mass of protoplasm that forms the fundamental unit of living matter **3** : container holding an electrolyte for generating electricity — **celled** *adj*

cel•lar \'selər\ *n* : room or area below ground

cel•lo \'chelō\ *n, pl* **-los** : bass member of the violin family — **cel•list** \-ist\ *n*

cel•lo•phane \'selə,fān\ *n* : thin transparent cellulose wrapping

cell phone *n* : portable cordless telephone for use in a system of radio transmitters

cel•lu•lar \'selyələr\ *adj* : relating to or consisting of cells

cel•lu•lose \'selyə,lōs\ *n* : complex plant carbohydrate

Cel•sius \'selsēəs\ *adj* : relating to a thermometer scale on which the freezing point of water is 0° and the boiling point is 100°

ce•ment \si'ment\ *n* **1** : powdery mixture of clay and limestone that hardens when wetted **2** : binding agent ~ *vb* : unite or cover with cement

cem•e•tery \'semə,terē\ *n, pl* **-ter•ies** : burial ground

cen•ser \'sensər\ *n* : vessel for burning incense

cen•sor \'sensər\ *n* : one with power to suppress anything objectionable (as in printed matter) ~ *vb* : be a censor of — **cen•so•ri•al** \sen'sōrēəl\ *adj* — **cen•sor•ship** \-,ship\ *n*

cen•so•ri•ous \sen'sōrēəs\ *adj* : critical — **cen•so•ri•ous•ly** *adv* — **cen•so•ri•ous•ness** *n*

cen•sure \'senchər\ *n* : official reprimand ~ *vb* **-sured; -sur•ing** : find blameworthy — **cen•sur•able** *adj*

cen•sus \'sensəs\ *n* : periodic population count — **census** *vb*

cent \'sent\ *n* : monetary unit equal to $\frac{1}{100}$ of a basic unit of value

cen•taur \'sen,tör\ *n* : mythological creature that is half man and half horse

cen•ten•ni•al \sen'tenēəl\ *n* : 100th anniversary — **centennial** *adj*

cen•ter \'sentər\ *n* **1** : middle point **2** : point of origin or greatest concentration **3** : region of concentrated population **4** : player near the middle of the team ~ *vb* **1** : place, fix, or concentrate at or around a center **2** : have a center — **cen•ter•piece** *n*

cen•ti•grade \'sentə,grād, 'sänt-\ *adj* : Celsius

cen•ti•me•ter \'sentə,mētər, 'sänt-\ *n* : $\frac{1}{100}$ meter

cen•ti•pede \'sentə,pēd\ *n* : long flat many-legged arthropod

cen•tral \'sentrəl\ *adj* **1** : constituting or being near a center **2** : essential or principal — **cen•tral•ly** *adv*

cen•tral•ize \-trə,līz\ *vb* **-ized; -iz•ing**

: bring to a central point or under central control — **cen·tral·i·za·tion** \ˌsentrələ'zāshən\ *n* — **cen·tral·iz·er** *n*

cen·tre \'sentər\ *chiefly Brit var of* CENTER

cen·trif·u·gal \sen'trifyəgəl, -'trifigəl\ *adj* : acting in a direction away from a center or axis

cen·tri·fuge \'sentrə,fyüj\ *n* : machine that separates substances by spinning

cen·trip·e·tal \sen'tripət³l\ *adj* : acting in a direction toward a center or axis

cen·tu·ri·on \sen'chùrēən, -'tùr-\ *n* : Roman military officer

cen·tu·ry \'senchərē\ *n, pl* **-ries** : 100 years

ce·ram·ic \sə'ramik\ *n* 1 *pl* : art or process of shaping and hardening articles from clay 2 : product of ceramics — **ceramic** *adj*

ce·re·al \'sirēəl\ *adj* : made of or relating to grain or to the plants that produce it ~ *n* 1 : grass yielding edible grain 2 : food prepared from a cereal grain

cer·e·bel·lum \ˌserə'beləm\ *n, pl* **-bellums** *or* **-bel·la** \-'belə\ : part of the brain controlling muscular coordination — **cer·e·bel·lar** \-ər\ *adj*

ce·re·bral \sə'rēbrəl, 'serə-\ *adj* 1 : relating to the brain, intellect, or cerebrum 2 : appealing to the intellect

cerebral palsy *n* : disorder caused by brain damage and marked esp. by defective muscle control

cer·e·brate \'serə,brāt\ *vb* **-brat·ed; -brat·ing** : think — **cer·e·bra·tion** \ˌserə'brāshən\ *n*

ce·re·brum \sə'rēbrəm, 'serə-\ *n, pl* **-brums** *or* **-bra** \-brə\ : part of the brain that contains the higher nervous centers

cer·e·mo·ny \'serə,mōnē\ *n, pl* **-nies** 1 : formal act prescribed by law, ritual, or convention 2 : prescribed procedures — **cer·e·mo·ni·al** \ˌserə'mōnēəl\ *adj or n* — **cer·e·mo·ni·ous** \-nēəs\ *adj*

ce·rise \sə'rēs\ *n* : moderate red

cer·tain \'sərt³n\ *adj* 1 : settled 2 : true 3 : specific but not named 4 : bound 5 : assured ~ *pron* : certain ones — **cer·tain·ly** *adv* — **cer·tain·ty** \-tē\ *n*

cer·tif·i·cate \sər'tifikət\ *n* : document establishing truth or fulfillment

cer·ti·fy \'sərtə,fī\ *vb* **-fied; -fy·ing** 1

: verify 2 : endorse — **cer·ti·fi·able** \-ˌfīəbəl\ *adj* — **cer·ti·fi·ably** \-blē\ *adv* — **cer·ti·fi·ca·tion** \ˌsərtəfə-'kāshən\ *n* — **cer·ti·fi·er** *n*

cer·ti·tude \'sərtə,tüd, -,tyüd\ *n* : state of being certain

cer·vix \'sərviks\ *n, pl* **-vi·ces** \-və,sēz\ *or* **-vix·es** 1 : neck 2 : narrow end of the uterus — **cer·vi·cal** \-vikəl\ *adj*

ce·sar·e·an \si'zarēən\ *n* : surgical operation to deliver a baby — **cesarean** *adj*

ce·si·um \'sēzēəm\ *n* : silver-white soft ductile chemical element

ces·sa·tion \se'sāshən\ *n* : a halting

ces·sion \'seshən\ *n* : a yielding

cess·pool \'ses,pül\ *n* : underground sewage pit

Cha·blis \'shab,lē; sha'blē\ *n, pl* **Chablis** \-,lēz, -'blēz\ : dry white wine

chafe \'chāf\ *vb* **chafed; chaf·ing** 1 : fret 2 : make sore by rubbing

chaff \'chaf\ *n* 1 : debris separated from grain 2 : something worthless

chaf·ing dish \'chāfiŋ-\ *n* : utensil for cooking at the table

cha·grin \shə'grin\ *n* : embarrassment or humiliation ~ *vb* : cause to feel chagrin

chain \'chān\ *n* 1 : flexible series of connected links 2 *pl* : fetters 3 : linked series ~ *vb* : bind or connect with a chain

chair \'cher\ *n* 1 : seat with a back 2 : position of authority or dignity 3 : chairman ~ *vb* : act as chairman of

chair·man \-mən\ *n* : presiding officer — **chair·man·ship** *n*

chair·wom·an \-ˌwùmən\ *n* : woman who is a presiding officer

chaise longue \'shāz'lôŋ\ *n, pl* **chaise longues** \-lôŋ, -'lôŋz\ : long chair for reclining

cha·let \sha'lā\ *n* : Swiss mountain cottage with overhanging roof

chal·ice \'chaləs\ *n* : eucharistic cup

chalk \'chòk\ *n* 1 : soft limestone 2 : chalky material used as a crayon ~ *vb* : mark with chalk — **chalky** *adj* — **chalk up** *vb* 1 : credit 2 : achieve

chalk·board *n* : blackboard

chal·lenge \'chalənj\ *vb* **-lenged; -leng·ing** 1 : dispute 2 : invite or dare to act or compete — **challenge** *n* — **chal·leng·er** *n*

cham·ber \'chāmbər\ *n* 1 : room 2 : enclosed space 3 : legislative meeting place or body **4** *pl* : judge's consultation room — **cham·bered** *adj*

cham·ber·maid *n* : bedroom maid

chamber music *n* : music by a small group for a small audience

cha·me·leon \kə'mēlyən\ *n* : small lizard whose skin changes color

cham·ois \'shamē\ *n, pl* **cham·ois** \-ē, -ēz\ **1** : goatlike antelope **2** : soft leather

¹**champ** \'champ, 'chämp\ *vb* : chew noisily

²**champ** \'champ\ *n* : champion

cham·pagne \sham'pān\ *n* : sparkling white wine

cham·pi·on \'champēən\ *n* **1** : advocate or defender **2** : winning contestant ~ *vb* : protect or fight for

cham·pi·on·ship \-,ship\ *n* **1** : title of a champion **2** : contest to pick a champion

chance \'chans\ *n* **1** : unpredictable element of existence **2** : opportunity **3** : probability **4** : risk **5** : raffle ticket ~ *vb* **chanced; chanc·ing 1** : happen **2** : encounter unexpectedly **3** : risk — **chance** *adj*

chan·cel \'chansəl\ *n* : part of a church around the altar

chan·cel·lery, chan·cel·lory \'chansələrē\ *n, pl* **-ler·ies** *or* **-lor·ies 1** : position of a chancellor **2** : chancellor's office

chan·cel·lor \-ələr\ *n* **1** : chief or high state official **2** : head of a university — **chan·cel·lor·ship** *n*

chan·cre \'shaŋkər\ *n* : skin ulcer esp. from syphilis

chancy \'chansē\ *adj* **chanc·i·er; -est** : risky

chan·de·lier \,shandə'lir\ *n* : hanging lighting fixture

chan·dler \'chandlər\ *n* : provisions dealer — **chan·dlery** *n*

change \'chānj\ *vb* **changed; chang·ing 1** : make or become different **2** : exchange **3** : give or receive change for ~ *n* **1** : a changing **2** : excess from a payment **3** : money in smaller denominations **4** : coins — **change·able** *adj* — **change·less** *adj* — **chang·er** *n*

chan·nel \'chan°l\ *n* **1** : deeper part of a waterway **2** : means of passage or communication **3** : strait **4** : broadcast frequency ~ *vb* **-neled** *or* **-nelled; -nel·ing** *or* **-nel·ling** : make or direct through a channel

chant \'chant\ *vb* : sing or speak in one tone — **chant** *n* — **chant·er** *n*

chan·tey, chan·ty \'shantē, 'chant-\ *n, pl* **-teys** *or* **-ties** : sailors' work song

Cha·nu·kah \'känəkə, 'hän-\ *var of* **HANUKKAH**

cha·os \'kā,äs\ *n* : complete disorder — **cha·ot·ic** \kā'ätik\ *adj* — **cha·ot·i·cal·ly** \-iklē\ *adv*

¹**chap** \'chap\ *n* : fellow

²**chap** *vb* **-pp-** : dry and crack open usu. from wind and cold

cha·pel \'chapəl\ *n* : private or small place of worship

chap·er·on, chap·er·one \'shapə,rōn\ *n* : older person who accompanies young people at a social gathering ~ *vb* **-oned; -on·ing** : act as chaperon at or for — **chap·er·on·age** \-ij\ *n*

chap·lain \'chaplən\ *n* : clergy member in a military unit or a prison — **chap·lain·cy** \-sē\ *n*

chap·ter \'chaptər\ *n* **1** : main book division **2** : branch of a society

char \'chär\ *vb* **-rr- 1** : burn to charcoal **2** : scorch

char·ac·ter \'kariktər\ *n* **1** : letter or graphic mark **2** : trait or distinctive combination of traits **3** : peculiar person **4** : fictional person — **char·ac·ter·i·za·tion** \,kariktərə'zāshən\ *n* — **char·ac·ter·ize** \'kariktə,rīz\ *vb*

char·ac·ter·is·tic \,kariktə'ristik\ *adj* : typical ~ *n* : distinguishing quality — **char·ac·ter·is·ti·cal·ly** \-tiklē\ *adv*

cha·rades \shə'rādz\ *n sing or pl* : pantomime guessing game

char·coal \'chär,kōl\ *n* : porous carbon prepared by partial combustion

chard \'chärd\ *n* : leafy vegetable

charge \'chärj\ *vb* **charged; charg·ing 1** : give an electric charge to **2** : impose a task or responsibility on **3** : command **4** : accuse **5** : rush forward in assault **6** : assume a debt for **7** : fix as a price ~ *n* **1** : excess or deficiency of electrons in a body **2** : tax **3** : responsibility **4** : accusation **5** : cost **6** : attack — **charge·able** *adj*

charg·er \-ər\ *n* : horse ridden in battle

char·i·ot \'charēət\ *n* : ancient 2-wheeled vehicle — **char·i·o·teer** \,charēə'tir\ *n*

cha·ris·ma \kə'rizmə\ *n* : special ability to lead — **char·is·mat·ic** \ˌkarəz-ˈmatik\ adj

char·i·ty \ˈcharətē\ n, pl **-ties** 1 : love for mankind 2 : generosity or leniency 3 : alms 4 : institution for relief of the needy — **char·i·ta·ble** \-əbəl\ adj — **char·i·ta·ble·ness** n — **char·i·ta·bly** \-blē\ adv

char·la·tan \ˈshärlətən\ n : impostor

charm \ˈchärm\ n 1 : something with magic power 2 : appealing trait 3 : small ornament ∼ vb : fascinate — **charm·er** n — **charm·ing** adj — **charm·ing·ly** adv

char·nel house \ˈchärn³l-\ n : place for dead bodies

chart \ˈchärt\ n 1 : map 2 : diagram ∼ vb 1 : make a chart of 2 : plan

char·ter \-ər\ n 1 : document granting rights 2 : constitution ∼ vb 1 : establish by charter 2 : rent — **char·ter·er** n

char·treuse \shär'trüz, -'trüs\ n : brilliant yellow green

char·wom·an \ˈchär,wümən\ n : cleaning woman

chary \ˈcharē\ adj **chari·er; -est** : cautious — **char·i·ly** \ˈcharəlē\ adv

¹**chase** \ˈchās\ vb **chased; chas·ing** 1 : follow trying to catch 2 : drive away — **chase** n — **chas·er** n

²**chase** vb **chased; chas·ing** : decorate (metal) by embossing or engraving

chasm \ˈkazəm\ n : gorge

chas·sis \ˈchasē, ˈshasē\ n, pl **chas·sis** \-ēz\ : supporting structural frame

chaste \ˈchāst\ adj **chast·er; chast·est** 1 : abstaining from all or unlawful sexual relations 2 : modest or decent 3 : severely simple — **chaste·ly** adv — **chaste·ness** n — **chas·ti·ty** \ˈchastətē\ n

chas·ten \ˈchās³n\ vb : discipline

chas·tise \chas'tīz\ vb **-tised; -tis·ing** 1 : punish 2 : censure — **chas·tise·ment** \-mənt, ˈchastəz-\ n

chat \ˈchat\ n : informal talk — **chat** vb — **chat·ty** \-ē\ adj

châ·teau \sha'tō\ n, pl **-teaus** \-'tōz\ or **-teaux** \-'tō, -'tōz\ 1 : large country house 2 : French vineyard estate

chat·tel \ˈchat³l\ n : item of tangible property other than real estate

chat·ter \ˈchatər\ vb 1 : utter rapidly succeeding sounds 2 : talk fast or too much — **chatter** n — **chat·ter·er** n

chat·ter·box n : incessant talker

chauf·feur \ˈshōfər, shō'fər\ n : hired car driver ∼ vb : work as a chauffeur

chau·vin·ism \ˈshōvə,nizəm\ n : excessive patriotism — **chau·vin·ist** \-vənist\ n — **chau·vin·is·tic** \ˌshōvə'nistik\ adj

cheap \ˈchēp\ adj 1 : inexpensive 2 : shoddy — **cheap** adv — **cheap·en** \ˈchēpən\ vb — **cheap·ly** adv — **cheap·ness** n

cheap·skate n : stingy person

cheat \ˈchēt\ n 1 : act of deceiving 2 : one that cheats ∼ vb 1 : deprive through fraud or deceit 2 : violate rules dishonestly — **cheat·er** n

check \ˈchek\ n 1 : sudden stoppage 2 : restraint 3 : test or standard for testing 4 : written order to a bank to pay money 5 : ticket showing ownership 6 : slip showing an amount due 7 : pattern in squares or fabric in such a pattern 8 : mark placed beside an item noted ∼ vb 1 : slow down or stop 2 : restrain 3 : compare or correspond with a source or original 4 : inspect or test for condition 5 : mark with a check 6 : leave or accept for safekeeping or shipment 7 : checker — **check in** vb : report one's arrival — **check out** vb : settle one's account and leave

¹**check·er** \-ər\ n : piece in checkers ∼ vb : mark with different colors or into squares

²**checker** n : one that checks

check·er·board \-ˌbōrd\ n : board of 64 squares of alternate colors

check·ers \ˈchekərz\ n : game for 2 played on a checkerboard

check·mate vb : thwart completely — **checkmate** n

check·point n : place where traffic is checked

check·up n : physical examination

ched·dar \ˈchedər\ n : hard smooth cheese

cheek \ˈchēk\ n 1 : fleshy side part of the face 2 : impudence — **cheeked** \ˈchēkt\ adj — **cheeky** adj

cheep \ˈchēp\ vb : utter faint shrill sounds — **cheep** n

cheer \ˈchir\ n 1 : good spirits 2 : food and drink for a feast 3 : shout of applause or encouragement ∼ vb 1 : give hope or courage to 2 : make or become glad 3 : urge on or applaud with shouts — **cheer·er** n — **cheer·ful** \-fəl\ adj — **cheer·ful·ly**

adv — **cheer·ful·ness** *n* — **cheer·lead·er** *n* — **cheer·less** *adj* — **cheer·less·ly** *adv* — **cheer·less·ness** *n*

cheery \'chirē\ *adj* **cheer·i·er; -est** : cheerful — **cheer·i·ly** *adv* — **cheer·i·ness** *n*

cheese \'chēz\ *n* : curd of milk usu. pressed and cured — **cheesy** *adj*

cheese·cloth *n* : lightweight coarse cotton gauze

chee·tah \'chētə\ *n* : spotted swift-moving African cat

chef \'shef\ *n* : chief cook

chem·i·cal \'kemikəl\ *adj* **1** : relating to chemistry **2** : working or produced by chemicals ~ *n* : substance obtained by chemistry — **chem·i·cal·ly** \-klē\ *adv*

che·mise \shə'mēz\ *n* **1** : woman's one-piece undergarment **2** : loose dress

chem·ist \'kemist\ *n* **1** : one trained in chemistry **2** *Brit* : pharmacist

chem·is·try \-istrē\ *n, pl* **-tries** : science that deals with the composition and properties of substances

che·mo·ther·a·py \‚kēmō'therəpē, ‚kemō-\ *n* : use of chemicals in the treatment of disease — **che·mo·ther·a·peu·tic** *adj*

che·nille \shə'nēl\ *n* : yarn with protruding pile or fabric of such yarn

cheque \'chek\ *chiefly Brit var of* CHECK 4

cher·ish \'cherish\ *vb* : hold dear

cher·ry \'cherē\ *n, pl* **-ries** : small fleshy fruit of a tree related to the roses or the tree or its wood

cher·ub \'cherəb\ *n* **1** *pl* **-u·bim** \-ə‚bim, -yə-\ : angel **2** *pl* **-ubs** : chubby child — **che·ru·bic** \chə-'rübik\ *adj*

chess \'ches\ *n* : game for 2 played on a checkerboard — **chess·board** *n* — **chess·man** *n*

chest \'chest\ *n* **1** : boxlike container **2** : part of the body enclosed by the ribs and breastbone — **chest·ed** *adj*

chest·nut \'ches‚nət\ *n* : nut of a tree related to the beech or the tree

chev·i·ot \'shevēət\ *n* **1** : heavy rough wool fabric **2** : soft-finished cotton fabric

chev·ron \'shevrən\ *n* : V-shaped insignia

chew \'chü\ *vb* : crush or grind with the teeth ~ *n* : something to chew —

chew·able *adj* — **chew·er** *n* — **chewy** *adj*

chic \'shēk\ *n* : smart elegance of dress or manner ~ *adj* **1** : stylish **2** : currently fashionable

chi·ca·nery \shik'ānərē\ *n, pl* **-ner·ies** : trickery

chick \'chik\ *n* : young chicken or bird

chick·a·dee \-ə‚dē\ *n* : small grayish American bird

chick·en \'chikən\ *n* **1** : common domestic fowl or its flesh used as food **2** : coward

chicken pox *n* : acute contagious virus disease esp. of children

chi·cle \'chikəl\ *n* : gum from a tropical evergreen tree

chic·o·ry \'chikərē\ *n, pl* **-ries** : herb used in salad or its dried ground root used to adulterate coffee

chide \'chīd\ *vb* **chid** \'chid\ *or* **chid·ed** \'chīdəd\; **chid** *or* **chid·den** \'chid⁰n\ *or* **chided**; **chid·ing** \'chīdiŋ\ : scold

chief \'chēf\ *n* : leader ~ *adj* **1** : highest in rank **2** : most important — **chief·dom** *n* — **chief·ly** *adv*

chief·tain \'chēftən\ *n* : chief

chif·fon \shif'än, 'shif‚-\ *n* : sheer fabric

chig·ger \'chigər\ *n* : bloodsucking mite

chi·gnon \'shēn‚yän\ *n* : knot of hair

chil·blain \'chil‚blān\ *n* : sore or inflamed swelling caused by cold

child \'chīld\ *n, pl* **chil·dren** \'chil-drən\ **1** : unborn or recently born person **2** : son or daughter — **child·bear·ing** *n or adj* — **child·birth** *n* — **child·hood** *n* — **child·ish** *adj* — **child·ish·ly** *adv* — **child·ish·ness** *n* — **child·less** *adj* — **child·less·ness** *n* — **child·like** *adj* — **child·proof** \-‚prüf\ *adj*

chili, chile, chil·li \'chilē\ *n, pl* **chil·ies** *or* **chil·es** *or* **chil·lies 1** : hot pepper **2** : spicy stew of ground beef, chilies, and beans

chill \'chil\ *vb* : make or become cold or chilly ~ *adj* : moderately cold ~ *n* **1** : feeling of coldness with shivering **2** : moderate coldness

chilly \-ē\ *adj* **chill·i·er; -est** : noticeably cold — **chill·i·ness** *n*

chime \'chīm\ *n* : set of tuned bells or their sound ~ *vb* : make bell-like sounds — **chime in** *vb* : break into or join in a conversation

chi•me•ra, chi•mae•ra \kī'mirə, kə-\ *n* **1** : imaginary monster **2** : illusion — **chi•me•ri•cal** \-'merikəl\ *adj*

chim•ney \'chimnē\ *n, pl* **-neys** **1** : passage for smoke **2** : glass tube around a lamp flame

chimp \'chimp, 'shimp\ *n* : chimpanzee

chim•pan•zee \,chim,pan'zē, ,shim-; chim'panzē, shim-\ *n* : small ape

chin \'chin\ *n* : part of the face below the mouth — **chin•less** *adj*

chi•na \'chīnə\ *n* **1** : porcelain ware **2** : domestic pottery

chin•chil•la \chin'chilə\ *n* : small So. American rodent with soft pearl-gray fur or this fur

chink \'chiŋk\ *n* : small crack ~ *vb* : fill chinks of

chintz \'chints\ *n* : printed cotton cloth

chip \'chip\ *n* **1** : small thin flat piece cut or broken off **2** : thin crisp morsel of food **3** : counter used in games **4** : flaw where a chip came off **5** : small slice of semiconductor containing electronic circuits ~ *vb* **-pp-** : cut or break chips from — **chip in** *vb* : contribute

chip•munk \-,məŋk\ *n* : small striped ground-dwelling rodent

chip•per \-ər\ *adj* : lively and cheerful

chi•rop•o•dy \kə'räpədē, shə-\ *n* : podiatry — **chi•rop•o•dist** \-ədist\ *n*

chi•ro•prac•tic \'kīrə,praktik\ *n* : system of healing based esp. on manipulation of body structures — **chi•ro•prac•tor** \-tər\ *n*

chirp \'chərp\ *n* : short sharp sound like that of a bird or cricket — **chirp** *vb*

chis•el \'chizəl\ *n* : sharp-edged metal tool ~ *vb* **-eled** *or* **-elled; -el•ing** *or* **-el•ling** **1** : work with a chisel **2** : cheat — **chis•el•er** \-ələr\ *n*

chit \'chit\ *n* : signed voucher for a small debt

chit•chat \-,chat\ *n* : casual conversation — **chitchat** *vb*

chiv•al•rous \'shivəlrəs\ *adj* **1** : relating to chivalry **2** : honest, courteous, or generous — **chiv•al•rous•ly** *adv* — **chiv•al•rous•ness** *n*

chiv•al•ry \-rē\ *n, pl* **-ries** **1** : system or practices of knighthood **2** : spirit or character of the ideal knight — **chi•val•ric** \shə'valrik\ *adj*

chive \'chīv\ *n* : herb related to the onion

chlo•ride \'klōr,īd\ *n* : compound of chlorine

chlo•ri•nate \-ə,nāt\ *vb* **-nat•ed; -nat•ing** : treat or combine with chlorine — **chlo•ri•na•tion** \,klōrə'nāshən\ *n*

chlo•rine \'klōr,ēn\ *n* : chemical element that is a heavy strong-smelling greenish yellow irritating gas

chlo•ro•form \'klōrə,fórm\ *n* : etherlike colorless heavy fluid ~ *vb* : anesthetize or kill with chloroform

chlo•ro•phyll \'klōrə,fil\ *n* : green coloring matter of plants

chock \'chäk\ *n* : wedge for blocking the movement of a wheel — **chock** *vb*

chock–full \'chək'fûl, 'chäk-\ *adj* : full to the limit

choc•o•late \'chäkələt, 'chók-\ *n* **1** : ground roasted cacao beans or a beverage made from them **2** : candy made of or with chocolate **3** : dark brown

choice \'chòis\ *n* **1** : act or power of choosing **2** : one selected **3** : variety offered for selection ~ *adj* **choic•er; choic•est** **1** : worthy of being chosen **2** : selected with care **3** : of high quality

choir \'kwīr\ *n* : group of singers esp. in church — **choir•boy** *n* — **choir•mas•ter** *n*

choke \'chōk\ *vb* **choked; chok•ing** **1** : hinder breathing **2** : clog or obstruct ~ *n* **1** : a choking or sound of choking **2** : valve for controlling air intake in a gasoline engine

chok•er \-ər\ *n* : tight necklace

cho•ler \'kälər, 'kō-\ *n* : bad temper — **cho•ler•ic** \'kälərik, kə'ler-\ *adj*

chol•era \'kälərə\ *n* : disease marked by severe vomiting and dysentery

cho•les•ter•ol \kə'lestə,ról, -,ról\ *n* : waxy substance in animal tissues

choose \'chüz\ *vb* **chose** \'chōz\; **cho•sen** \'chōz²n\; **choos•ing** **1** : select after consideration **2** : decide **3** : prefer — **choos•er** *n*

choosy; choos•ey \'chüzē\ *adj* **choos•ier; -est** : fussy in making choices

chop \'chäp\ *vb* **-pp-** **1** : cut by repeated blows **2** : cut into small pieces ~ *n* **1** : sharp downward blow **2** : small cut of meat often with part of a rib

chop·per \-ər\ *n* **1** : one that chops **2** : helicopter

chop·py \-ē\ *adj* **-pi·er; -est 1** : rough with small waves **2** : jerky or disconnected — **chop·pi·ly** *adv* — **chop·pi·ness** *n*

chops \'chäps\ *n pl* : fleshy covering of the jaws

chop·sticks *n pl* : pair of sticks used in eating in oriental countries

cho·ral \'kōrəl\ *adj* : relating to or sung by a choir or chorus or in chorus — **cho·ral·ly** *adv*

cho·rale \kə'ral, -'räl\ *n* **1** : hymn tune or harmonization of a traditional melody **2** : chorus or choir

¹chord \'kórd\ *n* : harmonious tones sounded together

²chord *n* **1** : cordlike anatomical structure **2** : straight line joining 2 points on a curve

chore \'chōr\ *n* **1** *pl* : daily household or farm work **2** : routine or disagreeable task

cho·re·og·ra·phy \ˌkōrē'ägrəfē\ *n, pl* **-phies** : art of composing and arranging dances — **cho·reo·graph** \'kōrēəˌgraf\ *vb* — **cho·re·og·ra·pher** \ˌkōrē'ägrəfər\ *n* — **cho·reo·graph·ic** \-ēə'grafik\ *adj*

cho·ris·ter \'kōrəstər\ *n* : choir singer

chor·tle \'chórt³l\ *vb* **-tled; -tling** : laugh or chuckle — **chortle** *n*

cho·rus \'kōrəs\ *n* **1** : group of singers or dancers **2** : part of a song repeated at intervals **3** : composition for a chorus ~ *vb* : sing or utter together

chose *past of* CHOOSE

cho·sen \'chōz³n\ *adj* : favored

¹chow \'chaủ\ *n* : food

²chow *n* : thick-coated muscular dog

chow·der \'chaủdər\ *n* : thick soup usu. of seafood and milk

chow mein \'chaủ'mān\ *n* : thick stew of shredded vegetables and meat

chris·ten \'kris³n\ *vb* **1** : baptize **2** : name — **chris·ten·ing** *n*

Chris·ten·dom \-dəm\ *n* : areas where Christianity prevails

Chris·tian \'krischən\ *n* : adherent of Christianity ~ *adj* : relating to or professing a belief in Christianity or Jesus Christ — **Chris·tian·ize** \'krischəˌnīz\ *vb*

Chris·ti·an·i·ty \ˌkrischē'anətē\ *n* : religion derived from the teachings of Jesus Christ

Christian name *n* : first name

Christ·mas \'krisməs\ *n* : December 25 celebrated as the birthday of Christ

chro·mat·ic \krō'matik\ *adj* **1** : relating to color **2** : proceeding by half steps of the musical scale

chrome \'krōm\ *n* : chromium or something plated with it

chro·mi·um \-ēəm\ *n* : a bluish white metallic element used esp. in alloys

chro·mo·some \'krōməˌsōm, -ˌzōm\ *n* : part of a cell nucleus that contains the genes — **chro·mo·som·al** \ˌkrōmə'sōməl, -'zō-\ *adj*

chron·ic \'kränik\ *adj* : frequent or persistent — **chron·i·cal·ly** \-iklē\ *adv*

chron·i·cle \'kränikəl\ *n* : history ~ *vb* **-cled; -cling** : record — **chron·i·cler** \-iklər\ *n*

chro·nol·o·gy \krə'näləjē\ *n, pl* **-gies** : list of events in order of their occurrence — **chron·o·log·i·cal** \ˌkrän³l-'äjikəl\ *adj* — **chron·o·log·i·cal·ly** \-iklē\ *adv*

chro·nom·e·ter \krə'nämətər\ *n* : very accurate timepiece

chrys·a·lis \'krisələs\ *n, pl* **chry·sal·i·des** \kris'aləˌdēz\ *or* **chrys·a·lis·es** : insect pupa enclosed in a shell

chry·san·the·mum \kris'anthəməm\ *n* : plant with showy flowers

chub·by \'chəbē\ *adj* **-bi·er; -est** : fat — **chub·bi·ness** *n*

¹chuck \'chək\ *vb* **1** : tap **2** : toss ~ *n* **1** : light pat under the chin **2** : toss

²chuck *n* **1** : cut of beef **2** : machine part that holds work or another part

chuck·le \'chəkəl\ *vb* **-led; -ling** : laugh quietly — **chuckle** *n*

chug \'chəg\ *n* : sound of a laboring engine ~ *vb* **-gg-** : work or move with chugs

chum \'chəm\ *n* : close friend ~ *vb* **-mm-** : be chums — **chum·my** \-ē\ *adj*

chump \'chəmp\ *n* : fool

chunk \'chəŋk\ *n* **1** : short thick piece **2** : sizable amount

chunky \-ē\ *adj* **chunk·i·er; -est 1** : stocky **2** : containing chunks

church \'chərch\ *n* **1** : building esp. for Christian public worship **2** : whole body of Christians **3** : denomination **4** : congregation — **church·go·er** *n* — **church·go·ing** *adj or n*

church·yard *n* : cemetery beside a church

churl \'chərl\ n : rude ill-bred person — **churl·ish** adj

churn \'chərn\ n : container in which butter is made ~ vb 1 : agitate in a churn 2 : shake violently

chute \'shüt\ n : trough or passage

chut·ney \'chətnē\ n, pl **-neys** : sweet and sour relish

chutz·pah \'hütspə, 'kut-, -spä\ n : nerve or insolence

ci·ca·da \sə'kādə\ n : stout-bodied insect with transparent wings

ci·der \'sīdər\ n : apple juice

ci·gar \sig'är\ n : roll of leaf tobacco for smoking

cig·a·rette \,sigə'ret, 'sigə,ret\ n : cut tobacco rolled in paper for smoking

cinch \'sinch\ n 1 : strap holding a saddle or pack in place 2 : sure thing — **cinch** vb

cin·cho·na \sin'kōnə\ n : So. American tree that yields quinine

cinc·ture \'siŋkchər\ n : belt or sash

cin·der \'sindər\ n 1 pl : ashes 2 : piece of partly burned wood or coal

cin·e·ma \'sinəmə\ n : movies or a movie theater — **cin·e·mat·ic** \,sinə-'matik\ adj

cin·na·mon \'sinəmən\ n : spice from an aromatic tree bark

ci·pher \'sīfər\ n 1 : zero 2 : code

cir·ca \'sərkə\ prep : about

cir·cle \'sərkəl\ n 1 : closed symmetrical curve 2 : cycle 3 : group with a common tie ~ vb **-cled; -cling** 1 : enclose in a circle 2 : move or revolve around

cir·cuit \'sərkət\ n 1 : boundary 2 : regular tour of a territory 3 : complete path of an electric current 4 : group of electronic components

cir·cu·itous \,sər'kyüətəs\ adj : circular or winding

cir·cuit·ry \'sərkətrē\ n, pl **-ries** : arrangement of an electric circuit

cir·cu·lar \'sərkyələr\ adj 1 : round 2 : moving in a circle ~ n : advertising leaflet — **cir·cu·lar·i·ty** \,sərkyə'larətē\ n

cir·cu·late \'sərkyə,lāt\ vb **-lat·ed; -lat·ing** : move or cause to move in a circle or from place to place or person to person — **cir·cu·la·tion** \,sər-kyə'lāshən\ n — **cir·cu·la·to·ry** \'sərkyələ,tōrē\ adj

cir·cum·cise \'sərkəm,sīz\ vb **-cised; -cis·ing** : cut off the foreskin of — **cir·cum·ci·sion** \,sərkəm'sizhən\ n

cir·cum·fer·ence \sər'kəmfrəns\ n : perimeter of a circle

cir·cum·flex \'sərkəm,fleks\ n : phonetic mark (as ^)

cir·cum·lo·cu·tion \,sərkəmlō'kyü-shən\ n : excessive use of words

cir·cum·nav·i·gate \,sərkəm'navə,gāt\ vb : sail completely around — **cir·cum·nav·i·ga·tion** n

cir·cum·scribe \'sərkəm,skrīb\ vb 1 : draw a line around 2 : limit

cir·cum·spect \'sərkəm,spekt\ adj : careful — **cir·cum·spec·tion** \,sərkəm'spekshən\ n

cir·cum·stance \'sərkəm,stans\ n 1 : fact or event 2 pl : surrounding conditions 3 pl : financial situation — **cir·cum·stan·tial** \,sərkəm'stan-chəl\ adj

cir·cum·vent \,sərkəm'vent\ vb : get around esp. by trickery — **cir·cum·ven·tion** \-'venchən\ n

cir·cus \'sərkəs\ n : show with feats of skill, animal acts, and clowns

cir·rho·sis \sə'rōsəs\ n, pl **-rho·ses** \-,sēz\ : fibrosis of the liver — **cir·rhot·ic** \-'rätik\ adj or n

cir·rus \'sirəs\ n, pl **-ri** \-,ī\ : wispy white cloud

cis·tern \'sistərn\ n : underground water tank

cit·a·del \'sitəd³l, -ə,del\ n : fortress

cite \'sīt\ vb **cit·ed; cit·ing** 1 : summon before a court 2 : quote 3 : refer to esp. in commendation — **ci·ta·tion** \sī'tāshən\ n

cit·i·zen \'sitəzən\ n : member of a country — **cit·i·zen·ry** \-rē\ n — **cit·i·zen·ship** n

cit·ron \'sitrən\ n : lemonlike fruit

cit·rus \'sitrəs\ n, pl **-rus** or **-rus·es** : evergreen tree or shrub grown for its fruit (as the orange or lemon)

city \'sitē\ n, pl **cit·ies** : place larger or more important than a town

civ·ic \'sivik\ adj : relating to citizenship or civil affairs

civ·ics \-iks\ n : study of citizenship

civ·il \'sivəl\ adj 1 : relating to citizens 2 : polite 3 : relating to or being a lawsuit — **civ·il·ly** adv

ci·vil·ian \sə'vilyən\ n : person not in a military, police, or fire-fighting force

ci·vil·i·ty \sə'vilətē\ n, pl **-ties** : courtesy

civ·i·li·za·tion \,sivələ'zāshən\ n 1

: high level of cultural development **2**
: culture of a time or place

civ•i•lize \\'siva,līz\\ *vb* **-lized; -liz•ing**
: raise from a primitive stage of cultural development — **civ•i•lized** *adj*

civil liberty *n* : freedom from arbitrary governmental interference — usu. pl.

civil rights *n pl* : nonpolitical rights of a citizen

civil service *n* : government service

civil war *n* : war among citizens of one country

clack \\'klak\\ *vb* : make or cause a clatter — **clack** *n*

clad \\'klad\\ *adj* : covered

claim \\'klām\\ *vb* **1** : demand or take as the rightful owner **2** : maintain ~ *n* **1** : demand of right or ownership **2** : declaration **3** : something claimed — **claim•ant** \\-ənt\\ *n*

clair•voy•ant \\klar'vóiənt\\ *adj* : able to perceive things beyond the senses — **clair•voy•ance** \\-əns\\ *n* — **clair•voy•ant** *n*

clam \\'klam\\ *n* : bivalve mollusk

clam•ber \\'klambər\\ *vb* : climb awkwardly

clam•my \\'klamē\\ *adj* **-mi•er; -est** : being damp, soft, and usu. cool — **clam•mi•ness** *n*

clam•or \\-ər\\ *n* **1** : uproar **2** : protest — **clamor** *vb* — **clam•or•ous** *adj*

clamp \\'klamp\\ *n* : device for holding things together — **clamp** *vb*

clan \\'klan\\ *n* : group of related families — **clan•nish** *adj* — **clan•nish•ness** *n*

clan•des•tine \\klan'destən\\ *adj* : secret

clang \\'klaŋ\\ *n* : loud metallic ringing — **clang** *vb*

clan•gor \\-ər, -gər\\ *n* : jumble of clangs

clank \\'klaŋk\\ *n* : brief sound of struck metal — **clank** *vb*

clap \\'klap\\ *vb* **-pp-** **1** : strike noisily **2** : applaud — ~ *n* **1** : loud crash **2** : noise made by clapping the hands

clap•board \\'klabərd, 'klap-, -,bōrd\\ *n* : narrow tapered board used for siding

clap•per \\'klapər\\ *n* : tongue of a bell

claque \\'klak\\ *n* **1** : group hired to applaud at a performance **2** : group of sycophants

clar•et \\'klarət\\ *n* : dry red wine

clar•i•fy \\'klarə,fī\\ *vb* **-fied; -fy•ing** : make or become clear — **clar•i•fi•ca•tion** \\,klarəfə'kāshən\\ *n*

clar•i•net \\,klarə'net\\ *n* : woodwind instrument shaped like a tube — **clar•i•net•ist, clar•i•net•tist** \\-ist\\ *n*

clar•i•on \\klarēən\\ *adj* : loud and clear

clar•i•ty \\'klarətē\\ *n* : clearness

clash \\'klash\\ *vb* **1** : make or cause a clash **2** : be in opposition or disharmony ~ *n* **1** : crashing sound **2** : hostile encounter

clasp \\'klasp\\ *n* **1** : device for holding things together **2** : embrace or grasp ~ *vb* **1** : fasten **2** : embrace or grasp

class \\'klas\\ *n* **1** : group of the same status or nature **2** : social rank **3** : course of instruction **4** : group of students — ~ *vb* : classify — **class•less** *adj* — **class•mate** *n* — **class•room** *n*

clas•sic \\'klasik\\ *adj* **1** : serving as a standard of excellence **2** : classical ~ *n* : work of enduring excellence and esp. of ancient Greece or Rome — **clas•si•cal** \\-ikəl\\ *adj* — **clas•si•cal•ly** \\-klē\\ *adv* — **clas•si•cism** \\'klasə,sizəm\\ *n* — **clas•si•cist** \\-sist\\ *n*

clas•si•fied \\'klasə,fīd\\ *adj* : restricted for security reasons

clas•si•fy \\-,fī\\ *vb* **-fied; -fy•ing** : arrange in or assign to classes — **clas•si•fi•ca•tion** \\,klasəfə'kāshən\\ *n* — **clas•si•fi•er** \\'klasə,fīər\\ *n*

clat•ter \\'klatər\\ *n* : rattling sound — **clatter** *vb*

clause \\'klóz\\ *n* **1** : separate part of a document **2** : part of a sentence with a subject and predicate

claus•tro•pho•bia \\,klóstrə'fōbēə\\ *n* : fear of closed or narrow spaces — **claus•tro•pho•bic** \\-bik\\ *adj*

clav•i•chord \\'klavə,kórd\\ *n* : early keyboard instrument

clav•i•cle \\'klavikəl\\ *n* : collarbone

claw \\'kló\\ *n* : sharp curved nail or process (as on the toe of an animal) ~ *vb* : scratch or dig — **clawed** *adj*

clay \\'klā\\ *n* : plastic earthy material — **clay•ey** \\-ē\\ *adj*

clean \\'klēn\\ *adj* **1** : free from dirt or disease **2** : pure or honorable **3** : thorough — ~ *vb* : make or become clean — **clean** *adv* — **clean•er** *n* — **clean•ly** \\-lē\\ *adv* — **clean•ness** *n*

clean•ly \\'klenlē\\ *adj* **-li•er; -est** : clean — **clean•li•ness** *n*

cleanse \\'klenz\\ *vb* **cleansed; cleans•ing** : make clean — **cleans•er** *n*

clear \\'klir\\ *adj* **1** : bright **2** : free from

clouds **3** : transparent **4** : easily heard, seen or understood **5** : free from doubt **6** : free from restriction or obstruction ~ *vb* **1** : make or become clear **2** : go away **3** : free from accusation or blame **4** : explain or settle **5** : net **6** : jump or pass without touching ~ *n* : clear space or part — **clear** *adv* — **clear·ance** \'klirəns\ *n*

clear·ing \'klirin\ *n* : land cleared of wood

clear·ly *adv* **1** : in a clear manner **2** : it is obvious that

cleat \'klēt\ *n* : projection that strengthens or prevents slipping

cleav·age \'klēvij\ *n* **1** : a splitting apart **2** : depression between a woman's breasts

¹**cleave** \'klēv\ *vb* **cleaved** \'klēvd\ or **clove** \'klōv\; **cleav·ing** : adhere

²**cleave** *vb* **cleaved** \'klēvd\; **cleav·ing** : split apart

cleav·er \'klēvər\ *n* : heavy chopping knife

clef \'klef\ *n* : sign on the staff in music to show pitch

cleft \'kleft\ *n* : crack

clem·ent \'klemənt\ *adj* **1** : merciful **2** : temperate or mild — **clem·en·cy** \-ənsē\ *n*

clench \'klench\ *vb* : hold fast **2** : close tightly

cler·gy \'klərjē\ *n* : body of religious officials — **cler·gy·man** \-jimən\ *n*

cler·ic \'klerik\ *n* : member of the clergy

cler·i·cal \-ikəl\ *adj* **1** : relating to the clergy **2** : relating to a clerk or office worker

clerk \'klərk, *Brit* 'klärk\ *n* **1** : official responsible for record-keeping **2** : person doing general office work **3** : salesperson in a store — **clerk** *vb* — **clerk·ship** *n*

clev·er \'klevər\ *adj* **1** : resourceful **2** : marked by wit or ingenuity — **clev·er·ly** *adv* — **clev·er·ness** *n*

clew *var of* CLUE

cli·ché \kli'shā\ *n* : trite phrase — **cli·chéd** \-'shād\ *adj*

click \'klik\ *n* : slight sharp noise ~ *vb* : make or cause to make a click

cli·ent \'klīənt\ *n* **1** : person who engages professional services **2** : customer

cli·en·tele \kliən'tel, klē-\ *n* : body of customers

cliff \'klif\ *n* : high steep face of rock

cli·mate \'klīmət\ *n* : average weather conditions over a period of years — **cli·mat·ic** \klī'matik\ *adj*

cli·max \'klī,maks\ *n* : the highest point ~ *vb* : come to a climax — **cli·mac·tic** \klī'maktik\ *adj*

climb \'klīm\ *vb* **1** : go up or down by use of hands and feet **2** : rise ~ *n* : a climbing — **climb·er** *n*

clinch \'klinch\ *vb* **1** : fasten securely **2** : settle **3** : hold fast or firmly — **clinch** *n* — **clinch·er** *n*

cling \'klin\ *vb* **clung** \'kləŋ\; **cling·ing 1** : adhere firmly **2** : hold on tightly

clin·ic \'klinik\ *n* : facility for diagnosis and treatment of outpatients — **clin·i·cal** \-əl\ *adj* — **clin·i·cal·ly** \-klē\ *adv*

clink \'kliŋk\ *vb* : make a slight metallic sound — **clink** *n*

clin·ker \'kliŋkər\ *n* : fused stony matter esp. in a furnace

¹**clip** \'klip\ *vb* **-pp-** : fasten with a clip ~ *n* : device to hold things together

²**clip** *vb* **-pp- 1** : cut or cut off **2** : hit ~ *n* **1** : clippers **2** : sharp blow **3** : rapid pace

clip·per \'klipər\ *n* **1** *pl* : implement for clipping **2** : fast sailing ship

clique \'klēk, 'klik\ *n* : small exclusive group of people

cli·to·ris \'klitərəs, kli'tòrəs\ *n, pl* **cli·to·ri·des** \-'tòrə,dēz\ : small organ at the front of the vulva

cloak \'klōk\ *n* **1** : loose outer garment **2** : something that conceals ~ *vb* : cover or hide with a cloak

clob·ber \'kläbər\ *vb* : hit hard

clock \'kläk\ *n* : timepiece not carried on the person ~ *vb* : record the time of

clock·wise \-,wīz\ *adv or adj* : in the same direction as a clock's hands move

clod \'kläd\ *n* **1** : lump esp. of earth **2** : dull insensitive person

clog \'kläg\ *n* **1** : restraining weight **2** : thick-soled shoe ~ *vb* **-gg- 1** : impede with a clog **2** : obstruct passage through **3** : become plugged up

clois·ter \'klòistər\ *n* **1** : monastic establishment **2** : covered passage ~ *vb* : shut away from the world

clone \'klōn\ *n* **1** : offspring produced from a single organism **2** : copy

¹**close** \'klōz\ *vb* **closed; clos·ing 1**

: shut **2** : cease operation **3** : terminate **4** : bring or come together ~ *n* : conclusion or end

²close \'klōs\ *adj* **clos•er; clos•est 1** : confining **2** : secretive **3** : strict **4** : stuffy **5** : having little space between items **6** : fitting tightly **7** : near **8** : intimate **9** : accurate **10** : nearly even — **close** *adv* — **close•ly** *adv* — **close•ness** *n*

clos•et \'kläzət, 'klòz-\ *n* : small compartment for household utensils or clothing ~ *vb* : take into a private room for a talk

clo•sure \'klōzhər\ *n* **1** : act of closing **2** : something that closes

clot \'klät\ *n* : dried mass of a liquid — **clot** *vb*

cloth \'klòth\ *n, pl* **cloths** \'klòthz, 'klòths\ **1** : fabric **2** : tablecloth

clothe \'klōth\ *vb* **clothed** *or* **clad** \'klad\; **cloth•ing** : dress

clothes \'klōthz, 'klōz\ *n pl* **1** : clothing **2** : bedclothes

cloth•ier \'klōthyər, -thēər\ *n* : maker or seller of clothing

cloth•ing \'klōthiŋ\ *n* : covering for the human body

cloud \'klaùd\ *n* **1** : visible mass of particles in the air **2** : something that darkens, hides, or threatens ~ *vb* : darken or hide — **cloud•i•ness** *n* — **cloud•less** *adj* — **cloudy** *adj*

cloud•burst *n* : sudden heavy rain

clout \'klaùt\ *n* **1** : blow **2** : influence ~ *vb* : hit forcefully

¹clove \'klōv\ *n* : section of a bulb

²clove *past of* CLEAVE

³clove *n* : dried flower bud of an East Indian tree used as a spice

clo•ver \'klōvər\ *n* : leguminous herb with usu. 3-part leaves

clo•ver•leaf *n, pl* **-leafs** *or* **-leaves** : highway interchange

clown \'klaùn\ *n* : funny costumed entertainer esp. in a circus ~ *vb* : act like a clown — **clown•ish** *adj* — **clown•ish•ly** *adv* — **clown•ish•ness** *n*

cloy \'klòi\ *vb* : disgust with excess — **cloy•ing•ly** \-iŋlē\ *adv*

club \'kləb\ *n* **1** : heavy wooden stick **2** : playing card of a suit marked with a black figure like a clover leaf **3** : group associated for a common purpose ~ *vb* **-bb-** : hit with a club

club•foot *n* : misshapen foot twisted out of position from birth — **club•foot•ed** \-¹fútəd\ *adj*

cluck \'klək\ *n* : sound made by a hen — **cluck** *vb*

clue \'klü\ *n* : piece of evidence that helps solve a problem ~ *vb* **clued; clue•ing** *or* **clu•ing** : provide with a clue

clump \'kləmp\ *n* **1** : cluster **2** : heavy tramping sound ~ *vb* : tread heavily

clum•sy \'kləmzē\ *adj* **-si•er; -est 1** : lacking dexterity, nimbleness, or grace **2** : tactless — **clum•si•ly** *adv* — **clum•si•ness** *n*

clung *past of* CLING

clunk•er \'kləŋkər\ *n* : old automobile

clus•ter \'kləstər\ *n* : group ~ *vb* : grow or gather in a cluster

clutch \'kləch\ *vb* : grasp ~ *n* **1** : grasping hand or claws **2** : control or power **3** : coupling for connecting two working parts in machinery

clut•ter \'klətər\ *vb* : fill with things that get in the way — **clutter** *n*

co- *prefix* : with, together, joint, or jointly

List of self-explanatory words with the prefix *co-*

coact	codesign	coexist
coactor	codevelop	coexistence
coauthor	codeveloper	coexistent
coauthorship	codirect	cofeature
cocaptain	codirector	cofinance
cochairman	codiscoverer	cofound
cochampion	codrive	cofounder
cocomposer	codriver	coheir
coconspirator	coedit	coheiress
cocreator	coeditor	cohost
codefendant	coexecutor	cohostess

coach \'kōch\ *n* **1** : closed 2-door 4-wheeled carriage **2** : railroad passenger car **3** : bus **4** : 2d-class air travel **5** : one who instructs or trains performers ~ *vb* : instruct or direct as a coach

co·ag·u·late \kō'agyə,lāt\ *vb* **-lat·ed; -lat·ing** : clot — **co·ag·u·lant** \-lənt\ *n* — **co·ag·u·la·tion** \-,agyə'lāshən\ *n*

coal \'kōl\ *n* **1** : ember **2** : black solid mineral used as fuel — **coal·field** *n*

co·alesce \,kōə'les\ *vb* **-alesced; -alesc·ing** : grow together — **co·ales·cence** \-'les°ns\ *n*

co·ali·tion \-'lishən\ *n* : temporary alliance

coarse \'kōrs\ *adj* **coars·er; coarsest 1** : composed of large particles **2** : rough or crude — **coarse·ly** *adv* — **coars·en** \-°n\ *vb* — **coarseness** *n*

coast \'kōst\ *n* : seashore ~ *vb* : move without effort — **coast·al** \-°l\ *adj*

coast·er \-ər\ *n* **1** : one that coasts **2** : plate or mat to protect a surface

coast guard *n* : military force that guards or patrols a coast — **coastguards·man** \'kōst,gärdzmən\ *n*

coast·line *n* : shape of a coast

coat \'kōt\ *n* **1** : outer garment for the upper body **2** : external growth of fur or feathers **3** : covering layer ~ *vb* : cover with a coat — **coat·ed** *adj* — **coat·ing** *n*

coax \'kōks\ *vb* : move to action or achieve by gentle urging or flattery

cob \'käb\ *n* : corncob

co·balt \'kō,bólt\ *n* : shiny silver-white magnetic metallic chemical element

cob·ble \'käbəl\ *vb* **cob·bled; cob·bling** : make or put together hastily

cob·bler \'käblər\ *n* **1** : shoemaker **2** : deep-dish fruit pie

cob·ble·stone *n* : small round paving stone

co·bra \'kōbrə\ *n* : venomous snake

cob·web \'käb,web\ *n* : network spun by a spider or a similar filament

co·caine \kō'kān, 'kō,kān\ *n* : drug obtained from the leaves of a So. American shrub (**co·ca** \'kōkə\)

co·chlea \'kōklēə, 'käk-\ *n, pl* **-chleas** *or* **-chle·ae** \-lē,ē, -,ī\ : the usu. spiral part of the inner ear — **cochle·ar** \-lēər\ *adj*

cock \'käk\ *n* **1** : male fowl **2** : valve or faucet ~ *vb* **1** : draw back the hammer of a firearm **2** : tilt to one side — **cock·fight** *n*

cock·a·too \'käkə,tü\ *n, pl* **-toos** : large Australian crested parrot

cock·eyed \'käk'īd\ *adj* **1** : tilted to one side **2** : slightly crazy

cock·le \'käkəl\ *n* : edible shellfish

cock·pit \'käk,pit\ *n* : place for a pilot, driver, or helmsman

cock·roach *n* : nocturnal insect often infesting houses

cock·tail \'käk,tāl\ *n* **1** : iced drink of liquor and flavorings **2** : appetizer

cocky \'käkē\ *adj* **cock·i·er; -est** : overconfident — **cock·i·ly** \-əlē\ *adv* — **cock·i·ness** *n*

co·coa \'kōkō\ *n* **1** : cacao **2** : powdered chocolate or a drink made from this

co·co·nut \'kōkə,nət\ *n* : large nutlike fruit of a tropical palm (**coconut palm**)

co·coon \kə'kün\ *n* : case protecting an insect pupa

cod \'käd\ *n, pl* **cod** : food fish of the No. Atlantic

cod·dle \'käd°l\ *vb* **-dled; -dling** : pamper

---

coinvent
coinventor
coinvestigator
coleader
comanagement
comanager
co-organizer
co-own
co-owner
copartner

copartnership
copresident
coprincipal
coprisoner
coproduce
coproducer
coproduction
copromoter
coproprietor
copublish

copublisher
corecipient
coresident
cosignatory
cosigner
cosponsor
costar
cowinner
coworker
cowrite

code \\'kōd\ *n* **1** : system of laws or rules **2** : system of signals

co·deine \\'kō,dēn\ *n* : narcotic drug used in cough remedies

cod·ger \\'käjər\ *n* : odd fellow

cod·i·cil \\'kädəsəl, -,sil\ *n* : postscript to a will

cod·i·fy \\'kädə,fī, 'kōd-\ *vb* **-fied; -fying** : arrange systematically — **cod·i·fi·ca·tion** \,kädəfə'kāshən, ,kōd-\ *n*

co·ed \\'kō,ed\ *n* : female student in a coeducational institution — **coed** *adj*

co·ed·u·ca·tion \,kō-\ *n* : education of the sexes together — **co·ed·u·ca·tion·al** *adj*

co·ef·fi·cient \,kōə'fishənt\ *n* **1** : number that is a multiplier of another **2** : number that serves as a measure of some property

co·erce \kō'ərs\ *vb* **-erced; -erc·ing** : force — **co·er·cion** \-'ərzhən, -shən\ *n* — **co·er·cive** \-'ərsiv\ *adj*

cof·fee \\'kófē\ *n* : drink made from the roasted and ground seeds (**coffee beans**) of a tropical shrub — **coffee·house** *n* — **cof·fee·pot** *n*

cof·fer \\'kófər\ *n* : box for valuables

cof·fin \-fən\ *n* : box for burial

cog \\'käg\ *n* : tooth on the rim of a gear — **cogged** \\'kägd\ *adj* — **cog·wheel** *n*

co·gent \\'kōjənt\ *adj* : compelling or convincing — **co·gen·cy** \-jənsē\ *n*

cog·i·tate \\'käjə,tāt\ *vb* **-tated; -tating** : think over — **cog·i·ta·tion** \,käjə'tāshən\ *n* — **cog·i·ta·tive** \\'käjə,tātiv\ *adj*

co·gnac \\'kōn,yak\ *n* : French brandy

cog·nate \\'käg,nāt\ *adj* : related — **cog·nate** *n*

cog·ni·tion \käg'nishən\ *n* : act or process of knowing — **cog·ni·tive** \\'kägnətiv\ *adj*

cog·ni·zance \\'kägnəzəns\ *n* : notice or awareness — **cog·ni·zant** \\'kägnəzənt\ *adj*

co·hab·it \kō'habət\ *vb* : live together as husband and wife — **co·hab·i·ta·tion** \-,habə'tāshən\ *n*

co·here \kō'hir\ *vb* **-hered; -her·ing** : stick together

co·her·ent \-'hirənt\ *adj* **1** : able to stick together **2** : logically consistent — **co·her·ence** \-əns\ *n* — **co·her·ent·ly** *adv*

co·he·sion \-'hēzhən\ *n* : a sticking together — **co·he·sive** \-siv\ *adj* —

co·he·sive·ly *adv* — **co·he·sive·ness** *n*

co·hort \\'kō,hort\ *n* **1** : group of soldiers **2** : companion

coif·fure \kwä'fyùr\ *n* : hair style

coil \\'kóil\ *vb* : wind in a spiral ~ *n* : series of loops (as of rope)

coin \\'kóin\ *n* : piece of metal used as money ~ *vb* **1** : make (a coin) by stamping **2** : create — **coin·age** \-ij\ *n* — **coin·er** *n*

co·in·cide \,kōən'sīd, 'kōən,sīd\ *vb* **-cid·ed; -cid·ing** **1** : be in the same place **2** : happen at the same time **3** : be alike — **co·in·ci·dence** \kō'in-sədəns\ *n* — **co·in·ci·dent** \-dənt\ *adj* — **co·in·ci·den·tal** \-,insə'dent³l\ *adj*

co·itus \\'kōətəs\ *n* : sexual intercourse — **co·ital** \-ət³l\ *adj*

coke \\'kōk\ *n* : fuel made by heating soft coal

co·la \\'kōlə\ *n* : carbonated soft drink

col·an·der \\'kələndər, 'käl-\ *n* : perforated utensil for draining food

cold \\'kōld\ *adj* **1** : having a low or below normal temperature **2** : lacking warmth of feeling **3** : suffering from lack of warmth ~ *n* **1** : low temperature **2** : minor respiratory illness — **cold·ly** *adv* — **cold·ness** *n* — **in cold blood** : with premeditation

cold–blood·ed *adj* **1** : cruel or merciless **2** : having a body temperature that varies with the temperature of the environment

cole·slaw \\'kōl,slò\ *n* : cabbage salad

col·ic \\'kälik\ *n* : sharp abdominal pain — **col·icky** *adj*

col·i·se·um \,kälə'sēəm\ *n* : arena

col·lab·o·rate \kə'labə,rāt\ *vb* **-rated; -rat·ing** **1** : work jointly with others **2** : help the enemy — **col·lab·o·ra·tion** \-,labə'rāshən\ *n* — **col·lab·o·ra·tor** \-'labə,rātər\ *n*

col·lapse \kə'laps\ *vb* **-lapsed; -laps·ing** **1** : fall in **2** : break down physically or mentally **3** : fold down ~ *n* : breakdown — **col·laps·ible** *adj*

col·lar \\'kälər\ *n* : part of a garment around the neck ~ *vb* **1** : seize by the collar **2** : grab — **col·lar·less** *adj*

col·lar·bone *n* : bone joining the breastbone and the shoulder blade

col·lards \\'kälərdz\ *n pl* : kale

col·late \kə'lāt; 'käl,āt, 'kōl-\ *vb* **-lat-**

ed; **-lat•ing 1** : compare carefully **2** : assemble in order

col•lat•er•al \kə'latərəl\ *adj* **1** : secondary **2** : descended from the same ancestors but not in the same line **3** : similar — ~ *n* : property used as security for a loan

col•league \'käl‚ēg\ *n* : associate

col•lect \kə'lekt\ *vb* **1** : bring, come, or gather together **2** : receive payment of ~ *adv or adj* : to be paid for by the receiver — **col•lect•ible,** **col•léct•able** *adj* — **col•lec•tion** \-'lek-shən\ *n* — **col•lec•tor** \-'lektər\ *n*

col•lec•tive \-tiv\ *adj* : denoting or shared by a group — ~ *n* : a cooperative unit — **col•lec•tive•ly** *adv*

col•lege \'kälij\ *n* : institution of higher learning granting a bachelor's degree — **col•le•gian** \kə'lējən\ *n* — **col•le•giate** \kə'lējət\ *adj*

col•lide \kə'līd\ *vb* **-lid•ed; -lid•ing** : strike together — **col•li•sion** \-'lizhən\ *n*

col•lie \'kälē\ *n* : large long-haired dog

col•loid \'käl‚ȯid\ *n* : tiny particles in suspension in a fluid — **col•loi•dal** \kə'lȯidᵊl\ *adj*

col•lo•qui•al \kə'lōkwēəl\ *adj* : used in informal conversation — **col•lo•qui•al•ism** \-ə‚lizəm\ *n*

col•lu•sion \kə'lüzhən\ *n* : secret cooperation for deceit — **col•lu•sive** \-'lüsiv\ *adj*

co•logne \kə'lōn\ *n* : perfumed liquid

¹**co•lon** \'kōlən\ *n, pl* **colons** *or* **co•la** \-lə\ : lower part of the large intestine — **co•lon•ic** \kō'länik\ *adj*

²**colon** *n, pl* **colons** : punctuation mark : used esp. to direct attention to following matter

col•o•nel \'kərnᵊl\ *n* : commissioned officer (as in the army) ranking next below a brigadier general

col•o•nize \'kälə‚nīz\ *vb* **-nized; -niz•ing 1** : establish a colony in **2** : settle — **col•o•ni•za•tion** \‚kälənə'zāshən\ *n* — **col•o•niz•er** *n*

col•on•nade \‚kälə'nād\ *n* : row of supporting columns

col•o•ny \'kälənē\ *n, pl* **-nies 1** : people who inhabit a new territory or the territory itself **2** : animals of one kind (as bees) living together — **co•lo•nial** \kə'lōnēəl\ *adj or n* — **col•o•nist** \'kälənist\ *n*

col•or \'kələr\ *n* **1** : quality of visible things distinct from shape that results

from light reflection **2** *pl* : flag **3** : liveliness ~ *vb* **1** : give color to **2** : blush — **col•or•fast** *adj* — **col•or•ful** *adj* — **col•or•less** *adj*

col•or–blind *adj* : unable to distinguish colors — **color blindness** *n*

col•ored \'kələrd\ *adj* **1** : having color **2** : of a race other than the white ~ *n, pl* **colored** *or* **coloreds** : colored person

co•los•sal \kə'läsəl\ *adj* : very large or great

co•los•sus \-səs\ *n, pl* **-si** \-'läs‚ī\ : something of great size or scope

colt \'kōlt\ *n* : young male horse — **colt•ish** *adj*

col•umn \'käləm\ *n* **1** : vertical section of a printed page **2** : regular feature article (as in a newspaper) **3** : pillar **4** : row (as of soldiers) — **co•lum•nar** \kə'ləmnər\ *adj* — **col•um•nist** \'käləmnist\ *n*

co•ma \'kōmə\ *n* : deep prolonged unconsciousness — **co•ma•tose** \-‚tōs, 'kämə-\ *adj*

comb \'kōm\ *n* **1** : toothed instrument for arranging the hair **2** : crest on a fowl's head — **comb** *vb* — **combed** \'kōmd\ *adj*

com•bat \kəm'bat, 'käm‚bat\ *vb* **-bat•ed** *or* **-bat•ted; -bat•ing** *or* **-bat•ting** : fight — **com•bat** \'käm‚bat\ *n* — **com•bat•ant** \kəm'batᵊnt\ *n* — **com•bat•ive** \kəm'bativ\ *adj*

com•bi•na•tion \‚kämbə'nāshən\ *n* **1** : process or result of combining **2** : code for opening a lock

com•bine \kəm'bīn\ *vb* **-bined; -bin•ing** : join together — ~ \'käm‚bīn\ *n* **1** : association for business or political advantage **2** : harvesting machine

com•bus•ti•ble \kəm'bəstəbəl\ *adj* : apt to catch fire — **com•bus•ti•bil•i•ty** \-‚bəstə'bilətē\ *n* — **combustible** *n*

com•bus•tion \-'bəschən\ *n* : process of burning

come \'kəm\ *vb* **came** \'kām\; **come; com•ing 1** : move toward or arrive at something **2** : reach a state **3** : originate or exist **4** : amount — **come clean** *vb* : confess — **come into** *vb* : acquire, achieve — **come off** *vb* : succeed — **come to** *vb* : regain consciousness — **come to pass** : happen — **come to terms** : reach an agreement

come·back n 1 : retort 2 : return to a former position — **come back** vb

co·me·di·an \kə'mēdēən\ n 1 : comic actor 2 : funny person 3 : entertainer specializing in comedy

co·me·di·enne \-,mēdē'en\ n : a woman who is a comedian

com·e·dy \'kämədē\ n, pl **-dies** 1 : an amusing play 2 : humorous entertainment

come·ly \'kəmlē\ adj **-li·er; -est** : attractive — **come·li·ness** n

com·et \'kämət\ n : small bright celestial body having a tail

com·fort \'kəmfərt\ n 1 : consolation 2 : well-being or something that gives it ~ vb 1 : give hope to 2 : console — **com·fort·able** \'kəmftəbəl, 'kəmfərt-\ adj — **com·fort·ably** \-blē\ adv

com·fort·er \'kəmfərtər\ n 1 : one that comforts 2 : quilt

com·ic \'kämik\ adj 1 : relating to comedy 2 : funny ~ n 1 : comedian 2 : sequence of cartoons — **com·i·cal** adj

com·ing \'kəmiŋ\ adj : next

com·ma \'kämə\ n : punctuation mark , used esp. to separate sentence parts

com·mand \kə'mand\ vb 1 : order 2 : control ~ n 1 : act of commanding 2 : an order given 3 : mastery 4 : troops under a commander — **com·man·dant** \'kämən,dant, -,dänt\ n

com·man·deer \,kämən'dir\ vb : seize by force

com·mand·er \kə'mandər\ n 1 : officer commanding an army or subdivision of an army 2 : commissioned officer in the navy ranking next below a captain

com·mand·ment \-'mandmənt\ n : order

command sergeant major n : noncommissioned officer in the army ranking above a first sergeant

com·mem·o·rate \kə'memə,rāt\ vb **-rat·ed; -rat·ing** : celebrate or honor — **com·mem·o·ra·tion** \-,memə'rāshən\ n — **com·mem·o·ra·tive** \-'memrətiv, -'memə,rāt-\ adj

com·mence \kə'mens\ vb **-menced; -menc·ing** : start

com·mence·ment \-mənt\ n 1 : beginning 2 : graduation ceremony

com·mend \kə'mend\ vb 1 : entrust 2 : recommend 3 : praise — **com-**

mend·able \-əbəl\ adj — **com·men·da·tion** \,kämən'dāshən, -,en-\ n

com·men·su·rate \kə'mensərət, -'mench-\ adj : equal in measure or extent

com·ment \'käm,ent\ n : statement of opinion or remark — **comment** vb

com·men·tary \-ən,terē\ n, pl **-tar·ies** : series of comments

com·men·ta·tor \-ən,tātər\ n : one who discusses news

com·merce \'kämərs\ n : business

com·mer·cial \kə'mərshəl\ adj : designed for profit or for mass appeal ~ n : broadcast advertisement — **com·mer·cial·ize** \-,īz\ vb — **com·mer·cial·ly** \-ē\ adv

com·min·gle \kə'miŋgəl\ vb : mix

com·mis·er·ate \kə'mizə,rāt\ vb **-at·ed; -at·ing** : sympathize — **com·mis·er·a·tion** \-,mizə'rāshən\ n

com·mis·sary \'kämə,serē\ n, pl **-sar·ies** : store esp. for military personnel

com·mis·sion \kə'mishən\ n 1 : order granting power or rank 2 : panel to judge, approve, or act 3 : the doing of an act 4 : agent's fee ~ vb 1 : confer rank or authority to or for 2 : request something be done

com·mis·sion·er \-shənər\ n 1 : member of a commission 2 : head of a government department

com·mit \kə'mit\ vb **-tt-** 1 : turn over to someone for safekeeping or confinement 2 : perform or do 3 : pledge — **com·mit·ment** n

com·mit·tee \kə'mitē\ n : panel that examines or acts on something

com·mo·di·ous \kə'mōdēəs\ adj : spacious

com·mod·i·ty \kə'mädətē\ n, pl **-ties** : article for sale

com·mo·dore \'kämə,dōr\ n 1 : former commissioned officer in the navy ranking next below a rear admiral 2 : officer commanding a group of merchant ships

com·mon \'kämən\ adj 1 : public 2 : shared by several 3 : widely known, found, or observed 4 : ordinary ~ n : community land — **com·mon·ly** adv — **in common** : shared together

com·mon·place \'kämən,plās\ n : cliché ~ adj : ordinary

common sense n : good judgment

com·mon·weal \-,wēl\ n : general welfare

com·mon·wealth \-,welth\ n : state

com·mo·tion \kə'mōshən\ *n* : disturbance

¹**com·mune** \kə'myün\ *vb* **-muned; -mun·ing** : communicate intimately

²**com·mune** \'käm,yün; kə'myün\ *n* : community that shares all ownership and duties — **com·mu·nal** \-ᵊl\ *adj*

com·mu·ni·cate \kə'myünə,kāt\ *vb* **-cat·ed; -cat·ing** 1 : make known 2 : transmit 3 : exchange information or opinions — **com·mu·ni·ca·ble** \-'myünikəbəl\ *adj* — **com·mu·ni·ca·tion** \-,myünə'kāshən\ *n* — **com·mu·ni·ca·tive** \-'myüni,kātiv, -kət-\ *adj*

Com·mu·nion \kə'myünyən\ *n* : Christian sacrament of partaking of bread and wine

com·mu·ni·qué \kə'myünə,kā, ,myünə'kā\ *n* : official bulletin

com·mu·nism \'kämyə,nizəm\ *n* 1 : social organization in which goods are held in common 2 *cap* : political doctrine based on revolutionary Marxist socialism — **com·mu·nist** \-nist\ *n or adj, often cap* — **com·mu·nis·tic** \,kämyə'nistik\ *adj, often cap*

com·mu·ni·ty \kə'myünətē\ *n, pl* **-ties** : body of people living in the same place under the same laws

com·mute \kə'myüt\ *vb* **-mut·ed; -mut·ing** 1 : reduce (a punishment) 2 : travel back and forth regularly ~ *n* : trip made in commuting — **com·mu·ta·tion** \,kämyə'tāshən\ *n* — **com·mut·er** *n*

¹**com·pact** \kəm'pakt, 'käm,pakt\ *adj* 1 : hard 2 : small or brief ~ *vb* : pack together ~ \'käm,pakt\ *n* 1 : cosmetics case 2 : small car — **com·pact·ly** *adv* — **com·pact·ness** *n*

²**com·pact** \'käm,pakt\ *n* : agreement

compact disc *n* : plastic-coated disc with laser-readable recorded music

com·pan·ion \kəm'panyən\ *n* 1 : close friend 2 : one of a pair — **com·pan·ion·able** *adj* — **com·pan·ion·ship** *n*

com·pa·ny \'kəmpənē\ *n, pl* **-nies** 1 : business organization 2 : group of performers 3 : guests 4 : infantry unit

com·par·a·tive \kəm'parətiv\ *adj* 1 : relating to or being an adjective or adverb form that denotes increase 2 : relative — **comparative** *n* — **com·par·a·tive·ly** *adv*

com·pare \kəm'par\ *vb* **-pared; -par·**

ing 1 : represent as similar 2 : check for likenesses or differences ~ *n* : comparison — **com·pa·ra·ble** \'kämprəbəl\ *adj*

com·par·i·son \kəm'parəsən\ *n* 1 : act of comparing 2 : change in the form and meaning of an adjective or adverb to show different levels of quality, quantity, or relation

com·part·ment \kəm'pärtmənt\ *n* : section or room

com·pass \'kəmpəs, 'käm-\ *n* 1 : scope 2 : device for drawing circles 3 : device for determining direction

com·pas·sion \kəm'pashən\ *n* : pity — **com·pas·sion·ate** \-ənət\ *adj*

com·pat·i·ble \-'patəbəl\ *adj* : harmonious — **com·pat·i·bil·i·ty** \-,patə'bilətē\ *n*

com·pa·tri·ot \kəm'pātrēət, -trē,ät\ *n* : fellow countryman

com·pel \kəm'pel\ *vb* **-ll-** : cause through necessity

com·pen·di·ous \kəm'pendēəs\ *adj* 1 : concise and comprehensive 2 : comprehensive

com·pen·di·um \-'pendēəm\ *n, pl* **-diums** *or* **-dia** \-dēə\ : summary

com·pen·sate \'kämpən,sāt\ *vb* **-sat·ed; -sat·ing** 1 : offset or balance 2 : repay — **com·pen·sa·tion** \,kämpən'sāshən\ *n* — **com·pen·sa·to·ry** \kəm'pensə,tōrē\ *adj*

com·pete \kəm'pēt\ *vb* **-pet·ed; -pet·ing** : strive to win — **com·pe·ti·tion** \,kämpə'tishən\ *n* — **com·pet·i·tive** \kəm'petətiv\ *adj* — **com·pet·i·tive·ness** *n* — **com·pet·i·tor** \kəm'petətər\ *n*

com·pe·tent \'kämpətənt\ *adj* : capable — **com·pe·tence** \-əns\ *n* — **com·pe·ten·cy** \-ənsē\ *n*

com·pile \kəm'pīl\ *vb* **-piled; -pil·ing** : collect or compose from several sources — **com·pi·la·tion** \,kämpə-'lāshən\ *n* — **com·pil·er** \kəm-'pīlər\ *n*

com·pla·cen·cy \kəm'plās°nsē\ *n* : self-satisfaction — **com·pla·cent** \-°nt\ *adj*

com·plain \kəm'plān\ *vb* 1 : express grief, pain, or discontent 2 : make an accusation — **com·plain·ant** *n* — **com·plain·er** *n*

com·plaint \-'plānt\ *n* 1 : expression of grief or discontent 2 : ailment 3 : formal accusation

com·ple·ment \'kämpləmənt\ *n* 1

: something that completes **2** : full number or amount ∼ \-₁mənt\ vb : complete — **com·ple·men·ta·ry** \₁kämplə'mentərē\ adj

com·plete \kəm'plēt\ adj -plet·er; -est **1** : having all parts **2** : finished **3** : total ∼ vb -plet·ed; -plet·ing **1** : make whole **2** : finish — **com·plete·ly** adv — **com·plete·ness** n — **com·ple·tion** \-'plēshən\ n

com·plex \käm'pleks, kəm-; 'käm-₁pleks\ adj **1** : having many parts **2** : intricate ∼ \'käm₁pleks\ n : psychological problem — **com·plex·i·ty** \kəm'pleksətē, käm-\ n

com·plex·ion \kəm'plekshən\ n : hue or appearance of the skin esp. of the face — **com·plex·ioned** adj

com·pli·cate \'kämplə₁kāt\ vb -cat·ed; -cat·ing : make complex or hard to understand — **com·pli·cat·ed** \-əd\ adj — **com·pli·ca·tion** \₁kämplə'kāshən\ n

com·plic·i·ty \kəm'plisətē\ n, pl -ties : participation in guilt

com·pli·ment \'kämpləmənt\ n **1** : flattering remark **2** pl : greeting ∼ \-₁ment\ vb : pay a compliment to

com·pli·men·ta·ry \₁kämplə'mentərē\ adj **1** : praising **2** : free

com·ply \kəm'plī\ vb -plied; -ply·ing : conform or yield — **com·pli·ance** \-əns\ n — **com·pli·ant** \-ənt\ n

com·po·nent \kəm'pōnənt, 'käm₁pō-\ n : part of something larger ∼ adj : serving as a component

com·port \kəm'pōrt\ vb **1** : agree **2** : behave — **com·port·ment** \-mənt\ n

com·pose \kəm'pōz\ vb -posed; -pos·ing **1** : create (as by writing) or put together **2** : calm **3** : set type — **com·pos·er** n — **com·po·si·tion** \₁kämpə'zishən\ n

com·pos·ite \käm'päzət, kəm-\ adj : made up of diverse parts — **composite** n

com·post \'käm₁pōst\ n : decayed organic fertilizing material

com·po·sure \kəm'pōzhər\ n : calmness

com·pote \'käm₁pōt\ n : fruits cooked in syrup

¹**com·pound** \'käm₁paủnd, käm'paủnd\ vb **1** : combine or add **2** : pay (interest) on principal and accrued interest ∼ \'käm₁paủnd\ adj : made up of 2

or more parts ∼ \'käm₁paủnd\ n : something that is compound

²**com·pound** \'käm₁paủnd\ n : enclosure

com·pre·hend \₁kämprē'hend\ vb **1** : understand **2** : include — **com·pre·hen·si·ble** \-'hensəbəl\ adj — **com·pre·hen·sion** \-'henchən\ n — **com·pre·hen·sive** \-siv\ adj

com·press \kəm'pres\ vb : squeeze together ∼ \'käm₁pres\ n : pad for pressing on a wound — **com·pres·sion** \-'preshən\ n — **com·pres·sor** \-'presər\ n

compressed air n : air under pressure greater than that of the atmosphere

com·prise \kəm'prīz\ vb -prised; -pris·ing **1** : contain or cover **2** : be made up of

com·pro·mise \'kämprə₁mīz\ vb -mised; -mis·ing : settle differences by mutual concessions — **compromise** n

comp·trol·ler \kən'trōlər, 'kämp₁trō-\ n : financial officer

com·pul·sion \kəm'pəlshən\ n **1** : coercion **2** : irresistible impulse — **com·pul·sive** \-siv\ adj — **com·pul·so·ry** \-'pəlsərē\ adj

com·punc·tion \-'pəŋkshən\ n : remorse

com·pute \-'pyüt\ vb -put·ed; -put·ing : calculate — **com·pu·ta·tion** \₁kämpyủ'tāshən\ n

com·put·er \kəm'pyütər\ n : electronic data processing machine — **com·put·er·i·za·tion** \-₁pyütərə'zā·shən\ n — **com·put·er·ize** \-'pyütə₁rīz\ vb

com·rade \'käm₁rad, -rəd\ n : companion — **com·rade·ship** n

¹**con** \'kän\ adv : against ∼ n : opposing side or person

²**con** vb -nn- : swindle

con·cave \kän'kāv, 'kän₁kāv\ adj : curved like the inside of a sphere — **con·cav·i·ty** \kän'kavətē\ n

con·ceal \kən'sēl\ vb : hide — **con·ceal·ment** n

con·cede \-'sēd\ vb -ced·ed; -ced·ing : grant

con·ceit \-'sēt\ n : excessively high opinion of oneself — **con·ceit·ed** \-əd\ adj

con·ceive \-'sēv\ vb -ceived; -ceiv·ing **1** : become pregnant **2** : think of — **con·ceiv·able** \-'sēvəbəl\ adj — **con·ceiv·ably** \-blē\ adv

con·cen·trate \'känsən,trāt\ vb **-trat·ed; -trat·ing 1** : gather together **2** : make stronger **3** : fix one's attention ~ n : something concentrated — **con·cen·tra·tion** \,känsən'trāshən\ n

con·cen·tric \kən'sentrik\ adj : having a common center

con·cept \'kän,sept\ n : thought or idea

con·cep·tion \kən'sepshən\ n **1** : act of conceiving **2** : idea

con·cern \kən'sərn\ vb **1** : relate to **2** : involve ~ n **1** : affair **2** : worry **3** : business — **con·cerned** \-'sərnd\ adj — **con·cern·ing** \-'sərniŋ\ prep

con·cert \'kän,sərt\ n **1** : agreement or joint action **2** : public performance of music — **con·cert·ed** \kən-'sərtəd\ adj

con·cer·ti·na \,känsər'tēnə\ n : accordionlike instrument

con·cer·to \kən'chertō\ n, pl **-ti** \-tē\ or **-tos** : orchestral work with solo instruments

con·ces·sion \-'seshən\ n **1** : act of conceding **2** : something conceded **3** : right to do business on a property

conch \'käŋk, 'känch\ n, pl **conchs** \'käŋks\ or **conch·es** \'känchəz\ : large spiral-shelled marine mollusk

con·cil·ia·to·ry \kən'silēə,tōrē\ adj : mollifying

con·cise \kən'sīs\ adj : said in few words — **con·cise·ly** adv — **con·cise·ness** n — **con·ci·sion** \kən'sizhən\ n

con·clave \'kän,klāv\ n : private meeting

con·clude \kən'klüd\ vb **-clud·ed; -clud·ing 1** : end **2** : decide — **con·clu·sion** \-'klüzhən\ n — **con·clu·sive** \-siv\ adj — **con·clu·sive·ly** adv

con·coct \kən'käkt, kän-\ vb : prepare or devise — **con·coc·tion** \-'käkshən\ n

con·com·i·tant \-'kämətənt\ adj : accompanying — **concomitant** n

con·cord \'kän,kord, 'kän-\ n : agreement

con·cor·dance \kən'kord³ns\ n **1** : agreement **2** : index of words — **con·cor·dant** \-³nt\ adj

con·course \'kän,kōrs\ n : open space where crowds gather

con·crete \kän'krēt, 'kän,krēt\ adj **1** : naming something real **2** : actual or substantial **3** : made of concrete ~ \'kän,krēt, kän'krēt\ n : hard building material made of cement, sand, gravel, and water

con·cre·tion \kän'krēshən\ n : hard mass

con·cu·bine \'käŋkyù,bīn\ n : mistress

con·cur \kən'kər\ vb **-rr-** : agree — **con·cur·rence** \-'kərəns\ n

con·cur·rent \-ənt\ adj : happening at the same time

con·cus·sion \kən'kəshən\ n **1** : shock **2** : brain injury from a blow

con·demn \-'dem\ vb **1** : declare to be wrong, guilty, or unfit for use **2** : sentence — **con·dem·na·tion** \,kän-,dem'nāshən\ n

con·dense \kən'dens\ vb **-densed; -dens·ing 1** : make or become more compact **2** : change from vapor to liquid — **con·den·sa·tion** \,kän-,den'sāshən, -dən-\ n — **con·dens·er** n

con·de·scend \,kändi'send\ vb **1** : lower oneself **2** : act haughtily — **con·de·scen·sion** \-'senchən\ n

con·di·ment \'kändəmənt\ n : pungent seasoning

con·di·tion \kən'dishən\ n **1** : necessary situation or stipulation **2** pl : state of affairs **3** : state of being ~ vb : put into proper condition — **con·di·tion·al** \kən'dishənəl\ adj — **con·di·tion·al·ly** \-ē\ adv

con·do·lence \kən'dōləns\ n : expression of sympathy — usu. pl.

con·do·min·i·um \,kändə'minēəm\ n, pl **-ums** : individually owned apartment

con·done \kən'dōn\ vb **-doned; -don·ing** : overlook or forgive

con·dor \'kändər, -,dor\ n : large western American vulture

con·du·cive \kən'düsiv, -'dyü-\ adj : tending to help or promote

con·duct \'kän,dəkt\ n **1** : management **2** : behavior ~ \kən'dəkt\ vb **1** : guide **2** : manage or direct **3** : be a channel for **4** : behave — **con·duc·tion** \-'dəkshən\ n — **con·duc·tive** \-'dəktiv\ adj — **con·duc·tiv·i·ty** \,kän,dək'tivətē\ n — **con·duc·tor** \-'dəktər\ n

con·duit \'kän,düət, -,dyü-\ n : channel (as for conveying fluid)

cone \'kōn\ n **1** : scaly fruit of pine

and related trees **2** : solid figure having a circular base and tapering sides

con·fec·tion \kən'fekshən\ *n* : sweet dish or candy — **con·fec·tion·er** \-shənər\ *n*

con·fed·er·a·cy \kən'fedərəsē\ *n, pl* **-cies 1** : league **2** *cap* : 11 southern states that seceded from the U.S. in 1860 and 1861

con·fed·er·ate \-rət\ *adj* **1** : united in a league **2** *cap* : relating to the Confederacy ~ **1** : ally **2** *cap* : adherent of the Confederacy ~ \-'fedə,rāt\ *vb* -**at·ed; -at·ing** : unite — **con·fed·er·a·tion** \-,fedə'rāshən\ *n*

con·fer \kən'fər\ *vb* **-rr- 1** : give **2** : meet to exchange views — **con·fer·ee** \,känfə'rē\ *n* — **con·fer·ence** \'känfərəns\ *n*

con·fess \kən'fes\ *vb* **1** : acknowledge or disclose one's misdeed, fault, or sin **2** : declare faith in — **con·fes·sion** \-'feshən\ *n* — **con·fes·sion·al** \-'feshənəl\ *n or adj*

con·fes·sor \kən'fesər, 2 also ' kän-,fes-\ *n* **1** : one who confesses **2** : priest who hears confessions

con·fet·ti \kən'fetē\ *n* : bits of paper or ribbon thrown in celebration

con·fi·dant \'känfə,dant, -,dänt\ *n* : one to whom secrets are confided

con·fide \kən'fīd\ *vb* **-fid·ed; -fid·ing** **1** : share private thoughts **2** : reveal in confidence

con·fi·dence \'känfədəns\ *n* **1** : trust **2** : self-assurance **3** : something confided — **con·fi·dent** \-dənt\ *adj* — **con·fi·den·tial** \,känfə'denchəl\ *adj* — **con·fi·den·tial·ly** \-ē\ *adv* — **con·fi·dent·ly** *adv*

con·fig·u·ra·tion \kən,figyə'rāshən\ *n* : arrangement

con·fine \kən'fīn\ *vb* **-fined; -fin·ing** **1** : restrain or restrict to a limited area **2** : imprison — **con·fine·ment** *n* — **con·fin·er** *n*

confines \'kän,fīnz\ *n pl* : bounds

con·firm \kən'fərm\ *vb* **1** : ratify **2** : verify **3** : admit as a full member of a church or synagogue — **con·fir·ma·tion** \,känfər'māshən\ *n*

con·fis·cate \'känfə,skāt\ *vb* **-cat·ed; -cat·ing** : take by authority — **con·fis·ca·tion** \,känfə'skāshən\ *n* — **con·fis·ca·to·ry** \kən'fiskə,tōrē\ *adj*

con·fla·gra·tion \,känflə'grāshən\ *n* : great fire

con·flict \'kän,flikt\ *n* **1** : war **2** : clash of ideas ~ \kən'flikt\ *vb* : clash

con·form \kən'fόrm\ *vb* **1** : make or be like **2** : obey — **con·for·mi·ty** \kən'fόrmətē\ *n*

con·found \kən'faund, kän-\ *vb* : confuse

con·front \kən'frənt\ *vb* : oppose or face — **con·fron·ta·tion** \,känfrən-'tāshən\ *n*

con·fuse \kən'fyüz\ *vb* **-fused; -fus·ing 1** : make mentally uncertain **2** : jumble — **con·fu·sion** \-'fyüzhən\ *n*

con·fute \-'fyüt\ *vb* **-fut·ed; -fut·ing** : overwhelm by argument

con·geal \kən'jēl\ *vb* **1** : freeze **2** : become thick and solid

con·ge·nial \kən'jēnēəl\ *adj* : kindred or agreeable — **con·ge·ni·al·i·ty** *n*

con·gen·i·tal \kən'jenət²l\ *adj* : existing from birth

con·gest \kən'jest\ *vb* : overcrowd or overfill — **con·ges·tion** \-'jeschən\ *n* — **con·ges·tive** \-'jestiv\ *adj*

con·glom·er·ate \kən'glämərət\ *adj* : made up of diverse parts ~ \-ə,rāt\ *vb* -**at·ed; -at·ing** : form into a mass ~ \-ərət\ *n* : diversified corporation — **con·glom·er·a·tion** \-,glämə'rāshən\ *n*

con·grat·u·late \kən'gracha,lāt, -'graj-\ *vb* **-lat·ed; -lat·ing** : express pleasure to for good fortune — **con·grat·u·la·tion** \-,gracha'lāshən, -,graj-\ *n* — **con·grat·u·la·to·ry** \-'grachələ,tōrē, -'graj-\ *adj*

con·gre·gate \'kängri,gāt\ *vb* **-gat·ed; -gat·ing** : assemble

con·gre·ga·tion \,kängri'gāshən\ *n* **1** : assembly of people at worship **2** : religious group — **con·gre·ga·tion·al** \-shənəl\ *adj*

con·gress \'kängrəs\ *n* : assembly of delegates or of senators and representatives — **con·gres·sio·nal** \kən'greshənəl, kän-\ *adj* — **con·gress·man** \'kängrəsmən\ *n* — **con·gress·wom·an** *n*

con·gru·ence \kən'grüəns, 'kängrəw-əns\ *n* : likeness — **con·gru·ent** \-ənt\ *adj*

con·gru·ity \kən'grüətē, kän-\ *n* : correspondence between things — **con·gru·ous** \'kängrəwəs\ *adj*

con·ic \'känik\ *adj* : relating to or like a cone — **con·i·cal** \-ikəl\ *adj*

co·ni·fer \'känəfər, 'kōn-\ *n* : cone-bearing tree — **co·nif·er·ous** \kō-'nifərəs\ *adj*

con·jec·ture \kən'jekchər\ *n or vb* : guess — **con·jec·tur·al** \-əl\ *adj*

con·join \kən'jóin\ *vb* : join together — **con·joint** \-'jóint\ *adj*

con·ju·gal \'känjigəl, kən'jü-\ *adj* : relating to marriage

con·ju·gate \'känjə,gāt\ *vb* **-gat·ed; -gat·ing** : give the inflected forms of (a verb) — **con·ju·ga·tion** \,känjə-'gāshən\ *n*

con·junc·tion \kən'jəŋkshən\ *n* **1** : combination **2** : occurrence at the same time **3** : a word that joins other words together — **con·junc·tive** \-tiv\ *adj*

con·jure \'känjər, 'kən-\ *vb* **-jured; -jur·ing** **1** : summon by sorcery **2** : practice sleight of hand **3** : entreat — **con·jur·er, con·ju·ror** \'känjərər, 'kən-\ *n*

con·nect \kə'nekt\ *vb* : join or associate — **con·nect·able** *adj* — **con·nec·tion** \-'nekshən\ *n* — **con·nec·tive** \-tiv\ *n or adj* — **con·nec·tor** *n*

con·nive \kə'nīv\ *vb* **-nived; -niv·ing** **1** : pretend ignorance of wrongdoing **2** : cooperate secretly — **con·niv·ance** *n*

con·nois·seur \,känə'sər, -'sur\ *n* : expert judge esp. of art

con·note \kə'nōt\ *vb* **-not·ed; -not·ing** : suggest additional meaning — **con·no·ta·tion** \,känə'tāshən\ *n*

con·nu·bi·al \kə'nübēəl, -'nyü-\ *adj* : relating to marriage

con·quer \'käŋkər\ *vb* : defeat or overcome — **con·quer·or** \-kərər\ *n*

con·quest \'kän,kwest, 'käŋ-\ *n* **1** : act of conquering **2** : something conquered

con·science \'känchəns\ *n* : awareness of right and wrong

con·sci·en·tious \,känchē'enchəs\ *adj* : honest and hard-working — **con·sci·en·tious·ly** *adv*

con·scious \'känchəs\ *adj* **1** : aware **2** : mentally awake or alert **3** : intentional — **con·scious·ly** *adv* — **con·scious·ness** *n*

con·script \kən'skript\ *vb* : draft for military service — **con·script** \'kän,skript\ *n* — **con·scrip·tion** \kən'skripshən\ *n*

con·se·crate \'känsə,krāt\ *vb* **-crat·ed; -crat·ing** **1** : declare sacred **2**

: devote to a solemn purpose — **con·se·cra·tion** \,känə'krāshən\ *n*

con·sec·u·tive \kən'sekyətiv\ *adj* : following in order — **con·sec·u·tive·ly** *adv*

con·sen·sus \-'sensəs\ *n* **1** : agreement in opinion **2** : collective opinion

con·sent \-'sent\ *vb* : give permission or approval — **consent** *n*

con·se·quence \'känsə,kwens\ *n* **1** : result or effect **2** : importance — **con·se·quent** \-kwənt, -,kwent\ *adj* — **con·se·quent·ly** *adv*

con·se·quen·tial \,känsə'kwenchəl\ *adj* : important

con·ser·va·tion \,känsər'vāshən\ *n* : planned management of natural resources — **con·ser·va·tion·ist** \-shən-ist\ *n*

con·ser·va·tive \kən'sərvətiv\ *adj* **1** : disposed to maintain the status quo **2** : cautious — **con·ser·va·tism** \-və,tizəm\ *n* — **conservative** *n* — **con·ser·va·tive·ly** *adv*

con·ser·va·to·ry \kən'sərvə,tōrē\ *n, pl* **-ries** : school for art or music

con·serve \-'sərv\ *vb* **-served; -serv·ing** : keep from wasting ~ \'kän-,sərv\ *n* : candied fruit or fruit preserves

con·sid·er \kən'sidər\ *vb* **1** : think about **2** : give thoughtful attention to **3** : think that — **con·sid·er·ate** \-'sidərət\ *adj* — **con·sid·er·ation** \-,sidə'rāshən\ *n*

con·sid·er·able \-'sidərəbəl\ *adj* **1** : significant **2** : noticeably large — **con·sid·er·a·bly** \-blē\ *adv*

con·sid·er·ing *prep* : taking notice of

con·sign \kən'sīn\ *vb* **1** : transfer **2** : send to an agent for sale — **con·sign·ee** \,känsə'nē, -,sī-; kən,sī-\ *n* — **con·sign·ment** \kən'sīnmənt\ *n* — **con·sign·or** \,känsə'nór, -,sī-; kən,sī-\ *n*

con·sist \kən'sist\ *vb* **1** : be inherent — used with *in* **2** : be made up — used with *of*

con·sis·ten·cy \-'sistənsē\ *n, pl* **-cies** **1** : degree of thickness or firmness **2** : quality of being consistent

con·sis·tent \-tənt\ *adj* : being steady and regular — **con·sis·tent·ly** *adv*

¹con·sole \kən'sōl\ *vb* **-soled; -sol·ing** : soothe the grief of — **con·so·la·tion** \,känsə'lāshən\ *n*

²con·sole \'kän,sōl\ *n* : cabinet or part with controls

con·sol·i·date \kən'sälə,dāt\ *vb* **-dat·ed; -dat·ing** : unite or compact — **con·sol·i·da·tion** \-,sälə'dāshən\ *n*

con·som·mé \,känsə'mā\ *n* : clear soup

con·so·nance \'känsənəns\ *n* : agreement or harmony — **con·so·nant** \-nənt\ *adj* — **con·so·nant·ly** *adv*

con·so·nant \-nənt\ *n* **1** : speech sound marked by constriction or closure in the breath channel **2** : letter other than *a, e, i, o* and *u* — **con·so·nan·tal** \,känsə'nant³l\ *adj*

con·sort \'kän,sȯrt\ *n* : spouse ~ \kən'sȯrt\ *vb* : keep company

con·spic·u·ous \kən'spikyəwəs\ *adj* : very noticeable — **con·spic·u·ous·ly** *adv*

con·spire \kən'spīr\ *vb* **-spired; -spir·ing** : secretly plan an unlawful act — **con·spir·a·cy** \-'spirəsē\ *n* — **con·spir·a·tor** \-'spirətər\ *n* — **con·spir·a·to·ri·al** \-,spirə'tōrēəl\ *adj*

con·sta·ble \'känstəbəl, 'kən-\ *n* : police officer

con·stab·u·lary \kən'stabyə,lerē\ *n, pl* **-lar·ies** : police force

con·stant \'känstənt\ *adj* **1** : steadfast or faithful **2** : not varying **3** : continually recurring ~ *n* : something unchanging — **con·stan·cy** \-stənsē\ *n* — **con·stant·ly** *adv*

con·stel·la·tion \,känstə'lāshən\ *n* : group of stars

con·ster·na·tion \-stər'nāshən\ *n* : amazed dismay

con·sti·pa·tion \,känstə'pāshən\ *n* : difficulty of defecation — **con·sti·pate** \'känstə,pāt\ *vb*

con·stit·u·ent \kən'stichəwənt\ *adj* **1** : component **2** : having power to elect ~ *n* **1** : component part **2** : one who may vote for a representative — **con·stit·u·en·cy** \-wənsē\ *n*

con·sti·tute \'känstə,tüt, -,tyüt\ *vb* **-tut·ed; -tut·ing 1** : establish **2** : be all or a basic part of

con·sti·tu·tion \,känstə'tüshən, -'tyü-\ *n* **1** : physical composition or structure **2** : the basic law of an organized body or the document containing it — **con·sti·tu·tion·al** \-əl\ *adj* — **con·sti·tu·tion·al·i·ty** \-,tüshə'nalətē, -,tyü-\ *n*

con·strain \kən'strān\ *vb* **1** : compel **2** : confine **3** : restrain — **con·straint** \-'strānt\ *n*

con·strict \-'strikt\ *vb* : draw or squeeze together — **con·stric·tion** \-'strikshən\ *n* — **con·stric·tive** \-'striktiv\ *adj*

con·struct \kən'strəkt\ *vb* : build or make — **con·struc·tion** \-'strək-shən\ *n* — **con·struc·tive** \-tiv\ *adj*

con·strue \kən'strü\ *vb* **-strued; -stru·ing** : explain or interpret

con·sul \'känsəl\ *n* **1** : Roman magistrate **2** : government commercial official in a foreign country — **con·sul·ar** \-ələr\ *adj* — **con·sul·ate** \-lət\ *n*

con·sult \kən'səlt\ *vb* **1** : ask the advice or opinion of **2** : confer — **con·sul·tant** \-ənt\ *n* — **con·sul·ta·tion** \,känsəl'tāshən\ *n*

con·sume \kən'süm\ *vb* **-sumed; -sum·ing** : eat or use up — **con·sum·able** *adj* — **con·sum·er** *n*

con·sum·mate \kən'səmət\ *adj* : complete or perfect ~ \'känsə,māt\ *vb* **-mat·ed; -mat·ing** : make complete — **con·sum·ma·tion** \,känsə'māshən\ *n*

con·sump·tion \kən'səmpshən\ *n* **1** : act of consuming **2** : use of goods **3** : tuberculosis — **con·sump·tive** \-tiv\ *adj or n*

con·tact \'kän,takt\ *n* **1** : a touching **2** : association or relationship **3** : connection or communication ~ *vb* **1** : come or bring into contact **2** : communicate with

con·ta·gion \kən'tājən\ *n* **1** : spread of disease by contact **2** : disease spread by contact — **con·ta·gious** \-jəs\ *adj*

con·tain \-'tān\ *vb* **1** : enclose or include **2** : have or hold within **3** : restrain — **con·tain·er** *n* — **con·tain·ment** *n*

con·tam·i·nate \kən'tamə,nāt\ *vb* **-nat·ed; -nat·ing** : soil or infect by contact or association — **con·tam·i·na·tion** \-,tamə'nāshən\ *n*

con·tem·plate \'käntəm,plāt\ *vb* **-plat·ed; -plat·ing** : view or consider thoughtfully — **con·tem·pla·tion** \,käntəm'plāshən\ *n* — **con·tem·pla·tive** \kən'templətiv; 'käntəm,plāt-\ *adj*

con·tem·po·ra·ne·ous \kən,tempə'rānēəs\ *adj* : contemporary

con·tem·po·rary \-'tempə,rerē\ *adj* **1** : occurring or existing at the same time **2** : of the same age — **contemporary** *n*

con·tempt \kən'tempt\ *n* **1** : feeling

of scorn **2** : state of being despised **3** : disobedience to a court or legislature — **con·tempt·ible** \-'tempt-əbəl\ adj

con·temp·tu·ous \-'tempchəwəs\ adj : feeling or expressing contempt — **con·temp·tu·ous·ly** adv

con·tend \-'tend\ vb **1** : strive against rivals or difficulties **2** : argue **3** : maintain or claim — **con·tend·er** n

¹**con·tent** \kən'tent\ adj : satisfied — vb : satisfy ~ n : ease of mind — **con·tent·ed** adj — **con·tent·ed·ly** adv — **con·tent·ed·ness** n — **con·tent·ment** n

²**con·tent** \'kän,tent\ n **1** pl : something contained **2** pl : subject matter (as of a book) **3** : essential meaning **4** : proportion contained

con·ten·tion \kən'tenchən\ n : state of contending — **con·ten·tious** \-chəs\ adj — **con·ten·tious·ly** adv

con·test \kən'test\ vb : dispute or challenge ~ \'kän,test\ n **1** : struggle **2** : game — **con·test·able** \-'testəbəl\ adj — **con·tes·tant** \-'testənt\ n

con·text \'kän,tekst\ n : words surrounding a word or phrase

con·tig·u·ous \kən'tigyəwəs\ adj : connected to or adjoining — **con·ti·gu·i·ty** \,käntə'gyüətē\ n

con·ti·nence \'känt³nəns\ n : self-restraint — **con·ti·nent** \-nənt\ adj

con·ti·nent \'känt³nənt\ n : great division of land on the globe — **con·ti·nen·tal** \,känt³n'ent³l\ adj

con·tin·gen·cy \kən'tinjənsē\ n, pl **-cies** : possible event

con·tin·gent \-jənt\ adj : dependent on something else ~ n : a quota from an area or group

con·tin·u·al \kən'tinyəwəl\ adj **1** : continuous **2** : steadily recurring — **con·tin·u·al·ly** \-ē\ adv

con·tin·ue \kən'tinyü\ vb **-tin·ued**; **-tin·u·ing 1** : remain in a place or condition **2** : endure **3** : resume after an intermission **4** : extend — **con·tin·u·ance** \-yəwəns\ n — **con·tin·u·ation** \-,tinyə'wāshən\ n

con·tin·u·ous \-'tinyəwəs\ adj : continuing without interruption — **con·ti·nu·i·ty** \,känt³n'üətē, -,'yü-\ n — **con·tin·u·ous·ly** adv

con·tort \kən'tort\ vb : twist out of shape — **con·tor·tion** \-'torshən\ n

con·tour \'kän,tûr\ n **1** : outline **2** pl : shape

con·tra·band \'käntrə,band\ n : illegal goods

con·tra·cep·tion \,käntrə'sepshən\ n : prevention of conception — **con·tra·cep·tive** \-'septiv\ adj or n

con·tract \'kän,trakt\ n : binding agreement ~ \kən'trakt; *1 usu* 'kän,trakt\ vb **1** : establish or undertake by contract **2** : become ill with **3** : make shorter — **con·trac·tion** \kən'trakshən\ n — **con·trac·tor** \'kän,traktər, kən'trak-\ n — **con·trac·tu·al** \kən'trakchəwəl\ adj — **con·trac·tu·al·ly** adv

con·tra·dict \,käntrə'dikt\ vb : state the contrary of — **con·tra·dic·tion** \-'dikshən\ n — **con·tra·dic·to·ry** \-'diktərē\ adj

con·tral·to \kən'traltō\ n, pl **-tos** : lowest female singing voice

con·trap·tion \kən'trapshən\ n : device or contrivance

con·trary \'kän,trerē; *4 often* kən-'trerē\ adj **1** : opposite in character, nature, or position **2** : mutually opposed **3** : unfavorable **4** : uncooperative or stubborn — **con·trar·i·ly** \-,trerəlē, -'trer-\ adv — **con·trari·wise** \-,wiz\ adv — **contrary** \'kän,trerē\ n

con·trast \'kän,trast\ n **1** : unlikeness shown by comparing **2** : unlike color or tone of adjacent parts ~ \kən-'trast\ vb **1** : show differences **2** : compare so as to show differences

con·tra·vene \,käntrə'vēn\ vb **-vened**; **-ven·ing** : go or act contrary to

con·trib·ute \kən'tribyət\ vb **-ut·ed**; **-ut·ing** : give or help along with others — **con·tri·bu·tion** \,käntrə-'byüshən\ n — **con·trib·u·tor** \kən-'tribyətər\ n — **con·trib·u·to·ry** \-yə,tōrē\ adj

con·trite \'kän,trīt, kən'trīt\ adj : repentant — **con·tri·tion** \kən'trish·ən\ n

con·trive \kən'trīv\ vb **-trived**; **-triv·ing 1** : devise or make with ingenuity **2** : bring about — **con·triv·ance** \-'trīvəns\ n — **con·triv·er** n

con·trol \-'trōl\ vb **-ll- 1** : exercise power over **2** : dominate or rule ~ n **1** : power to direct or regulate **2** : restraint **3** : regulating device — **con·trol·la·ble** adj — **con·trol·ler** \-'trōlər, 'kän,-\ n

con·tro·ver·sy \'käntrə‚vərsē\ *n, pl* **-sies** : clash of opposing views — **con·tro·ver·sial** \‚käntrə'vərshəl, -sēəl\ *adj*

con·tro·vert \'käntrə‚vərt, ‚käntrə'-\ *vb* : contradict — **con·tro·vert·ible** *adj*

con·tu·ma·cious \‚käntə'māshəs, -tyə-\ *adj* : rebellious

con·tu·me·ly \kən'tüməlē, 'käntü‚mēlē, -tyü-\ *n* : rudeness

con·tu·sion \kən'tüzhən, -tyü-\ *n* : bruise — **con·tuse** \-'tüz, -'tyüz\ *vb*

co·nun·drum \kə'nəndrəm\ *n* : riddle

con·va·lesce \‚känvə'les\ *vb* **-lesced; -lesc·ing** : gradually recover health — **con·va·les·cence** \-ᵊns\ *n* — **con·va·les·cent** \-ᵊnt\ *adj or n*

con·vec·tion \kən'vekshən\ *n* : circulation in fluids due to warmer portions rising and colder ones sinking — **con·vec·tion·al** \-'vekshənəl\ *adj* — **con·vec·tive** \-'vektiv\ *adj*

con·vene \kən'vēn\ *vb* **-vened; -ven·ing** : assemble or meet

con·ve·nience \-'vēnyəns\ *n* 1 : personal comfort or ease 2 : device that saves work

con·ve·nient \-nyənt\ *adj* 1 : suited to one's convenience 2 : near at hand — **con·ve·nient·ly** *adv*

con·vent \'känvənt, -‚vent\ *n* : community of nuns

con·ven·tion \kən'venchən\ *n* 1 : agreement esp. between nations 2 : large meeting 3 : body of delegates 4 : accepted usage or way of behaving — **con·ven·tion·al** \-'venchənəl\ *adj* — **con·ven·tion·al·ly** *adv*

con·verge \kən'vərj\ *vb* **-verged; -verg·ing** : approach a single point — **con·ver·gence** \-'vərjəns\ *n* — **con·ver·gent** \-jənt\ *adj*

con·ver·sant \-'vərsᵊnt\ *adj* : having knowledge and experience

con·ver·sa·tion \‚känvər'sāshən\ *n* : an informal talking together — **con·ver·sa·tion·al** \-shənəl\ *adj*

¹**con·verse** \kən'vərs\ *vb* **-versed; -vers·ing** : engage in conversation — **con·verse** \'kän‚vərs\ *n*

²**con·verse** \kən'vərs, 'kän‚vərs\ *adj* : opposite — **con·verse** \-'vərs, 'kän‚vərs\ *n* — **con·verse·ly** *adv*

con·ver·sion \kən'vərzhən\ *n* 1 : change 2 : adoption of religion

con·vert \kən'vərt\ *vb* 1 : turn from one belief or party to another 2 : change ~ \'kän‚vərt\ *n* : one who has undergone religious conversion — **con·vert·er, con·ver·tor** \kən-'vərtər\ *n* — **con·vert·ible** *adj*

con·vert·ible \kən'vərtəbəl\ *n* : automobile with a removable top

con·vex \kän'veks, 'kän‚-, kən'-\ *adj* : curved or rounded like the outside of a sphere — **con·vex·i·ty** \kən'veksətē, kän-\ *n*

con·vey \kən'vā\ *vb* **-veyed; -vey·ing** : transport or transmit — **con·vey·ance** \-'vāəns\ *n* — **con·vey·or** \-ər\ *n*

con·vict \kən'vikt\ *vb* : find guilty ~ \'kän‚vikt\ *n* : person in prison

con·vic·tion \kən'vikshən\ *n* 1 : act of convicting 2 : strong belief

con·vince \-'vins\ *vb* **-vinced; -vinc·ing** : cause to believe — **con·vinc·ing·ly** *adv*

con·viv·ial \-'vivyəl, -'vivēəl\ *adj* : cheerful or festive — **con·viv·i·al·i·ty** \-‚vivē'alətē\ *n*

con·voke \kən'vōk\ *vb* **-voked; -vok·ing** : call together to a meeting — **con·vo·ca·tion** \‚känvə'kāshən\ *n*

con·vo·lut·ed \'känvə‚lütəd\ *adj* 1 : intricately folded 2 : intricate

con·vo·lu·tion \‚känvə'lüshən\ *n* : voluted structure

con·voy \'kän‚vȯi, kən'vȯi\ *vb* : accompany for protection ~ \'kän‚vȯi\ *n* : group of vehicles or ships moving together

con·vul·sion \kən'vəlshən\ *n* : violent involuntary muscle contraction — **con·vulse** \-'vəls\ *vb* — **con·vul·sive** \-'vəlsiv\ *adj*

coo \'kü\ *n* : sound of a pigeon — **coo** *vb*

cook \'kük\ *n* : one who prepares food ~ *vb* : prepare food — **cook·book** *n* — **cook·er** *n* — **cook·ery** \-ərē\ *n* — **cook·ware** *n*

cook·ie, cooky \'kükē\ *n, pl* **-ies** : small sweet flat cake

cool \'kül\ *adj* 1 : moderately cold 2 : not excited 3 : unfriendly ~ *vb* : make or become cool ~ *n* 1 : cool time or place 2 : composure — **cool·ant** \-ənt\ *n* — **cool·er** *n* — **cool·ly** *adv* — **cool·ness** *n*

coo·lie \'külē\ *n* : unskilled laborer in or from the Far East

coop \'küp, 'küp\ *n* : enclosure usu.

for poultry ~ vb : confine in or as if in a coop

co-op \'kō,äp\ n : cooperative

coo-per \'küpər, 'kup-\ n : barrel maker — **cooper** vb

co-op-er-ate \kō'äpə,rāt\ vb : act jointly — **co-op-er-a-tion** \-,äpə-'rāshən\ n

co-op-er-a-tive \kō'äpərətiv, -'äpə,rāt-\ adj : willing to work with others ~ n : enterprise owned and run by those using its services

co-opt \kō'äpt\ vb 1 : elect as a colleague 2 : take over

co-or-di-nate \-'ord⁰nət\ adj : equal esp. in rank ~ n : any of a set of numbers used in specifying the location of a point on a surface or in space ~ \-⁰n,āt\ vb -nat-ed; -nat-ing 1 : make or become coordinate 2 : work or act together harmoniously — **co-or-di-nate-ly** adv — **co-or-di-na-tion** \-,ord⁰n'āshən\ n — **co-or-di-na-tor** \-⁰n,ātər\ n

coot \'küt\ n 1 : dark-colored ducklike bird 2 : harmless simple person

cop \'käp\ n : police officer

¹**cope** \'kōp\ n : cloaklike ecclesiastical vestment

²**cope** vb coped; cop-ing : deal with difficulties

co-pi-lot \'kō,pīlət\ n : assistant airplane pilot

cop-ing \'kōpiŋ\ n : top layer of a wall

co-pi-ous \'kōpēəs\ adj : very abundant — **co-pi-ous-ly** adv — **co-pi-ous-ness** n

cop-per \'käpər\ n 1 : malleable reddish metallic chemical element 2 : penny — **cop-pery** adj

cop-per-head n : largely coppery brown venomous snake

co-pra \'kōprə\ n : dried coconut meat

copse \'käps\ n : thicket

cop-u-la \'käpyələ\ n : verb linking subject and predicate — **cop-u-la-tive** \-,lātiv\ adj

cop-u-late \'käpyə,lāt\ vb -lat-ed; -lat-ing : engage in sexual intercourse — **cop-u-la-tion** \,käpyə'lāshən\ n

copy \'käpē\ n, pl cop-ies 1 : imitation or reproduction of an original 2 : writing to be set for printing ~ vb cop-ied; copy-ing 1 : make a copy of 2 : imitate — **copi-er** \-ər\ n — **copyist** n

copy-right n : sole right to a literary or artistic work ~ vb : get a copyright on

co-quette \kō'ket\ n : flirt

cor-al \'kórəl\ n 1 : skeletal material of colonies of tiny sea polyps 2 : deep pink — **coral** adj

cord \'kórd\ n 1 : usu. heavy string 2 : long slender anatomical structure 3 : measure of firewood equal to 128 cu. ft. 4 : small electrical cable ~ vb 1 : tie or furnish with a cord 2 : pile (wood) in cords

cor-dial \'kórjəl\ adj : warmly welcoming ~ n : liqueur — **cor-di-al-i-ty** \,kórjē'alətē, kórd'yal-\ n — **cor-dial-ly** \'kórjəlē\ adv

cor-don \'kórd⁰n\ n : encircling line of troops or police — **cordon** vb

cor-do-van \'kórdəvən\ n : soft fine-grained leather

cor-du-roy \'kórdə,rói\ n 1 : heavy ribbed fabric 2 pl : trousers of corduroy

core \'kōr\ n 1 : central part of some fruits 2 : inmost part ~ vb cored; cor-ing : take out the core of — **cor-er** n

cork \'kórk\ n 1 : tough elastic bark of a European oak (**cork oak**) 2 : stopper of cork ~ vb : stop up with a cork — **corky** adj

cork-screw n : device for drawing corks from bottles

cor-mo-rant \'kórmərənt, -,rant\ n : dark seabird

¹**corn** \'kórn\ n : cereal grass or its seeds ~ vb : cure or preserve in brine — **corn-meal** n — **corn-stalk** n — **corn-starch** n

²**corn** n : local hardening and thickening of skin

corn-cob n : axis on which the kernels of Indian corn are arranged

cor-nea \'kórnēə\ n : transparent part of the coat of the eyeball — **cor-ne-al** adj

cor-ner \'kórnər\ n 1 : point or angle formed by the meeting of lines or sides 2 : place where two streets meet 3 : inescapable position 4 : control of the supply of something ~ vb 1 : drive into a corner 2 : get a corner on 3 : turn a corner

cor-ner-stone n 1 : stone at a corner of a wall 2 : something basic

cor-net \kór'net\ n : trumpetlike instrument

cor·nice \'kornəs\ n : horizontal wall projection

cor·nu·co·pia \,kornə'kōpēə, -nyə-\ n : goat's horn filled with fruits and grain emblematic of abundance

co·rol·la \kə'rälə\ n : petals of a flower

cor·ol·lary \'korə,lerē\ n, pl **-lar·ies** 1 : logical deduction 2 : consequence or result

co·ro·na \kə'rōnə\ n : shining ring around the sun seen during eclipses

cor·o·nary \'korə,nerē\ adj : relating to the heart or its blood vessels ~ n 1 : thrombosis of an artery supplying the heart 2 : heart attack

cor·o·na·tion \,korə'nāshən\ n : crowning of a monarch

cor·o·ner \'korənər\ n : public official who investigates causes of suspicious deaths

¹**cor·po·ral** \'korpərəl\ adj : bodily

²**corporal** n : noncommissioned officer ranking next below a sergeant

cor·po·ra·tion \,korpə'rāshən\ n : legal creation with the rights and liabilities of a person — **cor·po·rate** \'korpərət\ adj

cor·po·re·al \kor'pōrēəl\ adj : physical or material — **cor·po·re·al·ly** adv

corps \'kōr\ n, pl **corps** \'kōrz\ 1 : subdivision of a military force 2 : working group

corpse \'korps\ n : dead body

cor·pu·lence \'korpyələns\ n : obesity — **cor·pu·lent** \-lənt\ adj

cor·pus \'korpəs\ n, pl **-po·ra** \-pərə\ 1 : corpse 2 : body of writings

cor·pus·cle \'kor,pəsəl\ n : blood cell

cor·ral \kə'ral\ n : enclosure for animals — **corral** vb

cor·rect \kə'rekt\ vb 1 : make right 2 : chastise ~ adj 1 : true or factual 2 : conforming to a standard — **cor·rec·tion** \-'rekshən\ n — **cor·rec·tive** \-'rektiv\ adj — **cor·rect·ly** adv — **cor·rect·ness** n

cor·re·late \'korə,lāt\ vb **-lat·ed; -lat·ing** : show a connection between — **cor·re·late** \-lət, -,lāt\ n — **cor·re·la·tion** \,korə'lāshən\ n

cor·rel·a·tive \kə'relətiv\ adj : regularly used together — **correlative** n

cor·re·spond \,korə'spänd\ vb 1 : match 2 : communicate by letter — **cor·re·spon·dence** \-'spändəns\ n — **cor·re·spond·ing·ly** \-'spändiŋlē\ adv

cor·re·spon·dent \-'spändənt\ n 1 : person one writes to 2 : reporter

cor·ri·dor \'korədər, -,dor\ n : passageway connecting rooms

cor·rob·o·rate \kə'räbə,rāt\ vb **-rat·ed; -rat·ing** : support with evidence — **cor·rob·o·ra·tion** \-,räbə'rāshən\ n

cor·rode \kə'rōd\ vb **-rod·ed; -rod·ing** : wear away by chemical action — **cor·ro·sion** \-'rōzhən\ n — **cor·ro·sive** \-'rōsiv\ adj or n

cor·ru·gate \'korə,gāt\ vb **-gat·ed; -gat·ing** : form into ridges and grooves — **cor·ru·gat·ed** adj — **cor·ru·ga·tion** \,korə'gāshən\ n

cor·rupt \kə'rəpt\ vb 1 : change from good to bad 2 : bribe ~ adj : morally debased — **cor·rupt·ible** adj — **cor·rup·tion** \-'rəpshən\ n

cor·sage \kor'säzh, -'säj\ n : bouquet worn by a woman

cor·set \'korsət\ n : woman's stiffened undergarment

cor·tege \kor'tezh, 'kor,-\ n : funeral procession

cor·tex \'kor,teks\ n, pl **-ti·ces** \'kortə,sēz\ or **-tex·es** : outer or covering layer of an organism or part (as the brain) — **cor·ti·cal** \'kortikəl\ adj

cor·ti·sone \'kortə,sōn, -,zōn\ n : adrenal hormone

cos·met·ic \käz'metik\ n : beautifying preparation ~ adj : relating to beautifying

cos·mic \'käzmik\ adj 1 : relating to the universe 2 : vast or grand

cos·mo·naut \'käzmə,not\ n : Soviet or Russian astronaut

cos·mo·pol·i·tan \,käzmə'pälət'n\ adj : belonging to all the world — **cosmopolitan** n

cos·mos \'käzməs, -,mōs, -,mäs\ n : universe

Cos·sack \'käs,ak, -ək\ n : Russian cavalryman

cost \'kost\ n 1 : amount paid for something 2 : loss or penalty ~ vb : **cost; cost·ing** 1 : require so much in payment 2 : cause to pay, suffer, or lose — **cost·li·ness** \-lēnəs\ n — **cost·ly** \-lē\ adj

cos·tume \'käs,tüm, -,tyüm\ n : clothing

co·sy \'kōzē\ var of COZY

cot \'kät\ n : small bed

cote \'kōt, 'kät\ n : small shed or coop

co·te·rie \'kōtə,rē, ,kōtə'-\ n : exclusive group of persons

co·til·lion \kō'tilyən\ *n* : formal ball

cot·tage \'kätij\ *n* : small house

cot·ton \'kät³n\ *n* : soft fibrous plant substance or thread or cloth made of it — **cot·ton·seed** *n* — **cot·tony** *adj*

cot·ton·mouth *n* : poisonous snake

couch \'kauch\ *vb* **1** : lie or place on a couch **2** : phrase ~ *n* : bed or sofa

couch potato *n* : one who spends a great deal of time watching television

cou·gar \'kügər, -gär\ *n* : large tawny wild American cat

cough \'kof\ *vb* : force air from the lungs with short sharp noises — **cough** *n*

could \'kud\ *past of* CAN

coun·cil \'kaunsəl\ *n* **1** : assembly or meeting **2** : body of lawmakers — **coun·cil·lor, coun·cil·or** \-sələr\ *n* — **coun·cil·man** \-mən\ *n* — **coun·cil·wom·an** *n*

coun·sel \'kaunsəl\ *n* **1** : advice **2** : deliberation **3** *pl* **-sel** : lawyer ~ *vb* **-seled** *or* **-selled; -sel·ing** *or* **-sel·ling** **1** : advise **2** : consult together — **coun·sel·or, coun·sel·lor** \-sələr\ *n*

¹count \'kaunt\ *vb* **1** : name or indicate one by one to find the total number **2** : recite numbers in order **3** : rely **4** : be of value or account ~ *n* **1** : act of counting or the total obtained by counting **2** : charge in an indictment — **count·able** *adj*

²count *n* : European nobleman

coun·te·nance \'kaunt³nəns\ *n* : face or facial expression ~ *vb* **-nanced; -nanc·ing** : allow or encourage

¹count·er \'kauntər\ *n* **1** : piece for reckoning or games **2** : surface over which business is transacted

²count·er *n* : one that counts

³coun·ter *vb* : oppose ~ *adv* : in an opposite direction ~ *n* : offsetting force or move ~ *adj* : contrary

counter- *prefix* **1** : contrary or opposite **2** : opposing **3** : retaliatory

coun·ter·act *vb* : lessen the force of — **coun·ter·ac·tive** *adj*

coun·ter·bal·ance *n* : balancing influence or weight ~ *vb* : oppose or balance

coun·ter·clock·wise *adv or adj* : opposite to the way a clock's hands move

coun·ter·feit \'kauntər,fit\ *vb* **1** : copy in order to deceive **2** : pretend ~ *adj* : spurious ~ *n* : fraudulent copy — **coun·ter·feit·er** *n*

coun·ter·mand \-,mand\ *vb* : supersede with a contrary order

coun·ter·pane \-,pān\ *n* : bedspread

coun·ter·part *n* : one that is similar or corresponds

coun·ter·point *n* : music with interwoven melodies

coun·ter·sign *n* : secret signal ~ *vb* : add a confirming signature to

count·ess \'kauntəs\ *n* : wife or widow of a count or an earl or a woman holding that rank in her own right

---

List of self-explanatory words with the prefix *counter-*

counteraccusation	counterevidence	counterreform
counteraggression	counterguerrilla	counterresponse
counterargue	counterinflationary	counterretaliation
counterassault	counterinfluence	counterrevolution
counterattack	countermeasure	counterrevolutionary
counterbid	countermove	counterstrategy
counterblockade	countermovement	counterstyle
counterblow	counteroffer	countersue
countercampaign	counterpetition	countersuggestion
countercharge	counterploy	countersuit
counterclaim	counterpower	countertendency
countercomplaint	counterpressure	counterterror
countercoup	counterpropaganda	counterterrorism
countercriticism	counterproposal	counterterrorist
counterdemand	counterprotest	counterthreat
counterdemonstration	counterquestion	counterthrust
counterdemonstrator	counterraid	countertrend
countereffort	counterrally	

count·less \-ləs\ *adj* : too many to be numbered

coun·try \'kəntrē\ *n, pl* **-tries** 1 : nation 2 : rural area ~ *adj* : rural — **coun·try·man** \-mən\ *n*

coun·try·side *n* : rural area or its people

coun·ty \'kaüntē\ *n, pl* **-ties** : local government division esp. of a state

coup \'kü\ *n, pl* **coups** \'küz\ 1 : brilliant sudden action or plan 2 : sudden overthrow of a government

coupe \'küp\ *n* : 2-door automobile with an enclosed body

cou·ple \'kəpəl\ *vb* **-pled; -pling** : link together ~ *n* 1 : pair 2 : two persons closely associated or married

cou·pling \'kəplin\ *n* : connecting device

cou·pon \'kü,pän, 'kyü-\ *n* : certificate redeemable for goods or a cash discount

cour·age \'kərij\ *n* : ability to conquer fear or despair — **cou·ra·geous** \kə'rājəs\ *adj*

cou·ri·er \'kúrēər, 'kərē-\ *n* : messenger

course \'kōrs\ *n* 1 : progress 2 : ground over which something moves 3 : part of a meal served at one time 4 : method of procedure 5 : subject taught in a series of classes ~ *vb* **coursed; cours·ing** 1 : hunt with dogs 2 : run speedily — **of course** : as might be expected

court \'kōrt\ *n* 1 : residence of a sovereign 2 : sovereign and his or her officials and advisers 3 : area enclosed by a building 4 : space marked for playing a game 5 : place where justice is administered ~ *vb* : woo — **court·house** *n* — **court·room** *n* — **court·ship** \-,ship\ *n*

cour·te·ous \'kərtēəs\ *adj* : showing politeness and respect for others — **cour·te·ous·ly** *adv*

cour·te·san \'kōrtəzən, 'kərt-\ *n* : prostitute

cour·te·sy \'kərtəsē\ *n, pl* **-sies** : courteous behavior

court·ier \'kōrtēər, 'kōrtyər\ *n* : person in attendance at a royal court

court·ly \'kōrtlē\ *adj* **-li·er; -est** : polite or elegant — **court·li·ness** *n*

court–mar·tial *n, pl* **courts–martial** : military trial court — **court–martial** *vb*

court·yard *n* : enclosure open to the sky that is attached to a house

cous·in \'kəz²n\ *n* : child of one's uncle or aunt

cove \'kōv\ *n* : sheltered inlet or bay

co·ven \'kəvən\ *n* : group of witches

cov·e·nant \'kəvənənt\ *n* : binding agreement — **cov·e·nant** \-nənt, -,nant\ *vb*

cov·er \'kəvər\ *vb* 1 : place something over or upon 2 : protect or hide 3 : include or deal with ~ *n* : something that covers — **cov·er·age** \-ərij\ *n*

cov·er·let \-lət\ *n* : bedspread

co·vert \'kō,vərt, 'kəvərt\ *adj* : secret ~ \'kəvərt, 'kō-\ *n* : thicket that shelters animals

cov·et \'kəvət\ *vb* : desire enviously — **cov·et·ous** *adj*

cov·ey \'kəvē\ *n, pl* **-eys** 1 : bird with her young 2 : small flock (as of quail)

¹**cow** \'kaü\ *n* : large adult female animal (as of cattle) — **cow·hide** *n*

²**cow** *vb* : intimidate

cow·ard \'kaüərd\ *n* : one who lacks courage — **cow·ard·ice** \-əs-\ *n* — **cow·ard·ly** *adv or adj*

cow·boy *n* : a mounted ranch hand who tends cattle

cow·er \'kaüər\ *vb* : shrink from fear or cold

cow·girl *n* : woman ranch hand who tends cattle

cowl \'kaül\ *n* : monk's hood

cow·lick \'kaü,lik\ *n* : turned-up tuft of hair that resists control

cow·slip \-,slip\ *n* : yellow flower

cox·swain \'käkən, -,swän\ *n* : person who steers a boat

coy \'kói\ *adj* : shy or pretending shyness

coy·ote \'kī,ōt, kī'ōtē\ *n, pl* **coy·otes** *or* **coyote** : small No. American wolf

coz·en \'kəz²n\ *vb* : cheat

co·zy \'kōzē\ *adj* **-zi·er; -est** : snug

crab \'krab\ *n* : short broad shellfish with pincers

crab·by \'krabē\ *adj* **-bi·er; -est** : cross

¹**crack** \'krak\ *vb* 1 : break with a sharp sound 2 : fail in tone 3 : break without completely separating ~ *n* 1 : sudden sharp noise 2 : witty remark 3 : narrow break 4 : sharp blow 5 : try

²**crack** *adj* : extremely proficient

crack·down *n* : disciplinary action — **crack down** *vb*

crack·er \-ər\ *n* : thin crisp bakery product

crack·le \'krakəl\ *vb* **-led; -ling** 1 : make snapping noises 2 : develop fine cracks in a surface — **crackle** *n*

crack·pot \'krak,pät\ *n* : eccentric

crack–up *n* : crash

cra·dle \'krād^əl\ *n* : baby's bed ~ *vb* **-dled; -dling** 1 : place in a cradle 2 : hold securely

craft \'kraft\ *n* 1 : occupation requiring special skill 2 : craftiness 3 *pl usu* **craft** : structure designed to provide transportation 4 *pl usu* **craft** : small boat — **crafts·man** \'kraftsmən\ *n* — **crafts·man·ship** \-,ship\ *n*

crafty \'kraftē\ *adj* **craft·i·er; -est** : sly — **craft·i·ness** *n*

crag \'krag\ *n* : steep cliff — **crag·gy** \-ē\ *adj*

cram \'kram\ *vb* **-mm-** 1 : eat greedily 2 : pack in tight 3 : study intensely for a test

cramp \'kramp\ *n* 1 : sudden painful contraction of muscle 2 *pl* : sharp abdominal pains ~ *vb* 1 : affect with cramp 2 : restrain

cran·ber·ry \'kran,berē\ *n* : red acid berry of a trailing plant

crane \'krān\ *n* 1 : tall wading bird 2 : machine for lifting heavy objects ~ *vb* **craned; cran·ing** : stretch one's neck to see

cra·ni·um \'krānēəm\ *n, pl* **-ni·ums** *or* **-nia** \-nēə\ : skull — **cra·ni·al** \-əl\ *adj*

crank \'krank\ *n* 1 : bent lever turned to operate a machine 2 : eccentric ~ *vb* : start or operate by turning a crank

cranky \'krankē\ *adj* **crank·i·er; -est** : irritable

cran·ny \'kranē\ *n, pl* **-nies** : crevice

craps \'kraps\ *n* : dice game

crash \'krash\ *vb* 1 : break noisily 2 : fall and hit something with noise and damage ~ *n* 1 : loud sound 2 : action of crashing 3 : failure

crass \'kras\ *adj* : crude or unfeeling

crate \'krāt\ *n* : wooden shipping container — **crate** *vb*

cra·ter \'krātər\ *n* : volcanic depression

cra·vat \krə'vat\ *n* : necktie

crave \'krāv\ *vb* **craved; crav·ing** : long for — **crav·ing** *n*

cra·ven \'krāvən\ *adj* : cowardly — **craven** *n*

craw·fish \'kró,fish\ *n* : crayfish

crawl \'król\ *vb* 1 : move slowly (as by drawing the body along the ground) 2 : swarm with creeping things ~ *n* : very slow pace

cray·fish \'krā,fish\ *n* : lobsterlike freshwater crustacean

cray·on \'krā,än, -ən\ *n* : stick of chalk or wax used for drawing or coloring — **crayon** *vb*

craze \'krāz\ *vb* **crazed; craz·ing** : make or become insane ~ *n* : fad

cra·zy \'krāzē\ *adj* **cra·zi·er; -est** 1 : mentally disordered 2 : wildly impractical — **cra·zi·ly** *adv* — **cra·zi·ness** *n*

creak \'krēk\ *vb or n* : squeak — **creaky** *adj*

cream \'krēm\ *n* 1 : yellowish fat-rich part of milk 2 : thick smooth sauce, confection, or cosmetic 3 : choicest part ~ *vb* : beat into creamy consistency — **creamy** *adj*

cream·ery \-ərē\ *n, pl* **-er·ies** : place where butter and cheese are made

crease \'krēs\ *n* : line made by folding — **crease** *vb*

cre·ate \krē'āt\ *vb* **-at·ed; -at·ing** : bring into being — **cre·ation** \krē-'āshən\ *n* — **cre·ative** \-'ātiv\ *adj* — **cre·ativ·i·ty** \,krēā'tivətē\ *n* — **cre·a·tor** \krē'ātər\ *n*

crea·ture \'krēchər\ *n* : lower animal or human being

cre·dence \'krēd^əns\ *n* : belief

cre·den·tials \kri'denchəlz\ *n pl* : evidence of qualifications or authority

cred·i·ble \'kredəbəl\ *adj* : believable — **cred·i·bil·i·ty** \,kredə'bilətē\ *n*

cred·it \'kredət\ *n* 1 : balance in a person's favor 2 : time given to pay for goods 3 : belief 4 : esteem 5 : source of honor ~ *vb* 1 : believe 2 : give credit to

cred·it·able \-əbəl\ *adj* : worthy of esteem or praise — **cred·it·ably** \-əblē\ *adv*

cred·i·tor \-ər\ *n* : person to whom money is owed

cred·u·lous \'krejələs\ *adj* : easily convinced — **cre·du·li·ty** \kri'dülətē, -'dyü-\ *n*

creed \'krēd\ *n* : statement of essential beliefs

creek \'krēk, 'krik\ *n* : small stream

creel \'krēl\ *n* : basket for carrying fish

creep \'krēp\ *vb* **crept** \'krept\; **creep·ing** 1 : crawl 2 : grow over a surface like ivy — **creep** *n* — **creep·er** *n*

cre·mate \'krē,māt\ *vb* **-mat·ed; -mat·ing** : burn up (a corpse) — **cre·ma·tion** \kri'māshən\ *n* — **cre·ma·to·ry** \'krēmə,tōrē, 'krem-\ *n*

cre·o·sote \'krēə,sōt\ *n* : oily wood preservative

crepe, crêpe \'krāp\ *n* : light crinkled fabric

cre·scen·do \krə'shendō\ *adv or adj* : growing louder — **crescendo** *n*

cres·cent \'kres²nt\ *n* : shape of the moon between new moon and first quarter

crest \'krest\ *n* **1** : tuft on a bird's head **2** : top of a hill or wave **3** : part of a coat of arms ~ *vb* : rise to a crest — **crest·ed** \-təd\ *adj*

crest·fall·en *adj* : sad

cre·tin \'krēt²n\ *n* : stupid person

cre·vasse \kri'vas\ *n* : deep fissure esp. in a glacier

crev·ice \'krevəs\ *n* : narrow fissure

crew \'krü\ *n* : body of workers (as on a ship) — **crew·man** \-mən\ *n*

crib \'krib\ *n* **1** : manger **2** : grain storage bin **3** : baby's bed ~ *vb* **-bb-** : put in a crib

crib·bage \'kribij\ *n* : card game scored by moving pegs on a board (**cribbage board**)

crick \'krik\ *n* : muscle spasm

¹**crick·et** \'krikət\ *n* : insect noted for the chirping of the male

²**cricket** *n* : bat and ball game played on a field with wickets

cri·er \'krīər\ *n* : one who calls out announcements

crime \'krīm\ *n* : serious violation of law

crim·i·nal \'krimən²l\ *adj* : relating to or being a crime or its punishment ~ *n* : one who commits a crime

crimp \'krimp\ *vb* : cause to become crinkled, wavy, or bent — **crimp** *n*

crim·son \'krimzən\ *n* : deep red — **crimson** *adj*

cringe \'krinj\ *vb* **cringed; cring·ing** : shrink in fear

crin·kle \'kriŋkəl\ *vb* **-kled; -kling** : wrinkle — **crinkle** *n* — **crin·kly** \-klē\ *adj*

crin·o·line \'krin²lən\ *n* **1** : stiff cloth **2** : full stiff skirt or petticoat

crip·ple \'kripəl\ *n* : disabled person ~ *vb* **-pled; -pling** : disable

cri·sis \'krīsəs\ *n, pl* **cri·ses** \-,sēz\ : decisive or critical moment

crisp \'krisp\ *adj* **1** : easily crumbled **2** : firm and fresh **3** : lively **4** : invigorating — **crisp** *vb* — **crisp·ly** *adv* — **crisp·ness** *n* — **crispy** *adj*

criss·cross \'kris,krós\ *n* : pattern of crossed lines ~ *vb* : mark with or follow a crisscross

cri·te·ri·on \krī'tirēən\ *n, pl* **-ria** \-ēə\ : standard

crit·ic \'kritik\ *n* : judge of literary or artistic works

crit·i·cal \-ikəl\ *adj* **1** : inclined to criticize **2** : being a crisis **3** : relating to criticism or critics — **crit·i·cal·ly** \-iklē\ *adv*

crit·i·cize \'kritə,sīz\ *vb* **-cized; -cizing 1** : judge as a critic **2** : find fault — **crit·i·cism** \-ə,sizəm\ *n*

cri·tique \krə'tēk\ *n* : critical estimate

croak \'krōk\ *n* : hoarse harsh cry (as of a frog) — **croak** *vb*

cro·chet \krō'shā\ *n* : needlework done with a hooked needle — **crochet** *vb*

crock \'kräk\ *n* : thick earthenware pot or jar — **crock·ery** \-ərē\ *n*

croc·o·dile \'kräkə,dīl\ *n* : large reptile of tropical waters

cro·cus \'krōkəs\ *n, pl* **-cus·es** : herb with spring flowers

crone \'krōn\ *n* : ugly old woman

cro·ny \'krōnē\ *n, pl* **-nies** : chum

crook \'krúk\ *n* **1** : bent or curved tool or part **2** : thief ~ *vb* : curve sharply

crook·ed \'krúkəd\ *adj* **1** : bent **2** : dishonest — **crook·ed·ness** *n*

croon \'krün\ *vb* : sing softly — **croon·er** *n*

crop \'kräp\ *n* **1** : pouch in the throat of a bird or insect **2** : short riding whip **3** : something that can be harvested ~ *vb* **-pp- 1** : trim **2** : appear unexpectedly — used with *up*

cro·quet \krō'kā\ *n* : lawn game of driving balls through wickets

cro·quette \-'ket\ *n* : mass of minced food deep-fried

cro·sier \'krōzhər\ *n* : bishop's staff

cross \'krós\ *n* **1** : figure or structure consisting of an upright and a cross piece **2** : interbreeding of unlike strains ~ *vb* **1** : intersect **2** : cancel **3** : go or extend across **4** : interbreed ~ *adj* **1** : going across **2** : contrary **3** : marked by bad temper — **cross·ing** *n* — **cross·ly** *adv*

cross•bow \-ˌbō\ *n* : short bow mounted on a rifle stock

cross•breed *vb* **-bred; -breed•ing** : hybridize

cross-ex•am•ine *vb* : question about earlier testimony — **cross-ex•am•i•na•tion** *n*

cross-eyed *adj* : having the eye turned toward the nose

cross-re•fer *vb* : refer to another place (as in a book) — **cross-ref•er•ence** *n*

cross•roads *n* : place where 2 roads cross

cross section *n* : representative portion

cross•walk *n* : path for pedestrians crossing a street

cross•ways *adv* : crosswise

cross•wise \-ˌwīz\ *adv* : so as to cross something — **crosswise** *adj*

crotch \'kräch\ *n* : angle formed by the parting of 2 legs or branches

crotch•ety \'krächətē\ *adj* : cranky, ill-natured

crouch \'krauch\ *vb* : stoop over — **crouch** *n*

croup \'krüp\ *n* : laryngitis of infants

crou•ton \'krü,tän\ *n* : bit of toast

¹crow \'krō\ *n* : large glossy black bird

²crow *vb* **1** : make the loud sound of the cock **2** : gloat ~ *n* : cry of the cock

crow•bar *n* : metal bar used as a pry or lever

crowd \'kraud\ *vb* : collect or cram together ~ *n* : large number of people

crown \'kraun\ *n* **1** : wreath of honor or victory **2** : royal headdress **3** : top or highest part ~ *vb* **1** : place a crown on **2** : honor — **crowned** \'kraund\ *adj*

cru•cial \'krüshəl\ *adj* : vitally important

cru•ci•ble \'krüsəbəl\ *n* : heat-resisting container

cru•ci•fix \'krüsə,fiks\ *n* : representation of Christ on the cross

cru•ci•fix•ion \ˌkrüsə'fikshən\ *n* : act of crucifying

cru•ci•fy \'krüsə,fī\ *vb* **-fied; -fy•ing 1** : put to death on a cross **2** : persecute

crude \'krüd\ *adj* **crud•er; -est 1** : not refined **2** : lacking grace or elegance ~ *n* : unrefined petroleum — **crude•ly** *adv* — **cru•di•ty** \-ətē\ *n*

cru•el \'krüəl\ *adj* **-el•er** *or* **-el•ler; -el•est** *or* **-el•lest** : causing suffering to others — **cru•el•ly** \-ē\ *adv* — **cru•el•ty** \tē\ *n*

cru•et \'krüət\ *n* : bottle for salad dressings

cruise \'krüz\ *vb* **cruised; cruis•ing 1** : sail to several ports **2** : travel at the most efficient speed — **cruise** *n*

cruis•er \'krüzər\ *n* **1** : warship **2** : police car

crumb \'krəm\ *n* : small fragment

crum•ble \'krəmbəl\ *vb* **-bled; -bling** : break into small pieces — **crum•bly** \-blē\ *adj*

crum•ple \'krəmpəl\ *vb* **-pled; -pling 1** : crush together **2** : collapse

crunch \'krənch\ *vb* : chew or press with a crushing noise ~ *n* : crunching sound — **crunchy** *adj*

cru•sade \krü'sād\ *n* **1** *cap* : medieval Christian expedition to the Holy Land **2** : reform movement — **crusade** *vb* — **cru•sad•er** *n*

crush \'krəsh\ *vb* **1** : squeeze out of shape **2** : grind or pound to bits **3** : suppress ~ *n* **1** : severe crowding **2** : infatuation

crust \'krəst\ *n* **1** : hard outer part of bread or a pie **2** : hard surface layer — **crust•al** *adj* — **crusty** *adj*

crus•ta•cean \ˌkrəs'tāshən\ *n* : aquatic arthropod having a firm shell

crutch \'krəch\ *n* : support for use by the disabled in walking

crux \'krəks, 'krüks\ *n*, *pl* **crux•es 1** : hard problem **2** : crucial point

cry \'krī\ *vb* **cried; cry•ing 1** : call out **2** : weep ~ *n*, *pl* **cries 1** : shout **2** : fit of weeping **3** : characteristic sound of an animal

crypt \'kript\ *n* : underground chamber

cryp•tic \'kriptik\ *adj* : enigmatic

cryp•tog•ra•phy \krip'tägrəfē\ *n* : coding and decoding of messages — **cryp•tog•ra•pher** \-fər\ *n*

crys•tal \'krist¹l\ *n* **1** : transparent quartz **2** : something (as glass) like crystal **3** : body formed by solidification that has a regular repeating atomic arrangement — **crys•tal•line** \-tələn\ *adj*

crys•tal•lize \-tə,līz\ *vb* **-lized; -liz•ing** : form crystals or a definite shape — **crys•tal•li•za•tion** \ˌkristələ'zāshən\ *n*

cub \'kəb\ *n* : young animal

cub•by•hole \'kəbē,hōl\ *n* : small confined space

cube \'kyüb\ *n* **1** : solid having 6 equal square sides **2** : product obtained by taking a number 3 times as a factor

~ vb **cubed; cub·ing 1** : raise to the 3d power **2** : form into a cube **3** : cut into cubes — **cu·bic** \'kyübik\ adj

cu·bi·cle \-bikəl\ n : small room

cu·bit \'kyübət\ n : ancient unit of length equal to about 18 inches

cuck·old \'kəkəld, 'kuk-\ n : man whose wife is unfaithful — **cuckold** vb

cuck·oo \'kükü, 'kuk-\ n, pl **-oos** : brown European bird ~ adj : silly

cu·cum·ber \'kyü,kəmbər\ n : fleshy fruit related to the gourds

cud \'kəd\ n : food chewed again by ruminating animals

cud·dle \'kəd°l\ vb **-dled; -dling** : lie close

cud·gel \'kəjəl\ n or vb : club

¹**cue** \'kyü\ n : signal — **cue** vb

²**cue** n : stick used in pool

¹**cuff** \'kəf\ n **1** : part of a sleeve encircling the wrist **2** : folded trouser hem

²**cuff** vb or n : slap

cui·sine \kwi'zēn\ n : manner of cooking

cu·li·nary \'kələ,nerē, 'kyülə-\ adj : of or relating to cookery

cull \'kəl\ vb : select

cul·mi·nate \'kəlmə,nāt\ vb **-nat·ed; -nat·ing** : rise to the highest point — **cul·mi·na·tion** \,kəlmə'nāshən\ n

cul·pa·ble \'kəlpəbəl\ adj : deserving blame

cul·prit \'kəlprət\ n : guilty person

cult \'kəlt\ n **1** : religious system **2** : faddish devotion — **cult·ist** n

cul·ti·vate \'kəltə,vāt\ vb **-vat·ed; -vat·ing 1** : prepare for crops **2** : foster the growth of **3** : refine — **cul·ti·va·tion** \,kəltə'vāshən\ n

cul·ture \'kəlchər\ n **1** : cultivation **2** : refinement of intellectual and artistic taste **3** : particular form or stage of civilization — **cul·tur·al** \'kəlchərəl\ adj — **cul·tured** \'kəlchərd\ adj

cul·vert \'kəlvərt\ n : drain crossing under a road or railroad

cum·ber·some \'kəmbərsəm\ adj : awkward to handle due to bulk

cu·mu·la·tive \'kyümyələtiv, -,lāt-\ adj : increasing by additions

cu·mu·lus \'kyümyələs\ n, pl **-li** \-,lī, -,lē\ : massive rounded cloud

cun·ning \'kənin\ adj **1** : crafty **2** : clever **3** : appealing ~ n **1** : skill **2** : craftiness

cup \'kəp\ n **1** : small drinking vessel **2** : contents of a cup **3** : a half pint ~ vb **-pp-** : shape like a cup — **cup·ful** n

cup·board \'kəbərd\ n : small storage closet

cup·cake n : small cake

cu·pid·i·ty \kyu'pidətē\ n, pl **-ties** : excessive desire for money

cu·po·la \'kyüpələ, -,lō\ n : small rooftop structure

cur \'kər\ n : mongrel dog

cu·rate \'kyürət\ n : member of the clergy — **cu·ra·cy** \-əsē\ n

cu·ra·tor \kyu'rātər\ n : one in charge of a museum or zoo

curb \'kərb\ n **1** : restraint **2** : raised edging along a street ~ vb : hold back

curd \'kərd\ n : coagulated milk

cur·dle \'kərd°l\ vb **-dled; -dling 1** : form curds **2** : sour

cure \'kyùr\ n **1** : recovery from disease **2** : remedy ~ vb **cured; cur·ing 1** : restore to health **2** : process for storage or use — **cur·able** adj

cur·few \'kər,fyü\ n : requirement to be off the streets at a set hour

cu·rio \'kyürē,ō\ n, pl **-ri·os** : rare or unusual article

cu·ri·ous \'kyùrēəs\ adj **1** : eager to learn **2** : strange — **cu·ri·os·i·ty** \,kyùrē'äsətē\ n — **cu·ri·ous·ness** n

curl \'kərl\ vb **1** : form into ringlets **2** : curve ~ n **1** : ringlet of hair **2** : something with a spiral form — **curl·er** n — **curly** adj

cur·lew \'kərlü, -lyü\ n, pl **-lews** or **-lew** : long-legged brownish bird

curli·cue \'kərli,kyü\ n : fanciful curve

cur·rant \'kərənt\ n **1** : small seedless raisin **2** : berry of a shrub

cur·ren·cy \'kərənsē\ n, pl **-cies 1** : general use or acceptance **2** : money

cur·rent \'kərənt\ adj : occurring in or belonging to the present ~ n **1** : swiftest part of a stream **2** : flow of electricity

cur·ric·u·lum \kə'rikyələm\ n, pl **-la** \-lə\ : course of study

¹**cur·ry** \'kərē\ vb **-ried; -ry·ing** : brush (a horse) with a wire brush (**cur·ry·comb** \-,kōm\) — **curry fa·vor** : seek favor by flattery

²**curry** n, pl **-ries** : blend of pungent spices or a food seasoned with this

curse \'kərs\ *n* **1** : a calling down of evil or harm upon one **2** : affliction ~ *vb* **cursed**; **curs·ing 1** : call down injury upon **2** : swear at **3** : afflict

cur·sor \'kərsər\ *n* : indicator on a computer screen

cur·so·ry \'kərsərē\ *adj* : hastily done

curt \'kərt\ *adj* : rudely abrupt — **curt·ly** *adv* — **curt·ness** *n*

cur·tail \kər'tāl\ *vb* : shorten — **cur·tail·ment** *n*

cur·tain \'kərt°n\ *n* : hanging screen that can be drawn back or raised — **curtain** *vb*

curt·sy, curt·sey \'kərtsē\ *n, pl* **-sies** *or* **-seys** : courteous bow made by bending the knees — **curtsy, curtsey** *vb*

cur·va·ture \'kərvə,chúr\ *n* : amount or state of curving

curve \'kərv\ *vb* **curved**; **curv·ing** : bend from a straight line or course ~ *n* **1** : a bending without angles **2** : something curved

cush·ion \'kùshən\ *n* **1** : soft pillow **2** : something that eases or protects ~ *vb* **1** : provide with a cushion **2** : soften the force of

cusp \'kəsp\ *n* : pointed end

cus·pid \'kəspəd\ *n* : a canine tooth

cus·pi·dor \'kəspə,dór\ *n* : spittoon

cus·tard \'kəstərd\ *n* : sweetened cooked mixture of milk and eggs

cus·to·dy \'kəstədē\ *n, pl* **-dies** : immediate care or charge — **cus·to·di·al** \,kəs'tōdēəl\ *adj* — **cus·to·di·an** \-dēən\ *n*

cus·tom \'kəstəm\ *n* **1** : habitual course of action **2** *pl* : import taxes ~ *adj* : made to personal order — **cus·tom·ar·i·ly** \,kəstə'merəlē\ *adv* — **cus·tom·ary** \'kəstə,merē\ *adj* — **custom–built** *adj* — **cus·tom–made** *adj*

cus·tom·er \'kəstəmər\ *n* : buyer

cut \'kət\ *vb* **cut**; **cut·ting 1** : penetrate or divide with a sharp edge **2** : experience the growth of (a tooth) through the gum **3** : shorten **4** : remove by severing **5** : intersect ~ *n* **1** : something separated by cutting **2** : reduction — **cut in** *vb* : thrust oneself between others

cu·ta·ne·ous \kyü'tānēəs\ *adj* : relating to the skin

cute \'kyüt\ *adj* **cut·er; -est** : pretty

cu·ti·cle \'kyütikəl\ *n* : outer layer (as of skin)

cut·lass \'kətləs\ *n* : short heavy curved sword

cut·lery \-lərē\ *n* : cutting utensils

cut·let \-lət\ *n* : slice of meat

cut·ter \'kətər\ *n* **1** : tool or machine for cutting **2** : small armed motorboat **3** : light sleigh

cut·throat *n* : murderer ~ *adj* : ruthless

-cy \sē\ *n suffix* **1** : action or practice **2** : rank or office **3** : body **4** : state or quality

cy·a·nide \'sīə,nīd, -nəd\ *n* : poisonous chemical salt

cy·ber- *comb form* : computer : computer network

cy·ber·space \'sībər,spās\ *n* : online world of the Internet

cy·cle \'sīkəl, *4 also* 'sikəl\ *n* **1** : period of time for a series of repeated events **2** : recurring round of events **3** : long period of time **4** : bicycle or motorcycle ~ *vb* **-cled; -cling** : ride a cycle — **cy·clic** \'sīklik, 'sik-\, **cy·cli·cal** \-əl\ *adj* — **cy·clist** \'sīklist, 'sik-\

cy·clone \'sī,klōn\ *n* : tornado — **cy·clon·ic** \sī'klänik\ *adj*

cy·clo·pe·dia, cy·clo·pae·dia \,sīklə-'pēdēə\ *n* : encyclopedia

cyl·in·der \'siləndər\ *n* **1** : long round body or figure **2** : rotating chamber in a revolver **3** : piston chamber in an engine — **cy·lin·dri·cal** \sə'lindri-kəl\ *adj*

cym·bal \'simbəl\ *n* : one of 2 concave brass plates clashed together

cyn·ic \'sinik\ *n* : one who attributes all actions to selfish motives — **cyn·i·cal** \-ikəl\ *adj* — **cyn·i·cism** \-ə,sizəm\ *n*

cy·no·sure \'sīnə,shùr, 'sin-\ *n* : center of attraction

cy·press \'sīprəs\ *n* : evergreen tree related to the pines

cyst \'sist\ *n* : abnormal bodily sac — **cys·tic** \'sistik\ *adj*

czar \'zär\ *n* : ruler of Russia until 1917 — **czar·ist** *n or adj*

D

d \'dē\ *n, pl* **d's** *or* **ds** \'dēz\ : 4th letter of the alphabet

¹dab \'dab\ *n* : gentle touch or stroke ~ *vb* **-bb-** : touch or apply lightly

²dab *n* : small amount

dab·ble \'dabəl\ *vb* **-bled; -bling 1** : splash **2** : work without serious effort — **dab·bler** \-blər\ *n*

dachs·hund \'däks,hùnt\ *n* : small dog with a long body and short legs

dad \'dad\ *n* : father

dad·dy \'dadē\ *n, pl* **-dies** : father

daf·fo·dil \'dafə,dil\ *n* : narcissus with trumpetlike flowers

daft \'daft\ *adj* : foolish — **daft·ness** *n*

dag·ger \'dagər\ *n* : knife for stabbing

dahl·ia \'dalyə, 'däl-\ *n* : tuberous herb with showy flowers

dai·ly \'dālē\ *adj* **1** : occurring, done, or used every day or every weekday **2** : computed in terms of one day ~ *n, pl* **-lies** : daily newspaper — **daily** *adv*

dain·ty \'dāntē\ *n, pl* **-ties** : something delicious ~ *adj* **-ti·er; -est** : delicately pretty — **dain·ti·ly** *adv* — **dain·ti·ness** *n*

dairy \'darē\ *n, pl* **-ies** : farm that produces or company that processes milk — **dairy·maid** *n* — **dairy·man** \-mən, -,man\ *n*

da·is \'dāəs\ *n* : raised platform (as for a speaker)

dai·sy \'dāzē\ *n, pl* **-sies** : tall leafy-stemmed plant bearing showy flowers

dale \'dāl\ *n* : valley

dal·ly \'dalē\ *vb* **-lied; -ly·ing 1** : flirt **2** : dawdle — **dal·li·ance** \-əns\ *n*

dal·ma·tian \dal'māshən\ *n* : large dog having a spotted white coat

¹dam \'dam\ *n* : female parent of a domestic animal

²dam *n* : barrier to hold back water — **dam** *vb*

dam·age \'damij\ *n* **1** : loss or harm due to injury **2** *pl* : compensation for loss or injury ~ *vb* **-aged; -ag·ing** : do damage to

dam·ask \'daməsk\ *n* : firm lustrous figured fabric

dame \'dām\ *n* : woman of rank or authority

damn \'dam\ *vb* **1** : condemn to hell **2** : curse — **dam·na·ble** \-nəbəl\ *adj* — **dam·na·tion** \dam'nāshən\ *n* — **damned** *adj*

damp \'damp\ *n* : moisture ~ *vb* **1** : reduce the draft in **2** : restrain **3** : moisten ~ *adj* : moist — **damp·ness** *n*

damp·en \'dampən\ *vb* **1** : diminish in activity or vigor **2** : make or become damp

damp·er \'dampər\ *n* : movable plate to regulate a flue draft

dam·sel \'damzəl\ *n* : young woman

dance \'dans\ *vb* **danced; danc·ing** : move rhythmically to music ~ *n* : act of dancing or a gathering for dancing — **danc·er** *n*

dan·de·li·on \'dand³l,īən\ *n* : common yellow-flowered herb

dan·der \'dandər\ *n* : temper

dan·druff \'dandrəf\ *n* : whitish thin dry scales of skin on the scalp

dan·dy \'dandē\ *n, pl* **-dies 1** : man too concerned with clothes **2** : something excellent ~ *adj* **-di·er; -est** : very good

dan·ger \'dānjər\ *n* **1** : exposure to injury or evil **2** : something that may cause injury — **dan·ger·ous** \'dānjərəs\ *adj*

dan·gle \'daŋgəl\ *vb* **-gled; -gling 1** : hang and swing freely **2** : be left without support or connection **3** : allow or cause to hang **4** : offer as an inducement

dank \'daŋk\ *adj* : unpleasantly damp

dap·per \'dapər\ *adj* : neat and stylishly dressed

dap·ple \'dapəl\ *vb* **-pled; -pling** : mark with colored spots

dare \'dar\ *vb* **dared; dar·ing 1** : have sufficient courage **2** : urge or provoke to contend — **dare** *n* — **dar·ing** \'darin\ *n or adj*

dare·dev·il *n* : recklessly bold person

dark \'därk\ *adj* **1** : having little or no light **2** : not light in color **3** : gloomy

~ *n* : absence of light — **dark·en** \-ən\ *vb* — **dark·ly** *adv* — **dark·ness** *n*

dar·ling \'därliŋ\ *n* **1** : beloved **2** : favorite ~ *adj* **1** : dearly loved **2** : very pleasing

darn \'därn\ *vb* : mend with interlacing stitches — **darn·er** *n*

dart \'därt\ *n* **1** : small pointed missile **2** *pl* : game of throwing darts at a target **3** : tapering fold in a garment **4** : quick movement ~ *vb* : move suddenly or rapidly

dash \'dash\ *vb* **1** : smash **2** : knock or hurl violently **3** : ruin **4** : perform or finish hastily **5** : move quickly ~ *n* **1** : sudden burst, splash, or stroke **2** : punctuation mark — **3** : tiny amount **4** : showiness or liveliness **5** : sudden rush **6** : short race **7** : dashboard

dash·board *n* : instrument panel

dash·ing \'dashiŋ\ *adj* : dapper and charming

das·tard \'dastərd\ *n* : one who sneakingly commits malicious acts

das·tard·ly \-lē\ *adj* : base or malicious

da·ta \'dātə, 'dat-, 'dät-\ *n sing or pl* : factual information

da·ta·base \-,bās\ *n* : data organized for computer search

¹**date** \'dāt\ *n* : edible fruit of a palm

²**date** *n* **1** : day, month, or year when something is done or made **2** : historical time period **3** : social engagement or the person one goes out with ~ *vb* **dat·ed; dat·ing** **1** : determine or record the date of **2** : have a date with **3** : originate — **to date** : up to now

dat·ed \-əd\ *adj* : old-fashioned

da·tum \'dātəm, 'dat-, 'dät-\ *n, pl* **-ta** \-ə\ *or* **-tums** : piece of data

daub \'dob\ *vb* : smear ~ *n* : something daubed on — **daub·er** *n*

daugh·ter \'dotər\ *n* : human female offspring

daugh·ter–in–law *n, pl* **daughters–in–law** : wife of one's son

daunt \'dont\ *vb* : lessen the courage of

daunt·less \-ləs\ *adj* : fearless

dav·en·port \'davən,pōrt\ *n* : sofa

daw·dle \'dōd'l\ *vb* **-dled; -dling** **1** : waste time **2** : loiter

dawn \'don\ *vb* **1** : grow light as the sun rises **2** : begin to appear, develop, or be understood ~ *n* **1** : first appearance (as of daylight)

day \'dā\ *n* **1** : period of light between one night and the next **2** : 24 hours **3** : specified date **4** : particular time or age **5** : period of work for a day — **day·light** *n* — **day·time** *n*

day·break *n* : dawn

day·dream *n* : fantasy of wish fulfillment — **daydream** *vb*

daylight saving time *n* : time one hour ahead of standard time

daze \'dāz\ *vb* **dazed; daz·ing** **1** : stun by a blow **2** : dazzle — **daze** *n*

daz·zle \'dazəl\ *vb* **-zled; -zling** **1** : overpower with light **2** : impress greatly — **dazzle** *n*

DDT \,dē,dē'tē\ *n* : long-lasting insecticide

dea·con \'dēkən\ *n* : subordinate church officer

dea·con·ess \'dēkənəs\ *n* : woman who assists in church ministry

dead \'ded\ *adj* **1** : lifeless **2** : unresponsive or inactive **3** : exhausted **4** : obsolete **5** : precise ~ *n, pl* **dead** **1** : one that is dead — usu. with the **2** : most lifeless time ~ *adv* **1** : completely **2** : directly — **dead·en** \'ded'n\ *vb*

dead·beat *n* : one who will not pay debts

dead end *n* : end of a street with no exit — **dead–end** *adj*

dead heat *n* : tie in a contest

dead·line *n* : time by which something must be finished

dead·lock *n* : struggle that neither side can win — **deadlock** *vb*

dead·ly \'dedlē\ *adj* **-li·er; -est** **1** : capable of causing death **2** : very accurate **3** : fatal to spiritual progress **4** : suggestive of death **5** : very great ~ *adv* : extremely — **dead·li·ness** *n*

dead·pan *adj* : expressionless — **deadpan** *n or vb or adv*

dead·wood *n* : something useless

deaf \'def\ *adj* : unable or unwilling to hear — **deaf·en** \-ən\ *vb* — **deaf·ness** *n*

deaf–mute *n* : deaf person unable to speak

deal \'dēl\ *n* **1** : indefinite quantity **2** : distribution of playing cards **3** : negotiation or agreement **4** : treatment received **5** : bargain ~ *vb* **dealt** \'delt\; **deal·ing** \'dēliŋ\ **1** : distribute playing cards **2** : be concerned with **3** : administer or deliver **4** : take action **5** : sell **6** : reach a state of acceptance — **deal·er** n — **deal·ing** n

dean \'dēn\ n **1** : head of a group of clergy members **2** : university or school administrator **3** : senior member

dear \'dir\ adj **1** : highly valued or loved **2** : expensive ~ n : loved one — **dear·ly** adv — **dear·ness** n

dearth \'dərth\ n : scarcity

death \'deth\ n **1** : end of life **2** : cause of loss of life **3** : state of being dead **4** : destruction or extinction — **death·less** adj — **death·ly** adj or adv

de·ba·cle \di'bäkəl, -'bakəl\ n : disaster or fiasco

de·bar \di'bär\ vb : bar from something

de·bark \-'bärk\ vb : disembark — **de·bar·ka·tion** \,dē,bär'kāshən\ n

de·base \di'bās\ vb : disparage — **de·base·ment** n

de·bate \-'bāt\ vb **-bat·ed; -bat·ing** : discuss a question by argument — **de·bat·able** adj — **debate** n — **de·bat·er** n

de·bauch \-'bȯch\ vb : seduce or corrupt — **de·bauch·ery** \-ərē\ n

de·bil·i·tate \-'bilə,tāt\ vb **-tat·ed; -tat·ing** : make ill or weak

de·bil·i·ty \-'bilətē\ n, pl **-ties** : physical weakness

deb·it \'debət\ n : account entry of a payment or debt ~ vb : record as a debit

deb·o·nair \,debə'nar\ adj : suave

de·bris \də'brē, dā-; 'dä,brē\ n, pl **-bris** \-'brēz, -,brēz\ : remains of something destroyed

debt \'det\ n **1** : sin **2** : something owed **3** : state of owing — **debt·or** \-ər\ n

de·bunk \dē'bəŋk\ vb : expose as false

de·but \'dā,byü, dā'byü\ n **1** : first public appearance **2** : formal entrance into society — **debut** vb — **deb·u·tante** \'debyü,tänt\ n

de·cade \'dek,ād, -əd; de'kād\ n : 10 years

dec·a·dence \'dekədəns, di'kād³ns\ n : deterioration — **dec·a·dent** \-ənt, -³nt\ adj or n

de·cal \'dē,kal, di'kal, 'dekəl\ n : picture or design for transfer from prepared paper

de·camp \di'kamp\ vb : depart suddenly

de·cant \di'kant\ vb : pour gently

de·cant·er \-ər\ n : ornamental bottle

de·cap·i·tate \di'kapə,tāt\ vb **-tat·ed; -tat·ing** : behead — **de·cap·i·ta·tion** \-,kapə'tāshən\ n

de·cay \di'kā\ vb **1** : decline in condition **2** : decompose — **decay** n

de·cease \-'sēs\ n : death — **decease** vb

de·ceit \-'sēt\ n **1** : deception **2** : dishonesty — **de·ceit·ful** \-fəl\ adj — **de·ceit·ful·ly** adv — **de·ceit·ful·ness** n

de·ceive \-'sēv\ vb **-ceived; -ceiv·ing** : trick or mislead — **de·ceiv·er** n

de·cel·er·ate \dē'selə,rāt\ vb **-at·ed; -at·ing** : slow down

De·cem·ber \di'sembər\ n : 12th month of the year having 31 days

de·cent \'dēs³nt\ adj **1** : good, right, or just **2** : clothed **3** : not obscene **4** : fairly good — **de·cen·cy** \-³nsē\ n — **de·cent·ly** adv

de·cep·tion \di'sepshən\ n **1** : act or fact of deceiving **2** : fraud — **de·cep·tive** \-'septiv\ adj — **de·cep·tive·ly** adv — **de·cep·tive·ness** n

de·cide \di'sīd\ vb **-cid·ed; -cid·ing 1** : make a choice or judgment **2** : bring to a conclusion **3** : cause to decide

de·cid·ed adj **1** : unquestionable **2** : resolute — **de·cid·ed·ly** adv

de·cid·u·ous \di'sijəwəs\ adj : having leaves that fall annually

dec·i·mal \'desəməl\ n : fraction in which the denominator is a power of 10 expressed by a point (**decimal point**) placed at the left of the numerator — **decimal** adj

de·ci·pher \di'sīfər\ vb : make out the meaning of — **de·ci·pher·able** adj

de·ci·sion \-'sizhən\ n **1** : act or result of deciding **2** : determination

de·ci·sive \-'sīsiv\ adj **1** : having the power to decide **2** : conclusive **3** : showing determination — **de·ci·sive·ly** adv — **de·ci·sive·ness** n

deck \'dek\ n **1** : floor of a ship **2** : pack of playing cards ~ vb **1** : array or dress up **2** : knock down

de·claim \di'klām\ vb : speak loudly or impressively — **dec·la·ma·tion** \,deklə'māshən\ n

de·clare \di'klar\ vb **-clared; -clar·ing 1** : make known formally **2** : state emphatically — **dec·la·ra·tion** \,deklə'rāshən\ n — **de·clar·a·tive** \di'klarətiv\ adj — **de·clar·a·to·ry** \di'klarə,tōrē\ adj — **de·clar·er** n

de·clen·sion \di'klenchən\ n : inflectional forms of a noun, pronoun, or adjective

de·cline \di'klīn\ vb **-clined; -clin·ing** 1 : turn or slope downward 2 : wane 3 : refuse to accept 4 : inflect ~ n 1 : gradual wasting away 2 : change to a lower state or level 3 : a descending slope — **dec·li·na·tion** \,dek-lə'nāshən\ n

de·code \dē'kōd\ vb : decipher (a coded message) — **de·cod·er** n

de·com·mis·sion \,dēkə'mishən\ vb : remove from service

de·com·pose \,dēkəm'pōz\ vb 1 : separate into parts 2 : decay — **de·com·po·si·tion** \dē,kämpə'zishən\ n

de·con·ges·tant \,dēkən'jestənt\ n : agent that relieves congestion

de·cor, dé·cor \dā'kȯr, 'dā,kȯr\ n : room design or decoration

dec·o·rate \'dekə,rāt\ vb **-rat·ed; -rat·ing** 1 : add something attractive to 2 : honor with a medal — **dec·o·ra·tion** \,dekə'rāshən\ n — **dec·o·ra·tive** \'dekərətiv\ adj — **dec·o·ra·tor** \'dekə,rātər\ n

de·co·rum \di'kōrəm\ n : proper behavior — **dec·o·rous** \'dekərəs, di-'kōrəs\ adj

de·coy \'dē,kȯi, di'-\ n : something that tempts or draws attention from another ~ vb : tempt

de·crease \di'krēs\ vb **-creased; -creas·ing** : grow or cause to grow less — **decrease** \'dē,krēs\ n

de·cree \di'krē\ n : official order — **de·cree** vb

de·crep·it \di'krepət\ adj : impaired by age

de·cre·scen·do \,dākrə'shendō\ adv or adj : with a decrease in volume

de·cry \di'krī\ vb : express strong disapproval of

ded·i·cate \'dedi,kāt\ vb **-cat·ed; -cat·ing** 1 : set apart for a purpose (as honor or worship) 2 : address to someone as a compliment — **ded·i·ca·tion** \,dedi'kāshən\ n — **ded·i·ca·to·ry** \'dedikə,tōrē\ adj

de·duce \di'düs, -'dyüs\ vb **-duced; -duc·ing** : derive by reasoning — **de·duc·ible** adj

de·duct \di'dəkt\ vb : subtract — **de·duct·ible** adj

de·duc·tion \-'dəkshən\ n 1 : subtrac-

tion 2 : reasoned conclusion — **de·duc·tive** \-'dəktiv\ adj

deed \'dēd\ n 1 : exploit 2 : document showing ownership ~ vb : convey by deed

deem \'dēm\ vb : think

deep \'dēp\ adj 1 : extending far or a specified distance down, back, within, or outward 2 : occupied 3 : dark and rich in color 4 : low in tone ~ adv 1 : deeply 2 : far along in time ~ n : deep place — **deep·en** \'dēpən\ vb — **deep·ly** adv

deep–seat·ed \-'sētəd\ adj : firmly established

deer \'dir\ n, pl deer : ruminant mammal with antlers in the male — **deer·skin** n

de·face \di'fās\ vb : mar the surface of — **de·face·ment** n — **de·fac·er** n

de·fame \di'fām\ vb **-famed; -fam·ing** : injure the reputation of — **def·a·ma·tion** \,defə'māshən\ n — **de·fam·a·to·ry** \di'famə,tōrē\ adj

de·fault \di'fȯlt\ n : failure in a duty — **default** vb — **de·fault·er** n

de·feat \di'fēt\ vb 1 : frustrate 2 : win victory over ~ n : loss of a battle or contest

def·e·cate \'defi,kāt\ vb **-cat·ed; -cat·ing** : discharge feces from the bowels — **def·e·ca·tion** \,defi'kāshən\ n

de·fect \'dē,fekt, di'fekt\ n : imperfection ~ \di'-\ vb : desert — **de·fec·tion** \-'fekshən\ n — **de·fec·tor** \-'fektər\ n

de·fec·tive \di'fektiv\ adj : faulty or deficient — **defective** n

de·fend \-'fend\ vb 1 : protect from danger or harm 2 : take the side of — **de·fend·er** n

de·fen·dant \-'fendənt\ n : person charged or sued in a court

de·fense \-'fens\ n 1 : act of defending 2 : something that defends 3 : party, group, or team that opposes another — **de·fense·less** adj — **de·fen·si·ble** adj — **de·fen·sive** adj or n

¹**de·fer** \di'fər\ vb **-rr-** : postpone — **de·fer·ment** \di'fərmənt\ n — **de·fer·ra·ble** \-əbəl\ adj

²**defer** vb **-rr-** : yield to the opinion or wishes of another — **def·er·ence** \'defrəns\ n — **def·er·en·tial** \,defə'renchəl\ adj

de·fi·ance \di'fīəns\ n : disposition to resist — **de·fi·ant** \-ənt\ adj

de·fi·cient \di'fishənt\ adj 1 : lacking

something necessary **2** : not up to standard — **de·fi·cien·cy** \-'fishən-sē\ n

def·i·cit \'defəsət\ n : shortage esp. in money

de·file \di'fīl\ vb -filed; -fil·ing **1** : make filthy or corrupt **2** : profane or dishonor — **de·file·ment** n

de·fine \di'fīn\ vb -fined; -fin·ing **1** : fix or mark the limits of **2** : clarify in outline **3** : set forth the meaning of — **de·fin·able** adj — **de·fin·ably** adv — **de·fin·er** n — **def·i·ni·tion** \defə'nishən\ n

def·i·nite \'defənət\ adj **1** : having distinct limits **2** : clear in meaning, intent, or identity **3** : typically designating an identified or immediately identifiable person or thing — **def·i·nite·ly** adv

de·fin·i·tive \di'finətiv\ adj **1** : conclusive **2** : authoritative

de·flate \di'flāt\ vb -flat·ed; -flat·ing **1** : release air or gas from **2** : reduce — **de·fla·tion** \-'flāshən\ n

de·flect \-'flekt\ vb : turn aside — **de·flec·tion** \-'flekshən\ n

de·fog \-'fög, -'fäg\ vb : remove condensed moisture from — **de·fog·ger** n

de·fo·li·ate \dē'fōlē,āt\ vb -at·ed; -at·ing : deprive of leaves esp. prematurely — **de·fo·li·ant** \-lēənt\ n — **de·fo·li·a·tion** \-,fōlē'āshən\ n

de·form \di'förm\ vb **1** : distort **2** : disfigure — **de·for·ma·tion** \,dē,för'māshən, ,defər-\ n — **de·for·mi·ty** \di'förmətē\ n

de·fraud \di'fröd\ vb : cheat

de·fray \-'frā\ vb : pay

de·frost \-'fröst\ vb **1** : thaw out **2** : free from ice — **de·frost·er** n

deft \'deft\ adj : quick and skillful — **deft·ly** adv — **deft·ness** n

de·funct \di'fəŋkt\ adj : dead

de·fy \-'fī\ vb -fied; -fy·ing **1** : challenge **2** : boldly refuse to obey

de·gen·er·ate \di'jenərət\ adj : degraded or corrupt ∼ n : degenerate person ∼ \-ə,rāt\ vb : become degenerate — **de·gen·er·a·cy** \-ərəsē\ n — **de·gen·er·a·tion** \-jenə'rāshən\ n — **de·gen·er·a·tive** \-'jenə,rātiv\ adj

de·grade \di'grād\ vb **1** : reduce from a higher to a lower rank or degree **2** : debase **3** : decompose — **de·grad-**

able \-əbəl\ adj — **deg·ra·da·tion** \,degrə'dāshən\ n

de·gree \di'grē\ n **1** : step in a series **2** : extent, intensity, or scope **3** : title given to a college graduate **4** : a 360th part of the circumference of a circle **5** : unit for measuring temperature

de·hy·drate \dē'hī,drāt\ vb **1** : remove water from **2** : lose liquid — **de·hy·dra·tion** \,dēhī'drāshən\ n

de·i·fy \'dēə,fī, 'dā-\ vb -fied; -fy·ing : make a god of — **de·i·fi·ca·tion** \,dēəfə'kāshən, ,dā-\ n

deign \'dān\ vb : condescend

de·i·ty \'dēətē, 'dā-\ n, pl -ties **1** cap : God **2** : a god or goddess

de·ject·ed \di'jektəd\ adj : sad — **de·jec·tion** \-shən\ n

de·lay \di'lā\ n : a putting off of something ∼ vb **1** : postpone **2** : stop or hinder for a time

de·lec·ta·ble \di'lektəbəl\ adj : delicious

del·e·gate \'deligət, -,gāt\ n : representative ∼ \-,gāt\ vb -gat·ed; -gat·ing **1** : entrust to another **2** : appoint as one's delegate — **del·e·ga·tion** \,deli'gāshən\ n

de·lete \di'lēt\ vb -let·ed; -let·ing : eliminate something written — **de·le·tion** \-'lēshən\ n

del·e·te·ri·ous \,delə'tirēəs\ adj : harmful

de·lib·er·ate \di'libərət\ adj **1** : determined after careful thought **2** : intentional **3** : not hurried ∼ \-ə,rāt\ vb -at·ed; -at·ing : consider carefully — **de·lib·er·ate·ly** adv — **de·lib·er·ate·ness** n — **de·lib·er·a·tion** \-,libə'rāshən\ n — **de·lib·er·a·tive** \-'libə,rātiv, -rət-\ adj

del·i·ca·cy \'delikəsē\ n, pl -cies **1** : something special and pleasing to eat **2** : fineness **3** : frailty

del·i·cate \'delikət\ adj **1** : subtly pleasing to the senses **2** : dainty and charming **3** : sensitive or fragile **4** : requiring fine skill or tact — **del·i·cate·ly** adv

del·i·ca·tes·sen \,delikə'tes²n\ n : store that sells ready-to-eat food

de·li·cious \di'lishəs\ adj : very pleasing esp. in taste or aroma — **de·li·cious·ly** adv — **de·li·cious·ness** n

1de·light \di'līt\ n **1** : great pleasure **2** : source of great pleasure ∼ vb **1** : take great pleasure **2** : satisfy greatly — **de·light·ful** \-fəl\ *adj* — **de·light·ful·ly** *adv*

de·lin·eate \di'linē,āt\ *vb* -eat·ed; -eat·ing : sketch or portray — **de·lin·ea·tion** \-,linē'āshən\ *n*

de·lin·quent \-'liŋkwənt\ *n* : delinquent person ~ *adj* **1** : violating duty or law **2** : overdue in payment — **de·lin·quen·cy** \-kwənsē\ *n*

de·lir·i·um \di'lirēəm\ *n* : mental disturbance — **de·lir·i·ous** \-ēəs\ *adj*

de·liv·er \di'livər\ *vb* **1** : set free **2** : hand over **3** : assist in birth **4** : send to an intended destination — **de·liv·er·ance** \-ərəns\ *n* — **de·liv·er·er** *n* — **de·liv·ery** \-ərē\ *n*

dell \'del\ *n* : small secluded valley

del·ta \'deltə\ *n* : triangle of land at the mouth of a river

de·lude \di'lüd\ *vb* -lud·ed; -lud·ing : mislead or deceive

del·uge \'delyüj\ *n* **1** : flood **2** : drenching rain ~ *vb* -uged; -ug·ing **1** : flood **2** : overwhelm

de·lu·sion \di'lüzhən\ *n* : false belief

de·luxe \di'lůks, -'ləks, -'lüks\ *adj* : very luxurious or elegant

delve \'delv\ *vb* delved; delv·ing **1** : dig **2** : seek information in records

dem·a·gogue, dem·a·gog \'demə,gäg\ *n* : politician who appeals to emotion and prejudice — **dem·a·gogu·ery** \-,gägərē\ *n* — **dem·a·gogy** \-,gägē, -,gäjē\ *n*

de·mand \di'mand\ *n* **1** : act of demanding **2** : something claimed as due **3** : ability and desire to buy **4** : urgent need ~ *vb* **1** : ask for with authority **2** : require

de·mar·cate \di'mär,kāt, 'dē,mär-\ *vb* -cat·ed; -cat·ing : mark the limits of — **de·mar·ca·tion** \,dē,mär'kā-shən\ *n*

de·mean \di'mēn\ *vb* : degrade

de·mean·or \-'mēnər\ *n* : behavior

de·ment·ed \-'mentəd\ *adj* : crazy

de·mer·it \-'merət\ *n* : mark given an offender

demi·god \'demi,gäd\ *n* : mythological being less powerful than a god

de·mise \di'mīz\ *n* **1** : death **2** : loss of status

demi·tasse \'demi,tas\ *n* : small cup of coffee

de·mo·bi·lize \di'mōbə,līz, dē-\ *vb* : disband from military service — **de-mo·bi·li·za·tion** \-,mōbələ'zāshən\ *n*

de·moc·ra·cy \di'mäkrəsē\ *n, pl* -cies **1** : government in which the supreme power is held by the people **2** : political unit with democratic government

dem·o·crat \'demə,krat\ *n* : adherent of democracy

dem·o·crat·ic \,demə'kratik\ *adj* : relating to or favoring democracy — **dem·o·crat·i·cal·ly** \-tiklē\ *adv* — **de·moc·ra·tize** \di'mäkrə,tīz\ *vb*

de·mol·ish \di'mälish\ *vb* **1** : tear down or smash **2** : put an end to — **de·mo·li·tion** \,demə'lishən, dē-\ *n*

de·mon \'dēmən\ *n* : evil spirit — **de·mon·ic** \di'mänik\ *adj*

dem·on·strate \'demən,strāt\ *vb* -strat·ed; -strat·ing **1** : show clearly or publicly **2** : prove **3** : explain — **de·mon·stra·ble** \di'mänstrəbəl\ *adj* — **de·mon·stra·bly** \-blē\ *adv* — **dem·on·stra·tion** \,demən'strā-shən\ *n* — **de·mon·stra·tive** \di-'mänstrətiv\ *adj or n* — **dem·on·stra·tor** \'demən,strātər\ *n*

de·mor·al·ize \di'mȯrə,līz\ *vb* : destroy the enthusiasm of

de·mote \di'mōt\ *vb* -mot·ed; -mot·ing : reduce to a lower rank — **de·mo·tion** \-'mōshən\ *n*

de·mur \di'mər\ *vb* -rr- : object — **de·mur** *n*

de·mure \di'myůr\ *adj* : modest — **de·mure·ly** *adv*

den \'den\ *n* **1** : animal's shelter **2** : hiding place **3** : cozy private little room

de·na·ture \dē'nāchər\ *vb* -tured; -tur·ing : make (alcohol) unfit for drinking

de·ni·al \di'nīəl\ *n* : rejection of a request or of the validity of a statement

den·i·grate \'deni,grāt\ *vb* -grat·ed; -grat·ing : speak ill of

den·im \'denəm\ *n* **1** : durable twilled cotton fabric **2** *pl* : pants of denim

den·i·zen \'denəzən\ *n* : inhabitant

de·nom·i·na·tion \di,nämə'nāshən\ *n* **1** : religious body **2** : value or size in a series — **de·nom·i·na·tion·al** \-shənəl\ *adj*

de·nom·i·na·tor \-'nämə,nātər\ *n* : part of a fraction below the line

de·note \di'nōt\ *vb* **1** : mark out plainly **2** : mean — **de·no·ta·tion** \,dēnō'tāshən\ *n* — **de·no·ta·tive** \'dēnō,tātiv, di'nōtətiv\ *adj*

de·noue·ment \ˌdā.nü'mäⁿ\ n : final outcome (as of a drama)

de·nounce \di'naúns\ vb **-nounced; -nounc·ing 1** : pronounce blameworthy or evil **2** : inform against

dense \'dens\ adj **dens·er; -est 1** : thick, compact, or crowded **2** : stupid — **dense·ly** adv — **dense·ness** n — **den·si·ty** \'densətē\ n

dent \'dent\ n : small depression — **dent** vb

den·tal \'dentᵊl\ adj : relating to teeth or dentistry

den·ti·frice \'dentəfrəs\ n : preparation for cleaning teeth

den·tin \'dentᵊn\, **den·tine** \'den,tēn, ˌden'-\ n : bonelike component of teeth

den·tist \'dentist\ n : one who cares for and replaces teeth — **den·tist·ry** n

den·ture \'denchər\ n : artificial teeth

de·nude \di'nüd, -'nyüd\ vb **-nud·ed; -nud·ing** : strip of covering

de·nun·ci·a·tion \di,nənsē'āshən\ n : act of denouncing

de·ny \-'nī\ vb **-nied; -ny·ing 1** : declare untrue **2** : disavow **3** : refuse to grant

de·odor·ant \dē'ōdərənt\ n : preparation to prevent unpleasant odors — **de·odor·ize** \-ˌrīz\ vb

de·part \di'pärt\ vb **1** : go away or away from **2** : die — **de·par·ture** \-'pärchər\ n

de·part·ment \di'pärtmənt\ n **1** : area of responsibility or interest **2** : functional division — **de·part·men·tal** \di,pärt'mentᵊl, ˌdē-\ adj

de·pend \di'pend\ vb **1** : rely for support **2** : be determined by or based on something else — **de·pend·abil·i·ty** \-,pendə'bilətē\ n — **de·pend·able** adj — **de·pen·dence** \di'pendəns\ n — **de·pen·den·cy** \-dənsē\ n — **de·pen·dent** \-ənt\ adj or n

de·pict \di'pikt\ vb : show by or as if by a picture — **de·pic·tion** \-'pikshən\ n

de·plete \di'plēt\ vb **-plet·ed; -plet·ing** : use up resources of — **de·ple·tion** \-'plēshən\ n

de·plore \-'plōr\ vb **-plored; -plor·ing** : regret strongly — **de·plor·able** \-əbəl\ adj

de·ploy \-'plói\ vb : spread out for battle — **de·ploy·ment** \-mənt\ n

de·port \di'pōrt\ vb **1** : behave **2** : send out of the country — **de·por-**

ta·tion \ˌdē,pōr'tāshən\ n — **de·port·ment** \di'pōrtmənt\ n

de·pose \-'pōz\ vb **-posed; -pos·ing 1** : remove (a ruler) from office **2** : testify — **de·po·si·tion** \ˌdepə'zishən, ˌdē-\ n

de·pos·it \di'päzət\ vb **-it·ed; -it·ing** : place esp. for safekeeping ~ n **1** : state of being deposited **2** : something deposited **3** : act of depositing **4** : natural accumulation — **de·pos·i·tor** \-'päzətər\ n

de·pos·i·to·ry \di'päzə,tōrē\ n, pl **-ries** : place for deposit

de·pot \I usu 'dēpō, 2 usu 'dēp-\ n **1** : place for storage **2** : bus or railroad station

de·prave \di'prāv\ vb **-praved; -prav·ing** : corrupt morally — **de·praved** adj — **de·prav·i·ty** \-'pravətē\ n

dep·re·cate \'depri,kāt\ vb **-cat·ed; -cat·ing 1** : express disapproval of **2** : belittle — **dep·re·ca·tion** \ˌdepri'kāshən\ n — **dep·re·ca·to·ry** \'depri,kə,tōrē\ adj

de·pre·ci·ate \di'prēshē,āt\ vb **-at·ed; -at·ing 1** : lessen in value **2** : belittle — **de·pre·ci·a·tion** \-,prēshē'āshən\ n

dep·re·da·tion \ˌdeprə'dāshən\ n : a laying waste or plundering — **dep·re·date** \'deprə,dāt\ vb

de·press \di'pres\ vb **1** : press down **2** : lessen the activity or force of **3** : discourage **4** : decrease the market value of — **de·pres·sant** \-ᵊnt\ n or adj — **de·pressed** adj — **de·pres·sive** \-iv\ adj or n — **de·pres·sor** \-ər\ n

de·pres·sion \di'preshən\ n **1** : act of depressing or state of being depressed **2** : depressed place **3** : period of low economic activity

de·prive \-'prīv\ vb **-prived; -priv·ing** : take or keep something away from — **de·pri·va·tion** \ˌdeprə'vāshən\ n

depth \'depth\ n, pl **depths 1** : something that is deep **2** : distance down from a surface **3** : distance from front to back **4** : quality of being deep

dep·u·ta·tion \ˌdepyə'tāshən\ n : delegation

dep·u·ty \'depyətē\ n, pl **-ties** : person appointed to act for another — **dep·u·tize** \-yə,tīz\ vb

de·rail \di'rāl\ vb : leave the rails — **de·rail·ment** n

de·range \-'rānj\ vb **-ranged; -rang-**

ing 1 : disarrange or upset 2 : make insane — **de·range·ment** n

der·by \'dǝrbē, Brit 'där-\ n, pl -bies 1 : horse race 2 : stiff felt hat with dome-shaped crown

de·reg·u·late \dē'regyǝˌlāt\ vb : remove restrictions on — **de·reg·u·la·tion** \-ˌregyǝ'lāshǝn\ n

der·e·lict \'derǝˌlikt\ adj 1 : abandoned 2 : negligent ~ n 1 : something abandoned 2 : bum — **der·e·lic·tion** \ˌderǝ'likshǝn\ n

de·ride \di'rīd\ vb -rid·ed; -rid·ing : make fun of — **de·ri·sion** \-'ri-zhǝn\ n — **de·ri·sive** \-'rīsiv\ adj — **de·ri·sive·ly** adv — **de·ri·sive·ness** n

de·rive \di'rīv\ vb -rived; -riv·ing 1 : obtain from a source or parent 2 : come from a certain source 3 : infer or deduce — **der·i·va·tion** \ˌderǝ-'vāshǝn\ n — **de·riv·a·tive** \di'rivǝtiv\ adj or n

der·ma·tol·o·gy \ˌdǝrmǝ'täläjē\ n : study of the skin and its disorders — **der·ma·tol·o·gist** \-jist\ n

de·rog·a·tive \di'rägǝtiv\ adj : derogatory

de·rog·a·to·ry \di'rägǝˌtōrē\ adj : intended to lower the reputation

der·rick \'derik\ n 1 : hoisting apparatus 2 : framework over an oil well

de·scend \di'send\ vb 1 : move or climb down 2 : derive 3 : extend downward 4 : appear suddenly (as in an attack) — **de·scen·dant, de·scen·dent** \-ǝnt\ adj or n — **de·scent** \di'sent\ n

de·scribe \-'skrīb\ vb -scribed; -scrib·ing : represent in words — **de·scrib·able** adj — **de·scrip·tion** \-'skripshǝn\ n — **de·scrip·tive** \-'skriptiv\ adj

de·scry \di'skrī\ vb -scried; -scry·ing : catch sight of

des·e·crate \'desiˌkrāt\ vb -crat·ed; -crat·ing : treat (something sacred) with disrespect — **des·e·cra·tion** \ˌdesi'krāshǝn\ n

de·seg·re·gate \dē'segrǝˌgāt\ vb : eliminate esp. racial segregation in — **de·seg·re·ga·tion** n

¹**des·ert** \'dezǝrt\ n : dry barren region — **desert** adj

²**de·sert** \di'zǝrt\ n : what one deserves

³**de·sert** \di'zǝrt\ vb : abandon — **de·sert·er** n — **de·ser·tion** \-'zǝrshǝn\ n

de·serve \-'zǝrv\ vb -served; -serv·ing : be worthy of

des·ic·cate \'desiˌkāt\ vb -cat·ed; -cat·ing : dehydrate — **des·ic·ca·tion** \ˌdesi'kāshǝn\ n

de·sign \di'zīn\ vb 1 : create and work out the details of 2 : make a pattern or sketch of ~ n 1 : mental project or plan 2 : purpose 3 : preliminary sketch 4 : underlying arrangement of elements 5 : decorative pattern — **de·sign·er** n

des·ig·nate \'dezigˌnāt\ vb -nat·ed; -nat·ing 1 : indicate, specify, or name 2 : appoint — **des·ig·na·tion** \ˌdezig'nāshǝn\ n

de·sire \di'zīr\ vb -sired; -sir·ing 1 : feel desire for 2 : request ~ n 1 : strong conscious impulse to have, be, or do something 2 : something desired — **de·sir·abil·i·ty** \-ˌzīrǝ-'bilǝtē\ n — **de·sir·able** \-'zīrǝbǝl\ adj — **de·sir·able·ness** n — **de·sir·ous** \-'zīrǝs\ adj

de·sist \di'zist, -'sist\ vb : stop

desk \'desk\ n : table esp. for writing and reading

des·o·late \'desǝlǝt, 'dez-\ adj 1 : lifeless 2 : disconsolate ~ \-ˌlāt\ vb -lat·ed; -lat·ing : lay waste — **des·o·la·tion** \ˌdesǝ'lāshǝn, ˌdez-\ n

de·spair \di'spar\ vb : lose all hope ~ n : loss of hope

des·per·a·do \ˌdespǝ'rädō, -'räd-\ n, pl -does or -dos : desperate criminal

des·per·ate \'despǝrǝt\ adj 1 : hopeless 2 : rash 3 : extremely intense — **des·per·ate·ly** adv — **des·per·a·tion** \ˌdespǝ'rāshǝn\ n

de·spi·ca·ble \di'spikǝbǝl, 'despik-\ adj : deserving scorn

de·spise \di'spīz\ vb -spised; -spis·ing : feel contempt for

de·spite \-'spīt\ prep : in spite of

de·spoil \di'spȯil\ vb : strip of possessions or value

de·spon·den·cy \-'spändǝnsē\ n : dejection — **de·spon·dent** \-dǝnt\ adj

des·pot \'despǝt, -ˌpät\ n : tyrant — **des·pot·ic** \des'pätik\ adj — **des·po·tism** \'despǝˌtizǝm\ n

des·sert \di'zǝrt\ n : sweet food, fruit, or cheese ending a meal

des·ti·na·tion \ˌdestǝ'nāshǝn\ n : place where something or someone is going

des·tine \'destən\ vb **-tined; -tin·ing**
1 : designate, assign, or determine in
advance **2** : direct

des·ti·ny \'destənē\ n, pl **-nies** : that
which is to happen in the future

des·ti·tute \'destə,tüt, -,tyüt\ adj **1**
: lacking something **2** : very poor
— **des·ti·tu·tion** \,destə'tüshən,
-'tyü-\ n

de·stroy \di'stroi\ vb : kill or put an
end to

de·stroy·er \-'stroiər\ n **1** : one that
destroys **2** : small speedy warship

de·struc·tion \-'strəkshən\ n **1** : action of destroying **2** : ruin — **de-
struc·ti·bil·i·ty** \-,strəktə'bilətē\ n
— **de·struc·ti·ble** \-'strəktəbəl\ adj
— **de·struc·tive** \-'strəktiv\ adj

de·sul·to·ry \'desəl,tōrē\ adj : aimless

de·tach \di'tach\ vb : separate

de·tached \-'tacht\ adj **1** : separate **2**
: aloof or impartial

de·tach·ment \-'tachmənt\ n **1** : separation **2** : troops or ships on special
service **3** : aloofness **4** : impartiality

de·tail \di'tāl, 'dē,tāl\ n : small item or
part ~ vb : give details of

de·tain \di'tān\ vb **1** : hold in custody
2 : delay

de·tect \di'tekt\ vb : discover — **de-
tect·able** adj — **de·tec·tion** \-'tek-
shən\ n — **de·tec·tor** \-tər\ n

de·tec·tive \-'tektiv\ n : one who investigates crime

dé·tente \dā'tä^nt\ n : relaxation of ten-
sions between nations

de·ten·tion \di'tenchən\ n : confinement

de·ter \-'tər\ vb **-rr-** : discourage or prevent — **de·ter·rence** \-əns\ n — **de-
ter·rent** \-ənt\ adj or n

de·ter·gent \di'tərjənt\ n : cleansing
agent

de·te·ri·o·rate \-'tirēə,rāt\ vb **-rat·ed;**
-rat·ing : make or become worse —
de·te·ri·o·ra·tion \-,tirēə'rāshən\ n

de·ter·mi·na·tion \di,tərmə'nāshən\
n **1** : act of deciding or fixing **2**
: firm purpose

de·ter·mine \-'tərmən\ vb **-mined;**
-min·ing **1** : decide on, establish, or
settle **2** : find out **3** : bring about as a
result

de·test \-'test\ vb : hate — **de·test-
able** adj — **de·tes·ta·tion** \,dē,tes-
'tāshən\ n

det·o·nate \'det^ən,āt\ vb **-nat·ed;**
-nat·ing : explode — **det·o·na·tion**

\,det^ən'āshən\ n — **det·o·na·tor**
\'det^ən,ātər\ n

de·tour \'dē,tůr\ n : temporary indirect
route — **detour** vb

de·tract \di'trakt\ vb : take away —
de·trac·tion \-'trakshən\ n — **de-
trac·tor** \-'traktər\ n

det·ri·ment \'detrəmənt\ n : damage
— **det·ri·men·tal** \,detrə'ment^l\
adj — **det·ri·men·tal·ly** adv

deuce \'düs, 'dyüs\ n **1** : 2 in cards or
dice **2** : tie in tennis **3** : devil — used
as an oath

deut·sche mark \'doichə-\ n : monetary unit of Germany

de·val·ue \dē'val,yü\ vb : reduce the
value of — **de·val·u·a·tion** n

dev·as·tate \'devə,stāt\ vb **-tat·ed;**
-tat·ing : ruin — **dev·as·ta·tion**
\,devə'stāshən\ n

de·vel·op \di'veləp\ vb **1** : grow, increase, or evolve gradually **2** : cause
to grow, increase, or reach full potential — **de·vel·op·er** n — **de·vel-
op·ment** n — **de·vel·op·men·tal**
\-,veləp'ment^l\ adj

de·vi·ate \'dēvē,āt\ vb **-at·ed; -at·ing**
: change esp. from a course or standard — **de·vi·ant** \-vēənt\ adj or n
— **de·vi·ate** \-vēət, -vē,āt\ n — **de-
vi·a·tion** \,dēvē'āshən\ n

de·vice \di'vīs\ n **1** : specialized piece
of equipment or tool **2** : design

dev·il \'devəl\ n **1** : personified
supreme spirit of evil **2** : demon **3**
: wicked person ~ vb **-iled** or **-illed;**
-il·ing or **-il·ling** **1** : season highly **2**
: pester — **dev·il·ish** \'devəlish\ adj
— **dev·il·ry** \'devəlrē\, **dev·il·try**
\-trē\ n

de·vi·ous \'dēvēəs\ adj : tricky

de·vise \di'vīz\ vb **-vised; -vis·ing** **1**
: invent **2** : plot **3** : give by will

de·void \-'vóid\ adj : entirely lacking

de·vote \di'vōt\ vb **-vot·ed; -vot·ing**
: set apart for a special purpose

de·vot·ed adj : faithful

dev·o·tee \,devə'tē, -'tā\ n : ardent follower

de·vo·tion \di'vōshən\ n **1** : prayer —
usu. pl. **2** : loyalty and dedication —
de·vo·tion·al \-shənəl\ adj

de·vour \di'vaůər\ vb : consume rav-
enously — **de·vour·er** n

de·vout \-'vaůt\ adj **1** : devoted to religion **2** : serious — **de·vout·ly** adv
— **de·vout·ness** n

dew \'dü, 'dyü\ *n* : moisture condensed at night — **dew·drop** *n* — **dewy** *adj*

dex·ter·ous \'dekstrəs\ *adj* : skillful with the hands — **dex·ter·i·ty** \dek-'sterətē\ *n* — **dex·ter·ous·ly** *adv*

dex·trose \'dek,strōs\ *n* : plant or blood sugar

di·a·be·tes \,dīə'bētēz, -'bētəs\ *n* : disorder in which the body has too little insulin and too much sugar — **di·a·bet·ic** \-'betik\ *adj or n*

di·a·bol·ic \-'bälik\, **di·a·bol·i·cal** \-ikəl\ *adj* : fiendish

di·a·crit·ic \-'kritik\ *n* : mark accompanying a letter and indicating a specific sound value — **di·a·crit·i·cal** \-'kritikəl\ *adj*

di·a·dem \'dīə,dem\ *n* : crown

di·ag·no·sis \,dīig'nōsəs, -əg-\ *n, pl* **-no·ses** \-,sēz\ : identifying of a disease from its symptoms — **di·ag·nose** \'dīig,nōs, -əg-\ *vb* — **di·ag·nos·tic** \,dīig'nästik, -əg-\ *adj*

di·ag·o·nal \dī'agənəl\ *adj* : extending from one corner to the opposite corner ∼ *n* : diagonal line, direction, or arrangement — **di·ag·o·nal·ly** *adv*

di·a·gram \'dīə,gram\ *n* : explanatory drawing or plan ∼ *vb* **-gramed** *or* **-grammed**; **-gram·ing** *or* **-gram·ming** : represent by a diagram — **di·a·gram·mat·ic** \,dīəgrə'matik\ *adj*

di·al \'dīəl\ *n* 1 : face of a clock, meter, or gauge 2 : control knob or wheel ∼ *vb* **-aled** *or* **-alled**; **-al·ing** *or* **-al·ling** : turn a dial to call, operate, or select

di·a·lect \'dīə,lekt\ *n* : variety of language confined to a region or group

di·a·logue \-,lȯg\ *n* : conversation

di·am·e·ter \dī'amətər\ *n* 1 : straight line through the center of a circle 2 : thickness

di·a·met·ric \,dīə'metrik\ **di·a·met·ri·cal** \-trikəl\ *adj* : completely opposite — **di·a·met·ri·cal·ly** \-iklē\ *adv*

di·a·mond \'dīmənd, 'dīə-\ *n* 1 : hard brilliant mineral that consists of crystalline carbon 2 : flat figure having 4 equal sides, 2 acute angles, and 2 obtuse angles 3 : playing card of a suit marked with a red diamond 4 : baseball field

di·a·per \'dīpər\ *n* : baby's garment for receiving bodily wastes ∼ *vb* : put a diaper on

di·a·phragm \'dīə,fram\ *n* 1 : sheet of muscle between the chest and abdominal cavity 2 : contraceptive device

di·ar·rhea \,dīə'rēə\ *n* : abnormally watery discharge from bowels

di·a·ry \'dīərē\ *n, pl* **-ries** : daily record of personal experiences — **di·a·rist** \'dīərist\ *n*

di·a·tribe \'dīə,trīb\ *n* : biting or abusive denunciation

dice \'dīs\ *n, pl* **dice** : die or a game played with dice ∼ *vb* **diced**; **dic·ing** : cut into small cubes

dick·er \'dikər\ *vb* : bargain

dic·tate \'dik,tāt\ *vb* **-tat·ed**; **-tat·ing** 1 : speak for a person or a machine to record 2 : command ∼ *n* : order — **dic·ta·tion** \dik'tāshən\ *n*

dic·ta·tor \'dik,tātər\ *n* : person ruling absolutely and often brutally — **dic·ta·to·ri·al** \,diktətōrēəl\ *adj* — **dic·ta·tor·ship** \dik'tātər,ship, 'dik,-\ *n*

dic·tion \'dikshən\ *n* 1 : choice of the best word 2 : precise pronunciation

dic·tio·nary \-shə,nerē\ *n, pl* **-nar·ies** : reference book of words with information about their meanings

dic·tum \'diktəm\ *n, pl* **-ta** \-tə\ : authoritative or formal statement

did *past of* DO

di·dac·tic \dī'daktik\ *adj* : intended to teach a moral lesson

¹**die** \'dī\ *vb* **died**; **dy·ing** \'dīiŋ\ 1 : stop living 2 : pass out of existence 3 : stop or subside 4 : long

²**die** \'dī\ *n* 1 *pl* **dice** \'dīs\ : small marked cube used in gambling 2 *pl* **dies** \'dīz\ : form for stamping or cutting

die·sel \'dēzəl, -səl\ *n* : engine in which high compression causes ignition of the fuel

di·et \'dīət\ *n* : food and drink regularly consumed (as by a person) ∼ *vb* : eat less or according to certain rules — **di·etary** \'dīə,terē\ *adj or n* — **di·et·er** *n*

di·e·tet·ics \,dīə'tetiks\ *n sing or pl* : science of nutrition — **di·e·tet·ic** *adj* — **di·e·ti·tian, di·e·ti·cian** \-'tishən\ *n*

dif·fer \'difər\ *vb* 1 : be unlike 2 : vary 3 : disagree — **dif·fer·ence** \'difrəns\ *n*

dif·fer·ent \-rənt\ *adj* : not the same — **dif·fer·ent·ly** *adv*

dif·fer·en·ti·ate \,difə'renchē,āt\ *vb* **-at·ed**; **-at·ing** 1 : make or become different **2** : attain a specialized adult form during development **3** : distinguish — **dif•fer•en•ti•a•tion** \-₁ren-chē'āshən\ n

dif•fi•cult \'difikəlt\ adj : hard to do, understand, or deal with

dif•fi•cul•ty \-₁kəltē\ n, pl **-ties 1** : difficult nature **2** : great effort **3** : something hard to do, understand, or deal with

dif•fi•dent \'difədənt\ adj : reserved — **dif•fi•dence** \-əns\ n

dif•fuse \dif'yüs\ adj **1** : wordy **2** : not concentrated ~ \-'yüz\ vb **-fused; -fus•ing** : pour out or spread widely — **dif•fu•sion** \-'yüzhən\ n

dig \'dig\ vb **dug** \'dəg\; **dig•ging 1** : turn up soil **2** : hollow out or form by removing earth **3** : uncover by turning up earth ~ n **1** : thrust **2** : cutting remark — **dig in** vb **1** : establish a defensive position **2** : begin working or eating — **dig up** vb : discover

¹**di•gest** \'dī₁jest\ n : body of information in shortened form

²**di•gest** \dī'jest, də-\ vb **1** : think over **2** : convert (food) into a form that can be absorbed **3** : summarize — **di•gest•ible** adj — **di•ges•tion** \-'jeschən\ n — **di•ges•tive** \-'jestiv\ adj

dig•it \'dijət\ n **1** : any of the figures 1 to 9 inclusive and usu. the symbol 0 **2** : finger or toe

dig•i•tal \-ʔl\ adj : providing information in numerical digits — **dig•i•tal•ly** adv

digital camera n : camera that records images as digital data instead of on film

dig•ni•fy \'dignə₁fī\ vb **-fied; -fy•ing** : give dignity or attention to

dig•ni•tary \-₁terē\ n, pl **-taries** : person of high position

dig•ni•ty \'dignətē\ n, pl **-ties 1** : quality or state of being worthy of honored **2** : formal reserve (as of manner)

di•gress \dī'gres, də-\ vb : wander from the main subject — **di•gres•sion** \-'greshən\ n

dike \'dīk\ n : earth bank or dam

di•lap•i•dat•ed \də'lapə₁dātəd\ adj : fallen into partial ruin — **di•lap•i•da•tion** \-₁lapə'dāshən\ n

di•late \dī'lāt, 'dī₁lāt\ vb **-lat•ed; -lat•ing** : swell or expand — **dil•a•ta•tion** \₁dilə'tāshən\ n — **di•la•tion** \dī'lāshən\ n

di•la•to•ry \'dilə₁tōrē\ adj **1** : delaying **2** : tardy or slow

di•lem•ma \də'lemə\ n **1** : undesirable choice **2** : predicament

dil•et•tante \'dilə₁tänt, -₁tant; ₁dilə'tänt, -'tant\ n, pl **-tantes** or **-tan•ti** \-'täntē, -'tantē\ : one who dabbles in a field of interest

dil•i•gent \'diləjənt\ adj : attentive and busy — **dil•i•gence** \-jəns\ n — **dil•i•gent•ly** adv

dill \'dil\ n : herb with aromatic leaves and seeds

dil•ly•dal•ly \'dilē₁dalē\ vb : waste time by delay

di•lute \dī'lüt, də-\ vb **-lut•ed; -lut•ing** : lessen the consistency or strength of by mixing with something else ~ adj : weak — **di•lu•tion** \-'lüshən\ n

dim \'dim\ adj **-mm- 1** : not bright or distinct **2** : having no luster **3** : not seeing or understanding clearly — **dim** vb — **dim•ly** adv — **dim•mer** n — **dim•ness** n

dime \'dīm\ n : U.S. coin worth ¹⁄₁₀ dollar

di•men•sion \də'menchən, dī-\ n **1** : measurement of extension (as in length, height, or breadth) **2** : extent — **di•men•sion•al** \-'menchənəl\ adj

di•min•ish \də'minish\ vb **1** : make less or cause to appear less **2** : dwindle

di•min•u•tive \də'minyətiv\ adj : extremely small

dim•ple \'dimpəl\ n : small depression esp. in the cheek or chin

din \'din\ n : loud noise

dine \'dīn\ vb **dined; din•ing** : eat dinner

din•er \'dīnər\ n **1** : person eating dinner **2** : railroad dining car or restaurant resembling one

din•ghy \'dinē, -gē, -kē\ n, pl **-ghies** : small boat

din•gy \'dinjē\ adj **-gi•er; -est 1** : dirty **2** : shabby — **din•gi•ness** n

din•ner \'dinər\ n : main daily meal

di•no•saur \'dīnə₁sòr\ n : extinct often huge reptile

dint \'dint\ n : force — in the phrase by dint of

di•o•cese \'dīəsəs, -₁sēz, -₁sēs\ n, pl **-ces•es** \-səz, 'dīə₁sēz\ : territorial jurisdiction of a bishop — **di·oc·e·san** \di'äsəsən, ˌdīə'sēzᵉn\ *adj or n*

dip \'dip\ *vb* **-pp-** 1 : plunge into a liquid 2 : take out with a ladle 3 : lower and quickly raise again 4 : sink or slope downward suddenly ∼ *n* 1 : plunge into water for sport 2 : sudden downward movement or incline — **dip·per** *n*

diph·the·ria \dif'thirēə\ *n* : acute contagious disease

diph·thong \'dif.thoŋ\ *n* : two vowel sounds joined to form one speech sound (as *ou* in *out*)

di·plo·ma \də'plōmə\ *n, pl* **-mas** : record of graduation from a school

di·plo·ma·cy \-məsē\ *n* 1 : business of conducting negotiations between nations 2 : tact — **dip·lo·mat** \'diplə.mat\ *n* — **dip·lo·mat·ic** \diplə'matik\ *adj*

dire \'dīr\ *adj* **dir·er; -est** 1 : very horrible 2 : extreme

di·rect \də'rekt, dī-\ *vb* 1 : address 2 : cause to move or to follow a certain course 3 : show (someone) the way 4 : regulate the activities or course of 5 : request with authority ∼ *adj* 1 : leading to or coming from a point without deviation or interruption 2 : frank — **direct** *adv* — **di·rect·ly** *adv* — **di·rect·ness** *n* — **di·rec·tor** \-tər\ *n*

direct current *n* : electric current flowing in one direction only

di·rec·tion \də'rekshən, dī-\ *n* 1 : supervision 2 : order 3 : course along which something moves — **di·rec·tion·al** \-shənəl\ *adj*

di·rec·tive \-tiv\ *n* : order

di·rec·to·ry \-tərē\ *n, pl* **-ries** : alphabetical list of names and addresses

dirge \'dərj\ *n* : funeral hymn

di·ri·gi·ble \'dirəjəbəl, də'rijə-\ *n* : airship

dirt \'dərt\ *n* 1 : mud, dust, or grime that makes something unclean 2 : soil

dirty \-ē\ *adj* **dirt·i·er; -est** 1 : not clean 2 : unfair 3 : indecent ∼ *vb* **dirt·ied; dirty·ing** : make or become dirty — **dirt·i·ness** *n*

dis·able \dis'ābəl\ *vb* **-abled; -abling** : make unable to function — **dis·abil·i·ty** \disə'bilətē\ *n*

dis·abuse \disə'byüz\ *vb* : free from error or misconception

dis·ad·van·tage \disəd'vantij\ *n*

: something that hinders success — **dis·ad·van·ta·geous** *adj*

dis·af·fect \disə'fekt\ *vb* : cause discontent in — **dis·af·fec·tion** *n*

dis·agree \disə'grē\ *vb* 1 : fail to agree 2 : differ in opinion — **dis·agree·ment** *n*

dis·agree·able \-əbəl\ *adj* : unpleasant

dis·al·low \disə'laù\ *vb* : refuse to admit or recognize

dis·ap·pear \disə'pir\ *vb* 1 : pass out of sight 2 : cease to be — **dis·ap·pear·ance** *n*

dis·ap·point \disə'pöint\ *vb* : fail to fulfill the expectation or hope of — **dis·ap·point·ment** *n*

dis·ap·prove \-ə'prüv\ *vb* 1 : condemn or reject 2 : feel or express dislike or rejection — **dis·ap·prov·al** *n* — **dis·ap·prov·ing·ly** *adv*

dis·arm \dis'ärm\ *vb* 1 : take weapons from 2 : reduce armed forces 3 : make harmless or friendly — **dis·ar·ma·ment** \-'ärməmənt\ *n*

dis·ar·range \disə'rānj\ *vb* : throw into disorder — **dis·ar·range·ment** *n*

dis·ar·ray \disə'rā\ *n* : disorder

dis·as·ter \diz'astər, dis-\ *n* : sudden great misfortune — **di·sas·trous** \-'astrəs\ *adj*

dis·avow \disə'vaù\ *vb* : deny responsibility for — **dis·avow·al** \-'vaùəl\ *n*

dis·band \dis'band\ *vb* : break up the organization of

dis·bar \dis'bär\ *vb* : expel from the legal profession — **dis·bar·ment** *n*

dis·be·lieve \disbi'lēv\ *vb* : hold not worthy of belief — **dis·be·lief** *n*

dis·burse \dis'bərs\ *vb* **-bursed; -burs·ing** : pay out — **dis·burse·ment** *n*

disc *var of* DISK

dis·card \dis'kärd, 'dis.kärd\ *vb* : get rid of as unwanted — **dis·card** \'dis.kärd\ *n*

dis·cern \dis'ərn, diz-\ *vb* : discover with the eyes or the mind — **dis·cern·ible** *adj* — **dis·cern·ment** *n*

dis·charge \dis'chärj, 'dis.chärj\ *vb* 1 : unload 2 : shoot 3 : set free 4 : dismiss from service 5 : let go or let off 6 : give forth fluid ∼ \'dis.-, dis'-\ *n* 1 : act of discharging 2 : a flowing out (as of blood) 3 : dismissal

dis·ci·ple \di'sīpəl\ *n* : one who helps spread another's teachings

dis·ci·pli·nar·i·an \ˌdisəplə'nerēən\ n : one who enforces order

dis·ci·pline \'disəplən\ n 1 : field of study 2 : training that corrects, molds, or perfects 3 : punishment 4 : control gained by obedience or training ~ vb -plined; -plin·ing 1 : punish 2 : train in self-control — **dis·ci·plin·ary** \'disəplə,nerē\ adj

dis·claim \dis'klām\ vb : disavow

dis·close \-'klōz\ vb : reveal — **dis·clo·sure** \-'klōzhər\ n

dis·col·or \dis'kələr\ vb : change the color of esp. for the worse — **dis·col·or·ation** \dis,kələ'rāshən\ n

dis·com·fit \dis'kəmfət\ vb : upset — **dis·com·fi·ture** \dis'kəmfə,chúr\ n

dis·com·fort \dis'kəmfərt\ n : uneasiness

dis·con·cert \ˌdiskən'sərt\ vb : upset

dis·con·nect \ˌdiskə'nekt\ vb : undo the connection of

dis·con·so·late \dis'känsələt\ adj : hopelessly sad

dis·con·tent \ˌdiskən'tent\ n : uneasiness of mind — **dis·con·tent·ed** adj

dis·con·tin·ue \ˌdiskən'tinyü\ vb : end — **dis·con·tin·u·ance** n — **dis·con·ti·nu·i·ty** \dis,käntə'nüətē, -'nyü-\ n — **dis·con·tin·u·ous** \ˌdiskən'tinyəwəs\ adj

dis·cord \'dis,kórd\ n : lack of harmony — **dis·cor·dant** \dis'kórd'nt\ adj — **dis·cor·dant·ly** adv

dis·count \'dis,kaúnt\ n : reduction from a regular price ~ \'dis,-, dis'-\ vb 1 : reduce the amount of 2 : disregard — **discount** adj — **dis·count·er** n

dis·cour·age \dis'kərij\ vb -aged; -ag·ing 1 : deprive of courage, confidence, or enthusiasm 2 : dissuade — **dis·cour·age·ment** n

dis·course \'dis,kórs\ n 1 : conversation 2 : formal treatment of a subject ~ \dis'-\ vb -coursed; -cours·ing : talk at length

dis·cour·te·ous \dis'kərtēəs\ adj : lacking courtesy — **dis·cour·te·ous·ly** adv — **dis·cour·te·sy** n

dis·cov·er \dis'kəvər\ vb 1 : make known 2 : obtain the first sight or knowledge of 3 : find out — **dis·cov·er·er** n — **dis·cov·ery** \-ə'rē\ n

dis·cred·it \dis'kredət\ vb 1 : disbelieve 2 : destroy confidence in — n 1 : loss of reputation 2 : disbelief — **dis·cred·it·able** adj

dis·creet \dis'krēt\ adj : capable of keeping a secret — **dis·creet·ly** adv

dis·crep·an·cy \dis'krepənsē\ n, pl -cies : difference or disagreement

dis·crete \dis'krēt, 'dis,-\ adj : individually distinct

dis·cre·tion \dis'kreshən\ n 1 : discreet quality 2 : power of decision or choice — **dis·cre·tion·ary** adj

dis·crim·i·nate \dis'krimə,nāt\ vb -nat·ed; -nat·ing 1 : distinguish 2 : show favor or disfavor unjustly — **dis·crim·i·na·tion** \-,krimə'nāshən\ n — **dis·crim·i·na·to·ry** \-'krimənə,tōrē\ adj

dis·cur·sive \dis'kərsiv\ adj : passing from one topic to another — **dis·cur·sive·ly** adv — **dis·cur·sive·ness** n

dis·cus \'diskəs\ n, pl -cus·es : disk hurled for distance in a contest

dis·cuss \dis'kəs\ vb : talk about or present — **dis·cus·sion** \-'kəshən\ n

dis·dain \dis'dān\ n : feeling of contempt ~ vb : look upon or reject with disdain — **dis·dain·ful** \-fəl\ adj — **dis·dain·ful·ly** adv

dis·ease \di'zēz\ n : condition of a body that impairs its functioning — **dis·eased** \-'zēzd\ adj

dis·em·bark \ˌdisəm'bärk\ vb : get off a ship — **dis·em·bar·ka·tion** \dis-,em,bär'kāshən\ n

dis·em·bod·ied \ˌdisəm'bädēd\ adj : having no substance or reality

dis·en·chant \ˌdis'n'chant\ vb : to free from illusion — **dis·en·chant·ment** n

dis·en·chant·ed \-'chantəd\ adj : disappointed

dis·en·gage \-'n'gāj\ vb : release — **dis·en·gage·ment** n

dis·en·tan·gle \-'n'taŋgəl\ vb : free from entanglement

dis·fa·vor \dis'fāvər\ n : disapproval

dis·fig·ure \dis'figyər\ vb : spoil the appearance of — **dis·fig·ure·ment** n

dis·fran·chise \dis'fran,chīz\ vb : deprive of the right to vote — **dis·fran·chise·ment** n

dis·gorge \dis'górj\ vb : spew forth

dis·grace \dis'grās\ vb : bring disgrace to ~ n 1 : shame 2 : cause of shame — **dis·grace·ful** \-fəl\ adj — **dis·grace·ful·ly** adv

dis·grun·tle \dis'grənt'l\ vb -tled; -tling : put in bad humor

dis·guise \dis'gīz\ vb -guised; -guis-

ing : hide the true identity or nature of ~ *n* : something that conceals

dis·gust \dis'gəst\ *n* : strong aversion ~ *vb* : provoke disgust — **dis·gust·ed·ly** *adv* — **dis·gust·ing·ly** *adv*

dish \'dish\ *n* **1** : vessel for serving food or the food it holds **2** : food prepared in a particular way ~ *vb* : put in a dish — **dish·cloth** *n* — **dish·rag** *n* — **dish·wash·er** *n* — **dish·wa·ter** *n*

dis·har·mo·ny \dis'härmənē\ *n* : lack of harmony — **dis·har·mo·ni·ous** \,dishär'mōnēəs\ *adj*

dis·heart·en \dis'härt°n\ *vb* : discourage

di·shev·el \di'shevəl\ *vb* **-eled** *or* **-elled; -el·ing** *or* **-el·ling** : throw into disorder — **di·shev·eled, di·shev·elled** *adj*

dis·hon·est \dis'änəst\ *adj* : not honest — **dis·hon·est·ly** *adv* — **dis·hon·es·ty** *n*

dis·hon·or \dis'änər\ *n or vb* : disgrace — **dis·hon·or·able** *adj* — **dis·hon·or·ably** *adv*

dis·il·lu·sion \,disə'lüzhən\ *vb* : to free from illusion — **dis·il·lu·sion·ment** *n*

dis·in·cli·na·tion \dis,inklə'nāshən\ *n* : slight aversion — **dis·in·cline** \,dis°n'klīn\ *vb*

dis·in·fect \,dis°n'fekt\ *vb* : destroy disease germs in or on — **dis·in·fec·tant** \-'fektənt\ *adj or n* — **dis·in·fec·tion** \-'fekshən\ *n*

dis·in·gen·u·ous \,dis°n'jenyəwəs\ *adj* : lacking in candor

dis·in·her·it \-°n'herət\ *vb* : prevent from inheriting property

dis·in·te·grate \dis'intə,grāt\ *vb* : break into parts or small bits — **dis·in·te·gra·tion** \dis,intə'grāshən\ *n*

dis·in·ter·est·ed \dis'intərəstəd, -,res-\ *adj* **1** : not interested **2** : not prejudiced — **dis·in·ter·est·ed·ness** *n*

dis·joint·ed \dis'jöintəd\ *adj* **1** : separated at the joint **2** : incoherent

disk \'disk\ *n* : something round and flat

dis·like \dis'līk\ *vb* : regard with dislike ~ *n* : feeling that something is unpleasant and to be avoided

dis·lo·cate \'dislō,kāt, dis'-\ *vb* : move out of the usual or proper place — **dis·lo·ca·tion** \,dislō'kāshən\ *n*

dis·lodge \dis'läj\ *vb* : force out of a place

dis·loy·al \dis'löiəl\ *adj* : not loyal — **dis·loy·al·ty** *n*

dis·mal \'dizməl\ *adj* : showing or causing gloom — **dis·mal·ly** *adv*

dis·man·tle \dis'mant°l\ *vb* **-tled; -tling** : take apart

dis·may \dis'mā\ *vb* **-mayed; -may·ing** : discourage — **dismay** *n*

dis·mem·ber \dis'membər\ *vb* : cut into pieces — **dis·mem·ber·ment** *n*

dis·miss \dis'mis\ *vb* **1** : send away **2** : remove from service **3** : put aside or out of mind — **dis·miss·al** *n*

dis·mount \dis'maúnt\ *vb* **1** : get down from something **2** : take apart

dis·obey \,disə'bā\ *vb* : refuse to obey — **dis·obe·di·ence** \-'bēdēəns\ *n* — **dis·obe·di·ent** \-ənt\ *adj*

dis·or·der \dis'órdər\ *n* **1** : lack of order **2** : breach of public order **3** : abnormal state of body or mind — **disorder** *vb* — **dis·or·der·li·ness** *n* — **dis·or·der·ly** *adj*

dis·or·ga·nize \dis'órgə,nīz\ *vb* : throw into disorder — **dis·or·ga·ni·za·tion** *n*

dis·own \dis'ōn\ *vb* : repudiate

dis·par·age \-'parij\ *vb* **-aged; -ag·ing** : say bad things about — **dis·par·age·ment** *n*

dis·pa·rate \dis'parət, 'dispərət\ *adj* : different in quality or character — **dis·par·i·ty** \dis'parətē\ *n*

dis·pas·sion·ate \dis'pashənət\ *adj* : not influenced by strong feeling — **dis·pas·sion·ate·ly** *adv*

dis·patch \dis'pach\ *vb* **1** : send **2** : kill **3** : attend to rapidly **4** : defeat ~ *n* **1** : message **2** : news item from a correspondent **3** : promptness and efficiency — **dis·patch·er** *n*

dis·pel \dis'pel\ *vb* **-ll-** : clear away

dis·pen·sa·ry \-'pensərē\ *n, pl* **-ries** : place where medical or dental aid is provided

dis·pen·sa·tion \,dispən'sāshən\ *n* **1** : system of principles or rules **2** : exemption from a rule **3** : act of dispensing

dis·pense \dis'pens\ *vb* **-pensed; -pens·ing** **1** : portion out **2** : make up and give out (remedies) — **dis·pens·er** *n* — **dispense with** : do without

dis·perse \-'pərs\ *vb* **-persed; -pers-**

ing : scatter — **dis·per·sal** \-'pərsəl\ n — **dis·per·sion** \-'pərzhən\ n

dis·place \-'plās\ vb 1 : expel or force to flee from home or native land 2 : take the place of — **dis·place·ment** \-mənt\ n

dis·play \-'plā\ vb : present to view — **display** n

dis·please \-'plēz\ vb : arouse the dislike of — **dis·plea·sure** \-'plezhər\ n

dis·port \dis'pōrt\ vb 1 : amuse 2 : frolic

dis·pose \dis'pōz\ vb **-posed; -pos·ing** 1 : give a tendency to 2 : settle — **dis·pos·able** \-'pōzəbəl\ adj — **dis·pos·al** \-'pōzəl\ n — **dis·pos·er** n — **dispose of** 1 : determine the fate, condition, or use of 2 : get rid of

dis·po·si·tion \,dispə'zishən\ n 1 : act or power of disposing of 2 : arrangement 3 : natural attitude

dis·pos·sess \,dispə'zes\ vb : deprive of possession or occupancy — **dis·pos·ses·sion** \-'zeshən\ n

dis·pro·por·tion \,disprə'pōrshən\ n : lack of proportion — **dis·pro·por·tion·ate** \-shənət\ adj

dis·prove \dis'prüv\ vb : prove false

dis·pute \dis'pyüt\ vb **-put·ed; -put·ing** 1 : argue 2 : deny the truth or rightness of 3 : struggle against or over ~ n : debate or quarrel — **dis·put·able** \-əbəl, 'dispyət-\ adj — **dis·pu·ta·tion** \dispyə'tāshən\ n

dis·qual·i·fy \dis'kwälə,fī\ vb : make ineligible — **dis·qual·i·fi·ca·tion** n

dis·qui·et \dis'kwīət\ vb : make uneasy or restless ~ n : anxiety

dis·re·gard \disri'gärd\ vb : pay no attention to ~ n : neglect

dis·re·pair \,disri'par\ n : need of repair

dis·rep·u·ta·ble \dis'repyətəbəl\ adj : having a bad reputation

dis·re·pute \disri'pyüt\ n : low regard

dis·re·spect \,disri'spekt\ n : lack of respect — **dis·re·spect·ful** adj

dis·robe \dis'rōb\ vb : undress

dis·rupt \dis'rəpt\ vb : throw into disorder — **dis·rup·tion** \-'rəpshən\ n — **dis·rup·tive** \-'rəptiv\ adj

dis·sat·is·fac·tion \dis,satəs'fakshən\ n : lack of satisfaction

dis·sat·is·fy \dis'satəs,fī\ vb : fail to satisfy

dis·sect \dis'sekt\ vb : cut into parts

esp. to examine — **dis·sec·tion** \-'sekshən\ n

dis·sem·ble \di'sembəl\ vb **-bled; -bling** : disguise feelings or intention — **dis·sem·bler** n

dis·sem·i·nate \di'semə,nāt\ vb **-nat·ed; -nat·ing** : spread around — **dis·sem·i·na·tion** \-,semə'nāshən\ n

dis·sen·sion \di'senchən\ n : discord

dis·sent \di'sent\ vb : object or disagree ~ n : difference of opinion — **dis·sent·er** n

dis·ser·ta·tion \disər'tāshən\ n : long written study of a subject

dis·ser·vice \dis'sərvəs\ n : injury

dis·si·dent \'disədənt\ n : one who differs openly with an establishment — **dis·si·dence** \-əns\ n — **dissident** adj

dis·sim·i·lar \dis'simələr\ adj : different — **dis·sim·i·lar·i·ty** \di,simə-'larətē\ n

dis·si·pate \'disə,pāt\ vb **-pat·ed; -pat·ing** 1 : break up and drive off 2 : squander — **dis·si·pa·tion** \disə-ə'pāshən\ n

dis·so·ci·ate \dis'ōsē,āt, -shē-\ vb **-at·ed; -at·ing** : separate from association — **dis·so·ci·a·tion** \dis,ōsē-'āshən, -shē-\ n

dis·so·lute \'disə,lüt\ adj : loose in morals or conduct

dis·so·lu·tion \disə'lüshən\ n : act or process of dissolving

dis·solve \di'zälv\ vb 1 : break up or bring to an end 2 : pass or cause to pass into solution

dis·so·nance \'disənəns\ n : discord — **dis·so·nant** \-nənt\ adj

dis·suade \di'swād\ vb **-suad·ed; -suad·ing** : persuade not to do something — **dis·sua·sion** \-'swāzhən\ n

dis·tance \'distəns\ n 1 : measure of separation in space or time 2 : reserve

dis·tant \-tənt\ adj 1 : separate in space 2 : remote in time, space, or relationship 3 : reserved — **dis·tant·ly** adv

dis·taste \dis'tāst\ n : dislike — **dis·taste·ful** adj

dis·tem·per \dis'tempər\ n : serious virus disease of dogs

dis·tend \dis'tend\ vb : swell out — **dis·ten·sion, dis·ten·tion** \-'tenchən\ n

dis·till \di'stil\ vb : obtain by distillation — **dis·til·late** \'distə,lāt, -lət\ n

— **dis·till·er** n — **dis·till·ery** \di-'stilərē\ n

dis·til·la·tion \distə'lāshən\ n : purification of liquid by evaporating then condensing

dis·tinct \dis'tiŋkt\ adj 1 : distinguishable from others 2 : readily discerned — **dis·tinc·tive** \-tiv\ adj — **dis·tinc·tive·ly** adv — **dis·tinc·tive·ness** n — **dis·tinct·ly** adv — **dis·tinct·ness** n

dis·tinc·tion \-'tiŋkshən\ n 1 : act of distinguishing 2 : difference 3 : special recognition

dis·tin·guish \-'tiŋgwish\ vb 1 : perceive as different 2 : set apart 3 : discern 4 : make outstanding — **dis·tin·guish·able** adj — **dis·tin·guished** \-gwisht\ adj

dis·tort \dis'tort\ vb : twist out of shape, condition, or true meaning — **dis·tor·tion** \-'torshən\ n

dis·tract \di'strakt\ vb : divert the mind or attention of — **dis·trac·tion** \-'strakshən\ n

dis·traught \dis'trot\ adj : agitated with mental conflict

dis·tress \-'tres\ n 1 : suffering 2 : misfortune 3 : state of danger or great need ~ vb : subject to strain or distress — **dis·tress·ful** adj

dis·trib·ute \-'tribyət\ vb -ut·ed; -ut·ing 1 : divide among many 2 : spread or hand out — **dis·tri·bu·tion** \distrə'byüshən\ n — **dis·trib·u·tive** \dis'tribyətiv\ adj — **dis·trib·u·tor** \-ər\ n

dis·trict \'dis,trikt\ n : territorial division

dis·trust \dis'trəst\ vb or n : mistrust — **dis·trust·ful** \-fəl\ adj

dis·turb \dis'tərb\ vb 1 : interfere with 2 : destroy the peace, composure, or order of — **dis·tur·bance** \-'tər-bəns\ n — **dis·turb·er** n

dis·use \dis'yüs\ n : lack of use

ditch \'dich\ n : trench ~ vb 1 : dig a ditch in 2 : get rid of

dith·er \'dithər\ n : highly nervous or excited state

dit·to \'ditō\ n, pl **-tos** : more of the same

dit·ty \'ditē\ n, pl **-ties** : short simple song

di·uret·ic \dīyü'retik\ adj : tending to increase urine flow — **diuretic** n

di·ur·nal \dī'ərn'l\ adj 1 : daily 2 : of or occurring in the daytime

di·van \'dī,van, di'-\ n : couch

dive \'dīv\ vb **dived** \'dīvd\ or **dove** \'dōv\; **dived**; **div·ing** 1 : plunge into water headfirst 2 : submerge 3 : descend quickly ~ n 1 : act of diving 2 : sharp decline — **div·er** n

di·verge \də'vərj, dī-\ vb **-verged**; **-verg·ing** 1 : move in different directions 2 : differ — **di·ver·gence** \-'vərjəns\ n — **di·ver·gent** \-jənt\ adj

di·vers \'dīvərz\ adj : various

di·verse \dī'vərs, də-, 'dī,vərs\ adj : involving different forms — **di·ver·si·fi·ca·tion** \də,vərsəfə'kāshən, dī-\ n — **di·ver·si·fy** \-'vərsə,fī\ vb — **di·ver·si·ty** \-sətē\ n

di·vert \də'vərt, dī-\ vb 1 : turn from a course or purpose 2 : distract 3 : amuse — **di·ver·sion** \-'vərzhən\ n

di·vest \dī'vest, də-\ vb : strip of clothing, possessions, or rights

di·vide \də'vīd\ vb **-vid·ed**; **-vid·ing** 1 : separate 2 : distribute 3 : share 4 : subject to mathematical division ~ n : watershed — **di·vid·er** n

div·i·dend \'divə,dend\ n 1 : individual share 2 : bonus 3 : number to be divided

div·i·na·tion \divə'nāshən\ n : practice of trying to foretell future events

di·vine \də'vīn\ adj **-vin·er**; **-est** 1 : relating to or being God or a god 2 : supremely good ~ n : clergy member ~ vb **-vined**; **-vin·ing** 1 : infer 2 : prophesy — **di·vine·ly** adv — **di·vin·er** n — **di·vin·i·ty** \də'vinətē\ n

di·vis·i·ble \-'vizəbəl\ adj : capable of being divided — **di·vis·i·bil·i·ty** \-,vizə'bilətē\ n

di·vi·sion \-'vizhən\ n 1 : distribution 2 : part of a whole 3 : disagreement 4 : process of finding out how many times one number is contained in another

di·vi·sive \də'vīsiv, -'vi-, -ziv\ adj : creating dissension

di·vi·sor \-'vīzər\ n : number by which a dividend is divided

di·vorce \də'vōrs\ n : legal breaking up of a marriage — **divorce** vb

di·vor·cée \-,vōr'sā, -'sē\ n : divorced woman

di·vulge \də'vəlj, dī-\ vb **-vulged**; **-vulg·ing** : reveal

diz·zy \'dizē\ adj **-zi·er**; **-est** 1 : having a sensation of whirling 2 : causing or caused by giddiness — **diz·zi·ly** adv — **diz·zi·ness** n

DNA \ˌdē,en'ā\ n : compound in cell nuclei that is the basis of heredity

do \'dü\ vb **did** \'did\; **done** \'dən\; **do·ing** \'düiŋ\; **does** \'dəz\ n **1** : work to accomplish (an action or task) **2** : behave **3** : prepare or fix up **4** : fare **5** : finish **6** : serve the needs or purpose of **7** — used as an auxiliary verb — **do·er** \'düər\ n — **do away with 1** : get rid of **2** : destroy — **do by** : deal with — **do in** vb **1** : ruin **2** : kill

doc·ile \'däsəl\ adj : easily managed — **do·cil·i·ty** \dä'silətē\ n

¹dock \'däk\ vb **1** : shorten **2** : reduce

²dock n **1** : berth between 2 piers to receive ships **2** : loading wharf or platform ~ vb : bring or come into dock — **dock·work·er** n

³dock n : place in a court for a prisoner

dock·et \'däkət\ n **1** : record of the proceedings in a legal action **2** : list of legal causes to be tried — **docket** vb

doc·tor \'däktər\ n **1** : person holding one of the highest academic degrees **2** : one (as a surgeon) skilled in healing arts ~ vb **1** : give medical treatment to **2** : repair or alter — **doc·tor·al** \-tərəl\ adj

doc·trine \'däktrən\ n : something taught — **doc·tri·nal** \-trən⁹l\ adj

doc·u·ment \'däkyəmənt\ n : paper that furnishes information or legal proof — **doc·u·ment** \-ˌment\ vb — **doc·u·men·ta·tion** \ˌdäkyəmən'tāshən\ n — **doc·u·ment·er** n

doc·u·men·ta·ry \ˌdäkyə'mentərē\ adj **1** : of or relating to documents **2** : giving a factual presentation — **documentary** n

dod·der \'dädər\ vb : become feeble usu. from age

dodge \'däj\ vb **dodged**; **dodg·ing 1** : move quickly aside or out of the way of **2** : evade — **dodge** n

do·do \'dōdō\ n, pl **-does** or **-dos 1** : heavy flightless extinct bird **2** : stupid person

doe \'dō\ n, pl **does** or **doe** : adult female deer — **doe·skin** \-ˌskin\ n

does pres 3d sing of DO

doff \'däf\ vb : remove

dog \'dȯg\ n : flesh-eating domestic mammal ~ vb **1** : hunt down or track like a hound **2** : harass — **dog-**

catch·er n — **dog·gy** \-ē\ n or adj — **dog·house** n

dog·ear \'dȯg,ir\ n : turned-down corner of a page — **dog-ear** vb — **dog-eared** \-ˌird\ adj

dog·ged \'dȯgəd\ adj : stubbornly determined

dog·ma \'dȯgmə\ n : tenet or code of beliefs

dog·ma·tism \-ˌtizəm\ n : unwarranted stubbornness of opinion — **dog·ma·tic** \dȯg'matik\ adj

dog·wood n : flowering tree

doi·ly \'dȯilē\ n, pl **-lies** : small decorative mat

do·ings \'düiŋz\ n pl : events

dol·drums \'dōldrəmz,'däl-\ n pl : spell of listlessness, despondency, or stagnation

dole \'dōl\ n : distribution esp. of money to the needy or unemployed — **dole out** vb : give out esp. in small portions

dole·ful \'dōlfəl\ adj : sad — **dole·ful·ly** adv

doll \'däl, 'dȯl\ n : small figure of a person used esp. as a child's toy

dol·lar \'dälər\ n : any of various basic monetary units (as in the U.S. and Canada)

dol·ly \'dälē\ n, pl **-lies** : small cart or wheeled platform

dol·phin \'dälfən\ n **1** : sea mammal related to the whales **2** : saltwater food fish

dolt \'dōlt\ n : stupid person — **dolt·ish** adj

-dom \dəm\ n suffix **1** : office or realm **2** : state or fact of being **3** : those belonging to a group

do·main \dō'mān, də-\ n **1** : territory over which someone reigns **2** : sphere of activity or knowledge

dome \'dōm\ n **1** : large hemispherical roof **2** : roofed stadium

do·mes·tic \də'mestik\ adj **1** : relating to the household or family **2** : relating and limited to one's own country **3** : tame ~ n : household servant — **do·mes·ti·cal·ly** \-tiklē\ adv

do·mes·ti·cate \-ti,kāt\ vb **-cat·ed**; **-cat·ing** : tame — **do·mes·ti·ca·tion** \-ˌmesti'kāshən\ n

dom·i·cile \'dämə,sīl, 'dō-; 'däməsəl\ n : home — **domicile** vb

dom·i·nance \'dämənəns\ n : control — **dom·i·nant** \-nənt\ adj

dom·i·nate \-₁nāt\ vb **-nat·ed; -nat·ing** 1 : have control over 2 : rise high above — **dom·i·na·tion** \₁dämə'nā-shən\ n

dom·i·neer \₁dämə'nir\ vb : exercise arbitrary control

do·min·ion \də'minyən\ n 1 : supreme authority 2 : governed territory

dom·i·no \'dämə₁nō\ n, pl **-noes** or **-nos** : flat rectangular block used as a piece in a game (**dominoes**)

don \'dän\ vb **-nn-** : put on (clothes)

do·nate \'dō₁nāt\ vb **-nat·ed; -nat·ing** : make a gift of — **do·na·tion** \dō'nāshən\ n

¹**done** \'dən\ past part of DO

²**done** adj 1 : finished or ended 2 : cooked sufficiently

don·key \'däŋkē, 'dəŋ-\ n, pl **-keys** : sturdy domestic ass

do·nor \'dōnər\ n : one that gives

doo·dle \'düd⁀l\ vb **-dled; -dling** : draw or scribble aimlessly — **doo·dle** n

doom \'düm\ n 1 : judgment 2 : fate 3 : ruin — **doom** vb

door \'dōr\ n : passage for entrance or a movable barrier that can open or close such a passage — **door·jamb** n — **door·knob** n — **door·mat** n — **door·step** n — **door·way** n

dope \'dōp\ n 1 : narcotic preparation 2 : stupid person 3 : information ~ vb **doped; dop·ing** : drug

dor·mant \'dōrmənt\ adj : not actively growing or functioning — **dor·man·cy** \-mənsē\ n

dor·mer \'dōrmər\ n : window built upright in a sloping roof

dor·mi·to·ry \'dōrmə₁tōrē\ n, pl **-ries** : residence hall (as at a college)

dor·mouse \'dōr₁maůs\ n : squirrel-like rodent

dor·sal \'dōrsəl\ adj : relating to or on the back — **dor·sal·ly** adv

do·ry \'dōrē\ n, pl **-ries** : flat-bottomed boat

dose \'dōs\ n : quantity (as of medicine) taken at one time ~ vb **dosed; dos·ing** : give medicine to — **dos·age** \'dōsij\ n

dot \'dät\ n 1 : small spot 2 : small round mark made with or as if with a pen ~ vb **-tt-** : mark with dots

dot·age \'dōtij\ n : senility

dote \'dōt\ vb **dot·ed; dot·ing** 1 : act feebleminded 2 : be foolishly fond

dou·ble \'dəbəl\ adj 1 : consisting of 2 members or parts 2 : being twice as great or as many 3 : folded in two ~ n 1 : something twice another 2 : one that resembles another ~ adv : doubly ~ vb **-bled; -bling** 1 : make or become twice as great 2 : fold or bend 3 : clench

dou·ble–cross vb : deceive by trickery — **dou·ble–cross·er** n

dou·bly \'dəblē\ adv : to twice the degree

doubt \'daůt\ vb 1 : be uncertain about 2 : mistrust 3 : consider unlikely ~ n 1 : uncertainty 2 : mistrust 3 : inclination not to believe — **doubt·ful** \-fəl\ adj — **doubt·ful·ly** adv — **doubt·less** \-ləs\ adv

douche \'düsh\ n : jet of fluid for cleaning a body part

dough \'dō\ n : stiff mixture of flour and liquid — **doughy** \'dōē\ adj

dough·nut \-₁nət\ n : small fried ring-shaped cake

dough·ty \'daůtē\ adj **-ti·er; -est** : able, strong, or valiant

dour \'důr, 'daůr\ adj 1 : severe 2 : gloomy or sullen — **dour·ly** adv

douse \'daůs, 'daůz\ vb **doused; dous·ing** 1 : plunge into or drench with water 2 : extinguish

¹**dove** \'dəv\ n : small wild pigeon

²**dove** \'dōv\ past of DIVE

dove·tail \'dəv₁tāl\ vb : fit together neatly

dow·a·ger \'daůijər\ n 1 : widow with wealth or a title 2 : dignified elderly woman

dowdy \'daůdē\ adj **dowd·i·er; -est** : lacking neatness and charm

dow·el \'daůəl\ n 1 : peg used for fastening two pieces 2 : wooden rod

dow·er \'daůər\ n : property given a widow for life ~ vb : supply with a dower

¹**down** \'daůn\ adv 1 : toward or in a lower position or state 2 : to a lying or sitting position 3 : as a cash deposit 4 : on paper ~ adj 1 : lying on the ground 2 : directed or going downward 3 : being at a low level ~ prep : toward the bottom of ~ vb 1 : cause to go down 2 : defeat

²**down** n : fluffy feathers

down·cast adj 1 : sad 2 : directed down

down·fall n : ruin or cause of ruin

down·grade n : downward slope ~ vb : lower in grade or position

down·heart·ed adj : sad

down·pour n : heavy rain

down·right adv : thoroughly ~ adj : absolute or thorough

downs \'daùnz\ n pl : rolling treeless uplands

down·size \'daùn,sīz\ vb : reduce in size

down·stairs adv : on or to a lower floor and esp. the main floor — **down·stairs** adj or n

down-to-earth adj : practical

down·town adv : to, toward, or in the business center of a town — **down·town** n or adj

down·trod·den \'daùn,träd³n\ adj : suffering oppression

down·ward \'daùnwərd\, **down·wards** \-wərdz\ adv : to a lower place or condition — **downward** adj

down·wind adv or adj : in the direction the wind is blowing

downy \'daùnē\ adj -i·er; -est : resembling or covered with down

dow·ry \'daúrē\ n, pl -ries : property a woman gives her husband in marriage

dox·ol·o·gy \däk'säləjē\ n, pl -gies : hymn of praise to God

doze \'dōz\ vb **dozed; doz·ing** : sleep lightly — **doze** n

doz·en \'dəz³n\ n, pl -ens or -en : group of 12 — **doz·enth** \-³nth\ adj

drab \'drab\ adj -bb- : dull — **drab·ly** adv — **drab·ness** n

dra·co·ni·an \drā'kōnēən, dra-\ adj, often cap : harsh, cruel

draft \'draft, 'dråft\ n 1 : act of drawing or hauling 2 : act of drinking 3 : amount drunk at once 4 : preliminary outline or rough sketch 5 : selection from a pool or the selection process 6 : order for the payment of money 7 : air current ~ vb 1 : select usu. on a compulsory basis 2 : make a preliminary sketch, version, or plan of ~ adj : drawn from a container — **draft·ee** \draf'tē, dråf-\ n — **drafty** \'draftē\ adj

drafts·man \'draftsmən, 'dråfts-\ n : person who draws plans

drag \'drag\ n 1 : something dragged over a surface or through water 2 : something that hinders progress or is boring 3 : act or an instance of dragging ~ vb -gg- 1 : haul 2 : move or

work with difficulty 3 : pass slowly 4 : search or fish with a drag — **drag·ger** n

drag·net \-,net\ n 1 : trawl 2 : planned actions for finding a criminal

dra·gon \'dragən\ n : fabled winged serpent

drag·on·fly n : large 4-winged insect

drain \'drān\ vb 1 : draw off or flow off gradually or completely 2 : exhaust ~ n : means or act of draining — **drain·age** \-ij\ n — **drain·er** n — **drain·pipe** n

drake \'drāk\ n : male duck

dra·ma \'drämə, 'dram-\ n 1 : composition for theatrical presentation esp. on a serious subject 2 : series of events involving conflicting forces — **dra·mat·ic** \drə'matik\ adj — **dra·mat·i·cal·ly** \-iklē\ adv — **dram·a·tist** \'dramətist, 'dräm-\ n — **dram·a·ti·za·tion** \,dramətə'zāshən, ,dräm-\ n — **dra·ma·tize** \'dramə,tīz, 'dräm-\ vb

drank past of DRINK

drape \'drāp\ vb **draped; drap·ing** 1 : cover or adorn with folds of cloth 2 : cause to hang in flowing lines or folds ~ n : curtain

drap·ery \'drāpərē\ n, pl -er·ies : decorative fabric hung esp. as a heavy curtain

dras·tic \'drastik\ adj : extreme or harsh — **dras·ti·cal·ly** \-tiklē\ adv

draught \'draft, draughty \'draftē\ chiefly Brit var of DRAFT, DRAFTY

draw \'drò\ vb **drew** \'drü\; **drawn** \'drön\; **draw·ing** 1 : move or cause to move (as by pulling) 2 : attract or provoke 3 : extract 4 : take or receive (as money) 5 : bend a bow in preparation for shooting 6 : leave a contest undecided 7 : sketch 8 : write out 9 : deduce ~ n 1 : act, process, or result of drawing 2 : tie — **draw out** 1 : cause to speak candidly — **draw up** 1 : write out 2 : pull oneself erect 3 : bring or come to a stop

draw·back n : disadvantage

draw·bridge n : bridge that can be raised

draw·er \'dròr, 'dròər\ n 1 : one that draws 2 : sliding boxlike compartment 3 pl : underpants

draw·ing \'dróiŋ\ n 1 : occasion of choosing by lot 2 : act or art of making a figure, plan, or sketch with lines 3 : something drawn

drawl \'drȯl\ *vb* : speak slowly — **drawl** *n*

dread \'dred\ *vb* : feel extreme fear or reluctance ∼ *n* : great fear ∼ *adj* : causing dread — **dread·ful** \-fəl\ *adj* — **dread·ful·ly** *adv*

dream \'drēm\ *n* 1 : series of thoughts or visions during sleep 2 : dreamlike vision 3 : something notable 4 : ideal ∼ *vb* **dreamed** \'dremt, 'drēmd\ *or* **dreamt** \'dremt\; **dream·ing** 1 : have a dream 2 : imagine — **dream·er** *n* — **dream·like** *adj* — **dreamy** *adj*

drea·ry \'drirē\ *adj* **-ri·er; -est** : dismal — **drea·ri·ly** \'drirəlē\ *adv*

¹**dredge** \'drej\ *n* : machine for removing earth esp. from under water — *vb* **dredged; dredg·ing** : dig up or search with a dredge — **dredg·er** *n*

²**dredge** *vb* **dredged; dredg·ing** : coat (food) with flour

dregs \'dregz\ *n pl* 1 : sediment 2 : most worthless part

drench \'drench\ *vb* : wet thoroughly

dress \'dres\ *vb* 1 : put clothes on 2 : decorate 3 : prepare (as a carcass) for use 4 : apply dressings, remedies, or fertilizer to ∼ *n* 1 : apparel 2 : single garment of bodice and skirt ∼ *adj* : suitable for a formal event — **dress·mak·er** *n* — **dress·mak·ing** *n*

dress·er \'dresər\ *n* : bureau with a mirror

dress·ing *n* 1 : act or process of dressing 2 : sauce or a seasoned mixture 3 : material to cover an injury

dressy \'dresē\ *adj* **dress·i·er; -est** 1 : showy in dress 2 : stylish

drew *past of* DRAW

drib·ble \'dribəl\ *vb* **-bled; -bling** 1 : fall or flow in drops 2 : drool — **dribble** *n*

drier *comparative of* DRY

driest *superlative of* DRY

drift \'drift\ *n* 1 : motion or course of something drifting 2 : mass piled up by wind 3 : general intention or meaning ∼ *vb* 1 : float or be driven along (as by a current) 2 : wander without purpose 3 : pile up under force — **drift·er** *n* — **drift·wood** *n*

¹**drill** \'dril\ *vb* 1 : bore with a drill 2 : instruct by repetition ∼ *n* 1 : tool for boring holes 2 : regularly practiced exercise — **drill·er** *n*

²**drill** *n* : seed-planting implement

³**drill** *n* : twill-weave cotton fabric

drily *var of* DRYLY

drink \'driŋk\ *vb* **drank** \'draŋk\; **drunk** \'drəŋk\ *or* **drank**; **drink·ing** 1 : swallow liquid 2 : absorb 3 : drink alcoholic beverages esp. to excess ∼ *n* 1 : beverage 2 : alcoholic liquor — **drink·able** *adj* — **drink·er** *n*

drip \'drip\ *vb* **-pp-** : fall or let fall in drops ∼ *n* 1 : a dripping 2 : sound of falling drops

drive \'drīv\ *vb* **drove** \'drōv\; **driv·en** \'drivən\; **driv·ing** 1 : urge or force onward 2 : direct the movement or course of 3 : compel 4 : cause to become 5 : propel forcefully ∼ *n* 1 : trip in a vehicle 2 : intensive campaign 3 : aggressive or dynamic quality 4 : basic need — **driv·er** *n*

drive-in *adj* : accommodating patrons in cars — **drive-in** *n*

driv·el \'drivəl\ *vb* **-eled** *or* **-elled; -el·ing** *or* **-el·ling** 1 : drool 2 : talk stupidly ∼ *n* : nonsense

drive·way *n* : usu. short private road from the street to a house

driz·zle \'drizəl\ *n* : fine misty rain — **drizzle** *vb*

droll \'drōl\ *adj* : humorous or whimsical — **droll·ery** *n* — **drol·ly** *adv*

drom·e·dary \'drämə,derē\ *n, pl* **-dar·ies** : speedy one-humped camel

drone \'drōn\ *n* 1 : male honeybee 2 : deep hum or buzz ∼ *vb* **droned; dron·ing** : make a dull monotonous sound

drool \'drül\ *vb* : let liquid run from the mouth

droop \'drüp\ *vb* 1 : hang or incline downward 2 : lose strength or spirit — **droop** *n* — **droopy** \-ē\ *adj*

drop \'dräp\ *n* 1 : quantity of fluid in one spherical mass 2 *pl* : medicine used by drops 3 : decline or fall 4 : distance something drops ∼ *vb* **-pp-** 1 : fall in drops 2 : let fall 3 : convey 4 : go lower or become less strong or less active — **drop·let** \-lət\ *n* — **drop back** *vb* : move toward the rear — **drop behind** : fail to keep up — **drop in** *vb* : pay an unexpected visit

drop·per *n* : device that dispenses liquid by drops

drop·sy \'dräpsē\ *n* : edema

dross \'dräs\ *n* : waste matter

drought \'draut\ *n* : long dry spell

¹**drove** \'drōv\ *n* : crowd of moving people or animals

²**drove** *past of* DRIVE

drown \'draún\ *vb* **1** : suffocate in water **2** : overpower or become overpowered

drowse \'draúz\ *vb* **drowsed; drowsing** : doze — **drowse** *n*

drowsy \'draúzē\ *adj* **drows·i·er; -est** : sleepy — **drows·i·ly** *adv* — **drows·i·ness** *n*

drub \'drəb\ *vb* **-bb-** : beat severely

drudge \'drəj\ *vb* **drudged; drudg·ing** : do hard or boring work — **drudge** *n* — **drudg·ery** \-ərē\ *n*

drug \'drəg\ *n* **1** : substance used as or in medicine **2** : narcotic ~ *vb* **-gg-** : affect with drugs — **drug·gist** \-ist\ *n* — **drug·store** *n*

dru·id \'drüəd\ *n* : ancient Celtic priest

drum \'drəm\ *n* **1** : musical drum that is a skin-covered cylinder beaten usu. with sticks **2** : drum-shaped object (as a container) ~ *vb* **-mm-** **1** : beat a drum **2** : drive, force, or bring about by steady effort — **drum·beat** *n* — **drum·mer** *n*

drum·stick *n* **1** : stick for beating a drum **2** : lower part of a fowl's leg

drunk \'drəŋk\ *adj* : having the faculties impaired by alcohol ~ *n* : one who is drunk — **drunk·ard** \'drəŋkərd\ *n* — **drunk·en** \-kən\ *adj* — **drunk·en·ly** *adv* — **drunk·en·ness** *n*

dry \'drī\ *adj* **dri·er** \'drīər\; **dri·est** \'drīəst\ **1** : lacking water or moisture **2** : thirsty **3** : marked by the absence of alcoholic beverages **4** : uninteresting **5** : not sweet ~ *vb* **dried; dry·ing** : make or become dry — **dry·ly** *adv* — **dry·ness** *n*

dry–clean *vb* : clean (fabrics) chiefly with solvents other than water — **dry cleaning** *n*

dry·er \'drīər\ *n* : device for drying

dry goods *n pl* : textiles, clothing, and notions

dry ice *n* : solid carbon dioxide

du·al \'düəl, 'dyü-\ *adj* : twofold — **du·al·ism** \-ə,lizəm\ *n* — **du·al·i·ty** \dü'alətē, dyü-\ *n*

dub \'dəb\ *vb* **-bb-** : name

du·bi·ous \'dübēəs, 'dyü-\ *adj* **1** : uncertain **2** : questionable — **du·bi·ous·ly** *adv* — **du·bi·ous·ness** *n*

du·cal \'dükəl, 'dyü-\ *adj* : relating to a duke or dukedom

duch·ess \'dəchəs\ *n* **1** : wife of a duke **2** : woman holding a ducal title

duchy \-ē\ *n, pl* **-ies** : territory of a duke or duchess

¹duck \'dək\ *n* : swimming bird related to the goose and swan ~ *vb* **1** : thrust or plunge under water **2** : lower the head or body suddenly **3** : evade — **duck·ling** \-liŋ\ *n*

²duck *n* : cotton fabric

duct \'dəkt\ *n* : canal for conveying a fluid — **duct·less** \-ləs\ *adj*

duc·tile \'dəkt²l\ *adj* : able to be drawn out or shaped — **duc·til·i·ty** \,dək-'tilətē\ *n*

dude \'düd, 'dyüd\ *n* **1** : dandy **2** : guy

dud·geon \'dəjən\ *n* : ill humor

due \'dü, 'dyü\ *adj* **1** : owed **2** : appropriate **3** : attributable **4** : scheduled ~ *n* **1** : something due **2** *pl* : fee ~ *adv* : directly

du·el \'düəl, 'dyü-\ *n* : combat between 2 persons — **duel** *vb* — **du·el·ist** *n*

du·et \dü'et, dyü-\ *n* : musical composition for 2 performers

due to *prep* : because of

dug *past of* DIG

dug·out \'dəg,aút\ *n* **1** : boat made by hollowing out a log **2** : shelter made by digging

duke \'dük, 'dyük\ *n* : nobleman of the highest rank — **duke·dom** *n*

dull \'dəl\ *adj* **1** : mentally slow **2** : blunt **3** : not brilliant or interesting — **dull** *vb* — **dul·lard** \'dələrd\ *n* — **dull·ness** *n* — **dul·ly** *adv*

du·ly \'dülē, 'dyü-\ *adv* : in a due manner or time

dumb \'dəm\ *adj* **1** : mute **2** : stupid — **dumb·ly** *adv*

dumb·bell \'dəm,bel\ *n* **1** : short bar with weights on the ends used for exercise **2** : stupid person

dumb·found, dum·found \,dəm-'faúnd\ *vb* : amaze

dum·my \'dəmē\ *n, pl* **-mies 1** : stupid person **2** : imitative substitute

dump \'dəmp\ *vb* : let fall in a pile ~ *n* : place for dumping something (as refuse) — **in the dumps** : sad

dump·ling \'dəmpliŋ\ *n* : small mass of boiled or steamed dough

dumpy \'dəmpē\ *adj* **dump·i·er; -est** : short and thick in build

¹dun \'dən\ *adj* : brownish gray

²dun *vb* **-nn-** : hound for payment of a debt

dunce \'dəns\ *n* : stupid person

dune \'dün, 'dyün\ *n* : hill of sand

dung \'dəŋ\ *n* : manure

dun·ga·ree \,dəŋgə'rē\ *n* **1** : blue denim **2** *pl* : work clothes made of dungaree

dun·geon \'dənjən\ *n* : underground prison

dunk \'dəŋk\ *vb* : dip or submerge temporarily in liquid

duo \'düō, 'dyüō\ *n, pl* **du·os** : pair

du·o·de·num \,düə'dēnəm, ,dyü-; du̇-'äd°nəm, dyu̇-\ *n, pl* **-na** \-'dēnə, -°nə\ *or* **-nums** : part of the small intestine nearest the stomach — **du·o·de·nal** \-'dēn°l, -°nəl\ *adj*

dupe \'düp, 'dyüp\ *n* : one easily deceived or cheated — **dupe** *vb*

du·plex \'dü,pleks, 'dyü-\ *adj* : double ∼ *n* : 2-family house

du·pli·cate \'düplikət, 'dyü-\ *adj* **1** : consisting of 2 identical items **2** : being just like another ∼ *n* : exact copy ∼ \-,kāt\ *vb* **-cat·ed; -cat·ing 1** : make an exact copy of **2** : repeat or equal — **du·pli·ca·tion** \,düpli-'kāshən, ,dyü-\ *n* — **du·pli·ca·tor** \'düpli,kātər, dyü-\ *n*

du·plic·i·ty \du̇'plisətē, ,dyü-\ *n, pl* **-ties** : deception

du·ra·ble \'du̇rəbəl, 'dyu̇r-\ *adj* : lasting a long time — **du·ra·bil·i·ty** \,du̇rə'bilətē, ,dyu̇r-\ *n*

du·ra·tion \du̇'rāshən, dyu̇-\ *n* : length of time something lasts

du·ress \du̇'res, dyu̇-\ *n* : coercion

dur·ing \'du̇riŋ, 'dyu̇r-\ *prep* **1** : throughout **2** : at some point in

dusk \'dəsk\ *n* : twilight — **dusky** *adj*

dust \'dəst\ *n* : powdered matter ∼ *vb* **1** : remove dust from **2** : sprinkle with fine particles — **dust·er** *n* — **dust·pan** *n* — **dusty** *adj*

du·ty \'dütē, 'dyü-\ *n, pl* **-ties** **1** : action required by one's occupation or position **2** : moral or legal obligation **3** : tax — **du·te·ous** \-əs\ *adj* — **du·ti·able** \-əbəl\ *adj* — **du·ti·ful** \'dütifəl, 'dyü-\ *adj*

DVD \,dē,vē'dē\ *n* : digital video disk

dwarf \'dwȯrf\ *n, pl* **dwarfs** \'dwȯrfs\ *or* **dwarves** \'dwȯrvz\ : one that is much below normal size ∼ *vb* **1** : stunt **2** : cause to seem smaller — **dwarf·ish** *adj*

dwell \'dwel\ *vb* **dwelt** \'dwelt\ *or* **dwelled** \'dweld, 'dwelt\; **dwell·ing 1** : reside **2** : keep the attention directed — **dwell·er** *n* — **dwell·ing** *n*

dwin·dle \'dwind°l\ *vb* **-dled; -dling** : become steadily less

dye \'dī\ *n* : coloring material ∼ *vb* **dyed; dye·ing** : give a new color to

dying *pres part of* DIE

dyke *var of* DIKE

dy·nam·ic \dī'namik\ *adj* **1** : relating to physical force producing motion **2** : energetic or forceful

dy·na·mite \'dīnə,mīt\ *n* : explosive made of nitroglycerin — **dynamite** *vb*

dy·na·mo \-,mō\ *n, pl* **-mos** : electrical generator

dy·nas·ty \'dīnəstē, -,nas-\ *n, pl* **-ties** : succession of rulers of the same family — **dy·nas·tic** \dī'nastik\ *adj*

dys·en·tery \'dis°n,terē\ *n, pl* **-ter·ies** : disease marked by diarrhea

dys·lex·ia \dis'leksēə\ *n* : disturbance of the ability to read — **dys·lex·ic** \-sik\ *adj*

dys·pep·sia \-'pepshə, -sēə\ *n* : indigestion — **dys·pep·tic** \-'peptik\ *adj or n*

dys·tro·phy \'distrəfē\ *n, pl* **-phies** : disorder involving nervous and muscular tissue

E

e \'ē\ *n, pl* **e's** *or* **es** \'ēz\ : 5th letter of the alphabet

e- *comb form* : electronic

each \'ēch\ *adj* : being one of the class named ∼ *pron* : every individual one ∼ *adv* : apiece

ea·ger \'ēgər\ *adj* : enthusiastic or anxious — **ea·ger·ly** *adv* — **ea·ger·ness** *n*

ea·gle \'ēgəl\ *n* : large bird of prey

-ean — see -AN

¹ear \'ir\ *n* : organ of hearing or the outer part of this — **ear·ache** *n* — **eared** *adj* — **ear·lobe** \-,lōb\ *n*

²ear n : fruiting head of a cereal

ear·drum n : thin membrane that receives and transmits sound waves in the ear

earl \'ərl\ n : British nobleman — **earl·dom** \-dəm\ n

ear·ly \'ərlē\ adj -li·er; -est 1 : relating to or occurring near the beginning or before the usual time 2 : ancient — **early** adv

ear·mark vb : designate for a specific purpose

earn \'ərn\ vb 1 : receive as a return for service 2 : deserve

ear·nest \'ərnəst\ n : serious state of mind — **earnest** adj — **ear·nest·ly** adv — **ear·nest·ness** n

earn·ings \'ərninz\ n pl : something earned

ear·phone n : device that reproduces sound and is worn over or in the ear

ear·ring n : earlobe ornament

ear·shot n : range of hearing

earth \'ərth\ n 1 : soil or land 2 : planet inhabited by man — **earth·li·ness** n — **earth·ly** adj — **earth·ward** \-wərd\ adv

earth·en \'ərthən\ adj : made of earth or baked clay — **earth·en·ware** \-,war\ n

earth·quake n : shaking or trembling of the earth

earth·worm n : long segmented worm

earthy \'ərthē\ adj **earth·i·er; -est** 1 : relating to or consisting of earth 2 : practical 3 : coarse — **earth·i·ness** n

ease \'ēz\ n 1 : comfort 2 : naturalness of manner 3 : freedom from difficulty ~ vb **eased; eas·ing** 1 : relieve from distress 2 : lessen the tension of 3 : make easier

ea·sel \'ēzəl\ n : frame to hold a painter's canvas

east \'ēst\ adv : to or toward the east ~ adj : situated toward or at or coming from the east ~ n 1 : direction of sunrise 2 cap : regions to the east — **east·er·ly** \'ēstərlē\ adv or adj — **east·ward** adv or adj — **east·wards** adv

Eas·ter \'ēstər\ n : church feast celebrating Christ's resurrection

east·ern \'ēstərn\ adj 1 cap : relating to a region designated East 2 : lying toward or coming from the east — **East·ern·er** n

easy \'ēzē\ adj **eas·i·er; -est** 1

: marked by ease 2 : lenient — **eas·i·ly** \'ēzəlē\ adv — **eas·i·ness** \-ēnəs\ n

easy·go·ing adj : relaxed and casual

eat \'ēt\ vb **ate** \'āt\; **eat·en** \'ēt²n\; **eat·ing** 1 : take in as food 2 : use up or corrode — **eat·able** adj or n — **eat·er** n

eaves \'ēvz\ n pl : overhanging edge of a roof

eaves·drop vb : listen secretly — **eaves·drop·per** n

ebb \'eb\ n 1 : outward flow of the tide 2 : decline ~ vb 1 : recede from the flood state 2 : wane

eb·o·ny \'ebənē\ n, pl -nies : hard heavy wood of tropical trees ~ adj 1 : made of ebony 2 : black

ebul·lient \i'bulyənt, -'bəl-\ adj : exuberant — **ebul·lience** \-yəns\ n

ec·cen·tric \ik'sentrik\ adj 1 : odd in behavior 2 : being off center — **eccentric** n — **ec·cen·tri·cal·ly** \-triklē\ adv — **ec·cen·tric·i·ty** \ek,sen'trisətē\ n

ec·cle·si·as·tic \ik,lēzē'astik\ n : clergyman

ec·cle·si·as·ti·cal \-tikəl\, **ecclesiastic** adj : relating to a church — **ec·cle·si·as·ti·cal·ly** \-tiklē\ adv

ech·e·lon \'eshə,län\ n 1 : steplike arrangement 2 : level of authority

echo \'ekō\ n, pl **ech·oes** : repetition of a sound caused by a reflection of the sound waves — **echo** vb

éclair \ā'klar\ n : custard-filled pastry

eclec·tic \e'klektik, i-\ adj : drawing or drawn from varied sources

eclipse \i'klips\ n : total or partial obscuring of one celestial body by another — **eclipse** vb

ecol·o·gy \i'käləjē, e-\ n, pl -gies : science concerned with the interaction of organisms and their environment — **eco·log·i·cal** \,ēkə'läjikəl, ,ek-\ adj — **eco·log·i·cal·ly** adv — **ecol·o·gist** \i'käləjist, e-\ n

eco·nom·ic \,ekə'nämik, ,ēkə-\ adj : relating to the producing and the buying and selling of goods and services

eco·nom·ics \-'nämiks\ n : branch of knowledge dealing with goods and services — **econ·o·mist** \i'känəmist\ n

econ·o·mize \i'känə,mīz\ vb -mized; -miz·ing : be thrifty — **econ·o·miz·er** n

econ·o·my \-əmē\ *n, pl* **-mies 1** : thrifty use of resources **2** : economic system — **eco·nom·i·cal** \ˌekə'nämikəl, ˌēkə-\ *adj* — **eco·nom·i·cal·ly** *adv* — **economy** *adj*

ecru \'ekrü, 'akrü\ *n* : beige

ec·sta·sy \'ekstəsē\ *n, pl* **-sies** : extreme emotional excitement — **ec·stat·ic** \ek'statik, ik-\ *adj* — **ec·stat·i·cal·ly** \-iklē\ *adv*

ec·u·men·i·cal \ˌekyə'menikəl\ *adj* : promoting worldwide Christian unity

ec·ze·ma \ig'zēmə, 'egzəmə, 'eksə-\ *n* : itching skin inflammation

¹-ed \d *after a vowel or* b, g, j, l, m, n, ŋ, r, th, v, z, zh; əd, id *after* d, t; t *after other sounds*\ *vb suffix or adj suffix* **1** — used to form the past participle of regular verbs **2** : having or having the characteristics of

²-ed *vb suffix* — used to form the past tense of regular verbs

ed·dy \'edē\ *n, pl* **-dies** : whirlpool — **eddy** *vb*

ede·ma \i'dēmə\ *n* : abnormal accumulation of fluid in the body tissues — **edem·a·tous** \-'demətəs\ *adj*

Eden \'ēd°n\ *n* : paradise

edge \'ej\ *n* **1** : cutting side of a blade **2** : line where something begins or ends ∼ *vb* **edged; edg·ing 1** : give or form an edge **2** : move gradually **3** : narrowly defeat — **edg·er** *n*

edge·wise \-ˌwīz\ *adv* : sideways

edgy \'ejē\ *adj* **edg·i·er; -est** : nervous — **edg·i·ness** *n*

ed·i·ble \'edəbəl\ *adj* : fit or safe to be eaten — **ed·i·bil·i·ty** \ˌedə'bilətē\ — **edible** *n*

edict \'ēˌdikt\ *n* : order or decree

ed·i·fi·ca·tion \ˌedəfə'kāshən\ *n* : instruction or information — **ed·i·fy** \'edəˌfī\ *vb*

ed·i·fice \'edəfəs\ *n* : large building

ed·it \'edət\ *vb* **1** : revise and prepare for publication **2** : delete — **ed·i·tor** \-ər\ *n* — **ed·i·tor·ship** *n*

edi·tion \i'dishən\ *n* **1** : form in which a text is published **2** : total number published at one time

ed·i·to·ri·al \ˌedə'tōrēəl\ *adj* **1** : relating to an editor or editing **2** : expressing opinion ∼ *n* : article (as in a newspaper) expressing the views of an editor — **ed·i·to·ri·al·ize** \-ēəˌlīz\ *vb* — **ed·i·to·ri·al·ly** *adv*

ed·u·cate \'ejəˌkāt\ *vb* **-cat·ed; -cat-**

ing 1 : give instruction to **2** : develop mentally and morally **3** : provide with information — **ed·u·ca·ble** \'ejəkəbəl\ *adj* — **ed·u·ca·tion** \ˌejə'kāshən\ *n* — **ed·u·ca·tion·al** \-shənəl\ *adj* — **ed·u·ca·tor** \-ər\ *n*

eel \'ēl\ *n* : snakelike fish

ee·rie \'irē\ *adj* **-ri·er; -est** : weird — **ee·ri·ly** \'irəlē\ *adv*

ef·face \i'fās, e-\ *vb* **-faced; -fac·ing** : obliterate by rubbing out — **ef·face·ment** *n*

ef·fect \i'fekt\ *n* **1** : result **2** : meaning **3** : influence **4** *pl* : goods or possessions ∼ *vb* : cause to happen — **in effect** : in substance

ef·fec·tive \i'fektiv\ *adj* **1** : producing a strong or desired effect **2** : being in operation — **ef·fec·tive·ly** *adv* — **ef·fec·tive·ness** *n*

ef·fec·tu·al \i'fekchəwəl\ *adj* : producing an intended effect — **ef·fec·tu·al·ly** *adv* — **ef·fec·tu·al·ness** *n*

ef·fem·i·nate \ə'femənət\ *adj* : having qualities more typical of women than men — **ef·fem·i·na·cy** \-nəsē\ *n*

ef·fer·vesce \ˌefər'ves\ *vb* **-vesced; -vesc·ing 1** : bubble and hiss as gas escapes **1** : show exhilaration — **ef·fer·ves·cence** \-'ves°ns\ *n* — **ef·fer·ves·cent** \-°nt\ *adj* — **ef·fer·ves·cent·ly** *adv*

ef·fete \e'fēt\ *adj* **1** : worn out **2** : weak or decadent **3** : effeminate

ef·fi·ca·cious \ˌefə'kāshəs\ *adj* : effective — **ef·fi·ca·cy** \'efikəsē\ *n*

ef·fi·cient \i'fishənt\ *adj* : working well with little waste — **ef·fi·cien·cy** \-ənsē\ *n* — **ef·fi·cient·ly** *adv*

ef·fi·gy \'efəjē\ *n, pl* **-gies** : usu. crude image of a person

ef·flu·ent \'eˌflüənt, e'flü-\ *n* : something that flows out — **effluent** *adj*

ef·fort \'efərt\ *n* **1** : a putting forth of strength **2** : use of resources toward a goal **3** : product of effort — **ef·fort·less** *adj* — **ef·fort·less·ly** *adv*

ef·fron·tery \i'frəntərē\ *n, pl* **-ter·ies** : insolence

ef·fu·sion \i'fyüzhən, e-\ *n* : a gushing forth — **ef·fu·sive** \-'fyüsiv\ *adj* — **ef·fu·sive·ly** *adv*

¹egg \'eg, 'āg\ *vb* : urge to action

²egg *n* **1** : rounded usu. hard-shelled reproductive body esp. of birds and reptiles from which the young hatches **2** : ovum — **egg·shell** *n*

egg·nog \-ˌnäg\ n : rich drink of eggs and cream

egg·plant n : edible purplish fruit of a plant related to the potato

ego \'ēgō\ n, pl **egos** : self-esteem

ego·cen·tric \ˌēgō'sentrik\ adj : self-centered

ego·tism \'ēgəˌtizəm\ n : exaggerated sense of self-importance — **ego·tist** \-tist\ n — **ego·tis·tic** \ˌēgə'tistik\, **ego·tis·ti·cal** \-tikəl\ adj — **ego·tis·ti·cal·ly** adv

egre·gious \i'grējəs\ adj : notably bad — **egre·gious·ly** adv

egress \'ēˌgres\ n : a way out

egret \'ēgrət, i'gret, 'egrət\ n : long-plumed heron

ei·der·down \'īdərˌdaùn\ n : soft down obtained from a northern sea duck (**eider**)

eight \'āt\ n 1 : one more than 7 2 : 8th in a set or series 3 : something having 8 units — **eight** adj or pron — **eighth** \'ātth\ adj or adv or n

eigh·teen \āt'tēn\ n : one more than 17 — **eigh·teen** adj or pron — **eigh·teenth** \-'tēnth\ adj or n

eighty \'ātē\ n, pl **eight·ies** : 8 times 10 — **eight·i·eth** \'ātēəth\ adj or n — **eighty** adj or pron

ei·ther \'ēthər, 'ī-\ adj 1 : both 2 : being the one or the other of two ~ pron : one of two or more ~ conj : one or the other

ejac·u·late \i'jakyəˌlāt\ vb **-lat·ed; -lat·ing** 1 : say suddenly 2 : eject a fluid (as semen) — **ejac·u·la·tion** \-ˌjakyə'lāshən\ n

eject \i'jekt\ vb : drive or throw out — **ejec·tion** \-'jekshən\ n

eke \'ēk\ vb **eked; ek·ing** : barely gain with effort — usu. with out

elab·o·rate \i'labərət\ adj 1 : planned in detail 2 : complex and ornate ~ \-əˌrāt\ vb **-rat·ed; -rat·ing** : work out in detail — **elab·o·rate·ly** adv — **elab·o·rate·ness** n — **elab·o·ra·tion** \-ˌlabə'rāshən\ n

elapse \i'laps\ vb **elapsed; elaps·ing** : slip by

elas·tic \i'lastik\ adj 1 : springy 2 : flexible ~ n 1 : elastic material 2 : rubber band — **elas·tic·i·ty** \-ˌlas'tisətē, ˌēˌlas-\ n

elate \i'lāt\ vb **elat·ed; elat·ing** : fill with joy — **ela·tion** \-'lāshən\ n

el·bow \'elˌbō\ n 1 : joint of the arm 2 : elbow-shaped bend or joint ~ vb : push aside with the elbow

el·der \'eldər\ adj : older ~ n 1 : one who is older 2 : church officer

el·der·ber·ry \'eldərˌberē\ n : edible black or red fruit of a tree or shrub bearing these

el·der·ly \'eldərlē\ adj : past middle age

el·dest \'eldəst\ adj : oldest

elect \i'lekt\ adj : elected but not yet in office ~ n **elect** pl : exclusive group ~ vb : choose esp. by vote — **elec·tion** \i'lekshən\ n — **elec·tive** \i'lektiv\ n or adj — **elec·tor** \i'lektər\ n — **elec·tor·al** \-tərəl\ adj

elec·tor·ate \i'lektərət\ n : body of persons entitled to vote

elec·tric \i'lektrik\ adj 1 or **elec·tri·cal** \-trikəl\ : relating to or run by electricity 2 : thrilling — **elec·tri·cal·ly** adv

elec·tri·cian \iˌlek'trishən\ n : person who installs or repairs electrical equipment

elec·tric·i·ty \-'trisətē\ n, pl **-ties** 1 : fundamental form of energy occurring naturally (as in lightning) or produced artificially 2 : electric current

elec·tri·fy \i'lektrəˌfī\ vb **-fied; -fy·ing** 1 : charge with electricity 2 : equip for use of electric power 3 : thrill — **elec·tri·fi·ca·tion** \-ˌlektrəfə'kāshən\ n

elec·tro·car·dio·gram \iˌlektrō'kärdēəˌgram\ n : tracing made by an electrocardiograph

elec·tro·car·dio·graph \-ˌgraf\ n : instrument for monitoring heart function

elec·tro·cute \i'lektrəˌkyüt\ vb **-cut·ed; -cut·ing** : kill by an electric shock — **elec·tro·cu·tion** \-ˌlektrə'kyüshən\ n

elec·trode \i'lekˌtrōd\ n : conductor at a nonmetallic part of a circuit

elec·trol·y·sis \iˌlek'träləsəs\ n 1 : production of chemical changes by passage of an electric current through a substance 2 : destruction of hair roots with an electric current — **elec·tro·lyt·ic** \-ˌtrə'litik\ adj

elec·tro·lyte \i'lektrəˌlīt\ n : nonmetallic electric conductor

elec·tro·mag·net \iˌlektrō'magnət\ n : magnet made using electric current

elec·tro·mag·ne·tism \-nəˌtizəm\ n : natural force responsible for interac-

tions between charged particles —
elec·tro·mag·net·ic \-mag'netik\
adj — **elec·tro·mag·net·i·cal·ly**
\-ik'lē\ *adv*

elec·tron \i'lek,trän\ *n* : negatively
charged particle within the atom

elec·tron·ic \i,lek'tränik\ *adj* : relating to or electrons or electronics —
elec·tron·i·cal·ly \-ik'lē\ *adv*

elec·tron·ics \-iks\ *n* : physics of electrons and their use esp. in devices

elec·tro·plate \i'lektrə,plāt\ *vb* : coat
(as with metal) by electrolysis

el·e·gance \'eligəns\ *n* : refined grace-
fulness — **el·e·gant** \-gənt\ *adj* —
el·e·gant·ly *adv*

el·e·gy \'eləjē\ *n, pl* **-gies** : poem expressing grief for one who is dead —
ele·gi·ac \,elə'jīək, -,ak\ *adj*

el·e·ment \'eləmənt\ *n* **1** *pl* : weather
conditions **2** : natural environment **3**
: constituent part **4** *pl* : simplest principles **5** : substance that has atoms of
only one kind — **el·e·men·tal** \,elə'-
ment'l\ *adj*

el·e·men·ta·ry \,elə'mentrē\ *adj* **1**
: simple **2** : relating to the basic subjects of education

el·e·phant \'eləfənt\ *n* : huge mammal
with a trunk and 2 ivory tusks

el·e·vate \'elə,vāt\ *vb* **-vat·ed; -vat·ing**
1 : lift up **2** : exalt

el·e·va·tion \,elə'vāshən\ *n* : height or
a high place

el·e·va·tor \'elə,vātər\ *n* **1** : cage or
platform for raising or lowering
something **2** : grain storehouse

elev·en \i'levən\ *n* **1** : one more than
10 **2** : 11th in a set or series **3**
: something having 11 units —
eleven *adj or pron* — **eleventh**
\-ənth\ *adj or n*

elf \'elf\ *n, pl* **elves** \'elvz\ : mischievous fairy — **elf·in** \'elfən\ *adj* —
elf·ish \'elfish\ *adj*

elic·it \i'lisət\ *vb* : draw forth

el·i·gi·ble \'eləjəbəl\ *adj* : qualified to
participate or to be chosen — **el·i·gi·
bil·i·ty** \,eləjə'bilətē\ *n*

elim·i·nate \i'limə,nāt\ *vb* **-nat·ed;
-nat·ing** : get rid of — **elim·i·na·tion**
\i,limə'nāshən\ *n*

elite \ā'lēt\ *n* : choice or select group

elix·ir \i'liksər\ *n* : medicinal solution

elk \'elk\ *n* : large deer

el·lipse \i'lips, e-\ *n* : oval

el·lip·sis \-'lipsəs\ *n, pl* **-lip·ses**
\-,sēz\ **1** : omission of a word **2**
: marks (as ...) to show omission

el·lip·ti·cal \-tikəl\, **el·lip·tic** \-tik\
adj **1** : relating to or shaped like an
ellipse **2** : relating to or marked by
ellipsis

elm \'elm\ *n* : tall shade tree

el·o·cu·tion \,elə'kyūshən\ *n* : art of
public speaking

elon·gate \ē'lôŋ,gāt\ *vb* **-gat·ed; -gat·
ing** : make or grow longer — **elon·
ga·tion** \,ē,lôŋ'gāshən\ *n*

elope \i'lōp\ *vb* **eloped; elop·ing** : run
away esp. to be married — **elope·
ment** *n* — **elop·er** *n*

el·o·quent \'eləkwənt\ *adj* : forceful
and persuasive in speech — **el·o·
quence** \-kwəns\ *n* — **el·o·quent·ly**
adv

else \'els\ *adv* **1** : in a different way,
time, or place **2** : otherwise ~ *adj* **1**
: other **2** : more

else·where *adv* : in or to another place

elu·ci·date \ē'lüsə,dāt\ *vb* **-dat·ed;
-dat·ing** : explain — **elu·ci·da·tion**
\i,lüsə'dāshən\ *n*

elude \ē'lüd\ *vb* **elud·ed; elud·ing**
: evade — **elu·sive** \ē'lüsiv\ *adj* —
elu·sive·ly *adv* — **elu·sive·ness** *n*

elves *pl of* ELF

ema·ci·ate \i'māshē,āt\ *vb* **-at·ed; -at·
ing** : become or make very thin —
ema·ci·a·tion \i,māsē'āshən, -shē-\
n

e-mail \'ē,māl\ *n* : message sent or received via computers

em·a·nate \'emə,nāt\ *vb* **-nat·ed;
-nat·ing** : come forth — **em·a·na·
tion** \,emə'nāshən\ *n*

eman·ci·pate \i'mansə,pāt\ *vb* **-pat·ed;
-pat·ing** : set free — **eman·ci·pa·
tion** \i,mansə'pāshən\ *n* — **eman·
ci·pa·tor** \i'mansə,pātər\ *n*

emas·cu·late \i'maskyə,lāt\ *vb* **-lat·ed;
-lat·ing** **1** : castrate **2** : weaken —
emas·cu·la·tion \i,maskyə'lāshən\
n

em·balm \im'bäm, -'bälm\ *vb* : preserve (a corpse) — **em·balm·er** *n*

em·bank·ment \im'baŋkmənt\ *n*
: protective barrier of earth

em·bar·go \im'bärgō\ *n, pl* **-goes**
: ban on trade — **embargo** *vb*

em·bark \-'bärk\ *vb* **1** : go on board a
ship or airplane **2** : make a start —
em·bar·ka·tion \,em,bär'kāshən\ *n*

em·bar·rass \im'barəs\ *vb* : cause distress and self-consciousness — **em·bar·rass·ment** n

em·bas·sy \'embəsē\ n, pl **-sies** : residence and offices of an ambassador

em·bed \im'bed\ vb **-dd-** : fix firmly

em·bel·lish \-'belish\ vb : decorate — **em·bel·lish·ment** n

em·ber \'embər\ n : smoldering fragment from a fire

em·bez·zle \im'bezəl\ vb **-zled; -zling** : steal (money) by falsifying records — **em·bez·zle·ment** n — **em·bez·zler** \-ələr\ n

em·bit·ter \im'bitər\ vb : make bitter

em·bla·zon \-'blāzᵊn\ vb : display conspicuously

em·blem \'embləm\ n : symbol — **em·blem·at·ic** \,emblə'matik\ adj

em·body \im'bädē\ vb **-bod·ied; -body·ing** : give definite form or expression to — **em·bodi·ment** \-'bädimənt\ n

em·boss \-'bäs, -'bòs\ vb : ornament with raised work

em·brace \-'brās\ vb **-braced; -brac·ing** **1** : clasp in the arms **2** : welcome **3** : include — **embrace** n

em·broi·der \-'bròidər\ vb : ornament with or do needlework — **em·broi·dery** \-ərē\ n

em·broil \im'bròil\ vb : involve in conflict or difficulties

em·bryo \'embrē,ō\ n : living being in its earliest stages of development — **em·bry·on·ic** \,embrē'änik\ adj

emend \ē'mend\ vb : correct — **emen·da·tion** \,ē,men'dāshən\ n

em·er·ald \'emrəld, 'emə-\ n : green gem ~ adj : bright green

emerge \i'mərj\ vb **emerged; emerg·ing** : rise, come forth, or appear — **emer·gence** \-'mərjəns\ n — **emer·gent** \-jənt\ adj

emer·gen·cy \i'mərjənsē\ n, pl **-cies** : condition requiring prompt action

em·ery \'emərē\ n, pl **-er·ies** : dark granular mineral used for grinding

emet·ic \i'metik\ n : agent that induces vomiting — **emetic** adj

em·i·grate \'emə,grāt\ vb **-grat·ed; -grat·ing** : leave a country to settle elsewhere — **em·i·grant** \-igrənt\ n — **em·i·gra·tion** \,emə'grāshən\ n

em·i·nence \'emənəns\ n **1** : prominence or superiority **2** : person of high rank

em·i·nent \-nənt\ adj : prominent — **em·i·nent·ly** adv

em·is·sary \'emə,serē\ n, pl **-sar·ies** : agent

emis·sion \ē'mishən\ n : substance discharged into the air

emit \ē'mit\ vb **-tt-** : give off or out

emol·u·ment \i'mälyəmənt\ n : salary or fee

emote \i'mōt\ vb **emot·ed; emot·ing** : express emotion

emo·tion \i'mōshən\ n : intense feeling — **emo·tion·al** \-shənəl\ adj — **emo·tion·al·ly** adv

em·per·or \'empərər\ n : ruler of an empire

em·pha·sis \'emfəsəs\ n, pl **-pha·ses** \-,sēz\ : stress

em·pha·size \-,sīz\ vb **-sized; -siz·ing** : stress

em·phat·ic \im'fatik, em-\ adj : uttered with emphasis — **em·phat·i·cal·ly** \-ik lē\ adv

em·pire \'em,pīr\ n : large state or a group of states

em·pir·i·cal \im'pirikəl\ adj : based on observation — **em·pir·i·cal·ly** \-iklē\ adv

em·ploy \im'plòi\ vb **1** : use **2** : occupy ~ n : paid occupation — **em·ploy·ee, em·ploye** \im,plòi'ē, -'plòi,ē\ n — **em·ploy·er** n — **em·ploy·ment** \-mənt\ n

em·pow·er \im'paùər\ vb : give power to — **em·pow·er·ment** n

em·press \'emprəs\ n **1** : wife of an emperor **2** : woman emperor

emp·ty \'emptē\ adj **1** : containing nothing **2** : not occupied **3** : lacking value, sense, or purpose ~ vb **-tied; -ty·ing** : make or become empty — **emp·ti·ness** \-tēnəs\ n

emu \'ēmyü\ n : Australian bird related to the ostrich

em·u·late \'emyə,lāt\ vb **-lat·ed; -lat·ing** : try to equal or excel — **em·u·la·tion** \,emyə'lāshən\ n

emul·si·fy \i'məlsə,fī\ vb **-fied; -fy·ing** : convert into an emulsion — **emul·si·fi·ca·tion** \i,məlsəfə'kāshən\ n — **emul·si·fi·er** \-'məlsə,fīər\ n

emul·sion \i'məlshən\ n **1** : mixture of mutually insoluble liquids **2** : light-sensitive coating on photographic film

-en \ən,ᵊn\ vb suffix **1** : become or cause to be **2** : cause or come to have

en·able \in'ābəl\ vb **-abled; -abling** : give power, capacity, or ability to

en·act \in'akt\ *vb* **1** : make into law **2** : act out — **en·act·ment** *n*

enam·el \in'amǝl\ *n* **1** : glasslike substance used to coat metal or pottery **2** : hard outer layer of a tooth **3** : glossy paint — **enamel** *vb*

en·am·or \in'amǝr\ *vb* : excite with love

en·camp \in'kamp\ *vb* : make camp — **en·camp·ment** *n*

en·case \in'kās\ *vb* : enclose in or as if in a case

-ence \ǝns,ᵊns\ *n suffix* **1** : action or process **2** : quality or state

en·ceph·a·li·tis \in,sefǝ'lītǝs\ *n, pl* **-lit·i·des** \-'litǝ,dēz\ : inflammation of the brain

en·chant \in'chant\ *vb* **1** : bewitch **2** : fascinate — **en·chant·er** *n* — **en·chant·ment** *n* — **en·chant·ress** \-'chantrǝs\ *n*

en·cir·cle \in'sǝrkǝl\ *vb* : surround

en·close \in'klōz\ *vb* **1** : shut up or surround **2** : include — **en·clo·sure** \in'klōzhǝr\ *n*

en·co·mi·um \en'kōmēǝm\ *n, pl* **-mi·ums** *or* **-mia** \-mēǝ\ : high praise

en·com·pass \in'kǝmpǝs, -'käm-\ *vb* : surround or include

en·core \'än,kōr\ *n* : further performance

en·coun·ter \in'kaùntǝr\ *vb* **1** : fight **2** : meet unexpectedly — **encounter** *n*

en·cour·age \in'kǝrij\ *vb* **-aged; -ag·ing 1** : inspire with courage and hope **2** : foster — **en·cour·age·ment** *n*

en·croach \in'krōch\ *vb* : enter upon another's property or rights — **en·croach·ment** *n*

en·crust \in'krǝst\ *vb* : form a crust on

en·cum·ber \in'kǝmbǝr\ *vb* : burden — **en·cum·brance** \-brǝns\ *n*

-en·cy \ǝnsē,ᵊn-\ *n suffix* : -ence

en·cyc·li·cal \in'siklikǝl, en-\ *n* : papal letter to bishops

en·cy·clo·pe·dia \in,sīklǝ'pēdēǝ\ *n* : reference work on many subjects — **en·cy·clo·pe·dic** \-'pēdik\ *adj*

end \'end\ *n* **1** : point at which something stops or no longer exists **2** : cessation **3** : purpose — **~** *vb* **1** : stop or finish **2** : be at the end of — **end·less** *adj* — **end·less·ly** *adv*

en·dan·ger \in'dānjǝr\ *vb* : bring into danger

en·dear \in'dir\ *vb* : make dear — **dear·ment** \-mǝnt\ *n*

en·deav·or \in'devǝr\ *vb or n* : attempt

end·ing \'endiŋ\ *n* : end

en·dive \'en,dīv\ *n* : salad plant

en·do·crine \'endǝkrǝn, -,krīn, -,krēn\ *adj* : producing secretions distributed by the bloodstream

en·dorse \in'dórs\ *vb* **-dorsed; -dors·ing 1** : sign one's name to **2** : approve — **en·dorse·ment** *n*

en·dow \in'daù\ *vb* **1** : furnish with funds **2** : furnish naturally — **en·dow·ment** *n*

en·dure \in'dúr, -'dyúr\ *vb* **-dured; -dur·ing 1** : last **2** : suffer patiently **3** : tolerate — **en·dur·able** *adj* — **en·dur·ance** \-ǝns\ *n*

en·e·ma \'enǝmǝ\ *n* : injection of liquid into the rectum

en·e·my \-mē\ *n, pl* **-mies** : one that attacks or tries to harm another

en·er·get·ic \,enǝr'jetik\ *adj* : full of energy or activity — **en·er·get·i·cal·ly** \-iklē\ *adv*

en·er·gize \'enǝr,jīz\ *vb* **-gized; -giz·ing** : give energy to

en·er·gy \'enǝrjē\ *n, pl* **-gies 1** : capacity for action **2** : vigorous action **3** : capacity for doing work

en·er·vate \'enǝr,vāt\ *vb* **-vat·ed; -vat·ing** : make weak or listless — **en·er·va·tion** \,enǝr'vāshǝn\ *n*

en·fold \in'fōld\ *vb* : surround or embrace

en·force \-'fórs\ *vb* **1** : compel **2** : carry out — **en·force·able** \-ǝbǝl\ *adj* — **en·force·ment** *n*

en·fran·chise \-'fran,chīz\ *vb* **-chised; -chis·ing** : grant voting rights to — **en·fran·chise·ment** \-,chīzmǝnt, -chǝz-\ *n*

en·gage \in'gāj\ *vb* **-gaged; -gag·ing 1** : participate or cause to participate **2** : bring or come into working contact **3** : bind by a pledge to marry **4** : hire **5** : bring or enter into conflict — **en·gage·ment** \-mǝnt\ *n*

en·gag·ing *adj* : attractive

en·gen·der \in'jendǝr\ *vb* **-dered; -der·ing** : create

en·gine \'enjǝn\ *n* **1** : machine that converts energy into mechanical motion **2** : locomotive

en·gi·neer \,enjǝ'nir\ *n* **1** : one trained in engineering **2** : engine operator **~** *vb* : lay out or manage as an engineer

en·gi·neer·ing \-iŋ\ *n* : practical application of science and mathematics

en·grave \in'grāv\ vb **-graved; -gra·ving** : cut into a surface — **en·grav·er** n — **en·grav·ing** n

en·gross \in'grōs\ vb : occupy fully

en·gulf \-'gəlf\ vb : swallow up

en·hance \-'hans\ vb **-hanced; -hanc·ing** : improve in value — **en·hance·ment** n

enig·ma \i'nigmə\ n : puzzle or mystery — **enig·mat·ic** \,enig'matik, ,ē-\ adj — **enig·mat·i·cal·ly** adv

en·join \in'jȯin\ vb **1** : command **2** : forbid

en·joy \i'jȯi\ vb : take pleasure in — **en·joy·able** adj — **en·joy·ment** n

en·large \in'lärj\ vb **-larged; -larg·ing** : make or grow larger — **en·large·ment** n — **en·larg·er** n

en·light·en \-'līt'n\ vb : give knowledge or spiritual insight to — **en·light·en·ment** n

en·list \-'list\ vb **1** : join the armed forces **2** : get the aid of — **en·list·ee** \-,lis'tē\ n — **en·list·ment** \-'list-mənt\ n

en·liv·en \in'līvən\ vb : give life or spirit to

en·mi·ty \'enmətē\ n, pl **-ties** : mutual hatred

en·no·ble \in'ōbəl\ vb **-bled; -bling** : make noble

en·nui \,än'wē\ n : boredom

enor·mi·ty \i'nȯrmətē\ n, pl **-ties 1** : great wickedness **2** : huge size

enor·mous \i'nȯrməs\ adj : great in size, number, or degree — **enor·mous·ly** adv — **enor·mous·ness** n

enough \i'nəf\ adj : adequate ~ adv **1** : in an adequate manner **2** : in a tolerable degree ~ pron : adequate number, quantity, or amount

en·quire \in'kwīr\, **en·qui·ry** \in-,kwīrē, in'-; 'inkwərē, 'in-\ var of INQUIRE, INQUIRY

en·rage \in'rāj\ vb : fill with rage

en·rich \-'rich\ vb : make rich — **en·rich·ment** n

en·roll, en·rol \-'rōl\ vb **-rolled; -rolling 1** : enter on a list **2** : become enrolled — **en·roll·ment** n

en route \än'rüt, en-, in-\ adv or adj : on or along the way

en·sconce \in'skäns\ vb **-sconced; -sconc·ing** : settle snugly

en·sem·ble \än'sämbəl\ n **1** : small group **2** : complete costume

en·shrine \in'shrīn\ vb **1** : put in a shrine **2** : cherish

en·sign \'ensən, 1 also 'en,sīn\ n **1** : flag **2** : lowest ranking commissioned officer in the navy

en·slave \in'slāv\ vb : make a slave of — **en·slave·ment** n

en·snare \-'snar\ vb : trap

en·sue \-'sü\ vb **-sued; -su·ing** : follow as a consequence

en·sure \-'shùr\ vb **-sured; -sur·ing** : guarantee

en·tail \-'tāl\ vb : involve as a necessary result

en·tan·gle \-'tangəl\ vb : tangle — **en·tan·gle·ment** n

en·ter \'entər\ vb **1** : go or come in or into **2** : start **3** : set down (as in a list)

en·ter·prise \'entər,prīz\ n **1** : an undertaking **2** : business organization **3** : initiative

en·ter·pris·ing \-,prīziŋ\ adj : showing initiative

en·ter·tain \,entər'tān\ vb **1** : treat or receive as a guest **2** : hold in mind **3** : amuse — **en·ter·tain·er** n — **en·ter·tain·ment** n

en·thrall, en·thral \in'thról\ vb **-thralled; -thrall·ing** : hold spellbound

en·thu·si·asm \-'thüzē,azəm, -'thyü-\ n : strong excitement of feeling or its cause — **en·thu·si·ast** \-,ast, -əst\ n — **en·thu·si·as·tic** \-,thüzē'astik, -,thyü-\ adj — **en·thu·si·as·ti·cal·ly** \-tiklē\ adv

en·tice \-'tīs\ vb **-ticed; -tic·ing** : tempt — **en·tice·ment** n

en·tire \in'tīr\ adj : complete or whole — **en·tire·ly** adv — **en·tire·ty** \-'tīrətē, -'tīrtē\ n

en·ti·tle \-'tīt'l\ vb **-tled; -tling 1** : name **2** : give a right to

en·ti·ty \'entətē\ n, pl **-ties** : something with separate existence

en·to·mol·o·gy \,entə'mäləjē\ n : study of insects — **en·to·mo·log·i·cal** \-mə'läjikəl\ adj — **en·to·mol·o·gist** \-'mäləjist\ n

en·tou·rage \,äntù'räzh\ n : retinue

en·trails \'entrəlz, -,trālz\ n pl : intestines

¹**en·trance** \'entrəns\ n **1** : act of entering **2** : means or place of entering — **en·trant** \'entrənt\ n

²**en·trance** \in'trans\ vb **-tranced; -tranc·ing** : fascinate or delight

en·trap \in'trap\ vb : trap — **en·trap·ment** n

en·treat \-'trēt\ vb : ask urgently — en·treaty \-'trētē\ n

en·trée, en·tree \'än,trā\ n : principal dish of the meal

en·trench \in'trench\ vb : establish in a strong position — en·trench·ment n

en·tre·pre·neur \,äntrəprə'nər\ n : organizer or promoter of an enterprise

en·trust \in'trəst\ vb : commit to another with confidence

en·try \'entrē\ n, pl -tries 1 : entrance 2 : an entering in a record or an item so entered

en·twine \in'twīn\ vb : twine together or around

enu·mer·ate \i'nümə,rāt, -'nyü-\ vb -at·ed; -at·ing 1 : count 2 : list — enu·mer·a·tion \i,nümə'rāshən, -,nyü-\ n

enun·ci·ate \ē'nənsē,āt\ vb -at·ed; -at·ing 1 : announce 2 : pronounce — enun·ci·a·tion \-,nənsē'āshən\ n

en·vel·op \in'veləp\ vb : surround — en·vel·op·ment n

en·ve·lope \'envə,lōp, 'än-\ n : paper container for a letter

en·vi·ron·ment \in'vīrənmənt\ n : surroundings — en·vi·ron·men·tal \-,vīrən'ment³l\ adj

en·vi·ron·men·tal·ist \-³list\ n : person concerned about the environment

en·vi·rons \in'vīrənz\ n pl : vicinity

en·vis·age \in'vizij\ vb -aged; -ag·ing : have a mental picture of

en·vi·sion \-'vizhən\ vb : picture to oneself

en·voy \'en,vȯi, 'än-\ n : diplomat

en·vy \'envē\ n 1 : resentful awareness of another's advantage 2 : object of envy ~ vb -vied; -vy·ing : feel envy toward or on account of — en·vi·able \-vēəbəl\ adj — en·vi·ous \-vēəs\ adj — en·vi·ous·ly adv

en·zyme \'en,zīm\ n : biological catalyst

eon \'ēən, ē,än\ n : indefinitely long time

ep·au·let \,epə'let\ n : shoulder ornament on a uniform

ephem·er·al \i'femərəl\ adj : short-lived

ep·ic \'epik\ n : long poem about a hero — epic adj

ep·i·cure \'epi,kyu̇r\ n : person with fastidious taste esp. in food and wine — ep·i·cu·re·an \,epikyu̇'rēən, -'kyu̇rē-\ n or adj

ep·i·dem·ic \,epə'demik\ adj : affecting many persons at one time — epidemic n

epi·der·mis \,epə'dərməs\ n : outer layer of skin

ep·i·gram \'epə,gram\ n : short witty poem or saying

ep·i·lep·sy \'epə,lepsē\ n, pl -sies : nervous disorder marked by convulsive attacks — ep·i·lep·tic \,epə'leptik\ adj or n

epis·co·pal \i'piskəpəl\ adj : governed by bishops

ep·i·sode \'epə,sōd, -,zōd\ n : occurrence — ep·i·sod·ic \,epə'sädik, -'zäd-\ adj

epis·tle \i'pisəl\ n : letter

ep·i·taph \'epə,taf\ n : inscription in memory of a dead person

ep·i·thet \'epə,thet, -,thət\ n : characterizing often abusive word or phrase

epit·o·me \i'pitəmē\ n 1 : summary 2 : ideal example — epit·o·mize \-,mīz\ vb

ep·och \'epək, 'ep,äk\ n : extended period — ep·och·al \'epəkəl, 'ep,äkəl\ adj

ep·oxy \'ep,äksē, ep'äksē\ n : synthetic resin used esp. in adhesives ~ vb -ox·ied or -oxyed; -oxy·ing : glue with epoxy

equa·ble \'ekwəbəl, 'ēkwə-\ adj : free from unpleasant extremes — eq·ua·bil·i·ty \,ekwə'bilətē, ,ē-\ n — equa·bly \-blē\ adv

equal \'ēkwəl\ adj : of the same quantity, value, quality, number, or status as another ~ n : one that is equal ~ vb equaled or equalled; equal·ing or equal·ling : be or become equal to — equal·i·ty \i'kwälətē\ n — equal·ize \'ēkwə,līz\ vb — equal·ly \'ēkwəlē\ adv

equa·nim·i·ty \,ēkwə'nimətē, ,ek-\ n, pl -ties : calmness

equate \i'kwāt\ vb equat·ed; equat·ing : treat or regard as equal

equa·tion \i'kwāzhən, -shən\ n : mathematical statement that two things are equal

equa·tor \i'kwātər\ n : imaginary circle that divides the northern and southern hemispheres — equa·to·ri·al \,ēkwə'tōrēəl, ,ek-\ adj

eques·tri·an \i'kwestrēən\ adj : relating to horseback riding ~ n : horseback rider

equi·lat·er·al \ˌēkwə'latərəl\ *adj* : having equal sides

equi·lib·ri·um \-'librēəm\ *n, pl* **-ri·ums** *or* **-ria** \-rēə\ : state of balance

equine \'ē,kwīn, 'ek,wīn\ *adj* : relating to the horse — **equine** *n*

equi·nox \'ēkwə,näks, 'ek-\ *n* : time when day and night are everywhere of equal length

equip \i'kwip\ *vb* **-pp-** : furnish with needed resources — **equip·ment** \-mənt\ *n*

eq·ui·ta·ble \'ekwətəbəl\ *adj* : fair

eq·ui·ty \'ekwətē\ *n, pl* **-ties** 1 : justice 2 : value of a property less debt

equiv·a·lent \i'kwivələnt\ *adj* : equal — **equiv·a·lence** \-ləns\ *n* — **equivalent** *n*

equiv·o·cal \i'kwivəkəl\ *adj* : ambiguous or uncertain

equiv·o·cate \i'kwivə,kāt\ *vb* **-cat·ed; -cat·ing** 1 : use misleading language 2 : avoid answering definitely — **equiv·o·ca·tion** \-,kwivə'kāshən\ *n*

1-er \ər\ *adj suffix or adv suffix* — used to form the comparative degree of adjectives and adverbs and esp. those of one or two syllables

2-er \ər\, **-ier** \ēər, yər\, **-yer** \yər\ *n suffix* 1 : one that is associated with 2 : one that performs or is the object of an action 3 : one that is

era \'irə, 'erə, 'ērə\ *n* : period of time associated with something

erad·i·cate \i'radə,kāt\ *vb* **-cat·ed; -cat·ing** : do away with

erase \i'rās\ *vb* **erased; eras·ing** : rub or scratch out — **eras·er** *n* — **era·sure** \i'rāshər\ *n*

ere \'er\ *prep or conj* : before

erect \i'rekt\ *adj* : not leaning or lying down ~ *vb* 1 : build 2 : bring to an upright position — **erec·tion** \i'rek-shən\ *n*

er·mine \'ərmən\ *n* : weasel with white winter fur or its fur

erode \i'rōd\ *vb* **erod·ed; erod·ing** : wear away gradually

ero·sion \i'rōzhən\ *n* : process of eroding

erot·ic \i'rätik\ *adj* : sexually arousing — **erot·i·cal·ly** \-iklē\ *adv* — **erot·i·cism** \i'rätə,sizəm\ *n*

err \'er, 'ər\ *vb* : be or do wrong

er·rand \'erənd\ *n* : short trip taken to do something often for another

er·rant \-ənt\ *adj* 1 : traveling about 2 : going astray

er·rat·ic \ir'atik\ *adj* 1 : eccentric 2 : inconsistent — **er·rat·i·cal·ly** \-iklē\ *adv*

er·ro·ne·ous \ir'ōnēəs, e'rō-\ *adj* : wrong — **er·ro·ne·ous·ly** *adv*

er·ror \'erər\ *n* 1 : something that is not accurate 2 : state of being wrong

er·satz \'er,säts\ *adj* : phony

erst·while \'ərst,hwīl\ *adv* : in the past ~ *adj* : former

er·u·di·tion \ˌerə'dishən, ˌeryə-\ *n* : great learning — **er·u·dite** \'erə,dīt, 'eryə-\ *adj*

erupt \i'rəpt\ *vb* : burst forth esp. suddenly and violently — **erup·tion** \i'rəpshən\ *n* — **erup·tive** \-tiv\ *adj*

-ery \ərē\ *n suffix* 1 : character or condition 2 : practice 3 : place of doing

1-es \əz, iz *after* s, z, sh, ch; z *after* v or a vowel\ *n pl suffix* — used to form the plural of some nouns

2-es *vb suffix* — used to form the 3d person singular present of some verbs

es·ca·late \'eskə,lāt\ *vb* **-lat·ed; -lat·ing** : become quickly larger or greater — **es·ca·la·tion** \ˌeskə'lāshən\ *n*

es·ca·la·tor \'eskə,lātər\ *n* : moving stairs

es·ca·pade \'eskə,pād\ *n* : mischievous adventure

es·cape \is'kāp\ *vb* **-caped; -cap·ing** : get away or get away from ~ *n* 1 : flight from or avoidance of something unpleasant 2 : leakage 3 : means of escape ~ *adj* : providing means of escape — **es·cap·ee** \is,kā'pē, ,es-\ *n*

es·ca·role \'eskə,rōl\ *n* : salad green

es·carp·ment \is'kärpmənt\ *n* : cliff

es·chew \is'chü\ *vb* : shun

es·cort \'es,kort\ *n* : one accompanying another — **es·cort** \is'kort, es-\ *vb*

es·crow \'es,krō\ *n* : deposit to be delivered upon fulfillment of a condition

esoph·a·gus \i'säfəgəs\ *n, pl* **-gi** \-,gī, -,jī\ : muscular tube connecting the mouth and stomach

es·o·ter·ic \ˌesə'terik\ *adj* : mysterious or secret

es·pe·cial·ly \is'peshəlē\ *adv* : particularly or notably

es·pi·o·nage \'espēə,näzh, -nij\ *n* : practice of spying

es·pous·al \is'pauzəl\ *n* 1 : betrothal 2 : wedding 3 : a taking up as a supporter — **es·pouse** \-'pauz\ *vb*

es·pres·so \e'presō\ *n, pl* **-sos** : strong steam-brewed coffee

es·py \is'pi\ *vb* **-pied; -py·ing** : catch sight of

es·quire \'es,kwīr\ *n* — used as a title of courtesy

-ess \əs, ,es\ *n suffix* : female

es·say \'es,ā\ *n* : literary composition ~ *vb* \e'sā, 'es,ā\ : attempt — **es·say·ist** \'es,āist\ *n*

es·sence \'es⁀ns\ *n* **1** : fundamental nature or quality **2** : extract **3** : perfume

es·sen·tial \i'senchəl\ *adj* : basic or necessary — **essential** *n* — **es·sen·tial·ly** *adv*

-est \əst, ist\ *adj suffix or adv suffix* — used to form the superlative degree of adjectives and adverbs and esp. those of 1 or 2 syllables

es·tab·lish \is'tablish\ *vb* **1** : bring into existence **2** : put on a firm basis **3** : cause to be recognized

es·tab·lish·ment \-mənt\ *n* **1** : business or a place of business **2** : an establishing or being established **3** : controlling group

es·tate \is'tāt\ *n* **1** : one's possessions **2** : large piece of land with a house

es·teem \is'tēm\ *n or vb* : regard

es·ter \'estər\ *n* : organic chemical compound

esthetic *var of* AESTHETIC

es·ti·ma·ble \'estəməbəl\ *adj* : worthy of esteem

es·ti·mate \'estə,māt\ *vb* **-mat·ed; -mat·ing** : judge the approximate value, size, or cost ~ \-mət\ *n* **1** : rough or approximate calculation **2** : statement of the cost of a job — **es·ti·ma·tion** \,estə'māshən\ *n* — **es·ti·ma·tor** \'estə,mātər\ *n*

es·trange \is'trānj\ *vb* **-tranged; -trang·ing** : make hostile — **es·trange·ment** *n*

es·tro·gen \'estrəjən\ *n* : hormone that produces female characteristics

es·tu·ary \'eschə,werē\ *n, pl* **-ar·ies** : arm of the sea at a river's mouth

et cet·era \et'setərə, -'setrə\ : and others esp. of the same kind

etch \'ech\ *vb* : produce by corroding parts of a surface with acid — **etch·er** *n* — **etch·ing** *n*

eter·nal \i'tərn⁀l\ *adj* : lasting forever — **eter·nal·ly** *adv*

eter·ni·ty \-nətē\ *n, pl* **-ties** : infinite duration

eth·ane \'eth,ān\ *n* : gaseous hydrocarbon

eth·a·nol \'ethə,nȯl, -,nōl\ *n* : alcohol

ether \'ēthər\ *n* : light flammable liquid used as an anesthetic

ethe·re·al \i'thirēəl\ *adj* **1** : celestial **2** : exceptionally delicate

eth·i·cal \'ethikəl\ *adj* **1** : relating to ethics **2** : honorable — **eth·i·cal·ly** *adv*

eth·ics \-iks\ *n sing or pl* **1** : study of good and evil and moral duty **2** : moral principles or practice

eth·nic \'ethnik\ *adj* : relating to races or groups of people with common customs ~ *n* : member of a minority ethnic group

eth·nol·o·gy \eth'näləjē\ *n* : study of the races of human beings — **eth·no·log·i·cal** \,ethnə'läjikəl\ *adj* — **eth·nol·o·gist** \eth'näləjist\ *n*

et·i·quette \'etikət, -,ket\ *n* : good manners

et·y·mol·o·gy \,etə'mäləjē\ *n, pl* **-gies** **1** : history of a word **2** : study of etymologies — **et·y·mo·log·i·cal** \-mə-'läjikəl\ *adj* — **et·y·mol·o·gist** \-'mäləjist\ *n*

eu·ca·lyp·tus \,yükə'liptəs\ *n, pl* **-ti** \-,tī\ *or* **-tus·es** : Australian evergreen tree

Eu·cha·rist \'yükərəst\ *n* : Communion — **eu·cha·ris·tic** \,yükə'ristik\ *adj*

eu·lo·gy \'yüləjē\ *n, pl* **-gies** : speech in praise — **eu·lo·gis·tic** \,yülə'jis-tik\ *adj* — **eu·lo·gize** \'yülə,jīz\ *vb*

eu·nuch \'yünək\ *n* : castrated man

eu·phe·mism \'yüfə,mizəm\ *n* : substitution of a pleasant expression for an unpleasant or offensive one — **eu·phe·mis·tic** \,yüfə'mistik\ *adj*

eu·pho·ni·ous \yü'fōnēəs\ *adj* : pleasing to the ear — **eu·pho·ny** \'yüfənē\ *n*

eu·pho·ria \yù'fōrēə\ *n* : elation — **eu·phor·ic** \-'fȯrik\ *adj*

eu·ro \'yùrō\ *n, pl* **euros** : common monetary unit of most of the European Union

eu·tha·na·sia \,yüthə'nāzhə, -zhēə\ *n* : mercy killing

evac·u·ate \i'vakyə,wāt\ *vb* **-at·ed; -at·ing** **1** : discharge wastes from the body **2** : remove or withdraw from — **evac·u·a·tion** \i,vakyə'wāshən\ *n*

evade \i'vād\ *vb* **evad·ed; evad·ing** : manage to avoid

eval·u·ate \i'valyə,wāt\ vb -at·ed;
-at·ing : appraise — **eval·u·a·tion**
\i,valyə'wāshən\ n

evan·gel·i·cal \,ē,van'jelikəl, ,evən-\
adj : relating to the Christian gospel

evan·ge·lism \i'vanjə,lizəm\ n : the
winning or revival of personal com-
mitments to Christ — **evan·ge·list**
\i'vanjəlist\ n — **evan·ge·lis·tic** \i,-
vanjə'listik\ adj

evap·o·rate \i'vapə,rāt\ vb -rat·ed;
-rat·ing 1 : pass off in or convert into
vapor 2 : disappear quickly — **evap-
o·ra·tion** \i,vapə'rāshən\ n —
evap·ora·tor \i'vapə,rātər\ n

eva·sion \i'vāzhən\ n : act or instance
of evading — **eva·sive** \i'vāsiv\ adj
— **eva·sive·ness** n

eve \'ēv\ n : evening

even \'ēvən\ adj 1 : smooth 2 : equal
or fair 3 : fully revenged 4 : divisible
by 2 ~ adv 1 : already 2 — used for
emphasis ~ vb : make or become
even — **even·ly** adv — **even·ness** n

eve·ning \'ēvniŋ\ n : early part of the
night

event \i'vent\ n 1 : occurrence 2
: noteworthy happening 3 : eventual-
ity — **event·ful** adj

even·tu·al \i'venchəwəl\ adj : later —
even·tu·al·ly adv

even·tu·al·i·ty \i,venchə'walətē\ n, pl
-ties : possible occurrence or outcome

ev·er \'evər\ adv 1 : always 2 : at any
time 3 : in any case

ev·er·green adj : having foliage that remains green — **evergreen** n

ev·er·last·ing \,evər'lastiŋ\ adj : lasting forever

ev·ery \'evrē\ adj 1 : being each one of
a group 2 : all possible

ev·ery·body \'evri,bädē, -bəd-\ pron
: every person

ev·ery·day adj : ordinary

ev·ery·one \-,wən\ pron : every person

ev·ery·thing pron : all that exists

ev·ery·where adv : in every place or
part

evict \i'vikt\ vb : force (a person) to
move from a property — **evic·tion**
\i'vikshən\ n

ev·i·dence \'evədəns\ n 1 : outward
sign 2 : proof or testimony

ev·i·dent \-ənt\ adj : clear or obvious
— **ev·i·dent·ly** \-ədəntlē, -ə,dent-\
adv

evil \'ēvəl\ adj evil·er or evil·ler; evil-

est or evil·lest : wicked ~ n 1 : sin
2 : source of sorrow or distress —
evil·do·er \,ēvəl'düər\ n — **evil·ly**
adv

evince \i'vins\ vb evinced; evinc·ing
: show

evis·cer·ate \i'visə,rāt\ vb -at·ed; -at-
ing : remove the viscera of — **evis-
cer·a·tion** \i,visə'rāshən\ n

evoke \i'vōk\ vb evoked; evok·ing
: call forth or up — **evo·ca·tion**
\ēvō'kāshən, ,evə-\ n — **evoc·a·
tive** \i'väkətiv\ adj

evo·lu·tion \,evə'lüshən\ n : process of
change by degrees — **evo·lu·tion·ary**
\-shə,nerē\ adj

evolve \i'välv\ vb evolved; evolv·ing
: develop or change by degrees

ewe \'yü\ n : female sheep

ew·er \'yüər\ n : water pitcher

ex·act \ig'zakt\ vb : compel to furnish
~ adj : precisely correct — **ex·act-
ing** adj — **ex·ac·tion** \-'zakshən\ n
— **ex·ac·ti·tude** \-'zakta,tüd,
-,tyüd\ n — **ex·act·ly** adv — **ex·act-
ness** n

ex·ag·ger·ate \ig'zaja,rāt\ vb -at·ed;
-at·ing : say more than is true —
ex·ag·ger·at·ed·ly adv — **ex·ag·ger-
a·tion** \-,zaja'rāshən\ n — **ex·ag·
ger·a·tor** \-'zajərātər\ n

ex·alt \ig'zólt\ vb : glorify — **ex·al·ta·
tion** \,eg,zól'tāshən, ,ek,sól-\ n

ex·am \ig'zam\ n : examination

ex·am·ine \-ən\ vb -ined; -in·ing 1
: inspect closely 2 : test by questioning — **ex·am·i·na·tion** \-,zamə-
'nāshən\ n

ex·am·ple \ig'zampəl\ n 1 : representative sample 2 : model 3 : problem
to be solved for teaching purposes

ex·as·per·ate \ig'zaspə,rāt\ vb -at·ed;
-at·ing : thoroughly annoy — **ex·as-
per·a·tion** \-,zaspə'rāshən\ n

ex·ca·vate \'ekskə,vāt\ vb -vat·ed;
-vat·ing : dig or hollow out — **ex·ca-
va·tion** \,ekskə'vāshən\ n — **ex·ca-
va·tor** \'ekskə,vātər\,n

ex·ceed \ik'sēd\ vb 1 : go or be beyond the limit of 2 : do better than

ex·ceed·ing·ly adv : extremely

ex·cel \ik'sel\ vb -ll- : do extremely
well or far better than

ex·cel·lence \'eksələns\ n : quality of
being excellent

ex·cel·len·cy \-lənsē\ n, pl -cies —
used as a title of honor

ex·cel·lent \'eksələnt\ *adj* : very good
— **ex·cel·lent·ly** *adv*

ex·cept \ik'sept\ *vb* : omit ~ *prep*
: excluding ~ *conj* : but — **ex·cep·tion** \-'sepshən\ *n*

ex·cep·tion·al \-'sepshənəl\ *adj* : superior — **ex·cep·tion·al·ly** *adv*

ex·cerpt \'ek,sərpt, 'eg,zərpt\ *n*
: brief passage ~ \ek'-, eg'-, 'ek,-, 'eg,-\ *vb* : select an excerpt

ex·cess \ik'ses, 'ek,ses\ *n* : amount left over — **excess** *adj* — **ex·ces·sive** \ik'sesiv\ *adj* — **ex·ces·sive·ly** *adv*

ex·change \iks'chānj, 'eks,chānj\ *n*
1 : the giving or taking of one thing in return for another 2 : marketplace esp. for securities ~ *vb* **-changed;**
-chang·ing : transfer in return for some equivalent — **ex·change·able** \iks'chānjəbəl\ *adj*

¹**ex·cise** \'ek,sīz, -,sīs\ *n* : tax

²**ex·cise** \ik'sīz\ *vb* **-cised; -cis·ing**
: cut out — **ex·ci·sion** \-'sizhən\ *n*

ex·cite \ik'sīt\ *vb* **-cit·ed; -cit·ing**
1 : stir up 2 : kindle the emotions of — **ex·cit·abil·i·ty** \-,sītə'bilətē\ *n* — **ex·cit·able** \-'sītəbəl\ *adj* — **ex·ci·ta·tion** \,eksə'tāshən, -ə-\ *n* — **ex·cit·ed·ly** *adv* — **ex·cite·ment** \ik'sītmənt\ *n*

ex·claim \iks'klām\ *vb* : cry out esp. in delight — **ex·cla·ma·tion** \,eksklə'māshən\ *n* — **ex·clam·a·to·ry** \iks'klamə,tōrē\ *adj*

exclamation point *n* : punctuation mark ! used esp. after an interjection or exclamation

ex·clude \iks'klüd\ *vb* **-clud·ed; -clud·ing** : leave out — **ex·clu·sion** \-'klüzhən\ *n*

ex·clu·sive \-'klüsiv\ *adj* 1 : reserved for particular persons 2 : stylish 3 : sole — **exclusive** *n* — **ex·clu·sive·ly** *adv* — **ex·clu·sive·ness** *n*

ex·com·mu·ni·cate \,ekskə'myünə,kāt\ *vb* : expel from a church — **ex·com·mu·ni·ca·tion** \-,myünə'kāshən\ *n*

ex·cre·ment \'ekskrəmənt\ *n* : bodily waste

ex·crete \ik'skrēt\ *vb* **-cret·ed; -cret·ing** : eliminate wastes from the body — **ex·cre·tion** \-'skrēshən\ *n* — **ex·cre·to·ry** \'ekskrə,tōrē\ *adj*

ex·cru·ci·at·ing \ik'skrüshē,ātiŋ\ *adj*
: intensely painful — **ex·cru·ci·at·ing·ly** *adv*

ex·cul·pate \'ekskəl,pāt\ *vb* **-pat·ed; -pat·ing** : clear from alleged fault

ex·cur·sion \ik'skərzhən\ *n* : pleasure trip

ex·cuse \ik'skyüz\ *vb* **-cused; -cus·ing** 1 : pardon 2 : release from an obligation 3 : justify ~ \-'skyüs\ *n*
1 : justification 2 : apology

ex·e·cute \'eksi,kyüt\ *vb* **-cut·ed; -cut·ing** 1 : carry out fully 2 : enforce 3 : put to death — **ex·e·cu·tion** \,eksi'kyüshən\ *n* — **ex·e·cu·tion·er** \-shənər\ *n*

ex·ec·u·tive \ig'zekyətiv\ *adj* : relating to the carrying out of decisions, plans, or laws ~ *n* 1 : branch of government with executive duties 2 : administrator

ex·ec·u·tor \-yətər\ *n* : person named in a will to execute it

ex·ec·u·trix \ig'zekyə,triks\ *n, pl* **ex·ec·u·tri·ces** \-,zekyə'trī,sēz\ *or* **ex·ec·u·trix·es** : woman executor

ex·em·pla·ry \ig'zemplərē\ *adj* : so commendable as to serve as a model

ex·em·pli·fy \-plə,fī\ *vb* **-fied; -fy·ing**
: serve as an example of — **ex·em·pli·fi·ca·tion** \-,zempləfə'kāshən\ *n*

ex·empt \ig'zempt\ *adj* : being free from some liability ~ *vb* : make exempt — **ex·emp·tion** \-'zempshən\ *n*

ex·er·cise \'eksər,sīz\ *n* 1 : a putting into action 2 : exertion to develop endurance or a skill 3 *pl* : public ceremony ~ *vb* **-cised; -cis·ing** 1 : exert 2 : engage in exercise — **ex·er·cis·er** *n*

ex·ert \ig'zərt\ *vb* : put into action — **ex·er·tion** \-'zərshən\ *n*

ex·hale \eks'hāl\ *vb* **-haled; -hal·ing**
: breathe out — **ex·ha·la·tion** \eks-hə'lāshən\ *n*

ex·haust \ig'zóst\ *vb* 1 : draw out or develop completely 2 : use up 3 : tire or wear out ~ *n* : waste steam or gas from an engine or a system for removing it — **ex·haus·tion** \-'zós-chən\ *n* — **ex·haus·tive** \-'zóstiv\ *adj*

ex·hib·it \ig'zibət\ *vb* : display esp. publicly ~ *n* 1 : act of exhibiting 2 : something exhibited — **ex·hi·bi·tion** \,eksə'bishən\ *n* — **ex·hib·i·tor** \ig'zibətər\ *n*

ex·hil·a·rate \ig'zilə,rāt\ *vb* **-rat·ed; -rat·ing** : thrill — **ex·hil·a·ra·tion** \-,zilə'rāshən\ *n*

ex·hort \ig-'zȯrt\ vb : urge earnestly — **ex·hor·ta·tion** \eks-.ȯr'tāshən, .egz-, -ər-\ n

ex·hume \igz'üm, -'yüm; 'iks'yüm, -'hyüm\ vb -humed; -hum·ing : dig up (a buried corpse) — **ex·hu·ma·tion** \eksyü'māshən, -hyü-; .egzü-, -zyü-\ n

ex·i·gen·cies \'eksəjənsēz, ig'zijən-\ n pl : requirements (as of a situation)

ex·ile \'egˌzīl, 'ekˌsīl\ n 1 : banishment 2 : person banished from his or her country — **exile** vb

ex·ist \ig'zist\ vb 1 : have real or actual being 2 : live — **ex·is·tence** \-əns\ n — **ex·is·tent** \-ənt\ adj

ex·it \'egzət, 'eksət\ n 1 : departure 2 : way out of an enclosed space 3 : way off an expressway — **exit** vb

ex·o·dus \'eksədəs\ n : mass departure

ex·on·er·ate \ig'zänəˌrāt\ vb -at·ed; -at·ing : free from blame — **ex·on·er·a·tion** \-ˌzänə'rāshən\ n

ex·or·bi·tant \ig'zȯrbətənt\ adj : exceeding what is usual or proper

ex·or·cise \'ekˌsȯrˌsiz, -sər-\ vb -cised; -cis·ing : drive out (as an evil spirit) — **ex·or·cism** \-ˌsizəm\ n — **ex·or·cist** \-ˌsist\ n

ex·ot·ic \ig'zätik\ adj : foreign or strange — **exotic** n — **ex·ot·i·cal·ly** \-iklē\ adv

ex·pand \ik'spand\ vb : enlarge

ex·panse \-'spans\ n : very large area

ex·pan·sion \-'spanchən\ n 1 : act or process of expanding 2 : expanded part

ex·pan·sive \-'spansiv\ adj 1 : tending to expand 2 : warmly benevolent 3 : of large extent — **ex·pan·sive·ly** adv — **ex·pan·sive·ness** n

ex·pa·tri·ate \ek'spātrēˌāt, -ət\ n : exile — **expatriate** \-ˌāt\ adj or vb

ex·pect \ik'spekt\ vb 1 : look forward to 2 : consider probable or one's due — **ex·pec·tan·cy** \-ənsē\ n — **ex·pec·tant** \-ənt\ adj — **ex·pec·tant·ly** adv — **ex·pec·ta·tion** \ekˌspek'tāshən\ n

ex·pe·di·ent \ik'spēdēənt\ adj : convenient or advantageous rather than right or just ~ n : convenient often makeshift means to an end

ex·pe·dite \'ekspəˌdīt\ vb -dit·ed; -dit·ing : carry out or handle promptly — **ex·pe·dit·er** n

ex·pe·di·tion \ekspə'dishən\ n : long journey for work or research or the people making this

ex·pe·di·tious \-əs\ adj : prompt and efficient

ex·pel \ik'spel\ vb -ll- : force out

ex·pend \-'spend\ vb 1 : pay out 2 : use up — **ex·pend·able** adj

ex·pen·di·ture \-'spendichər, -dəˌchur\ n : act of using or spending

ex·pense \ik'spens\ n : cost — **ex·pen·sive** \-'spensiv\ adj — **ex·pen·sive·ly** adv

ex·pe·ri·ence \ik'spirēəns\ n 1 : a participating in or living through an event 2 : an event that affects one 3 : knowledge from doing ~ vb -enced; -enc·ing : undergo

ex·per·i·ment \ik'sperəmənt\ n : test to discover something ~ vb : make experiments — **ex·per·i·men·tal** \-ˌsperə'ment°l\ adj — **ex·per·i·men·ta·tion** \-mən'tāshən\ n — **ex·per·i·men·ter** \-'sperəˌmentər\ n

ex·pert \'ekˌspərt\ adj : thoroughly skilled ~ n : person with special skill — **ex·pert·ly** adv — **ex·pert·ness** n

ex·per·tise \ekspər'tēz\ n : skill

ex·pi·ate \'ekspēˌāt\ vb : make amends for — **ex·pi·a·tion** \ekspē'āshən\ n

ex·pire \ik'spīr, ek-\ vb -pired; -pir·ing 1 : breathe out 2 : die 3 : end — **ex·pi·ra·tion** \ekspə'rāshən\ n

ex·plain \ik'splān\ vb 1 : make clear 2 : give the reason for — **ex·plain·able** \-əbəl\ adj — **ex·pla·na·tion** \eksplə'nāshən\ n — **ex·plan·a·to·ry** \ik'splanəˌtōrē\ adj

ex·ple·tive \'eksplətiv\ n : usu. profane exclamation

ex·pli·ca·ble \ek'splikəbəl, 'eksplik-\ adj : capable of being explained

ex·plic·it \ik'splisət\ adj : absolutely clear or precise — **ex·plic·it·ly** adv — **ex·plic·it·ness** n

ex·plode \ik'splōd\ vb -plod·ed; -plod·ing 1 : discredit 2 : burst or cause to burst violently 3 : increase rapidly

ex·ploit \'ekˌsplȯit\ n : heroic act ~ \ik'splȯit\ vb 1 : utilize 2 : use unfairly — **ex·ploi·ta·tion** \ekˌsplȯi-'tāshən\ n

ex·plore \ik'splōr\ vb -plored; -plor·ing : examine or range over thoroughly — **ex·plo·ra·tion** \eksplə-

'rāshən\ *n* — **ex·plor·ato·ry** \ik-'splōrə,tōrē\ *adj* — **ex·plor·er** *n*

ex·plo·sion \ik-'splōzhən\ *n* : process or instance of exploding

ex·plo·sive \-siv\ *adj* 1 : able to cause explosion 2 : likely to explode — **explosive** *n* — **ex·plo·sive·ly** *adv*

ex·po·nent \ik-'spōnənt, 'ek,spō-\ *n* 1 : mathematical symbol showing how many times a number is to be repeated as a factor 2 : advocate — **ex·po·nen·tial** \,ekspə'nenchəl\ *adj* — **ex·po·nen·tial·ly** *adv*

ex·port \ek'spōrt, 'ek,spōrt\ *vb* : send to foreign countries — **export** \'ek,-\ *n* — **ex·por·ta·tion** \,ek,spōr'tāshən\ *n* — **ex·port·er** \ek'spōrtər, 'ek,spōrt-\ *n*

ex·pose \ik'spōz\ *vb* **-posed; -pos·ing** 1 : deprive of shelter or protection 2 : subject (film) to light 3 : make known — **ex·po·sure** \-'spōzhər\ *n*

ex·po·sé, ex·po·se \,ekspō'zā\ *n* : exposure of something discreditable

ex·po·si·tion \,ekspə'zishən\ *n* : public exhibition

ex·pound \ik'spaúnd\ *vb* : set forth or explain in detail

¹**ex·press** \-'spres\ *adj* 1 : clear 2 : specific 3 : traveling at high speed with few stops — **express** *adv* or *n* — **ex·press·ly** *adv*

²**express** *vb* 1 : make known in words or appearance 2 : press out (as juice)

ex·pres·sion \-'spreshən\ *n* 1 : utterance 2 : mathematical symbol 3 : significant word or phrase 4 : look on one's face — **ex·pres·sive** \-'spresiv\ *adj* — **ex·pres·sive·ness** *n*

ex·press·way \ik'spres,wā\ *n* : highspeed divided highway with limited access

ex·pul·sion \ik'spəlshən\ *n* : an expelling or being expelled

ex·pur·gate \'ekspər,gāt\ *vb* **-gat·ed; -gat·ing** : censor — **ex·pur·ga·tion** \,ekspər'gāshən\ *n*

ex·qui·site \ek'skwizət, 'ekskwiz-\ *adj* 1 : flawlessly beautiful and delicate 2 : keenly discriminating

ex·tant \'ekstənt, ek'stant\ *adj* : existing

ex·tem·po·ra·ne·ous \,ek,stempə'rānēəs\ *adj* : impromptu — **ex·tem·po·ra·ne·ous·ly** *adv*

ex·tend \ik'stend\ *vb* 1 : stretch forth

or out 2 : prolong 3 : enlarge — **ex·tend·able** \-'stendəbəl\ *adj*

ex·ten·sion \-'stenchən\ *n* 1 : an extending or being extended 2 : additional part 3 : extra telephone line

ex·ten·sive \-'stensiv\ *adj* : of considerable extent — **ex·ten·sive·ly** *adv*

ex·tent \-'stent\ *n* : range, space, or degree to which something extends

ex·ten·u·ate \ik'stenyə,wāt\ *vb* **-at·ed; -at·ing** : lessen the seriousness of — **ex·ten·u·a·tion** \-,stenyə'wāshən\ *n*

ex·te·ri·or \ek'stirēər\ *adj* : external ~ *n* : external part or surface

ex·ter·mi·nate \ik'stərmə,nāt\ *vb* **-nat·ed; -nat·ing** : destroy utterly — **ex·ter·mi·na·tion** \-,stərmə'nāshən\ *n* — **ex·ter·mi·na·tor** \-'stərmə,nātər\ *n*

ex·ter·nal \ek'stərn³l\ *adj* : relating to or on the outside — **ex·ter·nal·ly** *adv*

ex·tinct \ik'stinkt\ *adj* : no longer existing — **ex·tinc·tion** \-'stinkshən\ *n*

ex·tin·guish \-'stingwish\ *vb* : cause to stop burning — **ex·tin·guish·able** *adj* — **ex·tin·guish·er** *n*

ex·tir·pate \'ekstər,pāt\ *vb* **-pat·ed; -pat·ing** : destroy

ex·tol \ik'stōl\ *vb* **-ll-** : praise highly

ex·tort \-'stort\ *vb* : obtain by force or improper pressure — **ex·tor·tion** \-'stórshən\ *n* — **ex·tor·tion·er** *n* — **ex·tor·tion·ist** *n*

ex·tra \'ekstrə\ *adj* 1 : additional 2 : superior — **extra** *n* or *adv*

extra- *prefix* : outside or beyond

ex·tract \ik'strakt\ *vb* 1 : pull out forcibly 2 : withdraw (as a juice) ~ \'ek,-\ *n* 1 : excerpt 2 : product (as a juice) obtained by extracting — **ex·tract·able** *adj* — **ex·trac·tion** \ik'strakshən\ *n* — **ex·trac·tor** \-tər\ *n*

ex·tra·cur·ric·u·lar \,ekstrəkə'rikyələr\ *adj* : lying outside the regular curriculum

ex·tra·dite \'ekstrə,dīt\ *vb* **-dit·ed; -dit·ing** : bring or deliver a suspect to a different jurisdiction for trial — **ex·tra·di·tion** \,ekstrə'dishən\ *n*

ex·tra·mar·i·tal \,ekstrə'marət³l\ *adj* : relating to sexual relations of a married person outside of the marriage

ex·tra·ne·ous \ek'strānēəs\ *adj* : not essential or relevant — **ex·tra·ne·ous·ly** *adv*

ex·traor·di·nary \ik'strórd³n,erē, ,ekstrə'ȯrd-\ *adj* : notably unusual or exceptional — **ex·traor·di·nari·ly** \ik‚strȯrd³n'erəlē, ‚ekstrə‚ȯrd-\ *adv*

ex·tra·sen·so·ry \‚ekstrə'sensərē\ *adj* : outside the ordinary senses

ex·tra·ter·res·tri·al \‚ekstrətə'restrēəl\ *n* : one existing or coming from outside the earth **~** *adj* : relating to an extraterrestrial

ex·trav·a·gant \ik'stravigənt\ *adj* : wildly excessive, lavish, or costly — **ex·trav·a·gance** \-gəns\ *n* — **ex·trav·a·gant·ly** *adv*

ex·trav·a·gan·za \-‚stravə'ganzə\ *n* : spectacular event

ex·tra·ve·hic·u·lar \‚ekstrəvē'hik-yələr\ *adj* : occurring outside a spacecraft

ex·treme \ik'strēm\ *adj* **1** : very great or intense **2** : very severe **3** : not moderate **4** : most remote **~** *n* **1** : extreme state **2** : something located at one end or the other of a range — **ex·treme·ly** *adv*

ex·trem·i·ty \-'stremətē\ *n, pl* **-ties 1** : most remote part **2** : human hand or foot **3** : extreme degree or state (as of need)

ex·tri·cate \'ekstrə‚kāt\ *vb* **-cat·ed; -cat·ing** : set or get free from an entanglement or difficulty — **ex·tri·ca·ble** \ik'strikəbəl, ek-; 'ekstrik-\ *adj* — **ex·tri·ca·tion** \‚ekstrə'kāshən\ *n*

ex·tro·vert \'ekstrə‚vərt\ *n* : gregarious person — **ex·tro·ver·sion** \‚ekstrə'vərzhən\ *n* — **ex·tro·vert·ed** \'ekstrə‚vərtəd\ *adj*

ex·trude \ik'strüd\ *vb* **-trud·ed; -trud·ing** : to force or push out

ex·u·ber·ant \ig'zübərənt\ *adj* : joyously unrestrained — **ex·u·ber·ance** \-rəns\ *n* — **ex·u·ber·ant·ly** *adv*

ex·ude \ig'züd\ *vb* **-ud·ed; -ud·ing 1** : discharge slowly through pores **2** : display conspicuously

ex·ult \ig'zəlt\ *vb* : rejoice — **ex·ul·tant** \-'zəlt³nt\ *adj* — **ex·ul·tant·ly** *adv* — **ex·ul·ta·tion** \‚eksəl'tāshən, ‚egzəl-\ *n*

-ey — see -Y

eye \'ī\ *n* **1** : organ of sight consisting of a globular structure (**eye·ball**) in a socket of the skull with thin movable covers (**eye·lids**) bordered with hairs (**eye·lash·es**) **2** : vision **3** : judgment **4** : something suggesting an eye **~** *vb* **eyed; eye·ing** or **ey·ing** : look at — **eye·brow** \-‚braù\ *n* — **eyed** \'īd\ *adj* — **eye·strain** *n*

eye·drop·per *n* : dropper

eye·glass·es *n pl* : glasses

eye·let \'īlət\ *n* **1** : hole (as in cloth) for a lacing or rope

eye·open·er *n* : something startling — **eye·open·ing** *adj*

eye·piece *n* : lens at the eye end of an optical instrument

eye·sight *n* : sight

eye·sore *n* : unpleasant sight

eye·tooth *n* : upper canine tooth

eye·wit·ness *n* : person who actually sees something happen

ey·rie \'īrē, or like AERIE\ *var of* AERIE

F

f \'ef\ *n, pl* **f's** or **fs** \'efs\ : 6th letter of the alphabet

fa·ble \'fābəl\ *n* **1** : legendary story **2** : story that teaches a lesson — **fa·bled** \-bəld\ *adj*

fab·ric \'fabrik\ *n* **1** : structure **2** : material made usu. by weaving or knitting fibers

fab·ri·cate \'fabri‚kāt\ *vb* **-cat·ed; -cat·ing 1** : construct **2** : invent — **fab·ri·ca·tion** \‚fabri'kāshən\ *n*

fab·u·lous \'fabyələs\ *adj* **1** : like, told

in, or based on fable **2** : incredible or marvelous — **fab·u·lous·ly** *adv*

fa·cade \fə'säd\ *n* **1** : principal face of a building **2** : false or superficial appearance

face \'fās\ *n* **1** : front or principal surface (as of the head) **2** : presence **3** : facial expression **4** : grimace **5** : outward appearance **~** *vb* **faced; fac·ing 1** : challenge or resist firmly or brazenly **2** : cover with different material **3** : sit or stand with the face toward **4** : have the front oriented toward — **faced** \'fāst\ adj — **face·less** adj — **fa·cial** \'fāshəl\ adj or n

face·down adv : with the face downward

face-lift \'fās,lift\ n **1** : cosmetic surgery on the face **2** : modernization

fac·et \'fasət\ n **1** : surface of a cut gem **2** : phase — **fac·et·ed** adj

fa·ce·tious \fə'sēshəs\ adj : jocular — **fa·ce·tious·ly** adv — **fa·ce·tious·ness** n

fac·ile \'fasəl\ adj **1** : easy **2** : fluent

fa·cil·i·tate \fə'silə,tāt\ vb **-tat·ed; -tat·ing** : make easier

fa·cil·i·ty \fə'silətē\ n, pl **-ties 1** : ease in doing or using **2** : something built or installed to serve a purpose or facilitate an activity

fac·ing \'fāsiŋ\ n : lining or covering or material for this

fac·sim·i·le \fak'siməlē\ n : exact copy

fact \'fakt\ n **1** : act or action **2** : something that exists or is real **3** : piece of information — **fac·tu·al** \'fakchəwəl\ adj — **fac·tu·al·ly** adv

fac·tion \'fakshən\ n : part of a larger group — **fac·tion·al·ism** \-shənə,- lizəm\ n

fac·tious \'fakshəs\ adj : causing discord

fac·ti·tious \fak'tishəs\ adj : artificial

fac·tor \'faktər\ n **1** : something that has an effect **2** : gene **3** : number used in multiplying

fac·to·ry \'faktərē\ n, pl **-ries** : place for manufacturing

fac·to·tum \fak'tōtəm\ n : person (as a servant) with varied duties

fac·ul·ty \'fakəltē\ n, pl **-ties 1** : ability to act **2** : power of the mind or body **3** : body of teachers or department of instruction

fad \'fad\ n : briefly popular practice or interest — **fad·dish** adj — **fad·dist** n

fade \'fād\ vb **fad·ed; fad·ing 1** : wither **2** : lose or cause to lose freshness or brilliance **3** : grow dim **4** : vanish

fag \'fag\ vb **-gg- 1** : drudge **2** : tire or exhaust

fag·ot, fag·got \'fagət\ n : bundle of twigs

Fahr·en·heit \'farən,hīt\ adj : relating to a thermometer scale with the boiling point at 212 degrees and the freezing point at 32 degrees

fail \'fāl\ vb **1** : decline in health **2** : die away **3** : stop functioning **4** : be unsuccessful **5** : become bankrupt **6** : disappoint **7** : neglect ~ n : act of failing

fail·ing n : slight defect in character or conduct ~ prep : in the absence or lack of

faille \'fīl\ n : closely woven ribbed fabric

fail·ure \'fālyər\ n **1** : absence of expected action or performance **2** : bankruptcy **3** : deficiency **4** : one that has failed

faint \'fānt\ adj **1** : cowardly or spiritless **2** : weak and dizzy **3** : lacking vigor **4** : indistinct ~ vb : lose consciousness ~ n : act or condition of fainting — **faint·heart·ed** adj — **faint·ly** adv — **faint·ness** n

¹**fair** \'far\ adj **1** : pleasing in appearance **2** : not stormy or cloudy **3** : just or honest **4** : conforming with the rules **5** : open to legitimate pursuit or attack **6** : light in color **7** : adequate — **fair·ness** n

²**fair** adv chiefly Brit : **FAIRLY**

³**fair** n : exhibition for judging or selling — **fair·ground** n

fair·ly \'farlē\ adv **1** : in a manner of speaking **2** : without bias **3** : somewhat

fairy \'farē\ n, pl **fair·ies** : usu. small imaginary being — **fairy tale** n

fairy·land \-,land\ n **1** : land of fairies **2** : beautiful or charming place

faith \'fāth\ n, pl **faiths** \'fāths, 'fāthz\ **1** : allegiance **2** : belief and trust in God **3** : confidence **4** : system of religious beliefs — **faith·ful** \-fəl\ adj — **faith·ful·ly** adv — **faith·ful·ness** n — **faith·less** adj — **faith·less·ly** adv — **faith·less·ness** n

fake \'fāk\ vb **faked; fak·ing 1** : falsify **2** : counterfeit ~ n : copy, fraud, or impostor ~ adj : not genuine — **fak·er** n

fa·kir \fə'kir\ n : wandering beggar of India

fal·con \'falkən, 'fȯl-\ n : small long-winged hawk used esp. for hunting — **fal·con·ry** \-rē\ n

fall \'fȯl\ vb **fell** \'fel\; **fall·en** \'fȯlən\; **fall·ing 1** : go down by gravity **2** : hang freely **3** : go lower **4** : be defeated or ruined **5** : commit a sin **6** : happen at a certain time **7** : become gradually ~ n **1** : act of falling **2**

: autumn **3** : downfall **4** *pl* : waterfall **5** : distance something falls

fal·la·cy \\'faləsē\\ *n, pl* **-cies 1** : false idea **2** : false reasoning — **fal·la·cious** \\fə'lāshəs\\ *adj*

fal·li·ble \\'faləbəl\\ *adj* : capable of making a mistake — **fal·li·bly** \\-blē\\ *adv*

fall·out *n* **1** : radioactive particles from a nuclear explosion **2** : secondary effects

fal·low \\'falō\\ *adj* **1** : plowed but not planted **2** : dormant — **fallow** *n or vb*

false \\'fols\\ *adj* **fals·er; fals·est 1** : not genuine, true, faithful, or permanent **2** : misleading — **false·ly** *adv* — **false·ness** *n* — **fal·si·fi·ca·tion** \\,fölsəfə'kāshən\\ *n* — **fal·si·fy** \\'fölsə,fī\\ *vb* — **fal·si·ty** \\'fölsətē\\ *n*

false·hood \\'föls,hud\\ *n* : lie

fal·set·to \\fol'setō\\ *n, pl* **-tos** : artificially high singing voice

fal·ter \\'föltər\\ *vb* **-tered; -ter·ing 1** : move unsteadily **2** : hesitate — **fal·ter·ing·ly** *adv*

fame \\'fām\\ *n* : public reputation — **famed** \\'fāmd\\ *adj*

fa·mil·ial \\fə'milyəl\\ *adj* : relating to a family

¹fa·mil·iar \\fə'milyər\\ *n* **1** : companion **2** : guardian spirit

²familiar *adj* **1** : closely acquainted **2** : forward **3** : frequently seen or experienced — **fa·mil·iar·i·ty** \\fə,mil'yarətē, -,milē'yar-\\ *n* — **fa·mil·iar·ize** \\fə'milyə,rīz\\ *vb* — **fa·mil·iar·ly** *adv*

fam·i·ly \\'famlē\\ *n, pl* **-lies 1** : persons of common ancestry **2** : group living together **3** : parents and children **4** : group of related individuals

fam·ine \\'famən\\ *n* : extreme scarcity of food

fam·ish \\'famish\\ *vb* : starve

fa·mous \\'fāməs\\ *adj* : widely known or celebrated

fa·mous·ly *adv* : very well

¹fan \\'fan\\ *n* : device for producing a current of air ~ *vb* **-nn- 1** : move air with a fan **2** : direct a current of air upon **3** : stir to activity

²fan *n* : enthusiastic follower or admirer

fa·nat·ic \\fə'natik\\, **fa·nat·i·cal** \\-ikəl\\ *adj* : excessively enthusiastic or devoted — **fanatic** *n* — **fa·nat·i·cism** \\-'natə,sizəm\\ *n*

fan·ci·er \\'fansēər\\ *n* : one devoted to raising a particular plant or animal

fan·cy \\'fansē\\ *n, pl* **-cies 1** : liking **2** : whim **3** : imagination ~ *vb* **-cied; -cy·ing 1** : like **2** : imagine — **fan·ci·er; -est 1** : not plain **2** : of superior quality — **fan·ci·ful** \\-sifəl\\ *adj* — **fan·ci·ful·ly** \\-fəlē\\ *adv* — **fan·ci·ly** *adv*

fan·dan·go \\fan'dangō\\ *n, pl* **-gos** : lively Spanish dance

fan·fare \\'fan,far\\ *n* **1** : a sounding of trumpets **2** : showy display

fang \\'faŋ\\ *n* : long sharp tooth

fan·light *n* : semicircular window

fan·ta·sia \\fan'tāzhə, -zēə; ,fan-tə'zēə\\ *n* : music written to fancy rather than to form

fan·tas·tic \\fan'tastik\\ *adj* **1** : imaginary or unrealistic **2** : exceedingly or unbelievably great — **fan·tas·ti·cal·ly** \\-tiklē\\ *adv*

fan·ta·sy \\'fantəsē\\ *n* **1** : imagination **2** : product (as a daydream) of the imagination **3** : fantasia — **fan·ta·size** \\'fantə,sīz\\ *vb*

FAQ *abbr* frequently asked questions

far \\'fär\\ *adv* **far·ther** \\-thər\\ *or* **fur·ther** \\'fər-\\: **far·thest** *or* **fur·thest** \\-thəst\\ **1** : at or to a distance **2** : much **3** : to a degree **4** : to an advanced point or extent — *adj* **farther** *or* **further; far·thest** *or* **furthest 1** : remote **2** : long **3** : being more distant

far·away *adj* : distant

farce \\'färs\\ *n* **1** : satirical comedy with an improbable plot **2** : ridiculous display — **far·ci·cal** \\-sikəl\\ *adj*

¹fare \\'far\\ *vb* **fared; far·ing** : get along

²fare *n* **1** : price of transportation **2** : range of food

fare·well \\far'wel\\ *n* **1** : wish of welfare at parting **2** : departure — **farewell** *adj*

far-fetched \\'fär'fecht\\ *adj* : improbable

fa·ri·na \\fə'rēnə\\ *n* : fine meal made from cereal grains

farm \\'färm\\ *n* : place where something is raised for food ~ *vb* **1** : use (land) as a farm **2** : raise plants or animals for food — **farm·er** *n* — **farm·hand** \\-,hand\\ *n* — **farm·house** *n* — **farm·ing** *n* — **farm·land** \\-,land\\ *n* — **farm·yard** *n*

far-off *adj* : remote in time or space

far·ri·er \\'färēər\\ *n* : blacksmith who shoes horses

far·row \'farō\ vb : give birth to a litter of pigs — **farrow** n

far·sight·ed adj 1 : better able to see distant things than near 2 : judicious or shrewd — **far·sight·ed·ness** n

far·ther \'färthər\ adv 1 : at or to a greater distance or more advanced point 2 : to a greater degree or extent ~ adj : more distant

far·ther·most adj : most distant

far·thest \'färthəst\ adj : most distant ~ adv 1 : to or at the greatest distance 2 : to the most advanced point 3 : by the greatest extent

fas·ci·cle \'fasikəl\ n 1 : small bundle 2 : division of a book published in parts — **fas·ci·cled** \-kəld\ adj

fas·ci·nate \'fas²n,āt\ vb -nat·ed; -nat·ing : transfix and hold spellbound — **fas·ci·na·tion** \,fas²n-'āshən\ n

fas·cism \'fash,izəm\ n : dictatorship that exalts nation and race — **fas·cist** \-ist\ n or adj — **fas·cis·tic** \fa'shis-tik\ adj

fash·ion \'fashən\ n 1 : manner 2 : prevailing custom or style ~ vb : form or construct — **fash·ion·able** \-ənəbəl\ adj — **fash·ion·ably** \-blē\ adv

¹**fast** \'fast\ adj 1 : firmly fixed, bound, or shut 2 : faithful 3 : moving or acting quickly 4 : indicating ahead of the correct time 5 : deep and undisturbed 6 : permanently dyed 7 : wild or promiscuous ~ adv 1 : so as to be secure or bound 2 : soundly or deeply 3 : swiftly

²**fast** vb : abstain from food or eat sparingly ~ n : act or time of fasting

fas·ten \'fas²n\ vb : attach esp. by pinning or tying — **fas·ten·er** n — **fas·ten·ing** n

fas·tid·i·ous \fas'tidēəs\ adj : hard to please — **fas·tid·i·ous·ly** adv — **fas·tid·i·ous·ness** n

fat \'fat\ adj -tt- 1 : having much fat 2 : thick ~ n : animal tissue rich in greasy or oily matter — **fat·ness** n — **fat·ten** \'fat²n\ vb — **fat·ty** adj or n

fa·tal \'fāt²l\ adj : causing death or ruin — **fa·tal·i·ty** \fā'talətē, fə-\ n — **fa·tal·ly** adv

fa·tal·ism \'fāt²l,izəm\ n : belief that fate determines events — **fa·tal·ist** \-ist\ n — **fa·tal·is·tic** \,fāt²l'istik\ adj — **fa·tal·is·ti·cal·ly** \-tiklē\ adv

fate \'fāt\ n 1 : principle, cause, or will

held to determine events 2 : end or outcome — **fat·ed** adj — **fate·ful** \-fəl\ adj — **fate·ful·ly** adv

fa·ther \'fäthər, 'fath-\ n 1 : male parent 2 cap : God 3 : originator — **fa·ther** vb — **fa·ther·hood** \-,hủd\ n — **fa·ther·land** \-,land\ n — **fa·ther·less** adj — **fa·ther·ly** adj

father–in–law n, pl **fa·thers–in–law** : father of one's spouse

fath·om \'fathəm\ n : nautical unit of length equal to 6 feet ~ vb : understand — **fath·om·able** adj — **fath·om·less** adj

fa·tigue \fə'tēg\ n 1 : weariness from labor or use 2 : tendency to break under repeated stress ~ vb -tigued; -tigu·ing : tire

fat·u·ous \'fachəwəs\ adj : foolish or stupid — **fat·u·ous·ly** adv — **fat·u·ous·ness** n

fau·cet \'fòsət, 'fäs-\ n : fixture for drawing off a liquid

fault \'fòlt\ n 1 : weakness in character 2 : something wrong or imperfect 3 : responsibility for something wrong 4 : fracture in the earth's crust ~ vb : find fault in or with — **fault·find·er** n — **fault·find·ing** n — **fault·i·ly** \'fòltəlē\ adv — **fault·less** adj — **fault·less·ly** adv — **faulty** adj

fau·na \'fònə\ n : animals or animal life esp. of a region — **fau·nal** \-²l\ adj

faux pas \'fō'pä\ n, pl **faux pas** \same or -'päz\ : social blunder

fa·vor \'fāvər\ n 1 : approval 2 : partiality 3 : act of kindness ~ vb : regard or treat with favor — **fa·vor·able** \'fāvərəbəl\ adj — **fa·vor·ably** \-blē\ adv

fa·vor·ite \'fāvərət\ n : one favored — **favorite** adj — **fa·vor·it·ism** \-,izəm\ n

¹**fawn** \'fòn\ vb : seek favor by groveling

²**fawn** n : young deer

faze \'fāz\ vb **fazed; faz·ing** : disturb the composure of

fear \'fir\ n : unpleasant emotion caused by expectation or awareness of danger ~ vb : be afraid of — **fear·ful** \-fəl\ adj — **fear·ful·ly** adv — **fear·less** adj — **fear·less·ly** adv — **fear·less·ness** n — **fear·some** \-səm\ adj

fea·si·ble \'fēzəbəl\ adj : capable of being done — **fea·si·bil·i·ty** \,fēzə'bilətē\ n — **fea·si·bly** \'fēzəblē\ adv

feast \'fēst\ n 1 : large or fancy meal 2

: religious festival ～ vb : eat plentifully

feat \'fēt\ n : notable deed

feath·er \'fethər\ n : one of the light horny outgrowths that form the external covering of a bird's body — **feather** vb — **feath·ered** \-ərd\ adj — **feath·er·less** adj — **feath·ery** adj

fea·ture \'fēchər\ n 1 : shape or appearance of the face 2 : part of the face 3 : prominent characteristic 4 : special attraction ～ vb : give prominence to — **fea·ture·less** adj

Feb·ru·ary \'febyə,werē, 'febə-, 'febrə-\ n : 2d month of the year having 28 and in leap years 29 days

fe·ces \'fē,sēz\ n pl : intestinal body waste — **fe·cal** \-kəl\ adj

feck·less \'fekləs\ adj : irresponsible

fe·cund \'fekənd, 'fē-\ adj : prolific — **fe·cun·di·ty** \fi'kəndətē, fe-\ n

fed·er·al \'fedrəl, -dərəl\ adj : of or constituting a government with power distributed between a central authority and constituent units — **fed·er·al·ism** \-rə,lizəm\ n — **fed·er·al·ist** \-list\ n or adj — **fed·er·al·ly** adv

fed·er·ate \'fedə,rāt\ vb -at·ed; -at·ing : join in a federation

fed·er·a·tion \,fedə'rāshən\ n : union of organizations

fe·do·ra \fi'dōrə\ n : soft felt hat

fed up adj : out of patience

fee \'fē\ n : fixed charge

fee·ble \'fēbəl\ adj -bler; -blest : weak or ineffective — **fee·ble·mind·ed** \,fēbəl'mīndəd\ adj — **fee·ble·mind·ed·ness** n — **fee·ble·ness** n — **fee·bly** \-blē\ adv

feed \'fēd\ vb fed \'fed\; feed·ing 1 : give food to 2 : eat 3 : furnish ～ n : food for livestock — **feed·er** n

feel \'fēl\ vb felt \'felt\; feel·ing 1 : perceive or examine through physical contact 2 : think or believe 3 : be conscious of 4 : seem 5 : have sympathy ～ n 1 : sense of touch 2 : quality of a thing imparted through touch — **feel·er** n

feel·ing \'fēliŋ\ n 1 : sense of touch 2 : state of mind 3 pl : sensibilities 4 : opinion

feet pl of FOOT

feign \'fān\ vb : pretend

feint \'fānt\ n : mock attack intended to distract attention — **feint** vb

fe·lic·i·tate \fi'lisə,tāt\ vb -tat·ed; -tat-

ing : congratulate — **fe·lic·i·ta·tion** \-,lisə'tāshən\ n

fe·lic·i·tous \fi'lisətəs\ adj : aptly expressed — **fe·lic·i·tous·ly** adv

fe·lic·i·ty \-'lisətē\ n, pl -ties 1 : great happiness 2 : pleasing faculty esp. in art or language

fe·line \'fē,līn\ adj : relating to cats — **feline** n

¹**fell** \'fel\ vb : cut or knock down

²**fell** past of FALL

fel·low \'felō\ n 1 : companion or associate 2 : man or boy — **fel·low·ship** \-,ship\ n

fel·low·man \,felō'man\ n : kindred human being

fel·on \'felən\ n : one who has committed a felony

fel·o·ny \'felənē\ n, pl -nies : serious crime — **fe·lo·ni·ous** \fə'lōnēəs\ adj

¹**felt** \'felt\ n : cloth made of pressed wool and fur

²**felt** past of FEEL

fe·male \'fē,māl\ adj : relating to or being the sex that bears young — **female** n

fem·i·nine \'femənən\ adj : relating to the female sex — **fem·i·nin·i·ty** \,femə'ninətē\ n

fem·i·nism \'femə,nizəm\ n : organized activity on behalf of women's rights — **fem·i·nist** \-nist\ n or adj

fe·mur \'fēmər\ n, pl fe·murs or fem·o·ra \'femərə\ : long bone of the thigh — **fem·o·ral** \'femərəl\ adj

fence \'fens\ n : enclosing barrier esp. of wood or wire ～ vb fenced; fenc·ing 1 : enclose with a fence 2 : practice fencing — **fenc·er** n

fenc·ing \'fensiŋ\ n 1 : combat with swords for sport 2 : material for building fences

fend \'fend\ vb : ward off

fend·er \'fendər\ n : guard over an automobile wheel

fen·nel \'fen³l\ n : herb related to the carrot

fer·ment \fər'ment\ vb : cause or undergo fermentation ～ \'fər,ment\ n : agitation

fer·men·ta·tion \,fərmən'tāshən, -,men-\ n : chemical decomposition of an organic substance in the absence of oxygen

fern \'fərn\ n : flowerless seedless green plant

fe·ro·cious \fə'rōshəs\ adj : fierce or savage — **fe·ro·cious·ly** adv — **fe·ro·**

cious·ness n — **fe·roc·i·ty** \-'räs-ətē\ n

fer·ret \'ferət\ n : white European polecat ~ vb : find out by searching

fer·ric \'ferik\, **fer·rous** \'ferəs\ adj : relating to or containing iron

fer·rule \'ferəl\ n : metal band or ring

fer·ry \'ferē\ vb **-ried; -ry·ing** : carry by boat over water ~ n, pl **-ries** : boat used in ferrying — **fer·ry·boat** n

fer·tile \'fərt²l\ adj **1** : producing plentifully **2** : capable of developing or reproducing — **fer·til·i·ty** \fər'tilətē\ n

fer·til·ize \'fərt²l,īz\ vb **-ized; -iz·ing** : make fertile — **fer·til·iza·tion** \,fərt²lə'zāshən\ n — **fer·til·iz·er** n

fer·vid \'fərvəd\ adj : ardent or zealous — **fer·vid·ly** adv

fer·vor \'fərvər\ n : passion — **fer·ven·cy** \-vənsē\ n — **fer·vent** \-vənt\ adj — **fer·vent·ly** adv

fes·ter \'festər\ vb **1** : form pus **2** : become more bitter or malignant

fes·ti·val \'festəvəl\ n : time of celebration

fes·tive \-tiv\ adj : joyous or happy — **fes·tive·ly** adv — **fes·tiv·i·ty** \fes'tivətē\ n

fes·toon \fes'tün\ n : decorative chain or strip hanging in a curve — **festoon** vb

fe·tal \'fēt²l\ adj : of, relating to, or being a fetus

fetch \'fech\ vb **1** : go or come after and bring or take back **2** : sell for

fetch·ing \'fechiŋ\ adj : attractive — **fetch·ing·ly** adv

fête \'fāt, 'fet\ n : lavish party ~ vb **fêt·ed; fêt·ing** : honor or commemorate with a fête

fet·id \'fetəd\ adj : having an offensive smell

fe·tish \'fetish\ n **1** : object believed to have magical powers **2** : object of unreasoning devotion or concern

fet·lock \'fet,läk\ n : projection on the back of a horse's leg above the hoof

fet·ter \'fetər\ n : chain or shackle for the feet — **fetter** vb

fet·tle \'fet²l\ n : state of fitness

fe·tus \'fētəs\ n : vertebrate not yet born or hatched

feud \'fyüd\ n : prolonged quarrel — **feud** vb

feu·dal \'fyüd²l\ adj : of or relating to feudalism

feu·dal·ism \-,izəm\ n : medieval political order in which land is granted in return for service — **feu·dal·is·tic** \,fyüd²l'istik\ adj

fe·ver \'fēvər\ n **1** : abnormal rise in body temperature **2** : state of heightened emotion — **fe·ver·ish** adj — **fe·ver·ish·ly** adv

few \'fyü\ pron : not many ~ adj : some but not many — often with a ~ n : small number — often with a

few·er \-ər\ pron : smaller number of things

fez \'fez\ n, pl **fez·zes** : round flat-crowned hat

fi·an·cé \,fē,än'sā\ n : man one is engaged to

fi·an·cée \,fē,än'sā\ n : woman one is engaged to

fi·as·co \fē'asko\ n, pl **-coes** : ridiculous failure

fi·at \'fēat, -,at, -,ät; 'fīat, -,at\ n : decree

fib \'fib\ n : trivial lie — **fib** vb — **fib·ber** n

fi·ber, fi·bre \'fībər\ n **1** : threadlike substance or structure (as a muscle cell or fine root) **2** : indigestible material in food **3** : element that gives texture or substance — **fi·brous** \-brəs\ adj

fi·ber·board n : construction material made of compressed fibers

fi·ber·glass n : glass in fibrous form in various products (as insulation)

fi·bril·la·tion \,fibrə'lāshən, ,fīb-\ n : rapid irregular contractions of heart muscle — **fib·ril·late** \'fibrə,lāt, 'fīb-\ vb

fib·u·la \'fibyələ\ n, pl **-lae** \-lē, -,lī\ or **-las** : outer of the two leg bones below the knee — **fib·u·lar** \-lər\ adj

fick·le \'fikəl\ adj : unpredictably changeable — **fick·le·ness** n

fic·tion \'fikshən\ n : a made-up story or literature consisting of these — **fic·tion·al** \-shənəl\ adj

fic·ti·tious \fik'tishəs\ adj : made up or pretended

fid·dle \'fid²l\ n : violin ~ vb **-dled; -dling 1** : play on the fiddle **2** : move the hands restlessly — **fid·dler** \'fidlər, -²lər\ n

fid·dle·sticks n : nonsense — used as an interjection

fi·del·i·ty \fə'delətē, fī-\ n, pl **-ties 1** : quality or state of being faithful **2** : quality of reproduction

fid•get \'fijət\ *n* **1** *pl* : restlessness **2** : one that fidgets ~ *vb* : move restlessly — **fid•gety** *adj*

fi•du•cia•ry \fə'düshē,erē, -'dyü-, -shərē\ *adj* : held or holding in trust — **fiduciary** *n*

field \'fēld\ *n* **1** : open country **2** : cleared land **3** : land yielding some special product **4** : sphere of activity **5** : area for sports **6** : region or space in which a given effect (as magnetism) exists ~ *vb* : put into the field — **field** *adj* — **field•er** *n*

fiend \'fēnd\ *n* **1** : devil **2** : extremely wicked person — **fiend•ish** *adj* — **fiend•ish•ly** *adv*

fierce \'firs\ *adj* **fierc•er; -est 1** : violently hostile or aggressive **2** : intense **3** : menacing looking — **fierce•ly** *adv* — **fierce•ness** *n*

fiery \'fīərē\ *adj* **fi•er•i•er; -est 1** : burning **2** : hot or passionate — **fi•eri•ness** \'fīərēnəs\ *n*

fi•es•ta \fē'estə\ *n* : festival

fife \'fīf\ *n* : small flute

fif•teen \fif'tēn\ *n* : one more than 14 — **fifteen** *adj or pron* — **fif•teenth** \-'tēnth\ *adj or n*

fifth \'fifth\ *n* **1** : one that is number 5 in a countable series **2** : one of 5 equal parts of something — **fifth** *adj or adv*

fif•ty \'fiftē\ *n, pl* **-ties** : 5 times 10 — **fif•ti•eth** \-tēəth\ *adj or n* — **fifty** *adj or pron*

fif•ty–fif•ty *adv or adj* : shared equally

fig \'fig\ *n* : pear-shaped edible fruit

fight \'fīt\ *vb* **fought** \'fòt\; **fight•ing 1** : contend against another in battle **2** : box : struggle ~ *n* **1** : hostile encounter **2** : boxing match **3** : verbal disagreement — **fight•er** *n*

fig•ment \'figmənt\ *n* : something imagined or made up

fig•u•ra•tive \'figyərətiv, -gə-\ *adj* : metaphorical — **fig•u•ra•tive•ly** *adv*

fig•ure \'figyər, -gər\ *n* **1** : symbol representing a number **2** *pl* : arithmetical calculations **3** : price **4** : shape or outline **5** : illustration **6** : pattern or design **7** : prominent person ~ *vb* **-ured; -ur•ing 1** : be important **2** : calculate — **fig•ured** *adj*

fig•u•rine \,figyə'rēn\ *n* : small statue

fil•a•ment \'filəmənt\ *n* : fine thread or threadlike part — **fil•a•men•tous** \,filə'mentəs\ *adj*

fil•bert \'filbərt\ *n* : edible nut of a European hazel

filch \'filch\ *vb* : steal furtively

¹file \'fīl\ *n* : tool for smoothing or sharpening ~ *vb* **filed; fil•ing** : rub or smooth with a file

²file *vb* **filed; fil•ing 1** : arrange in order **2** : enter or record officially ~ *n* : device for keeping papers in order

³file *n* : row of persons or things one behind the other ~ *vb* **filed; fil•ing** : march in file

fil•ial \'filēəl, 'filyəl\ *adj* : relating to a son or daughter

fil•i•bus•ter \'filə,bəstər\ *n* : long speeches to delay a legislative vote — **filibuster** *vb* — **fil•i•bus•ter•er** *n*

fil•i•gree \'filə,grē\ *n* : ornamental designs of fine wire — **fil•i•greed** \-,grēd\ *adj*

fill \'fil\ *vb* **1** : make or become full **2** : stop up **3** : feed **4** : satisfy **5** : occupy fully **6** : spread through ~ *n* **1** : full supply **2** : material for filling — **fill•er** *n* — **fill in** *vb* **1** : provide information for or for **2** : substitute

fil•let \'filət, fil'ā, 'fil,ā\ *n* : piece of boneless meat or fish ~ *vb* : cut into fillets

fill•ing *n* : material used to fill something

fil•ly \'filē\ *n, pl* **-lies** : young female horse

film \'film\ *n* **1** : thin skin or membrane **2** : thin coating or layer **3** : strip of material used in taking pictures **4** : movie ~ *vb* : make a movie of — **filmy** *adj*

film•strip *n* : strip of film with photographs for still projection

fil•ter \'filtər\ *n* **1** : device for separating matter from a fluid **2** : device (as on a camera lens) that absorbs light ~ *vb* **1** : pass through a filter **2** : remove by means of a filter — **fil•ter•able** *adj* — **fil•tra•tion** \fil'trāshən\ *n*

filth \'filth\ *n* : repulsive dirt or refuse — **filth•i•ness** *n* — **filthy** \'filthē\ *adj*

fin \'fin\ *n* **1** : thin external process controlling movement in an aquatic animal **2** : fin-shaped part (as on an airplane) **3** : flipper — **finned** \'find\ *adj*

fi•na•gle \fə'nāgəl\ *vb* **-gled; -gling** : get by clever or tricky means — **fi•na•gler** *n*

fi•nal \'fīn²l\ *adj* **1** : not to be changed

2 : ultimate **3** : coming at the end — **final** n — **fi·nal·ist** \'fīnᵊlist\ n — **fi·nal·i·ty** \fī'nalətē, fə-\ n — **fi·nal·ize** \-,īz\ vb — **fi·nal·ly** adv

fi·na·le \fə'nalē, fi'näl-\ n : last or climactic part

fi·nance \fə'nans, 'fī,nans\ n **1** pl : money resources **2** : management of money affairs ~ vb **-nanced; -nanc·ing 1** : raise funds for **2** : give necessary funds to **3** : sell on credit

fi·nan·cial \fə'nanchəl, fī-\ adj : relating to finance — **fi·nan·cial·ly** adv

fi·nan·cier \,finən'sir, ,fī,nan-\ n : person who invests large sums of money

finch \'finch\ n : songbird (as a sparrow or linnet) with a strong bill

find \'fīnd\ vb **found** \'faund\; **finding 1** : discover or encounter **2** : obtain by effort **3** : experience or feel **4** : gain or regain the use of **5** : decide on (a verdict) ~ n **1** : act or instance of finding **2** : something found — **find·er** n — **find·ing** n — **find out** vb : learn, discover, or verify something

fine \'fīn\ n : money paid as a penalty ~ vb **fined; fin·ing** : impose a fine on ~ adj **fin·er; -est 1** : free from impurity **2** : small or thin **3** : not coarse **4** : superior in quality or appearance ~ adv : finely — **fine·ly** adv — **fine·ness** n

fin·ery \'fīnərē\ n, pl **-er·ies** : showy clothing and jewels

fi·nesse \fə'nes\ n **1** : delicate skill **2** : craftiness — **finesse** vb

fin·ger \'fiŋgər\ n **1** : one of the 5 divisions at the end of the hand and esp. one other than the thumb **2** : something like a finger **3** : part of a glove for a finger ~ vb **1** : touch with the fingers **2** : identify as if by pointing — **fin·gered** adj — **fin·ger·nail** n — **fin·ger·tip** n

fin·ger·ling \-gərlin\ n : small fish

fin·ger·print n : impression of the pattern of marks on the tip of a finger — **fingerprint** vb

fin·icky \'finikē\ adj : excessively particular in taste or standards

fin·ish \'finish\ vb **1** : come or bring to an end **2** : use or dispose of entirely **3** : put a final coat or surface on ~ n **1** : end **2** : final treatment given a surface — **fin·ish·er** n

fi·nite \'fī,nīt\ adj : having definite limits

fink \'fiŋk\ n : contemptible person

fiord var of FJORD

fir \'fər\ n : evergreen tree or its wood

fire \'fīr\ n **1** : light or heat and esp. the flame of something burning **2** : destructive burning (as of a house) **3** : enthusiasm **4** : the shooting of weapons ~ vb **fired; fir·ing 1** : kindle **2** : stir up or enliven **3** : dismiss from employment **4** : shoot **5** : bake — **fire·bomb** n or vb — **fire·fight·er** n — **fire·less** adj — **fire·proof** adj or vb — **fire·wood** n

fire·arm n : weapon (as a rifle) that works by an explosion of gunpowder

fire·ball n **1** : ball of fire **2** : brilliant meteor

fire·boat n : boat equipped for fighting fire

fire·box n **1** : chamber (as of a furnace) that contains a fire **2** : fire-alarm box

fire·break n : cleared land for checking a forest fire

fire·bug n : person who deliberately sets destructive fires

fire·crack·er n : small firework that makes noise

fire·fight·er \'fir,fitər\ n : a person who fights fires

fire·fly n : night-flying beetle that produces a soft light

fire·place n : opening made in a chimney to hold an open fire

fire·plug n : hydrant

fire·side n **1** : place near the fire or hearth **2** : home ~ adj : having an informal quality

fire·trap n : place apt to catch on fire

fire·work n : device that explodes to produce noise or a display of light

¹**firm** \'fərm\ adj **1** : securely fixed in place **2** : strong or vigorous **3** : not subject to change **4** : resolute ~ vb : make or become firm — **firm·ly** adv — **firm·ness** n

²**firm** n : business enterprise

fir·ma·ment \'fərməmənt\ n : sky

first \'fərst\ adj **1** : being number one **2** : foremost ~ adv **1** : before any other **2** : for the first time ~ n **1** : number one **2** : one that is first — **first class** n — **first-class** adj or adv — **first·ly** adv — **first-rate** adj or adv

first aid n : emergency care

first lieutenant n : commissioned officer ranking next below a captain

first sergeant n **1** : noncommissioned

officer serving as the chief assistant to the commander of a military unit **2** : rank in the army below a sergeant major and in the marine corps below a master gunnery sergeant

firth \'fərth\ n : estuary

fis·cal \'fiskəl\ adj : relating to money — **fis·cal·ly** adv

fish \'fish\ n, pl **fish** or **fish·es** : water animal with fins, gills, and usu. scales ∼ vb **1** : try to catch fish **2** : grope — **fish·er** n — **fish·hook** n — **fish·ing** n

fish·er·man \-mən\ n : one who fishes

fish·ery \'fishərē\ n, pl **-er·ies** : fishing business or a place for this

fishy \'fishē\ adj **fish·i·er; -est 1** : relating to or like fish **2** : questionable

fis·sion \'fishən, 'fizh-\ n : splitting of an atomic nucleus — **fis·sion·able** \-ənəbəl\ adj

fis·sure \'fishər\ n : crack

fist \'fist\ n : hand doubled up — **fist·ed** \'fistəd\ adj — **fist·ful** \-,fūl\ n

fist·i·cuffs \'fisti,kəfs\ n pl : fist fight

¹**fit** \'fit\ n : sudden attack of illness or emotion

²**fit** adj **-tt- 1** : suitable **2** : qualified **3** : sound in body ∼ vb **-tt- 1** : be suitable to **2** : insert or adjust correctly **3** : make room for **4** : supply or equip **5** : belong ∼ n : state of fitting or being fitted — **fit·ly** adv — **fit·ness** n — **fit·ter** n

fit·ful \'fitfəl\ adj : restless — **fit·ful·ly** adv

fit·ting adj : suitable ∼ n : a small part

five \'fiv\ n **1** : one more than 4 **2** : 5th in a set or series **3** : something having 5 units — **five** adj or pron

fix \'fiks\ vb **1** : attach **2** : establish **3** : make right **4** : prepare **5** : improperly influence ∼ n **1** : predicament **2** : determination of location — **fix·er** n

fix·a·tion \fik'sāshən\ n : obsessive attachment — **fix·ate** \'fik,sāt\ vb

fixed \'fikst\ adj **1** : stationary **2** : settled — **fixed·ly** \'fiksədlē\ adv — **fixed·ness** \-nəs\ n

fix·ture \'fikschər\ n : permanent part of something

fizz \'fiz\ vb : make a hissing sound ∼ n : effervescence

fiz·zle \'fizəl\ vb **-zled; -zling 1** : fizz **2** : fail ∼ n : failure

fjord \fē'ord\ n : inlet of the sea between cliffs

flab \'flab\ n : flabby flesh

flab·ber·gast \'flabər,gast\ vb : astound

flab·by \'flabē\ adj **-bi·er; -est** : not firm — **flab·bi·ness** n

flac·cid \'flaksəd, 'flasəd\ adj : not firm

¹**flag** \'flag\ n : flat stone

²**flag** n **1** : fabric that is a symbol (as of a country) **2** : something used to signal ∼ vb **-gg-** : signal with a flag — **flag·pole** n — **flag·staff** n

³**flag** vb **-gg-** : lose strength or spirit

flag·el·late \'flajə,lāt\ vb **-lat·ed; -lat·ing** : whip — **flag·el·la·tion** \,flajə'lāshən\ n

flag·on \'flagən\ n : container for liquids

fla·grant \'flāgrənt\ adj : conspicuously bad — **fla·grant·ly** adv

flag·ship n : ship carrying a commander

flag·stone n : flag

flail \'flāl\ n : tool for threshing grain ∼ vb : beat with or as if with a flail

flair \'flar\ n : natural aptitude

flak \'flak\ n, pl **flak 1** : antiaircraft fire **2** : criticism

flake \'flāk\ n : small flat piece ∼ vb **flaked; flak·ing** : separate or form into flakes

flam·boy·ant \flam'boiənt\ adj : showy — **flam·boy·ance** \-əns\ n — **flam·boy·ant·ly** adv

flame \'flām\ n **1** : glowing part of a fire **2** : state of combustion **3** : burning passion — **flame** vb — **flam·ing** adj

fla·min·go \flə'miŋgō\ n, pl **-gos** : long-legged long-necked tropical water bird

flam·ma·ble \'flaməbəl\ adj : easily ignited

flange \'flanj\ n : rim

flank \'flaŋk\ n : side of something ∼ vb **1** : attack or go around the side of **2** : be at the side of

flan·nel \'flan²l\ n : soft napped fabric

flap \'flap\ n **1** : slap **2** : something flat that hangs loose ∼ vb **-pp- 1** : move (wings) up and down **2** : swing back and forth noisily

flap·jack \-,jak\ n : pancake

flare \'flar\ vb **flared; flar·ing** : become suddenly bright or excited ∼ n : blaze of light

flash \'flash\ vb **1** : give off a sudden flame or burst of light **2** : appear or pass suddenly ∼ n **1** : sudden burst of light or inspiration **2** : instant ~ *adj* : coming suddenly

flash•light *n* : small battery-operated light

flashy \'flashē\ *adj* **flash•i•er**; **-est** : showy — **flash•i•ly** *adv* — **flash•i•ness** *n*

flask \'flask\ *n* : flattened bottle

flat \'flat\ *adj* **-tt-** **1** : smooth **2** : broad and thin **3** : definite **4** : uninteresting **5** : deflated **6** : below the true pitch ~ *n* **1** : level surface of land **2** : flat note in music **3** : apartment **4** : deflated tire ~ *adv* **-tt-** **1** : exactly **2** : below the true pitch ~ *vb* **-tt-** : make flat — **flat•ly** *adv* — **flat•ness** *n* — **flat•ten** \-ᵊn\ *vb*

flat•car *n* : railroad car without sides

flat•fish *n* : flattened fish with eyes on the upper side

flat•foot *n, pl* **flat•feet** : foot condition in which the arch is flattened — **flat–foot•ed** *adj*

flat–out *adj* **1** : being maximum effort or speed **2** : downright

flat•ter \'flatər\ *vb* **1** : praise insincerely **2** : judge or represent too favorably — **flat•ter•er** *n* — **flat•tery** \'flatərē\ *n*

flat•u•lent \'flachələnt\ *adj* : full of gas — **flat•u•lence** \-ləns\ *n*

flat•ware *n* : eating utensils

flaunt \'flȯnt\ *vb* : display ostentatiously — **flaunt** *n*

fla•vor \'flāvər\ *n* **1** : quality that affects the sense of taste **2** : something that adds flavor ~ *vb* : give flavor to — **fla•vor•ful** *adj* — **fla•vor•ing** *n* — **fla•vor•less** *adj*

flaw \'flȯ\ *n* : fault — **flaw•less** *adj* — **flaw•less•ly** *adv* — **flaw•less•ness** *n*

flax \'flaks\ *n* : plant from which linen is made

flax•en \'flaksən\ *adj* : made of or like flax

flay \'flā\ *vb* **1** : strip off the skin of **2** : criticize harshly

flea \'flē\ *n* : leaping bloodsucking insect

fleck \'flek\ *vb or n* : streak or spot

fledg•ling \'flejliŋ\ *n* : young bird

flee \'flē\ *vb* **fled** \'fled\; **flee•ing** : run away

fleece \'flēs\ *n* : sheep's wool ~ *vb* **fleeced**; **fleec•ing** **1** : shear **2** : get money from dishonestly — **fleecy** *adj*

¹**fleet** \'flēt\ *vb* : pass rapidly ~ *adj*

: swift — **fleet•ing** *adj* — **fleet•ness** *n*

²**fleet** *n* : group of ships

fleet admiral *n* : commissioned officer of the highest rank in the navy

flesh \'flesh\ *n* **1** : soft parts of an animal's body **2** : soft plant tissue (as fruit pulp) — **fleshed** \'flesht\ *adj* — **fleshy** *adj* — **flesh out** *vb* : make fuller

flesh•ly \'fleshlē\ *adj* : sensual

flew *past of* FLY

flex \'fleks\ *vb* : bend

flex•i•ble \'fleksəbəl\ *adj* **1** : capable of being flexed **2** : adaptable — **flex•i•bil•i•ty** \fleksə'bilətē\ *n* — **flex•i•bly** \-səblē\ *adv*

flick \'flik\ *n* : light jerky stroke ~ *vb* **1** : strike lightly **2** : flutter

flick•er \'flikər\ *vb* **1** : waver **2** : burn unsteadily ~ *n* **1** : sudden movement **2** : wavering light

fli•er \'flīər\ *n* **1** : aviator **2** : advertising circular

¹**flight** \'flīt\ *n* **1** : act or instance of flying **2** : ability to fly **3** : a passing through air or space **4** : series of stairs — **flight•less** *adj*

²**flight** *n* : act or instance of running away

flighty \-ē\ *adj* **flight•i•er**; **-est** : capricious or silly — **flight•i•ness** *n*

flim•flam \'flim,flam\ *n* : trickery

flim•sy \-zē\ *adj* **-si•er**; **-est** **1** : not strong or well made **2** : not believable — **flim•si•ly** *adv* — **flim•si•ness** *n*

flinch \'flinch\ *vb* : shrink from pain

fling \'fliŋ\ *vb* **flung** \'fləŋ\; **fling•ing** **1** : move brusquely **2** : throw ~ *n* **1** : act or instance of flinging **2** : attempt **3** : period of self-indulgence

flint \'flint\ *n* : hard quartz that gives off sparks when struck with steel — **flinty** *adj*

flip \'flip\ *vb* **-pp-** **1** : cause to turn over quickly or many times **2** : move with a quick push ~ *adj* : insolent — **flip** *n*

flip•pant \'flipənt\ *adj* : not serious enough — **flip•pan•cy** \-ənsē\ *n*

flip•per \'flipər\ *n* : paddlelike limb (as of a seal) for swimming

flirt \'flərt\ *vb* **1** : be playfully romantic **2** : show casual interest ~ *n* : one who flirts — **flir•ta•tion** \flər'tāshən\ *n* — **flir•ta•tious** \-shəs\ *adj*

flit \'flit\ *vb* **-tt-** : dart

float \'flōt\ *n* **1** : something that floats **2** : vehicle carrying an exhibit ~ *vb*

1 : rest on or in a fluid without sinking **2** : wander **3** : finance by issuing stock or bonds — **float·er** n

flock \'fläk\ n : group of animals (as birds) or people ~ vb : gather or move as a group

floe \'flō\ n : mass of floating ice

flog \'fläg\ vb **-gg-** : beat with a rod or whip — **flog·ger** n

flood \'fləd\ n **1** : great flow of water over the land **2** : overwhelming volume ~ vb : cover or fill esp. with water — **flood·wa·ter** n

floor \'flōr\ n **1** : bottom of a room on which one stands **2** : story of a building **3** : lower limit ~ vb **1** : furnish with a floor **2** : knock down **3** : amaze — **floor·board** n — **floor·ing** \-iŋ\ n

floo·zy, floo·zie \'flüzē\ n, pl **-zies** : promiscuous young woman

flop \'fläp\ vb **-pp-** **1** : flap **2** : slump heavily **3** : fail — **flop** n

flop·py \'fläpē\ adj **-pi·er; -est** : soft and flexible

flo·ra \'flōrə\ n : plants or plant life of a region

flo·ral \'flōrəl\ adj : relating to flowers

flor·id \'flōrəd\ adj **1** : very flowery in style **2** : reddish

flo·rist \'flōrist\ n : flower dealer

floss \'fläs\ n **1** : soft thread for embroidery **2** : thread used to clean between teeth — **floss** vb

flo·ta·tion \flō'tāshən\ n : process or instance of floating

flo·til·la \flō'tilə\ n : small fleet

flot·sam \'flätsəm\ n : floating wreckage

¹flounce \'flaùns\ vb **flounced; flounc·ing** : move with exaggerated jerky motions — **flounce** n

²flounce n : fabric border or wide ruffle

¹floun·der \'flaùndər\ n, pl **flounder** or **flounders** : flatfish

²flounder vb **1** : struggle for footing **2** : proceed clumsily

flour \'flaùr\ n : finely ground meal ~ vb : coat with flour — **floury** adj

flour·ish \'flərish\ vb **1** : thrive **2** : wave threateningly ~ n **1** : embellishment **2** : fanfare **3** : wave **4** : showiness of action

flout \'flaùt\ vb : treat with disdain

flow \'flō\ vb **1** : move in a stream **2** : proceed smoothly and readily ~ n : uninterrupted stream

flow·er \'flaùər\ n **1** : showy plant

shoot that bears seeds **2** : state of flourishing ~ vb **1** : produce flowers **2** : flourish — **flow·ered** adj — **flow·er·less** adj — **flow·er·pot** n — **flow·ery** \-ē\ adj

flown past part of FLY

flu \'flü\ n **1** : influenza **2** : minor virus ailment

flub \'fləb\ vb **-bb-** : bungle — **flub** n

fluc·tu·ate \'fləkchə,wāt\ vb **-at·ed; -at·ing** : change rapidly esp. up and down — **fluc·tu·a·tion** \,fləkchə-'wāshən\ n

flue \'flü\ n : smoke duct

flu·ent \'flüənt\ adj : speaking with ease — **flu·en·cy** \-ənsē\ n — **flu·ent·ly** adv

fluff \'fləf\ n **1** : something soft and light **2** : blunder ~ vb **1** : make fluffy **2** : make a mistake — **fluffy** \-ē\ adj

flu·id \'flüəd\ adj : flowing ~ n : substance that can flow — **flu·id·i·ty** \flü'idətē\ n — **flu·id·ly** adv

fluid ounce n : unit of liquid measure equal to 1/16 pint

fluke \'flük\ n : stroke of luck

flume \'flüm\ n : channel for water

flung past of FLING

flunk \'fləŋk\ vb : fail in school work

flun·ky, flun·key \'fləŋkē\ n, pl **-kies** or **-keys** : lackey

flu·o·res·cence \,flùr'es°ns, ,flòr-\ n : emission of light after initial absorption — **flu·o·resce** \-'es\ vb — **flu·o·res·cent** \-'es°nt\ adj

flu·o·ri·date \'flórə,dāt, 'flùr-\ vb **-dat·ed; -dat·ing** : add fluoride to — **flu·o·ri·da·tion** \,flórə'dāshən, ,flùr-\ n

flu·o·ride \'flór,īd, 'flùr-\ n : compound of fluorine

flu·o·rine \'flùr,ēn, -ən\ n : toxic gaseous chemical element

flu·o·ro·car·bon \,flórō'kärbən, ,flùr-\ n : compound containing fluorine and carbon

flu·o·ro·scope \'flùrə,skōp\ n : instrument for internal examination — **flu·o·ro·scop·ic** \,flùrə'skäpik\ adj — **flu·o·ros·co·py** \flùr'äskəpē\ n

flur·ry \'flərē\ n, pl **-ries** **1** : light snowfall **2** : bustle **3** : brief burst of activity — **flurry** vb

¹flush \'fləsh\ vb : cause (a bird) to fly from cover

²flush n **1** : sudden flow (as of water) **2** : surge of emotion **3** : blush ~ vb **1**

: blush **2** : wash out with a rush of liquid ~ *adj* **1** : filled to overflowing **2** : of a reddish healthy color **3** : smooth or level **4** : abutting — **flush** *adv*

³**flush** *n* : cards of the same suit

flus·ter \'fləstər\ *vb* : upset — **fluster** *n*

flute \'flüt\ *n* **1** : pipelike musical instrument **2** : groove — **flut·ed** *adj* — **flut·ing** *n* — **flut·ist** \-ist\ *n*

flut·ter \'flətər\ *vb* **1** : flap the wings rapidly **2** : move with quick wavering or flapping motions **3** : behave in an agitated manner ~ *n* **1** : a fluttering **2** : state of confusion — **flut·tery** \-ərē\ *adj*

flux \'fləks\ *n* : state of continuous change

¹**fly** \'flī\ *vb* flew \'flü\ flown \'flōn\; **fly·ing 1** : move through the air with wings **2** : float or soar **3** : flee **4** : move or pass swiftly **5** : operate an airplane

²**fly** *n, pl* **flies** : garment closure

³**fly** *n, pl* **flies** : winged insect

fly·er *var of* FLIER

fly·pa·per *n* : sticky paper for catching flies

fly·speck *n* **1** : speck of fly dung **2** : something tiny

fly·wheel *n* : rotating wheel that regulates the speed of machinery

foal \'fōl\ *n* : young horse — **foal** *vb*

foam \'fōm\ *n* **1** : mass of bubbles on top of a liquid **2** : material of cellular form ~ *vb* : form foam — **foamy** *adj*

fob \'fäb\ *n* : short chain for a pocket watch

fo'c'sle *var of* FORECASTLE

fo·cus \'fōkəs\ *n, pl* **-ci** \-ˌsī\ **1** : point at which reflected or refracted rays meet **2** : adjustment (as of eyeglasses) for clear vision **3** : central point ~ *vb* : bring to a focus — **focal** \-kəl\ *adj* — **fo·cal·ly** *adv*

fod·der \'fädər\ *n* : food for livestock

foe \'fō\ *n* : enemy

fog \'fȯg, 'fäg\ *n* **1** : fine particles of water suspended near the ground **2** : mental confusion ~ *vb* **-gg-** : obscure or be obscured with fog — **fog·gy** *adj*

fog·horn *n* : warning horn sounded in a fog

fo·gy \'fōgē\ *n, pl* **-gies** : person with old-fashioned ideas

foi·ble \'fȯibəl\ *n* : minor character fault

¹**foil** \'fȯil\ *vb* : defeat ~ *n* : light fencing sword

²**foil** *n* **1** : thin sheet of metal **2** : one that sets off another by contrast

foist \'fȯist\ *vb* : force another to accept

¹**fold** \'fōld\ *n* **1** : enclosure for sheep **2** : group with a common interest

²**fold** *vb* **1** : lay one part over another **2** : embrace ~ *n* : part folded

fold·er \'fōldər\ *n* **1** : one that folds **2** : circular **3** : folded cover or envelope for papers

fol·de·rol \'fäldəˌräl\ *n* : nonsense

fo·liage \'fōlēij, -lij\ *n* : plant leaves

fo·lio \'fōlēˌō\ *n, pl* **-lios** : sheet of paper folded once

folk \'fōk\ *n, pl* **folk** *or* **folks** : people in general **2** *folks pl* : one's family ~ *adj* : relating to the common people

folk·lore *n* : customs and traditions of a people — **folk·lor·ist** *n*

folksy \'fōksē\ *adj* **folks·i·er;** **-est** : friendly and informal

fol·li·cle \'fälikəl\ *n* : small anatomical cavity or gland

fol·low \'fälō\ *vb* **1** : go or come after **2** : pursue **3** : obey **4** : proceed along **5** : keep one's attention fixed on **6** : result from — **fol·low·er** *n*

fol·low·ing \'fäləwiŋ\ *adj* : next ~ *n* : group of followers ~ *prep* : after

fol·ly \'fälē\ *n, pl* **-lies** : foolishness

fo·ment \fō'ment\ *vb* : incite

fond \'fänd\ *adj* **1** : strongly attracted **2** : affectionate **3** : dear — **fond·ly** *adv* — **fond·ness** *n*

fon·dle \'fänd'l\ *vb* **-dled;** **-dling** : touch lovingly

fon·due \fän'dü, -'dyü\ *n* : preparation of melted cheese

font \'fänt\ *n* **1** : baptismal basin **2** : fountain

food \'füd\ *n* : material eaten to sustain life

fool \'fül\ *n* **1** : stupid person **2** : jester ~ *vb* **1** : waste time **2** : meddle **3** : deceive — **fool·ery** \'fülərē\ *n* — **fool·ish** \'fülish\ *adj* — **fool·ish·ly** *adv* — **fool·ish·ness** *n* — **fool·proof** *adj*

fool·har·dy \'fülˌhärdē\ *adj* : rash — **fool·har·di·ness** *n*

foot \'füt\ *n, pl* **feet** \'fēt\ **1** : end part of a leg **2** : unit of length equal to ⅓ yard **3** : unit of verse meter **4** : bottom — **foot·age** \-ij\ *n* — **foot·ed** *adj* — **foot·path** *n* — **foot·print** —

foot·race n — **foot·rest** n — **foot·wear** n

foot·ball n : ball game played by 2 teams on a rectangular field

foot·bridge n : bridge for pedestrians

foot·hill n : hill at the foot of higher hills

foot·hold n : support for the feet

foot·ing n 1 : foothold 2 : basis

foot·lights n pl : stage lights along the floor

foot·lock·er n : small trunk

foot·loose adj : having no ties

foot·man \'fu̇tmən\ n : male servant

foot·note n : note at the bottom of a page

foot·step n 1 : step 2 : distance covered by a step 3 : footprint

foot·stool n : stool to support the feet

foot·work n : skillful movement of the feet (as in boxing)

fop \'fäp\ n : dandy — **fop·pery** \-ərē\ n — **fop·pish** adj

for \'fȯr\ prep 1 — used to show preparation or purpose 2 : because of 3 — used to show a reason 4 : in support of 5 : so as to support or help cure 6 : so as to be equal to 7 : concerning 8 : through the period of ~ conj : because

for·age \'fȯrij\ n : food for animals ~ vb **-aged; -ag·ing** 1 : hunt food 2 : search for provisions

for·ay \'fȯr‚ā\ n or vb : raid

¹**for·bear** \fȯr'bar\ vb **-bore** \-'bȯr\; **-borne** \-'bȯrn\; **-bear·ing** 1 : refrain from 2 : be patient — **for·bear·ance** \-'barəns\ n

²**forbear** var of FOREBEAR

for·bid \fər'bid\ vb **-bade** \-'bad, -'bād\ or **-bad** \-'bad\; **-bid·den** \-'bid²n\; **-bid·ding** 1 : prohibit 2 : order not to do something

for·bid·ding adj : tending to discourage

force \'fȯrs\ n 1 : exceptional strength or energy 2 : military strength 3 : body (as of persons) available for a purpose 4 : violence 5 : influence (as a push or pull) that causes motion ~ vb **forced; forc·ing** 1 : compel 2 : gain against resistance 3 : break open — **force·ful** \-fəl\ adj — **force·ful·ly** adv — **in force** 1 : in great numbers 2 : valid

for·ceps \'fȯrsəps\ n, pl **forceps** : surgical instrument for grasping objects

forc·ible \'fȯrsəbəl\ adj 1 : done by force 2 : showing force — **forc·i·bly** \-blē\ adv

ford \'fȯrd\ n : place to wade across a stream ~ vb : wade across

fore \'fȯr\ adv : in or toward the front ~ adj : being or coming before in time, place, or order ~ n : front

fore–and–aft adj : lengthwise

fore·arm \'fȯr‚ärm\ n : part of the arm between the elbow and the wrist

fore·bear \'fȯr‚bar\ n : ancestor

fore·bod·ing \fȯr'bōdiŋ\ n : premonition of disaster — **fore·bod·ing** adj

fore·cast \'fȯr‚kast\ vb **-cast; -cast·ing** : predict — **forecast** n — **fore·cast·er** n

fore·cas·tle \'fōksəl\ n : forward part of a ship

fore·close \fȯr'klōz\ vb : take legal measures to terminate a mortgage — **fore·clo·sure** \-'klōzhər\ n

fore·fa·ther \'fȯr‚fäthər\ n : ancestor

fore·fin·ger \'fȯr‚fiŋgər\ n : finger next to the thumb

fore·foot \'fȯr‚fu̇t\ n : front foot of a quadruped

fore·front \'fȯr‚frənt\ n : foremost position or place

¹**fore·go** \fȯr'gō\ vb **-went; -gone; -go·ing** : precede

²**forego** var of FORGO

fore·go·ing adj : preceding

fore·gone adj : determined in advance

fore·ground \'fȯr‚grau̇nd\ n : part of a scene nearest the viewer

fore·hand \'fȯr‚hand\ n : stroke (as in tennis) made with the palm of the hand turned forward — **forehand** adj

fore·head \'fȯrəd, 'fȯr‚hed\ n : part of the face above the eyes

for·eign \'fȯrən\ adj 1 : situated outside a place or country and esp. one's own country 2 : belonging to a different place or country 3 : not pertinent 4 : related to or dealing with other nations — **for·eign·er** \-ər\ n

fore·know \fȯr'nō\ vb **-knew; -known; -know·ing** : know beforehand — **fore·knowl·edge** n

fore·leg \'fȯr‚leg\ n : front leg

fore·lock \'fȯr‚läk\ n : front lock of hair

fore·man \'fȯrmən\ n 1 : spokesman of a jury 2 : workman in charge

fore·most \'fȯr‚mōst\ adj : first in time, place, or order — **foremost** adv

fore·noon \'fȯr‚nün\ n : morning

fo·ren·sic \fə'rensik\ adj : relating to courts or public speaking or debate

fo·ren·sics \-siks\ *n pl* : art or study of speaking or debating

fore·or·dain \ˌfȯrȯrˈdān\ *vb* : decree beforehand

fore·quar·ter \ˈfȯrˌkwȯrtər\ *n* : front half on one side of the body of a quadruped

fore·run·ner \ˈfȯrˌrənər\ *n* : one that goes before

fore·see \fȯrˈsē\ *vb* **-saw; -seen; -see·ing** : see or realize beforehand — **fore·see·able** *adj*

fore·shad·ow \fȯrˈshadō\ *vb* : hint or suggest beforehand

fore·sight \ˈfȯrˌsīt\ *n* : care or provision for the future — **fore·sight·ed** *adj* — **fore·sight·ed·ness** *n*

for·est \ˈfȯrəst\ *n* : large thick growth of trees and underbrush — **for·est·ed** \ˈfȯrəstəd\ *adj* — **for·est·er** \-əstər\ *n* — **for·est·land** \-ˌland\ *n* — **for·est·ry** \-əstrē\ *n*

fore·stall \fȯrˈstȯl, fȯr-\ *vb* : prevent by acting in advance

foreswear *var of* FORSWEAR

fore·taste \ˈfȯrˌtāst\ *n* : advance indication or notion ~ *vb* : anticipate

fore·tell \fȯrˈtel\ *vb* **-told; -tell·ing** : predict

fore·thought \ˈfȯrˌthȯt\ *n* : foresight

for·ev·er \fȯrˈevər\ *adv* **1** : for a limitless time **2** : always

for·ev·er·more \-ˌevərˈmȯr\ *adv* : forever

fore·warn \fȯrˈwȯrn\ *vb* : warn beforehand

fore·word \ˈfȯrwərd\ *n* : preface

for·feit \ˈfȯrfət\ *n* : something forfeited ~ *vb* : lose or lose the right to by an error or crime — **for·fei·ture** \-fəˌchùr\ *n*

¹forge \ˈfȯrj\ *n* : smithy ~ *vb* **forged; forg·ing 1** : form (metal) by heating and hammering **2** : imitate falsely esp. to defraud — **forg·er** *n* — **forg·ery** \-ərē\ *n*

²forge *vb* **forged; forg·ing** : move ahead steadily

for·get \fərˈget\ *vb* **-got** \-ˈgät\; **-got·ten** \-ˈgät³n\ *or* **-got; -get·ting 1** : be unable to think of or recall **2** : fail to think of at the proper time — **for·get·ta·ble** *adj* — **for·get·ful** \-fəl\ *adj* — **for·get·ful·ly** *adv*

forget–me–not *n* : small herb with blue or white flowers

for·give \fərˈgiv\ *vb* **-gave** \-ˈgāv\; **-giv·en** \-ˈgivən\; **-giv·ing** : pardon

— **for·giv·able** *adj* — **for·give·ness** *n*

for·giv·ing *adj* **1** : able to forgive **2** : allowing room for error or weakness

for·go, fore·go \fȯrˈgō\ *vb* **-went; -gone; -go·ing** : do without

fork \ˈfȯrk\ *n* **1** : implement with prongs for lifting, holding, or digging **2** : forked part **3** : a dividing into branches or a place where something branches ~ *vb* **1** : divide into branches **2** : move with a fork — **forked** \ˈfȯrkt, ˈfȯrkəd\ *adj*

fork·lift *n* : machine for lifting with steel fingers

for·lorn \fərˈlȯrn\ *adj* **1** : deserted **2** : wretched — **for·lorn·ly** *adv*

form \ˈfȯrm\ *n* **1** : shape **2** : set way of doing or saying something **3** : document with blanks to be filled in **4** : manner of performing with respect to what is expected **5** : mold **6** : kind or variety **7** : one of the ways in which a word is changed to show difference in use ~ *vb* **1** : give form or shape to **2** : train **3** : develop **4** : constitute — **form·a·tive** \ˈfȯrmətiv\ *adj* — **form·less** \-ləs\ *adj*

for·mal \ˈfȯrməl\ *adj* : following established custom ~ *n* : formal social event — **for·mal·i·ty** \fȯrˈmalətē\ *n* — **for·mal·ize** \ˈfȯrməˌlīz\ *vb* — **for·mal·ly** *adv*

form·al·de·hyde \fȯrˈmaldəˌhīd\ *n* : colorless pungent gas used as a preservative and disinfectant

for·mat \ˈfȯrˌmat\ *n* : general style or arrangement of something — **format** *vb*

for·ma·tion \fȯrˈmāshən\ *n* **1** : a giving form to something **2** : something formed **3** : arrangement

for·mer \ˈfȯrmər\ *adj* : coming before in time — **for·mer·ly** *adv*

for·mi·da·ble \ˈfȯrmədəbəl, fȯrˈmid-\ *adj* **1** : causing fear or dread **2** : very difficult — **for·mi·da·bly** \-blē\ *adv*

for·mu·la \ˈfȯrmyələ\ *n, pl* **-las** *or* **-lae** \-ˌlē, -ˌlī\ **1** : set form of words for ceremonial use **2** : recipe **3** : milk mixture for a baby **4** : group of symbols or figures briefly expressing information **5** : set form or method

for·mu·late \-ˌlāt\ *vb* **-lat·ed; -lat·ing** : design, devise — **for·mu·la·tion** \ˌfȯrmyəˈlāshən\ *n*

for·ni·ca·tion \ˌfȯrnəˈkāshən\ *n* : il-

licit sexual intercourse — **for·ni·cate**
\\'fórnə,kāt\\ vb — **for·ni·ca·tor**
\\-,kātər\\ n

for·sake \\fər'sāk\\ vb **-sook** \\-'súk\\;
-sak·en \\-'sākən\\; **-sak·ing** : renounce completely

for·swear \\fór'swar\\ vb **-swore;**
-sworn; -swear·ing 1 : renounce under oath 2 : perjure

for·syth·ia \\fər'sithēə\\ n : shrub grown
for its yellow flowers

fort \\'fórt\\ n 1 : fortified place 2 : permanent army post

forte \\'fórt, 'fór,tā\\ n : something at
which a person excels

forth \\'fórth\\ adv : forward

forth·com·ing adj 1 : coming or available soon 2 : open and direct

forth·right adj : direct — **forth·right·ly**
adv — **forth·right·ness** n

forth·with adv : immediately

for·ti·fy \\'fórtə,fī\\ vb **-fied; -fy·ing**
: make strong — **for·ti·fi·ca·tion**
\\,fórtəfə'kāshən\\ n

for·ti·tude \\'fórtə,tüd, -,tyüd\\ n : ability to endure

fort·night \\'fórt,nīt\\ n : 2 weeks —
fort·night·ly adj or adv

for·tress \\'fórtrəs\\ n : strong fort

for·tu·itous \\fór'tüətəs, -'tyü-\\ adj
: accidental

for·tu·nate \\'fórchənət\\ adj 1 : coming by good luck 2 : lucky — **for·tu·**
nate·ly adv

for·tune \\'fórchən\\ n 1 : prosperity at-
tained partly through luck 2 : good or
bad luck 3 : destiny 4 : wealth

for·tune-tell·er \\-,telər\\ n : one who
foretells a person's future — **for·**
tune-tell·ing \\-iŋ\\ n or adj

for·ty \\'fórtē\\ n, pl **forties** : 4 times 10
— **for·ti·eth** \\-ēəth\\ adj or n — **forty**
adj or pron

fo·rum \\'fórəm\\ n, pl **-rums** 1 : Roman marketplace 2 : medium for
open discussion

for·ward \\'fórwərd\\ adj : being near
or at or belonging to the front 2
: brash ~ adv : toward what is in
front ~ n : player near the front of
his team ~ vb 1 : help onward 2
: send on — **for·ward·er** \\-wərdər\\
— **for·ward·ness** n

for·wards \\'fórwərdz\\ adv : forward

fos·sil \\'fäsəl\\ n : preserved trace of an
ancient plant or animal ~ adj : being
or originating from a fossil — **fos·sil·**
ize vb

fos·ter \\'fóstər\\ adj : being, having, or
relating to substitute parents ~ vb
: help to grow or develop

fought past of FIGHT

foul \\'faúl\\ adj 1 : offensive 2
: clogged with dirt 3 : abusive 4 : wet
and stormy 5 : unfair ~ n : a breaking of the rules in a game ~ adv
: foully ~ vb 1 : make or become
foul or filthy 2 : tangle — **foul·ly** adv
— **foul-mouthed** \\-'maúthd,
-'maútht\\ adj — **foul·ness** n

fou·lard \\fu'lärd\\ n : lightweight silk

foul-up n : error or state of confusion

foul up vb : bungle

¹**found** \\'faúnd\\ past of FIND

²**found** vb : establish — **found·er** n

foun·da·tion \\faún'dāshən\\ n 1 : act
of founding 2 : basis for something
3 : endowed institution 4 : supporting
structure — **foun·da·tion·al** \\-shənəl\\
adj

foun·der \\'faúndər\\ vb : sink

found·ling \\'faúndliŋ\\ n : abandoned
infant that is found

found·ry \\'faúndrē\\ n, pl **-dries** : place
where metal is cast

fount \\'faúnt\\ n : fountain

foun·tain \\'faúnt'n\\ n 1 : spring of
water 2 : source 3 : artificial jet of
water

four \\'fór\\ n 1 : one more than 3 2
: 4th in a set or series 3 : something
having 4 units — **four** adj or pron

four·fold adj : quadruple — **four·fold**
adv

four·score adj : 80

four·some \\'fórsəm\\ n : group of 4

four·teen \\fór'tēn\\ n : one more than
13 — **fourteen** adj or pron — **four·**
teenth \\-'tēnth\\ adj or n

fourth \\'fórth\\ n 1 : one that is 4th 2
: one of 4 equal parts of something —
fourth adj or adv

fowl \\'faúl\\ n, pl **fowl** or **fowls** 1 : bird
2 : chicken

fox \\'fäks\\ n, pl **fox·es** 1 : small mammal related to wolves 2 : clever per-
son ~ vb : trick — **foxy** \\'fäksē\\ adj

fox·glove n : flowering plant that provides digitalis

fox·hole \\'fäks,hōl\\ n : pit for protection against enemy fire

foy·er \\'fóiər, 'fói,yā\\ n : entrance
hallway

fra·cas \\'frākəs, 'frak-\\ n, pl **-cas·es**
\\-əsəz\\ : brawl

frac·tion \\'frakshən\\ n 1 : number indicating one or more equal parts of a whole **2** : portion — **frac·tion·al** \-shənəl\ adj — **frac·tion·al·ly** adv

frac·tious \'frakshəs\ adj : hard to control

frac·ture \'frakchər\ n : a breaking of something — **fracture** vb

frag·ile \'frajəl, -,īl\ adj : easily broken — **fra·gil·i·ty** \frə'jilətē\ n

frag·ment \'fragmənt\ n : part broken off ~ \-,ment\ vb : break into parts — **frag·men·tary** \'fragmən,terē\ adj — **frag·men·ta·tion** \,fragmən'tāshən, -,men-\ n

fra·grant \'frāgrənt\ adj : sweet-smelling — **fra·grance** \-grəns\ n — **fra·grant·ly** adv

frail \'frāl\ adj : weak or delicate — **frail·ty** \-tē\ n

frame \'frām\ vb framed; fram·ing **1** : plan **2** : formulate **3** : construct or arrange **4** : enclose in a frame **5** : make appear guilty ~ n **1** : makeup of the body **2** : supporting or enclosing structure **3** : state or disposition (as of mind) — **frame·work** n

franc \'frank\ n : monetary unit (as of France)

fran·chise \'fran,chīz\ n **1** : special privilege **2** : the right to vote — **fran·chi·see** \,fran,chī'zē, -chə-\ n

fran·gi·ble \'franjəbəl\ adj : breakable — **fran·gi·bil·i·ty** \,franjə'bilətē\ n

¹**frank** \'frank\ adj : direct and sincere — **frank·ly** adv — **frank·ness** n

²**frank** vb : mark (mail) with a sign showing it can be mailed free ~ n : sign on franked mail

frank·furt·er \'frankfərtər, -,fərt-\, **frank·furt** \-fərt\ n : cooked sausage

frank·in·cense \'frankən,sens\ n : incense resin

fran·tic \'frantik\ adj : wildly excited — **fran·ti·cal·ly** \-iklē\ adv

fra·ter·nal \frə'tərnˀl\ adj **1** : brotherly **2** : of a fraternity — **fra·ter·nal·ly** adv

fra·ter·ni·ty \frə'tərnətē\ n, pl -ties : men's student social group

frat·er·nize \'fratər,nīz\ vb -nized; -niz·ing **1** : mingle as friends **2** : associate with members of a hostile group — **frat·er·ni·za·tion** \,fratərnə'zāshən\ n

frat·ri·cide \'fratrə,sīd\ n : killing of a sibling — **frat·ri·cid·al** \,fratrə'sīdˀl\ adj

fraud \'frȯd\ n : trickery — **fraud·u·**

lent \'frȯjələnt\ adj — **fraud·u·lent·ly** adv

fraught \'frȯt\ adj : full of or accompanied by something specified

¹**fray** \'frā\ n : fight

²**fray** vb **1** : wear by rubbing **2** : separate the threads of **3** : irritate

fraz·zle \'frazəl\ vb -zled; -zling : wear out ~ n : exhaustion

freak \'frēk\ n **1** : something abnormal or unusual **2** : enthusiast — **freak·ish** adj — **freak out** vb **1** : experience nightmarish hallucinations from drugs **2** : distress or become distressed

freck·le \'frekəl\ n : brown spot on the skin — **freckle** vb

free \'frē\ adj fre·er; fre·est **1** : having liberty or independence **2** : not taxed **3** : given without charge **4** : voluntary **5** : not in use **6** : not fastened ~ adv : without charge ~ vb freed; free·ing : set free — **free** adv — **free·born** adj — **free·dom** \'frēdəm\ n — **free·ly** adv

free·boo·ter \-,bütər\ n : pirate

free-for-all n : fight with no rules

free·load vb : live off another's generosity — **free·load·er** n

free·stand·ing adj : standing without support

free·way \'frē,wā\ n : expressway

free will n : independent power to choose — **free·will** adj

freeze \'frēz\ vb froze \'frōz\; fro·zen \'frōzˀn\; freez·ing **1** : harden into ice **2** : become chilled **3** : damage by frost **4** : stick fast **5** : become motionless **6** : fix at one stage or level ~ n **1** : very cold weather **2** : state of being frozen — **freez·er** n

freeze–dry vb : preserve by freezing then drying — **freeze–dried** adj

freight \'frāt\ n **1** : carrying of goods or payment for this **2** : shipped goods ~ vb : load or ship goods — **freight·er** n

french fry vb : fry in deep fat — **french fry** n

fre·net·ic \fri'netik\ adj : frantic — **fre·net·i·cal·ly** \-iklē\ adv

fren·zy \'frenzē\ n, pl -zies : violent agitation — **fren·zied** \-zēd\ adj

fre·quen·cy \'frēkwənsē\ n, pl -cies **1** : frequent or regular occurrence **2** : number of cycles or sound waves per second

fre·quent \'frēkwənt\ adj : happening

often ∼ \frē'kwent, 'frēkwənt\ vb
: go to habitually — **fre·quent·er** n
— **fre·quent·ly** adv

fres·co \'freskō\ n, pl **-coes** : painting
on fresh plaster

fresh \'fresh\ adj **1** : not salt **2** : pure
3 : not preserved **4** : not stale **5** : like
new **6** : insolent — **fres·hen** \-ən\
vb — **fresh·ly** adv — **fresh·ness** n

fresh·et \-ət\ n : overflowing stream

fresh·man \-mən\ n : first-year student

fresh·wa·ter \-mən\ n : water that is not salty

fret \'fret\ vb **-tt- 1** : worry or become
irritated **2** : fray **3** : agitate ∼ n **1**
: worn spot **2** : irritation — **fret·ful**
\-fəl\ adj — **fret·ful·ly** adv

fri·a·ble \'frīəbəl\ adj : easily pulverized

fri·ar \'frīər\ n : member of a religious
order

fri·ary \-ē\ n, pl **-ar·ies** : monastery of
friars

fric·as·see \'frikə,sē, ˌfrikə'-\ n
: meat stewed in a gravy ∼ vb **-seed**;
-see·ing : stew in gravy

fric·tion \'frikshən\ n **1** : a rubbing
between 2 surfaces **2** : clash of opinions — **fric·tion·al** adj

Fri·day \'frīdā\ n : 6th day of the week

friend \'frend\ n : person one likes —
friend·less \-ləs\ adj — **friend·li-
ness** \-lēnəs\ n — **friend·ly** adj —
friend·ship \-,ship\ n

frieze \'frēz\ n : ornamental band
around a room

frig·ate \'frigət\ n : warship smaller
than a destroyer

fright \'frīt\ n : sudden fear — **frigh·ten**
\-ᵊn\ vb — **fright·ful** \-fəl\ adj —
fright·ful·ly adv — **fright·ful·ness** n

frig·id \'frijəd\ adj : intensely cold —
fri·gid·i·ty frij'idətē\ n

frill \'fril\ n **1** : ruffle **2** : pleasing but
nonessential addition — **frilly** adj

fringe \'frinj\ n **1** : ornamental border
of short hanging threads or strips **2**
: edge — **fringe** vb

frisk \'frisk\ vb **1** : leap about **2**
: search (a person) esp. for weapons

frisky \'friskē\ adj **frisk·i·er; -est**
: playful — **frisk·i·ly** adv — **frisk·i-
ness** n

¹frit·ter \'fritər\ n : fried batter containing fruit or meat

²fritter vb : waste little by little

friv·o·lous \'frivələs\ adj : not important or serious — **fri·vol·i·ty** \friv-
'älətē\ n — **friv·o·lous·ly** adv

frizz \'friz\ vb : curl tightly — **frizz** n —
frizzy adj

fro \'frō\ adv : away

frock \'fräk\ n **1** : loose outer garment
2 : dress

frog \'frȯg, 'fräg\ n **1** : leaping amphibian **2** : hoarseness **3** : ornamental braid fastener **4** : small holder for
flowers

frog·man \-,man, -mən\ n : underwater swimmer

frol·ic \'frälik\ vb **-icked; -ick·ing**
: romp ∼ n : fun — **frol·ic·some**
\-səm\ adj

from \'frəm, 'främ\ prep — used to
show a starting point

frond \'fränd\ n : fern or palm leaf

front \'frənt\ n **1** : face **2** : behavior **3**
: main side of a building **4** : forward
part **5** : boundary between air masses
∼ vb **1** : have the main side adjacent
to something **2** : serve as a front —
fron·tal \-ᵊl\ adj

front·age \'frəntij\ n : length of
boundary line on a street

fron·tier \ˌfrən'tir\ n : outer edge of
settled territory — **fron·tiers·man**
\-'tirzmən\ n

fron·tis·piece \'frəntə,spēs\ n : illustration facing a title page

frost \'frȯst\ n **1** : freezing temperature
2 : ice crystals on a surface ∼ vb **1**
: cover with frost **2** : put icing on (a
cake) — **frosty** adj

frost·bite \-,bīt\ n : partial freezing of
part of the body — **frost·bit·ten**
\-,bitᵊn\ adj

frost·ing n : icing

froth \'frȯth\ n, pl **froths** \'frȯths,
'frȯthz\ : bubbles on a liquid —
frothy adj

fro·ward \'frōwərd\ adj : willful

frown \'fraun\ vb or n : scowl

frow·sy, frow·zy \'frauzē\ adj **-si·er** or
-zi·er; -est : untidy

froze past of FREEZE

frozen past part of FREEZE

fru·gal \'frügəl\ adj : thrifty — **fru·gal-
i·ty** \frü'galətē\ n — **fru·gal·ly** adv

fruit \'früt\ n **1** : usu. edible and sweet
part of a seed plant **2** : result ∼ vb
: bear fruit — **fruit·cake** n — **fruit·ed**
\-əd\ adj — **fruit·ful** adj — **fruit·ful-
ness** n — **fruit·less** adj — **fruit-
less·ly** adv — **fruity** adj

fru·ition \frü'ishən\ n : completion

frumpy \'frəmpē\ adj **frump·i·er; -est**
: dowdy

frus·trate \'frəs,trāt\ *vb* **-trat·ed; -trat·ing** **1** : block **2** : cause to fail — **frus·trat·ing·ly** *adv* — **frus·tra·tion** \,frəs'trāshən\ *n*

¹**fry** \'frī\ *vb* **fried; fry·ing** **1** : cook esp. with fat or oil **2** : be cooked by frying ∼ *n, pl* **fries** **1** : something fried **2** : social gathering with fried food

²**fry** *n, pl* **fry** : recently hatched fish

fud·dle \'fəd³l\ *vb* **-dled; -dling** : muddle

fud·dy-dud·dy \'fədē,dədē\ *n, pl* **-dies** : one who is old-fashioned or unimaginative

fudge \'fəj\ *vb* **fudged; fudg·ing** : cheat or exaggerate ∼ *n* : creamy candy

fu·el \'fyüəl\ *n* : material burned to produce heat or power ∼ *vb* **-eled** *or* **-elled; -el·ing** *or* **-el·ling** : provide with or take in fuel

fu·gi·tive \'fyüjətiv\ *adj* **1** : running away or trying to escape **2** : not lasting — **fugitive** *n*

-ful \'fəl\ *adj suffix* **1** : full of **2** : having the qualities of **3** : -able ∼ *n suffix* : quantity that fills

ful·crum \'fu̇lkrəm, 'fəl-\ *n, pl* **-crums** *or* **-cra** \-krə\ : support on which a lever turns

ful·fill, ful·fil \fu̇l'fil\ *vb* **-filled; -fil·ing** **1** : perform **2** : satisfy — **ful·fill·ment** *n*

¹**full** \'fu̇l\ *adj* **1** : filled **2** : complete **3** : rounded **4** : having an abundance of something ∼ *adv* : entirely ∼ *n* : utmost degree — **full·ness** *n* — **ful·ly** *adv*

²**full** *vb* : shrink and thicken woolen cloth — **full·er** *n*

full-fledged \'fu̇l'flejd\ *adj* : fully developed

ful·some \'fu̇lsəm\ *adj* : copious verging on excessive

fum·ble \'fəmbəl\ *vb* **-bled; -bling** : fail to hold something properly — **fumble** *n*

fume \'fyüm\ *n* : irritating gas ∼ *vb* **fumed; fum·ing** **1** : give off fumes **2** : show annoyance

fu·mi·gate \'fyümə,gāt\ *vb* **-gat·ed; -gat·ing** : treat with pest-killing fumes — **fu·mi·gant** \'fyümigənt\ *n* — **fu·mi·ga·tion** \,fyümə'gāshən\ *n*

fun \'fən\ *n* **1** : something providing amusement or enjoyment **2** : enjoyment ∼ *adj* : full of fun

func·tion \'fəŋkshən\ *n* **1** : special

purpose **2** : formal ceremony or social affair ∼ *vb* : have or carry on a function — **func·tion·al** \-shənəl\ *adj* — **func·tion·al·ly** *adv*

func·tion·ary \-shə,nerē\ *n, pl* **-ar·ies** : official

fund \'fənd\ *n* **1** : store **2** : sum of money intended for a special purpose **3** *pl* : available money ∼ *vb* : provide funds for

fun·da·men·tal \,fəndə'ment³l\ *adj* **1** : basic **2** : of central importance or necessity — **fundamental** *n* — **fun·da·men·tal·ly** *adv*

fu·ner·al \'fyünərəl\ *n* : ceremony for a dead person — **funeral** *adj* — **fu·ne·re·al** \fyü'nirēəl\ *adj*

fun·gi·cide \'fənjə,sīd, 'fəŋgə-\ *n* : agent that kills fungi — **fun·gi·cid·al** \,fənjə'sīd³l, ,fəŋgə-\ *adj*

fun·gus \'fəŋgəs\ *n, pl* **fun·gi** \'fən,jī, 'fəŋ,gī\ : lower plant that lacks chlorophyll — **fun·gal** \'fəŋgəl\ *adj* — **fun·gous** \-gəs\ *adj*

funk \'fəŋk\ *n* : state of depression

funky \'fəŋkē\ *adj* **funk·i·er; -est** : unconventional and unsophisticated

fun·nel \'fən³l\ *n* **1** : cone-shaped utensil with a tube for directing the flow of a liquid **2** : ship's smokestack ∼ *vb* **-neled; -nel·ing** : move to a central point or into a central channel

fun·nies \'fənēz\ *n pl* : section of comic strips

fun·ny \'fənē\ *adj* **-ni·er; -est** **1** : amusing **2** : strange

fur \'fər\ *n* **1** : hairy coat of a mammal **2** : article of clothing made with fur — **fur** *adj* — **furred** \'fərd\ *adj* — **fur·ry** \-ē\ *adj*

fur·bish \'fərbish\ *vb* : make lustrous or new looking

fu·ri·ous \'fyürēəs\ *adj* : fierce or angry — **fu·ri·ous·ly** *adv*

fur·long \'fər,lȯŋ\ *n* : a unit of distance equal to 220 yards

fur·lough \'fərlō\ *n* : authorized absence from duty — **furlough** *vb*

fur·nace \'fərnəs\ *n* : enclosed structure in which heat is produced

fur·nish \'fərnish\ *vb* **1** : provide with what is needed **2** : make available for use

fur·nish·ings \-iŋs\ *n pl* **1** : articles or accessories of dress **2** : furniture

fur·ni·ture \'fərnichər\ *n* : movable articles for a room

fu·ror \'fyu̇r,ȯr\ n 1 : anger 2 : sensational craze

fur·ri·er \'fərēər\ n : dealer in furs

fur·row \'fərō\ n 1 : trench made by a plow 2 : wrinkle or groove — **furrow** vb

fur·ther \'fərthər\ adv 1 : at or to a more advanced point 2 : more ~ adj : additional ~ vb : promote — **fur·ther·ance** \-ərəns\ n

fur·ther·more \'fərthər,mōr\ adv : in addition

fur·ther·most \-,mōst\ adj : most distant

fur·thest \'fərthəst\ adv or adj : farthest

fur·tive \'fərtiv\ adj : slyly or secretly done — **fur·tive·ly** adv — **fur·tive·ness** n

fu·ry \'fyu̇rē\ n, pl **-ries** 1 : intense rage 2 : violence

¹fuse \'fyüz\ n 1 : cord lighted to transmit fire to an explosive 2 usu **fuze** : device for exploding a charge ~ or **fuse** vb **fused** or **fuzed**; **fus·ing** or **fuz·ing** : equip with a fuse

²fuse vb **fused**; **fus·ing** 1 : melt and run together 2 : unite ~ n : electrical safety device — **fus·ible** adj

fu·se·lage \'fyüsə,läzh, -zə-\ n : main body of an aircraft

fu·sil·lade \'fyüsə,läd, -,lād, ,fyüsə'-, -zə-\ n : volley of fire

fu·sion \'fyüzhən\ n 1 : process of merging by melting 2 : union of atomic nuclei

fuss \'fəs\ n 1 : needless bustle or excitement 2 : show of attention 3 : objection or protest ~ vb : make a fuss

fuss·bud·get \-,bəjət\ n : one who fusses or is fussy about trifles

fussy \'fəsē\ adj **fuss·i·er**; **-est** 1 : irritable 2 : paying very close attention to details — **fuss·i·ly** adv — **fuss·i·ness** n

fu·tile \'fyüt³l, 'fyü,tīl\ adj : useless or vain — **fu·til·i·ty** \fyü'tilətē\ n

fu·ton \'fü,tän\ n : a cotton-filled mattress

fu·ture \'fyüchər\ adj : coming after the present ~ n 1 : time yet to come 2 : what will happen — **fu·tur·is·tic** \,fyüchə'ristik\ adj

fuze var of FUSE

fuzz \'fəz\ n : fine particles or fluff

fuzzy \-ē\ adj **fuzz·i·er**; **-est** 1 : covered with or like fuzz 2 : indistinct — **fuzz·i·ness** n

-fy \,fī\ vb suffix : make — **-fi·er** \,fīər\ n suffix

G

g \'jē\ n, pl **g's** or **gs** \'jēz\ 1 : 7th letter of the alphabet 2 : unit of gravitational force

gab \'gab\ vb **-bb-** : chatter — **gab** n — **gab·by** \'gabē\ adj

gab·ar·dine \'gabər,dēn\ n : durable twilled fabric

ga·ble \'gābəl\ n : triangular part of the end of a building — **ga·bled** \-bəld\ adj

gad \'gad\ vb **-dd-** : roam about

gad·fly n : persistently critical person

gad·get \'gajət\ n : device — **gad·get·ry** \'gajətrē\ n

gaff \'gaf\ n : metal hook for lifting fish — **gaff** vb

gaffe \'gaf\ n : social blunder

gag \'gag\ vb **-gg-** 1 : prevent from speaking or crying out by stopping up the mouth 2 : retch or cause to retch

~ n 1 : something that stops up the mouth 2 : laugh-provoking remark or act

gage var of GAUGE

gag·gle \'gagəl\ n : flock of geese

gai·ety \'gāətē\ n, pl **-eties** : high spirits

gai·ly \'gālē\ adv : in a gay manner

gain \'gān\ n 1 : profit 2 : obtaining of profit or possessions 3 : increase ~ vb 1 : get possession of 2 : win 3 : arrive at 4 : increase or increase in 5 : profit — **gain·er** n — **gain·ful** adj — **gain·ful·ly** adv

gain·say \gān'sā\ vb **-said** \-'sād, -'sed\; **-say·ing**; **-says** \-'sāz, -'sez\ : deny or dispute — **gain·say·er** n

gait \'gāt\ n : manner of walking or running — **gait·ed** adj

gal \'gal\ n : girl

ga·la \'gālə, 'galə, 'gälə\ n : festive celebration — **gala** adj

gal·axy \'galəksē\ n, pl **-ax·ies** : very large group of stars — **ga·lac·tic** \gə'laktik\ adj

gale \'gāl\ n 1 : strong wind 2 : outburst

¹gall \'gȯl\ n 1 : bile 2 : insolence

²gall n 1 : skin sore caused by chafing 2 : swelling of plant tissue caused by parasites ~ vb 1 : chafe 2 : irritate or vex

gal·lant \gə'lant, -'länt; 'galənt\ n : man very attentive to women ~ \'galənt; gə'lant, -'länt\ adj 1 : splendid 2 : brave 3 : polite and attentive to women — **gal·lant·ly** adv — **gal·lant·ry** \'galəntrē\ n

gall·blad·der n : pouch attached to the liver in which bile is stored

gal·le·on \'galyən\ n : large sailing ship formerly used esp. by the Spanish

gal·lery \'galərē\ n, pl **-ler·ies** 1 : outdoor balcony 2 : long narrow passage or hall 3 : room or building for exhibiting art 4 : spectators — **gal·ler·ied** \-rēd\ adj

gal·ley \'galē\ n, pl **-leys** 1 : old ship propelled esp. by oars 2 : kitchen of a ship or airplane

gal·li·um \'galēəm\ n : bluish white metallic chemical element

gal·li·vant \'galə,vant\ vb : travel or roam about for pleasure

gal·lon \'galən\ n : unit of liquid measure equal to 4 quarts

gal·lop \'galəp\ n : fast 3-beat gait of a horse — **gallop** vb — **gal·lop·er** n

gal·lows \'galōz\ n, pl **-lows** or **-lows·es** : upright frame for hanging criminals

gall·stone n : abnormal concretion in the gallbladder or bile passages

ga·lore \gə'lōr\ adj : in abundance

ga·losh \gə'läsh\ n : overshoe — usu. pl.

gal·va·nize \'galvə,nīz\ vb **-nized; -niz·ing** 1 : shock into action 2 : coat (iron or steel) with zinc — **gal·va·ni·za·tion** \,galvənə'zāshən\ n — **gal·va·niz·er** n

gam·bit \'gambit\ n 1 : opening tactic in chess 2 : stratagem

gam·ble \'gambəl\ vb **-bled; -bling** 1 : play a game for stakes 2 : bet 3 : take a chance ~ n : risky undertaking — **gam·bler** \-blər\ n

gam·bol \'gambəl\ vb **-boled** or **-bolled; -bol·ing** or **-bol·ling** : skip about in play — **gambol** n

game \'gām\ n 1 : playing activity 2 : competition according to rules 3 : animals hunted for sport or food ~ vb **gamed; gam·ing** : gamble ~ adj 1 : plucky 2 : lame — **game·ly** adv — **game·ness** n

game·cock n : fighting cock

game·keep·er n : person in charge of game animals or birds

gam·ete \gə'mēt, 'gam,ēt\ n : mature germ cell — **ga·met·ic** \gə'metik\ adj

ga·mine \ga'mēn\ n : charming tomboy

gam·ut \'gamət\ n : entire range or series

gamy or **gam·ey** \'gāmē\ adj **gam·i·er; -est** : having the flavor of game esp. when slightly tainted — **gam·i·ness** n

¹gan·der \'gandər\ n : male goose

²gander n : glance

gang \'gaŋ\ n 1 : group of persons working together 2 : group of criminals ~ vb : attack in a gang — with up

gan·gling \'gaŋgliŋ\ adj : lanky

gan·gli·on \'gaŋglēən\ n, pl **-glia** \-glēə\ : mass of nerve cells

gang·plank n : platform used in boarding or leaving a ship

gan·grene \'gaŋ,grēn, gaŋ'-, 'gaŋ-, gaŋ'-\ n : local death of body tissue — **gangrene** vb — **gan·gre·nous** \'gaŋgrənəs\ adj

gang·ster \'gaŋstər\ n : member of criminal gang

gang·way \-,wā\ n : passage in or out

gan·net \'ganət\ n : large fish-eating marine bird

gan·try \'gantrē\ n, pl **-tries** : frame structure supported over or around something

gap \'gap\ n 1 : break in a barrier 2 : mountain pass 3 : empty space

gape \'gāp\ vb **gaped; gap·ing** 1 : open widely 2 : stare with mouth open — **gape** n

ga·rage \gə'räzh, -'räj\ n : shelter or repair shop for automobiles ~ vb **-raged; -rag·ing** : put or keep in a garage

garb \'gärb\ n : clothing ~ vb : dress

gar·bage \'gärbij\ n 1 : food waste 2 : trash — **gar·bage·man** n

gar·ble \'gärbəl\ *vb* **-bled; -bling** : distort the meaning of

gar·den \'gärd³n\ *n* **1** : plot for growing fruits, flowers, or vegetables **2** : public recreation area ~ *vb* : work in a garden — **gar·den·er** \'gärd³nər\ *n*

gar·de·nia \gär'dēnyə\ *n* : tree or shrub with fragrant white or yellow flowers or the flower

gar·gan·tuan \gär'ganchəwən\ *adj* : having tremendous size or volume

gar·gle \'gärgəl\ *vb* **-gled; -gling** : rinse the throat with liquid — **gargle** *n*

gar·goyle \'gär‚goil\ *n* : waterspout in the form of a grotesque human or animal

gar·ish \'garish\ *adj* : offensively bright or gaudy

gar·land \'gärlənd\ *n* : wreath ~ *vb* : form into or deck with a garland

gar·lic \'gärlik\ *n* : herb with pungent bulbs used in cooking — **gar·licky** \-likē\ *adj*

gar·ment \'gärmənt\ *n* : article of clothing

gar·ner \'gärnər\ *vb* : acquire by effort

gar·net \'gärnət\ *n* : deep red mineral

gar·nish \'gärnish\ *vb* : add decoration to (as food) — **garnish** *n*

gar·nish·ee \‚gärni'shē\ *vb* **-eed; -ee·ing** : take (as a debtor's wages) by legal authority

gar·nish·ment \'gärnishmənt\ *n* : attachment of property to satisfy a creditor

gar·ret \'garət\ *n* : attic

gar·ri·son \'garəsən\ *n* : military post or the troops stationed there — **garrison** *vb*

gar·ru·lous \'garələs\ *adj* : talkative — **gar·ru·li·ty** \gə'rülətē\ *n* — **gar·ru·lous·ly** *adv* — **gar·ru·lous·ness** *n*

gar·ter \'gärtər\ *n* : band to hold up a stocking or sock

gas \'gas\ *n, pl* **gas·es** **1** : fluid (as hydrogen or air) that tends to expand indefinitely **2** : gasoline ~ *vb* **gassed; gas·sing 1** : treat with gas **2** : fill with gasoline — **gas·eous** \'gasēəs, 'gashəs\ *adj*

gash \'gash\ *n* : deep long cut — **gash** *vb*

gas·ket \'gaskət\ *n* : material or a part used to seal a joint

gas·light *n* : light of burning illuminating gas

gas·o·line \'gasə‚lēn, ‚gasə'-\ *n* : flammable liquid from petroleum

gasp \'gasp\ *vb* **1** : catch the breath audibly **2** : breathe laboriously — **gasp** *n*

gas·tric \'gastrik\ *adj* : relating to or located near the stomach

gas·tron·o·my \ga'stränəmē\ *n* : art of good eating — **gas·tro·nom·ic** \‚gastrə'nämik\ *adj*

gate \'gāt\ *n* : an opening for passage in a wall or fence — **gate·keep·er** *n* — **gate·post** *n*

gate·way *n* : way in or out

gath·er \'gathər\ *vb* **1** : bring or come together **2** : harvest **3** : pick up little by little **4** : deduce — **gath·er·er** *n* — **gath·er·ing** *n*

gauche \'gōsh\ *adj* : crude or tactless

gaudy \'gόdē\ *adj* **gaud·i·er; -est** : tastelessly showy — **gaud·i·ly** \'gόd³lē\ *adv* — **gaud·i·ness** *n*

gauge \'gāj\ *n* : instrument for measuring ~ *vb* **gauged; gaug·ing** : measure

gaunt \'gónt\ *adj* : thin or emaciated — **gaunt·ness** *n*

¹**gaunt·let** \-lət\ *n* **1** : protective glove **2** : challenge to combat

²**gauntlet** *n* : ordeal

gauze \'gόz\ *n* : thin often transparent fabric — **gauzy** *adj*

gave *past of* GIVE

gav·el \'gavəl\ *n* : mallet of a presiding officer, auctioneer, or judge

gawk \'gόk\ *vb* : stare stupidly

gawky \-ē\ *adj* **gawk·i·er; -est** : clumsy

gay \'gā\ *adj* **1** : merry **2** : bright and lively **3** : homosexual — **gay** *n*

gaze \'gāz\ *vb* **gazed; gaz·ing** : fix the eyes in a steady intent look — **gaze** *n* — **gaz·er** *n*

ga·zelle \gə'zel\ *n* : small swift antelope

ga·zette \-'zet\ *n* : newspaper

gaz·et·teer \‚gazə'tir\ *n* : geographical dictionary

gear \'gir\ *n* **1** : clothing **2** : equipment **3** : toothed wheel — **gear** *vb*

gear·shift *n* : mechanism by which automobile gears are shifted

geek \'gēk\ *n* : socially inept person

geese *pl of* GOOSE

gei·sha \'gāshə, 'gē-\ *n, pl* **-sha** *or* **-shas** : Japanese girl or woman trained to entertain men

gel·a·tin \'jelət³n\ *n* : sticky substance

obtained from animal tissues by boiling — **ge·lat·i·nous** \jə'lat'nəs\ *adj*

geld \'geld\ *vb* : castrate

geld·ing \-iŋ\ *n* : castrated horse

gem \'jem\ *n* : cut and polished valuable stone — **gem·stone** *n*

gen·der \'jendər\ *n* 1 : sex 2 : division of a class of words (as nouns) that determines agreement of other words

gene \'jēn\ *n* : segment of DNA that controls inheritance of a trait

ge·ne·al·o·gy \jēnē'äləjē, jen-, -'al-\ *n, pl* **-gies** : study of family pedigrees — **ge·ne·a·log·i·cal** \-ēə'läjikəl\ *adj* — **ge·ne·a·log·i·cal·ly** *adv* — **ge·ne·al·o·gist** \-ē'äləjist, -'al-\ *n*

genera *pl of* GENUS

gen·er·al \'jenrəl, 'jenə-\ *adj* 1 : relating to the whole 2 : applicable to all of a group 3 : common or widespread ~ *n* 1 : something that involves or is applicable to the whole 2 : commissioned officer in the army, air force, or marine corps ranking above a lieutenant general — **gen·er·al·ly** *adv* — **in general** : for the most part

gen·er·al·i·ty \jenə'ralətē\ *n, pl* **-ties** : general statement

gen·er·al·ize \'jenrə,līz, 'jenə-\ *vb* **-ized; -iz·ing** : reach a general conclusion esp. on the basis of particular instances — **gen·er·al·iza·tion** \jenrələ'zāshən, jenə-\ *n*

general of the air force : commissioned officer of the highest rank in the air force

general of the army : commissioned officer of the highest rank in the army

gen·er·ate \'jenə,rāt\ *vb* **-at·ed; -at·ing** : create or produce

gen·er·a·tion \jenə'rāshən\ *n* 1 : living beings constituting a single step in a line of descent 2 : production — **gen·er·a·tive** \'jenə,rātiv, -rət-\ *adj*

gen·er·a·tor \'jenə,rātər\ *n* 1 : one that generates 2 : machine that turns mechanical into electrical energy

ge·ner·ic \jə'nerik\ *adj* 1 : general 2 : not protected by a trademark 3 : relating to a genus — **generic** *n*

gen·er·ous \'jenərəs\ *adj* : freely giving or sharing — **gen·er·os·i·ty** \jenə'räsətē\ *n* — **gen·er·ous·ly** *adv* — **gen·er·ous·ness** *n*

ge·net·ics \jə'netiks\ *n* : biology dealing with heredity and variation — **ge-**

net·ic \-ik\ *adj* — **ge·net·i·cal·ly** *adv* — **ge·net·i·cist** \-'netəsist\ *n*

ge·nial \'jēnyəl\ *adj* : cheerful — **ge·nial·i·ty** \jēnē'alətē\ *n* — **ge·nial·ly** *adv*

ge·nie \'jēnē\ *n* : supernatural spirit that often takes human form

gen·i·tal \'jenət°l\ *adj* : concerned with reproduction — **gen·i·tal·ly** \-təlē\ *adv*

gen·i·ta·lia \jenə'tālyə\ *n pl* : external genital organs

gen·i·tals \'jenət°lz\ *n pl* : genitalia

ge·nius \'jēnyəs\ *n* 1 : single strongly marked capacity 2 : extraordinary intellectual power or a person having such power

geno·cide \'jenə,sīd\ *n* : systematic destruction of a racial or cultural group

genre \'zhänrə, 'zhä"rə\ *n* : category esp. of literary composition

gen·teel \jen'tēl\ *adj* : polite or refined

gen·tile \'jen,tīl\ *n* : person who is not Jewish — **gentile** *adj*

gen·til·i·ty \jen'tilətē\ *n, pl* **-ties** 1 : good birth and family 2 : good manners

gen·tle \'jent°l\ *adj* **-tler; -tlest** 1 : of a family of high social station 2 : not harsh, stern, or violent 3 : soft or delicate ~ *vb* **-tled; -tling** : make gentle — **gen·tle·ness** *n* — **gen·tly** *adv*

gen·tle·man \-mən\ *n* : man of good family or manners — **gen·tle·man·ly** *adv*

gen·tle·wom·an \-,wùmən\ *n* : woman of good family or breeding

gen·try \'jentrē\ *n, pl* **-tries** : people of good birth or breeding

gen·u·flect \'jenyə,flekt\ *vb* : bend the knee in worship — **gen·u·flec·tion** \jenyə'flekshən\ *n*

gen·u·ine \'jenyəwən\ *adj* : being the same in fact as in appearance — **gen·u·ine·ly** *adv* — **gen·u·ine·ness** *n*

ge·nus \'jēnəs\ *n, pl* **gen·era** \'jenərə\ : category of biological classification

ge·ode \'jē,ōd\ *n* : stone having a mineral-lined cavity

geo·des·ic \jēə'desik, -'dēs-\ *adj* : made of a framework of linked polygons

ge·og·ra·phy \jē'ägrəfē\ *n* 1 : study of the earth and its climate, products, and inhabitants 2 : natural features of a region — **ge·og·ra·pher** \-fər\ *n* — **geo·graph·ic** \jēə-**

'grafik\, **geo·graph·i·cal** \-ikəl\ adj — **geo·graph·i·cal·ly** adv

ge·ol·o·gy \jē'äləjē\ n : study of the history of the earth and its life esp. as recorded in rocks — **geo·log·ic** \jēə'läjik\, **geo·log·i·cal** \-ikəl\ — **geo·log·i·cal·ly** adv — **ge·ol·o·gist** \jē'äləjist\ n

ge·om·e·try \jē'ämətrē\ n, pl -tries : mathematics of the relations, properties, and measurements of solids, surfaces, lines, and angles — **geo·met·ric** \jēə'metrik\, **geo·met·ri·cal** \-rikəl\ adj

geo·ther·mal \jēo'thərməl\ adj : relating to or derived from the heat of the earth's interior

ge·ra·ni·um \jə'rānēəm\ n : garden plant with clusters of white, pink, or scarlet flowers

ger·bil \'jərbəl\ n : burrowing desert rodent

ge·ri·at·ric \jerē'atrik\ adj 1 : relating to aging or the aged 2 : old

ge·ri·at·rics \-triks\ n : medicine dealing with the aged and aging

germ \'jərm\ n 1 : microorganism 2 : source or rudiment

ger·mane \jər'mān\ adj : relevant

ger·ma·ni·um \-'mānēəm\ n : grayish white hard chemical element

ger·mi·cide \'jərmə,sīd\ n : agent that destroys germs — **ger·mi·cid·al** \,jərmə'sīd°l\ adj

ger·mi·nate \'jərmə,nāt\ vb -nat·ed; -nat·ing : begin to develop — **ger·mi·na·tion** \,jərmə'nāshən\ n

ger·ry·man·der \jerē'mandər, 'jerē,-, ,gerē'-, 'gerē,-\ vb : divide into election districts so as to give one political party an advantage — **gerry·mander** \n

ger·und \'jerənd\ n : word having the characteristics of both verb and noun

ge·sta·po \gə'stäpō\ n, pl -pos : secret police

ges·ta·tion \je'stāshən\ n : pregnancy or incubation — **ges·tate** \jes,tāt\ vb

ges·ture \'jeschər\ n 1 : movement of the body or limbs that expresses something 2 : something said or done for its effect on the attitudes of others — **ges·tur·al** \-chərəl\ adj — **gesture** vb

ge·sund·heit \gə'zu̇nt,hīt\ interj — used to wish good health to one who has just sneezed

get \'get\ vb **got** \'gät\; **got** or **got·ten** \'gät°n\; **get·ting** 1 : gain or be in possession of 2 : succeed in coming or going 3 : cause to come or go or to be in a certain condition or position 4 : become 5 : be subjected to 6 : understand 7 : be obliged — **get along** vb 1 : get by 2 : be on friendly terms — **get by** vb : meet one's needs

get·away \'getə,wā\ n 1 : escape 2 : a starting or getting under way

gey·ser \'gīzər\ n : spring that intermittently shoots out hot water and steam

ghast·ly \'gastlē\ adj -li·er; -est : horrible or shocking

gher·kin \'gərkən\ n : small pickle

ghet·to \'getō\ n, pl -tos or -toes : part of a city in which members of a minority group live

ghost \'gōst\ n : disembodied soul — **ghost·ly** adv

ghost·write vb -wrote; -writ·ten : write for and in the name of another — **ghost·writ·er** n

ghoul \'gül\ n : legendary evil being that feeds on corpses — **ghoul·ish** adj

GI \jē'ī\ n, pl **GI's** or **GIs** : member of the U.S. armed forces

gi·ant \'jīənt\ n 1 : huge legendary being 2 : something very large or very powerful — **giant** adj

gib·ber \'jibər\ vb -bered; -ber·ing : speak rapidly and foolishly

gib·ber·ish \'jibərish\ n : unintelligible speech or language

gib·bon \'gibən\ n : manlike ape

gibe \'jīb\ vb gibed; gib·ing : jeer at — **gibe** n

gib·lets \'jibləts\ n pl : edible fowl viscera

gid·dy \'gidē\ adj -di·er; -est 1 : silly 2 : dizzy — **gid·di·ness** n

gift \'gift\ n 1 : something given 2 : talent — **gift·ed** adj

gi·gan·tic \jī'gantik\ adj : very big

gig·gle \'gigəl\ vb -gled; -gling : laugh in a silly manner — **giggle** n — **gig·gly** \-əlē\ adj

gig·o·lo \'jigə,lō\ n, pl -los : man living on the earnings of a woman

Gi·la monster \'hēlə-\ n : large venomous lizard

gild \'gild\ vb **gild·ed** \'gildəd\ or **gilt** \'gilt\; **gild·ing** : cover with or as if with gold

gill \'gil\ n : organ of a fish for obtaining oxygen from water

gilt \'gilt\ *adj* : gold-colored ~ *n* : gold or goldlike substance on the surface of an object

gim·bal \'gimbəl, 'jim-\ *n* : device that allows something to incline freely

gim·let \'gimlət\ *n* : small tool for boring holes

gim·mick \'gimik\ *n* : new and ingenious scheme, feature, or device — **gim·mick·ry** *n* — **gim·micky** \-ikē\ *adj*

gimpy \'gimpē\ *adj* : lame

¹gin \'jin\ *n* : machine to separate seeds from cotton — **gin** *vb*

²gin *n* : clear liquor flavored with juniper berries

gin·ger \'jinjər\ *n* : pungent aromatic spice from a tropical plant — **gin·ger·bread** *n*

gin·ger·ly *adv* : very cautiously

ging·ham \'giŋəm\ *n* : cotton clothing fabric

gin·gi·vi·tis \,jinjə'vītəs\ *n* : inflammation of the gums

gink·go \'giŋkō\ *n, pl* **-goes** *or* **-gos** : tree of eastern China

gin·seng \'jin,siŋ, -,seŋ, -saŋ\ *n* : aromatic root of a Chinese herb

gi·raffe \jə'raf\ *n* : African mammal with a very long neck

gird \'gərd\ *vb* **gird·ed** \'gərdəd\ *or* **girt** \'gərt\; **gird·ing 1** : encircle or fasten with or as if with a belt **2** : prepare

gird·er \'gərdər\ *n* : horizontal supporting beam

gir·dle \'gərd²l\ *n* : woman's supporting undergarment ~ *vb* : surround

girl \'gərl\ *n* **1** : female child **2** : young woman **3** : sweetheart — **girl·hood** \-,hůd\ *n* — **girl·ish** *adj*

girl·friend *n* : frequent or regular female companion of a boy or man

girth \'gərth\ *n* : measure around something

gist \'jist\ *n* : main point or part

give \'giv\ *vb* **gave** \'gāv\; **giv·en** \'givən\; **giv·ing 1** : put into the possession or keeping of another **2** : pay **3** : perform **4** : contribute or donate **5** : produce **6** : utter **7** : yield to force, strain, or pressure ~ *n* : capacity or tendency to yield to force or strain — **give in** *vb* : surrender — **give out** *vb* : become used up or exhausted — **give up** *vb* **1** : let out of one's control **2** : cease from trying, doing, or hoping

give·away *n* **1** : unintentional betrayal **2** : something given free

giv·en \'givən\ *adj* **1** : prone or disposed **2** : having been specified

giz·zard \'gizərd\ *n* : muscular usu. horny-lined enlargement following the crop of a bird

gla·cial \'glāshəl\ *adj* **1** : relating to glaciers **2** : very slow — **gla·cial·ly** *adv*

gla·cier \'glāshər\ *n* : large body of ice moving slowly

glad \'glad\ *adj* **-dd- 1** : experiencing or causing pleasure, joy, or delight **2** : very willing — **glad·den** \-²n\ *vb* — **glad·ly** *adv* — **glad·ness** *n*

glade \'glād\ *n* : grassy open space in a forest

glad·i·a·tor \'gladē,ātər\ *n* : one who fought to the death for the entertainment of ancient Romans — **glad·i·a·to·ri·al** \,gladē'tōrēəl\ *adj*

glad·i·o·lus \,gladē'ōləs\ *n, pl* **-li** \-lē, -,lī\ : plant related to the irises

glam·our, glam·or \'glamər\ *n* : romantic or exciting attractiveness — **glam·or·ize** \-ə,rīz\ *vb* — **glam·or·ous** \-ərəs\ *adj*

glance \'glans\ *vb* **glanced; glanc·ing 1** : strike and fly off to one side **2** : give a quick look ~ *n* : quick look

gland \'gland\ *n* : group of cells that secretes a substance — **glan·du·lar** \'glanjələr\ *adj*

glans \'glanz\ *n, pl* **glan·des** \'glan-,dēz\ : conical vascular body forming the end of the penis or clitoris

glare \'glar\ *vb* **glared; glar·ing 1** : shine with a harsh dazzling light **2** : stare angrily ~ *n* **1** : harsh dazzling light **2** : angry stare

glar·ing \'glariŋ\ *adj* : painfully obvious — **glar·ing·ly** *adv*

glass \'glas\ *n* **1** : hard usu. transparent material made by melting sand and other materials **2** : something made of glass **3** *pl* : lenses used to correct defects of vision — **glass** *adj* — **glass·ful** \-,fůl\ *n* — **glass·ware** \-,war\ *n* — **glassy** *adj*

glass·blow·ing *n* : art of shaping a mass of molten glass by blowing air into it — **glass·blow·er** *n*

glau·co·ma \glaů'kōmə, glô-\ *n* : state of increased pressure within the eyeball

glaze \'glāz\ *vb* **glazed; glaz·ing 1**

: furnish with glass **2** : apply glaze to ~ n : glassy surface or coating

gla·zier \'glāzhər\ n : one who sets glass in window frames

gleam \'glēm\ n **1** : transient or partly obscured light **2** : faint trace ~ vb : send out gleams

glean \'glēn\ vb : collect little by little — **glean·able** adj — **glean·er** n

glee \'glē\ n : joy — **glee·ful** adj

glen \'glen\ n : narrow hidden valley

glib \'glib\ adj **-bb-** : speaking or spoken with ease — **glib·ly** adv

glide \'glīd\ vb **glid·ed; glid·ing** : move or descend smoothly and effortlessly — **glide** n

glid·er \'glīdər\ n **1** : winged aircraft having no engine **2** : swinging porch seat

glim·mer \'glimər\ vb : shine faintly or unsteadily ~ n **1** : faint light **2** : small amount

glimpse \'glimps\ vb **glimpsed; glimps·ing** : take a brief look at — **glimpse** n

glint \'glint\ vb : gleam or sparkle — **glint** n

glis·ten \'glis³n\ vb : shine or sparkle by reflection — **glisten** n

glit·ter \'glitər\ vb : shine with brilliant or metallic luster ~ n : small glittering ornaments — **glit·tery** adj

glitz \'glits\ n : extravagant showiness — **glitzy** \'glitsē\ adj

gloat \'glōt\ vb : think of something with triumphant delight

glob \'gläb\ n : large rounded lump

glob·al \'glōbəl\ adj : worldwide — **glob·al·ly** adv

globe \'glōb\ n **1** : sphere **2** : the earth or a model of it

glob·u·lar \'gläbyələr\ adj **1** : round **2** : made up of globules

glob·ule \'gläbyül\ n : tiny ball

glock·en·spiel \'gläkən,shpēl\ n : portable musical instrument consisting of tuned metal bars

gloom \'glüm\ n **1** : darkness **2** : sadness — **gloom·i·ly** adv — **gloom·i·ness** n — **gloomy** adj

glop \'gläp\ n : messy mass or mixture

glo·ri·fy \'glōrə,fī\ vb **-fied; -fy·ing** **1** : make to seem glorious **2** : worship — **glo·ri·fi·ca·tion** \,glōrəfə-'kāshən\ n

glo·ry \'glōrē\ n, pl **-ries** **1** : praise or honor offered in worship **2** : cause for praise or renown **3** : magnificence

4 : heavenly bliss ~ vb **-ried; -ry·ing** : rejoice proudly — **glo·ri·ous** \'glōrēəs\ adj — **glo·ri·ous·ly** adv

¹gloss \'gläs, 'glös\ n : luster — **gloss·i·ly** \-ə-lē\ adv — **gloss·i·ness** \-ēnəs\ n — **glossy** \-ē\ adj

gloss over vb **1** : mask the true nature of **2** : deal with only superficially

²gloss n : brief explanation or translation — vb : translate or explain

glos·sa·ry \'gläsərē, 'glös-\ n, pl **-ries** : dictionary — **glos·sar·i·al** \glä-'sarēəl, glö-\ adj

glove \'gləv\ n : hand covering with sections for each finger

glow \'glō\ vb **1** : shine with or as if with intense heat **2** : show exuberance ~ n : brightness or warmth of color or feeling

glow·er \'glaúər\ vb : stare angrily — **glower** n

glow-worm n : insect or insect larva that emits light

glu·cose \'glü,kōs\ n : sugar found esp. in blood, plant sap, and fruits

glue \'glü\ n : substance used for sticking things together — **glue** vb — **glu·ey** \'glüē\ adj

glum \'gləm\ adj **-mm-** **1** : sullen **2** : dismal

glut \'glət\ vb **-tt-** : fill to excess — **glut** n

glu·ten \'glüt³n\ n : gluey protein substance in flour

glu·ti·nous \'glüt³nəs\ adj : sticky

glut·ton \'glət³n\ n : one who eats to excess — **glut·ton·ous** \'glət³nəs\ adj — **glut·tony** \'glət³nē\ n

gnarled \'närld\ adj **1** : knotty **2** : gloomy or sullen

gnash \'nash\ vb : grind (as teeth) together

gnat \'nat\ n : small biting fly

gnaw \'nö\ vb : bite or chew on

gnome \'nōm\ n : dwarf of folklore — **gnom·ish** adj

gnu \'nü, 'nyü\ n, pl **gnu** or **gnus** : large African antelope

go \'gō\ vb **went** \'went\; **gone** \'gön, 'gän\; **go·ing** \'gōiŋ\; **goes** \'gōz\ **1** : move, proceed, run, or pass **2** : leave **3** : extend or lead **4** : sell or amount — with for **5** : happen **6** — used in present participle to show intent or imminent action **7** : become **8** : fit or harmonize **9** : belong ~ n, pl **goes** **1** : act or manner of going **2** : vigor **3** : attempt — **go back on** : betray — **go by the board** : be discarded — **go for** : favor — **go off** : explode — **go one better** : outdo — **go over 1** : examine **2** : study — **go to town** : be very successful — **on the go** : constantly active

goad \'gōd\ n : something that urges — **goad** vb

goal \'gōl\ n **1** : mark to reach in a race **2** : purpose **3** : object in a game through which a ball is propelled

goal·ie \'gōlē\ n : player who defends the goal

goal·keep·er n : goalie

goat \'gōt\ n : horned ruminant mammal related to the sheep — **goat·skin** n

goa·tee \gō'tē\ n : small pointed beard

gob \'gäb\ n : lump

¹gob·ble \'gäbəl\ vb **-bled; -bling** : eat greedily

²gobble vb **-bled; -bling** : make the noise of a turkey (**gobbler**)

gob·ble·dy·gook \'gäbəldē,guk, -'gük\ n : nonsense

gob·let \'gäblət\ n : large stemmed drinking glass

gob·lin \'gäblən\ n : ugly mischievous sprite

god \'gäd, 'gód\ n **1** cap : supreme being **2** : being with supernatural powers — **god·like** adj — **god·ly** adj

god·child n : person one sponsors at baptism — **god·daugh·ter** n — **god·son** n

god·dess \'gädəs, 'gód-\ n : female god

god·less \-ləs\ adj : not believing in God — **god·less·ness** n

god·par·ent n : sponsor at baptism — **god·fa·ther** n — **god·moth·er** n

god·send \-,send\ n : something needed that comes unexpectedly

goes pres 3d sing of GO

go·get·ter \'gō,getər\ n : enterprising person — **go-get·ting** \-iŋ\ adj or n

gog·gle \'gägəl\ vb **-gled; -gling** : stare wide-eyed

gog·gles \-əlz\ n pl : protective glasses

go·ings–on \,gōiŋz'òn, -'än\ n pl : events

goi·ter \'gòitər\ n : abnormally enlarged thyroid gland

gold \'gōld\ n : malleable yellow metallic chemical element — **gold·smith** \-,smith\ n

gold·brick \-,brik\ n : person who shirks duty — **goldbrick** vb

gold·en \'gōldən\ adj **1** : made of, containing, or relating to gold **2** : having the color of gold **3** : precious or favorable

gold·en·rod \'gōldən,räd\ n : herb having tall stalks with tiny yellow flowers

gold·finch \'gōld,finch\ n : yellow American finch

gold·fish \-,fish\ n : small usu. orange or golden carp

golf \'gälf, 'gólf\ n : game played by hitting a small ball (**golf ball**) with clubs (**golf clubs**) into holes placed in a field (**golf course**) — **golf** vb — **golf·er** n

go·nad \'gō,nad\ n : sex gland

gon·do·la \'gändələ (usual for 1), gän'dō-\ n **1** : long narrow boat used on the canals of Venice **2** : car suspended from a cable

gon·do·lier \,gändə'lir\ n : person who propels a gondola

gone \'gòn\ adj **1** : past **2** : involved

gon·er \'gònər\ n : hopeless case

gong \'gäŋ, 'gòŋ\ n : metallic disk that makes a deep sound when struck

gon·or·rhea \,gänə'rēə\ n : bacterial inflammatory venereal disease of the genital tract

goo \'gü\ n : thick or sticky substance — **goo·ey** \-ē\ adj

good \'gúd\ adj **bet·ter** \'betər\; **best** \'best\ **1** : satisfactory **2** : salutary **3** : considerable **4** : desirable **5** : well-behaved, kind, or virtuous ~ n **1** : something good **2** : benefit **3** pl : personal property **4** pl : wares ~ adv : well — **good–heart·ed** \-'härtəd\ adj — **good–look·ing** adj — **good–na·tured** adj — **good·ness** n — **for good** : forever

good–bye, good–by \gúd'bī\ n : parting remark

good–for–noth·ing n : idle worthless person

Good Friday n : Friday before Easter observed as the anniversary of the crucifixion of Christ

good·ly adj **-li·er; -est** : considerable

good·will n **1** : good intention **2** : kindly feeling

goody \'gúdē\ n, pl **good·ies** : something that is good esp. to eat

goody–goody adj : affectedly or annoyingly sweet or self-righteous — **goody–goody** n

goof \'güf\ vb **1** : blunder **2** : waste time — usu. with off or around — **goof** n — **goof–off** n

goofy \'güfē\ *adj* **goof·i·er; -est** : crazy — **goof·i·ness** *n*

goose \'güs\ *n, pl* **geese** \'gēs\ : large bird with webbed feet

goose·ber·ry \'güs,berē, 'güz-\ *n* : berry of a shrub related to the currant

goose bumps *n pl* : roughening of the skin caused by fear, excitement, or cold

goose·flesh *n* : goose bumps

goose pimples *n pl* : goose bumps

go·pher \'gōfər\ *n* : burrowing rodent

¹gore \'gōr\ *n* : blood

²gore *vb* **gored; gor·ing** : pierce or wound with a horn or tusk

gorge \'gōrj\ *n* : narrow ravine

²gorge *vb* **gorged; gorg·ing** : eat greedily

gor·geous \'gōrjəs\ *adj* : supremely beautiful

go·ril·la \gə'rilə\ *n* : African manlike ape

gory \'gōrē\ *adj* **gor·i·er; -est** : bloody

gos·hawk \'gäs,hók\ *n* : long-tailed hawk with short rounded wings

gos·ling \'gäzliŋ, 'gòz-\ *n* : young goose

gos·pel \'gäspəl\ *n* **1** : teachings of Christ and the apostles **2** : something accepted as infallible truth — **gospel** *adj*

gos·sa·mer \'gäsəmər, gäz-\ *n* **1** : film of cobweb **2** : light filmy substance

gos·sip \'gäsəp\ *n* **1** : person who reveals personal information **2** : rumor or report of an intimate nature ~ *vb* : spread gossip — **gos·sipy** \-ē-\ *adj*

got *past of* GET

Goth·ic \'gäthik\ *adj* : relating to a medieval style of architecture

gotten *past part of* GET

gouge \'gaüj\ *n* **1** : rounded chisel **2** : cavity or groove scooped out ~ *vb* **gouged; goug·ing 1** : cut or scratch a groove in **2** : overcharge

gou·lash \'gü,läsh, -,lash\ *n* : beef stew with vegetables and paprika

gourd \'gōrd, 'gürd\ *n* **1** : any of a group of vines including the cucumber, squash, and melon **2** : inedible hard-shelled fruit of a gourd

gour·mand \'gür,mänd\ *n* : person who loves good food and drink

gour·met \'gür,mā, gür'mā\ *n* : connoisseur of food and drink

gout \'gaüt\ *n* : disease marked by painful inflammation and swelling of the joints — **gouty** *adj*

gov·ern \'gəvərn\ *vb* **1** : control and direct policy in **2** : guide or influence strongly **3** : restrain — **govern·ment** \-ərmənt\ *n* — **gov·ern·men·tal** \,gəvər'ment³l\ *adj*

gov·ern·ess \'gəvərnəs\ *n* : female teacher in a private home

gov·er·nor \'gəvənər, 'gəvər-\ *n* **1** : head of a political unit **2** : automatic speed-control device — **gov·er·nor·ship** *n*

gown \'gaün\ *n* **1** : loose flowing outer garment **2** : woman's formal evening dress — **gown** *vb*

grab \'grab\ *vb* **-bb-** : take by sudden grasp — **grab** *n*

grace \'grās\ *n* **1** : unmerited divine assistance **2** : short prayer before or after a meal **3** : respite **4** : ease of movement or bearing ~ *vb* **graced; grac·ing 1** : honor **2** : adorn — **graceful** \-fəl\ *adj* — **grace·ful·ly** *adv* — **grace·ful·ness** *n* — **grace·less** *adj*

gra·cious \'grāshəs\ *adj* : marked by kindness and courtesy or charm and taste — **gra·cious·ly** *adv* — **gra·cious·ness** *n*

grack·le \'grakəl\ *n* : American blackbird

gra·da·tion \grā'dāshən, grə-\ *n* : step, degree, or stage in a series

grade \'grād\ *n* **1** : stage in a series, order, or ranking **2** : division of school representing one year's work **3** : mark of accomplishment in school **4** : degree of slope ~ *vb* **grad·ed; grad·ing 1** : arrange in grades **2** : make level or evenly sloping **3** : give a grade to — **grad·er** *n*

grade school *n* : school including the first 4 or 8 grades

gra·di·ent \'grādēənt\ *n* : slope

grad·u·al \'grajəwəl\ *adj* : going by steps or degrees — **grad·u·al·ly** *adv*

grad·u·ate \'grajəwət\ *n* : holder of a diploma ~ *adj* : of or relating to studies beyond the bachelor's degree ~ \-ə,wāt\ *vb* **-at·ed; -at·ing 1** : grant or receive a diploma **2** : mark with degrees of measurement — **grad·u·a·tion** \,grajə'wāshən\ *n*

graf·fi·to \grə'fētō, grə-\ *n, pl* **-ti** \-ē\ : inscription on a wall

graft \'graft\ *vb* : join one thing to another so that they grow together ~ *n*

1 : grafted plant **2** : the getting of money dishonestly or the money so gained — **graft·er** n

grain \'grān\ n **1** : seeds or fruits of cereal grasses **2** : small hard particle **3** : arrangement of fibers in wood — **grained** \'grānd\ adj — **grainy** adj

gram \'gram\ n : metric unit of weight equal to 1/1000 kilogram

gram·mar \'gramər\ n : study of words and their functions and relations in the sentence — **gram·mar·i·an** \grə-'mareən\ n — **gram·mat·i·cal** \-'matikəl\ adj — **gram·mat·i·cal·ly** adv

grammar school n : grade school

gra·na·ry \'grānərē, 'gran-\ n, pl -ries : storehouse for grain

grand \'grand\ adj **1** : large or striking in size or scope **2** : fine and imposing **3** : very good — **grand·ly** adv — **grand·ness** n

grand·child \-,chīld\ n : child of one's son or daughter — **grand·daugh·ter** n — **grand·son** n

gran·deur \'granjər\ n : quality or state of being grand

gran·dil·o·quence \gran'diləkwəns\ n : pompous speaking — **gran·dil·o·quent** \-kwənt\ adj

gran·di·ose \'grandē,ōs, ,grandē'-\ adj **1** : impressive **2** : affectedly splendid — **gran·di·ose·ly** adv

grand·par·ent \'grand,parənt\ n : parent of one's father or mother — **grand·fa·ther** \-,fäthər, -,fåth-\ n — **grand·moth·er** \-,məthər\ n

grand·stand \-,stand\ n : usu. roofed stand for spectators

grange \'grānj\ n : farmers association

gran·ite \'granət\ n : hard igneous rock

grant \'grant\ vb **1** : consent to **2** : give **3** : admit as true ~ n **1** : act of granting **2** : something granted — **grant·ee** \grant'ē\ n — **grant·er** \'grantər\ n — **grant·or** \-,or, -,ór\ n

gran·u·late \'granyə,lāt\ vb -lat·ed; -lat·ing : form into grains or crystals — **gran·u·la·tion** \granyə'lāshən\ n

gran·ule \'granyūl\ n : small particle — **gran·u·lar** \-yələr\ adj — **gran·u·lar·i·ty** \granyə'larətē\ n

grape \'grāp\ n : smooth juicy edible berry of a woody vine (**grape·vine**)

grape·fruit \-,früt\ n : large edible yellow-skinned citrus fruit

graph \'graf\ n : diagram that shows

relationships between things — **graph** vb

graph·ic \'grafik\ adj **1** : vividly described **2** : relating to the arts (**graphic arts**) of representation and printing on flat surfaces ~ n **1** : picture used for illustration **2** pl : computer screen display — **graph·i·cal·ly** \-iklē\ adv

graph·ite \'graf,īt\ n : soft carbon used for lead pencils and lubricants

grap·nel \'grapnəl\ n : small anchor with several claws

grap·ple \'grapəl\ vb -pled; -pling **1** : seize or hold with or as if with a hooked implement **2** : wrestle

grasp \'grasp\ vb **1** : take or seize firmly **2** : understand ~ n **1** : one's hold or control **2** : one's reach **3** : comprehension

grass \'gras\ n : plant with jointed stem and narrow leaves — **grassy** adj

grass·hop·per \-,häpər\ n : leaping plant-eating insect

grass·land n : land covered with grasses

grate \'grāt\ n **1** : grating **2** : frame of iron bars to hold burning fuel

²grate vb grat·ed; -ing **1** : pulverize by rubbing against something rough **2** : irritate — **grat·er** n — **grat·ing·ly** adv

grate·ful \'grātfəl\ adj : thankful or appreciative — **grate·ful·ly** adv — **grate·ful·ness** n

grat·i·fy \'gratə,fī\ vb -fied; -fy·ing : give pleasure to — **grat·i·fi·ca·tion** \gratəfə'kāshən\ n

grat·ing \'grātiŋ\ n : framework with bars across it

gra·tis \'gratəs, 'grät-\ adv or adj : free

grat·i·tude \'gratə,tüd, -,tyüd\ n : state of being grateful

gra·tu·itous \grə'tüətəs, -'tyü-\ adj **1** : free **2** : uncalled-for

gra·tu·ity \-ətē\ n, pl -ities : tip

¹grave \'grāv\ n : place of burial — **grave·stone** n — **grave·yard** n

²grave adj grav·er; grav·est **1** : threatening great harm or danger **2** : solemn — **grave·ly** adv — **grave·ness** n

grav·el \'gravəl\ n : loose rounded fragments of rock — **grav·el·ly** adj

grav·i·tate \'gravə,tāt\ vb -tat·ed; -tat·ing : move toward something

grav·i·ta·tion \,gravə'tāshən\ n : natural force of attraction that tends to draw bodies together — **grav·i·ta·tion·al** \-shənəl\ adj

grav·i·ty \'gravətē\ n, pl **-ties** 1 : serious importance 2 : gravitation

gra·vy \'grāvē\ n, pl **-vies** : sauce made from thickened juices of cooked meat

gray \'grā\ adj 1 : of the color gray 2 : having gray hair ~ n : neutral color between black and white ~ vb : make or become gray — **gray·ish** \-ish\ adj — **gray·ness** n

¹**graze** \'grāz\ vb **grazed; graz·ing** : feed on herbage or pasture — **graz·er** n

²**graze** vb **grazed; graz·ing** : touch lightly in passing

grease \'grēs\ n : thick oily material or fat ~ \'grēs, 'grēz\ vb **greased; greas·ing** : smear or lubricate with grease — **greasy** \'grēsē, -zē\ adj

great \'grāt\ adj 1 : large in size or number 2 : larger than usual — **great·ly** adv — **great·ness** n

grebe \'grēb\ n : diving bird related to the loon

greed \'grēd\ n : selfish desire beyond reason — **greed·i·ly** \-ᵊlē\ adv — **greed·i·ness** \-ēnəs\ n — **greedy** \'grēdē\ adj

green \'grēn\ adj 1 : of the color green 2 : unripe 3 : inexperienced ~ vb : become green ~ n 1 : color between blue and yellow 2 pl : leafy parts of plants — **green·ish** adj — **green·ness** n

green·ery \'grēnərē\ n, pl **-er·ies** : green foliage or plants

green·horn n : inexperienced person

green·house n : glass structure for the growing of plants

greet \'grēt\ vb 1 : address with expressions of kind wishes 2 : react to — **greet·er** n

greet·ing n 1 : friendly address on meeting 2 pl : best wishes

gre·gar·i·ous \gri'garēəs\ adj : social or companionable — **gre·gar·i·ous·ly** adv — **gre·gar·i·ous·ness** n

grem·lin \'gremlən\ n : small mischievous gnome

gre·nade \grə'nād\ n : small missile filled with explosive or chemicals

grew past of GROW

grey var of GRAY

grey·hound \'grā,haúnd\ n : tall slender dog noted for speed

grid \'grid\ n 1 : grating 2 : evenly spaced horizontal and vertical lines (as on a map)

grid·dle \'gridᵊl\ n : flat metal surface for cooking

grid·iron \'grid,īərn\ n 1 : grate for broiling 2 : football field

grief \'grēf\ n 1 : emotional suffering caused by or as if by bereavement 2 : disaster

griev·ance \'grēvəns\ n : complaint

grieve \'grēv\ vb **grieved; griev·ing** : feel or cause to feel grief or sorrow

griev·ous \'grēvəs\ adj 1 : oppressive 2 : causing grief or sorrow — **griev·ous·ly** adv

grill \'gril\ vb 1 : cook on a grill 2 : question intensely ~ n 1 : griddle 2 : informal restaurant

grille, grill \'gril\ n : grating forming a barrier or screen — **grill·work** n

grim \'grim\ adj **-mm-** 1 : harsh and forbidding in appearance 2 : relentless — **grim·ly** adv — **grim·ness** n

gri·mace \'griməs, grim'ās\ n : facial expression of disgust — **grimace** vb

grime \'grīm\ n : embedded or accumulated dirt — **grimy** adj

grin \'grin\ vb **-nn-** : smile so as to show the teeth — **grin** n

grind \'grīnd\ vb **ground** \'graúnd\; **grind·ing** 1 : reduce to powder 2 : wear down or sharpen by friction 3 : operate or produce by turning a crank ~ n : monotonous labor or routine — **grind·er** n — **grind·stone** \'grīn,stōn\ n

grip \'grip\ vb **-pp-** : seize or hold firmly ~ n 1 : grasp 2 : control 3 : device for holding

gripe \'grīp\ vb **griped; grip·ing** 1 : cause pains in the bowels 2 : complain — **gripe** n

grippe \'grip\ n : influenza

gris·ly \'grizlē\ adj **-li·er; -est** : horrible or gruesome

grist \'grist\ n : grain to be ground or already ground — **grist·mill** n

gris·tle \'grisəl\ n : cartilage — **gris·tly** \-lē\ adj

grit \'grit\ n 1 : hard sharp granule 2 : material composed of granules 3 : unyielding courage ~ vb **-tt-** : press with a grating noise — **grit·ty** adj

grits \'grits\ n pl : coarsely ground hulled grain

griz·zled \'grizəld\ adj : streaked with gray

groan \'grōn\ vb 1 : moan 2 : creak under a strain — **groan** n

gro·cer \'grōsər\ n : food dealer — **gro·cery** \'grōsrē, 'grōsh-, -ərē\ n

grog \'gräg\ n : rum diluted with water

grog·gy \-ē\ *adj* **-gi·er; -est** : dazed and unsteady on the feet — **grog·gi·ly** *adv* — **grog·gi·ness** *n*

groin \'grȯin\ *n* : juncture of the lower abdomen and inner thigh

grom·met \'grämət, 'grəm-\ *n* : eyelet

groom \'grüm, 'grům\ *n* **1** : one who cares for horses **2** : bridegroom ∼ *vb* **1** : clean and care for (as a horse) **2** : make neat or attractive **3** : prepare

groove \'grüv\ *n* **1** : long narrow channel **2** : fixed routine — **groove** *vb*

grope \'grōp\ *vb* **groped; grop·ing** : search for by feeling

gros·beak \'grōs,bēk\ *n* : finch with large conical bill

¹gross \'grōs\ *adj* **1** : glaringly noticeable **2** : bulky **3** : consisting of an overall total exclusive of deductions **4** : vulgar ∼ *n* : the whole before any deductions ∼ *vb* : earn as a total — **gross·ly** *adv* — **gross·ness** *n*

²gross *n, pl* **gross** : 12 dozen

gro·tesque \grō'tesk\ *adj* **1** : absurdly distorted or repulsive **2** : ridiculous — **gro·tesque·ly** *adv*

grot·to \'grätō\ *n, pl* **-toes** : cave

grouch \'graůch\ *n* : complaining person — **grouch** *vb* — **grouchy** *adj*

¹ground \'graůnd\ *n* **1** : bottom of a body of water **2** *pl* : sediment **3** : basis for something **4** : surface of the earth **5** : conductor that makes electrical connection with the earth or a framework ∼ *vb* **1** : force or bring down to the ground **2** : give basic knowledge to **3** : connect with an electrical ground — **ground·less** *adj*

²ground *past of* GRIND

ground·hog *n* : woodchuck

ground·wa·ter *n* : underground water

ground·work *n* : foundation

group \'grüp\ *n* : number of associated individuals ∼ *vb* : gather or collect into groups

grou·per \'grüpər\ *n* : large fish of warm seas

grouse \'graůs\ *n, pl* **grouse** *or* **grouses** : ground-dwelling game bird

grout \'graůt\ *n* : mortar for filling cracks — **grout** *vb*

grove \'grōv\ *n* : small group of trees

grov·el \'grävəl, 'grəv-\ *vb* **-eled** *or* **-elled; -el·ing** *or* **-el·ling** : abase oneself

grow \'grō\ *vb* **grew** \'grü\; **grown** \'grōn\; **grow·ing 1** : come into existence and develop to maturity **2** : be

able to grow **3** : advance or increase **4** : become **5** : cultivate — **grow·er** *n*

growl \'graůl\ *vb* : utter a deep threatening sound — **growl** *n*

grown–up \'grōn,əp\ *n* : adult — **grown–up** *adj*

growth \'grōth\ *n* **1** : stage in growing **2** : process of growing **3** : result of something growing

grub \'grəb\ *vb* **-bb- 1** : root out by digging **2** : search about ∼ *n* **1** : thick wormlike larva **2** : food

grub·by \'grəbē\ *adj* **-bi·er; -est** : dirty — **grub·bi·ness** *n*

grub·stake *n* : supplies for a prospector

grudge \'grəj\ *vb* **grudged; grudg·ing** : be reluctant to give ∼ *n* : feeling of ill will

gru·el \'grüəl\ *n* : thin porridge

gru·el·ing, gru·el·ling \-əliŋ\ *adj* : requiring extreme effort

grue·some \'grüsəm\ *adj* : horribly repulsive

gruff \'grəf\ *adj* : rough in speech or manner — **gruff·ly** *adv*

grum·ble \'grəmbəl\ *vb* **-bled; -bling** : mutter in discontent — **grum·bler** \-blər\ *n*

grumpy \-pē\ *adj* **grump·i·er; -est** : cross — **grump·i·ly** *adv* — **grump·i·ness** *n*

grunge \'grənj\ *n* **1** : something shabby, tattered, or dirty **2** : rock music expressing alienation and discontent — **grun·gy** \'grənjē\ *adj*

grun·ion \'grənyən\ *n* : fish of the California coast

grunt \'grənt\ *n* : deep guttural sound — **grunt** *vb*

gua·no \'gwänō\ *n* : excrement of seabirds used as fertilizer

guar·an·tee \,garən'tē\ *n* **1** : assurance of the fulfillment of a condition **2** : something given or held as a security ∼ *vb* **-teed; -tee·ing 1** : promise to be responsible for **2** : state with certainty — **guar·an·tor** \,garən'tór\ *n*

guar·an·ty \'garəntē\ *n, pl* **-ties 1** : promise to answer for another's failure to pay a debt **2** : guarantee **3** : pledge ∼ *vb* **-tied; -ty·ing** : guarantee

guard \'gärd\ *n* **1** : defensive position **2** : act of protecting **3** : an individual or group that guards against danger **4** : protective or safety device ∼ *vb* **1** : protect or watch over **2** : take precautions — **guard·house** n — **guard-room** n

guard·ian \'gärdēən\ n : one who has responsibility for the care of the person or property of another — **guardian·ship** n

gua·va \'gwävə\ n : shrubby tropical tree or its mildly acid fruit

gu·ber·na·to·ri·al \ˌgübənə'tōrēəl, ˌgyü-\ adj : relating to a governor

guer·ril·la, gue·ril·la \gə'rilə\ n : soldier engaged in small-scale harassing tactics

guess \'ges\ vb 1 : form an opinion from little evidence 2 : state correctly solely by chance 3 : think or believe — **guess** n

guest \'gest\ n 1 : person to whom hospitality (as of a house) is extended 2 : patron of a commercial establishment (as a hotel) 3 : person not a regular cast member who appears on a program

guf·faw \gə'fö, 'gəf،ö\ n : loud burst of laughter — **guf·faw** \gə'fö\ vb

guide \'gīd\ n 1 : one that leads or gives direction to another 2 : device on a machine to direct motion ~ vb **guid·ed; guid·ing** 1 : show the way to 2 : direct — **guid·able** adj — **guid·ance** \'gīd°ns\ n — **guide·book** n

guide·line \-ˌlīn\ n : summary of procedures regarding policy or conduct

guild \'gild\ n : association

guile \'gīl\ n : craftiness — **guile·ful** adj — **guile·less** adj — **guile·lessness** n

guil·lo·tine \'gilə,tēn, ˌgēyə'tēn, 'gēyə،-\ n : machine for beheading persons — **guillotine** vb

guilt \'gilt\ n 1 : fact of having committed an offense 2 : feeling of responsibility for offenses — **guilt·i·ly** adv — **guilt·i·ness** n — **guilty** \'giltē\ adj

guin·ea \'ginē\ n 1 : old gold coin of United Kingdom 2 : 21 shillings

guinea pig n : small So. American rodent

guise \'gīz\ n : external appearance

gui·tar \gə'tär, gi-\ n : 6-stringed musical instrument played by plucking

gulch \'gəlch\ n : ravine

gulf \'gəlf\ n 1 : extension of an ocean or a sea into the land 2 : wide gap

¹**gull** \'gəl\ n : seabird with webbed feet

²**gull** vb : make a dupe of ~ n : dupe — **gull·ible** adj

gul·let \'gələt\ n : throat

gul·ly \'gəlē\ n, pl **-lies** : trench worn by running water

gulp \'gəlp\ vb : swallow hurriedly or greedily — **gulp** n

¹**gum** \'gəm\ n : tissue along the jaw at the base of the teeth

²**gum** n 1 : sticky plant substance 2 : gum usu. of sweetened chicle prepared for chewing — **gum·my** adj

gum·bo \'gəmbō\ n : thick soup

gum·drop n : gumlike candy

gump·tion \'gəmpshən\ n : initiative

gun \'gən\ n 1 : cannon 2 : portable firearm 3 : discharge of a gun 4 : something like a gun ~ vb **-nn-** : hunt with a gun — **gun·fight** n — **gun·fight·er** n — **gun·fire** n — **gun·man** \-mən\ n — **gun·pow·der** n — **gun·shot** n — **gun·smith** n

gun·boat n : small armed ship

gun·ner \'gənər\ n : person who uses a gun

gun·nery sergeant \'gənərē-\ n : noncommissioned officer in the marine corps ranking next below a master sergeant

gun·ny·sack \'gənē،sak\ n : burlap sack

gun·sling·er \'gən،slipər\ n : skilled gunman in the old West

gun·wale \'gən°l\ n : upper edge of a boat's side

gup·py \'gəpē\ n, pl **-pies** : tiny tropical fish

gur·gle \'gərgəl\ vb **-gled; -gling** : make a sound like that of a flowing and gently splashing liquid — **gurgle** n

gu·ru \'gü،rü\ n, pl **-rus** 1 : personal religious teacher in Hinduism 2 : expert

gush \'gəsh\ vb : pour forth violently or enthusiastically — **gush·er** \'gəshər\ n

gushy \-ē\ adj **gush·i·er; -est** : effusively sentimental

gust \'gəst\ n 1 : sudden brief rush of wind 2 : sudden outburst — **gust** vb — **gusty** adj

gus·ta·to·ry \'gəstəˌtōrē\ adj : relating to the sense of taste

gus·to \'gəstō\ n : zest

gut \'gət\ n 1 pl : intestines 2 : digestive canal 3 pl : courage ~ vb **-tt-** : eviscerate

gut·ter \'gətər\ n : channel for carrying off rainwater

gut·tur·al \'gətərəl\ adj : sounded in the throat — **guttural** n

¹**guy** \ˈgī\ n : rope, chain, or rod attached to something to steady it — **guy** vb

²**guy** n : person

guz·zle \ˈgəzəl\ vb **-zled; -zling** : drink greedily

gym \ˈjim\ n : gymnasium

gym·na·si·um \jim'nāzēəm, -zhəm\ n, pl **-si·ums** or **-sia** \-zēə, -zhə\ : place for indoor sports

gym·nas·tics \jim'nastiks\ n : physical exercises performed in a gymnasium — **gym·nast** \ˈjim,nast\ n — **gym·nas·tic** adj

gy·ne·col·o·gy \ˌgīnəˈkäləjē, ˌjin-\ n : branch of medicine dealing with the diseases of women — **gy·ne·co·log·ic** \-ikəˈläjik\, **gy·ne·co·log·i·cal** \-ikəl\ adj — **gy·ne·col·o·gist** \-əˈkäləjist\ n

gyp \ˈjip\ n **1** : cheat **2** : trickery — **gyp** vb

gyp·sum \ˈjipsəm\ n : calcium-containing mineral

gy·rate \ˈjī,rāt\ vb **-rat·ed; -rat·ing** : revolve around a center — **gy·ra·tion** \jīˈrāshən\ n

gy·ro·scope \ˈjīrō,skōp\ n : wheel mounted to spin rapidly about an axis that is free to turn in various directions

H

h \ˈāch\ n, pl **h's** or **hs** \ˈāchəz\ : 8th letter of the alphabet

hab·er·dash·er \ˈhabər,dashər\ n : men's clothier — **hab·er·dash·ery** \-ərē\ n

hab·it \ˈhabət\ n **1** : monk's or nun's clothing **2** : usual behavior **3** : addiction — **hab·it–form·ing** adj

hab·it·able \-əbəl\ adj : capable of being lived in

hab·i·tat \ˈhabə,tat\ n : place where a plant or animal naturally occurs

hab·i·ta·tion \ˌhabəˈtāshən\ n **1** : occupancy **2** : dwelling place

ha·bit·u·al \həˈbichəwəl\ adj **1** : commonly practiced or observed **2** : doing, practicing, or acting by habit — **ha·bit·u·al·ly** adv

ha·bit·u·ate \həˈbichə,wāt\ vb **-at·ed; -at·ing** : accustom

ha·ci·en·da \ˌhāsēˈendə\ n : ranch house

¹**hack** \ˈhak\ vb **1** : cut with repeated irregular blows **2** : cough in a short dry manner **3** : manage successfully — **hack** n — **hack·er** n

²**hack** n **1** : horse or vehicle for hire **2** : saddle horse **3** : writer for hire — **hack** adj — **hack·man** \-mən\ n

hack·le \ˈhakəl\ n **1** : long feather on the neck or back of a bird **2** pl : hairs that can be erected **3** pl : temper

hack·ney \-nē\ n, pl **-neys 1** : horse for riding or driving **2** : carriage for hire

hack·neyed \-nēd\ adj : trite

hack·saw \ˈhak,sȯ\ n : saw for metal

had past of **HAVE**

had·dock \ˈhadək\ n, pl **haddock** : Atlantic food fish

Ha·des \ˈhādēz\ n **1** : mythological abode of the dead **2** often not cap : hell

haft \ˈhaft\ n : handle of a weapon or tool

hag \ˈhag\ n **1** : witch **2** : ugly old woman

hag·gard \ˈhagərd\ adj : worn or emaciated — **hag·gard·ly** adv

hag·gle \ˈhagəl\ vb **-gled; -gling** : argue in bargaining — **hag·gler** n

¹**hail** \ˈhāl\ n **1** : precipitation in small lumps of ice **2** : something like a rain of hail ~ vb : rain hail — **hail·stone** n — **hail·storm** n

²**hail** vb **1** : greet or salute **2** : summon ~ n : expression of greeting or praise — often used as an interjection

hair \ˈhar\ n : threadlike growth from the skin — **hair·brush** n — **hair·cut** n — **hair·dress·er** n — **haired** adj — **hair·i·ness** n — **hair·less** adj — **hair·pin** n — **hair·style** n — **hair·styl·ing** n — **hair·styl·ist** n — **hairy** adj

hair·breadth \-ˌbredth\, **hairs·breadth** \ˈharz-\ n : tiny distance or margin

hair·do \-ˌdü\ n, pl **-dos** : style of wearing hair

hair·line n **1** : thin line **2** : outline of the hair on the head

hair·piece *n* : toupee

hair–rais·ing *adj* : causing terror or astonishment

hake \'hāk\ *n* : marine food fish

hal·cy·on \'halsēən\ *adj* : prosperous or most pleasant

¹hale \'hāl\ *adj* : healthy or robust

²hale *vb* **haled; hal·ing 1** : haul **2** : compel to go

half \'haf, 'hȧf\ *n, pl* **halves** \'havz, 'hȧvz\ : either of 2 equal parts ~ *adj* **1** : being a half or nearly a half **2** : partial — **half** *adv*

half brother *n* : brother related through one parent only

half-heart·ed \-'härtəd\ *adj* : without enthusiasm — **half-heart·ed·ly** *adv*

half–life *n* : time for half of something to undergo a process

half sister *n* : sister related through one parent only

half·way *adj* : midway between 2 points — **half·way** *adv*

half–wit \-ˌwit\ *n* : foolish person — **half–wit·ted** \-ˌwitəd\ *adj*

hal·i·but \'haləbət\ *n, pl* **halibut** : large edible marine flatfish

hal·i·to·sis \ˌhalə'tōsəs\ *n* : bad breath

hall \'hȯl\ *n* **1** : large public or college or university building **2** : lobby **3** : auditorium

hal·le·lu·jah \ˌhalə'lüyə\ *interj* — used to express praise, joy, or thanks

hall·mark \'hȯlˌmärk\ *n* : distinguishing characteristic

hal·low \'halō\ *vb* : consecrate — **hallowed** \-ōd, -əwəd\ *adj*

Hal·low·een \ˌhaləˈwēn, ˌhäl-\ *n* : evening of October 31 observed esp. by children in merrymaking and masquerading

hal·lu·ci·na·tion \həˌlüsⁿ'āshən\ *n* : perception of objects that are not real — **hal·lu·ci·nate** \hə'lüsⁿˌāt\ *vb* — **hal·lu·ci·na·to·ry** \-'lüsⁿəˌtōrē\ *adj*

hal·lu·ci·no·gen \hə'lüsⁿəjən\ *n* : substance that induces hallucinations — **hal·lu·ci·no·gen·ic** \-ˌlüsⁿə'jenik\ *adj*

hall·way *n* : entrance hall

ha·lo \'hālō\ *n, pl* **-los** *or* **-loes** : circle of light appearing to surround a shining body

¹halt \'hȯlt\ *adj* : lame

²halt *vb* : stop or cause to stop — **halt** *n*

hal·ter \'hȯltər\ *n* **1** : rope or strap for leading or tying an animal **2** : brief blouse held up by straps ~ *vb* : catch (an animal) with a halter

halt·ing \'hȯltiŋ\ *adj* : uncertain — **halt·ing·ly** *adv*

halve \'hav, 'hȧv\ *vb* **halved; halv·ing 1** : divide into halves **2** : reduce to half

halves *pl of* HALF

ham \'ham\ *n* **1** : thigh — usu. pl. **2** : cut esp. of pork from the thigh **3** : showy actor **4** : amateur radio operator ~ *vb* **-mm-** : overplay a part — **ham** *adj*

ham·burg·er \'hamˌbərgər\, **ham·burg** \-ˌbərg\ *n* : ground beef or a sandwich made with this

ham·let \'hamlət\ *n* : small village

ham·mer \'hamər\ *n* **1** : hand tool for pounding **2** : gun part whose striking explodes the charge ~ *vb* : beat, drive, or shape with a hammer — **hammer out** *vb* : produce with effort

ham·mer·head *n* **1** : striking part of a hammer **2** : shark with a hammerlike head

ham·mock \'hamək\ *n* : swinging bed hung by cords at each end

¹ham·per \'hampər\ *vb* : impede

²hamper *n* : large covered basket

ham·ster \'hamstər\ *n* : stocky short-tailed rodent

ham·string \'hamˌstriŋ\ *vb* **-strung** \-ˌstrəŋ\; **-string·ing** \-ˌstriŋiŋ\ **1** : cripple by cutting the leg tendons **2** : make ineffective or powerless

hand \'hand\ *n* **1** : end of a front limb adapted for grasping **2** : side **3** : promise of marriage **4** : handwriting **5** : assistance or participation **6** : applause **7** : cards held by a player **8** : worker ~ *vb* : lead, assist, give, or pass with the hand — **hand·clasp** *n* — **hand·craft** *vb* — **hand·ful** *n* — **hand·gun** *n* — **hand·less** *adj* — **hand·made** *adj* — **hand·rail** *n* — **hand·saw** *n* — **hand·wo·ven** *adj* — **hand·writ·ing** *n* — **hand·writ·ten** *adj*

hand·bag *n* : woman's purse

hand·ball *n* : game played by striking a ball with the hand

hand·bill *n* : printed advertisement or notice distributed by hand

hand·book *n* : concise reference book

hand·cuffs *n pl* : locking bracelets that bind the wrists together — **handcuff** *vb*

hand·i·cap \'handēˌkap\ *n* **1** : advantage given or disadvantage imposed to equalize a competition **2** : disadvantage — **handicap** vb — **handicapped** adj — **handicapper** n

handicraft \'handē,kraft\ n **1** : manual skill **2** : article made by hand — **handicrafter** n

handiwork \-,wərk\ n : work done personally or by the hands

handkerchief \'haŋkərchəf, -,chēf\ n, pl **-chiefs** \-chəfs, -,chēfs\ : small piece of cloth carried for personal use

handle \'hand⁰l\ n : part to be grasped ~ vb **-dled; -dling 1** : touch, hold, or manage with the hands **2** : deal with **3** : deal or trade in — **handlebar** n — **handled** \-d⁰ld\ adj — **handler** \'handlər\ n

handmaid en n : female attendant

handout n : something given out

handpick vb : select personally

handshake n : clasping of hands (as in greeting)

handsome \'hansəm\ adj **-somer; -est 1** : sizable **2** : generous **3** : nice-looking — **handsomely** adv — **handsomeness** n

handspring n : somersault on the hands

handstand n : a balancing upside down on the hands

handy \'handē\ adj **handier; -est 1** : conveniently near **2** : easily used **3** : dexterous — **handily** adv — **handiness** n

handyman \-,man\ n : one who does odd jobs

hang \'haŋ\ vb hung \'həŋ\; **hanging 1** : fasten or remain fastened to an elevated point without support from below **2** : suspend by the neck until dead — past tense often *hanged* **3** : droop ~ n **1** : way a thing hangs **2** : an understanding of something — **hanger** n — **hanging** n

hangar \'haŋər\ n : airplane shelter

hangdog \'haŋ,dȯg\ adj : ashamed or guilty

hangman \-mən\ n : public executioner

hangnail n : loose skin near a fingernail

hangout n : place where one likes to spend time

hangover n : sick feeling following heavy drinking

hank \'haŋk\ n : coil or loop

hanker \'haŋkər\ vb : desire strongly — **hankering** n

hanky–panky \,haŋkē'paŋkē\ n : questionable or underhanded activity

hansom \'hansəm\ n : 2-wheeled covered carriage

Ha·nuk·kah \'känəkə, 'hän-\ n : 8-day Jewish holiday commemorating the rededication of the Temple of Jerusalem after its defilement by Antiochus of Syria

haphazard \hap'hazərd\ adj : having no plan or order — **haphazardly** adv

hapless \'hapləs\ adj : unfortunate — **haplessly** adv — **haplessness** n

happen \'hapən\ vb **1** : take place **2** : be fortunate to encounter something unexpectedly — often used with infinitive

happening \-əniŋ\ n : occurrence

happy \'hapē\ adj **-pier; -est 1** : fortunate **2** : content, pleased, or joyous — **happily** \'hapəlē\ adv — **happiness** n

harangue \hə'raŋ\ n : ranting or scolding speech — **harangue** vb — **haranguer** \-'raŋər\ n

harass \hə'ras, 'harəs\ vb **1** : disturb and impede by repeated raids **2** : annoy continually — **harassment** n

harbinger \'härbənjər\ n : one that announces or foreshadows what is coming

harbor \-bər\ n : protected body of water suitable for anchorage ~ vb **1** : give refuge to **2** : hold as a thought or feeling

hard \'härd\ adj **1** : not easily penetrated **2** : firm or definite **3** : close or searching **4** : severe or unfeeling **5** : strenuous or difficult **6** : physically strong or intense — **hard** adv — **hardness** n

harden \'härd⁰n\ vb : make or become hard or harder — **hardener** n

hardheaded \,härd'hedəd\ adj **1** : stubborn **2** : realistic — **hardheadedly** adv — **hardheadedness** n

hardhearted \-'härtəd\ adj : lacking sympathy — **hardheartedly** adv — **hardheartedness** n

hardly \'härdlē\ adv **1** : only just **2** : certainly not

hard–nosed \-,nōzd\ adj : tough or uncompromising

hardship \-,ship\ n : suffering or privation

hardtack \-,tak\ n : hard biscuit

hardware n **1** : cutlery or tools made

of metal **2** : physical components of a vehicle or apparatus

hard-wood \ n : wood of a broad-leaved usu. deciduous tree — **hardwood** adj

har-dy \'härdē\ adj **-di-er; -est** : able to withstand adverse conditions — **har-di-ly** adv — **har-di-ness** n

hare \'har\ n, pl **hare** or **hares** : long-eared mammal related to the rabbit

hare-brained \-,brānd\ adj : foolish

hare-lip n : deformity in which the upper lip is vertically split — **hare-lipped** \-,lipt\ adj

ha-rem \'harəm\ n : house or part of a house allotted to women in a Muslim household or the women and servants occupying it

hark \'härk\ vb : listen

har-le-quin \'härlikən, -kwən\ n : clown

har-lot \'härlət\ n : prostitute

harm \'härm\ n **1** : physical or mental damage **2** : mischief — vb : cause harm — **harm-ful** \-fəl\ adj — **harm-ful-ly** adv — **harm-ful-ness** n — **harm-less** adj — **harm-less-ly** adv — **harm-less-ness** n

har-mon-ic \här'mänik\ adj **1** : of or relating to musical harmony **2** : pleasing to hear — **har-mon-i-cal-ly** \-iklē\ adv

har-mon-i-ca \här'mänikə\ n : small wind instrument with metallic reeds

har-mo-ny \'härmənē\ n, pl **-nies 1** : musical combination of sounds **2** : pleasing arrangement of parts **3** : lack of conflict **4** : internal calm — **har-mo-ni-ous** \här'mōnēəs\ adj — **har-mo-ni-ous-ly** adv — **har-mo-ni-ous-ness** n — **har-mo-ni-za-tion** \,härmənə'zāshən\ n — **har-mo-nize** \'härmə,nīz\ vb

har-ness \'härnəs\ n : gear of a draft animal — vb **1** : put a harness on **2** : put to use

harp \'härp\ n : musical instrument with many strings plucked by the fingers — vb **1** : play on a harp **2** : dwell on a subject tiresomely — **harp-er** n — **harp-ist** n

har-poon \här'pün\ n : barbed spear used in hunting whales — **harpoon** vb — **har-poon-er** n

harp-si-chord \'härpsi,kord\ n : keyboard instrument with strings that are plucked

har-py \'härpē\ n, pl **-pies** : shrewish woman

har-row \'harō\ n : implement used to break up soil — vb **1** : cultivate with a harrow **2** : distress

har-ry \'harē\ vb **-ried; -ry-ing** : torment by or as if by constant attack

harsh \'härsh\ adj **1** : disagreeably rough **2** : severe — **harsh-ly** adv — **harsh-ness** n

har-um–scar-um \,harəm'skarəm\ adv : recklessly

har-vest \'härvəst\ n **1** : act or time of gathering in a crop **2** : mature crop — **harvest** vb — **har-vest-er** n

has pres 3d sing of HAVE

hash \'hash\ vb : chop into small pieces — n : chopped meat mixed with potatoes and browned

hasp \'hasp\ n : hinged strap fastener esp. for a door

has-sle \'hasəl\ n **1** : quarrel : struggle **3** : cause of annoyance — **hassle** vb

has-sock \'hasək\ n : cushion used as a seat or leg rest

haste \'hāst\ n **1** : rapidity of motion **2** : rash action **3** : excessive eagerness — **hast-i-ly** \'hāstəlē\ adv — **hast-i-ness** \-stēnəs\ n — **hasty** \-stē\ adj

has-ten \'hās^n\ vb : hurry

hat \'hat\ n : covering for the head

¹**hatch** \'hach\ n : small door or opening — **hatch-way** n

²**hatch** vb : emerge from an egg — **hatch-ery** \-ərē\ n

hatch-et \'hachət\ n : short-handled ax

hate \'hāt\ n : intense hostility and aversion — vb **hat-ed; hat-ing 1** : express or feel hate **2** : dislike — **hate-ful** \-fəl\ adj — **hate-ful-ly** adv — **hate-ful-ness** n — **hat-er** n

ha-tred \'hātrəd\ n : hate

hat-ter \'hatər\ n : one that makes or sells hats

haugh-ty \'hotē\ adj **-ti-er; -est** : disdainfully proud — **haugh-ti-ly** adv — **haugh-ti-ness** n

haul \'hol\ vb **1** : draw or pull **2** : transport or carry — n **1** : amount collected **2** : load or the distance it is transported — **haul-er** n

haunch \'honch\ n : hip or hindquarter — usu. pl.

haunt \'hont\ vb **1** : visit often **2** : visit or inhabit as a ghost — n : place frequented — **haunt-er** n — **haunt-ing-ly** adv

have \'hav, in sense 2 before "to" usu

haf\ *vb* **had** \'had\; **hav·ing** \'haviŋ\; **has** \'haz, *in sense 2 before "to" usu* 'has\ **1** : hold in possession, service, or affection **2** : be compelled or forced to **3** — used as an auxiliary with the past participle to form the present perfect, past perfect, or future perfect **4** : obtain or receive **5** : undergo **6** : cause to **7** : bear — **have to do with** : have in the way of connection or relation with or effect on

ha·ven \'hāvən\ *n* : place of safety

hav·oc \'havək\ *n* **1** : wide destruction **2** : great confusion

¹hawk \'hók\ *n* : bird of prey with a strong hooked bill and sharp talons

²hawk *vb* : offer for sale by calling out in the street — **hawk·er** *n*

haw·ser \'hózər\ *n* : large rope

haw·thorn \'hó,thòrn\ *n* : spiny shrub or tree with pink or white fragrant flowers

hay \'hā\ *n* : herbs (as grass) cut and dried for use as fodder — **hay** *vb* — **hay·loft** *n* — **hay·mow** \-,maù\ *n* — **hay·stack** *n*

hay·cock \'hā,käk\ *n* : small pile of hay

hay·rick \-,rik\ *n* : large outdoor stack of hay

hay·seed \'hā,sēd\ *n* : bumpkin

hay·wire *adj* : being out of order

haz·ard \'hazərd\ *n* **1** : source of danger **2** : chance ~ *vb* : venture or risk — **haz·ard·ous** *adj*

¹haze \'hāz\ *n* : fine dust, smoke, or light vapor in the air that reduces visibility

²haze *vb* **hazed; haz·ing** : harass by abusive and humiliating tricks

ha·zel \'hāzəl\ *n* **1** : shrub or small tree bearing edible nuts (**ha·zel·nuts**) **2** : light brown color

hazy \'hāzē\ *adj* **haz·i·er; -est 1** : obscured by haze **2** : vague or indefinite — **haz·i·ly** *adv* — **haz·i·ness** *n*

he \'hē\ *pron* **1** : that male one **2** : a or the person

head \'hed\ *n* **1** : front or upper part of the body **2** : mind **3** : upper or higher end **4** : director or leader **5** : place of leadership or honor ~ *adj* : principal or chief ~ *vb* **1** : provide with or form a head **2** : put, stand, or be at the head **3** : point or proceed in a certain direction — **head·ache** *n* — **head·band** *n* — **head·dress** *n* — **head·ed** *adj* — **head·first** *adv or adj* —

head·gear *n* — **head·less** *adj* — **head·rest** *n* — **head·ship** *n* — **head·wait·er** *n*

head·ing \-iŋ\ *n* **1** : direction in which a plane or ship heads **2** : something (as a title) standing at the top or beginning

head·land \'hedlənd, -,land\ *n* : promontory

head·light *n* : light on the front of a vehicle

head·line *n* : introductory line of a newspaper story printed in large type

head·long \-'lòŋ\ *adv* **1** : head foremost **2** : in a rash or reckless manner — **head·long** \-,lòŋ\ *adj*

head·mas·ter *n* : man who is head of a private school

head·mis·tress *n* : woman who is head of a private school

head·on *adj* : having the front facing in the direction of initial contact — **head·on** *adv*

head·phone *n* : an earphone held on by a band over the head — usu. pl.

head·quar·ters *n sing or pl* : command or administrative center

head·stone *n* : stone at the head of a grave

head·strong *adj* : stubborn or willful

head·wa·ters *n pl* : source of a stream

head·way *n* : forward motion

heady \'hedē\ *adj* **head·i·er; -est 1** : intoxicating **2** : shrewd

heal \'hēl\ *vb* : make or become sound or whole — **heal·er** *n*

health \'helth\ *n* : sound physical or mental condition

health·ful \-fəl\ *adj* : beneficial to health — **health·ful·ly** *adv* — **health·ful·ness** *n*

healthy \'helthē\ *adj* **health·i·er; -est** : enjoying or typical of good health — **health·i·ly** *adv* — **health·i·ness** *n*

heap \'hēp\ *n* : pile ~ *vb* : throw or lay in a heap

hear \'hir\ *vb* **heard** \'hərd\; **hear·ing** \'hiriŋ\ **1** : perceive by the ear **2** : heed **3** : learn

hear·ing *n* **1** : process or power of perceiving sound **2** : earshot **3** : session in which witnesses are heard

hear·ken \'härkən\ *vb* : give attention

hear·say *n* : rumor

hearse \'hərs\ *n* : vehicle for carrying the dead to the grave

heart \'härt\ *n* **1** : hollow muscular organ that keeps up the circulation of the blood **2** : playing card of a suit marked with a red heart **3** : whole personality or the emotional or moral part of it **4** : courage **5** : essential part — **heart-beat** n — **heart-ed** adj

heart-ache n : anguish of mind

heart-break n : crushing grief — **heart-break-er** n — **heart-break-ing** adj — **heart-bro-ken** adj

heart-burn n : burning distress in the heart area after eating

heart-en \'härt°n\ vb : encourage

hearth \'härth\ n **1** : area in front of a fireplace **2** : home — **hearth-stone** n

heart-less \'härtləs\ adj : cruel

heart-rend-ing \-,rendiŋ\ adj : causing intense grief or anguish

heart-sick adj : very despondent

heart-strings n pl : deepest emotions

heart-throb n : sweetheart

heart-warm-ing adj : inspiring sympathetic feeling

heart-wood n : central portion of wood

hearty \'härtē\ adj **heart-i-er**; **-est 1** : vigorously healthy **2** : nourishing — **heart-i-ly** adv — **heart-i-ness** n

heat \'hēt\ vb : make or become warm or hot ~ n **1** : condition of being hot **2** : form of energy that causes a body to rise in temperature **3** : intensity of feeling — **heat-ed-ly** adv — **heat-er** n

heath \'hēth\ n **1** : often evergreen shrubby plant of wet acid soils **2** : tract of wasteland — **heathy** adj

hea-then \'hēthən\ n, pl **-thens** or **-then** : uncivilized or godless person — **heathen** adj

heath-er \'hethər\ n : evergreen heath with lavender flowers — **heath-ery** adj

heat-stroke n : disorder that follows prolonged exposure to excessive heat

heave \'hēv\ vb **heaved** or **hove** \'hōv\; **heav-ing 1** : rise or lift upward **2** : throw **3** : rise and fall ~ n **1** : an effort to lift or raise **2** : throw

heav-en \'hevən\ n **1** pl : sky **2** : abode of the Deity and of the blessed dead **3** : place of supreme happiness — **heav-en-ly** adj — **heav-en-ward** adv or adj

heavy \'hevē\ adj **heavi-er**; **-est 1** : having great weight **2** : hard to bear **3** : greater than the average — **heav-i-ly** adv — **heavi-ness** n — **heavy-weight** n

heavy-du-ty adj : able to withstand unusual strain

heavy-set adj : stocky and compact in build

heck-le \'hekəl\ vb **-led**; **-ling** : harass with gibes — **heck-ler** \'heklər\ n

hec-tic \'hektik\ adj : filled with excitement, activity, or confusion — **hec-ti-cal-ly** \-tiklē\ adv

hedge \'hej\ n **1** : fence or boundary of shrubs or small trees **2** : means of protection ~ vb **hedged**; **hedg-ing 1** : protect oneself against loss **2** : evade the risk of commitment — **hedg-er** n

hedge-hog n : spiny mammal (as a porcupine)

he-do-nism \'hēd°n,izəm\ n : way of life devoted to pleasure — **he-do-nist** \-°nist\ n — **he-do-nis-tic** \,hēd°n-'istik\ adj

heed \'hēd\ vb : pay attention ~ n : attention — **heed-ful** \-fəl\ adj — **heed-ful-ly** adv — **heed-ful-ness** n — **heed-less** adj — **heed-less-ly** adv — **heed-less-ness** n

¹heel \'hēl\ n **1** : back of the foot **2** : crusty end of a loaf of bread **3** : solid piece forming the back of the sole of a shoe — **heel-less** \'hēlləs\ adj

²heel vb : tilt to one side

heft \'heft\ n : weight ~ vb : judge the weight of by lifting

hefty \'heftē\ adj **heft-i-er**; **-est** : big and bulky

he-ge-mo-ny \hi'jemənē\ n : preponderant influence over others

heif-er \'hefər\ n : young cow

height \'hīt, 'hītth\ n **1** : highest part or point **2** : distance from bottom to top **3** : altitude

height-en \'hīt°n\ vb : increase in amount or degree

hei-nous \'hānəs\ adj : shockingly evil — **hei-nous-ly** adv — **hei-nous-ness** n

heir \'ar\ n : one who inherits or is entitled to inherit property

heir-ess \'arəs\ n : female heir esp. to great wealth

heir-loom \'ar,lüm\ n : something handed on from one generation to another

held past of HOLD

he-li-cal \'helikəl, 'hē-\ adj : spiral

he-li-cop-ter \'helə,käptər, 'hē-\ n : aircraft supported in the air by rotors

he-lio-trope \'hēlyə,trōp\ n : garden

herb with small fragrant white or purple flowers

he·li·um \'hēlēəm\ *n* : very light nonflammable gaseous chemical element

he·lix \'hēliks\ *n, pl* **-li·ces** \'helə,sēz, 'hē-\ : something spiral

hell \'hel\ *n* **1** : nether world in which the dead continue to exist **2** : realm of the devil **3** : place or state of torment or destruction — **hell·ish** *adj*

hell·gram·mite \'helgrə,mīt\ *n* : aquatic insect larva

hel·lion \'helyən\ *n* : troublesome person

hel·lo \hə'lō, he-\ *n, pl* **-los** : expression of greeting

helm \'helm\ *n* : lever or wheel for steering a ship — **helms·man** \'helmzmən\ *n*

hel·met \'helmət\ *n* : protective covering for the head

help \'help\ *vb* **1** : supply what is needed **2** : be of use **3** : refrain from or prevent ~ *n* **1** : something that helps or a source of help **2** : one who helps another — **help·er** *n* — **help·ful** \-fəl\ *adj* — **help·ful·ly** *adv* — **help·ful·ness** *n* — **help·less** *adj* — **help·less·ly** *adv* — **help·less·ness** *n*

help·ing \'helpiŋ\ *n* : portion of food

help·mate *n* **1** : helper **2** : wife

help·meet \-,mēt\ *n* : helpmate

hel·ter-skel·ter \,heltər'skeltər\ *adv* : in total disorder

hem \'hem\ *n* : border of an article of cloth doubled back and stitched down ~ *vb* **-mm- 1** : sew a hem **2** : surround restrictively — **hem·line** *n*

he·ma·tol·o·gy \,hēmə'täləjē\ *n* : study of the blood and blood-forming organs — **he·ma·to·log·ic** \-mət⁰l-'äjik\ *adj* — **he·ma·tol·o·gist** \-'täləjist\ *n*

hemi·sphere \'hemə,sfir\ *n* : one of the halves of the earth divided by the equator into northern and southern parts (**northern hemisphere, southern hemisphere**) or by a meridian into eastern and western parts (**eastern hemisphere, western hemisphere**) — **hemi·spher·ic** \,hemə'sfirik, -'sfer-\, **hemi·spher·i·cal** \-'sfirikəl, -'sfer-\ *adj*

hem·lock \'hem,läk\ *n* **1** : poisonous herb related to the carrot **2** : evergreen tree related to the pines

he·mo·glo·bin \'hēmə,glōbən\ *n* : iron-containing compound found in red blood cells

he·mo·phil·ia \,hēmə'filēə\ *n* : hereditary tendency to severe prolonged bleeding — **he·mo·phil·i·ac** \-ē,ak\ *adj or n*

hem·or·rhage \'hemərij\ *n* : large discharge of blood — **hemorrhage** *vb* — **hem·or·rhag·ic** \,hemə'rajik\ *adj*

hem·or·rhoids \'hemə,ròidz\ *n pl* : swollen mass of dilated veins at or just within the anus

hemp \'hemp\ *n* : tall Asian herb grown for its tough fiber

hen \'hen\ *n* : female domestic fowl

hence \'hens\ *adv* **1** : away **2** : therefore **3** : from this source or origin

hence·forth *adv* : from this point on

hence·for·ward *adv* : henceforth

hench·man \'henchmən\ *n* : trusted follower

hen·na \'henə\ *n* : reddish brown dye from a tropical shrub used esp. on hair

hen·peck \'hen,pek\ *vb* : subject (one's husband) to persistent nagging

he·pat·ic \hi'patik\ *adj* : relating to or resembling the liver

hep·a·ti·tis \,hepə'tītəs\ *n, pl* **-tit·i·des** \-'titə,dēz\ : disease in which the liver becomes inflamed

her \'hər\ *adj* : of or relating to her or herself ~ \,ər, (')hər\ *pron objective case of* SHE

her·ald \'herəld\ *n* **1** : official crier or messenger **2** : harbinger ~ *vb* : give notice

her·ald·ry \'herəldrē\ *n, pl* **-ries** : practice of devising and granting stylized emblems (as for a family) — **he·ral·dic** \he'raldik, hə-\ *adj*

herb \'ərb, 'hərb\ *n* **1** : seed plant that lacks woody tissue **2** : plant or plant part valued for medicinal or savory qualities — **her·ba·ceous** \,ər'bā-shəs, ,hər-\ *adj* — **herb·age** \'ərbij, 'hər-\ *n* — **herb·al** \-bəl\ *n or adj* — **herb·al·ist** \-bəlist\ *n*

her·bi·cide \'ərbə,sīd, 'hər-\ *n* : agent that destroys plants — **her·bi·cid·al** \,ərbə'sīd⁰l, ,hər-\ *adj*

her·biv·o·rous \,ər'bivərəs, ,hər-\ *adj* : feeding on plants — **her·bi·vore** \'ərbə,vòr, 'hər-\ *n*

her·cu·le·an \,hərkyə'lēən, hər'kyü-lēən\ *adj* : of extraordinary power, size, or difficulty

herd \'hərd\ *n* : group of animals of

one kind ~ vb : assemble or move in a herd — **herd·er** n — **herds·man** \'hərdzmən\ n

here \'hir\ adv **1** : in, at, or to this place **2** : now **3** : at or in this point or particular **4** : in the present life or state ~ n : this place — **here·abouts** \'hirə,bauts\, **here·about** \-,baut\ adv

here·af·ter adv : in some future time or state ~ n : existence beyond earthly life

here·by adv : by means of this

he·red·i·tary \hə'redə,terē\ adj **1** : genetically passed or passable from parent to offspring **2** : passing by inheritance

he·red·i·ty \-atē\ n : the passing of characteristics from parent to offspring

here·in adv : in this

here·of adv : of this

here·on adv : on this

her·e·sy \'herəsē\ n, pl **-sies** : opinion or doctrine contrary to church dogma — **her·e·tic** \-,tik\ n — **he·re·ti·cal** \hə'retikəl\ adj

here·to adv : to this document

here·to·fore \'hirtü,fōr\ adv : up to this time

here·un·der adv : under this

here·un·to adv : to this

here·upon adv : on this

here·with adv **1** : with this **2** : hereby

her·i·tage \'herətij\ n **1** : inheritance **2** : birthright

her·maph·ro·dite \hər'mafrə,dīt\ n : animal or plant having both male and female reproductive organs — **hermaphrodite** adj — **her·maph·ro·dit·ic** \-,mafrə'ditik\ adj

her·met·ic \hər'metik\ adj : sealed airtight — **her·met·i·cal·ly** \-iklē\ adv

her·mit \'hərmət\ n : one who lives in solitude

her·nia \'hərnēə\ n, pl **-ni·as** or **-ni·ae** \-nē,ē, -nē,ī\ : protrusion of a bodily part through the weakened wall of its enclosure — **her·ni·ate** \-nē,āt\ vb

he·ro \'hērō, 'hirō\ n, pl **-roes** : one that is much admired or shows great courage — **he·ro·ic** \hi'rōik\ adj — **he·ro·i·cal·ly** \-iklē\ adv — **he·ro·ics** \-iks\ n pl — **her·o·ism** \'herə,wizəm\ n

her·o·in \'herəwən\ n : strongly addictive narcotic

her·o·ine \'herəwən\ n : woman of heroic achievements or qualities

her·on \'herən\ n : long-legged longbilled wading bird

her·pes \'hər,pēz\ n : virus disease characterized by the formation of blisters

her·pe·tol·o·gy \,hərpə'täləjē\ n : study of reptiles and amphibians — **her·pe·tol·o·gist** \-pə'täləjist\ n

her·ring \'heriŋ\ n, pl **-ring** or **-rings** : narrow-bodied Atlantic food fish

hers \'hərz\ pron : one or the ones belonging to her

her·self \hər'self\ pron : she, her — used reflexively or for emphasis

hertz \'herts, 'hərts\ n, pl **hertz** : unit of frequency equal to one cycle per second

hes·i·tant \'hezətənt\ adj : tending to hesitate — **hes·i·tance** \-tens\ n — **hes·i·tan·cy** \-tənsē\ n — **hes·i·tant·ly** adv

hes·i·tate \'hezə,tāt\ vb **-tat·ed; -tat·ing 1** : hold back esp. in doubt **2** : pause — **hes·i·ta·tion** \,hezə'tā·shən\ n

het·er·o·ge·neous \,hetərə'jēnēəs, -nyəs\ adj : consisting of dissimilar ingredients or constituents — **het·er·o·ge·ne·ity** \-jə'nēətē\ n — **het·er·o·ge·neous·ly** adv

het·er·o·sex·u·al \,hetərō'sekshəwəl\ adj : oriented toward the opposite sex — **heterosexual** n — **het·er·o·sex·u·al·i·ty** \-,seksha'walətē\ n

hew \'hyü\ vb **hewed; hewed** or **hewn** \'hyün\; **how·ing 1** : cut or shape with or as if with an ax **2** : conform strictly — **hew·er** n

hex \'heks\ vb : put an evil spell on — **hex** n

hexa·gon \'heksə,gän\ n : 6-sided polygon — **hex·ag·o·nal** \hek'sagən°l\ adj

hey·day \'hā,dā\ n : time of flourishing

hi·a·tus \hī'ātəs\ n : lapse in continuity

hi·ba·chi \hi'bächē\ n : brazier

hi·ber·nate \'hībər,nāt\ vb **-nat·ed; -nat·ing** : pass the winter in a torpid or resting state — **hi·ber·na·tion** \,hībər'nāshən\ n — **hi·ber·na·tor** \'hībər,nātər\ n

hic·cup \'hikəp\ vb **-cuped; -cup·ing** : to inhale spasmodically and make a peculiar sound ~ n pl : attack of hiccuping

hick \'hik\ n : awkward provincial person — **hick** adj

hick·o·ry \'hikərē\ n, pl **-ries** : No.

American hardwood tree — **hickory** *adj*

¹hide \'hīd\ *vb* **hid** \'hid\; **hid·den** \'hid'n\ *or* **hid**; **hid·ing** : put or remain out of sight — **hid·er** *n*

²hide *n* : animal skin

hide·bound \'hīd,baùnd\ *adj* : inflexible or conservative

hid·eous \'hidēəs\ *adj* : very ugly — **hid·eous·ly** *adv* — **hid·eous·ness** *n*

hie \'hī\ *vb* **hied**; **hy·ing** *or* **hie·ing** : hurry

hi·er·ar·chy \'hīə,rärkē\ *n, pl* **-chies** : persons or things arranged in a graded series — **hi·er·ar·chi·cal** \,hīə'rärkikəl\ *adj*

hi·ero·glyph·ic \,hīərə'glifik\ *n* : character in the picture writing of the ancient Egyptians

high \'hī\ *adj* **1** : having large extension upward **2** : elevated in pitch **3** : exalted in character **4** : of greater degree or amount than average **5** : expensive **6** : excited or stupefied by alcohol or a drug ~ *n* **1** : elevated point or level **2** : automobile gear giving the highest speed — **high·ly** *adv*

high·boy *n* : high chest of drawers on legs

high·brow \-,braù\ *n* : person of superior learning or culture — **highbrow** *adj*

high–definition *adj* : being or relating to a television system with twice as many scan lines per frame as a conventional system

high–flown *adj* : pretentious

high–hand·ed *adj* : willful and arrogant — **high–hand·ed·ly** *adv* — **high–hand·ed·ness** *n*

high·land \'hīlənd\ *n* : hilly country — **high·land·er** \-ləndər\ *n*

high·light *n* : event or detail of major importance ~ *vb* **1** : emphasize **2** : be a highlight of

high·ness \-nəs\ *n* **1** : quality or degree of being high **2** — used as a title (as for kings)

high–rise *adj* : having several stories

high school *n* : school usu. including grades 9 to 12 or 10 to 12

high–spir·it·ed *adj* : lively

high–strung \,hī'strəŋ\ *adj* : very nervous or sensitive

high·way *n* : public road

high·way·man \-mən\ *n* : one who robs travelers on a road

hi·jack \'hī,jak\ *vb* : steal esp. by commandeering a vehicle — **hijack** *n* — **hi·jack·er** *n*

hike \'hīk\ *vb* **hiked**; **hik·ing** **1** : raise quickly **2** : take a long walk ~ *n* **1** : long walk **2** : increase — **hik·er** *n*

hi·lar·i·ous \hi'larēəs, hī'-\ *adj* : extremely funny — **hi·lar·i·ous·ly** *adv* — **hi·lar·i·ty** \-ətē\ *n*

hill \'hil\ *n* : place where the land rises — **hill·side** *n* — **hill·top** *n* — **hilly** *adj*

hill·bil·ly \'hil,bilē\ *n, pl* **-lies** : person from a backwoods area

hill·ock \'hilək\ *n* : small hill

hilt \'hilt\ *n* : handle of a sword

him \'him\ *pron, objective case of* HE

him·self \him'self\ *pron* : he, him — used reflexively or for emphasis

¹hind \'hīnd\ *n* : female deer

²hind *adj* : back

hin·der \'hindər\ *vb* : obstruct or hold back

hind·most *adj* : farthest to the rear

hind·quar·ter *n* : back half of a complete side of a carcass

hin·drance \'hindrəns\ *n* : something that hinders

hind·sight *n* : understanding of an event after it has happened

Hin·du·ism \'hindü,izəm\ *n* : body of religious beliefs and practices native to India — **Hin·du** *n or adj*

hinge \'hinj\ *n* : jointed piece on which a swinging part (as a door) turns ~ *vb* **hinged**; **hing·ing** **1** : attach by or furnish with hinges **2** : depend

hint \'hint\ *n* **1** : indirect suggestion **2** : clue **3** : very small amount — **hint** *vb*

hin·ter·land \'hintər,land\ *n* : remote region

hip \'hip\ *n* : part of the body on either side just below the waist — **hip·bone** *n*

hip·po·pot·a·mus \,hipə'pätəməs\ *n, pl* **-mus·es** *or* **-mi** \-,mī\ : large thick-skinned African river animal

hire \'hīr\ *n* **1** : payment for labor **2** : employment **3** : one who is hired ~ *vb* **hired**; **hir·ing** : employ for pay

hire·ling \-liŋ\ *n* : one who serves another only for gain

hir·sute \'hər,süt, 'hir-\ *adj* : hairy

his \'hiz\ *adj* : of or belonging to him ~ *pron* : ones belonging to him

hiss \'his\ *vb* **1** : make a sibilant sound **2** : show dislike by hissing — **hiss** *n*

his·to·ri·an \his'tōrēən\ *n* : writer of history

his·to·ry \'histərē\ *n, pl* **-ries** **1** : chronological record of significant events **2** : study of past events **3** : an established record — **his·tor·ic** \his-'tör-ik\, **his·tor·i·cal** \-i-kəl\ *adj* — **his·tor·i·cal·ly** \-k-lē\ *adv*

his·tri·on·ics \‚histrē'äniks\ *n pl* : exaggerated display of emotion

hit \'hit\ *vb* **hit; hit·ting 1** : reach with a blow **2** : come or cause to come in contact **3** : affect detrimentally — *n* **1** : blow **2** : great success — **hit·ter** *n*

hitch \'hich\ *vb* **1** : move by jerks **2** : catch by a hook **3** : hitchhike — *n* **1** : jerk **2** : sudden halt

hitch·hike \'hich‚hīk\ *vb* : travel by securing free rides from passing vehicles — **hitch·hik·er** *n*

hith·er \'hithər\ *adv* : to this place

hith·er·to \-‚tü\ *adv* : up to this time

hive \'hīv\ *n* **1** : container housing honeybees **2** : colony of bees — **hive** *vb*

hives \'hīvz\ *n sing or pl* : allergic disorder with itchy skin patches

HMO \‚āch‚em'ō\ *n* : comprehensive health-care organization financed by clients

hoard \'hōrd\ *n* : hidden accumulation — **hoard** *vb* — **hoard·er** *n*

hoar·frost \'hōr‚fròst\ *n* : frost

hoarse \'hōrs\ *adj* **hoars·er; -est 1** : harsh in sound **2** : speaking in a harsh strained voice — **hoarse·ly** *adv* — **hoarse·ness** *n*

hoary \'hōrē\ *adj* **hoar·i·er; -est** : gray or white with age — **hoar·i·ness** *n*

hoax \'hōks\ *n* : act intended to trick or dupe — **hoax** *vb* — **hoax·er** *n*

hob·ble \'häbəl\ *vb* **-bled; -bling** : limp along — *n* : hobbling movement

hob·by \'häbē\ *n, pl* **-bies** : interest engaged in for relaxation — **hob·by·ist** \-ēist\ *n*

hob·gob·lin \'häb‚gäblən\ *n* **1** : mischievous goblin **2** : bogey

hob·nail \-‚nāl\ *n* : short nail for studding shoe soles — **hob·nailed** \-‚nāld\ *adj*

hob·nob \-‚näb\ *vb* **-bb-** : associate socially

ho·bo \'hōbō\ *n, pl* **-boes** : tramp

¹hock \'häk\ *n* : joint or region in the hind limb of a quadruped corresponding to the human ankle

²hock *n or vb* : pawn

hock·ey \'häkē\ *n* : game played on ice or a field by 2 teams

hod \'häd\ *n* : carrier for bricks or mortar

hodge·podge \'häj‚päj\ *n* : heterogeneous mixture

hoe \'hō\ *n* : long-handled tool for cultivating or weeding — **hoe** *vb*

hog \'hòg, 'häg\ *n* **1** : domestic adult swine **2** : glutton ~ *vb* : take selfishly — **hog·gish** *adj*

hogs·head \'hògz‚hed, 'hägz-\ *n* : large cask or barrel

hog·wash *n* : nonsense

hoist \'hòist\ *vb* : lift — *n* **1** : lift **2** : apparatus for hoisting

hok·ey \'hōkē\ *adj* **hok·i·er; -est 1** : tiresomely simple or sentimental **2** : phony

¹hold \'hōld\ *vb* **held** \'held\; **hold·ing 1** : possess **2** : restrain **3** : have a grasp on **4** : remain or keep in a particular situation or position **5** : contain **6** : regard **7** : cause to occur **8** : occupy esp. by appointment or election ~ *n* **1** : act or manner of holding **2** : restraining or controlling influence — **hold·er** *n* — **hold forth** : speak at length — **hold to** : adhere to — **hold with** : agree with

²hold *n* : cargo area of a ship

hold·ing \'hōldiŋ\ *n* : property owned — usu. pl.

hold·up *n* **1** : robbery at the point of a gun **2** : delay

hole \'hōl\ *n* **1** : opening into or through something **2** : hollow place (as a pit) **3** : den — **hole** *vb*

hol·i·day \'hälə‚dā\ *n* **1** : day of freedom from work **2** : vacation — **holiday** *vb*

ho·li·ness \'hōlēnəs\ *n* : quality or state of being holy — used as a title for a high religious official

ho·lis·tic \hō'listik\ *adj* : relating to a whole (as the body)

hol·ler \'hälər\ *vb* : cry out — **holler** *n*

hol·low \'hälō\ *adj* **-low·er** \-əwər\; **-est 1** : sunken **2** : having a cavity within **3** : sounding like a noise made in an empty place **4** : empty of value or meaning ~ *vb* : make or become hollow ~ *n* **1** : surface depression **2** : cavity — **hol·low·ness** *n*

hol·ly \'hälē\ *n, pl* **-lies** : evergreen tree or shrub with glossy leaves

hol·ly·hock \-‚häk, -‚hòk\ *n* : tall perennial herb with showy flowers

ho·lo·caust \'hälə‚kòst, 'hō-, 'hò-\ *n* : thorough destruction esp. by fire

hol·stein \'hōl,stēn, -,stīn\ n : large black-and-white dairy cow

hol·ster \'hōlstər\ n : case for a pistol

ho·ly \'hōlē\ adj -**li·er; -est 1** : sacred **2** : spiritually pure

hom·age \'ämij, 'hä-\ n : reverent regard

home \'hōm\ n **1** : residence **2** : congenial environment **3** : place of origin or refuge ∼ vb **homed; hom·ing** : go or return home — **home-bred** adj — **home·com·ing** n — **home-grown** adj — **home·land** \-,land\ n — **home·less** adj — **home·made** \-'mād\ adj

home·ly \-lē\ adj -**li·er; -est** : plain or unattractive — **home·li·ness** n

home·mak·er n : one who manages a household — **home·mak·ing** n

home·sick adj : longing for home — **home·sick·ness** n

home·spun \-,spən\ adj : simple

home·stead \-,sted\ n : home and land occupied and worked by a family — **home·stead·er** \-ər\ n

home·stretch n **1** : last part of a racetrack **2** : final stage

home·ward \-wərd\, **home·wards** \-wərdz\ adv : toward home — **homeward** adj

home·work n : school lessons to be done outside the classroom

hom·ey \'hōmē\ adj **hom·i·er; -est** : characteristic of home

ho·mi·cide \'hämə,sīd, 'hō-\ n : the killing of one human being by another — **hom·i·cid·al** \,hämə'sīd'l, ,hō-\ adj

hom·i·ly \'häməlē\ n, pl **-lies** : sermon

hom·i·ny \'hämənē\ n : type of processed hulled corn

ho·mo·ge·neous \,hōmə'jēnēəs, -nyəs\ adj : of the same or a similar kind — **ho·mo·ge·ne·i·ty** \-jə'nēətē\ n — **ho·mo·ge·neous·ly** adv

ho·mog·e·nize \hō'mäjə,nīz, hə-\ vb -**nized; -niz·ing** : make the particles in (as milk) of uniform size and even distribution — **ho·mog·e·ni·za·tion** \-,mäjənə'zāshən\ n — **ho·mog·e·niz·er** n

ho·mo·graph \'hämə,graf, 'hō-\ n : one of 2 or more words (as the noun conduct and the verb conduct) spelled alike but different in origin or meaning or pronunciation

hom·onym \'hämə,nim, 'hō-\ n **1** : homophone **2** : homograph **3** : one

of 2 or more words (as pool of water and pool the game) spelled and pronounced alike but different in meaning

ho·mo·phone \'hämə,fōn, 'hō-\ n : one of 2 or more words (as to, too, and two) pronounced alike but different in origin or meaning or spelling

Ho·mo sa·pi·ens \,hōmō'sapēənz, -'sā-\ n : humankind

ho·mo·sex·u·al \,hōmə'sekshəwəl\ adj : oriented toward one's own sex — **homosexual** n — **ho·mo·sex·u·al·i·ty** \-,seksha'walətē\ n

hone \'hōn\ vb : sharpen with or as if with an abrasive stone

hon·est \'änəst\ adj **1** : free from deception **2** : trustworthy **3** : frank — **hon·est·ly** adv — **hon·es·ty** \-əstē\ n

hon·ey \'hənē\ n, pl **-eys** : sweet sticky substance made by bees (**hon·ey-bees**) from the nectar of flowers

hon·ey·comb n : mass of 6-sided wax cells built by honeybees or something like it ∼ vb : make or become full of holes like a honeycomb

hon·ey·moon n : holiday taken by a newly married couple — **honey-moon** vb

hon·ey·suck·le \-,səkəl\ n : shrub or vine with flowers rich in nectar

honk \'häŋk, 'hȯŋk\ n : cry of a goose or a similar sound — **honk** vb — **honk·er** n

hon·or \'änər\ n **1** : good name **2** : outward respect or symbol of this **3** : privilege **4** : person of superior rank or position — used esp. as a title **5** : something or someone worthy of respect **6** : integrity ∼ vb **1** : regard with honor **2** : confer honor on **3** : fulfill the terms of — **hon·or·able** \'änərəbəl\ adj — **hon·or·ably** \-blē\ adv — **hon·or·ari·ly** \,änə'rerəlē\ adv — **hon·or·ary** \'änə,rerē\ adj — **hon·or·ee** \,änə'rē\ n

hood \'hud\ n **1** : part of a garment that covers the head **2** : covering over an automobile engine compartment — **hood·ed** adj

-hood \,hud\ n suffix **1** : state, condition, or quality **2** : individuals sharing a state or character

hood·lum \'hudləm, 'hud-\ n : thug

hood·wink \'hud,wiŋk\ vb : deceive

hoof \'huf, 'huf\ n, pl **hooves** \'huvz, 'huvz\ or **hoofs** : horny covering of the toes of some mammals (as horses or cattle) — **hoofed** \'hůft, 'hüft\ *adj*

hook \'hůk\ *n* : curved or bent device for catching, holding, or pulling ∼ *vb* : seize or make fast with a hook — **hook·er** *n*

hook·worm *n* : parasitic intestinal worm

hoo·li·gan \'hüligən\ *n* : thug

hoop \'hüp\ *n* : circular strip, figure, or object

hoot \'hüt\ *vb* **1** : shout in contempt **2** : make the cry of an owl — **hoot** *n* — **hoot·er** *n*

¹**hop** \'häp\ *vb* **-pp-** : move by quick springy leaps — **hop** *n*

²**hop** *n* : vine whose ripe dried flowers are used to flavor malt liquors

hope \'hōp\ *vb* **hoped; hop·ing** : desire with expectation of fulfillment ∼ *n* **1** : act of hoping **2** : something hoped for — **hope·ful** \-fəl\ *adj* — **hope·ful·ly** *adv* — **hope·ful·ness** *n* — **hope·less** *adj* — **hope·less·ly** *adv* — **hope·less·ness** *n*

hop·per \'häpər\ *n* : container that releases its contents through the bottom

horde \'hōrd\ *n* : throng or swarm

ho·ri·zon \hə'rīz³n\ *n* : apparent junction of earth and sky

hor·i·zon·tal \,hȯrə'zänt³l\ *adj* : parallel to the horizon — **hor·i·zon·tal·ly** *adv*

hor·mone \'hȯr,mōn\ *n* : cell product in body fluids that has a specific effect on other cells — **hor·mon·al** \hȯr'mōn³l\ *adj*

horn \'hȯrn\ *n* **1** : hard bony projection on the head of a hoofed animal **2** : brass wind instrument — **horned** *adj* — **horn·less** *adj*

hor·net \'hȯrnət\ *n* : large social wasp

horny \'hȯrnē\ *adj* **horn·i·er; -est** **1** : made of horn **2** : hard or callous **3** : sexually aroused

horo·scope \'hȯrə,skōp\ *n* : astrological forecast

hor·ren·dous \hȯ'rendəs\ *adj* : horrible

hor·ri·ble \'hȯrəbəl\ *adj* **1** : having or causing horror **2** : highly disagreeable — **hor·ri·ble·ness** *n* — **hor·ri·bly** \-blē\ *adv*

hor·rid \'hȯrəd\ *adj* : horrible — **hor·rid·ly** *adv*

hor·ri·fy \'hȯrə,fī\ *vb* **-fied; -fy·ing** : cause to feel horror

hor·ror \'hȯrər\ *n* **1** : intense fear, dread, or dismay **2** : intense repugnance **3** : something horrible

hors d'oeuvre \ȯr'dərv\ *n, pl* **hors d'oeuvres** \-'dərvz\ : appetizer

horse \'hȯrs\ *n* : large solid-hoofed domesticated mammal — **horse·back** *n or adv* — **horse·hair** *n* — **horse·hide** *n* — **horse·less** *adj* — **horse·man** \-mən\ *n* — **horse·man·ship** *n* — **horse·wom·an** *n* — **hors·ey, horsy** *adj*

horse·fly *n* : large fly with bloodsucking female

horse·play *n* : rough boisterous play

horse·pow·er *n* : unit of mechanical power

horse·rad·ish *n* : herb with a pungent root used as a condiment

horse·shoe *n* : U-shaped protective metal plate fitted to the rim of a horse's hoof

hor·ti·cul·ture \'hȯrtə,kəlchər\ *n* : science of growing fruits, vegetables, and flowers — **hor·ti·cul·tur·al** \,hȯrtə'kəlchərəl\ *adj* — **hor·ti·cul·tur·ist** \-rist\ *n*

ho·san·na \hō'zanə, -'zän-\ *interj* — used as a cry of acclamation and adoration — **hosanna** *n*

hose \'hōz\ *n* **1** *pl* **hose** : stocking or sock **2** *pl* **hos·es** : flexible tube for conveying fluids ∼ *vb* **hosed; hos·ing** : spray, water, or wash with a hose

ho·siery \'hōzhərē, 'hōzə-\ *n* : stockings or socks

hos·pice \'häspəs\ *n* **1** : lodging (as for travelers) maintained by a religious order **2** : facility or program for caring for dying persons

hos·pi·ta·ble \hä'spitəbəl, 'häs,pit-\ *adj* : given to generous and cordial reception of guests — **hos·pi·ta·bly** \-blē\ *adv*

hos·pi·tal \'häs,pit³l\ *n* : institution where the sick or injured receive medical care — **hos·pi·tal·iza·tion** \,häs,pit³lə'zāshən\ *n* — **hos·pi·tal·ize** \'häs,pit³l,īz\ *vb*

hos·pi·tal·i·ty \,häspə'talətē\ *n, pl* **-ties** : hospitable treatment, reception, or disposition

¹**host** \'hōst\ *n* **1** : army **2** : multitude

²**host** *n* : one who receives or entertains guests — **host** *vb*

³**host** *n* : eucharistic bread

hos·tage \'hästij\ *n* : person held to guarantee that promises be kept or demands met

hos·tel \'häst°l\ *n* : lodging for youth — **hos·tel·er** *n*

hos·tel·ry \-rē\ *n, pl* **-ries** : hotel

host·ess \'hōstəs\ *n* : woman who is host

hos·tile \'häst°l, -,tīl\ *adj* : openly or actively unfriendly or opposed to someone or something — **hostile** *n* — **hos·tile·ly** *adv* — **hos·til·i·ty** \häs'tilətē\ *n*

hot \'hät\ *adj* **-tt-** **1** : having a high temperature **2** : giving a sensation of heat or burning **3** : ardent **4** : pungent — **hot** *adv* — **hot·ly** *adv* — **hot·ness** *n*

hot·bed *n* : environment that favors rapid growth

hot dog *n* : frankfurter

ho·tel \hō'tel\ *n* : building where lodging and personal services are provided

hot·head·ed *adj* : impetuous — **hot·head** *n* — **hot·head·ed·ly** *adv* — **hot·head·ed·ness** *n*

hot·house *n* : greenhouse

hound \'haùnd\ *n* : long-eared hunting dog ~ *vb* : pursue relentlessly

hour \'aùər\ *n* **1** : 24th part of a day **2** : time of day — **hour·ly** *adv or adj*

hour·glass *n* : glass vessel for measuring time

house \'haùs\ *n, pl* **hous·es** \'haùzəz\ **1** : building to live in **2** : household **3** : legislative body **4** : business firm ~ \'haùz\ *vb* **housed; hous·ing** : provide with or take shelter — **house·boat** \'haùs,bōt\ *n* — **house·clean** \'haùs,klēn\ *vb* — **house·clean·ing** *n* — **house·ful** \-,fúl\ *n* — **house·maid** *n* — **house·wares** *n pl* — **house·work** *n*

house·bro·ken \-,brōkən\ *adj* : trained in excretory habits acceptable in indoor living

house·fly *n* : two-winged fly common about human habitations

house·hold \-,hōld\ *n* : those who dwell as a family under the same roof ~ *adj* **1** : domestic **2** : common or familiar — **house·hold·er** *n*

house·keep·ing \-,kēpiŋ\ *n* : care and management of a house or institution — **house·keep·er** *n*

house·warm·ing *n* : party to celebrate moving into a house

house·wife \'haùs,wīf\ *n* : married woman in charge of a household — **house·wife·ly** *adj* — **house·wif·ery** \-,wīfərē\ *n*

hous·ing \'haùziŋ\ *n* **1** : dwellings for people **2** : protective covering

hove *past of* HEAVE

hov·el \'həvəl, 'häv-\ *n* : small wretched house

hov·er \'həvər, 'häv-\ *vb* **1** : remain suspended in the air **2** : move about in the vicinity

how \'haù\ *adv* **1** : in what way or condition **2** : for what reason **3** : to what extent ~ *conj* : the way or manner in which

how·ev·er \haù'evər\ *conj* : in whatever manner ~ *adv* **1** : to whatever degree or in whatever manner **2** : in spite of that

how·it·zer \'haùətsər\ *n* : short cannon

howl \'haùl\ *vb* : emit a loud long doleful sound like a dog — **howl** *n* — **howl·er** *n*

hoy·den \'hȯid°n\ *n* : girl or woman of saucy or carefree behavior

hub \'həb\ *n* : central part of a circular object (as of a wheel) — **hub·cap** *n*

hub·bub \'həb,əb\ *n* : uproar

hu·bris \'hyübrəs\ *n* : excessive pride

huck·le·ber·ry \'həkəl,berē\ *n* **1** : shrub related to the blueberry or its berry **2** : blueberry

huck·ster \'həkstər\ *n* : peddler

hud·dle \'həd°l\ *vb* **-dled; -dling** **1** : crowd together **2** : confer — **huddle** *n*

hue \'hyü\ *n* : color or gradation of color — **hued** \'hyüd\ *adj*

huff \'həf\ *n* : fit of pique — **huffy** *adj*

hug \'həg\ *vb* **-gg-** **1** : press tightly in the arms **2** : stay close to — **hug** *n*

huge \'hyüj\ *adj* **hug·er; hug·est** : very large or extensive — **huge·ly** *adv* — **huge·ness** *n*

hu·la \'hülə\ *n* : Polynesian dance

hulk \'həlk\ *n* **1** : bulky or unwieldy person or thing **2** : old ship unfit for service — **hulk·ing** *adj*

hull \'həl\ *n* **1** : outer covering of a fruit or seed **2** : frame or body of a ship or boat ~ *vb* : remove the hulls of — **hull·er** *n*

hul·la·ba·loo \'hələbə,lü\ *n, pl* **-loos** : uproar

hum \'həm\ *vb* **-mm-** **1** : make a prolonged sound like that of the speech sound \m\ **2** : be busily active **3** : run smoothly **4** : sing with closed lips — **hum** *n* — **hum·mer** *n*

hu·man \'hyümən, 'yü-\ *adj* **1** : of or relating to the species people belong to **2** : by, for, or like people — **human** *n* — **hu·man·kind** *n* — **hu·man·ly** *adv* — **hu·man·ness** *n*

hu·mane \hyü'mān, ,yü-\ *adj* : showing compassion or consideration for others — **hu·mane·ly** *adv* — **hu·mane·ness** *n*

hu·man·ism \'hyümə,nizəm, 'yü-\ *n* : doctrine or way of life centered on human interests or values — **hu·man·ist** \-nist\ *n or adj* — **hu·man·is·tic** \,hyümə'nistik, ,yü-\ *adj*

hu·man·i·tar·i·an \hyü,manə'terēən, yü-\ *n* : person promoting human welfare — **humanitarian** *adj* — **hu·man·i·tari·an·ism** *n*

hu·man·i·ty \hyü'manətē, yü-\ *n, pl* **-ties 1** : human or humane quality or state **2** : the human race

hu·man·ize \'hyümə,nīz, 'yü-\ *vb* **-ized; -iz·ing** : make human or humane — **hu·man·iza·tion** \,hyümənə'zā-shən, ,yü-\ *n* — **hu·man·iz·er** *n*

hu·man·oid \'hyümə,nȯid, 'yü-\ *adj* : having human form — **humanoid** *n*

hum·ble \'həmbəl\ *adj* **-bler; -blest 1** : not proud or haughty **2** : not pretentious ~ *vb* **-bled; -bling** : make humble — **hum·ble·ness** *n* — **hum·bler** *n* — **hum·bly** \-blē\ *adv*

hum·bug \'həm,bəg\ *n* : nonsense

hum·drum \-,drəm\ *adj* : monotonous

hu·mid \'hyüməd, 'yü-\ *adj* : containing or characterized by moisture — **hu·mid·i·fi·ca·tion** \hyü,midəfə'kā-shən\ *n* — **hu·mid·i·fi·er** \-'midə-,fīər\ *n* — **hu·mid·i·fy** \-,fī\ *vb* — **hu·mid·ly** *adv*

hu·mid·i·ty \hyü'midətē, yü-\ *n, pl* **-ties** : atmospheric moisture

hu·mi·dor \'hyümə,dȯr, 'yü-\ *n* : humidified storage case (as for cigars)

hu·mil·i·ate \hyü'milē,āt, yü-\ *vb* **-at·ed; -at·ing** : injure the self-respect of — **hu·mil·i·at·ing·ly** *adv* — **hu·mil·i·ation** \-,milē'āshən\ *n*

hu·mil·i·ty \hyü'milətē, yü-\ *n* : humble quality or state

hum·ming·bird \'həmin,bərd\ *n* : tiny American bird that can hover

hum·mock \'həmək\ *n* : mound or knoll — **hum·mocky** \-məkē\ *adj*

hu·mor \'hyümər, 'yü-\ *n* **1** : mood **2** : quality of being laughably ludicrous or incongruous **3** : appreciation of what is ludicrous or incongruous **4** : something intended to be funny ~ *vb* : comply with the wishes or mood of — **hu·mor·ist** \-ərist\ *n* — **hu·mor·less** *adj* — **hu·mor·less·ly** *adv* — **hu·mor·less·ness** *n* — **hu·mor·ous** \'hyümərəs, 'yü-\ *adj* — **hu·mor·ous·ly** *adv* — **hu·mor·ous·ness** *n*

hump \'həmp\ *n* : rounded protuberance — **humped** *adj*

hump·back *n* : hunchback — **hump·backed** *adj*

hu·mus \'hyüməs, 'yü-\ *n* : dark organic part of soil

hunch \'hənch\ *vb* : assume or cause to assume a bent or crooked posture ~ *n* : strong intuitive feeling

hunch·back *n* **1** : back with a hump **2** : person with a crooked back — **hunch·backed** *adj*

hun·dred \'həndrəd\ *n, pl* **-dreds** *or* **-dred** : 10 times 10 — **hundred** *adj* — **hun·dredth** \-drədth\ *adj or n*

¹hung *past of* HANG

²hung *adj* : unable to reach a verdict

hun·ger \'həngər\ *n* **1** : craving or urgent need for food **2** : strong desire — **hunger** *vb* — **hun·gri·ly** \-grəlē\ *adv* — **hun·gry** *adj*

hunk \'həŋk\ *n* : large piece

hun·ker \'həŋkər\ *vb* : settle in for a sustained period — used with *down*

hunt \'hənt\ *vb* **1** : pursue for food or sport **2** : try to find ~ *n* **1** : act or instance of hunting — **hunt·er** *n*

hur·dle \'hərd²l\ *n* **1** : barrier to leap over in a race **2** : obstacle — **hurdle** *vb* — **hur·dler** *n*

hurl \'hərl\ *vb* : throw with violence — **hurl** *n* — **hurl·er** *n*

hur·rah \hù'rä, -'rȯ\ *interj* — used to express joy or approval

hur·ri·cane \'hərə,kān\ *n* : tropical storm with winds of 74 miles per hour or greater

hur·ry \'hərē\ *vb* **-ried; -ry·ing** : go or cause to go with haste ~ *n* : extreme haste — **hur·ried·ly** *adv* — **hur·ried·ness** *n*

hurt \'hərt\ *vb* **hurt; hurt·ing 1** : feel or cause pain **2** : do harm to ~ *n* **1** : bodily injury **2** : harm — **hurt·ful** \-fəl\ *adj* — **hurt·ful·ness** *n*

hur·tle \'hərt²l\ *vb* **-tled; -tling** : move rapidly or forcefully

hus·band \'həzbənd\ *n* : married man ~ *vb* : manage prudently

hus·band·ry \-bəndrē\ n 1 : careful use 2 : agriculture

hush \'həsh\ vb : make or become quiet ～ n : silence

husk \'həsk\ n : outer covering of a seed or fruit ～ vb : strip the husk from — **husk·er** n

¹**hus·ky** \'həskē\ adj -ki·er; -est : hoarse — **hus·ki·ly** adv — **hus·ki·ness** n

²**husky** adj -ki·er; -est : burly — **husk·i·ness** n

³**husky** n, pl **-kies** : working dog of the arctic

hus·sy \'həsē, -zē\ n, pl **-sies** 1 : brazen woman 2 : mischievous girl

hus·tle \'həsəl\ vb **-tled; -tling** 1 : hurry 2 : work energetically — **hustle** n — **hus·tler** \'həslər\ n

hut \'hət\ n : small often temporary dwelling

hutch \'həch\ n 1 : cupboard with open shelves 2 : pen for an animal

hy·a·cinth \'hīə,sinth\ n : bulbous herb grown for bell-shaped flowers

hy·brid \'hībrəd\ n : offspring of genetically differing parents — **hybrid** adj — **hy·brid·iza·tion** \,hībrədə'zāshən\ n — **hy·brid·ize** \'hībrəd,īz\ vb — **hy·brid·iz·er** n

hy·drant \'hīdrənt\ n : pipe from which water may be drawn to fight fires

hy·drau·lic \hī'drȯlik\ adj : operated by liquid forced through a small hole — **hy·drau·lics** \-liks\ n

hy·dro·car·bon \,hīdrə'kärbən\ n : organic compound of carbon and hydrogen

hy·dro·elec·tric \,hīdrōi'lektrik\ adj : producing electricity by waterpower — **hy·dro·elec·tric·i·ty** \-,lek-'trisətē\ n

hy·dro·gen \'hīdrəjən\ n : very light gaseous colorless odorless flammable chemical element

hydrogen bomb n : powerful bomb that derives its energy from the union of atomic nuclei

hy·dro·pho·bia \,hīdrə'fōbēə\ n : rabies

hy·dro·plane \'hīdrə,plān\ n : speedboat that skims the water

hy·drous \'hīdrəs\ adj : containing water

hy·e·na \hī'ēnə\ n : nocturnal carnivorous mammal of Asia and Africa

hy·giene \'hī,jēn\ n : conditions or practices conducive to health — **hy·gien·ic** \hī'jenik, -'jēn-; ,hījē'enik\ adj — **hy·gien·i·cal·ly** \-iklē\ adv — **hy·gien·ist** \hī'jēnist, -'jen-; 'hī,jēn-\ n

hy·grom·e·ter \hī'grämətər\ n : instrument for measuring atmospheric humidity

hying pres part of HIE

hymn \'him\ n : song of praise esp. to God — **hymn** vb

hym·nal \'himnəl\ n : book of hymns

hype \'hīp\ vb **hyped; hyp·ing** : publicize extravagantly — **hype** n

hyper- prefix 1 : above or beyond 2 : excessively or excessive

hy·per·bo·le \hī'pərbəlē\ n : extravagant exaggeration

hy·per·ten·sion \'hīpər,tenchən\ n : high blood pressure — **hy·per·ten·sive** \,hīpər'tensiv\ adj or n

hy·phen \'hīfən\ n : punctuation mark used to divide or compound words — **hyphen** vb

hy·phen·ate \'hīfə,nāt\ vb **-at·ed; -at·ing** : connect or divide with a hyphen — **hy·phen·ation** \,hīfə'nāshən\ n

hyp·no·sis \hip'nōsəs\ n, pl **-no·ses** \-,sēz\ : induced state like sleep in which the subject is responsive to suggestions of the inducer (**hyp·no·tist** \'hipnətist\) — **hyp·no·tism** \'hipnə,tizəm\ n — **hyp·no·tiz·able** \,hipnə'tīzəbəl\ adj — **hyp·no·tize** \'hipnə,tīz\ vb

---

List of self-explanatory words with the prefix hyper-

hyperacid	hyperenergetic	hypersensitive
hyperacidity	hyperexcitable	hypersensitiveness
hyperactive	hyperfastidious	hypersensitivity
hyperacute	hyperintense	hypersexual
hyperaggressive	hypermasculine	hypersusceptible
hypercautious	hypernationalistic	hypertense
hypercorrect	hyperreactive	hypervigilant
hypercritical	hyperrealistic	
hyperemotional	hyperromantic	

hyp·not·ic \hip'nätik\ *adj* : relating to hypnosis — **hypnotic** *n* — **hyp·not·i·cal·ly** \-iklē\ *adv*

hy·po·chon·dria \,hīpə'kändrēə\ *n* : morbid concern for one's health — **hy·po·chon·dri·ac** \-drē,ak\ *adj or n*

hy·poc·ri·sy \hip'äkrəsē\ *n, pl* **-sies** : a feigning to be what one is not — **hyp·o·crite** \'hipə,krit\ *n* — **hyp·o·crit·i·cal** \,hipə'kritikəl\ *adj* — **hyp·o·crit·i·cal·ly** *adv*

hy·po·der·mic \,hīpə'dərmik\ *adj* : administered or used in making an injection beneath the skin ~ *n* : hypodermic syringe

hy·pot·e·nuse \hī'pätə,nüs, -,nüz, -,nyüs, -,nyüz\ *n* : side of a right-angled triangle opposite the right angle

hy·poth·e·sis \hī'päthəsəs\ *n, pl* **-e·ses** \-,sēz\ : assumption made in order to test its consequences — **hy·poth·e·size** \-,sīz\ *vb* — **hy·po·thet·i·cal** \,hīpə'thetikəl\ *adj* — **hy·po·thet·i·cal·ly** *adv*

hys·ter·ec·to·my \,histə'rektəmē\ *n, pl* **-mies** : surgical removal of the uterus

hys·te·ria \his'terēə, -tir-\ *n* : uncontrollable fear or outburst of emotion — **hys·ter·i·cal** \-'terikəl\ *adj* — **hys·ter·i·cal·ly** *adv*

hys·ter·ics \-'teriks\ *n pl* : uncontrollable laughter or crying

I

i \'ī\ *n, pl* **i's** *or* **is** \'īz\ : 9th letter of the alphabet

I \'ī\ *pron* : the speaker

-ial *adj suffix* : of, relating to, or characterized by

-ian — see -AN

ibis \'ībəs\ *n, pl* **ibis** *or* **ibis·es** : wading bird with a down-curved bill

-ible — see -ABLE

ibu·pro·fen \,ībyū'prōfən\ *n* : drug used to relieve inflammation, pain, and fever

-ic \ik\ *adj suffix* : 1 : of, relating to, or being 2 : containing 3 : characteristic of 4 : marked by 5 : caused by

-ical \ikəl\ *adj suffix* : -ic — **-i·cal·ly** \iklē, -kəlē\ *adv suffix*

ice \'īs\ *n* : 1 : frozen water 2 : flavored frozen dessert ~ *vb* **iced; ic·ing** : 1 : freeze 2 : chill 3 : cover with icing

ice·berg \'īs,bərg\ *n* : large floating mass of ice

ice·box *n* : refrigerator

ice·break·er *n* : ship equipped to cut through ice

ice cream *n* : sweet frozen food

ice-skate *vb* : skate on ice — **ice skater** *n*

ich·thy·ol·o·gy \,ikthē'äləjē\ *n* : study of fishes — **ich·thy·ol·o·gist** \-jist\ *n*

ici·cle \'ī,sikəl\ *n* : hanging mass of ice

ic·ing \'īsiŋ\ *n* : sweet usu. creamy coating for baked goods

icon \'ī,kän\ *n* : 1 : religious image 2 : small picture on a computer screen identified with an available function

icon·o·clast \ī'känə,klast\ *n* : attacker of cherished beliefs or institutions — **icon·o·clasm** \-,klazəm\ *n*

icy \'īsē\ *adj* **ic·i·er; -est** : 1 : covered with or consisting of ice 2 : very cold — **ic·i·ly** *adv* — **ic·i·ness** *n*

id \'id\ *n* : unconscious instinctual part of the mind

idea \ī'dēə\ *n* : 1 : something imagined in the mind 2 : purpose or plan

ide·al \ī'dēəl\ *adj* : 1 : imaginary 2 : perfect ~ *n* : 1 : standard of excellence 2 : model 3 : aim — **ide·al·ly** *adv*

ide·al·ism \ī'dēə,lizəm\ *n* : adherence to ideals — **ide·al·ist** \-list\ *n* — **ide·al·is·tic** \ī,dēə'listik\ *adj* — **ide·al·is·ti·cal·ly** \-tiklē\ *adv*

ide·al·ize \ī'dēə,līz\ *vb* **-ized; -iz·ing** : think of or represent as ideal — **ide·al·iza·tion** \-,dēələ'zāshən\ *n*

iden·ti·cal \ī'dentikəl\ *adj* : 1 : being the same 2 : exactly or essentially alike

iden·ti·fi·ca·tion \ī,dentəfə'kāshən\ *n* : 1 : act of identifying 2 : evidence of identity

iden·ti·fy \ī'dentə,fī\ *vb* **-fied; -fy·ing** : 1 : associate 2 : establish the identity of — **iden·ti·fi·able** \ī,dentə'fīəbəl\ *adj* — **iden·ti·fi·er** \ī'dentə,fīər\ *n*

iden·ti·ty \ī'dentətē\ *n, pl* **-ties** : 1 : sameness of essential character 2

: individuality **3** : fact of being what is supposed

ide·ol·o·gy \ˌīdē'äləjē, id-\ n, pl **-gies** : body of beliefs — **ide·o·log·i·cal** \ˌīdēə'läjikəl, ˌid-\ adj

id·i·om \'idēəm\ n **1** : language peculiar to a person or group **2** : expression with a special meaning — **id·i·om·at·ic** \ˌidēə'matik\ adj — **id·i·om·at·i·cal·ly** \-iklē\ adv

id·i·o·syn·cra·sy \ˌidēō'siŋkrəsē\ n, pl -sies : personal peculiarity — **id·i·o·syn·crat·ic** \-ˌsin'kratik\ adj — **id·i·o·syn·crat·i·cal·ly** \-'kratiklē\ adv

id·i·ot \'idēət\ n : mentally retarded or foolish person — **id·i·o·cy** \-əsē\ n — **id·i·ot·ic** \ˌidē'ätik\ adj — **id·i·ot·i·cal·ly** \-iklē\ adv

idle \'īd°l\ adj **idler; idlest 1** : worthless **2** : inactive **3** : lazy ~ vb **idled; idling** : spend time doing nothing — **idle·ness** n — **idler** n — **idly** \'īdlē\ adv

idol \'īd°l\ n **1** : image of a god **2** : object of devotion — **idol·iza·tion** \ˌīd°lə'zāshən\ n — **idol·ize** \'īd°līz\ vb

idol·a·ter, idol·a·tor \ī'dälətər\ n : worshiper of idols — **idol·a·trous** \-trəs\ adj — **idol·a·try** \-trē\ n

idyll \'īd°l\ n : period of peace and contentment — **idyl·lic** \ī'dilik\ adj

-ier — see **-ER**

if \'if\ conj **1** : in the event that **2** : whether **3** : even though

-i·fy \ə₁fī\ vb suffix : -fy

ig·loo \'iglü\ n, pl **-loos** : hut made of snow blocks

ig·nite \ig'nīt\ vb **-nited; -nit·ing** : set afire or catch fire — **ig·nit·able** \-'nītəbəl\ adj

ig·ni·tion \ig'nishən\ n **1** : a setting on fire **2** : process or means of igniting fuel

ig·no·ble \ig'nōbəl\ adj : not honorable — **ig·no·bly** \-blē\ adv

ig·no·min·i·ous \ˌignə'minēəs\ adj **1** : dishonorable **2** : humiliating — **ig·no·min·i·ous·ly** adv — **ig·no·mi·ny** \'ignə₁minē, ig'nämənē\ n

ig·no·ra·mus \ˌignə'rāməs\ n : ignorant person

ig·no·rant \'ignərənt\ adj **1** : lacking knowledge **2** : showing a lack of knowledge or intelligence **3** : unaware — **ig·no·rance** \-rəns\ n — **ig·no·rant·ly** adv

ig·nore \ig'nōr\ vb **-nored; -nor·ing** : refuse to notice

igua·na \i'gwänə\ n : large tropical American lizard

ilk \'ilk\ n : kind

ill \'il\ adj **worse** \'wərs\; **worst** \'wərst\ **1** : sick **2** : bad **3** : rude or unacceptable **4** : hostile ~ adv **worse; worst 1** : with displeasure **2** : harshly **3** : scarcely **4** : badly ~ n **1** : evil **2** : misfortune **3** : sickness

il·le·gal \il'lēgəl\ adj : not lawful — **il·le·gal·i·ty** \ˌili'galətē\ n — **il·le·gal·ly** \il'lēgəlē\ adv

il·leg·i·ble \il'lejəbəl\ adj : not legible — **il·leg·i·bil·i·ty** \il,lejə'bilətē\ n — **il·leg·i·bly** \il'lejəblē\ adv

il·le·git·i·mate \ˌili'jitəmət\ adj **1** : born of unmarried parents **2** : illegal — **il·le·git·i·ma·cy** \-əməsē\ n — **il·le·git·i·mate·ly** adv

il·lic·it \il'lisət\ adj : not lawful — **il·lic·it·ly** adv

il·lim·it·able \il'limətəbəl\ adj : boundless — **il·lim·it·ably** \-blē\ adv

il·lit·er·ate \il'litərət\ adj : unable to read or write — **il·lit·er·a·cy** \-ərəsē\ n — **illiterate** n

ill-na·tured \-'nāchərd\ adj : cross — **ill-na·tured·ly** adv

ill·ness \'ilnəs\ n : sickness

il·log·i·cal \il'läjikəl\ adj : contrary to sound reasoning — **il·log·i·cal·ly** adv

ill-starred \'il'stärd\ adj : unlucky

il·lu·mi·nate \il'ümə₁nāt\ vb **-nat·ed; -nat·ing 1** : light up **2** : make clear — **il·lu·mi·nat·ing·ly** \-₁nātiŋlē\ adv — **il·lu·mi·na·tion** \-₁ümə'nāshən\ n

ill-use \-'yüz\ vb : abuse — **ill-use** \-'yüs\ n

il·lu·sion \il'üzhən\ n **1** : mistaken idea **2** : misleading visual image

il·lu·so·ry \il'üsərē, -'üz-\ adj : based on or producing illusion

il·lus·trate \'iləs₁trāt\ vb **-trat·ed; -trat·ing 1** : explain by example **2** : provide with pictures or figures — **il·lus·tra·tor** \-ər\ n

il·lus·tra·tion \ˌiləs'trāshən\ n **1** : example that explains **2** : pictorial explanation

il·lus·tra·tive \il'əstrətiv\ adj : designed to illustrate — **il·lus·tra·tive·ly** adv

il·lus·tri·ous \-trēəs\ adj : notably or

brilliantly outstanding — **il·lus·tri·ous·ness** n

ill will n : unfriendly feeling

im·age \'imij\ n 1 : likeness 2 : visual counterpart of an object formed by a lens or mirror 3 : mental picture ~ vb **-aged; -ag·ing** : create a representation of

im·ag·ery \'imijrē\ n 1 : images 2 : figurative language

imag·i·nary \im'ajə,nerē\ adj : existing only in the imagination

imag·i·na·tion \im,ajə'nāshən\ n 1 : act or power of forming a mental image 2 : creative ability — **imag·i·na·tive** \im'ajənativ, -ə,nātiv\ adj — **imag·i·na·tive·ly** adv

imag·ine \im'ajən\ vb **-ined; -in·ing** : form a mental picture of something not present — **imag·in·able** \-'ajənəbəl\ adj — **imag·in·ably** \-blē\ adv

im·bal·ance \im'baləns\ n : lack of balance

im·be·cile \'imbəsəl, -,sil\ n : idiot — imbecile, **im·be·cil·ic** \,imbə'silik\ adj — **im·be·cil·i·ty** \-'silətē\ n

im·bibe \im'bīb\ vb **-bibed; -bib·ing** : drink — **im·bib·er** n

im·bro·glio \im'brōlyō\ n, pl **-glios** : complicated situation

im·bue \-'byü\ vb **-bued; -bu·ing** : fill (as with color or a feeling)

im·i·tate \'imə,tāt\ vb **-tat·ed; -tat·ing** 1 : follow as a model 2 : mimic — **im·i·ta·tive** \-,tātiv\ adj — **im·i·ta·tor** \-ər\ n

im·i·ta·tion \,imə'tāshən\ n 1 : act of imitating 2 : copy — **imitation** adj

im·mac·u·late \im'akyələt\ adj : without stain or blemish — **im·mac·u·late·ly** adv

im·ma·te·ri·al \,imə'tirēəl\ adj 1 : spiritual 2 : not relevant — **im·ma·te·ri·al·i·ty** \-,tirē'alətē\ n

im·ma·ture \,imə'túr, -'tyúr\ adj : not yet mature — **im·ma·tu·ri·ty** \-ətē\ n

im·mea·sur·able \im'ezhərəbəl\ adj : indefinitely extensive — **im·mea·sur·ably** \-blē\ adv

im·me·di·a·cy \im'ēdēəsē\ n, pl **-cies** : quality or state of being urgent

im·me·di·ate \-ēət\ adj 1 : direct 2 : being next in line 3 : made or done at once 4 : not distant — **im·me·di·ate·ly** adv

im·me·mo·ri·al \,imə'mōrēəl\ adj : old beyond memory

im·mense \im'ens\ adj : vast — **im·mense·ly** adv — **im·men·si·ty** \-'ensətē\ n

im·merse \im'ərs\ vb **-mersed; -mers·ing** 1 : plunge or dip into liquid 2 : engross — **im·mer·sion** \-'ərzhən\ n

im·mi·grant \'imigrənt\ n : one that immigrates

im·mi·grate \'imə,grāt\ vb **-grat·ed; -grat·ing** : come into a place and take up residence — **im·mi·gra·tion** \,imə'grāshən\ n

im·mi·nent \'imənənt\ adj : ready to take place — **im·mi·nence** \-nəns\ n — **im·mi·nent·ly** adv

im·mo·bile \im'ōbəl\ adj : incapable of being moved — **im·mo·bil·i·ty** \,imō'bilətē\ n — **im·mo·bi·lize** \im'ōbə,līz\ vb

im·mod·er·ate \im'ädərət\ adj : not moderate — **im·mod·er·a·cy** \-ərəsē\ n — **im·mod·er·ate·ly** adv

im·mod·est \im'ädəst\ adj : not modest — **im·mod·est·ly** adv — **im·mod·es·ty** \-əstē\ n

im·mo·late \'imə,lāt\ vb **-lat·ed; -lat·ing** : offer in sacrifice — **im·mo·la·tion** \,imə'lāshən\ n

im·mor·al \im'órəl\ adj : not moral — **im·mo·ral·i·ty** \,imó'ralətē, ,imə-\ n — **im·mor·al·ly** adv

im·mor·tal \im'órt³l\ adj 1 : not mortal 2 : having lasting fame ~ n : one exempt from death or oblivion — **im·mor·tal·i·ty** \,im,ór'talətē\ n — **im·mor·tal·ize** \im'órt³l,īz\ vb

im·mov·able \im'üvəbəl\ adj 1 : stationary 2 : unyielding — **im·mov·abil·i·ty** \im,üvə'bilətē\ n — **im·mov·ably** adv

im·mune \im'yün\ adj : not liable esp. to disease — **im·mu·ni·ty** \im'yünətē\ n — **im·mu·ni·za·tion** \,imyənə'zāshən\ n — **im·mu·nize** \'imyə,nīz\ vb

im·mu·nol·o·gy \,imyə'näləjē\ n : science of immunity to disease — **im·mu·no·log·ic** \-yən°l'äjik\, **im·mu·no·log·i·cal** \-ikəl\ adj — **im·mu·nol·o·gist** \imyə'näləjist\ n

im·mu·ta·ble \im'yütəbəl\ adj : unchangeable — **im·mu·ta·bil·i·ty** \im,yütə'bilətē\ n — **im·mu·ta·bly** adv

imp \'imp\ n 1 : demon 2 : mischievous child

im·pact \im'pakt\ *vb* **1** : press close **2** : have an effect on ~ \'im,pakt\ *n* **1** : forceful contact **2** : influence

im·pact·ed \im'paktəd\ *adj* : wedged between the jawbone and another tooth

im·pair \im'par\ *vb* : diminish in quantity, value, or ability — **im·pair·ment** *n*

im·pa·la \im'palə\ *n, pl* **impalas** or **impala** : large African antelope

im·pale \im'pāl\ *vb* **-paled; -pal·ing** : pierce with something pointed

im·pal·pa·ble \im'palpəbəl\ *adj* : incapable of being felt — **im·pal·pa·bly** *adv*

im·pan·el \im'pan°l\ *vb* : enter in or on a panel

im·part \-'pärt\ *vb* : give from or as if from a store

im·par·tial \im'pärshəl\ *adj* : not partial — **im·par·tial·i·ty** \im,pärshē-'alətē\ *n* — **im·par·tial·ly** *adv*

im·pass·able \im'pasəbəl\ *adj* : not passable — **im·pass·ably** \-'pasəblē\ *adv*

im·passe \'im,pas\ *n* : inescapable predicament

im·pas·sioned \im'pashənd\ *adj* : filled with passion

im·pas·sive \im'pasiv\ *adj* : showing no feeling or interest — **im·pas·sive·ly** *adv* — **im·pas·siv·i·ty** \im,pas-'ivətē\ *n*

im·pa·tiens \im'pāshənz, -shəns\ *n* : annual herb with showy flowers

im·pa·tient \im'pāshənt\ *adj* : not patient — **im·pa·tience** \-shəns\ *n* — **im·pa·tient·ly** *adv*

im·peach \im'pēch\ *vb* **1** : charge (an official) with misconduct **2** : cast doubt on **3** : remove from office for misconduct — **im·peach·ment** *n*

im·pec·ca·ble \im'pekəbəl\ *adj* : faultless — **im·pec·ca·bly** *adv*

im·pe·cu·nious \,impi'kyünēəs\ *adj* : broke — **im·pe·cu·nious·ness** *n*

im·pede \im'pēd\ *vb* **-ped·ed; -ped·ing** : interfere with

im·ped·i·ment \-'pedəmənt\ *n* **1** : hindrance **2** : speech defect

im·pel \-'pel\ *vb* **-pelled; -pel·ling** : urge forward

im·pend \-'pend\ *vb* : be about to occur

im·pen·e·tra·ble \im'penətrəbəl\ *adj* : incapable of being penetrated or understood — **im·pen·e·tra·bil·i·ty** \im,penətrə'bilətē\ *n* — **im·pen·e·tra·bly** *adv*

im·pen·i·tent \im'penətənt\ *adj* : not penitent — **im·pen·i·tence** \-təns\ *n*

im·per·a·tive \im'perətiv\ *adj* **1** : expressing a command **2** : urgent ~ *n* **1** : imperative mood or verb form **2** : unavoidable fact, need, or obligation — **im·per·a·tive·ly** *adv*

im·per·cep·ti·ble \,impər'septəbəl\ *adj* : not perceptible — **im·per·cep·ti·bly** *adv*

im·per·fect \im'pərfikt\ *adj* : not perfect — **im·per·fec·tion** *n* — **im·per·fect·ly** *adv*

im·pe·ri·al \im'pirēəl\ *adj* **1** : relating to an empire or an emperor **2** : royal

im·pe·ri·al·ism \im'pirēə,lizəm\ *n* : policy of controlling other nations — **im·pe·ri·al·ist** \-list\ *n or adj* — **im·pe·ri·al·is·tic** \-,pirē'listik\ *adj* — **im·pe·ri·al·is·ti·cal·ly** \-tiklē\ *adv*

im·per·il \im'perəl\ *vb* **-iled** or **-illed; -il·ing** or **-il·ling** : endanger

im·pe·ri·ous \im'pirēəs\ *adj* : arrogant or domineering — **im·pe·ri·ous·ly** *adv*

im·per·ish·able \im'perishəbəl\ *adj* : not perishable

im·per·ma·nent \-'pərmənənt\ *adj* : not permanent — **im·per·ma·nent·ly** *adv*

im·per·me·able \-'pərmēəbəl\ *adj* : not permeable

im·per·mis·si·ble \,impər'misəbəl\ *adj* : not permissible

im·per·son·al \im'pərs°nəl\ *adj* : not involving human personality or emotion — **im·per·son·al·i·ty** \im,pərs°n-'alətē\ *n* — **im·per·son·al·ly** *adv*

im·per·son·ate \im'pərs°n,āt\ *vb* **-at·ed; -at·ing** : assume the character of — **im·per·son·a·tion** \-,pərs°n-'āshən\ *n* — **im·per·son·a·tor** \-'pərs°n,ātər\ *n*

im·per·ti·nent \im'pərt°nənt\ *adj* **1** : irrelevant **2** : insolent — **im·per·ti·nence** \-°nəns\ *n* — **im·per·ti·nent·ly** *adv*

im·per·turb·able \,impər'tərbəbəl\ *adj* : calm and steady

im·per·vi·ous \im'pərvēəs\ *adj* : incapable of being penetrated or affected

im·pet·u·ous \im'pechəwəs\ *adj* : impulsive — **im·pet·u·os·i·ty** \im,pechə'wäsətē\ *n* — **im·pet·u·ous·ly** *adv*

im·pe·tus \'impətəs\ *n* : driving force

im·pi·e·ty \im'pīətē\ *n* : quality or state of being impious

im·pinge \im'pinj\ *vb* **-pinged; -ping·ing** : encroach — **im·pinge·ment** \-mənt\ *n*

im·pi·ous \'impēəs, im'pī-\ adj : not pious

imp·ish \'impish\ adj : mischievous — **imp·ish·ly** adv — **imp·ish·ness** n

im·pla·ca·ble \im'plakəbəl, -'plā-\ adj : not capable of being appeased or changed — **im·pla·ca·bil·i·ty** \im-ˌplakə'bilətē, -ˌplā-\ n — **im·pla·ca·bly** \im'plakəblē\ adv

im·plant \im'plant\ vb 1 : set firmly or deeply 2 : fix in the mind or spirit ~ \'im‚plant\ n : something implanted in tissue — **im·plan·ta·tion** \ˌim-ˌplan'tāshən\ n

im·plau·si·ble \im'plózəbəl\ adj : not plausible — **im·plau·si·bil·i·ty** \im-ˌplózə'bilətē\ n

im·ple·ment \'impləmənt\ n : tool, utensil ~ \-ˌment\ vb : put into practice — **im·ple·men·ta·tion** \ˌimpləmən'tāshən\ n

im·pli·cate \'implə‚kāt\ vb -cat·ed; -cat·ing : involve

im·pli·ca·tion \ˌimplə'kāshən\ n 1 : an implying 2 : something implied

im·plic·it \im'plisət\ adj 1 : understood though only implied 2 : complete and unquestioning — **im·plic·it·ly** adv

im·plode \im'plōd\ vb -plod·ed; -plod·ing : burst inward — **im·plo·sion** \-'plōzhən\ n — **im·plo·sive** \-'plōsiv\ adj

im·plore \im'plōr\ vb -plored; -plor·ing : entreat

im·ply \-'plī\ vb -plied; -ply·ing : express indirectly

im·po·lite \ˌimpə'līt\ adj : not polite

im·pol·i·tic \im'päləˌtik\ adj : not politic

im·pon·der·a·ble \im'pändərəbəl\ adj : incapable of being precisely evaluated — **imponderable** n

¹im·port \im'pōrt\ vb 1 : mean 2 : bring in from an external source ~ \'im‚pōrt\ n 1 : meaning 2 : importance 3 : something imported — **im·por·ta·tion** \ˌim‚pōr'tāshən\ n — **im·port·er** n

im·por·tant \im'pōrtənt\ adj : having great worth, significance, or influence — **im·por·tance** \-ᵊns\ n — **im·por·tant·ly** adv

im·por·tu·nate \im'pōrchənət\ adj : troublesomely persistent or urgent

im·por·tune \ˌimpər'tün, -'tyün; im-'pōrchən\ vb -tuned; -tun·ing : urge or beg persistently — **im·por·tu·ni·ty** \ˌimpər'tünətē, -'tyü-\ n

ing 1 : establish as compulsory 2 : take unwarranted advantage of — **im·po·si·tion** \ˌimpə'zishən\ n

im·pos·ing \im'pōziŋ\ adj : impressive — **im·pos·ing·ly** adv

im·pos·si·ble \im'päsəbəl\ adj 1 : incapable of occurring 2 : enormously difficult — **im·pos·si·bil·i·ty** \im-ˌpäsə'bilətē\ n — **im·pos·si·bly** \im-'päsəblē\ adv

¹im·post \'im‚pōst\ n : tax

im·pos·tor, im·pos·ter \im'pästər\ n : one who assumes an identity or title to deceive — **im·pos·ture** \-'päs-chər\ n

im·po·tent \'impətənt\ adj : lacking power 2 : sterile — **im·po·tence** \-pətəns\ n — **im·po·ten·cy** \-ᵊnsē\ n — **im·po·tent·ly** adv

im·pound \im'paund\ vb : seize and hold in legal custody — **im·pound·ment** n

im·pov·er·ish \im'pävərish\ vb : make poor — **im·pov·er·ish·ment** n

im·prac·ti·ca·ble \im'praktikəbəl\ adj : not practicable

im·prac·ti·cal \-'praktikəl\ adj : not practical

im·pre·cise \ˌimpri'sīs\ adj : not precise — **im·pre·cise·ly** adv — **im·pre·cise·ness** n — **im·pre·ci·sion** \-'sizhən\ n

im·preg·na·ble \im'pregnəbəl\ adj : able to resist attack — **im·preg·na·bil·i·ty** \im‚pregnə'bilətē\ n

im·preg·nate \im'preg‚nāt\ vb -nat·ed; -nat·ing 1 : make pregnant 2 : cause to be filled, permeated, or saturated — **im·preg·na·tion** \ˌim-ˌpreg'nāshən\ n

im·pre·sa·rio \ˌimprə'särē‚ō\ n, pl -ri·os : one who sponsors an entertainment

¹im·press \im'pres\ vb 1 : apply with or produce by pressure 2 : press, stamp, or print in or upon 3 : produce a vivid impression of 4 : affect (as the mind) forcibly

²im·press \im'pres\ vb : force into naval service — **im·press·ment** n

im·pres·sion \im'preshən\ n 1 : mark made by impressing 2 : marked influence or effect 3 : printed copy 4 : vague notion or recollection — **im·pres·sion·able** \-'preshənəbəl\ adj

im·pres·sive \im'presiv\ adj : making a marked impression — **im·pres·sive·ly** adv — **im·pres·sive·ness** n

im·pri·ma·tur \ˌimprə'mä‚túr\ n : official approval (as of a publication by a censor)

im·print \im'print, 'im,-\ *vb* : stamp or mark by or as if by pressure ~ \'im,-\ *n* : something imprinted or printed

im·pris·on \im'priz'n\ *vb* : put in prison — **im·pris·on·ment** \-mənt\ *n*

im·prob·a·ble \im'präbəbəl\ *adj* : unlikely to be true or to occur — **im·prob·a·bil·i·ty** \im,präbə'bilətē\ *n* — **im·prob·a·bly** *adv*

im·promp·tu \im'prämptü, -tyü\ *adj* : not planned beforehand — **impromptu** *adv or n*

im·prop·er \im'präpər\ *adj* : not proper — **im·prop·er·ly** *adv*

im·pro·pri·ety \,imprə'prīətē\ *n, pl* **-eties** : state or instance of being improper

im·prove \im'prüv\ *vb* **-proved; -proving** : grow or make better — **im·prov·able** \-'prüvəbəl\ *adj* — **im·prove·ment** *n*

im·prov·i·dent \im'prävədənt\ *adj* : not providing for the future — **im·prov·i·dence** \-əns\ *n*

im·pro·vise \im'prə,vīz\ *vb* **-vised; -vising** : make, invent, or arrange offhand — **im·pro·vi·sa·tion** \im,prävə-'zāshən, ,imprəvə-\ *n* — **im·pro·vis·er, im·pro·vi·sor** \'imprə,vīzər\ *n*

im·pru·dent \im'prüd'nt\ *adj* : not prudent — **im·pru·dence** \-'ns\ *n*

im·pu·dent \'impyədənt\ *adj* : insolent — **im·pu·dence** \-əns\ *n* — **im·pu·dent·ly** *adv*

im·pugn \im'pyün\ *vb* : attack as false

im·pulse \'im,pəls\ *n* **1** : moving force **2** : sudden inclination

im·pul·sive \im'pəlsiv\ *adj* : acting on impulse — **im·pul·sive·ly** *adv* — **im·pul·sive·ness** *n*

im·pu·ni·ty \im'pyünətē\ *n* : exemption from punishment or harm

im·pure \im'pyur\ *adj* : not pure — **im·pu·ri·ty** \-'pyurətē\ *n*

im·pute \im'pyüt\ *vb* **-put·ed; -put·ing** : credit to or blame on a person or cause — **im·pu·ta·tion** \,impyə-'tāshən\ *n*

in \'in\ *prep* **1** — used to indicate location, inclusion, situation, or manner **2** : into **3** : during ~ *adv* : to or toward the inside ~ *adj* : located inside

in- \in\ *prefix* **1** : not **2** : lack of

in·ad·ver·tent \,inəd'vərt'nt\ *adj* : unintentional — **in·ad·ver·tence** \-'ns\ *n* — **in·ad·ver·ten·cy** \-'nsē\ *n* — **in·ad·ver·tent·ly** *adv*

in·alien·able \in'ālyənəbəl, -'ālēənə-\ *adj* : incapable of being transferred or given up — **in·alien·abil·i·ty** \-,ālyənə'bilətē, -'ālēənə-\ *n* — **in·alien·ably** *adv*

inane \in'ān\ *adj* **inan·er; -est** : silly or stupid — **inan·i·ty** \in'anətē\ *n*

in·an·i·mate \in'anəmət\ *adj* : not animate or animated — **in·an·i·mate·ly** *adv* — **in·an·i·mate·ness** *n*

in·ap·pre·cia·ble \,inə'prēshəbəl\ *adj* : too small to be perceived — **in·ap·pre·cia·bly** *adv*

in·ar·tic·u·late \,inär'tikyələt\ *adj* : without the power of speech or effective expression — **in·ar·tic·u·late·ly** *adv*

in·as·much as \,inaz'məchaz\ *conj* : because

in·at·ten·tion \,inə'tenchən\ *n* : failure to pay attention

in·au·gu·ral \in'ógyərəl, -gərəl\ *adj* : relating to an inauguration ~ *n* **1** : inaugural speech **2** : inauguration

in·au·gu·rate \in'ógyə,rāt, -gə-\ *vb* **-rat·ed; -rat·ing 1** : install in office **2** : start — **in·au·gu·ra·tion** \-,ógyə-'rāshən, -gə-\ *n*

in·board \'in,bórd\ *adv* : inside a vehicle or craft — **inboard** *adj*

in·born \'in,bórn\ *adj* : present from birth

in·bred \'in,bred\ *adj* : deeply ingrained in one's nature

in·breed·ing \'in,brēdiŋ\ *n* : interbreeding of closely related individuals — **in·breed** \-'brēd\ *vb*

in·cal·cu·la·ble \in'kalkyələbəl\ *adj*

List of self-explanatory words with the prefix *in-*

inability	inactivity	inadvisable
inaccessibility	inadequacy	inapparent
inaccessible	inadequate	inapplicable
inaccuracy	inadequately	inapposite
inaccurate	inadmissibility	inappositely
inaction	inadmissible	inappositeness
inactive	inadvisability	inappreciative

in·cal·cu·la·bly *adv* : too large to be calculated

in·can·des·cent \,inkən'des°nt\ *adj* **1** : glowing with heat **2** : brilliant — **in·can·des·cence** \-°ns\ *n*

in·can·ta·tion \,in,kan'tāshən\ *n* : use of spoken or sung charms or spells as a magic ritual

in·ca·pac·i·tate \,inkə'pasə,tāt\ *vb* **-tat·ed; -tat·ing** : disable

in·ca·pac·i·ty \,inkə'pasətē\ *n, pl* **-ties** : quality or state of being incapable

in·car·cer·ate \in'kärsə,rāt\ *vb* **-at·ed; -at·ing** : imprison — **in·car·cer·a·tion** \in,kärsə'rāshən\ *n*

in·car·nate \in'kärnət, -,nāt\ *adj* : having bodily form and substance — **in·car·nate** \-,nāt\ *vb* — **in·car·na·tion** \-,kär'nāshən\ *n*

in·cen·di·ary \in'sendē,erē\ *adj* **1** : pertaining to or used to ignite fire **2** : tending to excite — **incendiary** *n*

in·cense \'in,sens\ *n* : material burned to produce a fragrant odor or its smoke ~ \in'sens\ *vb* **-censed; -cens·ing** : make very angry

in·cen·tive \in'sentiv\ *n* : inducement to do something

in·cep·tion \in'sepshən\ *n* : beginning

in·ces·sant \in'ses°nt\ *adj* : continuing without interruption — **in·ces·sant·ly** *adv*

in·cest \'in,sest\ *n* : sexual intercourse between close relatives — **in·ces·tu·ous** \in'seschəwəs\ *adj*

inch \'inch\ *n* : unit of length equal to $\frac{1}{12}$ foot ~ *vb* : move by small degrees

in·cho·ate \in'kōət, 'inkə,wāt\ *adj* : new and not fully formed or ordered

in·ci·dent \'insədənt\ *n* : occurrence — **in·ci·dence** \-əns\ *n* — **incident** *adj*

in·ci·den·tal \,insə'dent°l\ *adj* **1** : subordinate, nonessential, or attendant **2** : met by chance ~ *n* **1** : something incidental **2** *pl* : minor expenses that are not itemized — **in·ci·den·tal·ly** *adv*

in·cin·er·ate \in'sinə,rāt\ *vb* **-at·ed;**

-at·ing : burn to ashes — **in·cin·er·a·tor** \-,rātər\ *n*

in·cip·i·ent \in'sipēənt\ *adj* : beginning to be or appear

in·cise \in'sīz\ *vb* **-cised; -cis·ing** : carve into

in·ci·sion \in'sizhən\ *n* : surgical cut

in·ci·sive \in'sīsiv\ *adj* : keen and discerning — **in·ci·sive·ly** *adv*

in·ci·sor \in'sīzər\ *n* : tooth for cutting

in·cite \in'sīt\ *vb* **-cit·ed; -cit·ing** : arouse to action — **in·cite·ment** *n*

in·ci·vil·i·ty \,insə'vilətē\ *n* : rudeness

in·clem·ent \in'klemənt\ *adj* : stormy — **in·clem·en·cy** \-ənsē\ *n*

in·cline \in'klīn\ *vb* **-clined; -clin·ing** **1** : bow **2** : tend toward an opinion **3** : slope ~ *n* : slope — **in·cli·na·tion** \inklə'nāshən\ *n* — **in·clin·er** *n*

inclose, inclosure *var of* ENCLOSE, ENCLOSURE

in·clude \in'klüd\ *vb* **-clud·ed; -clud·ing** : take in or comprise — **in·clu·sion** \in'klüzhən\ *n* — **in·clu·sive** \-'klüsiv\ *adj*

in·cog·ni·to \,in,käg'nētō, in'kägnə,tō\ *adv or adj* : with one's identity concealed

in·come \'in,kəm\ *n* : money gained (as from work or investment)

in·com·ing \'in,kəmiŋ\ *adj* : coming in

in·com·mu·ni·ca·do \,inkə,myünə'kädō\ *adv or adj* : without means of communication

in·com·pa·ra·ble \in'kämpərəbəl\ *adj* : eminent beyond comparison

in·com·pe·tent \in'kämpətənt\ *adj* : lacking sufficient knowledge or skill — **in·com·pe·tence** \-pətəns\ *n* — **in·com·pe·ten·cy** \-ənsē\ *n* — **incompetent** *n*

in·con·ceiv·able \,inkən'sēvəbəl\ *adj* **1** : impossible to comprehend **2** : unbelievable — **in·con·ceiv·ably** \-blē\ *adv*

in·con·gru·ous \in'käŋgrəwəs\ *adj* : inappropriate or out of place — **in·con·gru·i·ty** \,inkən'grüətē, -,kän-\ *n* — **in·con·gru·ous·ly** *adv*

in·con·se·quen·tial \,in,känsə'kwen-**

inapproachable	inartistically	inauthentic
inappropriate	inattentive	incapability
inappropriately	inattentively	incapable
inappropriateness	inattentiveness	incautious
inapt	inaudible	incoherence
inarguable	inaudibly	incoherent
inartistic	inauspicious	incoherently

chəl\ *adj* : unimportant — **in·con·se·quence** \in'känsə,kwens\ *n* — **in·con·se·quen·tial·ly** *adv*

in·con·sid·er·able \,inkən'sidərəbəl\ *adj* : trivial

in·con·sol·able \,inkən'sōləbəl\ *adj* : incapable of being consoled — **in·con·sol·ably** *adv*

in·con·ve·nience \,inkən'vēnyəns\ *n* 1 : discomfort 2 : something that causes trouble or annoyance ~ *vb* : cause inconvenience to — **in·con·ve·nient** \,inkən'vēnyənt\ *adj* — **in·con·ve·nient·ly** *adv*

in·cor·po·rate \in'kórpə,rāt\ *vb* -rat·ed; -rat·ing 1 : blend 2 : form into a legal body — **in·cor·po·rat·ed** *adj* — **in·cor·po·ra·tion** \-,kórpə'rāshən\ *n*

in·cor·ri·gi·ble \in'kórəjəbəl\ *adj* : incapable of being corrected or reformed — **in·cor·ri·gi·bil·i·ty** \in,kórəjə'bilətē\ *n*

in·crease \in'krēs, 'in,krēs\ *vb* -creased; -creas·ing : make or become greater ~ \'in,-, in'-\ *n* 1 : enlargement in size 2 : something added — **in·creas·ing·ly** \-'krēsiŋlē\ *adv*

in·cred·i·ble \in'kredəbəl\ *adj* : too extraordinary to be believed — **in·cred·i·bil·i·ty** \in,kredə'bilətē\ *n* — **in·cred·i·bly** \in'kredəblē\ *adv*

in·cred·u·lous \in'krejələs\ *adj* : skeptical — **in·cre·du·li·ty** \inkri-'dül·ətē, -'dyü-\ *n* — **in·cred·u·lous·ly** *adv*

in·cre·ment \'iŋkrəmənt, 'in-\ *n* : increase or amount of increase — **in·cre·men·tal** \iŋkrə'ment²l, ,in-\ *adj*

in·crim·i·nate \in'krimə,nāt\ *vb* -nat·ed; -nat·ing : show to be guilty of a crime — **in·crim·i·na·tion** \-,krimə-'nāshən\ *n* — **in·crim·i·na·to·ry** \-'krimənə,tōrē\ *adj*

in·cu·bate \'iŋkyə,bāt, 'in-\ *vb* -bat·ed; -bat·ing : keep (as eggs) under conditions favorable for development — **in·cu·ba·tion** \,iŋkyə'bāshən,

,in-\ *n* — **in·cu·ba·tor** \'iŋkyə,bātər, 'in-\ *n*

in·cul·cate \in'kəl,kāt, 'in,kəl-\ *vb* -cat·ed; -cat·ing : instill by repeated teaching — **in·cul·ca·tion** \,in,kəl-'kāshən\ *n*

in·cum·bent \in'kəmbənt\ *n* : holder of an office ~ *adj* : obligatory — **in·cum·ben·cy** \-bənsē\ *n*

in·cur \in'kər\ *vb* -rr- : become liable or subject to

in·cur·sion \in'kərzhən\ *n* : invasion

in·debt·ed \in'detəd\ *adj* : owing something — **in·debt·ed·ness** *n*

in·de·ci·sion \indi'sizhən\ *n* : inability to decide

in·deed \in'dēd\ *adv* : without question

in·de·fat·i·ga·ble \indi'fatigəbəl\ *adj* : not tiring — **in·de·fat·i·ga·bly** \-blē\ *adv*

in·def·i·nite \in'defənət\ *adj* 1 : not defining or identifying 2 : not precise 3 : having no fixed limit — **in·def·i·nite·ly** *adv*

in·del·i·ble \in'deləbəl\ *adj* : not capable of being removed or erased — **in·del·i·bly** *adv*

in·del·i·cate \in'delikət\ *adj* : improper — **in·del·i·ca·cy** \in'deləkəsē\ *n*

in·dem·ni·fy \in'demnə,fī\ *vb* -fied; -fy·ing : repay for a loss — **in·dem·ni·fi·ca·tion** \-,demnəfə'kāshən\ *n*

in·dem·ni·ty \in'demnətē\ *n, pl* -ties : security against loss or damage

¹**in·dent** \in'dent\ *vb* : leave a space at the beginning of a paragraph

²**indent** *vb* : force inward so as to form a depression or dent

in·den·ta·tion \,in,den'tashən\ *n* 1 : notch, recess, or dent 2 : action of indenting 3 : space at the beginning of a paragraph

in·den·ture \in'denchər\ *n* : contract binding one person to work for another for a given period — usu. in pl. ~ *vb* -tured; -tur·ing : bind by indentures

Independence Day *n* : July 4 observed as a legal holiday in commemoration

---

incombustible	incompletely	inconsiderately
incommensurate	incompleteness	inconsiderateness
incommodious	incomprehensible	inconsistency
incommunicable	inconclusive	inconsistent
incompatibility	incongruent	inconsistently
incompatible	inconsecutive	inconspicuous
incomplete	inconsiderate	inconspicuously

of the adoption of the Declaration of Independence in 1776

in·de·pen·dent \,ində'pendənt\ adj 1 : not governed by another 2 : not requiring or relying on something or somebody else 3 : not easily influenced — **in·de·pen·dence** \-dəns\ n — **independent** n — **in·de·pen·dent·ly** adv

in·de·ter·mi·nate \,indi'tərmənət\ adj : not definitely determined — **in·de·ter·mi·na·cy** \-nəsē\ n — **in·de·ter·mi·nate·ly** adv

in·dex \'in,deks\ n, pl **-dex·es** or **-di·ces** \-də,sēz\ 1 : alphabetical list of items (as topics in a book) 2 : a number that serves as a measure or indicator of something ~ vb 1 : provide with an index 2 : serve as an index of

index finger n : forefinger

in·di·cate \'ində,kāt\ vb **-cat·ed; -cat·ing** 1 : point out or to 2 : show indirectly 3 : state briefly — **in·di·ca·tion** \,ində'kāshən\ n — **in·di·ca·tor** \'ində,kātər\ n

in·dic·a·tive \in'dikətiv\ adj : serving to indicate

in·dict \in'dīt\ vb : charge with a crime — **in·dict·able** adj — **in·dict·ment** n

in·dif·fer·ent \in'difrənt\ adj 1 : having no preference 2 : showing neither interest nor dislike 3 : mediocre — **in·dif·fer·ence** \-'difrəns\ n — **in·dif·fer·ent·ly** adv

in·dig·e·nous \in'dijənəs\ adj : native to a particular region

in·di·gent \'indijənt\ adj : needy — **in·di·gence** \-jəns\ n

in·di·ges·tion \,indī'jeschən, -də-\ n : discomfort from inability to digest food

in·dig·na·tion \,indig'nāshən\ n : anger aroused by something unjust or unworthy — **in·dig·nant** \in'dignənt\ adj — **in·dig·nant·ly** adv

in·dig·ni·ty \in'dignətē\ n, pl **-ties** 1 : offense against self-respect 2 : humiliating treatment

in·di·go \'indi,gō\ n, pl **-gos** or **-goes**

1 : blue dye 2 : deep reddish blue color

in·di·rect \,ində'rekt, -dī-\ adj : not straight or straightforward — **in·di·rec·tion** \-'rekshən\ n — **in·di·rect·ly** adv — **in·di·rect·ness** n

in·dis·crim·i·nate \,indis'krimənət\ adj 1 : not careful or discriminating 2 : haphazard — **in·dis·crim·i·nate·ly** adv

in·dis·pens·able \,indis'pensəbəl\ adj : absolutely essential — **in·dis·pens·abil·i·ty** \-,pensə'bilətē\ n — **indispensable** n — **in·dis·pens·ably** \-'pensəblē\ adv

in·dis·posed \-'pōzd\ adj : slightly ill — **in·dis·po·si·tion** \in,dispə'zishən\ n

in·dis·sol·u·ble \,indis'älyəbəl\ adj : not capable of being dissolved or broken

in·di·vid·u·al \,ində'vijəwəl\ n 1 : single member of a category 2 : person — **individual** adj — **in·di·vid·u·al·ly** adv

in·di·vid·u·al·ist \-əwəlist\ n : person who is markedly independent in thought or action

in·di·vid·u·al·i·ty \-,vijə'walətē\ n : special quality that distinguishes an individual

in·di·vid·u·al·ize \-'vijəwə,līz\ vb **-ized; -iz·ing** 1 : make individual 2 : treat individually

in·doc·tri·nate \in'däktrə,nāt\ vb **-nat·ed; -nat·ing** : instruct in fundamentals (as of a doctrine) — **in·doc·tri·na·tion** \in,däktrə'nāshən\ n

in·do·lent \'indələnt\ adj : lazy — **in·do·lence** \-ləns\ n

in·dom·i·ta·ble \in'dämətəbəl\ adj : invincible — **in·dom·i·ta·bly** \-blē\ adv

in·door \'in'dōr\ adj : relating to the inside of a building

in·doors \in'dōrz\ adv : in or into a building

in·du·bi·ta·ble \in'dübətəbəl, -'dyü-\ adj : being beyond question — **in·du·bi·ta·bly** \-blē\ adv

in·duce \in'düs, -'dyüs\ *vb* **-duced; -duc·ing** **1** : persuade **2** : bring about — **in·duce·ment** *n* — **in·duc·er** *n*

in·duct \in'dəkt\ *vb* **1** : put in office **2** : admit as a member **3** : enroll (as for military service) — **in·duct·ee** \in-ˌdək'tē\ *n*

in·duc·tion \in'dəkshən\ *n* **1** : act or instance of inducting **2** : reasoning from particular instances to a general conclusion

in·duc·tive \in'dəktiv\ *adj* : reasoning by induction

in·dulge \in'dəlj\ *vb* **-dulged; -dulg·ing** : yield to the desire of or for — **in·dul·gence** \-'dəljəns\ *n* — **in·dul·gent** \-jənt\ *adj* — **in·dul·gent·ly** *adv*

in·dus·tri·al \in'dəstrēəl\ *adj* **1** : relating to industry **2** : heavy-duty — **in·dus·tri·al·ist** \-əlist\ *n* — **in·dus·tri·al·iza·tion** \-ˌdəstrēələ'zāshən\ *n* — **in·dus·tri·al·ize** \-'dəstrēəˌlīz\ *vb* — **in·dus·tri·al·ly** *adv*

in·dus·tri·ous \in'dəstrēəs\ *adj* : diligent or busy — **in·dus·tri·ous·ly** *adv* — **in·dus·tri·ous·ness** *n*

in·dus·try \'indəstrē\ *n, pl* **-tries** **1** : diligence **2** : manufacturing enterprises or activity

in·ebri·at·ed \in'ēbrēˌātəd\ *adj* : drunk — **in·ebri·a·tion** \-ˌēbrē'āshən\ *n*

in·ef·fa·ble \in'efəbəl\ *adj* : incapable of being expressed in words — **in·ef·fa·bly** \-blē\ *adv*

in·ept \in'ept\ *adj* **1** : inappropriate or foolish **2** : generally incompetent — **in·ep·ti·tude** \in'eptəˌtüd, -'tyüd\ *n* — **in·ept·ly** *adv* — **in·ept·ness** *n*

in·equal·i·ty \ˌini'kwälətē\ *n* : quality of being unequal or uneven

in·ert \in'ərt\ *adj* **1** : powerless to move or act **2** : sluggish — **in·ert·ly** *adv* — **in·ert·ness** *n*

in·er·tia \in'ərshə\ *n* : tendency of matter to remain at rest or in motion — **in·er·tial** \-shəl\ *adj*

in·es·cap·able \ˌinə'skāpəbəl\ *adj* : inevitable — **in·es·cap·ably** \-blē\ *adv*

in·es·ti·ma·ble \in'estəməbəl\ *adj* : incapable of being estimated — **in·es·ti·ma·bly** \-blē\ *adv*

in·ev·i·ta·ble \in'evətəbəl\ *adj* : incapable of being avoided or escaped — **in·ev·i·ta·bil·i·ty** \in,evətə'bilətē\ *n* — **in·ev·i·ta·bly** \in'evətəblē\ *adv*

in·ex·cus·able \ˌinik'skyüzəbəl\ *adj* : being without excuse or justification — **in·ex·cus·ably** \-blē\ *adv*

in·ex·haust·ible \ˌinig'zòstəbəl\ *adj* : incapable of being used up or tired out — **in·ex·haust·ibly** \-blē\ *adv*

in·ex·o·ra·ble \in'eksərəbəl\ *adj* : unyielding or relentless — **in·ex·o·ra·bly** *adv*

in·fal·li·ble \in'faləbəl\ *adj* : incapable of error — **in·fal·li·bil·i·ty** \in,falə'bilətē\ *n* — **in·fal·li·bly** *adv*

in·fa·mous \'infəməs\ *adj* : having the worst kind of reputation — **in·fa·mous·ly** *adv*

in·fa·my \-mē\ *n, pl* **-mies** : evil reputation

in·fan·cy \'infənsē\ *n, pl* **-cies** **1** : early childhood **2** : early period of existence

in·fant \'infənt\ *n* : baby

in·fan·tile \'infənˌtīl, -tᵊl, -ˌtēl\ *adj* **1** : relating to infants **2** : childish

in·fan·try \'infəntrē\ *n, pl* **-tries** : soldiers that fight on foot

in·fat·u·ate \in'fachəˌwāt\ *vb* **-at·ed; -at·ing** : inspire with foolish love or admiration — **in·fat·u·a·tion** \-ˌfachə'wāshən\ *n*

in·fect \in'fekt\ *vb* : contaminate with disease-producing matter — **in·fec·tion** \-'fekshən\ *n* — **in·fec·tious** \-shəs\ *adj* — **in·fec·tive** \-'fektiv\ *adj*

in·fer \in'fər\ *vb* **-rr-** : deduce — **in·fer·ence** \'infərəns\ *n* — **in·fer·en·tial** \ˌinfə'renchəl\ *adj*

in·fe·ri·or \in'firēər\ *adj* **1** : being lower in position, degree, rank, or

---

merit **2** : of lesser quality — **inferior** n — **in·fe·ri·or·i·ty** \in‚firē'órətē\ n

in·fer·nal \in'fərn°l\ adj : of or like hell — often used as a general expression of disapproval — **in·fer·nal·ly** adv

in·fer·no \in'fərnō\ n, pl -nos : place or condition suggesting hell

in·fest \in'fest\ vb : swarm or grow in or over — **in·fes·ta·tion** \‚in‚fes-'tāshən\ n

in·fi·del \'infəd°l, -fə‚del\ n : one who does not believe in a particular religion

in·fi·del·i·ty \‚infə'delətē, -fī-\ n, pl -ties : lack of faithfulness

in·field \'in‚fēld\ n : baseball field inside the base lines — **in·field·er** n

in·fil·trate \in'fil‚trāt, 'infil-\ vb -trat·ed; -trat·ing : enter or become established in without being noticed — **in·fil·tra·tion** \‚infil'trāshən\ n

in·fi·nite \'infənət\ adj **1** : having no limit or extending indefinitely **2** : vast — **infinite** n — **in·fi·nite·ly** adv — **in·fin·i·tude** \in'finə‚tüd, -tyüd\ n

in·fin·i·tes·i·mal \‚infinə'tesəməl\ adj : immeasurably small — **in·fin·i·tes·i·mal·ly** adv

in·fin·i·tive \in'finətiv\ n : verb form in English usu. used with to

in·fin·i·ty \in'finətē\ n, pl -ties **1** : quality or state of being infinite **2** : indefinitely great number or amount

in·firm \in'fərm\ adj : feeble from age — **in·fir·mi·ty** \-'fərmətē\ n

in·fir·ma·ry \in'fərmərē\ n, pl -ries : place for the care of the sick

in·flame \in'flām\ vb -flamed; -flam·ing **1** : excite to intense action or feeling **2** : affect or become affected with inflammation — **in·flam·ma·to·ry** \-'flamə‚tōrē\ adj

in·flam·ma·ble \in'flaməbəl\ adj : flammable

in·flam·ma·tion \‚inflə'māshən\ n : response to injury in which an affected area becomes red and painful and congested with blood

in·flate \in'flāt\ vb -flat·ed; -flat·ing **1** : swell or puff up (as with gas) **2** : expand or increase abnormally — **in·flat·able** adj

in·fla·tion \in'flāshən\ n **1** : act of inflating **2** : continual rise in prices — **in·fla·tion·ary** \-shə‚nerē\ adj

in·flec·tion \in'flekshən\ n **1** : change in pitch or loudness of the voice **2** : change in form of a word — **in·flect** \-'flekt\ vb — **in·flec·tion·al** \-'flek-shənəl\ adj

in·flict \in'flikt\ vb : give by or as if by hitting — **in·flic·tion** \-'flikshən\ n

in·flu·ence \'in‚flüəns\ n **1** : power or capacity of causing an effect in indirect or intangible ways ~ **2** : one that exerts influence ~ vb -enced; -enc·ing : affect or alter by influence — **in·flu·en·tial** \‚inflü'enchəl\ adj

in·flu·en·za \‚inflü'enzə\ n : acute very contagious virus disease

in·flux \'in‚fləks\ n : a flowing in

in·form \in'fórm\ vb : give information or knowledge to — **in·for·mant** \-ənt\ n — **in·form·er** n

in·for·mal \in'fórməl\ adj **1** : without formality or ceremony **2** : for ordinary or familiar use — **in·for·mal·i·ty** \‚infór'malətē, -fər-\ n — **in·for·mal·ly** adv

in·for·ma·tion \‚infər'māshən\ n : knowledge obtained from investigation, study, or instruction — **in·for·ma·tion·al** \-shənəl\ adj

in·for·ma·tive \in'fórmətiv\ adj : giving knowledge

in·frac·tion \in'frakshən\ n : violation

in·fra·red \‚infrə'red\ adj : being, relating to, or using radiation of wavelengths longer than those of red light — **infrared** n

in·fra·struc·ture \'infrə‚strəkchər\ n : foundation of a system or organization

in·fringe \in'frinj\ vb -fringed; -fring·ing : violate another's right or privilege — **in·fringe·ment** n

in·fu·ri·ate \in'fyúrē‚āt\ vb -at·ed; -at-

ing : make furious — **in·fu·ri·at·ing·ly** \-ˌātiŋlē\ adv

in·fuse \inˈfyüz\ vb -fused; -fus·ing 1 : instill a principle or quality in 2 : steep in liquid without boiling — **in·fu·sion** \-ˈfyüzhən\ n

¹-ing \iŋ\ vb suffix or adj suffix — used to form the present participle and sometimes an adjective resembling a present participle

²-ing n suffix 1 : action or process 2 : something connected with or resulting from an action or process

in·ge·nious \inˈjēnyəs\ adj : very clever — **in·ge·nious·ly** adv — **in·ge·nious·ness** n

in·ge·nue, **in·gé·nue** \ˈanjəˌnü, ˈän-; ˈaⁿzhə-, ˈäⁿ-\ n : naive young woman

in·ge·nu·ity \injəˈnüətē, -ˈnyü-\ n, pl **-ities** : skill or cleverness in planning or inventing

in·gen·u·ous \inˈjenyəwəs\ adj : innocent and candid — **in·gen·u·ous·ly** adv — **in·gen·u·ous·ness** n

in·gest \inˈjest\ vb : eat — **in·ges·tion** \-ˈjeschən\ n

in·gle·nook \ˈiŋgəlˌnúk\ n : corner by the fireplace

in·got \ˈiŋgət\ n : block of metal

in·grained \inˈgrānd\ adj : deep-seated

in·grate \ˈinˌgrāt\ n : ungrateful person

in·gra·ti·ate \inˈgrāshēˌāt\ vb -at·ed; -at·ing : gain favor for (oneself) — **in·gra·ti·at·ing** adj

in·gre·di·ent \inˈgrēdēənt\ n : one of the substances that make up a mixture

in·grown \ˈinˌgrōn\ adj : grown in and esp. into the flesh

in·hab·it \inˈhabət\ vb : live or dwell in — **in·hab·it·able** adj — **in·hab·it·ant** \-ətənt\ n

in·hale \inˈhāl\ vb -haled; -hal·ing : breathe in — **in·hal·ant** \-ənt\ n — **in·ha·la·tion** \inhəˈlāshən, ˌinə-\ n — **in·hal·er** n

in·here \inˈhir\ vb -hered; -her·ing : be inherent

in·her·ent \inˈhirənt, -ˈher-\ adj : being an essential part of something — **in·her·ent·ly** adv

in·her·it \inˈherət\ vb : receive from one's ancestors — **in·her·it·able** \-əbəl\ adj — **in·her·i·tance** \-ətəns\ n — **in·her·i·tor** \-ətər\ n

in·hib·it \inˈhibət\ vb : hold in check — **in·hi·bi·tion** \inhəˈbishən, ˌinə-\ n

in·hu·man \inˈhyümən, -ˈyü-\ adj : cruel or impersonal — **in·hu·man·i·ty** \-hyüˈmanətē, -yü-\ n — **in·hu·man·ly** adv — **in·hu·man·ness** n

in·im·i·cal \inˈimikəl\ adj : hostile or harmful — **in·im·i·cal·ly** adv

in·im·i·ta·ble \inˈimətəbəl\ adj : not capable of being imitated

in·iq·ui·ty \inˈikwətē\ n, pl **-ties** : wickedness — **in·iq·ui·tous** \-wətəs\ adj

ini·tial \inˈishəl\ adj 1 : of or relating to the beginning 2 : first ~ n : 1st letter of a word or name ~ vb -tialed or -tialled; -tial·ing or -tial·ling : put initials on — **ini·tial·ly** adv

ini·ti·ate \inˈishēˌāt\ vb -at·ed; -at·ing 1 : start 2 : induct into membership 3 : instruct in the rudiments of something — **initiate** \-ˈishēət\ n — **ini·ti·a·tion** \-ˌishēˈāshən\ n — **ini·ti·a·to·ry** \-ˈishēəˌtōrē\ adj

ini·tia·tive \inˈishətiv\ n 1 : first step 2 : readiness to undertake something on one's own

in·ject \inˈjekt\ vb : force or introduce into something — **in·jec·tion** \-ˈjekshən\ n

in·junc·tion \inˈjəŋkshən\ n : court writ requiring one to do or to refrain from doing a specified act

in·jure \ˈinjər\ vb -jured; -jur·ing : do damage, hurt, or a wrong to

in·ju·ry \ˈinjərē\ n, pl **-ries** 1 : act that injures 2 : hurt, damage, or loss sustained — **in·ju·ri·ous** \inˈjúrēəs\ adj

in·jus·tice \inˈjəstəs\ n : unjust act

ink \ˈiŋk\ n : usu. liquid and colored material for writing and printing ~ vb : put ink on — **ink·well** \-ˌwel\ n — **inky** adj

in·kling \ˈiŋkliŋ\ n : hint or idea

inexactly	inexpertness	inextricable
inexpedient	inexplicable	infeasibility
inexpensive	inexplicably	infeasible
inexperience	inexplicit	infelicitous
inexperienced	inexpressible	infelicity
inexpert	inexpressibly	infertile
inexpertly	inextinguishable	infertility

in·land \'in₁land, -lənd\ n : interior of a country — **inland** adj or adv

in–law \'in₁lò\ n : relative by marriage

in·lay \in'lā, 'in₁lā\ vb **-laid** \-'lād\; **-lay·ing** : set into a surface for decoration ~ \'in₁lā\ n 1 : inlaid work 2 : shaped filling cemented into a tooth

in·let \'in₁let, -lət\ n : small bay

in·mate \'in₁māt\ n : person confined to an asylum or prison

in me·mo·ri·am \₁inmə'mōrēəm\ prep : in memory of

in·most \'in₁mōst\ adj : deepest within

inn \'in\ n : hotel

in·nards \'inərdz\ n pl : internal parts

in·nate \in'āt\ adj 1 : inborn 2 : inherent — **in·nate·ly** adv

in·ner \'inər\ adj : being on the inside

in·ner·most \'inər₁mōst\ adj : farthest inward

in·ner·sole \₁inər'sōl\ n : insole

in·ning \'inin\ n : baseball team's turn at bat

inn·keep·er \'in₁kēpər\ n : owner of an inn

in·no·cent \'inəsənt\ adj 1 : free from guilt 2 : harmless 3 : not sophisticated — **in·no·cence** \-səns\ n — **innocent** n — **in·no·cent·ly** adv

in·noc·u·ous \in'äkyəwəs\ adj 1 : harmless 2 : inoffensive

in·no·va·tion \₁inə'vāshən\ n : new idea or method — **in·no·vate** \'inə₁vāt\ vb — **in·no·va·tive** \'inə₁vātiv\ adj — **in·no·va·tor** \-₁vātər\ n

in·nu·en·do \₁inyə'wendō\ n, pl **-dos** or **-does** : insinuation

in·nu·mer·a·ble \in'ümərəbəl, -'yüm-\ adj : countless

in·oc·u·late \in'äkyə₁lāt\ vb **-lat·ed**; **-lat·ing** : treat with something esp. to establish immunity — **in·oc·u·la·tion** \-₁äkyə'lāshən\ n

in·op·por·tune \in₁äpər'tün, -'tyün\ adj : inconvenient — **in·op·por·tune·ly** adv

in·or·di·nate \in'òrd²nət\ adj : unusual or excessive — **in·or·di·nate·ly** adv

in·or·gan·ic \₁in₁òr'ganik\ adj : made of mineral matter

in·pa·tient \'in₁pāshənt\ n : patient who stays in a hospital

in·put \'in₁pu̇t\ n : something put in — **input** vb

in·quest \'in₁kwest\ n : inquiry esp. before a jury

in·quire \in'kwīr\ vb **-quired**; **-quir·ing** 1 : ask 2 : investigate — **in·quir·er** n — **in·quir·ing·ly** adv — **in·qui·ry** \in₁kwīrē, in'kwīrē; 'inkwərē, 'in-\ n

in·qui·si·tion \₁inkwə'zishən, ₁in-\ n 1 : official inquiry 2 : severe questioning — **in·quis·i·tor** \in'kwizətər\ n — **in·quis·i·to·ri·al** \-₁kwizə-'tōrēəl\ adj

in·quis·i·tive \in'kwizətiv\ adj : curious — **in·quis·i·tive·ly** adv — **in·quis·i·tive·ness** n

in·road \'in₁rōd\ n : encroachment

in·rush \'in₁rəsh\ n : influx

in·sane \in'sān\ adj 1 : not sane 2 : absurd — **in·sane·ly** adv — **in·san·i·ty** \in'sanətē\ n

in·sa·tia·ble \in'sāshəbəl\ adj : incapable of being satisfied — **in·sa·tia·bil·i·ty** \-₁sāshə'bilətē\ n — **in·sa·tia·bly** adv

in·scribe \in'skrīb\ vb 1 : write 2 : engrave 3 : dedicate (a book) to someone — **in·scrip·tion** \-'skripshən\ n

in·scru·ta·ble \in'skrütəbəl\ adj : mysterious — **in·scru·ta·bly** adv

in·seam \'in₁sēm\ n : inner seam (of a garment)

in·sect \'in₁sekt\ n : small usu. winged animal with 6 legs

in·sec·ti·cide \in'sektə₁sīd\ n : insect poison — **in·sec·ti·cid·al** \in₁sektə-'sīd²l\ adj

in·se·cure \₁insi'kyu̇r\ adj 1 : uncertain 2 : unsafe 3 : fearful — **in·se·cure·ly** adv — **in·se·cu·ri·ty** \-'kyu̇rətē\ n

in·sem·i·nate \in'semə₁nāt\ vb **-nat·ed**; **-nat·ing** : introduce semen into

— in·sem·i·na·tion \-ₛsemə'nāshən\ n

in·sen·si·ble \in'sensəbəl\ adj 1 : unconscious 2 : unable to feel 3 : unaware — in·sen·si·bil·i·ty \-ₛsensə-'bilətē\ n — in·sen·si·bly adv

in·sen·tient \in'senchənt\ adj : lacking feeling — in·sen·tience \-chəns\ n

in·sert \in'sərt\ vb : put in — insert \'in,sərt\ n — in·ser·tion \-'sərshən\ n

in·set \'in,set\ vb inset or in·set·ted; in·set·ting : set in — inset n

in·shore \'in'shōr\ adj 1 : situated near shore 2 : moving toward shore ~ adv : toward shore

in·side \in'sīd, 'in,sīd\ n 1 : inner side 2 pl : innards ~ prep 1 : in or into the inside of 2 : within ~ adv 1 : on the inner side 2 : into the interior — inside adj — in·sid·er \-'sīdər\ n

inside of prep : inside

in·sid·i·ous \in'sidēəs\ adj 1 : treacherous 2 : seductive — in·sid·i·ous·ly adv — in·sid·i·ous·ness n

in·sight \'in,sīt\ n : understanding — in·sight·ful \in'sītfəl-\ adj

in·sig·nia \in'signēə\, in·sig·ne \-nē\ n, pl -nia or -ni·as : badge of authority or office

in·sin·u·ate \in'sinyə,wāt\ vb -at·ed; -at·ing 1 : imply 2 : bring in artfully — in·sin·u·a·tion \in,sinyə'wāshən\ n

in·sip·id \in'sipəd\ adj 1 : tasteless 2 : not stimulating — in·si·pid·i·ty \,insə'pidətē\ n

in·sist \in'sist\ vb : be firmly demanding — in·sis·tence \in'sistəns\ n — in·sis·tent \-tənt\ adj — in·sis·tent·ly adv

insofar as \,insō'färaz\ conj : to the extent that

in·sole \'in,sōl\ n : inside sole of a shoe

in·so·lent \'insələnt\ adj : contemptuously rude — in·so·lence \-ləns\ n

in·sol·vent \in'sälvənt\ adj : unable or insufficient to pay debts — in·sol·ven·cy \-vənsē\ n

in·som·nia \in'sämnēə\ n : inability to sleep — in·som·ni·ac \-nē-,ak\ n

in·so·much as \,insō'məchaz\ conj : inasmuch as

insomuch that conj : to such a degree that

in·sou·ci·ance \in'süsēəns, aⁿsü'syäⁿs\ n : lighthearted indifference — in·sou·ci·ant \in'süsēənt, aⁿsü'syäⁿ\ adj

in·spect \in'spekt\ vb : view closely and critically — in·spec·tion \-'spekshən\ n — in·spec·tor \-tər\ n

in·spire \in'spīr\ vb -spired; -spir·ing 1 : inhale 2 : influence by example 3 : bring about 4 : stir to action — in·spi·ra·tion \,inspə'rāshən\ n — in·spi·ra·tion·al \-'rāshənəl\ adj — in·spir·er n

in·stall, in·stal \in'stȯl\ vb -stalled; -stall·ing 1 : induct into office 2 : set up for use — in·stal·la·tion \,instə-'lāshən\ n

in·stall·ment \in'stȯlmənt\ n : partial payment

in·stance \'instəns\ n 1 : request or instigation 2 : example

in·stant \'instənt\ n : moment ~ adj 1 : immediate 2 : ready to mix — in·stan·ta·neous \,instən'tānēəs\ adj — in·stan·ta·neous·ly adv — in·stant·ly adv

in·stead \in'sted\ adv : as a substitute or alternative

instead of prep : as a substitute for or alternative to

in·step \'in,step\ n : part of the foot in front of the ankle

in·sti·gate \'instə,gāt\ vb -gat·ed; -gat·ing : incite — in·sti·ga·tion \,instə'gāshən\ n — in·sti·ga·tor \'instə,gātər\ n

in·still \in'stil\ vb -stilled; -still·ing : impart gradually

in·stinct \'in,stinkt\ n 1 : natural talent 2 : natural inherited or subconsciously motivated behavior — in·stinc·tive \in'stinktiv\ adj — in·stinc·tive·ly adv — in·stinc·tu·al \in'stinkchəwəl\ adj

in·sti·tute \'instə,tüt, -,tyüt\ vb -tuted; -tut·ing : establish, start, or organize ~ n 1 : organization promoting a cause 2 : school

in·sti·tu·tion \ˌinstə'tüshən, -'tyü-\ n 1 : act of instituting 2 : custom 3 : corporation or society of a public character — in·sti·tu·tion·al \-shənəl\ adj — in·sti·tu·tion·al·ize \-ˌīz\ vb — in·sti·tu·tion·al·ly adv

in·struct \in'strəkt\ vb 1 : teach 2 : give an order to — in·struc·tion \in'strəkshən\ n — in·struc·tion·al \-shənəl\ adj — in·struc·tive \in'strəktiv\ adj — in·struc·tor \in-'strəktər\ n — in·struc·tor·ship n

in·stru·ment \'instrəmənt\ n 1 : something that produces music 2 : means 3 : device for doing work and esp. precision work 4 : legal document — in·stru·men·tal \ˌinstrə-'mentʲl\ adj — in·stru·men·tal·ist \-ist\ n — in·stru·men·tal·i·ty \instrəmən'talətē, -ˌmen-\ n — in·stru·men·ta·tion \instrəmən'tā-shən, -ˌmen-\ n

in·sub·or·di·nate \ˌinsə'bórdᵊnət\ adj : not obeying — in·sub·or·di·na·tion \-ˌbórdᵊn'āshən\ n

in·suf·fer·able \in'səfərəbəl\ adj : unbearable — in·suf·fer·ably \-blē\ adv

in·su·lar \'insülər, -syü-\ adj 1 : relating to or residing on an island 2 : narrow-minded — in·su·lar·i·ty \ˌinsü'larətē, -syü-\ n

in·su·late \'insəˌlāt\ vb -lat·ed; -lat·ing : protect from heat loss or electricity — in·su·la·tion \ˌinsə'lāshən\ n — in·su·la·tor \'insəˌlātər\ n

in·su·lin \'insələn\ n : hormone used by diabetics

in·sult \in'səlt\ vb : treat with contempt ~ \'inˌsəlt\ n : insulting act or remark — in·sult·ing·ly \-inₑlē\ adv

in·su·per·a·ble \in'süpərəbəl\ adj : too difficult — in·su·per·a·bly \-blē\ adv

in·sure \in'shür\ vb -sured; -sur·ing 1 : guarantee against loss 2 : make certain — in·sur·able \-'əbəl\ adj — in·sur·ance \-əns\ n — in·sured \in'shürd\ n — in·sur·er n

in·sur·gent \in'sərjənt\ n : rebel — in·sur·gence \-jəns\ n — in·sur·gen·cy \-jənsē\ n — in·sur·gent adj

in·sur·mount·able \ˌinsər'mauntəbəl\

adj : too great to be overcome — in·sur·mount·ably \-blē\ adv

in·sur·rec·tion \ˌinsə'rekshən\ n : revolution — in·sur·rec·tion·ist n

in·tact \in'takt\ adj : undamaged

in·take \'inˌtāk\ n 1 : opening through which something enters 2 : act of taking in 3 : amount taken in

in·te·ger \'intijər\ n : number that is not a fraction and does not include a fraction

in·te·gral \'intigrəl\ adj : essential

in·te·grate \'intəˌgrāt\ vb -grat·ed; -grat·ing 1 : unite 2 : end segregation of or at — in·te·gra·tion \ˌintə-'grāshən\ n

in·teg·ri·ty \in'tegrətē\ n 1 : soundness 2 : adherence to a code of values 3 : completeness

in·tel·lect \'intʲlˌekt\ n : power of knowing or thinking — in·tel·lec·tu·al \ˌintʲl'ekchəwəl\ adj or n — in·tel·lec·tu·al·ism \-chəwəˌlizəm\ n — in·tel·lec·tu·al·ly adv

in·tel·li·gence \in'teləjəns\ n 1 : ability to learn and understand 2 : mental acuteness 3 : information

in·tel·li·gent \in'teləjənt\ adj : having or showing intelligence — in·tel·li·gent·ly adv

in·tel·li·gi·ble \in'teləjəbəl\ adj : understandable — in·tel·li·gi·bil·i·ty \-ˌteləjə'bilətē\ n — in·tel·li·gi·bly adv

in·tem·per·ance \in'tempərəns\ n : lack of moderation — in·tem·per·ate \-pərət\ adj — in·tem·per·ate·ness n

in·tend \in'tend\ vb : have as a purpose

in·tend·ed \-'tendəd\ n : engaged person — intended adj

in·tense \in'tens\ adj 1 : extreme 2 : deeply felt — in·tense·ly adv — in·ten·si·fi·ca·tion \-ˌtensəfə'kāshən\ n — in·ten·si·fy \-'tensəˌfī\ vb — in·ten·si·ty \in'tensətē\ n — in·ten·sive \in'tensiv\ adj — in·ten·sive·ly adv

¹in·tent \in'tent\ n : purpose — in·ten·tion \-'tenchən\ n — in·ten·tion·al \-'tenchənəl\ adj — in·ten·tion·al·ly adv

²intent adj : concentrated — in·tent·ly adv — in·tent·ness n

in·ter \in'tər\ vb -rr- : bury

---

inviable	invisibly	invulnerability
invisibility	involuntarily	invulnerable
invisible	involuntary	invulnerably

inter- *prefix* : between or among

in·ter·ac·tion \ˌintər'akshən\ *n* : mutual influence — **in·ter·act** \-'akt\ *vb* — **in·ter·ac·tive** *adj*

in·ter·breed \ˌintər'brēd\ *vb* -**bred** \-'bred\; -**breed·ing** : breed together

in·ter·ca·late \in'tərkəˌlāt\ *vb* -**lat·ed**; -**lat·ing** : insert — **in·ter·ca·la·tion** \ˌtərkə'lāshən\ *n*

in·ter·cede \ˌintər'sēd\ *vb* -**ced·ed**; -**ced·ing** : act to reconcile — **in·ter·ces·sion** \-'seshən\ *n* — **in·ter·ces·sor** \-'sesər\ *n*

in·ter·cept \ˌintər'sept\ *vb* : interrupt the progress of — **intercept** \'intərˌsept\ *n* — **in·ter·cep·tion** \ˌintər'sepshən\ *n* — **in·ter·cep·tor** \-'septər\ *n*

in·ter·change \ˌintər'chānj\ *vb* 1 : exchange 2 : change places ~ \'intərˌchānj\ *n* 1 : exchange 2 : junction of highways — **in·ter·change·able** \ˌintər'chānjəbəl\ *adj*

in·ter·course \'intərˌkōrs\ *n* 1 : relations between persons or nations 2 : copulation

in·ter·de·pen·dent \ˌintərdi'pendənt\ *adj* : mutually dependent — **in·ter·de·pen·dence** \-dəns\ *n*

in·ter·dict \ˌintər'dikt\ *vb* 1 : prohibit 2 : destroy or cut (an enemy supply line) — **in·ter·dic·tion** \-'dikshən\ *n*

in·ter·est \'intrəst, -tə,rest\ *n* 1 : right 2 : benefit 3 : charge for borrowed money 4 : readiness to pay special attention 5 : quality that causes interest ~ *vb* 1 : concern 2 : get the attention of — **in·ter·est·ing** *adj* — **in·ter·est·ing·ly** *adv*

in·ter·face \'intərˌfās\ *n* : common boundary — **in·ter·fa·cial** \ˌintər'fāshəl\ *adj*

in·ter·fere \ˌintər'fir\ *vb* -**fered**; -**fer·ing** 1 : collide or be in opposition 2

: try to run the affairs of others — **in·ter·fer·ence** \-'firəns\ *n*

in·ter·im \'intərəm\ *n* : time between — **interim** *adj*

in·te·ri·or \in'tirēər\ *adj* : being on the inside ~ *n* 1 : inside 2 : inland area

in·ter·ject \ˌintər'jekt\ *vb* : stick in between

in·ter·jec·tion \-'jekshən\ *n* : an exclamatory word — **in·ter·jec·tion·al·ly** \-shənəlē\ *adv*

in·ter·lace \ˌintər'lās\ *vb* : cross or cause to cross one over another

in·ter·lin·ear \ˌintər'linēər\ *adj* : between written or printed lines

in·ter·lock \ˌintər'läk\ *vb* 1 : interlace 2 : connect for mutual effect — **interlock** \'intərˌläk\ *n*

in·ter·lop·er \ˌintər'lōpər\ *n* : intruder or meddler

in·ter·lude \'intərˌlüd\ *n* : intervening period

in·ter·mar·ry \ˌintər'marē\ *vb* 1 : marry each other 2 : marry within a group — **in·ter·mar·riage** \-'marij\ *n*

in·ter·me·di·ary \ˌintər'mēdē,erē\ *n*, *pl* -**ar·ies** : agent between individuals or groups — **intermediary** *adj*

in·ter·me·di·ate \ˌintər'mēdēət\ *adj* : between extremes — **intermediate** *n*

in·ter·ment \in'tərmənt\ *n* : burial

in·ter·mi·na·ble \in'tərmənəbəl\ *adj* : endless — **in·ter·mi·na·bly** *adv*

in·ter·min·gle \ˌintər'miŋgəl\ *vb* : mingle

in·ter·mis·sion \ˌintər'mishən\ *n* : break in a performance

in·ter·mit·tent \-'mit'nt\ *adj* : coming at intervals — **in·ter·mit·tent·ly** *adv*

in·ter·mix \ˌintər'miks\ *vb* : mix together — **in·ter·mix·ture** \-'mikschər\ *n*

¹in·tern \'in,tərn, in'tərn\ *vb* : confine esp. during a war — **in·tern·ee** \ˌin,tər'nē\ *n* — **in·tern·ment** *n*

List of self-explanatory words with the prefix *inter-*

interagency	intercommunal	interfaculty
interatomic	intercommunity	interfamily
interbank	intercompany	interfiber
interborough	intercontinental	interfraternity
intercampus	intercounty	intergalactic
interchurch	intercultural	intergang
intercity	interdenominational	intergovernmental
interclass	interdepartmental	intergroup
intercoastal	interdivisional	interhemispheric
intercollegiate	interelectronic	interindustry
intercolonial	interethnic	interinstitutional

²in•tern \'in,tərn\ n : advanced student (as in medicine) gaining supervised experience ~ vb : act as an intern — in•tern•ship n

in•ter•nal \in'tərn°l\ adj 1 : inward 2 : inside of the body 3 : relating to or existing in the mind — in•ter•nal•ly adv

in•ter•na•tion•al \,intər'nashənəl\ adj : affecting 2 or more nations ~ n : something having international scope — in•ter•na•tion•al•ism \-,izəm\ n — in•ter•na•tion•al•ize \-,īz\ vb — in•ter•na•tion•al•ly adv

In•ter•net \'intər,net\ n : network that connects computer networks worldwide

in•ter•nist \'in,tərnist\ n : specialist in nonsurgical medicine

in•ter•play \'intər,plā\ n : interaction

in•ter•po•late \in'tərpə,lāt\ vb -lat•ed; -lat•ing : insert — in•ter•po•la•tion \-,tərpə'lāshən\ n

in•ter•pose \,intər'pōz\ vb -posed; -pos•ing 1 : place between 2 : intrude — in•ter•po•si•tion \-pə'zishən\ n

in•ter•pret \in'tərprət\ vb : explain the meaning of — in•ter•pre•ta•tion \in,tərprə'tāshən\ n — in•ter•pre•ta•tive \-'tərprə,tātiv\ adj — in•ter•pret•er n — in•ter•pre•tive \-'tərprətiv\ adj

in•ter•re•late \,intəri'lāt\ vb : have a mutual relationship — in•ter•re•lat•ed•ness \-'lātədnəs\ n — in•ter•re•la•tion \-'lāshən\ n — in•ter•re•la•tion•ship n

in•ter•ro•gate \in'terə,gāt\ vb -gat•ed; -gat•ing : question — in•ter•ro•ga•tion \-,terə'gāshən\ n — in•ter•rog•a•tive \,intə'rägətiv\ adj or n — in•ter•rog•a•tor \-'terə,gātər\ n — in•ter•rog•a•to•ry \,intə'rägə,tōrē\ adj

in•ter•rupt \,intə'rəpt\ vb : intrude so as to hinder or end continuity — in•ter-

rupt•er n — in•ter•rup•tion \-'rəpshən\ n — in•ter•rup•tive \-'rəptiv\ adv

in•ter•sect \,intər'sekt\ vb 1 : cut across or divide 2 : cross — in•ter•sec•tion \-'sekshən\ n

in•ter•sperse \,intər'spərs\ vb -spersed; -spers•ing : insert at intervals — in•ter•per•sion \-'spərzhən\ n

in•ter•stice \in'tərstəs\ n, pl -stic•es \-stə,sēz, -stəsəz\ : space between — in•ter•sti•tial \,intər'stishəl\ adj

in•ter•twine \,intər'twīn\ vb : twist together — in•ter•twine•ment n

in•ter•val \'intərvəl\ n 1 : time between 2 : space between

in•ter•vene \,intər'vēn\ vb -vened; -ven•ing 1 : happen between events 2 : intercede — in•ter•ven•tion \-'venchən\ n

in•ter•view \'intər,vyü\ n : a meeting to get information — interview vb — in•ter•view•er n

in•ter•weave \,intər'wēv\ vb -wove \-'wōv\; -wo•ven \-'wōvən\; -weav•ing : weave together — in•ter•wo•ven \-'wōvən\ adj

in•tes•tate \in'tes,tāt, -tət\ adj : not leaving a will

in•tes•tine \in'testən\ n : tubular part of the digestive system after the stomach including a long narrow upper part (small intestine) followed by a broader shorter lower part (large intestine) — in•toc•ti•nal \-tən°l\ adj

in•ti•mate \'intə,māt\ vb -mat•ed; -mat•ing : hint ~ \'intəmət\ adj 1 : very friendly 2 : suggesting privacy 3 : very personal ~ n : close friend — in•ti•ma•cy \'intəməsē\ n — in•ti•mate•ly adv — in•ti•ma•tion \,intə'māshən\ n

in•tim•i•date \in'timə,dāt\ vb -dat•ed;

-dat•ing : make fearful — **in•tim•i•da•tion** \-ˌtimə'dāshən\ n

in•to \'intü\ prep **1** : to the inside of **2** : to the condition of **3** : against

in•to•na•tion \ˌintō'nāshən\ n : way of singing or speaking

in•tone \in'tōn\ vb **-toned; -ton•ing** : chant

in•tox•i•cate \in'täkəˌkāt\ vb **-cat•ed; -cat•ing** : make drunk — **in•tox•i•cant** \-sikənt\ n or adj — **in•tox•i•ca•tion** \-ˌtäksə'kāshən\ n

in•tra•mu•ral \ˌintrə'myürəl\ adj : within a school

in•tran•si•gent \in'transəjənt\ adj : uncompromising — **in•tran•si•gence** \-jəns\ n — **intransigent** n

in•tra•ve•nous \ˌintrə'vēnəs\ adj : by way of the veins — **in•tra•ve•nous•ly** adv

in•trep•id \in'trepəd\ adj : fearless — **in•tre•pid•i•ty** \ˌintrə'pidətē\ n

in•tri•cate \'intrikət\ adj : very complex and delicate — **in•tri•ca•cy** \-trikəsē\ n — **in•tri•cate•ly** adv

in•trigue \in'trēg\ vb **-trigued; -trigu•ing 1** : scheme **2** : arouse curiosity of ∼ n : secret scheme — **in•trigu•ing•ly** \-inˌlē\ adv

in•trin•sic \in'trinzik, -sik\ adj : essential — **in•trin•si•cal•ly** \-ziklē, -si-\ adv

in•tro•duce \ˌintrə'düs, -'dyüs\ vb **-duced; -duc•ing 1** : bring in esp. for the 1st time **2** : cause to be acquainted **3** : bring to notice **4** : put in — **in•tro•duc•tion** \-'dəkshən\ n — **in•tro•duc•to•ry** \-'dəktərē\ adj

in•tro•spec•tion \ˌintrə'spekshən\ n : examination of one's own thoughts or feelings — **in•tro•spec•tive** \-'spektiv\ adj — **in•tro•spec•tive•ly** adv

in•tro•vert \'intrəˌvərt\ n : shy or reserved person — **in•tro•ver•sion** \ˌintrə'vərzhən\ n — **introvert** adj — **in•tro•vert•ed** \'intrəˌvərtəd\ adj

in•trude \in'trüd\ vb **-trud•ed; -trud•ing 1** : thrust in **2** : encroach — **in•trud•er** n — **in•tru•sion** \-'trüzhən\ n — **in•tru•sive** \-'trüsiv\ adj — **in•tru•sive•ness** n

in•tu•i•tion \ˌintü'ishən, -tyü-\ n : quick and ready insight — **in•tu•it** \in'tüət, -'tyü-\ vb — **in•tu•i•tive** \-ətiv\ adj — **in•tu•i•tive•ly** adv

in•un•date \'inənˌdāt\ vb **-dat•ed; -dat-**ing : flood — **in•un•da•tion** \ˌinən-'dāshən\ n

in•ure \in'ür, -'yür\ vb **-ured; -ur•ing** : accustom to accept something undesirable

in•vade \in'vād\ vb **-vad•ed; -vad•ing** : enter for conquest — **in•vad•er** n — **in•va•sion** \-'vāzhən\ n

¹in•val•id \in'valəd\ adj : not true or legal — **in•va•lid•i•ty** \ˌinvə'lidətē\ n — **in•val•id•ly** adv

²in•va•lid \'invələd\ adj : sickly ∼ n : one chronically ill

in•val•i•date \in'valəˌdāt\ vb : make invalid — **in•val•i•da•tion** \in,valə'dāshən\ n

in•valu•able \in'valyəwəbəl\ adj : extremely valuable

in•va•sive \in'vāsiv\ adj : involving entry into the body

in•vec•tive \in'vektiv\ n : abusive language — **invective** adj

in•veigh \in'vā\ vb : protest or complain forcefully

in•vei•gle \in'vāgəl, -'vē-\ vb **-gled; -gling** : win over or get by flattery

in•vent \in'vent\ vb **1** : think up **2** : create for the 1st time — **in•ven•tion** \-'venchən\ n — **in•ven•tive** \-'ventiv\ adj — **in•ven•tive•ness** n — **in•ven•tor** \-'ventər\ n

in•ven•to•ry \'invənˌtōrē\ n, pl **-ries 1** : list of goods **2** : stock — **inventory** vb

in•verse \in'vərs, 'in,vərs\ adj or n : opposite — **in•verse•ly** adv

in•vert \in'vərt\ vb **1** : turn upside down or inside out **2** : reverse — **in•ver•sion** \-'verzhən\ n

in•ver•te•brate \in'vərtəbrət, -ˌbrāt\ adj : lacking a backbone ∼ n : invertebrate animal

in•vest \in'vest\ vb **1** : give power or authority to **2** : endow with a quality **3** : commit money to someone else's use in hope of profit — **in•vest•ment** \-mənt\ n — **in•ves•tor** \-'vestər\ n

in•ves•ti•gate \in'vestəˌgāt\ vb **-gat•ed; -gat•ing** : study closely and systematically — **in•ves•ti•ga•tion** \-vestə'gāshən\ n — **in•ves•ti•ga•tive** \-'vestəˌgātiv\ adj — **in•ves•ti•ga•tor** \-'vestəˌgātər\ n

in•ves•ti•ture \in'vestəˌchúr, -chər\ n : act of establishing in office

in•vet•er•ate \in'vetərət\ adj : acting out of habit

in·vid·i·ous \in'vidēəs\ *adj* : harmful or obnoxious — **in·vid·i·ous·ly** *adv*

in·vig·o·rate \in'vigə,rāt\ *vb* **-rat·ed; -rat·ing** : give life and energy to — **in·vig·o·ra·tion** \-,vigə'rāshən\ *n*

in·vin·ci·ble \in'vinsəbəl\ *adj* : incapable of being conquered — **in·vin·ci·bil·i·ty** \in,vinsə'bilətē\ *n* — **in·vin·ci·bly** \in'vinsəblē\ *adv*

in·vi·o·la·ble \in'vīələbəl\ *adj* : safe from violation or desecration — **in·vi·o·la·bil·i·ty** \in,vīələ'bilətē\ *n*

in·vi·o·late \in'vīələt\ *adj* : not violated or profaned

in·vite \in'vīt\ *vb* **-vit·ed; -vit·ing** 1 : entice 2 : increase the likelihood of 3 : request the presence or participation of 4 : encourage — **in·vi·ta·tion** \,invə'tāshən\ *n* — **in·vit·ing** \in'vītiŋ\ *adj*

in·vo·ca·tion \,invə'kāshən\ *n* 1 : prayer 2 : incantation

in·voice \'in,vȯis\ *n* : itemized bill for goods shipped ~ *vb* **-voiced; -voic·ing** : bill

in·voke \in'vōk\ *vb* **-voked; -vok·ing** 1 : call on for help 2 : cite as authority 3 : conjure 4 : carry out

in·volve \in'välv\ *vb* **-volved; -volv·ing** 1 : draw in as a participant 2 : relate closely 3 : require as a necessary part 4 : occupy fully — **in·volve·ment** *n*

in·volved \-'välvd\ *adj* : intricate

in·ward \'inwərd\ *adj* : inside

²**in·ward, in·wards** \-wərdz\ *adv* : toward the inside, center, or inner being

in·ward·ly *adv* 1 : mentally or spiritually 2 : internally 3 : to oneself

io·dide \'īə,dīd\ *n* : compound of iodine

io·dine \'īə,dīn, -əd⁾n\ *n* 1 : nonmetallic chemical element 2 : solution of iodine used as an antiseptic

io·dize \'īə,dīz\ *vb* **-dized; -diz·ing** : treat with iodine or an iodide

ion \'īən, 'ī,än\ *n* : electrically charged particle — **ion·ic** \ī'änik\ *adj* — **ion·iz·able** \'īə,nīzəbəl\ *adj* — **ion·iza·tion** \,īənə'zāshən\ *n* — **ion·ize** \'īə,nīz\ *vb* — **ion·iz·er** \'īə,nīzər\ *n*

-ion *n suffix* 1 : act or process 2 : state or condition

ion·o·sphere \ī'änə,sfir\ *n* : layer of the upper atmosphere containing ionized gases — **ion·o·spher·ic** \ī,änə-'sfirik, -'sfer-\ *adj*

io·ta \ī'ōtə\ *n* : small quantity

IOU \,ī,ō'yü\ *n* : acknowledgment of a debt

IRA \,ī,är'ā\ *n* : individual retirement savings account

iras·ci·ble \i'rasəbəl, ī'ras-\ *adj* : marked by hot temper — **iras·ci·bil·i·ty** \-,asə'bilətē, -,ras-\ *n*

irate \ī'rāt\ *adj* : roused to intense anger — **irate·ly** *adv*

ire \'īr\ *n* : anger

ir·i·des·cence \,irə'des⁾ns\ *n* : rainbowlike play of colors — **ir·i·des·cent** \-⁾nt\ *adj*

iris \'īrəs\ *n, pl* **iris·es** *or* **iri·des** \'īrə,dēz, 'ir-\ 1 : colored part around the pupil of the eye 2 : plant with long leaves and large showy flowers

irk \'ərk\ *vb* : annoy — **irk·some** \-əm\ *adj* — **irk·some·ly** *adv*

iron \'īərn\ *n* 1 : heavy metallic chemical element 2 : something made of iron 3 : heated device for pressing clothes 4 : hardness, determination ~ *vb* : press or smooth out with an iron — **iron·ware** *n* — **iron·work** *n* — **iron·work·er** *n* — **iron·works** *n*

iron·clad \-'klad\ *adj* 1 : sheathed in iron armor 2 : strict or exacting

iron·ing \'īərniŋ\ *n* : clothes to be ironed

iron·wood \-,wùd\ *n* : tree or shrub with very hard wood or this wood

iro·ny \'īrənē\ *n, pl* **-nies** 1 : use of words to express the opposite of the literal meaning 2 : incongruity between the actual and expected result of events — **iron·ic** \ī'ränik\, **iron·i·cal** \-ikəl\ *adj* — **iron·i·cal·ly** \-iklē\ *adv*

ir·ra·di·ate \ir'ādē,āt\ *vb* **-at·ed; -at·ing** : treat with radiation — **ir·ra·di·a·tion** \-,ādē'āshən\ *n*

ir·ra·tio·nal \ir'ashənəl\ *adj* 1 : incapable of reasoning 2 : not based on reason — **ir·ra·tio·nal·i·ty** \ir,ashə-'nalətē\ *n* — **ir·ra·tio·nal·ly** *adv*

ir·rec·on·cil·able \ir,ekən'sīləbəl\ *adj* : impossible to reconcile — **ir·rec·on·cil·abil·i·ty** \-,sīlə'bilətē\ *n*

ir·re·cov·er·able \,iri'kəvərəbəl\ *adj* : not capable of being recovered — **ir·re·cov·er·ably** \-blē\ *adv*

ir·re·deem·able \,iri'dēməbəl\ *adj* : not redeemable

ir·re·duc·ible \,iri'düsəbəl, -'dyü-\ *adj* : not reducible — **ir·re·duc·ibly** \-blē\ *adv*

ir·re·fut·able \,iri'fyütəbəl, ir'refyət-\ *adj* : impossible to refute

ir·reg·u·lar \ir'egyələr\ *adj* : not regular or normal — **irregular** *n* — **ir·reg·u·lar·i·ty** \ir,egyə'larətē\ *n* — **ir·reg·u·lar·ly** *adv*

ir·rel·e·vant \ir'eləvənt\ *adj* : not relevant — **ir·rel·e·vance** \-vəns\ *n*

ir·re·li·gious \,iri'lijəs\ *adj* : not following religious practices

ir·rep·a·ra·ble \ir'epərəbəl\ *adj* : impossible to make good, undo, or remedy

ir·re·place·able \,iri'plāsəbəl\ *adj* : not replaceable

ir·re·press·ible \-'presəbəl\ *adj* : impossible to repress or control

ir·re·proach·able \-'prōchəbəl\ *adj* : blameless

ir·re·sist·ible \-'zistəbəl\ *adj* : impossible to successfully resist — **ir·re·sist·ibly** \-blē\ *adv*

ir·res·o·lute \ir'ezəlüt\ *adj* : uncertain — **ir·res·o·lute·ly** *adv* — **ir·res·o·lu·tion** \-,ezə'lüshən\ *n*

ir·re·spec·tive of \,iri'spektiv-\ *prep* : without regard to

ir·re·spon·si·ble \,iri'spänsəbəl\ *adj* : not responsible — **ir·re·spon·si·bil·i·ty** \-,spänsə'bilətē\ *n* — **ir·re·spon·si·bly** *adv*

ir·re·triev·able \,iri'trēvəbəl\ *adj* : not retrievable

ir·rev·er·ence \ir'evərəns\ *n* **1** : lack of reverence **2** : irreverent act or utterance — **ir·rev·er·ent** \-rənt\ *adj*

ir·re·vers·ible \,iri'vərsəbəl\ *adj* : incapable of being reversed

ir·rev·o·ca·ble \ir'evəkəbəl\ *adj* : incapable of being revoked — **ir·rev·o·ca·bly** \-blē\ *adv*

ir·ri·gate \'irə,gāt\ *vb* **-gat·ed; -gat·ing** : supply with water by artificial means — **ir·ri·ga·tion** \irə'gāshən\ *n*

ir·ri·tate \'irə,tāt\ *vb* **-tat·ed; -tat·ing** **1** : excite to anger **2** : make sore or inflamed — **ir·ri·ta·bil·i·ty** \,irətə'bilətē\ *n* — **ir·ri·ta·ble** \'irətəbəl\ *adj* — **ir·ri·ta·bly** \'irətəblē\ *adv* — **ir·ri·tant** \'irətənt\ *adj or n* — **ir·ri·tat·ing·ly** *adv* — **ir·ri·ta·tion** \irə'tāshən\ *n*

is *pres 3d sing of* BE

-ish \ish\ *adj suffix* **1** : characteristic of **2** : somewhat

Is·lam \is'läm, iz-, -'läm\ *n* : religious faith of Muslims — **Is·lam·ic** \-ik\ *adj*

is·land \'īlənd\ *n* : body of land surrounded by water — **is·land·er** \'īləndər\ *n*

isle \'īl\ *n* : small island

is·let \'īlət\ *n* : small island

-ism \,izəm\ *n suffix* **1** : act or practice **2** : characteristic manner **3** : condition **4** : doctrine

iso·late \'īsə,lāt\ *vb* **-lat·ed; -lat·ing** : place or keep by itself — **iso·la·tion** \,īsə'lāshən\ *n*

iso·met·rics \,īsə'metriks\ *n sing or pl* : exercise against unmoving resistance — **isometric** *adj*

isos·ce·les \ī'säsə,lēz\ *adj* : having 2 equal sides

iso·tope \'īsə,tōp\ *n* : species of atom of a chemical element — **iso·to·pic** \,īsə'täpik, -'tō-\ *adj*

is·sue \'ishü\ *vb* **-sued; -su·ing** **1** : go, come, or flow out **2** : descend from a specified ancestor **3** : emanate or result **4** : put forth or distribute officially \~ *n* **1** : action of issuing **2** : offspring **3** : result **4** : point of controversy **5** : act of giving out or printing **6** : quantity given out or printed — **is·su·ance** \'ishəwəns\ *n* — **is·su·er** *n*

-ist \ist\ *n suffix* **1** : one that does **2** : one that plays **3** : one that specializes in **4** : follower of a doctrine

isth·mus \'isməs\ *n* : narrow strip of land connecting 2 larger portions

it \'it\ *pron* **1** : that one — used of a lifeless thing or an abstract entity **2** — used as an anticipatory subject or object \~ *n* : player who tries to catch others (as in a game of tag)

ital·ic \ə'talik, i-, ī-\ *n* : style of type with slanting letters — **italic** *adj* — **ital·i·ci·za·tion** \ə,talasə'zāshən, i-, ī-\ *n* — **ital·i·cize** \ə'talə,sīz, i-, ī-\ *vb*

itch \'ich\ *n* **1** : uneasy irritating skin sensation **2** : skin disorder **3** : persistent desire — **itch** *vb* — **itchy** *adj*

item \'ītəm\ *n* **1** : particular in a list, account, or series **2** : piece of news — **item·iza·tion** \,ītəmə'zāshən\ *n* — **item·ize** \'ītə,mīz\ *vb*

itin·er·ant \ī'tinərənt, ə-\ *adj* : traveling from place to place

itin·er·ary \ī'tinə,rerē, ə-\ *n, pl* **-ar·ies** : route or outline of a journey

its \'its\ *adj* : relating to it

it·self \it'self\ *pron* : it — used reflexively or for emphasis

-ity \ətē\ *n suffix* : quality, state, or degree

-ive \iv\ *adj suffix* : that performs or tends toward an action

ivo·ry \īvərē\ *n, pl* **-ries 1** : hard creamy-white material of elephants' tusks **2** : pale yellow color

ivy \īvē\ *n, pl* **ivies** : trailing woody vine with evergreen leaves

-ize \īz\ *vb suffix* **1** : cause to be, become, or resemble **2** : subject to an action **3** : treat or combine with **4** : engage in an activity

J

j \jā\ *n, pl* **j's** *or* **js** \jāz\ : 10th letter of the alphabet

jab \jab\ *vb* **-bb-** : thrust quickly or abruptly ~ *n* : short straight punch

jab·ber \jabər\ *vb* : talk rapidly or unintelligibly — **jabber** *n*

jack \jak\ *n* **1** : mechanical device to raise a heavy body **2** : small flag **3** : small 6-pointed metal object used in a game (**jacks**) **4** : electrical socket ~ *vb* **1** : raise with a jack **2** : increase

jack·al \jakəl, -,ol\ *n* : wild dog

jack·ass *n* **1** : male ass **2** : stupid person

jack·et \jakət\ *n* : garment for the upper body

jack·ham·mer \jak,hamər\ *n* : pneumatic tool for drilling

jack·knife \jak,nīf\ *n* : pocketknife ~ *vb* : fold like a jackknife

jack-o'-lan·tern \jakə,lantərn\ *n* : lantern made of a carved pumpkin

jack·pot \jak,pät\ *n* : sum of money won

jack·rab·bit \-,rabət\ *n* : large hare of western No. America

jade \jād\ *n* : usu. green gemstone

jad·ed \jādəd\ *adj* : dulled or bored by having too much

jag·ged \jagəd\ *adj* : sharply notched

jag·uar \jag,wär, jagyə-\ *n* : black-spotted tropical American cat

jai alai \hī,lī\ *n* : game with a ball propelled by a basket on the hand

jail \jāl\ *n* : prison — **jail** *vb* — **jail·break** *n* — **jail·er**, **jail·or** *n*

ja·la·pe·ño \,hälə'pän,yō, -,pēnō\ *n* : Mexican hot pepper

ja·lopy \jə'läpē\ *n, pl* **-lopies** : dilapidated vehicle

jal·ou·sie \jaləsē\ *n* : door or window with louvers

jam \jam\ *vb* **-mm- 1** : press into a tight position **2** : cause to become wedged and unworkable ~ *n* **1** : crowded mass that blocks or impedes **2** : difficult situation **3** : thick sweet food made of cooked fruit

jamb \jam\ *n* : upright framing piece of a door

jam·bo·ree \,jambə'rē\ *n* : large festive gathering

jan·gle \jangəl\ *vb* **-gled; -gling** : make a harsh ringing sound — **jangle** *n*

jan·i·tor \janətər\ *n* : person who has the care of a building — **jan·i·to·ri·al** \,janə'tōrēəl\ *adj*

Jan·u·ary \janyə,werē\ *n* : 1st month of the year having 31 days

¹jar \jär\ *vb* **-rr- 1** : have a harsh or disagreeable effect **2** : vibrate or shake ~ *n* **1** : jolt **2** : painful effect

²jar *n* : wide-mouthed container

jar·gon \järgən, -,gän\ *n* : special vocabulary of a group

jas·mine \jazmən\ *n* : climbing shrub with fragrant flowers

jas·per \jaspər\ *n* : red, yellow, or brown opaque quartz

jaun·dice \jondəs\ *n* : yellowish discoloration of skin, tissues, and body fluids

jaun·diced \-dəst\ *adj* : exhibiting envy or hostility

jaunt \jont\ *n* : short pleasure trip

jaun·ty \jontē\ *adj* **-ti·er; -est** : lively in manner or appearance — **jaun·ti·ly** \jont'lē\ *adv* — **jaun·ti·ness** *n*

jave·lin \javələn\ *n* : light spear

jaw \jo\ *n* **1** : either of the bony or cartilaginous structures that support the mouth **2** : one of 2 movable parts for holding or crushing ~ *vb* : talk indignantly or at length — **jaw·bone** \-,bōn\ *n* — **jawed** \jod\ *adj*

jay \jā\ *n* : noisy brightly colored bird

jay·bird *n* : jay

jay·walk vb : cross a street carelessly — **jay·walk·er** n

jazz \'jaz\ vb : enliven ~ n 1 : kind of American music involving improvisation 2 : empty talk — **jazzy** adj

jeal·ous \'jeləs\ adj : suspicious of a rival or of one believed to enjoy an advantage — **jeal·ous·ly** adv — **jeal·ou·sy** \-əsē\ n

jeans \'jēnz\ n pl : pants made of durable twilled cotton cloth

jeep \'jēp\ n : 4-wheel army vehicle

jeer \'jir\ vb 1 : speak or cry out in derision 2 : ridicule ~ n : taunt

Je·ho·vah \ji'hōvə\ n : God

je·june \ji'jün\ adj : dull or childish

jell \'jel\ vb 1 : come to the consistency of jelly 2 : take shape

jel·ly \'jelē\ n, pl -lies : a substance (as food) with a soft somewhat elastic consistency — **jelly** vb

jel·ly·fish n : sea animal with a saucer-shaped jellylike body

jen·ny \'jenē\ n, pl -nies : female bird or donkey

jeop·ar·dy \'jepərdē\ n : exposure to death, loss, or injury — **jeop·ar·dize** \-ər,dīz\ vb

jerk \'jərk\ vb 1 : give a sharp quick push, pull, or twist 2 : move in short abrupt motions ~ n 1 : short quick pull or twist 2 : stupid or foolish person — **jerk·i·ly** adv — **jerky** adj

jer·kin \'jərkən\ n : close-fitting sleeveless jacket

jer·ry-built \'jerē,bilt\ adj : built cheaply and flimsily

jer·sey \'jərzē\ n, pl -seys 1 : plain knit fabric 2 : knitted shirt

jest \'jest\ n : witty remark — **jest** vb

jest·er \'jestər\ n : one employed to entertain a court

¹jet \'jet\ n : velvet-black coal used for jewelry

²jet vb -tt- 1 : spout or emit in a stream 2 : travel by jet ~ n 1 : forceful rush of fluid through a narrow opening 2 : jet-propelled airplane

jet–propelled adj : driven by an engine (**jet engine**) that produces propulsion (**jet propulsion**) by the rearward discharge of a jet of fluid

jet·sam \'jetsəm\ n : jettisoned goods

jet·ti·son \'jetəsən\ vb 1 : throw (goods) overboard 2 : discard — **jettison** n

jet·ty \'jetē\ n, pl -ties : pier or wharf

Jew \'jü\ n : one whose religion is Judaism — **Jew·ish** adj

jew·el \'jüəl\ n 1 : ornament of precious metal 2 : gem ~ vb -eled or -elled; -el·ing or -el·ling : adorn with jewels — **jew·el·er**, **jew·el·ler** \-ər\ — **jew·el·ry** \-rē\ n

jib \'jib\ n : triangular sail

jibe \'jīb\ vb jibed; jib·ing : be in agreement

jif·fy \'jifē\ n, pl -fies : short time

jig \'jig\ n : lively dance ~ vb -gg- : dance a jig

jig·ger \'jigər\ n : measure used in mixing drinks

jig·gle \'jigəl\ vb -gled; -gling : move with little quick jerks — **jiggle** n

jig·saw n : machine saw with a narrow blade that moves up and down

jilt \'jilt\ vb : drop (a lover) unfeelingly

jim·my \'jimē\ n, pl -mies : small crowbar ~ vb -mied; -my·ing : pry open

jim·son·weed \'jimsən,wēd\ n : coarse poisonous weed

jin·gle \'jiŋgəl\ vb -gled; -gling : make a light tinkling sound ~ n 1 : light tinkling sound 2 : short verse or song

jin·go·ism \'jiŋgō,izəm\ n : extreme chauvinism or nationalism — **jin·go·ist** \-ist\ n — **jin·go·is·tic** \,jiŋgō-'istik\ adj

jinx \'jiŋks\ n : one that brings bad luck — **jinx** vb

jit·ney \'jitnē\ n, pl -neys : small bus

jit·ters \'jitərz\ n pl : extreme nervousness — **jit·tery** \-ərē\ adj

job \'jäb\ n 1 : something that has to be done 2 : regular employment — **job·hold·er** n — **job·less** adj

job·ber \'jäbər\ n : middleman

jock·ey \'jäkē\ n, pl -eys : one who rides a horse in a race ~ vb -eyed; -ey·ing : manipulate or maneuver adroitly

jo·cose \jō'kōs\ adj : jocular

joc·u·lar \'jäkyələr\ adj : marked by jesting — **joc·u·lar·i·ty** \,jäkyə-'larətē\ n — **joc·u·lar·ly** adv

jo·cund \'jäkənd\ adj : full of mirth or gaiety

jodh·purs \'jädpərz\ n pl : riding breeches

¹jog \'jäg\ vb -gg- 1 : give a slight shake or push to 2 : run or ride at a slow pace ~ n 1 : slight shake 2 : slow pace — **jog·ger** n

²jog n : brief abrupt change in direction or line

join \'jóin\ vb 1 : come or bring together **2** : become a member of — **join·er** *n*

joint \'jȯint\ *n* **1** : point of contact between bones **2** : place where 2 parts connect **3** : often disreputable place ~ *adj* : common to 2 or more — **joint·ed** *adj* — **joint·ly** *adv*

joist \'jȯist\ *n* : beam supporting a floor or ceiling

joke \'jōk\ *n* : something said or done to provoke laughter ~ *vb* **joked; jok·ing** : make jokes — **jok·er** *n* — **jok·ing·ly** \'jōkiŋlē\ *adv*

jol·li·ty \'jälətē\ *n*, *pl* **-ties** : gaiety or merriment

jol·ly \'jälē\ *adj* **-li·er; -est** : full of high spirits

jolt \'jōlt\ *vb* **1** : move with a sudden jerky motion **2** : give a jolt to ~ *n* **1** : abrupt jerky blow or movement **2** : sudden shock — **jolt·er** *n*

jon·quil \'jänkwəl\ *n* : narcissus with white or yellow flowers

josh \'jäsh\ *vb* : tease or joke

jos·tle \'jäsəl\ *vb* **-tled; -tling** : push or shove

jot \'jät\ *n* : least bit ~ *vb* **-tt-** : write briefly and hurriedly

jounce \'jaúns\ *vb* **jounced; jounc·ing** : jolt — **jounce** *n*

jour·nal \'jərn°l\ *n* **1** : brief account of daily events **2** : periodical (as a newspaper)

jour·nal·ism \'jərn°l,izəm\ *n* : business of reporting or printing news — **jour·nal·ist** \-ist\ *n* — **jour·nal·is·tic** \,jərn°l'istik\ *adj*

jour·ney \'jərnē\ *n*, *pl* **-neys** : a going from one place to another ~ *vb* **-neyed; -ney·ing** : make a journey

jour·ney·man \-mən\ *n* : worker who has learned a trade and works for another person

joust \'jaúst\ *n* : combat on horseback between 2 knights with lances — **joust** *vb*

jo·vial \'jōvēəl\ *adj* : marked by good humor — **jo·vi·al·i·ty** \,jōvē'alətē\ *n* — **jo·vi·al·ly** \'jōvēəlē\ *adv*

¹**jowl** \'jaúl\ *n* : loose flesh about the lower jaw or throat

²**jowl** *n* **1** : lower jaw **2** : cheek

joy \'jȯi\ *n* **1** : feeling of happiness **2** : source of happiness — **joy** *vb* — **joy·ful** *adj* — **joy·ful·ly** *adv* — **joy·less** *adj* — **joy·ous** \'jȯiəs\ *adj* — **joy·ous·ly** *adv* — **joy·ous·ness** *n*

joy·ride *n* : reckless ride for pleasure — **joy·rid·er** *n* — **joy·rid·ing** *n*

ju·bi·lant \'jübələnt\ *adj* : expressing great joy — **ju·bi·lant·ly** *adv* — **ju·bi·la·tion** \,jübə'lāshən\ *n*

ju·bi·lee \'jübə,lē\ *n* **1** : 50th anniversary **2** : season or occasion of celebration

Ju·da·ism \'jüdə,izəm\ *n* : religion developed among the ancient Hebrews — **Ju·da·ic** \jü'dāik\ *adj*

judge \'jəj\ *vb* **judged; judg·ing 1** : form an opinion **2** : decide as a judge ~ *n* **1** : public official authorized to decide questions brought before a court **2** : one who gives an authoritative opinion — **judge·ship** *n*

judg·ment, judge·ment \'jəjmənt\ *n* **1** : decision or opinion given after judging **2** : capacity for judging — **judg·men·tal** \jəj'mentəl\ *adj* — **judg·men·tal·ly** *adv*

ju·di·ca·ture \'jüdikə,chùr\ *n* : administration of justice

ju·di·cial \jü'dishəl\ *adj* : relating to judicature or the judiciary — **ju·di·cial·ly** *adv*

ju·di·cia·ry \jü'dishē,erē, -'dishərē\ *n* : system of courts of law or the judges of them — **judiciary** *adj*

ju·di·cious \jü'dishəs\ *adj* : having or characterized by sound judgment — **ju·di·cious·ly** *adv*

ju·do \'jüdō\ *n* : form of wrestling — **judo·ist** *n*

jug \'jəg\ *n* : large deep container with a narrow mouth and a handle

jug·ger·naut \'jəgər,nȯt\ *n* : massive inexorable force or object

jug·gle \'jəgəl\ *vb* **-gled; -gling 1** : keep several objects in motion in the air at the same time **2** : manipulate for an often tricky purpose — **jug·gler** \'jəglər\ *n*

jug·u·lar \'jəgyələr\ *adj* : in or on the throat or neck

juice \'jüs\ *n* **1** : extractable fluid contents of cells or tissues **2** : electricity — **juic·er** *n* — **juic·i·ly** \'jüsəlē\ *adv* — **juic·i·ness** \-sēnəs\ *n* — **juicy** \'jüsē\ *adj*

ju·jube \'jü,jüb, 'jüjù,bē\ *n* : gummy candy

juke·box \'jük,bäks\ *n* : coin-operated machine for playing music recordings

ju·lep \'jüləp\ *n* : mint-flavored bourbon drink

Ju·ly \ju̇ˈlī\ *n* : 7th month of the year having 31 days

jum·ble \ˈjəmbəl\ *vb* **-bled; -bling** : mix in a confused mass — **jumble** *n*

jum·bo \ˈjəmbō\ *n, pl* **-bos** : very large version — **jumbo** *adj*

jump \ˈjəmp\ *vb* **1** : rise into or through the air esp. by muscular effort **2** : pass over **3** : give a start **4** : rise or increase sharply ~ *n* **1** : a jumping **2** : sharp sudden increase **3** : initial advantage

¹**jump·er** \ˈjəmpər\ *n* : one that jumps

²**jumper** *n* : sleeveless one-piece dress

jumpy \ˈjəmpē\ *adj* **jump·i·er; -est** : nervous or jittery

junc·tion \ˈjəŋkshən\ *n* **1** : a joining **2** : place or point of meeting

junc·ture \ˈjəŋkchər\ *n* **1** : joint or connection **2** : critical time or state of affairs

June \ˈjün\ *n* : 6th month of the year having 30 days

jun·gle \ˈjəŋgəl\ *n* : thick tangled mass of tropical vegetation

ju·nior \ˈjünyər\ *n* **1** : person who is younger or of lower rank than another **2** : student in the next-to-last year ~ *adj* : younger or lower in rank

ju·ni·per \ˈjünəpər\ *n* : evergreen shrub or tree

¹**junk** \ˈjəŋk\ *n* **1** : discarded articles **2** : shoddy product ~ *vb* : discard or scrap — **junky** *adj*

²**junk** *n* : flat-bottomed ship of Chinese waters

jun·ket \ˈjəŋkət\ *n* : trip made by an official at public expense

jun·ta \ˈhu̇ntə, ˈjəntə, ˈhəntə\ *n* : group of persons controlling a government

ju·ris·dic·tion \ju̇rəsˈdikshən\ *n* **1** : right or authority to interpret and apply the law **2** : limits within which authority may be exercised — **ju·ris·dic·tion·al** \-shənəl\ *adj*

ju·ris·pru·dence \-ˈprüdᵊns\ *n* **1** : system of laws **2** : science or philosophy of law

ju·rist \ˈju̇rist\ *n* : judge

ju·ry \ˈju̇rē\ *n, pl* **-ries** : body of persons sworn to give a verdict on a matter

just \ˈjəst\ *adj* **1** : reasonable **2** : correct or proper **3** : morally or legally right **4** : deserved ~ *adv* **1** : exactly **2** : very recently **3** : barely **4** : only **5** : quite **6** : possibly — **just·ly** *adv* — **just·ness** *n*

jus·tice \ˈjəstəs\ *n* **1** : administration of what is just **2** : judge **3** : administration of law **4** : fairness

jus·ti·fy \ˈjəstəˌfī\ *vb* **-fied; -fy·ing** : prove to be just, right, or reasonable — **jus·ti·fi·able** *adj* — **jus·ti·fi·ca·tion** \ˌjəstəfəˈkāshən\ *n*

jut \ˈjət\ *vb* **-tt-** : stick out

jute \ˈjüt\ *n* : strong glossy fiber from a tropical plant

ju·ve·nile \ˈjüvəˌnīl, -vənᵊl\ *adj* : relating to children or young people ~ *n* : young person

jux·ta·pose \ˈjəkstəˌpōz\ *vb* **-posed; -pos·ing** : place side by side — **jux·ta·po·si·tion** \ˌjəkstəpəˈzishən\ *n*

K

k \ˈkā\ *n, pl* **k's** *or* **ks** \ˈkāz\ : 11th letter of the alphabet

kai·ser \ˈkīzər\ *n* : German ruler

kale \ˈkāl\ *n* : curly cabbage

ka·lei·do·scope \kəˈlīdəˌskōp\ *n* : device containing loose bits of colored material reflecting in many patterns — **ka·lei·do·scop·ic** \-ˌlīdəˈskäpik\ *adj* — **ka·lei·do·scop·i·cal·ly** \-iklē\ *adv*

kan·ga·roo \ˌkaŋgəˈrü\ *n, pl* **-roos** : large leaping Australian mammal

ka·o·lin \ˈkāələn\ *n* : fine white clay

kar·a·o·ke \ˌkarēˈōkē\ *n* : device that plays accompaniments for singers

kar·at \ˈkarət\ *n* : unit of gold content

ka·ra·te \kəˈrätē\ *n* : art of self-defense by crippling kicks and punches

ka·ty·did \ˈkātēˌdid\ *n* : large American grasshopper

kay·ak \ˈkīˌak\ *n* : Eskimo canoe

ka·zoo \kəˈzü\ *n, pl* **-zoos** : toy musical instrument

keel \ˈkēl\ *n* : central lengthwise strip

on the bottom of a ship — **keeled** \'kēld\ *adj*

keen \'kēn\ *adj* 1 : sharp 2 : severe 3 : enthusiastic 4 : mentally alert — **keen·ly** *adv* — **keen·ness** *n*

keep \'kēp\ *vb* **kept** \'kept\; **keep·ing** 1 : perform 2 : guard 3 : maintain 4 : retain in one's possession 5 : detain 6 : continue in good condition 7 : refrain ~ *n* 1 : fortress 2 : means by which one is kept — **keep·er** *n*

keep·ing \'kēpiŋ\ *n* : conformity

keep·sake \'kēp,sāk\ *n* : souvenir

keg \'keg\ *n* : small cask or barrel

kelp \'kelp\ *n* : coarse brown seaweed

ken \'ken\ *n* : range of sight or understanding

ken·nel \'ken³l\ *n* : dog shelter — **kennel** *vb*

ker·chief \'kərchəf, -,chēf\ *n* : square of cloth worn as a head covering

ker·nel \'kərn³l\ *n* 1 : inner softer part of a seed or nut 2 : whole seed of a cereal 3 : central part

ker·o·sene, ker·o·sine \'kerə,sēn, ,kerə'-\ *n* : thin flammable oil from petroleum

ketch·up \'kechəp, 'ka-\ *n* : spicy tomato sauce

ket·tle \'ket³l\ *n* : vessel for boiling liquids

ket·tle·drum \-,drum\ *n* : brass or copper kettle-shaped drum

¹**key** \'kē\ *n* 1 : usu. metal piece to open a lock 2 : explanation 3 : lever pressed by a finger in playing an instrument or operating a machine 4 : leading individual or principle 5 : system of musical tones or pitch ~ *vb* : attune ~ *adj* : basic — **key·hole** *n* — **key up** *vb* : make nervous

²**key** *n* : low island or reef

key·board *n* : arrangement of keys

key·note \-,nōt\ *n* 1 : 1st note of a scale 2 : central fact, idea, or mood ~ *vb* 1 : set the keynote of 2 : deliver the major speech

key·stone *n* : wedge-shaped piece at the crown of an arch

kha·ki \'kakē, 'käk-\ *n* : light yellowish brown color

khan \'kän, 'kan\ *n* : Mongol leader

kib·butz \kib'üts, -'üts\ *n, pl* -**but·zim** \-,üt'sēm, -,üt-\ : Israeli communal farm or settlement

kib·itz·er \'kibətsər, kə'bit-\ *n* : one who offers unwanted advice — **kib·itz** \'kibəts\ *vb*

kick \'kik\ *vb* 1 : strike out or hit with the foot 2 : object strongly 3 : recoil ~ *n* 1 : thrust with the foot 2 : recoil of a gun 3 : stimulating effect — **kick·er** *n*

kid \'kid\ *n* 1 : young goat 2 : child ~ *vb* -**dd-** 1 : deceive as a joke 2 : tease — **kid·der** *n* — **kid·ding·ly** *adv*

kid·nap \'kid,nap\ *vb* -**napped** *or* -**naped** \-,napt\; -**nap·ping** *or* -**nap·ing** : carry a person away by illegal force — **kid·nap·per, kid·nap·er** *n*

kid·ney \'kidnē\ *n, pl* -**neys** : either of a pair of organs that excrete urine

kill \'kil\ *vb* 1 : deprive of life 2 : finish 3 : use up (time) ~ *n* : act of killing — **kill·er** *n*

kiln \'kil, 'kiln\ *n* : heated enclosure for burning, firing, or drying — **kiln** *vb*

ki·lo \'kēlō\ *n, pl* -**los** : kilogram

ki·lo·cy·cle \'kilə,sīkəl\ *n* : kilohertz

ki·lo·gram \'kēlə,gram, 'kilə-\ *n* : metric unit of weight equal to 2.2 pounds

ki·lo·hertz \'kilə,hərts, 'kēlə-, -,herts\ *n* : 1000 hertz

ki·lo·me·ter \kil'ämətər, 'kilə,mēt-\ *n* : 1000 meters

ki·lo·volt \'kilə,vōlt\ *n* : 1000 volts

kilo·watt \'kilə,wät\ *n* : 1000 watts

kilt \'kilt\ *n* : knee-length pleated skirt

kil·ter \'kiltər\ *n* : proper condition

ki·mo·no \kə'mōnō\ *n, pl* -**nos** : loose robe

kin \'kin\ *n* 1 : one's relatives 2 : kinsman

kind \'kīnd\ *n* 1 : essential quality 2 : group with common traits 3 : variety ~ *adj* 1 : of a sympathetic nature 2 : arising from sympathy — **kind·heart·ed** *adj* — **kind·ness** *n*

kin·der·gar·ten \'kindər,gärt³n\ *n* : class for young children — **kin·der·gart·ner** \-,gärtnər\ *n*

kin·dle \'kind³l\ *vb* -**dled; -dling** 1 : set on fire or start burning 2 : stir up

kin·dling \'kindliŋ, 'kinlən\ *n* : material for starting a fire

kind·ly \'kīndlē\ *adj* -**li·er; -est** : of a sympathetic nature ~ *adv* 1 : sympathetically 2 : courteously — **kind·li·ness** *n*

kin·dred \'kindrəd\ *n* 1 : related individuals 2 : kin ~ *adj* : of a like nature

kin·folk \'kin,fōk\, **kinfolks** *n pl* : kin

king \kiŋ\ *n* : male sovereign — **king·**

dom \-dəm\ n — **king·less** adj —
king·ly adj — **king·ship** n

king·fish·er \-ˌfishər\ n : bright-colored
crested bird

kink \'kiŋk\ n 1 : short tight twist or
curl 2 : cramp — **kinky** adj

kin·ship n : relationship

kins·man \'kinzmən\ n : male relative

kins·wom·an \-ˌwùmən\ n : female
relative

kip·per \'kipər\ n : dried or smoked
fish — **kipper** vb

kiss \'kis\ vb : touch with the lips as a
mark of affection — **kiss** n

kit \'kit\ n : set of articles (as tools or
parts)

kitch·en \'kichən\ n : room with cooking facilities

kite \'kit\ n 1 : small hawk 2 : covered
framework flown at the end of a
string

kith \'kith\ n : familiar friends

kit·ten \'kit²n\ n : young cat — **kit·ten·
ish** adj

¹**kit·ty** \'kitē\ n, pl **-ties** : kitten

²**kitty** n, pl **-ties** : fund or pool (as in a
card game)

kit·ty-cor·ner, kit·ty–cor·nered var of
CATERCORNER

ki·wi \'kē,wē\ n 1 : small flightless
New Zealand bird 2 : brownish egg-
shaped subtropical fruit

klep·to·ma·nia \ˌkleptə'mānēə\ n
: neurotic impulse to steal — **klep·to·
ma·ni·ac** \-nē,ak\ n

knack \'nak\ n 1 : clever way of doing
something 2 : natural aptitude

knap·sack \'nap,sak\ n : bag for carrying supplies on one's back

knave \'nāv\ n : rogue — **knav·ery**
\'nāvərē\ n — **knav·ish** \'nāvish\ adj

knead \'nēd\ vb 1 : work and press
with the hands 2 : massage —
knead·er n

knee \'nē\ n : joint in the middle part of
the leg — **kneed** \'nēd\ adj

knee-cap \'nē,kap\ n : bone forming
the front of the knee

kneel \'nēl\ vb **knelt** \'nelt\ or
kneeled; kneel·ing : rest on one's
knees

knell \'nel\ n : stroke of a bell

knew past of KNOW

knick·ers \'nikərz\ n pl : pants gath-
ered at the knee

knick·knack \'nik,nak\ n : small decorative object

knife \'nif\ n, pl **knives** \'nīvz\ : sharp

blade with a handle ∼ vb **knifed;
knif·ing** : stab or cut with a knife

knight \'nīt\ n 1 : mounted warrior of
feudal times 2 : man honored by a
sovereign ∼ vb : make a knight of —
knight·hood n — **knight·ly** adv

knit \'nit\ vb **knit** or **knit·ted; knit·ting**
1 : link firmly or closely 2 : form a
fabric by interlacing yarn or thread
∼ n : knitted garment — **knit·ter** n

knob \'näb\ n : rounded protuberance
or handle — **knobbed** \'näbd\ adj
— **knob·by** \'näbē\ adj

knock \'näk\ vb 1 : strike with a sharp
blow 2 : collide 3 : find fault with ∼
n : sharp blow — **knock out** vb
: make unconscious

knock·er n : device hinged to a door to
knock with

knoll \'nōl\ n : small round hill

knot \'nät\ n 1 : interlacing (as of
string) that forms a lump 2 : base of
a woody branch in the stem 3 : group
4 : one nautical mile per hour ∼ vb
-tt- : tie in or with a knot — **knot·ty**
adj

know \'nō\ vb **knew** \'nü, 'nyü\;
known \'nōn\; **know·ing** 1 : perceive directly or understand 2 : be
familiar with — **know·able** adj —
know·er n

know·ing \'nōiŋ\ adj : shrewdly and
keenly alert — **know·ing·ly** adv

knowl·edge \'nälij\ n 1 : understanding gained by experience 2 : range of
information — **knowl·edge·able** adj

knuck·le \'nəkəl\ n : rounded knob at a
finger joint

ko·ala \kō'älə\ n : gray furry Australian animal

kohl·ra·bi \kōl'rabē, -'räb-\ n, pl
-bies : cabbage that forms no head

Ko·ran \kə'ran, -'rän\ n : book of Islam containing revelations made to
Muhammad by Allah

ko·sher \'kōshər\ adj : ritually fit for
use according to Jewish law

kow·tow \kaù'taù, 'kaù,taù\ vb
: show excessive deference

kryp·ton \'krip,tän\ n : gaseous chemical element used in lamps

ku·dos \'kyü,däs, 'kü-, -,dōz\ n : fame
and renown

kum·quat \'kəm,kwät\ n : small citrus
fruit

Kwan·zaa, Kwan·za \'kwänzə\ n
: African-American festival held
from December 26 to January 1 ∼

L

l \'el\ *n, pl* **l's** *or* **ls** \'elz\ : 12th letter of the alphabet

lab \'lab\ *n* : laboratory

la·bel \'lābǝl\ *n* **1** : identification slip **2** : identifying word or phrase ~ *vb* **-beled** *or* **-belled;** — **bel·ing** *or* — **bel·ling** : put a label on

la·bi·al \'lābēǝl\ *adj* : of or relating to the lips

la·bor \'lābǝr\ *n* **1** : physical or mental effort **2** : physical efforts of childbirth **3** : task **4** : people who work manually ~ *vb* : work esp. with great effort — **la·bor·er** *n*

lab·o·ra·to·ry \'labrǝ,tōrē\ *n, pl* **-ries** : place for experimental testing

Labor Day *n* : 1st Monday in September observed as a legal holiday in recognition of working people

la·bo·ri·ous \lǝ'bōrēǝs\ *adj* : requiring great effort — **la·bo·ri·ous·ly** *adv*

lab·y·rinth \'labǝ,rinth\ *n* : maze — **lab·y·rin·thine** \,labǝ'rinthǝn\ *adj*

lace \'lās\ *n* **1** : cord or string for tying **2** : fine net usu. figured fabric ~ *vb* **laced; lac·ing 1** : tie **2** : adorn with lace — **lacy** \'lāsē\ *adj*

lac·er·ate \'lasǝ,rāt\ *vb* **-at·ed; -at·ing** : tear roughly — **lac·er·a·tion** \,lasǝ-'rāshǝn\ *n*

lach·ry·mose \'lakrǝ,mōs\ *adj* : tearful

lack \'lak\ *vb* : be missing or deficient in ~ *n* : deficiency

lack·a·dai·si·cal \,lakǝ'dāzikǝl\ *adj* : lacking spirit — **lack·a·dai·si·cal·ly** \-klē\ *adv*

lack·ey \'lakē\ *n, pl* **-eys 1** : footman or servant **2** : toady

lack·lus·ter \'lak,lǝstǝr\ *adj* : dull

la·con·ic \lǝ'känik\ *adj* : sparing of words — **la·con·i·cal·ly** \-iklē\ *adv*

lac·quer \'lakǝr\ *n* : glossy surface coating — **lacquer** *vb*

la·crosse \lǝ'krós\ *n* : ball game played with long-handled rackets

lac·tate \'lak,tāt\ *vb* **-tat·ed; -tat·ing** : secrete milk — **lac·ta·tion** \lak'tā-shǝn\ *n*

lac·tic \'laktik\ *adj* : relating to milk

la·cu·na \lǝ'künǝ, -'kyü-\ *n, pl* **-nae** \-,nē\ *or* **-nas** : blank space or missing part

lad \'lad\ *n* : boy

lad·der \'ladǝr\ *n* : device with steps or rungs for climbing

lad·en \'lād²n\ *adj* : loaded

la·dle \'lād²l\ *n* : spoon with a deep bowl **-ladle** *vb*

la·dy \'lādē\ *n, pl* **-dies 1** : woman of rank or authority **2** : woman

la·dy·bird \'lādē,bǝrd\ *n* : ladybug

la·dy·bug \-,bǝg\ *n* : brightly colored beetle

lag \'lag\ *vb* **-gg-** : fail to keep up ~ *n* **1** : a falling behind **2** : interval

la·ger \'lägǝr\ *n* : beer

lag·gard \'lagǝrd\ *adj* : slow ~ *n* : one that lags — **lag·gard·ly** *adv*

la·gniappe \'lan,yap\ *n* : bonus

la·goon \lǝ'gün\ *n* : shallow sound, channel, or pond near or connecting with a larger body of water

laid *past of* LAY

lain *past part of* LIE

lair \'lar\ *n* : den

lais·sez-faire \,les,ā'far\ *n* : doctrine opposing government interference in business

la·ity \'lāǝtē\ *n* : people of a religious faith who are not clergy members

lake \'lāk\ *n* : inland body of water

la·ma \'lämǝ\ *n* : Buddhist monk

lamb \'lam\ *n* : young sheep or its flesh used as food

lam·baste, lam·bast \lam'bāst, -'bast\ *vb* **1** : beat **2** : censure

lam·bent \'lambǝnt\ *adj* : light or bright — **lam·bent·ly** *adv*

lame \'lām\ *adj* **lam·er; lam·est 1** : having a limb disabled **2** : weak ~ *vb* **lamed; lam·ing** : make lame — **lame·ly** *adv* **-lame·ness** *n*

la·mé \lä'mā, la-\ *n* : cloth with tinsel threads

lame·brain \'lām,brān\ *n* : fool

la·ment \lǝ'ment\ *vb* **1** : mourn **2** : express sorrow for ~ *n* **1** : mourning **2** : complaint — **lam·en·ta·ble** \'lamǝn-tǝbǝl, lǝ'mentǝ-\ *adj* — **lam·en·ta·bly** \-blē\ *adv* — **lam·en·ta·tion** \,lamǝn'tāshǝn\ *n*

lam·i·nat·ed \'lamə₁nātəd\ *adj* : made of thin layers of material — **lam·i·nate** \-₁nāt\ *vt* — **lam·i·nate** \-nət\ *n or adj* — **lam·i·na·tion** \₁lamə'nā-shən\ *n*

lamp \'lamp\ *n* : device for producing light or heat

lam·poon \lam'pün\ *n* : satire — **lam·poon** *vb*

lam·prey \'lamprē\ *n, pl* **-preys** : sucking eellike fish

lance \'lans\ *n* : spear ~ *vb* **lanced; lanc·ing** : pierce or open with a lancet

lance corporal *n* : enlisted man in the marine corps ranking above a private first class and below a corporal

lan·cet \'lansət\ *n* : pointed surgical instrument

land \'land\ *n* 1 : solid part of the surface of the earth 2 : country ~ *vb* 1 : go ashore 2 : catch or gain 3 : touch the ground or a surface — **land·less** *adj* — **land·own·er** *n*

land·fill *n* : dump

land·ing \'landiŋ\ *n* 1 : action of one that lands 2 : place for loading passengers and cargo 3 : level part of a staircase

land·la·dy \'land₁lādē\ *n* : woman landlord

land·locked *adj* : enclosed by land

land·lord *n* : owner of property

land·lub·ber \-₁ləbər\ *n* : one with little sea experience

land·mark \-₁märk\ *n* 1 : object that marks a boundary or serves as a guide 2 : event that marks a turning point

land·scape \-₁skāp\ *n* : view of natural scenery ~ *vb* **-scaped; -scap·ing** : beautify a piece of land (as by decorative planting)

land·slide *n* 1 : slipping down of a mass of earth 2 : overwhelming victory

land·ward \'landwərd\ *adj* : toward the land — **landward** *adv*

lane \'lān\ *n* : narrow way

lan·guage \'langwij\ *n* : words and the methods of combining them for communication

lan·guid \'langwəd\ *adj* 1 : weak 2 : sluggish — **lan·guid·ly** *adv* — **lan·guid·ness** *n*

lan·guish \'langwish\ *vb* : become languid or discouraged

lan·guor \'langər\ *n* : listless indolence — **lan·guor·ous** *adj* — **lan·guor·ous·ly** *adv*

lank \'laŋk\ *adj* 1 : thin 2 : limp

lanky *adj* **lank·i·er; -est** : tall and thin

lan·o·lin \'lan²lən\ *n* : fatty wax from sheep's wool used in ointments

lan·tern \'lantərn\ *n* : enclosed portable light

¹**lap** \'lap\ *n* 1 : front part of the lower trunk and thighs of a seated person 2 : overlapping part 3 : one complete circuit completing a course (as around a track or pool) ~ *vb* **-pp-** : fold over

²**lap** *vb* **-pp-** 1 : scoop up with the tongue 2 : splash gently

lap·dog *n* : small dog

la·pel \lə'pel\ *n* : fold of the front of a coat

lap·i·dary \'lapə₁derē\ *n* : one who cuts and polishes gems ~ *adj* : relating to gems

lapse \'laps\ *n* 1 : slight error 2 : termination of a right or privilege 3 : interval ~ *vb* **lapsed; laps·ing** 1 : slip 2 : subside 3 : cease

lap·top \'lap₁täp\ *adj* : of a size that may be used on one's lap

lar·board \'lärbərd\ *n* : port side

lar·ce·ny \'lärs²nē\ *n, pl* **-nies** : theft — **lar·ce·nous** \'lärs²nəs\ *adj*

larch \'lärch\ *n* : tree like a pine that loses its needles

lard \'lärd\ *n* : pork fat

lar·der \'lärdər\ *n* : pantry

large \'lärj\ *adj* **larg·er; larg·est** : greater than average — **large·ly** *adv* — **large·ness** *n*

lar·gesse, lar·gess \lär'zhes, -'jes; 'lär₁-\ *n* : liberal giving

lar·i·at \'lärēət\ *n* : lasso

¹**lark** \'lärk\ *n* : small songbird

²**lark** *vb or n* : romp

lar·va \'lärvə\ *n, pl* **-vae** \-₁vē\ : wormlike form of an insect — **lar·val** \-vəl\ *adj*

lar·yn·gi·tis \₁larən'jītəs\ *n* : inflammation of the larynx

lar·ynx \'lariŋks\ *n, pl* **-ryn·ges** \lə'rin₁jēz\ *or* **-ynx·es** : upper part of the trachea — **la·ryn·ge·al** \₁larən'jēal, lə'rinjēal\ *adj*

la·sa·gna \lə'zänyə\ *n* : flat noodles baked usu. with tomato sauce, meat, and cheese

las·civ·i·ous \lə'sivēəs\ *adj* : lewd — **las·civ·i·ous·ness** *n*

la·ser \'lāzər\ *n* : device that produces an intense light beam

¹**lash** \'lash\ *vb* : whip ~ *n* 1 : stroke esp. of a whip 2 : eyelash

²**lash** *vb* : bind with a rope or cord

lass \'las\ *n* : girl

lass·ie \'lasē\ *n* : girl

las·si·tude \'lasə,tüd, -,tyüd\ *n* **1** : fatigue **2** : listlessness

las·so \'lasō, la'sü\ *n, pl* **-sos** *or* **-soes** : rope with a noose for catching livestock — **lasso** *vb*

¹last \'last\ *vb* : continue in existence or operation

²last *adj* **1** : final **2** : previous **3** : least likely ~ *adv* **1** : at the end **2** : most recently **3** : in conclusion ~ *n* : something that is last — **last·ly** *adv* — **at last** : finally

³last *n* : form on which a shoe is shaped

latch \'lach\ *vb* : catch or get hold ~ *n* : catch that holds a door closed

late \'lāt\ *adj* **lat·er; lat·est 1** : coming or staying after the proper time **2** : advanced toward the end **3** : recently deceased **4** : recent — **late** *adv* — **late·com·er** \-,kəmər\ *n* — **late·ly** *adv* — **late·ness** *n*

la·tent \'lāt⁰nt\ *adj* : present but not visible or expressed — **la·ten·cy** \-²nsē\ *n*

lat·er·al \'latərəl\ *adj* : on or toward the side — **lat·er·al·ly** *adv*

la·tex \'lā,teks\ *n, pl* **-ti·ces** \'lātə,sēz, 'lat-\ *or* **-tex·es** : emulsion of synthetic rubber or plastic

lath \'lath, 'lath\ *n, pl* **laths** *or* **lath** : building material (as a thin strip of wood) used as a base for plaster — **lath** *vb* — **lath·ing** \-iŋ\ *n*

lathe \'lāth\ *n* : machine that rotates material for shaping

lath·er \'lathər\ *n* : foam ~ *vb* : form or spread lather

lat·i·tude \'latə,tüd, -,tyüd\ *n* **1** : distance north or south from the earth's equator **2** : freedom of action

la·trine \lə'trēn\ *n* : toilet

lat·ter \'latər\ *adj* **1** : more recent **2** : being the second of 2 — **lat·ter·ly** *adv*

lat·tice \'latəs\ *n* : framework of crossed strips

laud *vb or n* : praise — **laud·able** *adj* — **laud·ably** *adv*

laugh \'laf, 'laf\ *vb* : show mirth, joy, or scorn with a smile and explosive sound — **laugh** *n* — **laugh·able** *adj* — **laugh·ing·ly** \-iŋlē\ *adv*

laugh·ing·stock \'lafiŋ,stäk, 'laf-\ *n* : object of ridicule

laugh·ter \'laftər, 'laf-\ *n* : action or sound of laughing

¹launch \'lonch\ *vb* **1** : hurl or send off **2** : set afloat **3** : start — **launch** *n* — **launch·er** *n*

²launch *n* : small open boat

laun·der \'londər\ *vb* : wash or iron fabrics — **laun·der·er** *n* — **laun·dress** \-drəs\ *n* — **laun·dry** \-drē\ *n*

lau·re·ate \'lorēət\ *n* : recipient of honors — **laureate** *adj*

lau·rel \'lorəl\ *n* **1** : small evergreen tree **2** : honor

la·va \'lävə, 'lav-\ *n* : volcanic molten rock

lav·a·to·ry \'lavə,tōrē\ *n, pl* **-ries** : bathroom

lav·en·der \'lavəndər\ *n* **1** : aromatic plant used for perfume **2** : pale purple color

lav·ish \'lavish\ *adj* : expended profusely ~ *vb* : expend or give freely — **lav·ish·ly** *adv* — **lav·ish·ness** *n*

law \'lo\ *n* **1** : established rule of conduct **2** : body of such rules **3** : principle of construction or procedure **4** : rule stating uniform behavior under uniform conditions **5** : lawyer's profession — **law·break·er** *n* — **law·giv·er** *n* — **law·less** *adj* — **law·less·ly** *adv* — **law·less·ness** *n* — **law·mak·er** *n* — **law·man** \-mən\ *n* — **law·suit** *n*

law·ful \'lofəl\ *adj* : permitted by law — **law·ful·ly** *adv*

lawn \'lon\ *n* : grass-covered yard

law·yer \'loyər\ *n* : legal practitioner

lax \'laks\ *adj* : not strict or tense — **lax·i·ty** \'laksətē\ *n* — **lax·ly** *adv*

lax·a·tive \'laksətiv\ *n* : drug relieving constipation

¹lay \'lā\ *vb* **laid** \'lād\; **lay·ing 1** : put or set down **2** : produce eggs **3** : bet **4** : impose as a duty or burden **5** : put forward ~ *n* : way something lies or is laid

²lay *past of* LIE

³lay *n* : song

⁴lay *adj* : of the laity — **lay·man** \-mən\ *n* — **lay·wom·an** \-,wùmən\ *n*

lay·er \'lāər\ *n* **1** : one that lays **2** : one thickness over or under another

lay·off \'lā,of\ *n* : temporary dismissal of a worker

lay·out \'lā,aùt\ *n* : arrangement

la·zy \'lāzē\ *adj* **-zi·er; -est** : disliking activity or exertion — **la·zi·ly** \'lāzəlē\ *adv* — **la·zi·ness** *n*

lea \'lē, 'lā\ *n* : meadow

leach \'lēch\ *vb* : remove (a soluble part) with a solvent

¹lead \'lēd\ *vb* **led** \'led\; **lead·ing 1** : guide on a way **2** : direct the activity of **3** : go at the head of **4** : tend to a definite result ~ *n* : position in front — **lead·er** \'lēd-ər\ *n* — **lead·er·less** *adj* — **lead·er·ship** *n*

²**lead** \'led\ *n* **1** : heavy bluish white chemical element **2** : marking substance in a pencil — **lead·en** \'led°n\ *adj*

leaf \'lēf\ *n, pl* **leaves** \'lēvz\ **1** : green outgrowth of a plant stem **2** : leaflike thing ~ *vb* **1** : produce leaves **2** : turn book pages — **leaf·age** \'lēfij\ *n* — **leafed** \'lēft\ *adj* — **leaf·less** *adj* — **leafy** *adj* — **leaved** \'lēfd\ *adj*

leaf·let \'lēflət\ *n* : pamphlet

¹**league** \'lēg\ *n* : unit of distance equal to about 3 miles

²**league** *n* : association for a common purpose — **league** *vb* — **leagu·er** *n*

leak \'lēk\ *vb* **1** : enter or escape through a leak **2** : become or make known ~ *n* : opening that accidentally admits or lets out a substance — **leak·age** \'lēkij\ *n* — **leaky** *adj*

¹**lean** \'lēn\ *vb* **1** : bend from a vertical position **2** : rely on for support **3** : incline in opinion — **lean** *n*

²**lean** *adj* **1** : lacking in flesh **2** : lacking richness — **lean·ness** \'lēnnəs\ *n*

leap \'lēp\ *vb* **leapt** *or* **leaped** \'lēpt, 'lept\; **leap·ing** : jump — **leap** *n*

leap year *n* : 366-day year

learn \'lərn\ *vb* **1** : gain understanding or skill by study or experience **2** : memorize **3** : find out — **learn·er** *n*

learn·ed \-əd\ *adj* : having great learning — **learn·ed·ness** *n*

learn·ing \-iŋ\ *n* : knowledge

lease \'lēs\ *n* : contract transferring real estate for a term and usu. for rent ~ *vb* **leased; leas·ing** : grant by or hold under a lease

leash \'lēsh\ *n* : line to hold an animal — **leash** *vb*

least \'lēst\ *adj* **1** : lowest in importance or position **2** : smallest **3** : scantiest ~ *n* : one that is least — ~ *adv* : in the smallest or lowest degree

leath·er \'lethər\ *n* : dressed animal skin — **leath·ern** \-ərn\ *adj* — **leath·ery** *adj*

¹**leave** \'lēv\ *vb* **left** \'left\; **leav·ing 1** : bequeath **2** : allow or cause to remain **3** : have as a remainder **4** : go away — ~ *n* **1** : permission **2** : authorized absence **3** : departure

²**leave** *vb* **leaved; leav·ing** : leaf

leav·en \'levən\ *n* : substance for producing fermentation ~ *vb* : raise dough with a leaven

leaves *pl of* LEAF

lech·ery \'lechərē\ *n* : inordinate indulgence in sex — **lech·er** \'lechər\ *n* — **lech·er·ous** \-chərəs\ *adj* — **lech·er·ous·ly** *adv* — **lech·er·ous·ness** *n*

lec·ture \'lekchər\ *n* **1** : instructive talk **2** : reprimand — **lecture** *vb* — **lec·tur·er** *n* — **lec·ture·ship** *n*

led *past of* LEAD

ledge \'lej\ *n* : shelflike projection

led·ger \'lejər\ *n* : account book

lee \'lē\ *n* : side sheltered from the wind — **lee** *adj*

leech \'lēch\ *n* : segmented freshwater worm that feeds on blood

leek \'lēk\ *n* : onionlike herb

leer \'lir\ *n* : suggestive or malicious look — **leer** *vb*

leery \'lirē\ *adj* : suspicious or wary

lees \'lēz\ *n pl* : dregs

lee·ward \'lēwərd, 'lüərd\ *adj* : situated away from the wind ~ *n* : the lee side

lee·way \'lē,wā\ *n* : allowable margin

¹**left** \'left\ *adj* : on the same side of the body as the heart ~ *n* : left hand — **left** *adv*

²**left** *past of* LEAVE

leg \'leg\ *n* **1** : limb of an animal that supports the body **2** : something like a leg **3** : clothing to cover the leg ~ *vb* **-gg-** : walk or run — **leg·ged** \'legəd\ *adj* — **leg·less** *adj*

leg·a·cy \'legəsē\ *n, pl* **-cies** : inheritance

le·gal \'lēgəl\ *adj* **1** : relating to law or lawyers **2** : lawful — **le·gal·is·tic** \,lēgə'listik\ *adj* — **le·gal·i·ty** \li-'galətē\ *n* — **le·gal·ize** \'lēgə,līz\ *vb* — **le·gal·ly** \-gəlē\ *adv*

leg·ate \'legət\ *n* : official representative

le·ga·tion \li'gāshən\ *n* **1** : diplomatic mission **2** : official residence and office of a diplomat

leg·end \'lejənd\ *n* **1** : story handed down from the past **2** : inscription **3** : explanation of map symbols — **leg·end·ary** \-ən,derē\ *adj*

leg·er·de·main \,lejərdə'mān\ *n* : sleight of hand

leg·ging, leg·gin \'legən, -in\ *n* : leg covering

leg·i·ble \'lejəbəl\ *adj* : capable of be-

ing read — **leg·i·bil·i·ty** \ˌlejə-
ˈbilətē\ *n* — **leg·i·bly** \ˈlejəblē\ *adv*
le·gion \ˈlējən\ *n* **1** : large army unit **2**
: multitude **3** : association of former
servicemen — **le·gion·ary** \-ˌerē\ *n*
— **le·gion·naire** \ˌlējənˈar\ *n*
leg·is·late \ˈlejəˌslāt\ *vb* **-lat·ed; -lat·**
ing : enact or bring about with laws
— **leg·is·la·tion** \ˌlejəˈslāshən\ *n* —
leg·is·la·tive \ˈlejəˌslātiv\ *adj* —
leg·is·la·tor \-ər\ *n*
leg·is·la·ture \ˈlejəˌslāchər\ *n* : organization with authority to make laws
le·git·i·mate \liˈjitəmət\ *adj* **1** : law-
fully begotten **2** : genuine **3** : conforming with law or accepted
standards — **le·git·i·ma·cy** \-məsē\
n — **le·git·i·mate·ly** *adv* — **le·git·i·**
mize \-ˌmīz\ *vb*
le·gume \ˈlegˌyüm, liˈgyüm\ *n* : plant
bearing pods — **le·gu·mi·nous**
\liˈgyümənəs\ *adj*
lei \ˈlā\ *n* : necklace of flowers
lei·sure \ˈlēzhər, lezh-, ˈlāzh-\ *n* **1**
: free time **2** : ease **3** : convenience
— **lei·sure·ly** *adj or adv*
lem·ming \ˈlemiŋ\ *n* : short-tailed rodent
lem·on \ˈlemən\ *n* : yellow citrus fruit
— **lem·ony** *adj*
lem·on·ade \ˌleməˈnād\ *n* : sweetened
lemon beverage
lend \ˈlend\ *vb* **lent** \ˈlent\; **lend·ing**
1 : give for temporary use **2** : furnish
— **lend·er** *n*
length \ˈleŋth\ *n* **1** : longest dimension **2** : duration in time **3** : piece to
be joined to others — **length·en**
\ˈleŋthən\ *vb* — **length·wise** *adv or*
adj — **lengthy** *adj*
le·nient \ˈlēnēənt, -nyənt\ *adj* : of
mild and tolerant disposition or effect
— **le·ni·en·cy** \ˈlēnēənsē -nyənsē\
n — **le·ni·ent·ly** *adv*
lens \ˈlenz\ *n* **1** : curved piece for
forming an image in an optical instrument **2** : transparent body in the eye
that focuses light rays
Lent \ˈlent\ *n* : 40-day period of penitence and fasting from Ash Wednesday to Easter — **Lent·en** \-ən\ *adj*
len·til \ˈlentᵊl\ *n* : legume with flat edible seeds
le·o·nine \ˈlēəˌnīn\ *adj* : like a lion
leop·ard \ˈlepərd\ *n* : large tawny
black-spotted cat

le·o·tard \ˈlēəˌtärd\ *n* : close-fitting
garment
lep·er \ˈlepər\ *n* : person with leprosy
lep·re·chaun \ˈleprəˌkän\ *n* : mischievous Irish elf
lep·ro·sy \ˈleprəsē\ *n* : chronic bacterial disease — **lep·rous** \-rəs\ *adj*
les·bi·an \ˈlezbēən\ *n* : female homosexual — **lesbian** *adj* — **les·bi·an·**
ism \-ˌizəm\ *n*
le·sion \ˈlēzhən\ *n* : abnormal area in
the body due to injury or disease
less \ˈles\ *adj* **1** : fewer **2** : of lower
rank, degree, or importance **3**
: smaller ~ *adv* : to a lesser degree
~ *n, pl* **less** : smaller portion ~
prep : minus — **less·en** \-ᵊn\ *vb*
-less \ləs\ *adj suffix* **1** : not having **2**
: unable to act or be acted on
les·see \leˈsē\ *n* : tenant under a lease
less·er \ˈlesər\ *adj* : of less size, quality, or significance
les·son \ˈlesᵊn\ *n* **1** : reading or exercise to be studied by a pupil **2** : something learned
les·sor \ˈlesˌȯr, leˈsȯr\ *n* : one who
transfers property by a lease
lest \ˌlest\ *conj* : for fear that
¹let \ˈlet\ *n* : hindrance or obstacle
²let *vb* **let; let·ting** **1** : cause to **2** : rent
3 : permit
-let \lət\ *n suffix* : small one
le·thal \ˈlēthəl\ *adj* : deadly — **le·thal·**
ly *adv*
leth·ar·gy \ˈlethərjē\ *n* **1** : drowsiness
2 : state of being lazy or indifferent
— **le·thar·gic** \liˈthärjik\ *adj*
let·ter \ˈletər\ *n* **1** : unit of an alphabet
2 : written or printed communication
3 *pl* : literature or learning **4** : literal
meaning ~ *vb* : mark with letters —
let·ter·er *n*
let·tuce \ˈletəs\ *n* : garden plant with
crisp leaves
leu·ke·mia \lüˈkēmēə\ *n* : cancerous
blood disease — **leu·ke·mic** \-mik\
adj or n
lev·ee \ˈlevē\ *n* : embankment to prevent flooding
lev·el \ˈlevəl\ *n* **1** : device for establishing a flat surface **2** : horizontal
surface **3** : position in a scale ~ *vb*
-eled *or* **-elled; -el·ing** *or* **-el·ling** **1**
: make flat or level **2** : aim **3** : raze
~ *adj* **1** : having an even surface **2**
: of the same height or rank — **lev·el·**
er *n* — **lev·el·ly** *adv* — **lev·el·ness** *n*
le·ver \ˈlevər, ˈlē-\ *n* : bar for prying or

dislodging something — **le·ver·age** \'levərij, 'lev-\ n

le·vi·a·than \li'vīəthən\ n 1 : large sea animal 2 : enormous thing

lev·i·ty \'levətē\ n : unseemly frivolity

levy \'levē\ n, pl **lev·ies** : imposition or collection of a tax ~ vb **lev·ied; levy·ing** 1 : impose or collect legally 2 : enlist for military service 3 : wage

lewd \'lüd\ adj 1 : sexually unchaste 2 : vulgar — **lewd·ly** adv — **lewd·ness** n

lex·i·cog·ra·phy \leksə'kägrəfē\ n : dictionary making — **lex·i·cog·ra·pher** \-fər\ n — **lex·i·co·graph·i·cal** \-kō'grafikəl\, **lex·i·co·graph·ic** \-ik\ adj

lex·i·con \'leksə,kän\ n, pl **-i·ca** \-sikə\ or **-icons** : dictionary

li·a·ble \'līəbəl\ adj 1 : legally obligated 2 : probable 3 : susceptible — **li·a·bil·i·ty** \,līə'bilətē\ n

li·ai·son \'lēə,zän, lē'ā-\ n 1 : close bond 2 : communication between groups

li·ar \'līər\ n : one who lies

li·bel \'lībəl\ n : action, crime, or an instance of injuring a person's reputation esp. by something written ~ vb **-beled** or **-belled; -bel·ing** or **-bel·ling** : make or publish a libel — **li·bel·er** n — **li·bel·ist** n — **li·bel·ous, li·bel·lous** \-bələs\ adj

lib·er·al \'librəl, 'libə-\ adj : not stingy, narrow, or conservative — **liberal** n — **lib·er·al·ism** \-,izəm\ n — **lib·er·al·i·ty** \,libə'ralətē\ n — **lib·er·al·ize** \'librə,līz, 'libə-\ vb — **lib·er·al·ly** \-rəlē\ adv

lib·er·ate \'libə,rāt\ vb **-at·ed; -at·ing** : set free — **lib·er·a·tion** \,libə'rāshən\ n — **lib·er·a·tor** \'libə,rātər\ n

lib·er·tine \'libər,tēn\ n : one who leads a dissolute life

lib·er·ty \'libərtē\ n, pl **-ties** 1 : quality or state of being free 2 : action going beyond normal limits

li·bi·do \lə'bēdō, -'bīd-\ n, pl **-dos** : sexual drive — **li·bid·i·nal** \lə-'bid²nəl\ adj — **li·bid·i·nous** \-əs\ adj

li·brary \'lī,brerē\ n, pl **-brar·ies** 1 : place where books are kept for use 2 : collection of books — **li·brar·i·an** \lī'brerēən\ n

li·bret·to \lə'bretō\ n, pl **-tos** or **-ti** \-ē\ : text of an opera — **li·bret·tist** \-ist\ n

lice pl of LOUSE

li·cense, li·cence \'līs²ns\ n 1 : legal permission to engage in some activity 2 : document or tag providing proof of a license 3 : irresponsible use

of freedom — **license** vb — **li·cens·ee** \,līs²n'sē\ n

li·cen·tious \lī'senchəs\ adj : disregarding sexual restraints — **li·cen·tious·ly** adv — **li·cen·tious·ness** n

li·chen \'līkən\ n : complex lower plant made up of an alga and a fungus

lic·it \'lisət\ adj : lawful

lick \'lik\ vb 1 : draw the tongue over 2 : beat ~ n 1 : stroke of the tongue 2 : small amount

lic·o·rice \'likərish, -rəs\ n : dried root of a European legume or candy flavored by it

lid \'lid\ n 1 : movable cover 2 : eyelid

1lie \'lī\ vb **lay** \'lā\; **lain** \'lān\; **ly·ing** \'līiŋ\ 1 : be in, rest in, or assume a horizontal position 2 : occupy a certain relative position ~ n : position in which something lies

2lie vb **lied; ly·ing** \'līiŋ\ : tell a lie ~ n : untrue statement

liege \'lēj\ n : feudal superior or vassal

lien \'lēn, 'lēən\ n : legal claim on the property of another

lieu·ten·ant \lü'tenənt\ n 1 : representative 2 : first lieutenant or second lieutenant 3 : commissioned officer in the navy ranking next below a lieutenant commander — **lieu·ten·an·cy** \-ənsē\ n

lieutenant colonel n : commissioned officer (as in the army) ranking next below a colonel

lieutenant commander n : commissioned officer in the navy ranking next below a commander

lieutenant general n : commissioned officer (as in the army) ranking next below a general

lieutenant junior grade n, pl **lieutenants junior grade** : commissioned officer in the navy ranking next below a lieutenant

life \'līf\ n, pl **lives** \'līvz\ 1 : quality that distinguishes a vital and functional being from a dead body or inanimate matter 2 : physical and mental experiences of an individual 3 : biography 4 : period of existence 5 : way of living 6 : liveliness — **life·less** adj — **life·like** adj

life·blood n : basic source of strength and vitality

life·boat n : boat for saving lives at sea

life·guard n : one employed to safeguard bathers

life·long adj : continuing through life

life·sav·ing *n* : art or practice of saving lives — **life·sav·er** \-,sāvər\ *n*

life·style \'līf,stīl\ *n* : a way of life

life·time *n* : duration of an individual's existence

lift \'lift\ *vb* 1 : move upward or cause to move upward 2 : put an end to — **lift** *n* — **lift·er** *n*

lift·off \'lift,óf\ *n* : vertical takeoff by a rocket

lig·a·ment \'ligəmənt\ *n* : band of tough tissue that holds bones together

lig·a·ture \'ligə,chùr, -chər\ *n* : something that binds or ties

¹**light** \'līt\ *n* 1 : radiation that makes vision possible 2 : daylight 3 : source of light 4 : public knowledge 5 : aspect 6 : celebrity 7 : flame for lighting ~ *adj* 1 : bright 2 : weak in color ~ *vb* **lit** \'lit\ *or* **light·ed**; **light·ing** 1 : make or become light 2 : cause to burn — **light·er** *n* — **light·ness** *n* — **light·proof** *adj*

²**light** *adj* : not heavy, serious, or abundant — **light** *adv* — **light·ly** *adv* — **light·ness** *n* — **light·weight** *adj*

³**light** *vb* **light·ed** *or* **lit** \'lit\; **light·ing** : settle or dismount

¹**light·en** \'līt°n\ *vb* 1 : make light or bright 2 : give out flashes of lightning

²**lighten** *vb* 1 : relieve of a burden 2 : become lighter

light·heart·ed \-'härtəd\ *adj* : free from worry — **light·heart·ed·ly** *adv* — **light·heart·ed·ness** *n*

light·house *n* : structure with a powerful light for guiding sailors

light·ning \'lītniŋ\ *n* : flashing discharge of atmospheric electricity

light–year \'līt,yir\ *n* : distance traveled by light in one year equal to about 5.88 trillion miles

lig·nite \'lig,nīt\ *n* : brownish black soft coal

¹**like** \'līk\ *vb* **liked**; **lik·ing** 1 : enjoy 2 : desire ~ *n* : preference — **lik·able**, **like·able** \'līkəbəl\ *adj*

²**like** *adj* : similar ~ *prep* 1 : similar or similarly to 2 : typical of 3 : such as ~ *n* : counterpart ~ *conj* : as or as if — **like·ness** *n* — **like·wise** *adv*

-like \,līk\ *adj comb form* : resembling or characteristic of

like·li·hood \'līklē,hùd\ *n* : probability

like·ly \'līklē\ *adj* **-li·er; -est** : probable 2 : believable ~ *adv* : in all probability

lik·en \'līkən\ *vb* : compare

lik·ing \'līkiŋ\ *n* : favorable regard

li·lac \'līlək, -,lak, -,läk\ *n* : shrub with clusters of fragrant pink, purple, or white flowers

lilt \'lilt\ *n* : rhythmical swing or flow

lily \'lilē\ *n, pl* **lil·ies** : tall bulbous herb with funnel-shaped flowers

lima bean \'līmə-\ *n* : flat edible seed of a plant or the plant itself

limb \'lim\ *n* 1 : projecting appendage used in moving or grasping 2 : tree branch — **limb·less** *adj*

lim·ber \'limbər\ *adj* : supple or agile ~ *vb* : make or become limber

lim·bo \'limbō\ *n, pl* **-bos** : place or state of confinement or oblivion

¹**lime** \'līm\ *n* : caustic white oxide of calcium

²**lime** *n* : small green lemonlike citrus fruit — **lime·ade** \-,ād\ *n*

lime·light *n* : center of public attention

lim·er·ick \'limərik\ *n* : light poem of 5 lines

lime·stone *n* : rock that yields lime when burned

lim·it \'limət\ *n* 1 : boundary 2 : something that restrains or confines ~ *vb* : set limits on — **lim·i·ta·tion** \,limə'tāshən\ *n* — **lim·it·less** *adj*

lim·ou·sine \'limə,zēn, ,limə'-\ *n* : large luxurious sedan

limp \'limp\ *vb* : walk lamely ~ *n* : limping movement or gait ~ *adj* : lacking firmness and body — **limp·ly** *adv* — **limp·ness** *n*

lim·pid \'limpəd\ *adj* : clear or transparent

lin·den \'lindən\ *n* : tree with large heart-shaped leaves

¹**line** \'līn\ *vb* **lined**; **lin·ing** : cover the inner surface of — **lin·ing** *n*

²**line** *n* 1 : cord, rope, or wire 2 : row or something like a row 3 : note 4 : course of action or thought 5 : state of agreement 6 : occupation 7 : limit 8 : transportation system 9 : long narrow mark ~ *vb* **lined**; **lin·ing** 1 : mark with a line 2 : place in a line 3 : form a line

lin·e·age \'linēij\ *n* : descent from a common ancestor

lin·e·al \'linēəl\ *adj* 1 : linear 2 : in a direct line of ancestry

lin·ea·ments \'linēəmənts\ *n pl* : features or contours esp. of a face

lin·e·ar \'linēər\ *adj* 1 : straight 2 : long and narrow

lin·en \'linən\ *n* **1** : cloth or thread made of flax **2** : household articles made of linen cloth

lin·er \'līnər\ *n* **1** : one that lines **2** : ship or airplane belonging to a line

line-up \'līn,əp\ *n* **1** : line of persons for inspection or identification **2** : list of players in a game

-ling \liŋ\ *n suffix* **1** : one linked with **2** : young, small, or minor one

lin·ger \'liŋgər\ *vb* : be slow to leave or act — **lin·ger·er** *n*

lin·ge·rie \,länjə'rā, ,laⁿzhə-, -'rē\ *n* : women's underwear

lin·go \'liŋgō\ *n, pl* **-goes** : usu. strange language

lin·guist \'liŋgwist\ *n* **1** : person skilled in speech or languages **2** : student of language — **lin·guis·tic** \liŋ-'gwistik\ *adj* — **lin·guis·tics** \-tiks\ *n pl*

lin·i·ment \'linəmənt\ *n* : liquid medication rubbed on the skin

link \'liŋk\ *n* **1** : connecting structure (as a ring of a chain) **2** : bond — **link** *vb* — **link·age** \-ij\ *n* — **link·er** *n*

li·no·leum \lə'nōlēəm\ *n* : floor covering with hard surface

lin·seed \'lin,sēd\ *n* : seeds of flax yielding an oil (**linseed oil**)

lint \'lint\ *n* : fine fluff or loose short fibers from fabric

lin·tel \'lint²l\ *n* : horizontal piece over a door or window

li·on \'līən\ *n* : large cat of Africa and Asia — **li·on·ess** \'līənəs\ *n*

li·on·ize \'līə,nīz\ *vb* **-ized; -iz·ing** : treat as very important — **li·on·iza·tion** \,līənə'zāshən\ *n*

lip \'lip\ *n* **1** : either of the 2 fleshy folds surrounding the mouth **2** : edge of something hollow — **lipped** \'lipt\ *adj* — **lip·read·ing** *n*

li·po·suc·tion \'lipə,səkshən, 'lī-\ *n* : surgical removal of fat deposits (as from the thighs)

lip·stick \'lip,stik\ *n* : stick of cosmetic to color lips

liq·ue·fy \'likwə,fī\ *vb* **-fied; -fy·ing** : make or become liquid — **liq·ue·fi·er** \'likwə,fīər\ *n*

li·queur \li'kər\ *n* : sweet or aromatic alcoholic liquor

liq·uid \'likwəd\ *adj* **1** : flowing freely like water **2** : neither solid nor gaseous **3** : of or convertible to cash — **liquid** *n* — **li·quid·i·ty** \lik'widətē\ *n*

liq·ui·date \'likwə,dāt\ *vb* **-dat·ed;**

-dat·ing 1 : pay off **2** : dispose of — **liq·ui·da·tion** \,likwə'dāshən\ *n*

li·quor \'likər\ *n* : liquid substance and esp. a distilled alcoholic beverage

lisp \'lisp\ *vb* : pronounce *s* and *z* imperfectly — **lisp** *n*

lis·some \'lisəm\ *adj* : supple or agile

¹list \'list\ *n* **1** : series of names or items ~ *vb* **1** : make a list of **2** : put on a list

²list *vb* : tilt or lean over ~ *n* : slant

lis·ten \'lis²n\ *vb* **1** : pay attention in order to hear **2** : heed — **lis·ten·er** \'lis²nər\ *n*

list·less \'listləs\ *adj* : having no desire to act — **list·less·ly** *adv* — **list·less·ness** *n*

lit \'lit\ *past of* LIGHT

lit·a·ny \'lit²nē\ *n, pl* **-nies 1** : prayer said as a series of responses to a leader **2** : long recitation

li·ter \'lētər\ *n* : unit of liquid measure equal to about 1.06 quarts

lit·er·al \'litərəl\ *adj* : being exactly as stated — **lit·er·al·ly** *adv*

lit·er·ary \'litə,rerē\ *adj* : relating to literature

lit·er·ate \'litərət\ *adj* : able to read and write — **lit·er·a·cy** \'litərəsē\ *n*

lit·er·a·ture \'litərə,chúr, -chər\ *n* : writings of enduring interest

lithe \'līth, 'lith\ *adj* **1** : supple **2** : graceful — **lithe·some** \-səm\ *adj*

litho·graph \'lithə,graf\ *n* : print from a drawing on metal or stone — **li·thog·ra·pher** \lith'ägrəfər, 'lithə,grafər\ *n* — **litho·graph·ic** \,lithə'grafik\ *adj* — **li·thog·ra·phy** \lith'ägrəfē\ *n*

lit·i·gate \'litə,gāt\ *vb* **-gat·ed; -gat·ing** : carry on a lawsuit — **lit·i·gant** \'litigənt\ *n* — **lit·i·ga·tion** \,litə'gā-shən\ *n* — **li·ti·gious** \lə'tijəs, li-\ *adj* — **li·ti·gious·ness** *n*

lit·mus \'litməs\ *n* : coloring matter that turns red in acid solutions and blue in alkaline

lit·ter \'litər\ *n* **1** : animal offspring of one birth **2** : stretcher **3** : rubbish **4** : material to absorb animal waste ~ *vb* **1** : give birth to young **2** : strew with litter

lit·tle \'lit³l\ *adj* **lit·tler** *or* **less** \'les\ *or* **less·er** \'lesər\; **lit·tlest** *or* **least** \'lēst\ **1** : not big **2** : not much **3** : not important ~ *adv* **less** \'les\; **least** \'lēst\ **1** : slightly **2** : not often ~ *n* : small amount — **lit·tle·ness** *n*

lit·ur·gy \'litərjē\ *n, pl* **-gies** : rite of

worship — **li·tur·gi·cal** \lə'tərjikəl\ *adj* — **li·tur·gi·cal·ly** \-klē\ *adv* — **lit·ur·gist** \'litərjist\ *n*

liv·able \'livəbəl\ *adj* : suitable for living in or with — **liv·a·bil·i·ty** \,livə-'bilətē\ *n*

¹live \'liv\ *vb* **lived; liv·ing 1** : be alive **2** : conduct one's life **3** : subsist **4** : reside

²live \'līv\ *adj* **1** : having life **2** : burning **3** : connected to electric power **4** : not exploded **5** : of continuing interest **6** : involving the actual presence of real people

live·li·hood \'līvlē,hud\ *n* : means of subsistence

live·long \'liv'lȯŋ\ *adj* : whole

live·ly \'līvlē\ *adj* **-li·er; -est** : full of life and vigor — **live·li·ness** *n*

liv·en \'līvən\ *vb* : enliven

liv·er \'livər\ *n* : organ that secretes bile

liv·ery \'livərē\ *n, pl* **-er·ies 1** : servant's uniform **2** : care of horses for pay — **liv·er·ied** \-rēd\ *adj* — **liv·ery·man** \-mən\ *n*

lives *pl of* LIFE

live·stock \'līv,stäk\ *n* : farm animals

liv·id \'livəd\ *adj* **1** : discolored by bruising **2** : pale **3** : enraged

liv·ing \'liviŋ\ *adj* : having life ~ *n* : livelihood

liz·ard \'lizərd\ *n* : reptile with 4 legs and a long tapering tail

lla·ma \'lämə\ *n* : So. American mammal related to the camel

load \'lōd\ *n* **1** : cargo **2** : supported weight **3** : burden **4** : a large quantity — usu. pl. ~ *vb* **1** : put a load on **2** : burden **3** : put ammunition in

¹loaf \'lōf\ *n, pl* **loaves** \'lōvz\ : mass of bread

²loaf *vb* : waste time — **loaf·er** *n*

loam \'lōm, 'lüm\ *n* : soil — **loamy** *adj*

loan \'lōn\ *n* **1** : money borrowed or its interest **2** : something lent temporarily **3** : grant of use ~ *vb* : lend

loath \'lōth, 'lōth\ *adj* : very reluctant

loathe \'lōth\ *vb* **loathed; loath·ing** : hate

loath·ing \'lōthiŋ\ *n* : extreme disgust

loath·some \'lōthsəm, 'lōth-\ *adj* : repulsive

lob \'läb\ *vb* **-bb-** : throw or hit in a high arc **-lob** *n*

lob·by \'läbē\ *n, pl* **-bies 1** : public waiting room at the entrance of a building **2** : persons lobbying ~ *vb*

-bied; -by·ing : try to influence legislators — **lob·by·ist** *n*

lobe \'lōb\ *n* : rounded part — **lo·bar** \'lōbar\ *adj* — **lobed** \'lōbd\ *adj*

lo·bot·o·my \lō'bätəmē\ *n, pl* **-mies** : surgical severance of nerve fibers in the brain

lob·ster \'läbstər\ *n* : marine crustacean with 2 large pincerlike claws

lo·cal \'lōkəl\ *adj* : confined to or serving a limited area — **local** *n* — **lo·cal·ly** *adv*

lo·cale \lō'kal\ *n* : setting for an event

lo·cal·i·ty \lō'kalətē\ *n, pl* **-ties** : particular place

lo·cal·ize \'lōkə,līz\ *vb* **-ized; -iz·ing** : confine to a definite place — **lo·cal·i·za·tion** \,lōkələ'zāshən\ *n*

lo·cate \'lō,kāt, lō'kāt\ *vb* **-cat·ed; -cat·ing 1** : settle **2** : find a site for **3** : discover the place of — **lo·ca·tion** \lō'kāshən\ *n*

¹lock \'läk\ *n* : tuft or strand of hair

²lock *n* **1** : fastener using a bolt **2** : enclosure in a canal to raise or lower boats ~ *vb* **1** : make fast with a lock **2** : confine **3** : interlock

lock·er \'läkər\ *n* : storage compartment

lock·et \'läkət\ *n* : small case worn on a necklace

lock·jaw *n* : tetanus

lock·out *n* : closing of a plant by an employer during a labor dispute

lock·smith \-,smith\ *n* : one who makes or repairs locks

lo·co·mo·tion \,lōkə'mōshən\ *n* : power of moving — **lo·co·mo·tive** \-'mōtiv\ *adj*

lo·co·mo·tive \-'mōtiv\ *n* : vehicle that moves railroad cars

lo·co·weed \'lōkō,wēd\ *n* : western plant poisonous to livestock

lo·cust \'lōkəst\ *n* **1** : migratory grasshopper **2** : cicada **3** : tree with hard wood or this wood

lo·cu·tion \lō'kyüshən\ *n* : way of saying something

lode \'lōd\ *n* : ore deposit

lode·stone *n* : magnetic rock

lodge \'läj\ *vb* **lodged; lodg·ing 1** : provide quarters for **2** : come to rest **3** : file ~ *n* **1** : special house (as for hunters) **2** : animal's den **3** : branch of a fraternal organization — **lodg·er** \'läjər\ *n* — **lodg·ing** *n* — **lodg·ment, lodge·ment** \-mənt\ *n*

loft \'lȯft\ *n* **1** : attic **2** : upper floor (as of a warehouse)

lofty \'lȯftē\ *adj* **loft·i·er; -est 1** : noble **2** : proud **3** : tall or high — **loft·i·ly** *adv* — **loft·i·ness** *n*

log \'lȯg, 'läg\ *n* **1** : unshaped timber **2** : daily record of a ship's or plane's progress ~ *vb* **-gg- 1** : cut (trees) for lumber **2** : enter in a log — **log·ger** \-ər\ *n*

log·a·rithm \'lȯgə̇rithəm, 'läg-\ *n* : exponent to which a base number is raised to produce a given number

loge \'lȯzh\ *n* : box in a theater

log·ger·head \'lȯgər,hed, 'läg-\ *n* : large Atlantic sea turtle — **at log·gerheads** : in disagreement

log·ic \'läjik\ *n* **1** : science of reasoning **2** : sound reasoning — **log·i·cal** \-ikəl\ *adj* — **log·i·cal·ly** *adv* — **lo·gi·cian** \lō'jishən\ *n*

lo·gis·tics \lō'jistiks\ *n sing or pl* : procurement and movement of people and supplies — **lo·gis·tic** *adj*

logo \'lȯgō, 'lōg-, 'läg-\ *n, pl* **log·os** \-ōz\ : advertising symbol

loin \'lȯin\ *n* **1** : part of the body on each side of the spine between the hip and lower ribs **2** *pl* : pubic regions

loi·ter \'lȯitər\ *vb* : remain around a place idly — **loi·ter·er** *n*

loll \'läl\ *vb* : lounge

lol·li·pop, lol·ly·pop \'läli,päp\ *n* : hard candy on a stick

lone \'lōn\ *adj* **1** : alone or isolated **2** : only — **lone·li·ness** *n* — **lone·ly** *adj* — **lon·er** \'lōnər\ *n*

lone·some \-səm\ *adj* : sad from lack of company — **lone·some·ly** *adv* — **lone·some·ness** *n*

long \'lȯn\ *adj* **lon·ger** \'lȯngər\; **long·est** \'lȯngəst\ **1** : extending far or for a considerable time **2** : having a specified length **3** : tedious **4** : well supplied — used with *on* ~ *adv* : for a long time ~ *n* : long period ~ *vb* : feel a strong desire — **long·ing** \lȯjin\ *n* — **long·ing·ly** *adv*

lon·gev·i·ty \län'jevətē\ *n* : long life

long·hand *n* : handwriting

long·horn *n* : cattle with long horns

lon·gi·tude \'länjə̇tüd, -ˌtyüd\ *n* : angular distance east or west from a meridian

lon·gi·tu·di·nal \ˌlänjə̇'tüd³nəl, -'tyüd-\ *adj* : lengthwise — **lon·gi·tu·di·nal·ly** *adv*

long·shore·man \'lȯn'shȯrmən\ *n* : one who loads and unloads ships

look \'lúk\ *vb* **1** : see **2** : seem **3** : direct one's attention **4** : face ~ *n* **1** : action of looking **2** : appearance of the face **3** : aspect — **look after** : take care of — **look for 1** : expect **2** : search for

look·out *n* **1** : one who watches **2** : careful watch

¹loom \'lüm\ *n* : frame or machine for weaving

²loom *vb* : appear large and indistinct or impressive

loon \'lün\ *n* : black-and-white diving bird

loo·ny, loo·ney \'lünē\ *adj* **-ni·er; -est** : crazy

loop \'lüp\ *n* **1** : doubling of a line that leaves an opening **2** : something like a loop **-loop** *vb*

loop·hole \'lüp,hōl\ *n* : means of evading

loose \'lüs\ *adj* **loos·er; -est 1** : not fixed tight **2** : not restrained **3** : not dense **4** : slack **5** : not exact ~ *vb* **loosed; loos·ing 1** : release **2** : untie or relax — **loose** *adv* — **loose·ly** *adv* — **loos·en** \'lüs³n\ *vb* — **loose·ness** *n*

loot \'lüt\ *n or vb* : plunder — **loot·er** *n*

lop \'läp\ *vb* **-pp-** : cut off

lope \'lōp\ *n* : bounding gait — **lope** *vb*

lop·sid·ed \'läp'sīdəd\ *adj* **1** : leaning to one side **2** : not symmetrical — **lop·sid·ed·ly** *adv* — **lop·sid·ed·ness** *n*

lo·qua·cious \lō'kwāshəs\ *adj* : very talkative — **lo·quac·i·ty** \-'kwasətē\ *n*

lord \'lȯrd\ *n* **1** : one with authority over others **2** : British nobleman

lord·ly \-lē\ *adj* **-li·er; -est** : haughty

lord·ship \-,ship\ *n* : rank of a lord

Lord's Supper *n* : Communion

lore \'lȯr\ *n* : traditional knowledge

lose \'lüz\ *vb* **lost** \'lȯst\; **los·ing** \'lüzin\ **1** : have pass from one's possession **2** : be deprived of **3** : waste **4** : be defeated in **5** : fail to keep to or hold **6** : get rid of — **los·er** *n*

loss \'lȯs\ *n* **1** : something lost **2** *pl* : killed, wounded, or captured soldiers **3** : failure to win

lost \'lȯst\ *adj* **1** : not used, won, or claimed **2** : unable to find one's way

lot \'lät\ *n* **1** : object used in deciding something by chance **2** : share **3** : fate **4** : plot of land **5** : much

loth \'lōth, 'lȯth\ *var of* **LOATH**

lo·tion \'lōshən\ *n* : liquid to rub on the skin

lot·tery \'lätərē\ *n, pl* **-ter·ies** : drawing of lots with prizes going to winners

lo·tus \'lōtəs\ *n* **1** : legendary fruit that causes forgetfulness **2** : water lily

loud \'laud\ *adj* **1** : high in volume of sound **2** : noisy **3** : obtrusive in color or pattern — **loud** *adv* — **loud·ly** *adv* — **loud·ness** *n*

loud·speak·er *n* : device that amplifies sound

lounge \'launj\ *vb* **lounged; loung·ing** : act or move lazily ~ *n* : room with comfortable furniture

lour \'lauər\ *var of* LOWER

louse \'laus\ *n, pl* **lice** \'līs\ : parasitic wingless usu. flat insect

lousy \'lauzē\ *adj* **lous·i·er; -est** : infested with lice **2** : not good — **lous·i·ly** *adv* — **lous·i·ness** *n*

lout \'laut\ *n* : stupid awkward person — **lout·ish** *adj* — **lout·ish·ly** *adv*

lou·ver, lou·vre \'lüvər\ *n* : opening having parallel slanted slats for ventilation or such a slat

love \'ləv\ *n* **1** : strong affection **2** : warm attachment **3** : beloved person ~ *vb* **loved; lov·ing** **1** : feel affection for **2** : enjoy greatly — **lov·able** \-əbəl\ *adj* — **love·less** *adj* — **lov·er** *n* — **lov·ing·ly** *adv*

love·lorn \-,lorn\ *adj* : deprived of love or of a lover

love·ly \'ləvlē\ *adj* **-li·er; -est** : beautiful — **love·li·ness** *n* — **lovely** *adv*

¹low \'lō\ *vb or n* : moo

²low *adj* **lower; low·est** **1** : not high or tall **2** : below normal level **3** : not loud **4** : humble **5** : sad **6** : less than usual **7** : falling short of a standard **8** : unfavorable ~ *n* **1** : something low **2** : automobile gear giving the slowest speed — **low** *adv* — **low·ness** *n*

low·brow \'lō,brau\ *n* : person with little taste or intellectual interest

¹low·er \'lauər\ *vb* **1** : scowl **2** : become dark and threatening

²low·er \'lōər\ *adj* : relatively low (as in rank)

³low·er \'lōər\ *vb* **1** : drop **2** : let descend **3** : reduce in amount

low·land \'lōlənd, -,land\ *n* : low flat country

low·ly \'lōlē\ *adj* **-li·er; -est** **1** : humble **2** : low in rank — **low·li·ness** *n*

loy·al \'loiəl\ *adj* : faithful to a country,

cause, or friend — **loy·al·ist** *n* — **loy·al·ly** *adv* — **loy·al·ty** \'loiəltē\ *n*

loz·enge \'läz°nj\ *n* : small medicated candy

lu·bri·cant \'lübrikənt\ *n* : material (as grease) to reduce friction

lu·bri·cate \-,kāt\ *vb* **-cat·ed; -cat·ing** : apply a lubricant to — **lu·bri·ca·tion** \,lübrə'kāshən\ *n* — **lu·bri·ca·tor** \'lübrə,kātər\ *n*

lu·cid \'lüsəd\ *adj* **1** : mentally sound **2** : easily understood — **lu·cid·i·ty** \lü-'sidətē\ *n* — **lu·cid·ly** *adv* — **lu·cid·ness** *n*

luck \'lək\ *n* **1** : chance **2** : good fortune — **luck·i·ly** *adv* — **luck·i·ness** *n* — **luck·less** *adj* — **lucky** *adj*

lu·cra·tive \'lükrətiv\ *adj* : profitable — **lu·cra·tive·ly** *adv* — **lu·cra·tive·ness** *n*

Lud·dite \'lə,dīt\ *n* : one who opposes technological change

lu·di·crous \'lüdəkrəs\ *adj* : comically ridiculous — **lu·di·crous·ly** *adv* — **lu·di·crous·ness** *n*

lug \'ləg\ *vb* **-gg-** : drag or carry laboriously

lug·gage \'ləgij\ *n* : baggage

lu·gu·bri·ous \lu'gübrēəs\ *adj* : mournful often to an exaggerated degree — **lu·gu·bri·ous·ly** *adv* — **lu·gu·bri·ous·ness** *n*

luke·warm \'lük'worm\ *adj* **1** : moderately warm **2** : not enthusiastic

lull \'ləl\ *vb* : make or become quiet or relaxed ~ *n* : temporary calm

lul·la·by \'lələ,bī\ *n, pl* **-bies** : song to lull children to sleep

lum·ba·go \,ləm'bāgō\ *n* : rheumatic back pain

lum·ber \'ləmbər\ *n* : timber dressed for use ~ *vb* : cut logs — **lum·ber·man** *n* — **lum·ber·yard** *n*

lum·ber·jack \-,jak\ *n* : logger

lu·mi·nary \'lümə,nerē\ *n, pl* **-nar·ies** : very famous person

lu·mi·nes·cence \,lümə'nes°ns\ *n* : low-temperature emission of light — **lu·mi·nes·cent** \-°nt\ *adj*

lu·mi·nous \'lümənəs\ *adj* : emitting light — **lu·mi·nance** \-nəns\ *n* — **lu·mi·nos·i·ty** \,lümə'näsətē\ *n* — **lu·mi·nous·ly** *adv*

lump \'ləmp\ *n* **1** : mass of irregular shape **2** : abnormal swelling ~ *vb* : heap together — **lump·ish** *adj* — **lumpy** *adj*

lu·na·cy \'lünəsē\ n, pl **-cies** : state of insanity

lu·nar \'lünər\ adj : of the moon

lu·na·tic \'lünə,tik\ adj : insane — **lunatic** n

lunch \'lənch\ n : noon meal ~ vb : eat lunch

lun·cheon \'lənchən\ n : usu. formal lunch

lung \'lən\ n : breathing organ in the chest — **lunged** \'ləŋd\ adj

lunge \'lənj\ n **1** : sudden thrust **2** : sudden move forward — **lunge** vb

lurch \'lərch\ n : sudden swaying — **lurch** vb

lure \'lür\ n **1** : something that attracts **2** : artificial fish bait ~ vb **lured; luring** : attract

lu·rid \'lürəd\ adj **1** : gruesome **2** : sensational — **lu·rid·ly** adv

lurk \'lərk\ vb : lie in wait

lus·cious \'ləshəs\ adj **1** : pleasingly sweet in taste or smell **2** : sensually appealing — **lus·cious·ly** adv — **luscious·ness** n

lush \'ləsh\ adj : covered with abundant growth

lust \'ləst\ n **1** : intense sexual desire **2** : intense longing — **lust** vb — **lustful** adj

lus·ter, lus·tre \'ləstər\ n **1** : brightness from reflected light **2** : magnificence — **lus·ter·less** adj — **lustrous** \-trəs\ adj

lusty \'ləstē\ adj **lust·i·er; -est** : full of vitality — **lust·i·ly** adv — **lust·i·ness** n

lute \'lüt\ n : pear-shaped stringed instrument — **lute·nist, lu·ta·nist** \'lüt³nist\ n

lux·u·ri·ant \,ləg'zhūrēənt, ,lək'shūr-\ adj **1** : growing plentifully **2** : rich and varied — **lux·u·ri·ance** \-ēəns\ n — **lux·u·ri·ant·ly** adv

lux·u·ri·ate \-ē,āt\ vb **-at·ed; -at·ing** : revel

lux·u·ry \'ləkshərē, 'ləgzh-\ n, pl **-ries** **1** : great comfort **2** : something adding to pleasure or comfort — **luxu·ri·ous** \,ləg'zhūrēəs, ,lək'shūr-\ adj — **lux·u·ri·ous·ly** adv

-ly \lē\ adv suffix **1** : in a specified way **2** : from a specified point of view

ly·ce·um \lī'sēəm, 'līsē-\ n : hall for public lectures

lye \'lī\ n : caustic alkaline substance

lying pres part of LIE

lymph \'limf\ n : bodily liquid consisting chiefly of blood plasma and white blood cells — **lym·phat·ic** \lim'fatik\ adj

lynch \'linch\ vb : put to death by mob action — **lynch·er** n

lynx \'liŋks\ n, pl **lynx** or **lynx·es** : wildcat

lyre \'līr\ n : ancient Greek stringed instrument

lyr·ic \'lirik\ adj **1** : suitable for singing **2** : expressing direct personal emotion ~ n **1** : lyric poem **2** pl : words of a song — **lyr·i·cal** \-ikəl\ adj

M

m \'em\ n, pl **m's** or **ms** \'emz\ : 13th letter of the alphabet

ma'am \'mam\ n : madam

ma·ca·bre \mə'käb, -'käbər, -'käbrə\ adj : gruesome

mac·ad·am \mə'kadəm\ n : pavement of cemented broken stone — **mac·ad·am·ize** \-,īz\ vb

mac·a·ro·ni \,makə'rōnē\ n : tube-shaped pasta

mac·a·roon \,makə'rün\ n : cookie of ground almonds or coconut

ma·caw \mə'kȯ\ n : large long-tailed parrot

¹**mace** \'mās\ n **1** : heavy spiked club **2** : ornamental staff as a symbol of authority

²**mace** n : spice from the fibrous coating of the nutmeg

ma·chete \mə'shetē\ n : large heavy knife

mach·i·na·tion \,makə'nāshən, ,mashə-\ n : plot or scheme — **machi·nate** \'makə,nāt, 'mash-\ vb

ma·chine \mə'shēn\ n : combination of mechanical or electrical parts ~ vb **-chined; -chin·ing** : modify by machine-operated tools — **ma·chin·able** adj — **ma·chin·ery** \-ərē\ n — **ma·chin·ist** n

mack·er·el \'makərəl\ *n, pl* **-el** *or* **-els** : No. Atlantic food fish

mack·i·naw \'makə,no\ *n* : short heavy plaid coat

mac·ra·mé \,makrə'mā\ *n* : coarse lace or fringe made by knotting

mac·ro \'makrō\ *adj* : very large

mac·ro·cosm \'makrə,käzəm\ *n* : universe

mad \'mad\ *adj* **-dd-** 1 : insane or rabid 2 : rash and foolish 3 : angry 4 : carried away by enthusiasm — **mad·den** \'mad°n\ *vb* — **mad·den·ing·ly** \'mad°niŋlē\ *adv* — **mad·ly** *adv* — **mad·ness** *n*

mad·am \'madəm\ *n, pl* **mes·dames** \mā'däm\ — used in polite address to a woman

ma·dame \mə'dam, *before a surname also* 'madəm\ *n, pl* **mes·dames** \mā'däm\ — used as a title for a woman not of English-speaking nationality

mad·cap \'mad,kap\ *adj* : wild or zany — **madcap** *n*

made *past of* MAKE

Ma·dei·ra \mə'dirə\ *n* : amber-colored dessert wine

ma·de·moi·selle \,madmwə'zel, -mə-'zel\ *n, pl* **ma·de·moi·selles** \-'zelz\ *or* **mes·de·moi·selles** \,mādmwə-'zel\ : an unmarried girl or woman — used as a title for a woman esp. of French nationality

mad·house *n* 1 : insane asylum 2 : place of great uproar or confusion

mad·man \-,man, -mən\ *n* : lunatic

mad·ri·gal \'madrigəl\ *n* : elaborate song for several voice parts

mad·wom·an \'mad,wumən\ *n* : woman who is insane

mael·strom \'mālstrəm\ *n* 1 : whirlpool 2 : tumult

mae·stro \'mīstrō\ *n, pl* **-stros** *or* **-stri** \-,strē\ : eminent composer or conductor

Ma·fia \'mäfēə\ *n* : secret criminal organization

ma·fi·o·so \,mäfē'ōsō\ *n, pl* **-si** \-sē\ : member of the Mafia

mag·a·zine \'magə,zēn\ *n* 1 : storehouse 2 : publication issued at regular intervals 3 : cartridge container in a gun

ma·gen·ta \mə'jentə\ *n* : deep purplish red color

mag·got \'magət\ *n* : wormlike fly larva — **mag·goty** *adj*

mag·ic \'majik\ *n* 1 : art of using supernatural powers 2 : extraordinary power or influence 3 : sleight of hand — **magic, mag·i·cal** \-ikəl\ *adj* — **mag·i·cal·ly** *adv* — **ma·gi·cian** \mə'jishən\ *n*

mag·is·te·ri·al \,majə'stirēəl\ *adj* 1 : authoritative 2 : relating to a magistrate

mag·is·trate \'majə,strāt\ *n* : judge — **mag·is·tra·cy** \-strəsē\ *n*

mag·ma \'magmə\ *n* : molten rock

mag·nan·i·mous \mag'nanəməs\ *adj* : noble or generous — **mag·na·nim·i·ty** \,magnə'nimətē\ *n* — **mag·nan·i·mous·ly** *adv*

mag·ne·sia \mag'nēzhə, -shə\ *n* : oxide of magnesium used as a laxative

mag·ne·sium \mag'nēzēəm, -zhəm\ *n* : silver-white metallic chemical element

mag·net \'magnət\ *n* 1 : body that attracts iron 2 : something that attracts — **mag·net·ic** \mag'netik\ *adj* — **mag·net·i·cal·ly** \-iklē\ *adv* — **mag·ne·tism** \'magnə,tizəm\ *n*

mag·ne·tite \'magnə,tīt\ *n* : black iron ore

mag·ne·tize \'magnə,tīz\ *vb* **-tized;** **-tiz·ing** 1 : attract like a magnet 2 : give magnetic properties to — **mag·ne·tiz·able** *adj* — **mag·ne·ti·za·tion** \,magnətə'zāshən\ *n* — **mag·ne·tiz·er** *n*

mag·nif·i·cent \mag'nifəsənt\ *adj* : splendid — **mag·nif·i·cence** \-səns\ *n* — **mag·nif·i·cent·ly** *adv*

mag·ni·fy \'magnə,fī\ *vb* **-fied;** **-fy·ing** 1 : intensify 2 : enlarge — **mag·ni·fi·ca·tion** \,magnəfə'kāshən\ *n* — **mag·ni·fi·er** \'magnə,fīər\ *n*

mag·ni·tude \'magnə,tüd, -,tyüd\ *n* 1 : greatness of size or extent 2 : quantity

mag·no·lia \mag'nōlyə\ *n* : shrub with large fragrant flowers

mag·pie \'mag,pī\ *n* : long-tailed black-and-white bird

ma·hog·a·ny \mə'hägənē\ *n, pl* **-nies** : tropical evergreen tree or its reddish brown wood

maid \'mād\ *n* 1 : unmarried young woman 2 : female servant

maid·en \'mād°n\ *n* : unmarried young woman ~ *adj* 1 : unmarried 2 : first — **maid·en·hood** \-,hùd\ *n* — **maid·en·ly** *adj*

maid·en·hair \-ˌhar\ *n* : fern with delicate feathery fronds

¹mail \'māl\ *n* 1 : something sent or carried in the postal system 2 : postal system — *vb* : send by mail — **mail·box** *n* — **mail·man** \-ˌman, -mən\ *n*

²mail *n* : armor of metal links or plates

maim \'mām\ *vb* : seriously wound or disfigure

main \'mān\ *n* 1 : force 2 : ocean 3 : principal pipe, duct, or circuit of a utility system — *adj* : chief — **main·ly** *adv*

main·frame \'mān,frām\ *n* : large fast computer

main·land \'mān,land, -lənd\ *n* : part of a country on a continent

main·stay *n* : chief support

main·stream *n* : prevailing current or direction of activity or influence — **mainstream** *adj*

main·tain \mān'tān\ *vb* 1 : keep in an existing state (as of repair) 2 : sustain 3 : declare — **main·tain·abil·i·ty** \-ˌtānə'bilətē\ *n* — **main·tain·able** \-'tānəbəl\ *adj* — **main·te·nance** \'mānt°nəns\ *n*

mai·tre d'hô·tel \ˌmātrədō'tel, ˌme-\ *n* : head of a dining room staff

maize \'māz\ *n* : corn

maj·es·ty \'majəstē\ *n, pl* **-ties** 1 : sovereign power or dignity — used as a title 2 : grandeur or splendor — **ma·jes·tic** \mə'jestik\ *adj* — **ma·jes·ti·cal·ly** \-tiklē\ *adv*

ma·jor \'mājər\ *adj* 1 : larger or greater 2 : noteworthy or conspicuous — *n* 1 : commissioned officer (as in the army) ranking next below a lieutenant colonel 2 : main field of study — *vb* **-jored; -jor·ing** : pursue an academic major

ma·jor·do·mo \ˌmājər'dōmō\ *n, pl* **-mos** : head steward

major general *n* : commissioned officer (as in the army) ranking next below a lieutenant general

ma·jor·i·ty \mə'jorətē\ *n, pl* **-ties** 1 : age of full civil rights 2 : quantity more than half

make \'māk\ *vb* **made** \'mād\; **mak·ing** 1 : cause to exist, occur, or appear 2 : fashion or manufacture 3 : formulate in the mind 4 : constitute 5 : prepare 6 : cause to be or become 7 : carry out or perform 8 : compel 9 : gain 10 : have an effect — used with *for* — *n* : brand — **mak·er** *n* —

make do *vb* : get along with what is available — **make good** *vb* 1 : repay 2 : succeed — **make out** *vb* 1 : draw up or write 2 : discern or understand 3 : fare — **make up** *vb* 1 : invent 2 : become reconciled 3 : compensate for

make–be·lieve *n* : a pretending to believe — *adj* : imagined or pretended

make·shift *n* : temporary substitute — **makeshift** *adj*

make·up \-ˌəp\ *n* 1 : way in which something is constituted 2 : cosmetics

mal·ad·just·ed \ˌmalə'jəstəd\ *adj* : poorly adjusted (as to one's environment) — **mal·ad·just·ment** \-'jəstmənt\ *n*

mal·adroit \ˌmalə'droit\ *adj* : clumsy or inept

mal·a·dy \'malədē\ *n, pl* **-dies** : disease or disorder

mal·aise \mə'lāz, ma-\ *n* : sense of being unwell

mal·a·mute \'malə,myüt\ *n* : powerful heavy-coated dog

mal·a·prop·ism \'malə,präp,izəm\ *n* : humorous misuse of a word

ma·lar·ia \mə'lerēə\ *n* : disease transmitted by a mosquito — **ma·lar·i·al** \-əl\ *adj*

ma·lar·key \mə'lärkē\ *n* : foolishness

mal·con·tent \ˌmalkən'tent\ *n* : discontented person — **malcontent** *adj*

male \'māl\ *adj* 1 : relating to the sex that performs a fertilizing function 2 : masculine — *n* : male individual — **male·ness** *n*

male·dic·tion \ˌmalə'dikshən\ *n* : curse

male·fac·tor \'malə,faktər\ *n* : one who commits an offense esp. against the law

ma·lef·i·cent \mə'lefəsənt\ *adj* : harmful

ma·lev·o·lent \mə'levələnt\ *adj* : malicious or spiteful — **ma·lev·o·lence** \-ləns\ *n*

mal·fea·sance \mal'fēz°ns\ *n* : misconduct by a public official

mal·for·ma·tion \ˌmalfor'māshən\ *n* : distortion or faulty formation — **mal·formed** \mal'formd\ *adj*

mal·func·tion \mal'fəŋkshən\ *vb* : fail to operate properly — **malfunction** *n*

mal·ice \'maləs\ *n* : desire to cause pain or injury to another — **ma·li·**

cious \mə'lishəs\ *adj* — **ma·li·cious·ly** *adv*

ma·lign \mə'līn\ *adj* 1 : wicked 2 : malignant ~ *vb* : speak evil of

ma·lig·nant \mə'lignənt\ *adj* 1 : harmful 2 : likely to cause death — **ma·lig·nan·cy** \-nənsē\ *n* — **ma·lig·nant·ly** *adv* — **ma·lig·ni·ty** \-nətē\ *n*

ma·lin·ger \mə'liŋgər\ *vb* : pretend illness to avoid duty — **ma·lin·ger·er** *n*

mall \'mȯl\ *n* 1 : shaded promenade 2 : concourse providing access to rows of shops

mal·lard \'malərd\ *n, pl* -**lard** *or* -**lards** : common wild duck

mal·lea·ble \'malēəbəl\ *adj* 1 : easily shaped 2 : adaptable — **mal·le·a·bil·i·ty** \malēə'bilətē\ *n*

mal·let \'malət\ *n* : hammerlike tool

mal·nour·ished \mal'nərisht\ *adj* : poorly nourished

mal·nu·tri·tion \malnu'trishən, -nyu-\ *n* : inadequate nutrition

mal·odor·ous \mal'ōdərəs\ *adj* : foul-smelling — **mal·odor·ous·ly** *adv* — **mal·odor·ous·ness** *n*

mal·prac·tice \-'praktəs\ *n* : failure of professional duty

malt \'mȯlt\ *n* : sprouted grain used in brewing

mal·treat \mal'trēt\ *vb* : treat badly — **mal·treat·ment** *n*

ma·ma, mam·ma \'mämə\ *n* : mother

mam·mal \'maməl\ *n* : warm-blooded vertebrate animal that nourishes its young with milk — **mam·ma·li·an** \mə'mālēən, ma-\ *adj or n*

mam·ma·ry \'mamərē\ *adj* : relating to the milk-secreting glands (**mammary glands**) of mammals

mam·mo·gram \'mamə,gram\ *n* : X-ray photograph of the breasts

mam·moth \'maməth\ *n* : large hairy extinct elephant ~ *adj* : enormous

man \'man\ *n, pl* **men** \'men\ 1 : human being 2 : adult male 3 : mankind ~ *vb* -**nn**- : supply with people for working — **man·hood** *n* — **man·hunt** *n* — **man·like** *adj* — **man·li·ness** *n* — **man·ly** *adj or adv* — **man–made** *adj* — **man·nish** *adj* — **man·nish·ly** *adv* — **man·nish·ness** *n* — **man–size, man–sized** *adj*

man·a·cle \'manikəl\ *n* : shackle for the hands or wrists — **manacle** *vb*

man·age \'manij\ *vb* -**aged; -ag·ing** 1 : control 2 : direct or carry on business or affairs 3 : cope — **man·age·abil-**

i·ty \manijə'bilətē\ *n* — **man·age·able** \'manijəbəl\ *adj* — **man·age·able·ness** *n* — **man·age·ably** \-blē\ *adv* — **man·age·ment** \'manijmənt\ *n* — **man·ag·er** \'manijər\ *n* — **man·a·ge·ri·al** \manə'jirēəl\ *adj*

man·da·rin \'mandərən\ *n* : Chinese imperial official

man·date \'man,dāt\ *n* : authoritative command

man·da·to·ry \'mandə,tōrē\ *adj* : obligatory

man·di·ble \'mandəbəl\ *n* : lower jaw — **man·dib·u·lar** \man'dibyələr\ *adj*

man·do·lin \mandə'lin, 'mandᵊlən\ *n* : stringed musical instrument

man·drake \'man,drāk\ *n* : herb with a large forked root

mane \'mān\ *n* : animal's neck hair — **maned** \'mānd\ *adj*

ma·neu·ver \mə'nüvər, -'nyü-\ *n* 1 : planned movement of troops or ships 2 : military training exercise 3 : clever or skillful move or action — **maneuver** *vb* — **ma·neu·ver·abil·i·ty** \-,nüvərə'bilətē, -,nyü-\ *n*

man·ful \'manfəl\ *adj* : courageous — **man·ful·ly** *adv*

man·ga·nese \'maŋgə,nēz, -,nēs\ *n* : gray metallic chemical element

mange \'mānj\ *n* : skin disease of domestic animals — **mangy** \'mānjē\ *adj*

man·ger \'mānjər\ *n* : feeding trough for livestock

man·gle \'maŋgəl\ *vb* -**gled; -gling** 1 : mutilate 2 : bungle — **man·gler** *n*

man·go \'maŋgō\ *n, pl* -**goes** : juicy yellowish red tropical fruit

man·grove \'man,grōv, 'maŋ-\ *n* : tropical tree growing in salt water

man·han·dle *vb* : handle roughly

man·hole *n* : entry to a sewer

ma·nia \'mānēə, -nyə\ *n* 1 : insanity marked by uncontrollable emotion or excitement 2 : excessive enthusiasm — **ma·ni·ac** \-nē,ak\ *n* — **ma·ni·a·cal** \mə'nīəkəl\ *adj* — **man·ic** \'manik\ *adj or n*

man·i·cure \'manə,kyúr\ *n* : treatment for the fingernails ~ *vb* -**cured; -cur·ing** 1 : do manicure work on 2 : trim precisely — **man·i·cur·ist** \-,kyúrist\ *n*

¹**man·i·fest** \'manə,fest\ *adj* : clear to the senses or to the mind ~ *vb* : make evident — **man·i·fes·ta·tion**

\,manəfə'stāshən\ *n* — **man·i·fest·ly** *adv*

²**manifest** *n* : invoice of cargo or list of passengers

man·i·fes·to \,manə'festō\ *n, pl* **-tos** *or* **-toes** : public declaration of policy or views

man·i·fold \'manə,fōld\ *adj* : marked by diversity or variety ∼ *n* : pipe fitting with several outlets for connections

ma·nila paper \mə'nilə-\ *n* : durable brownish paper

ma·nip·u·late \mə'nipyə,lāt\ *vb* **-lat·ed; -lat·ing 1** : treat or operate manually or mechanically **2** : influence esp. by cunning — **ma·nip·u·la·tion** \mə,nipyə'lāshən\ *n* — **ma·nip·u·la·tive** \-'nipyə,lātiv, -lətiv\ *adj* — **ma·nip·u·la·tor** \-,lātər\ *n*

man·kind \'man'kīnd\ *n* : human race

man·na \'manə\ *n* : something valuable that comes unexpectedly

manned \'mand\ *adj* : carrying or performed by a man

man·ne·quin \'manikən\ *n* : dummy used to display clothes

man·ner \'manər\ *n* **1** : kind **2** : usual way of acting **3** : artistic method **4** *pl* : social conduct

man·nered \-ərd\ *adj* **1** : having manners of a specified kind **2** : artificial

man·ner·ism \'manə,rizəm\ *n* : individual peculiarity of action

man·ner·ly \-lē\ *adj* : polite — **man·ner·li·ness** *n* — **mannerly** *adv*

man-of-war \,manə'wôr, -əv'wôr\ *n, pl* **men-of-war** \,men-\ : warship

man·or \'manər\ *n* : country estate — **ma·no·ri·al** \mə'nōrēəl\ *adj*

man·pow·er *n* : supply of people available for service

man·sard \'man,särd\ *n* : roof with two slopes on all sides and the lower slope the steeper

manse \'mans\ *n* : parsonage

man·ser·vant *n, pl* **men·ser·vants** : a male servant

man·sion \'manchən\ *n* : very big house

man·slaugh·ter *n* : unintentional killing of a person

man·tel \'mant³l\ *n* : shelf above a fireplace

man·tis \'mantəs\ *n, pl* **-tis·es** *or* **-tes** \'man,tēz\ : large green insect-eating insect with stout forelegs

man·tle \'mant³l\ *n* **1** : sleeveless cloak **2** : something that covers, enfolds, or envelops — **mantle** *vb*

man·tra \'mantrə\ *n* : mystical chant

man·u·al \'manyəwəl\ *adj* : involving the hands or physical force ∼ *n* : handbook — **man·u·al·ly** *adv*

man·u·fac·ture \,manyə'fakchər, ,manə-\ *n* : process of making wares by hand or by machinery ∼ *vb* **-tured; -tur·ing** : make from raw materials — **man·u·fac·tur·er** *n*

ma·nure \mə'nur, -'nyur\ *n* : animal excrement used as fertilizer

manu·script \'manyə,skript\ *n* **1** : something written or typed **2** : document submitted for publication

many \'menē\ *adj* **more** \'mōr\; **most** \'mōst\ : consisting of a large number — **many** *n or pron*

map \'map\ *n* : representation of a geographical area ∼ *vb* **-pp- 1** : make a map of **2** : plan in detail — **map·pa·ble** \-əbəl\ *adj* — **map·per** *n*

ma·ple \'māpəl\ *n* : tree with hard light-colored wood

mar \'mär\ *vb* **-rr-** : damage

mar·a·schi·no \,marə'skēnō, -'shē-\ *n, pl* **-nos** : preserved cherry

mar·a·thon \'marə,thän\ *n* **1** : long-distance race **2** : test of endurance — **mar·a·thon·er** \-,thänər\ *n*

ma·raud \mə'rod\ *vb* : roam about in search of plunder — **ma·raud·er** *n*

mar·ble \'märbəl\ *n* **1** : crystallized limestone **2** : small glass ball used in a children's game (**marbles**)

mar·bling \-bəliŋ\ *n* : intermixture of fat and lean in meat

march \'märch\ *vb* : move with regular steps or in a purposeful manner ∼ *n* **1** : distance covered in a march **2** : measured stride **3** : forward movement **4** : music for marching — **march·er** *n*

March *n* : 3d month of the year having 31 days

mar·chio·ness \'märshənəs\ *n* : woman holding the rank of a marquess

Mar·di Gras \'märdē,grä\ *n* : Tuesday before the beginning of Lent often observed with parades and merry-making

mare \'mar\ *n* : female horse

mar·ga·rine \'märjərən\ *n* : butter substitute made usu. from vegetable oils

mar·gin \'märjən\ *n* **1** : edge **2** : spare amount, measure, or degree

mar·gin·al \-jənəl\ *adj* **1** : relating to

or situated at a border or margin **2** : close to the lower limit of acceptability — **mar·gin·al·ly** adv

mari·gold \'mara₁gōld\ n : garden plant with showy flower heads

mar·i·jua·na \₁mara'wäna, -'hwä-\ n : intoxicating drug obtained from the hemp plant

ma·ri·na \ma'rēna\ n : place for mooring pleasure boats

mar·i·nate \'mara₁nāt\ vb **-nat·ed; -nat·ing** : soak in a savory sauce

ma·rine \ma'rēn\ adj **1** : relating to the sea **2** : relating to marines ~ n : infantry soldier associated with a navy

mar·i·ner \'maranar\ n : sailor

mar·i·o·nette \₁marēa'net\ n : puppet

mar·i·tal \'marat²l\ adj : relating to marriage

mar·i·time \'mara₁tīm\ adj : relating to the sea or commerce on the sea

mar·jo·ram \'märjaram\ n : aromatic mint used as a seasoning

mark \'märk\ n **1** : something aimed at **2** : something (as a line) designed to record position **3** : visible sign **4** : written symbol **5** : grade **6** : lasting impression **7** : blemish ~ vb **1** : designate or set apart by a mark or make a mark on **2** : characterize **3** : remark — **mark·er** n

marked \'märkt\ adj : noticeable — **mark·ed·ly** \'märkadlē\ adv

mar·ket \'märkat\ n **1** : buying and selling of goods or the place this happens **2** : demand for commodities **3** : store ~ vb : sell — **mar·ket·able** adj

mar·ket·place n **1** : market **2** : world of trade or economic activity

marks·man \'märksmən\ n : good shooter — **marks·man·ship** n

mar·lin \'märlən\ n : large oceanic fish

mar·ma·lade \'märma₁lād\ n : jam with pieces of fruit and rind

mar·mo·set \'märma₁set\ n : small bushy-tailed monkey

mar·mot \'märmət\ n : burrowing rodent

¹ma·roon \ma'rün\ vb : isolate without hope of escape

²maroon n : dark red color

mar·quee \mär'kē\ n : canopy over an entrance

mar·quess \'märkwəs\, **mar·quis** \'märkwəs, mär'kē\ n, pl **-quess·es**

or **-quis·es** or **-quis** : British noble ranking next below a duke

mar·quise \mär'kēz\ n, pl **mar·quises** \-'kēz, -'kēzəz\ : marchioness

mar·riage \'marij\ n **1** : state of being married **2** : wedding ceremony — **mar·riage·able** adj

mar·row \'marō\ n : soft tissue in the cavity of bone

mar·ry \'marē\ vb **-ried; -ry·ing 1** : join as husband and wife **2** : take or give in marriage — **mar·ried** adj or n

marsh \'märsh\ n : soft wet land — **marshy** adj

mar·shal \'märshəl\ n **1** : leader of ceremony **2** : usu. high military or administrative officer ~ vb **-shaled** or **-shalled; -shal·ing** or **-shal·ling 1** : arrange in order, rank, or position **2** : lead with ceremony

marsh·mal·low \'märsh₁melō, -₁malō\ n : spongy candy

mar·su·pi·al \mär'süpēəl\ n : mammal that nourishes young in an abdominal pouch — **marsupial** adj

mart \'märt\ n : market

mar·ten \'märt²n\ n, pl **-ten** or **-tens** : weasellike mammal with soft fur

mar·tial \'märshəl\ adj **1** : relating to war or an army **2** : warlike

mar·tin \'märt²n\ n : small swallow

mar·ti·net \₁märt²n'et\ n : strict disciplinarian

mar·tyr \'märtər\ n : one who dies or makes a great sacrifice for a cause ~ vb : make a martyr of — **mar·tyr·dom** \-dəm\ n

mar·vel \'märvəl\ vb **-veled** or **-velled; -vel·ing** or **-vel·ling** : feel surprise or wonder ~ n : something amazing — **mar·vel·ous, mar·vel·lous** \'märvələs\ adj — **mar·vel·ous·ly** adv — **mar·vel·ous·ness** n

Marx·ism \'märk₁sizəm\ n : political and social principles of Karl Marx — **Marx·ist** \-sist\ n or adj

mas·cara \mas'karə\ n : eye cosmetic

mas·cot \'mas₁kät, -kət\ n : one believed to bring good luck

mas·cu·line \'maskyələn\ adj : relating to the male sex — **mas·cu·lin·i·ty** \₁maskyə'linətē\ n

mash \'mash\ n **1** : crushed steeped grain for fermenting **2** : soft pulpy mass ~ vb **1** : reduce to a pulpy mass **2** : smash — **mash·er** n

mask \'mask\ n : disguise for the face

~ vb **1** : disguise **2** : cover to protect — **mask·er** n

mas·och·ism \'masə,kizəm, 'maz-\ n : pleasure in being abused — **mas·och·ist** \-kist\ n — **mas·och·is·tic** \,masə'kistik, ,maz-\ adj

ma·son \'mās°n\ n : workman who builds with stone or brick — **ma·son·ry** \-rē\ n

mas·quer·ade \,maskə'rād\ n **1** : costume party **2** : disguise ~ vb **-ad·ed; -ad·ing 1** : disguise oneself **2** : take part in a costume party — **mas·quer·ad·er** n

mass \'mas\ n **1** : large amount of matter or number of things **2** : expanse or magnitude **3** : great body of people — usu. pl. ~ vb : form into a mass — **mass·less** \-ləs\ adj — **massy** adj

Mass n : worship service of the Roman Catholic Church

mas·sa·cre \'masikər\ n : wholesale slaughter — **massacre** vb

mas·sage \mə'säzh, -'säj\ n : a rubbing of the body — **massage** vb

mas·seur \ma'sər\ n : man who massages

mas·seuse \-'sœz, -'süz\ n : woman who massages

mas·sive \'masiv\ adj **1** : being a large mass **2** : large in scope — **mas·sive·ly** adv — **mas·sive·ness** n

mast \'mast\ n : tall pole esp. for supporting sails — **mast·ed** adj

mas·ter \'mastər\ n **1** : male teacher **2** : holder of an academic degree between a bachelor's and a doctor's **3** : one highly skilled **4** : one in authority ~ vb **1** : subdue **2** : become proficient in — **mas·ter·ful** \-fəl\ adj — **mas·ter·ful·ly** adv — **mas·ter·ly** adj — **mas·tery** \'mastərē\ n

master chief petty officer n : petty officer of the highest rank in the navy

master gunnery sergeant n : noncommissioned officer in the marine corps ranking above a master sergeant

mas·ter·piece \'mastər,pēs\ n : great piece of work

master sergeant n **1** : noncommissioned officer in the army ranking next below a sergeant major **2** : noncommissioned officer in the air force ranking next below a senior master sergeant **3** : noncommissioned officer in the marine corps ranking next below a master gunnery sergeant

mas·ter·work n : masterpiece

mas·tic \'mastik\ n : pasty glue

mas·ti·cate \'mastə,kāt\ vb **-cat·ed; -cat·ing** : chew — **mas·ti·ca·tion** \,mastə'kāshən\ n

mas·tiff \'mastəf\ n : large dog

mas·to·don \'mastə,dän\ n : extinct elephantlike animal

mas·toid \'mas,tȯid\ n : bone behind the ear — **mastoid** adj

mas·tur·ba·tion \,mastər'bāshən\ n : stimulation of sex organs by hand — **mas·tur·bate** \'mastər,bāt\ vb

¹**mat** \'mat\ n **1** : coarse woven or plaited fabric **2** : mass of tangled strands **3** : thick pad ~ vb **-tt-** : form into a mat

²**mat** vb **-tt- 1** : make matte **2** : provide (a picture) with a mat ~ or **matt** or **matte** n : border around a picture

³**mat** var of MATTE

mat·a·dor \'matə,dȯr\ n : bullfighter

¹**match** \'mach\ n **1** : one equal to another **2** : one able to cope with another **3** : suitable pairing **4** : game **5** : marriage ~ vb **1** : set in competition **2** : marry **3** : be or provide the equal of **4** : fit or go together — **match·less** adj — **match·mak·er** n

²**match** n : piece of wood or paper material with a combustible tip

mate \'māt\ n **1** : companion **2** : subordinate officer on a ship **3** : one of a pair ~ vb **mat·ed; mat·ing 1** : fit together **2** : come together as a pair **3** : copulate

ma·te·ri·al \mə'tirēəl\ adj **1** : natural **2** : relating to matter **3** : important **4** : of a physical or worldly nature ~ n : stuff something is made of — **ma·te·ri·al·ly** adv

ma·te·ri·al·ism \mə'tirēə,lizəm\ n **1** : theory that matter is the only reality **2** : preoccupation with material and not spiritual things — **ma·te·ri·al·ist** \-list\ n or adj — **ma·te·ri·al·is·tic** \-,tirēə'listik\ adj

ma·te·ri·al·ize \mə'tirēə,līz\ vb **-ized; -iz·ing** : take or cause to take bodily form — **ma·te·ri·al·i·za·tion** \mə-,tirēələ'zāshən\ n

ma·té·ri·el, ma·te·ri·el \mə,tirē'el\ n : military supplies

ma·ter·nal \mə'tərn°l\ adj : motherly — **ma·ter·nal·ly** adv

ma·ter·ni·ty \mə'tərnətē\ n, pl **-ties 1** : state of being a mother **2** : hospital's childbirth facility ~ adj **1**

: worn during pregnancy **2** : relating to the period close to childbirth

math \\'math\ n : mathematics

math·e·mat·ics \,math∂'matiks\ n pl : science of numbers and of shapes in space — **math·e·mat·i·cal** \-ikəl\ adj — **math·e·mat·i·cal·ly** adv — **math·e·ma·ti·cian** \,mathəmə'tishən\ n

mat·i·nee, mat·i·née \,mat'n'ā\ n : afternoon performance

mat·ins \'mat'nz\ n : morning prayers

ma·tri·arch \'mātrē,ärk\ n : woman who rules a family — **ma·tri·ar·chal** \,mātrē'ärkəl\ adj — **ma·tri·ar·chy** \'mātrē,ärkē\ n

ma·tri·cide \'matrə,sīd\ n : murder of one's mother — **ma·tri·cid·al** \,matrə'sīdᵊl, ,mā-\ adj

ma·tric·u·late \mə'trikyə,lāt\ vb -lat·ed; -lat·ing : enroll in school — **ma·tric·u·la·tion** \-,trikyə'lāshən\ n

mat·ri·mo·ny \'matrə,mōnē\ n : marriage — **mat·ri·mo·ni·al** \,matrə'mōnēəl\ adj — **mat·ri·mo·ni·al·ly** adv

ma·trix \'mātriks\ n, pl -tri·ces \'mātrə,sēz, 'ma-\ or -trix·es \'mātriksəz\ : something (as a mold) that gives form, foundation, or origin to something else enclosed in it

ma·tron \'mātrən\ n 1 : dignified mature woman 2 : woman supervisor — **ma·tron·ly** adj

matte \'mat\ adj : not shiny

mat·ter \'matər\ n 1 : subject of interest 2 pl : circumstances 3 : trouble 4 : physical substance ∼ vb : be important

mat·tock \'matək\ n : a digging tool

mat·tress \'matrəs\ n : pad to sleep on

ma·ture \mə'túr, -'tyúr, -'chúr\ adj -tur·er; -est 1 : carefully considered 2 : fully grown or developed 3 : due for payment ∼ vb -tured; -tur·ing : become mature — **mat·u·ra·tion** \,machə'rāshən\ n — **ma·ture·ly** adv — **ma·tu·ri·ty** \-ətē\ n

maud·lin \'mȯdlən\ adj : excessively sentimental

maul \'mȯl\ n : heavy hammer ∼ vb 1 : beat 2 : handle roughly

mau·so·le·um \,mȯsə'lēəm, ,mȯzə-\ n, pl -leums or -lea \-'lēə\ : large above-ground tomb

mauve \'mōv, 'mȯv\ n : lilac color

ma·ven, ma·vin \'māvən\ n : expert

mav·er·ick \'mavrik\ n 1 : unbranded range animal 2 : nonconformist

maw \'mȯ\ n 1 : stomach 2 : throat, esophagus, or jaws

mawk·ish \'mȯkish\ adj : sickly sentimental — **mawk·ish·ly** adv — **mawk·ish·ness** n

max·im \'maksəm\ n : proverb

max·i·mum \'maksəməm\ n, pl -ma \-səmə\ or -mums 1 : greatest quantity 2 : upper limit 3 : largest number — **maximum** adj — **max·i·mize** \-sə,mīz\ vb

may \'mā\ verbal auxiliary, past **might** \'mīt\; pres sing & pl **may** 1 : have permission 2 : be likely to 3 — used to express desire, purpose, or contingency

May \'mā\ n : 5th month of the year having 31 days

may·ap·ple n : woodland herb having edible fruit

may·be \'mābē\ adv : perhaps

may·flow·er n : spring-blooming herb

may·fly n : fly with an aquatic larva

may·hem \'mā,hem, 'māəm\ n 1 : crippling or mutilation of a person 2 : needless damage

may·on·naise \'māə,nāz\ n : creamy white sandwich spread

may·or \'māər, 'mer\ n : chief city official — **may·or·al** \-əl\ adj — **may·or·al·ty** \-əltē\ n

maze \'māz\ n : confusing network of passages — **mazy** adj

ma·zur·ka \mə'zərkə\ n : Polish dance

me \'mē\ pron, objective case of I

mead \'mēd\ n : alcoholic beverage brewed from honey

mead·ow \'medō\ n : low-lying usu. level grassland — **mead·ow·land** \-,land\ n

mead·ow·lark n : songbird with a yellow breast

mea·ger, mea·gre \'mēgər\ adj 1 : thin 2 : lacking richness or strength — **mea·ger·ly** adv — **mea·ger·ness** n

¹**meal** \'mēl\ n 1 : food to be eaten at one time 2 : act of eating — **meal·time** n

²**meal** n : ground grain — **mealy** adj

¹**mean** \'mēn\ adj 1 : humble 2 : worthy of or showing little regard 3 : stingy 4 : malicious — **mean·ly** adv — **mean·ness** n

²**mean** \'mēn\ vb **meant** \'ment\; **mean·ing** \'mēniŋ\ 1 : intend 2 : serve to convey, show, or indicate 3 : be important

³**mean** n 1 : middle point 2 pl : some-

thing that helps gain an end **3** *pl* : material resources **4** : sum of several quantities divided by the number of quantities ~ *adj* : being a mean

me·an·der \mē'andər\ *vb* **-dered; -der·ing 1** : follow a winding course **2** : wander aimlessly — **meander** *n*

mean·ing \'mēnin\ *n* **1** : idea conveyed or intended to be conveyed **2** : aim — **mean·ing·ful** \-fəl\ *adj* — **mean·ing·ful·ly** *adv* — **mean·ing·less** *adj*

mean·time \'mēn,tīm\ *n* : intervening time — **meantime** *adv*

mean·while \-,hwīl\ *n* : meantime ~ *adv* **1** : meantime **2** : at the same time

mea·sles \'mēzəlz\ *n pl* : disease that is marked by red spots on the skin

mea·sly \'mēzlē\ *adj* **-sli·er; -est** : contemptibly small in amount

mea·sure \'mezhər, 'māzh-\ *n* **1** : moderate amount **2** : dimensions or amount **3** : something to show amount **4** : unit or system of measurement **5** : act of measuring **6** : means to an end ~ *vb* **-sured; -sur·ing 1** : find out or mark off size or amount of **2** : have a specified measurement — **mea·sur·able** \'mezhərəbəl, 'māzh-\ *adj* — **mea·sur·ably** \-blē\ *adv* — **mea·sure·less** *adj* — **mea·sure·ment** *n* — **mea·sur·er** *n*

meat \'mēt\ *n* **1** : food **2** : animal flesh used as food — **meat·ball** *n* — **meaty** *adj*

me·chan·ic \mi'kanik\ *n* : worker who repairs cars

me·chan·i·cal \mi'kanikəl\ *adj* **1** : relating to machines or mechanics **2** : involuntary — **me·chan·i·cal·ly** *adv*

me·chan·ics \-iks\ *n sing or pl* **1** : branch of physics dealing with energy and forces in relation to bodies **2** : mechanical details

mech·a·nism \'mekə,nizəm\ *n* **1** : piece of machinery **2** : technique for gaining a result **3** : basic processes producing a phenomenon — **mech·a·nis·tic** \,mekə'nistik\ *adj* — **mech·a·ni·za·tion** \,mekənə'zāshən\ *n* — **mech·a·nize** \'mekə,nīz\ *vb* — **mech·a·niz·er** *n*

med·al \'med°l\ *n* **1** : religious pin or pendant **2** : coinlike commemorative metal piece

med·al·ist, med·al·list \'med°list\ *n* : person awarded a medal

me·dal·lion \mə'dalyən\ *n* : large medal

med·dle \'med°l\ *vb* **-dled; -dling** : interfere — **med·dler** \'med°lər\ *n* — **med·dle·some** \'med°lsəm\ *adj*

me·dia \'mēdēə\ *n pl* : communications organizations

me·di·an \'mēdēən\ *n* : middle value in a range — **median** *adj*

me·di·ate \'mēdē,āt\ *vb* **-at·ed; -at·ing** : help settle a dispute — **me·di·a·tion** \,mēdē'āshən\ *n* — **me·di·a·tor** \'mēdē,ātər\ *n*

med·ic \'medik\ *n* : medical worker esp. in the military

med·i·ca·ble \'medikəbəl\ *adj* : curable

med·ic·aid \'medi,kād\ *n* : government program of medical aid for the poor

med·i·cal \'medikəl\ *adj* : relating to medicine — **med·i·cal·ly** \-klē\ *adv*

medi·care \'medi,ker\ *n* : government program of medical care for the aged

med·i·cate \'medə,kāt\ *vb* **-cat·ed; -cat·ing** : treat with medicine

med·i·ca·tion \,medə'kāshən\ *n* **1** : act of medicating **2** : medicine

med·i·cine \'medəsən\ *n* **1** : preparation used to treat disease **2** : science dealing with the cure of disease — **me·dic·i·nal** \mə'dis°nəl\ *adj* — **me·dic·i·nal·ly** *adv*

me·di·e·val, me·di·ae·val \,mēdē'ēvəl, ,med-, ,mid-; ,mē'dē-, ,me-, ,mi-\ *adj* : of or relating to the Middle Ages — **me·di·eval·ist** \-ist\ *n*

me·di·o·cre \,mēdē'ōkər\ *adj* : not very good — **me·di·oc·ri·ty** \-'äkrətē\ *n*

med·i·tate \'medə,tāt\ *vb* **-tat·ed; -tat·ing** : contemplate — **med·i·ta·tion** \,medə'tāshən\ *n* — **med·i·ta·tive** \'medə,tātiv\ *adj* — **med·i·ta·tive·ly** *adv*

me·di·um \'mēdēəm\ *n, pl* **-diums** or **-dia** \-ēə\ **1** : middle position or degree **2** : means of effecting or conveying something **3** : surrounding substance **4** : means of communication **5** : mode of artistic expression — **medium** *adj*

med·ley \'medlē\ *n, pl* **-leys** : series of songs performed as one

meek \'mēk\ *adj* **1** : mild-mannered **2** : lacking spirit — **meek·ly** *adv* — **meek·ness** *n*

meer·schaum \'mirshəm, -,shóm\ *n* : claylike tobacco pipe

¹**meet** \'mēt\ *vb* **met** \'met\; **meet·ing**

1 : run into 2 : join 3 : oppose 4 : assemble 5 : satisfy 6 : be introduced to ~ *n* : sports team competition

²**meet** *adj* : proper

meet•ing \'mētin\ *n* : a getting together — **meet•ing•house** *n*

mega•byte \'megə,bīt\ *n* : unit of computer storage capacity

mega•hertz \-,hərts, -,herts\ *n* : one million hertz

mega•phone \'megə,fōn\ *n* : cone-shaped device to intensify or direct the voice

mel•an•choly \'melən,kälē\ *n* : depression — **mel•an•chol•ic** \,melən-'kälik\ *adj* — **melancholy** *adj*

mel•a•no•ma \,melə'nōmə\ *n, pl* **-mas** : usu. malignant skin tumor

me•lee \'mā,lā, mā'lā\ *n* : brawl

me•lio•rate \'mēlyə,rāt, 'mēlēə-\ *vb* **-rat•ed; -rat•ing** : improve — **me•lio•ra•tion** \,mēlyə'rāshən, ,mēlēə-\ *n* — **me•lio•ra•tive** \'mēlyə,rātiv, 'mēlēə-\ *adj*

mel•lif•lu•ous \me'lifləwəs, mə-\ *adj* : sweetly flowing — **mel•lif•lu•ous•ly** *adv* — **mel•lif•lu•ous•ness** *n*

mel•low \'melō\ *adj* 1 : grown gentle or mild 2 : rich and full — **mellow** *vb* — **mel•low•ness** *n*

melo•dra•ma \'melə,drämə, -,dram-\ *n* : overly theatrical play — **melo•dra•mat•ic** \,melədrə'matik\ *adj* — **melo•dra•mat•i•cal•ly** \-tiklē\ *adv*

mel•o•dy \'melədē\ *n, pl* **-dies** 1 : agreeable sound 2 : succession of musical notes — **me•lod•ic** \mə-'lädik\ *adj* — **me•lod•i•cal•ly** \-iklē\ *adv* — **me•lo•di•ous** \mə'lōdēəs\ *adj* — **me•lo•di•ous•ly** *adv* — **me•lo•di•ous•ness** *n*

mel•on \'melən\ *n* : gourdlike fruit

melt \'melt\ *vb* 1 : change from solid to liquid usu. by heat 2 : dissolve or disappear gradually 3 : move or be moved emotionally

mem•ber \'membər\ *n* 1 : part of a person, animal, or plant 2 : one of a group 3 : part of a whole — **mem•ber•ship** \-,ship\ *n*

mem•brane \'mem,brān\ *n* : thin layer esp. in an organism — **mem•bra•nous** \-brənəs\ *adj*

me•men•to \mi'mentō\ *n, pl* **-tos** or **-toes** : souvenir

memo \'memō\ *n, pl* **mem•os** : memorandum

mem•oirs \'mem,wärz\ *n pl* : autobiography

mem•o•ra•bil•ia \,memərə'bilēə, -'bilyə\ *n pl* 1 : memorable things 2 : mementos

mem•o•ra•ble \'memərəbəl\ *adj* : worth remembering — **mem•o•ra•bil•i•ty** \,memərə'bilətē\ *n* — **mem•o•ra•ble•ness** *n* — **mem•o•ra•bly** \-blē\ *adv*

mem•o•ran•dum \,memə'randəm\ *n, pl* **-dums** or **-da** \-də\ : informal note

me•mo•ri•al \mə'mōrēəl\ *n* : something (as a monument) meant to keep remembrance alive — **memorial** *adj* — **me•mo•ri•al•ize** *vb*

Memorial Day *n* : last Monday in May or formerly May 30 observed as a legal holiday in commemoration of dead servicemen

mem•o•ry \'memrē, 'memə-\ *n, pl* **-ries** 1 : power of remembering 2 : something remembered 3 : commemoration 4 : time within which past events are remembered — **mem•o•ri•za•tion** \,memərə'zāshən\ *n* — **mem•o•rize** \'memə,rīz\ *vb* — **mem•o•riz•er** *n*

men *pl of* MAN

men•ace \'menəs\ *n* : threat of danger ~ *vb* **-aced; -ac•ing** 1 : threaten 2 : endanger — **men•ac•ing•ly** *adv*

me•nag•er•ie \mə'najərē\ *n* : collection of wild animals

mend \'mend\ *vb* 1 : improve 2 : repair 3 : heal — **mend** *n* — **mend•er** *n*

men•da•cious \men'dāshəs\ *adj* : dishonest — **men•da•cious•ly** *adv* — **men•dac•i•ty** \-'dasətē\ *n*

men•di•cant \'mendikənt\ *n* : beggar — **men•di•can•cy** \-kənsē\ *n* — **mendicant** *adj*

men•ha•den \men'hād°n, mən-\ *n, pl* **-den** : fish related to the herring

me•nial \'mēnēəl, -nyəl\ *adj* 1 : relating to servants 2 : humble ~ *n* : domestic servant — **me•ni•al•ly** *adv*

men•in•gi•tis \,menən'jītəs\ *n, pl* **-git•i•des** \-'jitə,dēz\ : disease of the brain and spinal cord

meno•pause \'menə,póz\ *n* : time when menstruation ends — **meno•paus•al** \,menə'pózəl\ *adj*

me•no•rah \mə'nōrə\ *n* : candelabrum used in Jewish worship

men•stru•a•tion \,menstrə'wāshən, men'strā-\ *n* : monthly discharge of blood from the uterus — **men•stru•al**

\'menstrəwəl\ *adj* — **men·stru·ate** \'menstrə,wāt, -,strāt\ *vb*

-ment \mənt\ *n suffix* **1** : result or means of an action **2** : action or process **3** : place of an action **4** : state or condition

men·tal \'ment^əl\ *adj* : relating to the mind or its disorders — **men·tal·i·ty** \men'talətē\ *n* — **men·tal·ly** *adv*

men·thol \'men,thȯl, -,thōl\ *n* : soothing substance from oil of peppermint — **men·tho·lat·ed** \-thə,lātəd\ *adj*

men·tion \'menchən\ *vb* : refer to — **mention** *n*

men·tor \'men,tȯr, 'mentər\ *n* : instructor

menu \'menyü\ *n* **1** : restaurant's list of food **2** : list of offerings

me·ow \mē'aù\ *n* : characteristic cry of a cat — **meow** *vb*

mer·can·tile \'mərkən,tēl, -,tīl\ *adj* : relating to merchants or trade

mer·ce·nary \'mərs^ən,erē\ *n, pl* **-nar·ies** : hired soldier ~ *adj* : serving only for money

mer·chan·dise \'mərchən,dīz, -,dīs\ *n* : goods bought and sold ~ *vb* **-dised; -dis·ing** : buy and sell — **mer·chan·dis·er** *n*

mer·chant \'mərchənt\ *n* : one who buys and sells

merchant marine *n* : commercial ships

mer·cu·ri·al \,mər'kyùrēəl\ *adj* : unpredictable — **mer·cu·ri·al·ly** *adv* — **mer·cu·ri·al·ness** *n*

mer·cu·ry \'mərkyərē\ *n* : heavy liquid metallic chemical element

mer·cy \'mərsē\ *n, pl* **-cies** **1** : show of pity or leniency **2** : divine blessing — **mer·ci·ful** \-sifəl\ *adj* — **mer·ci·ful·ly** *adv* — **mer·ci·less** \-siləs\ *adj* — **mer·ci·less·ly** *adv* — **mercy** *adj*

mere \'mir\ *adj, superlative* **mer·est** : nothing more than — **mere·ly** *adv*

merge \'mərj\ *vb* **merged; merg·ing** **1** : unite **2** : blend — **merg·er** \'mərjər\ *n*

me·rid·i·an \mə'ridēən\ *n* : imaginary circle on the earth's surface passing through the poles — **meridian** *adj*

me·ringue \mə'raŋ\ *n* : baked dessert topping of beaten egg whites

me·ri·no \mə'rēnō\ *n, pl* **-nos** **1** : kind of sheep **2** : fine soft woolen yarn

mer·it \'merət\ *n* **1** : praiseworthy quality **2** *pl* : rights and wrongs of a legal case ~ *vb* : deserve — **mer·i·to·ri·ous** \,merə'tōrēəs\ *adj* —

mer·i·to·ri·ous·ly *adv* — **mer·i·to·ri·ous·ness** *n*

mer·lot \mer'lō\ *n* : dry red wine

mer·maid \'mər,mād\ *n* : legendary female sea creature

mer·ry \'merē\ *adj* **-ri·er; -est** : full of high spirits — **mer·ri·ly** *adv* — **mer·ri·ment** \'merimənt\ *n* — **mer·ry·mak·er** \'merē,mākər\ *n* — **mer·ry·mak·ing** \'merē,mākin\ *n*

merry–go–round *n* : revolving amusement ride

me·sa \'māsə\ *n* : steep flat-topped hill

mes·dames *pl of* MADAM *or of* MADAME *or of* MRS.

mes·de·moi·selles *pl of* MADEMOI-SELLE

mesh \'mesh\ *n* **1** : one of the openings in a net **2** : net fabric **3** : working contact ~ *vb* : fit together properly — **meshed** \'mesht\ *adj*

mes·mer·ize \'mezmə,rīz\ *vb* **-ized; -iz·ing** : hypnotize

mess \'mes\ *n* **1** : meal eaten by a group **2** : confused, dirty, or offensive state ~ *vb* **1** : make dirty or untidy **2** : putter **3** : interfere — **messy** *adj*

mes·sage \'mesij\ *n* : news, information, or a command sent by one person to another

mes·sen·ger \'mes^ənjər\ *n* : one who carries a message or does an errand

Mes·si·ah \mə'sīə\ *n* **1** : expected deliverer of the Jews **2** : Jesus Christ **3** *not cap* : great leader

messieurs *pl of* MONSIEUR

Messrs. *pl of* MR.

mes·ti·zo \me'stēzō\ *n, pl* **-zos** : person of mixed blood

met *past of* MEET

me·tab·o·lism \mə'tabə,lizəm\ *n* : biochemical processes necessary to life — **met·a·bol·ic** \,metə'bälik\ *adj* — **me·tab·o·lize** \mə'tabə,līz\ *vb*

met·al \'met^əl\ *n* : shiny substance that can be melted and shaped and conducts heat and electricity — **me·tal·lic** \mə'talik\ *adj* — **met·al·ware** *n* — **met·al·work** *n* — **met·al·work·er** *n* — **met·al·work·ing** *n*

met·al·lur·gy \'met^əl,ərjē\ *n* : science of metals — **met·al·lur·gi·cal** \,met^əl-'ərjikəl\ *adj* — **met·al·lur·gist** \'met^əl,ərjist\ *n*

meta·mor·pho·sis \,metə'mȯrfəsəs\ *n, pl* **-pho·ses** \-,sēz\ : sudden and drastic change (as of form) — **meta·mor·phose** \-ˌfōz, -ˌfōs\ vb

met·a·phor \'metəˌfór, -fər\ n : use of a word denoting one kind of object or idea in place of another to suggest a likeness between them — **met·a·phor·i·cal** \ˌmetə'fórikəl\ adj

meta·phys·ics \ˌmetə'fiziks\ n : study of the causes and nature of things — **meta·phys·i·cal** \-'fizəkəl\ adj

mete \'mēt\ vb **met·ed; met·ing** : allot

me·te·or \'mētēər, -ē,ór\ n : small body that produces a streak of light as it burns up in the atmosphere

me·te·or·ic \ˌmētē'órik\ adj 1 : relating to a meteor 2 : sudden and spectacular — **me·te·or·i·cal·ly** \-iklē\ adv

me·te·or·ite \'mētēə,rīt\ n : meteor that reaches the earth

me·te·o·rol·o·gy \ˌmētēə'räləjē\ n : science of weather — **me·te·o·ro·log·ic** \ˌmētēˌórə'läjik\, **me·te·o·ro·log·i·cal** \-'läjikəl\ adj — **me·te·o·rol·o·gist** \-ēə'räləjist\ n

¹**me·ter** \'mētər\ n : rhythm in verse or music

²**meter** n : unit of length equal to 39.37 inches

³**meter** n : measuring instrument

meth·a·done \'methə,dōn\ n : synthetic addictive narcotic

meth·ane \'meth,ān\ n : colorless odorless flammable gas

meth·a·nol \'methə,nól, -,nōl\ n : volatile flammable poisonous liquid

meth·od \'methəd\ n 1 : procedure for achieving an end 2 : orderly arrangement or plan — **me·thod·i·cal** \mə'thädikəl\ adj — **me·thod·i·cal·ly** \-klē\ adv — **me·thod·i·cal·ness** n

me·tic·u·lous \mə'tikyələs\ adj : extremely careful in attending to details — **me·tic·u·lous·ly** adv — **me·tic·u·lous·ness** n

met·ric \'metrik\, **met·ri·cal** \-trikəl\ adj : relating to meter or the metric system — **met·ri·cal·ly** adv

metric system n : system of weights and measures using the meter and kilogram

met·ro·nome \'metrə,nōm\ n : instrument that ticks regularly to mark a beat in music

me·trop·o·lis \mə'träpələs\ n : major city — **met·ro·pol·i·tan** \ˌmetrə'pälətᵊn\ adj

met·tle \'metᵊl\ n : spirit or courage — **met·tle·some** \-səm\ adj

mez·za·nine \'mezᵊn,ēn, ˌmezᵊn'ēn\ n 1 : intermediate level between 2 main floors 2 : lowest balcony

mez·zo–so·pra·no \ˌmetsōsə'pranō, ˌmedz-\ n : voice between soprano and contralto

mi·as·ma \mī'azmə\ n 1 : noxious vapor 2 : harmful influence — **mi·as·mic** \-mik\ adj

mi·ca \'mīkə\ n : mineral separable into thin transparent sheets

mice pl of MOUSE

mi·cro \'mīkrō\ adj : very small

mi·crobe \'mī,krōb\ n : disease-causing microorganism — **mi·cro·bi·al** \mī-'krōbēəl\ adj

mi·cro·bi·ol·o·gy \ˌmīkrōbī'äləjē\ n : biology dealing with microscopic life — **mi·cro·bi·o·log·i·cal** \ˌmīkrō,bīə'läjikəl\ adj — **mi·cro·bi·ol·o·gist** \ˌmīkrōbī'äləjist\ n

mi·cro·com·put·er \'mīkrōkəm,pyütər\ n : small computer that uses a microprocessor

mi·cro·cosm \'mīkrə,käzəm\ n : one thought of as a miniature universe

mi·cro·film \-,film\ n : small film recording printed matter — **micro·film** vb

mi·crom·e·ter \mī'krämətər\ n : instrument for measuring minute distances

mi·cro·min·i·a·tur·ized \ˌmīkrō-'minēəchə,rīzd, -'minichə-\ adj : reduced to a very small size — **mi·cro·min·i·a·tur·iza·tion** \-,minēə,chùrə'zāshən, -,mini,chùr-, -chər-\ n

mi·cron \'mī,krän\ n : one millionth of a meter

mi·cro·or·gan·ism \ˌmīkrō'órgə,nizəm\ n : very tiny living thing

mi·cro·phone \'mīkrə,fōn\ n : instrument for changing sound waves into variations of an electric current

mi·cro·pro·ces·sor \'mīkrō,präsesər\ n : miniaturized computer processing unit on a single chip

mi·cro·scope \-,skōp\ n : optical device for magnifying tiny objects — **mi·cro·scop·ic** \ˌmīkrə'skäpik\ adj — **mi·cro·scop·i·cal·ly** adv — **mi·cros·copy** \mī'kräskəpē\ n

mi·cro·wave \'mīkrə,wāv\ n 1 : short radio wave 2 : oven that cooks food using microwaves ~ vb : heat or cook in a microwave oven — **mi·cro·wav·able, mi·cro·wave·able** \ˌmīkrə-ˈwāvəbəl\ *adj*

mid \ˈmid\ *adj* : middle — **mid·point** *n* — **mid·stream** *n* — **mid·sum·mer** *n* — **mid·town** *n or adj* — **mid·week** *n* — **mid·win·ter** *n* — **mid·year** *n*

mid·air *n* : a point in the air well above the ground

mid·day *n* : noon

mid·dle \ˈmid'l\ *adj* 1 : equally distant from the extremes 2 : being at neither extreme ~ *n* : middle part or point

Middle Ages *n pl* : period from about A.D. 500 to about 1500

mid·dle·man \-ˌman\ *n* : dealer or agent between the producer and consumer

mid·dling \ˈmidliŋ, -lən\ *adj* 1 : of middle or medium size, degree, or quality 2 : mediocre

midge \ˈmij\ *n* : very tiny fly

midg·et \ˈmijət\ *n* : very small person or thing

mid·land \ˈmidlənd, -ˌland\ *n* : interior of a country

mid·most *adj* : being nearest the middle — **midmost** *adv*

mid·night *n* : 12 o'clock at night

mid·riff \ˈmidˌrif\ *n* : mid-region of the torso

mid·ship·man \ˈmidˌshipmən, ˌmid-ˈship-\ *n* : student naval officer

midst \ˈmidst\ *n* : position close to or surrounded by others — **midst** *prep*

mid·way \ˈmidˌwā\ *n* : concessions and amusements at a carnival ~ *adv* : in the middle

mid·wife \ˈmidˌwif\ *n* : person who aids at childbirth — **mid·wife·ry** \midˈwifərē, -ˈwif-\ *n*

mien \ˈmēn\ *n* : appearance

miff \ˈmif\ *vb* : upset or peeve

¹**might** \ˈmīt\ *past of* MAY — used to express permission or possibility or as a polite alternative to *may*

²**might** *n* : power or resources

mighty \ˈmītē\ *adj* **might·i·er; -est** 1 : very strong 2 : great — **might·i·ly** *adv* — **might·i·ness** *n* — **mighty** *adv*

mi·graine \ˈmīˌgrān\ *n* : severe headache often with nausea

mi·grant \ˈmīgrənt\ *n* : one who moves frequently to find work

mi·grate \ˈmīˌgrāt\ *vb* **-grat·ed; -grat·ing** 1 : move from one place to another 2 : pass periodically from one region or climate to another — **mi·**

gra·tion \mīˈgrāshən\ *n* — **mi·gra·to·ry** \ˈmīgrəˌtōrē\ *adj*

mild \ˈmīld\ *adj* 1 : gentle in nature or behavior 2 : moderate in action or effect — **mild·ly** *adv* — **mild·ness** *n*

mil·dew \ˈmilˌdü, -ˌdyü\ *n* : whitish fungal growth — **mildew** *vb*

mile \ˈmīl\ *n* : unit of length equal to 5280 feet

mile·age \ˈmīlij\ *n* 1 : allowance per mile for traveling expenses 2 : amount or rate of use expressed in miles

mile·stone *n* : significant point in development

mi·lieu \mēlˈyü, -ˈyœ̄\ *n, pl* **-lieus** or **-lieux** \-ˈyüz, -ˈyœ̄\ : surroundings or setting

mil·i·tant \ˈmilətənt\ *adj* : aggressively active or hostile — **mil·i·tan·cy** \-tənsē\ *n* — **militant** *n* — **mil·i·tant·ly** *adv*

mil·i·ta·rism \ˈmilətəˌrizəm\ *n* : dominance of military ideals or of a policy of aggressive readiness for war — **mil·i·ta·rist** \-rist\ *n* — **mil·i·ta·ris·tic** \ˌmilətəˈristik\ *adj*

mil·i·tary \ˈmiləˌterē\ *adj* 1 : relating to soldiers, arms, or war 2 : relating to or performed by armed forces ~ *n* : armed forces or the people in them — **mil·i·tar·i·ly** \ˌmiləˈterəlē\ *adv*

mil·i·tate \-ˌtāt\ *vb* **-tat·ed; -tat·ing** : have an effect

mi·li·tia \məˈlishə\ *n* : civilian soldiers — **mi·li·tia·man** \-mən\ *n*

milk \ˈmilk\ *n* : white nutritive fluid secreted by female mammals for feeding their young ~ *vb* 1 : draw off the milk of 2 : draw something from as if by milking — **milk·er** *n* — **milk·i·ness** \-ēnəs\ *n* — **milky** *adj*

milk·man \-ˌman, -mən\ *n* : man who sells or delivers milk

milk·weed *n* : herb with milky juice

¹**mill** \ˈmil\ *n* 1 : building in which grain is ground into flour 2 : manufacturing plant 3 : machine used esp. for forming or processing ~ *vb* 1 : subject to a process in a mill 2 : move in a circle — **mill·er** *n*

²**mill** *n* : ¹⁄₁₀ cent

mil·len·ni·um \məˈlenēəm\ *n, pl* **-nia** \-ēə\ *or* **-niums** : a period of 1000 years

mil·let \ˈmilət\ *n* : cereal and forage grass with small seeds

mil·li·gram \ˈmiləˌgram\ *n* : ¹⁄₁₀₀₀ gram

mil·li·li·ter \-,lētər\ n : ¹⁄₁₀₀₀ liter

mil·li·me·ter \-,mētər\ n : ¹⁄₁₀₀₀ meter

mil·li·ner \'milənər\ n : person who makes or sells women's hats — **mil·li·nery** \-na,nerē\ n

mil·lion \'milyən\ n, pl **millions** or **million** : 1000 thousands — **million** adj — **mil·lionth** \-yənth\ adj or n

mil·lion·aire \,milyə'nar, 'milyə,nar\ n : person worth a million or more (as of dollars)

mil·li·pede \'milə,pēd\ n : longbodied arthropod with 2 pairs of legs on most segments

mill·stone n : either of 2 round flat stones used for grinding grain

mime \'mīm\ n 1 : mimic 2 : pantomime — **mime** vb

mim·eo·graph \'mimēə,graf\ n : machine for making many stencil copies — **mimeograph** vb

mim·ic \'mimik\ n : one that mimics ~ vb **-icked; -ick·ing** 1 : imitate closely 2 : ridicule by imitation — **mim·ic·ry** \'mimikrē\ n

min·a·ret \,minə'ret\ n : tower attached to a mosque

mince \'mins\ vb **minced; minc·ing** 1 : cut into small pieces 2 : choose (one's words) carefully 3 : walk in a prim affected manner

mind \'mīnd\ n 1 : memory 2 : the part of an individual that feels, perceives, and esp. reasons 3 : intention 4 : normal mental condition 5 : opinion 6 : intellectual ability ~ vb 1 : attend to 2 : obey 3 : be concerned about 4 : be careful — **mind·ed** adj — **mind·less** \'mīndləs\ adj — **mind·less·ly** adv — **mind·less·ness** n

mind·ful \-fəl\ adj : aware or attentive — **mind·ful·ly** adv — **mind·ful·ness** n

¹**mine** \'mīn\ pron : that which belongs to me

²**mine** \'mīn\ n 1 : excavation from which minerals are taken 2 : explosive device placed in the ground or water for destroying enemy vehicles or vessels that later pass over ~ vb **mined; min·ing** 1 : get ore from 2 : place military mines in — **mine·field** n — **min·er** n

min·er·al \'minərəl\ n 1 : crystalline substance not of organic origin 2 : useful natural substance (as coal) obtained from the ground — **mineral** adj

min·er·al·o·gy \,minə'räləjē, -'ral-\ n

: science dealing with minerals — **min·er·al·og·i·cal** \,minərə'läjikəl\ adj — **min·er·al·o·gist** \,minə-'räləjist, -'ral-\ n

min·gle \'miŋgəl\ vb **-gled; -gling** : bring together or mix

mini- comb form : miniature or of small dimensions

min·ia·ture \'minēə,chùr, 'mini,chùr, -chər\ n : tiny copy or very small version — **miniature** adj — **min·ia·tur·ist** \-,chùrist, -chər-\ n — **min·ia·tur·ize** \-ēəchə,rīz, -ichə-\ vb

mini·bike \'minē,bīk\ n : small motorcycle

mini·bus \-,bəs\ n : small bus

mini·com·put·er \-kəm,pyütər\ n : computer intermediate between a mainframe and a microcomputer in size and speed

mini·course \-,kōrs\ n : short course of study

min·i·mal \'minəməl\ adj : relating to or being a minimum — **min·i·mal·ly** adv

min·i·mize \'minə,mīz\ vb **-mized; -miz·ing** 1 : reduce to a minimum 2 : underestimate intentionally

min·i·mum \'minəməm\ n, pl **-ma** \-mə\ or **-mums** : lowest quantity or amount — **minimum** adj

min·ion \'minyən\ n 1 : servile dependent 2 : subordinate official

mini·se·ries \'minē,sirēz\ n : television story in several parts

mini·skirt \-,skərt\ n : very short skirt

min·is·ter \'minəstər\ n 1 : Protestant member of the clergy 2 : high officer of state 3 : diplomatic representative ~ vb : give aid or service — **min·is·te·ri·al** \,minə'stirēəl\ adj — **min·is·tra·tion** n

min·is·try \'minəstrē\ n, pl **-tries** 1 : office or duties of a minister 2 : body of ministers 3 : government department headed by a minister

mini·van \'minē,van\ n : small van

mink \'miŋk\ n, pl **mink** or **minks** : weasellike mammal or its soft brown fur

min·now \'minō\ n, pl **-nows** : small freshwater fish

¹**mi·nor** \'mīnər\ adj 1 : less in size, importance, or value 2 : not serious ~ n 1 : person not yet of legal age 2 : secondary field of academic specialization

mi·nor·i·ty \mə'nòrətē, mī-\ n, pl

-ties 1 : time or state of being a minor **2 :** smaller number (as of votes) **3 :** part of a population differing from others (as in race or religion)

min·strel \'minstrəl\ *n* **1 :** medieval singer of verses **2 :** performer in a program usu. of black American songs and jokes — **min·strel·sy** \-sē\ *n*

¹**mint** \'mint\ *n* **1 :** fragrant herb that yields a flavoring oil **2 :** mint-flavored piece of candy — **minty** *adj*

²**mint** *n* **1 :** place where coins are made **2 :** vast sum ∼ *adj* **:** unused — **mint** *vb* — **mint·er** *n*

min·u·et \ˌminyə'wet\ *n* **:** slow graceful dance

mi·nus \'mīnəs\ *prep* **:** diminished by **2 :** lacking ∼ *n* **:** negative quantity or quality

mi·nus·cule \'minəsˌkyül, min'əs-\, **min·is·cule** \'minəs-\ *adj* **:** very small

¹**min·ute** \'minət\ *n* **1 :** 60th part of an hour or of a degree **2 :** short time **3** *pl* **:** official record of a meeting

²**mi·nute** \mī'nüt, mə-, -'nyüt\ *adj* **-nut·er; -est 1 :** very small **2 :** marked by close attention to details — **mi·nute·ly** *adv* — **mi·nute·ness** *n*

mir·a·cle \'mirikəl\ *n* **1 :** extraordinary event taken as a sign of divine intervention in human affairs **2 :** marvel — **mi·rac·u·lous** \mə'rakyələs\ *adj* — **mi·rac·u·lous·ly** *adv*

mi·rage \mə'räzh\ *n* **:** distant illusion caused by atmospheric conditions (as in the desert)

mire \'mīr\ *n* **:** heavy deep mud ∼ *vb* **mired; mir·ing :** stick or sink in mire — **miry** *adj*

mir·ror \'mirər\ *n* **:** smooth surface (as of glass) that reflects images ∼ *vb* **:** reflect in or as if in a mirror

mirth \'mərth\ *n* **:** gladness and laughter — **mirth·ful** \-fəl\ *adj* — **mirth·ful·ly** *adv* — **mirth·ful·ness** *n* — **mirth·less** *adj*

mis·an·thrope \'misⁿn̩thrōp\ *n* **:** one who hates mankind — **mis·an·throp·ic** \misⁿn̩'thräpik\ *adj* — **mis·an·thro·py** \mis'anthrəpē\ *n*

mis·ap·pre·hend \ˌmisˌaprə'hend\ *vb* **:** misunderstand — **mis·ap·pre·hen·sion** *n*

mis·ap·pro·pri·ate \ˌmisə'prōprēˌāt\ *vb* **:** take dishonestly for one's own use — **mis·ap·pro·pri·a·tion** *n*

mis·be·got·ten \-bi'gätⁿn\ *adj* **1 :** illegitimate **2 :** ill-conceived

mis·be·have \ˌmisbi'hāv\ *vb* **:** behave improperly — **mis·be·hav·er** *n* — **mis·be·hav·ior** *n*

mis·cal·cu·late \mis'kalkyəˌlāt\ *vb* **:** calculate wrongly — **mis·cal·cu·la·tion** *n*

mis·car·ry \mis'karē, 'mis,karē\ *vb* **1 :** give birth prematurely before the fetus can survive **2 :** go wrong or be unsuccessful — **mis·car·riage** \-rij\ *n*

mis·ce·ge·na·tion \ˌmisˌejə'nāshən, ˌmisijə'nā-\ *n* **:** marriage between persons of different races

mis·cel·la·neous \ˌmisə'lānēəs\ *adj* **:** consisting of many things of different kinds — **mis·cel·la·neous·ly** *adv* — **mis·cel·la·neous·ness** *n*

mis·cel·la·ny \'misəˌlānē\ *n, pl* **-nies :** collection of various things

mis·chance \mis'chans\ *n* **:** bad luck

mis·chief \'mischəf\ *n* **:** conduct esp. of a child that annoys or causes minor damage

mis·chie·vous \'mischəvəs\ *adj* **1 :** causing annoyance or minor injury **2 :** irresponsibly playful — **mis·chie·vous·ly** *adv* — **mis·chie·vous·ness** *n*

mis·con·ceive \ˌmiskən'sēv\ *vb* **:** interpret incorrectly — **mis·con·cep·tion** *n*

mis·con·duct \mis'kändəkt\ *n* **1 :** mismanagement **2 :** bad behavior

mis·con·strue \ˌmiskən'strü\ *vb* **:** misinterpret — **mis·con·struc·tion** *n*

mis·cre·ant \'miskrēənt\ *n* **:** one who behaves criminally or viciously — **miscreant** *adj*

mis·deed \mis'dēd\ *n* **:** wrong deed

mis·de·mean·or \ˌmisdi'mēnər\ *n* **:** crime less serious than a felony

mi·ser \'mīzər\ *n* **:** person who hoards and is stingy with money — **mi·ser·li·ness** \-lēnəs\ *n* — **mi·ser·ly** *adj*

mis·er·a·ble \'mizərəbəl\ *adj* **1 :** wretchedly deficient **2 :** causing extreme discomfort **3 :** shameful — **mis·er·a·ble·ness** *n* — **mis·er·a·bly** \-blē\ *adv*

mis·ery \'mizərē\ *n, pl* **-er·ies :** suffering and want caused by distress or poverty

mis·fire \mis'fīr\ *vb* **1 :** fail to fire **2 :** miss an intended effect — **mis·fire** \'misˌfīr\ *n*

mis·fit \'misˌfit, mis'fit\ *n* **:** person poorly adjusted to his environment

mis·for·tune \mis'fȯrchən\ *n* **1** : bad luck **2** : unfortunate condition or event

mis·giv·ing \mis'givin\ *n* : doubt or concern

mis·guid·ed \mis'gīdəd\ *adj* : mistaken, uninformed, or deceived

mis·hap \'mis,hap\ *n* : accident

mis·in·form \,mis²n'fȯrm\ *vb* : give wrong information to — **mis·in·for·ma·tion** \,mis,infər'māshən\ *n*

mis·in·ter·pret \,mis²n'tərprət\ *vb* : understand or explain wrongly — **mis·in·ter·pre·ta·tion** \-,tərprə'tāshən\ *n*

mis·judge \mis'jəj\ *vb* : judge incorrectly or unjustly — **mis·judg·ment** *n*

mis·lay \mis'lā\ *vb* **-laid; -lay·ing** : misplace

mis·lead \mis'lēd\ *vb* **-led; -lead·ing** : lead in a wrong direction or into error — **mis·lead·ing·ly** *adv*

mis·man·age \mis'manij\ *vb* : manage badly — **mis·man·age·ment** *n*

mis·no·mer \mis'nōmər\ *n* : wrong name

mi·sog·y·nist \mə'säjənist\ *n* : one who hates or distrusts women — **mi·sog·y·nis·tic** \mə,säjə'nistik\ *adj* — **mi·sog·y·ny** \-nē\ *n*

mis·place \mis'plās\ *vb* : put in a wrong or unremembered place

mis·print \'mis,print, mis'-\ *n* : error in printed matter

mis·pro·nounce \,misprə'nauns\ *vb* : pronounce incorrectly — **mis·pro·nun·ci·a·tion** *n*

mis·quote \mis'kwōt\ *vb* : quote incorrectly — **mis·quo·ta·tion** \,miskwō'tāshən\ *n*

mis·read \mis'rēd\ *vb* **-read; -read·ing** : read or interpret incorrectly

mis·rep·re·sent \,mis,repri'zent\ *vb* : represent falsely or unfairly — **mis·rep·re·sen·ta·tion** *n*

mis·rule \mis'rül\ *vb* : govern badly ~ *n* **1** : bad or corrupt government **2** : disorder

¹miss \'mis\ *vb* **1** : fail to hit, reach, or contact **2** : notice the absence of **3** : fail to obtain **4** : avoid **5** : omit — **miss** *n*

²miss *n* : young unmarried woman or girl — often used as a title

mis·sal \'misəl\ *n* : book containing what is said at mass during the year

mis·shap·en \mis'shāpən\ *adj* : distorted

mis·sile \'misəl\ *n* : object (as a stone or rocket) thrown or shot

miss·ing \'misin\ *adj* : absent or lost

mis·sion \'mishən\ *n* **1** : ministry sent by a church to spread its teaching **2** : group of diplomats sent to a foreign country **3** : task

mis·sion·ary \'mishə,nerē\ *adj* : relating to religious missions ~ *n, pl* **-ar·ies** : person sent to spread religious faith

mis·sive \'misiv\ *n* : letter

mis·spell \mis'spel\ *vb* : spell incorrectly — **mis·spell·ing** *n*

mis·state \mis'stāt\ *vb* : state incorrectly — **mis·state·ment** *n*

mis·step \'mis,step\ *n* **1** : wrong step **2** : mistake

mist \'mist\ *n* : particles of water falling as fine rain

mis·take \mə'stāk\ *n* **1** : misunderstanding or wrong belief **2** : wrong action or statement — **mistake** *vb*

mis·tak·en \-'stākən\ *adj* : having a wrong opinion or incorrect information — **mis·tak·en·ly** *adv*

mis·ter \'mistər\ *n* : sir — used without a name in addressing a man

mis·tle·toe \'misəl,tō\ *n* : parasitic green shrub with waxy white berries

mis·treat \mis'trēt\ *vb* : treat badly — **mis·treat·ment** *n*

mis·tress \'mistrəs\ *n* **1** : woman in control **2** : a woman not his wife with whom a married man has recurrent sexual relations

mis·tri·al \mis'trīəl\ *n* : trial that has no legal effect

mis·trust \-'trəst\ *n* : lack of confidence ~ *vb* : have no confidence in — **mis·trust·ful** \-fəl\ *adj* — **mis·trust·ful·ly** *adv* — **mis·trust·ful·ness** *n*

misty \'mistē\ *adj* **mist·i·er; -est** **1** : obscured by mist **2** : tearful — **mist·i·ly** *adv* — **mist·i·ness** *n*

mis·un·der·stand \,mis,əndər'stand\ *vb* **1** : fail to understand **2** : interpret incorrectly

mis·un·der·stand·ing \-'standin\ *n* **1** : wrong interpretation **2** : disagreement

mis·use \mis'yüz\ *vb* **1** : use incorrectly **2** : mistreat — **misuse** \-'yüs\ *n*

mite \'mīt\ *n* **1** : tiny spiderlike animal **2** : small amount

mi·ter, mi·tre \'mītər\ *n* **1** : bishop's headdress **2** : angular joint in wood

~ vb -tered or -tred; -ter•ing or -tring \'mītəriŋ\ : bevel the ends of for a miter joint

mit•i•gate \'mitə,gāt\ vb -gat•ed; -gat•ing : make less severe — mit•i•ga•tion \,mitə'gāshən\ n — mit•i•ga•tive \'mitə,gātiv\ adj

mi•to•sis \mī'tōsəs\ n, pl -to•ses \-,sēz\ : process of forming 2 cell nuclei from one — mi•tot•ic \-'tätik\ adj

mitt \'mit\ n : mittenlike baseball glove

mit•ten \'mit°n\ n : hand covering without finger sections

mix \'miks\ vb : combine or join into one mass or group ~ n : commercially prepared food mixture — mix•able adj — mix•er n — mix up vb : confuse

mix•ture \'mikschər\ n : act or product of mixing

mix-up n : instance of confusion

mne•mon•ic \ni'mänik\ adj : relating to or assisting memory

moan \'mōn\ n : low prolonged sound of pain or grief — moan vb

moat \'mōt\ n : deep wide trench around a castle

mob \'mäb\ n 1 : large disorderly crowd 2 : criminal gang ~ vb -bb- : crowd around and attack or annoy

mo•bile \'mōbəl, -,bēl, -,bīl\ adj : capable of moving or being moved ~ \'mō,bēl\ n : suspended art construction with freely moving parts — mo•bil•i•ty \mō'bilətē\ n

mo•bi•lize \'mōbə,līz\ vb -lized; -liz•ing : assemble and make ready for war duty — mo•bi•li•za•tion \,mōbələ-'zāshən\ n

moc•ca•sin \'mäkəsən\ n 1 : heelless shoe 2 : venomous U.S. snake

mo•cha \'mōkə\ n 1 : mixture of coffee and chocolate 2 : dark brown color

mock \'mäk, 'mȯk\ vb 1 : ridicule 2 : mimic in derision ~ adj 1 : simulated 2 : phony — mock•er n — mock•ery \-ərē\ n — mock•ing•ly adv

mock•ing•bird \'mäkiŋ,bərd, 'mȯk-\ n : songbird that mimics other birds

mode \'mōd\ n 1 : particular form or variety 2 : style — mod•al \-°l\ adj — mod•ish \'mōdish\ adj

mod•el \'mäd°l\ n 1 : structural design 2 : miniature representation 3 : something worthy of copying 4 : one who poses for an artist or displays clothes

5 : type or design ~ vb -eled or -elled; -el•ing or -el•ling 1 : shape 2 : work as a model ~ adj 1 : serving as a pattern 2 : being a miniature representation of

mo•dem \'mōdəm, -,dem\ n : device by which a computer communicates with another computer over telephone lines

mod•er•ate \'mädərət\ adj : avoiding extremes ~ \'mädə,rāt\ vb -at•ed; -at•ing 1 : lessen the intensity of 2 : act as a moderator — moderate n — mod•er•ate•ly adv — mod•er•ate•ness n — mod•er•a•tion \,mädə-'rāshən\ n

mod•er•a•tor \'mädə,rātər\ n : one who presides

mod•ern \'mädərn\ adj : relating to or characteristic of the present — modern n — mo•der•ni•ty \mə-'dərnətē\ n — mod•ern•i•za•tion \,mädərnə'zāshən\ n — mod•ern•ize \'mädər,nīz\ vb — mod•ern•iz•er \'mädər,nīzər\ n — mod•ern•ly adv — mod•ern•ness n

mod•est \'mädəst\ adj 1 : having a moderate estimate of oneself 2 : reserved or decent in thoughts or actions 3 : limited in size, amount, or aim — mod•est•ly adv — mod•es•ty \-əstē\ n

mod•i•cum \'mädikəm\ n : small amount

mod•i•fy \'mädə,fī\ vb -fied; -fy•ing 1 : limit the meaning of 2 : change — mod•i•fi•ca•tion \,mädəfə'kāshən\ n — mod•i•fi•er \'mädə,fīər\ n

mod•u•lar \'mäjələr\ adj : built with standardized units — mod•u•lar•ized \-lə,rīzd\ adj

mod•u•late \'mäjə,lāt\ vb -lat•ed; -lat•ing 1 : keep in proper measure or proportion 2 : vary a radio wave — mod•u•la•tion \,mäjə'lāshən\ n — mod•u•la•tor \'mäjə,lātər\ n — mod•u•la•to•ry \-lə,tōrē\ adj

mod•ule \'mäjül\ n : standardized unit

mo•gul \'mōgəl\ n : important person

mo•hair \'mō,har\ n : fabric made from the hair of the Angora goat

moist \'mȯist\ adj : slightly or moderately wet — moist•en \'mȯis°n\ vb — moist•en•er \'mȯis°nər\ n — moist•ly adv — moist•ness n

mois•ture \'mȯischər\ n : small amount of liquid that causes dampness — **mois·tur·ize** \-chə,rīz\ vb — **mois·tur·iz·er** n

mo·lar \'mōlər\ n : grinding tooth — **molar** adj

mo·las·ses \mə'lasəz\ n : thick brown syrup from raw sugar

¹**mold** \'mōld\ n : crumbly organic soil

²**mold** n : frame or cavity for forming ∼ vb : shape in or as if in a mold — **mold·er** n

³**mold** n : surface growth of fungus ∼ vb : become moldy — **mold·i·ness** \'mōldēnəs\ n — **moldy** adj

mold·er \'mōldər\ vb : crumble

mold·ing \'mōldiŋ\ n : decorative surface, plane, or strip

¹**mole** \'mōl\ n : spot on the skin

²**mole** n : small burrowing mammal — **mole·hill** n

mol·e·cule \'mäli,kyül\ n : small particle of matter — **mo·lec·u·lar** \mə'lekyələr\ adj

mole·skin \-,skin\ n : heavy cotton fabric

mo·lest \mə'lest\ vb 1 : annoy or disturb 2 : force physical and usu. sexual contact on — **mo·les·ta·tion** \,mōl,es'tāshən, ,mäl-\ n — **mo·lest·er** n

mol·li·fy \'mälə,fī\ vb -**fied**; -**fy·ing** : soothe in temper — **mol·li·fi·ca·tion** \,mäləfə'kāshən\ n

mol·lusk, mol·lusc \'mäləsk\ n : shelled aquatic invertebrate — **mol·lus·can** \mə'ləskən\ n

mol·ly·cod·dle \'mälē,käd³l\ vb -**dled**; -**dling** : pamper

molt \'mōlt\ vb : shed hair, feathers, outer skin, or horns periodically — **molt** n — **molt·er** n

mol·ten \'mōlt³n\ adj : fused or liquefied by heat

mom \'mäm, 'məm\ n : mother

mo·ment \'mōmənt\ n 1 : tiny portion of time 2 : time of excellence 3 : importance

mo·men·tar·i·ly \,mōmən'terəlē\ adv 1 : for a moment 2 : at any moment

mo·men·tary \'mōmən,terē\ adj : continuing only a moment — **mo·men·tar·i·ness** n

mo·men·tous \mō'mentəs\ adj : very important — **mo·men·tous·ly** adv — **mo·men·tous·ness** n

mo·men·tum \-əm\ n, pl -**ta** \-ə\ or -**tums** : force of a moving body

mon·arch \'mänərk, -,ärk\ n : ruler of a kingdom or empire — **mo·nar·chi·cal** \mə'närkikəl\ adj

mon·ar·chist \'mänərkist\ n : believer in monarchical government — **mon·ar·chism** \-,kizəm\ n

mon·ar·chy \'mänərkē\ n, pl -**chies** : realm of a monarch

mon·as·tery \'mänə,sterē\ n, pl -**ter·ies** : house for monks

mo·nas·tic \mə'nastik\ adj : relating to monasteries, monks, or nuns — **monastic** n — **mo·nas·ti·cal·ly** \-tiklē\ adv — **mo·nas·ti·cism** \-tə,sizəm\ n

Mon·day \'məndā, -dē\ n : 2d day of the week

mon·e·tary \'mänə,terē, 'mən-\ adj : relating to money

mon·ey \'mənē\ n, pl -**eys** or -**ies** \'mənēz\ 1 : something (as coins or paper currency) used in buying 2 : wealth — **mon·eyed** \-ēd\ adj — **mon·ey·lend·er** n

mon·ger \'məŋgər, 'mäŋ-\ n : dealer

mon·gol·ism \'mäŋgə,lizəm\ n : congenital mental retardation — **Mon·gol·oid** \-gə,lóid\ adj or n

mon·goose \'män,güs, 'mäŋ-\ n, pl -**goos·es** : small agile mammal esp. of India

mon·grel \'mäŋgrəl, 'məŋ-\ n : offspring of mixed breed

mon·i·tor \'mänətər\ n 1 : student assistant 2 : television screen ∼ vb : watch or observe esp. for quality

monk \'məŋk\ n : member of a religious order living in a monastery — **monk·ish** adj

mon·key \'məŋkē\ n, pl -**keys** : small long-tailed arboreal primate ∼ vb 1 : fool 2 : tamper

mon·key·shines \-,shīnz\ n pl : pranks

monks·hood \'məŋks,hüd\ n : poisonous herb with showy flowers

mon·o·cle \'mänikəl\ n : eyeglass for one eye

mo·nog·a·my \mə'nägəmē\ n 1 : marriage with one person at a time 2 : practice of having a single mate for a period of time — **mo·nog·a·mist** \mə'nägəmist\ n — **mo·nog·a·mous** \-məs\ adj

mono·gram \'mänə,gram\ n : sign of identity made of initials — **mono·gram** vb

mono·graph \-,graf\ n : learned treatise

mono·lin·gual \,mänə'liŋgwəl\ adj : using only one language

mono·lith \'män°l,ith\ *n* **1** : single great stone **2** : single uniform massive whole — **mono·lith·ic** \,män°l-'ithik\ *adj*

mono·logue \'män°l,óg\ *n* : long speech — **mono·logu·ist** \-,ógist\, **mo·no·lo·gist** \mə'näləjist, 'män°l-,ógist\ *n*

mono·nu·cle·o·sis \,mänō,nüklē'ōsəs, -,nyü-\ *n* : acute infectious disease

mo·nop·o·ly \mə'näpəlē\ *n, pl* **-lies** **1** : exclusive ownership or control of a commodity **2** : one controlling a monopoly — **mo·nop·o·list** \-list\ *n* — **mo·nop·o·lis·tic** \mə,näpə'listik\ *adj* — **mo·nop·o·li·za·tion** \-lə-'zāshən\ *n* — **mo·nop·o·lize** \mə-'näpə,līz\ *vb*

mono·rail \'mänə,rāl\ *n* : single rail for a vehicle or a vehicle or system using it

mono·syl·lab·ic \,mänəsə'labik\ *adj* : consisting of or using words of only one syllable — **mono·syl·la·ble** \'mänə,siləbəl\ *n*

mono·the·ism \'mänōthē,izəm\ *n* : doctrine or belief that there is only one deity — **mono·the·ist** \-,thēist\ *n* — **mono·the·is·tic** \,mänōthē-'istik\ *adj*

mono·tone \'mänə,tōn\ *n* : succession of words in one unvarying tone

mo·not·o·nous \mə'nät°nəs\ *adj* **1** : sounded in one unvarying tone **2** : tediously uniform — **mo·not·o·nous·ly** *adv* — **mo·not·o·nous·ness** *n* — **mo·not·o·ny** \-°nē\ *n*

mon·ox·ide \mə'näk,sīd\ *n* : oxide containing one atom of oxygen in a molecule

mon·sieur \məs'yər, məsh-\ *n, pl* **mes·sieurs** \-,yərz, mā'syərz\ : man of high rank or station — used as a title for a man esp. of French nationality

mon·si·gnor \män'sēnyər\ *n, pl* **mon·si·gnors** *or* **mon·si·gno·ri** \,män-,sēn'yōrē\ : Roman Catholic prelate — used as a title

mon·soon \män'sün\ *n* : periodic rainy season

mon·ster \'mänstər\ *n* **1** : abnormal or terrifying animal **2** : ugly, wicked, or cruel person — **mon·stros·i·ty** \män'sträsətē\ *n* — **mon·strous** \'mänstrəs\ *adj* — **mon·strous·ly** *adv*

mon·tage \män'täzh\ *n* : artistic composition of several different elements

month \'mənth\ *n* : 12th part of a year — **month·ly** *adv or adj or n*

mon·u·ment \'mänyəmənt\ *n* : structure erected in remembrance

mon·u·men·tal \,mänyə'ment°l\ *adj* **1** : serving as a monument **2** : outstanding **3** : very great — **mon·u·men·tal·ly** *adv*

moo \'mü\ *vb* : make the noise of a cow — **moo** *n*

mood \'müd\ *n* : state of mind or emotion

moody \'müdē\ *adj* **mood·i·er; -est** **1** : sad **2** : subject to changing moods and esp. to bad moods — **mood·i·ly** \'müd°lē\ *adv* — **mood·i·ness** \-ēnəs\ *n*

moon \'mün\ *n* : natural satellite (as of earth) — **moon·beam** *n* — **moon·light** *n* — **moon·lit** *adj*

moon·light \-,līt\ *vb* **-ed; -ing** : hold a 2d job — **moon·light·er** *n*

moon·shine *n* **1** : moonlight **2** : meaningless talk **3** : illegally distilled liquor

¹**moor** \'mùr\ *n* : open usu. swampy wasteland — **moor·land** \-lənd, -,land\ *n*

²**moor** *vb* : fasten with line or anchor

moor·ing \-iŋ\ *n* : place where boat can be moored

moose \'müs\ *n, pl* **moose** : large heavy-antlered deer

moot \'müt\ *adj* : open to question

mop \'mäp\ *n* : floor-cleaning implement ~ *vb* **-pp-** : use a mop on

mope \'mōp\ *vb* **moped; mop·ing** : be sad or listless

mo·ped \'mō,ped\ *n* : low-powered motorbike

mo·raine \mə'rān\ *n* : glacial deposit of earth and stones

mor·al \'mórəl\ *adj* **1** : relating to principles of right and wrong **2** : conforming to a standard of right behavior **3** : relating to or acting on the mind, character, or will ~ *n* **1** : point of a story **2** *pl* : moral practices or teachings — **mor·al·ist** \'mórəlist\ *n* — **mor·al·is·tic** \,mórə'listik\ *adj* — **mor·al·i·ty** \mə'ralətē\ *n* — **mor·al·ize** \'mórə,līz\ *vb* — **mor·al·ly** *adv*

mo·rale \mə'ral\ *n* : emotional attitude

mo·rass \mə'ras\ *n* : swamp

mor·a·to·ri·um \,mórə'tōrēəm\ *n, pl* **-ri·ums** *or* **-ria** \-ēə\ : suspension of activity

mo·ray \'mór,ā, mə'rā\ *n* : savage eel

mor·bid \'mȯrbəd\ *adj* **1** : relating to disease **2** : gruesome — **mor·bid·i·ty** \mȯr'bidətē\ *n* — **mor·bid·ly** *adv* — **mor·bid·ness** *n*

mor·dant \'mȯrd²nt\ *adj* : sarcastic — **mor·dant·ly** *adv*

more \'mȯr\ *adj* **1** : greater **2** : additional ∼ *adv* **1** : in addition **2** : to a greater degree ∼ *n* **1** : greater quantity **2** : additional amount ∼ *pron* : additional ones

mo·rel \mə'rel\ *n* : pitted edible mushroom

more·over \mȯr'ōvər\ *adv* : in addition

mo·res \'mȯr,āz, -ēz\ *n pl* : customs

morgue \'mȯrg\ *n* : temporary holding place for dead bodies

mor·i·bund \'mȯrə,bənd\ *adj* : dying

morn \'mȯrn\ *n* : morning

morn·ing \'mȯrniŋ\ *n* : time from sunrise to noon

mo·ron \'mȯr,än\ *n* **1** : mentally retarded person **2** : very stupid person — **mo·ron·ic** \mə'ränik\ *adj* — **mo·ron·i·cal·ly** *adv*

mo·rose \mə'rōs\ *adj* : sullen — **mo·rose·ly** *adv* — **mo·rose·ness** *n*

mor·phine \'mȯr,fēn\ *n* : addictive painkilling drug

mor·row \'märō\ *n* : next day

Morse code \'mȯrs-\ *n* : code of dots and dashes or long and short sounds used for transmitting messages

mor·sel \'mȯrsəl\ *n* : small piece or quantity

mor·tal \'mȯrt²l\ *adj* **1** : causing or subject to death **2** : extreme — **mortal** *n* — **mor·tal·i·ty** \mȯr'talətē\ *n* — **mor·tal·ly** \'mȯrt²lē\ *adv*

mor·tar \'mȯrtər\ *n* **1** : strong bowl **2** : short-barreled cannon **3** : masonry material used to cement bricks or stones in place — **mortar** *vb*

mort·gage \'mȯrgij\ *n* : transfer of property rights as security for a loan — **mortgage** *vb* — **mort·gag·ee** \mȯrgi'jē\ *n* — **mort·ga·gor** \mȯrgi'jȯr\ *n*

mor·ti·fy \'mȯrtə,fī\ *vb* **-fied; -fy·ing** **1** : subdue by abstinence or self-inflicted pain **2** : humiliate — **mor·ti·fi·ca·tion** \mȯrtəfə'kāshən\ *n*

mor·tu·ary \'mȯrchə,werē\ *n, pl* **-ar·ies** : place where dead bodies are kept until burial

mo·sa·ic \mō'zāik\ *n* : inlaid stone decoration — **mosaic** *adj*

Mos·lem \'mäzləm\ *var of* MUSLIM

mosque \'mäsk\ *n* : building where Muslims worship

mos·qui·to \mə'skētō\ *n, pl* **-toes** : biting bloodsucking insect

moss \'mȯs\ *n* : green seedless plant — **mossy** *adj*

most \'mōst\ *adj* **1** : majority of **2** : greatest ∼ *adv* : to the greatest or a very great degree ∼ *n* : greatest amount ∼ *pron* : greatest number or part

-most \,mōst\ *adj suffix* : most : most toward

most·ly \'mōstlē\ *adv* : mainly

mote \'mōt\ *n* : small particle

mo·tel \mō'tel\ *n* : hotel with rooms accessible from the parking lot

moth \'mȯth\ *n* : small pale insect related to the butterflies

moth·er \'məthər\ *n* **1** : female parent **2** : source ∼ *vb* **1** : give birth to **2** : cherish or protect — **moth·er·hood** \-,hud\ *n* — **moth·er·land** \-,land\ *n* — **moth·er·less** *adj* — **moth·er·ly** *adj*

moth·er-in-law *n, pl* **mothers-in-law** : spouse's mother

mo·tif \mō'tēf\ *n* : dominant theme

mo·tion \'mōshən\ *n* **1** : act or instance of moving **2** : proposal for action ∼ *vb* : direct by a movement — **mo·tion·less** *adj* — **mo·tion·less·ly** *adv* — **mo·tion·less·ness** *n*

motion picture *n* : movie

mo·ti·vate \'mōtə,vāt\ *vb* **-vat·ed; -vat·ing** : provide with a motive — **mo·ti·va·tion** \,mōtə'vāshən\ *n* — **mo·ti·va·tor** \'mōtə,vātər\ *n*

mo·tive \'mōtiv\ *n* : cause of a person's action ∼ *adj* **1** : moving to action **2** : relating to motion — **mo·tive·less** *adj*

mot·ley \'mätlē\ *adj* : of diverse colors or elements

mo·tor \'mōtər\ *n* : unit that supplies power or motion ∼ *vb* : travel by automobile — **mo·tor·ist** \-ist\ *n* — **mo·tor·ize** \'mōtə,rīz\ *vb*

mo·tor·bike *n* : lightweight motorcycle

mo·tor·boat *n* : engine-driven boat

mo·tor·car *n* : automobile

mo·tor·cy·cle *n* : 2-wheeled automotive vehicle — **mo·tor·cy·clist** *n*

mo·tor·truck *n* : automotive truck

mot·tle \'mät²l\ *vb* **-tled; -tling** : mark with spots of different color

mot·to \'mätō\ *n, pl* **-toes** : brief guiding rule

mould \'mōld\ *var of* MOLD

mound \'maúnd\ *n* : pile (as of earth)

¹mount \'maúnt\ *n* : mountain

²mount *vb* 1 : increase in amount 2 : get up on 3 : put in position ~ *n* 1 : frame or support 2 : horse to ride — **mount·able** *adj* — **mount·er** *n*

moun·tain \'maúnt°n\ *n* : elevated land higher than a hill — **moun·tain·ous** \'maúnt°nəs\ *adj* — **moun·tain·top** *n*

moun·tain·eer \,maúnt°n'ir\ *n* : mountain resident or climber

moun·te·bank \'maúnti,baŋk\ *n* : impostor

mourn \'mōrn\ *vb* : feel or express grief — **mourn·er** *n* — **mourn·ful** \-fəl\ *adj* — **mourn·ful·ly** *adv* — **mourn·ful·ness** *n* — **mourn·ing** *n*

mouse \'maús\ *n, pl* mice \'mīs\ 1 : small rodent 2 : device for controlling cursor movement on a computer display — **mouse·trap** *n or vb* — **mousy, mous·ey** \'maúsē, -zē\ *adj*

mousse \'müs\ *n* 1 : light chilled dessert 2 : foamy hair-styling preparation

mous·tache \'məs,tash, məs'tash\ *var of* MUSTACHE

mouth \'maúth\ *n* : opening through which an animal takes in food ~ \'maúth\ *vb* 1 : speak 2 : repeat without comprehension or sincerity 3 : form soundlessly with the lips — **mouthed** \'maúthd, 'maútht\ *adj* — **mouth·ful** \-,fúl\ *n*

mouth·piece *n* 1 : part (as of a musical instrument) held in or to the mouth 2 : spokesman

mou·ton \'mü,tän\ *n* : processed sheepskin

move \'müv\ *vb* moved; mov·ing 1 : go or cause to go from one point to another 2 : change residence 3 : change or cause to change position 4 : take or cause to take action 5 : make a formal request 6 : stir the emotions ~ *n* 1 : act or instance of moving 2 : step taken to achieve a goal — **mov·able, move·able** \-əbəl\ *adj* — **move·ment** *n* — **mov·er** *n*

mov·ie \'müvē\ *n* : projected picture in which persons and objects seem to move

¹mow \'maú\ *n* : part of a barn where hay or straw is stored

²mow \'mō\ *vb* mowed; mowed *or* mown \'mōn\; mow·ing : cut with a machine — **mow·er** *n*

Mr. \'mistər\ *n, pl* Messrs. \'mesərz\ — conventional title for a man

Mrs. \'misəz, -səs, *esp South* 'mizəz, -əs\ *n, pl* Mes·dames \mā'däm, -'dam\ — conventional title for a married woman

Ms. \'miz\ *n* — conventional title for a woman

much \'məch\ *adj* more \'mōr\; most \'mōst\ : great in quantity, extent, or degree ~ *adv* more; most : to a great degree or extent ~ *n* : great quantity, extent, or degree

mu·ci·lage \'myüsəlij\ *n* : weak glue

muck \'mək\ *n* : manure, dirt, or mud — **mucky** *adj*

mu·cus \'myükəs\ *n* : slippery protective secretion of membranes (**mucous membranes**) lining body cavities — **mu·cous** \-kəs\ *adj*

mud \'məd\ *n* : soft wet earth — **mud·di·ly** \'məd°lē\ *adv* — **mud·di·ness** \-ēnəs\ *n* — **mud·dy** *adj or vb*

mud·dle \'məd°l\ *vb* -dled; -dling 1 : make, be, or act confused 2 : make a mess of — **muddle** *n* — **mud·dle·head·ed** \,məd°l'hedəd\ *adj*

mu·ez·zin \mü'ez°n, myü-\ *n* : Muslim who calls the hour of daily prayer

¹muff \'məf\ *n* : tubular hand covering

²muff *vb* : bungle — **muff** *n*

muf·fin \'məfən\ *n* : soft cake baked in a cup-shaped container

muf·fle \'məfəl\ *vb* -fled; -fling 1 : wrap up 2 : dull the sound of — **muf·fler** \'məflər\ *n*

muf·ti \'məftē\ *n* : civilian clothes

¹mug \'məg\ *n* : drinking cup ~ *vb* -gg- : make faces

²mug *vb* -gg- : assault with intent to rob — **mug·ger** *n*

mug·gy \'məgē\ *adj* -gi·er; -est : hot and humid — **mug·gi·ness** *n*

Mu·ham·mad·an \mō'hamədən, -'häm-; mü-\ *n* : Muslim — **Mu·ham·mad·an·ism** \-,izəm\ *n*

mu·lat·to \mù'lätō, -'lat-\ *n, pl* -toes *or* -tos : person of mixed black and white ancestry

mul·ber·ry \'məl,berē\ *n* : tree with small edible fruit

mulch \'məlch\ *n* : protective ground covering — **mulch** *vb*

mulct \'məlkt\ *n or vb* : fine

¹mule \'myül\ *n* 1 : offspring of a male ass and a female horse 2 : stubborn person — **mul·ish** \'myülish\ *adj* — **mul·ish·ly** *adv* — **mu·lish·ness** *n*

²**mule** *n* : backless shoe

mull \'məl\ *vb* : ponder

mul·let \'mələt\ *n, pl* -let *or* -lets : marine food fish

multi- *comb form* **1** : many or multiple **2** : many times over

mul·ti·far·i·ous \ˌməltə'farēəs\ *adj* : diverse

mul·ti·lat·er·al \ˌməlti'latərəl, -ˌtī-\ *adj* : having many sides or participants

mul·ti·lin·gual \-'lingwəl\ *adj* : knowing or using several languages — **mul·ti·lin·gual·ism** \-gwəˌlizəm\ *n*

mul·ti·na·tion·al \-'nashənəl\ *adj* **1** : relating to several nations or nationalities **2** : having divisions in several countries — **multinational** *n*

mul·ti·ple \'məltəpəl\ *adj* **1** : several or many **2** : various — **~** *n* : product of one number by another

multiple sclerosis \-sklə'rōsəs\ *n* : brain or spinal disease affecting muscle control

mul·ti·pli·ca·tion \ˌməltəplə'kāshən\ *n* **1** : increase **2** : short method of repeated addition

mul·ti·plic·i·ty \ˌməltə'plisətē\ *n, pl* -ties : great number or variety

mul·ti·ply \'məltəˌplī\ *vb* -plied; -plying **1** : increase in number **2** : perform multiplication — **mul·ti·pli·er** \-ˌplīər\ *n*

mul·ti·tude \'məltəˌtüd, -ˌtyüd\ *n*

: great number — **mul·ti·tu·di·nous** \ˌməltə'tüdʰnəs, -'tyü-\ *adj*

¹**mum** \'məm\ *adj* : silent

²**mum** *n* : chrysanthemum

mum·ble \'məmbəl\ *vb* -bled; -bling : speak indistinctly — **mumble** *n* — **mum·bler** *n*

mum·mer \'məmər\ *n* **1** : actor esp. in a pantomime **2** : disguised merrymaker — **mum·mery** *n*

mum·my \'məmē\ *n, pl* -mies : embalmed body — **mum·mi·fi·ca·tion** \ˌməmifə'kāshən\ *n* — **mum·mi·fy** \'məmiˌfī\ *vb*

mumps \'məmps\ *n sing or pl* : virus disease with swelling esp. of the salivary glands

munch \'mənch\ *vb* : chew

mun·dane \ˌmən'dān, 'mənˌ-\ *adj* **1** : relating to the world **2** : lacking concern for the ideal or spiritual — **mun·dane·ly** *adv*

mu·nic·i·pal \myù'nisəpəl\ *adj* : of or relating to a town or city — **mu·nic·i·pal·i·ty** \myùˌnisə'palətē\ *n*

mu·nif·i·cent \myù'nifəsənt\ *adj* : generous — **mu·nif·i·cence** \-səns\ *n*

mu·ni·tion \myù'nishən\ *n* : armaments

mu·ral \'myùrəl\ *adj* : relating to a wall — **~** *n* : wall painting — **mu·ra·list** *n*

mur·der \'mərdər\ *n* : unlawful killing of a person — **~** *vb* : commit a murder — **mur·der·er** *n* — **mur·der·ess** *n*

List of self-explanatory words with the prefix *multi-*

multiarmed	multifunction	multipurpose
multibarreled	multifunctional	multiracial
multibillion	multigrade	multiroom
multibranched	multiheaded	multisense
multibuilding	multihospital	multiservice
multicenter	multihued	multisided
multichambered	multilane	multispeed
multichannel	multilevel	multistage
multicolored	multimedia	multistep
multicounty	multimember	multistory
multicultural	multimillion	multisyllabic
multidimensional	multimillionaire	multitalented
multidirectional	multipart	multitrack
multidisciplinary	multipartite	multiunion
multidiscipline	multiparty	multiunit
multidivisional	multiplant	multiuse
multifaceted	multipolar	multivitamin
multifamily	multiproblem	multiwarhead
multifilament	multiproduct	multiyear

\-əs\ *n* — **mur·der·ous** \-əs\ *adj* — **mur·der·ous·ly** *adv*

murk \'mərk\ *n* : darkness — **murk·i·ly** \'mərkəlē\ *adv* — **murk·i·ness** \-kēnəs\ *n* — **murky** *adj*

mur·mur \'mərmər\ *n* **1** : muttered complaint **2** : low indistinct sound — **murmur** *vb* — **mur·mur·er** *n* — **mur·mur·ous** *adj*

mus·ca·tel \,məskə'tel\ *n* : sweet wine

mus·cle \'məsəl\ *n* **1** : body tissue capable of contracting to produce motion **2** : strength ~ *vb* **-cled; -cling** : force one's way — **mus·cled** *adj* — **mus·cu·lar** \'məskyələr\ *adj* — **mus·cu·lar·i·ty** \,məskyə'larətē\ *n*

muscular dystrophy *n* : disease marked by progressive wasting of muscles

mus·cu·la·ture \'məskyələ,chúr\ *n* : bodily muscles

¹**muse** \'myüz\ *vb* **mused; mus·ing** : ponder — **mus·ing·ly** *adv*

²**muse** *n* : source of inspiration

mu·se·um \myü'zēəm\ *n* : institution displaying objects of interest

mush \'məsh\ *n* **1** : corn meal boiled in water or something of similar consistency **2** : sentimental nonsense — **mushy** *adj*

mush·room \'məsh,rüm, -,rúm\ *n* : caplike organ of a fungus ~ *vb* : grow rapidly

mu·sic \'myüzik\ *n* : vocal or instrumental sounds — **mu·si·cal** \-zikəl\ *adj or n* — **mu·si·cal·ly** *adv*

mu·si·cian \myü'zishən\ *n* : composer or performer of music — **mu·si·cian·ly** *adj* — **mu·si·cian·ship** *n*

musk \'məsk\ *n* : strong-smelling substance from an Asiatic deer used in perfume — **musk·i·ness** \'məskēnəs\ *n* — **musky** *adj*

mus·kel·lunge \'məskə,lənj\ *n, pl* **-lunge** : large No. American pike

mus·ket \'məskət\ *n* : former shoulder firearm — **mus·ke·teer** \,məskə'tir\ *n*

musk·mel·on \'məsk,melən\ *n* : small edible melon

musk–ox \'məsk,äks\ *n* : shaggy-coated wild ox of the arctic

musk·rat \-,rat\ *n, pl* **-rat** *or* **-rats** : No. American aquatic rodent

Mus·lim \'məzləm, 'mús-, 'múz-\ *n* : adherent of Islam — **Muslim** *adj*

mus·lin \'məzlən\ *n* : cotton fabric

muss \'məs\ *n* : untidy state ~ *vb* : disarrange — **muss·i·ly** \'məsəlē\

adv — **muss·i·ness** \-ēnəs\ *n* — **mussy** *adj*

mus·sel \'məsəl\ *n* : edible mollusk

must \'məst\ *vb* — used as an auxiliary esp. to express a command, obligation, or necessity ~ \'məst\ *n* : something necessary

mus·tache \'məs,tash, məs-\ *n* : hair of the human upper lip

mus·tang \'məs,taŋ\ *n* : wild horse of Western America

mus·tard \'məstərd\ *n* : pungent yellow seasoning

mus·ter \'məstər\ *vb* **1** : assemble **2** : rouse ~ *n* : assembled group

musty \'məstē\ *adj* **mus·ti·er; -est** : stale — **mus·ti·ly** *adv* — **mus·ti·ness** *n*

mu·ta·ble \'myütəbəl\ *adj* : changeable — **mu·ta·bil·i·ty** \,myütə'bilətē\ *n*

mu·tant \'myüt²nt\ *adj* : relating to or produced by mutation — **mutant** *n*

mu·tate \'myü,tāt\ *vb* **-tat·ed; -tat·ing** : undergo mutation — **mu·ta·tive** \'myü,tātiv, 'myütət-\ *adj*

mu·ta·tion \myü'tāshən\ *n* : change in a hereditary character — **mu·ta·tion·al** *adj*

mute \'myüt\ *adj* **mut·er; mut·est 1** : unable to speak **2** : silent ~ *n* **1** : one who is mute **2** : muffling device ~ *vb* **mut·ed; mut·ing** : muffle — **mute·ly** *adv* — **mute·ness** *n*

mu·ti·late \'myüt²l,āt\ *vb* **-lat·ed; -lat·ing** : damage seriously (as by cutting off or altering an essential part) — **mu·ti·la·tion** \,myüt²l'āshən\ *n* — **mu·ti·la·tor** \'myüt²l,ātər\ *n*

mu·ti·ny \'myüt²nē\ *n, pl* **-nies** : rebellion — **mu·ti·neer** \,myüt²n'ir\ *n* — **mu·ti·nous** \'myüt²nəs\ *adj* — **mu·ti·nous·ly** *adv* — **mutiny** *vb*

mutt \'mət\ *n* : mongrel

mut·ter \'mətər\ *vb* **1** : speak indistinctly or softly **2** : grumble — **mutter** *n*

mut·ton \'mət²n\ *n* : flesh of a mature sheep — **mut·tony** *adj*

mu·tu·al \'myüchəwəl\ *adj* **1** : given or felt by one another in equal amount **2** : common — **mu·tu·al·ly** *adv*

muz·zle \'məzəl\ *n* **1** : nose and jaws of an animal **2** : muzzle covering to immobilize an animal's jaws **3** : discharge end of a gun ~ *vb* **-zled; -zling** : restrain with or as if with a muzzle

my \'mī\ *adj* **1** : relating to me or myself **2** — used interjectionally esp. to express surprise

my•nah, my•na \'mīnə\ *n* : dark crested Asian bird

my•o•pia \mī'ōpēə\ *n* : nearsightedness — **my•o•pic** \-'ōpik, -'äpik\ *adj* — **my•o•pi•cal•ly** *adv*

myr•i•ad \'mirēəd\ *n* : indefinitely large number — **myriad** *adj*

myrrh \'mər\ *n* : aromatic plant gum

myr•tle \'mərt°l\ *n* : shiny evergreen

my•self \mī'self\ *pron* : I, me — used reflexively or for emphasis

mys•tery \'mistərē\ *n, pl* **-ter•ies 1** : religious truth **2** : something not understood **3** : puzzling or secret quality or state — **mys•te•ri•ous** \mis-'tirēəs\ *adj* — **mys•te•ri•ous•ly** *adv* — **mys•te•ri•ous•ness** *n*

mys•tic \'mistik\ *adj* : mystical or mysterious ~ *n* : one who has mystical experiences — **mys•ti•cism** \-tə‚sizəm\ *n*

mys•ti•cal \'mistikəl\ *adj* **1** : spiritual **2** : relating to direct communion with God — **mys•ti•cal•ly** *adv*

mys•ti•fy \'mistə‚fī\ *vb* **-fied; -fy•ing** : perplex — **mys•ti•fi•ca•tion** \‚mistəfə'kāshən\ *n*

mys•tique \mis'tēk\ *n* : aura of mystery surrounding something

myth \'mith\ *n* **1** : legendary narrative explaining a belief or phenomenon **2** : imaginary person or thing — **myth•i•cal** \-ikəl\ *adj*

my•thol•o•gy \mith'äləjē\ *n, pl* **-gies** : body of myths — **myth•o•log•i•cal** \‚mithə'läjikəl\ *adj* — **my•thol•o•gist** \mith'äləjist\ *n*

N

n \'en\ *n, pl* **n's** *or* **ns** \'enz\ : 14th letter of the alphabet

nab \'nab\ *vb* **-bb-** : seize or arrest

na•cho \'nächō\ *n* : tortilla chip topped with a savory mixture and cheese and broiled

na•dir \'nā‚dir, 'nādər\ *n* : lowest point

¹nag \'nag\ *n* : old or decrepit horse

²nag *vb* **-gg- 1** : complain **2** : scold or urge continually **3** : be persistently annoying ~ *n* : one who nags habitually

na•iad \'nāəd, 'nī-, -‚ad\ *n, pl* **-ads** *or* **-ia•des** \-ə‚dēz\ : mythological water nymph

nail \'nāl\ *n* **1** : horny sheath at the end of each finger and toe **2** : pointed metal fastener ~ *vb* : fasten with a nail — **nail•er** *n*

na•ive, na•ïve \nä'ēv\ *adj* **-iv•er; -est 1** : innocent and unsophisticated **2** : easily deceived — **na•ive•ly** *adv* — **na•ive•ness** *n*

na•ive•té \nä‚ēvə'tā, nä'ēvə‚-\ *n* : quality or state of being naive

na•ked \'nākəd, 'nekəd\ *adj* **1** : having no clothes on **2** : uncovered **3** : plain or obvious **4** : unaided — **na•ked•ly** *adv* — **na•ked•ness** *n*

nam•by–pam•by \‚nambē'pambē\ *adj* : weak or indecisive

name \'nām\ *n* **1** : word by which a person or thing is known **2** : disparaging word for someone **3** : distinguished reputation ~ *vb* **named; nam•ing 1** : give a name to **2** : mention or identify by name **3** : nominate or appoint ~ *adj* **1** : relating to a name **2** : prominent — **name•able** *adj* — **name•less** *adj* — **name•less•ly** *adv*

name•ly \'nāmlē\ *adv* : that is to say

name•sake \-‚sāk\ *n* : one named after another

nano•tech•nol•o•gy \‚nanōtek'näləjē\ *n* : manipulation of materials on an atomic or molecular scale

¹nap \'nap\ *vb* **-pp- 1** : sleep briefly **2** : be off guard ~ *n* : short sleep

²nap *n* : soft downy surface — **nap•less** *adj* — **napped** \'napt\ *adj*

na•palm \'nä‚pälm, -‚päm\ *n* : gasoline in the form of a jelly

nape \'nāp, 'nap\ *n* : back of the neck

naph•tha \'nafthə\ *n* : flammable solvent

nap•kin \'napkən\ *n* : small cloth for use at the table

nar•cis•sism \'närsə‚sizəm\ *n* : self-love — **nar•cis•sist** \-sist\ *n or adj* — **nar•cis•sis•tic** \‚närsə'sistik\ *adj*

nar·cis·sus \när'sisəs\ *n, pl* **-cis·sus** *or* **-cis·sus·es** *or* **-cis·si** \-'sis,ī, -,ē\ : plant with flowers usu. borne separately

nar·cot·ic \när'kätik\ *n* : painkilling addictive drug — **narcotic** *adj*

nar·rate \'nar,āt\ *vb* **nar·rat·ed; nar·rat·ing** : tell (a story) — **nar·ra·tion** \na-'rāshən\ *n* — **nar·ra·tive** \'narətiv\ *n or adj* — **nar·ra·tor** \'nar,ātər\ *n*

nar·row \'narō\ *adj* 1 : of less than standard width 2 : limited 3 : not liberal 4 : barely successful ~ *vb* : make narrow — **nar·row·ly** *adv* — **nar·row·ness** *n*

nar·row-mind·ed \,narō'mīndəd\ *adj* : shallow, provincial, or bigoted

nar·rows \'narōz\ *n pl* : narrow passage

nar·whal \'när,hwäl, 'närwəl\ *n* : sea mammal with a tusk

nasal \'nāzəl\ *adj* : relating to or uttered through the nose — **na·sal·ly** *adv*

nas·tur·tium \nə'stərshəm, na-\ *n* : herb with showy flowers

nas·ty \'nastē\ *adj* **nas·ti·er; -est** 1 : filthy 2 : indecent 3 : malicious or spiteful 4 : difficult or disagreeable 5 : unfair — **nas·ti·ly** \'nastəlē\ *adv* — **nas·ti·ness** \-tēnəs\ *n*

na·tal \'nāt°l\ *adj* : relating to birth

na·tion \'nāshən\ *n* 1 : people of similar characteristics 2 : community with its own territory and government — **na·tion·al** \'nashənəl\ *adj or n* — **na·tion·al·ly** *adv* — **na·tion·hood** *n* — **na·tion·wide** *adj*

na·tion·al·ism \'nashənəl,izəm\ *n* : devotion to national interests, unity, and independence — **na·tion·al·ist** \-ist\ *n or adj* — **na·tion·al·is·tic** \,nashənəl'istik\ *adj*

na·tion·al·i·ty \,nashə'nalətē\ *n, pl* **-ties** 1 : national character 2 : membership in a nation 3 : political independence 4 : ethnic group

na·tion·al·ize \'nashənəl,īz\ *vb* **-ized; -iz·ing** 1 : make national 2 : place under government control — **na·tion·al·i·za·tion** \,nashənələ'zāshən\ *n*

na·tive \'nātiv\ *adj* 1 : belonging to a person at or by way of birth 2 : born or produced in a particular place ~ *n* : one who belongs to a country by birth

Na·tiv·i·ty \nə'tivətē, nā-\ *n, pl* **-ties** 1 : birth of Christ 2 *not cap* : birth

nat·ty \'natē\ *adj* **-ti·er; -est** : smartly dressed — **nat·ti·ly** \'nat°lē\ *adv*

nat·u·ral \'nachərəl\ *adj* 1 : relating to

or determined by nature 2 : not artificial 3 : simple and sincere 4 : lifelike ~ *n* : one having an innate talent — **nat·u·ral·ness** *n*

nat·u·ral·ism \'nachərə,lizəm\ *n* : realism in art and literature — **nat·u·ral·is·tic** \,nachərə'listik\ *adj*

nat·u·ral·ist \-list\ *n* 1 : one who practices naturalism 2 : student of animals or plants

nat·u·ral·ize \,līz\ *vb* **-ized; -iz·ing** 1 : become or cause to become established 2 : confer citizenship on — **nat·u·ral·i·za·tion** \,nachərələ'zāshən\ *n*

nat·u·ral·ly \'nachərəlē\ *adv* 1 : in a natural way 2 : as might be expected

na·ture \'nāchər\ *n* 1 : basic quality of something 2 : kind 3 : disposition 4 : physical universe 5 : natural environment

naught \'not, 'nät\ *n* 1 : nothing 2 : zero

naugh·ty \'notē, 'nät-\ *adj* **-ti·er; -est** 1 : disobedient or misbehaving 2 : improper — **naught·i·ly** \'not°lē, 'nät-\ *adv* — **naught·i·ness** \-ēnəs\ *n*

nau·sea \'nozēə, -shə\ *n* 1 : sickness of the stomach with a desire to vomit 2 : extreme disgust — **nau·seous** \-shəs, -zēəs\ *adj*

nau·se·ate \'nozē,āt, -zhē-, -sē-, -shē-\ *vb* **-at·ed; -at·ing** : affect or become affected with nausea — **nau·se·at·ing·ly** \-,ātinlē\ *adv*

nau·ti·cal \'notikəl\ *adj* : relating to ships and sailing — **nau·ti·cal·ly** *adv*

nau·ti·lus \'not°ləs\ *n, pl* **-lus·es** *or* **-li** \-°l,ī, -,ē\ : sea mollusk with a spiral shell

na·val \'nāvəl\ *adj* : relating to a navy

nave \'nāv\ *n* : central part of a church

na·vel \'nāvəl\ *n* : depression in the abdomen

nav·i·ga·ble \'navigəbəl\ *adj* : capable of being navigated — **nav·i·ga·bil·i·ty** \,navigə'bilətē\ *n*

nav·i·gate \'navə,gāt\ *vb* **-gat·ed; -gat·ing** 1 : sail on or through 2 : direct the course of — **nav·i·ga·tion** \,navə'gāshən\ *n* — **nav·i·ga·tor** \'navə,gātər\ *n*

na·vy \'nāvē\ *n, pl* **-vies** 1 : fleet 2 : nation's organization for sea warfare

nay \'nā\ *adv* : no — used in oral voting ~ *n* : negative vote

Na·zi \'nätsē, 'nat-\ *n* : member of a German fascist party from 1933 to 1945 — **Nazi** *adj* — **Na·zism** \'nät-,sizəm, 'nat-\, **Na·zi·ism** \-sē,izəm\ *n*

near \\'nir\ *adv* : at or close to ~ *prep* : close to ~ *adj* **1** : not far away **2** : very much like ~ *vb* : approach — **near·ly** *adv* — **near·ness** *n*

near·by \nir'bī, 'nir,bī\ *adv or adj* : near

near·sight·ed \'nir'sītəd\ *adj* : seeing well at short distances only — **near·sight·ed·ly** *adv* — **near·sight·ed·ness** *n*

neat \'nēt\ *adj* **1** : not diluted **2** : tastefully simple **3** : orderly and clean — **neat** *adv* — **neat·ly** *adv* — **neat·ness** *n*

neb·u·la \'nebyələ\ *n, pl* **-lae** \-,lē, -,lī\ : large cloud of interstellar gas — **neb·u·lar** \-lər\ *adj*

neb·u·lous \-ləs\ *adj* : indistinct

nec·es·sary \'nesə,serē\ *n, pl* **-saries** : indispensable item ~ *adj* **1** : inevitable **2** : compulsory **3** : positively needed — **nec·es·sar·i·ly** \,nesə-'serəlē\ *adv*

ne·ces·si·tate \ni'sesə,tāt\ *vb* **-tated; -tat·ing** : make necessary

ne·ces·si·ty \ni'sesətē\ *n, pl* **-ties 1** : very great need **2** : something that is necessary **3** : poverty **4** : circumstances that cannot be changed

neck \'nek\ *n* **1** : body part connecting the head and trunk **2** : part of a garment at the neck **3** : narrow part ~ *vb* : kiss and caress — **necked** \'nekt\ *adj*

neck·er·chief \'nekərchəf, -,chēf\ *n, pl* **-chiefs** \-chəfs, -,chēfs\ : cloth worn tied about the neck

neck·lace \'nekləs\ *n* : ornament worn around the neck

neck·tie *n* : ornamental cloth tied under a collar

nec·ro·man·cy \'nekrə,mansē\ *n* : art of conjuring up the spirits of the dead — **nec·ro·man·cer** \-sər\ *n*

ne·cro·sis \nə'krōsəs, ne-\ *n, pl* **-cro·ses** \-,sēz\ : death of body tissue

nec·tar \'nektər\ *n* : sweet plant secretion

nec·tar·ine \,nektə'rēn\ *n* : smooth-skinned peach

née, nee \'nā\ *adj* — used to designate a married woman by maiden name

need \'nēd\ *n* **1** : obligation **2** : lack of something or what is lacking **3** : poverty ~ *vb* **1** : be in want **2** : have cause for **3** : be under obligation — **need·ful** \-fəl\ *adj* — **need·less** *adj* — **need·less·ly** *adv* — **needy** *adj*

nee·dle \'nēd³l\ *n* **1** : pointed sewing implement or something like it **2** : movable bar in a compass **3** : hollow instrument for injecting or withdrawing material ~ *vb* **-dled; -dling** : incite to action by repeated gibes — **nee·dle·work** \-,wərk\ *n*

nee·dle·point \'nēd³l,pȯint\ *n* **1** : lace fabric **2** : embroidery on canvas — **needlepoint** *adj*

ne·far·i·ous \ni'farēəs\ *adj* : very wicked — **ne·far·i·ous·ly** *adv*

ne·gate \ni'gāt\ *vb* **-gat·ed; -gat·ing 1** : deny **2** : nullify — **ne·ga·tion** \-'gāshən\ *n*

neg·a·tive \'negətiv\ *adj* **1** : marked by denial or refusal **2** : showing a lack of something suspected or desirable **3** : less than zero **4** : having more electrons than protons **5** : having light and shadow images reversed ~ *n* **1** : negative word or vote **2** : a negative number **3** : negative photographic image — **neg·a·tive·ly** *adv* — **neg·a·tive·ness** *n* — **neg·a·tiv·i·ty** \,negə'tivətē\ *n*

ne·glect \ni'glekt\ *vb* **1** : disregard **2** : leave unattended to ~ *n* **1** : act of neglecting **2** : condition of being neglected — **ne·glect·ful** *adj*

neg·li·gee \,neglə'zhā\ *n* : woman's loose robe

neg·li·gent \'neglijənt\ *adj* : marked by neglect — **neg·li·gence** \-jəns\ *n* — **neg·li·gent·ly** *adv*

neg·li·gi·ble \'neglijəbəl\ *adj* : insignificant

ne·go·ti·ate \ni'gōshē,āt\ *vb* **-at·ed; -at·ing 1** : confer with another to settle a matter **2** : obtain cash for **3** : get through successfully — **ne·go·tia·ble** \-shəbəl, -shēə-\ *adj* — **ne·go·ti·a·tion** \-,gōshē'āshən, -shē'ā-\ *n* — **ne·go·ti·a·tor** \-'gōshē,ātər\ *n*

Ne·gro \'nēgrō\ *n, pl* **-groes** *sometimes offensive* : member of the dark-skinned race native to Africa — **Negro** *adj* — **Ne·groid** \'nē,grȯid\ *n or adj, often not cap*

neigh \'nā\ *n* : cry of a horse — **neigh** *vb*

neigh·bor \'nābər\ *n* **1** : one living nearby **2** : fellowman ~ *vb* : be near or next to — **neigh·bor·hood** \-,hud\ *n* — **neigh·bor·li·ness** *n* — **neigh·bor·ly** *adv*

nei·ther \'nēthər, 'nī-\ *pron or adj* : not the one or the other ~ *conj* **1** : not either **2** : nor

nem·e·sis \'neməsəs\ *n, pl* **-e·ses** \-ə,sēz\ **1** : old and usu. frustrating rival **2** : retaliation

ne·ol·o·gism \nē'älə,jizəm\ *n* : new word

ne·on \'nē,än\ *n* : gaseous colorless chemical element that emits a reddish glow in electric lamps — **neon** *adj*

neo·phyte \'nēə,fīt\ *n* : beginner

neph·ew \'nefyü, *chiefly Brit* 'nev-\ *n* : a son of one's brother, sister, brother-in-law, or sister-in-law

nep·o·tism \'nepə,tizəm\ *n* : favoritism shown in hiring a relative

nerd \'nərd\ *n* : one who is not stylish or socially at ease — **nerdy** *adj*

nerve \'nərv\ *n* **1** : strand of body tissue that connects the brain with other parts of the body **2** : self-control **3** : daring **4** *pl* : nervousness — **nerved** \'nərvd\ *adj* — **nerve·less** *adj*

ner·vous \'nərvəs\ *adj* **1** : relating to or made up of nerves **2** : easily excited **3** : timid or fearful — **ner·vous·ly** *adv* — **ner·vous·ness** *n*

nervy \'nərvē\ *adj* **nerv·i·er; -est** : insolent or presumptuous

-ness \nəs\ *n suffix* : condition or quality

nest \'nest\ *n* **1** : shelter prepared by a bird for its eggs **2** : place where eggs (as of insects or fish) are laid and hatched **3** : snug retreat **4** : set of objects fitting one inside or under another — *vb* : build or occupy a nest

nes·tle \'nesəl\ *vb* **-tled; -tling** : settle snugly (as in a nest)

¹net \'net\ *n* : fabric with spaces between strands or something made of this — *vb* **-tt-** : cover with or catch in a net

²net *adj* : remaining after deductions — *vb* **-tt-** : have as profit

neth·er \'nethər\ *adj* : situated below

net·tle \'net³l\ *n* : coarse herb with stinging hairs — *vb* **-tled; -tling** : provoke or vex — **net·tle·some** *adj*

net·work \-,wərk\ *n* : system of crossing or connected elements

neu·ral \'nùrəl, 'nyùr-\ *adj* : relating to a nerve

neu·ral·gia \nù'raljə, nyù-\ *n* : pain along a nerve — **neu·ral·gic** \-jik\ *adj*

neu·ri·tis \nù'rītəs, nyù-\ *n, pl* **-rit·i·des** \-'ritə,dēz\ *or* **-ri·tis·es** : inflammation of a nerve

neu·rol·o·gy \nù'räləjē, nyù-\ *n* : study of the nervous system — **neu·ro·log·i·cal** \,nùrə'läjikəl, ,nyùr-\, **neu·ro·log·ic** \-ik\ *adj* — **neu·rol·o·gist** \nù'räləjist, nyù-\ *n*

neu·ro·sis \nù'rōsəs, nyù-\ *n, pl* **-ro·ses** \-,sēz\ : nervous disorder

neu·rot·ic \nù'rätik, nyù-\ *adj* : relating to neurosis ~ *n* : unstable person — **neu·rot·i·cal·ly** *adv*

neu·ter \'nütər, 'nyü-\ *adj* : neither masculine nor feminine — *vb* : castrate or spay

neu·tral \-trəl\ *adj* **1** : not favoring either side **2** : being neither one thing nor the other **3** : not decided in color **4** : not electrically charged ~ *n* **1** : one that is neutral **2** : position of gears that are not engaged — **neu·tral·iza·tion** \,nütrələ'zāshən, ,nyü-\ *n* — **neu·tral·ize** \'nütrə,līz, 'nyü-\ *vb*

neu·tral·i·ty \nü'tralətē, nyü-\ *n* : state of being neutral

neu·tron \'nü,trän, 'nyü-\ *n* : uncharged atomic particle

nev·er \'nevər\ *adv* **1** : not ever **2** : not in any degree, way, or condition

nev·er·more *adv* : never again

nev·er·the·less *adv* : in spite of that

new \'nü, 'nyü\ *adj* **1** : not old or familiar **2** : different from the former **3** : recently discovered or learned **4** : not accustomed **5** : refreshed or regenerated **6** : being such for the first time ~ *adv* : newly — **new·ish** *adj* — **new·ness** *n*

new·born *adj* **1** : recently born **2** : born anew ~ *n, pl* **-born** *or* **-borns** : newborn individual

new·ly \-lē\ *adv* : recently

news \'nüz, 'nyüz\ *n* : report of recent events — **news·let·ter** *n* — **news·mag·a·zine** *n* — **news·man** \-mən, -,man\ *n* — **news·pa·per** *n* — **news·pa·per·man** \-,man\ *n* — **news·stand** *n* — **news·wom·an** \-,wùmən\ *n* — **news·wor·thy** *adj*

news·cast \-,kast\ *n* : broadcast of news — **news·cast·er** \-,kastər\ *n*

news·print *n* : paper made from wood pulp

newsy \'nüzē, 'nyü-\ *adj* **news·i·er; -est** : filled with news

newt \'nüt, 'nyüt\ *n* : small salamander

New Year *n* : New Year's Day

New Year's Day *n* : January 1 observed as a legal holiday

next \'nekst\ *adj* : immediately preceding or following ~ *adv* **1** : in the time or place nearest **2** : at the first time yet to come ~ *prep* : nearest to

nex·us \'neksəs\ *n, pl* **-us·es** \-səsəz\ *or* **-us** \-səs, -,süs\ : connection

nib \'nib\ *n* : pen point

nib·ble \'nibəl\ *vb* -**bled**; -**bling** : bite gently or bit by bit ~ *n* : small bite

nice \'nīs\ *adj* **nic·er**; **nic·est** 1 : fastidious 2 : very precise or delicate 3 : pleasing 4 : respectable — **nice·ly** *adv* — **nice·ness** *n*

nice·ty \'nīsətē\ *n*, *pl* -**ties** 1 : dainty or elegant thing 2 : fine detail 3 : exactness

niche \'nich\ *n* 1 : recess in a wall 2 : fitting place, work, or use

nick \'nik\ *n* 1 : small broken area or chip 2 : critical moment ~ *vb* : make a nick in

nick·el \'nikəl\ *n* 1 : hard silver-white metallic chemical element used in alloys 2 : U.S. 5-cent piece

nick·name \'nik,nām\ *n* : informal substitute name — **nickname** *vb*

nic·o·tine \'nikə,tēn\ *n* : poisonous and addictive substance in tobacco

niece \'nēs\ *n* : a daughter of one's brother, sister, brother-in-law, or sister-in-law

nig·gard·ly \'nigərdlē\ *adj* : stingy — **nig·gard** *n* — **nig·gard·li·ness** *n*

nig·gling \'nigəlin\ *adj* : petty and annoying

nigh \'nī\ *adv or adj or prep* : near

night \'nīt\ *n* 1 : period between dusk and dawn 2 : the coming of night — **night** *adj* — **night·ly** *adj or adv* — **night·time** *n*

night·clothes *n pl* : garments worn in bed

night·club \-,kləb\ *n* : place for drinking and entertainment open at night

night crawler *n* : earthworm

night·fall *n* : the coming of night

night·gown *n* : gown worn for sleeping

night·in·gale \'nīt²n,gāl, -in-\ *n* : Old World thrush that sings at night

night·mare \'nīt,mar\ *n* : frightening dream — **nightmare** *adj* — **night·mar·ish** \-,marish\ *adj*

night·shade \'nīt,shād\ *n* : group of plants that include poisonous forms and food plants (as the potato and eggplant)

nil \'nil\ *n* : nothing

nim·ble \'nimbəl\ *adj* -**bler**; -**blest** 1 : agile 2 : clever — **nim·ble·ness** *n* — **nim·bly** \-blē\ *adv*

nine \'nīn\ *n* 1 : one more than 8 2 : 9th in a set or series — **nine** *adj or pron* — **ninth** \'ninth\ *adj or pron*

nine·pins *n* : bowling game using 9 pins

nine·teen \nīn'tēn\ *n* : one more than 18 — **nineteen** *adj or pron* — **nine·teenth** \-'tēnth\ *adj or n*

nine·ty \'nīntē\ *n*, *pl* -**ties** : 9 times 10 — **nine·ti·eth** \-ēəth\ *adj or n* — **ninety** *adj or pron*

nin·ny \'ninē\ *n*, *pl* **nin·nies** : fool

¹**nip** \'nip\ *vb* -**pp-** 1 : catch hold of and squeeze tightly 2 : pinch or bite off 3 : destroy the growth or fulfillment of ~ *n* 1 : biting cold 2 : tang 3 : pinch or bite

²**nip** *n* : small quantity of liquor ~ *vb* -**pp-** : take liquor in nips

nip·per \'nipər\ *n* 1 : one that nips 2 *pl* : pincers 3 : small boy

nip·ple \'nipəl\ *n* : tip of the breast or something resembling it

nip·py \'nipē\ *adj* -**pi·er**; -**est** 1 : pungent 2 : chilly

nir·va·na \nir'vänə\ *n* : state of blissful oblivion

nit \'nit\ *n* : egg of a parasitic insect

ni·ter \'nītər\ *n* : potassium nitrate used in gunpowder or fertilizer or in curing meat

ni·trate \'nī,trāt, -trət\ *n* : chemical salt used esp. in curing meat

ni·tric acid \'nītrik-\ *n* : liquid acid used in making dyes, explosives, and fertilizers

ni·trite \-,trīt\ *n* : chemical salt used in curing meat

ni·tro·gen \'nītrəjən\ *n* : tasteless odorless gaseous chemical element

ni·tro·glyc·er·in, ni·tro·glyc·er·ine \,nītrō'glisərən\ *n* : heavy oily liquid used as an explosive and as a blood-vessel relaxer

nit·wit \'nit,wit\ *n* : stupid person

no \'nō\ *adv* 1 — used to express the negative 2 : in no respect or degree 3 : not so 4 — used as an interjection of surprise or doubt ~ *adj* 1 : not any 2 : not a ~ *n*, *pl* **noes** *or* **nos** \'nōz\ 1 : refusal 2 : negative vote

no·bil·i·ty \nō'bilətē\ *n* 1 : quality or state of being noble 2 : class of people of noble rank

no·ble \'nōbəl\ *adj* -**bler**; -**blest** 1 : illustrious 2 : aristocratic 3 : stately 4 : of outstanding character ~ *n* : nobleman — **no·ble·ness** *n* — **no·bly** *adv*

no·ble·man \-mən\ *n* : member of the nobility

no·ble·wom·an \-,wùmən\ *n* : a woman of noble rank

no·body \'nōbədē, -,bädē\ *pron* : no person ~ *n*, *pl* -**bod·ies** : person of no influence or importance

no–brain·er \'nō'brānər\ : something that requires a minimum of thought

noc·tur·nal \näk'tərnᵊl\ adj : relating to, occurring at, or active at night

noc·turne \'näk,tərn\ n : dreamy musical composition

nod \'näd\ vb **-dd- 1** : bend the head downward or forward (as in bowing or going to sleep or as a sign of assent) **2** : move up and down **3** : show by a nod of the head — **nod** n

node \'nōd\ n : stem part from which a leaf arises — **nod·al** \-ᵊl\ adj

nod·ule \'näjül\ n : small lump or swelling — **nod·u·lar** \'näjələr\ adj

no·el \nō'el\ n **1** : Christmas carol **2** cap : Christmas season

noes pl of NO

nog·gin \'nägən\ n **1** : small mug **2** : person's head

no·how \'nō,haú\ adv : in no manner

noise \'nóiz\ n : loud or unpleasant sound ∼ vb **noised; nois·ing** : spread by rumor — **noise·less** adj

— **noise·less·ly** adv — **noise·mak·er** n — **nois·i·ly** \'nóizəlē\ adv — **nois·i·ness** \-zēnəs\ n — **noisy** \'nóizē\ adj

noi·some \'nóisəm\ adj : harmful or offensive

no·mad \'nō,mad\ n : one who has no permanent home — **nomad** adj — **no·mad·ic** \nō'madik\ adj

no·men·cla·ture \'nōmən,klāchər\ n : system of names

nom·i·nal \'nämənᵊl\ adj **1** : being something in name only **2** : small or negligible — **nom·i·nal·ly** adv

nom·i·nate \'nämə,nāt\ vb **-nat·ed; -nat·ing** : propose or choose as a candidate — **nom·i·na·tion** \,nämə'nāshən\ n

nom·i·na·tive \'nämənətiv\ adj : relating to or being a grammatical case marking typically the subject of a verb — **nominative** n

nom·i·nee \,nämə'nē\ n : person nominated

non- \'nän, ,nän\ prefix **1** : not, reverse of, or absence of **2** : not important

---

List of self-explanatory words with the prefix *non-*

nonabrasive	noncombustible	nonelective
nonabsorbent	noncommercial	nonelectric
nonacademic	noncommunist	nonelectronic
nonaccredited	noncompliance	nonemotional
nonacid	nonconflicting	nonenforcement
nonaddictive	nonconforming	nonessential
nonadhesive	nonconsecutive	nonexclusive
nonadjacent	nonconstructive	nonexistence
nonadjustable	noncontagious	nonexistent
nonaffiliated	noncontrollable	nonexplosive
nonaggression	noncontroversial	nonfat
nonalcoholic	noncorrosive	nonfatal
nonaligned	noncriminal	nonfattening
nonappearance	noncritical	nonfictional
nonautomatic	noncumulative	nonflammable
nonbeliever	noncurrent	nonflowering
nonbinding	nondeductible	nonfunctional
nonbreakable	nondeferrable	nongovernmental
noncancerous	nondegradable	nongraded
noncandidate	nondelivery	nonhazardous
non-Catholic	nondemocratic	nonhereditary
non-Christian	nondenominational	nonindustrial
nonchurchgoer	nondestructive	nonindustrialized
noncitizen	nondiscrimination	noninfectious
nonclassical	nondiscriminatory	noninflationary
nonclassified	noneducational	nonintegrated
noncombat	nonelastic	nonintellectual
noncombatant	nonelected	noninterference

non·age \'nänij, 'nōnij\ *n* : period of youth and esp. legal minority

nonce \'näns\ *n* : present occasion ~ *adj* : occurring, used, or made only once

non·cha·lant \‚nänshə'länt\ *adj* : showing indifference — **non·cha·lance** \-'läns\ *n* — **non·cha·lant·ly** *adv*

non·com·mis·sioned officer \‚nänkə-'mishənd-\ *n* : subordinate officer in the armed forces appointed from enlisted personnel

non·com·mit·tal \‚nänkə'mit'l\ *adj* : indicating neither consent nor dissent

non·con·duc·tor *n* : substance that is a very poor conductor

non·con·form·ist *n* : one who does not conform to an established belief or mode of behavior — **non·con·for·mi·ty** *n*

non·de·script \‚nändi'skript\ *adj* : lacking distinctive qualities

none \'nən\ *pron* : not any ~ *adv* : not at all

non·en·ti·ty *n* : one of no consequence

none·the·less \‚nənthə'les\ *adv* : nevertheless

non·pa·reil \‚nänpə'rel\ *adj* : having no equal ~ *n* **1** : one who has no equal **2** : chocolate candy disk

non·par·ti·san *adj* : not influenced by political party bias

non·per·son *n* : person without social or legal status

non·plus \‚nän'pləs\ *vb* **-ss-** : perplex

non·pre·scrip·tion *adj* : available without a doctor's prescription

non·pro·lif·er·a·tion *adj* : aimed at ending increased use of nuclear arms

non·sched·uled *adj* : licensed to carry by air without a regular schedule

non·sense \'nän‚sens, -səns\ *n* : foolish or meaningless words or actions — **non·sen·si·cal** \nän'sensikəl\ *adj* — **non·sen·si·cal·ly** *adv*

non·sup·port *n* : failure in a legal obligation to provide for someone's needs

non·vi·o·lence *n* : avoidance of violence esp. in political demonstrations — **non·vi·o·lent** *adj*

---

nonintoxicating	nonpolitical	nonskier
noninvasive	nonpolluting	nonsmoker
non-Jewish	nonporous	nonsmoking
nonlegal	nonpregnant	nonspeaking
nonlethal	nonproductive	nonspecialist
nonliterary	nonprofessional	nonspecific
nonliving	nonprofit	nonstandard
nonmagnetic	nonracial	nonstick
nonmalignant	nonradioactive	nonstop
nonmedical	nonrated	nonstrategic
nonmember	nonrealistic	nonstudent
nonmetal	nonrecurring	nonsugar
nonmetallic	nonrefillable	nonsurgical
nonmilitary	nonrefundable	nonswimmer
nonmusical	nonreligious	nontaxable
nonnative	nonrenewable	nonteaching
nonnegotiable	nonrepresentative	nontechnical
nonobjective	nonresident	nontoxic
nonobservance	nonresponsive	nontraditional
nonorthodox	nonrestricted	nontransferable
nonparallel	nonreversible	nontropical
nonparticipant	nonsalable	nontypical
nonparticipating	nonscientific	nonunion
nonpaying	nonscientist	nonuser
nonpayment	nonsegregated	nonvenomous
nonperformance	non–self–governing	nonverbal
nonperishable	nonsexist	nonvoter
nonphysical	nonsexual	nonwhite
nonpoisonous	nonsignificant	nonworker

noo•dle \'nüd³l\ *n* : ribbon-shaped food paste

nook \'nùk\ *n* **1** : inside corner **2** : private place

noon \'nün\ *n* : middle of the day — **noon** *adj*

noon•day \-,dā\ *n* : noon

no one *pron* : no person

noon•time *n* : noon

noose \'nüs\ *n* : rope loop that slips down tight

nor \'nòr\ *conj* : and not — used esp. after *neither* to introduce and negate the 2d member of a series

norm \'nòrm\ *n* **1** : standard usu. derived from an average **2** : typical widespread practice or custom

nor•mal \'nòrməl\ *adj* : average, regular, or standard — **nor•mal•cy** \-sē\ *n* — **nor•mal•i•ty** \nòr'malitē\ *n* — **nor•mal•i•za•tion** \,nòrmələ'zāshən\ *n* — **nor•mal•ize** \'nòrmə,līz\ *vb* — **nor•mal•ly** *adv*

north \'nòrth\ *adv* : to or toward the north ∼ *adj* : situated toward, at, or coming from the north ∼ *n* **1** : direction to the left of one facing east **2** *cap* : regions to the north — **north•er•ly** \'nòrthərlē\ *adv or adj* — **north•ern** \-ərn\ *adj* — **North•ern•er** *n* — **north•ern•most** \-,mōst\ *adj* — **north•ward** \-wərd\ *adv or adj* — **north•wards** \-wərdz\ *adv*

north•east \nòrth'ēst\ *n* **1** : direction between north and east **2** *cap* : regions to the northeast — **northeast** *adj or adv* — **north•east•er•ly** \-ərlē\ *adv or adj* — **north•east•ern** \-ərn\ *adj*

northern lights *n pl* : aurora borealis

north pole *n* : northernmost point of the earth

north•west \-'west\ *n* **1** : direction between north and west **2** *cap* : regions to the northwest — **northwest** *adj or adv* — **north•west•er•ly** \-ərlē\ *adv or adj* — **north•west•ern** \-ərn\ *adj*

nose \'nōz\ *n* **1** : part of the face containing the nostrils **2** : sense of smell **3** : front part ∼ *vb* **nosed; nos•ing 1** : detect by smell **2** : push aside with the nose **3** : pry **4** : inch ahead — **nose•bleed** *n* — **nosed** \'nōzd\ *adj* — **nose out** *vb* : narrowly defeat

nose•gay \-,gā\ *n* : small bunch of flowers

nos•tal•gia \nä'staljə, nə-\ *n* : wistful yearning for something past — **nos•tal•gic** \-jik\ *adj*

nos•tril \'nästrəl\ *n* : opening of the nose

nos•trum \-trəm\ *n* : questionable remedy

nosy, nos•ey \'nōzē\ *adj* **nos•i•er; -est** : tending to pry

not \'nät\ *adv* — used to make a statement negative

no•ta•ble \'nōtəbəl\ *adj* **1** : noteworthy **2** : distinguished ∼ *n* : notable person — **no•ta•bil•i•ty** \nòtə'bilətē\ *n* — **no•ta•bly** \'nōtəblē\ *adv*

no•ta•rize \'nōtə,rīz\ *vb* **-rized; -riz•ing** : attest as a notary public

no•ta•ry public \'nōtərē-\ *n, pl* **-ries public** *or* **-ry publics** : public official who attests writings to make them legally authentic

no•ta•tion \nō'tāshən\ *n* **1** : note **2** : act, process, or method of marking things down

notch \'näch\ *n* : V-shaped hollow — **notch** *vb*

note \'nōt\ *vb* **not•ed; not•ing 1** : notice **2** : write down ∼ *n* **1** : musical tone **2** : written comment or record **3** : short informal letter **4** : notice or heed — **note•book** *n*

not•ed \'nōtəd\ *adj* : famous

note•wor•thy \-,wərthē\ *adj* : worthy of special mention

noth•ing \'nəthiŋ\ *pron* **1** : no thing **2** : no part **3** : one of no value or importance ∼ *adv* : not at all ∼ *n* **1** : something that does not exist **2** : zero **3** : one of little or no importance — **noth•ing•ness** *n*

no•tice \'nōtəs\ *n* **1** : warning or announcement **2** : attention ∼ *vb* **-ticed; -tic•ing** : take notice of — **no•tice•able** *adj* — **no•tice•ably** *adv*

no•ti•fy \'nōtə,fī\ *vb* **-fied; -fy•ing** : give notice of or to — **no•ti•fi•ca•tion** \,nōtəfə'kāshən\ *n*

no•tion \'nōshən\ *n* **1** : idea or opinion **2** : whim

no•to•ri•ous \nō'tōrēəs\ *adj* : widely and unfavorably known — **no•to•ri•e•ty** \,nōtə'rīətē\ *n* — **no•to•ri•ous•ly** *adv*

not•with•stand•ing \,nätwith'standiŋ, -with-\ *prep* : in spite of ∼ *adv* : nevertheless ∼ *conj* : although

nou•gat \'nügət\ *n* : nuts or fruit pieces in a sugar paste

nought \'nòt, 'nät\ *var of* NAUGHT

noun \'naùn\ *n* : word that is the name of a person, place, or thing

nour•ish \'nərish\ *vb* : promote the

growth of — **nour·ish·ing** adj — **nour·ish·ment** n

no·va \'nōvə\ n, pl **-vas** or **-vae** \-,vē, -,vī\ : star that suddenly brightens and then fades gradually

nov·el \'nävəl\ adj : new or strange ~ n : long invented prose story — **nov·el·ist** \-əlist\ n

nov·el·ty \'nävəltē\ n, pl **-ties** 1 : something new or unusual 2 : newness 3 : small manufactured article — usu. pl.

No·vem·ber \nō'vembər\ n : 11th month of the year having 30 days

nov·ice \'nävəs\ n 1 : one preparing to take vows in a religious order 2 : one who is inexperienced or untrained

no·vi·tiate \nō'vishət, nə-\ n : period or state of being a novice

now \'naù\ adv 1 : at the present time or moment 2 : forthwith 3 : under these circumstances ~ conj : in view of the fact ~ n : present time

now·a·days \'naùə,dāz\ adv : now

no·where \-,hwer\ adv : not anywhere — **no·where** n

nox·ious \'näkshəs\ adj : harmful

noz·zle \'näzəl\ n : device to direct or control a flow of fluid

nu·ance \'nü,äns, 'nyü-\ n : subtle distinction or variation

nub \'nəb\ n 1 : knob or lump 2 : gist

nu·bile \'nü,bīl, 'nyü-, -bəl\ adj 1 : of marriageable condition or age 2 : sexually attractive

nu·cle·ar \'nüklēər, 'nyü-\ adj 1 : relating to the atomic nucleus or atomic energy 2 : relating to a weapon whose power is from a nuclear reaction

nu·cle·us \'nüklēəs, 'nyü-\ n, pl **-clei** \-klē,ī\ : central mass or part (as of a cell or an atom)

nude \'nüd, 'nyüd\ adj **nud·er; nud·est** : naked ~ n : nude human figure — **nu·di·ty** \'nüdətē, 'nyü-\ n

nudge \'nəj\ vb **nudged; nudg·ing** : touch or push gently — **nudge** n

nud·ism \'nüd,izəm, 'nyü-\ n : practice of going nude — **nud·ist** \'nüdist, 'nyü-\ n

nug·get \'nəgət\ n : lump of gold

nui·sance \'nüs²ns, 'nyü-\ n : something annoying

null \'nəl\ adj : having no legal or binding force — **nul·li·ty** \'nələtē\ n

nul·li·fy \'nələ,fī\ vb **-fied; -fy·ing**

: make null or valueless — **nul·li·fi·ca·tion** \,nələfə'kāshən\ n

numb \'nəm\ adj : lacking feeling — **numb** vb — **numb·ly** adv — **numb·ness** n

num·ber \'nəmbər\ n 1 : total of individuals taken together 2 : indefinite total 3 : unit of a mathematical system 4 : numeral 5 : one in a sequence ~ vb 1 : count 2 : assign a number to 3 : comprise in number — **num·ber·less** adj

nu·mer·al \'nümərəl, 'nyü-\ n : conventional symbol representing a number

nu·mer·a·tor \'nümə,rātər, 'nyü-\ n : part of a fraction above the line

nu·mer·i·cal \nü'merikəl, nyü-\, **nu·mer·ic** \-'merik\ adj 1 : relating to numbers 2 : expressed in or involving numbers — **nu·mer·i·cal·ly** adv

nu·mer·ol·o·gy \nümə'räləjē, ,nyü-\ n : occult study of numbers — **nu·mer·ol·o·gist** \-jist\ n

nu·mer·ous \'nümərəs, 'nyü-\ adj : consisting of a great number

nu·mis·mat·ics \,nüməz'matiks, ,nyü-\ n : study or collection of monetary objects — **nu·mis·mat·ic** \-ik\ adj — **nu·mis·ma·tist** \nü'mizmətist, nyü-\ n

num·skull \'nəm,skəl\ n : stupid person

nun \'nən\ n : woman belonging to a religious order — **nun·nery** \-ərē\ n

nup·tial \'nəpshəl\ adj : relating to marriage or a wedding ~ n : marriage or wedding — usu. pl.

nurse \'nərs\ n 1 : one hired to care for children 2 : person trained to care for sick people ~ vb **nursed; nurs·ing** 1 : suckle 2 : care for

nurs·ery \'nərsərē\ n, pl **-er·ies** 1 : place where children are cared for 2 : place where young plants are grown

nursing home n : private establishment providing care for persons who are unable to care for themselves

nur·ture \'nərchər\ n 1 : training or upbringing 2 : food or nourishment ~ vb **-tured; -tur·ing** 1 : care for or feed 2 : educate

nut \'nət\ n 1 : dry hard-shelled fruit or seed with a firm inner kernel 2 : metal block with a screw hole through it 3 : foolish, eccentric, or crazy person 4 : enthusiast — **nut·crack·er** n — **nut·shell** n — **nut·ty** adj

nut·hatch \'nət,hach\ n : small bird

nut·meg \'nət,meg, -,māg\ n : nutlike aromatic seed of a tropical tree

nu·tri·ent \'nütrēənt, 'nyü-\ n : something giving nourishment — **nutrient** adj

nu·tri·ment \-trəmənt\ n : nutrient

nu·tri·tion \nü'trishən, nyü-\ n : act or process of nourishing esp. with food — **nu·tri·tion·al** \-'trishənəl\ adj — **nu·tri·tious** \-'trishəs\ adj — **nu·tri·tive** \'nütrətiv, 'nyü-\ adj

nuts \'nəts\ adj **1** : enthusiastic **2** : crazy

nuz·zle \'nəzəl\ vb **-zled; -zling 1** : touch with or as if with the nose **2** : snuggle

ny·lon \'nī,län\ n **1** : tough synthetic material used esp. in textiles **2** pl : stockings made of nylon

nymph \'nimf\ n **1** : lesser goddess in ancient mythology **2** : girl **3** : immature insect

O

o \'ō\ n, pl **o's** or **os** \'ōz\ **1** : 15th letter of the alphabet **2** : zero

O var of OH

oaf \'ōf\ n : stupid or awkward person — **oaf·ish** \'ōfish\ adj

oak \'ōk\ n, pl **oaks** or **oak** : tree bearing a thin-shelled nut or its wood — **oak·en** \'ōkən\ adj

oar \'ōr\ n : pole with a blade at the end used to propel a boat

oar·lock \-,läk\ n : u-shaped device for holding an oar

oa·sis \ō'āsəs\ n, pl **oa·ses** \-,sēz\ : fertile area in a desert

oat \'ōt\ n : cereal grass or its edible seed — **oat·cake** n — **oat·en** \-ᵊn\ adj — **oat·meal** n

oath \'ōth\ n, pl **oaths** \'ōthz, 'ōths\ **1** : solemn appeal to God as a pledge of sincerity **2** : profane utterance

ob·du·rate \'äbdûret, -dyû-\ adj : stubbornly resistant — **ob·du·ra·cy** \-rəsē\ n

obe·di·ent \ō'bēdēənt\ adj : willing to obey — **obe·di·ence** \-əns\ n — **obe·di·ent·ly** adv

obei·sance \ō'bēsəns, -'bās-\ n : bow of respect or submission

obe·lisk \'äbə,lisk\ n : 4-sided tapering pillar

obese \ōbēs\ adj : extremely fat — **obe·si·ty** \-'bēsətē\ n

obey \ō'bā\ vb **obeyed; obey·ing 1** : follow the commands or guidance of **2** : behave in accordance with

ob·fus·cate \'äbfə,skāt\ vb **-cat·ed; -cat·ing** : confuse — **ob·fus·ca·tion** \,äbfəs'kāshən\ n

obit·u·ary \ə'bichə,werē\ n, pl **-ar·ies** : death notice

¹ob·ject \'äbjikt\ n **1** : something that

may be seen or felt **2** : purpose **3** : noun or equivalent toward which the action of a verb is directed or which follows a preposition

²object \əb'jekt\ vb : offer opposition or disapproval — **ob·jec·tion** \-'jek-shən\ n — **ob·jec·tion·able** \-shənəbəl\ adj — **ob·jec·tion·ably** \-blē\ adv — **ob·jec·tor** \-'jektər\ n

ob·jec·tive \əb'jektiv\ adj **1** : relating to an object or end **2** : existing outside an individual's thoughts or feelings **3** : treating facts without distortion **4** : relating to or being a grammatical case marking objects ~ n : aim or end of action — **ob·jec·tive·ly** adv — **ob·jec·tive·ness** n — **ob·jec·tiv·i·ty** \,äb,jek'tivətē\ n

ob·li·gate \'äblə,gāt\ vb **-gat·ed; -gat·ing** : bind legally or morally — **ob·li·ga·tion** \,äblə'gāshən\ n — **oblig·a·to·ry** \ə'bligə,tōrē, 'äbligə-\ adj

oblige \ə'blīj\ vb **obliged; oblig·ing 1** : compel **2** : do a favor for — **oblig·ing** adj — **oblig·ing·ly** adv

oblique \ō'blēk, -'blīk\ adj **1** : lying at a slanting angle **2** : indirect — **oblique·ly** adv — **oblique·ness** n — **obliq·ui·ty** \-'blikwətē\ n

oblit·er·ate \ə'blitə,rāt\ vb **-at·ed; -at·ing** : completely remove or destroy — **oblit·er·a·tion** \-,blitə'rāshən\ n

obliv·i·on \ə'blivēən\ n **1** : state of having lost conscious awareness **2** : state of being forgotten

obliv·i·ous \-ēəs\ adj : not aware or mindful — with to or of — **obliv·i·ous·ly** adv — **obliv·i·ous·ness** n

ob·long \'äb,lȯŋ\ adj : longer in one direction than in the other with opposite sides parallel — **oblong** n

ob·lo·quy \'äbləkwē\ *n, pl* **-quies 1** : strongly condemning utterance **2** : bad repute

ob·nox·ious \äb'näkshəs, əb-\ *adj* : repugnant — **ob·nox·ious·ly** *adv* — **ob·nox·ious·ness** *n*

oboe \'ōbō\ *n* : slender woodwind instrument with a reed mouthpiece — **obo·ist** \'ō,bōist\ *n*

ob·scene \äb'sēn, əb-\ *adj* : repugnantly indecent — **ob·scene·ly** *adv* — **ob·scen·i·ty** \-'senətē\ *n*

ob·scure \äb'skyùr, əb-\ *adj* **1** : dim or hazy **2** : not well known **3** : vague ∼ *vb* : make indistinct or unclear — **ob·scure·ly** *adv* — **ob·scu·ri·ty** \-'skyùrətē\ *n*

ob·se·quies \'äbsəkwēz\ *n pl* : funeral or burial rites

ob·se·qui·ous \əb'sēkwēəs\ *adj* : excessively attentive or flattering — **ob·se·qui·ous·ly** *adv* — **ob·se·qui·ous·ness** *n*

ob·ser·va·to·ry \əb'zərvə,tōrē\ *n, pl* **-ries** : place for observing astronomical phenomena

ob·serve \əb'zərv\ *vb* **-served; -serving 1** : conform to **2** : celebrate **3** : see, watch, or notice **4** : remark — **ob·serv·able** *adj* — **ob·ser·vance** \-'zərvəns\ *n* — **ob·ser·vant** \-vənt\ *adj* — **ob·ser·va·tion** \ˌäbsər'vāshən, -zər-\ *n*

ob·sess \əb'ses\ *vb* : preoccupy intensely or abnormally — **ob·ses·sion** \äb'seshən, əb-\ *n* — **ob·ses·sive** \-'sesiv\ *adj* — **ob·ses·sive·ly** *adv*

ob·so·les·cent \ˌäbsə'les³nt\ *adj* : going out of use — **ob·so·les·cence** \-³ns\ *n*

ob·so·lete \ˌäbsə'lēt, 'äbsə,-\ *adj* : no longer in use

ob·sta·cle \'äbstikəl\ *n* : something that stands in the way or opposes

ob·stet·rics \əb'stetriks\ *n sing or pl* : branch of medicine that deals with childbirth — **ob·stet·ric** \-rik\, **ob·stet·ri·cal** \-rikəl\ *adj* — **ob·ste·tri·cian** \ˌäbstə'trishən\ *n*

ob·sti·nate \'äbstənət\ *adj* : stubborn — **ob·sti·na·cy** \-nəsē\ *n* — **ob·sti·nate·ly** *adv*

ob·strep·er·ous \əb'strepərəs\ *adj* : uncontrollably noisy or defiant — **ob·strep·er·ous·ness** *n*

ob·struct \əb'strəkt\ *vb* : block or impede — **ob·struc·tion** \-'strəkshən\

n — **ob·struc·tive** \-'strəktiv\ *adj* — **ob·struc·tor** \-tər\ *n*

ob·tain \əb'tān\ *vb* **1** : gain by effort **2** : be generally recognized — **ob·tain·able** *adj*

ob·trude \əb'trüd\ *vb* **-trud·ed; -truding 1** : thrust out **2** : intrude — **ob·tru·sion** \-'trüzhən\ *n* — **ob·tru·sive** \-'trüsiv\ *adj* — **ob·tru·sive·ly** *adv* — **ob·tru·sive·ness** *n*

ob·tuse \äb'tüs, əb-, -'tyüs\ *adj* **1** : slow-witted **2** : exceeding 90 but less than 180 degrees — **ob·tuse·ly** *adv* — **ob·tuse·ness** *n*

ob·verse \'äb,vərs, äb'-\ *n* : principal side (as of a coin)

ob·vi·ate \'äbvē,āt\ *vb* **-at·ed; -at·ing** : make unnecessary

ob·vi·ous \'äbvēəs\ *adj* : plain or unmistakable — **ob·vi·ous·ly** *adv* — **ob·vi·ous·ness** *n*

oc·ca·sion \ə'kāzhən\ *n* **1** : favorable opportunity **2** : cause **3** : time of an event **4** : special event ∼ *vb* : cause — **oc·ca·sion·al** \-'kāzhənəl\ *adj* — **oc·ca·sion·al·ly** *adv*

oc·ci·den·tal \ˌäksə'dent³l\ *adj* : western — **Occidental** *n*

oc·cult \ə'kəlt, 'äk,əlt\ *adj* **1** : secret or mysterious **2** : relating to supernatural agencies — **oc·cult·ism** \-'kəl-ˌtizəm\ *n* — **oc·cult·ist** \-'tist\ *n*

oc·cu·pan·cy \'äkyəpənsē\ *n, pl* **-cies** : an occupying

oc·cu·pant \-pənt\ *n* : one who occupies

oc·cu·pa·tion \ˌäkyə'pāshən\ *n* **1** : vocation **2** : action or state of occupying — **oc·cu·pa·tion·al** \-shənəl\ *adj* — **oc·cu·pa·tion·al·ly** *adv*

oc·cu·py \'äkyə,pī\ *vb* **-pied; -py·ing 1** : engage the attention of **2** : fill up **3** : take or hold possession of **4** : reside in — **oc·cu·pi·er** \-,pīər\ *n*

oc·cur \ə'kər\ *vb* **-rr- 1** : be found or met with **2** : take place **3** : come to mind

oc·cur·rence \ə'kərəns\ *n* : something that takes place

ocean \'ōshən\ *n* **1** : whole body of salt water **2** : very large body of water — **ocean·front** *n* — **ocean·going** *adj* — **oce·an·ic** \ˌōshē'anik\ *adj*

ocean·og·ra·phy \ˌōshə'nägrəfē\ *n* : science dealing with the ocean — **ocean·og·ra·pher** \-fər\ *n* — **ocean·o·graph·ic** \-nə'grafik\ *adj*

oce·lot \'äsə,lät, 'ōsə-\ *n* : medium-sized American wildcat

ocher, ochre \'ōkər\ *n* : red or yellow pigment

o'•clock \ə'kläk\ *adv* : according to the clock

oc•ta•gon \'äktə,gän\ *n* : 8-sided polygon — **oc•tag•o•nal** \äk'tagənəl\ *adj*

oc•tave \'äk'tiv\ *n* : musical interval of 8 steps or the notes within this interval

Oc•to•ber \äk'tōbər\ *n* : 10th month of the year having 31 days

oc•to•pus \'äktəpəs\ *n, pl* **-pus•es** *or* **-pi** \-,pī\ : sea mollusk with 8 arms

oc•u•lar \'äkyələr\ *adj* : relating to the eye

oc•u•list \'äkyəlist\ *n* **1** : ophthalmologist **2** : optometrist

odd \'äd\ *adj* **1** : being only one of a pair or set **2** : not divisible by two without a remainder **3** : additional to what is usual or to the number mentioned **4** : queer — **odd•ly** *adv* — **odd•ness** *n*

odd•i•ty \'ädətē\ *n, pl* **-ties** : something odd

odds \'ädz\ *n pl* **1** : difference by which one thing is favored **2** : disagreement **3** : ratio between winnings and the amount of the bet

ode \'ōd\ *n* : solemn lyric poem

odi•ous \'ōdēəs\ *adj* : hated — **odi•ous•ly** *adv* — **odi•ous•ness** *n*

odi•um \'ōdēəm\ *n* **1** : merited loathing **2** : disgrace

odor \'ōdər\ *n* : quality that affects the sense of smell — **odor•less** *adj* — **odor•ous** *adj*

od•ys•sey \'ädəsē\ *n, pl* **-seys** : long wandering

o'er \'ōr\ *adv or prep* : OVER

of \'əv, 'äv\ *prep* **1** : from **2** : distinguished by **3** : because of **4** : made or written by **5** : made with, being, or containing **6** : belonging to or connected with **7** : about **8** : that is **9** : concerning **10** : before

off \'óf\ *adv* **1** : from a place **2** : unattached or removed **3** : to a state of being no longer in use **4** : away from work **5** : at a distance in time or space ~ *prep* **1** : away from **2** : at the expense of **3** : not engaged in or abstaining from **4** : below the usual level of ~ *adj* **1** : not operating, or near to standard, or correct **2** : remote **3** : provided for

of•fal \'ófəl\ *n* **1** : waste **2** : viscera and trimmings of a butchered animal

of•fend \ə'fend\ *vb* **1** : sin or act in violation **2** : hurt, annoy, or insult — **of•fend•er** *n*

of•fense, of•fence \ə'fens, 'äf,ens\ *n* : attack, misdeed, or insult

of•fen•sive \ə'fensiv, 'äf,en-\ *adj* : causing offense ~ *n* : attack — **of•fen•sive•ly** *adv* — **of•fen•sive•ness** *n*

of•fer \'ófər\ *vb* **1** : present for acceptance **2** : propose **3** : put up (an effort) ~ *n* **1** : proposal **2** : bid — **of•fer•ing** *n*

of•fer•to•ry \'ófər,tōrē\ *n, pl* **-ries** : presentation of offerings or its musical accompaniment

off•hand *adv or adj* : without previous thought or preparation

of•fice \'ófəs\ *n* **1** : position of authority (as in government) **2** : rite **3** : place where a business is transacted — **of•fice•hold•er** *n*

of•fi•cer \'ófəsər\ *n* **1** : one charged with law enforcement **2** : one who holds an office of trust or authority **3** : one who holds a commission in the armed forces

of•fi•cial \ə'fishəl\ *n* : one in office ~ *adj* : authorized or authoritative — **of•fi•cial•dom** \-dəm\ *n* — **of•fi•cial•ly** *adv*

of•fi•ci•ant \ə'fishēənt\ *n* : clergy member who officiates at a religious rite

of•fi•ci•ate \ə'fishē,āt\ *vb* **-at•ed; -at•ing** : perform a ceremony or function

of•fi•cious \ə'fishəs\ *adj* : volunteering one's services unnecessarily — **of•fi•cious•ly** *adv* — **of•fi•cious•ness** *n*

off•ing \'ófiŋ\ *n* : future

off•set \'óf,set\ *vb* **-set; -set•ting** : provide an opposite or equaling effect to

off•shoot \'óf,shüt\ *n* : outgrowth

off•shore *adv* : at a distance from the shore ~ *adj* : moving away from or situated off the shore

off•spring \'óf,spriŋ\ *n, pl* **offspring** : one coming into being through animal or plant reproduction

of•ten \'ófən, 'óft-\ *adv* : many times — **of•ten•times, oft•times** *adv*

ogle \'ōgəl\ *vb* **ogled; ogling** : stare at lustily — **ogle** *n* — **ogler** \-ələr\ *n*

ogre \'ōgər\ *n* **1** : monster **2** : dreaded person

oh \'ō\ *interj* **1** — used to express an emotion **2** — used in direct address

ohm \'ōm\ *n* : unit of electrical resistance — **ohm•me•ter** \'ōm,mētər\ *n*

oil \'óil\ *n* **1** : greasy liquid substance

2 : petroleum ~ *vb* : put oil in or on
— **oil•er** \-ər\ *n* — **oil•i•ness** \'oilēnəs\ *n*
— **oily** \'oilē\ *adj*

oil•cloth *n* : cloth treated with oil or paint and used for coverings

oil•skin *n* : oiled waterproof cloth

oink \'oiŋk\ *n* : natural noise of a hog
— **oink** *vb*

oint•ment \'ointmənt\ *n* : oily medicinal preparation

OK *or* **okay** \ō'kā\ *adv or adj* : all right ~ *vb* **OK'd** *or* **okayed; OK'•ing** *or* **okay•ing** : approve ~ *n* : approval

okra \'ōkrə, *South also* -krē\ *n* : leafy vegetable with edible green pods

old \'ōld\ *adj* **1** : of long standing **2** : of a specified age **3** : relating to a past era **4** : having existed a long time — **old•ish** \'ōldish\ *adj*

old•en \'ōldən\ *adj* : of or relating to a bygone era

old–fash•ioned \-'fashənd\ *adj* **1** : out-of-date **2** : conservative

old maid *n* : spinster

old–tim•er \'ōld'tīmər\ *n* **1** : veteran **2** : one who is old

ole•an•der \'ōlē,andər\ *n* : poisonous evergreen shrub

oleo•mar•ga•rine \,ōlēō'märjərən\ *n* : margarine

ol•fac•to•ry \äl'faktərē, ōl-\ *adj* : relating to the sense of smell

oli•gar•chy \'älə,gärkē, 'ōlə-\ *n, pl* **-chies 1** : government by a few people **2** : those holding power in an oligarchy — **oli•garch** \-,gärk\ *n* — **oli•gar•chic** \,älə'gärkik, ,ōlə-\, **oli•gar•chi•cal** \-kikəl\ *adj*

ol•ive \'äliv, -əv\ *n* **1** : evergreen tree bearing small edible fruit or the fruit **2** : dull yellowish green color

om•buds•man \'äm,budzmən, äm-'budz-\ *n, pl* **-men** \-mən\ : complaint investigator

om•e•let, om•e•lette \'ämələt\ *n* : beaten eggs lightly fried and folded

omen \'ōmən\ *n* : sign or warning of the future

om•i•nous \'ämənəs\ *adj* : presaging evil — **om•i•nous•ly** *adv* — **om•i•nous•ness** *n*

omit \ō'mit\ *vb* **-tt- 1** : leave out **2** : fail to perform — **omis•si•ble** \ō-'misəbəl\ *adj* — **omis•sion** \-'mishən\ *n*

om•nip•o•tent \äm'nipətənt\ *adj* : almighty — **om•nip•o•tence** \-əns\ *n* — **om•nip•o•tent•ly** *adv*

om•ni•pres•ent \,ämni'prez²nt\ *adj* : ever-present — **om•ni•pres•ence** \-²ns\ *n*

om•ni•scient \äm'nishənt\ *adj* : all-knowing — **om•ni•science** \-əns\ *n* — **om•ni•scient•ly** *adv*

om•niv•o•rous \äm'nivərəs\ *adj* **1** : eating both meat and vegetables **2** : avid — **om•niv•o•rous•ly** *adv*

on \'ón, 'än\ *prep* **1** : in or to a position over and in contact with **2** : at or to **3** : about **4** : from **5** : with regard to **6** : in a state or process **7** : during the time of ~ *adv* **1** : in or into contact with **2** : forward **3** : into operation

once \'wəns\ *adv* **1** : one time only **2** : at any one time **3** : formerly ~ *n* : one time ~ *conj* : as soon as ~ *adj* : former — **at once 1** : simultaneously **2** : immediately

once–over *n* : swift examination

on•com•ing *adj* : approaching

one \'wən\ *adj* **1** : being a single thing **2** : being one in particular **3** : being the same in kind ~ *pron* **1** : certain indefinitely indicated person or thing **2** : a person in general ~ *n* **1** : 1st in a series **2** : single person or thing — **one•ness** *n*

oner•ous \'änərəs, 'ōnə-\ *adj* : imposing a burden

one•self \,wən'self\ *pron* : one's own self — usu. used reflexively or for emphasis

one–sid•ed \-'sīdəd\ *adj* **1** : occurring on one side only **2** : partial

one–time *adj* : former

one–way *adj* : made or for use in only one direction

on•go•ing *adj* : continuing

on•ion \'ənyən\ *n* : plant grown for its pungent edible bulb or this bulb

on•ly \'ōnlē\ *adj* : alone in its class ~ *adv* **1** : merely or exactly **2** : solely **3** : at the very least **4** : as a result ~ *conj* : but

on•set *n* : start

on•shore *adj* **1** : moving toward shore **2** : lying on or near the shore — **on•shore** *adv*

on•slaught \'än,slót, 'ón-\ *n* : attack

on•to \'óntü, 'än-\ *prep* : to a position or point on

onus \'ōnəs\ *n* : burden (as of obligation or blame)

on•ward \'ónwərd, 'än-\ *adv or adj* : forward

on•yx \'äniks\ *n* : quartz used as a gem

ooze \'üz\ *n* : soft mud ~ *vb* **oozed; ooz·ing** : flow or leak out slowly — **oozy** \'üzē\ *adj*

opac·i·ty \ō'pasətē\ *n* : quality or state of being opaque or an opaque spot

opal \'ōpal\ *n* : gem with delicate colors

opaque \ō'pāk\ *adj* **1** : blocking light **2** : not easily understood **3** : dull-witted — **opaque·ly** *adv*

open \'ōpən\ *adj* **1** : not shut or shut up **2** : not secret or hidden **3** : frank or generous **4** : extended **5** : free from controls **6** : not decided ~ *vb* **1** : make or become open **2** : make or become functional **3** : start ~ *n* : outdoors — **open·er** \-ər\ *n* — **open·ly** *adv* — **open·ness** *n*

open-hand·ed \-'handəd\ *adj* : generous — **open-hand·ed·ly** *adv*

open·ing \'ōpəniŋ\ *n* **1** : act or instance of making open **2** : something that is open **3** : opportunity

op·era \'äpərə, 'äprə\ *n* : drama set to music — **op·er·at·ic** \,äpə'ratik\ *adj*

op·er·a·ble \'äpərəbəl\ *adj* **1** : usable or in working condition **2** : suitable for surgical treatment

op·er·ate \'äpə,rāt\ *vb* -at·ed; -at·ing **1** : perform work **2** : perform an operation **3** : manage — **op·er·a·tor** \-,rātər\ *n*

op·er·a·tion \,äpə'rāshən\ *n* **1** : act or process of operating **2** : surgical work on a living body **3** : military action or mission — **op·er·a·tion·al** \-shənəl\ *adj*

op·er·a·tive \'äpərətiv, -,rāt-\ *adj* : working or having an effect

op·er·et·ta \,äpə'retə\ *n* : light opera

oph·thal·mol·o·gy \,äf,thal'mäləjē\ *n* : branch of medicine dealing with the eye — **oph·thal·mol·o·gist** \-jist\ *n*

opi·ate \'ōpēət, -pē,āt\ *n* : preparation or derivative of opium

opine \ō'pīn\ *vb* **opined; opin·ing** : express an opinion

opin·ion \ə'pinyən\ *n* **1** : belief **2** : judgment **3** : formal statement by an expert

opin·ion·at·ed \-yə,nātəd\ *adj* : stubborn in one's opinions

opi·um \'ōpēəm\ *n* : addictive narcotic drug that is the dried juice of a poppy

opos·sum \ə'päsəm\ *n* : common tree-dwelling nocturnal mammal

op·po·nent \ə'pōnənt\ *n* : one that opposes

op·por·tune \,äpər'tün, -'tyün\ *adj* : suitable or timely — **op·por·tune·ly** *adv*

op·por·tun·ism \-'tü,nizəm, -'tyü-\ *n* : a taking advantage of opportunities — **op·por·tun·ist** \-nist\ *n* — **op·por·tu·nis·tic** \-tü'nistik, -tyü-\ *adj*

op·por·tu·ni·ty \-'tünətē, -'tyü-\ *n, pl* -ties : favorable time

op·pose \ə'pōz\ *vb* -posed; -pos·ing **1** : place opposite or against something **2** : resist — **op·po·si·tion** \,äpə'zishən\ *n*

op·po·site \'äpəzət\ *n* : one that is opposed ~ *adj* **1** : set facing something that is at the other side or end **2** : opposed or contrary ~ *adj* : on opposite sides ~ *prep* : across from — **op·po·site·ly** *adv*

op·press \ə'pres\ *vb* **1** : persecute **2** : weigh down — **op·pres·sion** \ə'preshən\ *n* — **op·pres·sive** \-'presiv\ *adj* — **op·pres·sor** \-'presər\ *n*

op·pro·bri·ous \ə'prōbrēəs\ *adj* : expressing or deserving opprobrium — **op·pro·bri·ous·ly** *adv*

op·pro·bri·um \-brēəm\ *n* **1** : something that brings disgrace **2** : infamy

opt \'äpt\ *vb* : choose

op·tic \'äptik\ *adj* : relating to vision or the eye

op·ti·cal \'äptikəl\ *adj* : relating to optics, vision, or the eye

op·ti·cian \äp'tishən\ *n* : maker of or dealer in eyeglasses

op·tics \'äptiks\ *n pl* : science of light and vision

op·ti·mal \'äptəməl\ *adj* : most favorable — **op·ti·mal·ly** *adv*

op·ti·mism \'äptə,mizəm\ *n* : tendency to hope for the best — **op·ti·mist** \-mist\ *n* — **op·ti·mis·tic** \,äptə'mistik\ *adj* — **op·ti·mis·ti·cal·ly** *adv*

op·ti·mum \'äptəməm\ *n, pl* -ma \-mə\ : amount or degree of something most favorable to an end — **op·timum** *adj*

op·tion \'äpshən\ *n* **1** : ability to choose **2** : right to buy or sell a stock **3** : alternative — **op·tion·al** \-shənəl\ *adj*

op·tom·e·try \äp'tämətrē\ *n* : profession of examining the eyes — **op·tom·e·trist** \-trist\ *n*

op·u·lent \'äpyələnt\ *adj* : lavish — **op·u·lence** \-ləns\ *n* — **op·u·lent·ly** *adv*

opus \'ōpəs\ *n, pl* **opera** \'ōpərə, 'äpə-\ : work esp. of music

or \'ôr\ *conj* — used to indicate an alternative

-or \ər\ *n suffix* : one that performs an action

or·a·cle \'ôrəkəl\ *n* **1** : one held to give divinely inspired answers or revelations **2** : wise person or an utterance of such a person — **orac·u·lar** \'rakyələr\ *adj*

oral \'ôrəl\ *adj* **1** : spoken **2** : relating to the mouth — **oral·ly** *adv*

or·ange \'ôrinj\ *n* **1** : reddish yellow citrus fruit **2** : color between red and yellow — **or·ange·ade** \,ôrinj'ād\ *n*

orang·u·tan \ə'rəŋə,taŋ, -,tan\ *n* : large reddish brown ape

ora·tion \ə'rāshən\ *n* : elaborate formal speech

or·a·tor \'ôrətər\ *n* : one noted as a public speaker

or·a·to·rio \,ôrə'tōrē,ō\ *n, pl* **-ri·os** : major choral work

or·a·to·ry \'ôrə,tōrē\ *n* : art of public speaking — **or·a·tor·i·cal** \,ôrə'tôrikəl\ *adj*

orb \'ôrb\ *n* : spherical body

or·bit \'ôrbət\ *n* : path made by one body revolving around another ∼ *vb* : revolve around — **or·bit·al** \-ᵊl\ *adj* — **or·bit·er** *n*

or·chard \'ôrchərd\ *n* : place where fruit or nut trees are grown — **or·chard·ist** \-ist\ *n*

or·ches·tra \'ôrkəstrə\ *n* **1** : group of musicians **2** : front seats of a theater's main floor — **or·ches·tral** \ôr'kestrəl\ *adj* — **or·ches·tral·ly** *adv*

or·ches·trate \'ôrkə,strāt\ *vb* **-trat·ed; -trat·ing 1** : compose or arrange for an orchestra **2** : arrange or combine for best effect — **or·ches·tra·tion** \,ôrkə'strāshən\ *n*

or·chid \'ôrkəd\ *n* : plant with showy 3-petal flowers or its flower

or·dain \ôr'dān\ *vb* **1** : admit to the clergy **2** : decree

or·deal \ôr'dēl, 'ôr,dēl\ *n* : severely trying experience

or·der \'ôrdər\ *n* **1** : rank, class, or special group **2** : arrangement **3** : rule of law **4** : authoritative regulation or instruction **5** : working condition **6** : special request for a purchase or what is purchased ∼ *vb* **1** : arrange **2** : give an order to **3** : place an order for

or·der·ly \-lē\ *adj* **1** : being in order or

tidy **2** : well behaved ∼ *n, pl* **-lies 1** : officer's attendant **2** : hospital attendant — **or·der·li·ness** *n*

or·di·nal \'ôrdᵊnəl\ *n* : number indicating order in a series

or·di·nance \-ᵊnəns\ *n* : municipal law

or·di·nary \'ôrdᵊn,erē\ *adj* : of common occurrence, quality, or ability — **or·di·nar·i·ly** \,ôrdᵊn'erəlē\ *adv*

or·di·na·tion \,ôrdᵊn'āshən\ *n* : act of ordaining

ord·nance \'ôrdnəns\ *n* : military supplies

ore \'ôr\ *n* : mineral containing a valuable constituent

oreg·a·no \ə'regə,nō\ *n* : mint used as a seasoning and source of oil

or·gan \'ôrgan\ *n* **1** : air-powered or electronic keyboard instrument **2** : animal or plant structure with special function **3** : periodical

or·gan·ic \ôr'ganik\ *adj* **1** : relating to a bodily organ **2** : relating to living things **3** : relating to or containing carbon or its compounds **4** : relating to foods produced without the use of laboratory-made products — **or·gan·i·cal·ly** *adv*

or·gan·ism \'ôrgə,nizəm\ *n* : a living thing

or·gan·ist \'ôrgənist\ *n* : organ player

or·ga·nize \'ôrgə,nīz\ *vb* **-nized; -niz·ing** : form parts into a functioning whole — **or·ga·ni·za·tion** \,ôrgənə-'zāshən\ *n* — **or·ga·ni·za·tion·al** \-shənəl\ *adj* — **or·ga·niz·er** *n*

or·gasm \'ôr,gazəm\ *n* : climax of sexual excitement — **or·gas·mic** \ôr'gazmik\ *adj*

or·gy \'ôrjē\ *n, pl* **-gies** : unrestrained indulgence (as in sexual activity)

ori·ent \'ôrē,ent\ *vb* **1** : set in a definite position **2** : acquaint with a situation — **ori·en·ta·tion** \,ôrēən'tāshən\ *n*

ori·en·tal \,ôrē'entᵊl\ *adj* : Eastern — **Oriental** *n*

ori·fice \'ôrəfəs\ *n* : opening

or·i·gin \'ôrəjən\ *n* **1** : ancestry **2** : rise, beginning, or derivation from a source — **orig·i·nate** \ə'rijə,nāt\ *vb* — **orig·i·na·tor** \-ər\ *n*

orig·i·nal \ə'rijənəl\ *n* : something from which a copy is made ∼ *adj* **1** : first **2** : not copied from something else **3** : inventive — **orig·i·nal·i·ty** *n* — **orig·i·nal·ly** *adv*

ori·ole \'ôrē,ōl, -ēəl\ *n* : American songbird

or·na·ment \'ôrnəmənt\ *n* : something

that adorns ~ *vb* : provide with ornament — **or·na·men·tal** \ˌȯrnə'mentᵊl\ *adj* — **or·na·men·ta·tion** \-mən'tāshən\ *n*

or·nate \ȯr'nāt\ *adj* : elaborately decorated — **or·nate·ly** *adv* — **or·nate·ness** *n*

or·nery \'ȯrnərē, 'än-\ *adj* : irritable

or·ni·thol·o·gy \ˌȯrnə'thäləjē\ *n, pl* **-gies** : study of birds — **or·ni·tho·log·i·cal** \-thə'läjikəl\ *adj* — **or·ni·thol·o·gist** \-'thäləjist\ *n*

or·phan \'ȯrfən\ *n* : child whose parents are dead — **orphan** *vb* — **or·phan·age** \-anij\ *n*

or·tho·don·tics \ˌȯrthə'däntiks\ *n* : dentistry dealing with straightening teeth — **or·tho·don·tist** \-'däntist\ *n*

or·tho·dox \'ȯrthə,däks\ *adj* **1** : conforming to established doctrine **2** *cap* : of or relating to a Christian church originating in the Eastern Roman Empire — **or·tho·doxy** \-,däksē\ *n*

or·thog·ra·phy \ȯr'thägrəfē\ *n* : spelling — **or·tho·graph·ic** \ˌȯrthə'grafik\ *adj*

or·tho·pe·dics \ˌȯrthə'pēdiks\ *n sing or pl* : correction or prevention of skeletal deformities — **or·tho·pe·dic** \-ik\ *adj* — **or·tho·pe·dist** \-'pēdist\ *n*

-o·ry \ˌȯrē, ˌȯrē, ərē\ *adj suffix* **1** : of, relating to, or characterized by **2** : serving for, producing, or maintaining

os·cil·late \'äsə,lāt\ *vb* **-lat·ed; -lat·ing** : swing back and forth — **os·cil·la·tion** \ˌäsə'lāshən\ *n*

os·mo·sis \äz'mōsəs, äs-\ *n* : diffusion esp. of water through a membrane — **os·mot·ic** \-'mätik\ *adj*

os·prey \'äsprē, -ˌprā\ *n, pl* **-preys** : large fish-eating hawk

os·si·fy \'äsə,fī\ *vb* **-fied; -fy·ing** : make or become hardened or set in one's ways

os·ten·si·ble \ä'stensəbəl\ *adj* : seeming — **os·ten·si·bly** \-blē\ *adv*

os·ten·ta·tion \ˌästən'tāshən\ *n* : pretentious display — **os·ten·ta·tious** \-shəs\ *adj* — **os·ten·ta·tious·ly** *adv*

os·te·op·a·thy \ˌästē'äpəthē\ *n* : system of healing that emphasizes manipulation (as of joints) — **os·te·o·path** \'ästēə,path\ *n* — **os·te·o·path·ic** \ˌästēə'pathik\ *adj*

os·te·o·po·ro·sis \ˌästēōpə'rōsəs\ *n, pl* **-ro·ses** \-ˌsēz\ : condition characterized by fragile and porous bones

os·tra·cize \'ästrə,sīz\ *vb* **-cized; -ciz·ing** : exclude by common consent — **os·tra·cism** \-ˌsizəm\ *n*

os·trich \'ästrich, 'ȯs-\ *n* : very large flightless bird

oth·er \'əthər\ *adj* **1** : being the one left **2** : alternate **3** : additional ~ *pron* **1** : remaining one **2** : different one

oth·er·wise *adv* **1** : in a different way **2** : in different circumstances **3** : in other respects — **otherwise** *adj*

ot·ter \'ätər\ *n* : fish-eating mammal with webbed feet

ot·to·man \'ätəmən\ *n* : upholstered footstool

ought \'ȯt\ *verbal auxiliary* — used to express obligation, advisability, or expectation

ounce \'aůns\ *n* **1** : unit of weight equal to about 28.3 grams **2** : unit of capacity equal to about 29.6 milliliters

our \är, 'aůr\ *adj* : of or relating to us

ours \'aůrz, 'ärz\ *pron* : that which belongs to us

our·selves \är'selvz, aůr-\ *pron* : we, us — used reflexively or for emphasis

-ous \əs\ *adj suffix* : having or having the qualities of

oust \'aůst\ *vb* : expel or eject

oust·er \'aůstər\ *n* : expulsion

out \'aůt\ *adv* **1** : away from the inside or center **2** : beyond control **3** : to extinction, exhaustion, or completion **4** : in or into the open ~ *vb* : become known ~ *adj* **1** : situated outside **2** : absent ~ *prep* **1** : out through **2** : outward or along — **out·bound** *adj* — **out·build·ing** *n*

out·age \'aůtij\ *n* : period of no electricity

out·board \'aůt,bōrd\ *adv* : outside a boat or ship — **outboard** *adj*

out·break \'aůt,brāk\ *n* : sudden occurrence

out·burst \-ˌbərst\ *n* : violent expression of feeling

out·cast \-ˌkast\ *n* : person cast out by society

out·come \-ˌkəm\ *n* : result

out·crop \'aůt,kräp\ *n* : part of a rock stratum that appears above the ground — **outcrop** *vb*

out·cry \-ˌkrī\ *n* : loud cry

out·dat·ed \aůt'dātəd\ *adj* : out-of-date

out·dis·tance *vb* : go far ahead of

out·do \aůt'dü\ *vb* **-did** \-'did\; **-done** \-'dən\; **-do·ing** \-'düiŋ\; **-does** \-'dəz\ : do better than

out·doors \aút'dōrz\ *adv* : in or into the open air ~ *n* : open air — **out·door** *adj*

out·er \'aútər\ *adj* 1 : external 2 : farther out — **out·er·most** *adj*

out·field \'aút,fēld\ *n* : baseball field beyond the infield — **out·field·er** \-,fēldər\ *n*

out·fit \'aút,fit\ *n* 1 : equipment for a special purpose 2 : group ~ *vb* -tt- : equip — **out·fit·ter** *n*

out·go \'aút,gō\ *n, pl* **outgoes** : expenditure

out·go·ing \'aút,gōin\ *adj* 1 : retiring from a position 2 : friendly

out·grow \aút'grō\ *vb* -**grew** \-'grü\; -**grown** \-'grōn\; -**grow·ing** : grow faster than 2 : grow too large for

out·growth \'aút,grōth\ *n* 1 : product of growing out 2 : consequence

out·ing \'aútin\ *n* : excursion

out·land·ish \aút'landish\ *adj* : very strange — **out·land·ish·ly** *adv*

outlast *vb* : last longer than

out·law \'aút,lò\ *n* : lawless person ~ *vb* : make illegal

out·lay \'aút,lā\ *n* : expenditure

out·let \'aút,let, -lət\ *n* 1 : exit 2 : means of release 3 : market for goods 4 : electrical device that gives access to wiring

out·line \'aút,līn\ *n* 1 : line marking the outer limits 2 : summary ~ *vb* 1 : draw the outline of 2 : indicate the chief parts of

out·live \aút'liv\ *vb* : live longer than

out·look \'aút,lúk\ *n* 1 : viewpoint 2 : prospect for the future

out·ly·ing \'aút,līin\ *adj* : far from a central point

out·ma·neu·ver \,aútmə'nüvər, -'nyü-\ *vb* : defeat by more skillful maneuvering

out·mod·ed \aút'mōdəd\ *adj* : out-of-date

out·num·ber \-'nəmbər\ *vb* : exceed in number

out of *prep* 1 : out from within 2 : beyond the limits of 3 : among 4 — used to indicate absence or loss 5 : because of 6 : from or with

out–of–date *adj* : no longer in fashion or in use

out·pa·tient *n* : person treated at a hospital who does not stay overnight

out·post *n* : remote military post

out·put *n* : amount produced ~ *vb* -**put·ted** *or* -**put**; -**put·ting** : produce

out·rage \'aút,rāj\ *n* 1 : violent or shameful act 2 : injury or insult 3 : extreme anger ~ *vb* -**raged**; -**rag·ing** 1 : subject to violent injury 2 : make very angry

out·ra·geous \aút'rājəs\ *adj* : extremely offensive or shameful — **out·ra·geous·ly** *adv* — **out·ra·geous·ness** *n*

out·right *adv* 1 : completely 2 : instantly ~ *adj* 1 : complete 2 : given without reservation

out·set *n* : beginning

out·side \aút'sīd, 'aút,-\ *n* 1 : place beyond a boundary 2 : exterior 3 : utmost limit ~ *adj* 1 : outer 2 : coming from without 3 : remote ~ *adv* : on or to the outside ~ *prep* 1 : on or to the outside of 2 : beyond the limits of

outside of *prep* 1 : outside 2 : besides

out·sid·er \-'sīdər\ *n* : one who does not belong to a group

out·skirts *n pl* : outlying parts (as of a city)

out·smart \aút'smärt\ *vb* : outwit

out·source \'aút,sórs\ *vb* -**sourced**; -**sourc·ing** : obtain from an outside supplier

out·spo·ken *adj* : direct and open in speech — **out·spo·ken·ness** *n*

out·stand·ing *adj* 1 : unpaid 2 : very good — **out·stand·ing·ly** *adv*

out·strip \aút'strip\ *vb* 1 : go faster than 2 : surpass

¹**out·ward** \'aútwərd\ *adj* 1 : being toward the outside 2 : showing outwardly

²**outward, out·wards** \-wərdz\ *adv* : toward the outside — **out·ward·ly** *adv*

out·wit \aút'wit\ *vb* : get the better of by superior cleverness

ova *pl of* **OVUM**

oval \'ōvəl\ *adj* : egg-shaped — **oval** *n*

ova·ry \'ōvərē\ *n, pl* -**ries** 1 : egg-producing organ 2 : seed-producing part of a flower — **ovar·i·an** \ō'varēən\ *adj*

ova·tion \ō'vāshən\ *n* : enthusiastic applause

ov·en \'əvən\ *n* : chamber (as in a stove) for baking

over \'ōvər\ *adv* 1 : across 2 : upside down 3 : in excess or addition 4 : above 5 : at an end 6 : again ~ *prep* 1 : above in position or authority 2 : more than 3 : along, through, or across 4 : because of ~ *adj* 1 : upper 2 : remaining 3 : ended

over- *prefix* **1** : so as to exceed or surpass **2** : excessive or excessively

¹over•age \ˌōvər¹āj\ *adj* : too old

²over•age \¹ōvərij\ *n* : surplus

over•all \ˌōvər¹òl\ *adj* : including everything

over•alls \¹ōvərˌòlz\ *n pl* : pants with an extra piece covering the chest

over•awe *vb* : subdue by awe

over•bear•ing \-¹barin\ *adj* : arrogant

over•blown \-¹blōn\ *adj* : pretentious

over•board *adv* : over the side into the water

over•cast *adj* : clouded over ~ *n* : cloud covering

over•coat *n* : outer coat

over•come *vb* **-came** \-¹kām\; **-come; -com•ing 1** : defeat **2** : make helpless or exhausted

over•do *vb* **-did; -done; -do•ing; -does** : do too much

over•draft *n* : overdrawn sum

over•draw *vb* **-drew; -drawn; -draw•ing** : write checks for more than one's bank balance

over•flow \ˌōvər¹flō\ *vb* **1** : flood **2** : flow over — **overflow** \¹ōvərˌflō\ *n*

over•grow *vb* **-grew; -grown; -grow•ing** : grow over

over•hand *adj* : made with the hand brought down from above — **overhand** *adv* — **over•hand•ed** \-ˌhandəd\ *adv or adj*

over•hang *vb* **-hung; -hang•ing** : jut out over ~ *n* : something that overhangs

over•haul *vb* **1** : repair **2** : overtake

over•head \ˌōvər¹hed\ *adv* : aloft ~ \¹ōvərˌ-\ *adj* : situated above ~ \¹ōvərˌ-\ *n* : general business expenses

over•hear *vb* **-heard; -hear•ing** : hear without the speaker's knowledge

over•joyed *adj* : filled with joy

over•kill \¹ōvərˌkil\ *n* : large excess

over•land \-ˌland, -lənd\ *adv or adj* : by, on, or across land

over•lap *vb* : lap over — **overlap** \¹ōvərˌlap\ *n*

over•lay \ˌōvər¹lā\ *vb* **-laid; -lay•ing** : lay over or across — **over•lay** \¹ōvərˌlā\ *n*

over•look \ˌōvər¹lúk\ *vb* **1** : look down on **2** : fail to see **3** : ignore **4**

List of self-explanatory words with the prefix *over-*

overabundance	overcommit	overemphasis
overabundant	overcompensate	overemphasize
overachiever	overcomplicate	overenergetic
overactive	overconcern	overenthusiastic
overaggressive	overconfidence	overestimate
overambitious	overconfident	overexaggerate
overanalyze	overconscientious	overexaggeration
overanxiety	overconsume	overexcite
overanxious	overconsumption	overexcited
overarousal	overcontrol	overexercise
overassertive	overcook	overexert
overbake	overcorrect	overexertion
overbid	overcritical	overexpand
overbill	overcrowd	overexpansion
overbold	overdecorate	overexplain
overborrow	overdependence	overexploit
overbright	overdependent	overexpose
overbroad	overdevelop	overextend
overbuild	overdose	overextension
overburden	overdramatic	overexuberant
overbusy	overdramatize	overfamiliar
overbuy	overdress	overfatigued
overcapacity	overdrink	overfeed
overcapitalize	overdue	overfertilize
overcareful	overeager	overfill
overcautious	overeat	overfond
overcharge	overeducated	overgeneralization
overcivilized	overelaborate	overgeneralize
overclean	overemotional	overgenerous

: pardon **5** : supervise ∼ \'ōvər,-\ n
: observation point

over·ly \'ōvərlē\ adv : excessively

over·night adv **1** : through the night **2**
: suddenly — **overnight** adj

over·pass n : bridge over a road

over·pow·er vb : conquer

over·reach \,ōvər'rēch\ vb : try or
seek too much

over·ride vb -rode; -rid·den; -rid·ing
: neutralize action of

over·rule vb : rule against or set aside

over·run vb -ran; -run·ning **1** : swarm
or flow over **2** : go beyond ∼ n : an
exceeding of estimated costs

over·seas adv or adj : beyond or across
the sea

over·see \,ōvər'sē\ vb -saw; -seen;
-see·ing : supervise — **over·seer**
\'ōvər,siər\ n

over·shad·ow vb : exceed in importance

over·shoe n : protective outer shoe

over·shoot vb -shot; -shoot·ing
: shoot or pass beyond

over·sight n : inadvertent omission or
error

over·sleep vb -slept; -sleep·ing : sleep
longer than intended

over·spread vb -spread; -spread·ing
: spread over or above

over·state vb : exaggerate — **over·
state·ment** n

over·stay vb : stay too long

over·step vb : exceed

overt \ō'vərt, 'ō,vərt\ adj : not secret
— **overt·ly** adv

over·take vb -took; -tak·en; -tak·ing
: catch up with

over·throw \,ōvər'thrō\ vb -threw;
-thrown; -throw·ing **1** : upset **2**
: defeat — **over·throw** \'ōvər,-\ n

over·time n : extra working time —
overtime adv

over·tone n **1** : higher tone in a complex musical tone **2** : suggestion

over·ture \'ōvər,chúr, -chər\ n **1**
: opening offer **2** : musical introduction

over·turn vb **1** : turn over **2** : nullify

over·view n : brief survey

over·ween·ing \,ōvər'wēniŋ\ adj **1**
: arrogant **2** : excessive

over·whelm \,ōvər'hwelm\ vb : overcome completely — **over·whelm·
ing·ly** \-'hwelmiŋlē\ adv

over·wrought \,ōvər'rót\ adj : extremely excited

---

overglamorize	overparticular	overserious
overgraze	overpay	oversexed
overharvest	overpayment	oversimple
overhasty	overplay	oversimplify
overheat	overpopulated	oversolicitous
overidealize	overpraise	overspecialize
overimaginative	overprescribe	overspend
overimpress	overpressure	overstaff
overindebtedness	overprice	overstimulation
overindulge	overprivileged	overstock
overindulgence	overproduce	overstrain
overindulgent	overproduction	overstress
overinflate	overpromise	overstretch
overinsistent	overprotect	oversubtle
overintense	overprotective	oversupply
overintensity	overqualified	oversuspicious
overinvestment	overrate	oversweeten
overladen	overreact	overtax
overlarge	overreaction	overtighten
overlend	overrefined	overtip
overload	overregulate	overtired
overlong	overregulation	overtrain
overloud	overreliance	overtreat
overmedicate	overrepresented	overuse
overmodest	overrespond	overutilize
overmuch	overripe	overvalue
overobvious	oversaturate	overweight
overoptimistic	oversell	overwork
overorganize	oversensitive	overzealous

ovoid \'ō,void\, **ovoi-dal** \ō'void'l\ *adj* : egg-shaped

ovu-late \'ävyə,lāt, 'ōv-\ *vb* **-lat-ed; -lat-ing** : produce eggs from an ovary — **ovu-la-tion** \,ävyə'lāshən, ,ōv-\ *n*

ovum \'ōvəm\ *n, pl* **ova** \-və\ : female germ cell

owe \'ō\ *vb* **owed; ow-ing** **1** : have an obligation to pay **2** : be indebted to or for

owing to *prep* : because of

owl \'aül\ *n* : nocturnal bird of prey — **owl-ish** *adj* — **owl-ish-ly** *adv*

own \'ōn\ *adj* : belonging to oneself ~ *vb* **1** : have as property **2** : acknowl- edge ~ *pron* : one or ones belonging to oneself — **own-er** *n* — **own-er-ship** *n*

ox \'äks\ *n, pl* **ox-en** \'äksən\ : bovine mammal and esp. a castrated bull

ox-ide \'äk,sīd\ *n* : compound of oxygen

ox-i-dize \'äksə,dīz\ *vb* **-dized; -diz-ing** : combine with oxygen — **ox-i-da-tion** \,äksə'dāshən\ *n* — **ox-i-diz-er** *n*

ox-y-gen \'äksijən\ *n* : gaseous chemi-cal element essential for life

oys-ter \'öistər\ *n* : bivalve mollusk — **oys-ter-ing** \-riŋ\ *n*

ozone \'ō,zōn\ *n* : very reactive bluish form of oxygen

P

p \'pē\ *n, pl* **p's** *or* **ps** \'pēz\ : 16th let-ter of the alphabet

pace \'pās\ *n* **1** : walking step **2** : rate of progress ~ *vb* **paced; pac-ing** **1** : go at a pace **2** : cover with slow steps **3** : set the pace of

pace-mak-er *n* : electrical device to regulate heartbeat

pachy-derm \'paki,dərm\ *n* : elephant

pa-cif-ic \pə'sifik\ *adj* : calm or peace-ful

pac-i-fism \'pasə,fizəm\ *n* : opposition to war or violence — **pac-i-fist** \-fist\ *n or adj* — **pac-i-fis-tic** \,pasə'fistik\ *adj*

pac-i-fy \'pasə,fī\ *vb* **-fied; -fy-ing** : make calm — **pac-i-fi-ca-tion** \,pasəfə'kāshən\ *n* — **pac-i-fi-er** \'pasə,fīər\ *n*

pack \'pak\ *n* **1** : compact bundle **2** : group of animals ~ *vb* **1** : put into a container **2** : fill tightly or com-pletely **3** : send without ceremony — **pack-er** *n*

pack-age \'pakij\ *n* : items bundled to-gether ~ *vb* **-aged; -ag-ing** : enclose in a package

pack-et \'pakət\ *n* : small package

pact \'pakt\ *n* : agreement

pad \'pad\ *n* **1** : cushioning part or thing **2** : floating leaf of a water plant **3** : tablet of paper ~ *vb* **-dd-** **1** : fur-nish with a pad **2** : expand with need-less matter — **pad-ding** *n*

pad-dle \'pad'l\ *n* : implement with a flat blade ~ *vb* **-dled; -dling** : move, beat, or stir with a paddle

pad-dock \'padək\ *n* : enclosed area for racehorses

pad-dy \'padē\ *n, pl* **-dies** : wet land where rice is grown

pad-lock *n* : lock with a U-shaped catch — **padlock** *vb*

pae-an \'pēən\ *n* : song of praise

pa-gan \'pāgən\ *n or adj* : heathen — **pa-gan-ism** \-,izəm\ *n*

¹page \'pāj\ *n* : messenger ~ *vb* **paged; pag-ing** : summon by re-peated calls — **pag-er** *n*

²page *n* **1** : single leaf (as of a book) or one side of the leaf **2** : informa-tion at a single World Wide Web ad-dress

pag-eant \'pajənt\ *n* : elaborate spec-tacle or procession — **pag-eant-ry** \-əntrē\ *n*

pa-go-da \pə'gōdə\ *n* : tower with roofs curving upward

paid *past of* PAY

pail \'pāl\ *n* : cylindrical container with a handle — **pail-ful** \-,fúl\ *n*

pain \'pān\ *n* **1** : punishment or penalty **2** : suffering of body or mind **3** *pl* : great care ~ *vb* : cause or ex-perience pain — **pain-ful** \-fəl\ *adj* — **pain-ful-ly** *adv* — **pain-kill-er** *n* — **pain-kill-ing** *adj* — **pain-less** *adj* — **pain-less-ly** *adv*

pains·tak·ing \'pān,stākiŋ\ adj : taking pains — **painstaking** n — **pains·tak·ing·ly** adv

paint \'pānt\ vb 1 : apply color or paint to 2 : portray esp. in color ~ n : mixture of pigment and liquid — **paint·brush** n — **paint·er** n — **paint·ing** n

pair \'par\ n : a set of two ~ vb : put or go together as a pair

pa·ja·mas \pə'jäməz, -'jam-\ n pl : loose suit for sleeping

pal \'pal\ n : close friend

pal·ace \'paləs\ n 1 : residence of a chief of state 2 : mansion — **pa·la·tial** \pə'lāshəl\ adj

pal·at·able \'palətəbəl\ adj : agreeable to the taste

pal·ate \'palət\ n 1 : roof of the mouth 2 : taste — **pal·a·tal** \-ət³l\ adj

pa·la·ver \pə'lavər, -'läv-\ n : talk — **palaver** vb

¹**pale** \'pāl\ adj **pal·er; pal·est** 1 : lacking in color or brightness 2 : light in color or shade ~ vb **paled; pal·ing** : make or become pale — **pale·ness** n

²**pale** n 1 : fence stake 2 : enclosed place

pa·le·on·tol·o·gy \,pālē,än'täläjē\ n : branch of biology dealing with ancient forms of life known from fossils — **pa·le·on·tol·o·gist** \-,än'täläjist, -ən-\ n

pal·ette \'palət\ n : board on which paints are laid and mixed

pal·i·sade \,palə'sād\ n 1 : high fence 2 : line of cliffs

¹**pall** \'pól\ n 1 : cloth draped over a coffin 2 : something that produces gloom

²**pall** vb : lose in interest or attraction

pall·bear·er n : one who attends the coffin at a funeral

¹**pal·let** \'palət\ n : makeshift bed

²**pallet** n : portable storage platform

pal·li·ate \'palē,āt\ vb **-at·ed; -at·ing** 1 : ease without curing 2 : cover or conceal by excusing — **pal·li·a·tion** \,palē'āshən\ n — **pal·li·a·tive** \'palē-,ātiv\ adj or n

pal·lid \'paləd\ adj : pale

pal·lor \'palər\ n : paleness

¹**palm** \'päm, 'pälm\ n 1 : tall tropical tree crowned with large leaves 2 : symbol of victory

²**palm** n : underside of the hand ~ vb 1

: conceal in the hand 2 : impose by fraud

palm·ist·ry \'päməstrē, 'pälmə-\ n : reading a person's character or future in his palms — **palm·ist** \'pämist, 'pälm-\

palmy \'pämē, 'pälmē\ adj **palm·i·er; -est** : flourishing

pal·o·mi·no \,palə'mēnō\ n, pl **-nos** : light-colored horse

pal·pa·ble \'palpəbəl\ adj 1 : capable of being touched 2 : obvious — **pal·pa·bly** \-blē\ adv

pal·pi·tate \'palpə,tāt\ vb **-tat·ed; -tat·ing** : beat rapidly — **pal·pi·ta·tion** \,palpə'tāshən\ n

pal·sy \'pólzē\ n, pl **-sies** 1 : paralysis 2 : condition marked by tremor — **pal·sied** \-zēd\ adj

pal·try \'póltrē\ adj **-tri·er; -est** : trivial

pam·per \'pampər\ vb : spoil or indulge

pam·phlet \'pamflət\ n : unbound publication — **pam·phle·teer** \,pamflə-'tir\ n

pan \'pan\ n : broad, shallow, and open container ~ vb 1 : wash gravel in a pan to search for gold 2 : criticize severely

pan·a·cea \,panə'sēə\ n : remedy for all ills or difficulties

pan·cake n : fried flat cake

pan·cre·as \'paŋkrēəs, 'pan-\ n : gland that produces insulin — **pan·cre·at·ic** \,paŋkrē'atik, ,pan-\ adj

pan·da \'pandə\ n : black-and-white bearlike animal

pan·de·mo·ni·um \,pandə'mōnēəm\ n : wild uproar

pan·der \'pandər\ n 1 : pimp 2 : one who caters to others' desires or weaknesses ~ vb : act as a pander

pane \'pān\ n : sheet of glass

pan·e·gy·ric \,panə'jirik\ n : eulogistic oration — **pan·e·gyr·ist** \-'jirist\ n

pan·el \'pan³l\ n 1 : list of persons (as jurors) 2 : discussion group 3 : flat piece of construction material 4 : board with instruments or controls ~ vb **-eled** or **-elled; -el·ing** or **-el·ling** : decorate with panels — **pan·el·ing** n — **pan·el·ist** \-ist\ n

pang \'paŋ\ n : sudden sharp pain

pan·han·dle \'pan,hand³l\ vb **-dled; -dling** : ask for money on the street — **pan·han·dler** \-ər\ n

pan·ic \'panik\ *n* : sudden overpowering fright ~ *vb* **-icked; -ick·ing** : affect or be affected with panic — **pan·icky** \-ikē\ *adj*

pan·o·ply \'panəplē\ *n, pl* **-plies** 1 : full suit of armor 2 : impressive array

pan·o·ra·ma \,panə'ramə, -'räm-\ *n* : view in every direction — **pan·o·ram·ic** \-'ramik\ *adj*

pan·sy \'panzē\ *n, pl* **-sies** : low-growing garden herb with showy flowers

pant \'pant\ *vb* 1 : breathe with great effort 2 : yearn ~ *n* : panting sound

pan·ta·loons \,pant³l'ünz\ *n pl* : pants

pan·the·on \'panthē,än, -ən\ *n* 1 : the gods of a people 2 : group of famous people

pan·ther \'panthər\ *n* : large wild cat

pant·ies \'pantēz\ *n pl* : woman's or child's short underpants

pan·to·mime \'pantə,mīm\ *n* 1 : play without words 2 : expression by bodily or facial movements ~ *vb* : represent by pantomime

pan·try \'pantrē\ *n, pl* **-tries** : storage room for food and dishes

pants \'pants\ *n pl* 1 : 2-legged outer garment 2 : panties

pap \'pap\ *n* : soft food

pa·pa·cy \'pāpəsē\ *n, pl* **-cies** 1 : office of pope 2 : reign of a pope

pa·pal \'pāpəl\ *adj* : relating to the pope

pa·pa·ya \pə'pīə\ *n* : tropical tree with large yellow edible fruit

pa·per \'pāpər\ *n* 1 : pliable substance used to write or print on, to wrap things in, or to cover walls 2 : printed or written document 3 : newspaper — **paper** *adj or vb* — **pa·per·hang·er** *n* — **pa·per·weight** *n* — **pa·pery** \'pāpərē\ *adj*

pa·per·board *n* : cardboard

pa·pier–mâ·ché \,pāpərmə'shā, ,pap-,yāmə-, -mə-\ *n* : molding material of waste paper

pa·poose \pa'püs, pə-\ *n* : young child of American Indian parents

pa·pri·ka \pə'prēkə, pa-\ *n* : mild red spice from sweet peppers

pa·py·rus \pə'pīrəs\ *n, pl* **-rus·es** or **-ri** \-,rē, -,rī\ 1 : tall grasslike plant 2 : paper from papyrus

par \'pär\ *n* 1 : stated value 2 : common level 3 : accepted standard or normal condition — **par** *adj*

par·a·ble \'parəbəl\ *n* : simple story illustrating a moral truth

para·chute \'parə,shüt\ *n* : large umbrella-shaped device for making a descent through air — **parachute** *vb* — **para·chut·ist** \-,shütist\ *n*

pa·rade \pə'rād\ *n* 1 : pompous display 2 : ceremonial formation and march ~ *vb* **-rad·ed; -rad·ing** 1 : march in a parade 2 : show off

par·a·digm \'parə,dīm, -,dim\ *n* : model

par·a·dise \'parə,dīs, -,dīz\ *n* : place of bliss

par·a·dox \'parə,däks\ *n* : statement that seems contrary to common sense yet is perhaps true — **par·a·dox·i·cal** \,parə'däksikəl\ *adj* — **par·a·dox·i·cal·ly** *adv*

par·af·fin \'parəfən\ *n* : white waxy substance used esp. for making candles and sealing foods

par·a·gon \'parə,gän, -gən\ *n* : model of perfection

para·graph \'parə,graf\ *n* : unified division of a piece of writing ~ *vb* : divide into paragraphs

par·a·keet \'parə,kēt\ *n* : small slender parrot

par·al·lel \'parə,lel\ *adj* 1 : lying or moving in the same direction but always the same distance apart 2 : similar ~ *n* 1 : parallel line, curve, or surface 2 : line of latitude 3 : similarity ~ *vb* 1 : compare 2 : correspond to — **par·al·lel·ism** \-,izəm\ *n*

par·al·lel·o·gram \,parə'lelə,gram\ *n* : 4-sided polygon with opposite sides equal and parallel

pa·ral·y·sis \pə'raləsəs\ *n, pl* **-y·ses** \-,sēz\ : loss of function and esp. of voluntary motion — **par·a·lyt·ic** \,parə'litik\ *adj or n*

par·a·lyze \'parə,līz\ *vb* **-lyzed; -lyz·ing** : affect with paralysis — **par·a·lyz·ing·ly** *adv*

para·med·ic \,parə'medik\ *n* : person trained to provide initial emergency medical treatment

pa·ram·e·ter \pə'ramətər\ *n* : characteristic element — **para·met·ric** \,parə'metrik\ *adj*

par·a·mount \'parə,maunt\ *adj* : superior to all others

par·amour \'parə,mur\ *n* : illicit lover

para·noia \,parə'nöiə\ *n* : mental disorder marked by irrational suspicion — **para·noid** \\'parə,nóid\ adj or n

par·a·pet \'parəpət, -,pet\ n : protecting rampart in a fort

para·pher·na·lia \,parəfə'nālyə, -fər-\ n sing or pl : equipment

para·phrase \'parə,frāz\ n : restatement of a text giving the meaning in different words — **paraphrase** vb

para·ple·gia \,parə'plējə, -jēə\ n : paralysis of the lower trunk and legs — **para·ple·gic** \-jik\ adj or n

par·a·site \'parə,sīt\ n : organism living on another — **par·a·sit·ic** \,parə-'sitik\ adj — **par·a·sit·ism** \'parəse-,tizəm, -,sīt,iz-\ n

para·sol \'parə,sól\ n : umbrella used to keep off the sun

para·troops \-,trüps\ n pl : troops trained to parachute from an airplane — **para·troop·er** \-,trüpər\ n

par·boil \'pär,bóil\ vb : boil briefly

par·cel \'pärsəl\ n 1 : lot 2 : package ~ vb -celed or -celled; -cel·ing or -cel·ling : divide into portions

parch \'pärch\ vb : toast or shrivel with dry heat

parch·ment \'pärchmənt\ n : animal skin prepared to write on

par·don \'pärd'n\ n : excusing of an offense ~ vb : free from penalty — **par·don·able** \'pärd'nəbəl\ adj — **par·don·er** \-'nər\ n

pare \'par\ vb pared; par·ing 1 : trim off an outside part 2 : reduce as if by paring — **par·er** n

par·e·gor·ic \,parə'górik\ n : tincture of opium and camphor

par·ent \'parənt\ n : one that begets or brings up offspring — **par·ent·age** \-ij\ n — **pa·ren·tal** \pə'rent'l\ adj — **par·ent·hood** n

pa·ren·the·sis \pə'renthəsəs\ n, pl -the·ses \-,sēz\ 1 : word or phrase inserted in a passage 2 : one of a pair of punctuation marks ( ) — **par·en·thet·ic** \,parən'thetik\, **par·en·thet·i·cal** \-ikəl\ adj — **par·en·thet·i·cal·ly** adv

par·fait \pär'fā\ n : layered cold dessert

pa·ri·ah \pə'rīə\ n : outcast

par·ish \'parish\ n : local church community

pa·rish·io·ner \pə'rishənər\ n : member of a parish

par·i·ty \'parətē\ n, pl -ties : equality

park \'pärk\ n : land set aside for recreation or for its beauty ~ vb : leave a vehicle standing

par·ka \'pärkə\ n : usu. hooded heavy jacket

park·way \'pärk,wā\ n : broad landscaped thoroughfare

par·lance \'pärləns\ n : manner of speaking

par·lay \'pär,lā\ n : the risking of a stake plus its winnings — **parlay** vb

par·ley \'pärlē\ n, pl -leys : conference about a dispute — **parley** vb

par·lia·ment \'pärləmənt\ n : legislative assembly — **par·lia·men·tar·i·an** n — **par·lia·men·ta·ry** \,pärlə-'mentərē\ adj

par·lor \'pärlər\ n 1 : reception room 2 : place of business

pa·ro·chi·al \pə'rōkēəl\ adj 1 : relating to a church parish 2 : provincial — **pa·ro·chi·al·ism** \-ə,lizəm\ n

par·o·dy \'parədē\ n, pl -dies : humorous or satirical imitation — **parody** vb

pa·role \pə'rōl\ n : conditional release of a prisoner — **parole** vb — **pa·rol·ee** \-,rō'lē, -'rō,lē\ n

par·ox·ysm \'parək,sizəm, pə'räk-\ n : convulsion

par·quet \'pär,kā, pär'kā\ n : flooring of patterned wood inlay

par·ra·keet var of PARAKEET

par·rot \'parət\ n : bright-colored tropical bird

par·ry \'parē\ vb -ried; -ry·ing 1 : ward off a blow 2 : evade adroitly — **parry** n

parse \'pärs\ vb parsed; pars·ing : analyze grammatically

par·si·mo·ny \'pärsə,mōnē\ n : extreme frugality — **par·si·mo·ni·ous** \,pärsə'mōnēəs\ adj — **par·si·mo·ni·ous·ly** adv

pars·ley \'pärslē\ n : garden plant used as a seasoning or garnish

pars·nip \'pärsnəp\ n : carrotlike vegetable with a white edible root

par·son \'pärs'n\ n : minister

par·son·age \'pärs'nij\ n : parson's house

part \'pärt\ n 1 : one of the units into which a larger whole is divided 2 : function or role ~ vb 1 : take leave 2 : separate 3 : go away 4 : give up

par·take \pär'tāk, pər-\ vb -took; -tak·en; -tak·ing : have or take a share — **par·tak·er** n

par·tial \'pärshəl\ adj 1 : favoring one over another 2 : affecting a part only — **par·tial·i·ty** \pärshē'alotē\ n — **par·tial·ly** \'pärshəlē\ adv

par·tic·i·pate \pər'tisə,pāt, pär-\ vb -pat·ed; -pat·ing : take part in something — **par·tic·i·pant** \-pənt\ adj or n — **par·tic·i·pa·tion** \-,tisə'pāshən\ n — **par·tic·i·pa·to·ry** \-'tisəpə,tōrē\ adj

par·ti·ci·ple \'pärtə,sipəl\ n : verb form with functions of both verb and adjective — **par·ti·cip·i·al** \pärtə'sipēəl\ adj

par·ti·cle \'pärtikəl\ n : small bit

par·tic·u·lar \pär'tikyələr\ adj 1 : relating to a specific person or thing 2 : individual 3 : hard to please ∼ n : detail — **par·tic·u·lar·ly** adv

par·ti·san \'pärtəzən, -sən\ n 1 : adherent 2 : guerrilla — **partisan** adj — **par·ti·san·ship** n

par·tite \'pär,tīt\ adj : divided into parts

par·ti·tion \pər'tishən, pär-\ n 1 : distribution 2 : something that divides — **partition** vb

part·ly \'pärtlē\ adv : in some degree

part·ner \'pärtnər\ n 1 : associate 2 : companion 3 : business associate — **part·ner·ship** n

part of speech : class of words distinguished esp. according to function

par·tridge \'pärtrij\ n, pl -tridge or -tridg·es : stout-bodied game bird

par·ty \'pärtē\ n, pl -ties 1 : political organization 2 : participant 3 : company of persons esp. with a purpose 4 : social gathering

par·ve·nu \'pärvə,nü, -,nyü\ n : social upstart

pass \'pas\ vb 1 : move past, over, or through 2 : go away or die 3 : allow to elapse 4 : go unchallenged 5 : transfer or undergo transfer 6 : render a judgment 7 : occur 8 : enact 9 : undergo testing successfully 10 : be regarded 11 : decline ∼ n 1 : low place in a mountain range 2 : act of passing 3 : accomplishment 4 : permission to leave, enter, or move about — **pass·able** adj — **pass·ably** adv — **pass·er** n — **pass·er·by** n

pas·sage \'pasij\ n 1 : process of passing 2 : means of passing 3 : voyage 4 : right to pass 5 : literary selection — **pas·sage·way** n

pass·book n : bankbook

pas·sé \pa'sā\ adj : out-of-date

pas·sen·ger \'pasənjər\ n : traveler in a conveyance

pass·ing \'pasin\ n : death

pas·sion \'pashən\ n 1 : strong feeling esp. of anger, love, or desire 2 : object of affection or enthusiasm — **pas·sion·ate** \'pashənət\ adj — **pas·sion·ate·ly** adv — **pas·sion·less** adj

pas·sive \'pasiv\ adj 1 : not active but acted upon 2 : submissive — **passive** n — **pas·sive·ly** adv — **pas·siv·i·ty** \pa'sivətē\ n

Pass·over \'pas,ōvər\ n : Jewish holiday celebrated in March or April in commemoration of the Hebrews' liberation from slavery in Egypt

pass·port \'pas,pōrt\ n : government document needed for travel abroad

pass·word n 1 : word or phrase spoken to pass a guard 2 : sequence of characters needed to get into a computer system

past \'past\ adj 1 : ago 2 : just gone by 3 : having existed before the present 4 : expressing past time ∼ prep or adv : beyond ∼ n 1 : time gone by 2 : verb tense expressing time gone by 3 : past life

pas·ta \'pästə\ n : fresh or dried shaped dough

paste \'pāst\ n 1 : smooth ground food 2 : moist adhesive ∼ vb past·ed; past·ing : attach with paste — **pasty** adj

paste·board n : cardboard

pas·tel \pas'tel\ n : light color — **pastel** adj

pas·teur·ize \'paschə,rīz, 'pastə-\ vb -ized; -iz·ing : heat (as milk) so as to kill germs — **pas·teur·i·za·tion** \,paschərə'zāshən, ,pastə-\ n

pas·time \'pas,tīm\ n : amusement

pas·tor \'pastər\ n : priest or minister serving a church or parish — **pas·tor·ate** \-tərət\ n

pas·to·ral \'pastərəl\ adj 1 : relating to rural life 2 : of or relating to spiritual guidance or a pastor ∼ n : literary work dealing with rural life

pas·try \'pāstrē\ n, pl -ries : sweet baked goods

pas·ture \'paschər\ n : land used for grazing ∼ vb -tured; -tur·ing : graze

pat \'pat\ n 1 : light tap 2 : small mass

~ *vb* -tt- : tap gently ~ *adj or adv* **1** : apt or glib **2** : unyielding

patch \'pach\ *n* **1** : piece used for mending **2** : small area distinct from surrounding area ~ *vb* **1** : mend with a patch **2** : make of fragments **3** : repair hastily — **patchy** \-ē\ *adj*

patch·work *n* : something made of pieces of different materials, shapes, or colors

pate \'pāt\ *n* : crown of the head

pa·tel·la \pə'tela\ *n, pl* -**lae** \-'tel,ē, -,ī\ *or* -**las** : kneecap

pa·tent *adj* **1** \'pat'nt, 'pāt-\ : obvious \'pat-\ : protected by a patent ~ \'pat-\ *n* : document conferring or securing a right \'pat-\ *vb* : secure by patent — **pat·ent·ly** *adv*

pa·ter·nal \pə'tərn³l\ *adj* **1** : fatherly **2** : related through or inherited from a father — **pa·ter·nal·ly** *adv*

pa·ter·ni·ty \pə'tərnətē\ *n* : fatherhood

path \'path, 'pàth\ *n* **1** : trodden way **2** : route or course — **path·find·er** — **path·way** *n* — **path·less** *adj*

pa·thet·ic \pə'thetik\ *adj* : pitiful — **pa·thet·i·cal·ly** *adv*

pa·thol·o·gy \pə'thäləjē\ *n, pl* -**gies** **1** : study of disease **2** : physical abnormality — **path·o·log·i·cal** \,pathə·'läjikəl\ *adj* — **pa·thol·o·gist** \pə'thäləjist\ *n*

pa·thos \'pā,thäs\ *n* : element evoking pity

pa·tience \'pāshəns\ *n* : habit or fact of being patient

pa·tient \'pāshənt\ *adj* : bearing pain or trials without complaint ~ *n* : one under medical care — **pa·tient·ly** *adv*

pa·ti·na \pə'tēnə, 'patənə\ *n, pl* -**nas** \-nəz\ *or* -**nae** \-,nē, -,nī\ : green film formed on copper and bronze

pa·tio \'patē,ō, 'pät-\ *n, pl* -**ti·os** **1** : courtyard **2** : paved recreation area near a house

pa·tri·arch \'pātrē,ärk\ *n* **1** : man revered as father or founder **2** : venerable old man — **pa·tri·ar·chal** \,pātrē'ärkəl\ *adj* — **pa·tri·ar·chy** \-,ärkē\ *n*

pa·tri·cian \pə'trishən\ *n* : person of high birth — **patrician** *adj*

pat·ri·mo·ny \'patrə,mōnē\ *n* : something inherited — **pat·ri·mo·ni·al** \,patrə'mōnēəl\ *adj*

pa·tri·ot \'pātrēət, -,ät\ *n* : one who loves his or her country — **pa·tri·ot·**

ic \,pātrē'ätik\ *adj* — **pa·tri·ot·i·cal·ly** *adv* — **pa·tri·o·tism** \'pātrēə,tizəm\ *n*

pa·trol \pə'trōl\ *n* **1** : a going around for observation or security **2** : group on patrol ~ *vb* -ll- : carry out a patrol

pa·trol·man \-mən\ *n* : police officer

pa·tron \'pātrən\ *n* **1** : special protector **2** : wealthy supporter **3** : customer

pa·tron·age \'patrənij, 'pā-\ *n* **1** : support or influence of a patron **2** : trade of customers **3** : control of government appointments

pa·tron·ess \'pātrənəs\ *n* : woman who is a patron

pa·tron·ize \'pātrə,nīz, 'pa-\ *vb* -**ized**; -**iz·ing** **1** : be a customer of **2** : treat with condescension

¹**pat·ter** \'patər\ *vb* : talk glibly or mechanically ~ *n* : rapid talk

²**pat·ter** *vb* : pat or tap rapidly ~ *n* : quick succession of pats or taps

pat·tern \'patərn\ *n* **1** : model for imitation or making things **2** : artistic design **3** : noticeable formation or set of characteristics ~ *vb* : form according to a pattern

pat·ty \'patē\ *n, pl* -**ties** : small flat cake

pau·ci·ty \'pòsətē\ *n* : shortage

paunch \'pònch\ *n* : large belly — **paunchy** *adj*

pau·per \'pòpər\ *n* : poor person — **pau·per·ism** \-pə,rizəm\ *n* — **pau·per·ize** \-pə,rīz\ *vb*

pause \'pòz\ *n* : temporary stop ~ *vb* **paused; paus·ing** : stop briefly

pave \'pāv\ *vb* **paved; pav·ing** : cover to smooth or firm the surface — **pave·ment** \-mənt\ *n* — **pav·ing** *n*

pa·vil·ion \pə'vilyən\ *n* **1** : large tent **2** : light structure used for entertainment or shelter

paw \'pò\ *n* : foot of a 4-legged clawed animal ~ *vb* **1** : handle clumsily or rudely **2** : touch or strike with a paw

pawn \'pòn\ *n* **1** : goods deposited as security for a loan **2** : state of being pledged ~ *vb* : deposit as a pledge — **pawn·bro·ker** *n* — **pawn·shop** *n*

pay \'pā\ *vb* **paid** \'pād\; **pay·ing** **1** : make due return for goods or services **2** : discharge indebtedness for **3** : requite **4** : give freely or as fitting **5** : be profitable ~ *n* **1** : status of being paid **2** : something paid — **pay-**

able *adj* — **pay•check** *n* — **pay•ee** \pā'ē\ *n* — **pay•er** *n* — **pay•ment** *n*

PC \ˌpē'sē\ *n, pl* **PCs** *or* **PC's** : microcomputer

pea \'pē\ *n* : round edible seed of a leguminous vine

peace \'pēs\ *n* **1** : state of calm and quiet **2** : absence of war or strife — **peace•able** \-əbəl\ *adj* — **peace•ably** \-blē\ *adv* — **peace•ful** \-fəl\ *adj* — **peace•ful•ly** *adv* — **peace•keep•er** *n* — **peace•keep•ing** *n* — **peace•mak•er** *n* — **peace•time** *n*

peach \'pēch\ *n* : sweet juicy fruit of a flowering tree or this tree

pea•cock \'pē,käk\ *n* : brilliantly colored male pheasant

peak \'pēk\ *n* **1** : pointed or projecting part **2** : top of a hill **3** : highest level ~ *vb* : reach a maximum — **peak** *adj*

peak•ed \'pēkəd\ *adj* : sickly

peal \'pēl\ *n* : loud sound (as of ringing bells) ~ *vb* : give out peals

pea•nut \'pē,nət\ *n* : annual herb that bears underground pods or the pod or the edible seed inside

pear \'par\ *n* : fleshy fruit of a tree related to the apple

pearl \'pərl\ *n* : gem formed within an oyster — **pearly** \'pərlē\ *adj*

peas•ant \'pez²nt\ *n* : tiller of the soil — **peas•ant•ry** \-²ntrē\ *n*

peat \'pēt\ *n* : decayed organic deposit often dried for fuel — **peaty** *adj*

peb•ble \'pebəl\ *n* : small stone — **peb•bly** *adj*

pe•can \pi'kän, -'kan\ *n* : hickory tree bearing a smooth-shelled nut or the nut

pec•ca•dil•lo \ˌpekə'dilō\ *n, pl* **-loes** *or* **-los** : slight offense

¹**peck** \'pek\ *n* : unit of dry measure equal to 8 quarts

²**peck** *vb* : strike or pick up with the bill ~ *n* : quick sharp stroke

pec•tin \'pektən\ *n* : water-soluble plant substance that causes fruit jellies to set — **pec•tic** \-tik\ *adj*

pec•to•ral \'pektərəl\ *adj* : relating to the breast or chest

pe•cu•liar \pi'kyülyər\ *adj* **1** : characteristic of only one **2** : strange — **pe•cu•liar•i•ty** \-ˌkyül'yaratē, -ē'ar-\ *n* — **pe•cu•liar•ly** *adv*

pe•cu•ni•ary \pi'kyünē,erē\ *adj* : relating to money

ped•a•go•gy \'pedə,gōjē, -,gäj-\ *n* : art or profession of teaching — **ped•a•gog•ic** \ˌpedə'gäjik, -'gōj-\, **ped•a•**

gog•i•cal \-ikəl\ *adj* — **ped•a•gogue** \'pedə,gäg\ *n*

ped•al \'ped²l\ *n* : lever worked by the foot ~ *adj* : relating to the foot ~ *vb* : use a pedal

ped•ant \'ped²nt\ *n* : learned bore — **pe•dan•tic** \pi'dantik\ *adj* — **ped•ant•ry** \'ped²ntrē\ *n*

ped•dle \'ped²l\ *vb* **-dled; -dling** : offer for sale — **ped•dler** \'pedlər\ *n*

ped•es•tal \'pedəst²l\ *n* : support or foot of something upright

pe•des•tri•an \pə'destrēən\ *adj* **1** : ordinary **2** : walking ~ *n* : person who walks

pe•di•at•rics \ˌpēdē'atriks\ *n* : branch of medicine dealing with children — **pe•di•at•ric** \-trik\ *adj* — **pe•di•a•tri•cian** \ˌpēdēə'trishən\ *n*

ped•i•gree \'pedə,grē\ *n* : line of ancestors or a record of this

ped•i•ment \'pedəmənt\ *n* : triangular gablelike decoration of a building

peek \'pēk\ *vb* **1** : look furtively **2** : glance — **peek** *n*

peel \'pēl\ *vb* **1** : strip the skin or rind from **2** : lose the outer layer ~ *n* : skin or rind — **peel•ing** *n*

¹**peep** \'pēp\ *vb or n* : cheep

²**peep** *vb* **1** : look slyly **2** : begin to emerge ~ *n* : brief look — **peep•er** *n* — **peep•hole** *n*

¹**peer** \'pir\ *n* **1** : one's equal **2** : nobleman — **peer•age** \-ij\ *n*

²**peer** *vb* : look intently or curiously

peer•less \-ləs\ *adj* : having no equal

peeve \'pēv\ *vb* **peeved; peev•ing** : make resentful ~ *n* : complaint — **peev•ish** \-ish\ *adj* — **peev•ish•ly** *adv* — **peev•ish•ness** *n*

peg \'peg\ *n* : small pinlike piece ~ *vb* **-gg- 1** : put a peg into **2** : fix or mark with or as if with pegs

pei•gnoir \pān'wär, pen-\ *n* : negligee

pe•jo•ra•tive \pi'jórətiv\ *adj* : having a negative or degrading effect ~ *n* : a degrading word or phrase — **pe•jo•ra•tive•ly** *adv*

pel•i•can \'pelikən\ *n* : large-billed seabird

pel•la•gra \pə'lagrə, -'läg-\ *n* : protein-deficiency disease

pel•let \'pelət\ *n* : little ball — **pel•let•al** \-²l\ *adj* — **pel•let•ize** \-,īz\ *vb*

pell–mell \'pel'mel\ *adv* : in confusion or haste

pel·lu·cid \pə'lüsəd\ *adj* : very clear

¹pelt \'pelt\ *n* : skin of a fur-bearing animal

²pelt *vb* : strike with blows or missiles

pel·vis \'pelvəs\ *n, pl* **-vis·es** \-vəsəz\ *or* **-ves** \-¸vēz\ : cavity formed by the hip bones — **pel·vic** \-vik\ *adj*

¹pen \'pen\ *n* : enclosure for animals ~ *vb* **-nn-** : shut in a pen

²pen *n* : tool for writing with ink ~ *vb* **-nn-** : write

pe·nal \'pēn³l\ *adj* : relating to punishment

pe·nal·ize \'pēn³l¸īz, 'pen-\ *vb* **-ized; -iz·ing** : put a penalty on

pen·al·ty \'pen³ltē\ *n, pl* **-ties** **1** : punishment for crime **2** : disadvantage, loss, or hardship due to an action

pen·ance \'penəns\ *n* : act performed to show repentance

pence \'pens\ *pl of* PENNY

pen·chant \'penchənt\ *n* : strong inclination

pen·cil \'pensəl\ *n* : writing or drawing tool with a solid marking substance (as graphite) as its core ~ *vb* **-ciled** *or* **-cilled; -cil·ing** *or* **-cil·ling** : draw or write with a pencil

pen·dant \'pendənt\ *n* : hanging ornament

pen·dent, pen·dant \'pendənt\ *adj* : hanging

pend·ing \'pendiŋ\ *prep* : while awaiting ~ *adj* : not yet decided

pen·du·lous \'penjələs, -dyələs\ *adj* : hanging loosely

pen·du·lum \-ləm\ *n* : a hanging weight that is free to swing

pen·e·trate \'penə¸trāt\ *vb* **-trat·ed; -trat·ing** **1** : enter into **2** : permeate **3** : see into — **pen·e·tra·ble** \-trəbəl\ *adj* — **pen·e·tra·tion** \¸penə'trāshən\ *n* — **pen·e·tra·tive** \'penə¸trātiv\ *adj*

pen·guin \'pengwən, 'pen-\ *n* : short-legged flightless seabird

pen·i·cil·lin \¸penə'silən\ *n* : antibiotic usu. produced by a mold

pen·in·su·la \pə'ninsələ, -'ninchə-\ *n* : land extending out into the water — **pen·in·su·lar** \-lər\ *adj*

pe·nis \'pēnəs\ *n, pl* **-nes** \-¸nēz\ *or* **-nis·es** : male organ of copulation

pen·i·tent \'penətənt\ *adj* : feeling sorrow for sins or offenses ~ *n* : penitent person — **pen·i·tence** \-təns\ *n* — **pen·i·ten·tial** \¸penə'tenchəl\ *adj*

pen·i·ten·tia·ry \¸penə'tenchərē\ *n, pl* **-ries** : state or federal prison

pen·man·ship \'penmən¸ship\ *n* : art or practice of writing

pen·nant \'penənt\ *n* : nautical or championship flag

pen·ny \'penē\ *n, pl* **-nies** \-ēz\ *or* **pence** \'pens\ **1** : monetary unit equal to 1/100 pound **2** *pl* **-nies** : cent — **pen·ni·less** \'peniləs\ *adj*

pen·sion \'penchən\ *n* : retirement income ~ *vb* : pay a pension to — **pen·sion·er** *n*

pen·sive \'pensiv\ *adj* : thoughtful — **pen·sive·ly** *adv*

pent \'pent\ *adj* : confined

pen·ta·gon \'pentə¸gän\ *n* : 5-sided polygon — **pen·tag·o·nal** \pen-'tagən³l\ *adj*

pen·tam·e·ter \pen'tamətər\ *n* : line of verse containing 5 metrical feet

pent·house \'pent¸haús\ *n* : rooftop apartment

pen·u·ry \'penyərē\ *n* **1** : poverty **2** : thrifty or stingy manner — **pe·nu·ri·ous** \pə'núrēəs, -'nyúr-\ *adj*

pe·on \'pē¸än, -ən\ *n, pl* **-ons** *or* **-ones** \pā'ōnēz\ : landless laborer in Spanish America — **pe·on·age** \-ənij\ *n*

pe·o·ny \'pēənē\ *n, pl* **-nies** : garden plant having large flowers

peo·ple \'pēpəl\ *n, pl* **people** **1** *pl* : human beings in general **2** *pl* : human beings in a certain group (as a family) or community **3** *pl* **peoples** : tribe, nation, or race ~ *vb* **-pled; -pling** : constitute the population of

pep \'pep\ *n* : brisk energy ~ *vb* **pepped; pep·ping** : put pep into — **pep·py** *adj*

pep·per \'pepər\ *n* **1** : pungent seasoning from the berry (**peppercorn**) of a shrub **2** : vegetable grown for its hot or sweet fruit ~ *vb* : season with pepper — **pep·pery** \-ərē\ *adj*

pep·per·mint \-¸mint, -mənt\ *n* : pungent aromatic mint

pep·per·o·ni \¸pepə'rōnē\ *n* : spicy beef and pork sausage

pep·tic \'peptik\ *adj* : relating to digestion or the effect of digestive juices

per \'pər\ *prep* **1** : by means of **2** : for each **3** : according to

per·am·bu·late \pə'rambyə¸lāt\ *vb* **-lat·ed; -lat·ing** : walk — **per·am·bu·la·tion** \-¸rambyə'lāshən\ *n*

per·cale \pər'kāl, 'pər-; ,pər'kal\ n : fine woven cotton cloth

per·ceive \pər'sēv\ vb -ceived; -ceiv·ing 1 : realize 2 : become aware of through the senses — **per·ceiv·able** adj

per·cent \pər'sent\ adv : in each hundred ~ n, pl -cent or -cents 1 : one part in a hundred 2 : percentage

per·cent·age \pər'sentij\ n : part expressed in hundredths

per·cen·tile \pər'sen,tīl\ n : a standing on a scale of 0–100

per·cep·ti·ble \pər'septəbəl\ adj : capable of being perceived — **per·cep·ti·bly** \-blē\ adv

per·cep·tion \pər'sepshən\ n 1 : act or result of perceiving 2 : ability to understand

per·cep·tive \pər'septiv\ adj : showing keen perception — **per·cep·tive·ly** adv

¹**perch** \'pərch\ n : roost for birds ~ vb : roost

²**perch** n, pl perch or perch·es : freshwater spiny-finned food fish

per·co·late \'pərkə,lāt\ vb -lat·ed; -lat·ing : trickle or filter down through a substance — **per·co·la·tor** \-,lātər\ n

per·cus·sion \pər'kəshən\ n 1 : sharp blow 2 : musical instrument sounded by striking

pe·remp·to·ry \pə'remptərē\ adj 1 : imperative 2 : domineering — **pe·remp·to·ri·ly** \-tərəlē\ adv

pe·ren·ni·al \pə'renēəl\ adj 1 : present at all seasons 2 : continuing from year to year 3 : recurring regularly ~ n : perennial plant — **pe·ren·ni·al·ly** adv

per·fect \'pərfikt\ adj 1 : being without fault or defect 2 : exact 3 : complete ~ \pər'fekt\ vb : make perfect — **per·fect·ibil·i·ty** \pər,fektə'bilətē\ n — **per·fect·ible** \pər'fektəbəl\ adj — **per·fect·ly** adv — **per·fect·ness** n

per·fec·tion \pər'fekshən\ n 1 : quality or state of being perfect 2 : highest degree of excellence — **per·fec·tion·ist** \-shənist\ n

per·fid·i·ous \pər'fidēəs\ adj : treacherous — **per·fid·i·ous·ly** adv

per·fo·rate \'pərfə,rāt\ vb -rat·ed; -rat·ing : make a hole in — **per·fo·ra·tion** \,pərfə'rāshən\ n

per·force \pər'fōrs\ adv : of necessity

per·form \pər'fórm\ vb 1 : carry out 2 : do in a set manner 3 : give a performance — **per·form·er** n

per·for·mance \pər'fórməns\ n 1 : act or process of performing 2 : public presentation

per·fume \'pər,fyüm, pər'-\ n 1 : pleasant odor 2 : something that gives a scent ~ \pər'-, 'pər,-\ vb -fumed; -fum·ing : add scent to

per·func·to·ry \pər'fəŋktərē\ adj : done merely as a duty — **per·func·to·ri·ly** \-tərəlē\ adv

per·haps \pər'haps\ adv : possibly but not certainly

per·il \'perəl\ n : danger — **per·il·ous** adj — **per·il·ous·ly** adv

pe·rim·e·ter \pə'rimətər\ n : outer boundary of a body or figure

pe·ri·od \'pirēəd\ n 1 : punctuation mark . used esp. to mark the end of a declarative sentence or an abbreviation 2 : division of time 3 : stage in a process or development

pe·ri·od·ic \pirē'ädik\ adj : occurring at regular intervals — **pe·ri·od·i·cal·ly** adv

pe·ri·od·i·cal \,pirē'ädikəl\ n : newspaper or magazine

pe·riph·ery \pə'rifərē\ n, pl -er·ies : outer boundary — **pe·riph·er·al** \-ərəl\ adj

peri·scope \'perə,skōp\ n : optical instrument for viewing from a submarine

per·ish \'perish\ vb : die or spoil — **per·ish·able** \-əbəl\ adj or n

per·ju·ry \'pərjərē\ n : lying under oath — **per·jure** \'pərjər\ vb — **per·jur·er** n

¹**perk** \'pərk\ vb 1 : thrust (as the head) up jauntily 2 : freshen 3 : gain vigor or spirit — **perky** adj

²**perk** vb : percolate

³**perk** n : privilege or benefit in addition to regular pay

per·ma·nent \'pərmənənt\ adj : lasting ~ n : hair wave — **per·ma·nence** \-nəns\ n — **per·ma·nent·ly** adv

per·me·able \'pərmēəbəl\ adj : permitting fluids to seep through — **per·me·a·bil·i·ty** \,pərmēə'bilətē\ n

per·me·ate \'pərmē,āt\ vb -at·ed; -at·ing : seep through 2 : pervade — **per·me·ation** \,pərmē'āshən\ n

per·mis·si·ble \pər'misəbəl\ adj : that may be permitted

per·mis·sion \pər'mishən\ *n* : formal consent

per·mis·sive \pər'misiv\ *adj* : granting freedom esp. to excess — **per·mis·sive·ly** *adv* — **per·mis·sive·ness** *n*

per·mit \pər'mit\ *vb* **-tt-** 1 : approve 2 : make possible ∼ \'pər,-, pər'-\ *n* : license

per·ni·cious \pər'nishəs\ *adj* : very harmful — **per·ni·cious·ly** *adv*

per·ox·ide \pə'räk,sīd\ *n* : compound (as hydrogen peroxide) in which oxygen is joined to oxygen

per·pen·dic·u·lar \,pərpən'dikyələr\ *adj* 1 : vertical 2 : meeting at a right angle — **perpendicular** *n* — **per·pen·dic·u·lar·i·ty** \-,dikyə'larətē\ *n* — **per·pen·dic·u·lar·ly** *adv*

per·pe·trate \'pərpə,trāt\ *vb* **-trat·ed; -trat·ing** : be guilty of doing — **per·pe·tra·tion** \,pərpə'trāshən\ *n* — **per·pe·tra·tor** \'pərpə,trātər\ *n*

per·pet·u·al \pər'pechəwəl\ *adj* 1 : continuing forever 2 : occurring continually — **per·pet·u·al·ly** *adv* — **per·pe·tu·ity** \,pərpə'tüətē, -'tyü-\ *n*

per·pet·u·ate \pər'pecha,wāt\ *vb* **-at·ed; -at·ing** : make perpetual — **per·pet·u·a·tion** \-,pecha'wāshən\ *n*

per·plex \pər'pleks\ *vb* : confuse — **per·plex·i·ty** \-ətē\ *n*

per·se·cute \'pərsi,kyüt\ *vb* **-cut·ed; -cut·ing** : harass, afflict — **per·se·cu·tion** \,pərsi'kyüshən\ *n* — **per·se·cu·tor** \'pərsi,kyütər\ *n*

per·se·vere \,pərsə'vir\ *vb* **-vered; -ver·ing** : persist — **per·se·ver·ance** \-'virəns\ *n*

per·sist \pər'sist, -'zist\ *vb* 1 : go on resolutely in spite of difficulties 2 : continue to exist — **per·sis·tence** \-'sistəns, -'zis-\ *n* — **per·sis·ten·cy** \-tənsē\ *n* — **per·sis·tent** \-tənt\ *adj* — **per·sis·tent·ly** *adv*

per·son \'pərs³n\ *n* 1 : human being 2 : human being's body or individuality 3 : reference to the speaker, one spoken to, or one spoken of

per·son·able \'pərs³nəbəl\ *adj* : having a pleasing personality

per·son·age \'pərs³nij\ *n* : person of rank or distinction

per·son·al \'pərs³nəl\ *adj* 1 : relating to a particular person 2 : done in person 3 : affecting one's body 4 : offensive to a certain individual — **per·son·al·ly** *adv*

per·son·al·i·ty \,pərs³n'alətē\ *n, pl* **-ties** 1 : manner and disposition of an individual 2 : distinctive or well-known person

per·son·al·ize \'pərs³nə,līz\ *vb* **-ized; -iz·ing** : mark as belonging to a particular person

per·son·i·fy \pər'sänə,fī\ *vb* **-fied; -fy·ing** 1 : represent as a human being 2 : be the embodiment of — **per·son·i·fi·ca·tion** \-,sänəfə'kāshən\ *n*

per·son·nel \,pərs³n'el\ *n* : body of persons employed

per·spec·tive \pər'spektiv\ *n* 1 : apparent depth and distance in painting 2 : view of things in their true relationship or importance

per·spi·ca·cious \,pərspə'kāshəs\ *adj* : showing keen understanding or discernment — **per·spi·cac·i·ty** \-'kasətē\ *n*

per·spire \pər'spīr\ *vb* **-spired; -spir·ing** : sweat — **per·spi·ra·tion** \,pərspə'rāshən\ *n*

per·suade \pər'swād\ *vb* **-suad·ed; -suad·ing** : win over to a belief or course of action by argument or entreaty — **per·sua·sion** \pər'swāzhən\ *n* — **per·sua·sive** \-'swāsiv, -ziv\ *adj* — **per·sua·sive·ly** *adv* — **per·sua·sive·ness** *n*

pert \'pərt\ *adj* : flippant or irreverent

per·tain \pər'tān\ *vb* 1 : belong 2 : relate

per·ti·nent \'pərt³nənt\ *adj* : relevant — **per·ti·nence** \-³nəns\ *n*

per·turb \pər'tərb\ *vb* : make uneasy — **per·tur·ba·tion** \,pərtər'bāshən\ *n*

pe·ruse \pə'rüz\ *vb* **-rused; -rus·ing** : read attentively — **pe·rus·al** \-'rüzəl\ *n*

per·vade \pər'vād\ *vb* **-vad·ed; -vad·ing** : spread through every part of — **per·va·sive** \-'vāsiv, -ziv\ *adj*

per·verse \pər'vərs\ *adj* 1 : corrupt 2 : unreasonably contrary — **per·verse·ly** *adv* — **per·verse·ness** *n* — **per·ver·sion** \pər'vərzhən\ *n* — **per·ver·si·ty** \-'vərsətē\ *n*

per·vert \pər'vərt\ *vb* : corrupt or distort ∼ \'pər,-\ *n* : one that is perverted

pe·so \'pāsō\ *n, pl* **-sos** : monetary unit (as of Mexico)

pes·si·mism \'pesə,mizəm\ *n* : inclination to expect the worst — **pes·si·mist** \-,mist\ *n* — **pes·si·mis·tic** \,pesə'mistik\ *adj*

pest \'pest\ n 1 : nuisance 2 : plant or animal detrimental to humans or their crops — **pes·ti·cide** \'pestə̄ˌsīd\ n

pes·ter \'pestər\ vb **-tered; -ter·ing** : harass with petty matters

pes·ti·lence \'pestələns\ n : plague — **pes·ti·lent** \-lənt\ adj

pes·tle \'pesəl, 'pest²l\ n : implement for grinding substances in a mortar

pet \'pet\ n 1 : domesticated animal kept for pleasure 2 : favorite ~ vb **-tt-** : stroke gently or lovingly

pet·al \'pet²l\ n : modified leaf of a flower head

pe·tite \pə'tēt\ adj : having a small trim figure

pe·ti·tion \pə'tishən\ n : formal written request ~ vb : make a request — **pe·ti·tion·er** n

pet·ri·fy \'petrəˌfī\ vb **-fied; -fy·ing** 1 : change into stony material 2 : make rigid or inactive (as from fear) — **pet·ri·fac·tion** \ˌpetrə'fakshən\ n

pe·tro·leum \pə'trōlēəm\ n : raw oil obtained from the ground

pet·ti·coat \'petēˌkōt\ n : skirt worn under a dress

pet·ty \'petē\ adj **-ti·er; -est** 1 : minor 2 : of no importance 3 : narrow= minded or mean — **pet·ti·ly** \'petəlē\ adv — **pet·ti·ness** n

petty officer n : subordinate officer in the navy or coast guard

pet·u·lant \'pechələnt\ adj : irritable — **pet·u·lance** \-ləns\ n — **pet·u·lant·ly** adv

pe·tu·nia \pi'tünyə, -'tyü-\ n : tropical herb with bright flowers

pew \'pyü\ n : bench with a back used in a church

pew·ter \'pyütər\ n : alloy of tin used for household utensils

pH \ˌpē'āch\ n : number expressing relative acidity and alkalinity

pha·lanx \'fāˌlaŋks\ n, pl **-lanx·es** or **-lan·ges** \fə'lanˌjēz\ 1 : body (as of troops) in compact formation 2 pl **phalanges** : digital bone of the hand or foot

phal·lus \'faləs\ n, pl **-li** \'fal͟ī\ or **-lus·es** : penis — **phal·lic** adj

phan·ta·sy var of FANTASY

phan·tom \'fantəm\ n : something that only appears to be real — **phantom** adj

pha·raoh \'ferō, 'fārō\ n : ruler of ancient Egypt

phar·ma·ceu·ti·cal \ˌfärmə'sütikəl\ adj : relating to pharmacy or the making and selling of medicinal drugs — **pharmaceutical** n

phar·ma·col·o·gy \ˌfärmə'käləjē\ n : science of drugs esp. as related to medicinal uses — **phar·ma·co·log·i·cal** \-ikəl\ adj — **phar·ma·col·o·gist** \-'käləjist\ n

phar·ma·cy \'färməsē\ n, pl **-cies** 1 : art or practice of preparing and dispensing medical drugs 2 : drugstore — **phar·ma·cist** \-sist\ n

phar·ynx \'fariŋks\ n, pl **pha·ryn·ges** \fə'rinˌjēz\ : space behind the mouth into which the nostrils, esophagus, and windpipe open — **pha·ryn·ge·al** \fə'rinjəl, ˌfarən'jēəl\ adj

phase \'fāz\ n 1 : particular appearance or stage in a recurring series of changes 2 : stage in a process — **phase in** vb : introduce in stages — **phase out** vb : discontinue gradually

pheas·ant \'fez²nt\ n, pl **-ant** or **-ants** : long-tailed brilliantly colored game bird

phe·nom·e·non \fi'näməˌnän, -nən\ n, pl **-na** \-nə\ or **-nons** 1 : observable fact or event 2 pl **-nons** : prodigy — **phe·nom·e·nal** \-'nämən²l\ adj

phi·lan·der·er \fə'landərər\ n : one who makes love without serious intent

phi·lan·thro·py \fə'lanthrəpē\ n, pl **-pies** : charitable act or gift or an organization that distributes such gifts — **phil·an·throp·ic** \ˌfilən'thräpik\ adj — **phi·lan·thro·pist** \fə'lanthrəpist\ n

phi·lat·e·ly \fə'lat²lē\ n : collection and study of postage stamps — **phi·lat·e·list** \-²list\ n

phi·lis·tine \'filəˌstēn, fə'listən\ n : one who is smugly indifferent to intellectual or artistic values — **philistine** adj

philo·den·dron \ˌfilə'dendrən\ n, pl **-drons** or **-dra** \-drə\ : plant grown for its showy leaves

phi·los·o·pher \fə'läsəfər\ n 1 : reflective thinker 2 : student of philosophy

phi·los·o·phy \fə'läsəfē\ n, pl **-phies** 1 : critical study of fundamental beliefs 2 : sciences and liberal arts exclusive of medicine, law, and theology 3 : system of ideas 4 : sum of personal convictions — **phil·o·soph·ic** \ˌfilə'säfik\, **phil·o·soph·i-**

cal \-ikəl\ *adj* — **phil·o·soph·i·cal·ly** \-klē\ *adv* — **phi·los·o·phize** \fə'läsə‚fīz\ *vb*

phle·bi·tis \fli'bītəs\ *n* : inflammation of a vein

phlegm \'flem\ *n* : thick mucus in the nose and throat

phlox \'fläks\ *n*, *pl* **phlox** *or* **phlox·es** : herb grown for its flower clusters

pho·bia \'fōbēə\ *n* : irrational persistent fear

phoe·nix \'fēniks\ *n* : legendary bird held to burn itself to death and rise fresh and young from its ashes

phone \'fōn\ *n* : telephone ~ *vb* **phoned; phon·ing** : call on a telephone

pho·neme \'fō‚nēm\ *n* : basic distinguishable unit of speech — **pho·ne·mic** \fō'nēmik\ *adj*

pho·net·ics \fə'netiks\ *n* : study of speech sounds — **pho·net·ic** \-ik\ *adj* — **pho·ne·ti·cian** \‚fōnə'tishən\ *n*

pho·nics \'fäniks\ *n* : method of teaching reading by stressing sound values of syllables and words

pho·no·graph \'fōnə‚graf\ *n* : instrument that reproduces sounds from a grooved disc

pho·ny, pho·ney \'fōnē\ *adj* **-ni·er; -est** : not sincere or genuine — **phony** *n*

phos·phate \'fäs‚fāt\ *n* : chemical salt used in fertilizers — **phos·phat·ic** \fäs'fatik\ *adj*

phos·phor \'fäsfər\ *n* : phosphorescent substance

phos·pho·res·cence \‚fäsfə'resᵊns\ *n* : luminescence from absorbed radiation — **phos·pho·res·cent** \-ᵊnt\ *adj*

phos·pho·rus \'fäsfərəs\ *n* : poisonous waxy chemical element — **phos·phor·ic** \fäs'fórik, -'fär-\ *adj* — **phos·pho·rous** \'fäsfərəs, fäs·'fōrəs\ *adj*

pho·to \'fōtō\ *n*, *pl* **-tos** : photograph — **photo** *vb or adj*

pho·to·copy \'fōtə‚käpē\ *n* : photographic copy (as of a printed page) — **photocopy** *vb*

pho·to·elec·tric \‚fōtōi'lektrik\ *adj* : relating to an electrical effect due to the interaction of light with matter

pho·to·gen·ic \‚fōtə'jenik\ *adj* : suitable for being photographed

pho·to·graph \'fōtə‚graf\ *n* : picture taken by photography — **photograph** *vb* — **pho·tog·ra·pher** \fə'tägrəfər\ *n*

pho·tog·ra·phy \fə'tägrəfē\ *n* : process of using light to produce images on a sensitized surface — **pho·to·graph·ic** \‚fōtə'grafik\ *adj* — **pho·to·graph·i·cal·ly** *adv*

pho·to·syn·the·sis \‚fōtō'sinthəsəs\ *n* : formation of carbohydrates by chlorophyll-containing plants exposed to sunlight — **pho·to·syn·the·size** \-‚sīz\ *vb* — **pho·to·syn·thet·ic** \-sin'thetik\ *adj*

phrase \'frāz\ *n* **1** : brief expression **2** : group of related words that express a thought ~ *vb* **phrased; phras·ing** : express in a particular manner

phrase·ol·o·gy \‚frāzē'äləjē\ *n*, *pl* **-gies** : manner of phrasing

phy·lum \'fīləm\ *n*, *pl* **-la** \-lə\ : major division of the plant or animal kingdom

phys·i·cal \'fizikəl\ *adj* **1** : relating to nature **2** : material as opposed to mental or spiritual **3** : relating to the body ~ *n* : medical examination — **phys·i·cal·ly** \-klē\ *adv*

phy·si·cian \fə'zishən\ *n* : doctor of medicine

physician's assistant *n* : person certified to provide basic medical care under a physician's supervision

phys·i·cist \'fizəsist\ *n* : specialist in physics

phys·ics \'fiziks\ *n* : science that deals with matter and motion

phys·i·og·no·my \‚fizē'ägnəmē\ *n*, *pl* **-mies** : facial appearance esp. as a reflection of inner character

phys·i·ol·o·gy \‚fizē'äləjē\ *n* : functional processes in an organism — **phys·i·o·log·i·cal** \-ēə'läjikəl\, **phys·i·o·log·ic** \-ik\ *adj* — **phys·i·ol·o·gist** \-ē'äləjist\ *n*

phy·sique \fə'zēk\ *n* : build of a person's body

pi \'pī\ *n*, *pl* **pis** \'pīz\ : symbol π denoting the ratio of the circumference of a circle to its diameter or the ratio itself

pi·a·nist \pē'anist, 'pēənist\ *n* : one who plays the piano

pi·ano \pē'anō\ *n*, *pl* **-anos** : musical instrument with strings sounded by hammers operated from a keyboard

pi·az·za \pē'azə, -'äz-, -tsä\ *n*, *pl* **-zas** *or* **-ze** \-tsä\ : public square in a town

pic·a·yune \‚pikē'yün\ *adj* : trivial or petty

pic·co·lo \'pikə₁lō\ n, pl **-los** : small shrill flute

¹pick \'pik\ vb **1** : break up with a pointed instrument **2** : remove bit by bit **3** : gather by plucking **4** : select **5** : rob **6** : provoke **7** : unlock with a wire **8** : eat sparingly — n **1** : act of choosing **2** : choicest one — **pick·er** n — **pick up** vb **1** : improve **2** : put in order

²pick n : pointed digging tool

pick·ax n : pick

pick·er·el \'pikərəl\ n, pl **-el** or **-els** : small pike

pick·et \'pikət\ n **1** : pointed stake (as for a fence) **2** : worker demonstrating on strike ~ vb : demonstrate as a picket

pick·le \'pikəl\ n **1** : brine or vinegar solution for preserving foods or a food preserved in a pickle **2** : bad state — **pickle** vb

pick·pock·et \'pik₁päkət\ n : one who steals from pockets

pick·up \'pik₁əp\ n **1** : revival or acceleration **2** : light truck with an open body

pic·nic \'pik₁nik\ n : outing with food usu. eaten in the open ~ vb **-nicked; -nick·ing** : go on a picnic

pic·to·ri·al \pik'tōrēəl\ adj : relating to pictures

pic·ture \'pikchər\ n **1** : representation by painting, drawing, or photography **2** : vivid description **3** : copy **4** : movie ~ vb **-tured; -tur·ing** : form a mental image of

pic·tur·esque \₁pikchə'resk\ adj : attractive enough for a picture

pie \'pī\ n : pastry crust and a filling

pie·bald \'pī₁bȯld\ adj : blotched with white and black

piece \'pēs\ n **1** : part of a whole **2** : one of a group or set **3** : single item **4** : product of creative work ~ vb **pieced; piec·ing** : join into a whole

piece·meal \'pēs₁mēl\ adv or adj : gradually

pied \'pīd\ adj : colored in blotches

pier \'pir\ n **1** : support for a bridge span **2** : deck or wharf built out over water **3** : pillar

pierce \'pirs\ vb **pierced; pierc·ing 1** : enter or thrust into or through **2** : penetrate **3** : see through

pi·ety \'pīətē\ n, pl **-eties** : devotion to religion

pig \'pig\ n **1** : young swine **2** : dirty or greedy individual **3** : iron casting — **pig·gish** \-ish\ adj — **pig·let** \-lət\ n — **pig·pen** n — **pig·sty** n

pi·geon \'pijən\ n : stout-bodied short-legged bird

pi·geon·hole n : small open compartment for letters or documents ~ vb **1** : place in a pigeonhole **2** : classify

pig·gy·back \'pigē₁bak\ adv or adj : up on the back and shoulders

pig·head·ed \-'hedəd\ adj : stubborn

pig·ment \'pigmənt\ n : coloring matter — **pig·men·ta·tion** n

pig·my var of PYGMY

pig·tail n : tight braid of hair

¹pike \'pīk\ n, pl **pike** or **pikes** : large freshwater fish

²pike n : former weapon consisting of a long wooden staff with a steel point

³pike n : turnpike

pi·laf, pi·laff \pi'läf, 'pē₁läf\, **pi·lau** \pi'lō, -'lȯ; 'pēlō, -lȯ\ n : dish of seasoned rice

¹pile \'pīl\ n : supporting pillar driven into the ground

²pile n : quantity of things thrown on one another ~ vb **piled; pil·ing** : heap up, accumulate

³pile n : surface of fine hairs or threads — **piled** adj

piles \'pīls\ n pl : hemorrhoids

pil·fer \'pilfər\ vb : steal in small quantities

pil·grim \'pilgrəm\ n **1** : one who travels to a shrine or holy place in devotion **2** cap : one of the English settlers in America in 1620

pil·grim·age \-grəmij\ n : pilgrim's journey

pill \'pil\ n : small rounded mass of medicine — **pill·box** n

pil·lage \'pilij\ vb **-laged; -lag·ing** : loot and plunder — **pillage** n

pil·lar \'pilər\ n : upright usu. supporting column — **pil·lared** adj

pil·lo·ry \'pilərē\ n, pl **-ries** : wooden frame for public punishment with holes for the head and hands ~ vb **-ried; -ry·ing 1** : set in a pillory **2** : expose to public scorn

pil·low \'pilō\ n : soft cushion for the head — **pil·low·case** n

pi·lot \'pīlət\ n **1** : helmsman **2** : person licensed to take ships into and out of a port **3** : guide **4** : one that flies an aircraft or spacecraft ~ vb : act as pilot of — **pi·lot·less** adj

pi·men·to \pə'mentō\ n, pl **-tos** or **-to**
1 : allspice **2** : pimiento

pi·mien·to \pə'mentō, -'myen-\ n, pl **-tos** : mild red sweet pepper

pimp \'pimp\ n : man who solicits clients for a prostitute — **pimp** vb

pim·ple \'pimpəl\ n : small inflamed swelling on the skin — **pim·ply** \-pəlē\ adj

pin \'pin\ n **1** : fastener made of a small pointed piece of wire **2** : ornament or emblem fastened to clothing with a pin **3** : wooden object used as a target in bowling ~ vb **-nn- 1** : fasten with a pin **2** : hold fast or immobile — **pin·hole** n

pin·a·fore \'pinə,fōr\ n : sleeveless dress or apron fastened at the back

pin·cer \'pinsər\ n **1** pl : gripping tool with 2 jaws **2** : pincerlike claw

pinch \'pinch\ vb **1** : squeeze between the finger and thumb or between the jaws of a tool **2** : compress painfully **3** : restrict **4** : steal ~ n **1** : emergency **2** : painful effect **3** : act of pinching **4** : very small quantity

pin·cush·ion n : cushion for storing pins

¹pine \'pīn\ n : evergreen cone-bearing tree or its wood

²pine vb **pined; pin·ing 1** : lose health through distress **2** : yearn for intensely

pine·ap·ple n : tropical plant bearing an edible juicy fruit

pin·feath·er n : new feather just coming through the skin

¹pin·ion \'pinyən\ vb : restrain by binding the arms

²pinion n : small gear

¹pink \'piŋk\ n **1** : plant with narrow leaves and showy flowers **2** : highest degree

²pink n : light red color — **pink** adj — **pink·ish** adj

pink·eye n : contagious eye inflammation

pin·na·cle \'pinikəl\ n : highest point

pi·noch·le \'pē,nəkəl\ n : card game played with a 48-card deck

pin·point vb : locate, hit, or aim with great precision

pint \'pīnt\ n : 1/2 quart

pin·to \'pin,tō\ n, pl **pintos** : spotted horse or pony

pin·worm n : small parasitic intestinal worm

pi·o·neer \,pīə'nir\ n **1** : one that originates or helps open up a new line of thought or activity **2** : early settler ~ vb : act as a pioneer

pi·ous \'pīəs\ adj **1** : conscientious in religious practices **2** : affectedly religious — **pi·ous·ly** adv

pipe \'pīp\ n **1** : tube that produces music when air is forced through **2** : bagpipe **3** : long tube for conducting a fluid **4** : smoking tool ~ vb **piped; pip·ing 1** : play on a pipe **2** : speak in a high voice **3** : convey by pipes — **pip·er** n

pipe·line n **1** : line of pipe **2** : channel for information

pip·ing \'pīpiŋ\ n **1** : music of pipes **2** : narrow fold of material used to decorate edges or seams

pi·quant \'pēkənt\ adj **1** : tangy **2** : provocative or charming — **pi·quan·cy** \-kənsē\ n

pique \'pēk\ n : resentment ~ vb **piqued; piqu·ing 1** : offend **2** : arouse by provocation

pi·qué, pi·que \pi'kā\ n : durable ribbed clothing fabric

pi·ra·cy \'pīrəsē\ n, pl **-cies 1** : robbery on the seas **2** : unauthorized use of another's production or invention

pi·ra·nha \pə'ranyə, -'ränə\ n : small So. American fish with sharp teeth

pi·rate \'pīrət\ n : one who commits piracy — **pirate** vb — **pi·rat·i·cal** \pə'ratikəl, pī-\ adj

pir·ou·ette \,pirə'wet\ n : ballet turn on the toe or ball of one foot — **pirouette** vb

pis pl of PI

pis·ta·chio \pə'stashē,ō, -'stäsh-\ n, pl **-chios** : small tree bearing a greenish edible seed or its seed

pis·til \'pist²l\ n : female reproductive organ in a flower — **pis·til·late** \'pistə,lāt\ adj

pis·tol \'pist²l\ n : firearm held with one hand

pis·ton \'pistən\ n : sliding piece that receives and transmits motion usu. inside a cylinder

pit \'pit\ n **1** : hole or shaft in the ground **2** : sunken or enclosed place for a special purpose **3** : hell **4** : hollow or indentation ~ vb **-tt- 1** : form pits in **2** : become marred with pits

²**pit** *n* : stony seed of some fruits ∼ *vb* **-tt-** : remove the pit from

pit bull *n* : powerful compact dog bred for fighting

¹**pitch** \'pich\ *n* : resin from conifers — **pitchy** *adj*

²**pitch** *vb* **1** : erect and fix firmly in place **2** : throw **3** : set at a particular tone level **4** : fall headlong ∼ *n* **1** : action or manner of pitching **2** : degree of slope **3** : relative highness of a tone **4** : sales talk — **pitched** *adj*

¹**pitch·er** \'pichər\ *n* : container for liquids

²**pitcher** *n* : one that pitches (as in baseball)

pitch·fork *n* : long-handled fork for pitching hay

pit·e·ous \'pitēəs\ *adj* : arousing pity — **pit·e·ous·ly** *adv*

pit·fall \'pit,fȯl\ *n* : hidden danger

pith \'pith\ *n* **1** : spongy plant tissue **2** : essential or meaningful part — **pithy** *adj*

piti·able \'pitēəbəl\ *adj* : pitiful

piti·ful \'pitifəl\ *adj* **1** : arousing or deserving pity **2** : contemptible — **piti·ful·ly** *adv*

pit·tance \'pit⁰ns\ *n* : small portion or amount

pi·tu·i·tary \pə'tüə,terē, -'tyü-\ *adj* : relating to or being a small gland attached to the brain

pity \'pitē\ *n, pl* **pit·ies 1** : sympathetic sorrow **2** : something to be regretted ∼ *vb* **pit·ied; pity·ing** : feel pity for — **piti·less** *adj* — **piti·less·ly** *adv*

piv·ot \'pivət\ *n* : fixed pin on which something turns ∼ *vb* : turn on or as if on a pivot — **piv·ot·al** *adj*

pix·ie, pixy \'piksē\ *n, pl* **pix·ies** : mischievous sprite

piz·za \'pētsə\ *n* : thin pie of bread dough spread with a spiced mixture (as of tomatoes, cheese, and meat)

piz·zazz, piz·zazz \pə'zaz\ *n* : glamour

piz·ze·ria \,pētsə'rēə\ *n* : pizza restaurant

plac·ard \'plakərd, -,ärd\ *n* : poster ∼ *vb* : display placards in or on

pla·cate \'plā,kāt, 'plak,āt\ *vb* **-cat·ed; -cat·ing** : appease — **pla·ca·ble** \'plakəbəl, 'plākə-\ *adj*

place \'plās\ *n* **1** : space or room **2** : indefinite area **3** : a particular building, locality, area, or part **4** : relative position in a scale or sequence **5** : seat **6** : job ∼ *vb* **placed; plac·ing 1** : put in a place **2** : identify — **place·ment** *n*

pla·ce·bo \plə'sēbō\ *n, pl* **-bos** : something inactive prescribed as a remedy for its psychological effect

pla·cen·ta \plə'sentə\ *n, pl* **-tas** *or* **-tae** \-,ē\ : structure in a uterus by which a fetus is nourished — **pla·cen·tal** \-'sent⁰l\ *adj*

plac·id \'plasəd\ *adj* : undisturbed or peaceful — **pla·cid·i·ty** \pla'sidətē\ *n* — **plac·id·ly** *adv*

pla·gia·rize \'plājə,rīz\ *vb* **-rized; -riz·ing** : use (words or ideas) of another as if your own — **pla·gia·rism** \-,rizəm\ *n* — **pla·gia·rist** \-rist\ *n*

plague \'plāg\ *n* **1** : disastrous evil **2** : destructive contagious bacterial disease ∼ *vb* **plagued; plagu·ing 1** : afflict with disease or disaster **2** : harass

plaid \'plad\ *n* : woolen fabric with a pattern of crossing stripes or the pattern itself — **plaid** *adj*

plain \'plān\ *n* : expanse of relatively level treeless country ∼ *adj* **1** : lacking ornament **2** : not concealed or disguised **3** : easily understood **4** : frank **5** : not fancy or pretty — **plain·ly** *adv* — **plain·ness** \'plānnəs\ *n*

plain·tiff \'plāntəf\ *n* : complaining party in a lawsuit

plain·tive \'plāntiv\ *adj* : expressive of suffering or woe — **plain·tive·ly** *adv*

plait \'plāt, 'plat\ *n* **1** : pleat **2** : braid of hair or straw — **plait** *vb*

plan \'plan\ *n* **1** : drawing or diagram **2** : method for accomplishing something ∼ *vb* **-nn- 1** : form a plan of **2** : intend — **plan·less** *adj* — **plan·ner** *n*

¹**plane** \'plān\ *vb* **planed; plan·ing** : smooth or level off with a plane ∼ *n* : smoothing or shaping tool — **plan·er** *n*

²**plane** *n* **1** : level surface **2** : level of existence, consciousness, or development **3** : airplane ∼ *adj* **1** : flat **2** : dealing with flat surfaces or figures

plan·et \'planət\ *n* : celestial body that revolves around the sun — **plan·e·tary** \-ə,terē\ *adj*

plan·e·tar·i·um \,planə'terēəm\ *n, pl* **-iums** *or* **-ia** \-ēə\ : building or room housing a device to project images of celestial bodies

plank \'plaŋk\ *n* **1** : heavy thick board

2 : article in the platform of a political party — **plank·ing** n

plank·ton \'plaŋktən\ n : tiny aquatic animal and plant life — **plank·ton·ic** \plaŋk'tänik\ adj

plant \'plant\ vb **1** : set in the ground to grow **2** : place firmly or forcibly ~ n **1** : living thing without sense organs that cannot move about **2** : land, buildings, and machinery used esp. in manufacture

¹**plan·tain** \'plant°n\ n : short-stemmed herb with tiny greenish flowers

²**plantain** n : banana plant with starchy greenish fruit

plan·ta·tion \plan'tāshən\ n : agricultural estate usu. worked by resident laborers

plant·er \'plantər\ n **1** : plantation owner **2** : plant container

plaque \'plak\ n **1** : commemorative tablet **2** : film layer on a tooth

plas·ma \'plazmə\ n **1** : watery part of blood **2** : highly ionized gas — **plas·mat·ic** \plaz'matik\ adj

plasma TV n : television screen in which cells of plasma emit light upon receiving an electric current

plas·ter \'plastər\ n **1** : medicated dressing **2** : hardening paste for coating walls and ceilings ~ vb : cover with plaster — **plas·ter·er** n

plas·tic \'plastik\ adj : capable of being molded ~ n : material that can be formed into rigid objects, films, or filaments — **plas·tic·i·ty** \plas'tisətē\ n

plate \'plāt\ n **1** : flat thin piece **2** : plated metalware **3** : shallow usu. circular dish **4** : denture or the part of it that fits to the mouth **5** : something printed from an engraving ~ vb **plat·ed; plat·ing** : overlay with metal — **plat·ing** n

pla·teau \pla'tō\ n, pl **-teaus** or **-teaux** \-'tōz\ : large level area of high land

plat·form \'plat,form\ n **1** : raised flooring or stage **2** : declaration of principles for a political party

plat·i·num \'plat°nəm\ n : heavy grayish-white metallic chemical element

plat·i·tude \'platə,tüd, -,tyüd\ n : trite remark — **plat·i·tu·di·nous** \,platə-'tüd°nəs, -'tyüd-\ adj

pla·toon \plə'tün\ n : small military unit

platoon sergeant n : noncommissioned officer in the army ranking below a first sergeant

plat·ter \'platər\ n : large serving plate

platy·pus \'platipəs\ n : small aquatic egg-laying mammal

plau·dit \'plodət\ n : act of applause

plau·si·ble \'plozəbəl\ adj : reasonable or believeable — **plau·si·bil·i·ty** \,plozə'bilətē\ n — **plau·si·bly** \-blē\ adv

play \'plā\ n **1** : action in a game **2** : recreational activity **3** : light or fitful movement **4** : free movement **5** : stage representation of a drama ~ vb **1** : engage in recreation **2** : move or toy with aimlessly **3** : perform music **4** : act in a drama — **play·act·ing** n — **play·er** n — **play·ful** \-fəl\ adj — **play·ful·ly** adv — **play·ful·ness** n — **play·pen** n — **play·suit** n — **play·thing** n

play·ground n : place for children to play

play·house n **1** : theater **2** : small house for children to play in

playing card n : one of a set of 24 to 78 cards marked to show its rank and suit and used to play a game of cards

play·mate n : companion in play

play-off n : contest or series of contests to determine a champion

play·wright \-,rīt\ n : writer of plays

pla·za \'plazə, 'pläz-\ n **1** : public square **2** : shopping mall

plea \'plē\ n **1** : defendant's answer to charges **2** : urgent request

plead \'plēd\ vb **pleaded** \'plēdəd\ or **pled** \'pled\; **plead·ing 1** : argue for or against in court **2** : answer to a charge or indictment **3** : appeal earnestly — **plead·er** n

pleas·ant \'plez°nt\ adj **1** : giving pleasure **2** : marked by pleasing behavior or appearance — **pleas·ant·ly** adv — **pleas·ant·ness** n

pleas·ant·ries \-°ntrēz\ n pl : pleasant and casual conversation

please \'plēz\ vb **pleased; pleas·ing 1** : give pleasure or satisfaction to **2** : desire or intend

pleas·ing \'plēziŋ\ adj : giving pleasure — **pleas·ing·ly** adv

plea·sur·able \'plezhərəbəl\ adj : pleasant — **plea·sur·ably** \-blē\ adv

plea·sure \'plezhər\ n **1** : desire or inclination **2** : enjoyment **3** : source of delight

pleat \'plēt\ vb : arrange in pleats ～ n : fold in cloth

ple·be·ian \pli'bēən\ n : one of the common people ～ adj : ordinary

pledge \'plej\ n 1 : something given as security 2 : promise or vow ～ vb pledged; pledg·ing 1 : offer as or bind by a pledge 2 : promise

ple·na·ry \'plēnərē, 'plen-\ adj : full

pleni·po·ten·tia·ry \plenəpə'tenchərē, -'tenchē,erē\ n : diplomatic agent having full authority — **plenipotentiary** adj

plen·i·tude \'plenə,tüd, -,tyüd\ n 1 : completeness 2 : abundance

plen·te·ous \'plentēəs\ adj : existing in plenty

plen·ty \'plentē\ n : more than adequate number or amount — **plen·ti·ful** \'plentifəl\ adj — **plen·ti·ful·ly** adv

pleth·o·ra \'plethərə\ n : excess

pleu·ri·sy \'plúrəsē\ n : inflammation of the chest membrane

pli·able \'plīəbəl\ adj : flexible

pli·ant \'plīənt\ adj : flexible — **pli·an·cy** \-ənsē\ n

pli·ers \'plīərz\ n pl : pinching or gripping tool

¹**plight** \'plīt\ vb : pledge

²**plight** n : bad state

plod \'pläd\ vb -dd- 1 : walk heavily or slowly 2 : work laboriously and monotonously — **plod·der** n — **plod·ding·ly** \-iŋlē\ adv

plot \'plät\ n 1 : small area of ground 2 : ground plan 3 : main story development (as of a book or movie) 4 : secret plan for doing something ～ vb -tt- 1 : make a plot or plan of 2 : plan or contrive — **plot·ter** n

plo·ver \'pləvər, 'plōvər\ n, pl -ver or -vers : shorebird related to the sandpiper

plow, plough \'plaú\ n 1 : tool used to turn soil 2 : device for pushing material aside ～ vb 1 : break up with a plow 2 : cleave or move through like a plow — **plow·man** \-mən, -,man\ n

plow·share \-,sher\ n : plow part that cuts the earth

ploy \' plói\ n : clever maneuver

pluck \'plək\ vb 1 : pull off or out 2 : tug or twitch ～ n 1 : act or instance of plucking 2 : spirit or courage

plucky \'pləkē\ adj pluck·i·er; -est : courageous or spirited

plug \'pləg\ n 1 : something for seal-

ing an opening 2 : electrical connector at the end of a cord 3 : piece of favorable publicity ～ vb -gg- 1 : stop or make tight or secure by inserting a plug 2 : publicize

plum \'pləm\ n 1 : smooth-skinned juicy fruit 2 : fine reward

plum·age \'plümij\ n : feathers of a bird — **plum·aged** \-mijd\ adj

plumb \'pləm\ n : weight on the end of a line (**plumb line**) to show vertical direction ～ adv 1 : vertically 2 : completely ～ vb : sound or test with a plumb ～ adj : vertical

plumb·er \'pləmər\ n : one who repairs usu. water pipes and fixtures

plumb·ing \'pləmiŋ\ n : system of water pipes in a building

plume \'plüm\ n : large, conspicuous, or showy feather ～ vb plumed; plum·ing 1 : provide or deck with feathers 2 : indulge in pride — **plumed** \'plümd\ adj

plum·met \'pləmət\ vb : drop straight down

¹**plump** \'pləmp\ vb : drop suddenly or heavily ～ adv 1 : straight down 2 : in a direct manner

²**plump** adj : having a full rounded form — **plump·ness** n

plun·der \'pləndər\ vb : rob or take goods by force (as in war) ～ n : something taken in plundering — **plun·der·er** n

plunge \'plənj\ vb plunged; plung·ing 1 : thrust or drive with force 2 : leap or dive into water 3 : begin an action suddenly 4 : dip or move suddenly forward or down ～ n : act or instance of plunging — **plung·er** n

plu·ral \'plúrəl\ adj : relating to a word form denoting more than one — **plural** n

plu·ral·i·ty \plú'ralətē\ n, pl -ties : greatest number of votes cast when not a majority

plu·ral·ize \'plúrə,līz\ vb -ized; -iz·ing : make plural — **plu·ral·i·za·tion** \,plúrələ'zāshən\ n

plus \'pləs\ prep : with the addition of ～ n 1 : sign + (**plus sign**) in mathematics to indicate addition 2 : added or positive quantity 3 : advantage ～ adj : being more or in addition ～ conj : and

plush \'pləsh\ n : fabric with a long pile ～ adj : luxurious — **plush·ly** adv — **plushy** adj — **plush·ness** n

plu·toc·ra·cy \plü'täkrəsē\ n, pl **-cies**
1 : government by the wealthy 2 : a
controlling class of the wealthy —
plu·to·crat \'plütə,krat\ n — **plu·to·crat·ic** \,plütə'kratik\ adj

plu·to·ni·um \plü'tōnēəm\ n : radioactive chemical element

¹**ply** \'plī\ n, pl **plies** : fold, thickness, or
strand of which something is made

²**ply** vb **plied; ply·ing** 1 : use or work at
2 : keep supplying something to 3
: travel regularly usu. by sea

ply·wood n : sheets of wood glued and
pressed together

pneu·mat·ic \nü'matik, nyü-\ adj 1
: moved by air pressure 2 : filled with
compressed air — **pneu·mat·i·cal·ly**
adv

pneu·mo·nia \nü'mōnyə, nyü-\ n
: inflammatory lung disease

¹**poach** \'pōch\ vb : cook in simmering
liquid

²**poach** vb : hunt or fish illegally —
poach·er n

pock \'päk\ n : small swelling on the
skin or its scar — **pock·mark** n —
pock·marked adj

pock·et \'päkət\ n 1 : small open bag
sewn into a garment 2 : container or
receptacle 3 : isolated area or group
~ vb : put in a pocket — **pock·et·ful**
\-,fúl\ n

pock·et·book n 1 : purse 2 : financial
resources

pock·et·knife n : knife with a folding
blade carried in the pocket

pod \'päd\ n 1 : dry fruit that splits
open when ripe 2 : compartment on a
ship or craft

po·di·a·try \pə'dīətrē, pō-\ n : branch
of medicine dealing with the foot —
po·di·a·trist \pə'dīətrist, pō-\ n

po·di·um \'pōdēəm\ n, pl **-diums** or
-dia \-ēə\ : dais

po·em \'pōəm\ n : composition in
verse

po·et \'pōət\ n : writer of poetry

po·et·ry \'pōətrē\ n 1 : metrical writing 2 : poems — **po·et·ic** \pō'etik\,
po·et·i·cal \-ikəl\ adj

po·grom \'pōgrəm, pə'gräm,
'pägrəm\ n : organized massacre

poi·gnant \'póinyənt\ adj 1 : emotionally painful 2 : deeply moving —
poi·gnan·cy \-nyənsē\ n

poin·set·tia \póin'setēə, -'setə\ n
: showy tropical American plant

point \'póint\ n 1 : individual often es-

sential detail 2 : purpose 3 : particular place, time, or stage 4 : sharp end
5 : projecting piece of land 6 : dot or
period 7 : division of the compass 8
: unit of counting ~ vb 1 : sharpen
2 : indicate direction by extending a
finger 3 : direct attention to 4 : aim
— **point·ed·ly** \-ədlē\ adv — **point·less** adj

point-blank adj 1 : so close to a target
that a missile goes straight to it
2 : direct — **point-blank** adv

point·er \'póintər\ n 1 : one that
points out 2 : large short-haired hunting dog 3 : hint or tip

poise \'póiz\ vb **poised; pois·ing**
: balance ~ n : self-possessed calmness

poi·son \'póiz³n\ n : chemical that can
injure or kill ~ vb 1 : injure or kill
with poison 2 : apply poison to 3
: affect destructively — **poi·son·er** n
— **poi·son·ous** \'póiz³nəs\ adj

poke \'pōk\ vb **poked; pok·ing** 1
: prod 2 : dawdle ~ n : quick thrust

¹**pok·er** \'pōkər\ n : rod for stirring a fire

²**poker** n : card game for gambling

po·lar \'pōlər\ adj : relating to a geographical or magnetic pole

po·lar·ize \'pōlə,rīz\ vb **-ized; -iz·ing**
1 : cause to have magnetic poles 2
: break up into opposing groups —
po·lar·i·za·tion \,pōlərə'zāshən\ n

¹**pole** \'pōl\ n : long slender piece of
wood or metal

²**pole** n 1 : either end of the earth's axis
2 : battery terminal 3 : either end of a
magnet

pole·cat \'pōl,kat\ n, pl **polecats** or
polecat 1 : European carnivorous
mammal 2 : skunk

po·lem·ics \pə'lemiks\ n sing or pl
: practice of disputation — **po·lem·i·cal** \-ikəl\ adj — **po·lem·i·cist**
\-əsist\ n

po·lice \pə'lēs\ n, pl **police** 1 : department of government that keeps public order and enforces the laws 2
: members of the police ~ vb **-liced;
-lic·ing** : regulate and keep in order
— **po·lice·man** \-mən\ n — **po·lice·wom·an** n

police officer n : member of the police

¹**pol·i·cy** \'päləsē\ n, pl **-cies** : course of
action selected to guide decisions

²**policy** n, pl **-cies** : insurance contract —
pol·i·cy·hold·er n

po·lio \'pōlē,ō\ *n* : poliomyelitis — **po·lio** *adj*

po·lio·my·eli·tis \-,mīə'lītəs\ *n* : acute virus disease of the spinal cord

pol·ish \'pälish\ *vb* **1** : make smooth and glossy **2** : develop or refine ~ *n* **1** : shiny surface **2** : refinement

po·lite \pə'līt\ *adj* -**lit·er**; -**est** : marked by courteous social conduct — **po·lite·ly** *adv* — **po·lite·ness** *n*

pol·i·tic \'pälə,tik\ *adj* : shrewdly tactful

politically correct *adj* : seeking to avoid offending members of a different group

pol·i·tics \'pälə,tiks\ *n sing or pl* : practice of government and managing of public affairs — **po·lit·i·cal** \pə'litikəl\ *adj* — **po·lit·i·cal·ly** *adv* — **pol·i·ti·cian** \,pälə'tishən\ *n*

pol·ka \'pōlkə\ *n* : lively couple dance — **polka** *vb*

pol·ka dot \'pōkə,dät\ *n* : one of a series of regular dots in a pattern

poll \'pōl\ *n* **1** : head **2** : place where votes are cast — usu. pl. **3** : a sampling of opinion ~ *vb* **1** : cut off **2** : receive or record votes **3** : question in a poll — **poll·ster** \-stər\ *n*

pol·len \'pälən\ *n* : spores of a seed plant

pol·li·na·tion \pälə'nāshən\ *n* : the carrying of pollen to fertilize the seed — **pol·li·nate** \'pälə,nāt\ *vb* — **pol·li·na·tor** \-ər\ *n*

pol·lute \pə'lüt\ *vb* -**lut·ed**; -**lut·ing** : contaminating with waste products — **pol·lut·ant** \-'lüt²nt\ *n* — **pol·lut·er** *n* — **pol·lu·tion** \-'lüshən\ *n*

pol·ly·wog, pol·li·wog \'pälē,wäg\ *n* : tadpole

po·lo \'pōlō\ *n* : game played by 2 teams on horseback using long-handled mallets to drive a wooden ball

pol·ter·geist \'pōltər,gīst\ *n* : mischievous ghost

pol·troon \päl'trün\ *n* : coward

poly·es·ter \'pälē,estər\ *n* : synthetic fiber

po·lyg·a·my \pə'ligəmē\ *n* : marriage to several spouses at the same time — **po·lyg·a·mist** \-mist\ *n* — **po·lyg·a·mous** \-məs\ *adj*

poly·gon \'päli,gän\ *n* : closed plane figure with straight sides

poly·mer \'päləmər\ *n* : chemical compound of molecules joined in long strings — **po·lym·er·i·za·tion** \pə-

,limərə'zāshən\ *n* — **po·lym·er·ize** \pə'limə,rīz\ *vb*

poly·tech·nic \,päli'teknik\ *adj* : relating to many technical arts or applied sciences

poly·the·ism \'pälithē,izəm\ *n* : worship of many gods — **poly·the·ist** \-,thēist\ *adj or n*

poly·un·sat·u·rat·ed \,päle,ən'sachə-,rātəd\ *adj* : having many double or triple bonds in a molecule

pome·gran·ate \'päm,granət, 'pämə-\ *n* : tropical reddish fruit with many seeds

pom·mel \'pəməl, 'päm-\ *n* **1** : knob on the hilt of a sword **2** : knob at the front of a saddle ~ \'pəməl\ *vb* -**meled** *or* -**melled**; -**mel·ing** *or* -**mel·ling** : pummel

pomp \'pämp\ *n* **1** : brilliant display **2** : ostentation

pomp·ous \'pämpəs\ *adj* : pretentiously dignified — **pom·pos·i·ty** \päm-'päsətē\ *n* — **pomp·ous·ly** *adv*

pon·cho \'pänchō\ *n, pl* -**chos** : blanketlike cloak

pond \'pänd\ *n* : small body of water

pon·der \'pändər\ *vb* : consider

pon·der·ous \'pändərəs\ *adj* **1** : very heavy **2** : clumsy **3** : oppressively dull

pon·tiff \'päntəf\ *n* : pope — **pon·tif·i·cal** \pän'tifikəl\ *adj*

pon·tif·i·cate \pän'tifə,kāt\ *vb* -**cat·ed**; -**cat·ing** : talk pompously

pon·toon \pän'tün\ *n* : flat-bottomed boat or float

po·ny \'pōnē\ *n, pl* -**nies** : small horse

po·ny·tail \-,tāl\ *n* : hair arrangement like the tail of a pony

poo·dle \'püd²l\ *n* : dog with a curly coat

¹**pool** \'pül\ *n* **1** : small body of water **2** : puddle

²**pool** *n* **1** : amount contributed by participants in a joint venture **2** : game of pocket billiards ~ *vb* : combine in a common fund

poor \'pùr, 'pōr\ *adj* **1** : lacking material possessions **2** : less than adequate **3** : arousing pity **4** : unfavorable — **poor·ly** *adv*

¹**pop** \'päp\ *vb* -**pp-** **1** : move suddenly **2** : burst with or make a sharp sound **3** : protrude ~ *n* **1** : sharp explosive sound **2** : flavored soft drink

²**pop** *adj* : popular

pop·corn \'päp,kòrn\ *n* : corn whose

kernels burst open into a light mass when heated

pope \'pōp\ *n, often cap* : head of the Roman Catholic Church

pop·lar \'päplər\ *n* : slender quick-growing tree

pop·lin \'päplən\ *n* : strong plain-woven fabric with crosswise ribs

pop·over \'päp͵ōvər\ *n* : hollow muffin made from egg-rich batter

pop·py \'päpē\ *n, pl* **-pies** : herb with showy flowers

pop·u·lace \'päpyələs\ *n* **1** : common people **2** : population

pop·u·lar \'päpyələr\ *adj* **1** : relating to the general public **2** : widely accepted **3** : commonly liked — **pop·u·lar·i·ty** \͵päpyə'larətē\ *n* — **pop·u·lar·ize** \'päpyələ͵rīz\ *vb* — **pop·u·lar·ly** \-lərlē\ *adv*

pop·u·late \'päpyə͵lāt\ *vb* **-lat·ed; -lat·ing** : inhabit or occupy

pop·u·la·tion \͵päpyə'lāshən\ *n* : people or number of people in an area

pop·u·list \'päpyəlist\ *n* : advocate of the rights of the common people — **pop·u·lism** \-͵lizəm\ *n*

pop·u·lous \'päpyələs\ *adj* : densely populated — **pop·u·lous·ness** *n*

por·ce·lain \'pōrsələn\ *n* : fine-grained ceramic ware

porch \'pōrch\ *n* : covered entrance

por·cu·pine \'pōrkyə͵pīn\ *n* : mammal with sharp quills

¹**pore** \'pōr\ *vb* **pored; por·ing** : read attentively

²**pore** *n* : tiny hole (as in the skin) — **pored** *adj*

pork \'pōrk\ *n* : pig meat

pork barrel *n* : government projects benefiting political patrons

por·nog·ra·phy \pōr'nägrəfē\ *n* : depiction of erotic behavior intended to cause sexual excitement — **por·no·graph·ic** \͵pōrnə'grafik\ *adj*

po·rous \'pōrəs\ *adj* : permeable to fluids — **po·ros·i·ty** \pə'räsətē\ *n*

por·poise \'pōrpəs\ *n* **1** : small whale with a blunt snout **2** : dolphin

por·ridge \'pōrij\ *n* : soft boiled cereal

por·rin·ger \'pōrənjər\ *n* : low one-handled metal bowl or cup

¹**port** \'pōrt\ *n* **1** : harbor **2** : city with a harbor

²**port** *n* **1** : inlet or outlet (as in an engine) for a fluid **2** : porthole

³**port** *n* : left side of a ship or airplane looking forward — **port** *adj*

⁴**port** *n* : sweet wine

por·ta·ble \'pōrtəbəl\ *adj* : capable of being carried — **portable** *n*

por·tage \'pōrtij, pōr'täzh\ *n* : carrying of boats overland between navigable bodies of water or the route where this is done — **portage** *vb*

por·tal \'pōrt³l\ *n* : entrance

por·tend \pōr'tend\ *vb* : give a warning of beforehand

por·tent \'pōr͵tent\ *n* : something that foreshadows a coming event — **por·ten·tous** \pōr'tentəs\ *adj*

por·ter \'pōrtər\ *n* : baggage carrier

por·ter·house \-͵haüs\ *n* : choice cut of steak

port·fo·lio \pōrt'fōlē͵ō\ *n, pl* **-lios** **1** : portable case for papers **2** : office or function of a diplomat **3** : investor's securities

port·hole \'pōrt͵hōl\ *n* : window in the side of a ship or aircraft

por·ti·co \'pōrti͵kō\ *n, pl* **-coes** or **-cos** : colonnade forming a porch

por·tion \'pōrshən\ *n* : part or share of a whole ～ *vb* : divide into or allot portions

port·ly \'pōrtlē\ *adj* **-li·er; -est** : somewhat stout

por·trait \'pōrtrət, -͵trāt\ *n* : picture of a person — **por·trait·ist** \-ist\ *n* — **por·trai·ture** \'pōrtrə͵chùr\ *n*

por·tray \pōr'trā\ *vb* **1** : make a picture of **2** : describe in words **3** : play the role of — **por·tray·al** *n*

por·tu·la·ca \͵pōrchə'lakə\ *n* : tropical herb with showy flowers

pose \'pōz\ *vb* **posed; pos·ing** **1** : assume a posture or attitude **2** : propose **3** : pretend to be what one is not ～ *n* **1** : sustained posture **2** : pretense — **pos·er** *n*

posh \'päsh\ *adj* : elegant

po·si·tion \pə'zishən\ *n* **1** : stand taken on a question **2** : place or location **3** : status **4** : job — **position** *vb*

pos·i·tive \'päzətiv\ *adj* **1** : definite **2** : confident **3** : relating to or being an adjective or adverb form that denotes no increase **4** : greater than zero **5** : having a deficiency of electrons **6** : affirmative — **pos·i·tive·ly** *adv* — **pos·i·tive·ness** *n*

pos·se \'päsē\ *n* : emergency assistants of a sheriff

pos·sess \pə'zes\ vb **1** : have as property or as a quality **2** : control — **pos·ses·sion** \-'zeshən\ n — **pos·ses·sor** \-'zesər\ n

pos·ses·sive \pə'zesiv\ adj **1** : relating to a grammatical case denoting ownership **2** : jealous — **possessive** n — **pos·ses·sive·ness** n

pos·si·ble \'päsəbəl\ adj **1** : that can be done **2** : potential — **pos·si·bil·i·ty** \‚päsə'bilətē\ n — **pos·si·bly** adv

pos·sum \'päsəm\ n : opossum

¹**post** \'pōst\ n : upright stake serving to support or mark ~ vb : put up or announce by a notice

²**post** vb **1** : mail **2** : inform

³**post** n **1** : sentry's station **2** : assigned task **3** : army camp ~ vb : station

post- prefix : after or subsequent to

post·age \'pōstij\ n : fee for mail

post·al \'pōstᵊl\ adj : relating to the mail

post·card n : card for mailing a message

post·date \‚pōst'dāt\ vb : assign a date to that is later than the actual date of execution

post·er \'pōstər\ n : large usu. printed notice

pos·te·ri·or \pō'stirēər, pä-\ adj **1** : later **2** : situated behind ~ n : buttocks

pos·ter·i·ty \pä'sterətē\ n : all future generations

post·haste \'pōst'hāst\ adv : speedily

post·hu·mous \'päschəməs\ adj : occurring after one's death — **post·hu·mous·ly** adv

post·man \'pōstmən, -‚man\ n : mail carrier

post·mark n : official mark on mail — **postmark** vb

post·mas·ter n : chief of a post office

post me·ri·di·em \'pōstmə'ridēəm, -ē‚em\ adj : being after noon

post·mor·tem \‚pōst'mortəm\ adj : occurring or done after death ~ n **1** : medical examination of a corpse **2** : analysis after an event

post office n : agency or building for mail service

post·op·er·a·tive \‚pōst'äpərətiv, -'äpə‚rāt-\ adj : following surgery

post·paid adv : with postage paid by the sender

post·par·tum \-'pärtəm\ adj : following childbirth — **postpartum** adv

post·pone \-'pōn\ vb -**poned**; -**pon·ing** : put off to a later time — **post·pone·ment** n

post·script \'pōst‚skript\ n : added note

pos·tu·lant \'päschələnt\ n : candidate for a religious order

pos·tu·late \'päschə‚lāt\ vb -**lat·ed**; -**lat·ing** : assume as true ~ n : assumption

pos·ture \'päschər\ n : bearing of the body ~ vb -**tured**; -**tur·ing** : strike a pose

po·sy \'pōzē\ n, pl -**sies** : flower or bunch of flowers

pot \'pät\ n : rounded container ~ vb -**tt**- : place in a pot — **pot·ful** n

po·ta·ble \'pōtəbəl\ adj : drinkable

pot·ash \'pät‚ash\ n : white chemical salt of potassium used esp. in agriculture

po·tas·si·um \pə'tasēəm\ n : silver-white metallic chemical element

po·ta·to \pə'tātō\ n, pl -**toes** : edible plant tuber

List of self-explanatory words with the prefix post-

postadolescent	postgraduation	postpuberty
postattack	postharvest	postrecession
postbaccalaureate	posthospital	postretirement
postbiblical	postimperial	postrevolutionary
postcollege	postinaugural	postseason
postcolonial	postindustrial	postsecondary
postelection	postinoculation	postsurgical
postexercise	postmarital	posttreatment
postflight	postmenopausal	posttrial
postgame	postnatal	postvaccination
postgraduate	postnuptial	postwar
	postproduction	

pot·bel·ly n : paunch — **pot·bel·lied** adj

po·tent \'pōt²nt\ adj : powerful or effective — **po·ten·cy** \-²nsē\ n

po·ten·tate \'pōt²n‚tāt\ n : powerful ruler

po·ten·tial \pə'tenchəl\ adj : capable of becoming actual ~ n 1 : something that can become actual 2 : degree of electrification with reference to a standard — **po·ten·ti·al·i·ty** \pə‚tenchē'alətē\ n — **po·ten·tial·ly** adv

poth·er \'päthər\ n : fuss

pot·hole \'pät‚hōl\ n : large hole in a road surface

po·tion \'pōshən\ n : liquid medicine or poison

pot·luck n : whatever food is available

pot·pour·ri \‚pōpu̇'rē\ n 1 : mix of flowers, herbs, and spices used for scent 2 : miscellaneous collection

pot·shot n 1 : casual or easy shot 2 : random critical remark

pot·ter \'pätər\ n : pottery maker

pot·tery \'pätərē\ n, pl **-ter·ies** : objects (as dishes) made from clay

pouch \'pau̇ch\ n 1 : small bag 2 : bodily sac

poul·tice \'pōltəs\ n : warm medicated dressing — **poultice** vb

poul·try \'pōltrē\ n : domesticated fowl

pounce \'pau̇ns\ vb **pounced; pounc·ing** : spring or swoop upon and seize

¹**pound** \'pau̇nd\ n 1 : unit of weight equal to 16 ounces 2 : monetary unit (as of the United Kingdom) — **pound·age** \-ij\ n

²**pound** n : shelter for stray animals

³**pound** vb 1 : crush by beating 2 : strike heavily 3 : drill 4 : move along heavily

pour \'pōr\ vb 1 : flow or supply esp. copiously 2 : rain hard

pout \'pau̇t\ vb : look sullen — **pout** n

pov·er·ty \'pävərtē\ n 1 : lack of money or possessions 2 : poor quality

pow·der \'pau̇dər\ n : dry material of fine particles ~ vb : sprinkle or cover with powder — **pow·dery** adj

pow·er \'pau̇ər\ n 1 : position of authority 2 : ability to act 3 : one that has power 4 : physical might 5 : force or energy used to do work ~

vb : supply with power — **pow·er·ful** \-fəl\ adj — **pow·er·ful·ly** adv — **pow·er·less** adj

pow·er·house n : dynamic or energetic person

pow·wow \'pau̇‚wau̇\ n : conference

pox \'päks\ n, pl **pox** or **pox·es** : disease marked by skin rash

prac·ti·ca·ble \'praktikəbəl\ adj : feasible — **prac·ti·ca·bil·i·ty** \‚praktikə'bilətē\ n

prac·ti·cal \'praktikəl\ adj 1 : relating to practice 2 : virtual 3 : capable of being put to use 4 : inclined to action as opposed to speculation — **prac·ti·cal·i·ty** \‚prakti'kalətē\ n — **prac·ti·cal·ly** \'praktiklē\ adv

prac·tice, prac·tise \'praktəs\ vb **-ticed** or **-tised; -tic·ing** or **-tis·ing** 1 : perform repeatedly to become proficient 2 : do or perform customarily 3 : be professionally engaged in ~ n 1 : actual performance 2 : habit 3 : exercise for proficiency 4 : exercise of a profession

prac·ti·tio·ner \prak'tishənər\ n : one who practices a profession

prag·ma·tism \'pragmə‚tizəm\ n : practical approach to problems — **prag·mat·ic** \prag'matik\ adj — **prag·mat·i·cal·ly** adv

prai·rie \'prerē\ n : broad grassy rolling tract of land

praise \'prāz\ vb **praised; prais·ing** 1 : express approval of 2 : glorify — **praise** n — **praise·wor·thy** adj

prance \'prans\ vb **pranced; pranc·ing** 1 : spring from the hind legs 2 : swagger — **prance** n — **pranc·er** n

prank \'praŋk\ n : playful or mischievous act — **prank·ster** \-stər\ n

prate \'prāt\ vb **prat·ed; prat·ing** : talk long and foolishly

prat·fall \'prat‚fȯl\ n : fall on the buttocks

prat·tle \'prat²l\ vb **-tled; -tling** : babble — **prattle** n

prawn \'prȯn\ n : shrimplike crustacean

pray \'prā\ vb 1 : entreat 2 : ask earnestly for something 3 : address God or a god

prayer \'prer\ n 1 : earnest request 2 : an addressing of God or a god 3 : words used in praying — **prayer·ful** adj — **prayer·ful·ly** adv

praying mantis n : mantis

pre- *prefix* : before, prior to, or in advance

preach \'prēch\ *vb* **1** : deliver a sermon **2** : advocate earnestly — **preach•er** *n* — **preach•ment** *n*

pre•am•ble \'prē,ambəl\ *n* : introduction

pre•can•cer•ous \,prē'kansərəs\ *adj* : likely to become cancerous

pre•car•i•ous \pri'karēəs\ *adj* : dangerously insecure — **pre•car•i•ous•ly** *adv* — **pre•car•i•ous•ness** *n*

pre•cau•tion \pri'kȯshən\ *n* : care taken beforehand — **pre•cau•tion•ary** \-shə,nerē\ *adj*

pre•cede \pri'sēd\ *vb* **-ced•ed; -ced•ing** : be, go, or come ahead of — **prec•e•dence** \'presədəns, pri'sēd'ns\ *n*

prec•e•dent \'presədənt\ *n* : something said or done earlier that serves as an example

pre•cept \'prē,sept\ *n* : rule of action or conduct

pre•cinct \'prē,siŋkt\ *n* **1** : district of a city **2** *pl* : vicinity

pre•cious \'preshəs\ *adj* **1** : of great value **2** : greatly cherished **3** : affected

prec•i•pice \'presəpəs\ *n* : steep cliff

pre•cip•i•tate \pri'sipə,tāt\ *vb* **-tat•ed; -tat•ing** **1** : cause to happen quickly or abruptly **2** : cause to separate out of a liquid **3** : fall as rain, snow, or hail ~ *n* : solid matter precipitated from a liquid ~ \-'sipətət, -ə,tāt\ *adj* : unduly hasty — **pre•cip•i•tate•ly** *adv* — **pre•cip•i•tate•ness** *n* — **pre•cip•i•tous** \pri'sipətəs\ *adj* — **pre•cip•i•tous•ly** *adv*

pre•cip•i•ta•tion \pri,sipə'tāshən\ *n* **1** : rash haste **2** : rain, snow, or hail

pré•cis \prā'sē\ *n, pl* **pré•cis** \-'sēz\ : concise summary of essentials

pre•cise \pri'sīs\ *adj* **1** : definite **2** : highly accurate — **pre•cise•ly** *adv* — **pre•cise•ness** *n*

pre•ci•sion \pri'sizhən\ *n* : quality or state of being precise

pre•clude \pri'klüd\ *vb* **-clud•ed; -clud•ing** : make impossible

pre•co•cious \pri'kōshəs\ *adj* : exceptionally advanced — **pre•co•cious•ly** *adv* — **pre•coc•i•ty** \pri'käsətē\ *n*

pre•cur•sor \pri'kərsər\ *n* : harbinger

pred•a•to•ry \'predə,tōrē\ *adj* : preying upon others — **pred•a•tor** \'predətər\ *n*

pre•de•ces•sor \'predə,sesər, 'prēd-\ *n* : a previous holder of a position

pre•des•tine \prē'destən\ *vb* : settle beforehand — **pre•des•ti•na•tion** \-,destə'nāshən\ *n*

pre•dic•a•ment \pri'dikəmənt\ *n* : difficult situation

pred•i•cate \'predikət\ *n* : part of a sentence that states something about the subject ~ \'predə,kāt\ *vb* **-cat•ed; -cat•ing** **1** : affirm **2** : establish — **pred•i•ca•tion** \,predə-'kāshən\ *n*

pre•dict \pri'dikt\ *vb* : declare in advance — **pre•dict•abil•i•ty** \-,diktə'bilətē\ *n* — **pre•dict•able** \-'diktəbəl\ *adj* — **pre•dict•ably** \-blē\ *adv* — **pre•dic•tion** \-'dikshən\ *n*

pre•di•lec•tion \,pred'l'ekshən, ,prēd-\ *n* : established preference

pre•dis•pose \,prēdis'pōz\ *vb* : cause to be favorable or susceptible to something beforehand — **pre•dis•po•si•tion** \,prē,dispə'zishən\ *n*

pre•dom•i•nate \pri'dämə,nāt\ *vb* : be

List of self-explanatory words with the prefix *pre-*

preadmission	prebreakfast	preconception
preadolescence	precalculus	preconcert
preadolescent	precancel	precondition
preadult	precancellation	preconstructed
preanesthetic	preclear	preconvention
prearrange	preclearance	precook
prearrangement	precollege	precool
preassembled	precolonial	precut
preassign	precombustion	predawn
prebattle	precompute	predefine
prebiblical	preconceive	predeparture

superior — **pre·dom·i·nance** \-nəns\ n — **pre·dom·i·nant** \-nənt\ adj — **pre·dom·i·nant·ly** adv

pre·em·i·nent \prē'emənənt\ adj : having highest rank — **pre·em·i·nence** \-nəns\ n — **pre·em·i·nent·ly** adv

pre·empt \prē'empt\ vb 1 : seize for oneself 2 : take the place of — **pre·emp·tion** \-'empshən\ n — **pre·emp·tive** \-'emptiv\ adj

preen \'prēn\ vb : dress or smooth up (as feathers)

pre·fab·ri·cat·ed \'prē'fabrə̩kātəd\ adj : manufactured for rapid assembly elsewhere — **pre·fab·ri·ca·tion** \prē-̩fabri'kāshən\ n

pref·ace \'prefəs\ n : introductory comments ~ vb -aced; -ac·ing : introduce with a preface — **pref·a·to·ry** \'prefə̩tōrē\ adj

pre·fect \'prē̩fekt\ n : chief officer or judge — **pre·fec·ture** \-̩fekchər\ n

pre·fer \pri'fər\ vb -rr- 1 : like better 2 : bring (as a charge) against a person — **pref·er·a·ble** \'prefərəbəl\ adj — **pref·er·a·bly** adv — **pref·er·ence** \-ərəns\ n — **pref·er·en·tial** \prefə-'renchəl\ adj

pre·fer·ment \pri'fərmənt\ n : promotion

pre·fig·ure \prē'figyər\ vb : foreshadow

¹**pre·fix** \'prē̩fiks, prē'fiks\ vb : place before

²**pre·fix** \'prē̩fiks\ n : affix at the beginning of a word

preg·nant \'pregnənt\ adj 1 : containing unborn young 2 : meaningful — **preg·nan·cy** \-nənsē\ n

pre·hen·sile \prē'hensəl, -̩sīl\ adj : adapted for grasping

pre·his·tor·ic \̩prēhis'tórik\, **pre·his·tor·i·cal** \-ikəl\ adj : relating to the period before written history

prej·u·dice \'prejədəs\ n 1 : damage esp. to one's rights 2 : unreasonable attitude for or against something ~ vb -diced; -dic·ing 1 : damage 2 : cause to have prejudice — **prej·u·di·cial** \̩prejə'dishəl\ adj

prel·ate \'prelət\ n : clergy member of high rank — **prel·a·cy** \-əsē\ n

pre·lim·i·nary \pri'limə̩nerē\ n, pl -nar·ies : something that precedes or introduces — **preliminary** adj

pre·lude \'prel̩üd, -̩yüd; 'prā̩lüd\ n : introductory performance, event, or musical piece

pre·ma·ture \̩prēmə'tủər, -'tyủr, -'chủr\ adj : coming before the usual or proper time — **pre·ma·ture·ly** adv

pre·med·i·tate \pri'medə̩tāt\ vb : plan beforehand — **pre·med·i·ta·tion** \-̩medə'tāshən\ n

pre·mier \pri'mir, -'myir; 'prēmēər\ adj : first in rank or importance ~ n : prime minister — **pre·mier·ship** n

pre·miere \pri'myer, -'mir\ n : 1st performance ~ vb -miered; -mier·ing : give a 1st performance of

prem·ise \'preməs\ n 1 : statement made or implied as a basis of argument 2 pl : piece of land with the structures on it

pre·mi·um \'prēmēəm\ n 1 : bonus 2 : sum over the stated value 3 : sum paid for insurance 4 : high value

pre·mo·ni·tion \̩prēmə'nishən, ̩premə-\ n : feeling that something is about to happen — **pre·mon·i·to·ry** \pri'mänə̩tōrē\ adj

pre·oc·cu·pied \prē'äkyə̩pīd\ adj : lost in thought

pre·oc·cu·py \-̩pī\ vb : occupy the attention of — **pre·oc·cu·pa·tion** \prē-̩äkyə'pāshən\ n

---

predesignate	prefight	premarital
predetermine	preform	premenopausal
predischarge	pregame	premenstrual
predrill	preheat	premix
preelection	preinaugural	premodern
preelectric	preindustrial	premodify
preemployment	preinterview	premoisten
preestablish	prejudge	premold
preexist	prekindergarten	prenatal
preexistence	prelaunch	prenotification
preexistent	prelife	prenotify

pre•pare \pri'par\ *vb* **-pared; -par•ing**
1 : make or get ready often beforehand
2 : put together or compound — **prep-
a•ra•tion** \,prepə'rāshən\ *n* — **pre-
pa•ra•to•ry** \pri'parə,tōrē\ *adj* —
pre•pared•ness \-'parədnəs\ *n*

pre•pon•der•ant \pri'pändərənt\ *adj*
: having great weight, power, importance, or numbers — **pre•pon•der-
ance** \-rəns\ *n* — **pre•pon•der•ant-
ly** *adv*

prep•o•si•tion \,prepə'zishən\ *n* : word
that combines with a noun or pronoun
to form a phrase — **prep•o•si•tion•al**
\-'zishənəl\ *adj*

pre•pos•sess•ing \,prēpə'zesiŋ\ *adj*
: tending to create a favorable impression

pre•pos•ter•ous \pri'pästərəs\ *adj*
: absurd

pre•req•ui•site \prē'rekwəzət\ *n*
: something required beforehand —
prerequisite *adj*

pre•rog•a•tive \pri'rägətiv\ *n* : special
right or power

pre•sage \'presij, pri'sāj\ *vb* **-saged;**
-sag•ing 1 : give a warning of **2**
: predict — **pres•age** \'presij\ *n*

pres•by•ter \'prezbətər\ *n* : priest or
minister

pre•science \'prēshəns, 'presh-\ *n*
: foreknowledge of events — **pre-
scient** \-ənt\ *adj*

pre•scribe \pri'skrīb\ *vb* **-scribed;**
-scrib•ing 1 : lay down as a guide **2**
: direct the use of as a remedy

pre•scrip•tion \pri'skripshən\ *n*
: written direction for the preparation
and use of a medicine or the medicine
prescribed

pres•ence \'prezəns\ *n* **1** : fact or condition of being present **2** : appearance or bearing

¹pres•ent \'prezᵊnt\ *n* : gift

²pre•sent \pri'zent\ *vb* **1** : introduce **2**
: bring before the public **3** : make a
gift to or of **4** : bring before a court
for inquiry — **pre•sent•able** *adj* —
pre•sen•ta•tion \,prē,zen'tāshən,
,prezᵊn-\ *n* — **pre•sent•ment** \pri-
'zentmənt\ *n*

³pres•ent \'prezᵊnt\ *adj* : now existing,
in progress, or attending ∼ *n* : present time

pre•sen•ti•ment \pri'zentəmənt\ *n*
: premonition

pres•ent•ly \'prezᵊntlē\ *adv* **1** : soon
2 : now

present participle *n* : participle that
typically expresses present action

pre•serve \pri'zərv\ *vb* **-served; -serv-
ing 1** : keep safe from danger or
spoilage **2** : maintain ∼ *n* **1** : preserved fruit — often in pl. **2** : area for
protection of natural resources —
pres•er•va•tion \,prezər'vāshən\ *n*
— **pre•ser•va•tive** \pri'zərvativ\ *adj*
or n — **pre•serv•er** \-'zərvər\ *n*

pre•side \pri'zīd\ *vb* **-sid•ed; -sid•ing**
1 : act as chairman **2** : exercise control

pres•i•dent \'prezədənt\ *n* **1** : one
chosen to preside **2** : chief official (as
of a company or nation) — **pres•i-
den•cy** \-ənsē\ *n* — **pres•i•den•tial**
\,prezə'denchəl\ *adj*

press \'pres\ *n* **1** : crowded condition
2 : machine or device for exerting
pressure and esp. for printing **3**
: pressure **4** : printing or publishing
establishment **5** : news media and
esp. newspapers ∼ *vb* **1** : lie against
and exert pressure on **2** : smooth with
an iron or squeeze with something
heavy **3** : urge **4** : crowd **5** : force
one's way — **press•er** *n*

press•ing *adj* : urgent

pres•sure \'preshər\ *n* **1** : burden of
distress or urgent business **2** : direct

prenuptial	prepubertal	presale
preopening	prepublication	preschool
preoperational	prepunch	preseason
preoperative	prepurchase	preselect
preordain	prerecorded	preset
prepackage	preregister	preshrink
prepay	preregistration	preshrunk
preplan	prerehearsal	presoak
preprocess	prerelease	presort
preproduction	preretirement	prestamp
preprofessional	prerevolutionary	presterilize
preprogram	prerinse	prestrike

application of force — **pressure** vb — **pres·sur·i·za·tion** \ˌpreshərə-ˈzāshən\ n — **pres·sur·ize** \ˌ ˌīz\ vb

pres·ti·dig·i·ta·tion \ˌprestəˌdijə-ˈtāshən\ n : sleight of hand

pres·tige \presˈtēzh, -ˈtēj\ n : estimation in the eyes of people — **pres·ti·gious** \-ˈtijəs\ adj

pres·to \ˈprestō\ adv or adj : quickly

pre·sume \priˈzüm\ vb **-sumed; -sum·ing** 1 : assume authority without right to do so 2 : take for granted — **pre·sum·able** \-ˈzüməbəl\ adj — **pre·sum·ably** \-blē\ adv

pre·sump·tion \priˈzəmpshən\ n 1 : presumptuous attitude or conduct 2 : belief supported by probability — **pre·sump·tive** \-tiv\ adj

pre·sump·tu·ous \priˈzəmpchəwəs\ adj : too bold or forward — **pre·sump·tu·ous·ly** adv

pre·sup·pose \ˌprēsəˈpōz\ vb : take for granted — **pre·sup·po·si·tion** \ˌprēˌsəpəˈzishən\ n

pre·tend \priˈtend\ vb 1 : act as if something is real or true when it is not 2 : act in a way that is false 3 : lay claim — **pre·tend·er** n

pre·tense, pre·tence \ˈprēˌtens, priˈtens\ n 1 : insincere effort 2 : deception — **pre·ten·sion** \priˈtenchən\ n

pre·ten·tious \priˈtenchəs\ adj : overly showy or self-important — **pre·ten·tious·ly** adv — **pre·ten·tious·ness** n

pre·ter·nat·u·ral \ˌprētərˈnachərəl\ adj 1 : exceeding what is natural 2 : inexplicable by ordinary means — **pre·ter·nat·u·ral·ly** adv

pre·text \ˈprēˌtekst\ n : falsely stated purpose

pret·ty \ˈpritē, ˈpurt-\ adj **-ti·er; -est** : pleasing by delicacy or attractiveness ~ adv : in some degree ~ vb **-tied; -ty·ing** : make pretty — **pret·ti·ly** \ˈpritɝlē\ adv — **pret·ti·ness** n

pret·zel \ˈpretsəl\ n : twisted thin bread that is glazed and salted

pre·vail \priˈvāl\ vb 1 : triumph 2 : urge successfully 3 : be frequent, widespread, or dominant

prev·a·lent \ˈprevələnt\ adj : widespread — **prev·a·lence** \-ləns\ n

pre·var·i·cate \priˈvarəˌkāt\ vb **-cat·ed; -cat·ing** : deviate from the truth — **pre·var·i·ca·tion** \-ˌvarə-ˈkāshən\ n — **pre·var·i·ca·tor** \-ˈvarə-ˌkātər\ n

pre·vent \priˈvent\ vb : keep from happening or acting — **pre·vent·able** adj — **pre·ven·tion** \-ˈvenchən\ n — **pre·ven·tive** \-ˈventiv\ adj or n — **pre·ven·ta·tive** \-ˈventətiv\ adj or n

pre·view \ˈprēˌvyü\ vb : view or show beforehand — **preview** n

pre·vi·ous \ˈprēvēəs\ adj : having gone, happened, or existed before — **pre·vi·ous·ly** adv

prey \ˈprā\ n, pl **preys** 1 : animal taken for food by another 2 : victim ~ vb 1 : seize and devour animals as prey 2 : have a harmful effect on

price \ˈprīs\ n : cost ~ vb **priced; pric·ing** : set a price on

price·less \-ləs\ adj : too precious to have a price

pric·ey \ˈprīsē\ adj **pric·i·er; -est** : expensive

prick \ˈprik\ n 1 : tear or small wound made by a point 2 : something sharp or pointed ~ vb : pierce slightly with a sharp point — **prick·er** n

prick·le \ˈprikəl\ n 1 : small sharp spine or thorn 2 : slight stinging pain ~ vb **-led; -ling** : tingle — **prick·ly** \ˈpriklē\ adj

pride \ˈprīd\ n : quality or state of being proud ~ vb **prid·ed; prid·ing** : indulge in pride — **pride·ful** adj

priest \ˈprēst\ n : person having authority to perform the sacred rites of a religion — **priest·hood** n — **priest·li·ness** \-lēnəs\ n — **priest·ly** adj

priest·ess \ˈprēstəs\ n : woman who is a priest

prig \ˈprig\ n : one who irritates by rigid or pointed observance of proprieties — **prig·gish** \-ish\ adj — **prig·gish·ly** adv

prim \ˈprim\ adj **-mm-** : stiffly formal and proper — **prim·ly** adv — **prim·ness** n

---

presurgery	pretournament	prewar
presweeten	pretreat	prewash
pretape	pretreatment	prewrap
pretelevision	pretrial	

pri·mal \\'prīməl\ *adj* **1** : original or primitive **2** : most important

pri·ma·ry \\'prī,merē, 'prīmərē\ *adj* : first in order of time, rank, or importance ~ *n*, *pl* **-ries** : preliminary election — **pri·mar·i·ly** \prī'merəlē\ *adv*

primary school *n* : elementary school

pri·mate *n* **1** \\'prī,māt, -mət\ : highest-ranking bishop **2** \-,māt\ : mammal of the group that includes humans and monkeys

prime \\'prīm\ *n* : earliest or best part or period ~ *adj* : standing first (as in significance or quality) ~ *vb* **primed;** **prim·ing 1** : fill or load **2** : lay a preparatory coating on

prime minister *n* : chief executive of a parliamentary government

¹prim·er \\'primər\ *n* : small introductory book

²prim·er \\'prīmər\ *n* **1** : device for igniting an explosive **2** : material for priming a surface

pri·me·val \prī'mēvəl\ *adj* : relating to the earliest ages

prim·i·tive \\'primətiv\ *adj* **1** : relating to or characteristic of an early stage of development **2** : of or relating to a tribal people or culture ~ *n* : one that is primitive — **prim·i·tive·ly** *adv* — **prim·i·tive·ness** *n*

pri·mor·di·al \prī'mòrdēəl\ *adj* : primeval

primp \\'primp\ *vb* : dress or groom in a finicky manner

prim·rose \\'prim,rōz\ *n* : low herb with clusters of showy flowers

prince \\'prins\ *n* **1** : ruler **2** : son of a king or queen — **prince·ly** *adj*

prin·cess \\'prinsəs, -,ses\ *n* **1** : daughter of a king or queen **2** : wife of a prince

prin·ci·pal \\'prinsəpəl\ *adj* : most important ~ *n* **1** : leading person **2** : head of a school **3** : sum lent at interest — **prin·ci·pal·ly** *adv*

prin·ci·pal·i·ty \,prinsə'palətē\ *n*, *pl* **-ties** : territory of a prince

prin·ci·ple \\'prinsəpəl\ *n* **1** : general or fundamental law **2** : rule or code of conduct or devotion to such a code

print \\'print\ *n* **1** : mark or impression made by pressure **2** : printed state or form **3** : printed matter **4** : copy made by printing **5** : cloth with a figure stamped on it ~ *vb* **1** : produce impressions of (as from type)

2 : write in letters like those of printer's type — **print·able** *adj* — **print·er** *n*

print·ing \\'printiŋ\ *n* : art or business of a printer

print·out \\'print,aût\ *n* : printed output produced by a computer — **print out** *vb*

¹pri·or \\'prīər\ *n* : head of a religious house — **pri·o·ry** \\'prīərē\ *n*

²prior *adj* : coming before in time, order, or importance — **pri·or·i·ty** \prī'òrətē\ *n*

pri·or·ess \\'prīərəs\ *n* : nun who is head of a religious house

prism \\'prizəm\ *n* : transparent 3-sided object that separates light into colors — **pris·mat·ic** \priz'matik\ *adj*

pris·on \\'priz²n\ *n* : place where criminals are confined

pris·on·er \\'priz²nər\ *n* : person on trial or in prison

pris·sy \\'prisē\ *adj* **-si·er; -est** : overly prim — **pris·si·ness** *n*

pris·tine \\'pris,tēn, pris'-\ *adj* : pure

pri·va·cy \\'prīvəsē\ *n*, *pl* **-cies** : quality or state of being apart from others

pri·vate \\'prīvət\ *adj* **1** : belonging to a particular individual or group **2** : carried on independently **3** : withdrawn from company or observation ~ *n* : enlisted person of the lowest rank in the marine corps or of one of the two lowest ranks in the army — **pri·vate·ly** *adv*

pri·va·teer \,prīvə'tir\ *n* : private ship armed to attack enemy ships and commerce

private first class *n* : enlisted person ranking next below a corporal in the army and next below a lance corporal in the marine corps

pri·va·tion \prī'vāshən\ *n* : lack of what is needed for existence

priv·i·lege \\'privəlij\ *n* : right granted as an advantage or favor — **priv·i·leged** *adj*

privy \\'privē\ *adj* **1** : private or secret **2** : having access to private or secret information ~ *n*, *pl* **priv·ies** : outdoor toilet — **priv·i·ly** \\'privəlē\ *adv*

¹prize \\'prīz\ *n* **1** : something offered or striven for in competition or in contests of chance **2** : something very desirable — **prize** *adj* — **prize·win·ner** *n* — **prize·win·ning** *adj*

²prize *vb* **prized; priz·ing** : value highly

³prize *vb* **prized; priz·ing** : pry

prize·fight n : professional boxing match — **prize·fight·er** n — **prize·fight·ing** n

¹**pro** \'prō\ n : favorable argument or person ~ adv : in favor

²**pro** n or adj : professional

prob·a·ble \'präbəbəl\ adj : seeming true or real or to have a good chance of happening — **prob·a·bil·i·ty** \ˌpräbə'bilətē\ n — **prob·a·bly** \'präbəblē\ adv

pro·bate \'prō.bāt\ n : judicial determination of the validity of a will ~ vb -bat·ed; -bat·ing : establish by probate

pro·ba·tion \prō'bāshən\ n 1 : period of testing and trial 2 : freedom for a convict during good behavior under supervision — **pro·ba·tion·ary** \-shə.nerē\ adj — **pro·ba·tion·er** n

probe \'prōb\ n 1 : slender instrument for examining a cavity 2 : investigation ~ vb probed; prob·ing 1 : examine with a probe 2 : investigate

pro·bi·ty \'prōbətē\ n : honest behavior

prob·lem \'präbləm\ n 1 : question to be solved 2 : source of perplexity or vexation — **problem** adj — **prob·lem·at·ic** \ˌpräblə'matik\ adj — **prob·lem·at·i·cal** \-ikəl\ adj

pro·bos·cis \prə'bäsəs\ n, pl -cis·es also -ci·des \-ə.dēz\ : long flexible snout

pro·ce·dure \prə'sējər\ n 1 : way of doing something 2 : series of steps in regular order — **pro·ce·dur·al** \-'sējərəl\ adj

pro·ceed \prō'sēd\ vb 1 : come forth 2 : go on in an orderly way 3 : begin and carry on an action 4 : advance

pro·ceed·ing n 1 : procedure 2 pl : something said or done or its official record

pro·ceeds \'prō.sēdz\ n pl : total money taken in

pro·cess \'präs.es, 'prōs-\ n, pl -cess·es \-.esəz, -əsəz, -ə.sēz\ 1 : something going on 2 : natural phenomenon marked by gradual changes 3 : series of actions or operations directed toward a result 4 : summons 5 : projecting part ~ vb : subject to a process — **pro·ces·sor** \-ər\ n

pro·ces·sion \prə'seshən\ n : group moving along in an orderly way

pro·ces·sion·al \-'seshənəl\ n : music for a procession

pro·claim \prō'klām\ vb : announce publicly or with conviction — **proc·la·ma·tion** \ˌpräklə'māshən\ n

pro·cliv·i·ty \prō'klivətē\ n, pl -ties : inclination

pro·cras·ti·nate \prə'krastə.nāt\ vb -nat·ed; -nat·ing : put something off until later — **pro·cras·ti·na·tion** \-ˌkrastə'nāshən\ n — **pro·cras·ti·na·tor** \-'krastə.nātər\ n

pro·cre·ate \'prōkrē.āt\ vb -at·ed; -at·ing : produce offspring — **pro·cre·ation** \ˌprōkrē'āshən\ n — **pro·cre·ative** \'prōkrē.ātiv\ adj — **pro·cre·ator** \-.ātər\ n

proc·tor \'präktər\ n : supervisor of students (as at an examination) — **proctor** vb

pro·cure \prə'kyùr\ vb -cured; -cur·ing : get possession of — **pro·cur·able** \-'kyùrəbəl\ adj — **pro·cure·ment** n — **pro·cur·er** n

prod \'präd\ vb -dd- : push with or as if with a pointed instrument — **prod** n

prod·i·gal \'prädigəl\ adj : recklessly extravagant or wasteful — **prodigal** n — **prod·i·gal·i·ty** \ˌprädə'galətē\ n

pro·di·gious \prə'dijəs\ adj : extraordinary in size or degree — **pro·di·gious·ly** adv

prod·i·gy \'prädəjē\ n, pl -gies : extraordinary person or thing

pro·duce \prə'düs, -'dyüs\ vb -duced; -duc·ing 1 : present to view 2 : give birth to 3 : bring into existence ~ \'präd.üs, 'prōd-, -ˌyüs\ n 1 : product 2 : agricultural products — **pro·duc·er** \prə'düsər, -'dyü-\ n

prod·uct \'präd.əkt\ n 1 : number resulting from multiplication 2 : something produced

pro·duc·tion \prə'dəkshən\ n : act, process, or result of producing — **pro·duc·tive** \-'dəktiv\ adj — **pro·duc·tive·ness** n — **pro·duc·tiv·i·ty** \ˌprō.dək'tivətē, ˌprä-\ n

prof \'präf\ n : professor

pro·fane \prō'fān\ vb -faned; -fan·ing : treat with irreverence ~ adj 1 : not concerned with religion 2 : serving to debase what is holy — **pro·fane·ly** adv — **pro·fane·ness** n — **pro·fan·i·ty** \prō'fanətē\ n

pro·fess \prə'fes\ vb 1 : declare openly 2 : confess one's faith in — **pro·fessed·ly** \-ədlē\ adv

pro·fes·sion \prə'feshən\ n 1 : open

declaration of belief **2** : occupation requiring specialized knowledge and academic training

pro·fes·sion·al \prə'feshənəl\ *adj* **1** : of, relating to, or engaged in a profession **2** : playing sport for pay — **professional** *n* — **pro·fes·sion·al·ism** *n* — **pro·fes·sion·al·ize** *vb* — **pro·fes·sion·al·ly** *adv*

pro·fes·sor \prə'fesər\ *n* : university or college teacher — **pro·fes·so·ri·al** \ˌprōfə'sōrēəl, ˌpräfə-\ *adj* — **pro·fes·sor·ship** *n*

prof·fer \'präfər\ *vb* **-fered; -fer·ing** : offer — **proffer** *n*

pro·fi·cient \prə'fishənt\ *adj* : very good at something — **pro·fi·cien·cy** \-ənsē\ *n* — **proficient** *n* — **pro·fi·cient·ly** *adv*

pro·file \'prō,fīl\ *n* : picture in outline — **profile** *vb*

prof·it \'präfət\ *n* **1** : valuable return **2** : excess of the selling price of goods over cost ~ *vb* : gain a profit — **prof·it·able** \'präfətəbəl\ *adj* — **prof·it·ably** *adv* — **prof·it·less** *adj*

prof·i·teer \ˌpräfə'tir\ *n* : one who makes an unreasonable profit — **prof·iteer** *vb*

prof·li·gate \'präfligət, -lə,gāt\ *adj* **1** : shamelessly immoral **2** : wildly extravagant — **prof·li·ga·cy** \-gəsē\ *n* — **profligate** *n* — **prof·li·gate·ly** *adv*

pro·found \prə'faůnd\ *adj* **1** : marked by intellectual depth or insight **2** : deeply felt — **pro·found·ly** *adv* — **pro·fun·di·ty** \-'fəndətē\ *n*

pro·fuse \prə'fyüs\ *adj* : pouring forth liberally — **pro·fuse·ly** *adv* — **pro·fu·sion** \-'fyüzhən\ *n*

pro·gen·i·tor \prō'jenətər\ *n* : direct ancestor

prog·e·ny \'präjənē\ *n, pl* **-nies** : offspring

pro·ges·ter·one \prō'jestə,rōn\ *n* : female hormone

prog·no·sis \präg'nōsəs\ *n, pl* **-no·ses** \-ˌsēz\ : prospect of recovery from disease

prog·nos·ti·cate \präg'nästə,kāt\ *vb* **-cat·ed; -cat·ing** : predict from signs or symptoms — **prog·nos·ti·ca·tion** \-ˌnästə'kāshən\ *n* — **prog·nos·ti·ca·tor** \-'nästə,kātər\ *n*

pro·gram \'prō,gram, -grəm\ *n* **1** : outline of the order to be pursued or the subjects included (as in a performance) **2** : plan of procedure **3**

: coded instructions for a computer ~ *vb* **-grammed** *or* **-gramed; -gram·ming** *or* **-gram·ing** **1** : enter in a program **2** : provide a computer with a program — **pro·gram·ma·bil·i·ty** \ˌprō,gramə'bilətē\ *n* — **pro·gram·ma·ble** \'prō,gram`əbəl\ *adj* — **pro·gram·mer** \'prō,gramər\ *n*

prog·ress \'prägrəs, -,res\ *n* : movement forward or to a better condition ~ \prə'gres\ *vb* **1** : move forward **2** : improve — **pro·gres·sive** \-'gresiv\ *adj* — **pro·gres·sive·ly** *adv*

pro·gres·sion \prə'greshən\ *n* **1** : act of progressing **2** : continuous connected series

pro·hib·it \prō'hibət\ *vb* : prevent by authority

pro·hi·bi·tion \ˌprōə'bishən\ *n* **1** : act of prohibiting **2** : legal restriction on sale or manufacture of alcoholic beverages — **pro·hi·bi·tion·ist** \-'bishənist\ *n* — **pro·hib·i·tive** \prō'hibətiv\ *adj* — **pro·hib·i·tive·ly** *adv* — **pro·hib·i·to·ry** \-'hibə,tōrē\ *adj*

proj·ect \'präj,ekt, -ikt\ *n* : planned undertaking ~ \prə'jekt\ *vb* **1** : design or plan **2** : protrude **3** : throw forward — **pro·jec·tion** \-'jekshən\ *n*

pro·jec·tile \prə'jektᵊl\ *n* : missile hurled by external force

pro·jec·tor \-'jektər\ *n* : device for projecting pictures on a screen

pro·le·tar·i·an \ˌprōlə'terēən\ *n* : member of the proletariat — **proletarian** *adj*

pro·le·tar·i·at \-ēət\ *n* : laboring class

pro·lif·er·ate \prə'lifə,rāt\ *vb* **-at·ed; -at·ing** : grow or increase in number rapidly — **pro·lif·er·a·tion** \-,lifə'rāshən\ *n*

pro·lif·ic \prə'lifik\ *adj* : producing abundantly — **pro·lif·i·cal·ly** *adv*

pro·logue \'prō,lòg, -,läg\ *n* : preface

pro·long \prə'lòŋ\ *vb* : lengthen in time or extent — **pro·lon·ga·tion** \ˌprō,lòŋ'gāshən\ *n*

prom \'präm\ *n* : formal school dance

prom·e·nade \ˌprämə'nād, -'näd\ *n* **1** : leisurely walk **2** : place for strolling — **promenade** *vb*

prom·i·nence \'prämənəns\ *n* **1** : quality, state, or fact of being readily noticeable or distinguished **2** : something that stands out — **prom·i-**

nent \-nənt\ *adj* — **prom·i·nent·ly** *adv*

pro·mis·cu·ous \prə'miskyəwəs\ *adj* : having a number of sexual partners — **prom·is·cu·i·ty** \,prämis'kyüətē, ,prō,mis-\ *n* — **pro·mis·cu·ous·ly** *adv* — **pro·mis·cu·ous·ness** *n*

prom·ise \'präməs\ *n* **1** : statement that one will or will not do something **2** : basis for expectation — **promise** *vb* — **prom·is·so·ry** \-ə,sōrē\ *adj*

prom·is·ing \'präməsiŋ\ *adj* : likely to succeed — **prom·is·ing·ly** *adv*

prom·on·to·ry \'prämən,tōrē\ *n, pl* **-ries** : point of land jutting into the sea

pro·mote \prə'mōt\ *vb* **-mot·ed; -mot·ing 1** : advance in rank **2** : contribute to the growth, development, or prosperity of — **pro·mot·er** *n* — **pro·mo·tion** \-'mōshən\ *n* — **pro·mo·tion·al** \-'mōshənəl\ *adj*

¹**prompt** \'prämpt\ *vb* **1** : incite **2** : give a cue to (an actor or singer) — **prompt·er** *n*

²**prompt** *adj* : ready and quick — **prompt·ly** *adv* — **prompt·ness** *n*

prone \'prōn\ *adj* **1** : having a tendency **2** : lying face downward — **prone·ness** \'prōnnəs\ *n*

prong \'prȯŋ\ *n* : sharp point of a fork — **pronged** \'prȯŋd\ *adj*

pro·noun \'prō,naun\ *n* : word used as a substitute for a noun

pro·nounce \prə'nauns\ *vb* **-nounced; -nounc·ing 1** : utter officially or as an opinion **2** : say or speak esp. correctly — **pro·nounce·able** *adj* — **pro·nounce·ment** *n* — **pro·nun·ci·a·tion** \-,nənsē'āshən\ *n*

pro·nounced \-'naunst\ *adj* : decided

¹**proof** \'prüf\ *n* **1** : evidence of a truth or fact **2** : trial impression or print

²**proof** *adj* : designed for or successful in resisting or repelling

proof·read *vb* : read and mark corrections in — **proof·read·er** *n*

prop \'präp\ *vb* **-pp- 1** : support **2** : sustain — **prop** *n*

pro·pa·gan·da \,präpə'gandə, ,prōpə-\ *n* : the spreading of ideas or information to further or damage a cause — **pro·pa·gan·dist** \-dist\ *n* — **pro·pa·gan·dize** \-,dīz\ *vb*

prop·a·gate \'präpə,gāt\ *vb* **-gat·ed; -gat·ing 1** : reproduce biologically **2** : cause to spread — **prop·a·ga·tion** \,präpə'gāshən\ *n*

pro·pane \'prō,pān\ *n* : heavy flammable gaseous fuel

pro·pel \prə'pel\ *vb* **-ll-** : drive forward — **pro·pel·lant, pro·pel·lent** *n or adj*

pro·pel·ler \prə'pelər\ *n* : hub with revolving blades that propels a craft

pro·pen·si·ty \prə'pensətē\ *n, pl* **-ties** : particular interest or inclination

prop·er \'präpər\ *adj* **1** : suitable or right **2** : limited to a specified thing **3** : correct **4** : strictly adhering to standards of social manners, dignity, or good taste — **prop·er·ly** *adv*

prop·er·ty \'präpərtē\ *n, pl* **-ties 1** : quality peculiar to an individual **2** : something owned **3** : piece of real estate **4** : ownership

proph·e·cy \'präfəsē\ *n, pl* **-cies** : prediction

proph·e·sy \-,sī\ *vb* **-sied; -sy·ing** : predict — **proph·e·si·er** \-,sīər\ *n*

proph·et \'präfət\ *n* : one who utters revelations or predicts events — **proph·et·ess** \-əs\ *n* — **pro·phet·ic** \prə'fetik\ *adj* — **pro·phet·i·cal·ly** *adv*

pro·pin·qui·ty \prə'piŋkwətē\ *n* : nearness

pro·pi·ti·ate \prō'pishē,āt\ *vb* **-at·ed; -at·ing** : gain or regain the favor of — **pro·pi·ti·a·tion** \-,pishē'āshən\ *n* — **pro·pi·tia·to·ry** \-'pishēə,tōrē\ *adj*

pro·pi·tious \prə'pishəs\ *adj* : favorable

pro·po·nent \prə'pōnənt\ *n* : one who argues in favor of something

pro·por·tion \prə'pōrshən\ *n* **1** : relation of one part to another or to the whole with respect to magnitude, quantity, or degree **2** : symmetry **3** : share ～ *vb* : adjust in size in relation to others — **pro·por·tion·al** \-shənəl\ *adj* — **pro·por·tion·al·ly** *adv* — **pro·por·tion·ate** \-shənət\ *adj* — **pro·por·tion·ate·ly** *adv*

pro·pose \prə'pōz\ *vb* **-posed; -pos·ing 1** : plan or intend **2** : make an offer of marriage **3** : present for consideration — **pro·pos·al** \-'pōzəl\ *n*

prop·o·si·tion \,präpə'zishən\ *n* : something proposed ～ *vb* : suggest sexual intercourse to

pro·pound \prə'paund\ *vb* : set forth for consideration

pro·pri·etor \prə'prīətər\ *n* : owner — **pro·pri·etary** \prə'prīə,terē\ *adj* —

pro·pri·etor·ship n — **pro·pri·etress** \-'prīətrəs\ n

pro·pri·ety \prə'prīətē\ n, pl **-eties** : standard of acceptability in social conduct

pro·pul·sion \prə'pəlshən\ n 1 : action of propelling 2 : driving power — **pro·pul·sive** \-siv\ adj

pro·sa·ic \prō'zāik\ adj : dull

pro·scribe \prō'skrīb\ vb **-scribed; -scrib·ing** : prohibit — **pro·scrip·tion** \-'skripshən\ n

prose \'prōz\ n : ordinary language

pros·e·cute \'präsi,kyüt\ vb **-cut·ed; -cut·ing** 1 : follow to the end 2 : seek legal punishment of — **pros·e·cu·tion** \,präsi'kyüshən\ n — **pros·e·cu·tor** \'präsi,kyütər\ n

pros·e·lyte \'präsə,līt\ n : new convert — **pros·e·ly·tize** \'präsələ,tīz\ vb

pros·pect \'präs,pekt\ n 1 : extensive view 2 : something awaited 3 : potential buyer ~ vb : look for mineral deposits — **pro·spec·tive** \prə'spektiv, 'präs,pek-\ adj — **pro·spec·tive·ly** adv — **pros·pec·tor** \-,pektər, 'pek-\ n

pro·spec·tus \prə'spektəs\ n : introductory description of an enterprise

pros·per \'präspər\ vb : thrive or succeed — **pros·per·ous** \-pərəs\ adj

pros·per·i·ty \präs'perətē\ n : economic well-being

pros·tate \'präs,tāt\ n : glandular body about the base of the male urethra — **prostate** adj

pros·the·sis \präs'thēsəs, 'prästhə-\ n, pl **-the·ses** \-,sēz\ : artificial replacement for a body part — **pros·thet·ic** \präs'thetik\ adj

pros·ti·tute \'prästə,tüt, -,tyüt\ vb **-tut·ed; -tut·ing** 1 : offer sexual activity for money 2 : put to corrupt or unworthy purposes ~ n : one who engages in sexual activities for money — **pros·ti·tu·tion** \,prästə'tüshən, -'tyü-\ n

pros·trate \'präs,trāt\ adj : stretched out with face on the ground ~ vb **-trat·ed; -trat·ing** 1 : fall or throw (oneself) into a prostrate position 2 : reduce to helplessness — **pros·tra·tion** \präs'trāshən\ n

pro·tag·o·nist \prō'tagənist\ n : main character in a drama or story

pro·tect \prə'tekt\ vb : shield from injury — **pro·tec·tor** \-tər\ n

pro·tec·tion \prə'tekshən\ n 1 : act of protecting 2 : one that protects — **pro·tec·tive** \-'tektiv\ adj

pro·tec·tor·ate \-tərət\ n : state dependent upon the authority of another state

pro·té·gé \'prōtə,zhā\ n : one under the care and protection of an influential person

pro·tein \'prō,tēn\ n : complex combination of amino acids present in living matter

pro·test \'prō,test\ n 1 : organized public demonstration of disapproval 2 : strong objection ~ \prə'test\ vb 1 : assert positively 2 : object strongly — **pro·tes·ta·tion** \,prätəs'tāshən\ n — **pro·test·er, pro·tes·tor** \'prō-,testər\ n

Prot·es·tant \'prätəstənt\ n : Christian not of a Catholic or Orthodox church — **Prot·es·tant·ism** \'prätəstənt-,izəm\ n

pro·to·col \'prōtə,kól\ n : diplomatic etiquette

pro·ton \'prō,tän\ n : positively charged atomic particle

pro·to·plasm \'prōtə,plazəm\ n : complex colloidal living substance of plant and animal cells — **pro·to·plas·mic** \,prōtə'plazmik\ adj

pro·to·type \'prōtə,tīp\ n : original model

pro·to·zo·an \,prōtə'zōən\ n : single-celled lower invertebrate animal

pro·tract \prō'trakt\ vb : prolong

pro·trac·tor \-'traktər\ n : instrument for drawing and measuring angles

pro·trude \prō'trüd\ vb **-trud·ed; -trud·ing** : stick out or cause to stick out — **pro·tru·sion** \-'trüzhən\ n

pro·tu·ber·ance \prō'tübərəns, -'tyü-\ n : something that protrudes — **pro·tu·ber·ant** adj

proud \'praúd\ adj 1 : having or showing excessive self-esteem 2 : highly pleased 3 : having proper self-respect 4 : glorious — **proud·ly** adv

prove \'prüv\ vb proved; proved or prov·en \'prüvən\; prov·ing 1 : test by experiment or by a standard 2 : establish the truth of by argument or evidence 3 : turn out esp. after trial or test — **prov·able** \'prüvəbəl\ adj

prov·en·der \'prävəndər\ n : dry food for domestic animals

prov·erb \'präv,ərb\ n : short meaningful popular saying — **pro·ver·bi·al** \prə'vərbēəl\ adj

pro·vide \prə'vīd\ vb **-vid·ed; -vid·ing** 1 : take measures beforehand 2 : make a stipulation 3 : supply what is needed — **pro·vid·er** n

pro·vid·ed conj : if

prov·i·dence \'prävədəns\ n 1 often cap : divine guidance 2 cap : God 3 : quality of being provident

prov·i·dent \-ədənt\ adj : making provision for the future 2 : thrifty — **prov·i·dent·ly** adv

prov·i·den·tial \‚prävə'denchəl\ adj 1 : relating to Providence 2 : opportune

pro·vid·ing conj : provided

prov·ince \'prävəns\ n 1 : administrative district 2 pl : all of a country outside the metropolis 3 : sphere

pro·vin·cial \prə'vinchəl\ adj 1 : relating to a province 2 : limited in outlook — **pro·vin·cial·ism** \-‚izəm\ n

pro·vi·sion \prə'vizhən\ n 1 : act of providing 2 : stock of food — usu. in pl. 3 : stipulation ∼ vb : supply with provisions

pro·vi·sion·al \-'vizhənəl\ adj : provided for a temporary need — **pro·vi·sion·al·ly** adv

pro·vi·so \prə'vīzō\ n, pl **-sos** or **-soes** : stipulation

pro·voke \prə'vōk\ vb **-voked; -vok·ing** 1 : incite to anger 2 : stir up on purpose — **prov·o·ca·tion** \‚prävə'kāshən\ n — **pro·voc·a·tive** \prə'väkətiv\ adj

prow \'prau̇\ n : bow of a ship

prow·ess \'prau̇əs\ n 1 : valor 2 : extraordinary ability

prowl \'prau̇l\ vb : roam about stealthily — prowl n — **prowl·er** n

prox·i·mate \'präksəmət\ adj : very near

prox·im·i·ty \präk'simətē\ n : nearness

proxy \'präksē\ n, pl **prox·ies** : authority to act for another — **proxy** adj

prude \'prüd\ n : one who shows extreme modesty — **prud·ery** \'prüdərē\ n — **prud·ish** \'prüdish\ adj

pru·dent \'prüd²nt\ adj 1 : shrewd 2 : cautious 3 : thrifty — **pru·dence** \-²ns\ n — **pru·den·tial** \prü'denchəl\ adj — **pru·dent·ly** adv

¹**prune** \'prün\ n : dried plum

²**prune** vb **pruned; prun·ing** : cut off unwanted parts

pru·ri·ent \'prürēənt\ adj : lewd — **pru·ri·ence** \-ēəns\ n

¹**pry** \'prī\ vb **pried; pry·ing** : look closely or inquisitively

²**pry** vb **pried; pry·ing** : raise, move, or pull apart with a lever

psalm \'säm, 'sälm\ n : sacred song or poem — **psalm·ist** n

pseu·do·nym \'süd²n‚im\ n : fictitious name — **pseu·don·y·mous** \sü'dänəməs\ adj

pso·ri·a·sis \sə'rīəsəs\ n : chronic skin disease

psy·che \'sīkē\ n : soul or mind

psy·chi·a·try \sə'kīətrē, sī-\ n : branch of medicine dealing with mental, emotional, and behavioral disorders — **psy·chi·at·ric** \‚sīkē'atrik\ adj — **psy·chi·a·trist** \sə'kīətrist, sī-\ n

psy·chic \'sīkik\ adj 1 : relating to the psyche 2 : sensitive to supernatural forces ∼ n : person sensitive to supernatural forces — **psy·chi·cal·ly** adv

psy·cho·anal·y·sis \‚sīkōə'naləsəs\ n : study of the normally hidden content of the mind esp. to resolve conflicts — **psy·cho·an·a·lyst** \-'an²list\ n — **psy·cho·an·a·lyt·ic** \-‚an²l'itik\ adj — **psy·cho·an·a·lyze** \-'an²l‚īz\ vb

psy·chol·o·gy \sī'käləjē\ n, pl **-gies** 1 : science of mind and behavior 2 : mental and behavioral aspect (as of an individual) — **psy·cho·log·i·cal** \‚sīkə'läjikəl\ adj — **psy·cho·log·i·cal·ly** adv — **psy·chol·o·gist** \sī'käləjist\ n

psy·cho·path \'sīkə‚path\ n : mentally ill or unstable person — **psy·cho·path·ic** \‚sīkə'pathik\ adj

psy·cho·sis \sī'kōsəs\ n, pl **-cho·ses** \-‚sēz\ : mental derangement (as paranoia) — **psy·chot·ic** \-'kätik\ adj or n

psy·cho·so·mat·ic \‚sīkəsə'matik\ adj : relating to bodily symptoms caused by mental or emotional disturbance

psy·cho·ther·a·py \‚sīkō'therəpē\ n : treatment of mental disorder by psychological means — **psy·cho·ther·a·pist** \-pist\ n

pto·maine \'tō‚mān\ n : bacterial decay product

pu·ber·ty \'pyübərtē\ n : time of sexual maturity

pu·bic \'pyübik\ adj : relating to the lower abdominal region

pub·lic \'pəblik\ adj 1 : relating to the

people as a whole **2** : civic **3** : not private **4** : open to all **5** : well-known ∼ n : people as a whole — **pub·lic·ly** adv

pub·li·ca·tion \,pəbləˈkāshən\ n **1** : process of publishing **2** : published work

pub·lic·i·ty \pəˈblisətē\ n **1** : news information given out to gain public attention **2** : public attention

pub·li·cize \ˈpəbləˌsīz\ vb **-cized; -ciz·ing** : bring to public attention — **pub·li·cist** \-sist\ n

pub·lish \ˈpəblish\ vb **1** : announce publicly **2** : reproduce for sale esp. by printing — **pub·lish·er** n

puck·er \ˈpəkər\ vb : pull together into folds or wrinkles ∼ n : wrinkle

pud·ding \ˈpu̇diŋ\ n : creamy dessert

pud·dle \ˈpəd²l\ n : very small pool of water

pudgy \ˈpəjē\ adj **pudg·i·er; -est** : short and plump

pu·er·ile \ˈpyu̇rəl\ adj : childish

puff \ˈpəf\ vb **1** : blow in short gusts **2** : pant **3** : enlarge ∼ n **1** : short discharge (as of air) **2** : slight swelling **3** : something light and fluffy — **puffy** adj

pug \ˈpəg\ n : small stocky dog

pu·gi·lism \ˈpyüjəˌlizəm\ n : boxing — **pu·gi·list** \-list\ n — **pu·gi·lis·tic** \ˌpyüjəˈlistik\ adj

pug·na·cious \ˌpəgˈnāshəs\ adj : prone to fighting — **pug·nac·i·ty** \-ˈnasətē\ n

puke \ˈpyük\ vb **puked; puk·ing** : vomit — **puke** n

pul·chri·tude \ˈpəlkrəˌtüd, -ˌtyüd\ n : beauty — **pul·chri·tu·di·nous** \ˌpəlkrəˈtüd²nəs, -ˈtyüd-\ adj

pull \ˈpu̇l\ vb **1** : exert force so as to draw (something) toward or out **2** : move **3** : stretch or tear ∼ n **1** : act of pulling **2** : influence **3** : device for pulling something — **pull·er** n

pul·let \ˈpu̇lət\ n : young hen

pul·ley \ˈpu̇lē\ n, pl **-leys** : wheel with a grooved rim

Pull·man \ˈpu̇lmən\ n : railroad car with berths

pull·over \ˈpu̇lˌōvər\ adj : put on by being pulled over the head — **pullover** n

pul·mo·nary \ˈpu̇lməˌnerē, ˈpəl-\ adj : relating to the lungs

pulp \ˈpəlp\ n **1** : soft part of a fruit or

vegetable **2** : soft moist mass (as of mashed wood) — **pulpy** adj

pul·pit \ˈpu̇lˌpit\ n : raised desk used in preaching

pul·sate \ˈpəlˌsāt\ vb **-sat·ed; -sat·ing** : expand and contract rhythmically — **pul·sa·tion** \ˌpəlˈsāshən\ n

pulse \ˈpəls\ n : arterial throbbing caused by heart contractions — **pulse** vb

pul·ver·ize \ˈpəlvəˌrīz\ vb **-ized; -iz·ing** : beat or grind into a powder

pu·ma \ˈpümə, ˈpyü-\ n : cougar

pum·ice \ˈpəməs\ n : light porous volcanic glass used in polishing

pum·mel \ˈpəməl\ vb **-meled; -mel·ing** : beat

¹**pump** \ˈpəmp\ n : device for moving or compressing fluids ∼ vb **1** : raise (as water) with a pump **2** : fill by means of a pump — with up **3** : move like a pump — **pump·er** n

²**pump** n : woman's low shoe

pum·per·nick·el \ˈpəmpərˌnikəl\ n : dark rye bread

pump·kin \ˈpəŋkən, ˈpəmpkən\ n : large usu. orange fruit of a vine related to the gourd

pun \ˈpən\ n : humorous use of a word in a way that suggests two or more interpretations — **pun** vb

¹**punch** \ˈpənch\ vb **1** : strike with the fist **2** : perforate with a punch ∼ n : quick blow with the fist — **punch·er** n

²**punch** n : tool for piercing or stamping

³**punch** n : mixed beverage often including fruit juice

punc·til·i·ous \ˌpəŋkˈtilēəs\ adj : marked by precise accordance with conventions

punc·tu·al \ˈpəŋkchəwəl\ adj : prompt — **punc·tu·al·i·ty** \ˌpəŋkchəˈwalətē\ n — **punc·tu·al·ly** adv

punc·tu·ate \ˈpəŋkchəˌwāt\ vb **-at·ed; -at·ing** : mark with punctuation

punc·tu·a·tion \ˌpəŋkchəˈwāshən\ n : standardized marks in written matter to clarify the meaning and separate parts

punc·ture \ˈpəŋkchər\ n : act or result of puncturing ∼ vb **-tured; -tur·ing** : make a hole in

pun·dit \ˈpəndət\ n **1** : learned person **2** : expert or critic

pun·gent \ˈpənjənt\ adj : having a sharp or stinging odor or taste — **pun·gen·cy** \-jənsē\ n — **pun·gent·ly** adv

pun·ish \ˈpənish\ vb : impose a penalty

on or for — **pun·ish·able** adj — **pun·ish·ment** n

pu·ni·tive \'pyünətiv\ adj : inflicting punishment

pun·kin var of PUMPKIN

¹**punt** \'pənt\ n : long narrow flat‑bottomed boat ～ vb : propel (a boat) by pushing with a pole

²**punt** vb : kick a ball dropped from the hands ～ n : act of punting a ball

pu·ny \'pyünē\ adj **-ni·er; -est** : slight in power or size

pup \'pəp\ n : young dog

pu·pa \'pyüpə\ n, pl **-pae** \-ˌpē, -ˌpī\ or **-pas** : insect (as a moth) when it is in a cocoon — **pu·pal** \-pəl\ adj

¹**pu·pil** \'pyüpəl\ n : young person in school

²**pupil** n : dark central opening of the iris of the eye

pup·pet \'pəpət\ n : small doll moved by hand or by strings — **pup·pe·teer** \ˌpəpə'tir\ n

pup·py \'pəpē\ n, pl **-pies** : young dog

pur·chase \'pərchəs\ vb **-chased; -chas·ing** : obtain in exchange for money ～ n 1 : act of purchasing 2 : something purchased 3 : secure grasp — **pur·chas·er** n

pure \'pyúr\ adj **pur·er; pur·est** : free of foreign matter, contamination, or corruption — **pure·ly** adv

pu·ree \pyù'rā, -'rē\ n : thick liquid mass of food — **puree** vb

pur·ga·to·ry \'pərgəˌtōrē\ n, pl **-ries** : intermediate state after death for purification by expiating sins — **pur·ga·tor·i·al** \ˌpərgə'tōrēəl\ adj

purge \'pərj\ vb **purged; purg·ing** 1 : purify esp. from sin 2 : have or cause emptying of the bowels 3 : get rid of ～ n 1 : act or result of purging 2 : something that purges — **pur·ga·tive** \'pərgətiv\ adj or n

pu·ri·fy \'pyúrəˌfī\ vb **-fied; -fy·ing** : make or become pure — **pu·ri·fi·ca·tion** \ˌpyúrəfə'kāshən\ n — **pu·ri·fi·er** \-ˌfīər\ n

Pu·rim \'púrim\ n : Jewish holiday celebrated in February or March in commemoration of the deliverance of the Jews from the massacre plotted by Haman

pu·ri·tan \'pyúrətʰn\ n : one who practices or preaches a very strict moral code — **pu·ri·tan·i·cal** \ˌpyúrə‑'tanikəl\ adj — **pu·ri·tan·i·cal·ly** adv

pu·ri·ty \'pyúrətē\ n : quality or state of being pure

purl \'pərl\ n : stitch in knitting ～ vb : knit in purl stitch

pur·loin \pər'lóin, 'pərˌlóin\ vb : steal

pur·ple \'pərpəl\ n : bluish red color — **pur·plish** \'pərpəlish\ adj

pur·port \pər'pōrt\ vb : convey outwardly as the meaning ～ \'pərˌpōrt\ n : meaning — **pur·port·ed·ly** \-ədlē\ adv

pur·pose \'pərpəs\ n 1 : something (as a result) aimed at 2 : resolution ～ vb **-posed; -pos·ing** : intend — **pur·pose·ful** \-fəl\ adj — **pur·pose·ful·ly** adv — **pur·pose·less** adj — **pur·pose·ly** adv

purr \'pər\ n : low murmur typical of a contented cat — **purr** vb

¹**purse** \'pərs\ n 1 : bag or pouch for money and small objects 2 : financial resource 3 : prize money

²**purse** vb **pursed; purs·ing** : pucker

pur·su·ance \pər'süəns\ n : act of carrying out or into effect

pur·su·ant to \-'süənt-\ prep : according to

pur·sue \pər'sü\ vb **-sued; -su·ing** 1 : follow in order to overtake 2 : seek to accomplish 3 : proceed along 4 : engage in — **pur·su·er** n

pur·suit \pər'süt\ n 1 : act of pursuing 2 : occupation

pur·vey \pər'vā\ vb **-veyed; -vey·ing** : supply (as provisions) usu. as a business — **pur·vey·or** \-ər\ n

pus \'pəs\ n : thick yellowish fluid (as in a boil)

push \'púsh\ vb 1 : press against to move forward 2 : urge on or provoke ～ n 1 : vigorous effort 2 : act of pushing — **push·cart** n — **push·er** \'púshər\ n

pushy \'púshē\ adj **push·i·er; -est** : objectionably aggressive

pu·sil·lan·i·mous \ˌpyüsə'lanəməs\ adj : cowardly

pussy \'púsē\ n, pl **puss·ies** : cat

pus·tule \'pəschül\ n : pus‑filled pimple

put \'pút\ vb **put; put·ting** 1 : bring to a specified position or condition 2 : subject to pain, suffering, or death 3 : impose or cause to exist 4 : express 5 : cause to be used or employed — **put off** vb : postpone or delay — **put out** vb : bother or inconvenience —

put up *vb* **1** : prepare for storage **2** : lodge **3** : contribute or pay — **put up with** : endure

pu·tre·fy \'pyütrə,fī\ *vb* **-fied; -fy·ing** : make or become putrid — **pu·tre·fac·tion** \,pyütrə'fakshən\ *n*

pu·trid \'pyütrəd\ *adj* : rotten — **pu·trid·i·ty** \pyü'tridətē\ *n*

put·ty \'pətē\ *n, pl* **-ties** : doughlike cement — **putty** *vb*

puz·zle \'pəzəl\ *vb* **-zled; -zling** **1** : confuse **2** : attempt to solve — with *out* or *over* ~ *n* : something that confuses or tests ingenuity — **puz·zle·ment** *n* — **puz·zler** \-ələr\ *n*

pyg·my \'pigmē\ *n, pl* **-mies** : dwarf — **pygmy** *adj*

py·lon \'pī,län, -lən\ *n* : tower or tall post

pyr·a·mid \'pirə,mid\ *n* : structure with a square base and 4 triangular sides meeting at a point

pyre \'pīr\ *n* : material heaped for a funeral fire

py·ro·ma·nia \,pīrō'mānēə\ *n* : irresistible impulse to start fires — **py·ro·ma·ni·ac** \-nē,ak\ *n*

py·ro·tech·nics \,pīrə'tekniks\ *n pl* : spectacular display (as of fireworks) — **py·ro·tech·nic** \-nik\ *adj*

Pyr·rhic \'pirik\ *adj* : achieved at excessive cost

py·thon \'pī,thän, -thən\ *n* : very large constricting snake

Q

q \'kyü\ *n, pl* **q's** *or* **qs** \'kyüz\ : 17th letter of the alphabet

¹**quack** \'kwak\ *vb* : make a cry like that of a duck — **quack** *n*

²**quack** *n* : one who pretends to have medical or healing skill — **quack** *adj* — **quack·ery** \-ərē\ *n*

quad·ran·gle \'kwäd,rangəl\ *n* : rectangular courtyard

quad·rant \'kwädrənt\ *n* : 1/4 of a circle

quad·ri·lat·er·al \,kwädrə'latərəl\ *n* : 4-sided polygon

qua·drille \kwä'dril, kə-\ *n* : square dance for 4 couples

quad·ru·ped \'kwädrə,ped\ *n* : animal having 4 feet

qua·dru·ple \kwä'drüpəl, -'drəp-; 'kwädrəp-\ *vb* **-pled; -pling** \-pliŋ\ : multiply by 4 ~ *adj* : being 4 times as great or as many

qua·dru·plet \kwä'drəplət, -'drüp-; 'kwädrəp-\ *n* : one of 4 offspring born at one birth

quaff \'kwäf, 'kwaf\ *vb* : drink deeply or repeatedly — **quaff** *n*

quag·mire \'kwag,mīr, 'kwäg-\ *n* : soft land or bog

qua·hog \'kō,hòg, 'kwò-, 'kwō-, -,häg\ *n* : thick-shelled clam

¹**quail** \'kwāl\ *n, pl* **quail** *or* **quails** : short-winged plump game bird

²**quail** *vb* : cower in fear

quaint \'kwānt\ *adj* : pleasingly old-fashioned or odd — **quaint·ly** *adv* — **quaint·ness** *n*

quake \'kwāk\ *vb* **quaked; quak·ing** : shake or tremble ~ *n* : earthquake

qual·i·fi·ca·tion \,kwäləfə'kāshən\ *n* **1** : limitation or stipulation **2** : special skill or experience for a job

qual·i·fy \'kwälə,fī\ *vb* **-fied; -fy·ing** **1** : modify or limit **2** : fit by skill or training for some purpose **3** : become eligible — **qual·i·fied** *adj* — **qual·i·fi·er** \-,fīər\ *n*

qual·i·ty \'kwälətē\ *n, pl* **-ties** **1** : peculiar and essential character, nature, or feature **2** : excellence or distinction

qualm \'kwäm, 'kwälm, 'kwòm\ *n* : sudden feeling of doubt or uneasiness

quan·da·ry \'kwändrē\ *n, pl* **-ries** : state of perplexity or doubt

quan·ti·ty \'kwäntətē\ *n, pl* **-ties** **1** : something that can be measured or numbered **2** : considerable amount

quan·tum theory \'kwäntəm-\ *n* : theory in physics that radiant energy (as light) is composed of separate packets of energy

quar·an·tine \'kwòrən,tēn\ *n* **1** : restraint on the movements of persons or goods to prevent the spread of pests or disease **2** : place or period of quarantine — **quarantine** *vb*

quar·rel \'kwȯrəl\ n : basis of conflict — **quarrel** vb — **quar·rel·some** \-səm\ adj

¹**quar·ry** \'kwȯrē\ n, pl **-ries** : prey

²**quarry** n, pl **-ries** : excavation for obtaining stone — **quarry** vb

quart \'kwȯrt\ n : unit of liquid measure equal to .95 liter or of dry measure equal to 1.10 liters

quar·ter \'kwȯrtər\ n 1 : 1/4 part 2 : 1/4 of a dollar 3 : city district 4 pl : place to live esp. for a time 5 : mercy ~ vb : divide into 4 equal parts

quar·ter·ly \'kwȯrtərlē\ adv or adj : at 3-month intervals ~ n, pl **-lies** : periodical published 4 times a year

quar·ter·mas·ter n 1 : ship's helmsman 2 : army supply officer

quar·tet \kwȯr'tet\ n 1 : music for 4 performers 2 : group of 4

quar·to \'kwȯrtō\ n, pl **-tos** : book printed on pages cut 4 from a sheet

quartz \'kwȯrts\ n : transparent crystalline mineral

quash \'kwäsh, 'kwȯsh\ vb 1 : set aside by judicial action 2 : suppress summarily and completely

qua·si \'kwā,zī, -sī; 'kwäzē, 'kwäs-; 'kwāzē\ adj : similar or nearly identical

qua·train \'kwä,trān\ n : unit of 4 lines of verse

qua·ver \'kwāvər\ vb : tremble or trill — **quaver** n

quay \'kē, 'kā, 'kwā\ n : wharf

quea·sy \'kwēzē\ adj **-si·er; -est** : nauseated — **quea·si·ly** \-zəlē\ adv — **quea·si·ness** \-zēnəs\ n

queen \'kwēn\ n 1 : wife or widow of a king 2 : female monarch 3 : woman of rank, power, or attractiveness 4 : fertile female of a social insect — **queen·ly** adj

queer \'kwir\ adj : differing from the usual or normal — **queer·ly** adv — **queer·ness** n

quell \'kwel\ vb : put down by force

quench \'kwench\ vb 1 : put out 2 : satisfy (a thirst) — **quench·able** adj — **quench·er** n

quer·u·lous \'kwerələs, -yələs\ adj : fretful or whining — **quer·u·lous·ly** adv — **quer·u·lous·ness** n

que·ry \'kwirē, 'kwer-\ n, pl **-ries** : question — **query** vb

quest \'kwest\ n or vb : search

ques·tion \'kweschən\ n 1 : something asked 2 : subject for debate 3 : dispute ~ vb : ask questions 2 : doubt or dispute 3 : subject to analysis — **ques·tion·er** n

ques·tion·able \'kweschənəbəl\ adj 1 : not certain 2 : of doubtful truth or morality — **ques·tion·ably** \-blē\ adv

question mark n : a punctuation mark ? used esp. at the end of a sentence to indicate a direct question

ques·tion·naire \,kweschə'nar\ n : set of questions

queue \'kyü\ n 1 : braid of hair 2 : a waiting line ~ vb **queued; queu·ing** or **queue·ing** : line up

quib·ble \'kwibəl\ n : minor objection — **quibble** vb — **quib·bler** n

quick \'kwik\ adj 1 : rapid 2 : alert or perceptive ~ n : sensitive area of living flesh — **quick** adv — **quick·ly** adv — **quick·ness** n

quick·en \'kwikən\ vb 1 : come to life 2 : increase in speed

quick·sand n : deep mass of sand and water

quick·sil·ver n : mercury

qui·es·cent \kwī'es³nt\ adj : being at rest — **qui·es·cence** \-əns\ n

qui·et \'kwīət\ adj 1 : marked by little motion or activity 2 : gentle 3 : free from noise 4 : not showy 5 : secluded ~ vb : pacify — **quiet** adv or n — **qui·et·ly** adv — **qui·et·ness** n

qui·etude \'kwīə,tüd, -,tyüd\ n : quietness or repose

quill \'kwil\ n 1 : a large stiff feather 2 : porcupine's spine

quilt \'kwilt\ n : padded bedspread ~ vb : stitch or sew in layers with padding in between

quince \'kwins\ n : hard yellow applelike fruit

qui·nine \'kwī,nīn\ n : bitter drug used against malaria

quin·tes·sence \kwin'tes³ns\ n 1 : purest essence of something 2 : most typical example — **quin·tes·sen·tial** \,kwintə'senchəl\ adj — **quin·tes·sen·tial·ly** adv

quin·tet \kwin'tet\ n 1 : music for 5 performers 2 : group of 5

quin·tu·ple \kwin'tüpəl, -'tyüp-, -'təp-; 'kwintəp-\ adj : having 5 units or members 2 : being 5 times as great or as many — **quintuple** n or vb

quin·tu·plet \-plət\ *n* : one of 5 offspring at one birth

quip \'kwip\ *vb* **-pp-** : make a clever remark — **quip** *n*

quire \'kwīr\ *n* : 24 or 25 sheets of paper of the same size and quality

quirk \'kwərk\ *n* : peculiarity of action or behavior — **quirky** *adj*

quit \'kwit\ *vb* **quit; quit·ting** 1 : stop 2 : leave — **quit·ter** *n*

quite \'kwīt\ *adv* 1 : completely 2 : to a considerable extent

quits \'kwits\ *adj* : even or equal with another (as by repaying a debt)

¹**quiv·er** \'kwivər\ *n* : case for arrows

²**quiver** *vb* : shake or tremble — **quiver** *n*

quix·ot·ic \kwik'sätik\ *adj* : idealistic to an impractical degree — **quix·ot·i·cal·ly** \-tiklē\ *adv*

quiz \'kwiz\ *n, pl* **quiz·zes** : short test ~ *vb* **-zz-** : question closely

quiz·zi·cal \'kwizikəl\ *adj* 1 : teasing 2 : curious

quoit \'kóit, 'kwóit, 'kwät\ *n* : ring thrown at a peg in a game (**quoits**)

quon·dam \'kwändəm, -,dam\ *adj* : former

quo·rum \'kwōrəm\ *n* : required number of members present

quo·ta \'kwōtə\ *n* : proportional part or share

quotation mark *n* : one of a pair of punctuation marks " " or ' ' used esp. to indicate the beginning and the end of a quotation

quote \'kwōt\ *vb* **quot·ed; quot·ing** 1 : repeat (another's words) exactly 2 : state (a price) — **quot·able** *adj* — **quo·ta·tion** \kwō'tāshən\ *n* — **quote** *n*

quo·tient \'kwōshənt\ *n* : number obtained from division

R

r \'är\ *n, pl* **r's** *or* **rs** \'ärz\ : 18th letter of the alphabet

rab·bet \'rabət\ *n* : groove in a board

rab·bi \'rab,ī\ *n* : Jewish religious leader — **rab·bin·ic** \rə'binik\, **rab·bin·i·cal** \-ikəl\ *adj*

rab·bin·ate \'rabənət, -,nāt\ *n* : office of a rabbi

rab·bit \'rabət\ *n, pl* **-bit** *or* **-bits** : long-eared burrowing mammal

rab·ble \'rabəl\ *n* : mob

ra·bid \'rabəd\ *adj* 1 : violent 2 : fanatical 3 : affected with rabies — **ra·bid·ly** *adv*

ra·bies \'rābēz\ *n, pl* **rabies** : acute deadly virus disease

rac·coon \ra'kün\ *n, pl* **-coon** *or* **-coons** : tree-dwelling mammal with a black mask and a bushy ringed tail

¹**race** \'rās\ *n* 1 : strong current of water 2 : contest of speed 3 : election campaign ~ *vb* **raced; rac·ing** 1 : run in a race 2 : rush — **race·course** *n* — **rac·er** *n* — **race·track** *n*

²**race** *n* 1 : family, tribe, people, or nation of the same stock 2 : division of mankind based on hereditary traits — **ra·cial** \'rāshəl\ *adj* — **ra·cial·ly** *adv*

race·horse *n* : horse used for racing

rac·ism \'rās,izəm\ *n* : discrimination based on the belief that some races are by nature superior — **rac·ist** \-ist\ *n*

rack \'rak\ *n* 1 : framework for display or storage 2 : instrument that stretches the body for torture ~ *vb* : torture with or as if with a rack

¹**rack·et** \'rakət\ *n* : bat with a tight netting across an open frame

²**racket** *n* 1 : confused noise 2 : fraudulent scheme — **rack·e·teer** \,rakə'tir\ *n* — **rack·e·teer·ing** *n*

ra·con·teur \,rak,än'tər\ *n* : storyteller

racy \'rāsē\ *adj* **rac·i·er; -est** : risqué — **rac·i·ly** *adv* — **rac·i·ness** *n*

ra·dar \'rā,där\ *n* : radio device for determining distance and direction of distant objects

ra·di·al \'rādēəl\ *adj* : having parts arranged like rays coming from a common center — **ra·di·al·ly** *adv*

ra·di·ant \'rādēənt\ *adj* 1 : glowing 2 : beaming with happiness 3 : transmitted by radiation — **ra·di·ance** \-əns\ *n* — **ra·di·ant·ly** *adv*

ra·di·ate \'rādē,āt\ *vb* **-at·ed; -at·ing** 1 : issue rays or in rays 2 : spread from a center — **ra·di·a·tion** \,rādē-'āshən\ *n*

ra·di·a·tor \'rādē,ātər\ n : cooling or heating device

rad·i·cal \'radikəl\ adj 1 : fundamental 2 : extreme ~ n : person favoring extreme changes — **rad·i·cal·ism** \-,izəm\ n — **rad·i·cal·ly** adv

radii pl of RADIUS

ra·dio \'rādē,ō\ n, pl **-di·os** 1 : wireless transmission or reception of sound by means of electric waves 2 : radio receiving set ~ vb : send a message to by radio — **radio** adj

ra·dio·ac·tiv·i·ty \,rādēō,ak'tivətē\ n : property of an element that emits energy through nuclear disintegration — **ra·dio·ac·tive** — **radio** adj

ra·di·ol·o·gy \,rādē'äləjē\ n : medical use of radiation — **ra·di·ol·o·gist** \-jist\ n

rad·ish \'radish\ n : pungent fleshy root usu. eaten raw

ra·di·um \'rādēəm\ n : metallic radioactive chemical element

ra·di·us \'rādēəs\ n, pl **-dii** \-ē,ī\ 1 : line from the center of a circle or sphere to the circumference or surface 2 : area defined by a radius

ra·don \'rā,dän\ n : gaseous radioactive chemical element

raff·ish \'rafish\ adj : flashily vulgar — **raff·ish·ly** adv — **raff·ish·ness** n

raf·fle \'rafəl\ n : lottery among people who have bought tickets ~ vb **-fled; -fling** : offer in a raffle

¹**raft** \'raft\ n : flat floating platform ~ vb : travel or transport by raft

²**raft** n : large amount or number

raf·ter \'raftər\ n : beam supporting a roof

¹**rag** \'rag\ n : waste piece of cloth

²**rag** n : composition in ragtime

rag·a·muf·fin \'ragə,məfən\ n : ragged dirty person

rage \'rāj\ n 1 : violent anger 2 : vogue ~ vb **raged; rag·ing** 1 : be extremely angry or violent 2 : be out of control

rag·ged \'ragəd\ adj : torn — **rag·ged·ly** adv — **rag·ged·ness** n

ra·gout \ra'gü\ n : meat stew

rag·time n : syncopated music

rag·weed n : coarse weedy herb with allergenic pollen

raid \'rād\ n : sudden usu. surprise attack — **raid** vb — **raid·er** n

¹**rail** \'rāl\ n 1 : bar serving as a guard or barrier 2 : bar forming a track for wheeled vehicles 3 : railroad

²**rail** vb : scold someone vehemently — **rail·er** n

rail·ing \'rālin\ n : rail or a barrier of rails

rail·lery \'rālərē\ n, pl **-ler·ies** : good-natured ridicule

rail·road \'rāl,rōd\ n : road for a train laid with iron rails and wooden ties ~ vb : force something hastily — **rail·road·er** n — **rail·road·ing** n

rail·way \-,wā\ n : railroad

rai·ment \'rāmənt\ n : clothing

rain \'rān\ n 1 : water falling in drops from the clouds 2 : shower of objects ~ vb : fall as or like rain — **rain·coat** n — **rain·drop** n — **rain·fall** n — **rain·mak·er** n — **rain·mak·ing** n — **rain·storm** n — **rain·water** n — **rainy** adj

rain·bow \-,bō\ n : arc of colors formed by the sun shining through moisture

raise \'rāz\ vb **raised; rais·ing** 1 : lift 2 : arouse 3 : erect 4 : collect 5 : breed, grow, or bring up 6 : increase 7 : make light ~ n : increase esp. in pay — **rais·er** n

rai·sin \'rāz'n\ n : dried grape

ra·ja, ra·jah \'räjə\ n : Indian prince

¹**rake** \'rāk\ n : garden tool for smoothing or sweeping ~ vb **raked; rak·ing** 1 : gather, loosen, or smooth with or as if with a rake 2 : sweep with gunfire

²**rake** n : dissolute man

rak·ish \'rākish\ adj : smart or jaunty — **rak·ish·ly** adv — **rak·ish·ness** n

ral·ly \'ralē\ vb **-lied; -ly·ing** 1 : bring or come together 2 : revive or recover 3 : make a comeback ~ n, pl **-lies** 1 : act of rallying 2 : mass meeting

ram \'ram\ n 1 : male sheep 2 : beam used in battering down walls or doors ~ vb **-mm-** 1 : force or drive in or through 2 : strike against violently

RAM \'ram\ n : main internal storage area in a computer

ram·ble \'rambəl\ vb **-bled; -bling** : wander — **ramble** n — **ram·bler** \-blər\ n

ram·bunc·tious \ram'bənkshəs\ adj : unruly

ram·i·fi·ca·tion \,raməfə'kāshən\ n : consequence

ram·i·fy \'ramə,fī\ vb **-fied; -fy·ing** : branch out

ramp \'ramp\ n : sloping passage or connecting roadway

ram·page \'ram₁pāj, ram'pāj\ *vb* **-paged; -pag·ing** : rush about wildly ~ \'ram₁-\ *n* : violent or riotous action or behavior

ram·pant \'rampənt\ *adj* : widespread — **ram·pant·ly** *adv*

ram·part \'ram₁pärt\ *n* : embankment of a fortification

ram·rod *n* : rod used to load or clean a gun ~ *adj* : strict or inflexible

ram·shack·le \'ram₁shakəl\ *adj* : shaky

ran *past of* RUN

ranch \'ranch\ *n* **1** : establishment for the raising of cattle, sheep, or horses **2** : specialized farm ~ *vb* : operate a ranch — **ranch·er** *n*

ran·cid \'ransəd\ *adj* : smelling or tasting as if spoiled — **ran·cid·i·ty** \ran-'sidətē\ *n*

ran·cor \'raŋkər\ *n* : bitter deep-seated ill will — **ran·cor·ous** *adj*

ran·dom \'randəm\ *adj* : occurring by chance — **ran·dom·ly** *adv* — **ran·dom·ness** *n* — **at random** : without definite aim or method

ran·dom·ize \'randə₁mīz\ *vb* **-ized; -izing** : select, assign, or arrange in a random way

rang *past of* RING

range \'rānj\ *n* **1** : series of things in a row **2** : open land for grazing **3** : cooking stove **4** : variation within limits **5** : place for target practice **6** : extent ~ *vb* **ranged; rang·ing** **1** : arrange **2** : roam at large, freely, or over **3** : vary within limits

rang·er \'rānjər\ *n* : officer who manages and protects public lands

rangy \'rānjē\ *adj* **rang·i·er; -est** : being slender with long limbs — **rang·i·ness** *n*

¹rank \'raŋk\ *adj* **1** : vigorous in growth **2** : unpleasantly strong-smelling — **rank·ly** *adv* — **rank·ness** *n*

²rank *n* **1** : line of soldiers **2** : orderly arrangement **3** : grade of official standing **4** : position within a group ~ *vb* **1** : arrange in formation or according to class **2** : take or have a relative position

rank and file *n* : general membership

ran·kle \'raŋkəl\ *vb* **-kled; -kling** : cause anger, irritation, or bitterness

ran·sack \'ran₁sak\ *vb* : search through and rob

ran·som \'ransəm\ *n* : something demanded for the freedom of a captive

~ *vb* : gain the freedom of by paying a price — **ran·som·er** *n*

rant \'rant\ *vb* : talk or scold violently — **rant·er** *n* — **rant·ing·ly** *adv*

¹rap \'rap\ *n* : sharp blow or rebuke ~ *vb* **-pp-** : strike or criticize sharply

²rap *vb* **-pp-** : talk freely

ra·pa·cious \rə'pāshəs\ *adj* **1** : excessively greedy **2** : ravenous — **ra·pa·cious·ly** *adv* — **ra·pa·cious·ness** *n* — **ra·pac·i·ty** \-'pasətē\ *n*

¹rape \'rāp\ *n* : herb grown as a forage crop and for its seeds (**rape·seed**)

²rape *vb* **raped; rap·ing** : force to have sexual intercourse — **rape** *n* — **rap·er** *n* — **rap·ist** \'rāpist\ *n*

rap·id \'rapəd\ *adj* : very fast — **ra·pid·i·ty** \rə'pidətē\ *n* — **rap·id·ly** *adv*

rap·ids \-ədz\ *n pl* : place in a stream where the current is swift

ra·pi·er \'rāpēər\ *n* : narrow 2-edged sword

rap·ine \'rapən, -₁in\ *n* : plunder

rap·port \ra'pōr\ *n* : harmonious relationship

rapt \'rapt\ *adj* : engrossed — **rapt·ly** *adv* — **rapt·ness** *n*

rap·ture \'rapchər\ *n* : spiritual or emotional ecstasy — **rap·tur·ous** \-chərəs\ *adj* — **rap·tur·ous·ly** *adv*

¹rare \'rar\ *adj* **rar·er; -est** : having a portion relatively uncooked

²rare *adj* **rar·er; rar·est 1** : not dense **2** : unusually fine **3** : seldom met with — **rare·ly** *adv* — **rare·ness** *n* — **rar·i·ty** \'rarətē\ *n*

rar·e·fy \'rarə₁fī\ *vb* **-fied; -fy·ing** : make or become rare, thin, or less dense — **rar·e·fac·tion** \₁rarə'fakshən\ *n*

rar·ing \'rarən, -iŋ\ *adj* : full of enthusiasm

ras·cal \'raskəl\ *n* : mean, dishonest, or mischievous person — **ras·cal·i·ty** \ras'kalətē\ *n* — **ras·cal·ly** \'ras-kəlē\ *adj*

¹rash \'rash\ *adj* : too hasty in decision or action — **rash·ly** *adv* — **rash·ness** *n*

²rash *n* : a breaking out of the skin with red spots

rasp \'rasp\ *vb* **1** : rub with or as if with a rough file **2** : speak in a grating tone ~ *n* : coarse file

rasp·ber·ry \'raz₁berē\ *n* : edible red or black berry

rat \'rat\ *n* : destructive rodent larger than the mouse ~ *vb* : betray or inform on

ratch·et \'rachət\ *n* : notched device for allowing motion in one direction

rate \'rāt\ *n* 1 : quantity, amount, or degree measured in relation to some other quantity 2 : rank ~ *vb* **rat·ed; rat·ing** 1 : estimate or determine the rank or quality of 2 : deserve

rath·er \'rathər, 'rȧth-, 'rǟth-\ *adv* 1 : preferably 2 : on the other hand 3 : more properly 4 : somewhat

rat·i·fy \'ratə‚fī\ *vb* **-fied; -fy·ing** : approve and accept formally — **rat·i·fi·ca·tion** \‚ratəfə'kāshən\ *n*

rat·ing \'rātiŋ\ *n* : classification according to grade

ra·tio \'rāshēō\ *n*, *pl* **-tios** : relation in number, quantity, or degree between things

ra·tion \'rashən, 'rāshən\ *n* : share or allotment (as of food) ~ *vb* : use or allot sparingly

ra·tio·nal \'rashənəl\ *adj* 1 : having reason or sanity 2 : relating to reason — **ra·tio·nal·ly** *adv*

ra·tio·nale \‚rashə'nal\ *n* 1 : explanation of principles of belief or practice 2 : underlying reason

ra·tio·nal·ize \'rashənə‚līz\ *vb* **-ized; -iz·ing** : justify (as one's behavior or weaknesses) esp. to oneself — **ra·tio·nal·i·za·tion** \‚rashənələ'zāshən\ *n*

rat·tan \ra'tan, rə-\ *n* : palm with long stems used esp. for canes and wickerwork

rat·tle \'rat³l\ *vb* **-tled; -tling** 1 : make a series of clattering sounds 2 : say briskly 3 : confuse or upset ~ *n* 1 : series of clattering sounds 2 : something (as a toy) that rattles

rat·tler \'ratlər\ *n* : rattlesnake

rat·tle·snake *n* : American venomous snake with a rattle at the end of the tail

rat·ty \'ratē\ *adj* **rat·ti·er; -est** : shabby

rau·cous \'rȯkəs\ *adj* : harsh or boisterous — **rau·cous·ly** *adv* — **rau·cous·ness** *n*

rav·age \'ravij\ *n* : destructive effect ~ *vb* **-aged; -ag·ing** : lay waste — **rav·ag·er** *n*

rave \'rāv\ *vb* **raved; rav·ing** 1 : talk wildly in or as if in delirium 2 : talk with extreme enthusiasm ~ *n* 1 : act of raving 2 : enthusiastic praise

rav·el \'ravəl\ *vb* **-eled** *or* **-elled; -el·ing** *or* **-el·ling** 1 : unravel 2 : tangle ~ *n* 1 : something tangled 2 : loose thread

ra·ven \'rāvən\ *n* : large black bird ~ *adj* : black and shiny

rav·en·ous \'ravənəs\ *adj* : very hungry — **rav·en·ous·ly** *adv* — **rav·en·ous·ness** *n*

ra·vine \rə'vēn\ *n* : narrow steep-sided valley

rav·ish \'ravish\ *vb* 1 : seize and take away by violence 2 : overcome with joy or delight 3 : rape — **rav·ish·er** *n* — **rav·ish·ment** *n*

raw \'rȯ\ *adj* **raw·er** \'rȯər\; **raw·est** \'rȯəst\ 1 : not cooked 2 : not processed 3 : not trained 4 : having the surface rubbed off 5 : cold and damp 6 : vulgar — **raw·ness** *n*

raw·hide \'rȯ‚hīd\ *n* : untanned skin of cattle

ray \'rā\ *n* 1 : thin beam of radiant energy (as light) 2 : tiny bit

ray·on \'rā‚än\ *n* : fabric made from cellulose fiber

raze \'rāz\ *vb* **razed; raz·ing** : destroy or tear down

ra·zor \'rāzər\ *n* : sharp cutting instrument used to shave off hair

re- \rē, ‚rē, 'rē\ *prefix* 1 : again or anew 2 : back or backward

reach \'rēch\ *vb* 1 : stretch out 2 : touch or try to touch or grasp 3 : extend to or arrive at 4 : communicate with ~ *n* 1 : act of reaching 2 : distance one can reach 3 : ability to reach — **reach·able** *adj* — **reach·er** *n*

re·act \rē'akt\ *vb* 1 : act in response to some influence or stimulus 2 : undergo chemical change — **re·ac·tive** \-'aktiv\ *adj*

re·ac·tion \rē'akshən\ *n* 1 : action or emotion caused by and directly related or counter to another action 2 : chemical change

re·ac·tion·ary \-shə‚nerē\ *adj* : relat-

List of self-explanatory words with the prefix *re-*

reaccelerate	reacquire	readjustment
reaccept	reactivate	readmit
reacclimatize	reactivation	readopt
reaccredit	readdress	reaffirm
reacquaint	readjust	realign

ing to or favoring return to an earlier political order or policy — **reactionary** n

re·ac·tor \rē'aktər\ n 1 : one that reacts 2 : device for the controlled release of nuclear energy

read \'rēd\ vb **read** \'red\; **read·ing** \'rēdiŋ\ 1 : understand written language 2 : utter aloud printed words 3 : interpret 4 : study 5 : indicate ~ \'red\ adj : informed by reading — **read·a·bil·i·ty** \ˌrēdə'bilətē\ n — **read·able** adj — **read·ably** adv — **read·er** n — **read·er·ship** n

read·ing \'rēdiŋ\ n 1 : something read or for reading 2 : particular version, interpretation, or performance 3 : data indicated by an instrument

ready \'redē\ adj **read·i·er; -est** 1 : prepared or available for use or action 2 : willing to do something ~ vb **read·ied; ready·ing** : make ready ~ n : state of being ready — **read·i·ly** adv — **read·i·ness** n

re·al \'rēl\ adj 1 : relating to fixed or immovable things (as land) 2 : genuine 3 : not imaginary ~ adv : very — **re·al·ness** n — **for real** 1 : in earnest 2 : genuine

real estate n : property in houses and land

re·al·ism \'rēə,lizəm\ n 1 : disposition to deal with facts practically 2 : faithful portrayal of reality — **re·alist** \-list\ adj or n — **re·al·is·tic** \ˌrēə'listik\ adj — **re·al·is·ti·cal·ly** \-tiklē\ adv

re·al·i·ty \rē'alətē\ n, pl **-ties** 1 : quality or state of being real 2 : something real

re·al·ize \'rēə,līz\ vb **-ized; -iz·ing** 1 : make actual 2 : obtain 3 : be aware of — **re·al·iz·able** adj — **re·al·i·zation** \ˌrēələ'zāshən\ n

re·al·ly \'rēlē, 'ril-\ adv : in truth

realm \'relm\ n 1 : kingdom 2 : sphere

¹ream \'rēm\ n : quantity of paper that is 480, 500, or 516 sheets

²ream vb : enlarge, shape, or clean with a specially shaped tool (**reamer**)

reap \'rēp\ vb : cut or clear (as a crop) with a scythe or machine — **reap·er** n

¹rear \'rir\ vb 1 : raise upright 2 : breed or bring up 3 : rise on the hind legs

²rear n 1 : back 2 : position at the back of something ~ adj : being at the back — **rear·ward** \-wərd\ adj or adv

rear admiral n : commissioned officer in the navy or coast guard ranking next below a vice admiral

rea·son \'rēz³n\ n 1 : explanation or justification 2 : motive for action or belief 3 : power or process of thinking ~ vb 1 : use the faculty of reason 2 : try to persuade another — **reason·er** n — **rea·son·ing** \'rēz³niŋ\ n

rea·son·able \'rēz³nəbəl\ adj 1 : being within the bounds of reason 2 : inexpensive — **rea·son·able·ness** n — **rea·son·ably** \-blē\ adv

re·as·sure \ˌrēə'shúr\ vb : restore one's confidence — **re·as·sur·ance** \-'shúrəns\ n — **re·as·sur·ing·ly** adv

re·bate \'rē,bāt\ n : return of part of a payment — **rebate** n

reb·el \'rebəl\ n : one that resists authority ~ \ri'bel\ vb **-belled; -belling** 1 : resist authority 2 : feel or exhibit anger — **rebel** \'rebəl\ adj

re·bel·lion \ri'belyən\ n : resistance to authority and esp. to one's government

re·bel·lious \-yəs\ adj 1 : engaged in rebellion 2 : inclined to resist authority — **re·bel·lious·ly** adv — **re·bellious·ness** n

re·birth \'rē'bərth\ n 1 : new or second birth 2 : revival

re·bound \'rē'baúnd, ri-\ vb 1 : spring back on striking something 2 : recover from a reverse ~ \'rē,-\ n 1 : action of rebounding 2 : reaction to a reverse

re·buff \ri'bəf\ vb : refuse or repulse rudely — **rebuff** n

re·buke \-'byük\ vb **-buked; -buk·ing** : reprimand sharply — **rebuke** n

re·bus \'rēbəs\ n : riddle representing syllables or words with pictures

re·but \ri'bət\ vb **-but·ted; -but·ting** : refute — **re·but·ter** n

re·but·tal \-³l\ n : opposing argument

re·cal·ci·trant \ri'kalsətrənt\ adj 1 : stubbornly resisting authority 2 : re sistant to handling or treatment — **re·cal·ci·trance** \-trəns\ n

re·call \ri'kȯl\ vb 1 : call back 2 : remember 3 : revoke ~ \ri'-, 'rē,-\ n 1 : a summons to return 2 : remembrance 3 : act of revoking

re·cant \ri'kant\ vb : take back (something said) publicly

re·ca·pit·u·late \,rēkə'pichə,lāt\ vb : summarize — **re·ca·pit·u·la·tion** \-,pichə'lāshən\ n

re·cede \ri'sēd\ vb **-ced·ed; -ced·ing** 1 : move back or away 2 : slant backward

re·ceipt \-'sēt\ n 1 : act of receiving 2 : something (as payment) received — usu. in pl. 3 : writing acknowledging something received

re·ceive \ri'sēv\ vb **-ceived; -ceiv·ing** 1 : take in or accept 2 : greet or entertain (visitors) 3 : pick up radio waves and convert into sounds or pictures — **re·ceiv·able** adj

re·ceiv·er \ri'sēvər\ n 1 : one that receives 2 : one having charge of property or money involved in a lawsuit 3 : apparatus for receiving radio waves — **re·ceiv·er·ship** n

re·cent \'rēs°nt\ adj 1 : having lately come into existence 2 : of the present time or time just past — **re·cent·ly** adv — **re·cent·ness** n

re·cep·ta·cle \ri'septikəl\ n : container

re·cep·tion \ri'sepshən\ n 1 : act of receiving 2 : social gathering at which guests are formally welcomed

re·cep·tion·ist \-shənist\ n : person employed to greet callers

re·cep·tive \ri'septiv\ adj : open and responsive to ideas, impressions, or suggestions — **re·cep·tive·ly** adv — **re·cep·tive·ness** n — **re·cep·tiv·i·ty** \,rē,sep'tivətē\ n

re·cess \'rē,ses, ri'ses\ n 1 : indentation in a line or surface 2 : suspension of a session for rest ~ vb 1 : make a recess in or put into a recess 2 : interrupt a session for a recess

re·ces·sion \ri'seshən\ n 1 : departing procession 2 : period of reduced economic activity

rec·i·pe \'resə,pē\ n : instructions for making something

re·cip·i·ent \ri'sipēənt\ n : one that receives

re·cip·ro·cal \ri'siprəkəl\ adj 1 : affecting each in the same way 2 : so related that one is equivalent to the other — **re·cip·ro·cal·ly** adv — **re·ci·proc·i·ty** \,resə'präsətē\ n

re·cip·ro·cate \-,kāt\ vb : make a return for something done or given — **re·cip·ro·ca·tion** \-,siprə'kāshən\ n

re·cit·al \ri'sīt°l\ n 1 : public reading or recitation 2 : music or dance concert or exhibition by pupils — **re·cit·al·ist** \-°list\ n

rec·i·ta·tion \,resə'tāshən\ n : a reciting or recital

re·cite \ri'sīt\ vb **-cit·ed; -cit·ing** 1 : repeat verbatim 2 : recount — **re·cit·er** n

reck·less \'rekləs\ adj : lacking caution — **reck·less·ly** adv — **reck·less·ness** n

reck·on \'rekən\ vb 1 : count or calculate 2 : consider

reck·on·ing n 1 : act or instance of reckoning 2 : settling of accounts

re·claim \ri'klām\ vb 1 : change to a desirable condition 2 : obtain from a waste product or by-product 3 : demand or obtain the return of — **re·claim·able** adj — **rec·la·ma·tion** \,reklə'māshən\ n

re·cline \ri'klīn\ vb **-clined; -clin·ing** : lean backward or lie down

rec·luse \'rek,lüs, ri'klüs\ n : one who leads a secluded or solitary life

rec·og·ni·tion \,rekig'nishən\ n : act of recognizing or state of being recognized

re·cog·ni·zance \ri'känəzəns, -'käg-\ n : promise recorded before a court

rec·og·nize \'rekig,nīz\ vb 1 : identify as previously known 2 : take notice of 3 : acknowledge esp. with appreciation — **rec·og·niz·able** \'rekəg,nīzəbəl\ adj — **rec·og·niz·ably** \-blē\ adv

re·coil \ri'kȯil\ vb : draw or spring back ~ \'rē,-, ri'-\ n : action of recoiling

rec·ol·lect \,rekə'lekt\ vb : remember

rec·ol·lec·tion \ˌrekə'lekshən\ n 1 : act or power of recollecting 2 : something recollected

rec·om·mend \ˌrekə'mend\ vb 1 : present as deserving of acceptance or trial 2 : advise — **rec·om·mend·able** \-'mendəbəl\ adj

rec·om·men·da·tion \ˌrekəmən'dāshən\ n 1 : act of recommending 2 : something recommended or that recommends

rec·om·pense \'rekəmˌpens\ n : compensation — **recompense** vb

rec·on·cile \'rekənˌsīl\ vb -ciled; -cil·ing 1 : cause to be friendly again 2 : adjust or settle 3 : bring to acceptance — **rec·on·cil·able** adj — **rec·on·cile·ment** n — **rec·on·cil·er** n — **rec·on·cil·i·a·tion** \ˌrekənˌsilē-'āshən\ n

re·con·dite \'rekənˌdīt, ri'kän-\ adj 1 : hard to understand 2 : little known

re·con·di·tion \ˌrēkən'dishən\ vb : restore to good condition

re·con·nais·sance \ri'känəzəns, -səns\ n : exploratory survey of enemy territory

re·con·noi·ter, re·con·noi·tre \ˌrēkə-'nóitər, ˌrekə-\ vb -tered or -tred; -ter·ing or -tring : make a reconnaissance of

re·cord \ri'kórd\ vb 1 : set down in writing 2 : register permanently 3 : indicate 4 : preserve (as sound or images) for later reproduction ~ \'rekərd\ n 1 : something recorded 2 : best performance

re·cord·er \ri'kórdər\ n 1 : person or device that records 2 : wind instrument with finger holes

¹**re·count** \ri'kaúnt\ vb : relate in detail

²**re·count** \'rē-\ vb : count again — **re·count** \'rē-, ˌrē'-\ n

re·coup \ri'küp\ vb : make up for (an expense or loss)

re·course \'rēˌkórs, ri'-\ n : source of aid or a turning to such a source

re·cov·er \ri'kəvər\ vb 1 : regain position, poise, or health 2 : recoup — **re·cov·er·able** adj — **re·cov·ery** \-'kəvərē\ n

rec·re·a·tion \ˌrekrē'āshən\ n : a refreshing of strength or spirits as a change from work or study — **rec·re·a·tion·al** \-shənəl\ adj

re·crim·i·na·tion \riˌkrimə'nāshən\ n : retaliatory accusation — **re·crim·i·nate** vb

re·cruit \ri'krüt\ n : newly enlisted member ~ vb : enlist the membership or services of — **re·cruit·er** n — **re·cruit·ment** n

rect·an·gle \'rekˌtaŋgəl\ n : 4-sided figure with 4 right angles — **rect·an·gu·lar** \rek'taŋgyələr\ adj

rec·ti·fy \'rektəˌfī\ vb -fied; -fy·ing : make or set right — **rec·ti·fi·ca·tion** \ˌrektəfə'kāshən\ n

rec·ti·tude \'rektəˌtüd, -ˌtyüd\ n : moral integrity

rec·tor \'rektər\ n : pastor

rec·to·ry \'rektərē\ n, pl -ries : rector's residence

rec·tum \'rektəm\ n, pl -tums or -ta \-tə\ : last part of the intestine joining the colon and anus — **rec·tal** \-t²l\ adj

re·cum·bent \ri'kəmbənt\ adj : lying down

re·cu·per·ate \ri'küpəˌrāt, -'kyü-\ vb -at·ed; -at·ing : recover (as from illness) — **re·cu·per·a·tion** \-ˌküpə-'rāshən, -ˌkyü-\ n — **re·cu·per·a·tive** \-'küpərātiv, -'kyü-\ adj

re·cur \ri'kər\ vb -rr- 1 : return in thought or talk 2 : occur again — **re·cur·rence** \-'kərəns\ n — **re·cur·rent** \-ənt\ adj

re·cy·cle \rē'sīkəl\ vb : process (as glass or cans) in order to regain a material for human use — **re·cy·cla·ble** \-kələbəl\ adj

red \'red\ n 1 : color of blood or of the ruby 2 cap : communist — **red** adj — **red·dish** adj — **red·ness** n

red·den \'red²n\ vb : make or become red or reddish

re·deem \ri'dēm\ vb 1 : regain, free, or rescue by paying a price 2 : atone for 3 : free from sin 4 : convert into something of value — **re·deem·able** adj — **re·deem·er** n

re·demp·tion \-'dempshən\ n : act of

---

rebuild	recertification	recheck
rebury	recertify	rechristen
recalculate	rechannel	recirculate
recapture	recharge	recirculation
recast	rechargeable	reclassification

redeeming — **re·demp·tive** \-tiv\ adj — **re·demp·to·ry** \-tərē\ adj

red·head \-ˌhed\ n : one having red hair — **red·head·ed** \-ˈhedəd\ adj

red·o·lent \ˈredᵊlənt\ adj 1 : having a fragrance 2 : suggestive — **red·o·lence** \-əns\ n — **red·o·lent·ly** adv

re·dou·ble \rēˈdəbəl\ vb 1 : make twice as great in size or amount 2 : intensify

re·doubt \riˈdaut\ n : small fortification

re·doubt·able \-əbəl\ adj : arousing dread

re·dound \riˈdaund\ vb : have an effect

re·dress \riˈdres\ vb : set right ~ n 1 : relief or remedy 2 : compensation

red tape n : complex obstructive official routine

re·duce \riˈdüs, -ˈdyüs\ vb 1 : lessen 2 : put in a lower rank 3 : lose weight — **re·duc·er** n — **re·duc·ible** \-ˈdüsəbəl, -ˈdyü-\ adj

re·duc·tion \riˈdəkshən\ n 1 : act of reducing 2 : amount lost in reducing 3 : something made by reducing

re·dun·dant \riˈdəndənt\ adj : using more words than necessary — **re·dun·dan·cy** \-dənsē\ n — **re·dun·dant·ly** adv

red·wood n : tall coniferous timber tree

reed \ˈrēd\ n 1 : tall slender grass of wet areas 2 : elastic strip that vibrates to produce tones in certain wind instruments — **reedy** adj

reef \ˈrēf\ n : ridge of rocks or sand at or near the surface of the water

reek \ˈrēk\ n : strong or disagreeable fume or odor ~ vb : give off a reek

¹**reel** \ˈrēl\ n : revolvable device on which something flexible is wound or a quantity of something wound on it ~ vb 1 : wind on a reel 2 : pull in by reeling — **reel·able** adj — **reel·er** n

²**reel** vb 1 : whirl or waver as from a blow 2 : walk or move unsteadily ~ n : reeling motion

³**reel** n : lively dance

re·fer \riˈfər\ vb -rr- 1 : direct or send to some person or place 2 : submit for consideration or action 3 : have connection 4 : mention or allude to something — **re·fer·able** \ˈrefərəbəl, riˈfərə-\ adj — **re·fer·ral** \riˈfərəl\ n

ref·er·ee \ˌrefəˈrē\ n 1 : one to whom an issue is referred for settlement 2 : sports official ~ vb -eed; -ee·ing : act as referee

ref·er·ence \ˈrefərəns\ n 1 : act of referring 2 : a bearing on a matter 3 : consultation for information 4 : person who can speak for one's character or ability or a recommendation given by such a person

ref·er·en·dum \ˌrefəˈrendəm\ n, pl -da \-də\ or -dums : a submitting of legislative measures for voters' approval or rejection

re·fill \rēˈfil\ vb : fill again — **re·fill** \ˈrē-\ n — **re·fill·able** adj

re·fine \riˈfīn\ vb -fined; -fin·ing 1 : free from impurities or waste matter 2 : improve or perfect 3 : free or become free of what is coarse or uncouth — **re·fine·ment** \-mənt\ n — **re·fin·er** n

re·fin·ery \riˈfīnərē\ n, pl -er·ies : place for refining (as oil or sugar)

re·flect \riˈflekt\ vb 1 : bend or cast back (as light or heat) 2 : bring as a result 3 : cast reproach or blame 4 : ponder — **re·flec·tion** \-ˈflekshən\ n — **re·flec·tive** \-tiv\ adj — **re·flec·tor** \riˈflektər\ n

re·flex \ˈrēˌfleks\ n : automatic response to a stimulus ~ adj 1 : bent back 2 : relating to a reflex — **re·flex·ly** adv

re·flex·ive \riˈfleksiv\ adj : of or relating to an action directed back upon the doer or the grammatical subject — **reflexive** n — **re·flex·ive·ly** adv — **re·flex·ive·ness** n

re·form \riˈfȯrm\ vb : make or become better esp. by correcting bad habits — **reform** n — **re·form·able** adj — **re·for·ma·tive** \-ˈfȯrmətiv\ adj — **re·form·er** n

re·for·ma·to·ry \riˈfȯrməˌtōrē\ n, pl -ries : penal institution for reforming young offenders

re·fract \riˈfrakt\ vb : subject to refraction

---

re·frac·tion \-'frakshən\ *n* : the bending of a ray (as of light) when it passes from one medium into another — **re·frac·tive** \-tiv\ *adj*

re·frac·to·ry \ri'fraktərē\ *adj* : obstinate or unmanageable

re·frain \ri'frān\ *vb* : hold oneself back ∼ *n* : verse recurring regularly in a song — **re·frain·ment** *n*

re·fresh \ri'fresh\ *vb* 1 : make or become fresh or fresher 2 : supply or take refreshment — **re·fresh·er** *n* — **re·fresh·ing·ly** *adv*

re·fresh·ment \-mənt\ *n* 1 : act of refreshing 2 *pl* : light meal

re·frig·er·ate \ri'frijə,rāt\ *vb* -at·ed; -at·ing : chill or freeze (food) for preservation — **re·frig·er·ant** \-ərənt\ *adj or n* — **re·frig·er·a·tion** \-,frijə'rāshən\ *n* — **re·frig·er·a·tor** \-'frijə,rātər\ *n*

ref·uge \'ref,yüj\ *n* 1 : protection from danger 2 : place that provides protection

ref·u·gee \,refyü'jē\ *n* : person who flees for safety

re·fund \ri'fənd, 'rē,fənd\ *vb* : give or put back (money) ∼ \'rē,-\ *n* 1 : act of refunding 2 : sum refunded — **re·fund·able** *adj*

re·fur·bish \ri'fərbish\ *vb* : renovate

¹**re·fuse** \ri'fyüz\ *vb* -fused; -fus·ing : decline to accept, do, or give — **re·fus·al** \-'fyüzəl\ *n*

²**ref·use** \'ref,yüs, -,yüz\ *n* : worthless matter

re·fute \ri'fyüt\ *vb* -fut·ed; -fut·ing : prove to be false — **ref·u·ta·tion** \,refyü'tāshən\ *n* — **re·fut·er** \ri'fyütər\ *n*

re·gal \'rēgəl\ *adj* 1 : befitting a king 2 : stately — **re·gal·ly** *adv*

re·gale \ri'gāl\ *vb* -galed; -gal·ing 1 : entertain richly or agreeably 2 : delight

re·ga·lia \ri'gālyə\ *n pl* 1 : symbols of royalty 2 : insignia of an office or order 3 : finery

re·gard \ri'gärd\ *n* 1 : consideration 2 : feeling of approval and liking 3 *pl* : friendly greetings 4 : relation ∼ *vb*

1 : pay attention to 2 : show respect for 3 : have an opinion of 4 : look at 5 : relate to — **re·gard·ful** *adj* — **re·gard·less** *adj*

re·gard·ing *prep* : concerning

regardless of \ri'gärdləs-\ *prep* : in spite of

re·gen·er·ate \ri'jenərət\ *adj* 1 : formed or created again 2 : spiritually reborn ∼ \-'jenə,rāt\ *vb* 1 : reform completely 2 : replace (a lost body part) by new tissue growth 3 : give new life to — **re·gen·er·a·tion** \-,jenə'rāshən\ *n* — **re·gen·er·a·tive** \-'jenə,rātiv\ *adj* — **re·gen·er·a·tor** \-,rātər\ *n*

re·gent \'rējənt\ *n* 1 : person who rules during the childhood, absence, or incapacity of the sovereign 2 : member of a governing board — **re·gen·cy** \-jənsē\ *n*

re·gime \rā'zhēm, ri-\ *n* : government in power

reg·i·men \'rejəmən\ *n* : systematic course of treatment or training

reg·i·ment \'rejəmənt\ *n* : military unit ∼ \-,ment\ *vb* 1 : organize rigidly for control 2 : make orderly — **reg·i·men·tal** \,rejə'ment³l\ *adj* — **reg·i·men·ta·tion** \-mən'tāshən\ *n*

re·gion \'rējən\ *n* : indefinitely defined area — **re·gion·al** \'rējənəl\ *adj* — **re·gion·al·ly** *adv*

reg·is·ter \'rejəstər\ *n* 1 : record of items or details or a book for keeping such a record 2 : device to regulate ventilation 3 : counting or recording device 4 : range of a voice or instrument ∼ *vb* 1 : enter in a register 2 : record automatically 3 : get special care for mail by paying more postage

reg·is·trar \-,strär\ *n* : official keeper of records

reg·is·tra·tion \,rejə'strāshən\ *n* 1 : act of registering 2 : entry in a register

reg·is·try \'rejəstrē\ *n, pl* -tries 1 : enrollment 2 : place of registration 3 : official record book

re·gress \ri'gres\ *vb* : go or cause to go

---

recopy	rededication	rediscover
re-create	redefine	rediscovery
recross	redeposit	redissolve
redecorate	redesign	redistribute
rededicate	redevelop	redraft

back or to a lower level — **re·gres·sion** \-'greshən\ n — **re·gres·sive** adj

re·gret \ri'gret\ vb **-tt-** 1 : mourn the loss or death of 2 : be very sorry for ~ n 1 : sorrow or the expression of sorrow 2 pl : message declining an invitation — **re·gret·ful** \-fəl\ adj — **re·gret·ful·ly** adv — **re·gret·ta·ble** \-əbəl\ adj — **re·gret·ta·bly** \-blē\ adv — **re·gret·ter** n

reg·u·lar \'regyələr\ adj 1 : conforming to what is usual, normal, or average 2 : steady, uniform, or unvarying — **regular** n — **reg·u·lar·i·ty** \,regyə-'larətē\ n — **reg·u·lar·ize** \'regyələ-,rīz\ vb — **reg·u·lar·ly** adv

reg·u·late \'regyə,lāt\ vb **-lat·ed; -lat·ing** 1 : govern according to rule 2 : adjust to a standard — **reg·u·la·tive** \-,lātiv\ adj — **reg·u·la·tor** \-,lātər\ n — **reg·u·la·to·ry** \-lə,tōrē\ adj

reg·u·la·tion \,regyə'lāshən\ n 1 : act of regulating 2 : rule dealing with details of procedure

re·gur·gi·tate \rē'gərjə,tāt\ vb **-tat·ed; -tat·ing** : vomit — **re·gur·gi·ta·tion** \-,gərjə'tāshən\ n

re·ha·bil·i·tate \,rēhə'bilə,tāt\ vb **-tat·ed; -tat·ing** 1 : reinstate 2 : make good or usable again — **re·ha·bil·i·ta·tion** \-,bilə'tāshən\ n

re·hears·al \ri'hərsəl\ n : practice session or performance

re·hearse \-'hərs\ vb **-hearsed; -hears·ing** 1 : repeat or recount 2 : engage in a rehearsal of — **re·hears·er** n

reign \'rān\ n : sovereign's authority or rule ~ vb : rule as a sovereign

re·im·burse \,rēəm'bərs\ vb **-bursed; -burs·ing** : repay — **re·im·burs·able** adj — **re·im·burse·ment** n

rein \'rān\ n 1 : strap fastened to a bit to control an animal 2 : restraining influence ~ vb : direct by reins

re·in·car·na·tion \,rē,in,kär'nāshən\ n : rebirth of the soul — **re·in·car·nate** \rēin'kär,nāt\ vb

rein·deer \'rān,dir\ n : caribou

re·in·force \,rēən'fōrs\ vb : strengthen or support — **re·in·force·ment** n — **re·in·forc·er** n

re·in·state \,rēən'stāt\ vb : restore to a former position — **re·in·state·ment** n

re·it·er·ate \rē'itə,rāt\ vb : say again — **re·it·er·a·tion** \-,itə'rāshən\ n

re·ject \ri'jekt\ vb 1 : refuse to grant or consider 2 : refuse to admit, believe, or receive 3 : throw out as useless or unsatisfactory ~ \'rē-\ : rejected person or thing — **re·jec·tion** \-'jek-shən\ n

re·joice \ri'jóis\ vb **-joiced; -joic·ing** : feel joy — **re·joic·er** n

re·join vb 1 \rē'jóin\ : join again 2 \ri'-\ : say in answer

re·join·der \ri'jóindər\ n : answer

re·ju·ve·nate \ri'jüvə,nāt\ vb **-nat·ed; -nat·ing** : make young again — **re·ju·ve·na·tion** \-,jüvə'nāshən\ n

re·lapse \ri'laps, 'rē,laps\ n : recurrence of illness after a period of improvement ~ \ri'-\ vb : suffer a relapse

re·late \ri'lāt\ vb **-lat·ed; -lat·ing** 1 : give a report of 2 : show a connection between 3 : have a relationship — **re·lat·able** adj — **re·lat·er, re·la·tor** n

re·la·tion \-'lāshən\ n 1 : account 2 : connection 3 : relationship 4 : reference 5 pl : dealings — **re·la·tion·ship** \-,ship\ n : state of being related or interrelated

rel·a·tive \'relətiv\ n : person connected with another by blood or marriage ~ adj : considered in comparison with something else — **rel·a·tive·ly** adv — **rel·a·tive·ness** n

re·lax \ri'laks\ vb 1 : make or become less tense or rigid 2 : make less severe 3 : seek rest or recreation — **re·lax·er** n

re·lax·a·tion \,rē,lak'sāshən\ n 1 : lessening of tension 2 : recreation

re·lay \'rē,lā\ n : fresh supply (as of horses or people) arranged to relieve others ~ \'rē,-, ri'-\ vb **-layed; -lay·ing** : pass along in stages

re·lease \ri'lēs\ vb **-leased; -leas·ing** 1 : free from confinement or oppression 2 : relinquish 3 : permit publication, performance, exhibition, or

---

redraw	reengage	reequip
reemerge	reenlist	reestablish
reemergence	reenlistment	reestablishment
reemphasize	reenroll	reestimate
reenergize	reenter	reevaluate

sale **~** n **1** : relief from trouble **2** : discharge from an obligation **3** : act of releasing or what is released

rel·e·gate \'relə,gāt\ vb **-gat·ed; -gat·ing 1** : remove to some less prominent position **2** : assign to a particular class or sphere — **rel·e·ga·tion** \,relə-'gāshən\ n

re·lent \ri'lent\ vb : become less severe

re·lent·less \-ləs\ adj : mercilessly severe or persistent — **re·lent·less·ly** adv — **re·lent·less·ness** n

rel·e·vance \'reləvəns\ n : relation to the matter at hand — **rel·e·vant** \-vənt\ adj — **rel·e·vant·ly** adv

re·li·able \ri'līəbəl\ adj : fit to be trusted — **re·li·abil·i·ty** \-,līə'bilətē\ n — **re·li·able·ness** n — **re·li·ably** \-'līəblē\ adv

re·li·ance \ri'līəns\ n : act or result of relying

re·li·ant \ri'līənt\ adj : dependent

rel·ic \'relik\ n **1** : object venerated because of its association with a saint or martyr **2** : remaining trace

re·lief \ri'lēf\ n **1** : lightening of something oppressive **2** : welfare

re·lieve \ri'lēv\ vb **-lieved; -liev·ing 1** : free from a burden or distress **2** : release from a post or duty **3** : break the monotony of — **re·liev·er** n

re·li·gion \ri'lijən\ n **1** : service and worship of God **2** : set or system of religious beliefs — **re·li·gion·ist** n

re·li·gious \-'lijəs\ adj **1** : relating or devoted to an ultimate reality or deity **2** : relating to religious beliefs or observances **3** : faithful, fervent, or zealous — **re·li·gious·ly** adv

re·lin·quish \-'liŋkwish, -'lin-\ vb **1** : renounce **2** : let go of — **re·lin·quish·ment** n

rel·ish \'relish\ n **1** : keen enjoyment **2** : highly seasoned sauce (as of pickles) **~** vb : enjoy — **rel·ish·able** adj

re·live \rē'liv\ vb : live over again (as in the imagination)

re·lo·cate \'rē,lō,kāt, ,rēlō'kāt\ vb : move to a new location — **re·lo·ca·tion** \,rēlō'kāshən\ n

re·luc·tant \ri'ləktənt\ adj : feeling or showing doubt or unwillingness — **re·luc·tance** \ri'ləktəns\ n — **re·luc·tant·ly** adv

re·ly \ri'lī\ vb **-lied; -ly·ing** : place faith or confidence — often with on

re·main \ri'mān\ vb **1** : be left after others have been removed **2** : be something yet to be done **3** : stay behind **4** : continue unchanged

re·main·der \-'māndər\ n : that which is left over

re·mains \-'mānz\ n pl **1** : remaining part or trace **2** : dead body

re·mark \ri'märk\ vb : express as an observation **~** n : passing comment

re·mark·able \-'märkəbəl\ adj : extraordinary — **re·mark·able·ness** n — **re·mark·ably** \-blē\ adv

re·me·di·al \ri'mēdēəl\ adj : intended to remedy or improve

rem·e·dy \'remədē\ n, pl **-dies 1** : medicine that cures **2** : something that corrects an evil or compensates for a loss **~** vb **-died; -dy·ing** : provide or serve as a remedy for

re·mem·ber \ri'membər\ vb **1** : think of again **2** : keep from forgetting **3** : convey greetings from

re·mem·brance \-brəns\ n **1** : act of remembering **2** : something that serves to bring to mind

re·mind \ri'mīnd\ vb : cause to remember — **re·mind·er** n

rem·i·nisce \,remə'nis\ vb **-nisced; -nisc·ing** : indulge in reminiscence

rem·i·nis·cence \-'nis³ns\ n **1** : recalling of a past experience **2** : account of a memorable experience

rem·i·nis·cent \-³nt\ adj **1** : relating to reminiscence **2** : serving to remind — **rem·i·nis·cent·ly** adv

re·miss \ri'mis\ adj : negligent or careless in performance of duty — **re·miss·ly** adv — **re·miss·ness** n

re·mis·sion \ri'mishən\ n **1** : act of forgiving **2** : period of relief from or easing of symptoms of a disease

re·mit \ri'mit\ vb **-tt- 1** : pardon **2** : send money in payment

re·mit·tance \ri'mit³ns\ n : sum of money remitted

reevaluation	refloat	refuel
reexamination	refocus	regain
reexamine	refold	regrow
refinance	reformulate	regrowth
refire	refreeze	rehear

rem·nant \'remnənt\ n : small part or trace remaining

re·mod·el \rē'mädºl\ vb : alter the structure of

re·mon·strance \ri'mänstrəns\ n : act or instance of remonstrating

re·mon·strate \ri'män,strāt\ vb -strat·ed; -strat·ing : speak in protest, reproof, or opposition — **re·mon·stra·tion** \ri,män'strāshən, ,remən-\ n

re·morse \ri'mòrs\ n : distress arising from a sense of guilt — **re·morse·ful** adj — **re·morse·less** adj

re·mote \ri'mōt\ adj -mot·er; -est 1 : far off in place or time 2 : hard to reach or find 3 : acting, acted on, or controlled indirectly or from afar 4 : slight 5 : distant in manner — **re·mote·ly** adv — **re·mote·ness** n

re·move \ri'müv\ vb -moved; -mov·ing 1 : move by lifting or taking off or away 2 : get rid of — **re·mov·able** adj — **re·mov·al** \-vəl\ n — **re·mov·er** n

re·mu·ner·ate \ri'myünə,rāt\ vb -at·ed; -at·ing : pay — **re·mu·ner·a·tion** n — **re·mu·ner·a·tor** \-,rātər\ n

re·mu·ner·a·tive \ri'myünərətiv, -,rāt-\ adj : gainful

re·nais·sance \,renə'säns, -'zäns\ n : rebirth or revival

re·nal \'rēnºl\ adj : relating to the kidneys

rend \'rend\ vb rent \'rent\; rend·ing : tear apart forcibly

ren·der \'rendər\ vb 1 : extract by heating 2 : hand over or give up 3 : do (a service) for another 4 : cause to be or become

ren·dez·vous \'rändi,vü, -dā-\ n, pl **ren·dez·vous** \-,vüz\ 1 : place appointed for a meeting 2 : meeting at an appointed place — **-voused; -vous·ing** : meet at a rendezvous

ren·di·tion \ren'dishən\ n : version

ren·e·gade \'reni,gād\ n : deserter of one faith or cause for another

re·nege \ri'nig, -'neg, -'nēg, -'nāg\ vb -neged; -neg·ing : go back on a promise — **re·neg·er** n

re·new \ri'nü, -'nyü\ vb 1 : make or become new, fresh, or strong again 2 : begin again 3 : grant or obtain an extension of — **re·new·able** adj — **re·new·al** n — **re·new·er** n

re·nounce \ri'naúns\ vb -nounced; -nounc·ing : give up, refuse, or resign — **re·nounce·ment** n

ren·o·vate \'renə,vāt\ vb -vat·ed; -vat·ing : make like new again — **ren·o·va·tion** \,renə'vāshən\ n — **ren·o·va·tor** \'renə,vātər\ n

re·nown \ri'naún\ n : state of being widely known and honored — **renowned** \-'naúnd\ adj

¹**rent** \'rent\ n : money paid or due periodically for the use of another's property ~ vb : hold or give possession and use of for rent — **rent·al** n or adj — **rent·er** n

²**rent** n : a tear in cloth

re·nun·ci·a·tion \ri,nənsē'āshən\ n : act of renouncing

¹**re·pair** \ri'par\ vb : go

²**repair** vb : restore to good condition ~ n 1 : act or instance of repairing 2 : condition — **re·pair·er** n — **re·pair·man** \-,man\ n

rep·a·ra·tion \,repə'rāshən\ n : money paid for redress — usu. pl.

rep·ar·tee \,repər'tē\ n : clever replies

re·past \ri'past, 'rē,past\ n : meal

re·pa·tri·ate \rē'pātrē,āt\ vb -at·ed; -at·ing : send back to one's own country — **re·pa·tri·ate** \-trēət, -trē,āt\ n — **re·pa·tri·a·tion** \-,pātrē'āshən\ n

re·pay \rē'pā\ vb -paid; -pay·ing : pay back — **re·pay·able** adj — **re·pay·ment** n

re·peal \ri'pēl\ vb : annul by legislative action — **repeal** n — **re·peal·er** n

re·peat \ri'pēt\ vb : say or do again ~ n 1 : act of repeating 2 : something repeated — **re·peat·able** adj — **re·peat·ed·ly** adv — **re·peat·er** n

re·pel \ri'pel\ vb -pelled; -pel·ling 1 : drive away 2 : disgust — **re·pel·lent** \-'pelənt\ adj or n

re·pent \ri'pent\ vb 1 : turn from sin 2 : regret — **re·pen·tance** \ri'pentºns\ n — **re·pen·tant** \-ºnt\ adj

re·per·cus·sion \,rēpər'kəshən,

reheat
rehire
rehospitalization
rehospitalize
reidentify

reignite
reimplant
reimpose
reincorporate
reindict

reinfection
reinflate
reinject
reinjection
reinoculate

,rep-\ : effect of something done or said

rep·er·toire \'repər,twär\ n : pieces a company or performer can present

rep·er·to·ry \'repər,tōrē\ n, pl -ries 1 : repertoire 2 : theater with a resident company doing several plays

rep·e·ti·tion \,repə'tishən\ n : act or instance of repeating

rep·e·ti·tious \-'tishəs\ adj : tediously repeating — **rep·e·ti·tious·ly** adv — **rep·e·ti·tious·ness** n

re·pet·i·tive \ri'petətiv\ adj : repetitious — **re·pet·i·tive·ly** adv — **re·pet·i·tive·ness** n

re·pine \ri'pīn\ vb re·pined; re·pin·ing : feel or express discontent

re·place \ri'plās\ vb 1 : restore to a former position 2 : take the place of 3 : put something new in the place of — **re·place·able** adj — **re·place·ment** n — **re·plac·er** n

re·plen·ish \ri'plenish\ vb : stock or supply anew — **re·plen·ish·ment** n

re·plete \ri'plēt\ adj : full — **re·plete·ness** n — **re·ple·tion** \-'plēshən\ n

rep·li·ca \'replikə\ n : exact copy

rep·li·cate \'replə,kāt\ vb -cat·ed; -cat·ing : duplicate or repeat — **rep·li·cate** \-likət\ n — **rep·li·ca·tion** \-lə'kāshən\ n

re·ply \ri'plī\ vb -plied; -ply·ing : say or do in answer ~ n, pl -plies : answer

re·port \ri'pōrt\ n 1 : rumor 2 : statement of information (as events or causes) 3 : explosive noise ~ vb 1 : give an account of 2 : present an account of (an event) as news 3 : present oneself 4 : make known to authorities — **re·port·age** \ri'pōrtij, ,repər'täzh, ,rep,ôr'-\ n — **re·port·ed·ly** adv — **re·port·er** n — **re·por·to·ri·al** \,repər'tōrēəl\ adj

re·pose \ri'pōz\ vb -posed; -pos·ing : lay or lie at rest ~ n 1 : state of resting 2 : calm or peace — **re·pose·ful** adj

re·pos·i·to·ry \ri'päzə,tōrē\ n, pl -ries : place where something is stored

re·pos·sess \,rēpə'zes\ vb : regain possession and legal ownership of — **re·pos·ses·sion** \-'zeshən\ n

rep·re·hend \,repri'hend\ vb : censure — **rep·re·hen·sion** \-'henchən\ n

rep·re·hen·si·ble \-'hensəbəl\ adj : deserving condemnation — **rep·re·hen·si·bly** adv

rep·re·sent \,repri'zent\ vb 1 : serve as a sign or symbol of 2 : act or speak for 3 : describe as having a specified quality or character — **rep·re·sen·ta·tion** \,repri,zen'tāshən\ n

rep·re·sen·ta·tive \,repri'zentətiv\ adj 1 : standing or acting for another 2 : carried on by elected representatives ~ n 1 : typical example 2 : one that represents another 3 : member of usu. the lower house of a legislature — **rep·re·sen·ta·tive·ly** adv — **rep·re·sen·ta·tive·ness** n

re·press \ri'pres\ vb : restrain or suppress — **re·pres·sion** \-'preshən\ n — **re·pres·sive** \-'presiv\ adj

re·prieve \ri'prēv\ n 1 : a delay in punishment 2 : temporary respite — **re·prieve** vb

rep·ri·mand \'reprə,mand\ n : formal or severe criticism — **reprimand** vb

re·pri·sal \ri'prīzəl\ n : act in retaliation

re·prise \ri'prēz\ n : musical repetition

re·proach \ri'prōch\ n 1 : disgrace 2 : rebuke ~ vb : express disapproval to — **re·proach·ful** adj — **re·proach·ful·ly** adv — **re·proach·ful·ness** n

rep·ro·bate \'reprə,bāt\ n : scoundrel — **reprobate** adj

rep·ro·ba·tion \,reprə'bāshən\ n : strong disapproval

re·pro·duce \,rēprə'düs, -'dyüs\ vb 1 : produce again or anew 2 : produce offspring — **re·pro·duc·ible** \-'düsəbəl, -'dyü-\ adj — **re·pro·duc·tion** \-'dəkshən\ n — **re·pro·duc·tive** \-'dəktiv\ adj

re·proof \ri'prüf\ n : blame or censure for a fault

re·prove \ri'prüv\ vb -proved; -prov·ing : express disapproval to or of

rep·tile \'rept²l, -,tīl\ n : air-breathing scaly vertebrate — **rep·til·ian** \rep-'tilēən\ adj or n

reinsert	reintegrate	reinvestigate
reinsertion	reintegration	reinvestigation
reinspect	reinter	reinvigorate
reinstall	reintroduce	rejudge
reinstitute	reinvent	rekindle

re·pub·lic \ri'pəblik\ *n* : country with representative government

re·pub·li·can \-likən\ *adj* **1** : relating to or resembling a republic **2** : supporting a republic — **republican** *n* — **re·pub·li·can·ism** *n*

re·pu·di·ate \ri'pyüdē,āt\ *vb* **-at·ed; -at·ing** : refuse to have anything to do with — **re·pu·di·a·tion** \-,pyüdē'āshən\ *n*

re·pug·nant \ri'pəgnənt\ *adj* : contrary to one's tastes or principles — **re·pug·nance** \-nəns\ *n* — **re·pug·nant·ly** *adv*

re·pulse \ri'pəls\ *vb* **-pulsed; -puls·ing 1** : drive or beat back **2** : rebuff **3** : be repugnant to — **repulse** *n* — **re·pul·sion** \-'pəlshən\ *n*

re·pul·sive \-siv\ *adj* : arousing aversion or disgust — **re·pul·sive·ly** *adv* — **re·pul·sive·ness** *n*

rep·u·ta·ble \'repyətəbəl\ *adj* : having a good reputation — **rep·u·ta·bly** \-blē\ *adv*

rep·u·ta·tion \,repyə'tāshən\ *n* : one's character or public esteem

re·pute \ri'pyüt\ *vb* **-put·ed; -put·ing** : think of as being ∼ *n* : reputation — **re·put·ed** *adj* — **re·put·ed·ly** *adv*

re·quest \ri'kwest\ *n* : act or instance of asking for something or a thing asked for ∼ *vb* **1** : make a request of **2** : ask for — **re·quest·er** *n*

re·qui·em \'rekwēəm, 'rāk-\ *n* : Mass for a dead person or a musical setting for this

re·quire \ri'kwīr\ *vb* **-quired; -quir·ing 1** : insist on **2** : call for as essential — **re·quire·ment** *n*

req·ui·site \'rekwəzət\ *adj* : necessary — **requisite** *n*

req·ui·si·tion \,rekwə'zishən\ *n* : formal application or demand — **requisition** *vb*

re·quite \ri'kwīt\ *vb* **-quit·ed; -quit·ing** : make return for or to — **re·quit·al** \-'kwīt'l\ *n*

re·scind \ri'sind\ *vb* : repeal or cancel — **re·scis·sion** \-'sizhən\ *n*

res·cue \'reskyü\ *vb* **-cued; -cu·ing** : set free from danger or confinement — **rescue** *n* — **res·cu·er** *n*

re·search \ri'sərch, 'rē,sərch\ *n* : careful or diligent search esp. for new knowledge — **research** *vb* — **re·search·er** *n*

re·sem·ble \ri'zembəl\ *vb* **-sem·bled; -sem·bling** : be like or similar to — **re·sem·blance** \-'zembləns\ *n*

re·sent \ri'zent\ *vb* : feel or show annoyance at — **re·sent·ful** *adj* — **re·sent·ful·ly** *adv* — **re·sent·ment** *n*

res·er·va·tion \,rezər'vāshən\ *n* **1** : act of reserving or something reserved **2** : limiting condition

re·serve \ri'zərv\ *vb* **-served; -serv·ing 1** : store for future use **2** : set aside for special use ∼ *n* **1** : something reserved **2** : restraint in words or bearing **3** : military forces withheld from action or not part of the regular services — **re·served** *adj*

res·er·voir \'rezər,vwär, -,vwȯr, -,vȯr, -,vȯi\ *n* : place where something (as water) is kept in store

re·side \ri'zīd\ *vb* **-sid·ed; -sid·ing 1** : make one's home **2** : be present

res·i·dence \'rezədəns\ *n* **1** : act or fact of residing in a place **2** : place where one lives — **res·i·dent** \-ənt\ *adj or n* — **res·i·den·tial** \,rezə'denchəl\ *adj*

res·i·due \'rezə,dü, -,dyü\ *n* : part remaining — **re·sid·u·al** \ri'zijəwəl\ *adj*

re·sign \ri'zīn\ *vb* **1** : give up deliberately **2** : give (oneself) over without resistance — **res·ig·na·tion** \,rezig·'nāshən\ *n* — **re·sign·ed·ly** \-'zīnədlē\ *adv*

re·sil·ience \ri'zilyəns\ *n* : ability to recover or adjust easily

re·sil·ien·cy \-yənsē\ *n* : resilience

re·sil·ient \-yənt\ *adj* : elastic

res·in \'rez'n\ *n* : substance from the gum or sap of trees — **res·in·ous** *adj*

re·sist \ri'zist\ *vb* **1** : withstand the force or effect of **2** : fight against — **re·sist·ible** \-'zistəbəl\ *adj* — **re·sist·less** *adj*

re·sis·tance \ri'zistəns\ *n* **1** : act of resisting **2** : ability of an organism to

---

reknit
relabel
relandscape
relaunch
relearn

relight
reline
reload
remarriage
remarry

rematch
remelt
remobilize
remoisten
remold

resist disease **3** : opposition to electric current

re·sis·tant \-tənt\ adj : giving resistance

res·o·lute \'rezə,lüt\ adj : having a fixed purpose — **res·o·lute·ly** adv — **res·o·lute·ness** n

res·o·lu·tion \,rezə'lüshən\ n **1** : process of resolving **2** : firmness of purpose **3** : statement of the opinion, will, or intent of a body

re·solve \ri'zälv\ vb **-solved; -solv·ing 1** : find an answer to **2** : make a formal resolution ∼ n : something resolved **2** : steadfast purpose — **re·solv·able** adj

res·o·nant \'rez²nənt\ adj **1** : continuing to sound **2** : relating to intensification or prolongation of sound (as by a vibrating body) — **res·o·nance** \-əns\ n — **res·o·nant·ly** adv

re·sort \ri'zȯrt\ n **1** : source of help **2** : place to go for vacation ∼ vb **1** : go often or habitually **2** : have recourse

re·sound \ri'zaùnd\ vb : become filled with sound

re·sound·ing \-iŋ\ adj : impressive — **re·sound·ing·ly** adv

re·source \'rē,sȯrs, ri'sȯrs\ n **1** : new or reserve source **2** pl : available funds **3** : ability to handle situations — **re·source·ful** adj — **re·source·ful·ness** n

re·spect \ri'spekt\ n **1** : relation to something **2** : high or special regard **3** : detail ∼ vb : consider deserving of high regard — **re·spect·er** n — **re·spect·ful** adj — **re·spect·ful·ly** adv — **re·spect·ful·ness** n

re·spect·able \ri'spektəbəl\ adj **1** : worthy of respect **2** : fair in size, quantity, or quality — **re·spect·abil·i·ty** \-,spektə'bilətē\ n — **re·spect·ably** \-'spektəblē\ adv

re·spec·tive \-tiv\ adj : individual and specific

re·spec·tive·ly \-lē\ adv **1** : as relating to each **2** : each in the order given

res·pi·ra·tion \,respə'rāshən\ n : act or process of breathing — **re·spi·ra·to·ry** \'respərə,tȯrē, ri'spīrə-\ adj — **re·spire** \ri'spīr\ vb

res·pi·ra·tor \'respə,rātər\ n : device for artificial respiration

re·spite \'respət\ n : temporary delay or rest

re·splen·dent \ri'splendənt\ adj : shining brilliantly — **re·splen·dence** \-dəns\ n — **re·splen·dent·ly** adv

re·spond \ri'spänd\ vb **1** : answer **2** : react — **re·spon·dent** \-'spändənt\ n or adj — **re·spond·er** n

re·sponse \ri'späns\ n **1** : act of responding **2** : answer

re·spon·si·ble \ri'spänsəbəl\ adj **1** : answerable for acts or decisions **2** : able to fulfill obligations **3** : having important duties — **re·spon·si·bil·i·ty** \-,spänsə'bilətē\ n — **re·spon·si·ble·ness** n — **re·spon·si·bly** \-blē\ adv

re·spon·sive \-siv\ adj : quick to respond — **re·spon·sive·ly** adv — **re·spon·sive·ness** n

¹rest \'rest\ n **1** : sleep **2** : freedom from work or activity **3** : state of inactivity **4** : something used as a support ∼ vb **1** : get rest **2** : cease action or motion **3** : give rest to **4** : sit or lie fixed or supported **5** : depend — **rest·ful** adj — **rest·ful·ly** adv

²rest n : remainder

res·tau·rant \'restərənt, -tə,ränt\ n : public eating place

res·ti·tu·tion \,restə'tüshən, -'tyü-\ n : act or fact of restoring something or repaying someone

res·tive \'restiv\ adj : uneasy or fidgety — **res·tive·ly** adv — **res·tive·ness** n

rest·less \'restləs\ adj **1** : lacking or giving no rest **2** : always moving **3** : uneasy — **rest·less·ly** adv — **rest·less·ness** n

re·store \ri'stȯr\ vb **-stored; -stor·ing 1** : give back **2** : put back into use or into a former state — **re·stor·able** adj — **res·to·ra·tion** \,restə'rāshən\ n — **re·stor·ative** \ri'stȯrətiv\ n or adj — **re·stor·er** n

re·strain \ri'strān\ vb : limit or keep under control — **re·strain·able** adj — **re·strained** \-'strānd\ adj — **re·strain·ed·ly** \-'strānədlē\ adv — **re·strain·er** n

---

remotive | reoccurrence | reorient
rename | reoperate | repack
renegotiate | reorchestrate | repave
reoccupy | reorganization | rephotograph
reoccur | reorganize | replan

restraining order n : legal order directing one person to stay away from another

re·straint \-'strānt\ n **1** : act of restraining **2** : restraining force **3** : control over feelings

re·strict \ri'strikt\ vb **1** : confine within bounds **2** : limit use of — **re·stric·tion** \-'strikshən\ n — **re·stric·tive** adj — **re·stric·tive·ly** adv

re·sult \ri'zəlt\ vb : come about because of something else — ~ n **1** : thing that results **2** : something obtained by calculation or investigation — **re·sul·tant** \-'zəltᵊnt\ adj or n

re·sume \ri'züm\ vb -sumed; -sum·ing : return or take up again after interruption — **re·sump·tion** \-'zəmpshən\ n

ré·su·mé, **re·su·me**, **re·su·mé** \'rezə‚mā, ‚rezə'-\ n : summary of one's career and qualifications

re·sur·gence \ri'sərjəns\ n : a rising again — **re·sur·gent** \-jənt\ adj

res·ur·rect \‚rezə'rekt\ vb **1** : raise from the dead **2** : bring to attention or use again — **res·ur·rec·tion** \-'rekshən\ n

re·sus·ci·tate \ri'səsə‚tāt\ vb -tat·ed; -tat·ing : bring back from apparent death — **re·sus·ci·ta·tion** \ri‚səsə-'tāshən, ‚rē-\ n — **re·sus·ci·ta·tor** \-‚tātər\ n

re·tail \'rē‚tāl\ vb : sell in small quantities directly to the consumer — ~ n : business of selling to consumers — **retail** adj or adv — **re·tail·er** n

re·tain \ri'tān\ vb **1** : keep or hold onto **2** : engage the services of

re·tain·er n **1** : household servant **2** : retaining fee

re·tal·i·ate \ri'talē‚āt\ vb -at·ed; -at·ing : return (an injury) in kind — **re·tal·i·a·tion** \-‚talē'āshən\ n — **re·tal·ia·to·ry** \-'talyə‚tōrē\ adj

re·tard \ri'tärd\ vb : hold back — **re·tar·da·tion** \‚rē‚tär'dāshən, ri-\ n

re·tard·ed \ri'tärdəd\ adj : slow or limited in intellectual development

retch \'rech\ vb : try to vomit

re·ten·tion \ri'tenchən\ n **1** : state of being retained **2** : ability to retain — **re·ten·tive** \-'tentiv\ adj

ret·i·cent \'retəsənt\ adj : tending not to talk — **ret·i·cence** \-səns\ n — **ret·i·cent·ly** adv

ret·i·na \'retᵊnə\ n, pl -nas or -nae \-ᵊn‚ē\ : sensory membrane lining the eye — **ret·i·nal** \'retᵊnəl\ adj

ret·i·nue \'retᵊn‚ü, -‚yü\ n : attendants or followers of a distinguished person

re·tire \ri'tīr\ vb -tired; -tir·ing **1** : withdraw for privacy **2** : end a career **3** : go to bed — **re·tir·ee** \ri‚tī'rē\ n — **re·tire·ment** n

re·tir·ing \ri'tīrin\ adj : shy

re·tort \ri'tōrt\ vb : say in reply — ~ n : quick, witty, or cutting answer

re·trace \rē'trās\ vb : go over again or in reverse

re·tract \ri'trakt\ vb **1** : draw back or in **2** : withdraw a charge or promise — **re·tract·able** adj — **re·trac·tion** \-'trakshən\ n

re·treat \ri'trēt\ n **1** : act of withdrawing **2** : place of privacy or safety or meditation and study — ~ vb : make a retreat

re·trench \ri'trench\ vb : cut down (as expenses) — **re·trench·ment** n

ret·ri·bu·tion \‚retrə'byüshən\ n : retaliation — **re·trib·u·tive** \ri'tribyətiv\ adj — **re·trib·u·to·ry** \-yə‚tōrē\ adj

re·trieve \ri'trēv\ vb -trieved; -triev·ing **1** : search for and bring in game **2** : recover — **re·triev·able** adj — **re·triev·al** \-'trēvəl\ n

re·triev·er \-'trēvər\ n : dog for retrieving game

ret·ro·ac·tive \‚retrō'aktiv\ adj : made effective as of a prior date — **ret·ro·ac·tive·ly** adv

ret·ro·grade \'retrə‚grād\ adj **1** : moving backward **2** : becoming worse

ret·ro·gress \‚retrə'gres\ vb : move backward — **ret·ro·gres·sion** \-'greshən\ n

ret·ro·spect \'retrə‚spekt\ n : review of past events — **ret·ro·spec·tion** \‚retrə'spekshən\ n — **ret·ro·spec·tive** \-'spektiv\ adj — **ret·ro·spec·tive·ly** adv

replaster	repressurize	reread
replay	reprice	rereading
replot	reprint	rerecord
repolish	reprocess	reregister
repopulate	reprogram	reroof

re·turn \ri'tərn\ *vb* **1** : go or come back **2** : pass, give, or send back to an earlier possessor **3** : answer **4** : bring in as a profit **5** : give or do in return ∼ *n* **1** : act of returning or something returned **2** *pl* : report of balloting results **3** : statement of taxable income **4** : profit — **return** *adj* — **re·turn·able** *adj or n* — **re·turn·er** *n*

re·union \rē'yünyən\ *n* **1** : act of reuniting **2** : a meeting of persons after a separation

re·vamp \rē'vamp\ *vb* : renovate or revise

re·veal \ri'vēl\ *vb* **1** : make known **2** : show plainly

rev·eil·le \'revəlē\ *n* : military signal sounded about sunrise

rev·el \'revəl\ *vb* **-eled** *or* **-elled; -el·ing** *or* **-el·ling 1** : take part in a revel **2** : take great pleasure ∼ *n* : wild party or celebration — **rev·el·er, rev·el·ler** \-ər\ *n* — **rev·el·ry** \-rē\ *n*

rev·e·la·tion \revə'lāshən\ *n* **1** : act of revealing **2** : something enlightening or astonishing

re·venge \ri'venj\ *vb* : avenge ∼ *n* **1** : desire for retaliation **2** : act of retaliation — **re·venge·ful** *adj* — **re·veng·er** *n*

rev·e·nue \'revə,nü, -,nyü\ *n* : money collected by a government

re·ver·ber·ate \ri'vərbə,rāt\ *vb* **-at·ed; -at·ing** : resound in a series of echoes — **re·ver·ber·a·tion** \-,vərbə'rā·shən\ *n*

re·vere \ri'vir\ *vb* **-vered; -ver·ing** : show honor and devotion to — **rev·er·ence** \'revərəns\ *n* — **rev·er·ent** \-rənt\ *adj* — **rev·er·ent·ly** *adv*

rev·er·end \'revərənd\ *adj* : worthy of reverence ∼ *n* : clergy member

rev·er·ie \'revərē\ *n, pl* **-er·ies** : daydream

re·verse \ri'vərs\ *adj* **1** : opposite to a previous or normal condition **2** : acting in an opposite way ∼ *vb* **-versed; -vers·ing 1** : turn upside down or completely around **2** : change to the contrary or in the opposite direction ∼ *n* **1** : something contrary **2**

: change for the worse **3** : back of something — **re·ver·sal** \-səl\ *n* — **re·verse·ly** *adv* — **re·vers·ible** \-'vərsəbəl\ *adj*

re·vert \ri'vərt\ *vb* : return to an original type or condition — **re·ver·sion** \-'vərzhən\ *n*

re·view \ri'vyü\ *n* **1** : formal inspection **2** : general survey **3** : critical evaluation **4** : second or repeated study or examination ∼ *vb* **1** : examine or study again **2** : reexamine judicially **3** : look back over **4** : examine critically — **re·view·er** *n*

re·vile \ri'vīl\ *vb* **-viled; -vil·ing** : abuse verbally — **re·vile·ment** *n* — **re·vil·er** *n*

re·vise \-'vīz\ *vb* **-vised; -vis·ing 1** : look over something written to correct or improve **2** : make a new version of — **re·vis·able** *adj* — **revise** *n* — **re·vis·er, re·vi·sor** \-'vīzər\ *n* — **re·vi·sion** \-'vizhən\ *n*

re·viv·al \-'tīvəl\ *n* **1** : act of reviving or state of being revived **2** : evangelistic meeting

re·vive \-'tīv\ *vb* **-vived; -viv·ing** : bring back to life or consciousness or into use — **re·viv·er** *n*

rev·o·ca·tion \revə'kāshən\ *n* : act or instance of revoking

re·voke \ri'vōk\ *vb* **-voked; -vok·ing** : annul by recalling — **re·vok·er** *n*

re·volt \-'vōlt\ *vb* **1** : throw off allegiance **2** : cause or experience disgust or shock ∼ *n* : rebellion or revolution — **re·volt·er** *n*

re·volt·ing \-iŋ\ *adj* : extremely offensive — **re·volt·ing·ly** *adv*

rev·o·lu·tion \revə'lüshən\ *n* **1** : rotation **2** : progress in an orbit **3** : sudden, radical, or complete change (as overthrow of a government) — **rev·o·lu·tion·ary** \-shə,nerē\ *adj or n*

rev·o·lu·tion·ize \-shə,nīz\ *vb* **-ized; -iz·ing** : change radically — **rev·o·lu·tion·iz·er** *n*

re·volve \ri'välv\ *vb* **-volved; -volv·ing 1** : ponder **2** : move in an orbit **3** : rotate — **re·volv·able** *adj*

re·volv·er \ri'välvər\ *n* : pistol with a revolving cylinder

---

reroute	resegregate	resew
resalable	resell	reshoot
resale	resentence	reshow
reschedule	reset	resocialization
reseal	resettle	resod

re·vue \ri'vyü\ n : theatrical production of brief numbers

re·vul·sion \ri'vəlshən\ n : complete dislike or repugnance

re·ward \ri'word\ vb : give a reward to or for ~ n : something offered for service or achievement

re·write \rē'rīt\ vb **-wrote; -writ·ten; -writ·ing** : revise — **rewrite** n

rhap·so·dy \'rapsədē\ n, pl **-dies** 1 : expression of extravagant praise 2 : flowing free-form musical composition — **rhap·sod·ic** \rap'sädik\ adj — **rhap·sod·i·cal·ly** \-iklē\ adv — **rhap·so·dize** \'rapsə,dīz\ vb

rhet·o·ric \'retərik\ n : art of speaking or writing effectively — **rhe·tor·i·cal** \ri'tòrikəl\ adj — **rhet·o·ri·cian** \,retə'rishən\ n

rheu·ma·tism \'rümə,tizəm, 'rùm-\ n : disorder marked by inflammation or pain in muscles or joints — **rheu·mat·ic** \rù'matik\ adj

rhine·stone \'rīn,stōn\ n : a colorless imitation gem

rhi·no \'rīnō\ n, pl **-no** or **-nos** : rhinoceros

rhi·noc·er·os \ri'näsərəs\ n, pl **-noc·er·os·es** or **-noc·er·os** or **-noc·eri** \-'näsə,rī\ : large thick-skinned mammal with 1 or 2 horns on the snout

rho·do·den·dron \,rōdə'dendrən\ n : flowering evergreen shrub

rhom·bus \'rämbəs\ n, pl **-bus·es** or **-bi** \-,bī\ : parallelogram with equal sides

rhu·barb \'rü,bärb\ n : garden plant with edible stalks

rhyme \'rīm\ n 1 : correspondence in terminal sounds 2 : verse that rhymes

~ vb **rhymed; rhym·ing** : make or have rhymes

rhythm \'rithəm\ n : regular succession of sounds or motions — **rhyth·mic** \'rithmik\, **rhyth·mi·cal** \-mikəl\ adj — **rhyth·mi·cal·ly** adv

rhythm and blues n : popular music based on blues and black folk music

rib \'rib\ n 1 : curved bone joined to the spine 2 : riblike thing — vb **-bb- 1** : furnish or mark with ribs 2 : tease — **rib·ber** n

rib·ald \'ribəld\ adj : coarse or vulgar — **rib·ald·ry** \-əldrē\ n

rib·bon \'ribən\ n 1 : narrow strip of fabric used esp. for decoration 2 : strip of inked cloth (as in a typewriter)

ri·bo·fla·vin \,rībə'flāvən, 'rībə,-\ n : growth-promoting vitamin

rice \'rīs\ n, pl **rice** : starchy edible seeds of an annual cereal grass

rich \'rich\ adj 1 : having a lot of money or possessions 2 : valuable 3 : containing much sugar, fat, or seasoning 4 : abundant 5 : deep and pleasing in color or tone 6 : fertile — **rich·ly** adv — **rich·ness** n

rich·es \'richəz\ n pl : wealth

rick·ets \'rikəts\ n : childhood bone disease

rick·ety \'rikətē\ adj : shaky

rick·sha, rick·shaw \'rik,shò\ n : small covered 2-wheeled carriage pulled by one person

ric·o·chet \'rikə,shā, Brit also -,shet\ vb **-cheted** \-,shād\ or **-chet·ted** \-,shetəd\; **-chet·ing** \-,shāiŋ\ or **-chet·ting** \-,shetiŋ\ : bounce off at an angle — **ricochet** n

rid \'rid\ vb **rid; rid·ding** : make free of

---

resolidify	resynthesis	reupholster
restage	resynthesize	reusable
restart	retarget	reuse
restate	reteach	reutilize
restatement	retell	revaccinate
restimulate	retest	revaccination
restock	rethink	revisit
restructure	retighten	rewash
restudy	retrain	reweave
restyle	retranslate	rewind
resubmit	retransmit	rewire
resupply	retry	rewrap
resurface	retune	
resurvey	retype	

something unwanted — **rid·dance** \'rid²ns\ n

rid·den \'rid²n\ adj : overburdened with — used in combination

¹**rid·dle** \'rid²l\ n : puzzling question ~ vb **-dled; -dling** : speak in riddles

²**riddle** vb **-dled; -dling** : fill full of holes

ride \'rīd\ vb **rode** \'rōd\; **rid·den** \'rid²n\; **rid·ing** \'rīdiŋ\ **1** : be carried along **2** : sit on and cause to move **3** : travel over a surface **4** : tease or nag ~ n **1** : trip on an animal or in a vehicle **2** : mechanical device ridden for amusement

rid·er n **1** : one that rides **2** : attached clause or document — **rid·er·less** adj

ridge \'rij\ n **1** : range of hills **2** : raised line or strip **3** : line of intersection of 2 sloping surfaces — **ridgy** adj

rid·i·cule \'ridə,kyül\ vb : laugh at or make fun of — **ridicule** n

ri·dic·u·lous \rə'dikyələs\ adj : arousing ridicule — **ri·dic·u·lous·ly** adv — **ri·dic·u·lous·ness** n

rife \'rīf\ adj : abounding — **rife** adv

riff·raff \'rif,raf\ n : mob

¹**ri·fle** \'rīfəl\ vb **-fled; -fling** : ransack esp. with intent to steal — **ri·fler** \-flər\ n

²**rifle** n : long shoulder weapon with spiral grooves in the bore — **ri·fle·man** \-mən\ n — **ri·fling** n

rift \'rift\ n : separation — **rift** vb

¹**rig** \'rig\ vb **-gg- 1** : fit out with rigging **2** : set up esp. as a makeshift ~ n **1** : distinctive shape, number, and arrangement of sails and masts of a sailing ship **2** : equipment **3** : carriage with its horse

²**rig** vb **-gg-** : manipulate esp. by deceptive or dishonest means

rig·ging \'rigiŋ, -ən\ n : lines that hold and move the masts, sails, and spars of a sailing ship

right \'rīt\ adj **1** : meeting a standard of conduct **2** : correct **3** : genuine **4** : normal **5** : opposite of left ~ n **1** : something that is correct, just, proper, or honorable **2** : something to which one has a just claim **3** : something that is on the right side ~ adv **1** : according to what is right **2** : immediately **3** : completely **4** : on or to the right ~ vb **1** : restore to a proper state **2** : bring or become upright again — **right·er** n — **right·ness** n — **right·ward** \-wərd\ adv

right angle n : angle whose sides are perpendicular to each other — **right–**

an·gled \'rīt'aŋgəld\, **right–an·gle** \-gəl\ adj

righ·teous \'rīchəs\ adj : acting or being in accordance with what is just or moral — **righ·teous·ly** adv — **righ·teous·ness** n

right·ful \'rītfəl\ adj : lawful — **right·ful·ly** \-ē\ adv — **right·ful·ness** n

right·ly \'rītlē\ adv **1** : justly **2** : properly **3** : correctly

rig·id \'rijəd\ adj : lacking flexibility — **ri·gid·i·ty** \rə'jidətē\ n — **rig·id·ly** adv

rig·ma·role \'rigmə,rōl, 'rigə-\ n **1** : meaningless talk **2** : complicated often unnecessary procedure

rig·or \'rigər\ n : severity — **rig·or·ous** adj — **rig·or·ous·ly** adv

rig·or mor·tis \,rigər'mortəs\ n : temporary stiffness of muscles occurring after death

rile \'rīl\ vb **riled; ril·ing** : anger

rill \'ril\ n : small brook

rim \'rim\ n : edge esp. of something curved ~ vb **-mm-** : border

¹**rime** \'rīm\ n : frost — **rimy** \'rīmē\ adj

²**rime** var of RHYME

rind \'rīnd\ n : usu. hard or tough outer layer

¹**ring** \'riŋ\ n **1** : circular band used as an ornament or for holding or fastening **2** : something circular **3** : place for contest or display **4** : group with a selfish or dishonest aim ~ vb : surround — **ringed** \'riŋd\ adj — **ring·like** adj

²**ring** vb **rang** \'raŋ\; **rung** \'rəŋ\; **ring·ing 1** : sound resonantly when struck **2** : cause to make a metallic sound by striking **3** : resound **4** : call esp. by a bell ~ n **1** : resonant sound or tone **2** : act or instance of ringing

ring·er \'riŋər\ n **1** : one that sounds by ringing **2** : illegal substitute **3** : one that closely resembles another

ring·lead·er \'riŋ,lēdər\ n : leader esp. of troublemakers

ring·let n : long curl

ring·worm n : contagious skin disease caused by fungi

rink \'riŋk\ n : enclosed place for skating

rinse \'rins\ vb **rinsed; rins·ing 1** : cleanse usu. with water only **2** : treat (hair) with a rinse ~ n **1** : liquid used for rinsing — **rins·er** n

ri·ot \'rīət\ n **1** : violent public disorder **2** : random or disorderly profusion — **riot** vb — **ri·ot·er** n — **ri·ot·ous** adj

rip \'rip\ *vb* **-pp-** : cut or tear open **~** *n* : rent made by ripping — **rip·per** *n*

ripe \'rīp\ *adj* **rip·er; rip·est** : fully grown, developed, or prepared — **ripe·ly** *adv* — **rip·en** \'rīpən\ *vb* — **ripe·ness** *n*

rip–off *n* : theft — **rip off** *vb*

rip·ple \'ripəl\ *vb* **-pled; -pling** 1 : become lightly ruffled on the surface 2 : sound like rippling water — **ripple** *n*

rise \'rīz\ *vb* **rose** \'rōz\; **ris·en** \'riz²n\; **ris·ing** \'rīziŋ\ 1 : get up from sitting, kneeling, or lying 2 : take arms 3 : appear above the horizon 4 : ascend 5 : gain a higher position or rank 6 : increase **~** *n* 1 : act of rising 2 : origin 3 : elevation 4 : increase 5 : upward slope 6 : area of high ground — **ris·er** \'rīzər\ *n*

risk \'risk\ *n* : exposure to loss or injury — **risk** *vb* — **risk·i·ness** *n* — **risky** *adj*

ris·qué \ris'kā\ *adj* : nearly indecent

rite \'rīt\ *n* 1 : set form for conducting a ceremony 2 : liturgy of a church 3 : ceremonial action

rit·u·al \'richəwəl\ *n* : rite — **ritual** *adj* — **rit·u·al·ism** \-,izəm\ *n* — **rit·u·al·is·tic** \,richəwəl'istik\ *adj* — **rit·u·al·is·ti·cal·ly** \-'tiklē\ *adv* — **rit·u·al·ly** \'richəwəlē\ *adv*

ri·val \'rīvəl\ *n* 1 : competitor 2 : peer **~** *vb* **-valed** *or* **-valled; -val·ing** *or* **-val·ling** 1 : be in competition with 2 : equal — **rival** *adj* — **ri·val·ry** \-rē\ *n*

riv·er \'rivər\ *n* : large natural stream of water — **riv·er·bank** *n* — **riv·er·bed** *n* — **riv·er·boat** *n* — **riv·er·side** *n*

riv·et \'rivət\ *n* : headed metal bolt **~** *vb* : fasten with a rivet — **riv·et·er** *n*

riv·u·let \'rivyələt\ *n* : small stream

roach \'rōch\ *n* : cockroach

road \'rōd\ *n* : open way for vehicles, persons, and animals — **road·bed** *n* — **road·side** *n or adj* — **road·way** *n*

road·block *n* : obstruction on a road

road·run·ner *n* : large fast-running bird

roam \'rōm\ *vb* : wander

roan \'rōn\ *adj* : of a dark color sprinkled with white **~** *n* : animal with a roan coat

roar \'rōr\ *vb* : utter a full loud prolonged sound — **roar** *n* — **roar·er** *n*

roast \'rōst\ *vb* 1 : cook by dry heat 2 : criticize severely **~** *n* : piece of meat suitable for roasting — **roast** *adj* — **roast·er** *n*

rob \'räb\ *vb* **-bb-** 1 : steal from 2 : commit robbery — **rob·ber** *n*

rob·bery \'räbərē\ *n, pl* **-ber·ies** : theft of something from a person by use of violence or threat

robe \'rōb\ *n* 1 : long flowing outer garment 2 : covering for the lower body **~** *vb* **robed; rob·ing** : clothe with or as if with a robe

rob·in \'räbən\ *n* : No. American thrush with a reddish breast

ro·bot \'rō,bät, -bət\ *n* 1 : machine that looks and acts like a human being 2 : efficient but insensitive person — **ro·bot·ic** \rō'bätik\ *adj*

ro·bust \rō'bəst, 'rō,bəst\ *adj* : strong and vigorously healthy — **ro·bust·ly** *adv* — **ro·bust·ness** *n*

¹**rock** \'räk\ *vb* : sway or cause to sway back and forth **~** *n* 1 : rocking movement 2 : popular music marked by repetition and a strong beat

²**rock** *n* : mass of hard mineral material — **rock** *adj* — **rocky** *adj*

rock·er *n* 1 : curved piece on which a chair rocks 2 : chair that rocks

rock·et \'räkət\ *n* 1 : self-propelled firework or missile 2 : jet engine that carries its own oxygen **~** *vb* : rise abruptly and rapidly — **rock·et·ry** \-ətrē\ *n*

rod \'räd\ *n* 1 : straight slender stick 2 : unit of length equal to 5 yards

rode *past of* RIDE

ro·dent \'rōd²nt\ *n* : usu. small gnawing mammal

ro·deo \'rōdē,ō, rō'dāō\ *n, pl* **-de·os** : contest of cowboy skills

roe \'rō\ *n* : fish eggs

rogue \'rōg\ *n* : dishonest or mischievous person — **rogu·ery** \'rōgərē\ *n* — **rogu·ish** \'rōgish\ *adj* — **rogu·ish·ly** *adv* — **rogu·ish·ness** *n*

roil \'rȯil\ *vb* 1 : make cloudy or muddy by stirring up 2 : make angry

role \'rōl\ *n* 1 : part to play 2 : function

roll \'rōl\ *n* 1 : official record or list of names 2 : something rolled up or rounded 3 : bread baked in a small rounded mass 4 : sound of rapid drum strokes 5 : heavy reverberating sound 6 : rolling movement **~** *vb* 1 : move by turning over 2 : move on wheels 3 : flow in a continuous stream 4 : swing from side to side 5 : shape or be shaped in rounded form 6 : press with a roller

roll·er *n* 1 : revolving cylinder 2 : rod on which something is rolled up 3 : long heavy ocean wave

roller skate n : a skate with wheels instead of a runner — **roller–skate** vb

rol·lick·ing \'rälikiŋ\ adj : full of good spirits

Ro·man Catholic \'rōmən-\ n : member of a Christian church led by a pope — **Roman Catholic** adj — **Roman Catholicism** n

ro·mance \rō'mans, 'rō,mans\ n 1 : medieval tale of knightly adventure 2 : love story 3 : love affair ~ vb -manced; -manc·ing 1 : have romantic fancies 2 : have a love affair with — **ro·manc·er** n

ro·man·tic \rō'mantik\ adj 1 : visionary or imaginative 2 : appealing to one's emotions — **ro·man·ti·cal·ly** \-k.lē\ adv

romp \'rämp\ vb : play actively and noisily — **romp** n

roof \'rüf, 'rüf\ n, pl **roofs** \'rüfs, 'rüfs; 'rüvz, 'rüvz\ : upper covering part of a building ~ vb : cover with a roof — **roofed** \'rüft, 'rüft\ adj — **roof·ing** n — **roof·less** adj — **roof·top** n

¹rook \'rük\ n : crowlike bird

²rook vb : cheat

rook·ie \'rükē\ n : novice

room \'rüm, 'rúm\ n 1 : sufficient space 2 : partitioned part of a building ~ vb : occupy lodgings — **room·er** n — **room·ful** n — **roomy** adj

room·mate n : one sharing the same lodgings

roost \'rüst\ n : support on which birds perch ~ vb : settle on a roost

roost·er \'rüstər, 'rüs-\ n : adult male domestic chicken

¹root \'rüt, 'rút\ n 1 : leafless underground part of a seed plant 2 : rootlike thing or part 3 : source 4 : essential core ~ vb : form, fix, or become fixed by roots — **root·less** adj — **root·let** \-lət\ n — **root·like** adj

²root vb : turn up with the snout

³root \'rüt, 'rút\ vb : applaud or encourage noisily — **root·er** n

rope \'rōp\ n : large strong cord of strands of fiber ~ vb roped; rop·ing 1 : tie with a rope 2 : lasso

ro·sa·ry \'rōzərē\ n, pl -ries 1 : string of beads used in praying 2 : Roman Catholic devotion

¹rose past of RISE

²rose \'rōz\ n 1 : prickly shrub with bright flowers 2 : purplish red — **rose** adj — **rose·bud** n — **rose·bush** n

rose·mary \'rōz,merē\ n, pl **-mar·ies** : fragrant shrubby mint

ro·sette \rō'zet\ n : rose-shaped ornament

Rosh Ha·sha·nah \,räshhä'shänə, ,rōsh-\ n : Jewish New Year observed as a religious holiday in September or October

ros·in \'räz'n\ n : brittle resin

ros·ter \'rästər\ n : list of names

ros·trum \'rästrəm\ n, pl **-trums** or **-tra** \-trə\ : speaker's platform

rosy \'rōzē\ adj **ros·i·er; -est** 1 : of the color rose 2 : hopeful — **ros·i·ly** adv — **ros·i·ness** n

rot \'rät\ vb **-tt-** : undergo decomposition ~ n 1 : decay 2 : disease in which tissue breaks down

ro·ta·ry \'rōtərē\ adj 1 : turning on an axis 2 : having a rotating part

ro·tate \'rō,tāt\ vb **-tat·ed; -tat·ing** 1 : turn about an axis or a center 2 : alternate in a series — **ro·ta·tion** \rō'tāshən\ n — **ro·ta·tor** \'rō,tātər\ n

rote \'rōt\ n : repetition from memory

ro·tor \'rōtər\ n 1 : part that rotates 2 : system of rotating horizontal blades for supporting a helicopter

rot·ten \'rät'n\ adj 1 : having rotted 2 : corrupt 3 : extremely unpleasant or inferior — **rot·ten·ness** n

ro·tund \rō'tənd\ adj : rounded — **ro·tun·di·ty** \-'təndətē\ n

ro·tun·da \rō'təndə\ n : building or room with a dome

roué \rü'ā\ n : man given to debauched living

rouge \'rüzh, 'rüj\ n : cosmetic for the cheeks — **rouge** vb

rough \'rəf\ adj 1 : not smooth 2 : not calm 3 : harsh, violent, or rugged 4 : crudely or hastily done ~ n : rough state or something in that state ~ vb 1 : roughen 2 : manhandle 3 : make roughly — **rough·ly** adv — **rough·ness** n

rough·age \'rəfij\ n : coarse bulky food

rough·en \'rəfən\ vb : make or become rough

rough·neck \'rəf,nek\ n : rowdy

rou·lette \rü'let\ n : gambling game using a whirling numbered wheel

round \'raúnd\ adj 1 : having every part the same distance from the center 2 : cylindrical 3 : complete 4 : approximate 5 : blunt 6 : moving in or forming a circle ~ n 1 : round or curved thing **2** : series of recurring actions or events **3** : period of time or a unit of action **4** : fired shot **5** : cut of beef $\sim$ *vb* **1** : make or become round **2** : go around **3** : finish **4** : express as an approximation — **round·ish** *adj* — **round·ly** *adv* — **round·ness** *n*

²**round** *prep or adv* : around

round·about *adj* : indirect

round·up \'raùnd,əp\ *n* **1** : gathering together of range cattle **2** : summary — **round up** *vb*

rouse \'raùz\ *vb* **roused; rous·ing 1** : wake from sleep **2** : stir up

rout \'raùt\ *n* **1** : state of wild confusion **2** : disastrous defeat $\sim$ *vb* : defeat decisively

route \'rüt, 'raùt\ *n* : line of travel $\sim$ *vb* **rout·ed; rout·ing** : send by a selected route

rou·tine \rü'tēn\ *n* **1** : regular course of procedure **2** : an often repeated speech, formula, or part — **routine** *adj* — **rou·tine·ly** *adv*

rove \'rōv\ *vb* **roved; rov·ing** : wander or roam — **rov·er** *n*

¹**row** \'rō\ *vb* **1** : propel a boat with oars **2** : carry in a rowboat $\sim$ *n* : act of rowing — **row·boat** \-,bōt\ *n* — **row·er** \'rōər\ *n*

²**row** *n* : number of objects in a line

³**row** \'raù\ *n* : noisy quarrel — **row** *vb*

row·dy \'raùdē\ *adj* **-di·er; -est** : coarse or boisterous in behavior — **row·di·ness** *n* — **rowdy** *n*

roy·al \'rȯiəl\ *adj* : relating to or befitting a king $\sim$ *n* : person of royal blood — **roy·al·ly** *adv*

roy·al·ty \'rȯiəltē\ *n, pl* **-ties 1** : state of being royal **2** : royal persons **3** : payment for use of property

rub \'rəb\ *vb* **-bb- 1** : use pressure and friction on a body **2** : scour, polish, erase, or smear by pressure and friction **3** : chafe with friction $\sim$ *n* : difficulty

rub·ber \'rəbər\ *n* **1** : one that rubs **2** : waterproof elastic substance or something made of it — **rubber** *adj* — **rub·ber·ize** \-,īz\ *vb* — **rub·bery** *adj*

rub·bish \'rəbish\ *n* : waste or trash

rub·ble \'rəbəl\ *n* : broken fragments esp. of a destroyed building

ru·ble \'rübəl\ *n* : monetary unit of Russia

ru·by \'rübē\ *n, pl* **-bies** : precious red stone or its color — **ruby** *adj*

rud·der \'rədər\ *n* : steering device at the rear of a ship or aircraft

rud·dy \'rədē\ *adj* **-di·er; -est** : reddish — **rud·di·ness** *n*

rude \'rüd\ *adj* **rud·er; rud·est 1** : roughly made **2** : impolite — **rude·ly** *adv* — **rude·ness** *n*

ru·di·ment \'rüdəmənt\ *n* **1** : something not fully developed **2** : elementary principle — **ru·di·men·ta·ry** \,rüdə'mentərē\ *adj*

rue \'rü\ *vb* **rued; ru·ing** : feel regret for $\sim$ *n* : regret — **rue·ful** \-fəl\ *adj* — **rue·ful·ly** *adv* — **rue·ful·ness** *n*

ruf·fi·an \'rəfēən\ *n* : brutal person

ruf·fle \'rəfəl\ *vb* **-fled; -fling 1** : draw into or provide with pleats **2** : roughen the surface of **3** : irritate $\sim$ *n* : strip of fabric pleated on one edge — **ruf·fly** \'rəfəlē, -flē\ *adj*

rug \'rəg\ *n* : piece of heavy fabric used as a floor covering

rug·ged \'rəgəd\ *adj* **1** : having a rough uneven surface **2** : severe **3** : strong — **rug·ged·ly** *adv* — **rug·ged·ness** *n*

ru·in \'rüən\ *n* **1** : complete collapse or destruction **2** : remains of something destroyed — usu. in pl. **3** : cause of destruction $\sim$ *vb* **1** : destroy **2** : damage beyond repair **3** : bankrupt

ru·in·ous \'rüənəs\ *adj* : causing ruin — **ru·in·ous·ly** *adv*

rule \'rül\ *n* **1** : guide or principle for governing action **2** : usual way of doing something **3** : government **4** : straight strip (as of wood or metal) marked off in units for measuring $\sim$ *vb* **ruled; rul·ing 1** : govern **2** : give as a decision — **rul·er** *n*

rum \'rəm\ *n* : liquor made from molasses or sugarcane

rum·ble \'rəmbəl\ *vb* **-bled; -bling** : make a low heavy rolling sound — **rumble** *n*

ru·mi·nant \'rümənənt\ *n* : hoofed mammal (as a cow or deer) that chews the cud — **ruminant** *adj*

ru·mi·nate \'rümə,nāt\ *vb* **-nat·ed; -nat·ing** : contemplate — **ru·mi·na·tion** \,rümə'nāshən\ *n*

rum·mage \'rəmij\ *vb* **-maged; -mag·ing** : search thoroughly

rum·my \'rəmē\ *n* : card game

ru·mor \'rümər\ *n* **1** : common talk **2** : widespread statement not authenticated — **rumor** *vb*

rump \'rəmp\ *n* : rear part of an animal

rum·ple \'rəmpəl\ *vb* **-pled; -pling** : tousle or wrinkle — **rumple** *n*

rum·pus \'rəmpəs\ *n* : disturbance

run \'rən\ *vb* **ran** \'ran\; **run**; **run·ning** **1** : go rapidly or hurriedly **2** : enter a race or election **3** : operate **4** : continue in force **5** : flow rapidly **6** : take a certain direction **7** : manage **8** : incur ~ *n* **1** : act of running **2** : brook **3** : continuous series **4** : usual kind **5** : freedom of movement **6** : lengthwise ravel

run·around *n* : evasive or delaying action esp. in response to a request

run·away \'rənə‚wā\ *n* : fugitive ~ *adj* **1** : fugitive **2** : out of control

run·down *adj* : being in poor condition

¹rung *past part of* RING

²rung \'rəŋ\ *n* : horizontal piece of a chair or ladder

run·ner \'rənər\ *n* **1** : one that runs **2** : thin piece or part on which something slides **3** : slender creeping branch of a plant

run·ner–up *n, pl* **run·ners–up** : competitor who finishes second

run·ning \'rəniŋ\ *adj* **1** : flowing **2** : continuous

runt \'rənt\ *n* : small person or animal — **runty** *adj*

run·way \'rən‚wā\ *n* : strip on which aircraft land and take off

ru·pee \rü'pē, 'rü‚-\ *n* : monetary unit (as of India)

rup·ture \'rəpchər\ *n* **1** : breaking or tearing apart **2** : hernia ~ *vb* **-tured; -tur·ing** : cause or undergo rupture

ru·ral \'rürəl\ *adj* : relating to the country or agriculture

ruse \'rüs, 'rüz\ *n* : trick

¹rush \'rəsh\ *n* : grasslike marsh plant

²rush *vb* **1** : move forward or act with too great haste **2** : perform in a short time ~ *n* **1** : violent forward motion ~ *adj* : requiring speed — **rush·er** *n*

rus·set \'rəsət\ *n* **1** : reddish brown color **2** : a baking potato — **russet** *adj*

rust \'rəst\ *n* **1** : reddish coating on exposed iron **2** : reddish brown color — **rust** *vb* — **rusty** *adj*

rus·tic \'rəstik\ *adj* : relating to or suitable for the country or country dwellers ~ *n* : rustic person — **rus·ti·cal·ly** *adv*

rus·tle \'rəsəl\ *vb* **-tled; -tling 1** : make or cause a rustle **2** : forage food **3** : steal cattle from the range ~ *n* : series of small sounds — **rus·tler** \-ələr\ *n*

rut \'rət\ *n* **1** : track worn by wheels or feet **2** : set routine — **rut·ted** *adj*

ruth·less \'rüthləs\ *adj* : having no pity — **ruth·less·ly** *adv* — **ruth·less·ness** *n*

RV \‚är-'vē\ *n* recreational vehicle

rye \'rī\ *n* **1** : cereal grass grown for grain **2** : whiskey from rye

S

s \'es\ *n, pl* **s's** *or* **ss** \'esəz\ : 19th letter of the alphabet

¹-s \s *after sounds* f, k, k̲, p, t, th; əz *after sounds* ch, j, s, sh, z, zh; z *after other sounds*\ — used to form the plural of most nouns

²-s *vb suffix* — used to form the 3d person singular present of most verbs

Sab·bath \'sabəth\ *n* **1** : Saturday observed as a day of worship by Jews and some Christians **2** : Sunday observed as a day of worship by Christians

sa·ber, sa·bre \'sābər\ *n* : curved cavalry sword

sa·ble \'sābəl\ *n* **1** : black **2** : dark brown mammal or its fur

sab·o·tage \'sabə‚täzh\ *n* : deliberate destruction or hampering ~ *vb* **-taged; -tag·ing** : wreck through sabotage

sab·o·teur \‚sabə'tər\ *n* : person who sabotages

sac \'sak\ *n* : anatomical pouch

sac·cha·rin \'sakərən\ *n* : low-calorie artificial sweetener

sac·cha·rine \-ərən\ *adj* : nauseatingly sweet

sa·chet \sa'shā\ *n* : small bag with perfumed powder (**sachet powder**)

¹sack \'sak\ *n* : bag ~ *vb* : fire

²sack *vb* : plunder a captured place

²sack·cloth *n* : rough garment worn as a sign of penitence

sac·ra·ment \'sakrəmənt\ n : formal religious act or rite — **sac·ra·men·tal** \,sakrə'mentᵊl\ adj

sa·cred \'sākrəd\ adj 1 : set apart for or worthy of worship 2 : worthy of reverence 3 : relating to religion — **sa·cred·ly** adv — **sa·cred·ness** n

sac·ri·fice \'sakrə,fīs\ n 1 : the offering of something precious to a deity or the thing offered 2 : loss or deprivation ~ vb -ficed; -fic·ing : offer or give up as a sacrifice — **sac·ri·fi·cial** \,sakrə'fishəl\ adj

sac·ri·lege \'sakrəlij\ n : violation of something sacred — **sac·ri·le·gious** \,sakrə'lijəs, -'lējəs\ adj

sac·ro·sanct \'sakrō,saŋkt\ adj : sacred

sad \'sad\ adj -dd- 1 : affected with grief or sorrow 2 : causing sorrow — **sad·den** \'sadᵊn\ vb — **sad·ly** adv — **sad·ness** n

sad·dle \'sadᵊl\ n : seat for riding on horseback ~ vb -dled; -dling : put a saddle on

sa·dism \'sā,dizəm, 'sad,iz-\ n : delight in cruelty — **sa·dist** \'sādist, 'sad-\ n — **sa·dis·tic** \sə'distik\ adj — **sa·dis·ti·cal·ly** adv

sa·fa·ri \sə'färē, -'far-\ n : hunting expedition in Africa

safe \'sāf\ adj saf·er; saf·est 1 : free from harm 2 : providing safety ~ n : container to keep valuables safe — **safe·keep·ing** n — **safe·ly** adv

safe·guard n : measure or device for preventing accidents — **safeguard** vb

safe·ty \'sāftē\ n, pl -ties 1 : freedom from danger 2 : protective device

saf·flow·er \'saf,laůər\ n : herb with seeds rich in edible oil

saf·fron \'safrən\ n : orange powder from a crocus flower used in cooking

sag \'sag\ vb -gg- : droop, sink, or settle — **sag** n

sa·ga \'sägə\ n : story of heroic deeds

sa·ga·cious \sə'gāshəs\ adj : shrewd — **sa·gac·i·ty** \-'gasətē\ n

¹**sage** \'sāj\ adj : wise or prudent ~ n : wise man — **sage·ly** adv

²**sage** n : mint used in flavoring

sage·brush n : low shrub of the western U.S.

said past of SAY

sail \'sāl\ n 1 : fabric used to catch the wind and move a boat or ship 2 : trip on a sailboat ~ vb 1 : travel on a ship or sailboat 2 : move with ease or grace — **sail·boat** n — **sail·or** \'sālər\ n

sail·fish n : large fish with a very large dorsal fin

saint \'sānt, before a name ,sānt or sənt\ n : holy or godly person — **saint·ed** \-əd\ adj — **saint·hood** \-,hủd\ n — **saint·li·ness** n — **saint·ly** adj

¹**sake** \'sāk\ n 1 : purpose or reason 2 : one's good or benefit

²**sa·ke, sa·ki** \'säkē\ n : Japanese rice wine

sa·la·cious \sə'lāshəs\ adj : sexually suggestive — **sa·la·cious·ly** adv

sal·ad \'saləd\ n : dish usu. of raw lettuce, vegetables, or fruit

sal·a·man·der \'salə,mandər\ n : lizardlike amphibian

sa·la·mi \sə'lämē\ n : highly seasoned dried sausage

sal·a·ry \'salərē\ n, pl -ries : regular payment for services

sale \'sāl\ n 1 : transfer of ownership of property for money 2 : selling at bargain prices 3 **sales** pl : activities involved in selling — **sal·able, sale·able** \'sāləbəl\ adj — **sales·man** \-mən\ n — **sales·per·son** n — **sales·wom·an** n

sa·lient \'sālyənt\ adj : standing out conspicuously

sa·line \'sā,lēn, -,līn\ adj : containing salt — **sa·lin·i·ty** \sā'linətē, sə-\ n

sa·li·va \sə'līvə\ n : liquid secreted into the mouth — **sal·i·vary** \'salə,verē\ adj — **sal·i·vate** \-,vāt\ vb — **sal·i·va·tion** \,salə'vāshən\ n

sal·low \'salō\ adj : of a yellowish sickly color

sal·ly \'salē\ n, pl -lies 1 : quick attack on besiegers 2 : witty remark — **sally** vb

salmon \'samən\ n, pl **salmon** 1 : food fish with pink or red flesh 2 : deep yellowish pink color

sa·lon \sə'län, 'sal,än, sa'lōⁿ\ n : elegant room or shop

sa·loon \sə'lün\ n 1 : public cabin on a passenger ship 2 : barroom

sal·sa \'sólsə, 'säl-\ n : spicy sauce of tomatoes, onions, and hot peppers

salt \'sólt\ n 1 : white crystalline substance that consists of sodium and chlorine 2 : compound formed usu. from acid and metal — **salt** vb or adj — **salt·i·ness** n — **salty** adj

salt·wa·ter adj : relating to or living in salt water

sa·lu·bri·ous \sə'lübrēəs\ adj : good for health

sal·u·tary \'salyə,terē\ *adj* : health-giving or beneficial

sal·u·ta·tion \,salyə'tāshən\ *n* : greeting

sa·lute \sə'lüt\ *vb* **-lut·ed; -lut·ing** : honor by ceremony or formal movement — **salute** *n*

sal·vage \'salvij\ *n* : something saved from destruction ∼ *vb* **-vaged; -vag·ing** : rescue or save

sal·va·tion \sal'vāshən\ *n* : saving of a person from sin or danger

salve \'sav, 'sȧv\ *n* : medicinal ointment ∼ *vb* **salved; salv·ing** : soothe

sal·ver \'salvər\ *n* : small tray

sal·vo \'salvō\ *n, pl* **-vos** *or* **-voes** : simultaneous discharge of guns

same \'sām\ *adj* : being the one referred to ∼ *pron* : the same one or ones ∼ *adv* : in the same manner — **same·ness** *n*

sam·ple \'sampəl\ *n* : piece or part that shows the quality of a whole ∼ *vb* **-pled; -pling** : judge by a sample

sam·pler \'samplər\ *n* : piece of needlework testing skill in embroidering

san·a·to·ri·um \,sanə'tōrēəm\ *n, pl* **-riums** *or* **-ria** \-ēə\ : hospital for the chronically ill

sanc·ti·fy \'saŋktə,fī\ *vb* **-fied; -fy·ing** : make holy — **sanc·ti·fi·ca·tion** \,saŋktəfə'kāshən\ *n*

sanc·ti·mo·nious \,saŋktə'mōnēəs\ *adj* : hypocritically pious — **sanc·ti·mo·nious·ly** *adv*

sanc·tion \'saŋkshən\ *n* **1** : authoritative approval **2** : coercive measure — usu. pl ∼ *vb* : approve

sanc·ti·ty \'saŋktətē\ *n, pl* **-ties** : quality or state of being holy or sacred

sanc·tu·ary \'saŋkchə,werē\ *n, pl* **-ies** **1** : consecrated place **2** : place of refuge

sand \'sand\ *n* : loose granular particles of rock ∼ *vb* : smooth with an abrasive — **sand·bank** *n* — **sand·er** *n* — **sand·storm** *n* — **sandy** *adj*

san·dal \'sand'l\ *n* : shoe consisting of a sole strapped to the foot

sand·pa·per *n* : abrasive paper — **sandpaper** *vb*

sand·pip·er \-,pīpər\ *n* : long-billed shorebird

sand·stone *n* : rock made of naturally cemented sand

sand·wich \'sand,wich\ *n* **2** : or more slices of bread with a filling between them ∼ *vb* : squeeze or crowd in

sane \'sān\ *adj* **san·er; san·est 1** : mentally healthy **2** : sensible — **sane·ly** *adv*

sang *past of* SING

san·gui·nary \'saŋgwə,nerē\ *adj* : bloody

san·guine \'saŋgwən\ *adj* **1** : reddish **2** : cheerful

san·i·tar·i·um \,sanə'terēəm\ *n, pl* **-iums** *or* **-ia** \-ēə\ : sanatorium

san·i·tary \'sanə,terē\ *adj* **1** : relating to health **2** : free from filth or infective matter

san·i·ta·tion \,sanə'tāshən\ *n* : protection of health by maintenance of sanitary conditions

san·i·ty \'sanətē\ *n* : soundness of mind

sank *past of* SINK

¹sap \'sap\ *n* **1** : fluid that circulates through a plant **2** : gullible person

²sap *vb* **-pp- 1** : undermine **2** : weaken or exhaust gradually

sa·pi·ent \'sāpēənt, 'sapē-\ *adj* : wise — **sa·pi·ence** \-əns\ *n*

sap·ling \'sapliŋ\ *n* : young tree

sap·phire \'saf,īr\ *n* : hard transparent blue gem

sap·py \'sapē\ *adj* **-pi·er; -est 1** : full of sap **2** : overly sentimental

sap·suck·er \'sap,səkər\ *n* : small No. American woodpecker

sar·casm \'sär,kazəm\ *n* **1** : cutting remark **2** : ironical criticism or reproach — **sar·cas·tic** \sär'kastik\ *adj* — **sar·cas·ti·cal·ly** *adv*

sar·coph·a·gus \sär'käfəgəs\ *n, pl* **-gi** \-,gī, -,jī\ : large stone coffin

sar·dine \sär'dēn\ *n* : small fish preserved for use as food

sar·don·ic \sär'dänik\ *adj* : disdainfully humorous — **sar·don·i·cal·ly** *adv*

sa·rong \sə'roŋ, -'räŋ\ *n* : loose garment worn esp. by Pacific islanders

sar·sa·pa·ril·la \,saspə'rilə, ,särs-\ *n* : dried roots of a tropical American plant used esp. for flavoring or a carbonated drink flavored with this

sar·to·ri·al \sär'tōrēəl\ *adj* : relating to a tailor or men's clothes

¹sash \'sash\ *n* : broad band worn around the waist or over the shoulder

²sash *n, pl* **sash 1** : frame for a pane of glass in a door or window **2** : movable part of a window

sas·sa·fras \'sasə,fras\ *n* : No. American tree or its dried root bark

sassy \'sasē\ *adj* **sass·i·er; -est** : saucy

sat *past of* SIT

Sa·tan \'sāt³n\ n : devil — **sa·tan·ic** \sə-'tanik, sā-\ adj — **sa·tan·i·cal·ly** adv

satch·el \'sachəl\ n : small bag

sate \'sāt\ vb **sat·ed; sat·ing** : satisfy fully

sat·el·lite \'sat³l‚īt\ n 1 : toady 2 : body or object that revolves around a larger celestial body

sa·ti·ate \'sāshē‚āt\ vb **-at·ed; -at·ing** : sate — **sa·ti·ety** \sə'tīətē\ n

sat·in \'sat³n\ n : glossy fabric — **sat·iny** adj

sat·ire \'sa‚tīr\ n : literary ridicule done with humor — **sa·tir·ic** \sə'tirik\, **sa·tir·i·cal** \-ikəl\ adj — **sa·tir·i·cal·ly** adv — **sat·i·rist** \'satərist\ n — **sat·i·rize** \-ə‚rīz\ vb

sat·is·fac·tion \‚satəs'fakshən\ n : state of being satisfied — **sat·is·fac·to·ri·ly** \-'faktərəlē\ adv — **sat·is·fac·to·ry** \-'faktərē\ adj

sat·is·fy \'satəs‚fī\ vb **-fied; -fy·ing** 1 : make happy 2 : pay what is due to or on — **sat·is·fy·ing·ly** adv

sat·u·rate \'sachə‚rāt\ vb **-rat·ed; -rat·ing** : soak or charge thoroughly — **sat·u·ra·tion** \‚sachə'rāshən\ n

Sat·ur·day \'satərdā, -dē\ n : 7th day of the week

sat·ur·nine \'satər‚nīn\ adj : sullen

sa·tyr \'sātər, 'sat-\ n : pleasure-loving forest god of ancient Greece

sauce \'sȯs\ n : fluid dressing or topping for food — **sauce·pan** n

sau·cer \'sȯsər\ n : small shallow dish under a cup

saucy \'sasē, 'sȯsē\ adj **sauc·i·er; -est** : insolent — **sauc·i·ly** adv — **sauc·i·ness** n

sauer·kraut \'saůər‚kraůt\ n : finely cut and fermented cabbage

sau·na \'saůnə\ n : steam or dry heat bath or a room or cabinet used for such a bath

saun·ter \'sȯntər, 'sänt-\ vb : stroll

sau·sage \'sȯsij\ n : minced and highly seasoned meat

sau·té \sȯ'tā, sō-\ vb **-téed** or **-téd; -té·ing** : fry in a little fat — **sauté** n

sav·age \'savij\ adj 1 : wild 2 : cruel ~ n : person belonging to a primitive society — **sav·age·ly** adv — **sav·age·ness** n — **sav·age·ry** n

¹**save** \'sāv\ vb **saved; sav·ing** 1 : rescue from danger 2 : guard from destruction 3 : redeem from sin 4 : put aside as a reserve — **sav·er** n

²**save** prep : except

sav·ior, sav·iour \'sāvyər\ n 1 : one who saves 2 cap : Jesus Christ

sa·vor \'sāvər\ n : special flavor ~ vb : taste with pleasure — **sa·vory** adj

¹**saw** past of SEE

²**saw** \'sȯ\ n : cutting tool with teeth ~ vb **sawed; sawed** or **sawn; saw·ing** : cut with a saw — **saw·dust** \-‚dəst\ n — **saw·mill** n — **saw·yer** \-yər\ n

saw·horse n : support for wood being sawed

sax·o·phone \'saksə‚fōn\ n : wind instrument with a reed mouthpiece and usu. a bent metal body

say \'sā\ vb **said** \'sed\; **say·ing** \'sāiŋ\; **says** \'sez\ 1 : express in words 2 : state positively ~ n, pl **says** \'sāz\ 1 : expression of opinion 2 : power of decision

say·ing \'sāiŋ\ n : commonly repeated statement

scab \'skab\ n 1 : protective crust over a sore or wound 2 : worker taking a striker's job ~ vb **-bb-** 1 : become covered with a scab 2 : work as a scab — **scab·by** adj

scab·bard \'skabərd\ n : sheath for the blade of a weapon

scaf·fold \'skafəld, -‚ōld\ n 1 : raised platform for workmen 2 : platform on which a criminal is executed

scald \'skȯld\ vb 1 : burn with hot liquid or steam 2 : heat to the boiling point

¹**scale** \'skāl\ n : weighing device ~ vb **scaled; scal·ing** : weigh

²**scale** n 1 : thin plate esp. on the body of a fish or reptile 2 : thin coating or layer ~ vb **scaled; scal·ing** : strip of scales — **scaled** \'skāld\ adj — **scaleless** adj — **scaly** adj

³**scale** n 1 : graduated series 2 : size of a sample (as a model) in proportion to the size of the actual thing 3 : standard of estimation or judgment 4 : series of musical tones ~ vb **scaled; scal·ing** 1 : climb by a ladder 2 : arrange in a graded series

scal·lion \'skalyən\ n : bulbless onion

scal·lop \'skäləp, 'skal-\ n 1 : marine mollusk 2 : rounded projection on a border

scalp \'skalp\ n : skin and flesh of the head ~ vb 1 : remove the scalp from 2 : resell at a greatly increased price — **scalp·er** n

scal·pel \'skalpəl\ n : surgical knife

scamp \'skamp\ n : rascal

scam·per \'skampər\ *vb* : run nimbly — **scamper** *n*

scan \'skan\ *vb* **-nn-** 1 : read (verses) so as to show meter 2 : examine closely or hastily 3 : examine with a sensing device — **scan** *n* — **scan·ner** *n*

scan·dal \'skand°l\ *n* 1 : disgraceful situation 2 : malicious gossip — **scan·dal·ize** *vb* — **scan·dal·ous** *adj*

scant \'skant\ *adj* : barely sufficient ∼ *vb* : stint — **scant·i·ly** *adv* — **scanty** *adj*

scape·goat \'skāp₁gōt\ *n* : one that bears the blame for others

scap·u·la \'skapyələ\ *n, pl* **-lae** \-₁lē\ *or* **-las** : shoulder blade

scar \'skär\ *n* : mark where a wound has healed — **scar** *vb*

scar·ab \'skarəb\ *n* : large dark beetle or an ornament representing one

scarce \'skers\ *adj* **scarc·er; scarc·est** : lacking in quantity or number — **scar·ci·ty** \'skersətē\ *n*

scarce·ly \'skerslē\ *adv* 1 : barely 2 : almost not

scare \'sker\ *vb* **scared; scar·ing** : frighten — *n* : fright — **scary** *adj*

scare·crow \'sker₁krō\ *n* : figure for scaring birds from crops

scarf \'skärf\ *n, pl* **scarves** \'skärvz\ *or* **scarfs** : cloth worn about the shoulders or the neck

scar·let \'skärlət\ *n* : bright red color — **scarlet** *adj*

scarlet fever *n* : acute contagious disease marked by fever, sore throat, and red rash

scath·ing \'skāthiŋ\ *adj* : bitterly severe

scat·ter \'skatər\ *vb* 1 : spread about irregularly 2 : disperse

scav·en·ger \'skavənjər\ *n* 1 : person that collects refuse or waste 2 : animal that feeds on decayed matter — **scav·enge** \'skavənj\ *vb*

sce·nar·io \sə'narē₁ō, -'när-\ *n, pl* **-i·os** 1 : plot of a play or movie 2 : possible sequence of events

scene \'sēn\ *n* 1 : single situation in a play or movie 2 : stage setting 3 : view 4 : display of emotion — **sce·nic** \'sēnik\ *adj*

scen·ery \'sēnərē\ *n, pl* **-er·ies** 1 : painted setting for a stage 2 : picturesque view

scent \'sent\ *vb* 1 : smell 2 : fill with odor ∼ *n* 1 : odor 2 : sense of smell 3 : perfume — **scent·ed** \'sentəd\ *adj*

scep·ter \'septər\ *n* : staff signifying authority

scep·tic \'skeptik\ *var of* SKEPTIC

sched·ule \'skejül, *esp Brit* 'shedyül\ *n* : list showing sequence of events ∼ *vb* **-uled; -ul·ing** : make a schedule of

scheme \'skēm\ *n* 1 : crafty plot 2 : systematic design ∼ *vb* **schemed; schem·ing** : form a plot — **sche·mat·ic** \ski'matik\ *adj* — **schem·er** *n*

schism \'sizəm, 'skiz-\ *n* : split — **schis·mat·ic** \siz'matik, skiz-\ *n or adj*

schizo·phre·nia \₁skitsə'frēnēə\ *n* : severe mental illness — **schiz·oid** \'skit₁sóid\ *adj or n* — **schizo·phren·ic** \₁skitsə'frenik\ *adj or n*

schol·ar \'skälər\ *n* : student or learned person — **schol·ar·ly** *adj*

schol·ar·ship \-₁ship\ *n* 1 : qualities or learning of a scholar 2 : money given to a student to pay for education

scho·las·tic \skə'lastik\ *adj* : relating to schools, scholars, or scholarship

¹**school** \'skül\ *n* 1 : institution for learning 2 : pupils in a school 3 : group with shared beliefs ∼ *vb* : teach — **school·boy** *n* — **school·girl** *n* — **school·house** *n* — **school·mate** *n* — **school·room** *n* — **school·er** *n*

²**school** *n* : large number of fish swimming together

schoo·ner \'skünər\ *n* : sailing ship

sci·ence \'sīəns\ *n* : branch of systematic study esp. of the physical world — **sci·en·tif·ic** \₁sīən'tifik\ *adj* — **sci·en·tif·i·cal·ly** *adv* — **sci·en·tist** \'sīəntist\ *n*

scin·til·late \'sint°l₁āt\ *vb* **-lat·ed; -lat·ing** : flash — **scin·til·la·tion** \₁sint°l-'āshən\ *n*

scin·til·lat·ing *adj* : brilliantly lively or witty

sci·on \'sīən\ *n* : descendant

scis·sors \'sizərz\ *n pl* : small shears

scoff \'skäf\ *vb* : mock — **scoff·er** *n*

scold \'skōld\ *n* : person who scolds ∼ *vb* : criticize severely

scoop \'küp\ *n* : shovellike utensil ∼ *vb* 1 : take out with a scoop 2 : dig out

scoot \'küt\ *vb* : move swiftly

scoot·er \'skütər\ *n* : child's foot-propelled vehicle

¹**scope** \'skōp\ *n* 1 : extent 2 : room for development

²**scope** *n* : viewing device (as a microscope)

scorch \'skȯrch\ *vb* : burn the surface of

score \'skōr\ *n, pl* **scores 1** *or pl* **score** : twenty **2** : cut **3** : record of points made (as in a game) **4** : debt **5** : music of a composition ~ *vb* **scored; scor·ing 1** : record **2** : mark with lines **3** : gain in a game **4** : assign a grade to **5** : compose a score for — **score·less** *adj* — **scor·er** *n*

scorn \'skȯrn\ *n* : emotion involving both anger and disgust ~ *vb* : hold in contempt — **scorn·er** *n* — **scorn·ful** \-fəl\ *adj* — **scorn·ful·ly** *adv*

scor·pi·on \'skȯrpēən\ *n* : poisonous long-tailed animal

scoun·drel \'skaůndrəl\ *n* : villain

¹**scour** \'skaůər\ *vb* : examine thoroughly

²**scour** *vb* : rub in order to clean

scourge \'skərj\ *n* **1** : whip **2** : punishment ~ *vb* **scourged; scourg·ing 1** : lash **2** : punish severely

scout \'skaůt\ *vb* : inspect or observe to get information ~ *n* : person sent out to get information

scow \'skaů\ *n* : large flat-bottomed boat with square ends

scowl \'skaůl\ *vb* : make a frowning expression of displeasure — **scowl** *n*

scrag·gly \'skraglē\ *adj* : irregular or unkempt

scram \'skram\ *vb* **-mm-** : go away at once

scram·ble \'skrambəl\ *vb* **-bled; -bling 1** : clamber clumsily around **2** : struggle for possession of something **3** : mix together **4** : cook (eggs) by stirring during frying — **scramble** *n*

¹**scrap** \'skrap\ *n* **1** : fragment **2** : discarded material ~ *vb* **-pp-** : get rid of as useless

²**scrap** *vb* **-pp-** : fight — **scrap** *n* — **scrap·per** *n*

scrap·book *n* : blank book in which mementos are kept

scrape \'skrāp\ *vb* **scraped; scraping 1** : remove by drawing a knife over **2** : clean or smooth by rubbing **3** : draw across a surface with a grating sound **4** : damage by contact with a rough surface **5** : gather or proceed with difficulty ~ *n* **1** : act of scraping **2** : predicament — **scrap·er** *n*

scratch \'skrach\ *vb* **1** : scrape or dig with or as if with claws or nails **2** : cause to move gratingly **3** : delete by or as if by drawing a line through

~ *n* : mark or sound made in scratching — **scratchy** *adj*

scrawl \'skrȯl\ *vb* : write hastily and carelessly — **scrawl** *n*

scraw·ny \'skrȯnē\ *adj* **-ni·er; -est** : very thin

scream \'skrēm\ *vb* : cry out loudly and shrilly ~ *n* : loud shrill cry

screech \'skrēch\ *vb or n* : shriek

screen \'skrēn\ *n* **1** : device or partition used to protect or decorate **2** : surface on which pictures appear (as in movies) ~ *vb* : shield or separate with or as if with a screen

screw \'skrü\ *n* **1** : grooved fastening device **2** : propeller ~ *vb* **1** : fasten by means of a screw **2** : move spirally

screw·driv·er \'skrü,drīvər\ *n* : tool for turning screws

scrib·ble \'skribəl\ *vb* **-bled; -bling** : write hastily or carelessly — **scribble** *n* — **scrib·bler** \-ələr\ *n*

scribe \'skrīb\ *n* : one who writes or copies writing

scrimp \'skrimp\ *vb* : economize greatly

scrip \'skrip\ *n* **1** : paper money for less than a dollar **2** : certificate entitling one to something (as stock)

script \'skript\ *n* : text (as of a play)

scrip·ture \'skripchər\ *n* : sacred writings of a religion — **scrip·tur·al** \'skripchərəl\ *adj*

scroll \'skrōl\ *n* **1** : roll of paper for writing a document **2** : spiral or coiled design

scro·tum \'skrōtəm\ *n, pl* **-ta** \-ə\ *or* **-tums** : pouch containing the testes

scrounge \'skraůnj\ *vb* **scrounged; scroung·ing** : collect by or as if by foraging

¹**scrub** \'skrəb\ *n* : stunted tree or shrub or a growth of these — **scrub** *adj* — **scrub·by** *adj*

²**scrub** *vb* **-bb-** : clean or wash by rubbing — **scrub** *n*

scruff \'skrəf\ *n* : loose skin of the back of the neck

scrump·tious \'skrəmpshəs\ *adj* : delicious

scru·ple \'skrüpəl\ *n* : reluctance due to ethical considerations — **scruple** *vb* — **scru·pu·lous** \-pyələs\ *adj* — **scru·pu·lous·ly** *adv*

scru·ti·ny \'skrüt⁸nē\ *n, pl* **-nies** : careful inspection — **scru·ti·nize** \-⁸n₁īz\ *vb*

scud \'skəd\ *vb* **-dd-** : move speedily

scuff \'skəf\ vb : scratch, scrape, or wear away — **scuff** n

scuf·fle \'skəfəl\ vb **-fled; -fling 1** : struggle at close quarters **2** : shuffle one's feet — **scuffle** n

scull \'skəl\ n **1** : oar **2** : racing shell propelled with sculls ∼ vb : propel a boat by an oar over the stern

scul·lery \'skələrē\ n, pl **-ler·ies** : room for cleaning dishes and cookware

sculpt \'skəlpt\ vb : sculpture

sculp·ture \'skəlpchər\ n : work of art carved or molded ∼ vb **-tured; -tur·ing** : form as sculpture — **sculp·tor** \-tər\ n — **sculp·tur·al** \-chərəl\ adj

scum \'skəm\ n : slimy film on a liquid

scur·ri·lous \'skərələs\ adj : vulgar or abusive

scur·ry \'skərē\ vb **-ried; -ry·ing** : scamper

scur·vy \'skərvē\ n : vitamin-deficiency disease

¹scut·tle \'skətᵊl\ n : pail for coal

²scuttle vb **-tled; -tling** : sink (a ship) by cutting holes in its bottom

³scuttle vb **-tled; -tling** : scamper

scythe \'sīth\ n : tool for mowing by hand — **scythe** vb

sea \'sē\ n **1** : large body of salt water **2** : ocean **3** : rough water — **sea** adj — **sea·coast** n — **sea·food** n — **sea·port** n — **sea·shore** n — **sea·wa·ter** n

sea·bird n : bird frequenting the open ocean

sea·board n : country's seacoast

sea·far·er \-ˌfarər\ n : seaman — **sea·far·ing** \-ˌfariŋ\ adj or n

sea horse n : small fish with a horselike head

¹seal \'sēl\ n : large sea mammal of cold regions — **seal·skin** n

²seal n **1** : device for stamping a design **2** : something that closes ∼ vb **1** : affix a seal to **2** : close up securely **3** : determine finally — **seal·ant** \-ᵊnt\ n — **seal·er** n

sea lion n : large Pacific seal with external ears

seam \'sēm\ n **1** : line of junction of 2 edges **2** : layer of a mineral ∼ vb : join by sewing — **seam·less** adj

sea·man \'sēmən\ n **1** : one who helps to handle a ship **2** : naval enlisted man ranking next below a petty officer third class — **sea·man·ship** n

seaman apprentice n : naval enlisted man ranking next below a seaman

seaman recruit n : naval enlisted man of the lowest rank

seam·stress \'sēmstrəs\ n : woman who sews

seamy \'sēmē\ adj **seam·i·er; -est** : unpleasant or sordid

sé·ance \'sāˌäns\ n : meeting for communicating with spirits

sea·plane n : airplane that can take off from and land on the water

sear \'sir\ vb : scorch — **sear** n

search \'sərch\ vb **1** : look through **2** : seek — **search** n — **search·er** n — **search·light** n

search engine n : computer software used to search for specified information on the World Wide Web

sea·sick adj : nauseated by the motion of a ship — **sea·sick·ness** n

¹sea·son \'sēzᵊn\ n **1** : division of the year **2** : customary time for something — **sea·son·al** \'sēzᵊnəl\ adj — **sea·son·al·ly** adv

²season vb **1** : add spice to (food) **2** : make strong or fit for use — **sea·son·ing** \-ᵊniŋ\ n

sea·son·able \'sēznəbəl\ adj : occurring at a suitable time — **sea·son·ably** \-blē\ adv

seat \'sēt\ n **1** : place to sit **2** : chair, bench, or stool for sitting on **3** : place that serves as a capital or center ∼ vb **1** : place in or on a seat **2** : provide seats for

sea·weed n : marine alga

sea·wor·thy adj : strong enough to hold up to a sea voyage

se·cede \si'sēd\ vb **-ced·ed; -ced·ing** : withdraw from a body (as a nation)

se·clude \si'klüd\ vb **-clud·ed; -clud·ing** : shut off alone — **se·clu·sion** \si'klüzhən\ n

¹sec·ond \'sekənd\ adj : next after the 1st ∼ n **1** : one that is second **2** : one who assists (as in a duel) — **sec·ond, se·cond·ly** adv

²second n **1** : 60th part of a minute **2** : moment

sec·ond·ary \'sekənˌderē\ adj **1** : second in rank or importance **2** : coming after the primary or elementary

sec·ond·hand adj **1** : not original **2** : used before

second lieutenant n : lowest ranking commissioned officer of the army, air force, or marines

se·cret \'sēkrət\ adj **1** : hidden **2**

: kept from general knowledge — **se-cre-cy** \-krəsē\ *n* — **secret** *n* — **se-cre-tive** \'sēkrətiv, si'krēt-\ *adj* — **se-cret-ly** *adv*

sec-re-tar-i-at \₁sekrə'terēət\ *n* : administrative department

sec-re-tary \'sekrə₁terē\ *n, pl* **-tar-ies** 1 : one hired to handle correspondence and other tasks for a superior 2 : official in charge of correspondence or records 3 : head of a government department — **sec-re-tar-i-al** \₁sekrə-'terēəl\ *adj*

¹**se-crete** \si'krēt\ *vb* **-cret-ed; -cret-ing** : produce as a secretion

²**se-crete** \si'krēt, 'sēkrət\ *vb* **-cret-ed; -cret-ing** : hide

se-cre-tion \si'krēshən\ *n* 1 : process of secreting 2 : product of glandular activity

sect \'sekt\ *n* : religious group

sec-tar-i-an \sek'terēən\ *adj* 1 : relating to a sect 2 : limited in character or scope ~ *n* : member of a sect

sec-tion \'sekshən\ *n* : distinct part — **sec-tion-al** \-shənəl\ *adj*

sec-tor \'sektər\ *n* 1 : part of a circle between 2 radii 2 : distinctive part

sec-u-lar \'sekyələr\ *adj* 1 : not sacred 2 : not monastic

¹**se-cure** \si'kyùr\ *adj* **-cur-er; -est** : free from danger or loss ~ *vb* 1 : fasten safely 2 : get — **se-cure-ly** *adv*

se-cu-ri-ty \si'kyùrətē\ *n, pl* **-ties** 1 : safety 2 : something given to guarantee payment 3 *pl* : bond or stock certificates

se-dan \si'dan\ *n* 1 : chair carried by 2 men 2 : enclosed automobile

¹**se-date** \si'dāt\ *adj* : quiet and dignified — **se-date-ly** *adv*

²**sedate** *vb* **-dat-ed; -dat-ing** : dose with sedatives — **se-da-tion** \si'dāshən\ *n*

sed-a-tive \'sedətiv\ *adj* : serving to relieve tension ~ *n* : sedative drug

sed-en-tary \'sed³n₁terē\ *adj* : characterized by much sitting

sedge \'sej\ *n* : grasslike marsh plant

sed-i-ment \'sedəmənt\ *n* : material that settles to the bottom of a liquid or is deposited by water or a glacier — **sed-i-men-ta-ry** \₁sedə'mentərē\ *adj* — **sed-i-men-ta-tion** \-mən'tā-shən, -₁men-\ *n*

se-di-tion \si'dishən\ *n* : revolution against a government — **se-di-tious** \-əs\ *adj*

se-duce \si'düs, -'dyüs\ *vb* **-duced;**

-duc-ing 1 : lead astray 2 : entice to sexual intercourse — **se-duc-er** *n* — **se-duc-tion** \-'dəkshən\ *n* — **se-duc-tive** \-tiv\ *adj*

sed-u-lous \'sejələs\ *adj* : diligent

¹**see** \'sē\ *vb* **saw** \'sò\; **seen** \'sēn\; **see-ing** 1 : perceive by the eye 2 : have experience of 3 : understand 4 : make sure 5 : meet with or escort

²**see** *n* : jurisdiction of a bishop

seed \'sēd\ *n, pl* **seed** *or* **seeds** 1 : part by which a plant is propagated 2 : source ~ *vb* 1 : sow 2 : remove seeds from — **seed-less** *adj*

seed-ling \-liŋ\ *n* : young plant grown from seed

seedy \-ē\ *adj* **seed-i-er; -est** 1 : full of seeds 2 : shabby

seek \'sēk\ *vb* **sought** \'sòt\; **seek-ing** 1 : search for 2 : try to reach or obtain — **seek-er** *n*

seem \'sēm\ *vb* : give the impression of being — **seem-ing-ly** *adv*

seem-ly \-lē\ *adj* **seem-li-er; -est** : proper or fit

seep \'sēp\ *vb* : leak through fine pores or cracks — **seep-age** \'sēpij\ *n*

seer \'sēər\ *n* : one who foresees or predicts events

seer-suck-er \'sir₁səkər\ *n* : light puckered fabric

see-saw \'sē₁sò\ *n* : board balanced in the middle — **seesaw** *vb*

seethe \'sēth\ *vb* **seethed; seeth-ing** : become violently agitated

seg-ment \'segmənt\ *n* : division of a thing — **seg-ment-ed** \-₁mentəd\ *adj*

seg-re-gate \'segri₁gāt\ *vb* **-gat-ed; -gat-ing** 1 : cut off from others 2 : separate by races — **seg-re-ga-tion** \₁segri'gāshən\ *n*

seine \'sān\ *n* : large weighted fishing net ~ *vb* : fish with a seine

seis-mic \'sīzmik, 'sīs-\ *adj* : relating to an earthquake

seis-mo-graph \-mə₁graf\ *n* : apparatus for detecting earthquakes

seize \'sēz\ *vb* **seized; seiz-ing** : take by force — **sei-zure** \'sēzhər\ *n*

sel-dom \'seldəm\ *adv* : not often

se-lect \sə'lekt\ *adj* 1 : favored 2 : discriminating ~ *vb* : take by preference — **se-lec-tive** \-'lektiv\ *adj*

se-lec-tion \sə'lekshən\ *n* : act of selecting or thing selected

se-lect-man \si'lekt₁man, -mən\ *n* : New England town official

self \'self\ *n, pl* **selves** \'selvz\ : essential person distinct from others

self- *comb form* **1** : oneself or itself **2** : of oneself or itself **3** : by oneself or automatic **4** : to, for, or toward oneself

self-cen·tered *adj* : concerned only with one's own self

self-con·scious *adj* : uncomfortably aware of oneself as an object of observation — **self-con·scious·ly** *adv* — **self-con·scious·ness** *n*

self·ish \'selfish\ *adj* : excessively or exclusively concerned with one's own well-being — **self·ish·ly** *adv* — **self·ish·ness** *n*

self·less \'selfləs\ *adj* : unselfish — **self·less·ness** *n*

self-made *adj* : having succeeded by one's own efforts

self-righ·teous *adj* : strongly convinced of one's own righteousness

self·same \'self,sām\ *adj* : precisely the same

sell \'sel\ *vb* **sold** \'sōld\; **sell·ing 1** : transfer (property) esp. for money **2**

: deal in as a business **3** : be sold — **sell·er** *n*

selves *pl of* SELF

se·man·tic \si'mantik\ *adj* : relating to meaning in language — **se·man·tics** \-iks\ *n sing or pl*

sem·a·phore \'semə,fōr\ *n* **1** : visual signaling apparatus **2** : signaling by flags

sem·blance \'sembləns\ *n* : appearance

se·men \'sēmən\ *n* : male reproductive fluid

se·mes·ter \sə'mestər\ *n* : half a school year

semi- \,semi, 'sem-, -,ī\ *prefix* **1** : half **2** : partial

semi·co·lon \'semi,kōlən\ *n* : punctuation mark ;

semi·con·duc·tor *n* : substance between a conductor and a nonconductor in ability to conduct electricity — **semi·con·duct·ing** *adj*

semi·fi·nal *adj* : being next to the final — **semifinal** *n*

semi·for·mal *adj* : being or suitable for an occasion of moderate formality

---

List of self-explanatory words with the prefix *self-*

self–addressed	self–destructive	self–operating
self–administered	self–determination	self–pity
self–analysis	self–determined	self–portrait
self–appointed	self–discipline	self–possessed
self–assertive	self–doubt	self–possession
self–assurance	self–educated	self–preservation
self–assured	self–employed	self–proclaimed
self–awareness	self–employment	self–propelled
self–cleaning	self–esteem	self–propelling
self–closing	self–evident	self–protection
self–complacent	self–explanatory	self–reliance
self–conceit	self–expression	self–reliant
self–confessed	self–fulfilling	self–respect
self–confidence	self–fulfillment	self–respecting
self–confident	self–governing	self–restraint
self–contained	self–government	self–sacrifice
self–contempt	self–help	self–satisfaction
self–contradiction	self–image	self–satisfied
self–contradictory	self–importance	self–service
self–control	self–important	self–serving
self–created	self–imposed	self–starting
self–criticism	self–improvement	self–styled
self–defeating	self–indulgence	self–sufficiency
self–defense	self–indulgent	self–sufficient
self–denial	self–inflicted	self–supporting
self–denying	self–interest	self–taught
self–destruction	self–love	self–winding

sem·i·nal \'semən²l\ *adj* **1** : relating to seed or semen **2** : causing or influencing later development

sem·i·nar \'semə₁när\ *n* : conference or conferencelike study

sem·i·nary \'semə₁nerē\ *n, pl* **-nar·ies** : school and esp. a theological school — **sem·i·nar·i·an** \₁semə'nerēən\ *n*

sen·ate \'senət\ *n* : upper branch of a legislature — **sen·a·tor** \-ər\ *n* — **sen·a·to·ri·al** \₁senə'tōrēəl\ *adj*

send \'send\ *vb* **sent** \'sent\; **send·ing** **1** : cause to go **2** : propel — **send·er** *n*

se·nile \'sēn₁īl, 'sen-\ *adj* : mentally deficient through old age — **se·nil·i·ty** \si'nilətē\ *n*

se·nior \'sēnyər\ *adj* : older or higher ranking — **senior** *n* — **se·nior·i·ty** \₁sēn'yòrətē\ *n*

senior chief petty officer *n* : petty officer in the navy or coast guard ranking next below a master chief petty officer

senior master sergeant *n* : noncommissioned officer in the air force ranking next below a chief master sergeant

sen·sa·tion \sen'sāshən\ *n* **1** : bodily feeling **2** : condition of excitement or the cause of it — **sen·sa·tion·al** \-shənəl\ *adj*

sense \'sens\ *n* **1** : meaning **2** : faculty of perceiving something physical **3** : sound mental capacity ~ *vb* **sensed; sens·ing** **1** : perceive by the senses **2** : detect automatically — **sense·less** *adj* — **sense·less·ly** *adv*

sen·si·bil·i·ty \₁sensə'bilətē\ *n, pl* **-ties** : delicacy of feeling

sen·si·ble \'sensəbəl\ *adj* **1** : capable of sensing or being sensed **2** : aware or conscious **3** : reasonable — **sen·si·bly** \-blē\ *adv*

sen·si·tive \'sensətiv\ *adj* **1** : subject to excitation by or responsive to stimuli **2** : having power of feeling **3** : easily affected — **sen·si·tive·ness** *n* — **sen·si·tiv·i·ty** \₁sensə'tivətē\ *n*

sen·si·tize \'sensə₁tīz\ *vb* **-tized; -tiz·ing** : make or become sensitive

sen·sor \'sen₁sòr, -sər\ *n* : device that responds to a physical stimulus

sen·so·ry \'sensərē\ *adj* : relating to sensation or the senses

sen·su·al \'senchəwəl, -shəwəl\ *adj* **1** : pleasing the senses **2** : devoted to the pleasures of the senses — **sen·su·al·ist** *n* — **sen·su·al·i·ty** \₁senchə-'walətē\ *n* — **sen·su·al·ly** *adv*

sen·su·ous \'senchəwəs\ *adj* : having strong appeal to the senses

sent *past of* **SEND**

sen·tence \'sent²ns, -²nz\ *n* **1** : judgment of a court **2** : grammatically self-contained speech unit ~ *vb* **-tenced; -tenc·ing** : impose a sentence on

sen·ten·tious \sen'tenchəs\ *adj* : using pompous language

sen·tient \'senchēənt\ *adj* : capable of feeling

sen·ti·ment \'sentəmənt\ *n* **1** : belief **2** : feeling

sen·ti·men·tal \₁sentə'ment²l\ *adj* : influenced by tender feelings — **sen·ti·men·tal·ism** *n* — **sen·ti·men·tal·ist** *n* — **sen·ti·men·tal·i·ty** \-₁men-'talətē, -mən-\ *n* — **sen·ti·men·tal·ize** \-'ment²l₁īz\ *vb* — **sen·ti·men·tal·ly** *adv*

sen·ti·nel \'sent²nəl\ *n* : sentry

sen·try \'sentrē\ *n, pl* **-tries** : one who stands guard

se·pal \'sēpəl, 'sep-\ *n* : modified leaf in a flower calyx

sep·a·rate \'sepə₁rāt\ *vb* **-rat·ed; -rat·ing** **1** : set or keep apart **2** : become divided or detached ~ \'seprət, 'sepə-\ *adj* **1** : not connected or shared **2** : distinct from each other — **sep·a·ra·ble** \'sepərəbəl\ *adj* — **sep·a·rate·ly** *adv* — **sep·a·ra·tion** \₁sepə'rāshən\ *n* — **sep·a·ra·tor** \'sepə₁rātər\ *n*

se·pia \'sēpēə\ *n* : brownish gray

Sep·tem·ber \sep'tembər\ *n* : 9th month of the year having 30 days

sep·ul·chre, sep·ul·cher \'sepəlkər\ *n* : burial vault — **se·pul·chral** \sə'pəlkrəl\ *adj*

se·quel \'sēkwəl\ *n* **1** : consequence or result **2** : continuation of a story

se·quence \'sēkwəns\ *n* : continuous or connected series — **se·quen·tial** \si-'kwenchəl\ *adj* — **se·quen·tial·ly** *adv*

se·ques·ter \si'kwestər\ *vb* : segregate

se·quin \'sēkwən\ *n* : spangle

se·quoia \si'kwòiə\ *n* : huge California coniferous tree

sera *pl of* **SERUM**

ser·aph \'serəf\ *n, pl* **-a·phim** \-ə₁fim\ *or* **-aphs** : angel — **se·raph·ic** \sə'rafik\ *adj*

sere \'sir\ *adj* : dried up or withered

ser·e·nade \₁serə'nād\ *n* : music sung or played esp. to a woman being courted — **serenade** *vb*

ser·en·dip·i·ty \ˌserənˈdipətē\ n : good luck in finding things not sought for — **ser·en·dip·i·tous** \-əs\ adj

se·rene \səˈrēn\ adj : tranquil — **se·rene·ly** adv — **se·ren·i·ty** \sə-ˈrenətē\ n

serf \ˈsərf\ n : peasant obligated to work the land — **serf·dom** \-dəm\ n

serge \ˈsərj\ n : twilled woolen cloth

ser·geant \ˈsärjənt\ n : noncommissioned officer (as in the army) ranking next below a staff sergeant

sergeant first class n : noncommissioned officer in the army ranking next below a master sergeant

sergeant major n, pl **sergeants major** or **sergeant majors** 1 : noncommissioned officer serving as an enlisted adviser in a headquarters 2 : noncommissioned officer in the marine corps ranking above a first sergeant

se·ri·al \ˈsirēəl\ adj : being or relating to a series or sequence ~ n : story appearing in parts — **se·ri·al·ly** adv

se·ries \ˈsirēz\ n, pl **series** : number of things in order

se·ri·ous \ˈsirēəs\ adj 1 : subdued in appearance or manner 2 : sincere 3 : of great importance — **se·ri·ous·ly** adv — **se·ri·ous·ness** n

ser·mon \ˈsərmən\ n : lecture on religion or behavior

ser·pent \ˈsərpənt\ n : snake — **ser·pen·tine** \-pənˌtēn, -ˌtīn\ adj

ser·rat·ed \ˈserˌātəd\ adj : saw-toothed

se·rum \ˈsirəm\ n, pl **-rums** or **-ra** \-ə\ : watery part of blood

ser·vant \ˈsərvənt\ n : person employed for domestic work

serve \ˈsərv\ vb **served; serv·ing** 1 : work through or perform a term of service 2 : be of use 3 : prove adequate 4 : hand out (food or drink) 5 : be of service to — **serv·er** n

ser·vice \ˈsərvəs\ n 1 : act or means of serving 2 : meeting for worship 3 : branch of public employment or the persons in it 4 : set of dishes or silverware 5 : benefit ~ vb **-viced; -vic·ing** : repair — **ser·vice·able** adj — **ser·vice·man** \-ˌman, -mən\ n — **ser·vice·wom·an** n

ser·vile \ˈsərvəl, -ˌvīl\ adj : behaving like a slave — **ser·vil·i·ty** \ˌsər-ˈvilətē\ n

serv·ing \ˈsərviŋ\ n : helping

ser·vi·tude \ˈsərvəˌtüd, -ˌtyüd\ n : slavery

ses·a·me \ˈsesəmē\ n : annual herb or its seeds that are used in flavoring

ses·sion \ˈseshən\ n : meeting

set \ˈset\ vb **set; set·ting** 1 : cause to sit 2 : place 3 : settle, arrange, or adjust 4 : cause to be or do 5 : become fixed or solid 6 : sink below the horizon ~ adj : settled ~ n 1 : group classed together 2 : setting for the scene of a play or film 3 : electronic apparatus 4 : collection of mathematical elements — **set forth** vb : begin a trip — **set off** vb : set forth — **set out** vb : begin a trip or undertaking — **set up** vb 1 : assemble or erect 2 : cause

set·back n : reverse

set·tee \seˈtē\ n : bench or sofa

set·ter \ˈsetər\ n : large long-coated hunting dog

set·ting \ˈsetiŋ\ n : the time, place, and circumstances in which something occurs

set·tle \ˈsetᵊl\ vb **-tled; -tling** 1 : come to rest 2 : sink gradually 3 : establish in residence 4 : adjust or arrange 5 : calm 6 : dispose of (as by paying) 7 : decide or agree on — **set·tle·ment** \-mənt\ n — **set·tler** \ˈsetᵊlər\ n

sev·en \ˈsevən\ n : one more than 6 — **seven** adj or pron — **sev·enth** \-ənth\ adj or adv or n

sev·en·teen \ˌsevənˈtēn\ n : one more than 16 — **seventeen** adj or pron — **sev·en·teenth** \-ˈtēnth\ adj or n

sev·en·ty \ˈsevəntē\ n, pl **-ties** : 7 times 10 — **sev·en·ti·eth** \-tēəth\ adj or n — **seventy** adj or pron

sev·er \ˈsevər\ vb **-ered; -er·ing** : cut off or apart — **sev·er·ance** \ˈsevrəns, -vərəns\ n

sev·er·al \ˈsevrəl, ˈsevə-\ adj 1 : distinct 2 : consisting of an indefinite but not large number — **sev·er·al·ly** adv

se·vere \səˈvir\ adj **-ver·er; -est** 1 : strict 2 : restrained or unadorned 3 : painful or distressing 4 : hard to endure — **se·vere·ly** adv — **se·ver·i·ty** \-ˈverətē\ n

sew \ˈsō\ vb **sewed; sewn** \ˈsōn\ or **sewed; sew·ing** : join or fasten by stitches — **sew·ing** n

sew·age \ˈsüij\ n : liquid household waste

¹sew·er \ˈsōər\ n : one that sews

²sew·er \ˈsüər\ n : pipe or channel to carry off waste matter

sex \ˈseks\ n 1 : either of 2 divisions

into which organisms are grouped according to their reproductive roles or the qualities which differentiate them **2** : copulation — **sexed** \'sekst\ *adj* — **sex·less** *adj* — **sex·u·al** \'sek-shəwəl\ *adj* — **sex·u·al·i·ty** \,seksha-'walətē\ *n* — **sex·u·al·ly** *adv* — **sexy** *adj*

sex·ism \'sek,sizəm\ *n* : discrimination based on sex and esp. against women — **sex·ist** \'seksist\ *adj or n*

sex·tant \'sekstənt\ *n* : instrument for navigation

sex·tet \sek'stet\ *n* **1** : music for 6 performers **2** : group of 6

sex·ton \'sekstən\ *n* : church caretaker

shab·by \'shabē\ *adj* **-bi·er; -est 1** : worn and faded **2** : dressed in worn clothes **3** : not generous or fair — **shab·bi·ly** *adv* — **shab·bi·ness** *n*

shack \'shak\ *n* : hut

shack·le \'shakəl\ *n* : metal device to bind legs or arms ~ *vb* **-led; -ling** : bind or fasten with shackles

shad \'shad\ *n* : Atlantic food fish

shade \'shād\ *n* **1** : space sheltered from the light esp. of the sun **2** : gradation of color **3** : small difference **4** : something that shades ~ *vb* **shaded; shad·ing 1** : shelter from light and heat **2** : add shades of color to **3** : show slight differences esp. in color or meaning

shad·ow \'shadō\ *n* **1** : shade cast upon a surface by something blocking light **2** : trace **3** : gloomy influence ~ *vb* **1** : cast a shadow **2** : follow closely — **shad·owy** *adj*

shady \'shādē\ *adj* **shad·i·er; -est 1** : giving shade **2** : of dubious honesty

shaft \'shaft\ *n* **1** : long slender cylindrical part **2** : deep vertical opening (as of a mine)

shag \'shag\ *n* : shaggy tangled mat

shag·gy \'shagē\ *adj* **-gi·er; -est 1** : covered with long hair or wool **2** : not neat and combed

shake \'shāk\ *vb* **shook** \'shùk\; **shak·en** \'shākən\; **shak·ing 1** : move or cause to move quickly back and forth **2** : distress **3** : clasp (hands) as friendly gesture — **shake** *n* — **shak·er** \-ər\ *n*

shake-up *n* : reorganization

shaky \'shākē\ *adj* **shak·i·er; -est** : not sound, stable, or reliable — **shak·i·ly** *adv* — **shak·i·ness** *n*

shale \'shāl\ *n* : stratified rock

shall \'shal\ *vb, past* **should** \'shùd\; *pres sing & pl* **shall** — used as an auxiliary to express a command, futurity, or determination

shal·low \'shalō\ *adj* **1** : not deep **2** : not intellectually profound

shal·lows \-ōz\ *n pl* : area of shallow water

sham \'sham\ *adj or n or vb* : fake

sham·ble \'shambəl\ *vb* **-bled; -bling** : shuffle along — **sham·ble** *n*

sham·bles \'shambəlz\ *n* : state of disorder

shame \'shām\ *n* **1** : distress over guilt or disgrace **2** : cause of shame or regret ~ *vb* **shamed; sham·ing 1** : make ashamed **2** : disgrace — **shame·ful** \-fəl\ *adj* — **shame·ful·ly** \-ē\ *adv* — **shame·less** *adj* — **shame·less·ly** *adv*

shame·faced \'shām'fāst\ *adj* : ashamed

sham·poo \sham'pü\ *vb* : wash one's hair ~ *n, pl* **-poos** : act of or preparation used in shampooing

sham·rock \'sham,räk\ *n* : plant of legend with 3-lobed leaves

shank \'shaŋk\ *n* : part of the leg between the knee and ankle

shan·ty \'shantē\ *n, pl* **-ties** : hut

shape \'shāp\ *vb* **shaped; shap·ing** : form esp. in a particular structure or appearance ~ *n* **1** : distinctive appearance or arrangement of parts **2** : condition — **shape·less** \-ləs\ *adj* — **shape·li·ness** *n* — **shape·ly** *adj*

shard \'shärd\ *n* : broken piece

share \'sher\ *n* **1** : portion belonging to one **2** : interest in a company's stock ~ *vb* **shared; shar·ing** : divide or use with others — **share·hold·er** *n* — **shar·er** *n*

share·crop·per \-,kräpər\ *n* : farmer who works another's land in return for a share of the crop — **share·crop** *vb*

shark \'shärk\ *n* : voracious sea fish

sharp \'shärp\ *adj* **1** : having a good point or cutting edge **2** : alert, clever, or sarcastic **3** : vigorous or fierce **4** : having prominent angles or a sudden change in direction **5** : distinct **6** : higher than the true pitch ~ *adv* : exactly ~ *n* : sharp note — **sharp·ly** *adv* — **sharp·ness** *n*

sharp·en \'shärpən\ *vb* : make sharp — **sharp·en·er** \-ənər\ *n*

sharp·shoot·er *n* : expert marksman — **sharp·shoot·ing** *n*

shat·ter \'shatər\ *vb* : smash or burst into fragments — **shat·ter·proof** \-,prüf\ *adj*

shave \'shāv\ *vb* **shaved; shaved** or **shav·en** \'shāvən\; **shav·ing 1** : cut off with a razor **2** : make bare by cutting the hair from **3** : slice very thin ~ *n* : act or instance of shaving — **shav·er** *n*

shawl \'shȯl\ *n* : loose covering for the head or shoulders

she \'shē\ *pron* : that female one

sheaf \'shēf\ *n, pl* **sheaves** \'shēvz\ : bundle esp. of grain stalks

shear \'shir\ *vb* **sheared; sheared** or **shorn** \'shȯrn\; **shear·ing 1** : trim wool from **2** : cut off with scissorlike action

shears \'shirz\ *n pl* : cutting tool with 2 blades fastened so that the edges slide by each other

sheath \'shēth\ *n, pl* **sheaths** \'shēthz, 'shēths\ : covering (as for a blade)

sheathe \'shēth\ *vb* **sheathed; sheath·ing** : put into a sheath

shed \'shed\ *vb* **shed; shed·ding 1** : give off (as tears or hair) **2** : cause to flow or diffuse ~ *n* : small storage building

sheen \'shēn\ *n* : subdued luster

sheep \'shēp\ *n, pl* **sheep** : domesticated mammal covered with wool — **sheep·skin** *n*

sheep·ish \'shēpish\ *adj* : embarrassed by awareness of a fault

sheer \'shir\ *adj* **1** : pure **2** : very steep **3** : very thin or transparent

sheet \'shēt\ *n* : broad flat piece (as of cloth or paper)

sheikh, sheik \'shēk, 'shāk\ *n* : Arab chief — **sheikh·dom, sheik·dom** \-dəm\ *n*

shelf \'shelf\ *n, pl* **shelves** \'shelvz\ **1** : flat narrow structure used for storage or display **2** : sandbank or rock ledge

shell \'shel\ *n* **1** : hard or tough outer covering **2** : case holding explosive powder and projectile for a weapon **3** : light racing boat with oars ~ *vb* **1** : remove the shell of **2** : bombard — **shelled** \'sheld\ *adj* — **shell·er** *n*

shel·lac \shə'lak\ *n* : varnish ~ *vb* **-lacked; -lack·ing 1** : coat with shellac **2** : defeat — **shel·lack·ing** *n*

shell·fish *n* : water animal with a shell

shel·ter \'sheltər\ *n* : something that gives protection ~ *vb* : give refuge to

shelve \'shelv\ *vb* **shelved; shelv·ing 1** : place or store on shelves **2** : dismiss or put aside

she·nan·i·gans \shə'nanigənz\ *n pl* : mischievous or deceitful conduct

shep·herd \'shepərd\ *n* : one that tends sheep ~ *vb* : act as a shepherd or guardian

shep·herd·ess \'shepərdəs\ *n* : woman who tends sheep

sher·bet \'shərbət\, **sher·bert** \-bərt\ *n* : fruit-flavored frozen dessert

sher·iff \'sherəf\ *n* : county law officer

sher·ry \'sherē\ *n, pl* **-ries** : type of wine

shield \'shēld\ *n* **1** : broad piece of armor carried on the arm **2** : something that protects — **shield** *vb*

shier *comparative of* SHY

shiest *superlative of* SHY

shift \'shift\ *vb* **1** : change place, position, or direction **2** : get by ~ *n* **1** : loose-fitting dress **2** : an act or instance of shifting **3** : scheduled work period

shift·less \-ləs\ *adj* : lazy

shifty \'shiftē\ *adj* **shift·i·er; -est** : tricky or untrustworthy

shil·le·lagh \shə'lālē\ *n* : club or stick

shil·ling \'shiliŋ\ *n* : former British coin

shil·ly-shally \'shilē,shalē\ *vb* **-shallied; -shally·ing 1** : hesitate **2** : dawdle

shim·mer \'shimər\ *vb* or *n* : glimmer

shin \'shin\ *n* : front part of the leg below the knee ~ *vb* **-nn-** : climb by sliding the body close along

shine \'shīn\ *vb* **shone** \-'shōn\ or **shined; shin·ing 1** : give off or cause to give off light **2** : be outstanding **3** : polish ~ *n* : brilliance

shin·gle \'shiŋgəl\ *n* **1** : small thin piece used in covering roofs or exterior walls — **shingle** *vb*

shin·gles \'shiŋgəlz\ *n pl* : acute inflammation of spinal nerves

shin·ny \'shinē\ *vb* **-nied; -ny·ing** : shin

shiny \'shīnē\ *adj* **shin·i·er; -est** : bright or polished

ship \'ship\ *n* **1** : large oceangoing vessel **2** : aircraft or spacecraft ~ *vb* **-pp- 1** : put on a ship **2** : transport by carrier — **ship·board** *n* — **ship·build·er** *n* — **ship·per** *n* — **ship·wreck** *n* or *vb* — **ship·yard** *n*

-ship \,ship\ *n suffix* **1** : state, condition, or quality **2** : rank or profession

3 : skill **4** : something showing a state or quality

ship•ment \-mənt\ n : an act of shipping or the goods shipped

ship•ping \'shipiŋ\ n **1** : ships **2** : transportation of goods

ship-shape adj : tidy

shire \'shīr, in place-name compounds ,shir, shər\ n : British county

shirk \'shərk\ vb : evade — **shirk•er** n

shirr \'shər\ vb **1** : gather (cloth) by drawing up parallel lines of stitches **2** : bake (eggs) in a dish

shirt \'shərt\ n : garment for covering the torso — **shirt•less** adj

shiv•er \'shivər\ vb : tremble — **shiver** n — **shiv•ery** adj

shoal \'shōl\ n : shallow place (as in a river)

¹shock \'shäk\ n : pile of sheaves set up in a field

²shock n **1** : forceful impact **2** : violent mental or emotional disturbance **3** : effect of a charge of electricity **4** : depression of the vital bodily processes ~ vb **1** : strike with surprise, horror, or disgust **2** : subject to an electrical shock — **shock•proof** adj

³shock n : bushy mass (as of hair)

shod•dy \'shädē\ adj **-di•er**; **-est** : poorly made or done — **shod•di•ly** \'shäd°lē\ adv — **shod•di•ness** n

shoe \'shü\ n **1** : covering for the human foot **2** : horseshoe ~ vb **shod** \'shäd\; **shoe•ing** : put horseshoes on — **shoe•lace** n — **shoe•ma•ker** n

shone past of SHINE

shook past of SHAKE

shoot \'shüt\ vb **shot** \'shät\; **shoot•ing 1** : propel (as with an arrow or bullet) **2** : wound or kill with a missile **3** : discharge (a weapon) **4** : drive (as a ball) at a goal **5** : photograph **6** : move swiftly ~ n : new plant growth — **shoot•er** n

shop \'shäp\ n : place where things are made or sold ~ vb **-pp-** : visit stores — **shop•keep•er** n — **shop•per** n

shop•lift vb : steal goods from a store — **shop•lift•er** \-,liftər\ n

¹shore \'shōr\ n : land along the edge of water — **shore•line** n

²shore vb **shored**; **shor•ing** : prop up ~ n : something that props

shore•bird n : bird of the seashore

shorn past part of SHEAR

short \'short\ adj **1** : not long or tall or extending far **2** : brief in time **3** : curt **4** : not having or being enough ~ adv : curtly ~ n **1** pl : short drawers or trousers **2** : short circuit — **short•en** \-°n\ vb — **short•ly** adv — **short•ness** n

short•age \'shortij\ n : deficiency

short•cake n : dessert of biscuit with sweetened fruit

short•change vb : cheat esp. by giving too little change

short circuit n : abnormal electric connection — **short–circuit** vb

short•com•ing n : fault or failing

short•cut \-,kət\ n **1** : more direct route than that usu. taken **2** : quicker way of doing something

short•hand n : method of speed writing

short–lived \'short'livd, -,livd\ adj : of short life or duration

short•sight•ed adj : lacking foresight

shot \'shät\ n **1** : act of shooting **2** : attempt (as at making a goal) **3** : small pellets forming a charge **4** : range or reach **5** : photograph **6** : injection of medicine **7** : small serving of liquor — **shot•gun** n

should \'shud\ past of SHALL — used as an auxiliary to express condition, obligation, or probability

shoul•der \'shōldər\ n **1** : part of the body where the arm joins the trunk **2** : part that projects or lies to the side ~ vb : push with or bear on the shoulder

shoulder blade n : flat triangular bone at the back of the shoulder

shout \'shaut\ vb : give voice loudly — **shout** n

shove \'shəv\ vb **shoved**; **shov•ing** : push along or away — **shove** n

shov•el \'shəvəl\ n : broad tool for digging or lifting ~ vb **-eled** or **-elled**; **-el•ing** or **-el•ling** : take up or dig with a shovel

show \'shō\ vb **showed** \'shōd\; **shown** \'shōn\ or **showed**; **show•ing 1** : present to view **2** : reveal or demonstrate **3** : teach **4** : prove **5** : conduct or escort **6** : appear or be noticeable ~ n **1** : demonstrative display **2** : spectacle **3** : theatrical, radio, or television program — **show•case** n — **show off** vb **1** : display proudly **2** : act so as to attract attention — **show up** vb : arrive

show•down n : decisive confrontation

show•er \'shauər\ n **1** : brief fall of rain **2** : bath in which water sprinkles down on the person or a facility for such a bath **3** : party at which someone gets gifts ∼ *vb* **1** : rain or fall in a shower **2** : bathe in a shower — **show•ery** *adj*

showy \'shōē\ *adj* **show•i•er; -est** : very noticeable or overly elaborate — **show•i•ly** *adv* — **show•i•ness** *n*

shrap•nel \'shrapnəl\ *n, pl* **shrapnel** : metal fragments of a bomb

shred \'shred\ *n* : narrow strip cut or torn off ∼ *vb* **-dd-** : cut or tear into shreds

shrew \'shrü\ *n* **1** : scolding woman **2** : mouselike mammal — **shrew•ish** \-ish\ *adj*

shrewd \'shrüd\ *adj* : clever — **shrewd•ly** *adv* — **shrewd•ness** *n*

shriek \'shrēk\ *n* : shrill cry — **shriek** *vb*

shrill \'shril\ *adj* : piercing and high-pitched — **shril•ly** *adv*

shrimp \'shrimp\ *n* : small sea crustacean

shrine \'shrīn\ *n* **1** : tomb of a saint **2** : hallowed place

shrink \'shriŋk\ *vb* **shrank** \'shraŋk\; **shrunk** \'shrəŋk\ *or* **shrunk•en** \'shrəŋkən\; **shrink•ing 1** : draw back or away **2** : become smaller — **shrink•able** *adj*

shrink•age \'shriŋkij\ *n* : amount lost by shrinking

shriv•el \'shrivəl\ *vb* **-eled** *or* **-elled; -el•ing** *or* **-el•ling** : shrink or wither into wrinkles

shroud \'shraud\ *n* **1** : cloth put over a corpse **2** : cover or screen ∼ *vb* : veil or screen from view

shrub \'shrəb\ *n* : low woody plant — **shrub•by** *adj*

shrub•bery \'shrəbərē\ *n, pl* **-ber•ies** : growth of shrubs

shrug \'shrəg\ *vb* **-gg-** : hunch the shoulders up in doubt, indifference, or uncertainty — **shrug** *n*

shuck \'shək\ *vb* : strip of a shell or husk — **shuck** *n*

shud•der \'shədər\ *vb* : tremble — **shudder** *n*

shuf•fle \'shəfəl\ *vb* **-fled; -fling 1** : mix together **2** : walk with a sliding movement — **shuffle** *n*

shuf•fle•board \'shəfəl,bōrd\ *n* : game of sliding disks into a scoring area

shun \'shən\ *vb* **-nn-** : keep away from

shunt \'shənt\ *vb* : turn off to one side

shut \'shət\ *vb* **shut; shut•ting 1** : bar passage into or through (as by moving

a lid or door) **2** : suspend activity — **shut out** *vb* : exclude — **shut up** *vb* : stop or cause to stop talking

shut–in *n* : invalid

shut•ter \'shətər\ *n* **1** : movable cover for a window **2** : camera part that exposes film

shut•tle \'shət²l\ *n* **1** : part of a weaving machine that carries thread back and forth **2** : vehicle traveling back and forth over a short route ∼ *vb* **-tled; -tling** : move back and forth frequently

shut•tle•cock \'shət²l,käk\ *n* : light conical object used in badminton

shy \'shī\ *adj* **shi•er** *or* **shy•er** \'shīər\; **shi•est** *or* **shy•est** \'shīəst\ **1** : sensitive and hesitant in dealing with others **2** : wary **3** : lacking ∼ *vb* **shied; shy•ing** : draw back (as in fright) — **shy•ly** *adv* — **shy•ness** *n*

sib•i•lant \'sibələnt\ *adj* : having the sound of the *s* or the *sh* in *sash* — **sibilant** *n*

sib•ling \'sibliŋ\ *n* : brother or sister

sick \'sik\ *adj* **1** : not in good health **2** : nauseated **3** : relating to or meant for the sick — **sick•bed** *n* — **sick•en** \-ən\ *vb* — **sick•ly** *adj* — **sick•ness** *n*

sick•le \'sikəl\ *n* : curved short-handled blade

side \'sīd\ *n* **1** : part to left or right of an object or the torso **2** : edge or surface away from the center or at an angle to top and bottom or ends **3** : contrasting or opposing position or group — **sid•ed** *adj*

side•board *n* : piece of dining-room furniture for table service

side•burns \-,bərnz\ *n pl* : whiskers in front of the ears

side•long \'sīd,lòŋ\ *adv or adj* : to or along the side

side•show *n* : minor show at a circus

side•step *vb* **1** : step aside **2** : avoid

side•swipe \-,swīp\ *vb* : strike with a glancing blow — **sideswipe** *n*

side•track *vb* : lead aside or astray

side•walk *n* : paved walk at the side of a road

side•ways \-,wāz\ *adv or adj* **1** : to or from the side **2** : with one side to the front

sid•ing \'sīdiŋ\ *n* **1** : short railroad track **2** : material for covering the outside of a building

si•dle \'sīd²l\ *vb* **-dled; -dling** : move sideways or unobtrusively

siege \'sēj\ *n* : persistent attack (as on a fortified place)

si·es·ta \sē'estə\ *n* : midday nap

sieve \'siv\ *n* : utensil with holes to separate particles

sift \'sift\ *vb* **1** : pass through a sieve **2** : examine carefully — **sift·er** *n*

sigh \'sī\ *n* : audible release of the breath (as to express weariness) — **sigh** *vb*

sight \'sīt\ *n* **1** : something seen or worth seeing **2** : process, power, or range of seeing **3** : device used in aiming **4** : view or glimpse ~ *vb* : get sight of — **sight·ed** *adj* — **sight·less** *adj* — **sight-see·ing** *adj* — **sight-seer** \-,sēər\ *n*

sign \'sīn\ *n* **1** : symbol **2** : gesture expressing a command or thought **3** : public notice to advertise or warn **4** : trace ~ *vb* **1** : mark with or make a sign **2** : write one's name on — **sign·er** *n*

sig·nal \'signəl\ *n* **1** : sign of command or warning **2** : electronic transmission ~ *vb* -**naled** *or* -**nalled**; -**nal·ing** *or* -**nal·ling** : communicate or notify by signals ~ *adj* : distinguished

sig·na·to·ry \'signə,tōrē\ *n, pl* -**ries** : person or government that signs jointly with others

sig·na·ture \'signə,chúr\ *n* : one's name written by oneself

sig·net \'signət\ *n* : small seal

sig·nif·i·cance \sig'nifikəns\ *n* **1** : meaning **2** : importance — **sig·nif·i·cant** \-kənt\ *adj* — **sig·nif·i·cant·ly** *adv*

sig·ni·fy \'signə,fī\ *vb* -**fied**; -**fy·ing** **1** : show by a sign **2** : mean — **sig·ni·fi·ca·tion** \,signəfə'kāshən\ *n*

si·lence \'sīləns\ *n* : state of being without sound ~ *vb* -**lenced**; -**lenc·ing** : keep from making noise or sound — **si·lenc·er** *n*

si·lent \'sīlənt\ *adj* : having or producing no sound — **si·lent·ly** *adv*

sil·hou·ette \,silə'wet\ *n* : outline filled in usu. with black ~ *vb* -**ett·ed**; -**ett·ing** : represent by a silhouette

sil·i·ca \'silikə\ *n* : mineral found as quartz and opal

sil·i·con \'silikən, -,kän\ *n* : nonmetallic chemical element

silk \'silk\ *n* **1** : fine strong lustrous protein fiber from moth larvae (**silkworms** \-,wərmz\) **2** : thread or cloth made from silk — **silk·en** \'silkən\ *adj* — **silky** *adj*

sill \'sil\ *n* : bottom part of a window frame or a doorway

sil·ly \'silē\ *adj* **sil·li·er; -est** : foolish or stupid — **sil·li·ness** *n*

si·lo \'sīlō\ *n, pl* -**los** : tall building for storing animal feed

silt \'silt\ *n* : fine earth carried by rivers ~ *vb* : obstruct or cover with silt

sil·ver \'silvər\ *n* **1** : white ductile metallic chemical element **2** : silverware ~ *adj* : having the color of silver — **sil·very** *adj*

sil·ver·ware \-,war\ *n* : eating and serving utensils esp. of silver

sim·i·lar \'simələr\ *adj* : resembling each other in some ways — **sim·i·lar·i·ty** \,simə'larətē\ *n* — **sim·i·lar·ly** \'simələrlē\ *adv*

sim·i·le \'simə,lē\ *n* : comparison of unlike things using *like* or *as*

sim·mer \'simər\ *vb* : stew gently

sim·per \'simpər\ *vb* : give a silly smile — **simper** *n*

sim·ple \'simpəl\ *adj* -**pler; -plest** **1** : free from dishonesty, vanity, or pretense **2** : of humble origin or modest position **3** : not complex **4** : lacking education, experience, or intelligence — **sim·ple·ness** *n* — **sim·ply** \-plē\ *adv*

sim·ple·ton \'simpəltən\ *n* : fool

sim·plic·i·ty \sim'plisətē\ *n* : state or fact of being simple

sim·pli·fy \'simplə,fī\ *vb* -**fied**; -**fy·ing** : make easier — **sim·pli·fi·ca·tion** \,simpləfə'kāshən\ *n*

sim·u·late \'simyə,lāt\ *vb* -**lat·ed**; -**lat·ing** : create the effect or appearance of — **sim·u·la·tion** \,simyə'lāshən\ *n* — **sim·u·la·tor** \'simyə,lātər\ *n*

si·mul·ta·ne·ous \,sīməl'tānēəs\ *adj* : occurring or operating at the same time — **si·mul·ta·ne·ous·ly** *adv* — **simul·ta·ne·ous·ness** *n*

sin \'sin\ *n* : offense against God ~ *vb* -**nn-** : commit a sin — **sin·ful** \-fəl\ *adj* — **sin·less** *adj* — **sin·ner** *n*

since \'sins\ *adv* **1** : from a past time until now **2** : backward in time ~ *prep* **1** : in the period after **2** : continuously from ~ *conj* **1** : from the time when **2** : because

sin·cere \sin'sir\ *adj* -**cer·er; -cer·est** : genuine or honest — **sin·cere·ly** *adv* — **sin·cer·i·ty** \-'serətē\ *n*

si·ne·cure \'sīni,kyúr, 'sini-\ *n* : well-paid job that requires little work

sin·ew \'sinyü\ n 1 : tendon 2 : physical strength — **sin·ewy** adj

sing \'siŋ\ vb **sang** \'saŋ\ or **sung** \'səŋ\; **sung**; **sing·ing** : produce musical tones with the voice — **sing·er** n

singe \'sinj\ vb **singed**; **singe·ing** : scorch lightly

sin·gle \'siŋgəl\ adj 1 : one only 2 : unmarried ∼ n : separate one — **single·ness** n — **sin·gly** \-glē\ adv — **single out** vb : select or set aside

sin·gu·lar \'siŋgyələr\ adj 1 : relating to a word form denoting one 2 : outstanding or superior 3 : queer — **singular** n — **sin·gu·lar·i·ty** \siŋgyə-'larətē\ n — **sin·gu·lar·ly** \'siŋgyə-lərlē\ adv

sin·is·ter \'sinəstər\ adj : threatening evil

sink \'siŋk\ vb **sank** \'saŋk\ or **sunk** \'səŋk\; **sunk**; **sink·ing** 1 : submerge or descend 2 : grow worse 3 : make by digging or boring 4 : invest ∼ n : basin with a drain

sink·er \'siŋkər\ n : weight to sink a fishing line

sin·u·ous \'sinyəwəs\ adj : winding in and out — **sin·u·os·i·ty** \siŋyə-'wäsətē\ n — **sin·u·ous·ly** adv

si·nus \'sīnəs\ n : skull cavity usu. connecting with the nostrils

sip \'sip\ vb **-pp-** : drink in small quantities — **sip** n

si·phon \'sīfən\ n : tube that draws liquid by suction — **siphon** vb

sir \'sər\ n 1 — used before the first name of a knight or baronet 2 — used as a respectful form of address

sire \'sīr\ n : father ∼ vb **sired**; **sir·ing** : beget

si·ren \'sīrən\ n 1 : seductive woman 2 : wailing warning whistle

sir·loin \'sər,lȯin\ n : cut of beef

sirup var of SYRUP

si·sal \'sīsəl, -zəl\ n : strong rope fiber

sis·sy \'sisē\ n, pl **-sies** : timid or effeminate boy

sis·ter \'sistər\ n : female sharing one or both parents with another person — **sis·ter·hood** \-,hùd\ n — **sis·ter·ly** adj

sis·ter-in-law \'sis·tərs·in·law\ n : sister of one's spouse or wife of one's brother

sit \'sit\ vb **sat** \'sat\; **sit·ting** 1 : rest on the buttocks or haunches 2 : roost 3 : hold a session 4 : pose for a portrait 5 : have a location 6 : rest or fix in place — **sit·ter** n

site \'sīt\ n 1 : place 2 : Web site

sit·u·at·ed \'sicha,wātad\ adj : located

sit·u·a·tion \,sicha'wāshən\ n 1 : location 2 : condition 3 : job

six \'siks\ n : one more than 5 — **six** adj or pron — **sixth** \'siksth\ adj or adv or n

six·teen \siks'tēn\ n : one more than 15 — **sixteen** adj or pron — **six·teenth** \-'tēnth\ adj or n

six·ty \'sikstē\ n, pl **-ties** : 6 times 10 — **six·ti·eth** \-əth\ adj or n — **sixty** adj or pron

siz·able, size·able \'sīzəbəl\ adj : quite large — **siz·ably** \-blē\ adv

size \'sīz\ n : measurement of the amount of space something takes up ∼ vb : grade according to size

siz·zle \'sizəl\ vb **-zled**; **-zling** : fry with a hissing sound — **sizzle** n

skate \'skāt\ n 1 : metal runner on a shoe for gliding over ice 2 : roller skate — **skate** vb — **skat·er** n

skein \'skān\ n : loosely twisted quantity of yarn or thread

skel·e·ton \'skelət'n\ n : bony framework — **skel·e·tal** \-ət'l\ adj

skep·tic \'skeptik\ n : one who is critical or doubting — **skep·ti·cal** \-tikəl\ adj — **skep·ti·cism** \-tə,sizəm\ n

sketch \'skech\ n 1 : rough drawing 2 : short story or essay — **sketch** vb — **sketchy** adj

skew·er \'skyüər\ n : long pin for holding roasting meat — **skewer** vb

ski \'skē\ n, pl **skis** : long strip for gliding over snow or water — **ski** vb — **ski·er** n

skid \'skid\ n 1 : plank for supporting something or on which it slides 2 : act of skidding ∼ vb **-dd-** : slide sideways

skiff \'skif\ n : small boat

skill \'skil\ n : developed or learned ability — **skilled** \'skild\ adj — **skill·ful** \-fəl\ adj — **skill·ful·ly** adv

skil·let \'skilət\ n : pan for frying

skim \'skim\ vb **-mm-** 1 : take off from the top of a liquid 2 : read or move over swiftly ∼ adj : having the cream removed — **skim·mer** n

skimp \'skimp\ vb : give too little of something — **skimpy** adj

skin \'skin\ n 1 : outer layer of an animal body 2 : rind ∼ vb **-nn-** : take the skin from — **skin•less** adj — **skinned** adj — **skin•tight** adj

skin diving n : sport of swimming under water with a face mask and flippers

skin•flint \'skin,flint\ n : stingy person

skin•ny \'skinē\ adj -ni•er; -est : very thin

skip \'skip\ vb -pp- 1 : move with leaps 2 : read past or ignore — **skip** n

skip•per \'skipər\ n : ship's master — **skipper** vb

skir•mish \'skərmish\ n : minor combat — **skirmish** vb

skirt \'skərt\ n : garment or part of a garment that hangs below the waist ~ vb : pass around the edge of

skit \'skit\ n : brief usu. humorous play

skit•tish \'skitish\ adj : easily frightened

skulk \'skəlk\ vb : move furtively

skull \'skəl\ n : bony case that protects the brain

skunk \'skəŋk\ n : mammal that can forcibly eject an ill-smelling fluid

sky \'skī\ n, pl **skies** 1 : upper air 2 : heaven — **sky•line** n — **sky•ward** \-wərd\ adv or adj

sky•lark \'skī,lärk\ n : European lark noted for its song

sky•light n : window in a roof or ceiling

sky•rock•et n : shooting firework ~ vb : rise suddenly

sky•scrap•er \-,skrāpər\ n : very tall building

slab \'slab\ n : thick slice

slack \'slak\ adj 1 : careless 2 : not taut 3 : not busy ~ n 1 : part hanging loose 2 pl : casual trousers — **slack•en** vb — **slack•ly** adv — **slack•ness** n

slag \'slag\ n : waste from melting of ores

slain past part of SLAY

slake \'slāk\ vb **slaked; slak•ing** : quench

slam \'slam\ n : heavy jarring impact ~ vb -mm- : shut, strike, or throw violently and loudly

slan•der \'slandər\ n : malicious gossip ~ vb : hurt (someone) with slander — **slan•der•er** n — **slan•der•ous** adj

slang \'slaŋ\ n : informal nonstandard vocabulary — **slangy** adj

slant \'slant\ vb 1 : slope 2 : present with a special viewpoint ~ n : sloping direction, line, or plane

slap \'slap\ vb -pp- : strike sharply with the open hand — **slap** n

slash \'slash\ vb 1 : cut with sweeping strokes 2 : reduce sharply ~ n : gash

slat \'slat\ n : thin narrow flat strip

slate \'slāt\ n 1 : dense fine-grained layered rock 2 : roofing tile or writing tablet of slate 3 : list of candidates ~ vb **slat•ed; slat•ing** : designate

slat•tern \'slatərn\ n : untidy woman — **slat•tern•ly** adj

slaugh•ter \'slôtər\ n 1 : butchering of livestock for market 2 : great and cruel destruction of lives ~ vb : commit slaughter upon — **slaughter-house** n

slave \'slāv\ n : one owned and forced into service by another ~ vb **slaved; slav•ing** : work as or like a slave — **slave** adj — **slav•ery** \'slāvərē\ n

sla•ver \'slavər, 'slāv-\ vb or n : slobber

slav•ish \'slāvish\ adj : of or like a slave — **slav•ish•ly** adv

slay \'slā\ vb **slew** \'slü\; **slain** \'slān\; **slay•ing** : kill — **slay•er** n

slea•zy \'slēzē, 'slā-\ adj -zi•er; -est : shabby or shoddy

sled \'sled\ n : vehicle on runners — **sled** vb

¹**sledge** \'slej\ n : sledgehammer

²**sledge** n : heavy sled

sledge•ham•mer n : heavy long-handled hammer — **sledgehammer** adj or vb

sleek \'slēk\ adj : smooth or glossy — **sleek** vb

sleep \'slēp\ n : natural suspension of consciousness ~ vb **slept** \'slept\; **sleep•ing** : rest in a state of sleep — **sleep•er** n — **sleep•less** adj — **sleep•walk•er** n

sleepy \'slēpē\ adj **sleep•i•er; -est** 1 : ready for sleep 2 : quietly inactive — **sleep•i•ly** \'slēpəlē\ adv — **sleep•i•ness** \-pēnəs\ n

sleet \'slēt\ n : frozen rain — **sleet** vb — **sleety** adj

sleeve \'slēv\ n : part of a garment for the arm — **sleeve•less** adj

sleigh \'slā\ n : horse-drawn sled with seats ~ vb : drive or ride in a sleigh

sleight of hand \'slīt-\ : skillful manual manipulation or a trick requiring it

slen•der \'slendər\ adj 1 : thin esp. in physique 2 : scanty

sleuth \'slüth\ n : detective

slew \'slü\ past of SLAY

slice \'slīs\ n : thin flat piece ~ vb **sliced; slic•ing** : cut a slice from

slick \'slik\ adj 1 : very smooth 2 : clever — **slick** vb

slick•er \\'slikər\\ n : raincoat

slide \\'slīd\\ vb **slid** \\'slid\\; **slid•ing** \\'slīdiŋ\\ : move smoothly along a surface ~ n 1 : act of sliding 2 : surface on which something slides 3 : transparent picture for projection

slier comparative of SLY

sliest superlative of SLY

slight \\'slīt\\ adj 1 : slender 2 : frail 3 : small in degree ~ vb 1 : ignore or treat as unimportant — **slight** n — **slight•ly** adv

slim \\'slim\\ adj **-mm-** 1 : slender 2 : scanty ~ vb **-mm-** : make or become slender

slime \\'slīm\\ n : dirty slippery film (as on water) — **slimy** adj

sling \\'sliŋ\\ vb **slung** \\'sləŋ\\; **sling•ing** : hurl with or as if with a sling ~ n 1 : strap for swinging and hurling stones 2 : looped strap or bandage to lift or support

sling•shot n : forked stick with elastic bands for shooting pebbles

slink \\'sliŋk\\ vb **slunk** \\'sləŋk\\; **slink•ing** : move stealthily or sinuously — **slinky** adj

¹**slip** \\'slip\\ vb **-pp-** 1 : escape quietly or secretly 2 : slide along smoothly 3 : make a mistake 4 : to pass without being noticed or done 5 : fall off from a standard ~ n 1 : ship's berth 2 : sudden mishap 3 : mistake 4 : woman's undergarment

²**slip** n 1 : plant shoot 2 : small strip (as of paper)

slip•per \\'slipər\\ n : shoe that slips on easily

slip•pery \\'slipərē\\ adj **-peri•er**; **-est** 1 : slick enough to slide on 2 : tricky — **slip•peri•ness** n

slip•shod \\'slip,shäd\\ adj : careless

slit \\'slit\\ vb **slit**; **slit•ting** : make a slit in ~ n : long narrow cut

slith•er \\'slithər\\ vb : glide along like a snake — **slith•ery** adj

sliv•er \\'slivər\\ n : splinter

slob \\'släb\\ n : untidy person

slob•ber \\'släbər\\ vb : dribble saliva — **slobber** n

slo•gan \\'slōgən\\ n : word or phrase expressing the aim of a cause

sloop \\'slüp\\ n : one-masted sailboat

slop \\'släp\\ n : food waste for animal feed ~ vb **-pp-** : spill

slope \\'slōp\\ vb **sloped**; **slop•ing** : deviate from the vertical or horizontal ~ n : upward or downward slant

slop•py \\'släpē\\ adj **-pi•er**; **-est** 1 : muddy 2 : untidy

slot \\'slät\\ n : narrow opening

sloth \\'slòth, 'slōth\\ n, pl **sloths** \\with ths or thz\\ 1 : laziness 2 : slow-moving mammal — **sloth•ful** adj

slouch \\'slauch\\ n 1 : drooping posture 2 : lazy or incompetent person ~ vb : walk or stand with a slouch

¹**slough** \\'slü, 'slau\\ n : swamp

²**slough**, **sluff** \\'sləf\\ vb : cast off (old skin)

slov•en•ly \\'sləvənlē\\ adj : untidy

slow \\'slō\\ adj 1 : sluggish or stupid 2 : moving, working, or happening at less than usual speed ~ vb 1 : make slow 2 : go slower — **slow** adv — **slow•ly** adv — **slow•ness** n

sludge \\'sləj\\ n : slushy mass (as of treated sewage)

slug \\'sləg\\ n 1 : mollusk related to the snails 2 : bullet 3 : metal disk ~ vb **-gg-** : strike forcibly — **slug•ger** n

slug•gish \\'sləgish\\ adj : slow in movement or flow — **slug•gish•ly** adv — **slug•gish•ness** n

sluice \\'slüs\\ n : channel for water ~ vb **sluiced**; **sluic•ing** : wash in running water

slum \\'sləm\\ n : thickly populated area marked by poverty

slum•ber \\'sləmbər\\ vb or n : sleep

slump \\'sləmp\\ vb 1 : sink suddenly 2 : slouch — **slump** n

slung past of SLING

slunk past of SLINK

¹**slur** \\'slər\\ vb **-rr-** : run (words or notes) together — **slur** n

²**slur** n : malicious or insulting remark

slurp \\'slərp\\ vb : eat or drink noisily — **slurp** n

slush \\'sləsh\\ n : partly melted snow — **slushy** adj

slut \\'slət\\ n 1 : untidy woman 2 : lewd woman — **slut•tish** adj

sly \\'slī\\ adj **sli•er** \\'slīər\\; **sli•est** \\'slīəst\\ : given to or showing secrecy and deception — **sly•ly** adv — **sly•ness** n

¹**smack** \\'smak\\ n : characteristic flavor ~ vb : have a taste or hint

²**smack** vb 1 : move (the lips) so as to make a sharp noise 2 : kiss or slap with a loud noise ~ n 1 : sharp noise made by the lips 2 : noisy slap

³**smack** adv : squarely and sharply

⁴**smack** n : fishing boat

small \\'smòl\\ adj 1 : little in size or

amount **2** : few in number **3** : trivial — **small·ish** adj — **small·ness** n

small·pox \'smȯl,päks\ n : contagious virus disease

smart \'smärt\ vb **1** : cause or feel stinging pain **2** : endure distress ~ adj **1** : intelligent or resourceful **2** : stylish — **smart** n — **smart·ly** adv — **smart·ness** n

smash \'smash\ vb : break or be broken into pieces ~ n **1** : smashing blow **2** : act or sound of smashing

smat·ter·ing \'smatəriŋ\ n **1** : superficial knowledge **2** : small scattered number or amount

smear \'smir\ n : greasy stain ~ vb **1** : spread (something sticky) **2** : smudge **3** : slander

smell \'smel\ vb **smelled** \'smeld\ or **smelt** \'smelt\; **smell·ing** : **1** : perceive the odor of **2** : have or give off an odor ~ n **1** : sense by which one perceives odor **2** : odor — **smelly** adj

¹**smelt** \'smelt\ n, pl **smelts** or **smelt** : small food fish

²**smelt** vb : melt or fuse (ore) in order to separate the metal — **smelt·er** n

smile \'smīl\ n : facial expression with the mouth turned up usu. to show pleasure — **smile** vb

smirk \'smərk\ vb : wear a conceited smile — **smirk** n

smite \'smīt\ vb **smote** \'smōt\; **smitten** \'smit²n\ or **smote**; **smit·ing** \'smītiŋ\ **1** : strike heavily or kill **2** : affect strongly

smith \'smith\ n : worker in metals and esp. a blacksmith

smithy \'smithē\ n, pl **smith·ies** : a smith's workshop

smock \'smäk\ n : loose dress or protective coat

smog \'smäg, 'smȯg\ n : fog and smoke — **smog·gy** adj

smoke \'smōk\ n : sooty gas from burning ~ vb **smoked; smok·ing** **1** : give off smoke **2** : inhale the fumes of burning tobacco **3** : cure (as meat) with smoke — **smoke·less** adj — **smok·er** n — **smoky** adj

smoke·stack n : chimney through which smoke is discharged

smol·der, smoul·der \'smōldər\ vb **1** : burn and smoke without flame **2** : be suppressed but active — **smolder** n

smooth \'smüth\ adj **1** : having a surface without irregularities **2** : not jar-

ring or jolting ~ vb : make smooth — **smooth·ly** adv — **smooth·ness** n

smor·gas·bord \'smȯrgəs,bȯrd\ n : buffet consisting of many foods

smoth·er \'sməthər\ vb **1** : kill by depriving of air **2** : cover thickly

smudge \'sməj\ vb **smudged; smudg·ing** : soil or blur by rubbing ~ n **1** : thick smoke **2** : dirty spot

smug \'sməg\ adj **-gg-** : content in one's own virtue or accomplishment — **smug·ly** adv — **smug·ness** n

smug·gle \'sməgəl\ vb **-gled; -gling** : import or export secretly or illegally — **smug·gler** \'sməglər\ n

smut \'smət\ n **1** : something that soils **2** : indecent language or matter **3** : disease of plants caused by fungi — **smut·ty** adj

snack \'snak\ n : light meal

snag \'snag\ n : unexpected difficulty ~ vb **-gg-** : become caught on something that sticks out

snail \'snāl\ n : small mollusk with a spiral shell

snake \'snāk\ n : long-bodied limbless reptile — **snake·bite** n

snap \'snap\ vb **-pp-** **1** : bite at something **2** : utter angry words **3** : break suddenly with a sharp sound ~ n **1** : act or sound of snapping **2** : fastening that closes with a click **3** : something easy to do — **snap·per** n — **snap·pish** adj — **snap·py** adj

snap·drag·on n : garden plant with spikes of showy flowers

snap·shot \'snap,shät\ n : casual photograph

snare \'snar\ n : trap for catching game ~ vb : capture or hold with or as if with a snare

¹**snarl** \'snärl\ n : tangle ~ vb : cause to become knotted

²**snarl** vb or n : growl

snatch \'snach\ vb **1** : try to grab something suddenly **2** : seize or take away suddenly ~ n **1** : act of snatching **2** : something brief or fragmentary

sneak \'snēk\ vb : move or take in a furtive manner ~ n : one who acts in a furtive manner — **sneak·i·ly** \'snēkəlē\ adv — **sneak·ing·ly** adv — **sneaky** adj

sneak·er \'snēkər\ n : sports shoe

sneer \'snir\ vb : smile scornfully — **sneer** n

sneeze \'snēz\ vb **sneezed; sneez·ing**

: force the breath out with sudden and involuntary violence — **sneeze** n

snick·er \'snikər\ n : partly suppressed laugh — **snicker** vb

snide \'snīd\ adj : subtly ridiculing

sniff \'snif\ vb : draw air audibly up the nose **2** : detect by smelling — **sniff** n

snip \'snip\ n : fragment snipped off ~ vb **-pp-** : cut off by bits

¹**snipe** \'snīp\ n, pl **snipes** or **snipe** : game bird of marshy areas

²**snipe** vb **sniped; snip·ing** : shoot at an enemy from a concealed position — **snip·er** n

snips \'snips\ n pl : scissorslike tool

sniv·el \'snivəl\ vb **-eled** or **-elled; -el·ing** or **-el·ling 1** : have a running nose **2** : whine

snob \'snäb\ n : one who acts superior to others — **snob·bery** \-ərē\ n — **snob·bish** adj — **snob·bish·ly** adv — **snob·bish·ness** n

snoop \'snüp\ vb : pry in a furtive way ~ n : prying person

snooze \'snüz\ vb **snoozed; snooz·ing** : take a nap — **snooze** n

snore \'snōr\ vb **snored; snor·ing** : breathe with a hoarse noise while sleeping — **snore** n

snort \'snȯrt\ vb : force air noisily through the nose — **snort** n

snout \'snaůt\ n : long projecting muzzle (as of a swine)

snow \'snō\ n : crystals formed from water vapor ~ vb : fall as snow — **snow·ball** n — **snow·bank** n — **snow·drift** n — **snow·fall** n — **snow·plow** n — **snow·storm** n — **snowy** adj

snow·shoe n : frame of wood strung with thongs for walking on snow

snub \'snəb\ vb **-bb-** : ignore or avoid through disdain — **snub** n

¹**snuff** \'snəf\ vb : put out (a candle) — **snuff·er** n

²**snuff** vb : draw forcibly into the nose ~ n : pulverized tobacco

snug \'snəg\ adj **-gg- 1** : warm, secure, and comfortable **2** : fitting closely — **snug·ly** adv — **snug·ness** n

snug·gle \'snəgəl\ vb **-gled; -gling** : curl up comfortably

so \'sō\ adv **1** : in the manner or to the extent indicated **2** : in the same way **3** : therefore **4** : finally **5** : thus ~ conj : for that reason

soak \'sōk\ vb **1** : lie in a liquid **2** : absorb ~ n : act of soaking

soap \'sōp\ n : cleaning substance — **soap** vb — **soapy** adj

soar \'sōr\ vb : fly upward on or as if on wings

sob \'säb\ vb **-bb-** : weep with convulsive heavings of the chest — **sob** n

so·ber \'sōbər\ adj **1** : not drunk **2** : serious or solemn — **so·ber·ly** adv

so·bri·ety \sə'brīətē, sō-\ n : quality or state of being sober

soc·cer \'säkər\ n : game played by kicking a ball

so·cia·ble \'sōshəbəl\ adj : friendly — **so·cia·bil·i·ty** \ˌsōshə'bilətē\ n — **so·cia·bly** \'sōshəblē\ adv

so·cial \'sōshəl\ adj **1** : relating to pleasant companionship **2** : naturally living or growing in groups **3** : relating to human society ~ n : social gathering — **so·cial·ly** adv

so·cial·ism \'sōshəˌlizəm\ n : social system based on government control of the production and distribution of goods — **so·cial·ist** \'sōshəlist\ n or adj — **so·cial·is·tic** \ˌsōshə'listik\ adj

so·cial·ize \'sōshəˌlīz\ vb **-ized; -iz·ing 1** : regulate by socialism **2** : adapt to social needs **3** : participate in a social gathering — **so·cial·i·za·tion** \ˌsōshələ'zāshən\ n

social work n : services concerned with aiding the poor and socially maladjusted — **social worker** n

so·ci·ety \sə'sīətē\ n, pl **-et·ies 1** : companionship **2** : community life **3** : rich or fashionable class **4** : voluntary group

so·ci·ol·o·gy \ˌsōsē'äləjē\ n : study of social relationships — **so·ci·o·log·i·cal** \-ə'läjikəl\ adj — **so·ci·ol·o·gist** \-'äləjist\ n

¹**sock** \'säk\ n, pl **socks** or **sox** : short stocking

²**sock** vb or n : punch

sock·et \'säkət\ n : hollow part that holds something

sod \'säd\ n : turf ~ vb **-dd-** : cover with sod

so·da \'sōdə\ n **1** : carbonated water or a soft drink **2** : ice cream drink made with soda

sod·den \'säd³n\ adj **1** : lacking spirit **2** : soaked or soggy

so·di·um \'sōdēəm\ n : soft waxy silver white metallic chemical element

so·fa \'sōfə\ n : wide padded chair

soft \'sȯft\ adj **1** : not hard, rough, or harsh **2** : nonalcoholic — **soft·en**

\'sòfən\ *vb* — **soft·en·er** \-ənər\ *n* — **soft·ly** *adv* — **soft·ness** *n*

soft·ball *n* : game like baseball

soft·ware \'sòft,war\ *n* : computer programs

sog·gy \'sägē\ *adj* -**gi·er**; **-est** : heavy with moisture — **sog·gi·ness** \-ēnəs\ *n*

¹**soil** \'sòil\ *vb* : make or become dirty ~ *n* : embedded dirt

²**soil** *n* : loose surface material of the earth

so·journ \'sō,jərn, sō'jərn\ *n* : temporary stay ~ *vb* : reside temporarily

so·lace \'säləs\ *n or vb* : comfort

so·lar \'sōlər\ *adj* : relating to the sun or the energy in sunlight

sold *past of* SELL

sol·der \'sädər, 'sòd-\ *n* : metallic alloy melted to join metallic surfaces ~ *vb* : cement with solder

sol·dier \'sōljər\ *n* : person in military service ~ *vb* : serve as a soldier — **sol·dier·ly** *adj or adv*

¹**sole** \'sōl\ *n* : bottom of the foot or a shoe — **soled** *adj*

²**sole** *n* : flatfish caught for food

³**sole** *adj* : single or only — **sole·ly** *adv*

sol·emn \'säləm\ *adj* 1 : dignified and ceremonial 2 : highly serious — **so·lem·ni·ty** \sə'lemnətē\ *n* — **sol·emn·ly** *adv*

so·lic·it \sə'lisət\ *vb* : ask for — **so·lic·i·ta·tion** \-,lisə'tāshən\ *n*

so·lic·i·tor \sə'lisətər\ *n* 1 : one that solicits 2 : lawyer

so·lic·i·tous \sə'lisətəs\ *adj* : showing or expressing concern — **so·lic·i·tous·ly** *adv* — **so·lic·i·tude** \sə'lisə,tüd, -,tyüd\ *n*

sol·id \'säləd\ *adj* 1 : not hollow 2 : having 3 dimensions 3 : hard 4 : of good quality 5 : of one character ~ *n* 1 : 3-dimensional figure 2 : substance in solid form — **solid** *adv* — **so·lid·i·ty** \sə'lidətē\ *n* — **sol·id·ly** *adv* — **sol·id·ness** *n*

sol·i·dar·i·ty \sälə'darətē\ *n* : unity of purpose

so·lid·i·fy \sə'lidə,fī\ *vb* -**fied**; **-fy·ing** : make or become solid — **so·lid·i·fi·ca·tion** \-,lidəfə'kāshən\ *n*

so·lil·o·quy \sə'liləkwē\ *n, pl* -**quies** : dramatic monologue — **so·lil·o·quize** \-,kwīz\ *vb*

sol·i·taire \'sälə,tar\ *n* 1 : solitary gem 2 : card game for one person

sol·i·tary \-,terē\ *adj* 1 : alone 2 : secluded 3 : single

sol·i·tude \-,tüd, -,tyüd\ *n* : state of being alone

so·lo \'sōlō\ *n, pl* -**los** : performance by only one person ~ *adv* : alone — **solo** *adj or vb* — **so·lo·ist** *n*

sol·stice \'sälstəs\ *n* : time of the year when the sun is farthest north or south of the equator

sol·u·ble \'sälyəbəl\ *adj* 1 : capable of being dissolved 2 : capable of being solved — **sol·u·bil·i·ty** \,sälyə'bilətē\ *n*

so·lu·tion \sə'lüshən\ *n* 1 : answer to a problem 2 : homogeneous liquid mixture

solve \'sälv\ *vb* **solved**; **solv·ing** : find a solution for — **solv·able** *adj*

sol·vent \'sälvənt\ *adj* 1 : able to pay all debts 2 : dissolving or able to dissolve ~ *n* : substance that dissolves or disperses another substance — **sol·ven·cy** \-vənsē\ *n*

som·ber, som·bre \'sämbər\ *adj* 1 : dark 2 : grave — **som·ber·ly** *adv*

som·bre·ro \səm'brerō\ *n, pl* -**ros** : broad-brimmed hat

some \'səm\ *adj* 1 : one unspecified 2 : unspecified or indefinite number of 3 : at least a few or a little ~ *pron* : a certain number or amount

-**some** \səm\ *adj suffix* : characterized by a thing, quality, state, or action

some·body \'səmbədē, -,bäd-\ *pron* : some person

some·day \'səm,dā\ *adv* : at some future time

some·how \-,haú\ *adv* : by some means

some·one \-,wən\ *pron* : some person

som·er·sault \'səmər,sòlt\ *n* : body flip — **somersault** *vb*

some·thing \'səmthin\ *pron* : some undetermined or unspecified thing

some·time \'səm,tīm\ *adv* : at a future, unknown, or unnamed time

some·times \-,tīmz\ *adv* : occasionally

some·what \-,hwət, -,hwät\ *adv* : in some degree

some·where \-,hwer\ *adv* : in, at, or to an unknown or unnamed place

som·no·lent \'sämnələnt\ *adj* : sleepy — **som·no·lence** \-ləns\ *n*

son \'sən\ *n* : male offspring

so·nar \'sō,när\ *n* : device that detects and locates underwater objects using sound waves

so·na·ta \sə'nätə\ n : instrumental composition

song \'soṅ\ n : music and words to be sung

song·bird n : bird with musical tones

son·ic \'sänik\ adj : relating to sound waves or the speed of sound

son–in–law n, pl **sons–in–law** : husband of one's daughter

son·net \'sänət\ n : poem of 14 lines

so·no·rous \sə'nōrəs, 'sänərəs\ adj 1 : loud, deep, or rich in sound 2 : impressive — **so·nor·i·ty** \sə'nörətē\ n

soon \'sün\ adv 1 : before long 2 : promptly 3 : early

soot \'sut, 'sət, 'süt\ n : fine black substance formed by combustion — **sooty** adj

soothe \'süth\ vb **soothed; sooth·ing** : calm or comfort — **sooth·er** n

sooth·say·er \'süth,sāər\ n : prophet — **sooth·say·ing** \-iṅ\ n

sop \'säp\ n : conciliatory bribe, gift, or concession ~ vb **-pp-** 1 : dip in a liquid 2 : soak 3 : mop up

so·phis·ti·cat·ed \sə'fistə,kātəd\ adj 1 : complex 2 : wise, cultured, or shrewd in human affairs — **so·phis·ti·ca·tion** \-,fistə'kāshən\ n

soph·ist·ry \'säfəstrē\ n : subtly fallacious reasoning or argument — **sophist** \'säfist\ n

soph·o·more \'säf'm,ōr, 'säf,mōr\ n : 2d-year student

so·po·rif·ic \,säpə'rifik, ,sōp-\ adj : causing sleep or drowsiness

so·pra·no \sə'pranō\ n, pl **-nos** : highest singing voice

sor·cery \'sorsərē\ n : witchcraft — **sor·cer·er** \-rər\ n — **sor·cer·ess** \-rəs\ n

sor·did \'sordəd\ adj : filthy or vile — **sor·did·ly** adv — **sor·did·ness** n

sore \'sōr\ adj **sor·er; sor·est** 1 : causing pain or distress 2 : severe or intense 3 : angry ~ n : sore spot. infected spot on the body — **sore·ly** adv — **sore·ness** n

sor·ghum \'sorgəm\ n : forage grass

so·ror·i·ty \sə'rorətē\ n, pl **-ties** : women's student social group

¹**sor·rel** \'sörəl\ n : brownish orange to light brown color or an animal of this color

²**sorrel** n : herb with sour juice

sor·row \'särō\ n : deep distress, sadness, or regret or a cause of this — **sor·row·ful** \-fəl\ adj — **sor·row·ful·ly** adv

sor·ry \'särē\ adj **-ri·er; -est** 1 : feeling sorrow, regret, or penitence 2 : dismal

sort \'sort\ n 1 : kind 2 : nature ~ vb : classify — **out of sorts** : grouchy

sor·tie \'sortē, sor'tē\ n : military attack esp. against besiegers

SOS \,es,ō'es\ n : call for help

so–so \'sō'sō\ adj or adv : barely acceptable

sot \'sät\ n : drunkard — **sot·tish** adj

souf·flé \sü'flā\ n : baked dish made light with beaten egg whites

sought past of SEEK

soul \'sōl\ n 1 : immaterial essence of an individual life 2 : essential part 3 : person

soul·ful \'sōlfəl\ adj : full of or expressing deep feeling — **soul·ful·ly** adv

¹**sound** \'saund\ adj 1 : free from fault, error, or illness 2 : firm or hard 3 : showing good judgment — **sound·ly** adv — **sound·ness** n

²**sound** n 1 : sensation of hearing 2 : energy of vibration sensed in hearing 3 : something heard ~ vb 1 : make or cause to make a sound 2 : seem — **sound·less** adj — **sound·less·ly** adv — **sound·proof** adj or vb

³**sound** n : wide strait ~ vb 1 : measure the depth of (water) 2 : investigate

soup \'süp\ n : broth usu. containing pieces of solid food — **soupy** adj

sour \'saúər\ adj 1 : having an acid or tart taste 2 : disagreeable ~ vb : become or make sour — **sour·ish** adj — **sour·ly** adv — **sour·ness** n

source \'sōrs\ n 1 : point of origin 2 : one that provides something needed

souse \'saús\ vb **soused; sous·ing** 1 : pickle 2 : immerse 3 : intoxicate ~ n 1 : something pickled 2 : drunkard

south \'saúth\ adv : to or toward the south ~ adj : situated toward, at, or coming from the south ~ n 1 : direction to the right of sunrise 2 cap : regions to the south — **south·er·ly** \'sət̲hərlē\ adv or adj — **south·ern** \'sət̲hərn\ adj — **South·ern·er** n — **south·ern·most** \-,mōst\ adj — **south·ward** \'saúthwərd\ adv or adj — **south·wards** \-wərdz\ adv

south·east \saúth'ēst, naut saú'ēst\ n 1 : direction between south and east 2 cap : regions to the southeast — **southeast** adj or adv — **south·east-**

er·ly adv or adj — **south·east·ern** \-ərn\ adj

south pole n : the southernmost point of the earth

south·west \saùth'west, naut saò-'west\ n 1 : direction between south and west 2 cap : regions to the southwest — **southwest** adj or adv — **south·west·er·ly** adv or adj — **southwest·ern** \-ərn\ adj

sou·ve·nir \'süvə‚nir\ n : something that is a reminder of a place or event

sov·er·eign \'sävərən\ n 1 : supreme ruler 2 : gold coin of the United Kingdom ~ adj 1 : supreme 2 : independent — **sov·er·eign·ty** \-tē\ n

¹sow \'saù\ n : female swine

²sow \'sō\ vb sowed; sown \'sōn\ or sowed; sow·ing 1 : plant or strew with seed 2 : scatter abroad — **sow·er** \'sōər\ n

sox pl of SOCK

soy·bean \'sòi‚bēn\ n : legume with edible seeds

spa \'spä\ n : resort at a mineral spring

space \'spās\ n 1 : period of time 2 : area in, around, or between 3 : region beyond earth's atmosphere 4 : accommodations ~ vb spaced; **spac·ing** : place at intervals — **space·craft** n — **space·flight** n — **space·man** n — **space·ship** n

spa·cious \'spāshəs\ adj : large or roomy — **spa·cious·ly** adv — **spa·cious·ness** n

¹spade \'spād\ n or vb : shovel — **spade·ful** n

²spade n : playing card marked with a black figure like an inverted heart

spa·ghet·ti \spə'getē\ n : pasta strings

spam \'spam\ n : unsolicited commercial e-mail

span \'span\ n 1 : amount of time 2 : distance between supports ~ vb -nn- : extend across

span·gle \'spaŋgəl\ n : small disk of shining metal or plastic — **spangle** vb

span·iel \'spanyəl\ n : small or medium-sized dog with drooping ears and long wavy hair

spank \'spaŋk\ vb : hit on the buttocks with an open hand

¹spar \'spär\ n : pole or boom

²spar vb -rr- : practice boxing

spare \'spar\ adj 1 : held in reserve 2 : thin or scanty ~ vb spared; **spar·ing** 1 : reserve or avoid using 2 : avoid punishing or killing — **spare** n

spar·ing \'spariŋ\ adj : thrifty — **spar·ing·ly** adv

spark \'spärk\ n 1 : tiny hot and glowing particle 2 : smallest beginning or germ 3 : visible electrical discharge ~ vb 1 : emit or produce sparks 2 : stir to activity

spar·kle \'spärkəl\ vb -kled; -kling 1 : flash 2 : effervesce ~ n : gleam — **spark·ler** \-klər\ n

spar·row \'sparō\ n : small singing bird

sparse \'spärs\ adj spars·er; spars·est : thinly scattered — **sparse·ly** adv

spasm \'spazəm\ n 1 : involuntary muscular contraction 2 : sudden, violent, and temporary effort or feeling — **spas·mod·ic** \spaz'mädik\ adj — **spas·mod·i·cal·ly** adv

spas·tic \'spastik\ adj : relating to, marked by, or affected with muscular spasm — **spastic** n

¹spat \'spat\ past of SPIT

²spat n : petty dispute

spa·tial \'spāshəl\ adj : relating to space — **spa·tial·ly** adv

spat·ter \'spatər\ vb : splash with drops of liquid — **spatter** n

spat·u·la \'spachələ\ n : flexible knife-like utensil

spawn \'spòn\ vb 1 : produce eggs or offspring 2 : bring forth ~ n : egg cluster — **spawn·er** n

spay \'spā\ vb : remove the ovaries of (a female)

speak \'spēk\ vb spoke \'spōk\; spoken \'spōkən\; speak·ing 1 : utter words 2 : express orally 3 : address an audience 4 : use (a language) in talking — **speak·er** n

spear \'spir\ n : long pointed weapon ~ vb : strike or pierce with a spear

spear·head n : leading force, element, or influence — **spearhead** vb

spear·mint n : aromatic garden mint

spe·cial \'speshəl\ adj : unusual or unique 2 : particularly favored 3 : set aside for a particular use — **special** n — **spe·cial·ly** adv

spe·cial·ist \'speshəlist\ n 1 : person who specializes in a particular branch of learning or activity 2 : any of four enlisted ranks in the army corresponding to the grades of corporal through sergeant first class

spe·cial·ize \'speshə‚līz\ vb -ized; -iz·ing : concentrate one's efforts — **spe·cial·i·za·tion** \‚speshələ'zāshən\ n

spe·cial·ty \'speshəltē\ *n, pl* **-ties** : area or field in which one specializes

spe·cie \'spēshē, -sē\ *n* : money in coin

spe·cies \'spēshēz, -sēz\ *n, pl* **species** : biological grouping of closely related organisms

spe·cif·ic \spi'sifik\ *adj* : definite or exact — **spe·cif·i·cal·ly** *adv*

spec·i·fi·ca·tion \,spesəfə'kāshən\ *n* **1** : act or process of specifying **2** : detailed description of work to be done — usu. pl.

spec·i·fy \'spesə,fī\ *vb* **-fied; -fy·ing** : mention precisely or by name

spec·i·men \-əmən\ *n* : typical example

spe·cious \'spēshəs\ *adj* : apparently but not really genuine or correct

speck \'spek\ *n* : tiny particle or blemish — **speck** *vb*

speck·led \'spekəld\ *adj* : marked with spots

spec·ta·cle \'spektikəl\ *n* **1** : impressive public display **2** *pl* : eyeglasses

spec·tac·u·lar \spek'takyələr\ *adj* : sensational or showy

spec·ta·tor \'spek,tātər\ *n* : person who looks on

spec·ter, spec·tre \'spektər\ *n* **1** : ghost **2** : haunting vision

spec·tral \'spektrəl\ *adj* : relating to or resembling a specter or spectrum

spec·trum \'spektrəm\ *n, pl* **-tra** \-trə\ *or* **-trums** : series of colors formed when white light is dispersed into its components

spec·u·late \'spekyə,lāt\ *vb* **-lat·ed; -lat·ing** **1** : think about things yet unknown **2** : risk money in a business deal in hope of high profit — **spec·u·la·tion** \,spekyə'lāshən\ *n* — **spec·u·la·tive** \'spekyə,lātiv\ *adj* — **spec·u·la·tor** \-,lātər\ *n*

speech \'spēch\ *n* **1** : power, act, or manner of speaking **2** : talk given to an audience — **speech·less** *adj*

speed \'spēd\ *n* **1** : quality of being fast **2** : rate of motion or performance ~ *vb* **sped** \'sped\ *or* **speed·ed; speed·ing** : go at or excessive rate of speed — **speed·boat** *n* — **speed·er** *n* — **speed·i·ly** \'spēd'lē\ *adv* — **speed·up** \-,əp\ *n* — **speedy** *adj*

speed·om·e·ter \spi'dämətər\ *n* : instrument for indicating speed

¹**spell** \'spel\ *n* : influence of or like magic

²**spell** *vb* **1** : name, write, or print the letters of **2** : mean — **spell·er** *n*

³**spell** *vb* : substitute for or relieve (someone) ~ *n* **1** : turn at work **2** : period of time

spell·bound *adj* : held by a spell

spend \'spend\ *vb* **spent** \'spent\; **spend·ing** **1** : pay out **2** : cause or allow to pass — **spend·er** *n*

spend·thrift \'spend,thrift\ *n* : wasteful person

sperm \'spərm\ *n, pl* **sperm** *or* **sperms** : semen or a germ cell in it

spew \'spyü\ *vb* : gush out in a stream

sphere \'sfir\ *n* **1** : figure with every point on its surface at an equal distance from the center **2** : round body **3** : range of action or influence — **spher·i·cal** \'sfirikəl, 'sfer-\ *adj*

spher·oid \'sfir-\ *n* : spherelike figure

spice \'spīs\ *n* **1** : aromatic plant product for seasoning food **2** : interesting quality — **spice** *vb* — **spicy** *adj*

spi·der \'spīdər\ *n* : small insectlike animal with 8 legs — **spi·dery** *adj*

spig·ot \'spigət, 'spikət\ *n* : faucet

spike \'spīk\ *n* : very large nail ~ *vb* **spiked; spik·ing** : fasten or pierce with a spike — **spiked** \'spīkt\ *adj*

spill \'spil\ *vb* **1** : fall, flow, or run out unintentionally **2** : divulge ~ *n* **1** : act of spilling **2** : something spilled — **spill·able** *adj*

spill·way *n* : passage for surplus water

spin \'spin\ *vb* **spun** \'spən\; **spin·ning** **1** : draw out fiber and twist into thread **2** : form thread from a sticky body fluid **3** : revolve or cause to revolve extremely fast ~ *n* : rapid rotating motion — **spin·ner** *n*

spin·ach \'spinich\ *n* : garden herb with edible leaves

spi·nal \'spīn'l\ *adj* : relating to the backbone — **spi·nal·ly** *adv*

spinal cord *n* : thick strand of nervous tissue that extends from the brain along the back within the backbone

spin·dle \'spind'l\ *n* **1** : stick used for spinning thread **2** : shaft around which something turns

spin·dly \'spindlē\ *adj* : tall and slender

spine \'spīn\ *n* **1** : backbone **2** : stiff sharp projection on a plant or animal — **spine·less** *adj* — **spiny** *adj*

spin·et \'spinət\ *n* : small piano

spin·ster \'spinstər\ *n* : woman who has never married

spi·ral \'spīrəl\ *adj* : circling or winding around a single point or line — **spiral** n or vb — **spi·ral·ly** adv

spire \'spīr\ n : steeple — **spiry** adj

spir·it \'spirət\ n 1 : life-giving force 2 cap : presence of God 3 : ghost 4 : mood 5 : vivacity or enthusiasm 6 pl : alcoholic liquor ~ vb : carry off secretly — **spir·it·ed** adj — **spir·it·less** adj

spir·i·tu·al \'spirichəwəl\ adj 1 : relating to the spirit or sacred matters 2 : deeply religious ~ n : religious folk song — **spir·i·tu·al·i·ty** \,spirichə'walātē\ n — **spir·i·tu·al·ly** adv

spir·i·tu·al·ism \'spirichəwə,lizəm\ n : belief that spirits communicate with the living — **spir·i·tu·al·ist** \-list\ n or adj

¹**spit** \'spit\ n 1 : rod for holding and turning meat over a fire 2 : point of land that runs into the water

²**spit** vb **spit** or **spat** \'spat\; **spit·ting** : eject saliva from the mouth ~ n 1 : saliva 2 : perfect likeness

spite \'spīt\ n : petty ill will ~ vb **spit·ed**; **spit·ing** : annoy or offend — **spite·ful** \-fəl\ adj — **spite·ful·ly** adv — **in spite of** : in defiance or contempt of

spit·tle \'spit³l\ n : saliva

spit·toon \spi'tün\ n : receptacle for spit

splash \'splash\ vb : scatter a liquid on — **splash** n

splat·ter \'splatər\ vb : spatter — **splatter** n

splay \'splā\ vb : spread out or apart — **splay** n or adj

spleen \'splēn\ n 1 : organ for maintenance of the blood 2 : spite or anger

splen·did \'splendəd\ adj 1 : impressive in beauty or brilliance 2 : outstanding — **splen·did·ly** adv

splen·dor \'splendər\ n 1 : brilliance 2 : magnificence

splice \'splīs\ vb **spliced**; **splic·ing** : join (2 things) end to end — **splice** n

splint \'splint\ n 1 : thin strip of wood 2 : something that keeps an injured body part in place

splin·ter \'splintər\ n : thin needlelike piece ~ vb : break into splinters

split \'split\ vb **split**; **split·ting** : divide lengthwise or along a grain — **split** n

splotch \'splach\ n : blotch

splurge \'splərj\ vb **splurged**; **splurg·ing** : indulge oneself — **splurge** n

splut·ter \'splətər\ n : sputter — **splutter** vb

spoil \'spȯil\ n : plunder ~ vb **spoiled** \'spȯild, 'spȯilt\ or **spoilt** \'spȯilt\; **spoil·ing** : pillage 2 : ruin 3 : rot — **spoil·age** \'spȯilij\ n — **spoil·er** n

¹**spoke** \'spōk\ past of SPEAK

²**spoke** n : rod from the hub to the rim of a wheel

spo·ken past part of SPEAK

spokes·man \'spōksmən\ n : person who speaks for others

spokes·wom·an \-,wümən\ n : woman who speaks for others

sponge \'spənj\ n 1 : porous water‑absorbing mass that forms the skeleton of some marine animals 2 : sponge-like material used for wiping ~ vb **sponged**; **spong·ing** 1 : wipe with a sponge 2 : live at another's expense — **spongy** \'spənjē\ adj

spon·sor \'spänsər\ n : one who assumes responsibility for another or who provides financial support — **sponsor** vb — **spon·sor·ship** n

spon·ta·ne·ous \spän'tānēəs\ adj : done, produced, or occurring naturally or without planning — **spon·ta·ne·i·ty** \,späntən'ēətē\ n — **spon·ta·ne·ous·ly** \spän'tānēəslē\ adv

spoof \'spüf\ vb : make good-natured fun of — **spoof** n

spook \'spük\ n : ghost ~ vb : frighten — **spooky** adj

spool \'spül\ n : cylinder on which something is wound

spoon \'spün\ n : utensil consisting of a small shallow bowl with a handle — **spoon** vb — **spoon·ful** \-,fül\ n

spoor \'spu̇r, 'spȯr\ n : track or trail esp. of a wild animal

spo·rad·ic \spə'radik\ adj : occasional — **spo·rad·i·cal·ly** adv

spore \'spȯr\ n : primitive usu. one‑celled reproductive body

sport \'spȯrt\ vb 1 : frolic 2 : show off ~ n 1 : physical activity engaged in for pleasure 2 : jest 3 : person who shows good sportsmanship — **sport·ive** \-iv\ adj — **sporty** adj

sports·cast \'spȯrts,kast\ n : broadcast of a sports event — **sports·cast·er** \-,kastər\ n

sports·man \-mən\ n : one who enjoys hunting and fishing

sports·man·ship \-mən,ship\ n : ability to be gracious in winning or losing

spot \'spät\ n 1 : blemish 2 : distinctive small part 3 : location ~ vb **-tt-** 1 : mark with spots 2 : see or recognize ~ adj : made at random or in limited numbers — **spot·less** adj — **spot·less·ly** adv

spot·light n 1 : intense beam of light 2 : center of public interest — **spotlight** vb

spot·ty \'spätē\ adj -ti·er; -est : uneven in quality

spouse \'spaús\ n : one's husband or wife

spout \'spaút\ vb 1 : shoot forth in a stream 2 : say pompously ~ n 1 : opening through which liquid spouts 2 : jet of liquid

sprain \'sprān\ n : twisting injury to a joint — vb : injure with a sprain

sprat \'sprat\ n : small or young herring

sprawl \'spról\ vb : lie or sit with limbs spread out — **sprawl** n

¹**spray** \'sprā\ n : branch or arrangement of flowers

²**spray** n 1 : mist 2 : device that discharges liquid as a mist — **spray** vb — **spray·er** n

spread \'spred\ vb **spread**; **spreading** 1 : open up or unfold 2 : scatter or smear over a surface 3 : cause to be known or to exist over a wide area ~ n 1 : extent to which something is spread 2 : cloth cover 3 : something intended to be spread — **spread·er** n

spread-sheet \'spred,shēt\ n : accounting program for a computer

spree \'sprē\ n : burst of indulging in something

sprig \'sprig\ n : small shoot or twig

spright·ly \'sprītlē\ adj -li·er; -est : lively — **spright·li·ness** n

spring \'sprin\ vb **sprang** \'spran\ or **sprung** \'sprən\; **sprung**; **springing** 1 : move or grow quickly or by elastic force 2 : come from by descent 3 : make known suddenly ~ n 1 : source 2 : flow of water from underground 3 : season between winter and summer 4 : elastic body or device (as a coil of wire) 5 : leap 6 : elastic power — **springy** adj

sprin·kle \'sprinkəl\ vb -**kled**; -**kling** : scatter in small drops or particles ~ n : light rainfall — **sprin·kler** n

sprint \'sprint\ n : short run at top speed — **sprint** vb — **sprint·er** n

sprite \'sprīt\ n : elf or elfish person

sprock·et \'spräkət\ n : toothed wheel whose teeth engage the links of a chain

sprout \'spraút\ vb : send out new growth ~ n : plant shoot

¹**spruce** \'sprüs\ n : conical evergreen tree

²**spruce** adj **spruc·er**; **spruc·est** : neat and stylish in appearance ~ vb **spruced**; **spruc·ing** : make or become neat

spry \'sprī\ adj **spri·er** or **spry·er** \'sprīər\; **spri·est** or **spry·est** \'sprīəst\ : agile and active

spume \'spyüm\ n : froth

spun past of SPIN

spunk \'spənk\ n : courage — **spunky** adj

spur \'spər\ n 1 : pointed device used to urge on a horse 2 : something that urges to action 3 : projecting part ~ vb -**rr**- : urge on — **spurred** adj

spu·ri·ous \'spyúrēəs\ adj : not genuine

spurn \'spərn\ vb : reject

¹**spurt** \'spərt\ n : burst of effort, speed, or activity ~ vb : make a spurt

²**spurt** vb : gush out ~ n : sudden gush

sput·ter \'spətər\ vb 1 : talk hastily and indistinctly in excitement 2 : make popping sounds — **sputter** n

spy \'spī\ vb **spied**; **spy·ing** : watch or try to gather information secretly — **spy** n

squab \'skwäb\ n, pl **squabs** or **squab** : young pigeon

squab·ble \'skwäbəl\ n or vb : dispute

squad \'skwäd\ n : small group

squad·ron \'skwädrən\ n : small military unit

squal·id \'skwäləd\ adj : filthy or wretched

squall \'skwól\ n : sudden violent brief storm — **squally** adj

squa·lor \'skwälər\ n : quality or state of being squalid

squan·der \'skwändər\ vb : waste

square \'skwar\ n 1 : instrument for measuring right angles 2 : flat figure that has 4 equal sides and 4 right angles 3 : open area in a city 4 : product of number multiplied by itself ~ adj **squar·er**; **squar·est** 1 : being a square in form 2 : having sides meet at right angles 3 : multiplied by itself 4 : being a square unit of area 5 : honest ~ vb **squared**; **squar·ing** 1 : form into a square 2 : multiply (a number) by itself 3 : conform 4 : settle — **square·ly** adv

¹**squash** \'skwäsh, 'skwósh\ vb 1 : press flat 2 : suppress

²**squash** n, pl **squash·es** or **squash** : garden vegetable

squat \'skwät\ vb **-tt-** 1 : stoop or sit on one's heels 2 : settle on land one does not own ~ n : act or posture of squatting — adj **squat·ter**; **squat·test** : short and thick — **squat·ter** n

squawk \'skwȯk\ n : harsh loud cry — **squawk** vb

squeak \'skwēk\ vb : make a thin high-pitched sound — **squeak** n — **squeaky** adj

squeal \'skwēl\ vb 1 : make a shrill sound or cry 2 : protest — **squeal** n

squea·mish \'skwēmish\ adj : easily nauseated or disgusted

squeeze \'skwēz\ vb **squeezed**; **squeez·ing** 1 : apply pressure to 2 : extract by pressure — **squeeze** n — **squeez·er** n

squelch \'skwelch\ vb : suppress (as with a retort) — **squelch** n

squid \'skwid\ n, pl **squid** or **squids** : 10-armed long-bodied sea mollusk

squint \'skwint\ vb : look with the eyes partly closed — **squint** n or adj

squire \'skwīr\ n 1 : knight's aide 2 : country landholder 3 : lady's devoted escort ~ vb **squired**; **squir·ing** : escort

squirm \'skwərm\ vb : wriggle

squir·rel \'skwərəl\ n : rodent with a long bushy tail

squirt \'skwərt\ vb : eject liquid in a spurt — **squirt** n

stab \'stab\ n 1 : wound made by a pointed weapon 2 : quick thrust 3 : attempt ~ vb **-bb-** : pierce or wound with or as if with a pointed weapon

¹**sta·ble** \'stābəl\ n : building for domestic animals ~ vb **-bled**; **-bling** : keep in a stable

²**stable** adj **sta·bler**; **sta·blest** 1 : firmly established 2 : mentally and emotionally healthy 3 : steady — **sta·bil·i·ty** \stə'bilətē\ n — **sta·bil·iza·tion** \ˌstābələ'zāshən\ n — **sta·bi·lize** \'stābə,līz\ vb — **sta·bi·liz·er** n

stac·ca·to \stə'kätō\ adj : disconnected

stack \'stak\ n : large pile ~ vb : pile up

sta·di·um \'stādēəm\ n : outdoor sports arena

staff \'staf\ n, pl **staffs** \'stafs, stavz\ or **staves** \'stavz, 'stāvz\ 1 : rod or supporting cane 2 : people assisting a leader 3 : 5 horizontal lines on which music is written ~ vb : supply with workers — **staff·er** n

staff sergeant n : noncommissioned officer ranking next above a sergeant in the army, air force, or marine corps

stag \'stag\ n, pl **stags** or **stag** : male deer ~ adj : only for men ~ adv : without a date

stage \'stāj\ n 1 : raised platform for a speaker or performers 2 : theater 3 : step in a process ~ vb **staged**; **stag·ing** : produce (a play)

stage·coach n : passenger coach

stag·ger \'stagər\ vb 1 : reel or cause to reel from side to side 2 : overlap or alternate — **stagger** n — **stag·ger·ing·ly** adv

stag·nant \'stagnənt\ adj : not moving or active — **stag·nate** \-ˌnāt\ vb — **stag·na·tion** \stag'nāshən\ n

¹**staid** \'stād\ adj : sedate

²**staid** past of **STAY**

stain \'stān\ vb 1 : discolor 2 : dye (as wood) 3 : disgrace ~ n 1 : discolored area 2 : mark of guilt 3 : coloring preparation — **stain·less** adj

stair \'star\ n 1 : step in a series for going from one level to another 2 pl : flight of steps — **stair·way** n

stair·case n : series of steps with their framework

stake \'stāk\ n 1 : usu. small post driven into the ground 2 : bet 3 : prize in a contest ~ vb **staked**; **stak·ing** 1 : mark or secure with a stake 2 : bet

sta·lac·tite \stə'lak,tīt\ n : icicle-shaped deposit hanging in a cavern

sta·lag·mite \stə'lag,mīt\ n : icicle-shaped deposit on a cavern floor

stale \'stāl\ adj **stal·er**; **stal·est** 1 : having lost good taste and quality from age 2 : no longer new, strong, or effective — **stale·ness** n

stale·mate \'stāl,māt\ n : deadlock — **stalemate** vb

¹**stalk** \'stȯk\ vb 1 : walk stiffly or proudly 2 : pursue stealthily

²**stalk** n : plant stem — **stalked** \'stȯkt\ adj

¹**stall** \'stȯl\ n 1 : compartment in a stable 2 : booth where articles are sold

²**stall** vb : bring or come to a standstill unintentionally

³**stall** vb : delay, evade, or keep a situation going to gain advantage or time

stal·lion \'stalyən\ n : male horse

stal·wart \'stȯlwərt\ adj : strong or brave

sta·men \'stāmən\ n : flower organ that produces pollen

stam·i·na \'stamənə\ n : endurance

stam·mer \\'stamər\\ vb : hesitate in speaking — **stammer** n

stamp \\'stamp\\ vb 1 : pound with the sole of the foot or a heavy implement 2 : impress or imprint 3 : cut out with a die 4 : attach a postage stamp to ~ n 1 : device for stamping 2 : act of stamping 3 : government seal showing a tax or fee has been paid

stam·pede \stam'pēd\ n : headlong rush of frightened animals ~ vb -ped·ed; -ped·ing : flee in panic

stance \\'stans\\ n : way of standing

¹**stanch** \\'stȯnch, 'stänch\\ vb : stop the flow of (as blood)

²**stanch** var of STAUNCH

stan·chion \\'stanchən\\ n : upright support

stand \\'stand\\ vb **stood** \\'stu̇d\\; **standing** 1 : be at rest in or assume an upright position 2 : remain unchanged 3 : be steadfast 4 : maintain a relative position or rank 5 : set upright 6 : undergo or endure ~ n 1 : act or place of standing, staying, or resisting 2 : sales booth 3 : structure for holding something upright 4 : group of plants growing together 5 pl : tiered seats 6 : opinion or viewpoint

stan·dard \\'standərd\\ n 1 : symbolic figure or flag 2 : model, rule, or guide 3 : upright support — **standard** adj — **stan·dard·i·za·tion** \\ˌstandərdə'zāshən\\ n — **stan·dard·ize** \\'standərdˌīz\\ vb

standard time n : time established over a region or country

stand·ing \\'standiŋ\\ n 1 : relative position or rank 2 : duration

stand·still n : state of rest

stank past of STINK

stan·za \\'stanzə\\ n : division of a poem

¹**sta·ple** \\'stāpəl\\ n : U-shaped wire fastener — **staple** vb — **sta·pler** \-plər\ n

²**staple** n : chief commodity or item — **staple** adj

star \\'stär\\ n 1 : celestial body visible as a point of light 2 : 5- or 6-pointed figure representing a star 3 : leading performer ~ vb -rr- 1 : mark with a star 2 : play the leading role — **star·dom** \\'stärdəm\\ n — **star·less** adj — **star·light** n — **star·ry** adj

star·board \\'stärbərd\\ n : right side of a ship or airplane looking forward — **starboard** adj

starch \\'stärch\\ n : nourishing carbohydrate from plants also used in adhesives and laundering ~ vb : stiffen with starch — **starchy** adj

stare \\'star\\ vb **stared; star·ing** : look intently with wide-open eyes — **stare** n — **star·er** n

stark \\'stärk\\ adj 1 : absolute 2 : severe or bleak ~ adv : completely — **stark·ly** adv

star·ling \\'stärliŋ\\ n : bird related to the crows

start \\'stärt\\ vb 1 : twitch or jerk (as from surprise) 2 : perform or show performance of the first part of an action or process ~ n 1 : sudden involuntary motion 2 : beginning — **start·er** n

star·tle \\'stärt²l\\ vb -tled; -tling : frighten or surprise suddenly

starve \\'stärv\\ vb **starved; starv·ing** 1 : suffer or die from hunger 2 : kill with hunger — **star·va·tion** \stär'vāshən\ n

stash \\'stash\\ vb : store in a secret place for future use — **stash** n

state \\'stāt\\ n 1 : condition of being 2 : condition of mind 3 : nation or a political unit within it ~ vb **stat·ed; stat·ing** 1 : express in words 2 : establish — **state·hood** \-ˌhu̇d\ n

state·ly \\'stātlē\\ adj **-li·er; -est** : having impressive dignity — **state·li·ness** n

state·ment \\'stātmənt\\ n 1 : something stated 2 : financial summary

state·room n : private room on a ship

states·man \\'stātsmən\\ n : one skilled in government or diplomacy — **states·man·like** adj — **states·man·ship** n

stat·ic \\'statik\\ adj 1 : relating to bodies at rest or forces in equilibrium 2 : not moving 3 : relating to stationary charges of electricity ~ n : noise on radio or television from electrical disturbances

sta·tion \\'stāshən\\ n 1 : place of duty 2 : regular stop on a bus or train route 3 : social standing 4 : place where radio or television programs originate ~ vb : assign to a station

sta·tion·ary \\'stāshəˌnerē\\ adj 1 : not moving or not movable 2 : not changing

sta·tio·nery \\'stāshəˌnerē\\ n : letter paper with envelopes

sta·tis·tic \stə'tistik\ n : single item of statistics

sta·tis·tics \-tiks\ n pl : numerical facts collected for study — **sta·tis·ti·cal**

\-tikəl\ *adj* — **sta·tis·ti·cal·ly** *adv* — **stat·is·ti·cian** \statə'stishən\ *n*

stat·u·ary \'stachə‚werē\ *n, pl* **-ar·ies** : collection of statues

stat·ue \'stachü\ *n* : solid 3-dimensional likeness — **stat·u·ette** \stachə'wet\ *n*

stat·u·esque \stachə'wesk\ *adj* : tall and shapely

stat·ure \'stachər\ *n* **1** : height **2** : status gained by achievement

sta·tus \'stātəs, 'stat-\ *n* : relative situation or condition

sta·tus quo \-'kwō\ *n* : existing state of affairs

stat·ute \'stachüt\ *n* : law — **stat·u·to·ry** \'stachə‚tōrē\ *adj*

staunch \'stónch\ *adj* : steadfast — **staunch·ly** *adv*

stave \'stāv\ *n* : narrow strip of wood ~ *vb* **staved** *or* **stove** \'stōv\; **stav·ing** **1** : break a hole in **2** : drive away

staves *pl of* STAFF

¹**stay** \'stā\ *n* : support ~ *vb* **stayed; stay·ing** : prop up

²**stay** *vb* **stayed** \'stād\ *or* **staid** \'stād\; **stay·ing** **1** : pause **2** : remain **3** : reside **4** : stop or postpone **5** : satisfy for a time ~ *n* : a staying

stead \'sted\ *n* : one's place, job, or function — **in good stead** : to advantage

stead·fast \-‚fast\ *adj* : faithful or determined — **stead·fast·ly** *adv*

steady \'stedē\ *adj* **steadi·er; -est** **1** : firm in position or sure in movement **2** : calm or reliable **3** : constant **4** : regular ~ *vb* **stead·ied; steady·ing** : make or become steady — **steadi·ly** \'sted°lē\ *adv* — **steadi·ness** *n*

steak \'stāk\ *n* : thick slice of meat

steal \'stēl\ *vb* **stole** \'stōl\; **sto·len** \'stōlən\; **steal·ing** **1** : take and carry away wrongfully and with intent to keep **2** : move secretly or slowly

stealth \'stelth\ *n* : secret or unobtrusive procedure — **stealth·i·ly** \-thəlē\ *adv* — **stealthy** *adj*

steam \'stēm\ *n* : vapor of boiling water ~ *vb* : give off steam — **steam·boat** *n* — **steam·ship** *n* — **steamy** *adj*

steed \'stēd\ *n* : horse

steel \'stēl\ *n* : tough carbon-containing iron ~ *vb* : fill with courage — **steel** *adj* — **steely** *adj*

¹**steep** \'stēp\ *adj* : having a very sharp slope or great elevation — **steep·ly** *adv* — **steep·ness** *n*

²**steep** *vb* : soak in a liquid

stee·ple \'stēpəl\ *n* : usu. tapering church tower

stee·ple·chase *n* : race over hurdles

¹**steer** \'stir\ *n* : castrated ox

²**steer** *vb* **1** : direct the course of (as a ship or car) **2** : guide

steer·age \'stirij\ *n* : section in a ship for people paying the lowest fares

stein \'stīn\ *n* : mug

stel·lar \'stelər\ *adj* : relating to stars or resembling a star

¹**stem** \'stem\ *n* : main upright part of a plant ~ *vb* **-mm-** **1** : derive **2** : make progress against — **stem·less** *adj* — **stemmed** *adj*

²**stem** *vb* **-mm-** : stop the flow of

stem cell *n* : undifferentiated cell that may give rise to many different types of cells

stench \'stench\ *n* : stink

sten·cil \'stensəl\ *n* : printing sheet cut with letters to let ink pass through — **stencil** *vb*

ste·nog·ra·phy \stə'nägrəfē\ *n* : art or process of writing in shorthand — **ste·nog·ra·pher** \-fər\ *n* — **steno·graph·ic** \stenə'grafik\ *adj*

sten·to·ri·an \sten'tōrēən\ *adj* : extremely loud and powerful

step \'step\ *n* **1** : single action of a leg in walking or running **2** : rest for the foot in going up or down **3** : degree, rank, or stage **4** : way of walking ~ *vb* **-pp-** **1** : move by steps **2** : press with the foot

step- \'step-\ *comb form* : related by a remarriage and not by blood

step·lad·der *n* : light portable set of steps in a hinged frame

steppe \'step\ *n* : dry grassy treeless land esp. of Asia

-ster \stər\ *n suffix* **1** : one that does, makes, or uses **2** : one that is associated with or takes part in **3** : one that is

ste·reo \'sterē‚ō, 'stir-\ *n, pl* **-reos** : stereophonic sound system — **stereo** *adj*

ste·reo·phon·ic \sterēə'fänik, ‚stir-\ *adj* : relating to a 3-dimensional effect of reproduced sound

ste·reo·type \'sterēə‚tīp, 'stir-\ *n* : gross often mistaken generalization — **stereotype** *vb* — **ste·reo·typ·i·cal** \sterēə'tipikəl\ *adj* — **ste·reo·typi·cal·ly** *adv*

ste·reo·typed \'sterēə‚tīpt, 'stir-\ *adj* : lacking originality or individuality

ster·ile \'sterəl\ *adj* **1** : unable to bear fruit, crops, or offspring **2** : free from disease germs — **ste·ril·i·ty** \stə-'rilətē\ *n* — **ster·il·i·za·tion** \,sterələ-'zāshən\ *n* — **ster·il·ize** \-ə,līz\ *vb* — **ster·il·iz·er** *n*

ster·ling \'stərliŋ\ *adj* **1** : being or made of an alloy of 925 parts of silver with 75 parts of copper **2** : excellent

¹**stern** \'stərn\ *adj* : severe — **stern·ly** *adv* — **stern·ness** *n*

²**stern** *n* : back end of a boat

ster·num \'stərnəm\ *n, pl* **-nums** *or* **-na** \-nə\ : long flat chest bone joining the 2 sets of ribs

stetho·scope \'stethə,skōp\ *n* : instrument used for listening to sounds in the chest

ste·ve·dore \'stēvə,dōr\ *n* : worker who loads and unloads ships

stew \'stü, 'styü\ *n* **1** : dish of boiled meat and vegetables **2** : state of worry or agitation — **stew** *vb*

stew·ard \'stüərd, 'styü-\ *n* **1** : manager of an estate or an organization **2** : person on a ship or airliner who looks after passenger comfort — **stew·ard·ship** *n*

stew·ard·ess \-əs\ *n* : woman who is a steward (as on an airplane)

¹**stick** \'stik\ *n* **1** : cut or broken branch **2** : long thin piece of wood or something resembling it

²**stick** *vb* **stuck** \'stək\; **stick·ing** **1** : stab **2** : thrust or project **3** : hold fast to something **4** : attach **5** : become jammed or fixed

stick·er \'stikər\ *n* : adhesive label

stick·ler \'stiklər\ *n* : one who insists on exactness or completeness

sticky \'stikē\ *adj* **stick·i·er; -est** **1** : adhesive or gluey **2** : muggy **3** : difficult

stiff \'stif\ *adj* **1** : not bending easily **2** : tense **3** : formal **4** : strong **5** : severe — **stiff·en** \'stifən\ *vb* — **stiff·en·er** \-ənər\ *n* — **stiff·ly** *adv* — **stiff·ness** *n*

sti·fle \'stīfəl\ *vb* **-fled; -fling** : smother or suffocate **2** : suppress

stig·ma \'stigmə\ *n, pl* **-ma·ta** \stig-'mätə, 'stigmətə\ *or* **-mas** : mark of disgrace — **stig·ma·tize** \'stigmə-,tīz\ *vb*

stile \'stīl\ *n* : steps for crossing a fence

sti·let·to \stə'letō\ *n, pl* **-tos** *or* **-toes** : slender dagger

¹**still** \'stil\ *adj* **1** : motionless **2** : silent — *vb* : make or become still — *adv* **1** : without motion **2** : up to and during this time **3** : in spite of that — *n* : silence — **still·ness** *n*

²**still** *n* : apparatus used in distillation

still·born *adj* : born dead — **still·birth** *n*

stilt \'stilt\ *n* : one of a pair of poles for walking

stilt·ed \'stiltəd\ *adj* : not easy and natural

stim·u·lant \'stimyələnt\ *n* : substance that temporarily increases the activity of an organism — **stimulant** *adj*

stim·u·late \-,lāt\ *vb* **-lat·ed; -lat·ing** : make active — **stim·u·la·tion** \,stimyə'lāshən\ *n*

stim·u·lus \'stimyələs\ *n, pl* **-li** \-,lī\ : something that stimulates

sting \'stiŋ\ *vb* **stung** \'stəŋ\; **sting·ing** **1** : prick painfully **2** : cause to suffer acutely — *n* **1** : act of stinging or a resulting wound — **sting·er** *n*

stin·gy \'stinjē\ *adj* **stin·gi·er; -est** : not generous — **stin·gi·ness** *n*

stink \'stiŋk\ *vb* **stank** \'staŋk\ *or* **stunk** \'stəŋk\; **stunk; stink·ing** : have a strong offensive odor — **stink** *n* — **stink·er** *n*

stint \'stint\ *vb* : be sparing or stingy — *n* **1** : restraint **2** : quantity or period of work

sti·pend \'stī,pend, -pənd\ *n* : money paid periodically

stip·ple \'stipəl\ *vb* **-pled; -pling** : engrave, paint, or draw with dots instead of lines — **stipple** *n*

stip·u·late \'stipyə,lāt\ *vb* **-lat·ed; -lat·ing** : demand as a condition — **stip·u·la·tion** \,stipyə'lāshən\ *n*

stir \'stər\ *vb* **-rr-** **1** : move slightly **2** : prod or push into activity **3** : mix by continued circular movement — *n* : act or result of stirring

stir·rup \'stərəp\ *n* : saddle loop for the foot

stitch \'stich\ *n* **1** : loop formed by a needle in sewing **2** : sudden sharp pain — *vb* **1** : fasten or decorate with stitches **2** : sew

stock \'stäk\ *n* **1** : block or part of wood **2** : original from which others derive **3** : farm animals **4** : supply of goods **5** : money invested in a large business **6** *pl* : instrument of punishment like a pillory with holes for the feet or feet and hands — *vb* : provide with stock

stock·ade \stä'kād\ *n* : defensive or confining enclosure

stock·ing \'stäkiŋ\ *n* : close-fitting covering for the foot and leg

stock·pile *n* : reserve supply — **stock·pile** *vb*

stocky \'stäkē\ *adj* **stock·i·er; -est** : short and relatively thick

stock·yard *n* : yard for livestock to be slaughtered or shipped

stodgy \'stäjē\ *adj* **stodg·i·er; -est** **1** : dull **2** : old-fashioned

sto·ic \'stōik\, **sto·i·cal** \-ikəl\ *adj* : showing indifference to pain — **stoic** *n* — **sto·i·cal·ly** *adv* — **sto·i·cism** \'stōə,sizəm\ *n*

stoke \'stōk\ *vb* **stoked; stok·ing** : stir up a fire or supply fuel to a furnace — **stok·er** *n*

¹**stole** \'stōl\ *past of* STEAL

²**stole** *n* : long wide scarf

stolen *past part of* STEAL

stol·id \'stäləd\ *adj* : having or showing little or no emotion — **stol·id·ly** \'stälədlē\ *adv*

stom·ach \'stəmək, -ik\ *n* **1** : saclike digestive organ **2** : abdomen **3** : appetite or desire ~ *vb* : put up with — **stom·ach·ache** *n*

stomp \'stämp, 'stómp\ *vb* : stamp

stone \'stōn\ *n* **1** : hardened earth or mineral matter **2** : small piece of rock **3** : seed that is hard or has a hard covering ~ *vb* **stoned; ston·ing** : pelt or kill with stones — **stony** *adj*

stood *past of* STAND

stool \'stül\ *n* **1** : seat usu. without back or arms **2** : footstool **3** : discharge of feces

¹**stoop** \'stüp\ *vb* **1** : bend over **2** : lower oneself ~ *n* **1** : act of bending over **2** : bent position of shoulders

²**stoop** *n* : small porch at a house door

stop \'stäp\ *vb* **-pp- 1** : block an opening **2** : end or cause to end **3** : pause for rest or a visit in a journey ~ *n* **1** : plug **2** : act or place of stopping **3** : delay in a journey — **stop·light** *n* — **stop·page** \-ij\ *n* — **stop·per** *n*

stop·gap *n* : temporary measure or thing

stor·age \'stōrij\ *n* : safekeeping of goods (as in a warehouse)

store \'stōr\ *vb* **stored; stor·ing** : put aside for future use ~ *n* **1** : something stored **2** : retail business establishment — **store·house** *n* — **store·keep·er** *n* — **store·room** *n*

stork \'stórk\ *n* : large wading bird

storm \'stórm\ *n* **1** : heavy fall of rain or snow **2** : violent outbreak ~ *vb* **1** : rain or snow heavily **2** : rage **3** : make an attack against — **stormy** *adj*

¹**sto·ry** \'stōrē\ *n, pl* **-ries 1** : narrative **2** : report — **sto·ry·tell·er** *n*

²**story** *n, pl* **-ries** : floor of a building

stout \'staut\ *adj* **1** : firm or strong **2** : thick or bulky — **stout·ly** *adv* — **stout·ness** *n*

¹**stove** \'stōv\ *n* : apparatus for providing heat (as for cooking or heating)

²**stove** *past of* STAVE

stow \'stō\ *vb* **1** : pack in a compact mass **2** : put or hide away

strad·dle \'strad°l\ *vb* **-dled; -dling** : stand over or sit on with legs on opposite sides — **straddle** *n*

strafe \'strāf\ *vb* **strafed; straf·ing** : fire upon with machine guns from a low-flying airplane

strag·gle \'stragəl\ *vb* **-gled; -gling** : wander or become separated from others — **strag·gler** \-ələr\ *n*

straight \'strāt\ *adj* **1** : having no bends, turns, or twists **2** : just, proper, or honest **3** : neat and orderly ~ *adv* : in a straight manner — **straight·en** \'strāt°n\ *vb*

straight·for·ward \strāt'fórwərd\ *adj* : frank or honest

straight·way *adv* : immediately

¹**strain** \'strān\ *n* **1** : lineage **2** : trace

²**strain** *vb* **1** : exert to the utmost **2** : filter or remove by filtering **3** : injure by improper use ~ *n* **1** : excessive tension or exertion **2** : bodily injury from excessive effort — **strain·er** *n*

strait \'strāt\ *n* **1** : narrow channel connecting 2 bodies of water **2** *pl* : distress

strait·en \'strāt°n\ *vb* **1** : hem in **2** : make distressing or difficult

¹**strand** \'strand\ *vb* **1** : drive or cast upon the shore **2** : leave helpless

²**strand** *n* **1** : twisted fiber of a rope **2** : length of something ropelike

strange \'strānj\ *adj* **strang·er; strang·est 1** : unusual or queer **2** : new — **strange·ly** *adv* — **strange·ness** *n*

strang·er \'strānjər\ *n* : person with whom one is not acquainted

stran·gle \'straŋgəl\ *vb* **-gled; -gling** : choke to death — **stran·gler** \-glər\ *n*

stran·gu·la·tion \straŋgyə'lāshən\ *n* : act or process of strangling

strap \'strap\ n : narrow strip of flexible material used esp. for fastening ～ vb 1 : secure with a strap 2 : beat with a strap — **strap•less** n

strap•ping \'strapiŋ\ adj : robust

strat•a•gem \'stratəjəm, -,jem\ n : deceptive scheme or maneuver

strat•e•gy \'stratəjē\ n, pl **-gies** : carefully worked out plan of action — **strate•gic** \strə'tējik\ adj — **strat•e•gist** \'stratəjist\ n

strat•i•fy \'stratə,fī\ vb **-fied; -fy•ing** : form or arrange in layers — **strat•i•fi•ca•tion** \,stratəfə'kāshən\ n

strato•sphere \'stratə,sfir\ n : earth's atmosphere from about 7 to 31 miles above the surface

stra•tum \'strātəm, 'strat-\ n, pl **-ta** \'strātə, 'strat-\ : layer

straw \'strò\ n 1 : grass stems after grain is removed 2 : tube for drinking ～ adj : made of straw

straw•ber•ry \'strò,berē\ n : juicy red pulpy fruit

stray \'strā\ vb : wander or deviate ～ n : person or animal that strays ～ adj : separated from or not related to anything close by

streak \'strēk\ n 1 : mark of a different color 2 : narrow band of light 3 : trace 4 : run (as of luck) or series ～ vb 1 : form streaks in or on 2 : move fast

stream \'strēm\ n 1 : flow of water on land 2 : steady flow (as of water or air) ～ vb 1 : flow in a stream 2 : pour out streams

stream•er \'strēmər\ n : long ribbon or ribbonlike flag

stream•lined \-,līnd, -'līnd\ adj : made with contours to reduce air or water resistance 2 : simplified 3 : modernized — **streamline** vb

street \'strēt\ n : thoroughfare esp. in a city or town

street•car n : passenger vehicle running on rails in the streets

strength \'streŋth\ n 1 : quality of being strong 2 : toughness 3 : intensity

strength•en \'streŋthən\ vb : make, grow, or become stronger — **strength•en•er** \'streŋthənər\ n

stren•u•ous \'strenyəwəs\ adj 1 : vigorous 2 : requiring or showing energy — **stren•u•ous•ly** adv

stress \'stres\ n 1 : pressure or strain that tends to distort a body 2 : relative prominence given to one thing

among others 3 : state of physical or mental tension or something inducing it ～ vb : put stress on — **stress•ful** \'stresfəl\ adj

stretch \'strech\ vb 1 : spread or reach out 2 : draw out in length or breadth 3 : make taut 4 : exaggerate 5 : become extended without breaking ～ n : act of extending beyond normal limits

stretch•er \'strechər\ n : device for carrying a sick or injured person

strew \'strü\ vb **strewed; strewed** or **strewn** \'strün\; **strew•ing** 1 : scatter 2 : cover by scattering something over

strick•en \'strikən\ adj : afflicted with disease

strict \'strikt\ adj 1 : allowing no escape or evasion 2 : precise — **strict•ly** adv — **strict•ness** n

stric•ture \'strikchər\ n : hostile criticism

stride \'strīd\ vb **strode** \'strōd\; **strid•den** \'strid°n\; **strid•ing** : walk or run with long steps ～ n 1 : long step 2 : manner of striding

stri•dent \'strīd°nt\ adj : loud and harsh

strife \'strīf\ n : conflict

strike \'strīk\ vb **struck** \'strək\; **struck; strik•ing** \'strikiŋ\ 1 : hit sharply 2 : delete 3 : produce by impressing 4 : cause to sound 5 : afflict 6 : occur to or impress 7 : cause (a match) to ignite by rubbing 8 : refrain from working 9 : find 10 : take on (as a pose) ～ n 1 : act or instance of striking — **strik•er** n — **strike out** vb : start out vigorously — **strike up** vb : start

strik•ing \'strikiŋ\ adj : very noticeable — **strik•ing•ly** adv

string \'striŋ\ n 1 : line usu. of twisted threads 2 : series 3 pl : stringed instruments ～ vb **strung** \'strəŋ\; **string•ing** 1 : thread on or with a string 2 : hang or fasten by a string

stringed \'striŋd\ adj : having strings

strin•gent \'strinjənt\ adj : severe

stringy \'striŋē\ adj **string•i•er; -est** : tough or fibrous

¹**strip** \'strip\ vb **-pp-** 1 : take the covering or clothing from 2 : undress — **strip•per** n

²**strip** n : long narrow flat piece

stripe \'strip\ n : distinctive line or long narrow section ～ vb **striped**

\'strīpt\ : **strip•ing** : make stripes on — **striped** \'strīpt, 'strīpəd\ adj

strive \'strīv\ vb **strove** \'strōv\; **striven** \'strivən\ or **strived**; **striv•ing** \'strīvin\ 1 : struggle 2 : try hard

strode past of STRIDE

stroke \'strōk\ vb **stroked**; **strok•ing** : rub gently ~ n 1 : act of swinging or striking 2 : sudden action

stroll \'strōl\ vb : walk leisurely — **stroll** n — **stroll•er** n

strong \'strȯn\ adj 1 : capable of exerting great force or of withstanding stress or violence 2 : healthy 3 : zealous — **strong•ly** adv

strong•hold n : fortified place

struck past of STRIKE

struc•ture \'strəkchər\ n 1 : building 2 : arrangement of elements ~ vb **-tured; -tur•ing** : make into a structure — **struc•tur•al** \-chərəl\ adj

strug•gle \'strəgəl\ vb **-gled; -gling** 1 : make strenuous efforts to overcome an adversary 2 : proceed with great effort ~ n 1 : strenuous effort 2 : intense competition for superiority

strum \'strəm\ vb **-mm-** : play (a musical instrument) by brushing the strings with the fingers

strum•pet \'strəmpət\ n : prostitute

strung past of STRING

strut \'strət\ vb **-tt-** : walk in a proud or showy manner ~ n 1 : proud walk 2 : supporting bar or rod

strych•nine \'strik,nīn, -nən, -,nēn\ n : bitter poisonous substance

stub \'stəb\ n : short end or section ~ vb **-bb-** : strike against something

stub•ble \'stəbəl\ n : short growth left after cutting — **stub•bly** adj

stub•born \'stəbərn\ adj 1 : determined not to yield 2 : hard to control — **stub•born•ly** adv — **stub•born•ness** n

stub•by \'stəbē\ adj : short, blunt, and thick

stuc•co \'stəkō\ n, pl **-cos** or **-coes** : plaster for coating outside walls — **stuc•coed** \'stəkōd\ adj

stuck past of STICK

stuck–up \'stək'əp\ adj : conceited

¹stud \'stəd\ n : male horse kept for breeding

²stud n 1 : upright beam for holding wall material 2 : projecting nail, pin, or rod ~ vb **-dd-** : supply or dot with studs

stu•dent \'stüd³nt, 'styü-\ n : one who studies

stud•ied \'stədēd\ adj : premeditated

stu•dio \'stüdē,ō, 'styü-\ n, pl **-dios** 1 : artist's workroom 2 : place where movies are made or television or radio shows are broadcast

stu•di•ous \'stüdēəs, 'styü-\ adj : devoted to study — **stu•di•ous•ly** adv

study \'stədē\ n, pl **stud•ies** 1 : act or process of learning about something 2 : branch of learning 3 : careful examination 4 : room for reading or studying ~ vb **stud•ied; study•ing** : apply the attention and mind to a subject

stuff \'stəf\ n 1 : personal property 2 : raw or fundamental material 3 : unspecified material or things ~ vb : fill by packing things in — **stuff•ing** n

stuffy \'stəfē\ adj **stuff•i•er; -est** 1 : lacking fresh air 2 : unimaginative or pompous

stul•ti•fy \'stəltə,fī\ vb **-fied; -fy•ing** 1 : cause to appear foolish 2 : impair or make ineffective 3 : have a dulling effect on

stum•ble \'stəmbəl\ vb **-bled; -bling** 1 : lose one's balance or fall in walking or running 2 : speak or act clumsily 3 : happen by chance — **stumble** n

stump \'stəmp\ n : part left when something is cut off ~ vb : confuse — **stumpy** adj

stun \'stən\ vb **-nn-** 1 : make senseless or dizzy by or as if by a blow 2 : bewilder

stung past of STING

stunk past of STINK

stun•ning \'stənin\ adj 1 : astonishing or incredible 2 : strikingly beautiful — **stun•ning•ly** adv

¹stunt \'stənt\ vb : hinder the normal growth or progress of

²stunt n : spectacular feat

stu•pe•fy \'stüpə,fī, 'styü-\ vb **-fied; -fy•ing** 1 : make insensible by or as if by drugs 2 : amaze

stu•pen•dous \stu'pendəs, styü-\ adj : very big or impressive — **stu•pendous•ly** adv

stu•pid \'stüpəd, 'styü-\ adj : not sensible or intelligent — **stu•pid•i•ty** \stü'pidətē, styü-\ n — **stu•pid•ly** adv

stu•por \'stüpər, 'styü-\ n : state of being conscious but not aware or sensible

stur•dy \'stərdē\ adj **-di•er; -est**

: strong — **stur·di·ly** \'stərdəlē\ adv — **stur·di·ness** n

stur·geon \'stərjən\ n : fish whose roe is caviar

stut·ter \'stətər\ vb or n : stammer

¹**sty** \'stī\ n, pl **sties** : pig pen

²**sty, stye** \'stī\ n, pl **sties** or **styes** : inflamed swelling on the edge of an eyelid

style \'stīl\ n 1 : distinctive way of speaking, writing, or acting 2 : elegant or fashionable way of living ∼ vb **styled; styl·ing** 1 : name 2 : give a particular design or style to — **styl·ish** \'stīlish\ adj — **styl·ish·ly** adv — **styl·ish·ness** n — **styl·ist** \-ist\ n — **styl·ize** \'stīəl‚īz\ vb

sty·lus \'stīləs\ n, pl **-li** \'stīl‚ī\ 1 : pointed writing tool 2 : phonograph needle

sty·mie \'stīmē\ vb **-mied; -mie·ing** : block or frustrate

suave \'swäv\ adj : well-mannered and gracious — **suave·ly** adv

¹**sub** \'səb\ n or vb : substitute

²**sub** n : submarine

sub- \‚səb, 'səb, 'səb\ prefix 1 : under or beneath 2 : subordinate or secondary 3 : subordinate portion of 4 : with repetition of a process so as to form, stress, or deal with subordinate parts or relations 5 : somewhat 6 : nearly

sub·con·scious \‚səb'känchəs\ adj : existing without conscious awareness ∼ n : part of the mind concerned with subconscious activities — **sub·con·scious·ly** adv

sub·di·vide \‚səbdə'vīd, 'səbdə‚vīd\ vb 1 : divide into several parts 2 : divide (land) into building lots — **sub·di·vi·sion** \-'vizhən, -‚vizh-\ n

sub·due \səb'dü, -'dyü\ vb **-dued;**

-du·ing 1 : bring under control 2 : reduce the intensity of

sub·ject \'səbjikt\ n 1 : person under the authority of another 2 : something being discussed or studied 3 : word or word group about which something is said in a sentence ∼ adj 1 : being under one's authority 2 : prone 3 : dependent on some condition or act ∼ \səb'jekt\ vb 1 : bring under control 2 : cause to undergo — **sub·jec·tion** \-'jekshən\ n

sub·jec·tive \‚səb'jektiv\ adj : deriving from an individual viewpoint or bias — **sub·jec·tive·ly** adv — **sub·jec·tiv·i·ty** \-‚jek'tivətē\ n

sub·ju·gate \'səbji‚gāt\ vb **-gat·ed; -gat·ing** : bring under one's control — **sub·ju·ga·tion** \‚səbji'gāshən\ n

sub·junc·tive \səb'jənktiv\ adj : relating to a verb form which expresses possibility or contingency — **subjunctive** n

sub·let \'səb‚let\ vb **-let; -let·ting** : rent (a property) from a lessee

sub·lime \sə'blīm\ adj : splendid — **sub·lime·ly** adv

sub·ma·rine \'səbmə‚rēn, ‚səbmə'-\ adj : existing, acting, or growing under the sea ∼ n : underwater boat

sub·merge \səb'mərj\ vb **-merged; -merg·ing** : put or plunge under the surface of water — **sub·mer·gence** \-'mərjəns\ n — **sub·mers·ible** \-'mərsəbəl\ adj or n — **sub·mer·sion** \-'mərzhən\ n

sub·mit \səb'mit\ vb **-tt-** 1 : yield 2 : give or offer — **sub·mis·sion** \-'mishən\ n — **sub·mis·sive** \-'misiv\ adj

sub·nor·mal \‚səb'nórməl\ adj : falling below what is normal

sub·or·di·nate \sə'bórdənət\ adj : lower

List of self-explanatory words with the prefix sub-

subacute	subcategory	subdean
subagency	subclass	subdepartment
subagent	subclassification	subdistrict
subarctic	subclassify	subentry
subarea	subcommission	subfamily
subatmospheric	subcommittee	subfreezing
subaverage	subcommunity	subgroup
subbase	subcomponent	subhead
subbasement	subcontract	subheading
subbranch	subcontractor	subhuman
subcabinet	subculture	subindex

in rank **~** *n* : one that is subordinate **~** \sə'bórd°n‚āt\ *vb* **-nat•ed; -nating** : place in a lower rank or class — **sub•or•di•na•tion** \-‚bórd°n'āshən\ *n*

sub•poe•na \sə'pēnə\ *n* : summons to appear in court **~** *vb* **-naed; -na•ing** : summon with a subpoena

sub•scribe \səb'skrīb\ *vb* **-scribed; -scrib•ing 1** : give consent or approval **2** : agree to support or to receive and pay for — **sub•scrib•er** *n*

sub•scrip•tion \səb'skripshən\ *n* : order for regular receipt of a publication

sub•se•quent \'səbsikwənt, -sə‚kwent\ *adj* : following after — **sub•se•quently** \-‚kwentlē, -kwənt-\ *adv*

sub•ser•vi•ence \səb'sərvēəns\ *n* : obsequious submission — **sub•ser•vi•ent** \-ənt\ *adj*

sub•side \səb'sīd\ *vb* **-sid•ed; -sid•ing** : die down in intensity

sub•sid•iary \səb'sidē‚erē\ *adj* **1** : furnishing support **2** : of secondary importance **~** *n* : company controlled by another company

sub•si•dize \'səbsə‚dīz\ *vb* **-dized; -diz•ing** : aid with a subsidy

sub•si•dy \'səbsədē\ *n, pl* **-dies** : gift of supporting funds

sub•sist \səb'sist\ *vb* : acquire the necessities of life — **sub•sis•tence** \-'sistəns\ *n*

sub•stance \'səbstəns\ *n* **1** : essence or essential part **2** : physical material **3** : wealth

sub•stan•dard \‚səb'standərd\ *adj* : falling short of a standard or norm

sub•stan•tial \səb'stanchəl\ *adj* **1** : plentiful **2** : considerable — **substan•tial•ly** *adv*

sub•stan•ti•ate \səb'stanchē‚āt\ *vb* **-at•ed; -at•ing** : verify — **sub•stanti•a•tion** \-‚stanchē'āshən\ *n*

sub•sti•tute \'səbstə‚tūt, -‚tyūt\ *n* : replacement **~** *vb* **-tut•ed; -tut•ing** : put or serve in place of another — **substitute** *adj* — **sub•sti•tu•tion** \‚səbstə'tūshən, -'tyū-\ *n*

sub•ter•fuge \'səbtər‚fyūj\ *n* : deceptive trick

sub•ter•ra•nean \‚səbtə'rānēən\ *adj* : lying or being underground

sub•ti•tle \'səb‚tīt°l\ *n* : movie caption

sub•tle \'sət°l\ *adj* **-tler** \-°lr\; **-tlest** \-ist\ **1** : hardly noticeable **2** : clever — **sub•tle•ty** \-tē\ *n* — **subt•ly** \-°lē\ *adv*

sub•tract \səb'trakt\ *vb* : take away (as one number from another) — **subtrac•tion** \-'trakshən\ *n*

sub•urb \'səb‚ərb\ *n* : residential area adjacent to a city — **sub•ur•ban** \sə'bərbən\ *adj or n* — **sub•ur•banite** \-bə‚nīt\ *n*

sub•vert \səb'vərt\ *vb* : overthrow or ruin — **sub•ver•sion** \-'vərzhən\ *n* — **sub•ver•sive** \-'vərsiv\ *adj*

sub•way \'səb‚wā\ *n* : underground electric railway

suc•ceed \sək'sēd\ *vb* **1** : follow (someone) in a job, role, or title **2** : attain a desired object or end

suc•cess \-'ses\ *n* **1** : favorable outcome **2** : gaining of wealth and fame **3** : one that succeeds — **success•ful** \-fəl\ *adj* — **suc•cess•ful•ly** *adv*

suc•ces•sion \sək'seshən\ *n* **1** : order, act, or right of succeeding **2** : series

suc•ces•sive \-'sesiv\ *adj* : following in order — **suc•ces•sive•ly** *adv*

suc•ces•sor \-'sesər\ *n* : one that succeeds another

suc•cinct \sək'siŋkt, sə'siŋkt\ *adj* : brief — **suc•cinct•ly** *adv* — **succinct•ness** *n*

suc•cor \'səkər\ *n or vb* : help

---

subindustry	subpolar	substage
sublease	subprincipal	subsurface
sublethal	subprocess	subsystem
sublevel	subprogram	subtemperate
subliterate	subproject	subtheme
subnetwork	subregion	subtopic
suboceanic	subsea	subtotal
suborder	subsection	subtreasury
subpar	subsense	subtype
subpart	subspecialty	subunit
subplot	subspecies	subvariety

suc·co·tash \'sǝkǝ,tash\ *n* : beans and corn cooked together

suc·cu·lent \'sǝkyǝlǝnt\ *adj* : juicy — **suc·cu·lence** \-lǝns\ *n* — **succulent** *n*

suc·cumb \sǝ'kǝm\ *vb* 1 : yield 2 : die

such \'sǝch\ *adj* 1 : of this or that kind 2 : having a specified quality — **such** *pron or adv*

suck \'sǝk\ *vb* 1 : draw in liquid with the mouth 2 : draw liquid from by or as if by mouth — **suck** *n*

suck·er \'sǝkǝr\ *n* : one that sucks or clings 2 : easily deceived person

suck·le \'sǝkǝl\ *vb* **-led; -ling** : give or draw milk from the breast or udder

suck·ling \'sǝkliŋ\ *n* : young unweaned mammal

su·crose \'sü,krōs, -,krōz\ *n* : cane or beet sugar

suc·tion \'sǝkshǝn\ *n* 1 : act of sucking 2 : act or process of drawing in by partially exhausting the air

sud·den \'sǝd'n\ *adj* 1 : happening unexpectedly 2 : steep 3 : hasty — **sud·den·ly** *adv* — **sud·den·ness** *n*

suds \'sǝdz\ *n pl* : soapy water esp. when frothy — **sudsy** \'sǝdzē\ *adj*

sue \'sü\ *vb* **sued; su·ing** 1 : petition 2 : bring legal action against

suede, suède \'swād\ *n* : leather with a napped surface

su·et \'süǝt\ *n* : hard beef fat

suf·fer \'sǝfǝr\ *vb* 1 : experience pain, loss, or hardship 2 : permit — **suf·fer·er** *n*

suf·fer·ing \-ǝriŋ\ *n* : pain or hardship

suf·fice \sǝ'fīs\ *vb* **-ficed; -fic·ing** : be sufficient

suf·fi·cient \sǝ'fishǝnt\ *adj* : adequate — **suf·fi·cien·cy** \-ǝnsē\ *n* — **sufficiently** *adv*

suf·fix \'sǝf,iks\ *n* : letters added at the end of a word — **suffix** \'sǝfiks, sǝ'fiks\ *vb* — **suf·fix·a·tion** \,sǝf,ik-'sāshǝn\ *n*

suf·fo·cate \'sǝfǝ,kāt\ *vb* **-cat·ed; -cat·ing** : suffer or die or cause to die from lack of air — **suf·fo·cat·ing·ly** *adv* — **suf·fo·ca·tion** \,sǝfǝ'kāshǝn\ *n*

suf·frage \'sǝfrij\ *n* : right to vote

suf·fuse \sǝ'fyüz\ *vb* **-fused; -fus·ing** : spread over or through

sug·ar \'shügǝr\ *n* : sweet substance ~ *vb* : mix, cover, or sprinkle with sugar — **sug·ar·cane** *n* — **sug·ary** *adj*

sug·gest \sǝ'jest, sǝg-\ *vb* 1 : put

into someone's mind 2 : remind one by association of ideas — **sug·gest·ible** \-'jestǝbǝl\ *adj* — **sug·ges·tion** \-'jeschǝn\ *n*

sug·ges·tive \-'jestiv\ *adj* : suggesting something improper — **sug·ges·tive·ly** *adv* — **sug·ges·tive·ness** *n*

sui·cide \'süǝ,sīd\ *n* 1 : act of killing oneself purposely 2 : one who commits suicide — **sui·cid·al** \,süǝ-'sīd'l\ *adj*

suit \'süt\ *n* 1 : action in court to recover a right or claim 2 : number of things used or worn together 3 : one of the 4 sets of playing cards ~ *vb* 1 : be appropriate or becoming to 2 : meet the needs of — **suit·abil·i·ty** \,sütǝ-'bilǝtē\ *n* — **suit·able** \'sütǝbǝl\ *adj* — **suit·ably** *adv*

suit·case *n* : case for a traveler's clothing

suite \'swēt, *for 2 also* 'süt\ *n* 1 : group of rooms 2 : set of matched furniture

suit·or \'sütǝr\ *n* : one who seeks to marry a woman

sul·fur \'sǝlfǝr\ *n* : nonmetallic yellow chemical element — **sul·fu·ric** \,sǝl-'fyürik\ *adj* — **sul·fu·rous** \-'fyürǝs, 'sǝlfǝrǝs, 'sǝlfyǝ-\ *adj*

sulk \'sǝlk\ *vb* : be moodily silent or irritable — **sulk** *n*

sulky \'sǝlkē\ *adj* : inclined to sulk ~ *n* : light 2-wheeled horse-drawn cart — **sulk·i·ly** \'sǝlkǝlē\ *adv* — **sulk·i·ness** \-kēnǝs\ *n*

sul·len \'sǝlǝn\ *adj* 1 : gloomily silent 2 : dismal — **sul·len·ly** *adv* — **sul·len·ness** *n*

sul·ly \'sǝlē\ *vb* **-lied; -ly·ing** : cast doubt or disgrace on

sul·tan \'sǝlt'n\ *n* : sovereign of a Muslim state — **sul·tan·ate** \-,āt\ *n*

sul·try \'sǝltrē\ *adj* **-tri·er; -est** 1 : very hot and moist 2 : sexually arousing

sum \'sǝm\ *n* 1 : amount 2 : gist 3 : result of addition ~ *vb* **-mm-** : find the sum of

su·mac \'shü,mak, 'sü-\ *n* : shrub with spikes of berries

sum·ma·ry \'sǝmǝrē\ *adj* 1 : concise 2 : done without delay or formality ~ *n, pl* **-ries** : concise statement — **sum·mar·i·ly** \sǝ'merǝlē, 'sǝmǝrǝlē\ *adv* — **sum·ma·rize** \'sǝmǝ,rīz\ *vb*

sum·ma·tion \,sǝ'māshǝn\ *n* : a summing up esp. in court

sum·mer \'sǝmǝr\ *n* : season in which

the sun shines most directly — **sum-mery** adj

sum·mit \'səmət\ n 1 : highest point 2 : high-level conference

sum·mon \'səmən\ vb 1 : send for or call together 2 : order to appear in court — **sum·mon·er** n

sum·mons \'səmənz\ n, pl **sum·mons·es** : an order to answer charges in court

sump·tu·ous \'səmpchəwəs\ adj : lavish

sun \'sən\ n 1 : shining celestial body around which the planets revolve 2 : light of the sun ~ vb -nn- : expose to the sun — **sun·beam** n — **sun·block** n — **sun·burn** n or vb — **sun·glass·es** n pl — **sun·light** n — **sun·ny** adj — **sun·rise** n — **sun·set** n — **sun·shine** n — **sun·tan** n

sun·dae \'sənˌdā\ n : ice cream with topping

Sun·day \'sənˌdā, -dē\ n : 1st day of the week

sun·di·al \-ˌdīəl\ n : device for showing time by the sun's shadow

sun·dries \'səndrēz\ n pl : various small articles

sun·dry \-drē\ adj : several

sun·fish n : perchlike freshwater fish

sun·flow·er n : tall plant grown for its oil-rich seeds

sung past of SING

sunk past of SINK

sunk·en \'səŋkən\ adj 1 : submerged 2 : fallen in

sun·spot n : dark spot on the sun

sun·stroke n : heatstroke from the sun

sup \'səp\ vb -pp- : eat the evening meal

super \'süpər\ adj : very fine

super- \ˌsüpər, ˈsü-\ prefix 1 : higher in quantity, quality, or degree than 2 : in addition 3 : exceeding a norm 4 : in excessive degree or intensity 5 : surpassing others of its kind 6 : situated above, on, or at the top of 7 : more inclusive than 8 : superior in status or position

su·perb \su̇'pərb\ adj : outstanding — **su·perb·ly** adv

su·per·cil·ious \ˌsüpər'silēəs\ adj : haughtily contemptuous

su·per·fi·cial \ˌsüpər'fishəl\ adj : relating to what is only apparent — **su·per·fi·ci·al·i·ty** \-ˌfishē'alətē\ n — **su·per·fi·cial·ly** adv

su·per·flu·ous \su̇'pərfləwəs\ adj : more than necessary — **su·per·flu·i·ty** \ˌsüpər'flüətē\ n

su·per·im·pose \ˌsüpərim'pōz\ vb : lay over or above something

su·per·in·tend \ˌsüpərin'tend\ vb : have charge and oversight of — **su·per·in·ten·dence** \-'tendəns\ n — **su·per·in·ten·den·cy** \-dənsē\ n — **su·per·in·ten·dent** \-dənt\ n

su·pe·ri·or \su̇'pirēər\ adj 1 : higher, better, or more important 2 : haughty — **superior** n — **su·pe·ri·or·i·ty** \-ˌpirē'órətē\ n

su·per·la·tive \su̇'pərlətiv\ adj 1 : relating to or being an adjective or adverb form that denotes an extreme level 2 : surpassing others — **superlative** n — **su·per·la·tive·ly** adv

su·per·mar·ket \'süpərˌmärkət\ n : self-service grocery store

---

List of self-explanatory words with the prefix super-

superabundance	supergovernment	superport
superabundant	supergroup	superpowerful
superambitious	superhero	superrich
superathlete	superheroine	supersalesman
superbomb	superhuman	superscout
superclean	superintellectual	supersecrecy
supercolossal	superintelligence	supersecret
superconvenient	superintelligent	supersensitive
supercop	superman	supersize
superdense	supermodern	supersized
supereffective	superpatriot	superslick
superefficiency	superpatriotic	supersmooth
superefficient	superpatriotism	supersoft
superfast	superplane	superspecial
supergood	superpolite	superspecialist

su·per·nat·u·ral \ˌsüpərˈnachərəl\ *adj* : beyond the observable physical world — **su·per·nat·u·ral·ly** *adv*

su·per·pow·er \ˈsüpərˌpaůər\ *n* : politically and militarily dominant nation

su·per·sede \ˌsüpərˈsēd\ *vb* **-sed·ed; sed·ing** : take the place of

su·per·son·ic \-ˈsänik\ *adj* : faster than the speed of sound

su·per·sti·tion \ˌsüpərˈstishən\ *n* : beliefs based on ignorance, fear of the unknown, or trust in magic — **su·per·sti·tious** \-əs\ *adj*

su·per·struc·ture \ˈsüpərˌstrəkchər\ *n* : something built on a base or as a vertical extension

su·per·vise \ˈsüpərˌvīz\ *vb* **-vised; -vis·ing** : have charge of — **su·per·vi·sion** \ˌsüpərˈvizhən\ *n* — **su·per·vi·sor** \ˈsüpərˌvīzər\ *n* — **su·per·vi·so·ry** \ˌsüpərˈvīzərē\ *adj*

su·pine \süˈpīn\ *adj* **1** : lying on the back **2** : indifferent or abject

sup·per \ˈsəpər\ *n* : evening meal

sup·plant \səˈplant\ *vb* : take the place of

sup·ple \ˈsəpəl\ *adj* **-pler; -plest** : able to bend easily

sup·ple·ment \ˈsəpləmənt\ *n* : something that adds to or makes up for a lack — **supplement** *vb* — **sup·ple·men·tal** \ˌsəpləˈmentʾl\ *adj* — **sup·ple·men·ta·ry** \-ˈmentərē\ *adj*

sup·pli·ant \ˈsəplēənt\ *n* : one who supplicates

sup·pli·cate \ˈsəpləˌkāt\ *vb* **-cat·ed; -cat·ing** **1** : pray to God **2** : ask earnestly and humbly — **sup·pli·cant** \-likənt\ *n* — **sup·pli·ca·tion** \ˌsəpləˈkāshən\ *n*

sup·ply \səˈplī\ *vb* **-plied; -ply·ing** : furnish ~ *n, pl* **-plies** **1** : amount needed or available **2** *pl* : provisions — **sup·pli·er** \-ˈplīər\ *n*

sup·port \səˈpōrt\ *vb* **1** : take sides with **2** : provide with food, clothing, and shelter **3** : hold up or serve as a foundation for — **support** *n* — **sup·port·able** *adj* — **sup·port·er** *n*

sup·pose \səˈpōz\ *vb* **-posed; -pos-** ing **1** : assume to be true **2** : expect **3** : think probable — **sup·po·si·tion** \ˌsəpəˈzishən\ *n*

sup·pos·i·to·ry \səˈpäzəˌtōrē\ *n, pl* **-ries** : medicated material for insertion (as into the rectum)

sup·press \səˈpres\ *vb* **1** : put an end to by authority **2** : keep from being known **3** : hold back — **sup·pres·sant** \səˈpresʾnt\ *n* — **sup·pres·sion** \-ˈpreshən\ *n*

su·prem·a·cy \süˈpreməsē\ *n, pl* **-cies** : supreme power or authority

su·preme \süˈprēm\ *adj* **1** : highest in rank or authority **2** : greatest possible — **su·preme·ly** *adv*

Supreme Being *n* : God

sur·charge \ˈsərˌchärj\ *n* **1** : excessive load or burden **2** : extra fee or cost

sure \ˈshür\ *adj* **sur·er; sur·est** **1** : confident **2** : reliable **3** : not to be disputed **4** : bound to happen ~ *adv* : surely — **sure·ness** *n*

sure·ly \ˈshürlē\ *adv* **1** : in a sure manner **2** : without doubt **3** : indeed

sure·ty \ˈshürətē\ *n, pl* **-ties** **1** : guarantee **2** : one who gives a guarantee for another person

surf \ˈsərf\ *n* : waves that break on the shore ~ *vb* : ride the surf — **surfboard** *n* — **surf·er** *n* — **surf·ing** *n*

sur·face \ˈsərfəs\ *n* **1** : the outside of an object **2** : outward aspect ~ *vb* **-faced; -fac·ing** : rise to the surface

sur·feit \ˈsərfət\ *n* **1** : excess **2** : excessive indulgence (as in food or drink) **3** : disgust caused by excess ~ *vb* : feed, supply, or indulge to the point of surfeit

surge \ˈsərj\ *vb* **surged; surg·ing** : rise and fall in or as if in waves ~ *n* : sudden increase

sur·geon \ˈsərjən\ *n* : physician who specializes in surgery

sur·gery \ˈsərjərē\ *n, pl* **-ger·ies** : medical treatment involving cutting open the body

sur·gi·cal \ˈsərjikəl\ *adj* : relating to surgeons or surgery — **sur·gi·cal·ly** *adv*

superspy	superstrong	superthin
superstar	supersystem	supertight
superstate	supertanker	superweapon
superstrength	superthick	superwoman

sur·ly \'sərlē\ adj **-li·er; -est** : having a rude nature — **sur·li·ness** n

sur·mise \sər'mīz\ vb **-mised; -mis·ing** : guess — **surmise** n

sur·mount \-'maúnt\ vb **1** : prevail over **2** : get to or be the top of

sur·name \'sər,nām\ n : family name

sur·pass \sər'pas\ vb : go beyond or exceed — **sur·pass·ing·ly** adv

sur·plice \'sərpləs\ n : loose white outer ecclesiastical vestment

sur·plus \'sər,pləs\ n : quantity left over

sur·prise \sə'prīz, sər-\ vb **-prised; -pris·ing 1** : come upon or affect unexpectedly **2** : amaze — **surprise** n — **sur·pris·ing** adj — **sur·pris·ing·ly** adv

sur·ren·der \sə'rendər\ vb : give up oneself or a possession to another ~ n : act of surrendering

sur·rep·ti·tious \,sərəp'tishəs\ adj : done, made, or acquired by stealth — **sur·rep·ti·tious·ly** adv

sur·rey \'sərē\ n, pl **-reys** : horse-drawn carriage

sur·ro·gate \'sərəgāt, -gət\ n : substitute

sur·round \sə'raúnd\ vb : enclose on all sides

sur·round·ings \sə'raúndiŋz\ n pl : objects, conditions, or area around something

sur·veil·lance \sər'vāləns, -'vālyəns, -'vāəns\ n : careful watch

sur·vey \sər'vā\ vb **-veyed; -vey·ing 1** : look over and examine closely **2** : make a survey of (as a tract of land) ~ \'sər,-\ n, pl **-veys 1** : inspection **2** : process of measuring (as land) — **sur·vey·or** \-ər\ n

sur·vive \sər'vīv\ vb **-vived; -viv·ing 1** : remain alive or in existence **2** : outlive or outlast — **sur·viv·al** n — **sur·vi·vor** \-'vīvər\ n

sus·cep·ti·ble \sə'septəbəl\ adj : likely to allow or be affected by something — **sus·cep·ti·bil·i·ty** \-,septə'bilətē\ n

sus·pect \'səs,pekt, sə'spekt\ adj : regarded with suspicion **2** : questionable ~ \'səs,pekt\ n : one who is suspected (as of a crime) ~ \sə'spekt\ vb **1** : have doubts of **2** : believe guilty without proof **3** : guess

sus·pend \sə'spend\ vb **1** : temporarily stop or keep from a function or job **2** : withhold (judgment) temporarily **3** : hang

sus·pend·er \sə'spendər\ n : one of 2 supporting straps holding up trousers and passing over the shoulders

sus·pense \sə'spens\ n : excitement and uncertainty as to outcome — **suspense·ful** adj

sus·pen·sion \sə'spenchən\ n : act of suspending or the state or period of being suspended

sus·pi·cion \sə'spishən\ n **1** : act of suspecting something **2** : trace

sus·pi·cious \-əs\ adj **1** : arousing suspicion **2** : inclined to suspect — **sus·pi·cious·ly** adv

sus·tain \sə'stān\ vb **1** : provide with nourishment **2** : keep going **3** : hold up **4** : suffer **5** : support or prove

sus·te·nance \'səstənəns\ n **1** : nourishment **2** : something that sustains or supports

svelte \'sfelt\ adj : slender and graceful

swab \'swäb\ n **1** : mop **2** : wad of absorbent material for applying medicine ~ vb **-bb-** : use a swab on

swad·dle \'swädʰl\ vb **-dled; -dling** \'swädʰliŋ\ : bind (an infant) in bands of cloth

swag·ger \'swagər\ vb **-gered; -ger·ing 1** : walk with a conceited swing **2** : boast — **swagger** n

¹**swal·low** \'swälō\ n : small migratory bird

²**swallow** vb **1** : take into the stomach through the throat **2** : envelop or take in **3** : accept too easily — **swallow** n

swam past of SWIM

swamp \'swämp\ n : wet spongy land ~ vb : deluge (as with water) — **swampy** adj

swan \'swän\ n : white long-necked swimming bird

swap \'swäp\ vb **-pp-** : trade — **swap** n

swarm \'swórm\ n **1** : mass of honeybees leaving a hive to start a new colony **2** : large crowd ~ vb : gather in a swarm

swar·thy \'swórthē, -thē\ adj **-thi·er; -est** : dark in complexion

swash·buck·ler \'swäsh,bəklər\ n : swaggering or daring soldier or adventurer — **swash·buck·ling** \-,bəkliŋ\ adj

swat \'swät\ vb **-tt-** : hit sharply — **swat** n — **swat·ter** n

swatch \'swäch\ n : sample piece (as of fabric)

swath \'swäth, 'swóth\, **swathe**

\\'swäth, 'swȯth, 'swȧth\ *n* : row or path cut (as through grass)

swathe \\'swāth, 'swȯth, 'swȧth\ *vb* **swathed; swath·ing** : wrap with or as if with a bandage

sway \\'swā\ *vb* **1** : swing gently from side to side **2** : influence ∼ *n* **1** : gentle swinging from side to side **2** : controlling power or influence

swear \\'swar\ *vb* **swore** \\'swōr\; **sworn** \\'swōrn\; **swear·ing 1** : make or cause to make a solemn statement under oath **2** : use profane language — **swear·er** *n* — **swear·ing** *n*

sweat \\'swet\ *vb* **sweat** *or* **sweat·ed; sweat·ing 1** : excrete salty moisture from skin glands **2** : form drops of moisture on the surface **3** : work or cause to work hard — **sweat** *n* — **sweaty** *adj*

sweat·er \\'swetər\ *n* : knitted jacket or pullover

sweat·shirt \\'swet,shərt\ *n* : loose collarless heavy cotton jersey pullover

sweep \\'swēp\ *vb* **swept** \\'swept\; **sweep·ing 1** : remove or clean by a brush or a single forceful wipe (as of the hand) **2** : move with speed and force (as of the hand) **3** : move or extend in a wide curve ∼ *n* **1** : a clearing off or away **2** : single forceful wipe or swinging movement **3** : scope — **sweep·er** *n* — **sweep·ing** *adj*

sweep·stakes \\'swēp,stāks\ *n, pl* **sweep·stakes** : contest in which the entire prize may go to the winner

sweet \\'swēt\ *adj* **1** : being or causing the pleasing taste typical of sugar **2** : not stale or spoiled **3** : not salted **4** : pleasant **5** : much loved ∼ *n* : something sweet — **sweet·en** \\'swēt⁰n\ *vb* — **sweet·ly** *adv* — **sweet·ness** *n* — **sweet·en·er** \\-⁰nər\ *n*

sweet·heart *n* : person one loves

sweet potato *n* : sweet yellow edible root of a tropical vine

swell \\'swel\ *vb* **swelled; swelled** *or* **swol·len** \\'swōlən\; **swell·ing 1** : enlarge **2** : bulge **3** : fill or be filled with emotion ∼ *n* **1** : long rolling ocean wave **2** : condition of bulging — **swell·ing** *n*

swel·ter \\'sweltər\ *vb* : be uncomfortable from excessive heat

swept *past of* SWEEP

swerve \\'swərv\ *vb* **swerved; swerv·ing** : move abruptly aside from a course — **swerve** *n*

¹swift \\'swift\ *adj* **1** : moving with great speed **2** : occurring suddenly — **swift·ly** *adv* — **swift·ness** *n*

²swift *n* : small insect-eating bird

swig \\'swig\ *vb* **-gg-** : drink in gulps — **swig** *n*

swill \\'swil\ *vb* : swallow greedily ∼ *n* **1** : animal food of refuse and liquid **2** : garbage

swim \\'swim\ *vb* **swam** \\'swam\; **swum** \\'swəm\; **swim·ming 1** : propel oneself in water **2** : float in or be surrounded with a liquid **3** : be dizzy ∼ *n* : act or period of swimming — **swim·mer** *n*

swin·dle \\'swind³l\ *vb* **-dled; -dling** \\-iŋ\ : cheat (someone) of money or property — **swindle** *n* — **swin·dler** \\-ər\ *n*

swine \\'swīn\ *n, pl* **swine** : short-legged hoofed mammal with a snout — **swin·ish** \\'swīnish\ *adj*

swing \\'swiŋ\ *vb* **swung** \\'swəŋ\; **swing·ing 1** : move or cause to move rapidly in an arc **2** : sway or cause to sway back and forth **3** : hang so as to sway or sag **4** : turn on a hinge or pivot **5** : manage or handle successfully ∼ *n* **1** : act or instance of swinging **2** : swinging movement (as in trying to hit something) **3** : suspended seat for swinging — **swing** *adj* — **swing·er** *n*

swipe \\'swīp\ *n* : strong sweeping blow — *vb* **swiped; swip·ing 1** : strike or wipe with a sweeping motion **2** : steal esp. with a quick movement

swirl \\'swərl\ *vb* : move or cause to move in a circle — **swirl** *n*

swish \\'swish\ *n* : hissing, sweeping, or brushing sound — **swish** *vb*

switch \\'swich\ *n* **1** : slender flexible whip or twig **2** : blow with a switch **3** : shift, change, or reversal **4** : device that opens or closes an electrical circuit — *vb* **1** : punish or urge on with a switch **2** : change or reverse roles, positions, or subjects **3** : operate a switch of

switch·board *n* : panel of switches to make and break telephone connections

swiv·el \\'swivəl\ *vb* **-eled** *or* **-elled; -eling** *or* **-el·ling** : swing or turn on a pivot — **swivel** *n*

swollen *past part of* SWELL

swoon \\'swün\ *vb* : faint — **swoon** *n*

swoop \\'swüp\ *vb* : make a swift diving attack — **swoop** *n*

sword \'sòrd\ n : thrusting or cutting weapon with a long blade

sword•fish n : large ocean fish with a long swordlike projection

swore past of SWEAR

sworn past part of SWEAR

swum past part of SWIM

swung past of SWING

syc•a•more \'sikə,mōr\ n : shade tree

sy•co•phant \'sikəfənt\ n : servile flatterer — **syc•o•phan•tic** \,sikə-'fantik\ adj

syl•la•ble \'siləbəl\ n : unit of a spoken word — **syl•lab•ic** \sə'labik\ adj

syl•la•bus \'siləbəs\ n, pl **-bi** \-,bī\ or **-bus•es** : summary of main topics (as of a course of study)

syl•van \'silvən\ adj 1 : living or located in a wooded area 2 : abounding in woods

sym•bol \'simbəl\ n : something that represents or suggests another thing — **sym•bol•ic** \sim'bälik\ adj — **sym•bol•i•cal•ly** adv

sym•bol•ism \'simbə,lizəm\ n : representation of meanings with symbols

sym•bol•ize \'simbə,līz\ vb **-ized; -iz•ing** : serve as a symbol of — **sym•bol•i•za•tion** \,simbələ'zāshən\ n

sym•me•try \'simətrē\ n, pl **-tries** : regularity and balance in the arrangement of parts — **sym•met•ri•cal** \sə'metrikəl\ adj — **sym•met•ri•cal•ly** adv

sym•pa•thize \'simpə,thīz\ vb **-thized; -thiz•ing** : feel or show sympathy — **sym•pa•thiz•er** n

sym•pa•thy \'simpəthē\ n, pl **-thies** 1 : ability to understand or share the feelings of another 2 : expression of sorrow for another's misfortune — **sym•pa•thet•ic** \,simpə'thetik\ adj — **sym•pa•thet•i•cal•ly** adv

sym•pho•ny \'simfənē\ n, pl **-nies** : composition for an orchestra or the orchestra itself — **sym•phon•ic** \sim'fänik\ adj

sym•po•sium \sim'pōzēəm\ n, pl **-sia** \-zēə\ or **-siums** : conference at which a topic is discussed

symp•tom \'simptəm\ n : unusual feeling or reaction that is a sign of disease — **symp•tom•at•ic** \,simptə-'matik\ adj

syn•a•gogue, syn•a•gog \'sinə,gäg, -,gòg\ n : Jewish house of worship

syn•chro•nize \'siŋkrə,nīz, 'sin-\ vb **-nized; -niz•ing** 1 : occur or cause to occur at the same instant 2 : cause to agree in time — **syn•chro•ni•za•tion** \,siŋkrənə'zāshən, ,sin-\ n

syn•co•pa•tion \,siŋkə'pāshən, ,sin-\ n : shifting of the regular musical accent to the weak beat — **syn•co•pate** \'siŋkə,pāt, 'sin-\ vb

syn•di•cate \'sindikət\ n : business association ~ \-də,kāt\ vb **-cat•ed; -cat•ing** 1 : form a syndicate 2 : publish through a syndicate — **syn•di•ca•tion** \,sində'kāshən\ n

syn•drome \'sin,drōm\ n : particular group of symptoms

syn•onym \'sinə,nim\ n : word with the same meaning as another — **syn•on•y•mous** \sə'nänəməs\ adj — **syn•on•y•my** \-mē\ n

syn•op•sis \sə'näpsəs\ n, pl **-op•ses** \-,sēz\ : condensed statement or outline

syn•tax \'sin,taks\ n : way in which words are put together — **syn•tac•tic** \sin'taktik\, **syn•tac•ti•cal** \-tikəl\ adj

syn•the•sis \'sinthəsəs\ n, pl **-the•ses** \-,sēz\ : combination of parts or elements into a whole — **syn•the•size** \-,sīz\ vb

syn•thet•ic \sin'thetik\ adj : artificially made — **synthetic** n — **syn•thet•i•cal•ly** adv

syph•i•lis \'sifələs\ n : venereal disease

sy•ringe \sə'rinj, 'sirinj\ n : plunger device for injecting or withdrawing liquids

syr•up \'sərəp, 'sirəp\ n : thick sticky sweet liquid — **syr•upy** adj

sys•tem \'sistəm\ n 1 : arrangement of units that function together 2 : regular order — **sys•tem•at•ic** \,sistə'matik\ adj — **sys•tem•at•i•cal•ly** adv — **sys•tem•a•tize** \'sistəmə,tīz\ vb

sys•tem•ic \sis'temik\ adj : relating to the whole body

T

t \'tē\ *n, pl* t's *or* ts \'tēz\ : 20th letter of the alphabet

tab \'tab\ *n* 1 : short projecting flap 2 *pl* : careful watch

tab·by \'tabē\ *n, pl* -bies : domestic cat

tab·er·na·cle \'tabər,nakəl\ *n* : house of worship

ta·ble \'tābəl\ *n* 1 : piece of furniture having a smooth slab fixed on legs 2 : supply of food 3 : arrangement of data in columns 4 : short list — ta·ble·cloth *n* — ta·ble·top *n* — ta·ble·ware *n* — tab·u·lar \'tabyələr\ *adj*

tab·leau \'tab,lō\ *n, pl* -leaux \-,lōz\ 1 : graphic description 2 : depiction of a scene by people in costume

ta·ble·spoon *n* 1 : large serving spoon 2 : measuring spoon holding 1/2 fluid ounce — ta·ble·spoon·ful \-,fu̇l\ *n*

tab·let \'tablət\ *n* 1 : flat slab suited for an inscription 2 : collection of sheets of paper glued together at one edge 3 : disk-shaped pill

tab·loid \'tab,lȯid\ *n* : newspaper of small page size

ta·boo \ta-'bü, ta-\ *adj* : banned esp. as immoral or dangerous — taboo *n or vb*

tab·u·late \'tabyə,lāt\ *vb* -lat·ed; -lat·ing : put in the form of a table — tab·u·la·tion \,tabyə'lāshən\ *n* — tab·u·la·tor \'tabyə,lātər\ *n*

tac·it \'tasət\ *adj* : implied but not expressed — tac·it·ly *adv* — tac·it·ness *n*

tac·i·turn \'tasə,tərn\ *adj* : not inclined to talk

tack \'tak\ *n* 1 : small sharp nail 2 : course of action ~ *vb* 1 : fasten with tacks 2 : add on

tack·le \'takəl, *naut often* 'tāk-\ *n* 1 : equipment 2 : arrangement of ropes and pulleys 3 : act of tackling ~ *vb* -led; -ling 1 : seize or throw down 2 : start dealing with

¹tacky \'takē\ *adj* tack·i·er; -est : sticky to the touch

²tacky *adj* tack·i·er; -est : cheap or gaudy

tact \'takt\ *n* : sense of the proper thing to say or do — tact·ful \-fəl\ *adj* —

tact·ful·ly *adv* — tact·less *adj* — tact·less·ly *adv*

tac·tic \'taktik\ *n* : action as part of a plan

tac·tics \'taktiks\ *n sing or pl* 1 : science of maneuvering forces in combat 2 : skill of using available means to reach an end — tac·ti·cal \-tikəl\ *adj* — tac·ti·cian \tak'tishən\ *n*

tac·tile \'takt²l, -,tīl\ *adj* : relating to or perceptible through the sense of touch

tad·pole \'tad,pōl\ *n* : larval frog or toad with tail and gills

taf·fe·ta \'tafətə\ *n* : crisp lustrous fabric (as of silk)

taf·fy \'tafē\ *n, pl* -fies : candy stretched until porous

¹tag \'tag\ *n* : piece of hanging or attached material ~ *vb* -gg- 1 : provide or mark with a tag 2 : follow closely

²tag *n* : children's game of trying to catch one another ~ *vb* : touch a person in tag

tail \'tāl\ *n* 1 : rear end or a growth extending from the rear end of an animal 2 : back or last part 3 : the reverse of a coin ~ *vb* : follow — tailed \'tāld\ *adj* — tail·less *adj*

tail·gate \-,gāt\ *n* : hinged gate on the back of a vehicle that can be lowered for loading ~ *vb* -gat·ed; -gat·ing : drive too close behind another vehicle

tail·light *n* : red warning light at the back of a vehicle

tai·lor \'tālər\ *n* : one who makes or alters garments ~ *vb* 1 : fashion or alter (clothes) 2 : make or adapt for a special purpose

tail·spin *n* : spiral dive by an airplane

taint \'tānt\ *vb* : affect or become affected with something bad and esp. decay ~ *n* : trace of decay or corruption

take \'tāk\ *vb* took \'tu̇k\; tak·en \'tākən\; tak·ing 1 : get into one's possession 2 : become affected by 3 : receive into one's body (as by eating) 4 : pick out or remove 5 : use for transportation 6 : need or make use of **7** : lead, carry, or cause to go to another place **8** : undertake and do, make, or perform ~ *n* : amount taken — **take-over** *n* — **tak-er** *n* — **take advantage of** : profit by — **take exception** : object — **take off** *vb* **1** : remove **2** : go away **3** : mimic **4** : begin flight — **take over** *vb* : assume control or possession of or responsibility for — **take place** : happen

take-off *n* : act or instance of taking off

talc \'talk\ *n* : soft mineral used in making toilet powder (**tal-cum powder** \'talkəm-\)

tale \'tāl\ *n* **1** : story or anecdote **2** : falsehood

tal-ent \'talənt\ *n* : natural mental or creative ability — **tal-ent-ed** *adj*

tal-is-man \'taləsmən, -əz-\ *n, pl* **-mans** : object thought to act as a charm

talk \'tök\ *vb* **1** : express one's thoughts in speech **2** : discuss **3** : influence to a position or course of action by talking ~ *n* **1** : act of talking **2** : formal discussion **3** : rumor **4** : informal lecture — **talk-a-tive** \-ətiv\ *adj* — **talk-er** *n*

tall \'töl\ *adj* : extending to a great or specified height — **tall-ness** *n*

tal-low \'talō\ *n* : hard white animal fat used esp. in candles

tal-ly \'talē\ *n, pl* **-lies** : recorded amount ~ *vb* **-lied; -ly-ing** **1** : add or count up **2** : match

tal-on \'talən\ *n* : bird's claw

tam \'tam\ *n* : tam-o'-shanter

tam-bou-rine \,tambə'rēn\ *n* : small drum with loose disks at the sides

tame \'tām\ *adj* **tam-er; tam-est** **1** : changed from being wild to being controllable by man **2** : docile **3** : dull ~ *vb* **tamed; tam-ing** : make or become tame — **tam-able, tame-able** *adj* — **tame-ly** *adv* — **tam-er** *n*

tam-o'-shan-ter \'tamə,shantər\ *n* : Scottish woolen cap with a wide flat circular crown

tamp \'tamp\ *vb* : drive down or in by a series of light blows

tam-per \'tampər\ *vb* : interfere so as to change for the worse

tan \'tan\ *vb* **-nn-** **1** : change (hide) into leather esp. by soaking in a liquid containing tannin **2** : make or become brown (as by exposure to the sun) ~ *n* **1** : brown skin color induced by the

sun **2** : light yellowish brown — **tan-ner** *n* — **tan-nery** \'tanərē\ *n*

tan-dem \'tandəm\ *adv* : one behind another

tang \'taŋ\ *n* : sharp distinctive flavor — **tangy** *adj*

tan-gent \'tanjənt\ *adj* : touching a curve or surface at only one point ~ *n* **1** : tangent line, curve, or surface **2** : abrupt change of course — **tan-gen-tial** \tan'jenchəl\ *adj*

tan-ger-ine \'tanjə,rēn, ,tanjə'-\ *n* : deep orange citrus fruit

tan-gi-ble \'tanjəbəl\ *adj* **1** : able to be touched **2** : substantially real — **tan-gi-bly** *adv*

tan-gle \'taŋgəl\ *vb* **-gled; -gling** : unite in intricate confusion ~ *n* : tangled twisted mass

tan-go \'taŋgō\ *n, pl* **-gos** : dance of Latin-American origin — **tango** *vb*

tank \'taŋk\ *n* **1** : large artificial receptacle for liquids **2** : armored military vehicle — **tank-ful** *n*

tan-kard \'taŋkərd\ *n* : tall one-handled drinking vessel

tank-er \'taŋkər\ *n* : vehicle or vessel with tanks for transporting a liquid

tan-nin \'tanən\ *n* : substance of plant origin used in tanning and dyeing

tan-ta-lize \'tant°l,īz\ *vb* **-lized; -liz-ing** : tease or torment by keeping something desirable just out of reach — **tan-ta-liz-er** *n* — **tan-ta-liz-ing-ly** *adv*

tan-ta-mount \'tantə,maunt\ *adj* : equivalent in value or meaning

tan-trum \'tantrəm\ *n* : fit of bad temper

¹**tap** \'tap\ *n* **1** : faucet **2** : act of tapping ~ *vb* **-pp-** **1** : pierce so as to draw off fluid **2** : connect into — **tap-per** *n*

²**tap** *vb* **-pp-** : rap lightly ~ *n* **1** : light stroke or its sound

tape \'tāp\ *n* **1** : narrow flexible strip (as of cloth, plastic, or metal) **2** : tape measure ~ *vb* **taped; tap-ing** **1** : fasten with tape **2** : record on tape

tape measure *n* : strip of tape marked in units for use in measuring

ta-per \'tāpər\ *n* **1** : slender wax candle **2** : gradual lessening of width in a long object ~ *vb* **1** : make or become smaller toward one end **2** : diminish gradually

tap-es-try \'tapəstrē\ *n, pl* **-tries** : heavy handwoven ruglike wall hanging

tape-worm *n* : long flat intestinal worm

tap-i-o-ca \,tapē'ōkə\ *n* : a granular starch used esp. in puddings

tar \'tär\ n : thick dark sticky liquid distilled (as from coal) ~ vb -rr- : treat or smear with tar

ta·ran·tu·la \tə'ranchələ, -'rantᵊlə\ n : large hairy usu. harmless spider

tar·dy \'tärdē\ adj -di·er; -est : late — **tar·di·ly** \'tärdᵊlē\ adv — **tar·di·ness** n

tar·get \'tärgət\ n 1 : mark to shoot at 2 : goal to be achieved ~ vb 1 : make a target of 2 : establish as a goal

tar·iff \'tarəf\ n 1 : duty or rate of duty imposed on imported goods 2 : schedule of tariffs, rates, or charges

tar·nish \'tärnish\ vb : make or become dull or discolored — **tarnish** n

tar·pau·lin \tär'pólən, 'tärpə-\ n : waterproof protective covering

¹**tar·ry** \'tarē\ vb -ried; -ry·ing : be slow in leaving

²**tar·ry** \'tärē\ adj : resembling or covered with tar

¹**tart** \'tärt\ adj 1 : pleasantly sharp to the taste 2 : caustic — **tart·ly** adv — **tart·ness** n

²**tart** n : small pie

tar·tan \'tärtᵊn\ n : woolen fabric with a plaid design

tar·tar \'tärtər\ n : hard crust on the teeth

task \'task\ n : assigned work

task·mas·ter n : one that burdens another with labor

tas·sel \'tasəl, 'täs-\ n : hanging ornament made of a bunch of cords fastened at one end

taste \'tāst\ vb **tast·ed; tast·ing** n 1 : test or determine the flavor of 2 : eat or drink in small quantities 3 : have a specific flavor ~ n 1 : small amount tasted 2 : bit 3 : special sense that identifies sweet, sour, bitter, or salty qualities 4 : individual preference 5 : critical appreciation of quality — **taste·ful** \-fəl\ adj — **taste·ful·ly** adv — **taste·less** adj — **taste·less·ly** adv — **tast·er** n

tasty \'tāstē\ adj **tast·i·er; -est** : pleasing to the sense of taste — **tast·i·ness** n

tat·ter \'tatər\ n 1 : part torn and left hanging 2 pl : tattered clothing ~ vb : make or become ragged

tat·tle \'tatᵊl\ vb -tled; -tling : inform on someone — **tat·tler** n

tat·tle·tale n : one that tattles

tat·too \ta'tü\ vb : mark the skin with indelible designs or figures — **tattoo** n

taught past of TEACH

taunt \'tónt\ n : sarcastic challenge or insult — **taunt** vb — **taunt·er** n

taut \'tót\ adj : tightly drawn — **taut·ly** adv — **taut·ness** n

tav·ern \'tavərn\ n : establishment where liquors are sold to be drunk on the premises

taw·dry \'tódrē\ adj -dri·er; -est : cheap and gaudy — **taw·dri·ly** \'tódrəlē\ adv

taw·ny \'tónē\ adj -ni·er; -est : brownish orange

tax \'taks\ vb 1 : impose a tax on 2 : charge 3 : put under stress ~ n 1 : charge by authority for public purposes 2 : strain — **tax·able** adj — **tax·a·tion** \tak'sāshən\ n — **tax·pay·er** n — **tax·pay·ing** adj

taxi \'taksē\ n, pl **tax·is** \-sēz\ : automobile transporting passengers for a fare ~ vb **tax·ied; taxi·ing** or **taxy·ing; tax·is** or **tax·ies** 1 : transport or go by taxi 2 : move along the ground before takeoff or after landing

taxi·cab \'taksē‚kab\ n : taxi

taxi·der·my \'taksə‚dərmē\ n : skill or job of stuffing and mounting animal skins — **taxi·der·mist** \-mist\ n

tea \'tē\ n : cured leaves of an oriental shrub or a drink made from these — **tea·cup** n — **tea·pot** n

teach \'tēch\ vb **taught** \'tót\; **teach·ing** 1 : tell or show the fundamentals or skills of something 2 : cause to know the consequences 3 : impart knowledge of — **teach·able** adj — **teach·er** n — **teach·ing** n

teak \'tēk\ n : East Indian timber tree or its wood

tea·ket·tle \'tē‚ketᵊl\ n : covered kettle with a handle and spout for boiling water

teal \'tēl\ n, pl **teal** or **teals** : small short-necked wild duck

team \'tēm\ n 1 : draft animals harnessed together 2 : number of people organized for a game or work ~ vb : form or work together as a team — **team** adj — **team·mate** n — **team·work** n

team·ster \'tēmstər\ n 1 : one that drives a team of animals 2 : one that drives a truck

¹**tear** \'tir\ n : drop of salty liquid that moistens the eye — **tear·ful** \-fəl\ adj — **tear·ful·ly** adv

²**tear** \'tar\ vb **tore** \'tōr\; **torn** \'tórn\; **tear·ing** 1 : separate or pull apart by

force **2** : move or act with violence or haste ~ *n* : act or result of tearing

tease \'tēz\ *vb* **teased; teas·ing** : annoy by goading, coaxing, or tantalizing ~ *n* **1** : act of teasing or state of being teased **2** : one that teases

tea·spoon \'tē,spün\ *n* **1** : small spoon for stirring or sipping **2** : measuring spoon holding 1/6 fluid ounce — **tea-spoon·ful** \-,fül\ *n*

teat \'tēt\ *n* : protuberance through which milk is drawn from an udder or breast

tech·ni·cal \'teknikəl\ *adj* **1** : having or relating to special mechanical or scientific knowledge **2** : by strict interpretation of rules — **tech·ni·cal·ly** *adv*

tech·ni·cal·i·ty \,teknə'kalətē\ *n, pl* **-ties** : detail meaningful only to a specialist

technical sergeant *n* : noncommissioned officer in the air force ranking next below a master sergeant

tech·ni·cian \tek'nishən\ *n* : person with the technique of a specialized skill

tech·nique \tek'nēk\ *n* : manner of accomplishing something

tech·nol·o·gy \tek'näləjē\ *n, pl* **-gies** : applied science — **tech·no·log·i·cal** \,teknə'läjikəl\ *adj*

te·dious \'tēdēəs\ *adj* : wearisome from length or dullness — **te·dious·ly** *adv* — **te·dious·ness** *n*

te·di·um \'tēdēəm\ *n* : tedious state or quality

tee \'tē\ *n* : mound or peg on which a golf ball is placed before beginning play — **tee** *vb*

teem \'tēm\ *vb* : become filled to overflowing

teen·age \'tēn,āj\, **teen·aged** \-,ājd\ *adj* : relating to people in their teens — **teen·ag·er** \-,ājər\ *n*

teens \'tēnz\ *n pl* : years 13 to 19 in a person's life

tee·pee *var of* TEPEE

tee·ter \'tētər\ *vb* **1** : move unsteadily **2** : seesaw — **teeter** *n*

teeth *pl of* TOOTH

teethe \'tēth\ *vb* **teethed; teeth·ing** : grow teeth

tele·cast \'teli,kast\ *vb* **-cast; -cast-ing** : broadcast by television — **tele-cast** *n* — **tele·cast·er** *n*

tele·com·mu·ni·ca·tion \'teləkəmyünə-'kāshən\ *n* : communication at a distance (as by radio or telephone)

tele·gram \'telə,gram\ *n* : message sent by telegraph

tele·graph \-,graf\ *n* : system for communication by electrical transmission of coded signals ~ *vb* : send by telegraph — **te·leg·ra·pher** \tə'legrəfər\ *n* — **tele·graph·ic** \,telə'grafik\ *adj*

te·lep·a·thy \tə'lepəthē\ *n* : apparent communication without known sensory means — **tele·path·ic** \,telə-'pathik\ *adj* — **tele·path·i·cal·ly** *adv*

tele·phone \'telə,fōn\ *n* : instrument or system for electrical transmission of spoken words ~ *vb* **-phoned; -phon·ing** : communicate with by telephone — **tele·phon·er** *n*

tele·scope \-,skōp\ *n* : tube-shaped optical instrument for viewing distant objects ~ *vb* **-scoped; -scop·ing** : slide or cause to slide inside another similar section — **tele·scop·ic** \,telə-'skäpik\ *adj*

tele·vise \'telə,vīz\ *vb* **-vised; -vis·ing** : broadcast by television

tele·vi·sion \-,vizhən\ *n* : transmission and reproduction of images by radio waves

tell \'tel\ *vb* **told** \'tōld\; **tell·ing** **1** : count **2** : relate in detail **3** : reveal **4** : give information or an order to **5** : find out by observing

tell·er \'telər\ *n* **1** : one that relates or counts **2** : bank employee handling money

te·mer·i·ty \tə'merətē\ *n, pl* **-ties** : boldness

temp \'temp\ *n* **1** : temperature **2** : temporary worker

tem·per \'tempər\ *vb* **1** : dilute or soften **2** : toughen ~ *n* **1** : characteristic attitude or feeling **2** : toughness **3** : disposition or control over one's emotions

tem·per·a·ment \'tempərəmənt\ *n* : characteristic frame of mind — **tem-per·a·men·tal** \,temprə'ment³l\ *adj*

tem·per·ance \'temprəns\ *n* : moderation in or abstinence from indulgence and esp. the use of intoxicating drink

tem·per·ate \'tempərət\ *adj* : moderate

tem·per·a·ture \'tempər,chúr, -prə-,chúr, -chər\ *n* **1** : degree of hotness or coldness **2** : fever

tem·pest \'tempəst\ *n* : violent storm — **tem·pes·tu·ous** \tem'peschəwəs\ *adj*

¹tem·ple \'tempəl\ *n* : place of worship

²**temple** n : flattened space on each side of the forehead

tem·po \'tempō\ n, pl **-pi** \-ˌpē\ or **-pos** : rate of speed

tem·po·ral \'tempərəl\ adj : relating to time or to secular concerns

tem·po·rary \'tempəˌrerē\ adj : lasting for a short time only — **tem·po·rar·i·ly** \ˌtempə'rerəlē\ adv

tempt \'tempt\ vb 1 : coax or persuade to do wrong 2 : attract or provoke — **tempt·er** n — **tempt·ing·ly** adv — **tempt·ress** \'temptrəs\ n

temp·ta·tion \temp'tāshən\ n 1 : act of tempting 2 : something that tempts

ten \'ten\ n 1 : one more than 9 2 : 10th in a set or series 3 : thing having 10 units — **ten** adj or pron — **tenth** \'tenth\ adj or adv or n

ten·a·ble \'tenəbəl\ adj : capable of being held or defended — **ten·a·bil·i·ty** \ˌtenə'bilətē\ n

te·na·cious \tə'nāshəs\ adj 1 : holding fast 2 : retentive — **te·na·cious·ly** adv — **te·nac·i·ty** \tə'nasətē\ n

ten·ant \'tenənt\ n : one who occupies a rented dwelling — **ten·an·cy** \-ənsē\ n

¹**tend** \'tend\ vb : take care of or supervise something

²**tend** vb 1 : move in a particular direction 2 : show a tendency

ten·den·cy \'tendənsē\ n, pl **-cies** : likelihood to move, think, or act in a particular way

¹**ten·der** \'tendər\ adj 1 : soft or delicate 2 : expressing or responsive to love or sympathy 3 : sensitive (as to touch) — **ten·der·ly** adv — **ten·der·ness** n

²**tend·er** \'tendər\ n 1 : one that tends 2 : boat providing transport to a larger ship 3 : vehicle attached to a steam locomotive for carrying fuel and water

³**tend·er** n 1 : offer of a bid for a contract 2 : something that may be offered in payment — **tender** vb

ten·der·ize \'tendəˌrīz\ vb **-ized; -iz·ing** : make (meat) tender — **ten·der·iz·er** \'tendəˌrīzər\ n

ten·der·loin \'tendərˌlȯin\ n : tender beef or pork strip from near the backbone

ten·don \'tendən\ n : cord of tissue attaching muscle to bone — **ten·di·nous** \-dənəs\ adj

ten·dril \'tendrəl\ n : slender coiling growth of some climbing plants

ten·e·ment \'tenəmənt\ n 1 : house divided into apartments 2 : shabby dwelling

te·net \'tenət\ n : principle of belief

ten·nis \'tenəs\ n : racket-and-ball game played across a net

ten·or \'tenər\ n 1 : general drift or meaning 2 : highest natural pitch male voice

ten·pin \'tenˌpin\ n : bottle-shaped pin bowled at in a game (**tenpins**)

¹**tense** \'tens\ n 1 : distinct verb form that indicates time

²**tense** adj **tens·er; tens·est** : stretched tight 2 : marked by nervous tension — **tense** vb — **tense·ly** adv — **tense·ness** n — **ten·si·ty** \'tensətē\ n

ten·sile \'tensəl, -ˌsīl\ adj : relating to tension

ten·sion \'tenchən\ n 1 : tense condition 2 : state of mental unrest or of potential hostility or opposition

tent \'tent\ n : collapsible shelter

ten·ta·cle \'tentikəl\ n : long flexible projection of an insect or mollusk — **ten·ta·cled** \-kəld\ adj — **ten·tac·u·lar** \ten'takyələr\ adj

ten·ta·tive \'tentətiv\ adj : subject to change or discussion — **ten·ta·tive·ly** adv

ten·u·ous \'tenyəwəs\ adj 1 : not dense or thick 2 : flimsy or weak — **ten·u·ous·ly** adv — **ten·u·ous·ness** n

ten·ure \'tenyər\ n : act, right, manner, or period of holding something — **ten·ured** \-yərd\ adj

te·pee \'tēˌpē\ n : conical tent

tep·id \'tepəd\ adj : moderately warm

term \'tərm\ n 1 : period of time 2 : mathematical expression 3 : special word or phrase 4 pl : conditions 5 pl : relations ∼ vb : name

ter·mi·nal \'tərmən³l\ n 1 : end 2 : device for making an electrical connection 3 : station at end of a transportation line — **terminal** adj

ter·mi·nate \'tərməˌnāt\ vb **-nat·ed; -nat·ing** : bring or come to an end — **ter·mi·na·ble** \-nəbəl\ adj — **ter·mi·na·tion** \ˌtərmə'nāshən\ n

ter·mi·nol·o·gy \ˌtərmə'näləjē\ n : terms used in a particular subject

ter·mi·nus \'tərmənəs\ n, pl **-ni** \-ˌnī\ or **-nus·es** 1 : end 2 : end of a transportation line

ter·mite \'tərˌmīt\ n : wood-eating insect

tern \'tərn\ n : small sea bird

ter·race \'terəs\ n 1 : balcony or patio 2 : bank with a flat top ∼ vb **-raced; -rac·ing** : landscape in a series of banks

ter·ra–cot·ta \,terə'kätə\ n : reddish brown earthenware

ter·rain \tə'rān\ n : features of the land

ter·ra·pin \'terəpən\ n : No. American turtle

ter·rar·i·um \tə'rareəm\ n, pl **-ia** \-ēə\ or **-i·ums** : container for keeping plants or animals

ter·res·tri·al \tə'restrēəl\ adj 1 : relating to the earth or its inhabitants 2 : living or growing on land

ter·ri·ble \'terəbəl\ adj 1 : exciting terror 2 : distressing 3 : intense 4 : of very poor quality — **ter·ri·bly** \-blē\ adv

ter·ri·er \'terēər\ n : small dog

ter·rif·ic \tə'rifik\ adj 1 : exciting terror 2 : extraordinary

ter·ri·fy \'terə,fī\ vb **-fied; -fy·ing** : fill with terror — **ter·ri·fy·ing·ly** adv

ter·ri·to·ry \'terə,tōrē\ n, pl **-ries** : particular geographical region — **ter·ri·to·ri·al** \,terə'tōrēəl\ adj

ter·ror \'terər\ n : intense fear and panic or a cause of this

ter·ror·ism \-,izəm\ n : systematic covert warfare to produce terror for political coercion — **ter·ror·ist** \-ist\ adj or n

ter·ror·ize \-,īz\ vb **-ized; -iz·ing** 1 : fill with terror 2 : coerce by threat or violence

ter·ry \'terē\ n, pl **-ries** : absorbent fabric with a loose pile

terse \'tərs\ adj **ters·er; ters·est** : concise — **terse·ly** adv — **terse·ness** n

ter·tia·ry \'tərshē,erē\ adj : of 3d rank, importance, or value

test \'test\ n : examination or evaluation ∼ vb : examine by a test — **test·er** n

tes·ta·ment \'testəmənt\ n 1 cap : division of the Bible 2 : will — **tes·ta·men·ta·ry** \,testə'mentərē\ adj

tes·ti·cle \'testikəl\ n : testis

tes·ti·fy \'testə,fī\ vb **-fied; -fy·ing** 1 : give testimony 2 : serve as evidence

tes·ti·mo·ni·al \,testə'mōnēəl\ n 1 : favorable recommendation 2 : tribute — **testimonial** adj

tes·ti·mo·ny \'testə,mōnē\ n, pl **-nies** : statement given as evidence in court

tes·tis \'testəs\ n, pl **-tes** \-,tēz\ : male reproductive gland

tes·ty \'testē\ adj **-ti·er; -est** : easily annoyed

tet·a·nus \'tet³nəs\ n : bacterial disease producing violent spasms

à tête à tête \,tätə'tät\ adv : privately ∼ n : private conversation ∼ adj : private

teth·er \'tethər\ n : leash ∼ vb : restrain with a leash

text \'tekst\ n 1 : author's words 2 : main body of printed or written matter on a page 3 : textbook 4 : scriptural passage used as the theme of a sermon 5 : topic — **tex·tu·al** \'tekschəwəl\ adj

text·book \-,buk\ n : book on a school subject

tex·tile \'tek,stīl, 'tekst³l\ n : fabric

tex·ture \'tekschər\ n 1 : feel and appearance of something 2 : structure

than \'than\ conj or prep — used in comparisons

thank \'thank\ vb : express gratitude to

thank·ful \-fəl\ adj : giving thanks — **thank·ful·ly** adv — **thank·ful·ness** n

thank·less adj : not appreciated

thanks \'thanks\ n pl : expression of gratitude

Thanks·giv·ing \thanks'givin\ n : 4th Thursday in November observed as a legal holiday for giving thanks for divine goodness

that \'that\ pron, pl **those** \'thōz\ 1 : something indicated or understood 2 : the one farther away ∼ adj, pl **those** : being the one mentioned or understood or farther away ∼ conj or pron — used to introduce a clause ∼ adv : to such an extent

thatch \'thach\ vb : cover with thatch ∼ n : covering of matted straw

thaw \'thò\ vb : melt or cause to melt — **thaw** n

the \thə, before vowel sounds usu thē\ definite article : that particular one ∼ adv — used before a comparative or superlative

the·ater, the·atre \'thēətər\ n 1 : building or room for viewing a play or movie 2 : dramatic arts

the·at·ri·cal \thē'atrikəl\ adj 1 : relating to the theater 2 : involving exaggerated emotion

thee \'thē\ pron, archaic objective case of THOU

theft \'theft\ n : act of stealing

their \\'ther\\ *adj* : relating to them

theirs \\'theərz\\ *pron* : their one or ones

the·ism \\'thē,izəm\\ *n* : belief in the existence of a god or gods — **the·ist** \-ist\ *n or adj* — **the·is·tic** \thē-'istik\ *adj*

them \\'them\\ *pron, objective case of* THEY

theme \\'thēm\\ *n* **1** : subject matter **2** : essay **3** : melody developed in a piece of music — **the·mat·ic** \thi-'matik\ *adj*

them·selves \thəm'selvz, them-\ *pron sg* : they, them — used reflexively or for emphasis

then \\'then\\ *adv* **1** : at that time **2** : soon after that **3** : in addition **4** : in that case **5** : consequently ~ *n* : that time ~ *adj* : existing at that time

thence \\'thens, 'thens\\ *adv* : from that place or fact

the·oc·ra·cy \thē'äkrəsē\ *n, pl* **-cies** : government by officials regarded as divinely inspired — **the·o·crat·ic** \,thēə'kratik\ *adj*

the·ol·o·gy \thē'äləjē\ *n, pl* **-gies** : study of religion — **the·o·lo·gian** \,thēə'lōjən\ *n* — **the·o·log·i·cal** \-'läjikəl\ *adj*

the·o·rem \\'thēərəm, 'thirəm\\ *n* : provable statement of truth

the·o·ret·i·cal \,thēə'retikəl\ *adj* : relating to or being theory — **the·o·ret·i·cal·ly** *adv*

the·o·rize \\'thēə,rīz\\ *vb* **-rized; -riz·ing** : put forth theories — **the·o·rist** *n*

the·o·ry \\'thēərē, 'thirē\\ *n, pl* **-ries** **1** : general principles of a subject **2** : plausible or scientifically acceptable explanation **3** : judgment, guess, or opinion

ther·a·peu·tic \,therə'pyütik\ *adj* : offering or relating to remedy — **ther·a·peu·ti·cal·ly** *adv*

ther·a·py \\'therəpē\\ *n, pl* **-pies** : treatment for mental or physical disorder — **ther·a·pist** \-pist\ *n*

there \\'thar\\ *adv* **1** : in, at, or to that place **2** : in that respect ~ *pron* — used to introduce a sentence or clause ~ *n* : that place or point

there·abouts, there·about \,therə'baúts, 'therə,-, -'baút\ *adv* : near that place, time, number, or quantity

there·af·ter \thar'aftər\ *adv* : after that

there·by \thar'bī, 'thar,bī\ *adv* **1** : by that means **2** : connected with or with reference to that

there·fore \\'thar,fōr\\ *adv* : for that reason

there·in \thar'in\ *adv* **1** : in or into that place, time, or thing **2** : in that respect

there·of \-'əv, -'äv\ *adv* **1** : of that or it **2** : from that

there·upon \'tharə,pón, -,pän; ,tharə-'pón, -'pän\ *adv* **1** : on that matter **2** : therefore **3** : immediately after that

there·with \thar'with, -'with\ *adv* : with that

ther·mal \\'thərməl\\ *adj* : relating to, caused by, or conserving heat — **ther·mal·ly** *adv*

ther·mo·dy·nam·ics \,thərmōdī-'namiks\ *n* : physics of heat

ther·mom·e·ter \thər'mämətər\ *n* : instrument for measuring temperature — **ther·mo·met·ric** \,thərmə-'metrik\ *adj*

ther·mos \\'thərməs\\ *n* : double-walled bottle used to keep liquids hot or cold

ther·mo·stat \\'thərmə,stat\\ *n* : automatic temperature control — **ther·mo·stat·ic** \,thərmə'statik\ *adj* — **ther·mo·stat·i·cal·ly** *adv*

the·sau·rus \thi'sórəs\ *n, pl* **-sau·ri** \-'sór,ī\ *or* **-sau·rus·es** \-'sórəsəz\ : book of words and esp. synonyms

these *pl of* THIS

the·sis \\'thēsəs\\ *n, pl* **the·ses** \'thē-,sēz\ **1** : proposition to be argued for **2** : essay embodying results of original research

thes·pi·an \\'thespēən\\ *adj* : dramatic ~ *n* : actor

they \\'thā\\ *pron* **1** : those ones **2** : people in general

thi·a·mine \\'thīəmən, -,mēn\\ *n* : essential vitamin

thick \\'thik\\ *adj* **1** : having relatively great mass from front to back or top to bottom **2** : viscous ~ *n* : most crowded or thickest part — **thick·ly** *adv* — **thick·ness** *n*

thick·en \\'thikən\\ *vb* : make or become thick — **thick·en·er** \-ənər\ *n*

thick·et \\'thikət\\ *n* : dense growth of bushes or small trees

thick–skinned \-'skind\ *adj* : insensitive to criticism

thief \\'thēf\\ *n, pl* **thieves** \'thēvz\ : one that steals

thieve \\'thēv\\ *vb* **thieved; thiev·ing** : steal — **thiev·ery** *n*

thigh \\'thī\\ *n* : upper part of the leg

thigh·bone \\'thī,bōn\\ *n* : femur

thim·ble \\'thimbəl\\ *n* : protective cap

for the finger in sewing — **thim·ble·ful** n

thin \'thin\ adj **-nn- 1** : having relatively little mass from front to back or top to bottom **2** : not closely set or placed **3** : relatively free flowing **4** : lacking substance, fullness, or strength ∼ vb **-nn-** : make or become thin — **thin·ly** adv — **thin·ness** n

thing \'thiŋ\ n **1** : matter of concern **2** : event or act **3** : object **4** pl : possessions

think \'thiŋk\ vb **thought** \'thȯt\; **think·ing 1** : form or have in the mind **2** : have as an opinion **3** : ponder **4** : devise by thinking **5** : imagine — **think·er** n

thin–skinned adj : extremely sensitive to criticism

third \'thərd\ adj **1** : being number 3 in a countable series ∼ n **1** : one that is third **2** : one of 3 equal parts — **third, third·ly** adv

third dimension n : thickness or depth — **third–dimensional** adj

third world n : less developed nations of the world

thirst \'thərst\ n **1** : dryness in mouth and throat **2** : intense desire ∼ vb : feel thirst — **thirsty** adj

thir·teen \thər'tēn\ n : one more than 12 — **thirteen** adj or pron — **thir·teenth** \-'tēnth\ adj or n

thir·ty \'thərtē\ n, pl **thirties** : 3 times 10 — **thir·ti·eth** \-ēəth\ adj or n — **thirty** adj or pron

this \'this\ pron, pl **these** \'thēz\ : something close or under immediate discussion ∼ adj, pl **these** : being the one near, present, just mentioned, or more immediately under observation ∼ adv : to such an extent or degree

this·tle \'thisəl\ n : tall prickly herb

thith·er \'thithər\ adv : to that place

thong \'thȯŋ\ n : strip of leather or hide

tho·rax \'thȯr,aks\ n, pl **-rax·es** or **-races** \'thȯrə,sēz\ **1** : part of the body between neck and abdomen **2** : middle of 3 divisions of an insect body — **tho·rac·ic** \thə'rasik\ adj

thorn \'thȯrn\ n : sharp spike on a plant or a plant bearing these — **thorny** adj

thor·ough \'thərō\ adj : omitting or overlooking nothing — **thor·ough·ly** adv — **thor·ough·ness** n

thor·ough·bred \'thərə,bred\ n **1** cap : light speedy racing horse **2** : one of excellent quality — **thoroughbred** adj

thor·ough·fare \'thərə,far\ n : public road

those pl of THAT

thou \'thaů\ pron, archaic : you

though \'thō\ adv : however ∼ conj **1** : despite the fact that **2** : granting that

thought \'thȯt\ past of THINK n **1** : process of thinking **2** : serious consideration **3** : idea

thought·ful \-fəl\ adj **1** : absorbed in or showing thought **2** : considerate of others — **thought·ful·ly** adv — **thought·ful·ness** n

thought·less \-ləs\ adj **1** : careless or reckless **2** : lacking concern for others — **thought·less·ly** adv

thou·sand \'thauz²nd\ n, pl **-sands** or **-sand** : 10 times 100 — **thousand** adj — **thou·sandth** \-²nth\ adj or n

thrash \'thrash\ vb **1** : thresh **2** : beat **3** : move about violently — **thrash·er** n

thread \'thred\ n **1** : fine line of fibers **2** : train of thought **3** : ridge around a screw ∼ vb **1** : pass thread through **2** : put together on a thread **3** : make one's way through or between

thread·bare adj **1** : worn so that the thread shows **2** : trite

threat \'thret\ n **1** : expression of intention to harm **2** : thing that threatens

threat·en \'thret²n\ vb **1** : utter threats **2** : show signs of being near or impending — **threat·en·ing·ly** adv

three \'thrē\ n **1** : one more than 2 **2** : 3d in a set or series — **three** adj or pron

three·fold \'thrē,fōld\ adj : triple — **three·fold** \-'fōld\ adv

three·score adj : being 3 times 20

thresh \'thresh, 'thrash\ vb : beat to separate grain — **thresh·er** n

thresh·old \'thresh,ōld\ n **1** : sill of a door **2** : beginning stage

threw past of THROW

thrice \'thrīs\ adv : 3 times

thrift \'thrift\ n : careful management or saving of money — **thrift·i·ly** \'thriftəlē\ adv — **thrifty** adj

thrill \'thril\ vb **1** : have or cause to have a sudden sharp feeling of excitement **2** : tremble — **thrill** n — **thrill·er** n — **thrill·ing·ly** adv

thrive \'thrīv\ vb **throve** \'thrōv\ or

thrived; thriv·en \'thrivən\ 1 : grow vigorously 2 : prosper

throat \'thrōt\ n 1 : front part of the neck 2 : passage to the stomach — **throat·ed** adj — **throaty** adj

throb \'thräb\ vb **-bb-** : pulsate — **throb** n

throe \'thrō\ n 1 : pang or spasm 2 pl : hard or painful struggle

throne \'thrōn\ n : chair representing power or sovereignty

throng \'thrȯŋ\ n or vb : crowd

throt·tle \'thrät°l\ vb **-tled; -tling** : choke ~ n : valve regulating volume of fuel and air delivered to engine cylinders

through \'thrü\ prep 1 : into at one side and out at the other side of 2 : by way of 3 : among, between, or all around 4 : because of 5 : throughout the time of ~ \'thrü\ adv 1 : from one end or side to the other 2 : from beginning to end 3 : to the core 4 : into the open ~ adj 1 : going directly from origin to destination 2 : finished

through·out \thrü'aút\ adv 1 : everywhere 2 : from beginning to end ~ prep 1 : in or to every part of 2 : during the whole of

throve past of THRIVE

throw \'thrō\ vb **threw** \'thrü\; **thrown** \'thrōn\; **throw·ing** 1 : propel through the air 2 : cause to fall or fall off 3 : put suddenly in a certain position or condition 4 : move quickly as if throwing 5 : put on or off hastily — **throw** n — **throw·er** \'thrōər\ n — **throw up** vb : vomit

thrush \'thrəsh\ n : songbird

thrust \'thrəst\ vb **thrust; thrust·ing** 1 : shove forward 2 : stab or pierce — **thrust** n

thud \'thəd\ n : dull sound of something falling — **thud** vb

thug \'thəg\ n : ruffian or gangster

thumb \'thəm\ n 1 : short thick division of the hand opposing the fingers 2 : glove part for the thumb ~ vb : leaf through with the thumb — **thumb·nail** n

thump \'thəmp\ vb : strike with something thick or heavy causing a dull sound — **thump** n

thun·der \'thəndər\ n : sound following lightning — **thunder** vb — **thun·der·clap** n — **thun·der·ous** \'thəndərəs\ adj — **thun·der·ous·ly** adv

thun·der·bolt \-,bōlt\ n : discharge of lightning with thunder

thun·der·show·er \'thəndər,shaúər\ n : shower with thunder and lightning

thun·der·storm n : storm with thunder and lightning

Thurs·day \'thərzdā, -dē\ n : 5th day of the week

thus \'thəs\ adv 1 : in this or that way 2 : to this degree or extent 3 : because of this or that

thwart \'thwȯrt\ vb : block or defeat

thy \'thī\ adj, archaic : your

thyme \'tīm, 'thīm\ n : cooking herb

thy·roid \'thī,rȯid\ adj : relating to a large endocrine gland (**thyroid gland**)

thy·self \thī'self\ pron, archaic : yourself

ti·ara \tē'arə, -'är-\ n : decorative formal headband

tib·ia \'tibēə\ n, pl **-i·ae** \-ē,ē\ : bone between the knee and ankle

tic \'tik\ n : twitching of facial muscles

¹**tick** \'tik\ n : small 8-legged bloodsucking animal

²**tick** n 1 : light rhythmic tap or beat 2 : check mark ~ vb 1 : make ticks 2 : mark with a tick 3 : operate

tick·er \'tikər\ n 1 : something (as a watch) that ticks 2 : telegraph instrument that prints on paper tape

tick·et \'tikət\ n 1 : tag showing price, payment of a fee or fare, or a traffic offense 2 : list of candidates ~ vb : put a ticket on

tick·ing \'tikiŋ\ n : fabric covering of a mattress

tick·le \'tikəl\ vb **-led; -ling** 1 : please or amuse 2 : touch lightly causing uneasiness, laughter, or spasmodic movements — **tickle** n

tick·lish \'tiklish\ adj 1 : sensitive to tickling 2 : requiring delicate handling — **tick·lish·ness** n

tid·al wave \'tīd°l-\ n : high sea wave following an earthquake

tid·bit \'tid,bit\ n : choice morsel

tide \'tīd\ n : alternate rising and falling of the sea ~ vb **tid·ed; tid·ing** : be enough to allow (one) to get by for a time — **tid·al** \'tīd°l\ adj — **tide·wa·ter** n

tid·ings \'tīdiŋz\ n pl : news or message

ti·dy \'tīdē\ adj **-di·er; -est** 1 : well ordered and cared for 2 : large or substantial — **ti·di·ness** n — **tidy** vb

tie \'tī\ *n* **1** : line or ribbon for fastening, uniting, or closing **2** : cross support to which railroad rails are fastened **3** : uniting force **4** : equality in score or tally or a deadlocked contest **5** : necktie ~ *vb* **tied; ty•ing** *or* **tie•ing 1** : fasten or close by wrapping and knotting a tie **2** : form a knot in **3** : gain the same score or tally as an opponent

tier \'tir\ *n* : one of a steplike series of rows

tiff \'tif\ *n* : petty quarrel — **tiff** *vb*

ti•ger \'tīgər\ *n* : very large black-striped cat — **ti•ger•ish** \-gərish\ *adj* — **ti•gress** \-grəs\ *n*

tight \'tīt\ *adj* **1** : fitting close together esp. so as not to allow air or water in **2** : held very firmly **3** : taut **4** : fitting too snugly **5** : difficult **6** : stingy **7** : evenly contested **8** : low in supply — **tight** *adv* — **tight•en** \-ᵊn\ *vb* — **tight•ly** *adv* — **tight•ness** *n*

tights \'tīts\ *n pl* : skintight garments

tight•wad \'tīt,wäd\ *n* : stingy person

tile \'tīl\ *n* : thin piece of stone or fired clay used on roofs, floors, or walls ~ *vb* : cover with tiles

¹till \'til\ *prep or conj* : until

²till *vb* : cultivate (soil) — **till•able** *adj*

³till *n* : money drawer

¹till•er \'tilər\ *n* : one that cultivates soil

²till•er \'tilər\ *n* : lever for turning a boat's rudder

tilt \'tilt\ *vb* : cause to incline ~ *n* : slant

tim•ber \'timbər\ *n* **1** : cut wood for building **2** : large squared piece of wood **3** : wooded land or trees for timber ~ *vb* : cover, frame, or support with timbers — **tim•bered** *adj* — **tim•ber•land** \-,land\ *n*

tim•bre \'tambər, 'tim-\ *n* : sound quality

time \'tīm\ *n* **1** : period during which something exists or continues or can be accomplished **2** : point at which something happens **3** : customary hour **4** : age **5** : tempo **6** : moment, hour, day, or year as indicated by a clock or calendar **7** : one's experience during a particular period ~ *vb* **timed; tim•ing 1** : arrange or set the time of **2** : determine or record the time, duration, or rate of — **time•keep•er** *n* — **time•less** *adj* — **time•less•ness** *n* — **time•li•ness** *n* — **time•ly** *adv* — **tim•er** *n*

time•piece *n* : device to show time

times \'tīmz\ *prep* : multiplied by

time•ta•ble \'tīm,tābəl\ *n* : table of departure and arrival times

tim•id \'timəd\ *adj* : lacking in courage or self-confidence — **ti•mid•i•ty** \tə'midətē\ *n* — **tim•id•ly** *adv*

tim•o•rous \'timərəs\ *adj* : fearful — **tim•o•rous•ly** *adv* — **tim•o•rous•ness** *n*

tim•pa•ni \'timpənē\ *n pl* : set of kettledrums — **tim•pa•nist** \-nist\ *n*

tin \'tin\ *n* **1** : soft white metallic chemical element **2** : metal food can

tinc•ture \'tiŋkchər\ *n* : alcoholic solution of a medicine

tin•der \'tindər\ *n* : substance used to kindle a fire

tine \'tīn\ *n* : one of the points of a fork

tin•foil \'tin,fȯil\ *n* : thin metal sheeting

tinge \'tinj\ *vb* **tinged; tinge•ing** *or* **ting•ing** \'tinjiŋ\ **1** : color slightly **2** : affect with a slight odor ~ *n* : slight coloring or flavor

tin•gle \'tiŋgəl\ *vb* **-gled; -gling** : feel a ringing, stinging, or thrilling sensation — **tingle** *n*

tin•ker \'tiŋkər\ *vb* : experiment in or repairing something — **tin•ker•er** *n*

tin•kle \'tiŋkəl\ *vb* **-kled; -kling** : make or cause to make a high ringing sound — **tinkle** *n*

tin•sel \'tinsəl\ *n* : decorative thread or strip of glittering metal or paper

tint \'tint\ *n* **1** : slight or pale coloration **2** : color shade ~ *vb* : give a tint to

ti•ny \'tīnē\ *adj* **-ni•er; -est** : very small

¹tip \'tip\ *vb* **-pp- 1** : overturn **2** : lean ~ *n* : act or state of tipping

²tip *n* : pointed end of something ~ *vb* **-pp- 1** : furnish with a tip **2** : cover the tip of

³tip *n* : small sum given for a service performed ~ *vb* : give a tip to

⁴tip *n* : piece of confidential information ~ *vb* **-pp-** : give confidential information to

tip-off \'tip,ȯf\ *n* : indication

tip•ple \'tipəl\ *vb* **-pled; -pling** : drink intoxicating liquor esp. habitually or excessively — **tip•pler** *n*

tip•sy \'tipsē\ *adj* **-si•er; -est** : unsteady or foolish from alcohol

tip•toe \'tip,tō\ *n* : the toes of the feet ~ *adv or adj* : supported on tiptoe ~ *vb* **-toed; -toe•ing** : walk quietly or on tiptoe

tip–top *n* : highest point ~ *adj* : excellent

ti•rade \tī'rād, 'tī,-\ *n* : prolonged speech of abuse

¹**tire** \'tīr\ *vb* **tired; tir•ing** 1 : make or become weary 2 : wear out the patience of — **tire•less** *adj* — **tire•less•ly** *adv* — **tire•some** \-səm\ *adj* — **tire•some•ly** *adv*

²**tire** *n* : rubber cushion encircling a car wheel

tired \'tīrd\ *adj* : weary

tis•sue \'tishü\ *n* 1 : soft absorbent paper 2 : layer of cells forming a basic structural element of an animal or plant body

ti•tan•ic \tī'tanik, tə-\ *adj* : gigantic

ti•ta•ni•um \tī'tānēəm, tə-\ *n* : gray light strong metallic chemical element

tithe \'tīth\ *n* : tenth part paid or given esp. for the support of a church — **tithe** *vb* — **tith•er** *n*

tit•il•late \'tit²l,āt\ *vb* **-lat•ed; -lat•ing** : excite pleasurably — **tit•il•la•tion** \,tit²l'āshən\ *n*

ti•tle \'tīt²l\ *n* 1 : legal ownership 2 : distinguishing name 3 : designation of honor, rank, or office 4 : championship — **ti•tled** *adj*

tit•ter \'titər\ *n* : nervous or affected laugh — **titter** *vb*

tit•u•lar \'tichələr\ *adj* 1 : existing in title only 2 : relating to or bearing a title

tiz•zy \'tizē\ *n, pl* **tizzies** : state of agitation or worry

TNT \,tē,en'tē\ *n* : high explosive

to \'tü\ *prep* 1 : in the direction of 2 : at, on, or near 3 : resulting in 4 : before or until 5 — used to show a relationship or object of a verb 6 — used with an infinitive ~ *adv* 1 : forward 2 : to a state of consciousness

toad \'tōd\ *n* : tailless leaping amphibian

toad•stool \-,stül\ *n* : mushroom esp. when inedible or poisonous

toady \'tōdē\ *n, pl* **toad•ies** : one who flatters to gain favors — **toady** *vb*

toast \'tōst\ *vb* 1 : make (as a slice of bread) crisp and brown 2 : drink in honor of someone or something ~ *n* 1 : toasted sliced bread 2 : act of drinking in honor of someone — **toast•er** *n*

to•bac•co \tə'bakō\ *n, pl* **-cos** : broadleaved herb or its leaves prepared for smoking or chewing

to•bog•gan \tə'bägən\ *n* : long flatbottomed light sled ~ *vb* : coast on a toboggan

to•day \tə'dā\ *adv* 1 : on or for this day 2 : at the present time ~ *n* : present day or time

tod•dle \'täd²l\ *vb* **-dled; -dling** : walk with tottering steps like a young child — **toddle** *n* — **tod•dler** \'täd²lər\ *n*

to–do \tə'dü\ *n, pl* **to–dos** \-'düz\ : disturbance or fuss

toe \'tō\ *n* : one of the 5 end divisions of the foot — **toe•nail** *n*

tof•fee, tof•fy \'tòfē, 'tä-\ *n, pl* **toffees** *or* **toffies** : candy made of boiled sugar and butter

to•ga \'tōgə\ *n* : loose outer garment of ancient Rome

to•geth•er \tə'gethər\ *adv* 1 : in or into one place or group 2 : in or into contact or association 3 : at one time 4 : as a group — **to•geth•er•ness** *n*

togs \'tägz, 'tògz\ *n pl* : clothing

toil \'tòil\ *vb* : work hard and long — **toil** *n* — **toil•er** *n* — **toil•some** *adj*

toi•let \'tòilət\ *n* 1 : dressing and grooming oneself 2 : bathroom 3 : water basin to urinate and defecate in

to•ken \'tōkən\ *n* 1 : outward sign or expression of something 2 : small part representing the whole 3 : piece resembling a coin

told *past of* TELL

tol•er•a•ble \'tälərəbəl\ *adj* 1 : capable of being endured 2 : moderately good — **tol•er•a•bly** \-blē\ *adv*

tol•er•ance \'tälərəns\ *n* 1 : lack of opposition for beliefs or practices differing from one's own 2 : capacity for enduring 3 : allowable deviation — **tol•er•ant** *adj* — **tol•er•ant•ly** *adv*

tol•er•ate \'tälə,rāt\ *vb* **-at•ed; -at•ing** 1 : allow to be or to be done without opposition 2 : endure or resist the action of — **tol•er•a•tion** \,tälə'rāshən\ *n*

¹**toll** \'tōl\ *n* 1 : fee paid for a privilege or service 2 : cost of achievement in loss or suffering — **toll•booth** *n* — **toll•gate** *n*

²**toll** *vb* 1 : cause the sounding of (a bell) 2 : sound with slow measured strokes ~ *n* : sound of a tolling bell

tom•a•hawk \'tämə,hòk\ *n* : light ax used as a weapon by American Indians

to•ma•to \tə'mātō, -'mät-\ *n, pl* **-toes** : tropical American herb or its fruit

tomb \'tüm\ *n* : house, vault, or grave for burial

tom·boy \'täm‚bȯi\ *n* : girl who behaves in a manner usu. considered boyish

tomb·stone *n* : stone marking a grave

tom·cat \'täm‚kat\ *n* : male cat

tome \'tōm\ *n* : large or weighty book

to·mor·row \tə'märō\ *adv* : on or for the day after today — **tomorrow** *n*

tom-tom \'täm‚täm\ *n* : small-headed drum beaten with the hands

ton \'tən\ *n* : unit of weight equal to 2000 pounds

tone \'tōn\ *n* **1** : vocal or musical sound **2** : sound of definite pitch **3** : manner of speaking that expresses an emotion or attitude **4** : color quality **5** : healthy condition **6** : general character or quality ～ *vb* : soften or muffle — often used with *down* — **ton·al** \-ᵊl\ *adj* — **to·nal·i·ty** \tō'nalətē\ *n*

tongs \'tänz, 'tȯnz\ *n pl* : grasping device of 2 joined or hinged pieces

tongue \'tən\ *n* **1** : fleshy movable organ of the mouth **2** : language **3** : something long and flat and fastened at one end — **tongued** \'tənd\ *adj* — **tongue·less** *adj*

ton·ic \'tänik\ *n* : something (as a drug) that invigorates or restores health — **tonic** *adj*

to·night \tə'nīt\ *adv* : on this night ～ *n* : present or coming night

ton·sil \'tänsəl\ *n* : either of a pair of oval masses in the throat — **ton·sil·lec·to·my** \‚tänsə'lektəmē\ *n* — **ton·sil·li·tis** \-'lītəs\ *n*

too \'tü\ *adv* **1** : in addition **2** : excessively

took *past of* TAKE

tool \'tül\ *n* : device worked by hand ～ *vb* : shape or finish with a tool

tool·bar \'tül‚bär\ *n* : strip of icons on a computer display providing quick access to pictured functions

toot \'tüt\ *vb* : sound or cause to sound esp. in short blasts — **toot** *n*

tooth \'tüth\ *n, pl* **teeth** \'tēth\ **1** : one of the hard structures in the jaws for chewing **2** : one of the projections on the edge of a gear wheel — **tooth·ache** *n* — **tooth·brush** *n* — **toothed** \'tütht\ *adj* — **tooth·less** *adj* — **tooth·paste** *n* — **tooth·pick** *n*

tooth·some \'tüthsəm\ *adj* **1** : delicious **2** : attractive

¹**top** \'täp\ *n* **1** : highest part or level of something **2** : lid or covering ～ *vb* **-pp- 1** : cover with a top **2** : surpass **3** : go over the top of ～ *adj* : being at the top — **topped** *adj*

²**top** *n* : spinning toy

to·paz \'tō‚paz\ *n* : hard gem

top·coat *n* : lightweight overcoat

top·ic \'täpik\ *n* : subject for discussion or study

top·i·cal \-ikəl\ *adj* **1** : relating to or arranged by topics **2** : relating to current or local events — **top·i·cal·ly** *adv*

top·most \'täp‚mōst\ *adj* : highest of all

top-notch \-'näch\ *adj* : of the highest quality

to·pog·ra·phy \tə'pägrəfē\ *n* **1** : art of mapping the physical features of a place **2** : outline of the form of a place — **to·pog·ra·pher** \-fər\ *n* — **top·o·graph·ic** \‚täpə'grafik\, **top·o·graph·i·cal** \-ikəl\ *adj*

top·ple \'täpəl\ *vb* **-pled; -pling** : fall or cause to fall

top·sy-tur·vy \‚täpsē'tərvē\ *adv or adj* **1** : upside down **2** : in utter confusion

torch \'tȯrch\ *n* : flaming light — **torch·bear·er** *n* — **torch·light** *n*

tore *past of* TEAR

tor·ment \'tȯr‚ment\ *n* : extreme pain or anguish or a source of this ～ *vb* **1** : cause severe anguish to **2** : harass — **tor·men·tor** \-ər\ *n*

torn *past part of* TEAR

tor·na·do \tȯr'nādō\ *n, pl* **-does** *or* **-dos** : violent destructive whirling wind

tor·pe·do \tȯr'pēdō\ *n, pl* **-does** : self-propelled explosive submarine missile ～ *vb* : hit with a torpedo

tor·pid \'tȯrpəd\ *adj* **1** : having lost motion or the power of exertion **2** : lacking vigor — **tor·pid·i·ty** \tȯr'pidətē\ *n*

tor·por \'tȯrpər\ *n* : extreme sluggishness or lethargy

torque \'tȯrk\ *n* : turning force

tor·rent \'tȯrənt\ *n* **1** : rushing stream **2** : tumultuous outburst — **tor·ren·tial** \tȯ'renchəl, tə-\ *adj*

tor·rid \'tȯrəd\ *adj* **1** : parched with heat **2** : impassioned

tor·sion \'tȯrshən\ *n* : a twisting or being twisted — **tor·sion·al** \'tȯrshənəl\ *adj* — **tor·sion·al·ly** *adv*

tor·so \'tȯrsō\ *n, pl* **-sos** *or* **-si** \-‚sē\ : trunk of the human body

tor·til·la \tȯr'tēyə\ *n* : round flat cornmeal or wheat flour bread

tor·toise \'tȯrtəs\ *n* : land turtle

tor·tu·ous \'tȯrchəwəs\ *adj* 1 : winding 2 : tricky

tor·ture \'tȯrchər\ *n* 1 : use of pain to punish or force 2 : agony ∼ *vb* **-tured; -tur·ing** : inflict torture on — **tor·tur·er** *n*

toss \'tȯs, 'täs\ *vb* 1 : move to and fro or up and down violently 2 : throw with a quick light motion 3 : move restlessly — **toss** *n*

toss–up *n* 1 : a deciding by flipping a coin 2 : even chance

tot \'tät\ *n* : small child

to·tal \'tōtᵊl\ *n* : entire amount ∼ *vb* **-taled** *or* **-talled; -tal·ing** *or* **-tal·ling** 1 : add up 2 : amount to — **total** *adj* — **to·tal·ly** *adv*

to·tal·i·tar·i·an \tō,talə'terēən\ *adj* : relating to a political system in which the government has complete control over the people — **totalitarian** *n* — **to·tal·i·tar·i·an·ism** \-ēə,nizəm\ *n*

to·tal·i·ty \tō'talətē\ *n, pl* **-ties** : whole amount or entirety

tote \'tōt\ *vb* **tot·ed; tot·ing** : carry

to·tem \'tōtəm\ *n* : often carved figure used as a family or tribe emblem

tot·ter \'tätər\ *vb* 1 : sway as if about to fall 2 : stagger

touch \'təch\ *vb* 1 : make contact with so as to feel 2 : be or cause to be in contact 3 : take into the hands or mouth 4 : treat or mention a subject 5 : relate or concern 6 : move to sympathetic feeling ∼ *n* 1 : light stroke 2 : act or fact of touching or being touched 3 : sense of feeling 4 : trace 5 : state of being in contact — **touch up** *vb* : improve with minor changes

touch·down \'təch,daủn\ *n* : scoring of 6 points in football

touch·stone *n* : test or criterion of genuineness or quality

touchy \'təchē\ *adj* **touch·i·er; -est** 1 : easily offended 2 : requiring tact

tough \'təf\ *adj* 1 : strong but elastic 2 : not easily chewed 3 : severe or disciplined 4 : stubborn ∼ *n* : rowdy — **tough·ly** *adv* — **tough·ness** *n*

tough·en \'təfən\ *vb* : make or become tough

tou·pee \tü'pā\ *n* : small wig for a bald spot

tour \'tủr\ *n* 1 : period of time spent at work or on an assignment 2 : journey with a return to the starting point ∼ *vb* : travel over to see the sights — **tour·ist** \'tủrist\ *n*

tour·na·ment \'tủrnəmənt, 'tər-\ *n* 1 : medieval jousting competition 2 : championship series of games

tour·ney \-nē\ *n, pl* **-neys** : tournament

tour·ni·quet \'tủrnikət, 'tər-\ *n* : tight bandage for stopping blood flow

tou·sle \'taủzəl\ *vb* **-sled; -sling** : dishevel (as someone's hair)

tout \'taủt, 'tüt\ *vb* : praise or publicize loudly

tow \'tō\ *vb* : pull along behind — **tow** *n*

to·ward, to·wards \'tōrd, tə'wȯrd, 'tȯrdz, tə'wȯrdz\ *prep* 1 : in the direction of 2 : with respect to 3 : in part payment on

tow·el \'taủəl\ *n* : absorbent cloth or paper for wiping or drying

tow·er \'taủər\ *n* : tall structure ∼ *vb* : rise to a great height — **tow·ered** \'taủərd\ *adj* — **tow·er·ing** *adj*

tow·head \'tō,hed\ *n* : person having whitish blond hair — **tow·head·ed** \-,hedəd\ *adj*

town \'taủn\ *n* 1 : small residential area 2 : city — **towns·peo·ple** \'taủnz-,pēpəl\ *n pl*

town·ship \'taủn,ship\ *n* 1 : unit of local government 2 : 36 square miles of U.S. public land

tox·ic \'täksik\ *adj* : poisonous — **tox·ic·i·ty** \täk'sisətē\ *n*

tox·in \'täksən\ *n* : poison produced by an organism

toy \'tȯi\ *n* : something for a child to play with ∼ *vb* : amuse oneself or play with something ∼ *adj* 1 : designed as a toy 2 : very small

¹**trace** \'trās\ *vb* **traced; trac·ing** 1 : mark over the lines of (a drawing) 2 : follow the trail or the development of ∼ *n* 1 : track 2 : tiny amount or residue — **trace·able** *adj* — **trac·er** *n*

²**trace** *n* : line of a harness

tra·chea \'trākēə\ *n, pl* **-che·ae** \-kē,ē\ : windpipe — **tra·che·al** \-kēəl\ *adj*

track \'trak\ *n* 1 : trail left by wheels or footprints 2 : racing course 3 : train rails 4 : awareness of a progression 5 : looped belts propelling a vehicle ∼ *vb* 1 : follow the trail of 2 : make tracks on — **track·er** *n*

track–and–field *adj* : relating to athletic contests of running, jumping, and throwing events

¹**tract** \'trakt\ *n* 1 : stretch of land 2 : system of body organs

²**tract** *n* : pamphlet of propaganda

trac·ta·ble \'traktəbəl\ *adj* : easily controlled

trac·tion \'trakshən\ *n* : gripping power to permit movement — **trac·tion·al** \-shənəl\ *adj* — **trac·tive** \'traktiv\ *adj*

trac·tor \'traktər\ *n* **1** : farm vehicle used esp. for pulling **2** : truck for hauling a trailer

trade \'trād\ *n* **1** : one's regular business **2** : occupation requiring skill **3** : the buying and selling of goods **4** : act of trading ∼ *vb* **trad·ed; trad·ing** **1** : give in exchange for something **2** : buy and sell goods **3** : be a regular customer — **trades·peo·ple** \'trādz,pēpəl\ *n pl*

trade–in \'trād,in\ *n* : an item traded to a merchant at the time of a purchase

trade·mark \'trād,märk\ *n* : word or mark identifying a manufacturer — **trademark** *vb*

trades·man \'trādzmən\ *n* : shopkeeper

tra·di·tion \trə'dishən\ *n* : belief or custom passed from generation to generation — **tra·di·tion·al** \-'dishənəl\ *adj* — **tra·di·tion·al·ly** *adv*

tra·duce \trə'düs, -'dyüs\ *vb* **-duced; -duc·ing** : lower the reputation of — **tra·duc·er** *n*

traf·fic \'trafik\ *n* **1** : business dealings **2** : movement along a route ∼ *vb* : do business — **traf·fick·er** *n* — **traffic light** *n*

trag·e·dy \'trajədē\ *n, pl* **-dies 1** : serious drama describing a conflict and having a sad end **2** : disastrous event

trag·ic \'trajik\ *adj* : being a tragedy — **trag·i·cal·ly** *adv*

trail \'trāl\ *vb* **1** : hang down and drag along the ground **2** : draw along behind **3** : follow the track of **4** : dwindle ∼ *n* **1** : something that trails **2** : path or evidence left by something

trail·er \'trālər\ *n* **1** : vehicle intended to be hauled **2** : dwelling designed to be towed to a site

train \'trān\ *n* **1** : trailing part of a gown **2** : retinue or procession **3** : connected series **4** : group of linked railroad cars ∼ *vb* **1** : cause to grow as desired **2** : make or become prepared or skilled **3** : point — **train·ee** *n* — **train·er** *n* — **train·load** *n*

traipse \'trāps\ *vb* **traipsed; traips·ing** : walk

trait \'trāt\ *n* : distinguishing quality

trai·tor \'trātər\ *n* : one who betrays a trust or commits treason — **trai·tor·ous** *adj*

tra·jec·to·ry \trə'jektərē\ *n, pl* **-ries** : path of something moving through air or space

tram·mel \'traməl\ *vb* **-meled** *or* **-melled; -mel·ing** *or* **-mel·ling** : impede — **trammel** *n*

tramp \'tramp\ *vb* **1** : walk or hike **2** : tread on ∼ *n* : beggar or vagrant

tram·ple \'trampəl\ *vb* **-pled; -pling** : walk or step on so as to bruise or crush — **trample** *n* — **tram·pler** \-plər\ *n*

tram·po·line \,trampə'lēn, 'trampə,-\ *n* : resilient sheet or web supported by springs and used for bouncing — **tram·po·lin·ist** \-'ist\ *n*

trance \'trans\ *n* **1** : sleeplike condition **2** : state of mystical absorption

tran·quil \'traŋkwəl, 'tran-\ *adj* : quiet and undisturbed — **tran·quil·ize** \-kwə,līz\ *vb* — **tran·quil·iz·er** *n* — **tran·quil·li·ty, tran·quil·i·ty** \tran-'kwilətē, traŋ-\ *n* — **tran·quil·ly** *adv*

trans·act \trans'akt, tranz-\ *vb* : conduct (business)

trans·ac·tion \-'akshən\ *n* **1** : business deal **2** *pl* : records of proceedings

tran·scend \trans'end\ *vb* : rise above or surpass — **tran·scen·dent** \-'endənt\ *adj* — **tran·scen·den·tal** \,trans,en'dent²l, -ən-\ *adj*

tran·scribe \trans'krīb\ *vb* **-scribed; -scrib·ing** : make a copy, arrangement, or recording of — **tran·scrip·tion** \trans'kripshən\ *n*

tran·script \'trans,kript\ *n* : official copy

tran·sept \'trans,ept\ *n* : part of a church that crosses the nave at right angles

trans·fer \trans'fər, 'trans,fər\ *vb* **-rr- 1** : move from one person, place, or situation to another **2** : convey ownership of **3** : print or copy by contact **4** : change to another vehicle or transportation line ∼ \'trans,fər\ *n* **1** : act or process of transferring **2** : one that transfers or is transferred **3** : ticket permitting one to transfer — **trans·fer·able** \trans'fərəbəl\ *adj* — **trans·fer·al** \-əl\ *n* — **trans·fer·ence** \-əns\ *n*

trans·fig·ure \trans'figyər\ *vb* **-ured; -ur·ing 1** : change the form or appearance of **2** : glorify — **trans·fig·u·ra·tion** \ˌtrans·figyə'rāshən\ n

trans·fix \trans'fiks\ vb **1** : pierce through **2** : hold motionless

trans·form \-'form\ vb **1** : change in structure, appearance, or character **2** : change (an electric current) in potential or type — **trans·for·ma·tion** \ˌtransfər'māshən\ n — **trans·form·er** \trans'formər\ n

trans·fuse \trans'fyüz\ vb **-fused; -fus·ing 1** : diffuse into or through **2** : transfer (as blood) into a vein — **trans·fu·sion** \-'fyüzhən\ n

trans·gress \trans'gres, tranz-\ vb : sin — **trans·gres·sion** \-'greshən\ n — **trans·gres·sor** \-'gresər\ n

tran·sient \'tranchənt\ adj : not lasting or staying long — **transient** n — **tran·sient·ly** adv

tran·sis·tor \tranz'istər, trans-\ n : small electronic device used in electronic equipment — **tran·sis·tor·ize** \-tə‚rīz\ vb

tran·sit \'transət, 'tranz-\ n **1** : movement over, across, or through **2** : local and esp. public transportation **3** : surveyor's instrument

tran·si·tion \trans'ishən, tranz-\ n : passage from one state, stage, or subject to another — **tran·si·tion·al** \-'ishənəl\ adj

tran·si·to·ry \'transə‚tōrē, 'tranz-\ adj : of brief duration

trans·late \trans'lāt, tranz-\ vb **-lat·ed; -lat·ing** : change into another language — **trans·lat·able** adj — **trans·la·tion** \-'lāshən\ n — **trans·la·tor** \-'lātər\ n

trans·lu·cent \trans'lüs³nt, tranz-\ adj : not transparent but clear enough to allow light to pass through — **trans·lu·cence** \-³ns\ n — **trans·lu·cen·cy** \-³nsē\ n — **trans·lu·cent·ly** adv

trans·mis·sion \-'mishən\ n **1** : act or process of transmitting **2** : system of gears between a car engine and drive wheels

trans·mit \-'mit\ vb **-tt- 1** : transfer from one person or place to another **2** : pass on by inheritance **3** : broadcast — **trans·mis·si·ble** \-'misəbəl\ adj — **trans·mit·ta·ble** \-'mitəbəl\ adj — **trans·mit·tal** \-'mit³l\ n — **trans·mit·ter** n

tran·som \'transəm\ n : often hinged window above a door

trans·par·ent \trans'parənt\ adj **1**

: clear enough to see through **2** : obvious — **trans·par·en·cy** \-ənsē\ n — **trans·par·ent·ly** adv

tran·spire \trans'pīr\ vb **-spired; -spir·ing** : take place — **tran·spi·ra·tion** \ˌtranspə'rāshən\ n

trans·plant \trans'plant\ vb **1** : dig up and move to another place **2** : transfer from one body part or person to another — **transplant** \'trans‚-\ n — **trans·plan·ta·tion** \ˌtrans‚plan'tāshən\ n

trans·port \trans'pōrt\ vb **1** : carry or deliver to another place **2** : carry away by emotion ~ \'trans‚-\ n **1** : act of transporting **2** : rapture **3** : ship or plane for carrying troops or supplies — **trans·por·ta·tion** \ˌtranspər'tāshən\ n — **trans·port·er** n

trans·pose \trans'pōz\ vb **-posed; -pos·ing** : change the position, sequence, or key — **trans·po·si·tion** \ˌtranspə'zishən\ n

trans·ship \tran'ship, trans-\ vb : transfer from one mode of transportation to another — **trans·ship·ment** n

trans·verse \trans'vərs, tranz-\ adj : lying across — **transverse** \'trans‚vərs, 'tranz-\ n — **trans·verse·ly** adv

trap \'trap\ n **1** : device for catching animals **2** : something by which one is caught unawares **3** : device to allow one thing to pass through while keeping other things out ~ vb **-pp-** : catch in a trap — **trap·per** n

trap·door \'trap‚dor\ n : door in a floor or roof

tra·peze \tra'pēz\ n : suspended bar used by acrobats

trap·e·zoid \'trapə‚zȯid\ n : plane 4-sided figure with 2 parallel sides — **trap·e·zoi·dal** \ˌtrapə'zȯid³l\ adj

trap·pings \'trapiŋz\ n pl **1** : ornamental covering **2** : outward decoration or dress

trash \'trash\ n : something that is no good — **trashy** adj

trau·ma \'traumə, 'trȯ-\ n : bodily or mental injury — **trau·mat·ic** \trə'matik, trȯ-, trau-\ adj

tra·vail \trə'vāl, 'trav‚āl\ n : painful work or exertion ~ vb : labor hard

trav·el \'travəl\ vb **-eled** or **-elled; -el·ing** or **-el·ling 1** : take a trip or tour **2** : move or be carried from point to point ~ n : journey — often pl. — **trav·el·er, trav·el·ler** n

tra·verse \tra'vərs, tra'vərs, 'travərs\ *vb* **-versed; -vers·ing** : go or extend across — **tra·verse** \'travərs\ *n*

trav·es·ty \'travəstē\ *n, pl* **-ties** : imitation that makes crude fun of something — **travesty** *vb*

trawl \'trȯl\ *vb* : fish or catch with a trawl ⁓ *n* : large cone-shaped net — **trawl·er** *n*

tray \'trā\ *n* : shallow flat-bottomed receptacle for holding or carrying something

treach·er·ous \'trechərəs\ *adj* : disloyal or dangerous — **treach·er·ous·ly** *adv*

treach·ery \'trechərē\ *n, pl* **-er·ies** : betrayal of a trust

tread \'tred\ *vb* **trod** \'träd\; **trod·den** \'träd³n\ *or* **trod; tread·ing** **1** : step on or over **2** : walk **3** : press or crush with the feet ⁓ *n* **1** : way of walking **2** : sound made in walking **3** : part on which a thing runs

trea·dle \'tred³l\ *n* : foot pedal operating a machine — **treadle** *vb*

tread·mill *n* **1** : mill worked by walking persons or animals **2** : wearisome routine

trea·son \'trēz³n\ *n* : attempt to overthrow the government — **trea·son·able** \'trēz³nəbəl\ *adj* — **trea·son·ous** \-³nəs\ *adj*

trea·sure \'trezhər, 'trāzh-\ *n* **1** : wealth stored up **2** : something of great value ⁓ *vb* **-sured; -sur·ing** : keep as precious

trea·sur·er \'trezhərər, 'trāzh-\ *n* : officer who handles funds

trea·sury \'trezhərē, 'trāzh-\ *n, pl* **-sur·ies** : place or office for keeping and distributing funds

treat \'trēt\ *vb* **1** : have as a topic **2** : pay for the food or entertainment of **3** : act toward or regard in a certain way **4** : give medical care to ⁓ *n* **1** : food or entertainment paid for by another **2** : something special and enjoyable — **treat·ment** \-mənt\ *n*

trea·tise \'trētəs\ *n* : systematic written exposition or argument

trea·ty \'trētē\ *n, pl* **-ties** : agreement between governments

tre·ble \'trebəl\ *n* **1** : highest part in music **2** : upper half of the musical range ⁓ *adj* : triple in number or amount ⁓ *vb* **-bled; -bling** : make triple — **tre·bly** *adv*

tree \'trē\ *n* : tall woody plant ⁓ *vb*

treed; tree·ing : force up a tree — **tree·less** *adj*

trek \'trek\ *n* : difficult trip ⁓ *vb* **-kk-** : make a trek

trel·lis \'treləs\ *n* : structure of crossed strips

trem·ble \'trembəl\ *vb* **-bled; -bling** **1** : shake from fear or cold **2** : move or sound as if shaken

tre·men·dous \tri'mendəs\ *adj* : amazingly large, powerful, or excellent — **tre·men·dous·ly** *adv*

trem·or \'tremər\ *n* : a trembling

trem·u·lous \'tremyələs\ *adj* : trembling or quaking

trench \'trench\ *n* : long narrow cut in land

tren·chant \'trenchənt\ *adj* : sharply perceptive

trend \'trend\ *n* : prevailing tendency, direction, or style ⁓ *vb* : move in a particular direction — **trendy** \'trendē\ *adj*

trep·i·da·tion \,trepə'dāshən\ *n* : nervous apprehension

tres·pass \'trespəs, -,pas\ *n* **1** : sin **2** : unauthorized entry onto someone's property ⁓ *vb* **1** : sin **2** : enter illegally — **tres·pass·er** *n*

tress \'tres\ *n* : long lock of hair

tres·tle \'tresəl\ *n* **1** : support with a horizontal piece and spreading legs **2** : framework bridge

tri·ad \'trī,ad, -əd\ *n* : union of 3

tri·age \trē'äzh, 'trē,äzh\ *n* : system of dealing with cases (as patients) according to priority guidelines intended to maximize success

tri·al \'trīəl\ *n* **1** : hearing and judgment of a matter in court **2** : source of great annoyance **3** : test use or experimental effort — **trial** *adj*

tri·an·gle \'trī,aŋgəl\ *n* : plane figure with 3 sides and 3 angles — **tri·an·gu·lar** \trī'aŋgyələr\ *adj*

tribe \'trīb\ *n* : social group of numerous families — **trib·al** \'trībəl\ *adj* — **tribes·man** \'trībzmən\ *n* — **tribes·peo·ple** \-,pēpəl\ *n pl*

trib·u·la·tion \,tribyə'lāshən\ *n* : suffering from oppression

tri·bu·nal \trī'byün³l, tri-\ *n* **1** : court **2** : something that decides

trib·u·tary \'tribyə,terē\ *n, pl* **-tar·ies** : stream that flows into a river or lake

trib·ute \'trib,yüt\ *n* **1** : payment to acknowledge submission **2** : tax **3** : gift or act showing respect

trick \'trik\ *n* **1** : scheme to deceive **2** : prank **3** : deceptive or ingenious feat **4** : mannerism **5** : knack **6** : tour of duty ~ *vb* : deceive by cunning — **trick·ery** \-ərē\ *n* — **trick·ster** \-stər\ *n*

trick·le \'trikəl\ *vb* **-led; -ling** : run in drops or a thin stream — **trickle** *n*

tricky \'trikē\ *adj* **trick·i·er; -est 1** : inclined to trickery **2** : requiring skill or caution

tri·cy·cle \'trī,sikəl\ *n* : 3-wheeled bicycle

tri·dent \'trīd°nt\ *n* : 3-pronged spear

tri·en·ni·al \'trī'enēəl\ *adj* : lasting, occurring, or done every 3 years — **triennial** *n*

tri·fle \'trīfəl\ *n* : something of little value or importance ~ *vb* **-fled; -fling 1** : speak or act in a playful or flirting way **2** : toy — **tri·fler** *n*

tri·fling \'trīfliŋ\ *adj* : trivial

trig·ger \'trigər\ *n* : finger-piece of a firearm lock that fires the gun ~ *vb* : set into motion — **trigger** *adj* — **trig·gered** \-ərd\ *adj*

trig·o·nom·e·try \,trigə'nämətrē\ *n* : mathematics dealing with triangular measurement — **trig·o·no·met·ric** \-nə'metrik\ *adj*

trill \'tril\ *n* **1** : rapid alternation between 2 adjacent tones **2** : rapid vibration in speaking ~ *vb* : utter in or with a trill

tril·lion \'trilyən\ *n* : 1000 billions — **trillion** *adj* — **tril·lionth** \-yənth\ *adj or n*

tril·o·gy \'triləjē\ *n, pl* **-gies** : 3-part literary or musical composition

trim \'trim\ *vb* **-mm- 1** : decorate **2** : make neat or reduce by cutting ~ *adj* **-mm-** : neat and compact ~ *n* **1** : state or condition **2** : ornaments — **trim·ly** *adv* — **trim·mer** *n*

trim·ming \'trimiŋ\ *n* : something that ornaments or completes

Trin·i·ty \'trinətē\ *n* : divine unity of Father, Son, and Holy Spirit

trin·ket \'triŋkət\ *n* : small ornament

trio \'trēō\ *n, pl* **tri·os 1** : music for 3 performers **2** : group of 3

trip \'trip\ *vb* **-pp- 1** : step lightly **2** : stumble or cause to stumble **3** : make or cause to make a mistake **4** : release (as a spring or switch) ~ *n* **1** : journey **2** : stumble **3** : drug-induced experience

tri·par·tite \trī'pär,tīt\ *adj* : having 3 parts or parties

tripe \'trīp\ *n* **1** : animal's stomach used as food **2** : trash

tri·ple \'tripəl\ *vb* **-pled; -pling** : make 3 times as great ~ *n* : group of 3 ~ *adj* **1** : having 3 units **2** : being 3 times as great or as many

trip·let \'triplət\ *n* **1** : group of 3 **2** : one of 3 offspring born together

trip·li·cate \'triplikət\ *adj* : made in 3 identical copies ~ *n* : one of 3 copies

tri·pod \'trī,päd\ *n* : a stand with 3 legs — **tripod, tri·po·dal** \'tripəd°l, 'trī,päd-\ *adj*

tri·sect \'trī,sekt, trī'-\ *vb* : divide into 3 usu. equal parts — **tri·sec·tion** \'trī,sekshən\ *n*

trite \'trīt\ *adj* **trit·er; trit·est** : commonplace

tri·umph \'trīəmf\ *n, pl* **-umphs** : victory or great success ~ *vb* : obtain or celebrate victory — **tri·um·phal** \trī'əmfəl\ *adj* — **tri·um·phant** \-fənt\ *adj* — **tri·um·phant·ly** *adv*

tri·um·vi·rate \trī'əmvərət\ *n* : ruling body of 3 persons

triv·et \'trivət\ *n* **1** : 3-legged stand **2** : stand to hold a hot dish

triv·ia \'trivēə\ *n sing or pl* : unimportant details

triv·i·al \'trivēəl\ *adj* : of little importance — **triv·i·al·i·ty** \trivē'alətē\ *n*

trod *past of* TREAD

trod·den *past part of* TREAD

troll \'trōl\ *n* : dwarf or giant of folklore inhabiting caves or hills

trol·ley \'trälē\ *n, pl* **-leys** : streetcar run by overhead electric wires

trol·lop \'träləp\ *n* : untidy or immoral woman

trom·bone \träm'bōn, 'träm,-\ *n* : musical instrument with a long sliding tube — **trom·bon·ist** \-'bōnist, -,bō-\ *n*

troop \'trüp\ *n* **1** : cavalry unit **2** *pl* : soldiers **3** : collection of people or things ~ *vb* : move or gather in crowds

troop·er \'trüpər\ *n* **1** : cavalry soldier **2** : police officer on horseback or state police officer

tro·phy \'trōfē\ *n, pl* **-phies** : prize gained by a victory

trop·ic \'träpik\ *n* **1** : either of the 2 parallels of latitude one 23½ degrees north of the equator (**tropic of Cancer** \-'kansər\) and one 23½ degrees south of the equator (**tropic of Cap·ri·corn** \-'kaprə,korn\) **2** pl : region lying between the tropics — **tropic, trop·i·cal** \-ikəl\ adj

trot \'trät\ n : moderately fast gait esp. of a horse with diagonally paired legs moving together ~ vb **-tt-** : go at a trot — **trot·ter** n

troth \'träth, 'tröth, 'tröth\ n **1** : pledged faithfulness **2** : betrothal

trou·ba·dour \'trübə,dor\ n : medieval lyric poet

trou·ble \'trəbəl\ vb **-bled; -bling 1** : disturb **2** : afflict **3** : make an effort ~ n **1** : cause of mental or physical distress **2** : effort — **trou·ble·mak·er** n — **trou·ble·some** adj — **trou·ble·some·ly** adv

trough \'tróf\ n, pl **troughs** \'tröfs, 'tróvz\ **1** : narrow container for animal feed or water **2** : long channel or depression (as between waves)

trounce \'trauns\ vb **trounced; trounc·ing** : thrash, punish, or defeat severely

troupe \'trüp\ n : group of stage performers — **troup·er** n

trou·sers \'trauzərz\ n pl : long pants — **trouser** adj

trous·seau \'trüsö, trü'sö\ n, pl **-seaux** \-söz, -'söz\ or **-seaus** : bride's collection of clothing and personal items

trout \'traút\ n, pl **trout** : freshwater food and game fish

trow·el \'traúəl\ n **1** : tool for spreading or smoothing **2** : garden scoop — **trowel** vb

troy \'trói\ n : system of weights based on a pound of 12 ounces

tru·ant \'trüənt\ n : student absent from school without permission — **tru·an·cy** \-ənse\ n — **truant** adj

truce \'trüs\ n : agreement to halt fighting

truck \'trək\ n **1** : wheeled frame for moving heavy objects **2** : automotive vehicle for transporting heavy loads ~ vb : transport on a truck — **truck·er** n — **truck·load** n

truck·le \'trəkəl\ vb **-led; -ling** : yield slavishly to another

tru·cu·lent \'trəkyələnt\ adj : aggressively self-assertive — **tru·cu·lence** \-ləns\ n — **tru·cu·lent·ly** adv

trudge \'trəj\ vb **trudged; trudg·ing** : walk or march steadily and with difficulty

true \'trü\ adj **tru·er; tru·est 1** : loyal

2 : in agreement with fact or reality **3** : genuine ~ adv **1** : truthfully **2** : accurately ~ vb **trued; true·ing** : make balanced or even — **tru·ly** adv

true–blue adj : loyal

truf·fle \'trəfəl\ n **1** : edible fruit of an underground fungus **2** : ball-shaped chocolate candy

tru·ism \'trü,izəm\ n : obvious truth

trump \'trəmp\ n : card of a designated suit any of whose cards will win over other cards ~ vb : take with a trump

trumped–up \'trəmpt'əp\ adj : made-up

trum·pet \'trəmpət\ n : tubular brass wind instrument with a flaring end ~ vb **1** : blow a trumpet **2** : proclaim loudly — **trum·pet·er** n

trun·cate \'trən,kāt, 'trən-\ vb **-cat·ed; -cat·ing** : cut short — **trun·ca·tion** \,trən'kāshən\ n

trun·dle \'trənd²l\ vb **-dled; -dling** : roll along

trunk \'trənk\ n **1** : main part (as of a body or tree) **2** : long muscular nose of an elephant **3** : storage chest **4** : storage space in a car **5** pl : shorts

truss \'trəs\ vb : bind tightly ~ n **1** : set of structural parts forming a framework **2** : appliance worn to hold a hernia in place

trust \'trəst\ n **1** : reliance on another **2** : assured hope **3** : credit **4** : property held or managed in behalf of another **5** : combination of firms that reduces competition **6** : something entrusted to another's care **7** : custody ~ vb **1** : depend **2** : hope **3** : entrust **4** : have faith in — **trust·ful** \-fəl\ adj — **trust·ful·ly** adv — **trust·ful·ness** n — **trust·worth·i·ness** n — **trust·wor·thy** adj

trust·ee \,trəs'tē\ n : person holding property in trust — **trust·ee·ship** n

trusty \'trəstē\ adj **trust·i·er; -est** : dependable

truth \'trüth\ n, pl **truths** \'trüthz, 'trüths\ **1** : real state of things **2** : true or accepted statement **3** : agreement with fact or reality — **truth·ful** \-fəl\ adj — **truth·ful·ly** adv — **truth·ful·ness** n

try \'trī\ vb **tried; try·ing 1** : conduct the trial of **2** : put to a test **3** : strain **4** : make an effort at ~ n, pl **tries** : act of trying

try·out n : competitive test of performance esp. for athletes or actors — **try out** vb

tryst \'trist, 'trīst\ *n* : secret rendezvous of lovers

tsar \'zär, 'tsär, 'sär\ *var of* CZAR

T-shirt \'tē,shərt\ *n* : collarless pullover shirt with short sleeves

tub \'təb\ *n* **1** : wide bucketlike vessel **2** : bathtub

tu·ba \'tübə, 'tyü-\ *n* : large low-pitched brass wind instrument

tube \'tüb, 'tyüb\ *n* **1** : hollow cylinder **2** : round container from which a substance can be squeezed **3** : airtight circular tube of rubber inside a tire **4** : electronic device consisting of a sealed usu. glass container with electrodes inside — **tubed** \'tübd, 'tyübd\ *adj* — **tube·less** *adj*

tu·ber \'tübər, 'tyü-\ *n* : fleshy underground growth (as of a potato) — **tu·ber·ous** \-rəs\ *adj*

tu·ber·cu·lo·sis \tü,bərkyə'lōsəs, tyü-\ *n, pl* **-lo·ses** \-,sēz\ : bacterial disease esp. of the lungs — **tu·ber·cu·lar** \-'bərkyələr\ *adj* — **tu·ber·cu·lous** \-ləs\ *adj*

tub·ing \'tübiŋ, 'tyü-\ *n* : series or arrangement of tubes

tu·bu·lar \'tübyələr, 'tyü-\ *adj* : of or like a tube

tuck \'tək\ *vb* **1** : pull up into a fold **2** : put into a snug often concealing place **3** : make snug in bed — with *in* or *in* : fold in a cloth

tuck·er \'təkər\ *vb* : fatigue

Tues·day \'tüzdā, 'tyüz-, -dē\ *n* : 3d day of the week

tuft \'təft\ *n* : clump (as of hair or feathers) — **tuft·ed** \'təftəd\ *adj*

tug \'təg\ *vb* **-gg-** **1** : pull hard **2** : move by pulling — *n* **1** : act of tugging **2** : tugboat

tug·boat *n* : boat for towing or pushing ships through a harbor

tug-of-war \,təgə'wor\ *n, pl* **tugs-of-war** : pulling contest between 2 teams

tu·ition \tü'ishən, tyü-\ *n* : cost of instruction

tu·lip \'tüləp, 'tyü-\ *n* : herb with cup-shaped flowers

tum·ble \'təmbəl\ *vb* **-bled; -bling 1** : perform gymnastic feats of rolling and turning **2** : fall or cause to fall suddenly **3** : toss — *n* : act of tumbling

tum·bler \'təmblər\ *n* **1** : acrobat **2** : drinking glass **3** : obstruction in a lock that can be moved (as by a key)

tu·mid \'tüməd, 'tyü-\ *adj* : turgid

tum·my \'təmē\ *n, pl* **-mies** : belly

tu·mor \'tümər, 'tyü-\ *n* : abnormal and useless growth of tissue — **tu·mor·ous** *adj*

tu·mult \'tü,məlt, 'tyü-\ *n* **1** : uproar **2** : violent agitation of mind or feelings — **tu·mul·tu·ous** \tü'məlchəwəs, tyü-\ *adj*

tun \'tən\ *n* : large cask

tu·na \'tünə, 'tyü-\ *n, pl* **-na** *or* **-nas** : large sea food fish

tun·dra \'təndrə\ *n* : treeless arctic plain

tune \'tün, 'tyün\ *n* **1** : melody **2** : correct musical pitch **3** : harmonious relationship — *vb* **tuned; tuning 1** : bring or come into harmony **2** : adjust in musical pitch **3** : adjust a receiver so as to receive a broadcast **4** : put in first-class working order — **tun·able** *adj* — **tune·ful** \-fəl\ *adj* — **tun·er** *n*

tung·sten \'təŋstən\ *n* : metallic element used for electrical purposes and in hardening alloys (as steel)

tu·nic \'tünik, 'tyü-\ *n* **1** : ancient knee-length garment **2** : hip-length blouse or jacket

tun·nel \'tən³l\ *n* : underground passageway — *vb* **-neled** *or* **-nelled; -nel·ing** *or* **-nel·ling** : make a tunnel through or under something

tur·ban \'tərbən\ *n* : wound headdress worn esp. by Muslims

tur·bid \'tərbəd\ *adj* **1** : dark with stirred-up sediment **2** : confused — **tur·bid·i·ty** \,tər'bidətē\ *n*

tur·bine \'tərbən, -,bīn\ *n* : engine turned by the force of gas or water on fan blades

tur·bo·jet \'tərbō,jet\ *n* : airplane powered by a jet engine having a turbine-driven air compressor or the engine itself

tur·bo·prop \'tərbō,präp\ *n* : airplane powered by a propeller turned by a jet engine-driven turbine

tur·bu·lent \'tərbyələnt\ *adj* **1** : causing violence or disturbance **2** : marked by agitation or tumult — **tur·bu·lence** \-ləns\ *n* — **tur·bu·lent·ly** *adv*

tu·reen \tə'rēn, tyü-\ *n* : deep bowl for serving soup

turf \'tərf\ *n* : upper layer of soil bound by grass and roots

tur·gid \'tərjəd\ *adj* **1** : swollen **2** : too highly embellished in style — **tur·gid·i·ty** \,tər'jidətē\ *n*

tur·key \'tərkē\ *n, pl* **-keys** : large American bird raised for food

tur·moil \'tər,móil\ *n* : extremely agitated condition

turn \'tərn\ *vb* **1** : move or cause to move around an axis **2** : twist (a mechanical part) to operate **3** : wrench **4** : cause to face or move in a different direction **5** : reverse the sides or surfaces of **6** : upset **7** : go around **8** : become or cause to become **9** : seek aid from a source **~** *n* **1** : act or instance of turning **2** : change **3** : place at which something turns **4** : place, time, or opportunity to do something in order — **turn·er** *n* — **turn down** *vb* : decline to accept — **turn in** *vb* **1** : deliver or report to authorities **2** : go to bed — **turn off** *vb* : stop the functioning of — **turn out** *vb* **1** : expel **2** : produce **3** : come together **4** : prove to be in the end — **turn over** *vb* : transfer — **turn up** *vb* **1** : discover or appear **2** : happen unexpectedly

turn·coat *n* : traitor

tur·nip \'tərnəp\ *n* : edible root of an herb

turn·out \'tərn,aůt\ *n* **1** : gathering of people for a special purpose **2** : size of a gathering

turn·over *n* **1** : upset or reversal **2** : filled pastry **3** : volume of business **4** : movement (as of goods or people) into, through, and out of a place

turn·pike \'tərn,pīk\ *n* : expressway on which tolls are charged

turn·stile \-,stīl\ *n* : post with arms pivoted on the top that allows people to pass one by one

turn·ta·ble *n* : platform that turns a phonograph record

tur·pen·tine \'tərpən,tīn\ *n* : oil distilled from pine-tree resin and used as a solvent

tur·pi·tude \'tərpə,tüd, -,tyüd\ *n* : inherent baseness

tur·quoise \'tər,kóiz, -,kwóiz\ *n* : blue or greenish gray gemstone

tur·ret \'tərət\ *n* **1** : little tower on a building **2** : revolving tool holder or gun housing

tur·tle \'tərtᵊl\ *n* : reptile with the trunk enclosed in a bony shell

tur·tle·dove *n* : wild pigeon

tur·tle·neck *n* : high close-fitting collar that can be turned over or a sweater or shirt with this collar

tusk \'təsk\ *n* : long protruding tooth (as of an elephant) — **tusked** \'təskt\ *adj*

tus·sle \'təsəl\ *n or vb* : struggle

tu·te·lage \'tütᵊlij, 'tyüt-\ *n* **1** : act of protecting **2** : instruction esp. of an individual

tu·tor \'tütər, 'tyü-\ *n* : private teacher **~** *vb* : teach usu. individually

tux·e·do \,tək'sēdō\ *n, pl* **-dos** *or* **-does** : semiformal evening clothes for a man

TV \,tē'vē, 'tē,vē\ *n* : television

twain \'twān\ *n* : two

twang \'twaŋ\ *n* **1** : harsh sound like that of a plucked bowstring **2** : nasal speech or resonance **~** *vb* : sound or speak with a twang

tweak \'twēk\ *vb* : pinch and pull playfully — **tweak** *n*

tweed \'twēd\ *n* **1** : rough woolen fabric **2** *pl* : tweed clothing — **tweedy** *adj*

tweet \'twēt\ *n* : chirping note — **tweet** *vb*

twee·zers \'twēzərz\ *n pl* : small pincerlike tool

twelve \'twelv\ *n* **1** : one more than 11 **2** : 12th in a set or series **3** : something having 12 units — **twelfth** \'twelfth\ *adj or n* — **twelve** *adj or pron*

twen·ty \'twentē\ *n, pl* **-ties** : 2 times 10 — **twen·ti·eth** \-ēəth\ *adj or n* — **twenty** *adj or pron*

twen·ty–twen·ty, 20–20 *adj* : being vision of normal sharpness

twice \'twīs\ *adv* **1** : on 2 occasions **2** : 2 times

twig \'twig\ *n* : small branch — **twig·gy** *adj*

twi·light \'twī,līt\ *n* : light from the sky at dusk or dawn — **twilight** *adj*

twill \'twil\ *n* : fabric with a weave that gives an appearance of diagonal lines in the fabric

twilled \'twild\ *adj* : made with a twill weave

twin \'twin\ *n* : either of 2 offspring born together **~** *adj* **1** : born with one another or as a pair at one birth **2** : made up of 2 similar parts

twine \'twin\ *n* : strong twisted thread **~** *vb* **twined; twin·ing** **1** : twist together **2** : coil about a support — **twin·er** *n* — **twiny** *adj*

twinge \'twinj\ *vb* **twinged; twing·ing** *or* **twinge·ing** : affect with or feel a sudden sharp pain **~** *n* : sudden sharp stab (as of pain)

twin·kle \'twiŋkəl\ *vb* **-kled; -kling**

: shine with a flickering light **~** n 1
: wink 2 : intermittent shining —
twin·kler \-klər\ n

twirl \'twərl\ vb : whirl round **~** n 1
: act of twirling 2 : coil — **twirl·er** n

twist \'twist\ vb 1 : unite by winding
(threads) together 2 : wrench 3
: move in or have a spiral shape 4
: follow a winding course **~** n 1 : act
or result of twisting 2 : unexpected
development

twist·er \'twistər\ n : tornado

¹twit \'twit\ n : fool

²twit vb **-tt-** : taunt

twitch \'twich\ vb : move or pull with a
sudden motion **~** n : act of twitching

twit·ter \'twitər\ vb : make chirping
noises **~** n : small intermittent noise

two \'tü\ n, pl **twos** 1 : one more than
one 2 : the 2d in a set or series 3
: something having 2 units — **two** adj
or pron

two·fold \'tü,fōld\ adj : double — **two·**
fold \-'fōld\ adv

two·some \'tüsəm\ n : couple

-ty n suffix : quality, condition, or degree

ty·coon \tī'kün\ n : powerful and successful businessman

tying pres part of TIE

tyke \'tīk\ n : small child

tym·pa·num \'timpənəm\ n, pl **-na**
\-nə\ : eardrum or the cavity which it
closes externally — **tym·pan·ic**
\tim'panik\ adj

type \'tīp\ n 1 : class, kind, or group
set apart by common characteristics
2 : special design of printed letters
~ vb **typed; typ·ing** 1 : write with a

typewriter 2 : identify or classify as a
particular type

type·writ·er n : keyboard machine that
produces printed material by striking
a ribbon with raised letters — **type·**
write vb

ty·phoid \'tī,fȯid, tī'-\ adj : relating to
or being a communicable bacterial
disease (**typhoid fever**)

ty·phoon \tī'fün\ n : hurricane of the
western Pacific ocean

ty·phus \'tīfəs\ n : severe disease with
fever, delirium, and rash

typ·i·cal \'tipikəl\ adj : having the
essential characteristics of a group —
typ·i·cal·i·ty \,tipə'kalətē\ n — **typ·**
i·cal·ly adv — **typ·i·cal·ness** n

typ·i·fy \'tipə,fī\ vb **-fied; -fy·ing** : be
typical of

typ·ist \'tīpist\ n : one who operates a
typewriter

ty·pog·ra·phy \tī'pägrəfē\ n 1 : art of
printing with type 2 : style, arrangement, or appearance of printed matter
— **ty·po·graph·ic** \,tīpə'grafik\, **ty·**
po·graph·i·cal \-ikəl\ adj — **ty·po·**
graph·i·cal·ly adv

ty·ran·ni·cal \tə'ranikəl, tī-\ adj : relating to a tyrant — **ty·ran·ni·cal·ly** adv

tyr·an·nize \'tirə,nīz\ vb **-nized; -niz·**
ing : rule or deal with in the manner
of a tyrant — **tyr·an·niz·er** n

tyr·an·ny \'tirənē\ n, pl **-nies** : unjust
use of absolute governmental power

ty·rant \'tīrənt\ n : harsh ruler having
absolute power

ty·ro \'tīrō\ n, pl **-ros** : beginner

tzar \'zär, 'tsär, 'sär\ var of CZAR

U

u \'yü\ n, pl **u's** or **us** \'yüz\ : 21st letter of the alphabet

ubiq·ui·tous \yü'bikwətəs\ adj : om-
nipresent — **ubiq·ui·tous·ly** adv —
ubiq·ui·ty \-wətē\ n

ud·der \'ədər\ n : animal sac containing milk glands and nipples

ug·ly \'əglē\ adj **ug·li·er; -est** 1 : offensive to look at 2 : mean or quar-
relsome — **ug·li·ness** n

uku·le·le \,yükə'lālē\ n : small 4-string
guitar

ul·cer \'əlsər\ n : eroded sore — **ul·cer·**
ous adj

ul·cer·ate \'əlsə,rāt\ vb **-at·ed; -at·ing**
: become affected with an ulcer — **ul·**
cer·a·tion \,əlsə'rāshən\ n — **ul·**
cer·a·tive \'əlsə,rātiv\ adj

ul·na \'əlnə\ n : bone of the forearm
opposite the thumb

ul·te·ri·or \,əl'tirēər\ adj : not revealed

ul·ti·mate \'əltəmət\ adj : final, maximum, or extreme — **ultimate** n — **ul·**
ti·mate·ly adv

ul·ti·ma·tum \ˌəltə'mātəm, -'mät-\ *n*, *pl* **-tums** *or* **-ta** \-ə\ : final proposition or demand carrying or implying a threat

ul·tra·vi·o·let \ˌəltrə'vīələt\ *adj* : having a wavelength shorter than visible light

um·bi·li·cus \ˌəmbə'līkəs, ˌəm'bili-\ *n*, *pl* **-li·ci** \-bə'līˌkī, -ˌsī; -'bilaˌkī, -ˌkē\ *or* **-li·cus·es** : small depression on the abdominal wall marking the site of the cord (**umbilical cord**) that joins the unborn fetus to its mother — **um·bil·i·cal** \ˌəm'bilikəl\ *adj*

um·brage \'əmbrij\ *n* : resentment

um·brel·la \ˌəm'brelə\ *n* : collapsible fabric device to protect from sun or rain

um·pire \'əmˌpīr\ *n* **1** : arbitrator **2** : sport official — **umpire** *vb*

ump·teen \'əmp'tēn\ *adj* : very numerous — **ump·teenth** \-'tēnth\ *adj*

un- \ˌən, 'ən\ *prefix* **1** : not **2** : opposite of

un·ac·cus·tomed *adj* **1** : not customary **2** : not accustomed

un·af·fect·ed *adj* **1** : not influenced or changed by something **2** : natural and sincere — **un·af·fect·ed·ly** *adv*

unan·i·mous \yü'nanəməs\ *adj* **1** : showing no disagreement **2** : formed with the agreement of all — **una·nim·i·ty** \ˌyünə'nimətē\ *n* — **unan·i·mous·ly** *adv*

un·armed *adj* : not armed or armored

un·as·sum·ing *adj* : not bold or arrogant

un·at·tached *adj* **1** : not attached **2** : not married or engaged

un·aware *adv* : unawares ~ *adj* : not aware

un·awares \ˌənə'warz\ *adv* **1** : without warning **2** : unintentionally

un·bal·anced *adj* **1** : not balanced **2** : mentally unstable

un·beat·en *adj* : not beaten

un·be·com·ing *adj* : not proper or suitable — **un·be·com·ing·ly** *adv*

un·be·liev·able *adj* **1** : improbable **2** : superlative — **un·be·liev·ably** *adv*

un·bend *vb* **-bent; -bend·ing** : make or become more relaxed and friendly

un·bend·ing *adj* : formal and inflexible

un·bind *vb* **-bound; -bind·ing** : remove bindings from **2** : release

un·bolt *vb* : open or unfasten by withdrawing a bolt

un·born *adj* : not yet born

un·bo·som *vb* : disclose thoughts or feelings

un·bowed \ˌən'baud\ *adj* : not defeated or subdued

un·bri·dled \ˌən'brīd°ld\ *adj* : unrestrained

un·bro·ken *adj* : not damaged **2** : not interrupted

un·buck·le *vb* : unfasten the buckle of

un·bur·den *vb* : relieve (oneself) of anxieties

un·but·ton *vb* : unfasten the buttons of

un·called–for *adj* : too harsh or rude for the occasion

un·can·ny \ˌən'kanē\ *adj* **1** : weird **2** : suggesting superhuman powers — **un·can·ni·ly** \-'kan'lē\ *adv*

un·ceas·ing *adj* : never ceasing — **un·ceas·ing·ly** *adv*

un·cer·e·mo·ni·ous *adj* : acting without ordinary courtesy — **un·cer·e·mo·ni·ous·ly** *adv*

un·cer·tain *adj* **1** : not determined, sure, or definitely known **2** : subject to chance or change — **un·cer·tain·ly** *adv* — **un·cer·tain·ty** *n*

List of self-explanatory words with the prefix *un-*

unable	unannounced	unbearable
unabridged	unanswered	unbiased
unacceptable	unanticipated	unbranded
unaccompanied	unappetizing	unbreakable
unaccounted	unappreciated	uncensored
unacquainted	unapproved	unchallenged
unaddressed	unarguable	unchangeable
unadorned	unarguably	unchanged
unadulterated	unassisted	unchanging
unafraid	unattended	uncharacteristic
unaided	unattractive	uncharged
unalike	unauthorized	unchaste
unambiguous	unavailable	uncivilized
unambitious	unavoidable	unclaimed

un·chris·tian adj : not consistent with Christian teachings

un·cle \'əŋkəl\ n 1 : brother of one's father or mother 2 : husband of one's aunt

un·clean adj : not clean or pure — **un·clean·ness** n

un·clog vb : remove an obstruction from

un·coil vb : release or become released from a coiled state

un·com·mit·ted adj : not pledged to a particular allegiance or course of action

un·com·mon adj 1 : rare 2 : superior — **un·com·mon·ly** adv

un·com·pro·mis·ing adj : not making or accepting a compromise

un·con·cerned adj 1 : disinterested 2 : not anxious or upset — **un·con·cerned·ly** adv

un·con·di·tion·al adj : not limited in any way — **un·con·di·tion·al·ly** adv

un·con·scio·na·ble adj : shockingly unjust or unscrupulous — **un·con·scio·na·bly** adv

un·con·scious adj 1 : not awake or aware of one's surroundings 2 : not consciously done ~ n : part of one's mental life that one is not aware of — **un·con·scious·ly** adv — **un·con·scious·ness** n

un·con·sti·tu·tion·al adj : not according to or consistent with a constitution

un·con·trol·la·ble adj : incapable of being controlled — **un·con·trol·la·bly** adv

un·count·ed adj : countless

un·couth \ˌən'küth\ adj : rude and vulgar

un·cov·er vb 1 : reveal 2 : expose by removing a covering

unc·tion \'əŋkshən\ n 1 : rite of anointing 2 : exaggerated or insincere earnestness

unc·tu·ous \'əŋkchəwəs\ adj 1 : oily 2 : insincerely smooth in speech or manner — **unc·tu·ous·ly** adv

un·cut adj 1 : not cut down, into, off, or apart 2 : not shaped by cutting 3 : not abridged

un·daunt·ed adj : not discouraged — **un·daunt·ed·ly** adv

un·de·ni·able adj : plainly true — **un·de·ni·ably** adv

un·der \'əndər\ adv : below or beneath something ~ prep 1 : lower than and sheltered by 2 : below the surface of 3 : covered or concealed by 4 : subject to the authority of 5 : less than ~ adj 1 : lying below or beneath 2 : subordinate 3 : less than usual, proper, or desired

un·der·age \ˌəndər'āj\ adj : of less than legal age

un·der·brush \'əndərˌbrəsh\ n : shrubs and small trees growing beneath large trees

un·der·clothes \'əndərˌklōz, -ˌklōthz\ n pl : underwear

un·der·cloth·ing \-ˌklōthiŋ\ n : underwear

un·der·cov·er \ˌəndər'kəvər\ adj : employed or engaged in secret investigation

un·der·cur·rent \'əndərˌkərənt\ n : hidden tendency or opinion

un·der·cut \ˌəndər'kət\ vb -cut; -cut·ting : offer to sell or to work at a lower rate than

un·der·de·vel·oped \ˌəndərdi'veləpt\ adj : not normally or adequately developed esp. economically

---

unclear	unconventionally	undeserving
uncleared	unconverted	undesirable
unclothed	uncooked	undetected
uncluttered	uncooperative	undetermined
uncombed	uncoordinated	undeveloped
uncomfortable	uncovered	undeviating
uncomfortably	uncultivated	undifferentiated
uncomplimentary	undamaged	undignified
unconfirmed	undated	undisturbed
unconsummated	undecided	undivided
uncontested	undeclared	undomesticated
uncontrolled	undefeated	undrinkable
uncontroversial	undemocratic	unearned
unconventional	undependable	uneducated

un·der·dog \'əndər,dȯg\ n : contestant given least chance of winning

un·der·done \,əndər'dən\ adj : not thoroughly done or cooked

un·der·es·ti·mate \,əndər'estə,māt\ vb : estimate too low

un·der·ex·pose \,əndərik'spōz\ vb : give less than normal exposure to — **un·der·ex·po·sure** n

un·der·feed \,əndər'fēd\ vb **-fed; -feed·ing** : feed inadequately

un·der·foot \,əndər'fu̇t\ adv 1 : under the feet 2 : in the way of another

un·der·gar·ment \'əndər,gärmənt\ n : garment to be worn under another

un·der·go \,əndər'gō\ vb **-went** \-'went\; **-gone; -go·ing** 1 : endure 2 : go through (as an experience)

un·der·grad·u·ate \,əndər'grajəwət\ n : university or college student

un·der·ground \,əndər'graùnd\ adv 1 : beneath the surface of the earth 2 : in secret ~ \'əndər,-\ adj 1 : being or growing under the surface of the ground 2 : secret ~ \'əndər,-\ n : secret political movement or group

un·der·growth \'əndər'grōth\ n : low growth on the floor of a forest

un·der·hand \'əndər,hand\ adv or adj 1 : with secrecy and deception 2 : with the hand kept below the waist

un·der·hand·ed \,əndər'handəd\ adj or adv : underhand — **un·der·hand·ed·ly** adv — **un·der·hand·ed·ness** n

un·der·line \'əndər,līn\ vb 1 : draw a line under 2 : stress — **underline** n

un·der·ling \'əndərliŋ\ n : inferior

un·der·ly·ing \,əndər,līiŋ\ adj : basic

un·der·mine \,əndər'mīn\ vb 1 : excavate beneath 2 : weaken or wear away secretly or gradually

un·der·neath \,əndər'nēth\ prep : directly under ~ adv 1 : below a surface or object 2 : on the lower side

un·der·nour·ished \,əndər'nərisht\ adj : insufficiently nourished — **un·der·nour·ish·ment** n

un·der·pants \'əndər,pants\ n pl : short undergarment for the lower trunk

un·der·pass \-,pas\ n : passageway crossing underneath another

un·der·pin·ning \'əndər,piniŋ\ n : support

un·der·priv·i·leged adj : poor

un·der·rate \,əndər'rāt\ vb : rate or value too low

un·der·score \'əndər,skōr\ vb 1 : underline 2 : emphasize — **underscore** n

un·der·sea \,əndər'sē\ adj : being, carried on, or used beneath the surface of the sea ~ \,əndər'sē\, **un·der·seas** \-'sēz\ adv : beneath the surface of the sea

un·der sec·re·tary n : deputy secretary

un·der·sell \,əndər'sel\ vb **-sold; -sell·ing** : sell articles cheaper than

un·der·shirt \'əndər,shərt\ n : shirt worn as underwear

un·der·shorts \'əndər,shȯrts\ n pl : short underpants

un·der·side \'əndər,sīd, ,əndər'sīd\ n : side or surface lying underneath

un·der·sized \,əndər'sīzd\ adj : unusually small

un·der·stand \,əndər'stand\ vb **-stood** \-'stu̇d\; **-stand·ing** 1 : be aware of the meaning of 2 : deduce 3 : have a sympathetic attitude — **un·der·stand·able** \-'standəbəl\ adj — **un·der·stand·ably** \-blē\ adv

un·der·stand·ing \,əndər'standiŋ\ n 1 : intelligence 2 : ability to compre-

unemotional	unfavorably	ungrammatical
unending	unfeigned	unharmed
unendurable	unfilled	unhealthful
unenforceable	unfinished	unheated
unenlightened	unflattering	unhurt
unethical	unforeseeable	unidentified
unexcitable	unforeseen	unimaginable
unexciting	unforgivable	unimaginative
unexplainable	unforgiving	unimportant
unexplored	unfulfilled	unimpressed
unfair	unfurnished	uninformed
unfairly	ungenerous	uninhabited
unfairness	ungentlemanly	uninjured
unfavorable	ungraceful	uninsured

hend and judge **3** : mutual agreement ~ *adj* : sympathetic

un·der·state \ˌəndərˈstāt\ *vb* **1** : represent as less than is the case **2** : state with restraint — **un·der·state·ment** *n*

un·der·stood \ˌəndərˈstud\ *adj* **1** : agreed upon **2** : implicit

un·der·study \ˈəndərˌstədē, ˌəndərˈ-\ *vb* : study another actor's part in order to substitute — **understudy** \ˈəndərˌ-\ *n*

un·der·take \ˌəndərˈtāk\ *vb* **-took; -tak·en; -tak·ing 1** : attempt (a task) or assume (a responsibility) **2** : guarantee

un·der·tak·er \ˈəndərˌtākər\ *n* : one in the funeral business

un·der·tak·ing \ˈəndərˌtākiŋ, ˌəndərˈ-\ *n* **1** : something (as work) that is undertaken **2** : promise

under–the–counter *adj* : illicit

un·der·tow \ˈəndərˌtō\ *n* : low or subdued tone or utterance

un·der·tow \-ˌtō\ *n* : current beneath the waves that flows seaward

un·der·val·ue \ˌəndərˈvalyü\ *vb* : value too low

un·der·wa·ter \-ˈwotər, -ˈwät-\ *adj* : being or used below the surface of the water — **underwater** *adv*

under way *adv* : in motion or in progress

un·der·wear \ˈəndərˌwar\ *n* : clothing worn next to the skin and under ordinary clothes

un·der·world \ˈəndərˌwərld\ *n* **1** : place of departed souls **2** : world of organized crime

un·der·write \ˈəndərˌrīt, ˌəndərˈ-\ *vb* **-wrote; -writ·ten; -writ·ing 1** : provide insurance for **2** : guarantee financial support of — **un·der·writ·er** *n*

un·dies \ˈəndēz\ *n pl* : underwear

un·do *vb* **-did; -done; -do·ing 1** : unfasten **2** : reverse **3** : ruin — **un·do·ing** *n*

un·doubt·ed *adj* : certain — **un·doubt·ed·ly** *adv*

un·dress *vb* : remove one's clothes ~ *n* : state of being naked

un·due *adj* : excessive — **un·du·ly** *adv*

un·du·late \ˈənjəˌlāt\ *vb* **-lat·ed; -lat·ing** : rise and fall regularly — **un·du·la·tion** \ˌənjəˈlāshən\ *n*

un·dy·ing *adj* : immortal or perpetual

un·earth *vb* : dig up or discover

un·earth·ly *adj* : supernatural

un·easy *adj* **1** : awkward or embarrassed **2** : disturbed or worried — **un·eas·i·ly** *adv* — **un·eas·i·ness** *n*

un·em·ployed *adj* : not having a job — **un·em·ploy·ment** *n*

un·equal *adj* : not equal or uniform — **un·equal·ly** *adv*

un·equaled, un·equalled *adj* : having no equal

un·equiv·o·cal *adj* : leaving no doubt — **un·equiv·o·cal·ly** *adv*

un·err·ing *adj* : infallible — **un·err·ing·ly** *adv*

un·even *adj* **1** : not smooth **2** : not regular or consistent — **un·even·ly** *adv* — **un·even·ness** *n*

un·event·ful *adj* : lacking interesting or noteworthy incidents — **un·event·ful·ly** *adv*

un·ex·pect·ed \ˌənikˈspektəd\ *adj* : not expected — **un·ex·pect·ed·ly** *adv*

un·fail·ing *adj* : steadfast — **un·fail·ing·ly** *adv*

un·faith·ful *adj* : not loyal — **un·faith·ful·ly** *adv* — **un·faith·ful·ness** *n*

un·fa·mil·iar *adj* **1** : not well known **2** : not acquainted — **un·fa·mil·iar·i·ty** *n*

---

unintelligent	unknowing	unmolested
unintelligible	unknowingly	unmotivated
unintelligibly	unknown	unmoving
unintended	unleavened	unnamed
unintentional	unlicensed	unnecessarily
unintentionally	unlikable	unnecessary
uninterested	unlimited	unneeded
uninteresting	unlovable	unnoticeable
uninterrupted	unmanageable	unnoticed
uninvited	unmarked	unobjectionable
unjust	unmarried	unobservable
unjustifiable	unmerciful	unobservant
unjustified	unmercifully	unobtainable
unjustly	unmerited	unobtrusive

un·fas·ten vb : release a catch or lock

un·feel·ing adj : lacking feeling or compassion — **un·feel·ing·ly** adv

un·fit adj : not suitable — **un·fit·ness** n

un·flap·pa·ble \ˌən¹flapəbəl\ adj : not easily upset or panicked — **un·flap·pa·bly** adv

un·fold vb 1 : open the folds of 2 : reveal 3 : develop

un·for·get·ta·ble adj : memorable — **un·for·get·ta·bly** adv

un·for·tu·nate adj 1 : not lucky or successful 2 : deplorable — **unfortunate** n — **un·for·tu·nate·ly** adv

un·found·ed adj : lacking a sound basis

un·freeze vb **-froze; -fro·zen; -freez·ing** : thaw

un·friend·ly adj : not friendly or kind — **un·friend·li·ness** n

un·furl vb : unfold or unroll

un·gain·ly adj : clumsy — **un·gain·li·ness** n

un·god·ly adj : wicked — **un·god·li·ness** n

un·grate·ful adj : not thankful for favors — **un·grate·ful·ly** adv — **un·grate·ful·ness** n

un·guent \¹əŋgwənt, ¹ən-\ n : ointment

un·hand vb : let go

un·hap·py adj 1 : unfortunate 2 : sad — **un·hap·pi·ly** adv — **un·hap·pi·ness** n

un·healthy adj 1 : not wholesome 2 : not well

un·heard–of \ˌən¹hərdəv, -ˌäv\ adj : unprecedented

un·hinge \ˌən¹hinj\ vb 1 : take from the hinges 2 : make unstable esp. mentally

un·hitch vb : unfasten

un·ho·ly adj : sinister or shocking — **un·ho·li·ness** n

un·hook vb : release from a hook

uni·cel·lu·lar \ˌyüni¹selyələr\ adj : having or consisting of a single cell

uni·corn \¹yüniˌkórn\ n : legendary animal with one horn in the middle of the forehead

uni·cy·cle \¹yüniˌsīkəl\ n : pedal-powered vehicle with only a single wheel

uni·di·rec·tion·al \ˌyünidə¹rekshənəl, -dī-\ adj : working in only a single direction

uni·form \¹yünəˌfórm\ adj : not changing or showing any variation ∼ n : distinctive dress worn by members of a particular group — **uni·for·mi·ty** \ˌyünə¹fórmətē\ n — **uni·form·ly** adv

uni·fy \¹yünəˌfī\ vb **-fied; -fy·ing** : make into a coherent whole — **uni·fi·ca·tion** \ˌyünəfə¹kāshən\ n

uni·lat·er·al \ˌyünə¹latərəl\ adj : having, affecting, or done by one side only — **uni·lat·er·al·ly** adv

un·im·peach·able adj : blameless

un·in·hib·it·ed adj : free of restraint — **un·in·hib·it·ed·ly** adv

union \¹yünyən\ n 1 : act or instance of joining 2 or more things into one or the state of being so joined 2 : confederation of nations or states 3 : organization of workers (**labor union, trade union**)

union·ize \¹yünyəˌnīz\ vb **-ized; -iz·ing** : form into a labor union — **union·iza·tion** \ˌyünyənə¹zāshən\ n

unique \yü¹nēk\ adj 1 : being the only one of its kind 2 : very unusual — **unique·ly** adv — **unique·ness** n

uni·son \¹yünəsən, -nəzən\ n 1 : sameness in pitch 2 : exact agreement

unit \¹yünət\ n 1 : smallest whole

unobtrusively	unpleasantness	unproven
unofficial	unpopular	unprovoked
unopened	unpopularity	unpunished
unopposed	unposed	unqualified
unorganized	unpredictability	unquenchable
unoriginal	unpredictable	unquestioning
unorthodox	unpredictably	unreachable
unorthodoxy	unprejudiced	unreadable
unpaid	unprepared	unready
unpardonable	unpretentious	unrealistic
unpatriotic	unproductive	unreasonable
unpaved	unprofitable	unreasonably
unpleasant	unprotected	unrefined
unpleasantly	unproved	unrelated

number **2** : definite amount or quantity used as a standard of measurement **3** : single part of a whole — **unit** adj

unite \yu̇-'nīt\ vb **unit·ed; unit·ing** : put or join together

uni·ty \'yü-nə-tē\ n, pl **-ties 1** : quality or state of being united or a unit **2** : harmony

uni·ver·sal \,yü-nə-'vər-səl\ adj **1** : relating to or affecting everyone or everything **2** : present or occurring everywhere — **uni·ver·sal·ly** adv

uni·verse \'yü-nə-,vərs\ n : the complete system of all things that exist

uni·ver·si·ty \,yü-nə-'vər-sə-tē\ n, pl **-ties** : institution of higher learning

un·kempt \,ən-'kempt\ adj : not neat or combed

un·kind adj : not kind or sympathetic — **un·kind·li·ness** n — **un·kind·ly** adv — **un·kind·ness** n

un·law·ful adj : illegal — **un·law·ful·ly** adv

un·leash vb : free from control or restraint

un·less \ən-'les\ conj : except on condition that

un·like \,ən-'līk, 'ən-,līk\ adj **1** : not similar **2** : not equal ∼ prep : different from — **un·like·ly** \ən-'līk-lē\ — **un·like·ness** \-nəs\ n — **un·like·li·hood** \-lē-hu̇d\ n

un·load vb **1** : take (cargo) from a vehicle, vessel, or plane **2** : take a load from **3** : discard

un·lock vb **1** : unfasten through release of a lock **2** : release or reveal

un·lucky adj **1** : experiencing bad luck **2** : likely to bring misfortune — **un·luck·i·ly** adv

un·mis·tak·able adj : not capable of being mistaken or misunderstood — **un·mis·tak·ably** adv

un·moved adj **1** : not emotionally affected **2** : remaining in the same place or position

un·nat·u·ral adj **1** : not natural or spontaneous **2** : abnormal — **un·nat·u·ral·ly** adv — **un·nat·u·ral·ness** n

un·nerve vb : deprive of courage, strength, or steadiness

un·oc·cu·pied adj **1** : not busy **2** : not occupied

un·pack vb **1** : remove (things packed) from a container **2** : remove the contents of (a package)

un·par·al·leled adj : having no equal

un·plug vb **1** : unclog **2** : disconnect from an electric circuit by removing a plug

un·prec·e·dent·ed adj : unlike or superior to anything known before

un·prin·ci·pled adj : unscrupulous

un·ques·tion·able adj : acknowledged as beyond doubt — **un·ques·tion·ably** adv

un·rav·el vb **1** : separate the threads of **2** : solve

un·re·al adj : not real or genuine — **un·re·al·i·ty** n

un·rea·son·ing adj : not using or being guided by reason

un·re·lent·ing adj : not yielding or easing — **un·re·lent·ing·ly** adv

un·rest n : turmoil

un·ri·valed or **un·ri·valled** adj : having no rival

un·roll vb **1** : unwind a roll of **2** : become unrolled

un·ruf·fled adj : not agitated or upset

un·ruly \,ən-'rü-lē\ adj : not readily con-

---

unreliable	unsatisfactory	unsolved
unremembered	unsatisfied	unsophisticated
unrepentant	unscented	unsound
unrepresented	unscheduled	unsoundly
unrequited	unseasoned	unsoundness
unresolved	unseen	unspecified
unresponsive	unselfish	unspoiled
unrestrained	unselfishly	unsteadily
unrestricted	unselfishness	unsteadiness
unrewarding	unshaped	unsteady
unripe	unshaven	unstructured
unsafe	unskillful	unsubstantiated
unsalted	unskillfully	unsuccessful
unsanitary	unsolicited	unsuitable

un·rul·i·ness n

un·scathed \ˌən'skāthd\ adj : unharmed

un·sci·en·tif·ic adj : not in accord with the principles and methods of science

un·screw vb : loosen or remove by withdrawing screws or by turning

un·scru·pu·lous adj : being or acting in total disregard of conscience, ethical principles, or rights of others — **un·scru·pu·lous·ly** adv — **un·scru·pu·lous·ness** n

un·seal vb : break or remove the seal of

un·sea·son·able adj : not appropriate or usual for the season — **un·sea·son·ably** adv

un·seem·ly \ˌən'sēmlē\ adj : not polite or in good taste — **un·seem·li·ness** n

un·set·tle vb : disturb — **un·set·tled** adj

un·sight·ly \ˌən'sītlē\ adj : not attractive

un·skilled adj : not having or requiring a particular skill

un·snap vb : loosen by undoing a snap

un·speak·able \ˌən'spēkəbəl\ adj : extremely bad — **un·speak·ably** \-blē\ adv

un·sta·ble adj 1 : not mentally or physically balanced 2 : tending to change

un·stop vb 1 : unclog 2 : remove a stopper from

un·stop·pa·ble \ˌən'stäpəbəl\ adj : not capable of being stopped

un·strung \ˌən'strəŋ\ adj : nervously tired or anxious

un·sung \ˌən'səŋ\ adj : not celebrated in song or verse

un·tan·gle vb 1 : free from a state of being tangled 2 : find a solution to

un·think·able \ˌən'thiŋkəbəl\ adj : not to be thought of or considered possible

un·think·ing adj : careless — **un·think·ing·ly** adv

un·tie vb -tied; -ty·ing or -tie·ing : open by releasing ties

un·til \ˌən'til\ prep : up to the time of ~ conj : to the time that

un·time·ly adj 1 : premature 2 : coming at an unfortunate time

un·to \ˌən'tü, 'ən,-\ prep : to

un·told adj 1 : not told 2 : too numerous to count

un·to·ward \ˌən'tōrd\ adj 1 : difficult to manage 2 : inconvenient

un·truth n 1 : lack of truthfulness 2 : lie

un·used adj 1 \ˌən'yüst, -'yüzd\ : not accustomed 2 \-'yüzd\ : not used

un·well adj : sick

un·wieldy \ˌən'wēldē\ adj : too big or awkward to manage easily

un·wind vb -wound; -wind·ing 1 : undo something that is wound 2 : become unwound 3 : relax

un·wit·ting adj 1 : not knowing 2 : not intended — **un·wit·ting·ly** adv

un·wont·ed adj 1 : unusual 2 : not accustomed by experience

un·wrap vb : remove the wrappings from

un·writ·ten adj : made or passed on only in speech or through tradition

un·zip vb : zip open

up \'əp\ adv 1 : in or to a higher position or level 2 : from beneath a surface or level 3 : in or into an upright position 4 : out of bed 5 : to or with greater intensity 6 : into existence, evidence, or knowledge 7 : away 8 — used to indicate a degree of success, completion, or finality 9 : in or

---

unsuitably	untreated	unwelcome
unsuited	untrue	unwholesome
unsupervised	untrustworthy	unwilling
unsupported	untruthful	unwillingly
unsure	unusable	unwillingness
unsurprising	unusual	unwise
unsuspecting	unvarying	unwisely
unsweetened	unverified	unworkable
unsympathetic	unwanted	unworthy
untamed	unwarranted	unworthiness
untanned	unwary	unworthy
untidy	unwavering	unyielding
untouched	unweaned	
untrained	unwed	

into parts ~ *adj* **1** : in the state of having risen **2** : raised to or at a higher level **3** : moving, inclining, or directed upward **4** : in a state of greater intensity **5** : at an end ~ *vb* **upped** *or in l* **up** ; **upped** ; **up-ping** ; **ups** *or in l* **up 1** : act abruptly **2** : move or cause to move upward ~ *prep* **1** : to, toward, or at a higher point of **2** : along or toward the beginning of

up-braid \əp'brād\ *vb* : criticize or scold

up-bring-ing \'əp,briŋiŋ\ *n* : process of bringing up and training

up-com-ing \əp'kəmiŋ\ *adj* : approaching

up-date \əp'dāt\ *vb* : bring up to date — **update** \'əp,dāt\ *n*

up-end \əp'end\ *vb* **1** : stand or rise on end **2** : overturn

up-grade \'əp,grād\ *n* **1** : upward slope **2** : increase ~ \'əp,-, ,əp'-\ *vb* : raise to a higher position

up-heav-al \əp'hēvəl\ *n* **1** : a heaving up (as of part of the earth's crust) **2** : violent change

up-hill \əp'hil\ *adv* : upward on a hill or incline ~ \'əp,-\ *adj* **1** : going up **2** : difficult

up-hold \əp'hōld\ *vb* -**held**; -**hold-ing** : support or defend — **up-hold-er** *n*

up-hol-ster \əp'hōlstər\ *vb* : cover (furniture) with padding and fabric (**up-hol-stery** \-stərē\) — **up-hol-ster-er** *n*

up-keep \'əp,kēp\ *n* : act or cost of keeping up or maintaining

up-land \'əplənd, -,land\ *n* : high land — **upland** *adj*

up-lift \əp'lift\ *vb* **1** : lift up **2** : improve the condition or spirits of — **up-lift** \'əp,-\ *n*

up-on \ə'pȯn, -'pän\ *prep* : on

up-per \'əpər\ *adj* : higher in position, rank, or order ~ *n* : top part of a shoe

upper-hand *n* : advantage

up-per-most \'əpər,mōst\ *adv* : in or into the highest or most prominent position — **uppermost** *adj*

pi-pi-ty \'əpətē\ *adj* : acting with a manner of undue importance

up-right \'əp,rīt\ *adj* **1** : vertical **2** : erect in posture **3** : morally correct ~ *n* : something that stands upright — **upright** *adv* — **up-right-ly** *adv* — **up-right-ness** *n*

up-ris-ing \'əp,rīziŋ\ *n* : revolt

up-roar \'əp,rōr\ *n* : state of commotion or violent disturbance

up-roar-i-ous \,əp'rōrēəs\ *adj* **1** : marked by uproar **2** : extremely funny — **up-roar-i-ous-ly** *adv*

up-root \,əp'rüt, -'ru̇t\ *vb* : remove by or as if by pulling up by the roots

up-set \,əp'set\ *vb* -**set**; -**set-ting 1** : force or be forced out of the usual position **2** : disturb emotionally or physically ~ \'əp,-\ *n* **1** : act of throwing into disorder **2** : minor physical disorder ~ *adj* : emotionally disturbed or agitated

up-shot \'əp,shät\ *n* : final result

up-side down \,əp,sīd'dau̇n\ *adv* **1** : turned so that the upper and lower parts are reversed **2** : in or into confusion or disorder — **upside-down** *adj*

up-stairs \'əp,starz, ,əp'-\ *adv* : up the stairs or to the next floor ~ *adj* : situated on the floor above ~ *n sing or pl* : part of a building above the ground floor

up-stand-ing \,əp'standiŋ, 'əp,-\ *adj* : honest

up-start \,əp'stärt\ *n* : one who claims more personal importance than is warranted — **up-start** *adj*

up-swing \'əp,swiŋ\ *n* : marked increase (as in activity)

up-tight \'əp'tīt\ *adj* **1** : tense **2** : angry **3** : rigidly conventional

up-to-date *adj* : current — **up-to-date-ness** *n*

up-town \'əp,tau̇n\ *n* : upper part of a town or city — **uptown** *adj or adv*

up-turn \'əp,tərn\ *n* : improvement or increase

up-ward \'əpwərd\, **up-wards** \-wərdz\ *adv* **1** : in a direction from lower to higher **2** : toward a higher or greater state or number ~ *adj* : directed toward or situated in a higher place — **up-ward-ly** *adv*

up-wind \,əp'wind\ *adv or adj* : in the direction from which the wind is blowing

ura-ni-um \yu̇'rānēəm\ *n* : metallic radioactive chemical element

ur-ban \'ərbən\ *adj* : characteristic of a city

ur-bane \,ər'bān\ *adj* : polished in manner — **ur-ban-i-ty** \,ər'banətē\ *n*

ur-ban-ite \'ərbə,nīt\ *n* : city dweller

ur-chin \'ərchən\ *n* : mischievous youngster

-ure *n suffix* : act or process

ure•thra \yù'rēthrə\ *n, pl* -thras *or* -thrae \-,thrē\ : canal that carries off urine from the bladder — **ure•thral** \-thrəl\ *adj*

urge \'ərj\ *vb* **urged; urging** **1** : earnestly plead for or insist on (an action) **2** : try to persuade **3** : impel to a course of activity ~ *n* : force or impulse that moves one to action

ur•gent \'ərjənt\ *adj* **1** : calling for immediate attention **2** : urging insistently — **ur•gen•cy** \-jənsē\ *n* — **ur•gent•ly** *adv*

uri•nal \'yùrən°l\ *n* : receptacle to urinate in

uri•nate \'yùrə,nāt\ *vb* -nat•ed; -nat•ing : discharge urine — **uri•na•tion** \,yùrə'nāshən\ *n*

urine \'yùrən\ *n* : liquid waste material from the kidneys — **uri•nary** \-ə,nerē\ *adj*

URL \,yù,är'el\ *n* : address on the Internet

urn \'ərn\ *n* **1** : vaselike or cuplike vessel on a pedestal **2** : large coffee pot

us \'əs\ *pron, objective case of* WE

us•able \'yüzəbəl\ *adj* : suitable or fit for use — **us•abil•i•ty** \,yüzə'bilətē\ *n*

us•age \'yüsij, -zij\ *n* **1** : customary practice **2** : way of doing or of using something

use \'yüs\ *n* **1** : act or practice of putting something into action **2** : state of being used **3** : way of using **4** : privilege, ability, or power to use something **5** : utility or function **6** : occasion or need to use ~ \'yüz\ *vb* **used** \'yüzd; "used to" *usu* 'yüstə\; **us•ing** \'yüziŋ\ **1** : put into action or service **2** : consume **3** : behave toward **4** : to make use of **5** — used in the past tense with *to* to indicate a former practice — **use•ful** \'yüsfəl\ *adj* — **use•ful•ly** *adv* — **use•ful•ness** *n*

— **use•less** \'yüsləs\ *adj* — **use•less•ly** *adv* — **use•less•ness** *n* — **us•er** *n*

used \'yüzd\ *adj* : not new

ush•er \'əshər\ *n* : one who escorts people to their seats ~ *vb* : conduct to a place

ush•er•ette \,əshə'ret\ *n* : woman or girl who is an usher

usu•al \'yüzhəwəl\ *adj* : being what is expected according to custom or habit — **usu•al•ly** \'yüzhəwəlē\ *adv*

usurp \yù'sərp, -'zərp\ *vb* : seize and hold by force or without right — **usur•pa•tion** \,yüsər'pāshən, -zər-\ *n* — **usurp•er** *n*

usu•ry \'yüzhərē\ *n, pl* -ries **1** : lending of money at excessive interest or the rate or amount of such interest — **usu•rer** \-zhərər\ *n* — **usu•ri•ous** \yù'zhùrēəs\ *adj*

uten•sil \yù'tensəl\ *n* **1** : eating or cooking tool **2** : useful tool

uter•us \'yütərəs\ *n, pl* **uteri** \-ə,rī\ : organ for containing and nourishing an unborn offspring — **uter•ine** \-,rīn, -rən\ *adj*

util•i•tar•i•an \yü,tilə'terēən\ *adj* : being or meant to be useful rather than beautiful

util•i•ty \yù'tilətē\ *n, pl* -ties **1** : usefulness **2** : regulated business providing a public service (as electricity)

uti•lize \'yüt°l,īz\ *vb* -lized; -liz•ing : make use of — **uti•li•za•tion** \,yüt°lə-'zāshən\ *n*

ut•most \'ət,mōst\ *adj* **1** : most distant **2** : of the greatest or highest degree or amount — **utmost** *n*

uto•pia \yù'tōpēə\ *n* : place of ideal perfection — **uto•pi•an** \-pēən\ *adj or n*

ut•ter \'ətər\ *adj* : absolute ~ *vb* : express with the voice — **ut•ter•er** \-ərər\ *n* — **ut•ter•ly** *adv*

ut•ter•ance \'ətərəns\ *n* : what one says

V

v \'vē\ *n, pl* **v's** *or* **vs** \'vēz\ : 22d letter of the alphabet

va•can•cy \'vākənsē\ *n, pl* -cies **1** : state of being vacant **2** : unused or unoccupied place or office

va•cant \-kənt\ *adj* **1** : not occupied, filled, or in use **2** : devoid of thought or expression — **va•cant•ly** *adv*

va•cate \-,kāt\ *vb* -cat•ed; -cat•ing **1** : annul **2** : leave unfilled or unoccupied

va·ca·tion \vā'kāshən, və-\ n : period of rest from routine — **vacation** vb — **va·ca·tion·er** n

vac·ci·nate \'vaksə,nāt\ vb **-nat·ed; -nat·ing** : administer a vaccine usu. by injection

vac·ci·na·tion \,vaksə'nāshən\ n : act of or the scar left by vaccinating

vac·cine \vak'sēn, 'vak,-\ n : substance to induce immunity to a disease

vac·il·late \'vasə,lāt\ vb **-lat·ed; -lat·ing** : waver between courses or opinions — **vac·il·la·tion** \,vasə'lāshən\ n

vac·u·ous \'vakyəwəs\ adj 1 : empty 2 : dull or inane — **va·cu·i·ty** \va-'kyüətē, və-\ n — **vac·u·ous·ly** adv — **vac·u·ous·ness** n

vac·u·um \'vak,yüm, -yəm\ n, pl **vac·u·ums** or **vac·ua** \-yəwə\ : empty space with no air ~ vb : clean with a vacuum cleaner

vacuum cleaner n : appliance that cleans by suction

vag·a·bond \'vagə,bänd\ n : wanderer with no home — **vagabond** adj

va·ga·ry \'vāgərē, və'gerē\ n, pl **-ries** : whim

va·gi·na \və'jīnə\ n, pl **-nae** \-,nē\ or **-nas** : canal that leads out from the uterus — **vag·i·nal** \'vajən°l\ adj

va·grant \'vāgrənt\ n : person with no home and no job — **va·gran·cy** \-grənsē\ n — **vagrant** adj

vague \'vāg\ adj **vagu·er; vagu·est** : not clear, definite, or distinct — **vague·ly** adv — **vague·ness** n

vain \'vān\ adj 1 : of no value 2 : unsuccessful 3 : conceited — **vain·ly** adv

va·lance \'valəns, 'vāl-\ n : border drapery

vale \'vāl\ n : valley

vale·dic·to·ri·an \,valə,dik'tōrēən\ n : student giving the farewell address at commencement

vale·dic·to·ry \-'diktərē\ adj : bidding farewell — **valedictory** n

va·lence \'vāləns\ n : degree of combining power of a chemical element

val·en·tine \'valən,tīn\ n : sweetheart or a card sent to a sweetheart or friend on St. Valentine's Day

va·let \'valət, 'val,ā, va'lā\ n : male personal servant

val·iant \'valyənt\ adj : brave or heroic — **val·iant·ly** adv

val·id \'valəd\ adj 1 : proper and legally binding 2 : founded on truth or fact — **va·lid·i·ty** \və'lidətē, va-\ n — **val·id·ly** adv

val·i·date \'valə,dāt\ vb **-dat·ed; -dat·ing** : establish as valid — **val·i·da·tion** \,valə'dāshən\ n

va·lise \və'lēs\ n : suitcase

val·ley \'valē\ n, pl **-leys** : long depression between ranges of hills

val·or \'valər\ n : bravery or heroism — **val·or·ous** \'valərəs\ adj

valu·able \'valyəwəbəl\ adj 1 : worth a lot of money 2 : being of great importance or use — **valuable** n

val·u·a·tion \,valyə'wāshən\ n 1 : act or process of valuing 2 : market value of a thing

val·ue \'valyü\ n 1 : fair return or equivalent for something exchanged 2 : how much something is worth 3 : distinctive quality (as of a color or sound) 4 : guiding principle or ideal — usu. pl. ~ vb **val·ued; valu·ing** 1 : estimate the worth of 2 : appreciate the importance of — **val·ue·less** adj — **val·u·er** n

valve \'valv\ n : structure or device to control flow of a liquid or gas — **valved** \'valvd\ adj — **valve·less** adj

vam·pire \'vam,pīr\ n 1 : legendary night-wandering dead body that sucks human blood 2 : bat that feeds on the blood of animals

¹**van** \'van\ n : vanguard

²**van** n : enclosed truck

va·na·di·um \və'nādēəm\ n : soft ductile metallic chemical element

van·dal \'vand°l\ n : person who willfully defaces or destroys property — **van·dal·ism** \-,izəm\ n — **van·dal·ize** \-,īz\ vb

vane \'vān\ n : bladelike device designed to be moved by force of the air or water

van·guard \'van,gärd\ n 1 : troops moving at the front of an army 2 : forefront of an action or movement

va·nil·la \və'nilə\ n : a flavoring made from the pods of a tropical orchid or this orchid

van·ish \'vanish\ vb : disappear suddenly

van·i·ty \'vanətē\ n, pl **-ties** 1 : futility or something that is futile 2 : undue pride in oneself 3 : makeup case or table

van·quish \'vaŋkwish, 'van-\ vb 1

: overcome in battle or in a contest **2** : gain mastery over

van·tage \'vantij\ *n* : position of advantage or perspective

va·pid \'vapəd, 'vāpəd\ *adj* : lacking spirit, liveliness, or zest — **va·pid·i·ty** \va'pidətē\ *n* — **vap·id·ly** \'vapədlē\ *adv* — **vap·id·ness** *n*

va·por \'vāpər\ *n* **1** : fine separated particles floating in and clouding the air **2** : gaseous form of an ordinarily liquid substance — **va·por·ous** \-pərəs\ *adj*

va·por·ize \'vāpə₊rīz\ *vb* **-ized; -iz·ing** : convert into vapor — **va·por·i·za·tion** \₊vāpərə'zāshən\ *n* — **va·por·iz·er** *n*

var·i·able \'verēəbəl\ *adj* : apt to vary — **var·i·abil·i·ty** \₊verēə'bilətē\ *n* — **var·i·able** *n* — **var·i·ably** *adv*

var·i·ance \'verēəns\ *n* **1** : instance or degree of variation **2** : disagreement or dispute **3** : legal permission to build contrary to a zoning law

var·i·ant \-ənt\ *n* : something that differs from others of its kind — **variant** *adj*

vari·a·tion \₊verē'āshən\ *n* : instance or extent of varying

var·i·cose \'varə₊kōs\ *adj* : abnormally swollen and dilated

var·ied \'verēd\ *adj* : showing variety — **var·ied·ly** *adv*

var·ie·gat·ed \'verēə₊gātəd\ *adj* : having patches, stripes, or marks of different colors — **var·ie·gate** \-₊gāt\ *vb* — **var·ie·ga·tion** \₊verēə'gāshən\ *n*

va·ri·ety \və'rīətē\ *n, pl* **-et·ies 1** : state of being different **2** : collection of different things **3** : something that differs from others of its kind

var·i·ous \'verēəs\ *adj* : being many and unlike — **var·i·ous·ly** *adv*

var·nish \'värnish\ *n* : liquid that dries to a hard glossy protective coating ~ *vb* : cover with varnish

var·si·ty \'värsətē\ *n, pl* **-ties** : principal team representing a school

vary \'verē\ *vb* **var·ied; vary·ing 1** : alter **2** : make or be of different kinds

vas·cu·lar \'vaskyələr\ *adj* : relating to a channel for the conveyance of a body fluid (as blood or sap)

vase \'vās, 'vāz\ *n* : tall usu. ornamental container to hold flowers

vas·sal \'vasəl\ *n* **1** : one acknowledging another as feudal lord **2** : one in

a dependent position — **vas·sal·age** \-əlij\ *n*

vast \'vast\ *adj* : very great in size, extent, or amount — **vast·ly** *adv* — **vast·ness** *n*

vat \'vat\ *n* : large tub- or barrel-shaped container

vaude·ville \'vȯdvəl, 'väd-, 'vōd-, -₊vil, -əvəl, -ə₊vil\ *n* : stage entertainment of unrelated acts

¹vault \'vȯlt\ *n* **1** : masonry arch **2** : usu. underground storage or burial room ~ *vb* : form or cover with a vault — **vault·ed** *adj* — **vaulty** *adj*

²vault *vb* : spring over esp. with the help of the hands or a pole ~ *n* : act of vaulting — **vault·er** *n*

vaunt \'vȯnt\ *vb* : boast — **vaunt** *n*

veal \'vēl\ *n* : flesh of a young calf

veer \'vir\ *vb* : change course esp. gradually — **veer** *n*

veg·e·ta·ble \'vejtəbəl, 'vejə-\ *adj* **1** : relating to or obtained from plants **2** : like that of a plant ~ *n* **1** : plant **2** : plant grown for food

veg·e·tar·i·an \₊vejə'terēən\ *n* : person who eats no meat — **vegetarian** *adj* — **veg·e·tar·i·an·ism** \-ē₊nizəm\ *n*

veg·e·tate \'vejə₊tāt\ *vb* **-tat·ed; -tat·ing** : lead a dull inert life

veg·e·ta·tion \₊vejə'tāshən\ *n* : plant life — **veg·e·ta·tion·al** \-shənəl\ *adj* — **veg·e·ta·tive** \'vejə₊tātiv\ *adj*

ve·he·ment \'vēəmənt\ *adj* : showing strong esp. violent feeling — **ve·he·mence** \-məns\ *n* — **ve·he·ment·ly** *adv*

ve·hi·cle \'vē₊hikəl, 'vēəkəl\ *n* **1** : medium through which something is expressed, applied, or administered **2** : structure for transporting something esp. on wheels — **ve·hic·u·lar** \vē'hikyələr\ *adj*

veil \'vāl\ *n* **1** : sheer material to hide something or to cover the face and head **2** : something that hides ~ *vb* : cover with a veil

vein \'vān\ *n* **1** : rock fissure filled with deposited mineral matter **2** : vessel that carries blood toward the heart **3** : sap-carrying tube in a leaf **4** : distinctive element or style of expression — **veined** \'vānd\ *adj*

ve·loc·i·ty \və'läsətē\ *n, pl* **-ties** : speed

ve·lour, ve·lours \və'lủr\ *n, pl* **velours** \-'lủrz\ : fabric with a velvetlike pile

vel·vet \'velvət\ *n* : fabric with a short soft pile — **velvet** *adj* — **vel·vety** *adj*

ve·nal \'vēn°l\ *adj* : capable of being corrupted esp. by money — **ve·nal·i·ty** \vi'nalətē\ *n* — **ve·nal·ly** *adv*

vend \'vend\ *vb* : sell — **vend·ible** *adj* — **ven·dor** \'vendər\ *n*

ven·det·ta \ven'detə\ *n* : feud marked by acts of revenge

ve·neer \və'nir\ *n* 1 : thin layer of fine wood glued over a cheaper wood 2 : superficial display ~ *vb* : overlay with a veneer

ven·er·a·ble \'venərəbəl\ *adj* : deserving of respect

ven·er·ate \'venə,rāt\ *vb* **-at·ed; -at·ing** : respect esp. with reverence — **ven·er·a·tion** \,venə'rāshən\ *n*

ve·ne·re·al disease \və'nirēəl-\ *n* : contagious disease spread through copulation

ven·geance \'venjəns\ *n* : punishment in retaliation for an injury or offense

venge·ful \'venjfəl\ *adj* : filled with a desire for revenge — **venge·ful·ly** *adv*

ve·nial \'vēnēəl\ *adj* : capable of being forgiven

ven·i·son \'venəsən, -əzən\ *n* : deer meat

ven·om \'venəm\ *n* 1 : poison secreted by certain animals 2 : ill will — **ven·om·ous** \-əməs\ *adj*

vent \'vent\ *vb* 1 : provide with or let out at a vent 2 : give expression to ~ *n* : opening for passage or for relieving pressure

ven·ti·late \'vent°l,āt\ *vb* **-lat·ed; -lat·ing** : allow fresh air to circulate through — **ven·ti·la·tion** \,vent°l'āshən\ *n* — **ven·ti·la·tor** \'vent°l,ātər\ *n*

ven·tri·cle \'ventrikəl\ *n* : heart chamber that pumps blood into the arteries

ven·tril·o·quist \ven'trilə,kwist\ *n* : one who can make the voice appear to come from another source — **ven·tril·o·quism** \-,kwizəm\ *n* — **ven·tril·o·quy** \-kwē\ *n*

ven·ture \'venchər\ *vb* **-tured; -tur·ing** 1 : risk or take a chance on 2 : put forward (an opinion) ~ *n* : speculative business enterprise

ven·ture·some \-səm\ *adj* : brave or daring — **ven·ture·some·ly** *adv* — **ven·ture·some·ness** *n*

ven·ue \'venyü\ *n* : scene of an action or event

ve·rac·i·ty \və'rasətē\ *n, pl* **-ties** : truthfulness or accuracy — **ve·ra·cious** \və'rāshəs\ *adj*

ve·ran·da, ve·ran·dah \və'randə\ *n* : large open porch

verb \'vərb\ *n* : word that expresses action or existence

ver·bal \'vərbəl\ *adj* 1 : having to do with or expressed in words 2 : oral 3 : relating to or formed from a verb — **ver·bal·i·za·tion** \,vərbələ'zāshən\ *n* — **ver·bal·ize** \'vərbə,līz\ *vb* — **ver·bal·ly** \-ē\ *adv*

verbal auxiliary *n* : auxiliary verb

ver·ba·tim \vər'bātəm\ *adv or adj* : using the same words

ver·biage \'vərbēij\ *n* : excess of words

ver·bose \vər'bōs\ *adj* : using more words than are needed — **ver·bos·i·ty** \-'bäsətē\ *n*

ver·dant \'vərd°nt\ *adj* : green with growing plants — **ver·dant·ly** *adv*

ver·dict \'vərdikt\ *n* : decision of a jury

ver·dure \'vərjər\ *n* : green growing vegetation or its color

verge \'vərj\ *vb* **verged; verg·ing** : be almost on the point of happening or doing something ~ *n* 1 : edge 2 : threshold

ver·i·fy \'verə,fī\ *vb* **-fied; -fy·ing** : establish the truth, accuracy, or reality of — **ver·i·fi·able** *adj* — **ver·i·fi·ca·tion** \,verəfə'kāshən\ *n*

ver·i·ly \'verəlē\ *adv* : truly or confidently

veri·si·mil·i·tude \,verəsə'milə,tüd\ *n* : appearance of being true

ver·i·ta·ble \'verətəbəl\ *adj* : actual or true — **ver·i·ta·bly** *adv*

ver·i·ty \'verətē\ *n, pl* **-ties** : truth

ver·mi·cel·li \,vərmə'chelē, -'sel-\ *n* : thin spaghetti

ver·min \'vərmən\ *n, pl* **vermin** : small animal pest

ver·mouth \vər'müth\ *n* : dry or sweet wine flavored with herbs

ver·nac·u·lar \vər'nakyələr\ *adj* : relating to a native language or dialect and esp. its normal spoken form ~ *n* : vernacular language

ver·nal \'vərn°l\ *adj* : relating to spring

ver·sa·tile \'vərsət°l\ *adj* : having many abilities or uses — **ver·sa·til·i·ty** \,vərsə'tilətē\ *n*

¹**verse** \'vərs\ *n* 1 : line or stanza of poetry 2 : poetry 3 : short division of a chapter in the Bible

²**verse** *vb* **versed; versing** : make familiar by experience, study, or practice

ver·sion \'vərzhən\ *n* 1 : translation of the Bible 2 : account or description from a particular point of view

ver·sus \'vərsəs\ *prep* : opposed to or against

ver·te·bra \'vərtəbrə\ n, pl **-brae** \-,brā, -,brē\ or **-bras** : segment of the backbone — **ver·te·bral** \vər'tēbrəl, 'vərtə-\ adj

ver·te·brate \'vərtəbrət, -,brāt\ n : animal with a backbone — **vertebrate** adj

ver·tex \'vər,teks\ n, pl **ver·ti·ces** \'vərtə,sēz\ 1 : point of intersection of lines or surfaces 2 : highest point

ver·ti·cal \'vərtikəl\ adj : rising straight up from a level surface — **vertical** n — **ver·ti·cal·i·ty** \,vərtə-'kalətē\ n — **ver·ti·cal·ly** adv

ver·ti·go \'vərti,gō\ n, pl **-goes** or **-gos** : dizziness

verve \'vərv\ n : liveliness or vividness

very \'verē\ adj **veri·er; -est** 1 : exact 2 : exactly suitable 3 : mere or bare 4 : precisely the same ~ adv 1 : to a high degree 2 : in actual fact

ves·i·cle \'vesikəl\ n : membranous cavity — **ve·sic·u·lar** \və'sikyələr\ adj

ves·pers \'vespərz\ n pl : late afternoon or evening worship service

ves·sel \'vesəl\ n 1 : a container (as a barrel, bottle, bowl, or cup) for a liquid 2 : craft for navigation esp. on water 3 : tube in which a body fluid is circulated

¹vest \'vest\ vb 1 : give a particular authority, right, or property to 2 : clothe with or as if with a garment

²vest n : sleeveless garment usu. worn under a suit coat

ves·ti·bule \'vestə,byül\ n : enclosed entrance — **ves·tib·u·lar** \ve'sti-byələr\ adj

ves·tige \'vestij\ n : visible trace or remains — **ves·ti·gial** \ve'stijēəl\ adj — **ves·ti·gial·ly** adv

vest·ment \'vestmənt\ n : clergy member's garment

ves·try \'vestrē\ n, pl **-tries** : church storage room for garments and articles

vet·er·an \'vetərən\ n 1 : former member of the armed forces 2 : person with long experience — **veteran** adj

Veterans Day n : 4th Monday in October or formerly November 11 observed as a legal holiday in commemoration of the end of war in 1918 and 1945

vet·er·i·nar·i·an \,vetərən'erēən\ n

: doctor of animals — **vet·er·i·nary** \'vetərən,erē\ adj

ve·to \'vētō\ n, pl **-toes** 1 : power to forbid and esp. the power of a chief executive to prevent a bill from becoming law 2 : exercise of the veto ~ vb 1 : forbid 2 : reject a legislative bill

vex \'veks\ vb **vexed; vex·ing** : trouble, distress, or annoy — **vex·a·tion** \vek'sāshən\ n — **vex·a·tious** \-shəs\ adj

via \'vīə, 'vēə\ prep : by way of

vi·a·ble \'vīəbəl\ adj 1 : capable of surviving or growing 2 : practical or workable — **vi·a·bil·i·ty** \,vīə'bilətē\ n — **vi·a·bly** \'vīəblē\ adv

via·duct \'vīə,dəkt\ n : elevated roadway or railway bridge

vi·al \'vīəl\ n : small bottle

vi·brant \'vībrənt\ adj 1 : vibrating 2 : pulsing with vigor or activity 3 : sounding from vibration — **vi·bran·cy** \-brənsē\ n

vi·brate \'vī,brāt\ vb **-brat·ed; -brat·ing** 1 : move or cause to move quickly back and forth or side to side 2 : respond sympathetically — **vi·bra·tion** \vī'brāshən\ n — **vi·bra·tor** \'vī-,brātər\ n — **vi·bra·to·ry** \'vībrə-,tōrē\ adj

vic·ar \'vikər\ n : parish clergy member — **vi·car·i·ate** \-ēət\ n

vi·car·i·ous \vī'karēəs\ adj : sharing in someone else's experience through imagination or sympathetic feelings — **vi·car·i·ous·ly** adv — **vi·car·i·ous·ness** n

vice \'vīs\ n 1 : immoral habit 2 : depravity

vice- \,vīs\ prefix : one that takes the place of

vice admiral n : commissioned officer in the navy or coast guard ranking above a rear admiral

vice·roy \'vīs,rói\ n : provincial governor who represents the sovereign

vice ver·sa \,vīsi'vərsə, ,vīs'vər-\ adv : with the order reversed

vi·cin·i·ty \və'sinətē\ n, pl **-ties** : surrounding area

vi·cious \'vishəs\ adj 1 : wicked 2

List of self-explanatory words with the prefix *vice-*

vice–chancellor	vice presidency	vice presidential
vice–consul	vice president	vice–regent

: savage **3** : malicious — **vi·cious·ly** *adv* — **vi·cious·ness** *n*

vi·cis·si·tude \və'sisə,tüd, vī-, -,tyüd\ *n* : irregular, unexpected, or surprising change — usu. used in pl.

vic·tim \'viktəm\ *n* : person killed, hurt, or abused

vic·tim·ize \'viktə,mīz\ *vb* **-ized; -iz·ing** : make a victim of — **vic·tim·i·za·tion** \,viktəmə'zāshən\ *n* — **vic·tim·iz·er** \'viktə,mīzər\ *n*

vic·tor \'viktər\ *n* : winner

Vic·to·ri·an \vik'tōrēən\ *adj* : relating to the reign of Queen Victoria of England or the art, taste, or standards of her time — ~ *n* : one of the Victorian period

vic·to·ri·ous \vik'tōrēəs\ *adj* : having won a victory — **vic·to·ri·ous·ly** *adv*

vic·to·ry \'viktərē\ *n, pl* **-ries** : success in defeating an enemy or opponent or in overcoming difficulties

vict·uals \'vit²lz\ *n pl* : food

vid·eo \'vidē,ō\ *adj* : relating to the television image

vid·eo·cas·sette \,vidē,ōkə'set\ *n* : cassette containing videotape

vid·eo·tape \'vidēō,tāp\ *vb* : make a recording of (a television production) on special tape — **videotape** *n*

vie \'vī\ *vb* **vied; vy·ing** : contend — **vi·er** \'vīər\ *n*

view \'vyü\ *n* **1** : process of seeing or examining **2** : opinion **3** : area of landscape that can be seen **4** : range of vision **5** : purpose or object ~ *vb* **1** : look at **2** : think about or consider — **view·er** *n*

view·point *n* : position from which something is considered

vig·il \'vijəl\ *n* **1** : day of devotion before a religious feast **2** : act or time of keeping awake **3** : long period of keeping watch (as over a sick or dying person)

vig·i·lant \'vijələnt\ *adj* : alert esp. to avoid danger — **vig·i·lance** \-ləns\ *n* — **vig·i·lant·ly** *adv*

vig·i·lan·te \,vijə'lantē\ *n* : one of a group independent of the law working to suppress crime

vi·gnette \vin'yet\ *n* : short descriptive literary piece

vig·or \'vigər\ *n* **1** : energy or strength **2** : intensity or force — **vig·or·ous** \'vigərəs\ *adj* — **vig·or·ous·ly** *adv* — **vig·or·ous·ness** *n*

vile \'vīl\ *adj* **vil·er; vil·est** : thoroughly

bad or contemptible — **vile·ly** *adv* — **vile·ness** *n*

vil·i·fy \'vilə,fī\ *vb* **-fied; -fy·ing** : speak evil of — **vil·i·fi·ca·tion** \,viləfə-'kāshən\ *n* — **vil·i·fi·er** \'vilə,fīər\ *n*

vil·la \'vilə\ *n* : country estate

vil·lage \'vilij\ *n* : small country town — **vil·lag·er** *n*

vil·lain \'vilən\ *n* : bad person — **vil·lain·ess** \-ənəs\ *n* — **vil·lainy** *n*

vil·lain·ous \-ənəs\ *adj* : evil or corrupt — **vil·lain·ous·ly** *adv* — **vil·lain·ous·ness** *n*

vim \'vim\ *n* : energy

vin·di·cate \'vində,kāt\ *vb* **-cat·ed; -cat·ing** **1** : avenge **2** : exonerate **3** : justify — **vin·di·ca·tion** \,vində-'kāshən\ *n* — **vin·di·ca·tor** \'vində-,kātər\ *n*

vin·dic·tive \vin'diktiv\ *adj* : seeking or meant for revenge — **vin·dic·tive·ly** *adv* — **vin·dic·tive·ness** *n*

vine \'vīn\ *n* : climbing or trailing plant

vin·e·gar \'vinigər\ *n* : acidic liquid obtained by fermentation — **vin·e·gary** \-gərē\ *adj*

vine·yard \'vinyərd\ *n* : plantation of grapevines

vin·tage \'vintij\ *n* **1** : season's yield of grapes or wine **2** : period of origin — ~ *adj* : of enduring interest

vi·nyl \'vīn²l\ *n* : strong plastic

vi·o·la \vē'ōlə\ *n* : instrument of the violin family tuned lower than the violin — **vi·o·list** \-list\ *n*

vi·o·late \'vīə,lāt\ *vb* **-lat·ed; -lat·ing** **1** : act with disrespect or disregard of **2** : rape **3** : desecrate — **vi·o·la·tion** \,vīə'lāshən\ *n* — **vi·o·la·tor** \'vīə-,lātər\ *n*

vi·o·lence \'vīələns\ *n* : intense physical force that causes or is intended to cause injury or destruction — **vi·o·lent** \-lənt\ *adj* — **vi·o·lent·ly** *adv*

vi·o·let \'vīələt\ *n* **1** : small flowering plant **2** : reddish blue

vi·o·lin \,vīə'lin\ *n* : bowed stringed instrument — **vi·o·lin·ist** \-nist\ *n*

VIP \,vē,ī'pē\ *n, pl* **VIPs** \-'pēz\ : very important person

vi·per \'vīpər\ *n* **1** : venomous snake **2** : treacherous or malignant person

vi·ra·go \və'rägō, -'rä-; 'virə,gō\ *n, pl* **-goes** *or* **-gos** : shrew

vi·ral \'vīrəl\ *adj* : relating to or caused by a virus

vir·gin \'vərjən\ *n* **1** : unmarried woman **2** : a person who has never

had sexual intercourse ~ *adj* **1**
: chaste **2** : natural and unspoiled —
vir·gin·al \-əl\ *adj* — **vir·gin·al·ly**
adv — **vir·gin·i·ty** \vər'jinətē\ *n*

vir·gule \'vərgyül\ *n* : mark/used esp.
to denote "or" or "per"

vir·ile \'virəl\ *adj* : masculine — **vi·ril·i·ty** \və'rilətē\ *n*

vir·tu·al \'vərchəwəl\ *adj* : being in
effect but not in fact or name — **vir·tu·al·ly** *adv*

vir·tue \'vərchü\ *n* **1** : moral excellence **2** : effective or commendable
quality **3** : chastity

vir·tu·os·i·ty \,vərchə'wäsətē\ *n, pl*
-ties : great skill (as in music)

vir·tu·o·so \,vərchə'wōsō, -zō\ *n,
pl* **-sos** *or* **-si** \-,sē, -,zē\ : highly
skilled performer esp. of music —
virtuoso *adj*

vir·tu·ous \'vərchəwəs\ *adj* **1** : morally
good **2** : chaste — **vir·tu·ous·ly** *adv*

vir·u·lent \'virələnt, -yələnt\ *adj* **1**
: extremely severe or infectious **2**
: full of malice — **vir·u·lence** \-ləns\
n — **vir·u·lent·ly** *adv*

vi·rus \'vīrəs\ *n* **1** : tiny disease-
causing agent **2** : a computer program that performs a malicious action (as destroying data)

vi·sa \'vēzə, -sə\ *n* : authorization to
enter a foreign country

vis·age \'vizij\ *n* : face

vis·cera \'visərə\ *n pl* : internal bodily
organs esp. of the trunk

vis·cer·al \'visərəl\ *adj* **1** : bodily **2**
: instinctive **3** : deeply or crudely
emotional — **vis·cer·al·ly** *adv*

vis·cid \'visəd\ *adj* : viscous — **vis·cid·i·ty** \vis'didətē\ *n*

vis·count \'vī,kaůnt\ *n* : British nobleman ranking below an earl and above
a baron

vis·count·ess \-əs\ *n* **1** : wife of a viscount **2** : woman with rank of a viscount

vis·cous \'viskəs\ *adj* : having a thick
or sticky consistency — **vis·cos·i·ty** \vis'käsətē\ *n*

vise \'vīs\ *n* : device for clamping
something being worked on

vis·i·bil·i·ty \,vizə'bilətē\ *n, pl* **-ties**
: degree or range to which something
can be seen

vis·i·ble \'vizəbəl\ *adj* **1** : capable of
being seen **2** : manifest or apparent
— **vis·i·bly** *adv*

vi·sion \'vizhən\ *n* **1** : vivid picture

seen in a dream or trance or in the
imagination **2** : imaginative foresight **3** : power
of seeing ~ *vb* : imagine

vi·sion·ary \'vizhə,nerē\ *adj* **1** : given
to dreaming or imagining **2** : illusory
3 : not practical ~ *n* : one with great
dreams or projects

vis·it \'vizət\ *vb* **1** : go or come to see
2 : stay with for a time as a guest **3**
: cause or be a reward, affliction, or
punishment ~ *n* : short stay as a
guest — **vis·it·able** *adj* — **vis·i·tor**
\-ər\ *n*

vis·i·ta·tion \,vizə'tāshən\ *n* **1** : official visit **2** : divine punishment or favor **3** : severe trial

vi·sor \'vīzər\ *n* **1** : front piece of a
helmet **2** : part (as on a cap or car
windshield) that shades the eyes

vis·ta \'vistə\ *n* : distant view

vi·su·al \'vizhəwəl\ *adj* **1** : relating to
sight **2** : visible — **vi·su·al·ly** *adv*

vi·su·al·ize \'vizhəwə,līz\ *vb* **-ized;
-iz·ing** : form a mental image of
— **vi·su·al·i·za·tion** \,vizhəwələ'zā·shən\ *n* — **vi·su·al·iz·er** \'vizhəwə·,līzər\ *n*

vi·tal \'vīt²l\ *adj* **1** : relating to, necessary for, or characteristic of life **2**
: full of life and vigor **3** : fatal **4**
: very important — **vi·tal·ly** *adv*

vi·tal·i·ty \vī'talətē\ *n, pl* **-ties 1** : life
force **2** : energy

vital signs *n pl* : body's pulse rate, respiration, temperature, and usu. blood
pressure

vi·ta·min \'vītəmən\ *n* : natural organic
substance essential to health

vi·ti·ate \'vishē,āt\ *vb* **-at·ed; -at·ing 1**
: spoil or impair **2** : invalidate — **vi·ti·a·tion** \,vishē'āshən\ *n* — **vi·ti·a·tor** \'vishē,ātər\ *n*

vit·re·ous \'vitrēəs\ *adj* : relating to or
resembling glass

vit·ri·ol \'vitrēəl\ *n* : something caustic,
corrosive, or biting — **vit·ri·ol·ic**
\,vitrē'älik\ *adj*

vi·tu·per·ate \vī'tüpə,rāt, və, -'tyü-\ *vb*
-at·ed; -at·ing : abuse in words — **vi·tu·per·a·tion** \-,tüpə'rāshən, -,tyü\
n — **vi·tu·per·a·tive** \-'tüpərətiv,
-'tyü-, -pə,rāt-\ *adj* — **vi·tu·per·a·tive·ly** *adv*

vi·va·cious \vəvāshəs, vī-\ *adj* : lively
— **vi·va·cious·ly** *adv* — **vi·va·cious·ness** *n* — **vi·vac·i·ty** \-'vasətē\ *n*

viv·id \'vivəd\ *adj* **1** : lively **2** : brilliant **3** : intense or sharp — **viv·id·ly** *adv* — **viv·id·ness** *n*

viv·i·fy \'viv·ə‚fī\ *vb* **-fied; -fy·ing** : give life or vividness to

vivi·sec·tion \‚vivə'sekshən, 'vivə‚-\ *n* : experimental operation on a living animal

vix·en \'viksən\ *n* **1** : scolding woman **2** : female fox

vo·cab·u·lary \vō'kabyə‚lerē\ *n, pl* **-lar·ies 1** : list or collection of words **2** : stock of words used by a person or about a subject

vo·cal \'vōkəl\ *adj* **1** : relating to or produced by or for the voice **2** : speaking out freely and usu. emphatically

vocal cords *n pl* : membranous folds in the larynx that are important in making vocal sounds

vo·cal·ist \'vōkəlist\ *n* : singer

vo·cal·ize \-‚līz\ *vb* **-ized; -iz·ing** : give vocal expression to

vo·ca·tion \vō'kāshən\ *n* : regular employment — **vo·ca·tion·al** \-shən-əl\ *adj*

vo·cif·er·ous \vō'sifərəs\ *adj* : noisy and insistent — **vo·cif·er·ous·ly** *adv*

vod·ka \'vädkə\ *n* : colorless distilled grain liquor

vogue \'vōg\ *n* : brief but intense popularity — **vogu·ish** \'vōgish\ *adj*

voice \'vȯis\ *n* **1** : sound produced through the mouth by humans and many animals **2** : power of speaking **3** : right of choice or opinion ~ *vb* **voiced; voic·ing** : express in words — **voiced** \'vȯist\ *adj*

void \'vȯid\ *adj* **1** : containing nothing **2** : lacking — with *of* **3** : not legally binding ~ *n* **1** : empty space **2** : feeling of hollowness ~ *vb* **1** : discharge (as body waste) **2** : make (as a contract) void — **void·able** *adj* — **void·er** *n*

vol·a·tile \'välət‚l\ *adj* **1** : readily vaporizing at a relatively low temperature **2** : likely to change suddenly — **vol·a·til·i·ty** \‚välə'tilətē\ *n* — **vol·a·til·ize** \'välət‚l‚īz\ *vb*

vol·ca·no \väl'kānō\ *n, pl* **-noes** or **-nos** : opening in the earth's crust from which molten rock and steam come out — **vol·ca·nic** \-'kanik\ *adj*

vo·li·tion \vō'lishən\ *n* : free will — **vo·li·tion·al** \-'lishənəl\ *adj*

vol·ley \'välē\ *n, pl* **-leys 1** : flight of missiles (as arrows) **2** : simultaneous shooting of many weapons

vol·ley·ball *n* : game of batting a large ball over a net

volt \'vōlt\ *n* : unit for measuring the force that moves an electric current

volt·age \-'vōltij\ *n* : quantity of volts

vol·u·ble \'välyəbəl\ *adj* : fluent and smooth in speech — **vol·u·bil·i·ty** \‚välyə'bilətē\ *n* — **vol·u·bly** \'väl-yəblē\ *adv*

vol·ume \'välyəm\ *n* **1** : book **2** : space occupied as measured by cubic units **3** : amount **4** : loudness of a sound

vo·lu·mi·nous \və'lümənəs\ *adj* : large or bulky

vol·un·tary \'välən‚terē\ *adj* **1** : done, made, or given freely and without expecting compensation **2** : relating to or controlled by the will — **vol·un·tar·i·ly** *adv*

vol·un·teer \‚välən'tir\ *n* : person who offers to help or work without expecting payment or reward ~ *vb* **1** : offer or give voluntarily **2** : offer oneself as a volunteer

vo·lup·tuous \və'ləpchəwəs\ *adj* **1** : luxurious **2** : having a full and sexually attractive figure — **vo·lup·tu·ous·ly** *adv* — **vo·lup·tuous·ness** *n*

vom·it \'vämət\ *vb* : throw up the contents of the stomach — **vomit** *n*

voo·doo \'vüdü\ *n, pl* **voodoos 1** : religion derived from African polytheism and involving sorcery **2** : one who practices voodoo **3** : charm or fetish used in voodoo — **voodoo** *adj* — **voo·doo·ism** \-‚izəm\ *n*

vo·ra·cious \vȯ'rāshəs, və-\ *adj* : greedy or exceedingly hungry — **vo·ra·cious·ly** *adv* — **vo·ra·cious·ness** *n* — **vo·rac·i·ty** \-'rasətē\ *n*

vor·tex \'vȯr‚teks\ *n, pl* **vor·ti·ces** \'vȯrtə‚sēz\ : whirling liquid

vo·ta·ry \'vōtərē\ *n, pl* **-ries 1** : devoted participant, adherent, admirer, or worshiper

vote \'vōt\ *n* **1** : individual expression of preference in choosing or reaching a decision **2** : right to indicate one's preference or the preference expressed ~ *vb* **vot·ed; vot·ing 1** : cast a vote **2** : choose or defeat by vote — **vote·less** *adj* — **vot·er** *n*

vo·tive \'vōtiv\ *adj* : consisting of or expressing a vow, wish, or desire

vouch \'vau̇ch\ *vb* : give a guarantee or personal assurance

vouch·er \'vau̇chər\ *n* : written record

or receipt that serves as proof of a transaction

vouch·safe \vaůch'sāf\ vb **-safed; -saf·ing** : grant as a special favor

vow \vaů\ n : solemn promise to do something or to live or act a certain way — **vow** vb

vow·el \'vaůəl\ n **1** : speech sound produced without obstruction or friction in the mouth **2** : letter representing such a sound

voy·age \'vȯiij\ n : long journey esp. by water or through space ~ vb **-aged; -ag·ing** : make a voyage — **voy·ag·er** n

vul·ca·nize \'vəlkə,nīz\ vb **-nized; -niz·ing** : treat (as rubber) to make more elastic or stronger

vul·gar \'vəlgər\ adj **1** : relating to the common people **2** : lacking refinement **3** : offensive in manner or language — **vul·gar·ism** \-,rizəm\ n — **vul·gar·ize** \-,rīz\ vb — **vul·gar·ly** adv

vul·gar·i·ty \,vəl'garətē\ n, pl **-ties 1** : state of being vulgar **2** : vulgar language or act

vul·ner·a·ble \'vəlnərəbəl\ adj : susceptible to attack or damage — **vul·ner·a·bil·i·ty** \,vəlnərə'bilətē\ n — **vul·ner·a·bly** adv

vul·ture \'vəlchər\ n : large flesh-eating bird

vul·va \'vəlvə\ n, pl **-vae** \-,vē, -,vī\ : external genital parts of the female

vying pres part of VIE

W

w \'dəbəl,yü\ n, pl **w's** or **ws** \-,yüz\ : 23d letter of the alphabet

wad \'wäd\ n **1** : little mass **2** : soft mass of fibrous material **3** : pliable plug to retain a powder charge **4** : considerable amount ~ vb **1** : form into a wad **2** : stuff with a wad

wad·dle \'wäd'l\ vb **-dled; -dling** : walk with short steps swaying from side to side — **waddle** n

wade \'wād\ vb **wad·ed; wad·ing 1** : step in or through (as water) **2** : move with difficulty — **wade** n — **wad·er** n

wa·fer \'wāfər\ n **1** : thin crisp cake or cracker **2** : waferlike thing

waf·fle \'wäfəl\ n : crisped cake of batter cooked in a hinged utensil (**waffle iron**) ~ vb : vacillate

waft \'wäft, 'waft\ vb : cause to move lightly by wind or waves — **waft** n

¹wag \'wag\ vb **-gg-** : sway or swing from side to side or to and fro — **wag** n

²wag n : wit — **wag·gish** adj

wage \'wāj\ vb **waged; wag·ing** : engage in ~ n **1** : payment for labor or services **2** : compensation

wa·ger \'wājər\ n or vb : bet

wag·gle \'wagəl\ vb **-gled; -gling** : wag — **waggle** n

wag·on \'wagən\ n **1** : 4-wheeled ve-

hicle drawn by animals **2** : child's 4-wheeled cart

waif \'wāf\ n : homeless child

wail \'wāl\ vb **1** : mourn **2** : make a sound like a mournful cry — **wail** n

wain·scot \'wānskət, -,skōt, -,skät\ n : usu. paneled wooden lining of an interior wall — **wainscot** vb

waist \'wāst\ n **1** : narrowed part of the body between chest and hips **2** : waistlike part — **waist·line** n

wait \'wāt\ vb **1** : remain in readiness or expectation **2** : delay **3** : attend as a waiter ~ n **1** : concealment **2** : act or period of waiting

wait·er \'wātər\ n : person who serves others at tables

wait·per·son \'wāt,pərsən\ n : a waiter or waitress

wait·ress \'wātrəs\ n : woman who serves others at tables

waive \'wāv\ vb **waived; waiv·ing** : give up claim to

waiv·er \'wāvər\ n : act of waiving right, claim, or privilege

¹wake \'wāk\ vb **woke** \'wōk\; **wo·ken** \'wōkən\; **wak·ing 1** : keep watch **2** : bring or come back to consciousness after sleep ~ n **1** : state of being awake **2** : watch held over a dead body

²wake n : track left by a ship

wake·ful \'wākfəl\ *adj* : not sleeping or able to sleep — **wake·ful·ness** *n*

wak·en \'wākən\ *vb* : wake

wale \'wāl\ *n* : ridge on cloth

walk \'wok\ *vb* **1** : move or cause to move on foot **2** : pass over, through, or along by walking ~ *n* **1** : a going on foot **2** : place or path for walking **3** : distance to be walked **4** : way of living **5** : way of walking **6** : slow 4-beat gait of a horse — **walk·er** *n*

wall \'wol\ *n* **1** : structure for defense or for enclosing something **2** : upright enclosing part of a building or room **3** : something like a wall ~ *vb* : provide, separate, surround, or close with a wall — **walled** \'wold\ *adj*

wal·la·by \'wäləbē\ *n, pl* **-bies** : small or medium-sized kangaroo

wal·let \'wälət\ *n* : pocketbook with compartments

wall·flow·er *n* **1** : mustardlike plant with showy fragrant flowers **2** : one who remains on the sidelines of social activity

wal·lop \'wäləp\ *n* **1** : powerful blow **2** : ability to hit hard ~ *vb* **1** : beat soundly **2** : hit hard

wal·low \'wälō\ *vb* **1** : roll about in deep mud **2** : indulge oneself excessively ~ *n* : place for wallowing

wall·pa·per *n* : decorative paper for walls — **wallpaper** *vb*

wal·nut \'wol,nət\ *n* **1** : nut with a furrowed shell and adherent husk **2** : tree on which this nut grows or its brown wood

wal·rus \'wolrəs, 'wäl-\ *n, pl* **-rus** *or* **-rus·es** : large seallike mammal of northern seas having ivory tusks

waltz \'wolts\ *n* : gliding dance to music having 3 beats to the measure or the music — **waltz** *vb*

wam·pum \'wämpəm\ *n* : strung shell beads used by No. American Indians as money

wan \'wän\ *adj* **-nn-** : sickly or pale — **wan·ly** *adv* — **wan·ness** *n*

wand \'wänd\ *n* : slender staff

wan·der \'wändər\ *vb* **1** : move about aimlessly **2** : stray **3** : become delirious — **wan·der·er** *n*

wan·der·lust \'wändər,ləst\ *n* : strong urge to wander

wane \'wān\ *vb* **waned; wan·ing** **1** : grow smaller or less **2** : lose power, prosperity, or influence — **wane** *n*

wan·gle \'waŋgəl\ *vb* **-gled; -gling** : obtain by sly or devious means

want \'wont\ *vb* **1** : lack **2** : need **3** : desire earnestly ~ *n* **1** : deficiency **2** : dire need **3** : something wanted

want·ing \-iŋ\ *adj* **1** : not present or in evidence **2** : falling below standards **3** : lacking in ability ~ *prep* **1** : less or minus **2** : without

wan·ton \'wont²n\ *adj* **1** : lewd **2** : having no regard for justice or for others' feelings, rights, or safety ~ *n* : lewd or immoral person ~ *vb* : be wanton — **wan·ton·ly** *adv* — **wan·ton·ness** *n*

wa·pi·ti \'wäpətē\ *n, pl* **-ti** *or* **-tis** : elk

war \'wor\ *n* **1** : armed fighting between nations **2** : state of hostility or conflict **3** : struggle between opposing forces or for a particular end ~ *vb* **-rr-** : engage in warfare — **war·less** \-ləs\ *adj* — **war·time** *n*

war·ble \'worbəl\ *n* **1** : melodious succession of low pleasing sounds **2** : musical trill ~ *vb* **-bled; -bling** : sing or utter in a trilling way

war·bler \'worblər\ *n* **1** : small thrush-like singing bird **2** : small bright-colored insect-eating bird

ward \'word\ *n* **1** : a guarding or being under guard or guardianship **2** : division of a prison or hospital **3** : electoral or administrative division of a city **4** : person under protection of a guardian or a law court ~ *vb* : turn aside — **ward·ship** *n*

¹**-ward** \word\ *adj suffix* **1** : that moves, tends, faces, or is directed toward **2** : that occurs or is situated in the direction of

²**-ward, -wards** *adv suffix* **1** : in a (specified) direction **2** : toward a (specified) point, position, or area

war·den \'word²n\ *n* **1** : guardian **2** : official charged with supervisory duties or enforcement of laws **3** : official in charge of a prison

ward·er \'wordər\ *n* : watchman or warden

ward·robe \'word,rōb\ *n* **1** : clothes closet **2** : collection of wearing apparel

ware \'war\ *n* **1** : articles for sale — often *pl.* **2** : items of fired clay

ware·house \-,haus\ *n* : place for storage of merchandise — **warehouse** *vb* — **ware·house·man** \-mən\ *n* — **ware·hous·er** \-,hauzər, -sər\ *n*

war•fare \'wȯr.far\ *n* **1** : military operations between enemies **2** : struggle

war•head \-.hed\ *n* : part of a missile holding the explosive material

war•like *adj* : fond of, relating to, or used in war

warm \'wȯrm\ *adj* **1** : having or giving out moderate or adequate heat **2** : serving to retain heat **3** : showing strong feeling **4** : giving a pleasant impression of warmth, cheerfulness, or friendliness ~ *vb* **1** : make or become warm **2** : give warmth or energy to **3** : experience feelings of affection **4** : become increasingly ardent, interested, or competent — **warm•er** *n* — **warm•ly** *adv* — **warm up** *vb* : make ready by preliminary activity

war•mon•ger \'wȯr.məŋgər, -.mäŋ-\ *n* : one who attempts to stir up war

warmth \'wȯrmth\ *n* **1** : quality or state of being warm **2** : enthusiasm

warn \'wȯrn\ *vb* **1** : put on guard **2** : notify in advance — **warn•ing** \-iŋ\ *n or adj*

warp \'wȯrp\ *n* **1** : lengthwise threads in a woven fabric **2** : twist ~ *vb* **1** : twist out of shape **2** : lead astray **3** : distort

war•rant \'wȯrant, 'wär-\ *n* **1** : authorization **2** : legal writ authorizing action ~ *vb* **1** : declare or maintain positively **2** : guarantee **3** : approve **4** : justify

warrant officer *n* : officer in the armed forces ranking next below a commissioned officer **2** : commissioned officer in the navy or coast guard ranking below an ensign

war•ran•ty \'wȯrantē, 'wär-\ *n, pl* **-ties** : guarantee of the integrity of a product

war•ren \'wȯran, 'wär-\ *n* : area where rabbits are bred and kept

war•rior \'wȯryar, 'wȯrēar, 'wärē-, 'wäryar\ *n* : man engaged or experienced in warfare

war•ship \'wȯr.ship\ *n* : naval vessel

wart \'wȯrt\ *n* **1** : small projection on the skin caused by a virus **2** : wartlike protuberance — **warty** *adj*

wary \'warē\ *adj* **war•i•er; -est** : careful in guarding against danger or deception

was *past 1st & 3d sing of* BE

wash \'wȯsh, 'wäsh\ *vb* **1** : cleanse with or as if with a liquid (as water) **2** : wet thoroughly with liquid **3** : flow along the border of **4** : flow in a stream **5** : move or remove by or as if by the action of water **6** : cover or daub lightly with a liquid **7** : undergo laundering ~ *n* **1** : act of washing or being washed **2** : articles to be washed **3** : surging action of water or disturbed air — **wash•able** \-əbəl\ *adj*

wash•board *n* : grooved board to scrub clothes on

wash•bowl *n* : large bowl for water for washing hands and face

wash•cloth *n* : cloth used for washing one's face and body

washed–up \'wȯsht'əp, 'wäsht-\ *adj* : no longer capable or usable

wash•er \'wȯshər, 'wäsh-\ *n* **1** : machine for washing **2** : ring used around a bolt or screw to ensure tightness or relieve friction

wash•ing \'wȯshiŋ, 'wäsh-\ *n* : articles to be washed

Washington's Birthday *n* : the 3d Monday in February or formerly February 22 observed as a legal holiday

wash•out *n* **1** : washing out or away of earth **2** : failure

wash•room *n* : bathroom

wasp \'wäsp, 'wȯsp\ *n* : slender-bodied winged insect related to the bees and having a formidable sting

wasp•ish \'wäspish, 'wȯs-\ *adj* : irritable

was•sail \'wäsəl, wä'säl\ *n* **1** : toast to someone's health **2** : liquor drunk on festive occasions **3** : riotous drinking — **wassail** *vb*

waste \'wāst\ *n* **1** : sparsely settled or barren region **2** : act or an instance of wasting **3** : refuse (as garbage or rubbish) **4** : material (as feces) produced but not used by a living body ~ *vb* **wast•ed; wast•ing 1** : ruin **2** : spend or use carelessly **3** : lose substance or energy ~ *adj* **1** : wild and uninhabited **2** : being of no further use — **wast•er** *n* — **waste•ful** \-fəl\ *adj* — **waste•ful•ly** *adv* — **waste•ful•ness** *n*

waste•bas•ket \-.baskət\ *n* : receptacle for refuse

waste•land \-.land, -lənd\ *n* : barren uncultivated land

wast•rel \'wāstrəl, 'wästrəl\ *n* : one who wastes

watch \'wäch, 'wȯch\ *vb* **1** : be or stay awake intentionally **2** : be on the lookout for danger **3** : observe **4** : keep oneself informed about ~ *n* : act of keeping awake to guard **2** : close observation **3** : one that watches **4** : period of duty on a ship or those on duty during this period **5** : timepiece carried on the person — **watch•er** n

watch•dog n **1** : dog kept to guard property **2** : one that protects

watch•ful \-fəl\ adj : steadily attentive — **watch•ful•ly** adv — **watch•ful•ness** n

watch•man \-mən\ n : person assigned to watch

watch•word n **1** : secret word used as a signal **2** : slogan

wa•ter \'wȯtər, 'wät-\ n **1** : liquid that descends as rain and forms rivers, lakes, and seas **2** : liquid containing or resembling water ~ vb **1** : supply with or get water **2** : dilute with or as if with water **3** : form or secrete watery matter

water buffalo n : common oxlike often domesticated Asian buffalo

wa•ter•col•or n **1** : paint whose liquid part is water **2** : picture made with watercolors

wa•ter•course n : stream of water

wa•ter•cress \-ˌkres\ n : perennial salad plant with white flowers

wa•ter•fall n : steep descent of the water of a stream

wa•ter•fowl n **1** : bird that frequents the water **2 waterfowl** pl : swimming game birds

wa•ter•front n : land fronting a body of water

water lily n : aquatic plant with floating leaves and showy flowers

wa•ter•logged \-ˌlȯgd, -ˌlägd\ adj : filled or soaked with water

wa•ter•mark n **1** : mark showing how high water has risen **2** : a marking in paper visible under light ~ vb : mark (paper) with a watermark

wa•ter•mel•on n : large fruit with sweet juicy usu. red pulp

water moccasin n : venomous snake of the southeastern U.S.

wa•ter•pow•er n : power of moving water used to run machinery

wa•ter•proof adj : not letting water through ~ vb : make waterproof — **wa•ter•proof•ing** n

wa•ter•shed \-ˌshed\ n **1** : dividing ridge between two drainage areas or one of these areas

water ski n : ski used on water when the

wearer is towed — **wa•ter•ski** vb — **wa•ter-ski•er** n

wa•ter•spout n **1** : pipe from which water is spouted **2** : tornado over a body of water

wa•ter•tight adj **1** : so tight as not to let water in **2** : allowing no possibility for doubt or uncertainty

wa•ter•way n : navigable body of water

wa•ter•works n pl : system by which water is supplied (as to a city)

wa•tery \'wȯtərē, 'wät-\ adj **1** : containing, full of, or giving out water **2** : being like water **3** : soft and soggy

watt \'wät\ n : unit of electric power — **watt•age** \'wätij\ n

wat•tle \'wät²l\ n **1** : framework of flexible branches used in building **2** : fleshy process hanging usu. about the head or neck (as of a bird) — **wat•tled** \-²ld\ adj

wave \'wāv\ vb **waved; wav•ing 1** : flutter **2** : signal with the hands **3** : wave to and fro with the hand **4** : curve up and down like a wave ~ n **1** : moving swell on the surface of water **2** : wave-like shape **3** : waving motion **4** : surge **5** : disturbance that transfers energy from point to point — **wave•let** \-lət\ n — **wave•like** adj — **wavy** adj

wave•length \'wāv,leŋth\ n **1** : distance from crest to crest in the line of advance of a wave **2** : line of thought that reveals a common understanding

wa•ver \'wāvər\ vb **1** : fluctuate in opinion, allegiance, or direction **2** : flicker **3** : falter — **waver** n — **wa•ver•er** n — **wa•ver•ing•ly** adv

¹wax \'waks\ n **1** : yellowish plastic substance secreted by bees **2** : substance like beeswax ~ vb : treat or rub with wax esp. for polishing

²wax vb **1** : grow larger **2** : become

wax•en \'waksən\ adj : made of or resembling wax

waxy \'waksē\ adj **wax•i•er; -est** : made of, full of, or resembling wax

way \'wā\ n **1** : thoroughfare for travel or passage **2** : route **3** : course of action **4** : method **5** : detail **6** : usual or characteristic state of affairs **7** : condition **8** : distance **9** : progress along a course — **by the way** : in a digression — **by the way of 1** : for the purpose of **2** : by the route through — **out of the way** : remote

way•bill n : paper that accompanies a

way·far·er \'wā,farər\ n : traveler esp. on foot — **way·far·ing** \-,farin\ adj

way·lay \'wā,lā\ vb -**laid** \-,lād\; -**lay·ing** : lie in wait for

way·side n : side of a road

way·ward \'wāwərd\ adj **1** : following one's own capricious inclinations **2** : unpredictable

we \'wē\ pron — used of a group that includes the speaker or writer

weak \'wēk\ adj **1** : lacking strength or vigor **2** : deficient in vigor of mind or character **3** : of less than usual strength **4** : not having or exerting authority — **weak·en** \'wēkən\ vb — **weak·ly** adv

weak·ling \-lin\ n : person who is physically, mentally, or morally weak

weak·ly \'wēklē\ adj : feeble

weak·ness \-nəs\ n **1** : quality or state of being weak **2** : fault **3** : object of special liking

wealth \'welth\ n **1** : abundant possessions or resources **2** : profusion

wealthy \'welthē\ adj **wealth·i·er; -est** : having wealth

wean \'wēn\ vb **1** : accustom (a young mammal) to take food by means other than nursing **2** : free from dependence

weap·on \'wepən\ n **1** : something (as a gun) that may be used to fight with **2** : means by which one contends against another — **weap·on·less** adj

wear \'war\ vb **wore** \'wōr\; **worn** \'wōrn\; **wear·ing 1** : use as an article of clothing or adornment **2** : carry on the person **3** : show an appearance of **4** : decay by use or by scraping **5** : lessen the strength of **6** : endure use ~ n **1** : act of wearing **2** : clothing **3** : lasting quality **4** : result of use — **wear·able** \'warəbəl\ adj — **wear·er** n — **wear out** vb **1** : make or become useless by wear **2** : tire

wea·ri·some \'wirēsəm\ adj : causing weariness — **wea·ri·some·ly** adv — **wea·ri·some·ness** n

wea·ry \'wirē\ adj -**ri·er; -est 1** : worn out in strength, freshness, or patience **2** : expressing or characteristic of weariness ~ vb -**ried; -ry·ing** : make or become weary — **wea·ri·ly** adv — **wea·ri·ness** n

wea·sel \'wēzəl\ n : small slender flesh-eating mammal

weath·er \'wethər\ n : state of the atmosphere ~ vb **1** : expose to or endure the action of weather **2** : endure

weath·er-beat·en adj : worn or damaged by exposure to the weather

weath·er·man \-,man\ n : one who forecasts and reports the weather

weath·er·proof adj : able to withstand exposure to weather — **weather-proof** vb

weather vane n : movable device that shows the way the wind blows

weave \'wēv\ vb **wove** \'wōv\ or **weaved; wo·ven** \'wōvən\ or **weaved; weav·ing 1** : form by interlacing strands of material **2** : to make as if by weaving together parts **3** : follow a winding course ~ n : pattern or method of weaving — **weav·er** n

web \'web\ n **1** : cobweb **2** : animal or plant membrane **3** : network **4** cap : **WORLD WIDE WEB** ~ vb -**bb**- : cover or provide with a web — **webbed** \'webd\ adj

web·bing \'webin\ n : strong closely woven tape

Web site n : group of World Wide Web pages available online

wed \'wed\ vb -**dd**- **1** : marry **2** : unite

wed·ding \'wedin\ n : marriage ceremony and celebration

wedge \'wej\ n : V-shaped object used for splitting, raising, forcing open, or tightening ~ vb **wedged; wedg·ing 1** : tighten or split with a wedge **2** : force into a narrow space

wed·lock \'wed,läk\ n : marriage

Wednes·day \'wenzdā, -dē\ n : 4th day of the week

wee \'wē\ adj : very small

weed \'wēd\ n : unwanted plant ~ vb **1** : remove weeds **2** : get rid of — **weed·er** n — **weedy** adj

weeds n pl : mourning clothes

week \'wēk\ n **1** : 7 successive days **2** : calendar period of 7 days beginning with Sunday and ending with Saturday **3** : the working or school days of the calendar week

week·day \'wēk,dā\ n : any day except Sunday and often Saturday

week·end \-,end\ n : Saturday and Sunday ~ vb : spend the weekend

week·ly \'wēklē\ adj : occurring, appearing, or done every week ~ n, pl -**lies** : weekly publication — **weekly** adv

weep \'wēp\ vb **wept** \'wept\; **weep-**

ing : shed tears — **weep·er** *n* — **weepy** *adj*

wee·vil \'wēvəl\ *n* : small injurious beetle with a long head usu. curved into a snout — **wee·vily, wee·vil·ly** \'wēvəlē\ *adj*

weft \'weft\ *n* : crosswise threads or yarn in weaving

weigh \'wā\ *vb* **1** : determine the heaviness of **2** : have a specified weight **3** : consider carefully **4** : raise (an anchor) off the sea floor **5** : press down or burden

weight \'wāt\ *n* **1** : amount that something weighs **2** : relative heaviness **3** : heavy object **4** : burden or pressure **5** : importance ~ *vb* **1** : load with a weight **2** : oppress — **weight·less** \-ləs\ *adj* — **weight·less·ness** *n* — **weighty** \'wātē\ *adj*

weird \'wird\ *adj* **1** : unearthly or mysterious **2** : strange — **weird·ly** *adv* — **weird·ness** *n*

wel·come \'welkəm\ *vb* **-comed; -com·ing** : accept or greet cordially ~ *adj* : received or permitted gladly ~ *n* : cordial greeting or reception

weld \'weld\ *vb* : unite by heating, hammering, or pressing ~ *n* : union by welding — **weld·er** *n*

wel·fare \'wel,far\ *n* **1** : prosperity **2** : government aid for those in need

¹**well** \'wel\ *n* **1** : spring **2** : hole sunk in the earth to obtain a natural deposit (as of oil) **3** : source of supply **4** : open space extending vertically through floors ~ *vb* : flow forth

²**well** *adv* **bet·ter** \'betər\; **best** \'best\ **1** : in a good or proper manner **2** : satisfactorily **3** : fully **4** : intimately **5** : considerably ~ *adj* **1** : satisfactory **2** : prosperous **3** : desirable **4** : healthy

well–adjusted \,welə'jəstəd\ *adj* : well-balanced

well–ad·vised \,weləd'vīzd\ *adj* : prudent

well–balanced \'wel'balənst\ *adj* **1** : evenly balanced **2** : emotionally or psychologically sound

well–be·ing \'wel'bēiŋ\ *n* : state of being happy, healthy, or prosperous

well–bred \-'bred\ *adj* : having good manners

well–done *adj* **1** : properly performed **2** : cooked thoroughly

well–heeled \-'hēld\ *adj* : financially well-off

well–mean·ing *adj* : having good intentions

well–nigh *adv* : nearly

well–off *adj* : being in good condition esp. financially

well–read \-'red\ *adj* : well informed through reading

well–round·ed \-'raundəd\ *adj* : broadly developed

well–spring *n* : source

well–to–do \,weltə'dü\ *adj* : prosperous

welsh \'welsh, 'welch\ *vb* **1** : avoid payment **2** : break one's word

Welsh rabbit *n* : melted often seasoned cheese poured over toast or crackers

Welsh rare·bit \-'rarbət\ *n* : Welsh rabbit

welt \'welt\ *n* **1** : narrow strip of leather between a shoe upper and sole **2** : ridge raised on the skin usu. by a blow ~ *vb* : hit hard

wel·ter \'weltər\ *vb* **1** : toss about **2** : wallow ~ *n* : confused jumble

wen \'wen\ *n* : abnormal growth or cyst

wench \'wench\ *n* : young woman

wend \'wend\ *vb* : direct one's course

went *past of* GO

wept *past of* WEEP

were *past 2d sing, past pl, or past subjunctive of* BE

were·wolf \'wer,wulf, 'wir-, 'wər-\ *n*, *pl* **-wolves** \-,wulvz\ : person held to be able to change into a wolf

west \'west\ *adv* : to or toward the west ~ *adj* : situated toward or at or coming from the west ~ *n* **1** : direction of sunset **2** *cap* : regions to the west — **west·er·ly** \'westərlē\ *adv or adj* — **west·ward** \-wərd\ *adv or adj* — **west·wards** \-wərdz\ *adv*

west·ern \'westərn\ *adj* **1** *cap* : of a region designated West **2** : lying toward or coming from the west — **West·ern·er** *n*

wet \'wet\ *adj* **-tt- 1** : consisting of or covered or soaked with liquid **2** : not dry ~ *n* : moisture ~ *vb* **-tt-** : make or become moist — **wet·ly** *adv* — **wet·ness** *n*

whack \'hwak\ *vb* : strike sharply ~ *n* **1** : sharp blow **2** : proper working order **3** : chance **4** : try

¹**whale** \'hwāl\ *n, pl* **whales** *or* **whale** : large marine mammal ~ *vb* **whaled; whal·ing** : hunt for whales — **whaleboat** *n* — **whal·er** *n*

²**whale** *vb* **whaled; whal·ing** : strike or hit vigorously

whale•bone *n* : horny substance attached to the upper jaw of some large whales (**whalebone whales**)

wharf \'hwȯrf\ *n, pl* **wharves** \'hwȯrvz\ : structure alongside which boats lie to load or unload

what \'hwät\ *pron* **1** — used to inquire the identity or nature of something **2** : that which **3** : whatever ~ *adv* : in what respect ~ *adj* **1** — used to inquire about the identity or nature of something **2** : how remarkable or surprising **3** : whatever

what•ev•er \hwät'evər\ *pron* **1** : anything or everything that **2** : no matter what ~ *adj* : of any kind at all

what•not \'hwät,nät\ *pron* : any of various other things that might be mentioned

what•so•ev•er \,hwätsō'evər\ *pron or adj* : whatever

wheal \'hwēl\ *n* : a welt on the skin

wheat \'hwēt\ *n* : cereal grain that yields flour — **wheat•en** *adj*

whee•dle \'hwēd'l\ *vb* **-dled; -dling** : coax or tempt by flattery

wheel \'hwēl\ *n* **1** : disk or circular frame capable of turning on a central axis **2** : device of which the main part is a wheel ~ *vb* **1** : convey or move on wheels or a wheeled vehicle **2** : rotate **3** : turn so as to change direction — **wheeled** *adj* — **wheel•er** *n* — **wheel•less** *adj*

wheel•bar•row \-,barō\ *n* : one-wheeled vehicle for carrying small loads

wheel•base *n* : distance in inches between the front and rear axles of an automotive vehicle

wheel•chair *n* : chair mounted on wheels esp. for the use of disabled persons

wheeze \'hwēz\ *vb* **wheezed; wheezing** : breathe with difficulty and with a whistling sound — **wheeze** *n* — **wheezy** *adj*

whelk \'hwelk\ *n* : large sea snail

whelp \'hwelp\ *n* : one of the young of various carnivorous mammals (as a dog) ~ *vb* : bring forth whelps

when \'hwen\ *adv* — used to inquire about or designate a particular time ~ *conj* **1** : at or during the time that **2** : every time that **3** : if **4** : although ~ *pron* : what time

whence \'hwens\ *adv or conj* : from what place, source, or cause

when•ev•er \hwen'evər\ *conj or adv* : at whatever time

where \'hwer\ *adv* **1** : at, in, or to what place **2** : at, in, or to what situation, position, direction, circumstances, or respect ~ *conj* **1** : at, in, or to what place, position, or circumstance **2** : at, in, or to which place ~ *n* : place

where•abouts \-ə,baúts\ *adv* : about where ~ *n sing or pl* : place where a person or thing is

where•as \hwer'az\ *conj* **1** : while on the contrary **2** : since

where•by *conj* : by, through, or in accordance with which

where•fore \'hwer,fōr\ *adv* **1** : why **2** : therefore ~ *n* : reason

where•in \hwer'in\ *adv* : in what respect

where•of \-'əv, -äv\ *conj* : of what, which, or whom

where•up•on \'hwerə,pȯn, -,pän\ *conj* **1** : on which **2** : and then

wher•ev•er \hwer'evər\ *adv* : where ~ *conj* : at, in, or to whatever place or circumstance

where•with•al \'hwerwith,ȯl, -with-\ *n* : resources and esp. money

whet \'hwet\ *vb* **-tt-** **1** : sharpen by rubbing (as with a stone) **2** : stimulate — **whet•stone** *n*

whether \'hwethər\ *conj* **1** : if it is or was true that **2** : if it is or was better **3** : whichever is the case

whey \'hwā\ *n* : watery part of sour milk

which \'hwich\ *adj* **1** : being what one or ones out of a group **2** : whichever ~ *pron* **1** : which one or ones **2** : whichever

which•ev•er \hwich'evər\ *pron or adj* : no matter what one

whiff \'hwif\ *n* **1** : slight gust **2** : inhalation of odor, gas, or smoke **3** : slight trace ~ *vb* : inhale an odor

while \'hwīl\ *n* **1** : period of time **2** : time and effort used ~ *conj* **1** : during the time that **2** : as long as **3** : although ~ *vb* **whiled; whil•ing** : cause to pass esp. pleasantly

whim \'hwim\ *n* : sudden wish, desire, or change of mind

whim•per \'hwimpər\ *vb* : cry softly — **whimper** *n*

whim•si•cal \'hwimzikəl\ *adj* **1** : full of whims **2** : erratic — **whim•si•cal•i•ty** \,hwimzə'kalətē\ *n* — **whim•si•cal•ly** *adv*

whim·sy, whim·sey \'hwimzē\ *n, pl* **-sies** *or* **-seys 1** : whim **2** : fanciful creation

whine \'hwīn\ *vb* **whined; whin·ing 1** : utter a usu. high-pitched plaintive cry **2** : complain — **whine** *n* — **whin·er** *n* — **whiny** *adj*

whin·ny \'hwinē\ *vb* **-nied; -ny·ing** : neigh — **whinny** *n*

whip \'hwip\ *vb* **-pp- 1** : move quickly **2** : strike with something slender and flexible **3** : defeat **4** : incite **5** : beat into a froth **~** *n* **1** : flexible device used for whipping **2** : party leader responsible for discipline **3** : thrashing motion — **whip·per** *n*

whip·cord *n* **1** : thin tough cord **2** : cloth made of hard-twisted yarns

whip·lash *n* : injury from a sudden sharp movement of the neck and head

whip·per·snap·per \'hwipər,snapər\ *n* : small, insignificant, or presumptuous person

whip·pet \'hwipət\ *n* : small swift dog often used for racing

whip·poor·will \'hwipər,wil\ *n* : American nocturnal bird

whir \'hwər\ *vb* **-rr-** : move, fly, or revolve with a whir **~** *n* : continuous fluttering or vibratory sound

whirl \'hwərl\ *vb* **1** : move or drive in a circle **2** : spin **3** : move or turn quickly **4** : reel **~** *n* **1** : rapid circular movement **2** : state of commotion or confusion **3** : try

whirl·pool *n* : whirling mass of water having a depression in the center

whirl·wind *n* : whirling wind storm

whisk \'hwisk\ *n* **1** : quick light sweeping or brushing motion **2** : usu. wire kitchen implement for beating **~** *vb* **1** : move or convey briskly **2** : beat **3** : brush lightly

whisk broom *n* : small broom

whis·ker \'hwiskər\ *n* **1** *pl* : beard **2** : long bristle or hair near an animal's mouth — **whis·kered** \-kərd\ *adj*

whis·key, whis·ky \'hwiskē\ *n, pl* **-keys** *or* **-kies** : liquor distilled from a fermented mash of grain

whis·per \'hwispər\ *vb* **1** : speak softly **2** : tell by whispering **~** *n* **1** : soft low sound **2** : rumor

whist \'hwist\ *n* : card game

whis·tle \'hwisəl\ *n* **1** : device by which a shrill sound is produced **2** : shrill clear sound made by a whistle or through the lips **~** *vb* **-tled; -tling**

1 : make or utter a whistle **2** : signal or call by a whistle **3** : produce by whistling — **whis·tler** *n*

whis·tle-blow·er \'hwisəl,blōər\ *n* : informer

whis·tle-stop *n* : brief political appearance

whit \'hwit\ *n* : bit

white \'hwīt\ *adj* **whit·er; -est 1** : free from color **2** : of the color of new snow or milk **3** : having light skin **~** *n* **1** : color of maximum lightness **2** : white part or thing **3** : person who is light-skinned — **white·ness** *n* — **whit·ish** *adj*

white blood cell *n* : blood cell that does not contain hemoglobin

white·cap \'hwīt,kap\ *n* : wave crest breaking into white foam

white-col·lar *adj* : relating to salaried employees with duties not requiring protective or work clothing

white elephant *n* : something costly but of little use or value

white·fish \'hwīt,fish\ *n* : freshwater food fish

whit·en \'hwīt³n\ *vb* : make or become white — **whit·en·er** \'hwīt³nər\ *n*

white slave *n* : woman or girl held unwillingly for purposes of prostitution — **white slavery** *n*

white·tail \'hwīt,tāl\ *n* : No. American deer

white·wash *vb* **1** : whiten with a composition (as of lime and water) **2** : gloss over or cover up faults or wrongdoing — **whitewash** *n*

whith·er \'hwithər\ *adv* **1** : to what place **2** : to what situation, position, degree, or end

¹**whit·ing** \'hwītiŋ\ *n* : usu. light or silvery food fish

²**whiting** *n* : pulverized chalk or limestone

whit·tle \'hwit³l\ *vb* **-tled; -tling 1** : pare **2** : shape by paring **3** : reduce gradually

whiz, whizz \'hwiz\ *vb* **-zz-** : make a sound like a speeding object — **whiz, whizz** *n*

who \'hü\ *pron* **1** : what or which person or persons **2** : person or persons that **3** — used to introduce a relative clause

who·dun·it \hü'dənət\ *n* : detective or mystery story

who·ev·er \hü'evər\ *pron* : no matter who

whole \'hōl\ *adj* **1** : being in healthy or

sound condition **2** : having all its parts or elements **3** : constituting the total sum of ~ *n* **1** : complete amount or sum **2** : something whole or entire — **on the whole 1** : considering all circumstances **2** : in general — **whole·ness** *n*

whole·heart·ed \'hōl'härtəd\ *adj* : sincere

whole number *n* : integer

whole·sale *n* : sale of goods in quantity usu. for resale by a retail merchant ~ *adj* **1** : of or relating to wholesaling **2** : performed on a large scale ~ *vb* **-saled; -sal·ing** : sell at wholesale — **whole·sal·er** *n* — **whole·sale** *adv*

whole·some \-səm\ *adj* **1** : promoting mental, spiritual, or bodily health **2** : healthy — **whole·some·ness** *n*

whole wheat *adj* : made of ground entire wheat kernels

whol·ly \'hōlē\ *adv* **1** : totally **2** : solely

whom \'hüm\ *pron, objective case of* WHO

whom·ev·er \hüm'evər\ *pron, objective case of* WHOEVER

whoop \'hwüp, 'hwúp, 'hüp, 'húp\ *vb* : shout loudly ~ *n* : shout

whooping cough *n* : infectious disease marked by convulsive coughing fits

whop·per \'hwäpər\ *n* **1** : something unusually large or extreme of its kind **2** : monstrous lie

whop·ping \'hwäpiŋ\ *adj* : extremely large

whore \'hōr\ *n* : prostitute

whorl \'hwórl, 'hwərl\ *n* : spiral — **whorled** *adj*

whose \'hüz\ *adj* : of or relating to whom or which ~ *pron* : whose one or ones

who·so·ev·er \hüsō'evər\ *pron* : whoever

why \'hwī\ *adv* : for what reason, cause, or purpose ~ *conj* **1** : reason for which **2** : for which ~ *n, pl* **whys** : reason ~ *interj* — used esp. to express surprise

wick \'wik\ *n* : cord that draws up oil, tallow, or wax to be burned

wick·ed \'wikəd\ *adj* **1** : morally bad **2** : harmful or troublesome **3** : very unpleasant **4** : very impressive — **wick·ed·ly** *adv* — **wick·ed·ness** *n*

wick·er \'wikər\ *n* **1** : small pliant branch **2** : wickerwork — **wicker** *adj*

wick·er·work *n* : work made of wickers

wick·et \'wikət\ *n* **1** : small gate, door,

or window **2** : frame in cricket or arch in croquet

wide \'wīd\ *adj* **wid·er; wid·est 1** : covering a vast area **2** : measured at right angles to the length **3** : having a great measure across **4** : opened fully **5** : far from the thing in question ~ *adv* **wid·er; wid·est 1** : over a great distance **2** : so as to leave considerable space between **3** : fully — **wide·ly** *adv* — **wid·en** \'wīd²n\ *vb*

wide–awake *adj* : alert

wide–eyed *adj* **1** : having the eyes wide open **2** : amazed **3** : naive

wide·spread *adj* : widely extended

wid·ow \'widō\ *n* : woman who has lost her husband by death and has not married again ~ *vb* : cause to become a widow — **wid·ow·hood** *n*

wid·ow·er \'widəwər\ *n* : man who has lost his wife by death and has not married again

width \'width\ *n* **1** : distance from side to side **2** : largeness of extent **3** : measured and cut piece of material

wield \'wēld\ *vb* **1** : use or handle esp. effectively **2** : exert — **wield·er** *n*

wie·ner \'wēnər\ *n* : frankfurter

wife \'wīf\ *n, pl* **wives** \'wīvz\ : married woman — **wife·hood** *n* — **wife·less** *adj* — **wife·ly** *adj*

wig \'wig\ *n* : manufactured covering of hair for the head

wig·gle \'wigəl\ *vb* **-gled; -gling 1** : move with quick jerky or shaking movements **2** : wriggle — **wiggle** *n* — **wig·gler** *n*

wig·gly \-əlē\ *adj* **1** : tending to wiggle **2** : wavy

wig·wag \'wig,wag\ *vb* : signal by a flag or light waved according to a code

wig·wam \'wig,wäm\ *n* : American Indian hut consisting of a framework of poles overlaid with bark, rush mats, or hides

wild \'wīld\ *adj* **1** : living or being in a state of nature and not domesticated or cultivated **2** : unrestrained **3** : turbulent **4** : crazy **5** : uncivilized **6** : erratic ~ *n* **1** : wilderness **2** : undomesticated state ~ *adv* : without control — **wild·ly** *adv* — **wild·ness** *n*

wild·cat \-,kat\ *n* : any of various undomesticated cats (as a lynx) ~ *adj* **1** : not sound or safe **2** : unauthorized

wil·der·ness \'wildərnəs\ *n* : uncultivated and uninhabited region

wild·fire \'wīld͵fīr\ *n* : sweeping and destructive fire

wild·fowl *n* : game waterfowl

wild·life \'wīld͵līf\ *n* : undomesticated animals

wile \'wīl\ *n* : trick to snare or deceive ~ *vb* **wiled; wil·ing** : lure

will \'wil\ *vb, past* **would** \'wùd\; *pres sing & pl* **will** 1 : wish 2 — used as an auxiliary verb to express (1) desire or willingness (2) customary action (3) simple future time (4) capability (5) determination (6) probability (7) inevitability or (8) a command 3 : dispose of by a will ~ *n* 1 : often determined wish 2 : act, process, or experience of willing 3 : power of controlling one's actions or emotions 4 : legal document disposing of property after death

will·ful, wil·ful \'wilfəl\ *adj* 1 : governed by will without regard to reason 2 : intentional — **will·ful·ly** *adv*

will·ing \'wiliŋ\ *adj* 1 : inclined or favorably disposed in mind 2 : prompt to act 3 : done, borne, or accepted voluntarily or without reluctance — **will·ing·ly** *adv* — **will·ing·ness** *n*

will-o'-the-wisp \͵wiləthə'wisp\ *n* 1 : light that appears at night over marshy grounds 2 : misleading or elusive goal or hope

wil·low \'wilō\ *n* : quick-growing shrub or tree with flexible shoots

wil·lowy \'wiləwē\ *adj* : gracefully tall and slender

will·pow·er \'wil͵paùər\ *n* : energetic determination

wil·ly-nil·ly \͵wilē'nilē\ *adv or adj* : without regard for one's choice

wilt \'wilt\ *vb* 1 : lose or cause to lose freshness and become limp esp. from lack of water 2 : grow weak

wily \'wīlē\ *adj* **wil·i·er; -est** : full of craftiness — **wil·i·ness** *n*

win \'win\ *vb* **won** \'wən\; **win·ning** 1 : get possession of esp. by effort 2 : gain victory in battle or a contest 3 : make friendly or favorable ~ *n* : victory

wince \'wins\ *vb* **winced; winc·ing** : shrink back involuntarily — **wince** *n*

winch \'winch\ *n* : machine for hoisting or pulling with a drum around which rope is wound — **winch** *vb*

¹**wind** \'wind\ *n* 1 : movement of the air 2 : breath 3 : gas in the stomach or intestines 4 : air carrying a scent 5

: intimation ~ *vb* 1 : get a scent of 2 : cause to be out of breath

²**wind** \'wīnd\ *vb* **wound** \'waùnd\; **wind·ing** 1 : have or follow a curving course 2 : move or lie to encircle 3 : encircle or cover with something pliable 4 : tighten the spring of ~ *n* : turn or coil — **wind·er** *n*

wind·break \-͵brāk\ *n* : trees and shrubs to break the force of the wind

wind·break·er \-͵brākər\ *n* : light weather-resistant jacket

wind·fall \'wind͵fòl\ *n* 1 : thing blown down by wind 2 : unexpected benefit

wind instrument *n* : musical instrument (as a flute or horn) sounded by wind and esp. by the breath

wind·lass \'windləs\ *n* : winch esp. for hoisting anchor

wind·mill \'wind͵mil\ *n* : machine worked by the wind turning vanes

win·dow \'windō\ *n* 1 : opening in the wall of a building to let in light and air 2 : pane in a window 3 : span of time for something 4 : area of a computer display — **win·dow·less** *adj*

win·dow-shop *vb* : look at the displays in store windows — **win·dow-shop·per** *n*

wind·pipe \'wind͵pīp\ *n* : passage for the breath from the larynx to the lungs

wind·shield \'-͵shēld\ *n* : transparent screen in front of the occupants of a vehicle

wind-up \'wīnd͵əp\ *n* : end — **wind up** *vb*

wind·ward \'windwərd\ *adj* : being in or facing the direction from which the wind is blowing ~ *n* : direction from which the wind is blowing

windy \'windē\ *adj* **wind·i·er; -est** 1 : having wind 2 : indulging in useless talk

wine \'wīn\ *n* 1 : fermented grape juice 2 : usu. fermented juice of a plant product (as fruit) used as a beverage ~ *vb* : treat to or drink wine

wing \'wiŋ\ *n* 1 : movable paired appendage for flying 2 : winglike thing 3 *pl* : area at the side of the stage out of sight 4 : faction ~ *vb* 1 : fly 2 : propel through the air — **winged** *adj* — **wing·less** *adj* — **on the wing** : in flight — **under one's wing** : in one's charge or care

wink \'wiŋk\ *vb* 1 : close and open the eyes quickly 2 : avoid seeing or noticing something 3 : twinkle 4 : close and open one eye quickly as a signal or hint ~ n 1 : brief sleep 2 : act of winking 3 : instant — **wink·er** n

win·ner \'winər\ n : one that wins

win·ning \-iŋ\ n 1 : victory 2 : money won at gambling ~ adj 1 : victorious 2 : charming

win·now \'winō\ vb 1 : remove (as chaff) by a current of air 2 : sort or separate something

win·some \'winsəm\ adj 1 : causing joy 2 : cheerful or gay — **win·some·ly** adv — **win·some·ness** n

win·ter \'wintər\ n : season between autumn and spring ~ adj : sown in autumn for harvest the next spring or summer — **win·ter·time** n

win·ter·green \'wintər,grēn\ n : low heathlike evergreen plant with red berries

win·try \'wintrē\ adj **win·tri·er; -est** 1 : characteristic of winter 2 : cold in feeling

wipe \'wīp\ vb **wiped; wip·ing** 1 : clean or dry by rubbing 2 : remove by rubbing 3 : erase completely 4 : destroy 5 : pass over a surface ~ n : act or instance of wiping — **wip·er** n

wire \'wīr\ n 1 : thread of metal 2 : work made of wire 3 : telegram or cablegram ~ vb 1 : provide with wire 2 : bind or mount with wire 3 : telegraph — **wire·less** adj

wire·less \-ləs\ n, chiefly Brit : radio

wire·tap vb : connect into a telephone or telegraph wire to get information — **wiretap** n — **wire·tap·per** n

wir·ing \'wīriŋ\ n : system of wires

wiry \'wīrē\ adj **wir·i·er** \'wīrēər\; **-est** 1 : resembling wire 2 : slender yet strong and sinewy — **wir·i·ness** n

wis·dom \'wizdəm\ n 1 : accumulated learning 2 : good sense

wisdom tooth n : last tooth on each half of each human jaw

¹wise \'wīz\ n : manner

²wise adj **wis·er; wis·est** 1 : having or showing wisdom, good sense, or good judgment 2 : aware of what is going on — **wise·ly** adv

wise·crack n : clever, smart, or flippant remark ~ vb : make a wisecrack

wish \'wish\ vb 1 : have a desire 2 : express a wish concerning 3 : request ~ n 1 : a wishing or desire 2 : expressed will or desire

wish·bone n : forked bone in front of the breastbone in most birds

wish·ful \-fəl\ adj 1 : expressive of a wish 2 : according with wishes rather than fact

wishy–washy \'wishē,wȯshē, -,wäsh-\ adj : weak or insipid

wisp \'wisp\ n 1 : small bunch of hay or straw 2 : thin strand, strip, fragment, or streak 3 : something frail, slight, or fleeting — **wispy** adj

wis·te·ria \wis'tirēə\ n : pealike woody vine with long clusters of flowers

wist·ful \'wistfəl\ adj : full of longing — **wist·ful·ly** adv — **wist·ful·ness** n

wit \'wit\ n 1 : reasoning power 2 : mental soundness — usu. pl. 3 : quickness and cleverness in handling words and ideas 4 : talent for clever remarks or one noted for witty remarks — **wit·less** adj — **wit·less·ly** adv — **wit·less·ness** n — **wit·ted** adj

witch \'wich\ n 1 : person believed to have magic power 2 : ugly old woman ~ vb : bewitch

witch·craft \'wich,kraft\ n : power or practices of a witch

witch·ery \'wichərē\ n, pl **-er·ies** 1 : witchcraft 2 : charm

witch ha·zel \'wich,hāzəl\ n 1 : shrub having small yellow flowers in fall 2 : alcoholic lotion made from witch hazel bark

witch–hunt n 1 : searching out and persecution of supposed witches 2 : harassment esp. of political opponents

with \'with, 'with\ prep 1 : against, to, or toward 2 : in support of 3 : because of 4 : in the company of 5 : having 6 : despite 7 : containing 8 : by means of

with·draw \with'drȯ, with-\ vb **-drew** \-'drü\; **-drawn** \-'drȯn\; **-draw·ing** \-'drȯiŋ\ 1 : take back or away 2 : call back or retract 3 : go away 4 : terminate one's participation in or use of — **with·draw·al** \-'drȯəl\ n

with·drawn \with'drȯn\ adj : socially detached and unresponsive

with·er \'withər\ vb 1 : shrivel 2 : lose or cause to lose energy, force, or freshness

with·ers \'withərz\ n pl : ridge between the shoulder bones of a horse

with·hold \with'hōld, with-\ vb **-held** \-'held\; **-hold·ing** 1 : hold back 2 : refrain from giving

with·in \with'in, with-\ adv 1 : in or into the interior 2 : inside oneself ~

prep **1** : in or to the inner part of **2** : in the limits or compass of

with·out \with'aut, with-\ *prep* **1** : outside **2** : lacking **3** : unaccompanied or unmarked by — **without** *adv*

with·stand \with'stand, with-\ *vb* **-stood** \-'stud\; **-stand·ing** : oppose successfully

wit·ness \'witnəs\ *n* **1** : testimony **2** : one who testifies **3** : one present at a transaction to testify that it has taken place **4** : one who has personal knowledge or experience **5** : something serving as proof ~ *vb* **1** : bear witness **2** : act as legal witness of **3** : furnish proof of **4** : be a witness of **5** : be the scene of

wit·ti·cism \'witə,sizəm\ *n* : witty saying or phrase

wit·ting \'witiŋ\ *adj* : intentional — **wit·ting·ly** *adv*

wit·ty \'witē\ *adj* **-ti·er; -est** : marked by or full of wit — **wit·ti·ly** \'witᵊlē\ *adv* — **wit·ti·ness** *n*

wives *pl of* WIFE

wiz·ard \'wizərd\ *n* **1** : magician **2** : very clever person — **wiz·ard·ry** \-ərdrē\ *n*

wiz·ened \'wiz'nd\ *adj* : dried up

wob·ble \'wäbəl\ *vb* **-bled; -bling** : move or cause to move with an irregular rocking motion **2** : tremble **3** : waver — **wobble** *n* — **wob·bly** \'wäbəlē\ *adj*

woe \'wō\ *n* **1** : deep suffering **2** : misfortune

woe·be·gone \'wōbi,gȯn\ *adj* : exhibiting woe, sorrow, or misery

woe·ful \'wōfəl\ *adj* **1** : full of woe **2** : bringing woe — **woe·ful·ly** *adv*

woke *past of* WAKE

woken *past part of* WAKE

wolf \'wülf\ *n, pl* **wolves** \'wülvz\ : large doglike predatory mammal ~ *vb* : eat greedily — **wolf·ish** *adj*

wol·fram \'wülfrəm\ *n* : tungsten

wol·ver·ine \,wülvə'rēn\ *n, pl* **-ines** : flesh-eating mammal related to the weasels

wom·an \'wumən\ *n, pl* **wom·en** \'wimən\ **1** : adult female person **2** : womankind **3** : feminine nature — **wom·an·hood** \-,hud\ *n* — **wom·an·ish** *adj*

wom·an·kind \-,kīnd\ *n* : females of the human race

wom·an·ly \-lē\ *adj* : having qualities characteristic of a woman — **wom·an·li·ness** \-lēnəs\ *n*

womb \'wüm\ *n* : uterus

won *past of* WIN

won·der \'wəndər\ *n* **1** : cause of astonishment or surprise **2** : feeling (as of astonishment) aroused by something extraordinary ~ *vb* **1** : feel surprise **2** : feel curiosity or doubt

won·der·ful \'wəndərfəl\ *adj* **1** : exciting wonder **2** : unusually good — **won·der·ful·ly** *adv* — **won·der·ful·ness** *n*

won·der·land \-,land, -lənd\ *n* **1** : fairylike imaginary realm **2** : place that excites admiration or wonder

won·der·ment \-mənt\ *n* : wonder

won·drous \'wəndrəs\ *adj* : wonderful — **won·drous·ly** *adv* — **won·drous·ness** *n*

wont \'wȯnt, 'wōnt\ *adj* : accustomed ~ *n* : habit — **wont·ed** *adj*

woo \'wü\ *vb* : try to gain the love or favor of — **woo·er** *n*

wood \'wud\ *n* **1** : dense growth of trees usu. smaller than a forest — often *pl.* **2** : hard fibrous substance of trees and shrubs beneath the bark **3** : wood prepared for some use (as burning) ~ *adj* **1** : wooden **2** : suitable for working with wood **3** *or* **woods** \'wudz\ : living or growing in woods — **wood·chop·per** *n* — **wood·pile** *n* — **wood·shed** *n*

wood·bine \'wud,bīn\ *n* : climbing vine

wood·chuck \-,chək\ *n* : thick-bodied grizzled animal of No. America

wood·craft *n* **1** : skill and practice in matters relating to the woods **2** : skill in making articles from wood

wood·cut \-,kət\ *n* **1** : relief printing surface engraved on wood **2** : print from a woodcut

wood·ed \'wudəd\ *adj* : covered with woods

wood·en \'wud'n\ *adj* **1** : made of wood **2** : lacking resilience **3** : lacking ease, liveliness or interest — **wood·en·ly** *adv* — **wood·en·ness** *n*

wood·land \-lənd, -,land\ *n* : land covered with trees

wood·peck·er \'wud,pekər\ *n* : brightly marked bird with a hard bill for drilling into trees

woods·man \'wudzmən\ *n* : person who works in the woods

wood·wind \'wud,wind\ *n* : one of a

group of wind instruments (as a flute or oboe)

wood•work *n* : work (as interior house fittings) made of wood

woody \'wȯdē\ *adj* **wood•i•er; -est** 1 : abounding with woods 2 : of, containing, or like wood fibers — **wood•i•ness** *n*

woof \'wȯf\ *n* : weft

wool \'wȯl\ *n* 1 : soft hair of some mammals and esp. the sheep 2 : something (as a textile) made of wool — **wooled** \'wȯld\ *adj*

wool•en, wool•len \'wȯlən\ *adj* 1 : made of wool 2 : relating to the manufacture of woolen products ∼ *n* 1 : woolen fabric 2 : woolen garments — usu. pl.

wool•gath•er•ing *n* : idle daydreaming

wool•ly \'wȯlē\ *adj* **-li•er; -est** 1 : of, relating to, or bearing wool 2 : consisting of or resembling wool 3 : confused or turbulent

woo•zy \'wüzē\ *adj* **-zi•er; -est** 1 : confused 2 : somewhat dizzy, nauseated, or weak — **woo•zi•ness** *n*

word \'wərd\ *n* 1 : brief remark 2 : speech sound or series of speech sounds that communicates a meaning 3 : written representation of a word 4 : order 5 : news 6 : promise 7 *pl* : dispute ∼ *vb* : express in words — **word•less** *adj*

word•ing \'wərdiŋ\ *n* : verbal expression

word processing *n* : production of structured and printed documents through a computer program (**word processor**) — **word process** *vb*

wordy \'wərdē\ *adj* **word•i•er; -est** : using many words — **word•i•ness** *n*

wore *past of* WEAR

work \'wərk\ *n* 1 : labor 2 : employment 3 : task 4 : something (as an artistic production) produced by mental effort or physical labor 5 *pl* : place where industrial labor is done 6 *pl* : moving parts of a mechanism 7 : workmanship ∼ *adj* 1 : suitable for wear while working 2 : used for work ∼ *vb* **worked** \'wərkt\ *or* **wrought** \'rȯt\; **work•ing** 1 : bring to pass 2 : create by expending labor upon 3 : bring or get into a form or condition 4 : set or keep in operation 5 : solve 6 : cause to labor 7 : arrange 8 : excite 9 : labor 10 : perform work regularly for wages 11 : function according to plan or design 12 : produce a desired

effect — **work•bench** *n* — **work•man** \-mən\ *n* — **work•room** *n* — **in the works** : in preparation

work•able \'wərkəbəl\ *adj* 1 : capable of being worked 2 : feasible — **work•able•ness** *n*

work•a•day \'wərkə,dā\ *adj* 1 : relating to or suited for working days 2 : ordinary

work•a•hol•ic \,wərkə'hȯlik, -'häl-\ *n* : compulsive worker

work•day \'wərk,dā\ *n* 1 : day on which work is done 2 : period of time during which one is working

work•er \'wərkər\ *n* : person who works esp. for wages

work•horse *n* 1 : horse used for hard work 2 : person who does most of the work of a group task

work•house *n* : place of confinement for persons who have committed minor offenses

work•ing \'wərkiŋ\ *adj* 1 : adequate to allow work to be done 2 : adopted or assumed to help further work or activity ∼ *n* : operation — usu. used in pl.

work•ing•man \'wərkiŋ,man\ *n* : worker

work•man•like \-,līk\ *adj* : worthy of a good workman

work•man•ship \-,ship\ *n* 1 : art or skill of a workman 2 : quality of a piece of work

work•out \'wərk,aút\ *n* : exercise to improve one's fitness

work out *vb* 1 : bring about by effort 2 : solve 3 : develop 4 : to be successful 5 : perform exercises

work•shop *n* 1 : small establishment for manufacturing or handicrafts 2 : seminar emphasizing exchange of ideas and practical methods

world \'wərld\ *n* 1 : universe 2 : earth with its inhabitants and all things upon it 3 : people in general 4 : great number or quantity 5 : class of persons or their sphere of interest

world•ly \'wərldlē\ *adj* 1 : devoted to this world and its pursuits rather than to religion 2 : sophisticated — **world•li•ness** *n*

world•ly-wise *adj* : possessing understanding of human affairs

world•wide *adj* : extended throughout the entire world — **worldwide** *adv*

World Wide Web *n* : part of the Internet accessible through a browser

worm \'wərm\ *n* 1 : earthworm or a

similar animal **2** *pl* : disorder caused by parasitic worms ∼ *vb* **1** : move or cause to move in a slow and indirect way **2** : to free from worms — **wormy** *adj*

worm–wood \'wərm,wu̇d\ *n* **1** : aromatic woody herb (as sagebrush) **2** : something bitter or grievous

worn *past part of* WEAR

worn–out \'wȯrn'au̇t\ *adj* : exhausted or used up by or as if by wear

wor•ri•some \'wərēsəm\ *adj* **1** : causing worry **2** : inclined to worry

wor•ry \'wərē\ *vb* **-ried; -ry•ing** **1** : shake and mangle with the teeth **2** : disturb **3** : feel or express anxiety ∼ *n, pl* **-ries 1** : anxiety **2** : cause of anxiety — **wor•ri•er** *n*

worse \'wərs\ *adj, comparative of* BAD *or of* ILL **1** : bad or evil in a greater degree **2** : more unwell ∼ *n* **1** : one that is worse **2** : greater degree of badness ∼ *adv comparative of* BAD *or of* ILL : in a worse manner

wors•en \'wərs²n\ *vb* : make or become worse

wor•ship \'wərshəp\ *n* **1** : reverence toward a divine being or supernatural power **2** : expression of reverence **3** : extravagant respect or devotion ∼ *vb* **-shiped** *or* **-shipped; -ship•ing** *or* **-ship•ping 1** : honor or reverence **2** : perform or take part in worship — **wor•ship•er, wor•ship•per** *n*

worst \'wərst\ *adj, superlative of* BAD *or of* ILL **1** : most bad, evil, ill, or corrupt **2** : most unfavorable, unpleasant, or painful ∼ *n* : one that is worst ∼ *adv superlative of* ILL *or of* BAD *or* BADLY : to the extreme degree of badness ∼ *vb* : defeat

wor•sted \'wu̇stəd, 'wərstəd\ *n* : smooth compact wool yarn or fabric made from such yarn

worth \'wərth\ *prep* **1** : equal in value to **2** : deserving of ∼ *n* **1** : monetary value **2** : value of something measured by its qualities **3** : moral or personal merit

worth•less \-ləs\ *adj* **1** : lacking worth **2** : useless — **worth•less•ness** *n*

worth•while \-'hwil\ *adj* : being worth the time or effort spent

wor•thy \'wərthē\ *adj* **-thi•er; -est 1** : having worth or value **2** : having sufficient worth ∼ *n, pl* **-thies** : worthy person — **wor•thi•ly** *adv* — **wor•thi•ness** *n*

would \'wu̇d\ *past of* WILL — used to express **(1)** preference **(2)** intent **(3)** habitual action **(4)** contingency **(5)** probability or **(6)** a request

would–be \'wu̇d'bē\ *adj* : desiring or pretending to be

¹wound \'wu̇nd\ *n* **1** : injury in which the skin is broken **2** : mental hurt ∼ *vb* : inflict a wound to or in

²wound \'wau̇nd\ *past of* WIND

wove *past of* WEAVE

woven *past part of* WEAVE

wrack \'rak\ *n* : ruin

wraith \'rāth\ *n, pl* **wraiths** \'rāths, 'rāthz\ **1** : ghost **2** : insubstantial appearance

wran•gle \'raŋgəl\ *vb or n* : quarrel — **wran•gler** *n*

wrap \'rap\ *vb* **-pp- 1** : cover esp. by winding or folding **2** : envelop and secure for transportation or storage **3** : enclose, surround, or conceal wholly **4** : coil, fold, draw, or twine about something ∼ *n* **1** : wrapper or wrapping **2** : outer garment (as a shawl)

wrap•per \'rapər\ *n* **1** : that in which something is wrapped **2** : one that wraps

wrap•ping *n* : something used to wrap an object

wrath \'rath\ *n* : violent anger — **wrath•ful** \-fəl\ *adj*

wreak \'rēk\ *vb* **1** : inflict **2** : bring about

wreath \'rēth\ *n, pl* **wreaths** \'rēthz, 'rēths\ : something (as boughs) intertwined into a circular shape

wreathe \'rēth\ *vb* **wreathed; wreath•ing 1** : shape into or take on the shape of a wreath **2** : decorate or cover with a wreath

wreck \'rek\ *n* **1** : broken remains (as of a ship or vehicle) after heavy damage **2** : something disabled or in a state of ruin **3** : an individual who has become weak or infirm **4** : action of breaking up or destroying something ∼ *vb* : ruin or damage by breaking up

wreck•age \'rekij\ *n* **1** : act of wrecking **2** : remains of a wreck

wreck•er \-ər\ *n* **1** : automotive vehicle for removing disabled cars **2** : one that wrecks or tears down and removes buildings

wren \'ren\ *n* : small mostly brown singing bird

wrench \'rench\ *vb* **1** : pull with violent twisting or force **2** : injure or disable by a violent twisting or straining ~ *n* **1** : forcible twisting **2** : tool for exerting a twisting force

wrest \'rest\ *vb* **1** : pull or move by a forcible twisting movement **2** : gain with difficulty ~ *n* : forcible twist

wres•tle \'resəl, 'ras-\ *vb* **-tled; -tling** **1** : scuffle with and attempt to throw and pin an opponent **2** : compete against in wrestling **3** : struggle (as with a problem) ~ *n* : action or an instance of wrestling — **wres•tler** \'reslər, 'ras-\ *n*

wres•tling \'reslin\ *n* : sport in which 2 opponents try to throw and pin each other

wretch \'rech\ *n* **1** : miserable unhappy person **2** : vile person

wretch•ed \'rechəd\ *adj* **1** : deeply afflicted, dejected, or distressed **2** : grievous **3** : inferior — **wretch•ed•ly** *adv* — **wretch•ed•ness** *n*

wrig•gle \'rigəl\ *vb* **-gled; -gling** **1** : twist and turn restlessly **2** : move along by twisting and turning — **wrig•gle** *n* — **wrig•gler** \'rigələr\ *n*

wring \'rin\ *vb* **wrung** \'rən\; **wring•ing** **1** : squeeze or twist out moisture **2** : get by or as if by twisting or pressing **3** : twist together in anguish **4** : pain — **wring•er** *n*

wrin•kle \'rinkəl\ *n* : crease or small fold on a surface (as in the skin or in cloth) ~ *vb* **-kled; -kling** : develop or cause to develop wrinkles — **wrin•kly** \-kəlē\ *adj*

wrist \'rist\ *n* : joint or region between the hand and the arm

writ \'rit\ *n* **1** : something written **2** : legal order in writing

write \'rīt\ *vb* **wrote** \'rōt\; **writ•ten** \'rit⁸n\; **writ•ing** \'rītin\ **1** : form letters or words on a surface **2** : form the letters or the words of (as on paper) **3** : make up and set down for others to read **4** : write a letter to — **write off** *vb* : cancel

writ•er \'rītər\ *n* : one that writes esp. as a business or occupation

writhe \'rīth\ *vb* **writhed; writh•ing** : twist and turn this way and that

writ•ing \'rītin\ *n* **1** : act of one that writes **2** : handwriting **3** : something written or printed

wrong \'rȯn\ *n* **1** : unfair or unjust act **2** : something that is contrary to justice **3** : state of being or doing wrong ~ *adj* **wrong•er** \'rȯnər\; **wrong•est** \'rȯnəst\ **1** : sinful **2** : not right according to a standard **3** : unsuitable **4** : incorrect ~ *adv* **1** : in a wrong direction or manner **2** : incorrectly ~ *vb* **wronged; wrong•ing** **1** : do wrong to **2** : treat unjustly — **wrong•ly** *adv*

wrong•do•er \-'düər\ *n* : one who does wrong — **wrong•do•ing** \-'düin\ *n*

wrong•ful \-fəl\ *adj* **1** : wrong **2** : illegal — **wrong•ful•ly** *adv* — **wrong•ful•ness** *n*

wrong•head•ed \'rȯn'hedəd\ *adj* : stubborn in clinging to wrong opinion or principles — **wrong•head•ed•ly** *adv* — **wrong•head•ed•ness** *n*

wrote *past of* WRITE

wrought \'rȯt\ *adj* **1** : formed **2** : hammered into shape **3** : deeply stirred

wrung *past of* WRING

wry \'rī\ *adj* **wri•er** \'rīər\; **wri•est** \'rīəst\ **1** : turned abnormally to one side **2** : twisted **3** : cleverly and often ironically humorous — **wry•ly** *adv* — **wry•ness** *n*

X

x \'eks\ *n*, *pl* **x's** *or* **xs** \'eksəz\ **1** : 24th letter of the alphabet **2** : unknown quantity ~ *vb* **x-ed; x-ing** *or* **x'ing** : cancel with a series of x's — usu. with *out*

xe•non \'zē,nän,'zen,än\ *n* : heavy gaseous chemical element

xe•no•pho•bia \,zenə'fōbēə, ,zēn-\ *n*

: fear and hatred of foreign people and things — **xe•no•phobe** \'zenə,fōb, 'zēn-\ *n*

Xmas \'krisməs\ *n* : Christmas

x-ra•di•a•tion *n* **1** : exposure to X rays **2** : radiation consisting of X rays

x-ray \'eks,rā\ *vb* : examine, treat, or photograph with X rays

X ray *n* **1** : radiation of short wavelength that is able to penetrate solids **2** : photograph taken with X rays — **X–ray** *adj*

xy·lo·phone \'zīlə,fōn\ *n* : musical instrument with wooden bars that are struck — **xy·lo·phon·ist** \-,fōnist\ *n*

Y

y \'wī\ *n*, *pl* **y's** *or* **ys** \'wīz\ : 25th letter of the alphabet

¹-y \ē\ *adj suffix* **1** : composed or full of **2** : like **3** : performing or apt to perform an action

²-y \ē\ *n suffix*, *pl* **-ies 1** : state, condition, or quality **2** : activity, place of business, or goods dealt with **3** : whole group

yacht \'yät\ *n* : luxurious pleasure boat — *vb* : race or cruise in a yacht

ya·hoo \'yähü, 'yä-\ *n*, *pl* **-hoos** : uncouth or stupid person

yak \'yak\ *n* : big hairy Asian ox

yam \'yam\ *n* **1** : edible root of a tropical vine **2** : deep orange sweet potato

yam·mer \'yamər\ *vb* **1** : whimper **2** : chatter — **yammer** *n*

yank \'yaŋk\ *n* : strong sudden pull — **yank** *vb*

Yank \'yaŋk\ *n* : Yankee

Yan·kee \'yaŋkē\ *n* : native or inhabitant of New England, the northern U.S., or the U.S.

yap \'yap\ *vb* **-pp- 1** : yelp **2** : chatter — **yap** *n*

¹yard \'yärd\ *n* **1** : 3 feet **2** : long spar for supporting and spreading a sail — **yard·age** \-ij\ *n*

²yard *n* **1** : enclosed roofless area **2** : grounds of a building **3** : work area

yard·arm \'yärd,ärm\ *n* : end of the yard of a square-rigged ship

yard·stick *n* **1** : measuring stick 3 feet long **2** : standard for judging

yar·mul·ke \'yäməkə, 'yär-, -məl-\ *n* : a small brimless cap worn by Jewish males in a synagogue

yarn \'yärn\ *n* **1** : spun fiber for weaving or knitting **2** : tale

yaw \'yó\ *vb* : deviate erratically from a course — **yaw** *n*

yawl \'yól\ *n* : sailboat with 2 masts

yawn \'yón\ *vb* : open the mouth wide — *n* : deep breath through a wide-open mouth — **yawn·er** *n*

ye \'yē\ *pron* : you

yea \'yā\ *adv* **1** : yes **2** : truly — *n* : affirmative vote

year \'yir\ *n* **1** : period of about 365 days **2** *pl* : age

year·book *n* : annual report of the year's events

year·ling \'yirliŋ, 'yərlən\ *n* : one that is or is rated as a year old

year·ly \'yirlē\ *adj* : annual — **yearly** *adv*

yearn \'yərn\ *vb* **1** : feel desire esp. for what one cannot have **2** : feel tenderness or compassion

yearn·ing \-iŋ\ *n* : tender or urgent desire

yeast \'yēst\ *n* : froth or sediment in sugary liquids containing a tiny fungus and used in making alcoholic liquors and as a leaven in baking — **yeasty** *adj*

yell \'yel\ *vb* : utter a loud cry — **yell** *n*

yel·low \'yelō\ *adj* **1** : of the color yellow **2** : sensational **3** : cowardly — *vb* : make or turn yellow — *n* **1** : color of lemons **2** : yolk of an egg — **yel·low·ish** \'yeləwish\ *adj*

yellow fever *n* : virus disease marked by prostration, jaundice, fever, and often hemorrhage

yellow jacket *n* : wasp with yellow stripes

yelp \'yelp\ *vb* : utter a sharp quick shrill cry — **yelp** *n*

yen \'yen\ *n* : strong desire

yeo·man \'yōmən\ *n* **1** : attendant or officer in a royal or noble household **2** : small farmer **3** : naval petty officer with clerical duties — **yeo·man·ry** \-rē\ *n*

-yer — see -ER

yes \'yes\ *adv* : — used to express consent or agreement — *n* : affirmative answer

ye·shi·va, ye·shi·vah \yə'shēvə\ *n*, *pl* **yeshivas** *or* **ye·shi·voth** \-,shē'vót, -'vōth\ : Jewish school

yes–man \'yes,man\ *n* : person who agrees with every opinion or suggestion of a boss

yes·ter·day \'yestərdē\ *adv* **1** : on the

day preceding today **2** : only a short time ago — *n* **1** : day last past **2** : time not long past

yet \'yet\ *adv* **1** : in addition **2** : up to now **3** : so soon as now **4** : nevertheless ~ *conj* : but

yew \'yü\ *n* : evergreen tree or shrubs with dark stiff poisonous needles

yield \'yēld\ *vb* **1** : surrender **2** : grant **3** : bear as a crop **4** : produce **5** : cease opposition or resistance ~ *n* : quantity produced or returned

yo•del \'yōd°l\ *vb* **-deled** *or* **-delled; -del•ing** *or* **-del•ling** : sing by abruptly alternating between chest voice and falsetto — **yodel** *n* — **yo•del•er** \'yōd°lər\ *n*

yo•ga \'yōgə\ *n* : system of exercises for attaining bodily or mental control and well-being

yo•gi \'yōgē\ *n* : person who practices yoga

yo•gurt \'yōgərt\ *n* : fermented slightly acid soft food made from milk

yoke \'yōk\ *n* **1** : neck frame for coupling draft animals or for carrying loads **2** : clamp **3** : slavery **4** : tie or link **5** : piece of a garment esp. at the shoulder ~ *vb* **yoked; yok•ing 1** : couple with a yoke **2** : join

yo•kel \'yōkəl\ *n* : naive and gullible country person

yolk \'yōk\ *n* : yellow part of an egg — **yolked** \'yōkt\ *adj*

Yom Kip•pur \,yōmki'pu̇r, ,yäm-, -'kipər\ *n* : Jewish holiday observed in September or October with fasting and prayer as a day of atonement

yon \'yän\ *adj or adv* : yonder

yon•der \'yändər\ *adv* : at or to that place ~ *adj* : distant

yore \'yōr\ *n* : time long past

you \'yü\ *pron* **1** : person or persons addressed **2** : person in general

young \'yəŋ\ *adj* **youn•ger** \'yəŋgər\; **youn•gest** \'yəŋgəst\ **1** : being in the first or an early stage of life, growth, or development **2** : recently come into being **3** : youthful ~ *n, pl* **young** : persons or animals that are young — **young•ish** \-ish\ *adj*

young•ster \-stər\ *n* **1** : young person **2** : child

your \yər, 'yu̇r, 'yōr\ *adj* : relating to you or yourself

yours \'yu̇rz, 'yōrz\ *pron* : the ones belonging to you

your•self \yər'self\ *pron, pl* **your•selves** \-'selvz\ : you — used reflexively or for emphasis

youth \'yüth\ *n, pl* **youths** \'yüthz, 'yüths\ **1** : period between childhood and maturity **2** : young man **3** : young persons **4** : state or quality of being young, fresh, or vigorous

youth•ful \'yüthfəl\ *adj* **1** : relating to or appropriate to youth **2** : young **3** : vigorous and fresh — **youth•ful•ly** *adv* — **youth•ful•ness** *n*

yowl \'yau̇l\ *vb* : utter a loud long mournful cry — **yowl** *n*

yo-yo \'yō,yō\ *n, pl* **-yos** : toy that falls from or rises to the hand as it unwinds and rewinds on a string

yuc•ca \'yəkə\ *n* : any of several plants related to the lilies that grow in dry regions

yule \'yül\ *n* : Christmas — **yule•tide** \-,tīd\ *n*

yum•my \'yəmē\ *adj* **-mi•er; -est** : highly attractive or pleasing

Z

z \'zē\ *n, pl* **z's** *or* **zs** : 26th letter of the alphabet

za•ny \'zānē\ *n, pl* **-nies 1** : clown **2** : silly person ~ *adj* **-ni•er; -est** : crazy or foolish — **za•ni•ly** *adv* — **za•ni•ness** *n*

zeal \'zēl\ *n* : enthusiasm

zeal•ot \'zelət\ *n* : fanatical partisan

zeal•ous \'zeləs\ *adj* : filled with zeal — **zeal•ous•ly** *adv* — **zeal•ous•ness** *n*

ze•bra \'zēbrə\ *n* : horselike African mammal marked with light and dark stripes

zeit•geist \'tsīt,gīst, 'zīt-\ *n* : general spirit of an era

ze•nith \'zēnəth\ *n* : highest point

zeph•yr \'zefər\ n : gentle breeze

zep•pe•lin \'zepələn\ n : rigid airship like a blimp

ze•ro \'zērō\ n, pl **-ros 1** : number represented by the symbol 0 or the symbol itself **2** : starting point **3** : lowest point ∼ adj : having no size or quantity

zest \'zest\ n **1** : quality of enhancing enjoyment **2** : keen enjoyment — **zest•ful** \-fəl\ adj — **zest•ful•ly** adv — **zest•ful•ness** n

zig•zag \'zig,zag\ n : one of a series of short sharp turns or angles ∼ adj : having zigzags ∼ adv : in or by a zigzag path ∼ vb **-gg-** : proceed along a zigzag path

zil•lion \'zilyən\ n : large indeterminate number

zinc \'ziŋk\ n : bluish white crystaline metallic chemical element

zing \'ziŋ\ n **1** : shrill humming noise **2** : energy — **zing** vb

zin•nia \'zinēə, 'zēnyə\ n : American herb widely grown for its showy flowers

¹zip \'zip\ vb **-pp-** : move or act with speed ∼ n : energy

²zip vb **-pp-** : close or open with a zipper

zip code n : number that identifies a U.S. postal delivery area

zip•per \'zipər\ n : fastener consisting of 2 rows of interlocking teeth

zip•py \'zipē\ adj **-pi•er; -est** : brisk

zir•con \'zər,kän\ n : zirconium-containing mineral sometimes used in jewelry

zir•co•ni•um \,zər'kōnēəm\ n : corrosion-resistant gray metallic element

zith•er \'zithər, 'zith-\ n : stringed musical instrument played by plucking

zi•ti \'zētē\ n, pl **ziti** : short tubular pasta

zo•di•ac \'zōdē,ak\ n : imaginary belt in the heavens encompassing the paths of the planets and divided into 12 signs used in astrology — **zo•di•a•cal** \zō'dīəkəl\ adj

zom•bie \'zämbē\ n : person thought to have died and been brought back to life without free will

zon•al \'zōnᵊl\ adj : of, relating to, or having the form of a zone — **zon•al•ly** adv

zone \'zōn\ n **1** : division of the earth's surface based on latitude and climate **2** : distinctive area ∼ vb **zoned; zon•ing 1** : mark off into zones **2** : reserve for special purposes — **zo•na•tion** \zō'nāshən\ n

zoo \'zü\ n, pl **zoos** : collection of living animals usu. for public display — **zoo•keep•er** n

zo•ol•o•gy \zō'äləjē\ n : science of animals — **zo•o•log•i•cal** \,zōə'läjikəl\ adj — **zo•ol•o•gist** \zō'äləjist\ n

zoom \'züm\ vb **1** : move with a loud hum or buzz **2** : move or increase with great speed — **zoom** n

zuc•chi•ni \zu'kēnē\ n, pl **-ni** or **-nis** : summer squash with smooth cylindrical dark green fruits

zwie•back \'swēbak, 'swī-, 'zwē-, 'zwī-\ n : biscuit of baked, sliced, and toasted bread

zy•gote \'zī,gōt\ n : cell formed by the union of 2 sexual cells — **zy•got•ic** \zī'gätik\ adj

Abbreviations

Most of these abbreviations have been given in one form. Variation in use of periods, in type, and in capitalization is frequent and widespread (as *mph, MPH, m.p.h., Mph*).

abbr abbreviation
AC alternating current
acad academic, academy
AD in the year of our Lord
adj adjective
adv adverb, advertisement
advt advertisement
AF air force, audio frequency
agric agricultural, agriculture
AK Alaska
aka also known as
AL, Ala Alabama
alg algebra
Alta Alberta
a.m., AM before noon
Am, Amer America, American
amp ampere
amt amount
anc ancient
anon anonymous
ans answer
ant antonym
APO army post office
approx approximate, approximately
Apr April
apt apartment, aptitude
AR Arkansas
arith arithmetic
Ariz Arizona
Ark Arkansas
art article, artificial
assn association
assoc associate, associated, association
asst assistant
ATM automated teller machine
att attached, attention, attorney
attn attention
atty attorney
Aug August
auth authentic, author, authorized
aux, auxil auxiliary
av avoirdupois
AV audiovisual
ave avenue
avg average

AZ Arizona
BA bachelor of arts
bal balance
bar barometer, barrel
bbl barrel, barrels
BC before Christ, British Columbia
BCE before Christian Era, before Common Era
bet between
biog biographer, biographical, biography
biol biologic, biological, biologist, biology
bldg building
blvd boulevard
BO backorder, best offer, body odor, box office, branch office
Brit Britain, British
bro brother, brothers
bros brothers
BS bachelor of science
Btu British thermal unit
bu bureau, bushel
c carat, cent, centimeter, century, chapter, circa, cup
C Celsius, centigrade
ca circa
CA, Cal, Calif California
cal calendar, caliber, calorie
Can, Canad Canada, Canadian
cap capacity, capital, capitalize, capitalized
Capt captain
CB citizens band
CDT central daylight time
cen central
cert certificate, certification, certified, certify
cf compare
chap chapter
chem chemistry
cir circle, circuit, circular, circumference
civ civil, civilian
cm centimeter
co company, county

CO Colorado
c/o care of
COD cash on delivery, collect on delivery
col colonial, colony, color, colored, column, counsel
Col colonel, Colorado
Colo Colorado
comp comparative, compensation, compiled, compiler, composition, compound, comprehensive, comptroller
cong congress, congressional
conj conjunction
Conn Connecticut
cont continued
contr contract, contraction
corp corporal, corporation
corr corrected, correction
cp compare, coupon
CPR cardiopulmonary resuscitation
cr credit, creditor
CSA Confederate States of America
CST central standard time
ct carat, cent, count, court
CT central time, certified teacher, Connecticut
cu cubic
cur currency, current
CZ Canal Zone
d penny
DA district attorney
dag dekagram
dal dekaliter
dam dekameter
dbl double
DC direct current, District of Columbia
DDS doctor of dental science, doctor of dental surgery
DE Delaware
dec deceased, decrease
Dec December
deg degree
Del Delaware
Dem Democrat, Democratic
dept department
det detached, detachment, detail, determine
dg decigram
dia, diam diameter
diag diagonal, diagram
dict dictionary
dif, diff difference
dim dimension, diminished
dir director
disc discount
dist distance, district

div divided, dividend, division, divorced
dl deciliter
dm decimeter
DMD doctor of dental medicine
DOB date of birth
doz dozen
DP data processing
dr dram, drive, drum
Dr doctor
DST daylight saving time
DUI driving under the influence
DWI driving while intoxicated
dz dozen
e east, eastern, excellent
ea each
ecol ecological, ecology
econ economics, economist, economy
EDT eastern daylight time
e.g. for example
EKG electrocardiogram, electrocardiograph
elec electric, electrical, electricity
elem elementary
eng engine, engineer, engineering
Eng England, English
esp especially
EST eastern standard time
ET eastern time
et al and others
etc et cetera
ex example, express, extra
exec executive
f false, female, feminine
F, Fah, Fahr Fahrenheit
Feb February
fed federal, federation
fem female, feminine
FL, Fla Florida
fl oz fluid ounce
FPO fleet post office
fr father, friar, from
Fri Friday
ft feet, foot, fort
fut future
FYI for your information
g gram
Ga, GA Georgia
gal gallery, gallon
gen general
geog geographic, geographical, geography
geol geologic, geological, geology
geom geometric, geometrical, geometry
gm gram
GMT Greenwich mean time

GOP Grand Old Party (Republican)
gov government, governor
govt government
GP general practice, general practitioner
gr grade, grain, gram
gram grammar, grammatical
gt great
GU Guam
hd head
hf half
hgt height
hgwy highway
HI Hawaii
hist historian, historical, history
hon honor, honorable, honorary
hr here, hour
HS high school
ht height
HT Hawaii time
hwy highway
i intransitive, island, isle
Ia, IA Iowa
ICU intensive care unit
ID Idaho, identification
i.e. that is
IL, Ill Illinois
imp imperative, imperfect
in inch
IN Indiana
inc incomplete, incorporated
ind independent
Ind Indian, Indiana
inf infinitive
int interest
interj interjection
intl, intnl international
ital italic, italicized
Jan January
JD juvenile delinquent
jour journal, journeyman
JP justice of the peace
jr, jun junior
JV junior varsity
Kan, Kans Kansas
kg kilogram
km kilometer
KS Kansas
kW kilowatt
Ky, KY Kentucky
l late, left, liter, long
L large
La Louisiana
LA Los Angeles, Louisiana
lat latitude
lb pound
lg large, long
lib liberal, librarian, library

long longitude
m male, masculine, meter, mile
M medium
MA Massachusetts
Man Manitoba
Mar March
masc masculine
Mass Massachusetts
math mathematical, mathematician
max maximum
Md Maryland
MD doctor of medicine, Maryland
MDT mountain daylight time
Me, ME Maine
med medium
mg milligram
mgr manager
MI, Mich Michigan
mid middle
min minimum, minor, minute
Minn Minnesota
misc miscellaneous
Miss Mississippi
ml milliliter
mm millimeter
MN Minnesota
mo month
Mo, MO Missouri
Mon Monday
Mont Montana
mpg miles per gallon
mph miles per hour
MRI magnetic resonance imaging
MS Mississippi
MST mountain standard time
mt mount, mountain
MT Montana, mountain time
n neuter, north, northern, noun
NA North America, not applicable
nat national, native, natural
natl national
naut nautical
NB New Brunswick
NC North Carolina
ND, N Dak North Dakota
NE, Neb, Nebr Nebraska
neg negative
neut neuter
Nev Nevada
Nfld Newfoundland
NH New Hampshire
NJ New Jersey
NM, N Mex New Mexico
no north, number
Nov November
NR not rated
NS Nova Scotia
NV Nevada

NWT Northwest Territories
NY New York
NYC New York City
O Ohio
obj object, objective
occas occasionally
Oct October
off office, officer, official
OH Ohio
OJ orange juice
OK, Okla Oklahoma
ON, Ont Ontario
opp opposite
OR, Ore, Oreg Oregon
orig original, originally
oz ounce, ounces
p page
Pa Pennsylvania
PA Pennsylvania, public address
PAC political action committee
par paragraph, parallel
part participle, particular
pass passenger, passive
pat patent
PC percent, politically correct, post-card
pd paid
PD police department
PDT Pacific daylight time
PE physical education
PEI Prince Edward Island
Penn, Penna Pennsylvania
pg page
PIN personal identification number
pk park, peak, peck
pkg package
pl place, plural
p.m., PM afternoon
PMS premenstrual syndrome
PO post office
Port Portugal, Portuguese
pos position, positive
poss possessive
pp pages
PQ Province of Quebec
pr pair, price, printed
PR public relations, Puerto Rico
prep preposition
pres present, president
prob probable, probably, problem
prof professor
pron pronoun
prov province
PS postscript, public school
PST Pacific standard time
psych psychology
pt part, payment, pint, point
PT Pacific time, physical therapy

pvt private
qr quarter
qt quantity, quart
Que Quebec
quot quotation
r right, river
rd road, rod, round
RDA recommended daily allowance, recommended dietary allowance
recd received
reg region, register, registered, regular
rel relating, relative, religion
rep report, reporter, representative, re-public
Rep Republican
res residence
rev reverse, review, revised, revision, revolution
Rev reverend
RFD rural free delivery
RI Rhode Island
rm room
RPM revolutions per minute
RR railroad, rural route
RSVP please reply
rt right
rte route
s small, south, southern
SA South America
SASE self-addressed stamped enve-lope
Sask Saskatchewan
Sat Saturday
SC South Carolina
sci science, scientific
SD, S Dak South Dakota
secy secretary
sen senate, senator, senior
Sept, Sep September
sing singular
sm small
so south, southern
soph sophomore
sp spelling
spec special, specifically
specif specific, specifically
SPF sun protection factor
sq square
sr senior
Sr sister
SSN Social Security number
SSR Soviet Socialist Republic
st street
St saint
std standard
subj subject
Sun Sunday

supt superintendent
SWAT Special Weapons and Tactics
syn synonym
t teaspoon, temperature, ton, transitive, troy, true
T tablespoon
tbs, tbsp tablespoon
TD touchdown
tech technical, technician, technology
Tenn Tennessee
terr territory
Tex Texas
Th, Thu, Thur, Thurs Thursday
TN Tennessee
trans translated, translation, translator
tsp teaspoon
Tu, Tue, Tues Tuesday
TX Texas
UK United Kingdom
UN United Nations
univ universal, university
US United States
USA United States of America
USSR Union of Soviet Socialist Republics

usu usual, usually
UT Utah
UV ultraviolet
v verb, versus
Va, VA Virginia
var variant, variety
vb verb
VG very good
VI Virgin Islands
vol volume, volunteer
VP vice president
vs versus
Vt, VT Vermont
w west, western
WA, Wash Washington
Wed Wednesday
WI, Wis, Wisc Wisconsin
wk week, work
wt weight
WV, W Va West Virginia
WY, Wyo Wyoming
XL extra large, extra long
yd yard
yr year, younger, your
YT Yukon Territory